MAKE THE MOST OF YOUR TIME ON EARTH

THE ROUGH GUIDE TO THE WORLD

Fully updated fourth edition

ROUGH GUIDES

Publishing information

This fourth edition published 2019 by Apa Publications Ltd
1st Floor, Mill House, 8 Mill Street, London SE1 2BA

Distribution

UK, Ireland and Europe

Apa Publications (UK) Ltd; sales@roughguides.com

United States and Canada

Ingram Publisher Services; ips@ingramcontent.com

Australia and New Zealand

Woodslane; info@woodslane.com.au

Southeast Asia

Apa Publications (SN) Pte; sales@roughguides.com

Worldwide

Apa Publications (UK) Ltd; sales@roughguides.com

Special Sales, Content Licensing and CoPublishing

Rough Guides can be purchased in bulk quantities at discounted prices. We can create special editions, personalised jackets and corporate imprints tailored to your needs. sales@roughguides.com.

roughguides.com

Printed in Poland by Pozkal

A catalogue record for this book is available from the British Library

The publishers and authors have done their best to ensure the accuracy and currency of all the information in
Make the Most of Your Time on Earth, however, they can accept no responsibility
for any loss, injury, or inconvenience sustained by any traveller as a result of information or advice contained in the guide.

Credits and acknowledgements

Editor: Joanna Reeves

Assistant editors: Tom Fleming, Siobhan Warwicker, Aimee White
Commissioning editors: Rebecca Hallett, Georgia Stephens

Managing editor: Rachel Lawrence
Picture editor and cover photo research: Aude Vauconsant
Cartography: Katie Bennett
Proofreaders: Jan McCann, Stewart Wild
Head of DTP and Pre-Press: Dan May

Thanks to all our writers and photographers, credited at the back of
the book, for their great ideas, fine writing and beautiful pictures.

CONTENTS

INTRODUCTION

What makes the ultimate travel experience? Is it something as simple as stumbling across that perfect undiscovered restaurant where you can feast on traditional food among locals? Or is it that dream adventure that takes you outside your comfort zone and pushes you to new limits? We asked our Rough Guide writers to share their most inspirational experiences – to inspire yours. Wildly different, the accounts all had one thing in common: authenticity. Each and every one pushed travel a bit further, either through opening a path to new territories, forging fresh routes across established ones or offering a new way of looking at the world.

It might be the all-encompassing awe of discovering an ancient city like Volubilis or defying gravity at China's Hanging Temple, or the sheer exhilaration of paragliding against a dramatic Matterhorn backdrop. It could be humbling wildlife encounters, from hippo-spotting in the Bijagós Islands to glimpsing jaguars in the Paraguayan Pantanal, or it might be appreciating natural wonders in all their diverse glory: Pamukkale's shallow staircase of thermal pools, the towering giants of Sequoia National Park, the churning waters of Devil's Pool in Zambia.

A shift to conscious travel sees people make better-informed decisions, not only booking trips that are unique but those that benefit local people and places too. Travellers are heading off the beaten track in an attempt to prevent popular places being "loved to death", whether that be wild camping in the Oman desert, going off-grid in northern Saskatchewan or exploring unchartered fjords in wild East Greenland.

That's not to say travel always has to be pushing yourself to extremes – you can have a life-changing experience from something as wonderfully unassuming as clawing for clams on Île de Noirmoutier or getting lost in the golden streets of Valletta.

Some experiences in this book are easy to undertake, others require planning and expertise. Some are rare events that happen once every few years; many are daily occurrences. Every single one, though, is a personal recommendation. For this fourth edition, we've added more than one hundred and fifty new experiences from around the globe. We hope that they truly inspire you to make the most of your time on Earth.

Joanna Reeves, Editor

SHETLAND
ISLES

ORKNEY
ISLANDS

WESTERN
ISLES

012 **015**

024

ATLANTIC
OCEAN

S C O T L A N D

023

NORTH
SEA

020

053 **033** **045**

004 029

021

017

NORTHERN
IRELAND

048

008 **011**

047

036

ISLE OF
MAN

040

IRISH
SEA

009

032

038

018

044

I R E L A N D

039

031

037

049

E N G L A N D

025

050

006

WALES

035 **052** **010**

005

043 **051** **028**

002

CELTIC
SEA

026 **027**

022 034

041

019 **014**

001

003

013

054

016

030

042

English Channel

007

046

ISLES OF
SCILLY

GUERNSEY

JERSEY F R A N C E

BRITAIN & IRELAND
001–054

Which is the real Britain and Ireland? The tradition-rich home of Welsh choirs, Oxford colleges and Georgian spa towns? The open expanses of green Connemara hills, vast Norfolk beaches and rearing Scottish highlands? Or the culture-packed buzz of its fast-paced cities? The answer, happily, is all of them. Layered with centuries of history, peppered with iconic attractions and well stocked with regional delicacies, Britain and Ireland juggle old and new to thrilling and sometimes eccentric effect, whether you're staying in an off-grid treehouse in Wales, walking in Hockney's landscapes on the Yorkshire Wolds Way, admiring street art in Manchester and London or cycling the North Coast 500 in Scotland.

001 In celebration of the oyster

ENGLAND I've always loved Whitstable, the arty fishing town on Kent's northern coast, with its shingle shore, its beach huts, its huge skies and its workaday bustle – and its oysters, which have been harvested in these estuarine waters since Roman times. So here I am, the archetypal "Down From Londoner" as locals call us, come to celebrate these ancient, sea-salty delicacies at Whitstable's annual Oyster Festival.

Heralding a week of ceilidhs and crabbing competitions, tug-o-wars and dog shows, the festival starts with the stately Landing of the Oysters, when fishermen carry baskets of freshly caught creatures from sea to shore to present them for blessing. Having witnessed this peculiarly moving scene, I follow the carnival parade of giant sea beasts and excited schoolkids through town before ducking off to the harbour. In the cool of the fish market I discover enormous prawns, silvery sardines and tiny tiger-striped clams shifting on their icy beds – and, of course, the celebrated oysters, heaped on wooden carts. Natives being out of season, these are Rock oysters, their gnarled, algae-tinged shells as dark, cold and heavy as tombstones.

Nearby, at the seafront, serious-faced shuckers deftly gouge open shells and flip the meat, mermaid tattoos writhing on their arms as they prepare plates for the feeding frenzy. This is not refined food. Silt smears the cold marble slabs while grit-flecked brine swooshes out of primeval-looking shells. The oysters themselves are colossal, their flesh gleaming and smooth, laced with delicate black frills. I grab a plate, plus a lemon quarter, and tip them back, savouring that surprising hit, mineral and creamy, a slurp of the ocean.

Next I head to the *Old Neptune*, Whitstable's pub on the beach, for a pint of oyster stout. Dark and cold, with a salty caramel bite, it's the perfect drink for today. Just yards away, silvery waves klonk hard against the shingle, churning up speckled shells before retreating with a shimmery whisper. Even without its Oyster Festival, Whitstable has a lot to celebrate.

Samantha Cook
is a writer and editor based in London. She is the author of the Rough Guides to New Orleans and Chick Flicks, and co-author of the Rough Guides to Kent, Sussex & Surrey, London and Vintage London.

The Globe Theatre: Shakespeare as it should be

002

ENGLAND It's standing-room only in 'the pit' at Shakespeare's Globe on London's South Bank, a reconstruction of the original theatre a few hundred metres away at which Shakespeare's theatre company, the Lord Chamberlain's Men, performed from 1599. Here in "this wooden O", as Henry V calls it, hard wooden seats encircle the 'thrust' stage, but you get the best atmosphere if you take your place in the pit, standing in the footsteps of the Elizabethan and Jacobean 'groundlings' who paid a penny apiece.

The cheap seats are also the best seats. This close up, Shakespeare cannot be dusty or distant. The performances are energized, physical, exhilarating. Audience and actors can see each other clear as day. The modern Globe's first artistic director, Mark Rylance, has said that he found himself on stage here "thinking of the audience as other actors". This is a participatory, democratic theatre experience. There's a terrific camaraderie, as both actors and audience tacitly agree to ignore the roar of that aeroplane flying overhead or those first drops of rain from the summer sky.

There's also a real intimacy in those moments when Shakespeare lays bare the inner sinews of human thought and emotion. Only here do you have the chance to eyeball Hamlet as he contemplates 'self-slaughter', Lady Macbeth as she tries to wash the imagined blood from her hands. With no elaborate sets, no darkened auditorium, it is only by the joint act of imagining that other worlds are conjured on stage.

The play ends, and the actors stamp out a valedictory jig on the bare wooden stage. It's a euphoric moment, and a Globe trademark, bringing tragedies, comedies and histories to a close in the same vein: inclusive, exuberant, joyous.

003

The burning barrels of Ottery St Mary

ENGLAND On the fifth of November, the small town of Ottery St Mary in Devon is brought to a standstill for an ancient tradition that has nothing to do with Guy Fawkes. While the rest of the country celebrates with fireworks, the crowds in Ottery cheer as locals run through the temporarily car-free streets with huge, flaming tar barrels hefted onto their shoulders. One of the biggest bonfires in the South West burns on the banks of the River Otter.

Thought to have originated in the sixteenth or seventeenth century, the reasons behind the celebration have been lost to antiquity. The main theory is that it began as a pagan ritual to cleanse the streets and ward off evil spirits, although many long-time residents have their own theories. Some families have carried the barrels for generations, and see it as a rite of passage.

The night begins around 5.30pm, when the first barrel is lit in front of a public house (each barrel is sponsored by a local pub), with sixteen more throughout the night; the smallest are light enough for children to carry, while the heaviest is a mighty 66lb. So far, women aren't allowed to participate and it can feel like a bit of a lads' game, but hopefully that will change in the future.

The night is rough, ready and dangerous: this is not a spectacle put on for tourists. In fact, to carry a flaming barrel you must be born and bred in Ottery and deemed ready by the current Barrel Rollers.

It certainly is a sight to behold: the streets and pubs jam-packed, people cheering and shouting as a Barrel Roller propels through the crowd, head bent beneath the weight as the dancing flames and roiling smoke reach skywards. Then the barrel is passed on and the former carrier will more often than not be faced with the new conundrum of slapping out the flames encasing the thick, hessian-sacking gloves they wear to protect their hands. Hair is singed, skin blistered, clothes ruined, but their broad smiles hold strong.

004 | Gigging in Glasgow

SCOTLAND Pop stars, travelling from coach to bar and from plane to arena, are notoriously oblivious about the city they happen to be performing in. There are countless stories of frontmen bellowing "Hello, Detroit!" when they're actually in Toronto. But some places have a genuine buzz about them. London is fine, but all too often its crowds sit back and wait to be impressed. If you want real passion, vibrant venues and bands who really play out of their skin, Glasgow is where it's at.

Scotland's biggest city has an alternative rock pedigree that few can match. Primal Scream, Franz Ferdinand, the Jesus & Mary Chain, Simple Minds, Snow Patrol and Belle & Sebastian have all sprung from a city that *Time* magazine has described as Europe's "secret capital" of rock music. Its gig scene, which stretches from gritty pubs to arty student haunts, marvellous church halls to cavernous arenas, is enthusiastic, vociferous and utterly magnetic. Nice 'N' Sleazy and King Tut's Wah Wah Hut (where Alan McGee first spotted Oasis) are legendary in their own right, but if one venue really defines the city, it's the Barrowland.

Opened in the 1930s as a ballroom, the Barrowland was the hunting ground of the killer known as "Bible John" in the late sixties. It's still a fairly rough-and-ready place – the Barras market is just outside, and its location in the Celtic heartland of Glasgow's East End makes it a favoured venue for rambunctious traditional bands. Shane McGowan's been there, drinking lurid cocktails, his slurred vocals drowned out by a roaring crowd. So have Keane, flushed with early success and looking bemused at the small fights that broke out near the front at their performance.

Of course, most gigs finish without the drama getting violent. With a 2000-person capacity that's atmospheric but intimate, and without any seats or barriers to get in the way of the music or the pogoing, the Barrowland is a wonderful place to see a live performance, full of energy and expectation. You could have witnessed PJ Harvey transfix the crowd, the Streets provoke wall-to-wall grins, the Mars Volta prompt walkouts, Leftfield fill the space with spine-shaking bass and the Libertines perform their epic, edgy, reunion gig. This is the stuff of music legend. Head to the Barrowland and be part of it.

005 | Getting away from it all on Skellig Michael

IRELAND The jagged twin pyramids of the Skellig Islands rise abruptly out of the Atlantic Ocean, six miles off the southwest tip of Ireland. Little Skellig is a teeming, noisy bird sanctuary, home to around 50,000 gannets and now officially full (the excess have had to move to another island off County Wexford). In tranquil contrast, neighbouring Skellig Michael shelters one of the most remarkable hermitages in the world.

In the late seventh or early eighth century, a monastery was somehow built on this inhospitable outcrop, in imitation of the desert communities of the early Church fathers – and, indeed, continuing the practices of Ireland's druids, who would spend long periods alone in the wilderness. Its design is a miracle of ingenuity and devotion. On small artificial terraces, the dry-stone beehive huts were ringed by sturdy outer walls, which deflected the howling winds and protected the vegetable patch made of bird droppings; channels crisscrossed the settlement to funnel rainwater into cisterns. Monks – up to fifteen of them at a time – lived

here for nearly five hundred years, withstanding anything the Atlantic could throw at them – including numerous Viking raids. In the twelfth century, however, a climatic change made the seas even rougher, while pressure was brought to bear on old, independent monasteries such as Skellig Michael to conform, and eventually the fathers adopted the Augustinian rule and moved to the mainland.

The beauty of a visit to the island is that it doesn't require a huge leap to imagine how the monks might have lived. You still cross over from the mainland on small, slow boats, huddling against the spray. From the quay, 650 steps climb almost vertically to the monastery, whose cells, chapels and refectory remain largely intact after 1300 years. The island even has residents, at least in the summer: friendly guides, employed by the Office of Public Works to give talks to visitors, sometimes stay out here for weeks at a time, making the most of the spiritual solitude.

006 | Bat-spotting on the River Cam

ENGLAND Visitors to Cambridge often come pre-programmed with a vision of themselves punting idyllically along the Backs, untroubled as a cloudless sky. Unfortunately, the reality can be more like a waterborne scrum: unscrupulous touts, mega-punts lashed together, and cacophonous collisions. For a more original twist on this most 'Cambridge' of pursuits, take to the river by night. Head upstream along its quietest, unlit stretch, away from the city. And look out for bats.

'Bat safari' tours run on summer nights on the stretch of river heading out towards Grantchester Meadows. Gathering at the boat yard by the Mill Pond just before dusk, passengers – some bat enthusiasts, most novices – are equipped with warm blankets and a bat detector. This converts the bats' echolocation signals, which they use to orientate themselves and locate insects, into frequencies humans can hear. Each

boat is helmed by a bat expert from the Wildlife Trust, and propelled by a 'punt chauffeur'.

Bat numbers in the UK are declining, but here the supply is plentiful. Dusty college attics make perfect roosting places, apparently. As night falls, the bats emerge to devour the evening swarms of insects. A common pipistrelle bat consumes three thousand insects in a night. Twilight is breakfast-time, and they're ravenous.

The bats are – or can be – a pretext, really, for an idyllic journey. All signs of civilization give way to dark skies and silence as you leave the city. Progress is slow and stately. The water splashes gently against the sides of the boat. Torches sweep the mist-topped waters to illumine bats skimming the surface. Weeping willows drip from the riverbank; tree branches are outlined against the starry sky.

Just don't tell all the other punters...

A play among the elements

007

ENGLAND Although it gives the impression of being much older, the Minack Theatre only dates back to the 1930s. Rowena Cade decided to carve a stage into the cliffs near the small Cornish village of Porthcurno, all so *The Tempest* could be experienced among the elements. It took her and her gardener, Billy Rawlings, and some local craftsmen just six months of work before the first play was put on for the public.

While it's a treat to see any type of performance at the Minack, it's apparent in every lovingly placed stone that it was designed to give Shakespeare's works the grand stage they deserve. Few things can compare to passing a summer's evening watching one of the playwright's iconic works here; the crash of the waves echoing behind the dialogue, the light of the moon glittering on the sea for a backdrop. It's a raw and rewarding experience, a thrillingly literal vision of all the world as a stage.

Though it's what makes the experience so unique, sitting out among the elements is something you need to be prepared for. The cliffs of Cornwall are famed for their blustery weather, so warm clothing is a must, and you might want to bring a cushion for your stony seat. But once you're wrapped up and sipping a hot drink, you'll find it all adds to the cosy atmosphere and enhances the feeling of camaraderie in the audience.

The Minack Theatre is open year-round, even when there aren't performances, giving everyone a chance to wander the steps and stand on the stage. You can also visit the Rowena Cade exhibition, which shows the staggering hard work and ingenuity that went into making the Minack, and the passion that brought it to life.

After your visit make time to explore the surrounding area, where you can enjoy beautiful cliff walks, the pale sands and clear water of Porthcurno beach, and sleepy Porthcurno village. The Porthcurno Telegraph Museum is surprisingly interesting – submarine cables from all over the world ended here, making this quiet village the British government's hub of telegraphic communication for decades.

008 | Wandering around Borrowdale in the Lake District

ENGLAND Eighteenth-century Romantic poet Thomas Gray described the narrowest part of Borrowdale – the so-called Jaws of Borrowdale – as "a menacing ravine whose rocks might, at any time, fall and crush a traveller". Gray obviously didn't get out much, for more than anything Borrowdale is characterized by its sylvan beauty, the once glaciated hills smoothed off by the ancient ice. Some have dubbed it the most beautiful valley in England, and it's easy to see why on the gentle walks that weave across the flat valley floor. Some of the best are around Derwentwater, its mountain backdrop, wooded slopes and quaint ferry service making it one of the prettiest lakes in the area.

Ever since Victorian times, visitors have flocked to the Bowder Stone, a 2000-tonne glacial erratic probably carried south from Scotland in the last Ice Age. This cube of andesitic lava is perched so precariously on one edge that it looks ready to topple at any moment. Wooden steps give access to its 30ft summit where the rock has been worn smooth by hundreds of thousands of feet.

Immediately north, a circular walk takes in an area boasting the densest concentration of superb views in the Lake District. The most spectacular is from Walla Crag – vistas stretch over Derwentwater up to the Jaws of Borrowdale.

North of the Bowder Stone, a small tumbling stream is spanned by Ashness Bridge, an ancient stone-built structure designed for packhorses. With its magnificent backdrop of Derwentwater and the rugged beauty of the northern fells, it's one of the most photographed scenes in the entire Lake District.

009 | Walking in Hockney's landscapes on the Yorkshire Wolds Way

ENGLAND They call it England's quietest National Trail. But unlike many of the other long-distance walking routes that thread through the country, it has no mountains to climb and no coastlines to negotiate. Instead, what the Yorkshire Wolds Way offers is 79 miles of rolling chalk uplands and tucked-away villages – a genuine escape from the rush and clamour of the daily grind. It's a glorious walk, winding from the banks of the River Humber to the seaside town of Filey, but remains completely overshadowed by better-known trails. Which is, of course, the attraction.

Quiet? Definitely, although the description says as much about the path that the trail traces – down hushed holloways and along snaffled-away dales – as it does about the scarcity of walkers. The serene topography of the region was enough to ensnare the artist David Hockney decades ago. The Yorkshireman might be famed for his vivid, sun-washed California paintings – and he's lived in LA on and off since the 1960s – but his roots often drawn him back to the deep, agricultural landscapes of the Wolds.

Hockney's Yorkshire-based works capture the seasonal alterations of the woods and farmlands. Walk the trail in early summer and you'll discover the rainbow-bright palette of natural colours he portrays in works like *Going Up Garrowby Hill*. Come in late winter, meanwhile, and you'll encounter the more spectral, grey-skied character of paintings such as *Bigger Trees Near Warter*.

On a more tangible note, hike the route at any time of year and you'll be treated to prime English countryside with all the trimmings: roaming beech woods, busy birdlife and yawning views over far-off cities. Be warned, too, that the route is studded with the kind of half-hidden rural pubs that it takes serious will-power to leave. Fuel up on comforting classics, washed down with pints of Yorkshire ale, in between long, undulating hikes. Assuming you do manage to prise yourself away from the likes of *The Gait Inn* in Millington or the time-stuck *Cross Keys Inn* in Thixendale, then – as they say in these parts – by heck, you'll be glad of the walk.

010 | Get a taste of English history at Pudding Club

ENGLAND In 1985, in a burst of English eccentricity, a group of gastronomes in the Cotswolds formed a club to combat one of the great threats facing the world: the looming extinction of the Great British Pudding. They continue to fight that good fight today, and you can support them by going along to a club meeting and celebrating Britain's delicious, stodgy contributions to the dessert menu.

Of course, when they say "pudding" they mean it in the English, rather than the American, sense. If you arrive expecting something creamy and blancmange-like, you'll go home hungry, but if you're craving some kind of baked, steamed or boiled cake – always served with custard – you'll end up with the opposite problem.

The illustrious club meets every week in the *Three Ways House Hotel*, in the typically charming Cotswolds village of Mickleton. Arrive early for a walk around the village, and maybe a visit to the Arts and Crafts garden at nearby Hidcote manor house.

When your stomach's growling, head back to *Three Ways House* for a light meal, after which the main event begins: the Parade of Seven Puddings. There's always a well-known favourite in the mix, whether a deliciously gooey Sticky Toffee Pudding or an eyebrow-raising Spotted Dick, but in keeping with the club's driving force, you're sure to be introduced to some unfamiliar recipes. Perhaps there'll be a Sussex Pond (a tangy pudding with a whole lemon in the middle), Blackberry Exeter (with an autumnal apple and blackberry filling), or College Pudding (dense and currant-studded).

You have to finish each serving before moving onto the next one, but so long as you stick to that rule, you can eat until you're about to burst.

011 | Hiking the Pennine Way

ENGLAND After two weeks' walking through rain and shine (and with moods to match), the final day of the Pennine Way, Britain's oldest and longest long-distance footpath, is upon you: a 27-mile marathon over the desolate Cheviot Hills. It's a challenging finale but the narcotic effects of mounting euphoria ought to numb your multiple aches. Anyway, if you're one of the few who've made it this far, you'll not give up now.

The Pennine Way begins at the village of Edale in Derbyshire's Peak District and meanders 270 miles north to Kirk Yetholm beneath the Cheviot Hills and a mile across the Scottish border. Along its course, it leads through some of England's most beautiful and least crowded countryside. In the early stages, it passes the birthplace of the English Industrial Revolution, and today stone slabs from the derelict mills and factories have been recycled into winding causeways over the once notorious moorland peat bogs. This is Brontë country, too, grim on a dank, misty day but bleakly inspiring when the cloud lifts.

The mires subside to become the rolling green pastures and dry-stone walls of the Yorkshire Dales that rise up to striking peaks like the 2278ft-high Pen-y-ghent – the "Mountain of the Winds".

The limestone Dales in turn become the wilder northern Pennines, where no one forgets stumbling onto the astounding glaciated abyss of High Cup Nick. The Way's final phase begins with an invigorating stage along the 2000-year-old Hadrian's Wall before ending with the calf-wrenching climax over the Cheviots.

Walking the wilds is exhilarating but staying in pretty villages along the way is also a highlight. Again and again you'll find yourself transported back to a bygone rural idyll of village shops, church bells and, of course, pubs. Memories of mud and glory will pass before your eyes as you stagger the last few yards onto Kirk Yetholm's village green, stuff your reviled backpack in the bin and turn towards the inviting bar at the *Border Hotel*.

012 | Sandwood Bay: Britain's most mysterious beach

SCOTLAND Cape Wrath: a name that epitomizes nature at its harshest, land and sea at their most unforgiving. In fact, the name Wrath denotes a "turning point" in Old Norse, and the Vikings regarded this stockade of vertical rock in the most northwesterly corner of Scotland as a milestone in their ocean-going voyages. As such, they were surely among the first travellers to come under the spell of Sandwood Bay, the Cape's most elemental stretch of coastline.

Here, across a mile-long breach in the headland, blow Britain's most remote sands, flanked by epic dunes and a slither of shimmering loch; a beach of such austere and unexpected elegance, scoured so relentlessly by the Atlantic and located in such relative isolation, that it scarcely seems part of the Scottish mainland at all. The freestanding impudence of the hulking stack of stone that is Am Buachaille ("the Herdsman"), rearing some 240ft out of the sea off the bay's southern tip, is fantastical in itself.

Even on the clearest of summer days, when shoals of cumuli race shadows across the foreshore, you are unlikely to encounter other visitors save for the odd sandpiper. You might not be entirely alone, though; whole galleons are said to be buried in the sand, and a cast of mermaids, ghostly pirates and grumbling sailors has filled accounts of the place for as long as people have frequented it. Though the last mermaid sighting was in 1900 (attributed to a local shepherd, Alexander Gunn, who famously stuck by his story till death), the sheer scale and magnetism of the Sandwood panorama – accessible only on foot via a desolate, four-mile path – may just throw you a supernatural encounter of your own.

Whether you camp wild in the haunted ruins of an old crofter's cottage, or merely stroll the sand in the teeth of an untrammelled westerly, the presence of the bay is undeniable. Or maybe it's just the feeling that you're standing at the edge of the known world, a turning point between the familiar and the inexplicable.

013 | Cycling in the New Forest

ENGLAND Covering a wedge of land between Bournemouth, South-ampton and the English Channel, the New Forest offers some of Britain's most exhilarating cycling country, with a chance to lose yourself amid a network of roads, gravelled paths and bridleways, and more than 100 miles of car-free cycle tracks. Here, you can indulge your wild side, surrounded by a leafy world remote from modern-day stresses.

Spring brings budding growth to the area and the ground is swathed in delicate colour, while autumn paints the forest in gorgeous hues of red, yellow and brown. Your travels will take you past tidy thatched cottages along quiet wooded lanes and on to exposed heathland with magnificent views and dotted with deer. The 40 miles/hr speed limit on forest roads makes for a safe and unhassled ride, picnic spots are

ubiquitous, and the occasional country pub provides more substantial refreshment on leisurely pit stops.

This national park has been a protected wilderness for nigh on a thousand years: William the Conqueror appropriated the area as a hunting reserve (his son, William Rufus, was killed here by an arrow in an apparent accident). The area has changed little since Norman times and is a superb place to spot wildlife: amid terrain ranging from thick woodland to bogs, heath and grassland, the forest is home to around 1300 fallow, roe, red and sika deer, not to mention some 3000 wild ponies, and numerous sheep, cattle, pigs and donkeys.

Park up the car and pedal off; go fast or take your time; map out routes or ride at random – you're the boss on this invigorating escape into freedom.

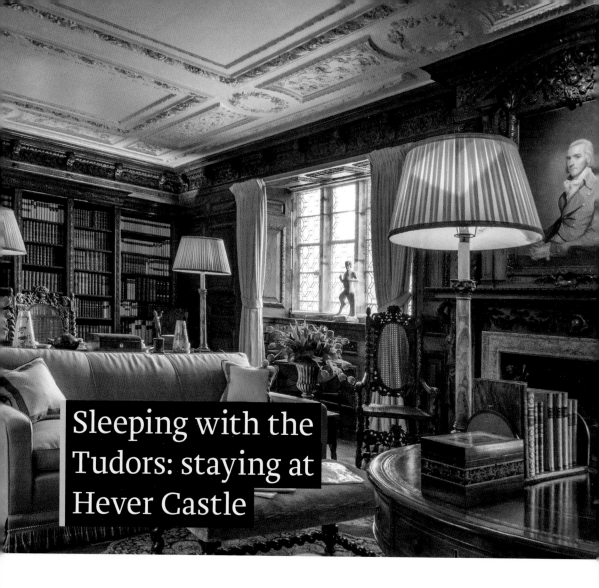

Sleeping with the Tudors: staying at Hever Castle

014

ENGLAND You'd have to be hard-hearted not to feel moved at Hever Castle, the fine fortified manor house in Kent that served as the childhood home of the unfortunate Anne Boleyn. Among the few of her effects to survive, on show in the extravagantly wood-panelled interior, is the poignantly inscribed illustrated prayer book that went with her to the executioner's block. The only drawback: you need to share the castle with the tourists.

To soak up the period atmosphere away from the hurly-burly, book a stay in the Astor Wing, part of the magnificent "Tudor extension" painstakingly added using only traditional methods and materials during the castle's renovation a century ago – and now open to the public as an opulent B&B. As you soak in regal luxury in your clawfoot bath, spare a thought for the ghost of poor Anne, said to drift silently across the bridge over the River Eden just a stone's throw away.

Cycling the North Coast 500

015

SCOTLAND The appeal of a bucket-list cycling trip is there to see in oodles of best-of lists, books and annual sporting events. The North Coast 500, or Route 66 with midges as it's been dubbed, is the newest of the lot, leaving the country's Central Belt behind for the heathery hills and glens of Caithness, Sutherland and Ross. After the one-two punch of the glorious landscape and notoriously unpredictable weather, there follows a greatest hits of Scottish icons to lure you off the road – spooky ruins, fairy-tale glens, toothy castles, rugged fairways and shingle-sand beaches. They're all in place, with whisky distilleries seemingly at every turn.

For those not familiar with Scotland's Highland geography, the route follows a 500-mile circuit beginning and ending in Inverness, the self-named capital of the north. You can start anywhere and bike in either direction, but the easiest route is to travel anticlockwise, heading towards the flatish east coast first, before the squiggly road climbs into the higgedly-piggedly hills of the west coast. A steely, determined spirit is more important than calves of steel, but you'll need to be prepared to cycle around 65 miles a day between hotels, B&Bs and campsites. At first, the route races through Wick and John O'Groats, past such iconic sights as the world-class Glenmorangie Distillery at Tain, Dunrobin Castle and the Castle of Mey, where the late Queen Mother used to holiday every summer. It then curves along a lonesome belt of sea-whipped coast, before looping southwest via Durness and Lochinver in the shadow of the sugar dome-topped summit of Suilven.

Before the homeward sprint, the villages of Ullapool and Torridon appear in quick succession, the spaces in between as much of a stage set as anything Shakespeare dreamt up in Macbeth. There are ancient sandstone hills, framed by snaggle-toothed ruins, and rampant moorland stretching to the horizon. Small wonder those who have completed it say once is never enough.

016 | Rambling on Dartmoor

ENGLAND In the middle of that most genteel of counties, Devon, it comes as something of a shock to encounter the 365 square miles of raw granite, barren bogland and rippling seas of heather that make up Dartmoor. The feeling of space is intimidating. If you want to declutter your mind and energize your body, the recipe is simple: invest in a pair of hiking boots, switch off your mobile and set out on an adventure into the primitive heart of Britain. The briefest of journeys onto the moor is enough to take in the dusky umbers of the landscape, flecked by yellow gorse and purple heather and threaded by flashes of moorland stream, all washed in a moist and misty light. Even the gathering haze that precedes rain appears otherworldly, while the moor under a mantle of snow and illuminated by a crisp wintry light is spellbinding.

Your walk will take you from picturesque, hideaway hamlets such as Holne and Buckland-in-the-Moor to bare wilderness and blasted crag within a few strides. There are some surprising examples of architecture, too, including the authentically Norman Okehampton Castle and the wholly fake Castle Drogo, built by Lutyens in the early twentieth century in the style of a medieval fortress. But by far the most stirring man-made relics to be found are the Bronze and Iron Age remains, a surprising testimony to the fact that this desolate expanse once hummed with activity: easily accessible are the grand hut circles of Grimspound, where Conan Doyle set a scene from his Sherlock Holmes yarn, *The Hound of the Baskervilles*.

The best way to explore is on an organized walk led by a knowledgeable guide. These will often focus on a theme, perhaps birdwatching, or orienteering, or painting. It's a first-rate way to get to grips with the terrain and discover facets of this vast landscape that you'd never encounter on your own. Alternatively, simply equip yourself with a decent map and seek out your own piece of Dartmoor. You may not see another soul for miles, but you'll soon absorb its slow, soothing rhythm.

017 | Horsing about at the Common Ridings

SCOTLAND The Common Ridings of the Scottish Border towns of Hawick, Selkirk, Jedburgh and Lauder are among Britain's best-kept secrets – an equestrian extravaganza that combines the danger of Pamplona's Fiesta de San Fermin and the drinking of Munich's Oktoberfest. Commemorating the days when the Scots needed early warnings of attacks from their expansionist neighbours, the focus of each event is a dawn horseback patrol of the commons and fields that mark each town's boundaries. Selkirk may boast the largest number of riders, and Lauder might be the oldest event, but Hawick is always the first – and the best attended – of them all.

At dawn on each day of the ridings, a colourful and incredibly noisy drum and fife band marches around the streets to shake people from their sleep and, more importantly, to allow plenty of time for the riders, and virtually the entire town population, to get down to the pub – they open at 6am – and stock up on the traditional breakfast of "Curds and Cream" (rum and milk). Suitably fortified, over two hundred riders – many of them exquisitely attired in cream jodhpurs, black riding boots, tweed jackets and white silk neckerchiefs – mount their horses and gallop at breakneck speed around the ancient lanes and narrow streets of town, before heading out into the fields to continue the racing in a slightly more organized manner.

By early evening, and with the racing done for the day, the spectators and riders stagger back into Hawick to reacquaint themselves with the town's pubs, an activity that most people approach with gusto. Stumbling out onto the street at well past midnight, you should have just enough time for an hour or two of shuteye before the fife band strikes up once more and it's time to do it all over again.

018 | Getting to the art of the matter in Manchester

ENGLAND Head into Manchester's hip Northern Quarter and you'll need your eyes peeled and your wits about you. Not because you're in physical danger (the vibe's too cool for that) but because there's such a wealth of urban art here that you won't want to miss a trick. Look up, look down and all around, on walls, doorways, rooftops and pavements, and you'll see that the red brick and grey skies are leavened with bold, quirky or just plain lovely pieces of public art.

Start by getting your bearings. Even the street signs are artworks; ceramic letters in a specially created typeface, Cypher – white on blue for the streets running east/west, blue on white for those heading north/south. Then kick off at legendary indie bazaar Afflecks, where a galvanized steel tree stretches along a side wall and seven glorious mosaics celebrate city icons – Morrissey, Man U and *Corrie*, of course, but also Danger Mouse, Factory Records, Vimto, Warburton's, Emmeline Pankhurst and more. Glance down and you'll see snatches of a specially commissioned Lemn Sissay poem, *Flags*, which trots along a full mile's worth of pavement; then look up again at *Big Horn*, a twisted steel sculpture – half snake, half saxophone – wrapped around the remains of a listed building.

Everywhere there's joyous graffiti art. Just across from Afflecks is a massive, whole-building mural of the four elements, created by the renowned Subism art collective and brought to life by the folk trotting up and down its fire escape. Check out nearby Stevenson Square, where every three months local artists get free rein to transform the walls of a former public toilet – always an event.

You can't miss the giant blue-tit mural on Newton Street, but harder to spot are the terracotta parrots and other ornamental birds perched on buildings around Tib Street, a nod to the many pet shops formerly resident here. Once you know to look, you'll notice endless things to make you stop, smile and reflect. And when darkness falls and the spray paint fades from view, you can enjoy the quarter's other big draw – its nightlife.

019 | Climb the highest lighthouse in Britain

ENGLAND Its tower stands almost 100ft tall, but what really lifts Old Light above the rest of Britain's lighthouses is the 400ft hulk of granite on which it's perched. Set on the wild island of Lundy, eleven miles off the Devon coast, Old Light's great height ended up crippling it: the lantern spent much of its time obscured by soupy fogs and was replaced in 1897 by lower lights at the north and south of the island.

Old Light may be in retirement, but it's still the highest lighthouse in Britain, and visitors can reap the rewards of its failure with a visit to its lofty lamp chamber. Climb the 147 narrow, stone steps and ease into a deckchair to take in the dizzying panorama of the island plummeting into a gaping ocean. Or venture up at sunset to witness orange skies silhouetting the surrounding coastlines of Wales, Cornwall, Devon and Somerset.

The Lundy experience begins as you slip away from the mainland aboard *Oldenburg*. If you're lucky, dolphins will ride the bow wave, or you might spot a basking shark. You disembark in a place with only a handful of permanent residents and little regard for modern trappings. Walking is the only means of transport – which you may come to regret when tackling the gruelling incline to the verdant plateau that caps the island.

Lundy is Norse for "Puffin Island" and these bright-beaked birds can be spotted during April and May. Wildlife is far from sparse at other times of year, though, with seals hauling themselves onto rocks above which kittiwakes, fulmars and shags soar. Lundy ponies, Soay sheep and feral deer roam the wild terrain, and in the kelp forests of the surrounding sea lies one of only three Marine Nature Reserves in the UK.

Come on a day-trip if you must, but once the ferry leaves, the island really turns on its magic. Rest your head in a converted pigsty, a castle or the keeper's quarters of the lighthouse. Or better yet, in a place where there's no electricity after midnight, be a true Robinson Crusoe and camp out under the stars.

020 | Playing the Old Course at St Andrews

SCOTLAND There are several courses where you have to play a round at least once to call yourself a true golf devotee (Pine Valley, Pebble Beach and Augusta National to name but a few), but the Old Course at St Andrews is still "the one". Just walking out onto the first tee sends shivers down the spine, as you think how many feet, legendary or otherwise, have squared up to send a ball hurtling into the blustery winds before you.

St Andrews is the home of golf – the game's equivalent to Wembley or Wimbledon, a venue that is part of the mythology of the sport. The contemporary view may be that golf courses should be manufactured, created and sculpted, but St Andrews had a very different designer of sorts, in the form of nature itself. Here, the landscape is the course. It may not have the charm or the aesthetics of its American counterparts but it has real character. There's barely a tree to be seen, so the atmosphere is quite different from many modern courses. Similarly, there's little water around aside from Swilcan Burn, which has to be traversed on the 18th fairway, and the adjacent bruise-black waters of the North Sea.

This perceived lack of obstacles doesn't mean there's little to test the most experienced of players, though; the course is filled with hidden humps, bumps and dips, and there are man-made challenges, too – the infamous Road Hole Bunker on the 17th being the most notorious.

They've been teeing off here for around three hundred years and you'd guess it hasn't changed much, which is one of the things that makes this such a unique sporting experience. Be sure to take a local caddie, though – that way, he can worry about whether you should be using a 9-iron or a pitching wedge, and you can concentrate on absorbing the significance of it all.

021 | Sunset cruising around the Farne Islands

ENGLAND Seahouses, on the Northumberland coast, has all the trappings of a traditional English seaside town. However, if you look beyond the amusement arcades, hotels, and fish and chips, and head down to the harbour, you'll discover an entirely different world is to be found just a couple of miles out to sea. At the harbour, vendors in their huts compete for custom, all offering boat tours around one of the UK's natural gems: the craggy archipelago that is the Farne Islands.

Taking a boat and drawing closer to the islands across the expanse of water which separates them from the mainland, it becomes apparent that they're teeming with wildlife: 100,000 seabirds nest upon them each year, while grey seals loll about through all four seasons, giving birth to their young in the autumn. The islands are famed for attracting puffins in their droves between early spring and summer, but there's plenty more avian activity besides. Kittiwakes, guillemots, common terns, cormorants, shags, oystercatchers, and many more occupy the dolerite rocks; their cacophonous din making you feel a very long way from Seahouses.

The islands themselves are maintained by the National Trust, and between April and October certain boats are licensed to drop passengers for an even closer look. The sunset cruises, which run between May and September, don't do this, but on a summer's day you do get to watch the sun disappear behind the horizon as you sail, casting a beautiful light across the water. It's difficult to imagine a more perfect framing for the islands, or for Bamburgh Castle looking back towards the mainland.

ENGLAND It starts sometime in August, when the first of the after-party posters materialize along Ladbroke Grove and the plink-plonk rhythms of steelband rehearsals filter through the clamour of Portobello market. By the time the crowd barriers appear on street corners and the shop-owners begin covering their windows with party-scarred plywood, the feeling of anticipation is almost tangible: Carnival is coming. These familiar old streets are about to be transformed into a wash of colour, sound, movement and pure, unadulterated joy that makes this huge street festival the highlight of London's party calendar.

Carnival Sunday morning, and in streets eerily emptied of cars, sound-system guys, still bleary-eyed from the excesses of last night's warm-up parties, wire up their towering stacks of speakers, while fragrant smoke wafts from the stalls of early-bird jerk chicken chefs. And then a bass line trembles through the morning air, and

the trains begin to disgorge crowds of revellers, dressed to impress and brandishing their whistles and horns. Some head straight for the sound systems, spending the entire day moving from one to the other and stopping wherever the music takes them. Streets lined by mansion blocks become canyons of sound, and all you can see is a moving sea of people, jumping and blowing whistles as wave after wave of music ripples through the air.

But the backbone of Carnival is mas (masquerade), the parade of costumed bands that winds its way through the centre of the event. Crowds line up along the route, and Ladbroke Grove becomes a seething throng of floats and flags, sequins and feathers, as the mas bands cruise along, their members dancing up a storm to the tunes bouncing from the music trucks. And for the next two days, the only thing that matters is the delicious, anarchic freedom of dancing on the London streets.

022

Hitting the streets for the Notting Hill Carnival

Trundling along the West Highland Railway

SCOTLAND Even in a country as scenic as Scotland, you might not expect to combine travelling by train with classic views of the Scottish Highlands; the tracks are down in the glens, after all, tracing the lower contours of the steep-sided scenery. On the other hand, you might have to crane your neck occasionally, but at least you don't have to keep your eyes on the road. And you can always get out for a wander; some of the stations on the West Highland line are so remote that no public road connects them, and at each stop, a handful of deerstalkers, hikers, mountain bikers, photographers or day-trippers might get on or off. It'll be a few hours until the next train comes along, but that's not a problem. There's a lot to take in.

The scenery along the West Highland Railway is both epic in its breadth and compelling in its imagery. You travel at a very sedate pace in a fairly workaday train carriage from the centre of Glasgow and its bold Victorian buildings, along the banks of the gleaming Clyde estuary, up the thickly wooded loch shores of Argyll, across the desolate heathery bogs of Rannoch Moor and deep into the grand natural architecture of the Central Highlands, their dappled birch forests fringing verdant green slopes and mist-enveloped peaks.

After a couple of hours, the train judders gently into the first of its destinations, Fort William, set at the foot of Britain's highest peak, Ben Nevis. The second leg of the journey is a gradual pull towards the Hebrides. At Glenfinnan, the train glides over an impressive 21-arch viaduct, most famous these days for conveying Harry Potter on the *Hogwarts Express*. Not long afterwards, the line reaches the coast, where there are snatched glimpses of bumpy islands and silver sands, before you pull into the fishing port of Mallaig, with seagulls screeching overhead in the stiff, salty breeze, and the silhouette of Skye emerging from across the sea.

SCOTLAND Is this the oddest scheduled domestic flight in Britain? Picture yourself on a twenty-seater propeller plane that takes off from Glasgow and lands an hour later directly on the beach at Barra, the southernmost island of the Western Isles, also known as the Outer Hebrides. There is no official airstrip, nor are there even any lights on the sand, and the flight times shift to fit in with the tide tables, because at high tide the runway is submerged.

Even if Barra were a dreary destination, the flight would be worth taking simply for the glorious views it gives of Scotland's beautiful west coast and the islands of Mull, Skye, Rum and Eigg. It's probably also a rare flight on which the person who demonstrates the safety procedures then turns around, gets into the cockpit and flies the plane.

The Western Isles is the only part of Britain – and one of only a few in the world – where you can experience a truly stunning landscape in solitude; a hundred-mile-long archipelago consisting of a million exquisitely beautiful acres with a population that would leave Old Trafford stadium two-thirds empty.

Give yourself a week to drive slowly up through the island chain, from Barra to Eriskay, site of the famous "Whisky Galore" shipwreck (both the real and the fictional one), then South Uist to Benbecula, to North Uist, and finally to Harris and Lewis. Some islands are linked by causeways (all of which have "Beware: Otters Crossing" traffic signs), others by car ferries. Stop if you can at *Scarista House*, a gourmet paradise set alongside a vast, perpetually empty white sandy beach in the midst of a walker's Eden.

025 | Exploring the Divine in modern times

ENGLAND In Norfolk, it can feel like there's a church around every corner – and it's no surprise. With over 650 in total, no county has more, and there's nowhere in the world with a greater concentration of medieval churches. The county capital, Norwich, manages to squeeze in over seventy churches, 32 of them medieval, and two cathedrals – it's almost greedy. They're a perfect way to explore the area's history, see some fascinating art and architecture, and marvel at centuries-old graffiti.

While there's a great sense of pride in this heritage, the fact remains that not as many people need to use the churches for worship or as community spaces now; in fact, past censuses have marked Norwich out as England's least religious city. But rather than letting these amazing buildings crumble, trusts stepped in to restore and maintain the churches. Thanks to the Norwich Historic Churches Trust, you might peer into one of the city's churches and see a circus-skills class in progress, or an exhibition, antiques sale, a puppet show, play or concert.

Beyond Norwich, the Churches Conservation Trust works to give new life to religious buildings whose congregations have shrunk too much to maintain them. One of the most innovative uses to which the Trust has put the churches is as sustainable, unusual, unique camping accommodation – or "champing", as it's been called. Though the selection of churches varies, recent hits in Norfolk have included St Michael the Archangel in Booton, kitted out with camping lanterns, battery candles, fold-out camp beds, camping chairs and cushions for overnight guests.

While it's a bit younger than the county's medieval churches, having been built in the nineteenth century, St Michael's packs in plenty of history and intriguing facts. The architect, Reverend Whitwell Elwin, was a descendent of Pocahontas and friend of Darwin. He had no formal training, which may explain some of the building's more weird and wonderful elements, such as the minaret-like towers. He also had a lot of very attractive friends, if the windows are anything to go by – all the angels were modelled on women he knew. No wonder the imaginative English architect Sir Edwin Lutyens called the church "very naughty but built in the right spirit". It's truly a masterpiece, and one of the most memorable places to spend the night you could imagine.

026 | Into the valley: hearing a Welsh choir

WALES The road into Senghenydd from the imposing Welsh castle town of Caerphilly snakes along the side of a steep slope that drops into a rocky valley below. Lined with red-toned terraced houses constructed from local stone, the village almost clings to the hillside, and though coal mining died here long ago, the landscape still bears its scars. You may need to pause on the high street to allow stray sheep to cross the road – this is one of Britain's most rural corners.

Senghenydd is home to the Aber Valley Male Voice Choir, and though the choir gives concerts all over the world, it is here in the village's ex-servicemen's club that the sound is created and honed to perfection. The 59 men, many of them second- or third-generation choristers, perform everything from sombre hymns to *Bohemian Rhapsody*. Singing in both English and Welsh, their voices swell in four-part harmonies, as rich and complex as an orchestra.

Male voice choirs are a Welsh institution, part of the lives of thousands of working men from Snowdonia to the Rhondda. The choirs grew from the companionship and community spirit forged by the men who worked down the mines of the south and the quarries of the north.

Times have changed, but they are still going strong. The choir in Senghenydd practises twice a week (the men come as much for the camaraderie as for the music), and visitors are welcome to drop in on a rehearsal – an intimate and moving experience. The high proportion of silver hair in the choir ranks might raise concern about whether the younger generation will carry on the tradition. But with nearly 150 male voice choirs in a land just short of three million people, this unique part of Welsh life seems in no danger of disappearing.

027

Daydreaming in Oxford

ENGLAND Christchurch meadow at dusk and the timing is impeccable. The light is perfect – the harsh midday sun has softened, and now, rather than glinting off the spires and turrets of Merton and Corpus Christi colleges, it seems almost to embrace them, revealing their sharp angles and intricate carvings. They jut proudly above the quiet parklands and sports grounds, and the majestic Tom Tower of Christchurch presides graciously over it all. The noise of the city centre (just minutes to the north) has melted away completely. This is the University of Oxford at its best; the time when clichés about "dreaming spires" don't seem so overblown after all.

Such fleeting glimpses of this centuries-old seat of learning, right in the midst of a thoroughly modern city, are both disarming and exhilarating. For a brief time, the colleges shed any contemporary associations and you can imagine what it would have been like to study here, long before cars clogged the narrow streets and camera-toting tourists swarmed among the cloisters. The spires acquire a greater significance, appearing to reach up, high into the sky, almost signifying the pursuit of knowledge.

Back at ground level there's plenty more to stimulate the imagination. Wander down Oxford's narrow alleys and into its quiet corners, where you'll feel the presence of generations of scholars who've gone before. Duck into the *Eagle and Child* pub, where J.R.R. Tolkien and C.S. Lewis hobnobbed; stroll the echoing walkways of Magdalen College, through which comedian Dudley Moore and Nobel Laureate Seamus Heaney rushed to tutorials; and visit the cavernous dining hall at Christchurch, where the likes of John Locke and Albert Einstein once ate, but which is now more famous as Hogwarts' hall in the *Harry Potter* films. In Oxford, however, facts are far better than fiction.

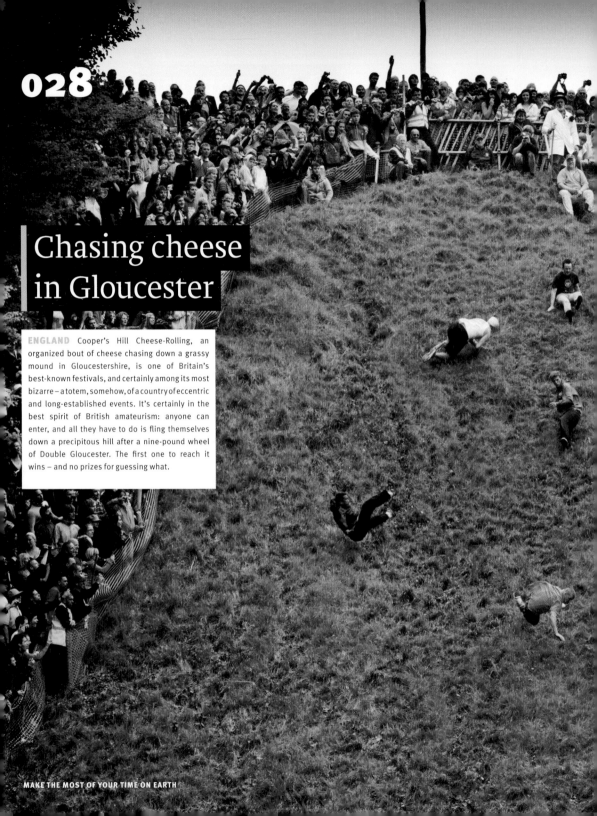

Chasing cheese in Gloucester

ENGLAND Cooper's Hill Cheese-Rolling, an organized bout of cheese chasing down a grassy mound in Gloucestershire, is one of Britain's best-known festivals, and certainly among its most bizarre – a totem, somehow, of a country of eccentric and long-established events. It's certainly in the best spirit of British amateurism: anyone can enter, and all they have to do is fling themselves down a precipitous hill after a nine-pound wheel of Double Gloucester. The first one to reach it wins – and no prizes for guessing what.

029

Tackling the velodrome in Glasgow

SCOTLAND There are no brakes. The gears are fixed. Your shoes are clipped into the pedals and don't clip out with ease. You're essentially attached to your bike. Then there's the question of how to slow it down. If it weren't for the words on the Sir Chris Hoy Velodrome website, that it "isn't just for elite athletes", you might be tempted to flee.

Riding at Glasgow's velodrome proves to be a revelation. There's no denying the impressive surroundings. But getting around it, at a human rather than superhuman pace, isn't as hard as it looks. The glossy 820ft (250m) track allows you to reach speeds of nearly 50 miles/hr. It's easy enough to brake without brakes, and with the words "it's easier if you go faster" ringing in your ears it's just a case of facing the fear. Soon even novice track cyclists are riding above the top line of those once-intimidating sloping sides. It's nothing but exhilarating.

030 | Watching starling murmurations in Brighton

ENGLAND You're not sure what it is at first. A rain cloud, maybe? Perhaps a shadow? But it's moving too fast, swirling and swooping and diving; contracting and expanding, almost as though it's alive – and then you hear the wings. It's a murmuration. Towards the end of each year, around forty thousand starlings arrive from as far away as Scandinavia to join their native cousins and converge on the derelict frame of Brighton's West Pier, in what's thought to be one of the most sensational roosts in the UK. They do it to keep warm and to exchange information, but mostly they do it for safety – imagine trying to pick out an individual bird in this vast, hypnotizing flock.

In the early evening, just before dusk, step out onto Brighton's pebbly beach and head west to the hulking great frame of the burnt pier – before long you'll see them. The birds will gradually start appearing from different directions: a couple here, a group there, coming together and flowing rhythmically against the orange sky. This is one of the most staggering natural displays on the planet. And then, as if there's been some invisible cue, they'll shoot downwards all at once to rest for the night.

The seafront base of Riddle & Finns, Brighton's renowned local seafood chain, is just across from the crumbling pier, and it's the perfect spot to finish watching the sunset over an aperitif. Sit down at a table for two beside the window with a plate of pan-fried scallops or hand-carved smoked salmon, and take in the view down over the pebbles and out to sea.

031 | Be enchanted by Holkham's magic

ENGLAND Is Holkham Bay in north Norfolk the best beach in Britain? It must certainly be the broadest. At high tide, you follow the private road from Holkham Hall, walk through a stretch of woods and expect to find the sea at your feet. But it is – literally – miles away: two miles at the very least, shimmering beyond a huge expanse of dunes, pools, flat sands and salt marsh. It's a wonderfully dramatic setting – this was the location for Gwyneth Paltrow's walk along the sands, as Viola, at the end of *Shakespeare in Love*.

The amazing thing about Holkham is that, even with the filming of a Hollywood movie in full swing, you could have wandered onto the beach and not noticed. It is that big. You saunter off from the crowds near the road's end and within a few minutes you're on your own, splashing through tidal pools, picking up the odd shell, or, if it's warm enough, diving into the sea. You can walk along the beach all the way to Wells (to the east) or Overy Staithe (west), or drop back from the sea and follow trails through woods of Corsican pines. Just beware going out onto the sandbanks when there's a rising tide; it comes in alarmingly fast.

Birdlife is exceptional around Holkham – which is a protected reserve – and you'll see colonies of pink-footed and Brent geese in winter, as well as oystercatchers, little terns and many other birds. And if you head down the coast to Cley-next-the-Sea or to Blakeney, you'll find even more riches, accompanied by rows of twitchers, camped behind binoculars. Take time to walk out to the hides at Cley Marshes, or for a boat ride to Blakeney Point, where you can watch the common and grey seals basking on the mud.

032 | Winning the prehistoric lottery

IRELAND Every year in Ireland, thousands of people do the Newgrange lottery. Entry is by application form, with the draw made in October by local schoolchildren. And the prize? The lucky winners are invited to a bleak, wintry field in the middle of County Meath on the longest night of the year, to huddle into a dank and claustrophobic tunnel and wait for the sun to come up.

It's not just any old field, though, but part of Brú na Boinne, one of Europe's most important archeological sites. A slow bend in the River Boyne cradles this extraordinary landscape of some forty Neolithic mounds, which served not only as graves but also as spiritual and ceremonial meeting places for the locals, five thousand years ago.

The tunnel belongs to the most famous passage mound, Newgrange, which stretches over 273ft in diameter, weighs 200,000 tons in total and is likely to have taken forty years to build. The lottery winners get to experience the annual astronomical event for which the tomb's passage was precisely and ingeniously designed: through a roofbox over the entrance, the first rays of the rising sun on the winter solstice shine unerringly into the burial chamber in the heart of the mound, 65ft away at the end of the passage.

Not everyone gets to win the lottery, of course, so throughout the year as part of an entertaining guided tour of the mound, visitors are shown a simulation of the solstice dawn in the central chamber. Once you've taken the tour and seen the impressive visitor centre, the perfect complement is to drive nineteen miles west to the Loughcrew Cairns, a group of thirty similar mounds that are largely unexcavated. Here, you borrow a torch and the key to the main passage tomb, Cairn T, and you'll almost certainly have the place to yourself. With views of up to sixteen counties on a clear day, you can let your imagination run wild in an unspoilt and enigmatic landscape.

Calling in the heavies at the Highland Games

SCOTLAND Throughout Scotland, not just in the Highlands, summer signals the onset of the Highland Games, from the smallest village get-togethers to the Giant Cowal Highland Gathering in Dunoon, which draws a crowd of around 20,000. Urbanites might blanch at the idea of alfresco Scottish country dancing, but with dog trials, tractors, fudge stalls and more cute animals than you could toss a caber at, the Highland Games are a guaranteed paradise for kids.

It's thought that the games originated in the eleventh century as a means of selecting soldiers through trials of strength and endurance. These events were formalized in the nineteenth century, partly as a result of Queen Victoria's romantic attachment to Highland culture: a culture that had in reality been brutally extinguished following the defeat of the Jacobites at Culloden.

The military origins of the games are recalled in displays of muscle- power by bulky bekilted local men, from tossing the caber (tree trunk) to hurling hammers and stones, and pitching bales of straw over a raised pole. Music and dance are also integral to the games, with pipe bands and small girls – kitted out in waistcoats, kilts and long woolly socks – performing reels and sword dances. You might also see showjumping, as well as sheepdogs being put through their paces, while the agricultural shows feature prize animals, from sleek ponies with intricate bows tied in their manes and tails to curly-horned rams.

034

Walk London's hidden highways

ENGLAND Go to Venice or Amsterdam, and you can hardly cross a street without tumbling into a canal. In London, you have to dig deeper. The Regent's Canal stretches from chichi Maida Vale the Thames-side Limehouse, cutting past London Zoo's aviaries, Camden's pop kids, Islington restaurants and Hackney high-rises on its way. Built in the early nineteenth century to connect London's docks with the grand Union Canal to Birmingham, its traffic was almost entirely lost to truck and rail by the 1950s.

Now (mostly) cleaned up, the canal and its tributaries feel like a wonderfully novel way to delve into a compelling, overexposed city. That's in part down to its submerged nature: much of its length is below street level, hidden by overgrown banks. Spend time by the water's edge and you feel utterly removed from the road and rail bridges above. When the route rises up or spews you back onto the street momentarily, you catch a brief glimpse of people seemingly oblivious to the green serpent that stretches across their city.

It's not all idyllic: for every lovely patch of reeds of or drifting duck, there's a bobbing beer can or the unmistakable judder of traffic. Stroll the busier stretches on a summer Sunday, when the walkers, cyclists and barges are out, and te canal can feel more like a major thoroughfare than an escape route. But this is a dynamic, breathing space: its energy is what makes it so vital, and makes the moments of quiet feel so special.

There are countless highlights: the spire of St Pancras station, soaring over a surprisingly secluded corner near revitalized King's Cross; Mile End's pictureesque nature reserve; and the bridges and whafs that connect Limehouse to the Isle of Dogs. The poet Paul Verlaine throught the isle's vast docks and warehouses classical in their majesty, calling them "astonishing...Tyre and Carthage all rolled in to one". Turned into smart flats or left to crumble, they are no longer the heartbeat of an industrial nation, but with their forgotten corners and fascinating history, they still feel magical.

035

Wacky races: the festivals of Llanwrtyd Wells

WALES Bathtubbing? Wife-carrying? No one does wacky quite like the Welsh, it seems, at least not like the natives of Llanwrtyd Wells. Each year, a series of bonkers events takes places that belies this small town's sleepy appearance – indeed, with a population of just over six hundred, it can justifiably claim to be the smallest town in Britain.

The event that kick-started all this lunacy, back in the 1980s – and purely arose as the result of a local bet – is the lung-busting Man versus Horse Marathon, a brutal 24-mile, multi-terrain endurance challenge between man and beast. And yep, you guessed correctly, the horse normally wins. The big competition nowadays, though it only occurs once every two years, is the eyebrow-raising World Alternative Games.

Conceived in 2012 as an antidote to the Olympic Games in London, it involves more than sixty madcap events. Utterly pointless, all of them, though try telling that to the legions of well-honed finger jousters, gravy wrestlers and backwards runners who descend upon the town in their

hundreds (sometimes thousands) in search of fame and glory, of sorts. Perhaps the most famous event, in August, is no less batty; it's the World Bog Snorkelling Championships, in which competitors, kitted out in flippers and goggles, have to complete two lengths of a murky, 180ft-long trench cut though a peat bog. The record, just for the record, currently stands at one minute twenty-two seconds, set in 2014.

The last, and possibly daftest, event of the year is the wonderfully named Real Ale Wobble, which involves two days of combined mountain biking and beer drinking – and even that, unsurprisingly, tends to appeal to the less serious-minded cyclist, or the most serious-minded drinker, depending upon which way you look at it. Either way, you're unlikely to be surprised to learn that this one is strictly non-competitive. Perhaps the best thing about all these events is that anyone is free to participate – so what are you waiting for?

036

Burning rubber at the Isle of Man TT

ENGLAND For fifty weeks of the year, the Isle of Man is a sleepy little place. Locals leave their doors unlocked, they stop to chat in the street, and they know the name of their next-door neighbour's cat. But for two weeks in summer, everything changes, as forty thousand visitors – with twelve thousand motorcycles – cross the Irish Sea and turn this quiet island into a rubber-burning, beer-swilling, eardrum-bursting maelstrom of a motorcycle festival.

The TT (Tourist Trophy) has been screeching round the Isle of Man for a hundred years, but only came about thanks to the island's political peculiarity. The Isle of Man is a Crown Dependency, but not a part of the UK or the EU – it has its own parliament and its own laws. And so when, in the early days of the automobile, the UK forbade motor racing on its public roads and imposed a speed limit of 20 miles/hr, race organizers made their way over the water.

And they've never left, although the race they devised in 1907 would be impossible to initiate today. It's the kind of nerve-tingling event that drives health and safety officers to drink: the 37-mile Mountain Course, which competitors lap several times, is no carefully cambered track – it's an ordinary road that winds its way through historic towns, screams along country roads, climbs up hills and takes in two hundred bends, many of which are not lined by grass or pavement but by bone-mashing brick walls. And the fastest riders complete the course at an average speed of 120 miles/hr.

Sad to say, they don't all reach the finish line. Around two hundred riders have taken their final tumble on the roads of the TT, and islanders will delight in describing the details to you over a pint of local Bushey's beer. They'll also tell you that, while many of their fellow Manx folk love the adrenaline, the triumph and the tragedy of those two weeks in summer, others are less enthusiastic. The combination of road closures and roistering bikers drives these malcontents to blow the dust from their door keys, to lock up their homes and seek refuge elsewhere – taking their daughters with them.

037

Barging down the Barrow

IRELAND There's a point on the River Barrow in County Kildare, about halfway between the country towns of Athy and Carlow, when you realize that you're in the middle of absolutely nowhere. A quick flick of the engine into neutral and you're surrounded by silence, nothing but the soothing slosh of water as the barge's bow glides slowly through the reeds. Flanked on both sides by trees and rolling fields of verdant emerald green, there's only one thing to do: sit back and soak up the solitude.

For nearly two hundred years, steel-boarded barges have plied the Grand Canal network, first transporting peat to Dublin and beyond, and latterly ferrying holidaymakers through the languid countryside. A week spent cruising along the Grand Canal and down the River Brrow, one of the most beautiful navigable stretches in Europe, is time spent recharging the soul: after a few early-morning maintenance checks, just undo the moorings, start up the engine and off you go, slowly chugging your way to the next ruined castle or cosy local.

Idle days make for idle ways, and the beauty of barging is that you have to do very little to keep your 30ft vessel on the straight and narrow. Manoeuvring thorugh a set of double locks without taking the whole thing with you provides a brief lull in the langour – racks have to be cranked, sluices oopened and pawls closed, all while the driver holds the barge steady to avoid getting beached on the back sill – but the rest of the day is spent cruising the backwaters of middle Ireland at a leisurely five miles/hr.

But if you're going to get nowhere fast, there can surely be fewer places better than the Barrow. Yellow iris, cuckoo flower and heavily scented meadowsweet line the river banks, herons let your barge get tantalizingly close before launching off across the water, and there's a traditional pub at every turn, each serving finer Guiness than the last.

038 | Watching the hurling at Croke Park

IRELAND The player leaps like a basketball star through a crowd of desperate opponents and flailing sticks. Barely visible to the naked eye, the arcing ball somehow lodges in his upstretched palm. Dropping to the ground, he shimmies his way out of trouble, the ball now delicately balanced on the flat end of his hurley, then bang! With a graceful, scything pull, he slots the ball through the narrow uprights, seventy yards away.

Such is the stuff of Irish boyhood dreams, an idealized sequence of hurling on continual rewind. With similarities to lacrosse and hockey – though it's not really like either – hurling is a thrilling mix of athleticism, timing, outrageous bravery and sublime skill. Said to be the fastest team game in the world, it can be readily enjoyed by anyone with an eye for sport.

The best place to watch a match is Dublin's vast Croke Park, the iconic headquarters of the GAA (Gaelic Athletic Association).

In this magnificent, 80,000-seater stadium, you'll experience all the colour, banter and passion of inter-county rivalry. And before the game, you can visit the excellent GAA Museum to get up to speed on hurling and its younger brother, Gaelic football, ancient sports whose renaissance was entwined with the struggle for Irish independence. Here, you'll learn about the first Bloody Sunday in 1920, when British troops opened fire on a match at this very ground, killing twelve spectators and one of the players. You'll be introduced to the modern-day descendants of Cúchulain, the greatest warrior-hero of Irish mythology, who is said to have invented hurling: star players of the last century including flat-capped Christy Ring of Cork and more recent icons such as Kilkenny's D.J. Carey. And finally, you can attempt to hit a hurling ball yourself – after a few fresh-air shots, you'll soon appreciate the intricate skills the game requires.

039 | Walking the walls of Conwy Castle

WALES Up on Conwy Castle's battlements the wind whips around the eight solid towers that have stood on this rocky knoll for over seven hundred years. It's a superb spot with long views out across the surrounding landscape, but look down from the castle's magnificent curtain walls and you'll also see all the elements that combined to make Conwy one of the most impressive fortresses of its day.

The castle occupies an important site, beside the tidal mud flats of the Conwy Estuary where pearl mussels have been harvested for centuries. To the south lie the northern peaks of Snowdonia, the mountains where the Welsh have traditionally sought refuge from invaders such as the Norman English, who built this castle around 1283.

Conwy formed a crucial link in Edward I's "Iron Ring" of eight castles around North Wales, designed to finally crush the last vestiges of Welsh resistance to his rule. Gazing upon this imposing fortress, which

took just five years to build and is still largely intact, it isn't hard to understand why he was successful.

A key part of the castle's design was its integration with the town, so that the two could support each other, and from the battlements a three-quarter-mile ring of intact town walls, punctuated with 21 towers, loops out from the base of the castle, encircling Conwy's old town. For centuries, the Welsh were forced to live outside the town walls while the English prospered within; the latter left behind a fine legacy in the form of the fourteenth-century half-timbered Aberconwy House and Plas Mawr, Britain's best-preserved Elizabethan town house.

Finish off by heading into town and walking a circuit of the 30ft-high town walls. Start at the highest point (tower 13), where you get a superb view across the slate roofs of the town to the castle, and wander down towards the river where a pint on the quay outside the *Liverpool Arms* is *de rigueur* on a fine evening.

040 | Let there be light: Blackpool's Illuminations

ENGLAND When autumn knocks, the temperature begins to drop and other resorts are shutting up shop, one seaside town switches on. From the end of August until early November, the Blackpool Illuminations light up the seafront – and if you've a penchant for gaudy, nostalgic, none-too-highbrow fun, you should get your coat on and come.

Comprising around a million lights, the glittering display stretches six miles from north to south, passing all three piers and the iconic Blackpool Tower. Garlands and overhead displays festoon the main drag, some magical (fairy crowns), others mystifying (eyeballs), but easily the best section is around the "Cliffs" area at Bispham, where some forty large tableaux deliver the oohs and aahs. You'll find a giant Noddy and Big Ears, Daleks, a Mad Hatter's Tea Party and the Teddy Bears' Picnic (this last some 25 years old and endearingly down at heel), as well as a less garish World War I tribute and an incongruously intellectual installation on the human brain.

The route is a fair old schlep on foot, but you can drive it (in bumper-to-bumper traffic), take a horse and carriage (pricey), or, best of all, hop on one of the heritage trams that trundle along the seafront, the most spectacular lit up to look like ocean liners or locomotives.

The lights come on at dusk, but Blackpool offers plenty to feast your eyes on during the day, too. Check out The Great Promenade Show, a series of site-specific contemporary sculptures along the prom, including *They Shoot Horses, Don't They?*, a giant rotating mirror ball that's a nod to the resort's ballroom heritage. And don't miss The Comedy Carpet outside the Tower, a brilliant typographic display of jokes and catchphrases from around one thousand comedians and writers.

Amazingly, the whole experience is free. All you'll need to buy is a tram ticket, a bag of salty chips and a novelty stick of rock. And never mind if it rains – the lights look even more gorgeous shimmering in the puddles.

041

Follow in the footsteps of kings and queens at Bath Spa

ENGLAND For almost twenty years at the end of the last century, Britain's most famous spa town had no thermal baths. The opening of the new Thermae Bath Spa in 2006, at the centre of this World Heritage City, was therefore a watershed in Bath's history. Once the haunt of the Roman elite who founded the city 2000 years ago, and later frequented by British royalty including Elizabeth I and Charles II, Britain's only natural thermal spa boasts a uniquely soothing atmosphere with gentle lighting and curative vapours, the surrounding grandeur testament to the importance given to these therapeutic waters.

The spa's centrepiece is its rooftop pool, where on cold winter evenings you can enjoy majestic views of Bath's Abbey and its genteel Georgian architecture through wisps of rising steam from the pool's 33.5°C water. The Celts thought that the goddess Sul was the force behind the spring, but we now know that the waters probably fell as rain in the nearby Mendip Hills some 10,000 years ago, before being pushed 1.5 miles upwards through bedrock and limestone to arrive at the pools enriched with minerals and hot enough to treat respiratory, muscular and skin problems.

The spa's remarkable design contrasts existing listed Georgian buildings and colonnades with contemporary glass curves and fountains, employing local Bath stone to impressive effect. The covered Minerva Bath provides thermal water jets for shoulder massage, while separate steam rooms offer eucalyptus, mint and lavender scents and there is a giant thermal shower to reinvigorate the soul.

When you've had your fill of rest and relaxation, the old Roman Baths nearby are well worth a visit, too – they offer one of the world's best-preserved insights into Roman culture, complete with authentic Latin graffiti.

Finding heaven on Earth in Cornwall

042

ENGLAND A disused clay pit may seem like an odd location for Britain's very own ecological paradise, but then everything about Cornwall's Eden Project is refreshingly far from conventional. From the conception of creating a unique ecosystem that could showcase the diversity of the world's plant life, through to the execution – a series of bulbous, alien-like, geodesic biomes wedged into the hillside of a crater – the designers have never been anything less than innovative.

The gigantic humid Rainforest Biome, the largest conservatory in the world, is kept at a constant temperature of 30°c. Besides housing lofty trees and creepers that scale its full 160ft height, the biome takes visitors on an interesting journey through tropical agriculture from coffee growing to the banana trade, to rice production and finding a cure for leukaemia. There's even a life-size replica of a bamboo Malaysian jungle home, and a spectacular treetop Canopy Walkway.

The smaller Mediterranean Biome reconstitutes the Mediterranean, California and parts of South Africa under one roof (unusually composed of Teflon-coated "ETFE cushions"), showing how regions like these have been cultivated for centuries in order to fill the world's supermarket shelves. There's also a well-informed introduction to the evils of the tobacco trade, and the centrepiece is a joyful homage to the god of wine, Bacchus, with wild, twisting sculptural installations of a Bacchanalian orgy surrounded by vines. The outdoor garden continues the focus on sustainable ethics, with a handful of inspiring allotments alongside an eye-opening sculpture made from waste.

Perhaps all this research and construction represents how future generations will exist? You'd better Adam'n'Eve-it. Maybe we've already taken our chunk of the apple, or maybe, with a visit to the Eden Project, we've enough information to create change in our everyday lives and look after our very own biome: planet Earth.

043 | Folking out under the hills

WALES Convertibles sell better in Britain than in much of the Mediterranean. That might make it sound like the inhabitants of this damp island are stupid. A kinder explanation is that they just enjoy the sunshine when it comes – an impression that will have struck anyone who's attended a pop festival in the UK with the force of a stage diver. Tales of rains that swallow tents at Glastonbury and turn Bestival into a treacherous mudbath acquire legendary proportions. When the sun shines and the right band is on stage, people tell fewer stories, but the smiles are as broad as they come. And Green Man, which has had its share of blissful warmth and endless drizzle, is the pick of the festive crop.

Located between Abergavenny and the Brecon Beacons, its estate location feels classically picturesque, but hills rear around the site, giving it that touch of the wilderness. Green Man's capacity (20,000 at last count) is big enough to bestow a sense of occasion but small enough to mean you might manage to find your tent and your friends,

which will prove a relief to anyone who's spent hours trekking back and forth around Glastonbury's acres. There's no big branding here, and the staff spend more time helping you out than telling you what you can't do – even the toilets are decidedly bearable. Green Man also manages the neat trick of being at once family- and hedonist-friendly – the DJ tent booms through the witching hours, but kids will enjoy the stalls, gardens and Little Folk children's area.

Indeed, while many festivals that try to be all things to all people end up tying themselves in knots, Green Man pulls out some crackers. There aren't many stadium headliners here, but the intriguing assortment of folk veterans, psychedelic hipsters and bluesy rockers has been picked by organizers who care deeply about their music. They've seen Animal Collective get the crowd frugging to swelling math-rock, Richard Thompson play nimble songs of love and loss, Bon Iver bring his Vermont laments to a sunny Saturday and Natural Milk Hotel inspire a joyful indie singalong. Worth the risk of rain? You bet.

044 | Following the Oyster Trail in Galway

IRELAND A canny bit of marketing may lie behind the origins of the Galway International Oyster Festival, but Ireland's longest-running and greatest gourmet extravaganza continues to celebrate the arrival of the new oyster season in the finest way possible: with a three-day furore of drinking, dancing and crustacean guzzling.

Just after midday in Eyre Square, Galway's mayor cracks open the first oyster of the season, knocks it back in one gulp, and declares the festival officially open – just as he or she has done since the 1950s, when the festival's devisers were searching for something that could extend the tourist season into September. A parade of marching bands, vintage cars, oyster openers, dignitaries and the like then makes its way down the town's main street and along the bank of the River Corrib, its destination the festival marquee, and the World Oyster Opening Championship.

All this pomp, however, is purely a sideshow, albeit a colourful one, to the weekend's main attraction, the Guinness Oyster Trail – the real backbone of the party and one of the greatest Irish pub crawls ever devised. The Trail consists of some thirty boozers dotted around the town, each providing a host of live music, comedy and dance acts over the entire period and, more importantly, offering free oysters with a pint of Guinness – every pub on the Oyster Trail employs a full-time oyster-opener throughout the weekend, who frantically and ceaselessly liberates the delicious creatures from their shells.

The traditional objective is to down a pint and a couple of oysters in every pub along the Trail over the three days – that's around thirty pints and up to one hundred oysters. If you can do this and still make it down for breakfast on the Sunday morning, you need never prove yourself again.

045 | Soaking up the Edinburgh Festival

SCOTLAND People talk about culture vultures flocking to the Edinburgh Festival in August, but the truth is that for an event this big you need the stamina of an ox, the appetite of a hippo and the nocturnal characteristics of an owl. The sheer scale and diversity of what's going on in the Scottish capital each August can be hard to digest properly – over half a dozen separate festivals take place simultaneously featuring thousands of different shows in more than two hundred venues. Not to mention the street acts, the buskers, the bizarrely dressed leafleters – and the simple fascination to be had just watching it all swirl around you.

How do you do the Festival without fear of disappointment or exhaustion? Book early for something significant in the International Festival, perhaps one of the world's great philharmonic orchestras at the Usher Hall. Wander into the tented Book Festival in gracious Charlotte Square and enjoy a reading and erudite discussion with a favourite author. As for the Fringe Festival, take a chance on an

intriguing-sounding piece of theatre by a company you've never heard of in a venue you struggle to find. After all, you've scoured the reviews in the papers over a couple of cappuccinos in a pleasant café and found a four-star show you can fit in before the new film by that director you've admired for a while.

Pick up a last-minute offer on cheap tickets for a comedian you've seen do a nearly hilarious slot on telly, then join the crowds shuffling up the Royal Mile to the nightly Military Tattoo, thrilling its multinational audience with pomp, ceremony and massed pipe bands, rounded off with fireworks crashing around the castle's battlements.

Time for more? There's probably a risqué cabaret going on at one of the Fringe venues, or a crazy Hungarian folk band stomping its way into the wee small hours in a folk club. But if you're going to do it all again tomorrow, then find a quiet corner of a cosy, wood-panelled pub and order a dram of whisky. Good stuff, this culture.

046 | Enjoying the seasons of the Scillies

ENGLAND It's no exaggeration to say that, from London, you can get to the Caribbean more quickly than to the Scillies. But then, that's part of the appeal. You take the night train down to Penzance and then hop on the *Scillonian* ferry (not for the queasy) or the helicopter out over the Atlantic.

What awaits depends very much on the weather. The Scillies out of season are bracing, as wind and rain batter these low island outcrops. Wrapped in waterproofs, you can still have fun, squelching over wet bracken and spongy turf to odd outcrops of ruined castles, or picking through the profusion of shells on the beaches. And if you can afford a room at the *Hell Bay Hotel* on Bryher, then you can top off the day with a first-rate meal while gazing at original sculptures and paintings by Barbara Hepworth and Ivor Hitchens.

In summer, when the sun's out, it's a very different scene, and you can swim, go boating, even learn to scuba dive – the water is crystal clear and there are numerous wrecks. It can be a cheap holiday, too, since for only a few pounds you can pitch a tent at the Bryher campsite and enjoy one of the loveliest views in Europe. From there, wander down to the *Fraggle Rock* pub for a pint and a crab sandwich, and then, if the tide's right, wade across to the neighbouring island of Tresco, and explore the subtropical Abbey Gardens.

Bryher's a favourite of many. Scilly-fans are fiercely loyal. But you can have as good a time on St Martin's, which has arguably the best beaches, or on the diminutive St Agnes, with its wind-sculpted granite and a brilliantly sited pub, *The Turk's Head*. St Mary's has its devotees, too, but with the islands' main town, regular roads and cars, it lacks essential isolated romance. For that, you'll need to go to Bryher.

047 | Walking in the mountains of Mourne

NORTHERN IRELAND The mountains rise above the seaside town of Newcastle like green giants, with Slieve Donard the highest, almost 3000ft above the sandy strand of Dundrum Bay. Donard is just one of more than twenty peaks in County Down's Kingdom of Mourne (as the tourist office likes to call it), with a dozen of them towering over 2000ft. Conveniently grouped together in a range that is just seven miles broad and about fourteen miles long, they are surprisingly overlooked – especially by many locals. On foot, in a landscape with no interior roads, you feel as if you have reached a magical oasis of high ground, a pure space that is part *Finian's Rainbow* and part Middle Earth.

Cutting across the heart of the Mournes is a dry-stone wall, part of a 22-mile barrier built in the 1920s to keep livestock out of the water catchment for the Silent Valley Reservoir. When a mist rolls off the sea, or a rain squall hits hard, the wall is a shelter, and a guide.

This is a wet place where the Glen River flows from the flanks of Slieve Commedagh and through Donard Wood. Some slopes are bog, and ragged black-faced sheep shelter behind clumps of golden gorse. Up here, peregrines ride on the wind and sharp-beaked ravens hope to scavenge the corpse of a lamb or two. Tied to the earth, you can follow the Brandy Pad, a scenic smugglers' track leading over the mountains from the Bloody River through Hare's Gap and down again to Clonachullion. This is ancient land, and prehistoric cairns and stone graves – said to mark the resting place of Irish chiefs – dot the hills, peering through the mist to meet you.

048 | Staking claims: a tour of the Belfast murals

NORTHERN IRELAND Mention the Falls Road and Shankill districts of Belfast, and up flash images of bitter sectarian street battles between the pro-British, Protestant Loyalists and the pro-Irish, largely Catholic Republicans. These close neighbours have long used wall paintings to stake territorial claims, and now that Belfast is firmly on the tourist agenda, the murals have become a star attraction.

Walking west from central Belfast to the Republican Falls Road, you can't miss the huge painted images adorning almost all end-terrace walls. Some are tributes to the fallen, while others commemorate specific incidents such as the 1981 prison hunger strike when Bobby Sands, along with nine comrades, became a Republican martyr. Elsewhere, "Free Ireland" slogans depict wrists shackled by manacles labelled "Made in Britain". The message could hardly be clearer.

A few steps up the side streets north of the Falls Road you hit the Peace Line, a fortified boundary of razor wire and CCTV cameras that separates the road from Loyalist Shankill.

There's an altogether more militaristic feel to Shankill, with guns on almost every mural. Union Jacks are ubiquitous, even on the kerbstones, and one whole housing estate is ringed by red, white and blue kerbing. Most murals also bear the red hand of Ulster, which forms the centrepiece of the Ulster Flag and features on the emblems of both the UVF and UDA paramilitary organizations.

In these districts, passions run high and you'd think it would feel unsettling being a rubbernecking tourist in a place that has witnessed so much bloodshed. But most people are just pleased that you're interested. If you feel at all intimidated or want a deeper insight, opt for one of the excellent taxi tours that visit both Falls Road and Shankill.

Mountain biking Welsh trails

049

WALES It's not often that the modest mountains of Wales can compete with giants like the Alps or the Rockies, but when it comes to mountain biking, the trails that run through the craggy peaks of Snowdonia, the high moorlands of the Cambrian Mountains, and the deep, green valleys of South Wales are more than a match for their loftier counterparts. Indeed, the International Mountain Biking Association has long rated Wales as one of the planet's top destinations.

Over the last decade or so, a series of purpose-built mountain-biking centres has been created throughout the country, providing world-class riding for everyone from rank beginner through to potential-world-cup downhiller. From easy, gently undulating trails along former rail lines that once served the heavy industry of the South Wales valleys, to the steep, rooty, rocky single tracks that run through the cloud-shadowed hills of North Wales, this is mountain biking at its finest.

Take a centre such as Coed-y-Brenin in Snowdonia National Park. You can ride all day here through deep pine forests, beside tumbling cascades, and alongside open pastures whose vistas stretch from the blue-green water of the Irish Sea to the misty mountaintops of the Snowdon range – and that just covers a couple of trails at only one of seven mountain-bike centres located around the country.

The tracks have been designed to be ridden year-round – despite the country's (somewhat) undeserved reputation for inclement weather, Welsh trails, like Welsh riders, can deal with anything that's thrown at them, and they remain open in all conditions. That's not to say you should wait for the next downpour – hit the trails when the sun is shining, when the views stretch far into the distance, and you'll begin to understand why this really is some of the finest mountain biking on Earth.

Staying off the grid in a treehouse

050

WALES First you'll see the staircase, its wooden steps spiralling up past broad leaves and low-hanging branches to the forest canopy above. Then you'll spot the treehouse: a low, curved pod nestled thirty feet in the air with two round windows, which almost lend it the expression of a great, wooden owl. This is Gwdy Hw – "owl" in Welsh. It's one of six owned by Living Room Treehouses, set on a 200-acre organic sheep farm deep in the Welsh valleys, just south of Snowdonia National Park.

Rattle across the rickety rope bridge – it's impossible to cross it elegantly – and slide open the glass door. Inside, you'll see a comfy double bed and rudimentary kitchen, as well as a wood-burning stove surrounded by flickering tealights. Rustle up a quick lunch, keeping a keen eye out for thieving squirrels, and enjoy it as you take in the forest views from the wooden deck. But you might not spend much time up here with all the distractions down below, namely the rope swing across

the stream, and the hammock swinging gently in the breeze – the perfect place for relaxing with a book.

When you're ready to explore farther, all you have to do is head down the hill and across the bridge. Pick up some locally made honey and jams from the little cupboard beside the road, leaving a few coins in the honesty box, and embark on the pleasant, winding hike up Glyndwr's Way for a picnic atop Moel Eiddew – also known locally as Power Mountain. Take in the sweeping views over the valleys: the pastoral, beautifully green landscape divided by hedges and dotted with sheep.

All of Living Room's treehouses are off-grid and eco-friendly, featuring alfresco showers heated by the wood-burning stoves, as well as ingenious Swedish compost loos that sit high in the treetops.

When the sun begins to dip, you can light some candles, sit back on the deck with a mug of hot chocolate, and keep a watchful eye for owls.

051 | Surfing the Severn Bore

ENGLAND Autumn mist swirls across the placid waters of the River Severn, and a kingfisher flits along the river bank in a spark of colour. Gradually, from downriver, a noise like the murmuring of a distant crowd develops into a roar, then suddenly a mighty wall of brown water appears across the entire width of the river, topped here and there by a creamy curl where the wave is racing to get ahead of itself.

This is the Severn Bore, one of the longest and biggest tidal bores in the world. It's a startling spectacle when you're watching from the river bank. If you're actually in the river, it can be terrifying.

The river, though, is where you'll be if you choose to surf the Bore. Since the sixties, surfers from all over the world have made their way to the Severn to catch this remarkable wave. It occurs on the biggest tides of the year when Atlantic waters from the Bristol Channel surge up the Severn Estuary at as much as twelve miles/hr and become funnelled between the ever-narrowing river banks to create one of Britain's most bizarre natural phenomena.

If the equinoxes coincide with big Atlantic swells, the wave may be as much as 6ft high, tearing off overhanging tree branches, sweeping away sections of river bank and providing a ride that can last for several miles. It's a challenge even for a competent surfer. Non-surfers will want to stay bankside, from where the Bore is simply a strange and magnificent sight.

052 | Hoarding books in Hay-on-Wye

WALES Though a drive through the electrically green countryside that surrounds Hay-on-Wye makes for a perfectly lovely afternoon, a more potent draw is the sleepy Welsh town's mouthwatering amount of printed matter: with over a million books crammed into its ageing stores, quaint, cobblestoned Hay-on-Wye (Y Gelli, in Welsh) is a bibliophilic Mecca to be reckoned with. Dusty volumes are packed in like sardines, some of them in shops tucked away down alleyways verdant with moss and mildew. Mouldering British cookbooks fight for shelf space with plant-taxonomy guides, romance novels and pricey but lavishly produced first editions.

To unearth these treasures the intrepid bookhunter need only meander into one of the many bookshops that liberally dot the town. Mystery aficionados should check out Murder & Mayhem, while a visit to The Poetry Bookshop is *de rigueur* for fans of verse.

One of the largest and most diverse collections can be found at the Hay Cinema Bookshop. Here, an enchanting mix of rickety mini staircases, two sprawling floors and a labyrinthine series of rooms loosely divided by subject matter creates a unique book-browsing space that seems to exist outside of the space-time continuum for the way in which it can so wholly consume an afternoon.

Stay long enough and your faith that there's an underlying logic to the bookshelves' progression from "Fifteenth-century Russian History" to "British Water Fowl" to "Erotica" will grow wonderfully, psychotically strong.

053 | Nature's architects: the Beaver Trial in Argyll

SCOTLAND It's not an everyday sighting, but when you do catch a glimpse, it really is a special moment. Once widespread in the United Kingdom, by the sixteenth century beavers were practically hunted to extinction. In 2009, however, a colony from Norway was reintroduced into Knapdale Forest – a magnificent ancient woodland in the heart of Argyll – and it's now possible to see these elusive creatures going about their business once more. If you're lucky.

Monitored by a team of ecologists, the Scottish Beaver Trial is just that, a trial, and so far it has been a success. To date, some fourteen babies (kits) have been born, but it's the beavers' impact on the landscape that has been most impressive, from the creation of new habitats for other species (for example, by establishing new pools for insects and birds) to the control of water flow in the lochs. Their presence has caught the imagination of the public too, judging by the sharp increase in visitor numbers to the region. The project has not been without its critics, however, with some suggestion that the animals are damaging the local habitats through, for example, unnecessary or excessive tree-felling. Either way, it'll be up to the government to decide whether the trial remains a viable long-term venture.

So what are the chances of a sighting? Your best bet is to visit at either dawn or dusk. Make your way from the interpretation centre in Barnluasgan, following the trail to Dubh Loch and a viewing platform, to discover the first evidence of beaver enterprise – a remarkable 59ft-long dam, just one of several dotted around the three lochs that these industrious architects inhabit. All around you'll see sharply gnawed tree stumps protruding from the water's edge, and garage-sized lodges, each one a chaotic tangle of severed branches, wood and mud – wattle and daub by any other name. Bring binoculars, midge repellent and refreshments – and be prepared to wait. And wait. That moment when a slick, black head emerges from the water before merrily going about its business, either chomping away at the nearest stump or hastily re.arranging its lodge, is worth every minute.

Gunpowder, treason and plot: bonfire night in Lewes

054

ENGLAND The first week of November sees one of the eccentric English's most irresponsible, unruly and downright dangerous festivals – Bonfire Night. Up and down the country, human effigies are burned in back gardens and fireworks are set off – all in the name of Guy Fawkes' foiled attempt to blow up the Houses of Parliament in 1605 – but in the otherwise peaceful market town of Lewes, things are taken to extremes. Imagine a head-on collision between Halloween and Mardi Gras and you're well on your way to picturing Bonfire Night, Lewes-style.

Throughout the evening, smoke fills the Lewes air, giving the steep and narrow streets an eerie, almost medieval feel. As the evening draws on, rowdy torch-lit processions make their way through the streets, pausing to hurl barrels of burning tar into the River Ouse before dispersing to their own part of town to stoke up their bonfires.

Establishment propaganda in the aftermath of the so-called Gunpowder Plot ensured that Fawkes' name was forever associated with treason and treachery, and that "bone fires" – featuring burnings in effigy of villains of the day – became inextricably linked with his name. As the societies head for their own bonfires, they are each trailed by huge papier-mâché figures. Crammed full of fireworks themselves, these "guys" are defended by a number of "prelates", who fearlessly bat the rockets thrown at them by members of rival societies back into the crowd.

Forget the limp burgers of mainstream displays and lame sparklers suitable for use at home – for a real pyrotechnic party, Lewes is king.

Need to know

001 Whitstable's Oyster Festival is held in July or Aug. For more, see ⓦ whitstableoysterfestival.co.uk.

002 Outdoor performances at Shakespeare's Globe run in the summer from April to October. Standing tickets available; visit ⓦ shakespearesglobe.com.

003 Information can be found at the official website, ⓦ tarbarrels.co.uk, but updates are usually posted on ⓦ facebook.com/tarbarrels or ⓦ twitter.com/ottery-tarbarrel.

004 The Barrowland is at 244 Gallowgate, Glasgow (ⓦ barrowland-ballroom.co.uk).

005 Boats run out to the Skelligs (ⓦ skelligislands.com), usually May–Sept, from several points on the Kerry coast, including Portmagee.

006 Bat safari tours are run by Scudamores; visit ⓦ scudamores.com. Tours run on Friday and Saturday evenings, typically from May to late September.

007 Entry to the theatre is £5; performances are individually priced. Further details on pricing, access and how to get there can be found at ⓦ minack.com.

008 Borrowdale (ⓦ nationatrust.org.uk/borrowdale) is in the heart of the Lake District, running south of Keswick for eight miles. Parking is limited so catch the local bus from Keswick.

009 Visit the official National Trail website for advice, information and details of accommodation options along the route – they're mainly pubs and B&Bs ⓦ nationaltrail.co.uk/yorkshire-wolds-way.

010 Book ahead for Pudding Club meetings at ⓦ puddingclub.com. To book a stay in one of the themed rooms, go to ⓦ threewayshousehotel.com/pudding_club. For information on Hidcote Manor, see ⓦ nationaltrust.org.uk/hidcote.

011 Most people walk the Pennine Way in two to three weeks, covering daily distances of 12 to 20 miles. For more, see ⓦ nationaltrail.co.uk/pennine-way.

012 Cape Wrath is used as an MOD air bombing range and access is restricted at times; see ⓦ visitcapewrath .com and ⓦ johnmuirtrust.org for more information.

013 You can rent bikes at several points throughout the New Forest. See ⓦ thenewforest.co.uk for more details.

014 Rooms at Hever Castle (ⓦ hevercastle.co.uk) start at £110.

015 The North Coast 500 website has cycle itineraries, accommodation and more; ⓦ northcoast500.com

016 Contact the High Moorland Visitor Centre (ⓦ dartmoor-npa.gov.uk) for details.

017 The Common Ridings are usually held in June. For more details, see ⓦ hawickcommonriding.co.uk.

018 It's a short walk to the Northern Quarter from Manchester's Piccadilly train station. Afflecks is open daily (ⓦ afflecks.com). For info on the Stevenson Square art project, check the website ⓦ outhousemcr .thecolouringbox.co.uk.

019 Depart from Ilfracombe or Bideford on board the MS Oldenburg between April and Oct, which runs several times a week. From Nov to March a helicopter service runs from Hartland Point on Mondays and Fridays. See ⓦ landmarktrust.org.uk/lundyisland.

020 Check details on ⓦ standrews.com.

021 Trips are available all year round from Seahouses Harbour, NE68 7RN; for more information on tour providers see ⓦ nationaltrust.org.uk/farne-islands.

022 See ⓦ nhcarnival.org for information on the carnival.

023 Trains run from Glasgow on the West Highland Line to Fort William and then onto Mallaig (5hr). See ⓦ scotrail.co.uk.

024 See ⓦ isleofbarra.com for more information on Barra; for more on Scarista House see ⓦ scarista-house.com.

025 Find out more about the Churches Conservation Trust at ⓦ visitchurches.org.uk, and about the Norwich Historic Churches Trust at ⓦ nhct-norwich.org. As most churches are unheated, champing only happens in the warmer months; book at ⓦ champing.co.uk.

026 For more information on the Aber Valley Male Voice Choir, see ⓦ aber-valleymvc.co.uk.

027 Oxford is easily accessible by bus from Victoria Coach Station (1hr 30min; check ⓦ nationalexpress.com for schedules) or train from Paddington and Marylebone stations (1hr; for details see ⓦ nationalrail.co.uk).

028 Cooper's Hill Cheese-Rolling (ⓦ facebook.com/BrockworthCheeseRoll) starts at noon on the end-of-May bank holiday Mon.

029 The Sir Chris Hoy Velodrome is part of Glasgow's Emirates Arena (ⓦ emiratesarena.co.uk).

030 Visit Brighton in December for the best chance of seeing the starling murmurations. For more information, check ⓦ brighton-hove.gov.uk.

031 For a picnic lunch on the beach, stock up at the wonderful Picnic Fayre deli in Cley-next-the-Sea (ⓦ picnicfayre.co.uk).

032 The Brú na Boinne visitor centre is 10km southwest of Drogheda in County Meath. For more, see ⓦ worldheritageireland.ie. The Loughcrew Cairns, near Oldcastle, are accessible only with your own transport – pick up the key for Cairn T from the coffee shop at Loughcrew Gardens (ⓦ loughcrew.com).

033 Highland Games are held from May to Sept – the big gatherings include Braemar (ⓦ braemargathering .org) and Cowal (ⓦ cowalgathering.com).

034 The London Canal Museum, 12–13 New Wharf Rd (ⓦ canalmuseum.org.uk), is worth a look. Good tube stops from which to explore the canal include Warwick Avenue, Camden Town, Angel, Mile End and Limehouse.

035 Four daily trains stop at Llanwrtyd Wells en route between Shrewsbury and Swansea. Details of all events can be found at ⓦ worldalternativegames.com and ⓦ www.green-events.co.uk.

036 TT race week is held at the end of May/early June; for more information, see ⓦ iomtt.com.

037 For more information on the Barrow itself, and for details of barge rental companies, see ⓦ iwai.ie.

038 See ⓦ crokepark.ie or ⓦ gaa.ie.

039 Entry hours and admission fees to Conwy Castle are detailed on ⓦ cadw.wales.gov.uk.

040 The Illuminations run for nine weeks from the end of Aug to early Nov. For light-up times and details of tram tickets check ⓦ visitblackpool.com/illuminations.

041 See ⓦ thermaebathspa.com for more details.

042 For more information, take a look at ⓦ eden project.com, or the unofficial, but useful, ⓦ eden-project.co.uk.

043 Green Man takes place every year in Aug. See ⓦ greenman.net for more details.

044 See ⓦ galwayoysterfest.com.

045 For more on Edinburgh's festivals and the Military Tattoo, go to ⓦ eif.co.uk or ⓦ edintattoo.co.uk.

046 From June to Sept, you need to book well ahead for accommodation – especially for the Hell Bay Hotel on Bryher (ⓦ hellbay.co.uk).

047 ⓦ mournelive.com is a useful resource.

048 Big E's Belfast Taxi Tours at 2 Berkley Ct, Crumlin; ℡ 07968 477924.

049 For information on the best riding in Wales, see ⓦ mbwales.com or ⓦ visitwales.co.uk/active.

050 Visit ⓦ living-room.co to check availability. Try booking in spring, when the forest floor is blanketed with bluebells.

051 The largest bores occur at the two equinoxes, in March and Sept. See ⓦ severn-bore.co.uk.

052 Hay-on-Wye straddles the English–Welsh border, twenty miles from Hereford. Murder & Mayhem, 5 Lion St (ⓦ hay-on-wyebooks.com); The Poetry Bookshop, Ice House, Brook St (ⓦ poetrybookshop.co.uk); Hay Cinema Bookshop, Castle St (ⓦ haycinemabookshop .co.uk).

053 The interpretation centre in Barnluasgan is four miles from the village of Cairnbaan, where there is good accommodation and food available. All info on the site can be found at ⓦ scottishbeavers.org.uk.

054 Bonfire Night is on Nov 5, unless this falls on a Sun, when it moves to Nov 6. For more information, see ⓦ lewesbonfirecouncil.org.uk.

WESTERN EUROPE
055–117

With the likes of France, Belgium, Germany and Switzerland all vying to tempt a visit, Western Europe would be a place apart even if all you wanted to do was eat, drink, sleep and repeat. And that's before you turn to the dizzying spread of heritage attractions – from Maastricht's architecture, Loire châteaux and Amsterdam's canals to Swiss mountain railways, Normandy's landing beaches and the Berlin Wall – and an events calendar that takes in the likes of Munich's Oktoberfest, Monaco's Grand Prix and Montreux's Jazz Festival. You can go paragliding in the Swiss Alps, bathe in the Baltic or claw for clams on Île de Noirmoutier – the hard part is choosing what to prioritize.

055 Hiking the Berlin Wall

GERMANY It was almost 25 years after the collapse of the Berlin Wall that I decided to walk its entire length. As a six-year resident of the former East of the German capital, I had noticed the ways in which the structure – or rather its absence – still influenced everything from attitudes, as with the so-called *Mauer im Kopf*, or Wall in the Mind, to architecture. Save for a few well-known remnants, the Wall itself has pretty much disappeared, but its place is now occupied by the Berlin Wall Trail. Laid out in 2006, this hiking and cycling trail traces the original 160km path of the Wall's former border fortifications.

Featuring an impressive 600 signs, 100 maps and 17 info boards, the trail can be conveniently divided into 14 individual sections, each accessible via public transportation at both start and end, and varying from 7km to 21 km in length. That makes it possible either to choose one part of the trail to enjoy, or to do the whole thing in segments. I began my own pilgrimage close to home at Bernauer Strasse, a 1.4km outdoor memorial that highlights points where escape tunnels were once dug, fatalities occurred and inconveniently situated churches destroyed. Even though I already knew the route was not a straight line through the city centre, only as I walked did I realize quite how barmily zig-zaggy it was, shooting off at seemingly random angles as it followed the old district boundaries to turn West Berlin into an isolated "island" within East Germany.

To my pleasant surprise, the trail proved to be a hugely rewarding recreational hike in its own right, passing through nature reserves, pine-filled forests and past the shimmering lakes that encircle the city. But much as I enjoyed the scenery, there was always a poignant memorial site or a section where the city edge seemed simply to stop and give out to East-facing wastelands or vistas. By the time I returned to my starting point, my understanding of one of the world's most famous structures had been immeasurably sharpened.

Paul Sullivan

has written and contributed to over a dozen major travel guides, published numerous articles internationally and penned three books on music. He lives in Berlin where he runs photography workshops and edits a sustainable travel website, ⓦSlowTravelBerlin.com.

FRANCE A monumentally graceful section of the Roman aqueduct that once supplied Nîmes with fresh water, the Pont du Gard is an iconic structure, a tribute not only to the engineering prowess of its creators, but also, with its lofty, elegant triple-tiered arches, to their aesthetic sensibilities. Now mostly vanished, the aqueduct originally cut boldly through the countryside for a staggering 50km, across hills, through a tunnel and over rivers. The bridge has endured, though, providing inspiration for the masons and architects who, over the centuries, travelled from all over France to see it, meticulously carving their names and home towns into the weathered, pale gold stone.

A fancy visitor centre gives you the lowdown on the construction of the bridge, but a better way to get up close and personal to this architectural marvel is to follow the hundreds of visitors who descend on a sunny day: make for the rocky banks of the River Gard,

don your swimming gear and take to the water. The tiers of arches rise high above you and to either side, with just one of the six lower arches making a superbly confident step across the river. Propelled by the gentle current of the reassuringly shallow Gard, you can float right under the arch, which casts a dense shadow onto the turquoise water. Beyond the bridge the river widens, and fearless kids leap from the rocks adjoining the aqueduct into the deepening waters, while families tuck into lavish picnics on the banks.

The splendour of the Pont du Gard made eighteenth-century philosopher and aqueduct enthusiast Jean-Jacques Rousseau wish he'd been born a Roman – perhaps he chose to ignore the fact that the bridge was built by slave labour. Better to be a twenty-first-century visitor – the only labour you'll have to expend is a bit of backstroke as you look up at what is still, after 2000 years, one of France's most imposing monuments.

057 | Kaffee und Kuchen in a Viennese Kaffeehaus

AUSTRIA As refined as afternoon tea and as sacred as the Japanese tea ceremony, *Kaffee und Kuchen* – coffee and cake – is the most civilized of Viennese rituals. It is not an experience to be rushed, and should you try, the archetypal grumpy Viennese waiter will surely sabotage your efforts. *Kaffee und Kuchen* is as much a cultural as a culinary experience. Each café is a destination in its own right: the grand, nineteenth-century *Café Central*, the suave *Café Landtmann* and the gloomy, bohemian *Café Hawelka* are as distinct from each other as *Topfenstrudel* is from *Gugelhupf*. In these memorable surroundings, there are newspapers to be read and, very likely, fevered artistic or political discussions to be had. Trotsky, it is said, planned world revolution over *Kaffee und Kuchen* in Vienna, though the contrast between the revolutionary intent and the bourgeois trappings must have been richly comic.

The coffee-and-cake culture is unique to Austria. For coffee, you may order a cappuccino, but you'll endear yourself to your waiter if instead you go for a *Mélange*, which is the closest Austrian equivalent. The choice is bewildering: there are *Einspänner, kleiner* or *grosser Brauner*, and even the *Kaisermélange* with egg yolk and brandy. Whatever you order, you'll most likely also get a small glass of water with your coffee.

The cakes are made with care from high-quality ingredients. It doesn't make them any healthier, but at least it ensures that the assault on your arteries is likely to be an enjoyable one. *Apfelstrudel* and the unexpectedly bitter chocolate *Sachertorte* are reliable and ubiquitous, ideally eaten with a heap of *schlagobers* (whipped cream) on the side. More exotic creations include the multilayered almond-sponge *Esterhazytorte* and the caramel-topped *Dobostorte*.

For all their sugary delights, an air of gloom pervades many Viennese cafés: part nostalgia for vanished imperial glories but also surely an acknowledgement of the transitory nature of sensual pleasure. Because finishing a hot, pungently sour cherry strudel is a small death, the last delicious forkful as full of sorrow and yearning as any symphony by Mahler.

058 | Mud, glorious mud

THE NETHERLANDS You can wallow in it, make pies with it, even smear it all over your face. But in the Netherlands they have a different use for mud. They walk across it for fun, striking out from the coast of Friesland at low tide to the Wadden Islands, a string of four islands between 10km and 20km offshore: an energetic pastime that goes right to the heart of the Dutch fascination with water and, well, primeval ooze.

It's a tough but rewarding pastime, and one you're not allowed to do on your own. Only experienced guides are allowed to cross the mud flats: the depth of the stuff is variable and the tides inconsistent – sometimes there's not much margin for error between tides – and in any case despite all the mud there are always deep channels left behind, even at low tide, and it pays to know where they are. You also have to get up early: most group treks start around 6am, and can take anything from three to six hours to reach their final destination. You need to be properly equipped: knee-high socks and high-top trainers are a good idea, as is a warm sweater and cagoule; and a complete change of clothes stashed in a watertight pack. It's freezing when you start and can be pretty hot by the time you finish, so dress in layers. But above all wear shorts; whatever happens, you're going to get covered in mud, so you may as well not weigh yourself down with mud-caked trousers.

Real hard-cases go to Terschelling, one of the prettiest and liveliest islands, but at 18km and six hours also by far the most gruelling choice, especially as for a lot of the time you're wading through water rather than mud; in fact they don't let you try it unless you've already completed the easier trip to Ameland, which takes about half the time and manages mostly to avoid the water. On the other side, a tractor will take you to a café in the main village where you can devour one of the best and hardest-earned late breakfasts of your life.

059 | Petit Train Jaune: following the narrow-gauge road

FRANCE As small and perfectly formed as its wind-in-the-hair views are vast, the fondly named Petit Train Jaune ("Little Yellow Train") has been pitting narrow-gauge track against the vertiginous rock of deepest French Catalonia for a century and counting.

It's best enjoyed in summer, when at least one of the spartan, buttercup-yellow carriages travels open-topped, while the squeamish can still savour spectacular vistas from the enclosed comfort of a gleaming modern counterpart. Not so much a train journey as a slow-motion roller-coaster ride, its 63km route, climbing from medieval Villefranche-de-Conflent on the Têt Valley floor to the heights of La Tour-de-Carol on the Pyrenean frontier with Spain, is a vital resource for remote communities and a magnet for tourists.

Dwarfed by sun-baked limestone colossi and cleaving to ever more impossibly narrow ledges, it offers a hugely exhilarating perspective of the country's lesser-known, ravishingly wild scenery, shadowed by the magisterial bulk of Pic du Canigou. Better still, the train proceeds on its three-hour journey at the kind of speed (55km/hr maximum) conducive to actually appreciating it all, or even getting off at one of the tiny stations to explore.

Idyllically sited hot springs, many known only to locals, steam all over this area; near the request-stop of Thuès-les-Bains especially, you might spot dripping villagers crossing the tracks, clearly judging their natural hot-tub eyrie to be worth the risk. If, after a soak, you have the energy to hike up the opposite side of the valley, enchanting hamlets like Canaveilles and Llar offer tantalizing views of the journey still to come. The train crosses this chasm twice on its way up to Mont Louis, France's highest fortified town: via a sliver of track atop a slender stone aqueduct and across a vertigo-inducing suspension bridge.

Once you've crested Bolquère – France's loftiest station, 1.5km above the Mediterranean – your ride pans out over the plateau of Cerdagne, which basks in an incredible 3000 hours of annual sunshine. Here, near journey's end, you're almost in Spain, even as the train's red-trimmed livery – not to mention the continuity of the Pyrenean landscape – makes the distinction superfluous.

GERMANY Carved balconies like lace, swaggering villas in spacious gardens and an absurdly long pier. Who would have expected "Herring Village" to be so glitzy? Indeed, who would have imagined such *Bäderarchitektur* (spa architecture) in a backwater like Usedom, a little-known island in the Baltic Sea? Yet during the latter half of the nineteenth century, as German aristocracy went crazy for seawater spa cures, Heringsdorf and adjacent Ahlbeck morphed from fishing villages to become the St-Tropez of the Baltic. When Kaiser Friedrich Wilhelm III began holidaying here, earning the villages their collective name *Kaiserbäder* (Emperor's spas), the Prussian elite followed.

Aristocrats and industrialists set aside six weeks every summer to wet an ankle in *Badewanne Berlins* ("Berlin's bathtub"). You can almost smell the moustache wax along Delbrückstrasse in Heringsdorf. A des-res of its day, synonymous with status, the promenade is a glimpse of the Second Empire at the height of its pomp. Mosaics glitter in the pediment of Neoclassical Villa Oechler at No. 5; it doesn't stretch the imagination far to visualize the glittering garden balls hosted before the palatial colonnades of Villa

Oppenheim, while the Kaiser himself took tea at Villa Staudt located at No. 6. Only breeze-block architecture bequeathed by the GDR in the centre spoils things here – top apparatchiks built hotel blocks for workers and took the grand villas for themselves.

Reunification has returned health cures and gloss to the resorts; Ahlbeck in particular has emerged as a stylish spa retreat for Berlin's city slickers. If you sit in a traditional *Strandkörbe* wicker seat, scrunching sugar-white sand between your toes – imperial villas on one side, Germans promenading continental Europe's longest pier on the other – you'd be forgiven for thinking the *Kaiserbäder* are back to normal. Not quite.

Usedom has acquired a new reputation of late. In 2008 the world's first nudist flights landed at its airport and a minor diplomatic spat occurred when Poles strolled across the newly dismantled border to see sizzling sausages of a very unexpected kind. Sure, *Freikörperkultur* (literally "Free Body Culture") is restricted to specified areas, but you can almost hear the Kaiser splutter into his schnapps.

Bathing in the Baltic

Having a beer in Brussels

061

BELGIUM Don't just ask for a beer in Belgium – your request will be met with a blank stare. Because no one produces such a wide range of beers as they do here: there are lagers, wheat beers, dark amber ales, strong beers brewed by Trappist monks, fruit beers and even beers mixed with grapes. Some beers are fermented in the cask, others in the bottle and corked champagne-like. And each beer has its own glass, specifically developed to enhance the enjoyment of that particular brew.

Brussels is the best place to try them all, including its own beery speciality, Lambic, a flattish concoction that is brewed in open barrels and fermented with the naturally occurring yeasts in the air of the Payottenland (the area around Brussels). It's not much changed from the stuff they drank in Bruegel's time, and a few glasses is enough to have you behaving like one of the peasants in his paintings – something you can do to your heart's content at *La Bécasse*, down an alley not far from the Grand-Place, or at the *Cantillon Brewery* in the Anderlecht district, where they still brew beer using these old methods, and which you can visit on regular tours.

You can taste another potent brew, Gueuze, a sparkling, cidery affair, at *La Mort Subite*, a dodgy-sounding name for a comfortable fin-de-siècle café. Your ale will be served with brisk efficiency by one of the ancient staff, and while you sip it you can munch on cubes of cheese with celery salt or cold meats like jellied pigs' cheeks.

After this aperitif, make your way to *In't Spinnekopke*, a restaurant that cooks everything in beer, and has lots to drink as well, or just head for *Delirium*, which serves over two thousand different types of beer, a quarter of which are Belgian.

062 | The melancholy charm of the world's most famous cemetery

FRANCE In 1900, a few days before he passed away, Oscar Wilde declared he was "fighting a duel to the death" with the wallpaper in his St-Germain hotel room. "One or other of us," he remarked, "has to go." The author's final resting place – Division 89 in Père-Lachaise, one of the world's largest and most famous cemeteries – seems far more likely to have met with his approval. Home to a string of notables including composer Frédéric Chopin, singer Edith Piaf, playwright Molière, and authors Marcel Proust and Honoré de Balzac, Père-Lachaise sits proudly on a hill in eastern Paris, exerting a distinct melancholic charm. Covering more than 47,000 square metres and boasting its own street signs and cobbled paths, the "city of the dead" attracts around two million visitors a year.

Wilde's tomb – marked by a Pharaonic winged messenger, designed by Jacob Epstein – attracts a steady stream of admirers, many of whom show their affection for the acerbic poet by leaving a lipstick kiss or scrawled tribute on it. A sober verse from *The Ballad of Reading Gaol*, which Wilde wrote after serving two years' hard labour for gross indecency, is inscribed on the tomb, while the messenger's missing appendage is reputedly used as a paperweight in the cemetery director's office. The grave of Doors singer Jim Morrison is protected from similarly adoring fans – who leave behind smouldering cigarettes, candles and flowers – by a security guard.

The most poignant monuments in Père-Lachaise, however, are found in Division 97, the *"coin des martyrs"*. Here, amid neatly tended flower gardens and towering trees, are moving memorials to Resistance fighters and victims of Nazi concentration camps. Nearby, in Division 76, a modest plaque on a stone wall, the *Mur des Fédérés*, marks where, after a dramatic chase through the cemetery, the final 147 troops of the 72-day Paris Commune uprising were lined up and executed in 1871; the spot remains a potent symbol for the Left. Visit first thing in the morning, and you can wander undisturbed among the graves and enjoy the sweeping views of Paris in peace.

063 | Climb the Reichstag's great glass dome

GERMANY Berlin may be young, trendy and tremendously zeitgeisty, but from inside the Reichstag's glass dome, it's impossible not to reflect on how modern Germany has had to absorb some very dark chapters in its history.

This building is one of history's survivors. Opened in 1894, it survived the Reichstag fire of 1933, which gave the pretext for Hitler to bring in emergency powers and later to bypass parliament altogether. It survived being almost completely gutted when the Red Army took Berlin in April 1945; look out for the graffiti scrawled by Soviet soldiers and uncovered during the 1990s restoration. And it survived the division of Germany, when the GDR moved its political capital to Bonn and the building fell into disuse.

Like Berlin itself, the Reichstag has not just endured but risen from the ashes: with its nineteenth-century base topped with the glass and steel dome added in 1999 by British architect Norman Foster, it is now among the most iconic landmarks on the city's ever-changing skyline.

Climb the dome's spiral ramps for a clear bird's-eye view of Berlin laid out beneath you: its streets fanning out, its skyline teeming with cranes. Nearby, you'll see the Brandenburg Gate; a little further off, Alexanderplatz, the heart of old East Berlin. Look up at the portico above the steps to the main entrance, and you'll see the words inscribed there in 1916 in Gothic script: DEM DEUTSCHEN VOLKE, "to the German people".

Today, the same idea is expressed through the glass panels at the centre of the dome which give a view down onto the legislative chamber. The people are literally above Germany's lawmakers, holding them accountable. It's a powerful image, and a powerful place to pause in this buzzing, still-changing city.

064 | Getting naked in Cap d'Agde

FRANCE Awkward to pronounce, difficult to place on a map and virtually impossible to describe to friends when you return home, Cap d'Agde's legendary nudist resort has to be one of the world's most unique places to stay. Of a size and scale befitting a small town, the Cap offers an ostentatious expression of alternative living. But this is no sect. The 60,000-odd naked people who come here during the height of summer often have nothing more in common than sunburnt bottoms and a desire to express themselves in unconventional ways.

The resort's sprawling campsite is generally the domain of what the French like to call *bios*: the hardy souls who arrive at the Cap when the nights are still chilly and leave when the last leaves have fallen from the trees. They love their body hair as much as they hate their clothes, are invariably the naked ones in the queue at the post office, and don't mind the odd strand of spaghetti getting tangled up in their short and curlies at lunch. These textile-loathing *bios* share the Cap with a very different breed, who are occasionally found at the campsite, but usually prefer the privacy of apartments or hotel rooms. During the day, these libertines gather at the northern end of the Cap's 2km-long beach. For them, being naked is a fashion statement as much as a philosophy: smooth bodies, strategically placed tattoos and intimate piercings are the order of the day – and sex on the beach is not necessarily a cocktail.

In the evenings, the *bios* prefer to play a game of pétanque, cook dinner and go to bed early. Meanwhile, as the last camp stoves are cooling down, a few couples might be spotted slipping out of the campsite dressed in leather, PVC, lacy lingerie and thigh-high stiletto boots to join the throngs of more adventurous debauchees who congregate nightly in the Cap's bars, restaurants and notoriously wild swingers' clubs for a night of uninhibited fun and frolicking.

FRANCE Rugby in France has a clearly defined heartland. Cast an eye at the locations of the 30 clubs that make up the sport's top two divisions, and you'll notice that only two are based in the north of the country – and both of those, in Paris. Of the remaining 28, 16 are in the free-spirited cities and country towns of the southwest. The region takes enthusiasm for rugby to a near-obsessive level, and there's nowhere better than Toulouse, home to Europe's most trophy-laden team, to get a taste for the local passion.

Southern France is not short of other fiercely supported club sides – most obviously, the highly successful Toulon in the southeast. It's in the southwest, however, where rugby was first popularized by British wine merchants towards the end of the nineteenth century, that the sport's history hangs heaviest. Match days in Toulouse are ebullient, bibulous affairs. If you're lucky enough to snare a ticket for a big game, you'll witness the crowd at its flag-waving, drum-thumping most vociferous, with the pre- and post-match atmosphere at its liveliest in the drinking holes of the riverside Place Saint-Pierre. Unlike certain other parts of the world, rugby here transcends the class system.

If you're in Toulouse outside rugby season, head for *De Danu*, a popular bar east of the town centre that's still run by a one-time Toulouse lock forward. Covered in shirts and memorabilia – and, if you're lucky, manned by a 2m-tall former pro – it's a great place to meet local fans.

And if you're really keen on seeing just how deep rugby's roots go in these parts, journey west out of town to the Chapelle Notre-Dame-du-Rugby, in the woods north of Bayonne. Fully consecrated, the church and its stained-glass windows are adorned with rugby scenes, used boots and other match-day memorabilia. There's even a statue of the Virgin being handed a rugby ball.

065

Tap into rugby passion in Toulouse

066 | Lounging aboard the Glacier Express

SWITZERLAND The Swiss are often chided for not being much good at, say, football, jokes or wars – but two things they do better than just about anyone are mountains and trains. Combine the two, and you're onto a winner.

So you're booked on the Glacier Express; you arrive at St Moritz under pristine-blue morning skies, and your state-of-the-art panoramic carriage awaits. Vast windows extend from knee level right up around the top of the coach; from any seat the views are all-encompassing. As the train gets going, you feel as though you're not so much a passenger, stuck behind glass, as a traveller, engaged in the scenery.

The journey starts under sparkling sunshine beside the River Inn, whose waters tumble east to join the Danube. Here, amid the wild Alpine forests, it's the slenderest of mountain brooks. Every sightline is dominated by sky-blue, snow-white and pine-green.

By mid-morning, you're rolling beside the young Rhine, crossable here by a single stepping stone. As forests, wild gorges, snowy peaks and huddled villages trundle past, the train climbs effortlessly into the bleak high country, above the tree line. After lunch, you down a warming schnapps as you crest the Oberalp Pass – 2033m above sea level, though dwarfed by a thousand more metres of craggy cliffs. On the other side, the snow lies thick on the village roofs below.

By mid-afternoon, the carriage is quiet: fingers are laced over bellies and there are a few yawns. But still the scenery is compulsive: one moment you're gazing down into a bottomless ravine, the next you're craning your neck to take in the soaring summits, framed against a still-perfect Alpine blue sky. As the train pulls into the little village of Zermatt, you catch your first glimpse of the iconic, pyramidal Matterhorn. It's time to celebrate your arrival – with a Toblerone, naturally.

067 | The Friedrichsbad: the best baths in Baden-Baden

GERMANY Time does strange things in southwest Germany. Even before Einstein hit on his Theory of Relativity in Ülm, Mark Twain had realized something was up after taking to the waters in the smart spa town of Baden-Baden. "Here at the Friedrichsbad," he wrote, "you lose track of time within ten minutes and track of the world within twenty."

Nearly 2000 years after the Romans tapped curative waters in this corner of the Black Forest, Twain swore that he left his rheumatism in Baden-Baden (literally, the "Baths of Baden"). England physios also considered Friedrichsbad sessions good enough to fast-track the return of injured striker Wayne Rooney for the World Cup in 2006. But regardless of whether a visit to the Roman-Irish mineral baths is for relaxation or rheumatism, as Twain noted, minutes melt into hours once inside.

Midway through the full sixteen-stage programme, schedules are mere memories as you float in the circular pool of the Kuppelbad, whose marble walls and columns, creamy caryatids and sculpted cupola make it seem more minor Renaissance cathedral than spa centrepiece. By the final stage, time is meaningless and locations are a blur, as you

drift prune-like and dozy between a sequence of mineral water baths, showers, scrubs and saunas of ever-decreasing temperatures.

If time warps inside the Friedrichsbad, the spa itself is a throwback to when Baden-Baden was a high rollers' playground – Kaisers and Tsars flocked here for the summer season, Queen Victoria promenaded parks planted in ball-gown colours, Strauss and Brahms staged gala concerts, and Dostoevsky tried his luck in a Versailles-styled casino. With such esteemed visitors, the town's steam room suddenly looked rather frumpy. So in 1877, Grand Duke Friedrich I cut the opening ribbons to his spa, the most modern bathing house in Europe but with all the palatial trimmings: hand-painted tiles, and arches and colonnades that alluded to the decadence of antiquity.

Be warned: for all its stately appearance, you need to leave your inhibitions at the Friedrichsbad door: bathing is nude and frequently mixed. Which can be just as much of a shock as the penultimate plunge into 18°C waters. Or the realization as you emerge tingling and light-headed that, actually, the three hours you thought you spent inside were in fact five.

068 | Impressionist paintings at the Musée d'Orsay

FRANCE Forget the Louvre, it's not a patch on the Musée d'Orsay – or so you'll be told. Maybe this is down to continued bitterness towards futuristic glass pyramids, but it's probably more about the understated elegance of the Musée d'Orsay itself. Located in a renovated Belle Époque railway station, the museum displays a splendid collection of vibrant impressionist canvases in much more intimate surroundings, right up under the roof in a wing whose attic-like feel is far less formal and imposing than the Louvre.

A wander through the compact impressionist and post-impressionist galleries provides an astonishingly comprehensive tour of the best paintings of the period, the majority of them easily recognizable classics like Van Gogh's *Starry Night* or Renoir's *Dance at Le Moulin de la Galette*. Even better, these are paintings you can really engage with, their straightforward style and vibrant, life-like scenes drawing you into the

stories they tell. It's easy to forget where you are and, transfixed, reach out a finger to trace the chunky swirls of paint that make up Van Gogh's manic skies; you might even catch yourself imitating the movements of Degas' delicate ballerinas as they dance across the walls, sweeping their arms in arcs above their heads and pointing their tiny toes.

When the intricate grandeur of Monet's *Rouen Cathedral* looms above you and reinstates a sense of decorum, it's almost as if you were standing beneath the imposing bulk of the mighty church itself. Exhilaration returns as you're transported to the tropics by Gauguin's disarming Tahitian maids, who eye you coyly from the depths of the jungle. But don't get so caught up in the stories that you forget the incredible artistic prowess on display; stick your nose right up to Seurat's dotted *Cirque*, then inch slowly backwards and, as the yellow-clad acrobats appear with their white horse, you'll feel the immense genius of the pioneer of pointillism.

Skiing the Streif

AUSTRIA It never looked this icy on TV. And it certainly never looked this steep. But then cameras have a way of warping reality: they make people look ever so slightly bigger, and they make downhill-skiing runs look a lot, lot tamer.

And Kitzbühel's "Streif" is far from tame. A legendary downhill course that makes up one third of the Hahnenkammrennen, the most popular series of races on the skiing World Cup circuit, Streif is a challenging run in the same way that Everest is a difficult climb.

Buoyed by the bravado of a late-night *Glühwein*, you have somehow talked yourself into giving it a crack. But now your legs are gone, and you can't seem to shake the image of an alpine rescue team scraping you off the slopes. 3, 2, 1. And you plunge down the slope, scooping up powder in the widest snowplough the course has ever seen. The Mausefalle

(Mousetrap) is swiftly negotiated – too swiftly for your liking – and you're on your way, the rushing wind making your eyes stream as you whizz through Steilhang and down Alte Schneise. Perfect edging and exact timing are the keys to success here. Most amateurs have neither, and sure enough you skitter across an icy patch, your trailing ski almost catching an edge. There isn't time to think of the mess you'd have made if it had done.

Building up sufficient speed to carry you through Brückenschuß and Gschößwiese, a section of the course most commentators maliciously describe as "flat", you descend on the Hausbergkante – a jump, followed by a difficult left-hand turn over a large rise in the terrain – and then it's down the Rasmusleitn, to the finish line. You punch the air and wave to the imaginary crowd. Piece of cake.

070 | Hunting for tarte flambée in Alsace

FRANCE Without doubt the most *formidable* of Alsace's culinary exports, the *tarte flambée* is known in German-speaking countries as *Flammkuchen* – the name translates roughly as "cooked in the flames" in both languages. A thin-crust pizza made with *crème fraîche*, sliced onions and smoked *lardons*, it's traditionally baked in a very hot wood-burning oven, and served as a first course or an appetizer, preferably with a glass of chilled Alsatian white wine, in cosy local taverns known as *Winstubs* (wine lounges).

Although you can try them at myriad places, most visitors will wind up in Strasbourg. There you can check out *L'Epicerie*, a small but buzzy place with a rustic atmosphere, where they sell all kinds of delicious *tartines*, including *tarte flambée*, or for something more traditional, head to *L'Ancienne Douane*, a former customs house with a pleasant spacious riverside terrace and great beers on tap. *Bon appetit!*

071 | Ars Electronica Centre: losing grip on reality

AUSTRIA Pegging yourself as the Museum of the Future is, in our ever-changing world, bold. Brash, even. And that's exactly what the Ars Electronica Centre in Linz is. Dedicated to new technology, and its influence within the realms of art, few museums on Earth have their fingers quite as firmly on the pulse.

The Ars features over fifty interactive installations, from warring robots to displays that enable you to create your own cyberspace project, but everyone comes here for the CAVE (Cave Automatic Visual Environment), the only exhibition of its kind that's open to the public. This room, measuring – cutely enough – 3m cubed, is at the cutting-edge of virtual reality; the simulation uses technology so advanced – 3-D projections dance across the walls and along the floor, as you navigate through virtual solar systems and across artificial landscapes – that you feel like you're part of the installation.

072 | Dining in the dark in Zürich

SWITZERLAND The rise of social media has changed the way we eat, with what looks good on Instagram often dictating food and restaurant choices. Switzerland isn't immune to this trend, but *Blindekuh*, the world's first restaurant in the dark is.

Set up 20 years ago to provide steady employment for Zürich's blind and visually impaired population – and to challenge sighted people to plunge into their world for the duration of a three-course meal – the restaurant is a fully immersive experience in every sense. You're hand-led to the table; you hear waiters pitter-patter behind you; catch the echoing clink of cutlery at a table somewhere in the all-consuming darkness; mix up sweet, sour, salty and bitter flavours in your mouth.

Eating here is akin to dining with a blindfold on, but you'll also have your eyes opened at the same time.

FRANCE The French call the Loire the "last wild river in France" for its winter habit of destructive flooding. In summer, however, it's hard to imagine anything gentler or more cultivated. The river meanders placidly between golden sandbanks where little white terns wheel and dive and herons fish in the shallows. At the water's edge stand grey-leaved willows and tall, fluttery poplars. The climate is idyllically temperate, vines comb the hillsides on all sides, and every kilometre or two brings another village built in creamy tufa stone, huddled around its church, or another well-to-do little town overlooked by a resplendent château.

Two hundred years ago the Loire thrummed with river traffic, but these days the freight has all taken to the roads and railways, leaving the old stone quays blissfully empty. New traffic, however, is returning to the banks. A delightful cycle network, *La Loire à Vélo* ("The Loire by bike"), now runs for some 800km – on minor roads or dedicated paths, and always at an easy gradient – from the hills above Sancerre, where you can try exquisite Sauvignon Blanc wines and *crottin de chavignol* goat's cheese, westwards to the Atlantic coast below Nantes, where refreshing Muscadet and mussels await.

As you pedal from provincial hotel to *chambre d'hôte* (bed and breakfast), perhaps staying at or visiting the odd Renaissance-masterpiece château here and there, you can pause to sample regional specialities: the little battered whitebait-like fish of *friture de Loire*, mushrooms grown in local caves, and endless goat's cheeses ranging from creamy fresh to the well-aged and truly goaty. Then there are the wines: the fresh reds of Chinon and Bourgueil, redolent of raspberries and violets; Anjou's summery rosé; the joyful sparklers of Vouvray and Saumur; and the deep, honeyed sweet whites made with the Chenin Blanc grape. Pedalling and picnicking: there's no finer way to taste the slow pace of rural France.

Pedalling and picnicking along the Loire

Climbing Mont st-Michel

074

FRANCE Wondrously unique yet as recognizable as the Eiffel Tower, Mont St-Michel, with its harmonious blend of natural and man-made beauty, has been drawing tourists and pilgrims alike to the Normandy coast for centuries. Soaring some 80m up from the waters of the bay that bears its name, this glowering granite islet has an entire commune clinging improbably to its steep boulders, its tiers of buildings topped by a magnificent Benedictine abbey.

From a few kilometres away, the sheer scale of the Mont makes a surreal contrast with the rural tranquillity of Normandy – a startling welcome for the first-time visitor. And as you approach along the modern bridge that connects the Mont to the rest of France, the grandeur of this UNESCO World Heritage Site becomes all the more apparent. Up close, the narrow, steepening streets offer an architectural history lesson, with Romanesque and Gothic buildings seemingly built one on top of the other.

Perched at the summit is the abbey itself, gushingly described by Guy de Maupassant as "the most wonderful Gothic building ever made for God on this earth". Although the first church was founded here in 709, today's abbey was constructed between the eleventh and thirteenth centuries, under Norman and subsequently French patronage. And as much as it's an aesthetic delight, the abbey is also a place of serenity: less than a third of the 3.5 million tourists that flock here each year actually climb all the way up to see it, and it remains a perfect place to be still and contemplate the Mont's glorious isolation.

Looking out from Mont St-Michel, as you watch the tides rolling in around its base – "like a galloping horse", said Victor Hugo – you can understand why medieval pilgrims would risk drowning to reach it, and why no invading force has ever succeeded in capturing the rock. It's a panorama to be savoured – as fine a sight as that of the Mont itself, and one that'll stay with you for a long time.

075 | Snow wonder: podding it up in the Swiss Alps

SWITZERLAND You can barely see *Whitepod*, a zero-impact, luxury "camp", until you're almost upon it, so well is it camouflaged against the deep snows of this tranquil forest setting, high in the Alps and far from any roads.

Each of the pods – eight of which make up the camp – is a mini geodesic dome sheathed in white canvas, a sturdy igloo-shaped construction that's set on a raised wooden platform. But this is no wilderness campsite: the emphasis here is squarely on contemporary five-star comforts. Inside each pod – heated by its own wood-burning stove – you get a proper king-size bed with multiple fluffy down covers and comfortable armchairs, along with an iPod and designer toiletries.

So far, so typical of the ski industry – hardly the world's most environmentally sound, with all those snow cannon and piste-grooming machines, not to mention Alpine traffic jams. *Whitepod*, however, is different: no concrete is used in the pods, so there is no impact on the ground beneath, and everything is sourced locally, from the logs to the solar power to the organic food.

For showers, meals and relaxing with other guests, you cross to the wooden chalet in the centre of the site, which has been updated inside – all soft lighting, comfortable lounging and chic designer touches. The atmosphere is great – out in the wild woods, boasting spectacular views of the mountains, yet with every comfort taken care of in an understated, oh-so-Swiss way.

076 | One Ring to rule them all

GERMANY Guests who quite possibly have waited ten years for tickets to the Bayreuth Festival approach expectantly up a hillside. At the top a flag rises and falls in the breeze, a large letter W emblazoned on it. Groups gather outside to take in the last fresh air they will breathe for several hours, sparkling in their very best – you will never have seen so many diamonds. The atmosphere is eager and anticipatory, but certainly not light-hearted. Richard Wagner saw attending his operas as more than entertainment. It's also a ritual, part of an almost sacred experience.

Held annually, the festival was conceived by Richard Wagner not just to showcase his work but to restore a spiritual dimension to materialistic European culture. The Festspielhaus building itself is an enclosed amphitheatre, built on a relative shoestring in brick and wood as Wagner's patrons couldn't afford more substantial materials. In spite of this, it has superb acoustics – Wagner, who designed it, would not have settled for anything less. Inside, there are no boxes

or balconies in the white-columned auditorium, just a single rake of seating for 1800 spectators. Seats are wooden and hard (many people bring cushions) and the acts are long. Wagner dispensed with the idea of a bell to call the audience to their seats. Instead, fifteen minutes before each act begins, a small brass ensemble plays a fanfare based on a key phrase from the upcoming act. They repeat it again twice, at ten and five minutes before the curtain rises.

The lights dim – Wagner revolutionized opera production by insisting on no distracting illumination in the auditorium – and the orchestra, hidden below a curved wooden canopy, begins. *Das Rheingold*, which opens Wagner's mighty *Ring Cycle*, is always played without interval and usually lasts two and a half hours. There will be four evenings like this, fifteen hours of uncompromising, highly emotional music each night. Whatever your feelings about Wagner the man, you will emerge from each performance of his music a changed person.

077 | Beach bar-hopping in Hamburg

GERMANY Move over Paris Plage. Although media reports heap praise upon its strip of sun, Seine and sand, the North European city that has a better claim to be the spiritual home of the urban beach is Hamburg. Every April tens of thousands of tonnes of sand are imported as miniature seaside paradises appear in the heart of Germany's second city. The doors open at the end of May and so begins another summer of beach bar-hopping Hamburg-style.

Having spent their weekends on sandy strips beside the River Elbe since the late nineteenth century, Hamburg residents have long known about urban beach culture. But the reason why no other German city does the *Stadtstrand* (city beach) with such panache comes down to character. That Hamburg is simultaneously a sophisticated media metropolis and a rollicking port city produces a beach bar scene that ranges from glamour to grunge without sacrificing the key element – good times. Think sand, sausages and *Strandkörbe* (traditional wicker seats) to a soundtrack of funk and house beats. Ibiza it is not, but then nor is it trying to be.

Your flip-flops on, head to the river in port-turned-nightlife district St Pauli to begin at *StrandPauli*. A year-round institution near the ferry port, it combines retro lampshades, castaway style and views of the second-largest container port in Europe – Hamburg in a nutshell.

Next stop west on the beach bar crawl is slicker *Hamburg City Beach Club*, all potted palms, day beds and aviator sunglasses, from where it's a short walk to the former docks in Altona. Behind the beach volleyball pitch are relaxed *Hamburg del Mar* and *Lago Bay*, which aspires towards Ibiza but scores most for a small swimming pool. A tip wherever you go: sunset is popular, so arrive early, buy a drink and settle in.

Not that it's all imported sand and urban chic. At the end of the road in Övelgönne further west still is *Altona's Strandperle*. Sure it's a glorified shack, but no one minds when it's on a genuine river beach to make Paris Plage look like a glorified sandpit. Now, what was the German for "*c'est magnifique*"?

078

Paragliding by the mighty Matterhorn

SWITZERLAND There aren't many mountains as iconic as the Matterhorn. It's big. It's brawny. It's beautifully formed. The peak's triangular bulk has adorned a million postcards and a million more Toblerone bars, which means that doing almost anything under its gaze is going to be memorable. But paragliding here? Riding the currents and turning slow circles in the air while the early-morning sun burns the last rags of cloud away from the Swiss Alps and the valley floor below: file under downright unforgettable.

You don't need to be a pro to give it a go. In fact, if you've never tried the sport before, it's hard to imagine a more impressive natural amphitheatre to start than this ineffably scenic pocket of Switzerland. A tandem flight means you can leave the technical stuff to someone else while you revel in the wraparound views. And regardless of how long it then takes you to touch back down in the town of Zermatt, it can only be too soon.

079 | Champagne tasting in Épernay

FRANCE Champagne is an exclusive drink, in all senses of the word, what with its upmarket associations and the fact that it can be made only from the grapes grown in the Champagne region of northern France. The centre of champagne production is Épernay, a town that's made much of its association with the fizzy stuff, and where all the *maisons* of the well-known brands are lined up along the appropriately named Avenue de Champagne.

All of these champagne houses offer tours and tastings, and one of the best places to indulge is at the *maison* of Moët et Chandon, arguably the best-known brand in the world. The splendid, cathedral-like cellars afford suitable dignity to this most regal of drinks, while the multilingual guides divulge the complexities of blending different grapes and vintages to maintain a consistency of flavour from one year to the next. During the tasting, an enthusiastic sommelier explains the subtleties of flavour in the different *cuvées*, and although the whole experience can feel rather impersonal, it's nonetheless an essential part of any visit to the region.

For an altogether more exclusive experience, head 15km or so north of Épernay to the village of Bligny. Here, the eighteenth-century Château de Bligny is the only one in France still producing its own champagne, and you can call ahead to arrange a private tour.

Driving through the wrought-iron gates and up the scrunchy gravel driveway, a sense of understated class strikes you immediately, and things only get classier as you're taken through the tastefully furnished rooms and vaulted cellars, and shown the family's cherished collection of champagne flutes. A tasting of several prize-winning vintages, taken in the opulent drawing room, is of course included. As you savour your second glass, you'll doubtless conclude that there's no better place to get a flavour of the heady world of champagne than the home ground of this "drink of kings".

080 | Gathering friends for a Swiss fondue

SWITZERLAND No one takes cheese as seriously as the Swiss. Elsewhere, cheese is one element within a more complex meal. In Switzerland, cheese is the meal – and fondue is the classic cheese feast. Pick a cold night and gather some friends: fondue is a sociable event, designed to ward off the Alpine chill with hot comfort food, warming alcohol and good company. No Swiss would dream of tackling one alone. In French, *fondre* means "to melt": fondue essentially comprises a pot of molten cheese that is brought to the table and kept bubbling over a tiny burner. To eat it, you spear a little cube of bread or chunk of potato with a long fork, swirl it through the cheese, twirl off the trailing ends and pop it into your mouth.

Those are the basics. But you'll find there's a whole ritual surrounding fondue consumption that most Swiss take alarmingly seriously. To start with, no one can agree on ingredients: the classic style is a *moitié-moitié*, or "half-and-half" – a mixture of Gruyère and Emmental – but many folk insist on nutty Vacherin Fribourgeois playing a part, and hardy types chuck in a block of stinking Appenzeller. Then there's the issue of what kind of alcohol to glug into the pot: kirsch (cherry spirit) is common, but French-speaking Swiss prefer white wine, while German speakers from the Lake Constance orchards stick firmly to cider.

Once that's decided and the pot is bubbling, everyone drinks a toast, the Swiss way: with direct eye contact as you say the other person's name – no mumbling or general clinking allowed! Then give your bread a good vigorous spin through the cheese (it helps stop the mixture separating), but lose it off your fork and the drinks are on you.

If the whole thing sounds like a recipe for a stomach ache, you'd be spot-on: imagine roughly 250g of molten cheese solidifying inside you. There's a reason for the traditional *coup du milieu* – everyone downing a shot of alcohol halfway through the meal: if it doesn't help things settle, at least it masks the discomfort.

081 | Brave the heights of Bonifacio

CORSICA A mere 11km separate the northernmost extremity of Sardinia from the iconic white cliffs of Bonifacio, on Corsica's wild southern tip. In fine weather, the straits can seem languid, like a lake of sapphire-coloured oil. But when the weather is up, the ferry crossing from Santa Teresa di Gallura is altogether different, and the ferocity of the currents ripping through this treacherous sea lane will remind you that, to generations of mariners, Bonifacio was a symbol of salvation.

Rearing vertically from the waves, the striated chalk escarpments form a wall of dazzling brilliance, even on the dullest, stormiest day. A row of ancient Genoese houses squeezes close to their edge, looking aloof and not a little smug – despite the fact the chalk beneath them has crumbled away in colossal chunks, leaving the structures hanging precariously over expanses of cobalt sea and razor-sharp rock.

As the ferry rounds the harbour mouth, the waves grow suddenly still, and it seems to glide the last couple of hundred metres into port. Under the vast, sand-coloured ramparts of Bonifacio's citadel, tourists stroll along a quayside lined with luxury yachts and pretty stone tenements sporting pastel-painted shutters. Wafts of coffee, grilled fish and freshly baked bread drift out of the waterfront cafés as you climb up the steps of the Montée Rastello to the *haute ville*.

Most people are in a hurry to peek inside the gateway at the top, at the narrow alleyways, tiny cobbled squares and delicate campanile of the Église Sainte-Marie-Majeur. But the town never looks quite as wonderful as it does from the cliffs around it. Follow the path that strikes left of the Montée into the maquis, an ocean of scrub rolling away to the mountains inland, and – as your ferry pitches and rolls its way out of the harbour – you'll be rewarded with one of the most magnificent seascapes in the entire Mediterranean.

082 | Getting groovy at the Montreux Jazz Festival

SWITZERLAND Backed by craggy hills and jutting out into the eastern tip of Lake Geneva, Montreux's setting is almost as stylish as its famous festival. But then few things are quite as cool as the Montreux Jazz Festival, one of Europe's most prestigious music events and a showcase for emerging talent as much as well-established stars.

This is jazz, but not as you may know it – everything from hip-hop to acid jazz, gospel, techno, reggae and African jazz gets an airing, and you can groove the days away on samba and salsa boats that head out onto the town's lake every afternoon. Jazz runs deep in Montreux – one of the venues is called the Miles Davis Hall – and the festival continues to expand and diversify, featuring a bewildering range of workshops and an A-List line-up. Herbie Hancock and John McLaughlin are just two of the more regular artists from a cast of around two thousand.

083 | Schloss Neuschwanstein, the ultimate fairy-tale castle

GERMANY If you could only visit one castle in the world, then Schloss Neuschwanstein has to be it. Boldly perched on a rocky outcrop high above the Bavarian village of Hohenschwangau, the *schloss* lords it over some of the most spectacular countryside in the country. It looks every bit the storybook castle, a forest of capped grey granite turrets rising from a monumental edifice. And the all-important intriguing background? Built in 1869 as a refuge from reality by King Ludwig II, a crazed monarch who compared himself to the mythical medieval "Grail King" Parzival, Neuschwanstein ticks that box, too.

084 | Riding Europe's most scenic railway

SWITZERLAND From Machu Picchu to Angkor Wat, UNESCO World Heritage sites generally don't move about much. But the Rhaetian Railway is a special case: 128km of spectacularly engineered line, weaving through 55 tunnels and nearly two hundred viaducts and bridges.

As you pull into one snowbound village after the other, you understand what UNESCO were getting at when they hailed the railway for "overcoming the isolation" of the local settlements. Still, the mountain gods rule: distant buildings look frozen in dumb amazement; church spires seem rather pathetic; you half-expect birds to simply disappear mid-flight – *poof* – so puny do they appear against this backdrop.

So too does the train: as it rounds precipitous corners, you find yourself leaning to right its balance. But relaxation comes: with the heating soporifically cosy, and the train ever climbing – Tiefencastel 884m, Samedan 1705m – your head swims sweetly and you find yourself assenting to the magic of the ride.

Downing a stein or ten at the Oktoberfest

GERMANY The world's largest public festival, the Munich Oktoberfest, kicks off on the penultimate Saturday in September and keeps pumping day after day for a full two weeks. Known locally as the "Wies'n" after the sprawling Theresienwiese park in which it takes place, it was first held to celebrate the wedding of local royalty but is now an unadulterated celebration of beer and Bavarian life, attracting almost six million visitors and seeing as many million litres of beer disappear in sixteen days.

At the heart of the festival are fourteen enormous beer tents where boisterous crowds sit at long benches, elbow to elbow, draining one huge litre-capacity glass or "*stein*" after another. If you're up for annihilation, head to the Hofbrau tent at a weekend, go for the ten-*stein* challenge and join in with the thousands of young bloods braying for beer. If you actually want to remember your time in Munich, or to encounter some real Germans, pitch up midweek and take in two or three of the other beer tents. Whenever and wherever you go, you can count on one thing for sure – within two *steins* you'll be laughing with your neighbours like long-lost buddies and banging the table in time with the Oompah bands.

The busiest time to visit Oktoberfest is the first weekend, when the "Grand Entry of the Oktoberfest Landlords and Breweries" starts the whole thing off as participants attired in Bavarian finery (lederhosen, basically), decorated carriages, curvaceous waitresses on horse-drawn floats and booming brass bands from each of the beer tents parade through town, joined by several thousand thirsty locals and international party-goers.

The local mayor gets things going by tapping the first barrel of Oktoberfest beer at the park's entrance and declaring "Ozapftis", which means "it's been tapped", but translates more accurately as, "Why doesn't everybody get as wasted as possible in my town for the next two weeks and don't worry about the mess because we'll clear up?" Huge cheers rise up from the crowd as the mad dash to the cavernous beer tents begins.

Canoeing down the Dordogne

FRANCE Have you ever fancied paddling in speckled sunlight past ancient châteaux and honey-hued villages, stopping off for a spot of gentle sightseeing and ending the day with a well-earned gastronomic extravaganza? If so, then canoeing down the Dordogne River in southwest France is just the ticket.

For a 170km stretch from Argentat down to Mauzac, the river provides classic canoeing. The scenery is glorious and varied, there are umpteen first-class sights within a stone's throw of the water, and the choice of accommodation ranges from convivial campsites and rustic village inns to luxury hotels in converted châteaux. The free-flowing river also offers a variety of canoeing conditions to suit beginners upwards, and though it's hardly whitewater rafting, some of the Dordogne's rapids are sufficiently challenging, particularly in spring and early summer, to give at least a *frisson* of excitement.

Keen canoeists should start at Argentat, from where it takes roughly ten days to paddle downstream. The river here is fast, fun and more or less crowd-free. Beyond Beaulieu the current eases back as the river widens, and the first limestone outcrops and sandy beaches – perfect for a picnic lunch – start to appear. Souillac marks the beginning of the most famous – and busiest – stretch of river. If you can only spare one day, then paddle from Souillac, or Domme, to Beynac where the river loops beneath beetling cliffs from which medieval fortresses keep watch from their dizzying eyries. At water level you glide past walnut orchards, duck farms and houses drenched in geraniums.

The crowds fall behind as you slip past Beynac. There are fewer sights and the scenery is more mellow, though the Dordogne has one final treat in store at Limeuil where it splits into two great channels that meander across the floodplain. Leave your canoe behind and head for the limestone cliffs for a bird's-eye view of this classic Dordogne scene.

087 | On the glittering trail of Klimt in Vienna

AUSTRIA Known for its lavish balls and even more lavish cakes, Vienna is overflowing with art. If there's one image that encapsulates the city, it's of an elegant, gold-clad muse staring out at the viewer with an unsettling beauty. No, not Conchita Wurst, but the women of Gustav Klimt's paintings. A tour of his artworks not only takes you to Vienna's finest galleries, but provides a window on the city at the beginning of the twentieth century.

In 1897, a group of artists frustrated with the constraints of Vienna's cultural establishment formed "The Secession" movement. Klimt was their first president, and their headquarters was a bold statement of *Jugendstil* (youth style), a simple white building topped with a golden dome. Displayed inside, Klimt's *Beethoven Frieze* (1902) depicts the quest for happiness. Its parade of strange characters – including Death, Madness, Lasciviousness and Wantonness – are all obstacles to true joy, which is found, in the last panel, through art, poetry and music in the form of Beethoven's Ninth Symphony.

Klimt bridged the avant-garde and traditional decorative arts. He trained at what's now the Museum of Applied Art (MAK), where you can see sketches for his *Stoclet Frieze* alongside objects by contemporaries in the Wiener Werkstätte. Early in his career, he also helped to decorate several public buildings with murals. In the Kunsthistorisches Museum, distinctive Klimt figures, nestled between the columns of the grand stairwell, usher you into one of the world's greatest art collections.

To see Klimt's most famous works, visit the Belvedere. The collection includes landscapes, portraits of society beauties, and richly decorated icons such as the mesmerizing *Judith* (1901) and, of course, *The Kiss* (1908), its full-on bling and sensuous subject still arresting, however many dodgy reproductions you've seen.

But Klimt – and Vienna – are not mere decoration. The Leopold Museum, an essential last stop, owns Klimt's late masterpiece, the brilliantly disturbing *Death and Life* (1910–15). Fittingly, it's shown alongside numerous paintings by his successor Egon Schiele, whose work brutally exposes the psychological unease lurking in the city Freud called home, an unease that simmers beneath the surface of Klimt's own perfectly gilded canvases.

088 | Cycling in the Dutch countryside

THE NETHERLANDS If you like the idea of cycling, but would rather cut off both arms and legs than bike up a mountain, then perhaps the Netherlands is the perfect place for you – especially if you're also scared of traffic.

The most cycle-friendly nation in the world, Holland has a fantastically well-integrated network of 26 well-signposted, long-distance or LF (*landelijke fietroutes*) paths, which connect up the entire country.

As you never have to go near a main road, the cycle paths make it straightforward for even the rawest cycling greenhorns to get around by bike, and to enjoy its underrated and sometimes swooningly beautiful vast skies, endlessly flat pastures and huge expanses of water.

The Netherlands is a small country, and it's easy to cover 50km or so a day, maybe more if you're fit enough and have a decent bike. If you're not planning to go very far, then you'll be OK using a sit-up-and-beg Dutch-style bike, gearless and with back-pedal brakes, which are only really suitable for short distances.

The one thing holding you back may be the wind, which can whip across the Dutch dykes and polders. But there's nothing quite like the refreshing feeling of your first Heineken of the evening after a long day's cycle ride. *Tot ziens!*

089 | Taste the wines of the Moselle Valley

GERMANY Clinging to the winding banks of the River Moselle, along with those of its tributaries, the Ruwer and the Saar, the 242km Moselle Wine Route runs from the western town of Perl to Koblenz, where the Moselle converges with the Rhine. Among the most prestigious of Germany's thirteen officially designated wine regions, it's also one of the largest, with over six thousand wine growers cultivating 88 million vines across some 126,000 acres of vineyards.

All impossibly steep terraced vineyards, teetering hilltop castles and palaces, and atmospheric German villages, the Moselle Valley is highly scenic in itself. Although grapes like Müller-Thurgau and the fruity and full-bodied Bacchus are cultivated here – and even fruity Blauer Spätburgunder (Pinot Noir) – the area is especially famous for its Rieslings. Taking up just over half of the slopes, they are truly inspiring wines, some of the best in the world in fact: light and crisp, low in alcohol and high in acidity, with subtle, flowery aromas.

Due to the lay of the land, in which gradients can reach as much as 68 percent, most of the work is still done by hand, from pruning and weeding to the harvest itself. You can learn precisely what's involved by visiting local producers; the best known include Piesporter Goldtröpfchen, Brauneberger Juffer and Trittenheimer Apotheke.

Marked with signs bearing three bunches of grapes and a letter "M", the Moselle Wine Route also features around 75 historic towns, including Traben-Trarbach, with its impressive Art Nouveau architecture; Cochem, home to picturesque medieval streets and a fine riverfront promenade; and Bernkastel-Kues, which has an attractive market square and still bears traces of its former existence as a Roman settlement.

Dedicated hiking and cycling trails lead through the whole region, while wine and music festivals – not least the Moselle Music Festival – take place throughout the summer and autumn.

090 | Washing it down with cider in Normandy

FRANCE Normandy is to cider what Bordeaux is to wine. Sparkling, crisp and refreshing, it's the perfect foil to the artery-clogging food that Normans also do rather well – and as some of France's best food and drink comes from the rolling hills and green meadows of Normandy's Pays d'Auge, dining at a country restaurant in these parts is an experience not to miss.

The bottle of cider plonked down by your waiter may look as distinguished as a fine champagne, but don't stand on ceremony: open it quickly and take a good swig while it's still cold.

Norman cider is typically sweeter and less alcoholic than its English cousin, with an invigorating fizz that tickles the back of the throat and bubbles up through the nose. Be sure to try a *kir normand*: cider mixed with cassis – a sophisticated and deliciously French take on that old student favourite, "snakebite and black".

Make sure that you have a full glass ready for the arrival of your *andouilles* starter: although it won't necessarily enhance the taste of assorted blood and guts in a sausage, a generous gulp of cider will help get it down. Pork and cider, on the other hand, is one of the classic combinations of Norman cooking. Opt for some pork chops to follow and they come drowned in a thick, deliciously satisfying sauce with as much cream in it as cider.

At this point, you may be offered the *trou normand*: a shot of Calvados apple brandy that helps digestion, apparently by lighting a fire in the pit of your stomach that burns through even the toughest *andouilles*' intestines. The *trou* clears just enough room for a slice of Camembert or Pont-l'Evêque, two of the famous cheeses produced in the Pays d'Auge, before you can finally leave the table, full and just a bit wobbly.

091 | Chewy times on Bregenzerwald's Cheese Street

AUSTRIA Despite the name, Bregenzerwald's *KäseStrasse* (Cheese Street) in Austria's Vorarlberg region is not a marked route along a specific road. Instead it denotes an association of cheese-related industries – around two hundred partners in all – that are united in cultivating, maintaining and promoting the highest standards of regional cheese production. Visitors can thus gain insights about cheese and other regional food production via operations that range from dairies, farms and private cheese makers to butchers, bakers and museums.

By far the best way to explore the area is by hiking. Bregenzerwald is a splendid rural landscape in itself, dotted with lush Alpine meadows, picturesque farms and traditional wooden-shingled farmhouses. The "route" spans an area of around 100km, with each venue marked by the distinctive *KäseStrasse* logo. As you explore, you're likely to come across everything from the Alpine Dairy Farming Museum in Hittisau, where you can see a 300-year-old dairy kitchen and learn about cheese-making and milk processing (guided tours available), to romantic mountain

inns (*hütte*). There are also some surprisingly modern spots, such as the Käsekeller Lingenau, demonstrating how cheese is matured, and KäseMolke Metzler, which produces natural remedies and cosmetics from whey.

Then, of course, there are the fantastic restaurants (*gasthöfe*), where you can sample dishes like the delicious macaroni cheese-esque concoction *Käseknopfel*. To be registered in the association, each restaurant has to have at least five different cheese dishes on its menu, and use a minimum of five Bregenzerwald cheeses.

In terms of when to visit, the summer is of course best for warm weather, while the region's *KäseHerbst* season (the "fifth season"), from mid-September to the end of October, is a popular time to host traditional festivals. Culture vultures may also be delighted to learn that the region hosts two excellent annual music events: an Opera Festival in Bregenz, and the Schubertiade, which takes place in the charming village of Schwarzenberg.

092 | Playboys and petrolheads: the Monaco Grand Prix

MONACO From the hotel-sized yachts in the harbour to the celebrity-filled Casino, the Grand Prix in Monaco is more than a motor race – it's a three-day playboy paradise. The Monaco crown is still the most sought-after in motor-racing circles, although today's event is as much a showcase for the richest men and women on the planet as it is for the drivers.

Set among the winding streets of the world's second-smallest and most densely populated principality, this is the most glamorous and high-profile date on the Formula One calendar. Attracting a global television audience of millions, the cars roar their way around the city centre at four times the speed the streets were designed for. The circuit is blessed with some of the most historic and memorable corners in motor racing: St Devote, Mirabeau, La Rascasse, Casino and, of course, the Tunnel. Part of Monaco's appeal is its renowned difficulty. Three-times Formula One World Champion Nelson Piquet memorably

described tackling the circuit as like "riding a bicycle around your living room".

Watching this gladiatorial spectacle around the Portier corner – one of the few possible, if unlikely, overtaking points on the course – is particularly thrilling, seeing the cars' flaming exhausts before they disappear into the Tunnel, and hearing the echoing engines roar behind. But one of the best and cheapest places to watch the race is the standing-only Secteur Rocher, a grassy area on a hill above the last corner – La Rascasse – at the circuit's western end, which offers fine views and attracts the most passionate F1 supporters. The cars look pretty small from up here, but watching them sweep past is exhilarating. And afterwards you can climb down for a stroll or drive around the circuit, which is reopened to traffic every evening: just don't imagine you're Michael Schumacher – the normal speed limit still applies.

093
Gorging on chocolates in Brussels

BELGIUM The Maya may have invented chocolate long ago, but Belgium is today its world headquarters, and nowhere more so than Brussels, whose temples to the art of the brown stuff are second to none. It's not just a tourist thing, although within the vicinity of the Grand-Place you could be forgiven for thinking so. Chocolate is massively popular in Belgium, and even the smallest town has at least a couple of chocolate shops; in fact, the country has two thousand all told, and produces 172,000 tonnes of chocolate every year. You may think that this would make for a nation of obese lardcakes, especially as Belgium's other favourite thing is beer (not even mentioning the country's obsession with *pommes frites*). However, whatever your doctor may tell you, chocolate in moderation is quite healthy. It reduces cholesterol and is easily digested; some claim it's an aphrodisiac as well.

So what are you waiting for? Everyone has their favourite chocolatier – some swear by *Neuhaus*, while others rely on good old *Leonidas*, which has a shop on every corner in Brussels – but *Godiva*

is perhaps the best-known Belgian name, formed in the early 1900s by Joseph Draps, one of whose descendants now runs a chocolate museum on the Grand-Place.

Once you've checked that out (and gobbled down a few free samples), make for the elegant Place du Grand Sablon, with not only a *Godiva* outlet, but also the stylish shop of *Pierre Marcolini*, who produces some of the best chocs in the city, if not the world. *Wittamer*, also on Place du Grand Sablon, doesn't just do chocolates, and in fact you can sip coffee and munch on a chocolate-covered choux pastry at its rather nice café; you're probably best off saving that big box of *Wittamer*'s delicious pralines for later... though trying just a few now surely can't hurt.

If you're not feeling queasy quite yet, stop at *Planète Chocolate*, on rue du Lombard, where you can find the city's most exotic and adventurous flavours – pepper, rose, various kinds of tea – as well as watch the chocolate-making process in action, followed by (what else?) the obligatory tasting. Moderation be damned.

The tiny French city that packs a mighty punch

FRANCE The ingredients for a great European weekend break are simple. You'll need a walkable city centre, a handful of excellent restaurants, some cool bars and a sprinkling of interesting attractions. Lyon, one of France's most delightful small cities and the country's culinary capital, ticks all these boxes – and more.

Lyon is a delight to wander. You'll spend most of your time between the ancient alleys of Vieux Lyon and the grander streets of the Presqu'île, perhaps with forays into the appealingly gritty district of Croix-Rousse. You'll rarely find yourself walking for more than half an hour, with plenty of food and drink spots for stops en route.

With more than two thousand restaurants and a prestigious culinary history stretching back to the nineteenth century, Lyon easily ranks as one of the top foodie destinations in Europe. Visit traditional *bouchons* for dishes such as *andouillette* and *tarte aux pralines*; call by the city's indoor market, the Halles de Lyon Paul Bocuse; and stop at one of the market bars for locally cured charcuterie and a light Beaujolais red.

A vibrant bar scene is also emerging: natural wine bar *Chateauneuf du Peuple* is one of the coolest places to drink, with a range of unusual bottles from boutique producers. You'll find award-winning cocktails at speakeasy-style *L'Antiquaire*, while the speciality coffee scene is starting to flourish at hip little cafés such as Mokxa and Le Tigre.

There's a good dose of culture, too. A clutch of excellent museums includes the standout Musée des Confluences, devoted to science and anthropology, and Musée des Beaux-Arts, featuring works from the likes of Rubens and Rembrandt. Elsewhere, you'll find exhibitions by big names such as Yoko Ono and Andy Warhol in the Renzo Piano-designed Musée d'Art Contemporain (MAC).

You'll also find plenty of things to do for free. The whole city is UNESCO-listed, with the Basilique Notre-Dame, Roman amphitheatres and ancient *traboules* (secret passages once used by silk manufacturers) just a few of the fascinating sights that are free to explore.

095 | Eating bouillabaisse on Marseille's Vieux Port

FRANCE Loved and maligned in equal measure, multicultural Marseille is urban France at its most forceful – it's noisy and streetwise, edgy and energetic, wild-eyed and wonderful. The city's blend of different influences and ethnicities gives it more claim than most to being the proverbial "melting pot" – and that term can also apply to the delicious, ingredient-busy fish broth that is its most famous culinary creation. Nice might have its *ratatouille* and Dijon its *boeuf bourguignon*, but Marseille has its *bouillabaisse*.

Originally concocted by local fishermen as a thrown-together stew made up of unsold leftovers from the day's catch – usually incorporating the bony rockfish – the dish has been greatly refined over the years. Most versions now contain at least three different kinds of fish, while in its more elaborate form you might find weever fish, John Dory, gurnerfish, eel, anglerfish, lobster and sometimes more besides, not to mention an extensive list of herbs, spices and vegetables. Even eating the dish has become ritualized – you're served the bouillon, or broth, with garlic-rubbed bread as a starter, before the fish and other ingredients arrive as a separate course. It's pricy when it's done well, but makes for a very worthwhile splurge.

Bouillabaisse is best sampled at one of the harbourside restaurants around Marseille's imposing Vieux Port. Fittingly, there's also a daily open-air fish market here, where you can still watch the morning haul being transferred from boat to stall. *Restaurant Le Miramar*, overlooking the scene, is often hailed as the city's definitive *bouillabaisse* outlet, partly because it's spent close to fifty years wooing discerning seafood diners. It even offers *bouillabaisse* cookery lessons on the third Thursday of each month, where you'll have the chance to see just how much time and effort – and, for that matter, how much marine life – goes into Marseille's trademark blow-out.

096 | Freewheeling in the Upper Danube Valley

GERMANY When Germans wax lyrical about the Rhine and Bavarian Alps, they're just trying to keep you out of the Upper Danube Valley. Few visitors know that Strauss's beloved Blue Danube waltzes into the picture in the Black Forest; and fewer still know that one of its most awe-inspiring stretches is tucked away in rural Swabia.

Here, limestone pinnacles and cave-riddled crags entice you to look up. Looking up, however, may be tempting, but it can also be treacherous when you're on a bike. Lose your balance and you may barely manage to escape a head-on collision with a cliff. Breathtaking – in every sense of the word. Freewheeling from Fridingen, you follow the loops and bends of the Danube River through evergreen valleys speckled with purple thistles. There's something special about a place that, for all its beauty, remains untouched by tourism. Aside perhaps from the odd farmer bidding you "*Guten Tag*", you can be alone in this Daliesque landscape; where surreal rock formations and deep crevasses punctuate shady pine and birch forests. Soft breezes blow across the cliffs, and you can hear the distant hammering of woodpeckers.

Pull up at a bend in the river, and pause to dangle your toes in the tingling water, streaked pink and gold. Towering 200m above is the gravity-defying Burg Bronnen, a medieval castle clinging precipitously to a rocky outcrop and seemingly hanging on for dear life. No way are you going to lug your bike up there.

No matter, you can still make it to the Benedictine abbey in Beuron if you notch it up a gear. Then again, why bother? Out here in the sticks, time no longer matters. Why not just slip back into your saddle, and carry on slowly tracing the curves of the Danube, gazing at an ever-shifting landscape as the late-afternoon sun silhouettes turrets, pinnacles and treetops?

097 | Ice and spice at Liège's Christmas market

BELGIUM Sugar and spice and all things nice, plus hand-warming cups of *escargots* (snails), sugary waffles, chocolate-filled crêpes and beer galore. Christmas doesn't come just one day a year in Belgium: for the whole month of December, Yuletide markets cover the country's cobblestoned squares. Liège – an ancient Walloon city an hour southeast of Brussels – hosts the largest, oldest and best.

In 1989, Liège established the "Village de Noël", a collection of over two hundred wooden chalets bedecked with twinkling fairy lights and dressed with cottonwool "snow". Over 1.5 million visitors come from all over Europe to sample the array of culinary treats on offer: from vast pans of steaming *tartiflette*, bun-sheathed and mustard-laden hot dogs, freshly shucked oysters and huge rounds of stinky cheese, to spicy mulled wine, windpipe-warming *peket* (locally made gin) and hefty Belgian beers.

Kids wrap their tongues around striped candy canes and head-sized lollipops, while their parents stock up on artisanal Christmas gifts such as hand-blown glass baubles, carved wooden toys, Peruvian woollen hats and mittens, Canadian fur stoles, Moroccan lamps, ceramic bowls, handmade soaps and jewellery, and home-made jams and oils.

Once all the treats have been digested, it's time to ride the giant Ferris wheel, strap on some skates and slide onto the ice rink, or race each other on the toboggan run.

Come weekends, bands of musicians wend their way through the streets playing carols, while balloon sculptors, dancing troupes and choirs take to centre stage to entertain scarf- and coat-clad families, all rosy cheeks and frosty breath.

As the night darkens and the mercury plummets, visitors cluster closer around the patio heaters provided by the makeshift bars, sipping on ever-stronger tipples before finally heading off in search of a late-night plate of *boulets à la liègeoise* (meatballs doused in sweet Liège syrup).

098 | Communing with Carnac's prehistoric past

FRANCE Created around 3300 BC, Carnac's three alignments of over two thousand menhirs comprise the greatest concentration of standing stones in the world. Come here in the summer and you'll encounter crowds and boundary ropes. But visit during the winter and you can wander among them freely – and if you arrive just after sunrise, when the mist still clings to the coast, you'll be accompanied by nothing but the birds and the sounds of the local farms waking up.

Just to the north of town, where the stones of Le Ménec alignment are at their tallest, you can walk between broken megalithic walls that stand twice your height. Stretching for more than 100m from one side to the other and extending for over 1km, the rows of stones might first seem part of a vast art installation. Each is weathered and worn by five thousand years of wild Atlantic storms, and their stark individuality provides a compelling contrast to the symmetry of the overall arrangement. But it's hard to believe there wasn't something religious about them.

It's possible that the stones had some sort of ritual significance, linked to the numerous tombs and dolmens in the area; or they may have been the centre of a mind-blowing system to measure the precise movements of the moon – we simply don't know.

At the northwest end of the third and final alignment, Kerlescan, don't turn back as most visitors do. Keep walking to where the stones peter out in the thick, damp woodland of Petit Ménec, and the moss- and lichen-smothered menhirs seem even more enchanting, half hidden in the leaves. There's something rather stirring about these megalithic monuments, and something mystical – the sense of being in a spiritual place. And the knowledge that they were placed here for reasons we don't understand sends shivers down your spine.

099 | Clawing for clams on Île de Noirmoutier

FRANCE It's quite some time after sunrise – and at least one *café au lait* and *pain au chocolat* in – when you head through the pine trees to Plage des Sableaux, on the laidback, unassuming little island, perched at the top of the Vendée region. You clutch your regulatory clam claw and carry an optimistically large wire basket. At low tide it seems the whole island, and their *grandmaman*, has the same idea: to dig for something fishy for dinner.

The ocean is so far out the shoreline is no longer even visible, the beach a vast expanse of shimmering wet sand, pockets of water reflecting the flat, pale blue sky, back at itself. People are silhouetted against the low morning sun; dark shapes bent over, kneeling or slowly but purposefully moving, heads down, searching out new spots to try their luck. You can hear the chalky clack of shell against shell, as each briny find is tossed into a basket. It looks easy. Relaxing, even.

Half-hour and an aching back and empty bucket later, it's time to copy the locals. Concentrating on the shallow pools around small rocks you look for the telltale air bubbles. Using your hands, you scoop the gloopy silty sand, sifting with your fingers to reveal the clams below. Nothing in the rules about fingers.

So you end up with not exactly a full basket, but enough to cook up a big pan of *spaghetti alle vongole*, the sauce an explosion of fresh, plump tomatoes zinging with garlic, and those soft meaty clams with their hint of the ocean – washed down with a glass or two of something crisp and white, of course.

100 | Taking a dip in Berlin's lakes

GERMANY Well known to locals but often a complete surprise to visitors, the dozens of lakes that surround Berlin provide a wonderful escape during the warmer months from the heat and bustle of the city. They come in all shapes and sizes, ranging from the largest, the Grosser Muggelsee, to several much smaller lakes that can be tricky to find without local help.

Some lakes, known as *Strandbäder*, or beach baths, have official lidos and swimming areas that charge small entry fees but offer well-kept amenities such as toilets and changing rooms, snack kiosks (usually selling sausages, ice cream, beer and soft drinks), and sometimes beach shops.

The most famous of these, the 2.7-square-kilometre Grosser Wannsee in the southwest of the city, has been luring the punters for over a hundred years, and has even had a famous song written about it – Conny Froboess' *Pack die Badehose ein*. With its long, sandy beach, capable of holding up to fifty thousand people, wicker chairs (*Strandkorben*) and much-loved water, it's an easy and enticing place to spend the entire day, even if you simply slurp ice cream and watch the yachts drift by.

The equivalent in the Eastern suburbs is the aforementioned Grosser Muggelsee, which covers 7.4 square kilometres, and the Strandbad Muggelsee, which has a small spa, leafy gardens and a large FKK (nudist) beach. The lake resort of Friedrichshagen is alongside, as is the neighbouring Kleiner Muggelsee, which also has its own beach.

Other recommended city lakes – some have official lidos, some are more "natural" – include Tegelersee, Schlactensee, Gross Glienicker See, Leipnitzsee, Bernsteinsee and Lietzensee. Although most are accessible within an hour by public transport, a venerable Berlin tradition involves packing your swimming gear and a picnic into your bike basket and using pedal power to find your own little seaside paradise. Alternatively, it's also possible to explore the lakes via the 66-Lakes-Trail, which also passes through some of Brandenburg's wonderful woodlands, heaths and meadows.

The Cathar castles of Languedoc-Roussillon

FRANCE It's hard to forget the first time you catch a glimpse of the Château de Peyrepertuse. In fact, it takes a while before you realize that this really is a castle, not just some fantastic rock formation sprouting from the mountaintop. But it's no mirage – 800 years ago, men really did haul slabs of stone up here to build one of the most hauntingly beautiful fortresses in Europe.

War was frequent in medieval France, and life often violent. The point of castles, obviously enough, was to provide a degree of protection from all that. Location was all-important – and the Cathar lords of Languedoc-Roussillon took this to ludicrous extremes, building their fortresses in seemingly impossible places. How they even laid foundations boggles the mind.

Approach on foot, from the village of Duilhac, and Peyrepertuse is a staggering sight. Improbably perched on the edge of a long, rocky ridge, it's surrounded by a sheer drop of several hundred metres, and its outer walls cleverly follow the contours of the mountain, snaking around the summit like a stone viper. Inside, at the lower end, is the main keep, a solid grey cube of rock that looks like it could withstand a battering from smart bombs, never mind medieval cannon. But to really appreciate the fortress, you have to get closer.

It's a sweaty hour-long hike to the top, but when you clamber through the main entrance and onto the upper keep, the views from the battlements are stupendous: here, where the mountain ends in a vast, jagged stub of granite, there are no walls – you'd need wings to attack from this side.

Ironically, even castles like this couldn't protect the Cathars. In the early thirteenth century, this Christian cult was virtually exterminated after forty years of war and a series of massacres that were brutal even by medieval standards. Peyrepertuse surrendered in 1240, but the fact that it still survives, as impressive now as it must have been centuries ago, is testament to the Cathars' ingenious building skills and their passionate struggle for religious freedom.

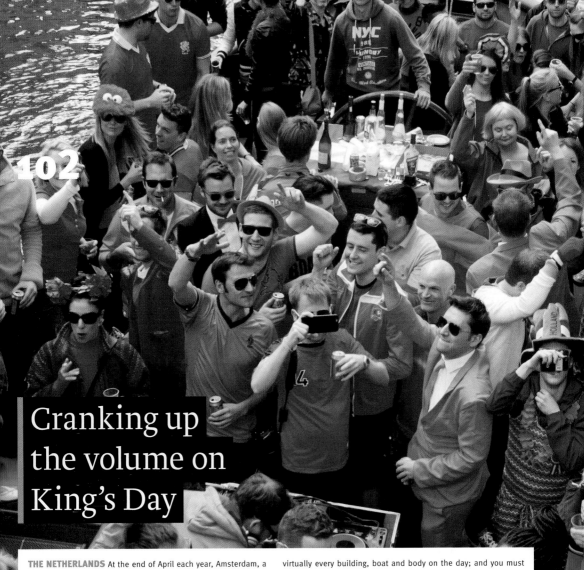

Cranking up the volume on King's Day

THE NETHERLANDS At the end of April each year, Amsterdam, a city famed for its easy-going, fun-loving population, manages to crank the party volume a few notches higher in a street party that blasts away for a full 24 hours. Held to celebrate the official birthday of the Dutch monarch, King's Day is traditionally the one time each year when the police are forbidden from interfering with any activity, no matter how outrageous; and, of course, it's always a challenge to see where they really draw the line.

Stages piled high with huge sound systems take over every available open space, blasting out the beats all day and night – the main stages are on Rembrandtplein and particularly Thorbeckplein, Leidseplein, Nieuwmarkt and Museumplein – and whatever your inclination, you'll find enough beer-chugging, pill-popping and red-hot partying to satisfy the most voracious of appetites. There are only two rules: you must dress as ridiculously as possible, preferably in orange, the Dutch national colour, which adorns virtually every building, boat and body on the day; and you must drink enough beer not to care.

The extensive and picturesque canals are Amsterdam's pride and joy, and King's Day makes the most of them. Boating restrictions are lifted (or perhaps just ignored) and everyone goes bananas on the water – rowing boats, barges and old fishing vessels, crammed full of people, crates of beer and booming sound systems, pound their way along the canals like entrants in some particularly disorganized aquatic carnival. Your mission is to get on board, as they're a great way to get around – pick one with good tunes and people you like the look of.

Alternatively, just hang out with everyone else and watch the boats come and go: crowds gather on the larger bridges and canal junctions to cheer as each bizarre vessel passes. Prinsengracht is a good canal to pick, with Reguliersgracht and Prinsengracht a particularly chaotic and enjoyable intersection.

103 | Paying your respects in Normandy

FRANCE Apart from the German stronghold of Pointe du Hoc, where gleeful kids take time out from building sandcastles to clamber over the rubble of battered bunkers, and the seafront at Arromanches, where parts of a floating harbour towed from England now lies in ruins just offshore, the D-Day landing beaches – Sword, Juno, Gold, Omaha and Utah – hold few traces of their bloody past.

It's almost as though the cheery banality of summertime in the seaside towns along this stretch of the Norman coast is deliberately intended to mask the painful memories of June 6, 1944. The beaches are dotted with gaily painted wooden bathing huts; the odd windsurfer braves the choppy waters; walkers ramble along the dunes; families up from Paris eat *moules frites* at beachside terraces – all a far cry from the terrible events of the day itself.

But while the sands are consumed by summer's frivolity, the cemeteries built to bury the D-Day dead serve as sanctuaries for those who don't want to forget. Visitors shuffle in silence across the well-manicured lawns of the American burial ground on a cliff overlooking Omaha, where rows of perfectly aligned white crosses sweep down to the cliff's edge and appear to continue for kilometres into the sea. In the church-like peace and tranquillity, broken only by the cries of seagulls, uniformed veterans remember fallen comrades and lost husbands and fathers. Even the children, too young to understand the sacrifices made, are humbled by the solemnity of their surroundings, affording only glancing and indifferent looks at the kites swirling in the breeze before returning to the poignantly simple crosses that have made the grown-ups so quiet.

104 | The jewel of Berry: Cathédrale St-Etienne

FRANCE A flat plain at the very heart of France, stranded between the verdant Loire Valley and the abundant hillsides of Burgundy, the Berry region has become a byword for provincial obscurity. This is *La France profonde*, the cherished "deep France", whose peasant traditions continue to resist the modernization that threatens – so they say – to engulf the nation. You can drive a long way here without seeing any more than open fields and modest farmhouses.

As you approach the miniature regional capital of Bourges, however, a mighty landmark begins to reveal itself. Looming over the fields, allotments and low houses is a vast Gothic cathedral, its perfect skeleton of flying buttresses and keel-like roof giving it the look of a huge ship in dry dock. A stupendous relic of the inexorable, withdrawing tide of power and belief, its preposterous size and wealth of detailing prove that the Berry was not always a backwater. In the early thirteenth century, when the cathedral was built, this was a powerful and wealthy region – and Bourges' archbishops wanted all the world to know it.

At the foot of the impossibly massive west front, five great portals yawn open, their deep arches fringed by sculptures. You could spend hours gazing at the central portal, which depicts the Last Judgement in appalling detail, complete with snake-tailed and wing-arsed devils, and damned souls – some wearing bishops' mitres – screaming from the bottom of boiling cauldrons.

Inside, the prevailing mood is one of quieter awe. The magnificent nave soars to an astonishing 38m, and is ringed by two tall aisles. No matter where you look, smooth-as-bone columns power their way from marble floor to tent-like vault, their pale stone magically dappled with colours cast by some of Europe's finest, oldest and deepest-hued stained glass.

Behind the high altar, at the very heart of the cathedral and at the very centre of France, the apse holds these jewels of the Berry: precious panels of coloured glass, their images of the Crucifixion, the Last Judgement, the Apocalypse and of Joseph and his coat glowing like gemstones.

105 | Marooned on Sein: the island at the edge of the world

FRANCE Of the many isolated islands dotted off the coast of Brittany, the tiny, flat-as-a-pancake Île de Sein has to be the most romantic and mysterious. A slender sliver, silhouetted against the sunset, Sein lies 8km west of the rocky Pointe du Raz, Brittany's westernmost promontory. Nowhere rising more than 6m above the surrounding sea, for much of its 2.5km length the island is little broader than the concrete breakwater that serves as its central spine. Each fresh tide seems likely to wash right over the land, and its very grip on existence seems so tenuous it's hard to believe anyone could survive here. However, a couple of hundred islanders make their living from the sea, fishing for scallops, lobster and crayfish. Indeed, the island has long been inhabited; Roman sources tell of a shrine served by nine virgin priestesses, and it's said to have been the last refuge of the Druids in Brittany.

Setting off to Sein on a misty morning feels like sailing off the edge of the world. Having picked their way along a chain of lonely lighthouses, ferries draw in at the island's one tight-knit village, hunched with its back to the open ocean. There are no cars – the rugged stone houses snuggle so close that no vehicle could squeeze between them – and even bicycles are not permitted.

Although low tide uncovers a small sandy beach in one of the harbours, there's little to the village itself, and most visitors stride off to enjoy the ravishing coastal scenery, where land, sea and sky meld together in a whirl of white surf. The tiny agricultural terraces of the eastern tip, connected by a pencil-thin natural causeway, have long been overgrown with sparse yellow broom – you'll probably have the place to yourself as you explore the myriad rock pools. A longer walk west leads to the Phare de Goulenez lighthouse; though it's not open to visitors, the lighthouse is an oddly comforting presence here at the very edge of the island, as the ocean claws and drags at the black, seaweed-strewn boulders, and the screaming seagulls return from their forays over the infinite Atlantic.

106 | Going to the medieval movies

FRANCE A world apart from piles of old stones, paintings of curly-wigged fat men or pungent-smelling châteaux, seeing the Bayeux Tapestry is more like going to the movies than trotting round a traditional tourist sight. Wrapped around a half-lit wall like a medieval IMAX theatre, it's protected by a glass case and dim lighting, while a deep, movie-trailer voice gives a blow-by-blow headphone commentary of the kings, shipwrecks and gory battles depicted in the comic-strip-like scenes.

The nuns who are thought to have embroidered this 70m strip of linen, which chronicles William of Normandy's 1066 conquest of England, could hardly have guessed that, nearly a millennium later, people would be lining up to marvel at their meticulous artwork and impeccable storytelling.

Like Shakespeare's plays, however, the Bayeux Tapestry is one of history's timeless treasures. Okay, so the characters are two-dimensional, the ancient colours hardly HD and the scenes

difficult to decipher without the commentary, but it's captivating nonetheless. William looks every bit the superhero on the back of his huge horse, while King Harold, with his dastardly moustache, appears the archetypal villain, his arrow in the eye a just dessert.

The wonderful detail adds intriguing layers to the main theme: the appearance of Halley's Comet as a bad omen when Harold is crowned king builds up the suspense, while the apparent barbecuing of kebabs on the beach has led some historians to argue that the tapestry is considerably newer than generally thought. Whether this is true is of no great importance – the images are as engrossing now as they ever were, and on exiting the theatre, even the staunchest of Brits might feel enthused enough to be secretly pleased that a brave Frenchman crossed the Channel to give Harold his comeuppance. And in this way, the Bayeux Tapestry has lost none of its power as one of the finest pieces of propaganda the world has ever seen.

107 | Joining the Gilles at Binche Carnival

BELGIUM Taking place in February or March, the four-hundred-year-old Binche Carnival is a magic combination of the country's national preoccupation with beer – outdoor beer tents are stacked high with a huge variety of Belgian brews – and a bizarre tradition that dates back to the Middle Ages.

The spectacular March of the Gilles is a parade of six hundred peculiarly and identically dressed men – the Gilles – strange, giant-like figures who dominate this event, all wearing the same wax masks, along with green glasses and moustaches, apparently in the style of Napoleon III. On Mardi Gras, groups of Gilles gather in the Grand-Place to dance around in a huge circle, or *rondeau*, holding hands and

tapping their wooden-clogged feet in time to the beat of the drum. The drummers, or *tamboureurs*, are situated in the middle of the circle, as is a smaller *rondeau* of petits Gilles. Get inside the circle if you can; here, you're perfectly placed to get dragged in with the Gilles as they head into the town hall for the ritual removal of their masks. In the afternoon, they emerge to lead the Grand Parade, sporting tall hats, elaborately adorned with ostrich feathers, and clutching wooden baskets filled with oranges, which they throw with gusto into the crowd, covering everyone in blood-red juice and pulp. Be warned, though, that this ferocious "battle" is a decidedly one-sided affair – it's not done to throw them back.

108 | Wine-tasting in Bordeaux

FRANCE Margaux, Pauillac, Sauternes, St-Émilion – some of the world's most famous wines come from the vineyards that encircle Bordeaux. So famous, in fact, that until recently, most châteaux didn't bother with marketing their wines. But times are changing: faced with greater competition and falling demand, more and more are opening their doors to the public. It has never been easier to visit these châteaux and sample the wines aptly described as "bottled sunlight".

There's plenty of choice, from top-rank names such as Mouton-Rothschild and Palmer to small, family-run concerns. Some make their wine according to time-honoured techniques, others are ultra high-tech, with gleaming, computer-controlled vats and automated bottling lines. There are a growing number of organic producers, too. All are equally rewarding. During the visit you'll learn about soil types and grape varieties, about fermentation, clarification and the long, complicated process which transforms grapes into wine.

Though you rarely get to see inside the châteaux themselves, several of the estates offer other attractions to draw in the punters, ranging from wine or wine-related museums to introductory wine-tasting classes (this being France, you can sometimes sign up children for the latter, too). And because not everyone is here for the wine alone, there are also art galleries, sculpture parks, hot-air balloon trips and, around St-Émilion, underground quarries to explore.

All visits, nevertheless, end in the tasting room. In top-rank châteaux, an almost reverential hush descends as the bottles are lovingly poured out. The aficionados swirl glasses and sniff the aromas, take a sip, savour it and then spit it out. If you feel like it, an appreciative nod always goes down well. And often, you will feel like it – because despite all the detailed scientific explanations of how they're produced, the taste of these wines suggests that magic still plays a part.

On
the art
trail
on the
Côte d'Azur

FRANCE Like most of Renoir's work, it's instantly appealing, with a dazzling range of colour and a warmth that radiates out from the canvas. A hazy farmhouse at the end of a driveway, framed by leafy trees and bathed in sunny pastel tones, *La Ferme des Collettes* is one of the artist's most famous paintings, perfectly evoking a hot, balmy day in the south of France.

But what makes this watercolour extra special is its location: it's one of eleven on show in the actual *ferme* depicted in the painting, a mansion in Cagnes-sur-Mer where the celebrated Impressionist lived and worked from 1907 until his death, and which is now the Musée Renoir. Step outside and you step right into the picture, bathed in the same bright light and warm Mediterranean air.

And then there's Picasso. Probably the greatest painter of the twentieth century, he spent a prolific year at the Château Grimaldi in Antibes, a short drive south of Nice. Now the Musée Picasso, it's packed with work from that period – the creative energy of *Ulysses and his*

Sirens, a 4m-high representation of the Greek hero tied to the mast of his ship, is simply overwhelming. But it's hard to stare at something this intense for long, and you'll soon find yourself drifting to the windows – and the same spectacular view of the ocean that inspired Picasso sixty years ago.

Ever since pointillist Paul Signac beached his yacht at St-Tropez in the 1880s, the Côte d'Azur has inspired more writers, sculptors and painters than almost anywhere on the planet. If you want to follow in their footsteps, Nice is the place to start, home to Henri Matisse for much of his life. Resist the temptations of the palm-fringed promenade and head inland to the Musée Matisse, a striking maroon-toned building set in the heart of an olive grove. Among the exotic works on display, *Nature morte aux grenades* offers a powerful insight into the intense emotional connection Matisse established with this part of France, his vibrant use of raw, bold colour contrasting beautifully with the rough, almost clumsy, style.

Floating through vineyards on a luxury barge

110

FRANCE Craving slow travel? This is it: mornings on a French Country Waterways cruise through Burgundy spent reclining on a sunwarmed deck, the only sound the quiet slurp of water against the side of the boat. The views are equally soothing: vineyards with fat grapes fan out in all directions and, occasionally, a local slowly pedals by on the towpath.

The full trip aboard the luxury barge is around 120km, which you could cover in a short drive; instead, it's spread out over six languid days. While "barge" may bring to mind industrial freighters belching smoke,

this is the opposite end of the spectrum – a five-star floating hotel and restaurant gliding along leafy canals and waterways of the Saône. Highlights along the way include the Château de la Rochepot, crowned by Burgundian multicoloured glazed tiles; the medieval capital of Beaune; and small, family-run wineries.

Come evening, the most important activity is to do nothing much at all – the hypnotic movement of a barge is a powerful sedative, especially after a glass of Burgundy red. Slow travel, indeed.

111 | Exploring architecture in Maastricht

THE NETHERLANDS Compared to other European cities, Maastricht might seem small and laidback, but the capital of Limburg packs an aesthetic and cultural punch that often takes visitors by surprise. Inhabited since Roman times, and sliced in half by the River Maas, the city was an important centre for trade and manufacturing during the medieval era, and has emerged as a vibrant cosmopolitan place where lifestyles, food and culture have been intriguingly impacted by German, Dutch and Belgian influences.

The architecture of the city is especially interesting to explore. Scattered amid the leafy squares and cobbled streets of the handsome Old Town, you'll find a host of Roman and medieval eye-candy, from the Onze Lieve Vrouwebasiliek church, which incorporates sections constructed from Roman walls, to Pieter Post's seventeenth-century Town Hall, dominating Markt, and thirteenth-century town gates such as Helpoort. There are also of course many old churches, such as the seventeenth-century Gothic Sint-Janskerk church with its soaring 71m spire.

Across Rene Greisch's modern Hoeg Brog, however, things get more modern. The Céramique district, circling out from the main Plein 1992 square, was built in the 1990s by an array of international starchitects. It spans the glass, wood and aluminium Centre Céramique – a former biscuit factory – the Stoa residential development by Swiss architects Luigi Snozzi and Aurelop Galfetti, and La Fortezza, a handsome geometric apartment and office complex by Swiss architect Mario Botta. Just south of the city, the idiosyncratic tower of the Bonnefanten Museum, built by Italian theorist and architect Aldo Rossi, is not only a prominent landmark, but also a fantastic museum in its own right, with both Old Masters and contemporary art.

Recent mixes of the modern and the medieval have more recently created spectacular results, namely the striking *Kruisheren Hotel*, set in a Gothic cloister that dates from the fifteenth century, and the Selexyz Dominicanen, a bookshop housed in a thirteenth-century Dominican church that comprises a three-storey "walk-in" black steel bookcase, and which won the Lensvelt de Architect Interior Prize (2007).

112 | Volcano-hopping in the Auvergne

FRANCE While the lush, low-lying countryside of the Loire and the mellow hills of the Dordogne might be more celebrated French landscapes, the craggy volcanoes and plunging valleys of the less-visited Auvergne will leave any visitor smitten. Rural and remote, the Auvergne holds an incredible eighty volcanoes – all dormant – in its Chaîne des Puys, their perfectly shaped green cones strung out in a row, north to south, like the spine of a slumbering stegosaurus.

Though it's not the highest volcano hereabouts, the mighty Puy de Dôme (1645m) is the iconic local emblem, long venerated by the Auvergnats. The remains of a Roman temple dedicated to Mercury recall its early importance, and it was a popular hiking destination among nineteenth-century tourists.

Cars are banned, but you can either walk the time-honoured route to the top in around an hour, or take the new Panoramique des Dômes electric rack railway, which glides through the clouds to the summit in twenty minutes, giving you time to admire the staggering views.

This being France, there's a gourmet restaurant at the top, but you're best off taking a picnic of bread and Saint-Nectaire cheese (as served at the table of Louis XIV, no less) and enjoying the top-of-the-world views. Grassy slopes, dotted with wildflowers, roll on as far as the eye can see, while paragliders dropping into the void add drama. The regional capital, Clermont-Ferrand, sits a mere 10km away, its cathedral spire just visible from your mountaintop perch.

The volcanoes are not the Auvergne's only highs. Driving in the region is a delight; the narrow roads snake round the undulating landscape, and only the tinkling of cowbells disturbs the absolute peace. Nestled among the volcanoes are scenic lakes carved out of craters, and dramatic rocky gorges. For many, though, the volcanoes' most notable influence has been on the local cuisine: thanks to the ultra-fertile soil, the food is sublime. An Auvergnat favourite is *truffade*, a dish of potatoes cooked in goose fat and stirred with gooey cheese: rib-sticking fare that gives you the heft you'll need to scale mountains.

113 | Taking flight at Angel Mountain

SWITZERLAND Place a map of Switzerland on a dartboard, and Engelberg ("Angel Mountain") will more or less form the bull's-eye. An unpretentious Alpine resort known mainly for its cheese-making monks, it transforms itself into an energetic winter venue for the annual Ski Jumping World Cup each December.

Most people know this most demented of sports solely from the Winter Olympics; for UK viewers, it will forever be associated with the bespectacled also-ran Eddie "The Eagle" Edwards. While Olympic ski jumps tend to be concrete white elephants, however, rarely used once the medals are dished out, in Engelberg the jump comes au naturel: thanks to a quirk of geology, it boasts a vertiginous 125m run that culminates in a perfectly shaped launch pad.

Come December, and the smell of *glühwein* and the sound of cowbells fill the air as 20,000 spectators arrive for two days of airborne thrills. Dozens of steel-thighed lunatics from Osaka to Oslo queue to lock

their skis into icy grooves, put their heads between their knees and let gravity do the rest. Big screens relay the action as these neoprene-clad superheroes take flight for several seconds, skis splayed in the classic V shape, before landing with a thwack and a cheer from the crowd.

For the more conventional downhill fan, Engelberg offers a smorgasbord of off-piste routes and challenging intermediate runs, and thanks to the glacier-capped Mount Titlis the season here lasts all the way from October to May. You'll also find James Bond-style thrills at the local Snow X-park, a race track for snowmobiles where you can pretend to be pursued by evil henchmen at 100km/hr.

If all that sounds rather too exhausting, then settle in for a movie at the European Outdoor Film Tour, which rolls into town along with the Ski Jumping World Cup. Instead of popcorn, film fans enjoy bowls of steaming *raclette*, wrap themselves in cosy blankets and snuggle up for a night under the stars in front of the big screen.

114 | Lord it in the Loire Valley

FRANCE You can't translate the word "château". "Castle" is too warlike, "palace" too regal – and besides, they're all so different: some are grim and broken keeps, others lofty Gothic castles or exquisite Renaissance manor houses. Many are elegant country residences whose tall, shuttered windows overlook swathes of rolling parkland. And a few – the finest – are magnificent royal jewels set in acre upon acre of prime hunting forest.

Today, the aristocracy no longer lords it over every last village in France, but a surprising number still cling to their ancestral homes. Some eke out a living offering tours, and the most fascinating châteaux are not always the grandest palaces but the half-decrepit country homes of faded aristocrats who will show off every stick of furniture, or tell you stories of their ancestors in the very chapel where they themselves will one day be buried.

Some owners, enticingly, even offer bed and breakfast. You get a vividly personal sense of France's patrician past when you wake up and see the moonlight shining through the curtains of your original, seventeenth-century four-poster – as at the Château de Brissac in Anjou. Or when you gaze from your leaded window down an ancient forest ride in the Manoir de la Rémonière in Touraine, or draw a chair up to the giant stone bedroom fireplace at the perfectly tumbledown Château de Chémery, near Blois.

As for the great royal residences, most are now cold and empty. National monuments like Chambord, a "hunting lodge" with a chimney for every day of the year, or Fontainebleau, where the *Mona Lisa* once hung in the royal bathroom, are the stunning but faded fruits of a noble culture that cherished excellence and had the money to pay for it in spades. But thanks to the tourist trade, many châteaux are recovering their former glory. The French state now scours auction houses all over the world for the fine furnishings flogged off by the wagon-load after the Revolution. Once empty and echoing, the royal palaces will soon be gilded once more – if not, perhaps, occupied.

115 | Exploring the prehistoric cave art of Pech Merle

FRANCE Imagine a cave in total darkness. Then a tiny flame from a tar torch appears, piercing the blackness, and a small party of men carrying ochre pigment and charcoal crawl through the labyrinth. They select a spot on the cold, damp walls and start to paint, using nothing but their hands and a vivid imagination. Finished, they gather their torches and leave their work to the dark.

Until now. A mind-blowing 25,000 years later, you can stand in the Grotte de Pech Merle and admire this same astonishing painting: two horses, the right-hand figure with a bold, naturalistic outline that contrasts with the decidedly abstract black dots – two hundred of them – that fill up its body and surround the head. The whole thing is circled, enigmatically, by six handprints, while a red fish positioned above its back adds to the sense of the surreal.

Short of inventing a time machine, this is the closest you'll get to the mind of Stone Age man. And it's this intimacy, enhanced by the cool dimness of the cave, that makes a visit here so overwhelming. Unlike Lascaux in the Dordogne, Pech Merle allows visitors to view the original art, and the so-called dotted horses are just the best-known of the cave's mesmerizing ensemble of seven hundred paintings, finger drawings and engravings of bison, mammoths and horses.

It was once common to think of prehistoric peoples as brutish, shaggy-haired cavemen waving clubs, but some 30,000 years ago here in France, they were busy creating the world's first naturalistic and abstract art. No one's sure just why they made these paintings, but it's possible that the tranquil, womb-like caves were sacred places linked to fertility cults, the drawings divided into male and female symbols suffused with Paleolithic mythology.

New theories, however, suggest something far more prosaic: that the paintings were made primarily by teenage boys who had the subjects of hunting and women foremost on their minds. Perhaps Pech Merle's most poignant treasure backs this up – the footprint of an adolescent boy, captured in clay as he left the cave one evening, some 25,000 years ago.

116 | Going underground in the Casemates du Bock

LUXEMBOURG The network of dark, damp tunnels below Luxembourg City's tenth-century castle – the Rocher du Bock – remains a clear legacy of the country's strategic position within Europe. Narrow stone staircases twist down underground, leading into a maze of cave-like chambers and passageways.

The Spanish began the casemates in 1644, carving them out of the rock to house soldiers and cannons – fortifications upon which successive European powers continued to build. Eventually spanning 23km, the tunnels were partially destroyed after military withdrawal, though they later provided vital shelter for the people of Luxembourg during both world wars. Now a UNESCO World Heritage Site, what remains of the underground ramparts is eerie, claustrophobic and utterly fascinating.

117 | Tasting wines that are fit for a prince

LIECHTENSTEIN Sandwiched between Switzerland and Austria, the principality of Liechtenstein may be pint-sized, but it has plenty of treats up its Alpine sleeves. There's the scenic mountain backdrop, for one, and the appealingly stodgy cuisine – the highlight being *käsknöpfle* (cheese-laden dumplings), which are as good a way as any to line your stomach for a visit to the prince's wine cellars.

Prince Hans-Adam II, resident of the mountaintop medieval castle that looks down imperiously on the state's capital, Vaduz, boasts one of the finest vineyards in the Rhine Valley, with optimum conditions for growing Pinot Noir and Chardonnay.

If you fail to score a personal invitation to the castle, a visit to the prince's Hofkellerei winery for a tasting of its fine vintages is a highly satisfying second best.

Need to know

055 For information on the Berlin Wall Trail and its various sections, visit Ⓦ berlin.de/mauer/mauerweg.

056 For more information, visit Ⓦ pontdugard.fr.

057 *Café Central*, 1, Herrengasse 14 (Ⓦ palaisevents.at); *Café Landtmann*, 1, Dr-Karl-Lueger-Ring 4 (Ⓦ landtmann .at); *Café Hawelka*, 1, Dorotheergasse 6 (Ⓦ hawelka.at).

058 For more information, and to organize tours, see Ⓦ www.wadlopen.net or Ⓦ wadlopen.com.

059 See Ⓦ sncf.com for timetable and fares. Note that the original open-topped carriages only run during the summer, and that many smaller stations are request stops only.

060 Usedom (Ⓦ kaiserbaeder-auf-usedom.de) is 2hr 30min by car or train from Berlin; change at Züssow to reach Heringsdorf and Ahlbeck by rail.

061 *La Bécasse*, rue de Tabora 11 (Ⓦ alabecasse.com); *Cantillon Brewery*, rue Gheude 56 (Ⓦ cantillon.be); *La Mort Subite*, rue Montagne-aux-Herbes Potagères 7 (Ⓦ alamortsubite.com); *In't Spinnekopke*, Place Jardin aux Fleurs 1 (Ⓦ spinnekopke.be); *Delirium*, Impasse de la Fidelité 4a (Ⓦ deliriumvillage.com).

062 Père-Lachaise cemetery is open daily; for a virtual tour, see Ⓦ pere-lachaise.com. Nearest metro stations are Père-Lachaise and Philippe-Auguste. For more info, visit Ⓦ parisinfo.com and Ⓦ paris.fr.

063 The Reichstag dome and roof terrace are open 8am–midnight daily; tickets are free, and must be booked online in advance at Ⓦ bundestag.de.

064 Cap d'Agde is 60km southwest of Montpellier. For more information, visit Ⓦ naturist.de.

065 Match tickets are usually available at least three weeks in advance. Buy them at Ⓦ stadetoulousain.fr or in person at the club store at rue Alsace Lorraine 73.

066 The *Glacier Express* runs daily between St Moritz and Zermatt: full details at Ⓦ glacierexpress.ch.

067 For details of opening times and massage costs, see Ⓦ carasana.de.

068 Check Ⓦ musee-orsay.fr for entry prices and opening times.

069 The Streif run can be found in the resort of Kitzbühel (Ⓦ kitzbuhel.com); the nearest airport is Munich.

070 *L'Epicerie* is at rue du Vieux Seigle 6 in Strasbourg (Ⓦ lepicerie-strasbourg.com), and *L'Ancienne Douane* at rue de la Douane 6 (Ⓦ anciennedouane.fr).

071 Find opening times, prices and other information on the Ars Electronica Centre at Ⓦ ars.electronica.art.

072 *Blindekuh* is at 148 Mühlebachstrasse, Zürich; check Ⓦ blindekuh.ch for opening hours, or call ☎ +41 44 421 5050.

073 Détours de Loire (Ⓦ locationdevelos.com) will drop you off, with bikes, at the location of your choice. See Ⓦ loireavelo.fr for more.

074 For more information, visit Ⓦ abbaye-mont-saint-michel.fr, Ⓦ ot-montsaintmichel.com, and Ⓦ bienvenueaumontsaintmichel.com.

075 *Whitepod* is located near Villars, in southwestern Switzerland (Ⓦ whitepod.com).

076 Tickets for the Bayreuth Festival can be ordered online at Ⓦ bayreuther-festspiele.de, from the start of the preceding Sept.

077 Beach bars open from noon to midnight between May and Sept. *StrandPauli* is at Hafenstr. 89 (Ⓦ strandpauli.de); *Hamburg City Beach Club* at Grosse Elbstr. 279; *Hamburg del Mar* (Ⓦ hamburg-del-mar.de) and *Lago Bay* (Ⓦ lago.cc) at Van-der-Smissen-Str. 4; and *Altona's Strandperle* at Schulberg 2.

078 Fly Zermatt offers tandem paragliding flights in view of the Matterhorn year-round, including equipment and instruction; Ⓦ flyzermatt.com. Wear warm clothing, even in summer.

079 Épernay's tourist office (Ⓦ ot-epernay.fr) has information on touring the town's champagne houses.

080 Fribourg is the best place to try a classic-style *moitié-moitié*; the pick of the bunch is the excellent *Gothard* at rue du Pont-Muré 18 (Ⓦ le-gothard.ch).

081 Ferries from Santa Teresa di Gallura in Sardinia run daily, all year. Corsica has an airport at Figari, 17km north of Bonifacio. For more, go to Ⓦ bonifacio.fr.

082 Ⓦ montreuxjazzfestival.com holds information on schedules, tickets and everything else.

083 The castle is a 20min walk from Hohenschwangau, in south Bavaria. See Ⓦ neuschwanstein.de.

084 For information and tickets go to Ⓦ rhb.ch/en/home.

085 For more info, check out Ⓦ oktoberfest.de.

086 Numerous canoe rental companies operate at various points along the Dordogne during summer. For more details, visit Ⓦ canoe-kayak-dordogne.com or Ⓦ canoe-france.com.

087 All museums listed are in central Vienna; to do them all justice, give yourself at least two days. See Ⓦ secession.at, Ⓦ mak.at, Ⓦ khm.at, Ⓦ belvedere.at, Ⓦ leopoldmuseum.org and Ⓦ wien.info for more.

088 For more information, visit Ⓦ nederlandfietsland .nl. The Dutch motoring organization, the ANWB, publishes cycle maps that cover the whole country.

089 For an English-language overview of the route, a downloadable brochure and an accommodation booking service, visit Ⓦ mosellandtouristik.de. The Moselle Music Festival takes place between June and Oct annually (Ⓦ moselmusikfestival.de).

090 The Route du Cidre is a 40km loop in the Pays d'Auge; see Ⓦ calvados-tourisme.com.

091 For tours of the Farming Museum in Hittisau, contact Ⓦ hittisau.at. The Bregenz Opera Festival (Ⓦ bregenzerfestspiele.com) takes place in July/Aug (dates vary each year), while Schwarzenberg's two-part Schubertiad (Ⓦ schubertiade.at) runs just before and afterwards, usually in June and Sept.

092 The Monaco Grand Prix is held each May. For tickets, visit Ⓦ formula1.com or Ⓦ monaco-grand-prix .com.

093 *Godiva*, Place du Grand Sablon 47–48 (Ⓦ godiva. com); *Pierre Marcolini*, rue des Minimes 1 (Ⓦ eu. marcolini.com); *Wittamer*, Place du Grand Sablon 12 (Ⓦ wittamer.com); and *Planète Chocolate*, rue du Lombard 24 (Ⓦ planetechocolat.be).

094 Find out more about Lyon at Ⓦ en.lyon-france. com.

095 Visit Ⓦ marseille-tourisme.com/en/ for city information. *Restaurant Le Miramar* details its *bouillabaisse* recipe, and lessons, at Ⓦ lemiramar.fr.

096 Trails in the Upper Danube Valley are mostly flat and well signposted. Valley Bike (Ⓦ valleybike.de) in Hausen am Tal near Beuron rents mountain bikes to visitors.

097 The Christmas Village (Ⓦ villagedenoel.be) is held on Place St Lambert and Place du Marché de Liège from the end of Nov to 30 Dec. Entrance is free; open daily 11am–8pm.

098 The Route des Alignements follows the course of the three main alignments. There's a visitor centre at the Alignement du Ménec (Ⓦ menhirs-carnac. fr).

099 An hour's drive from Nantes Atlantique Airport, Île de Noirmoutier can be reached by bridge 24/7 or causeway (accessible only at low tide). There are several beaches good for shellfish, including Plage des Sableaux, La Guérinière and L'Herbaudière.

100 For more information on the 66-Lakes-Trail, visit Ⓦ bit.ly/66LakesTrail. For a full list of the city's municipal pools and beaches, visit Ⓦ berlinerbaeder.de.

101 The Château de Peyrepertuse (Ⓦ chateaupeyrepertuse.com) sits above the village of Duilhac.

102 Amsterdam's main clubs lay on special King's Day nights – pick up a copy of the free listings magazine *NL20* (Ⓦ o2omagazine.nl) when you arrive.

103 The Normandy landing beaches stretch west from the mouth of the River Orne near Caen to the Cotentin Peninsula south of Cherbourg. The Caen Memorial offers informative tours (Ⓦ memorial-caen.fr).

104 The Cathédrale de St-Etienne is open daily (Ⓦ bourges-cathedrale.fr).

105 Daily ferries (Ⓦ pennarbed.fr) make the hour-long crossing to Sein from Audierne on the mainland. The island has a lovely inexpensive hotel, the *d'Armen* (Ⓦ hotel-armen.net), which has a good restaurant.

106 See Ⓦ bayeuxmuseum.com for hours and prices.

107 For more info, visit Ⓦ carnavaldebinche.be.

108 Local tourist offices and Maisons du Vin provide lists of producers offering vineyard visits. Most visits are free, though more famous châteaux may charge a small fee. See also Ⓦ chateau-mouton-rothschild.com and Ⓦ chateau-palmer.com.

109 For more information, visit Ⓦ cagnes-tourisme .com or Ⓦ www.musee-matisse-nice.org.

110 French Country Waterways offers a variety of routes through France, including in Alsace-Lorraine, Champagne and Burgundy, from April to October. For more information, visit Ⓦ fcwl.com.

111 Bonnefanten Museum is at Avenue Céramique 250 (Ⓦ bonnefanten.nl); *Kruisheren Hotel* at Kruisherengang 19 (Ⓦ oostwegelcollection.nl); and Selexyz Dominicanen at Dominicanenkerkstraat 1 (☎ +31 43 321 08 25).

112 The closest airports are Clermont-Ferrand, Rodez and Lyon. Trains from Paris run direct to Clermont-Ferrand. Ⓦ panoramiquedesdomes.fr has details of times and fares of the electric railway.

113 Engelberg is connected to Lucerne by the Zentralbahn railway (40min). The Ski Jumping World Cup (Ⓦ weltcup-engelberg.ch/en) and European Film Tour (Ⓦ eoft.eu) take place annually around Dec 20. See Ⓦ engelberg.ch for accommodation and ski-pass deals.

114 *Château de Brissac*, Brissac-Quincé (Ⓦ chateaubrissac.fr); *Château de Chémery*, Loir-et-Cher (Ⓦ chateau dechemery.fr); *Manoir de la Rémonière*, near Azay-le-Rideau (Ⓦ manoirdelaremoniere.com).

115 The Grotte de Pech Merle (Ⓦ pechmerle.com) is two hours' drive north of Toulouse.

116 The Casemates du Bock are open daily between March and Oct. For more details, see Ⓦ visitluxembourg.com.

117 Tours of the winery are available for ten people or more; see Ⓦ hofkellerei.li for details.

123
152 MADEIRA

148
149

CANARY ISLANDS

146 125
155

Bay of Biscay

FRANCE

ANDORRA

160 119
141   158
        120
   156   145
                     122
                     144
                     150
ATLANTIC   124
OCEAN
138   BALEARIC
131   SEA   MENO

                                   MALLORCA
PORTUGAL   SPAIN 132   121
                                   BALEARI
           130   ISLANDS
139   147
128   IBIZA
153

                                   MEDITERRANEAN
126   SEA
135

118   129   136
157   140 137   133
     151
Gulf of
Cadiz   ALBORAN
              Strait of   SEA
              Gibraltar

                    MOROCCO   ALGERIA

159 127
AZORES 134
       142

THE IBERIAN PENINSULA
118–160

The Iberian peninsula is big on pride, aflame with colour, and blessed, above all else, with an insatiable appetite for a long night out. With cities as culturally colossal as Barcelona, Lisbon and Madrid to shout about – not to mention islands as diverse as Madeira, the Azores, the Canaries and the Balearics – Spain and Portugal can claim world-class status in everything from art, sport and architecture to hiking, food and beaches. The countries' legendary festival roster ranges from the momentous Tomatina to the electronica-led Benicàssim, while landscapes vary from the wilds of the Tabernas Desert to the pinnacles of the Picos de Europa. And, from zipwiring across the Spain-Portugal border to hiking Andalucía's seldom-trodden Camino Mozárabe, you're not short on adventure, either.

118 Hiking the Rota Vicentina

PORTUGAL We had barely got going on our hike when my ankle rolled to the side and I tumbled over. My guide, José Granja, came across to check that I was OK. "You know, you need to taste the floor sometimes," he said, peering at me as we got going again. "I fell off my bike once. As I lay there, I saw an ant." He held a finger close to his face as if to inspect it. "I thought, I might as well make the most of being there, because I'd never throw myself to the ground on purpose."

José's spiritually flavoured interpretation of my roll in the dust came back to me later. After three days sampling the twin prongs of the Rota Vicentina walking trail, which runs for 340km through Portugal's southwest, I was pleasantly bone-weary and, yes, feeling pretty in touch with my surroundings.

First there'd been the gentle, inland Historical Way, passing goats whose tinny bells chimed in unison to weave rich blankets of sound. Here we encountered no one but an old farmer chasing his cows. "Ai! Ai!" he shouted, followed by a volley of curses as one animal strayed and he stumbled down the hillside in pursuit. We ate sandwiches of moist, dense Alentejo bread and splashed in Pego das Pias, one of many swimming holes associated with female spirits called *mouras encantadas*.

The aromas were potent. José taught me that the main note came from the region's emblematic plant, *esteva* (also known as rockrose), whose five purple dots are likened locally to the wounds of Christ. Its leaves are sticky and give a smell as sweet as lipgloss, with citrus undercurrents.

The winds that gusted across the big-skied Fisherman's Path whipped up the complex fragrance of the clifftop scrub. As we watched storks feed their wriggling young on precarious rocky eyries, Nicolau da Costa told me about *perceives* (goose barnacles), plucked off the rocks at low tide by bodyboard-paddling fishermen. Clearly a treat worth making an effort for – much like the Rota Vicentina itself.

Neil McQuillian
is a food, travel and short story writer, and a freelance editor for Rough Guides. His work has appeared in *Time Out, The Independent's Traveller* supplement, *The Sunday Times Travel* magazine, *Wallpaper** and *Uncommon London*.

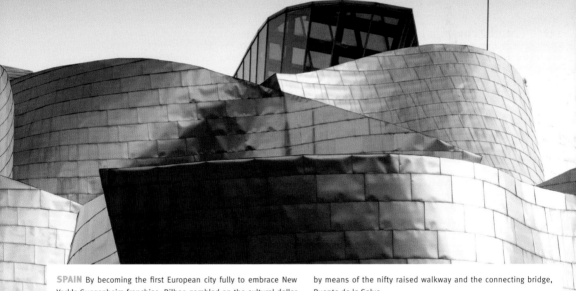

Gawping at the Guggenheim

SPAIN By becoming the first European city fully to embrace New York's Guggenheim franchise, Bilbao gambled on the cultural dollar and won. In the process, it transformed itself from a briny, rusting behemoth into a modern art mecca. Architect Frank O. Gehry was briefed to draw the gaze of the world; his response was an audacious, ingenious conflation of Bilbao's past and future, a riverine citadel moulded from titanium and limestone, steel and glass.

Up close, the building appears as an urban planner's daydream gone delightfully wrong; viewed from the opposite bank of the river, it assumes the guise of a gilded, glittering ark. But it all depends on your mood and the notoriously unpredictable Basque weather: on other days it broods like a computer-generated *Marie Celeste*, or glints rudely like a capricious cross between Monty Python and El Dorado. Gehry extends the aquatic theme by subsuming Bilbao's historic waterway into his design, so you can also take its measure

by means of the nifty raised walkway and the connecting bridge, Puente de la Salve.

Beside the main entrance, Jeff Koons' *Puppy*, an oversized, overstuffed floral statue, sits lost in an eternal siesta. Even the entrance is surreal, descending into the museum's huge atrium and voluminous galleries where, inevitably, the contents are rarely afforded quite as much attention as the surroundings. Amid the rotated collections of Abstract Expressionism and Pop Art, interactive installations and excitable knots of foreign students, the powers that be continue to hope that the wordless horror of Picasso's *Guernica* will one day become the centrepiece. That still languishes in Madrid, but *Guernica* or no, every city and its satellite is now clamouring for a piece of the Guggenheim action – stand up Guadalajara, sit down Rio. Spain, however, remains the titanium template, proof that Bilbao's ship has finally come in.

120 | Seeing stars in San Sebastián

SPAIN Visitors who make their way to the genteel resort of San Sebastián (known as Donostia), in Spain's Basque region, tend to have one thing on their mind: food. Within the country, Euskadi – as the Basque area is known – has always been recognized as serving Spain's finest cuisine. The city in fact boasts the most impressive per capita concentration of Michelin stars in the world, a recognition that its deep-rooted gastronomic tradition has finally come of age.

Juan Mari Arzak is widely regarded as the man who kicked it all off, back in the 1970s. Long the holder of three of those cherished stars, his *Arzak* restaurant remains the parlour-informal, family-friendly temple of audacious yet almost always recognizably Basque food; a meal here is a thrilling affair.

Deftly incorporating line-caught fruits of the Cantabrian sea, the flora and fauna of the Basque countryside, and flavours from further afield, Arzak and his daughter Elena are as likely to cook with smoked chocolate, cardamom, dry ice-assisted sauces and ash-charred vinaigrette as the signature truffles and foie gras. Bold, subversive takes on Spanish classics – strawberry gazpacho anyone? – confound and exhilarate, while longstanding favourites like truffle-distilled poached egg are so flawlessly presented you'll hesitate to slice into them. And despite the gourmet prices, the ratio of gregarious locals to foodie pilgrims means there's little scope for snobbery.

Still, if cost is an issue, you can experience San Sebastián's epicurean passions by way of a *txikiteo*, the Basque version of a tapas crawl. You can taste your way through a succession of tempting *pintxos* – their name for the baroque miniatures on offer – at hearteningly unpretentious bars such as *Txepetxa*, *Etxaniz* and *La Cuchara de San Telmo*, in the Casco Viejo (old town). Marinated anchovies with sea urchin roe, papaya or spider crab salad, tumblers of viscous garlic broth and earthy wild mushroom confit come with a tiny price tag – just a few euros – but with lasting reward.

121 | Trundle through Mallorca on the Tren de Sóller

SPAIN Some rail journeys span continents. Others are more modest, at least in terms of their length. This 28km saunter across one of Spain's major holiday islands is very much in the latter category – although it's anything but inconsequential. The line, which snakes from capital city Palma de Mallorca in the south up to the valley-slung town of Sóller, has been in place since 1911, and showcases the rampant, broad-shouldered scenery that makes Mallorca such a pull for outdoor-lovers.

The antique narrow-gauge locomotives that ply the rails today – all burnished wood, picture windows and leather seats – are predominantly loaded with pleasure-trippers, but this wasn't always the case. The line was originally created to transport citrus fruits from the orchards of the north to the capital, during an era when the equivalent trip by road took a full day. The rail journey, by contrast, takes just under an hour from one terminus to the other.

If you thought Mallorca was all package holidays and *pintxos*, it's a fine wake-up call. That the line is here at all is an impressive feat, burrowing as it does through the broad-beamed mountains of the UNESCO-listed Serra de Tramuntana, a range still marked with millennia-old farming terraces.

The opening stretch as you depart Palma is textbook Spanish suburbia, but things soon ramp up, initially through the almond groves and lime trees of the flatlands then among the huge clefts of rock that mark the foothills of the Serra. The line overcomes the natural barrier of the mountains themselves by virtue of a series of inclines and rock-chiselled tunnels, the longest of which stretches to almost 3km in length – although the stupendous valley panorama that emerges on the other side makes this view-starved section more than worthwhile.

And the best part? Come journey's end, when you sidle into Sóller in the Balearic sunshine, you can be smug in the knowledge that you've got the return journey to come.

122 | Modernismo and mañana: Gaudí's Sagrada Família

SPAIN If you've ever been at the mercy of a Spanish tradesman, or merely tried to buy a litre of milk after midday, you'll know that the Iberian concept of time is not just slightly elastic but positively twangy. The master of twang, however, has to be Antoni Gaudí i Cornet, the Catalan architect whose *pièce de résistance* is famously still under construction more than a century after he took the project on: "My client is not in a hurry" was his jocular riposte to the epic timescale.

Conceived as a riposte to secular radicalism, the Temple Expiatori de la Sagrada Família consumed the final decade and a half of a life that had become increasingly reclusive. Gaudí couldn't have imagined that a new millennium would find his creation feted as a wonder of the postmodern world, symbolic of a Barcelona reborn and the single most popular tourist attraction in Spain.

Craning your neck up to the totemic, honeycomb-Gothic meltdown of the Sagrada Família's towers today, it's perhaps not so difficult to believe that Gaudí was a nature-loving vegetarian as well as an ardent Catholic and nationalist. By subsuming the organic intricacy of cellular life, his off-kilter *modernismo* wields a hypnotic, outlandish power, a complexity of design that entwines itself around your grey matter in a single glance. Which is half its charm; if you don't fancy dodging sweaty tourists and piles of mosaics in progress, simply take a constitutional around the exterior. Personally masterminded by Gaudí before his death, the Nativity facade garlands its virgin birth with microcosmic stone flora, a stark contrast to the Cubist austerity of the recently completed Passion facade.

The main reward for venturing inside is an elevator ride up one of the towers, a less tiring, crowded and claustrophobic experience than taking the stairs (hundreds of them!), which leaves you with sufficient energy to goggle at the city through a prism of threaded stone and ceramics.

Tobogganing without snow

MADEIRA However you make the 560m climb up to Monte, the hillside town that hangs quietly over Madeira's verdant capital, Funchal, there's only one real choice when it comes to getting back down again. Well, you could test your driving skills on the impossibly steep streets, or risk vertigo as you dangle high above eucalyptus trees in a flimsy-looking cable car, but neither option is as downright wacky as taking a toboggan.

There's no snow, of course – this is a subtropical paradise – but thanks to some typically resourceful thinking you're not going to need it, as the road becomes your black run, and instead of using the latest winter sports gear, you'll be hurtling towards sea level in a giant wicker basket.

Tobogganing might seem an unlikely pursuit for Madeira, an island that's better known for sleepy resorts than extreme sports. But ever since the first wooden sledge made the 6km journey between Monte and Funchal in 1850, the ride has been picking up

speed. In fact, it's now one of the island's biggest draws. So when you find yourself at the bottom of the stairs that lead to Nossa Senhora do Monte, an imposing white church in the heart of town, look out for the swarm of tourists and take your place in the queue.

This is where the fun begins, and where you'll meet the two guys who'll be pushing your toboggan. They're locals, with bright white clothes and sun-dried skin. Usually, they're smoking. But when it's their turn to guide a sledge through the streets they spring into life, throwing their weight behind the job. At first, progress is slow. Then gravity takes over, powering you to speeds of up to 48 km/hr, and their only mission is to stop you pounding into cars, frightened dogs and any other obstacles that weave in front of your basket.

When you think you're going too fast to stop (there aren't any real brakes here), your wheezing guides will dig their rubber boots into the tarmac – giving you the first chance to jump out, look down and admire the sparkling blue Atlantic that stretches out before you.

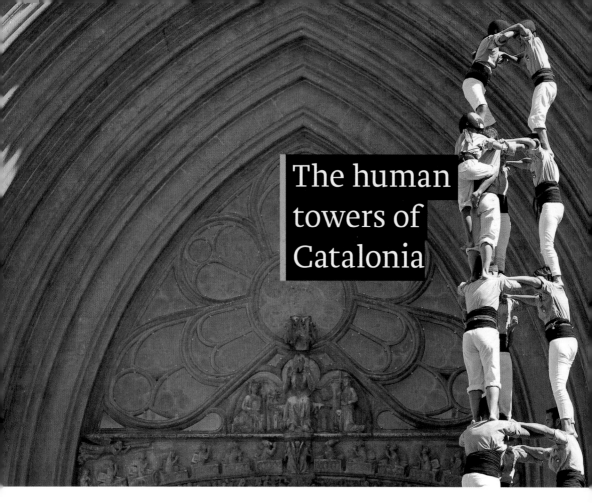

The human towers of Catalonia

SPAIN There is something mesmerizing yet terrifying about watching people, of all ages and sizes, climb atop one another to build a human tower. The tradition of building *castells* goes back around 200 years and stems from a Valencian dance that would end with a group of men creating a pillar of people by standing on each other's shoulders.

After it caught on in the town of Valls in Catalonia, numerous groups, or *colles*, popped up to recreate these pillars as a way to earn money. Fast-forward to modern Spain, and the practice is now essentially a national obsession. Today, more than one hundred *colles* exist and there are entire TV shows and magazines dedicated to following what is now a highly competitive sport.

The teams compete throughout the year at various festivals in Catalonia, but the climax comes at the biennial Concurs de Castells in Tarragona, when thousands of participants – and an equal number of spectators – descend on the Roman city for the largest gathering of human towers.

Inside the city's former bullring, the tension is almost palpable as *colles* from around Catalonia compete to build the most impressive structures. The stadium sits in silence, breathing on pause, as the towers are gradually built upwards from a base of tightly packed people. A ripple of cheers and applause carries through the crowd as a child, referred to as the *enxaneta*, scurries to the top of the tower to crown it, then shimmies down again, like a koala descending a tree.

A gripping phenomenon, indeed, *castells* are so much more than an exciting sport. Not only is it an important part of Catalan culture and heritage, but the towers themselves are also an astonishing feat of engineering. Each *colla* has a technical team at its core responsible for calculating how to build the most stable structure. It's a highly complex task, and not uncommon for a tower to collapse and for its parts – the people – to suffer broken bones.

It's distressing to see them tumble, but a pertinent reminder of just how brave the players are when they dust themselves off and climb again.

125 | Crossing Gran Canaria on foot

CANARY ISLANDS Thanks to its winter sun, long sandy beaches and string of purpose-built resorts, the island of Gran Canaria has become a hugely popular year-round holiday spot. If you're after nothing more than a suntan and a few cocktails, that's all well and good.

All too few travellers, however, realize that its heady natural splendour also makes the third largest of the Canary Islands a wonderful hiking destination. As a result, you only have to strap on your boots and head off into the hills, and you may well find that you have the trails to yourself.

Many of the island's designated treks explore its stupendous volcanic highlands, but the most comprehensive is Gran Canaria's very own end-to-end walk. Stretching 75km from the southern coastline to the north – and taking three days at a reasonable hiking pace – it leads you over lofty hill passes, into raw gorges, through cool pine forests, among sun-battered cactus groves and past citrus orchards hung heavy with fruit.

Although this cross-island hike is a relatively new initiative, the path that it follows is anything but. For much of the way, today's walkers are in fact retracing a centuries-old pilgrimage route that has long connected two of the island's holiest churches – Tunte in the centre and Galdar in the far north – and that section has been prefixed with a further day-hike to make it into a full coast-to-coast trek.

The trail passes through some sleepy, time-forgotten towns and villages (thankfully well stocked with beds, hot meals and cold beer), and finishes within a short drive of enjoyable capital city Las Palmas. The whole thing is billed as the island's own version of the Camino de Santiago, but while it's unquestionably a pilgrimage of sorts, you certainly don't need to see it as a spiritual quest to enjoy the drama of the journey.

Discover the secret patios of Córdoba

SPAIN The Moors may have left Spain over 500 years ago, but vestiges of their culture still exist in the Spanish language, cuisine and Islamic-style architecture. One place where this is more evident than others, is Córdoba. This Andalucían city often records some of the hottest temperatures in Europe, so to combat the heat, the Moors built Moroccan-style houses with central courtyards and water features. This tradition continued well after they left, and today the city has become famous for its picturesque patios. For most of the year, these oasis-like courtyards are hidden behind stone walls and heavy wooden doors; however, each May, residents open them up to the public during the Festival of the Patios of Córdoba.

Inscribed by UNESCO on its list of Intangible World Heritage, the festival starts at the end of April with a parade known as 'The Battle of the Flowers'. Thousands of carnations are thrown into the air, while floats decorated with arches and paper flowers wind their way through the streets. This is followed by the Fiesta de las Cruces (Festival of the May Crosses), when giant flower-adorned crosses are set up in squares across the city.

The festival culminates in the much-anticipated patio competition. With the sweet-scented smells of orange blossom and jasmine swirling through the air, and armed with a festival map, visitors can get the opportunity to see inside many of Córdoba's private patios.

It feels almost wrong to be invading these clandestine spaces, but you'll soon realise you're more than welcome. Locals go all out in decorating their patios for the occasion, filling them with colourful flower pots and petals delicately strewn across water features. Many even welcome visitors with wine, eager to share their artistic floral creations. During the week, a winner is crowned and a prize awarded for the best patio of the year.

127 | Geothermal cuisine: tucking into traditional Azorean food

AZORES Scattered like shards across a million square kilometres of the North Atlantic, west of Portugal, the nine islands of the Azores are unmistakably volcanic. For now, this green and breezy archipelago is snoozing in the temperate embrace of the Gulf Stream; the last significant onshore eruptions were in 1811. However, over thirty of its volcanoes remain active, and regular tremors and underwater seismic events serve to remind that every crag, crater and cave was sculpted by geothermal forces.

This might seem like a perilous place to live, but Azorean foodies embrace their role as volcano-dwellers, growing hothouse pineapples, bananas, guavas and passionfruit in the fertile soil and harvesting plump, meaty clams from volcanic lagoons. In the picturesque caldera village of Furnas on São Miguel, famous for its hot springs, they take things further by using natural volcanic energy to slow-cook a stew that's a signature local dish, *cozido das Furnas*. To make it, the chef lines a heavy pot with layers of meat, vegetables,

chorizo and blood sausage, covers it and lowers it into a steamy hollow in the ground to simmer for five or six hours. Order this hearty dish at a local restaurant, and you may be invited to the springs to watch the pot being unearthed.

At *Canto da Doca*, a casual, contemporary place, you can enjoy a little DIY volcanic cooking. Waiters bring a platter of fresh meat, squid, tuna, vegetables and sauces to your table, along with a piping-hot slab of lava stone. You drop morsels onto the slab one by one to cook, inhaling the delicious aromas as they sizzle. When the temperature dips, a fresh slab will miraculously appear.

While traditional Azorean cooking tends to be solid peasant grub – regional cheese to start, stewed or grilled meat or seafood as a main course, custardy puddings, fragrant Azorean tea as a pick-me-up – there's a move afoot to bring out the islands' gourmet side. Check out 10 Fest Azores, an annual ten-day gastronomic festival featuring Michelin-starred chefs from all over the world.

128 | Tram 28: taking a ride through Lisbon's historic quarters

PORTUGAL Just as you should arrive in Venice by boat, it is best to approach Lisbon on a tram, from the point where many people leave it for good: at Prazeres, by the city's picturesque main cemetery. Get a taxi to the suburban terminus of tram 28 for one of the most atmospheric public-transport rides in the world: a slow-motion roller coaster into the city's historic heart.

Electric trams first served Lisbon in 1901, though the route 28 fleet are remodelled 1930s versions. The polished wood interiors are gems of craftsmanship, from the grooved wooden floors to the shiny seats and sliding window panels. And the operators don't so much drive the trams as handle them like ancient caravels, adjusting pulleys and levers as the streetcar pitches and rolls across Lisbon's wavy terrain. As tram 28 rumbles past the towering dome of the Estrela Basilica, remember the famous bottoms that have probably sat exactly where you are: the writers Pessoa and Saramago, the singer Mariza, footballers Figo and Eusebio.

You reach central Lisbon at the smart Chiado district, glimpses of the steely Tagus flashing into view between the terracotta roof tiles and church spires. Suddenly you pitch steeply downhill, the tram hissing and straining against the gradients of Rua Vitor Cordon, before veering into the historic downtown Baixa district. Shoppers pile in and it's standing room only for newcomers, but those already seated can admire the row of traditional shops selling sequins and beads along Rua da Conceição through the open windows.

Now you climb past Lisbon's ancient cathedral and skirt the hilltop castle, the vistas across the Tagus estuary below truly dazzling. The best bit of the ride is yet to come, though: a weaving, grinding climb through the Alfama district, Lisbon's village-within-a-city where most roads are too narrow for cars. Entering Rua das Escolas Gerais, the street is just over tram width, its shopfronts so close that you can almost lean out and take a tin of sardines off the shelves.

129 | Crossing borders by zipwire

SPAIN & PORTUGAL There are many different ways to cross a border – by boat, by bridge, by car, by bike, on foot – but there's currently only one place on Earth where you can zipwire over an international frontier.

A heart-stopping ride that reaches speeds of up to 80km an hour, Límitezero crosses from the Spanish town of Sanlúcar de Guadiana in Andalucía over the Guadiana river to the pretty Portuguese village of Alcoutim in the Algarve. The 720m trip may only last less than a minute, but you'll gain an hour, so don't forget to change your watch on arrival.

At the Límitezero office in central Sanlúcar you'll be kitted up in harnesses and safety helmets, then taken in a 4WD up to the departure platform, high above the town. Take some time to check out the fantastic

views from here over the surrounding countryside, the river, and the two whitewashed villages which face each other from different countries across the wide Guadiana. Once the gate on the departure platform opens, you're off on an exhilarating ride down the hillside, swooping over boats moored in the river, and flying over the tips of the olive trees, before landing in a field in Portugal an hour earlier than you left.

Before you take the short boat trip back across the river to Spain, spend some time exploring the laidback village of Alcoutim, with its narrow cobbled streets and alleyways, attractive fourteenth-century castle with views over the town's rooftops and the river, or chill out with a drink or meal at one of the pretty riverfront cafés in the main square. And if the ride has got you all hot and bothered, you can even cool off and have a swim at the local Pego Fundo river beach.

130 | Discovering the spoils of the conquistadors

SPAIN In any account of Extremadura's history, a neat parallel is usually drawn between the austerity of the landscape and the savagery of the conquistadors who were born and raised here. The alternately broiling and bitterly cold plains hold an allure that's hard to shake off, and the contrast with the towns is striking. Both Trujillo and Cáceres remain synonymous with conquistador plunder, rich in lavish *solares* (mansions) built by New World returnees. Cáceres is UNESCO-protected, but Trujillo is even prettier, and its sons more infamous. This was the birthplace of Francisco Pizarro, illiterate conqueror of Peru and scourge of the Incas.

While Francisco's bronze likeness coolly surveys the Plaza Mayor, the legacy of his less bloodthirsty half-brother, Hernando, is more imposing. His Palacio de la Conquista lords it over the square, its richly ornamented facade adorned with a doomed Atahualpa (the last Inca ruler) and spuriously sage-like busts of both Pizarro siblings – the ultimate expression of local *hombres* made good. Nearby is the Palacio de Orellana-Pizarro, transformed from a fortress into a conquistador's des res by Francisco's cousin Juan, and crowned by an exquisite Renaissance balcony.

Keeping it in the family was important in Cáceres: the town's most impressive mansion, the Casa de Toledo-Moctezuma, is a work of mannerist indulgence and august grandeur, a place with royal Aztec connections where the son of conquistador Juan Cano (an acolyte of Hernán Cortés) and Doña Isabel (daughter of the Mexican emperor) settled down with his Spanish bride. Across the old town, the gorgeous honeyed-gothic facade of the Casa de los Golfínes de Abajo dates back to the years immediately prior to the New World voyages.

These days, the wealth of the Indies arrives in the form of sweet music: the world music jamboree that is WOMAD flings open its doors in Cáceres for four days each May. With consummate irony, it's possible to bask in balmy Latin American sounds, surrounded by mansions financed by Latin American gold.

131 | Stop! It's hammer time at the Festa de São João

PORTUGAL The old cliché that Porto works while Lisbon plays is redundant on June 23, when Portugal's second city teaches the capital a thing or two about having fun. The Festa de São João is a magnificent display of midsummer madness – one giant street party, where bands of hammer-wielding lunatics roam the town, and every available outdoor space in Porto is given over to a full night of eating, drinking and dancing to welcome in the city's saint's day.

By the evening, the *tripeiros*, as the residents of Porto are known, are already in the party mood. A tide of whistle-blowing, hammer-wielding revellers begins to seep down the steep streets towards the river. No one seems to know the origin of the tradition of hitting people on the head on this day, but what was customarily a rather harmless pat with a leek has evolved into a somewhat firmer clout with a plastic hammer. You should know that everyone has a plastic hammer, and everyone wants to hit someone else with it.

People start to dance to the live music by the Rio Douro while it's still light, banging their hammers on metal café tables to the rhythm of Latin and African sounds. Elsewhere, live music performances vary from pop and rock to traditional folk music and choral singing, and as darkness falls, exploding fireworks thunder through the night sky above the glowing neon of the port wine lodges over the Douro.

Midnight sees the inevitable climax of fireworks, but the night is far from over. As dawn approaches, the emphasis shifts further west to the beach of Praia dos Ingleses in the suburb of Foz do Douro. Here, there's space to participate in the tradition of lighting bonfires for São João, with youths challenging each other to jump over the largest flames. As the beach party rumbles on, pace yourself and before you know it the crowds will start to thin slightly and the first signs of daylight will appear on the horizon. Congratulations. You've made it through to the day of São João itself.

132 | Portraits and purgatory at the Prado

SPAIN Opened in 1819 at the behest of Ferdinand VII, Madrid's El Prado has long been one of the world's premier art galleries, with a collection so vast only a fraction of its paintings can be exhibited at any one time. Among those treasures – gleaned largely from the salons of the Spanish nobility – are half of the complete works of Diego Velázquez, virtuoso court painter to Felipe IV. Such was the clamour surrounding a 1990 exhibition that half a million people filed through the turnstiles; those locked out clashed with civil guards. What Velázquez himself would've made of it all is hard to say; in his celebrated masterpiece *Las Meninas*, he peers out inscrutably from behind his own canvas, cleverly dissolving the boundaries between viewer and viewed, superimposing scene upon reflected scene.

The works of Francisco de Goya are equally revolutionary, ranging from sensuous portraiture to piercing documents of personal and political trauma. It's hard to imagine public disorder over his infamous *Pinturas Negras*, nor do they attract the spectatorial logjams of *Las Meninas*, yet they're not works you'll forget in a hurry. The terrible magnetism of paintings like *The Colossus* and *Saturn Devouring One of His Sons* is easier to comprehend in the context of their creation, as the last will and testament of a deaf and disillusioned old man, fearful of his own flight into madness. Originally daubed on the walls of his farmhouse, the black paintings take to extremes motifs that Goya had pioneered: *Tres de Mayo* is unflinching in depicting the tawdry horror of war, its faceless Napoleonic executioners firing a fusillade that echoes into the twenty-first century.

133 | Going for your guns in Almería

SPAIN The only genuine desert in Europe, Almería's merciless canyons and moonscape gulches did, once upon a time in the Spanish Wild West, play host to Hollywood. Back in the Sixties, Spaghetti Western don Sergio Leone shot his landmark trilogy here, climaxing with *The Good, the Bad and the Ugly*. Since that golden era, the place has enjoyed the occasional flash of former glories: Alex Cox revisited the terrain in the Eighties with his all-star spaghetti parody *Straight to Hell*, and Sean Connery pitched up for *Indiana Jones and the Last Crusade*.

Spanish director Alex de la Iglesia's critically acclaimed *800 Bullets* actually subsumed the rise and fall of Almerían cinema into its plot, centring on the Fort Bravo studios/Texas Hollywood, where the most authentic film-set experience is still to be had. It's a gloriously eerie, down-at-heel place, which, likely as not, you'll have to yourself. Unfortunately, there's no explanation as to which sets were used in which films, but the splintered wood, fading paintwork and general dilapidation certainly feels genuine. A wholesale Mexican compound complete with a blinding white mission chapel is the atmospheric centrepiece; close your eyes and you can just about smell the gunpowder.

A couple of kilometres down the road is Mini-Hollywood, the sanitized big daddy of the region's three film-set theme parks, with a must-see museum of original poster art. And Leone diehards will want to complete the tour with a visit to nearby Western Leone, which houses the extant debris of the man's masterpiece, *Once Upon a Time in the West*. Hopelessly romantic cowboys (and girls) can even take a four-day horseriding tour into the desert, scouting various locations amid breathtakingly desolate scenery.

134 | Braving the wild Atlantic deeps

AZORES For many divers, after logging plentiful dives on tropical reefs, the time comes when they hanker for something beyond sun-lit shallows. Something rawer and wilder. Something oceanic. That's where the Azores come in.

Among Europe's finest diving destinations, the nine volcanic islands hide in plain sight in the mid-Atlantic, 1500km from Lisbon and 3900km from New York. That location makes this Portuguese archipelago a mid-ocean roadhouse for Atlantic and Caribbean species alike: sardines, octopus and moray eels, but also loggerhead turtles, parrotfish and barracuda. And because the islands spike almost vertically from the seabed, the world's largest pelagic species are found inshore: blue sharks, oceanic whitetips, whale sharks, giant manta rays, dolphins and a third of the world's whale species.

Factor in subaquatic lavascapes, visibility extending up to 50m (no river run-off clouds the seas), water warmed by the Gulf Stream to 16–22°C and the complete absence of the crowds that plague the Caribbean or Red Sea, and you have dive nirvana.

Diving makes a perfect fit for the recent – long overdue – rebranding of the Azores as a haven for active travellers. São Miguel, the largest and most accessible island, holds enough dive sites to keep you underwater for a week. You don't even have to stray far from its pocket-sized capital, Ponta Delgada. Within fifteen minutes of the harbour, the wreck of the *Dori* – which survived the D-Day landings but sank due to poorly loaded cargo in 1964 – lies surrounded by barracuda, alien-eyed octopuses and fireworms resembling Rio carnival dancers. An hour away, in the Caloura Marine Reserve, there's an extraordinary underwater "city" composed of lava arches and caves – Baixa das Castanhetas, where lava tubes vanish into the deep.

And that's just for starters. Experienced divers can take connecting flights to swim with whale sharks off Santa Maria, or, even better, hang off a dive-line off Pico, in wild open ocean the colour of ink, and watch the blue sharks and huge rays circle. For first timers, it's both nerve-wracking and exhilarating. Isn't that what proper ocean diving is all about?

135 | Marvelling inside the Mezquita

SPAIN La Mezquita: a name that evokes the mystery and grace of Córdoba's famous monument so much more seductively than the English translation. It's been a while since the Great Mosque was used as such (1236, to be exact), but at one time this was not only the largest mosque in the city – dwarfing a thousand others – but in all al-Andalus and nigh-on the entire world.

Almost a millennium later, its hallucinatory interior, a dreamscape of candy-striped arches piled upon arches, sifting light from shadow, still hushes the garrulous into silence and the jaded into awe. Since the Christians took over it's been mostly shadow, yet at one time the Mezquita's dense grove of recycled Roman columns was open to the sunlight, creating a generous, arboreal harmony with its courtyard and wider social environment. Today's visitors still enter through that same orange-blossom compound, the Patio de los Naranjos, proceeding through the Puerta de las Palmas where they doff their caps rather than removing their shoes. As your eyes adjust to the gloom, you're confronted with a jasper and marble forest, so constant, fluid and deceptively symmetrical in design that its ingenious system of secondary supporting arches barely registers. Gradually, the resourcefulness of the Muslim architects sinks in, the way they improvised on the inadequacy of their salvaged pillars, inversely propping up the great weight of the roof arches and ceiling.

That first flush of wonder ebbs slightly once you stumble upon an edifice that's clearly out of step with the Moorish scheme of things, if gracious enough in its own right. In 1523, despite fierce local opposition, the more zealous Christians finally got their revenge by tearing out the Mosque's heart and erecting a Renaissance cathedral. Carlos V's verdict was damning: "you have destroyed something that was unique in the world". Thankfully they left intact the famous Mihrab, a prayer niche of sublime perfection braided by Byzantine mosaics and roofed with a single block of marble. Like the Mezquita itself, its beauty transcends religious difference.

Pray Macarena! Easter in Seville

SPAIN The Spanish flock may be wavering but, being Catholic and proud, they take their religious festivals as seriously as they did in the days when a pointy hat meant the Inquisition. "Semana Santa" – Holy Week – is the most spectacular of all the Catholic celebrations, and the Andalucian city of Seville carries it off with unrivalled pomp and ceremony. Conceived as an extravagant antidote to Protestant asceticism, the festivities were designed to steep the common man in the Passion of Christ, and the intention remains the same today – the dazzling climax to months of preparation.

You don't need to be a Christian to appreciate the outlandish spectacle or the exquisitely choreographed attention to detail. Granted, if you're not expecting it, the sight of massed hooded penitents can be disorientating and not a little disturbing – rows of eyes opaque with concentration, feet stepping slavishly in time with brass and percussion. Holy Week, though, is also about the *pasos*, or floats, elaborate slow-motion platforms graced with piercing, tottering images of Jesus and the Virgin Mary, swathed in lavish Sevillano finery.

All across Seville, crowds hold their collective breath as they anticipate the moment when their local church doors are thrown back and the *paso* commences its unsteady journey, the *costaleros* (or bearers) sweating underneath, hidden from view. With almost sixty *cofradías*, or brotherhoods, all mounting their own processions between Palm Sunday and Good Friday, the city assumes the guise of a sacred snakes-and-ladders board, crisscrossed by caped, candlelit columns at all hours of the day and night, heavy with the ambrosial scent of incense and orange blossom, and pierced by the plaintive lament of the *saetas*, unaccompanied flights of religious song sung by locals on their balconies.

Regardless of where the processions start, they all converge on Calle Sierpes, the commercial thoroughfare jammed with families who've paid for a front-seat view. From here they proceed to the cathedral, where on Good Friday morning the whole thing reaches an ecstatic climax with the appearance of "La Macarena", the protector of Seville's bullfighters long before she graced the pop charts.

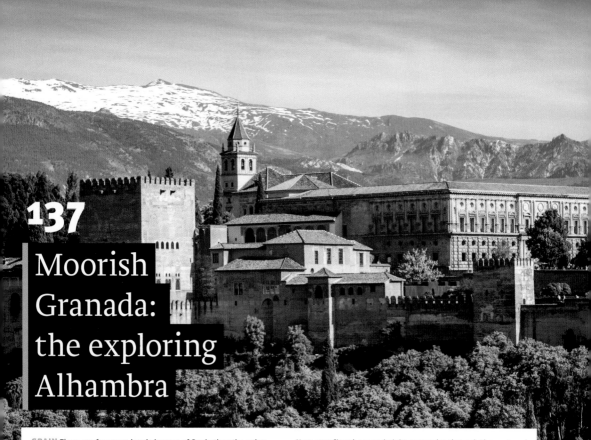

137

Moorish Granada: the exploring Alhambra

SPAIN There are few more iconic images of Spain than the ochre-tinted enclave of the Alhambra, towering out of an elm-wooded hillside above Granada, a snowy Sierra Nevada behind. By the time the last Moorish prince, Boabdil, surrendered his palace in 1492, scolded by his mother with the immortal line "Do not weep like a woman for what you could not defend like a man", a succession of Nasrid rulers had expanded upon the bare bones of the Alcazaba (or citadel). In doing so they created an exalted wonder of the world, elevating its inhabitants with voluptuous waterways and liberating inscriptions.

Yet its current status as the country's most revered monument is due at least in part to Washington Irving, a sometime American diplomat in Madrid who's better known for writing *The Legend of Sleepy Hollow*. In the mid-nineteenth century, when no one gave the place a second glance, Irving recognized its faded glamour, completing his *Tales of the Alhambra* in the abandoned palace.

Now over five thousand visitors wander through the restored complex each day, its chambers and gardens once again alive with cosmopolitan chatter if not free-flowing verse. No amount of words, however, can approximate the sensual charge of seeing the Palacios Nazaríes, the best-preserved palace of the Nasrid dynasty, for the first time. As a building, the palace's function was to concentrate the mind on the oneness of God, and nowhere is this more apparent than the Patio de los Leones courtyard. Here Arabic calligraphy sweeps across the stucco with unparalleled grace, stalactite vaulting dazzles in its intricate irregularity and white marble lions guard a symbolic representation of paradise. The sweet irony is that none of it was built to last, its simple adobe and wood in harmony with the elements and in stark contrast to the Alcazaba fortress opposite, the impregnable-looking towers of which have defined the Granada skyline for centuries.

138 | Port wine tasting in Vila Nova de Gaia

PORTUGAL Portugal's most famous tipple is best sampled in its birthplace, the attractive riverside suburb of Vila Nova de Gaia, where traditional wine lodges have been making port for more than three hundred years. Today dozens of port lodges stretch up the steep riverbanks, their well-known names – Croft, Sandeman and Cockburn's among them – splashed across every rooftop, facade and advertising hoarding.

Many of them run a guided tour of the port-making process, including a look round the vast subterranean cellars where the port is stored in giant vats, a trip to the ageing room, and sometimes a small museum. The still-working, cavernous cellars of Graham's, for example, house some two thousand barrels of ageing port, plus row-upon-row of bottles from great vintages, while its museum displays historic artefacts such as invoices to Winston Churchill for his favourite drink.

The highlight of all the tours, of course, is the tasting, which often takes place in a vaulted room, such as at Ferreira; on a terrace overlooking the Douro river (Graham's); or in a pretty garden (Taylor's). Tastings usually include two or three ports, but most lodges allow you to upgrade to sample some of the more prestigious vintages, while others offer cheese and port pairings. All the tours are pretty informative so, whichever you choose, you'll soon know your tawny from your ruby or your white – and have a good idea about the best vintages.

And if you still haven't had enough, stroll along the atmospheric riverfront to one of the tasting houses that offer port, chocolate and olive oil tastings – settle in and admire the views of the *barcos rabelos*, historic wooden boats that were used to bring the grapes down from the Douro vineyards to the wine lodges, with the pretty Ribeiro district beyond, whose ancient buildings and steep alleys tumble down the opposite bank.

139 | Exploring mystical Sintra

PORTUGAL Inspiration for a host of writers – including Lord Byron and William Beckford – Sintra, the former summer retreat of Portuguese monarchs, is dotted with palaces and surrounded by a series of wooded ravines.

Now one of Europe's finest UNESCO World Heritage sites, Sintra has been a centre for cult worship for centuries: the early Celts named it Mountain of the Moon after one of their gods, and the hills are scattered with ley lines and mysterious tombs. Locals say batteries drain noticeably faster here, and light bulbs pop with monotonous regularity. Some claim it is because of the angle of iron in the rocks, others that it's all part of the mystical powers that lurk in Sintra's hills and valleys. There are certainly plenty of geographical and meteorological quirks: house-sized boulders litter the landscape as if thrown by giants, while a white

cloud – affectionately known as "the queen's fart" – regularly hovers over Sintra's palaces even on the clearest summer day.

The fairy-tale Palácio da Pena on the heights above town, with its dizzy views over the surrounding woodlands, looks like something from *Shrek*, complete with elaborate walkways, domes and drawbridges. Inside, its kitsch decor is kept just as it was when Portugal's last monarch, Manuel, fled at the birth of the republic, in 1910.

Quinta da Regaleira, a private estate from the beginning of the twentieth century, is no less extraordinary. The gardens of this landowner's mansion hide the Initiation Well, entered via a revolving stone door. Inside, a moss-covered spiral staircase leads to a subterranean tunnel that resurfaces by a lake – a bizarre and mysterious place, which, like all of Sintra, shelters tales as fantastical as the buildings.

140 | Hiking the 'other' Camino in Andalucía

SPAIN On Roman trade routes, passing stone waymarkers and abandoned monasteries, the Camino Mozárabe troops north from Malaga to Córdoba and beyond. You have reached the halfway point, and the path ahead is wonderfully quiet.

Pilgrims come to Spain in their hundreds of thousands each year, with the majority committed to the Camino de Santiago, the Homerian traverse to St James' tomb in Santiago de Compostela in the north. Yet there is one biblical problem about the world's most popular long-distance hike: it is uncomfortably crowded and overrun by an inescapable mass of sweating, camera-ready tour groups. At the latest count, numbers tipped over 300,000 last year.

This is not a concern for those on the seldom-trodden Camino Mozárabe in Andalucía. The 417km route welcomes just 600-odd pilgrims each year, and problems sourcing accommodation and table reservations vanish. You won't want for scenery or history, either. The route is named after the Christians who lived within the former Islamic kingdom of Al-Andalus (Andalucía today), tackling the cultures of three

religions (Jews, Christians and Muslims) who lived and conquered its lands. It's a strikingly rugged region, too, punctuated by citrus-scented landscapes and olive groves.

Drawing a finger along the map is the quickest way to highlight the journey's memory-bank moments. Malaga's Santiago Church, where Pablo Picasso was baptized; the rugged massif of the El Torcal de Antequera nature reserve; the fortress town of Antequera, where you can stop for a lunch of *porra* (gazpacho with orange) and *zarangollo* (paprika-scrambled eggs); Zuheros, a hilltop hamlet crowned by an Arabic watchtower. And the grand finale towards the end: the medieval city of Córdoba, home to the tenth-century Mezquita, Europe's most strikingly beautiful mosque-church.

For the committed, the trail continues north, joining other Camino tributaries from Granada and Seville on one final, united march to St James' tomb. But the most spiritually uplifting section is on the walk to Córdoba. Because here, the tranquillity and lack of hustle makes it feel like you have all of southern Spain to yourself.

141 | A cheese pilgrimage in the Picos

SPAIN Good roads – not to mention an incongruous funicular subway and a wildly vertiginous cable car – may have hurtled the Picos de Europa into the twenty-first century, but these jagged, time-lost mountains uphold many ancient traditions. Slashed through by dramatic gorges and splashed with wildflowers, refreshed by frequent showers and shaded by drifting clouds, the Picos produce some of the world's finest blue cheeses, using methods unchanged for centuries.

Mention the Picos to any gastronome, and you'll be met with a blissed-out sigh. These ugly-pug cheeses – gnarled, grey-green and unutterably pungent – provide the most sensuous of eating, layered with taste from the deep, dark, nutty base notes to the zingy penicillin kick. The richness. The complex luxuriance. Flavours so transcendental they inspire pilgrimages to the source.

Picking your way along high mountain paths, across steep slopes of silvery scree where only the clatter of goat bells disrupts the silence, you spot dark recesses in the limestone far above. Within these mysterious caves, the blue cheeses bide their time for months, ageing to perfection in the damp and chilly gloom. Guided tours of certain caves, in Spanish only, enable you to enter a portal into the past.

Or you could simply eat. Supper at the friendly *Begona Pension*, in the one-horse village of Posada de Valdeon, ends with a grand finale – a thick grey smear on a white china plate. This is Valdeon cheese, blended with butter and a slosh of *orujo*, the local firewater – sophisticated, seductive and earthy. Pair it with bread or spread it on an apple slice, and match it with a strong, fruity red. You'd pay the earth for this kind of flavour matching in a Michelin-starred restaurant. Here? A handful of euros.

The uncrowned king of the blue cheeses, however, dwells in the caves of Cabrales in Asturias. Pockmarked, veined and mottled with natural mould, Cabrales couples a devastatingly strong, macho aroma with a surprisingly mellow, almost spicy taste. In the riverside town of Arenas de Cabrales, it dominates every menu – rice with mushrooms and Cabrales; Cabrales with clams; Cabrales in solitary splendour. Cheese lovers rejoice – the holy grail has been found.

142 | Taking a dip in the iron-rich thermal pool in the Parque Terra Nostra

AZORES The waters of the open-air Thermal Water Pool in Parque Terra Nostra on the island of São Miguel are thought to work wonders for your health. It takes a little courage to test this out, since the colour of the water (let's call it mulligatawny soup) is so unusual. But if you take the plunge, you'll find it warm and supremely soothing. It's particularly appealing on spring and autumn mornings, when a faint mist may hover over the surface.

The colour is down to the essential mineral content – iron, in particular, but also calcium, magnesium and other trace elements considered good for the skin – while the temperature is regulated by the natural thermal springs which have attracted hydrotherapy fans to this handsome valley for generations. The springs supply the pool with water at a pretty constant 35–40°C.

To enhance the rejuvenating effect, the pool is spacious and its surroundings sublime. It was built in 1780 by an American Honorary Consul and Azores aficionado, Thomas Hickling, as a centrepiece for his private park and mountain retreat. Today, Parque Terra Nostra is a historic botanical garden full of azaleas, hydrangeas, waterlilies and mature ornamental trees, many of them planted during the nineteenth century.

The Azores' temperate climate allows subtropical trees and shrubs to flourish. Wander around, and you'll discover giant monkey puzzle trees, sequoias, tree ferns, cycads and a grove of century-old ginkgo biloba trees that turn golden in winter. Among the park's defining flourishes are its Azorean Endemic and Native Flora Garden and one of the world's largest collections of camellias, numbering over six hundred, some unique and bred by the current head gardener.

Once the waters of the thermal pool have worked their magic, simply waft up a flight of Regency steps and you'll find refreshment of another sort: set back from the pool is the *Terra Nostra Garden Hotel*, a gracious spa hotel with Art Deco touches and a formal but relaxing restaurant which uses herbs from the garden in its recipes.

143 | Surreal life at the Dalí museum

SPAIN Nothing prepares you for the sheer volume of outwardly respectable, smart-casual tourists crowding desperately around the unwholesome creations of Catalonia's most eccentric, outrageous and egotistical son. Within a salmon-pink, egg-topped palace in the heart of Figueres, class and generation gaps dissolve as young and old aim their cameras at a siren-like Queen of Persia riding barefoot atop an Al Capone car. In the back seat, wan and hollow-chested passengers look like they have tussled with triffids once too often.

As the irreverence of the exhibits triggers an irreverence of the spirit, a funhouse *frisson* supplants standard gallery politesse. Frumpy pensioners queue to climb a staircase and gape at a distorted approximation of Mae West's face; gangling students compete to interpret an incongruous Duke Ellington LP sleeve, an Alice Cooper hologram and a gilded monkey skeleton; and designer-tagged señoritas jostle for position to crane their necks, point and click at a kitsch, fleshy-footed self-portrait reaching for the heavens.

Even if you're only dimly aware of Dalí's liquefied Surrealism, an hour in the man's domain will convince you that queasy paintings like the candle-faced *Cosmic Athletes* were dredged from one of the most singular subconscious minds of the twentieth century, one unhitched from the Surrealist vanguard in favour of his own, brilliantly christened "paranoiac-critical" method.

Like Gaudí before him, Salvador Dalí's monument was also his last, reclusive refuge. The man is actually buried in the crypt, right below your feet, and it's easy to imagine his moustachioed ghost prowling the half-moon corridors, bug-eyed and impish, revelling in the knowledge that his lurid mausoleum is Spain's most sought-after art spectacular after the Prado.

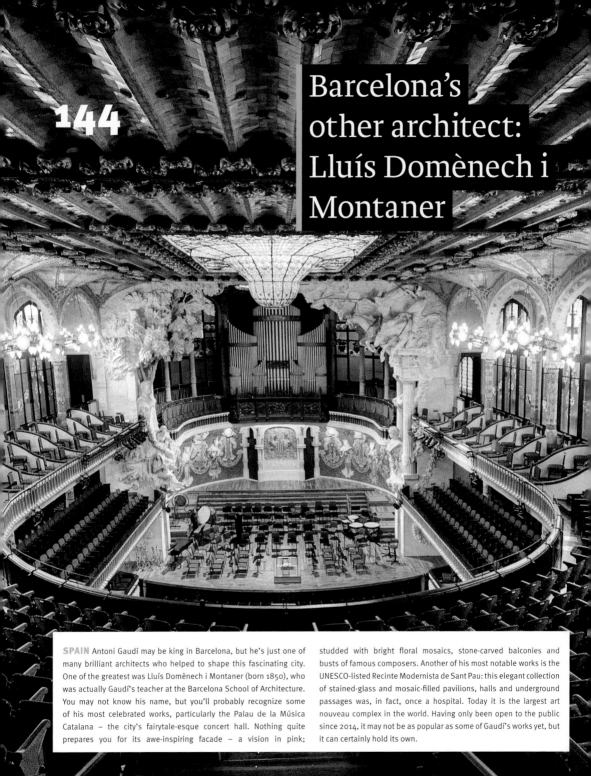

Barcelona's other architect: Lluís Domènech i Montaner

SPAIN Antoni Gaudí may be king in Barcelona, but he's just one of many brilliant architects who helped to shape this fascinating city. One of the greatest was Lluís Domènech i Montaner (born 1850), who was actually Gaudí's teacher at the Barcelona School of Architecture. You may not know his name, but you'll probably recognize some of his most celebrated works, particularly the Palau de la Música Catalana – the city's fairytale-esque concert hall. Nothing quite prepares you for its awe-inspiring facade – a vision in pink;

studded with bright floral mosaics, stone-carved balconies and busts of famous composers. Another of his most notable works is the UNESCO-listed Recinte Modernista de Sant Pau: this elegant collection of stained-glass and mosaic-filled pavilions, halls and underground passages was, in fact, once a hospital. Today it is the largest art nouveau complex in the world. Having only been open to the public since 2014, it may not be as popular as some of Gaudí's works yet, but it can certainly hold its own.

Hiking in the Pyrenees

SPAIN Soaring and plunging amid a rarefied conclave of snow-veined peaks near the French border, Catalunya's Parc Nacional d'Aigüestortes i Estany de Sant Maurici encompasses one of the most bracingly handsome stretches of the Pyrenean range.

Apart from the hydroelectric works that preclude wider official status, the park remains unspoiled habitat for such singular fauna as the Alpine marmot and the Pyrenean desman, an aquatic mole that forages in glacial streams. The entire 140-square-kilometre reach is studded with high-altitude lakes, fir and pine trees blanketing the lower slopes, beneath barbarous granite pinnacles reaching 2400m.

Assuming you approach from the east at Espot, you'll save blistered feet by negotiating the lengthy paved road into the park by 4WD-taxi. Once that ends, a network of trails fans out from the cobalt waters of the Estany de Sant Maurici, with convenient refuges at several intersections. Bisected by a main road and tunnel, the range then lunges westwards towards the equally impressive Parque Nacional de Ordesa y Monte Perdido, which gets the nod from UNESCO and the attention of climbers looking to tackle its vertigo-stricken, Wild West-gone-alpine canyons, thundering with glacial meltwater in late spring.

Anyone with a less adventurous head for heights can admire the limestone strangeness from the depths of the Ordesa Gorge, where an unusual east–west orientation funnels in damp Atlantic air and supports unexpectedly lush vegetation; access is most common from the west, via the village of Torla. Some 10km further south, Añisclo, an equally breathtaking and much quieter canyon, can be accessed via a minor road turning off at Sarvisé. Sequestered in its hulking gorge wall is the hermitage of San Urbez, bearing witness to the days when the park was an untrammelled wilderness, home to mystics rather than wardens.

146 | Stargazing in central Tenerife

CANARY ISLANDS Gaze heavenward on a clear, moonless light in Teide National Park, and you'll be astounded by constellations so vivid you feel as though you could reach out and touch them. It's enough to make anyone light-headed.

There's another reason to feel dizzy, of course. Wherever you are in the park, you're surprisingly high up. At 3718m, the peak of El Teide – the volcanic cone that's Tenerife's dramatic centrepiece – is the highest point on Spanish territory, while even the *Parador de Cañadas del Teide* in the crater below stands at 2146m. The journey to this point typically starts at sea level and can take barely an hour by car – an exhilarating climb, by any standard.

Thanks to both Teide's altitude and its latitude, close to the Tropic of Cancer but out of the path of tropical storms, the skies are naturally clear. Light pollution is low, too: this sculpted desert of timeworn lava is 7km, as the crow flies, from the nearest small town.

Teide is perfectly placed to study the sun – its observatory is equipped with Europe's finest solar telescopes – and its popularity among stargazers is on the rise. In 2013 the park was awarded Starlight Reserve and Starlight Tourist Destination status by the UNESCO-backed Starlight Foundation. With its international credentials in the bag, Tenerife is keen to attract more astro-tourists.

With a small telescope or even binoculars, you can enjoy superb views from the Parador or from Montaña Guajara, a nearby peak on the crater rim. For an even bigger buzz, you can take the cable car up to the peak of El Teide to spend a night at the *Altavista del Teide Refuge*, 3270m up.

As a bonus, Starmus, a festival of astronomy, art and music, offers the chance to mingle with stars of a different sort – in 2014, Stephen Hawking delivered the keynote and Brian May, Richard Dawkins and a galaxy of astronauts were among the speakers.

147 | Painting the town red at La Tomatina

SPAIN On the last Wednesday of every August, 130,000 kilos of over-ripe tomatoes are hurled around the tiny town of Buñol until the alleyways are ankle-deep in squelching fruit. What started in the 1940s as an impromptu food fight between friends has turned into one of the most bizarre and downright infantile fiestas on Earth, a summer spectacular in which thirty thousand or so finger-twitching participants try to dispose of the entire EU tomato mountain by way of a massive hour-long food fight.

Locals, young and old, spend the morning attaching protective plastic sheeting to their house fronts, draping them over the balconies and bolting closed the shutters. By midday, the plaza and surrounding streets are brimming to the edges with overheated humans, and the chant of "To-ma-te, To-ma-te" begins to ring out.

As the church clock chimes noon, dozens of trucks rumble into the plaza, disgorging their messy ammunition onto the dusty streets. And

then all hell breaks loose. There are no allies, no protection, nowhere to hide; everyone – man or woman, young or old – is out for themselves. The first five minutes is tough going: the tomatoes are surprisingly hard and they actually hurt until they have been thrown a few times. Some are fired head-on at point-blank range, others sneakily aimed from behind, and the skilled lobber might get one to splat straight onto the top of your head. After what seems like an eternity, the battle dies down as the tomatoes disintegrate into an unthrowable mush. The combatants slump exhausted into a dazed ecstasy, grinning inanely at one another and basking in the glory of the battle. But the armistice is short-lived as another truck rumbles into the square to deposit its load. Battle commences once more, until the next load of ammunition is exhausted. Six trucks come and go before the final ceasefire. All in all, it only lasts about an hour, but it's probably the most stupidly childish hour you'll ever enjoy as an adult.

148 | The art of lava: César Manrique's Lanzarote

CANARY ISLANDS Nature has treated Lanzarote harshly over the centuries. Violent volcanic eruptions have ripped the island apart, leaving much of its surface area twisted, charred and strewn with lava. Gaze up at the mighty Timanfaya cone and you feel connected to the centre of the Earth.

To César Manrique (1919–92), Lanzarote's influential painter, sculptor, designer and conservationist, the island's otherworldly lava landscapes were an inspiration. His abstract paintings – some of which hang in MIAC (Museo Internacional de Arte Contemporáneo) in Arrecife's Castillo de San José and FCM (Fundación César Manrique) in the Taro de Tahíche – are powerfully suggestive of furiously boiling rock. Manrique's greatest legacy is a circuit of large-scale artistic and architectural creations, designed on Lanzarote in the 1960s. Taking the island's stark natural aesthetic as a starting point, he moulded and enhanced sections of the terrain into public works of avant-garde art: sculptures, galleries, gardens and meeting places.

The Taro de Tahíche – Manrique's former home – nestles into a lava flow from the 1730s and is a fascinating building to visit. Its facade resembles a traditional Canarian house, but step inside and you find yourself in a light-drenched, glass-walled space hung with greats such as Picasso and Miró. Panoramic windows offer lava views so dramatic they threaten to upstage the paintings. Downstairs there's a perfect ornamental pool and a playboy lair sculpted out of natural caves.

A tour of Manrique's Lanzarote will take you to the Juguetes del Viento, jaunty mechanical sculptures which rotate in the brisk Atlantic breeze; the Jardín de Cactus, Manrique's flamboyant cactus garden; the Mirador del Río, a clifftop lookout; and *El Diablo*, a volcano-powered restaurant. Best of all is the *Jameos del Agua*, deep in the island's northern volcanic badlands. Here, Manrique transformed a series of roofless lava caves and a mysterious subterranean lagoon into a strikingly imaginative rock-walled restaurant, bar and rendezvous.

CANARY ISLANDS As climates change, tastes shift and appetites for distinctive bouquets grow, more and more vineyards are popping up in the unlikeliest of places. But who would have thought you could grow vines on a volcanic island with no freshwater springs, rivers or streams?

La Geria and Masdache in central Lanzarote, where vivid green vines thrive in sculpted fields of black lava, is perhaps the most unusual wine region in the world. Both beautiful and functional, Lanzarote's volcanic vineyards have been described as a perfect synthesis of art and engineering.

After a major eruption in 1730 smothered the most fertile valleys, the islanders, forced to rethink their farming methods, discovered that volcanic gravel trapped just enough morning dew to sustain a limited number of vines. By sheltering each plant in a hollow, edged with a *zoco* – a low, crescent-shaped wall of lava stones – they could protect the grapes from the scorchingly salty prevailing winds.

Little by little, they perfected their technique, and sweet, fortified Lanzarote malmsey – a favourite tipple in England in Shakespeare's day – became a respected speciality wine once more. It's been joined by a series of crisp white *malvasía*, rosés, cavas and reds.

Since Lanzarote's seventeen *bodegas* (wineries) are so boutique, few bottles of wine leave the island other than in visitors' luggage. But it's easy to sample some while you're here. Local restaurants make a point of championing their favourite *bodegas*, several of which have tasting rooms for anyone keen to buy wine at source.

At the oldest *bodega* of all, *El Grifo* in Masdache, you can take a short tour of the vineyards and visit an atmospheric museum of wine-making paraphernalia, complete with impressively dusty bottles, before sampling their famous *malvasía*.

Alternatively, for a relaxed afternoon in the winelands, make for *El Chupadero* in La Geria, an off-the-beaten-track wine bar with a rustic interior, gleaming white walls and inland Lanzarote's trademark crisp, arty vibe. Take a table outside, order some tapas and enjoy a glass or two of your latest favourite variety as the sun dips behind the volcanoes, tinging the horizon with fire.

149

Wine-tasting in Lanzarote's volcanic vineyards

Browsing La Boqueria

SPAIN It happens to most newcomers: noses flare, eyes widen and pulses quicken upon entering La Boqueria, Barcelona's cathedral to *comida fresca* (fresh food). Pass through the handsome Modernista cast-iron gateway and you're rapidly sucked in by the raw, noisy energy of the cavernous hall, the air dense with the salty tang of the sea and freshly spilled blood.

As they say in these parts, if you can't find it in La Boqueria, you can't find it anywhere: pyramids of downy peaches face whole cow heads – their eyes rolled back – and hairy curls of *rabo de toro* (bulls' tails). Pale-pink piglets are strung up by their hind legs, snouts pointing south, while *dorada* (sea bream) twitch on beds of ice next to a tangle of black eels.

The Mercat de Sant Josep, as it's officially called, was built in 1836 on the site of a former convent, though records show that there had been a market here since the thirteenth century. Its devotees are as diverse as the offerings: bargain-hunting grandmas rooting through dusty bins; *gran cocineros* (master chefs) from around Europe palming aubergines and holding persimmons up to the light; and droves of wide-eyed visitors weaving through the hubbub. At its core, though, La Boqueria is a family affair. Ask for directions and you might be told to turn right at Pili's place, then left at the Oliveros brothers. More than half of the stalls – and attendant professions – have been passed down through generations for over a century.

When it comes time to eat, do it here. The small bar-restaurants tucked away in La Boqueria may be low on frills, but they serve some of the finest market-fresh Catalan fare in the city. Flames lick over the dozens of orders crammed onto the tiny grill at *Pinotxo*, a bustling bar that has been around since 1940. Pull up a stool, and choose from the day's specials that are rattled off by various members of the extended family, like the affable, seventy-something Juanito. Tuck into bubbling *samfaina*, a Catalan ratatouille, or try *cap i pota*, stewed head and hoof of pig. As the afternoon meal winds down, Juanito walks the bar, topping up glasses from a jug of red wine. There's a toast – "Salud!" – and then everyone takes long, warming swallows, as all around the shuttered market sighs to a close.

151 | A drop of the bard's stuff: drinking sherry Spanish-style

SPAIN Sixteenth-century England might not have proved so green and pleasant for Spain's Armada, but at least Shakespeare was busy lauding its wine. Falstaff's avowal of the properties of "sherris-sack" should probably be taken with a *pellizco* of salt, but there's nothing quite like a chilled glass of fino in the Andalucían shade. The vineyards from which it derives are among the oldest on Earth, surviving the disapproval of Moorish rulers, the ravages of civil war and a phylloxera epidemic, only to face a twenty-first-century market saturated with trendy New World competition.

Downsized but unbowed, they still occupy the famous sherry triangle bounded by the southwestern towns of Jerez de la Frontera, San Lúcar de Barrameda and El Puerto de Santa María, intent on attracting a younger, hipper market. And why not; the sickly cream sherries

mouldering in British cupboards are a world away from the lithe tang of a fino or bleached-dry manzanilla, which dance on the palate and flirt coquettishly with tapas.

When it comes to sprucing up sherry's rather fusty image (at least outside Spain), González Byass have been leading the way with their rebranding of the famed Tio Pepe. Their cobbled lanes and dim, vaulted cellars are among the oldest in Jerez, one of the most atmospheric – if touristy – places to sample a fino or an almond-nutty amontillado straight from the *bota* (sherry cask); you can even anoint your soles with some of their hallowed grapes during the September harvest. And if you're still hankering after the kind of tipple granny used to pour, nose out the chocolatey bitter-richness of a dry oloroso instead. Falstaff would approve.

152 | Above the clouds on Pico Ruivo

MADEIRA A local challenge involves building a snowman on your bonnet, then driving to the beach for a swim before it melts. There are not many places where you can be in the mountains at ten in the morning and bathing in the sea by eleven, but such is the height of Madeira's peaks that in winter this is often possible.

More often associated with dazzling flora and year-round sunshine, Madeira also boasts some of Europe's most dramatic mountain ranges. Long-extinct volcanic peaks jut to nearly 2000m above the warm Atlantic waters, and one of the island's greatest walks is a dizzy footpath linking its highest points.

The walk to the island's highest peak, Pico Ruivo, is well signed and immediately dramatic, following a high ridge across a volcanic landscape. Skeletal bones of basalt columns and sills jut out of the soft, reddish ferrous soil, but as you climb, the scenery is far from

barren. In summer, the path is lined with miniature pink geraniums, weird interlocking leaves of house leeks and the contorted trunks of ancient heather trees.

The 11km path is endlessly varied, sometimes following steps up steep inclines, or skirting cliffs along terrifyingly narrow (but thankfully fenced) ledges. Despite the cool mountain air, you soon feel the heat of the high sun, and it can be thirsty work, though you can shelter in caves, once used by shepherds. At times, the track passes through rock tunnels hewn through dramatic outcrops.

After some five hours, you reach a government rest house just below the final ascent to Pico Ruivo. At 1862m, this is as high as you can go on Madeira. On clear days it's possible to see both the north and south coasts of the Portuguese island from here, though more often the view is over a fluffy landscape of billowing clouds.

153 | Clearing your calendar for bacalhau

PORTUGAL Whole window displays on Lisbon's Rua do Arsenal are lined with what looks like crinkly grey cardboard. The smell is far from alluring, but from these humble slabs of cod the Portuguese are able to conjure up an alleged 365 different recipes for *bacalhau*, one for each day of the year.

Reassuringly, none of this mummified fish dates back to when it first became popular in the 1500s, when the Corte Real brothers sailed as far as Newfoundland for its rich cod banks. To preserve the fish for the journey back, the brothers salted and dried it – the result was an instant hit both with Portuguese landlubbers and navigators, who could safely store it for their long explorations of the New World.

Nowadays, *bacalhau* is Portugal's national dish, served in just about every restaurant in the country and every family home on Christmas Day. Even in Setúbal – where harbour restaurants are stacked with the fresh variety – salted cod appears on most menus, bathed in water for up to two days, and then its skin and bones pulled

away from the swelled and softened flesh, before being boiled and strained into a fishy goo.

Some *bacalhau* dishes can be an acquired taste. At first, the stolid *bacalhau com grau* (boiled with chickpeas) that's the staple restaurant dish in the mosaic-paved old town of Cascais can seem unappetizing. But start with *rissóis de bacalhau* (cod rissoles), commonly served as a bar snack, and you'll soon be hooked. Move on to *bacalhau com natas* (baked with cream) or *bacalhau a brás* (with fried potatos, olives and egg) and there's no looking back.

With fourteen *bacalhau* options on its menu, *Sabores a Bacalhau*, in Lisbon's Parque das Nações, is a good place to start. In a restaurant swathed in decorative *azulejos* tiles appropriately showing sea creatures, a waiter solemnly declares, "Bacalhau is like the Kama Sutra. There may be hundreds of different variations, but you get to know the two or three types that are enjoyable!". Only the Portuguese could compare *bacalhau* with sex, but you can't argue that it's good.

Cycling for the soul: el Camino de Santiago

154

SPAIN Traditionally, pilgrimage meant hoofing it, wayfaring the hard way. Yet most Catholic authorities will tell you there's nothing particularly sinful about making it easier on yourself. You could roughly trace Spain's Camino de Santiago, or Way of St James, by car … but then taking full advantage of the fringe benefits – discounted accommodation and gorgeous red wine – would prove difficult. The answer? Get on your bike.

With reasonable fitness and not a little tenacity, the mantra of "two wheels good, four wheels bad" can take you a long way, on a religious pilgrimage route that pretty much patented European tourism back in the Middle Ages. The most popular section begins at the Pyrenean monastery of Roncesvalles, rolling right across northwestern Spain to the stunning (and stunningly wet) Galician city of Santiago de Compostela, where the presence of St James's mortal remains defines the whole exercise. Pack your mac, but spare a thought for the pre-Gortex, pre-Penny-Farthing millions who tramped through history, walking the proverbial five hundred miles to fall down at Santiago's door.

Bikers can expect a slight spiritual snag: you have to complete 200km to qualify for a reprieve from purgatory (twice the minimum for walkers). By the time you're hurtling down to Pamplona with a woody, moist Basque wind in your hair, though, purgatory will be the last thing on your mind. Granted, the vast, windswept plains between Burgos and León hold greater potential for torment, but by then you'll have crossed the Ebro and perhaps taken a little detour to linger amid the vineyards of La Rioja, fortifying your weary pins with Spain's most acclaimed wine.

The Camino was in fact responsible for spreading Rioja's reputation, as pilgrims used to slake their thirst at the monastery of Santo Domingo de la Calzada. The medieval grapevine likewise popularized the route's celebrated Romanesque architecture; today many monasteries, convents and churches house walkers and cyclists.

Once you're past the Cebreiro pass and into Celtic-green Galicia, rolling past hand-ploughed plots and slate-roofed villages, even a bike seems newfangled amid rhythms that have scarcely changed since the remains of St James first turned up in 813.

155 | Hiking the ancient forests of La Gomera

CANARY ISLANDS Despite being an easy ferry ride from Tenerife, La Gomera, the smallest of Spain's Canary Islands, is one of Europe's most remote corners. Indeed, a number of 1960s American draft dodgers sought refuge in this secluded spot, and it remains a perfect place to get away from it all. In its centre the ancient forests of the Parque Nacional de Garajonay unfold, a tangled mass of moss-cloaked laurel trees thriving among swirling mists to produce an eerie landscape straight out of a Tolkien novel.

The park is best explored along the rough paths that twist between the many labyrinthine root systems. Embark on its finest hike, a 9km trek that's manageable in about four hours if you use a bus or taxi to access the start (a road intersection called Pajarito) and finish points. The lush route takes in the island's central peak, Garajonay; from its summit, you can enjoy immense views looking out over dense tree canopy to neighbouring islands, including Tenerife's towering volcano Mount Teide – at 3718m, Spain's highest point. From Garajonay's peak, follow a crystal-clear stream through thick, dark forest to the cultivated terraces around the hamlet of El Cedro.

Here you can camp, get a basic room or even rent a no-frills cottage – but be sure at least to pause at its rustic bar. Settled on a wooden bench, try some thick watercress soup that's sprinkled with the traditional bread-substitute *gofio*, a flour made from roasted grains.

Beyond El Cedro the valley opens up to the craggy and precipitous landscape that surrounds the town of Hermigua. The terrain around here is so difficult that for centuries a whistling language thrived as a means of communication. These days, however, catching a bus back to your base – via dizzyingly steep hillside roads – is an easy matter.

156 | Waging wine war in La Rioja

SPAIN For grape gourmets, it might seem a terrible waste of wine, but each year several villages in La Rioja spend an entire day soaking each other in the stuff. One of the truly great events of the Spanish summer, the Wine War (La Batalla del Vino) is the modern-day remnant of ancient feuds between the wine town of Haro and its Riojan neighbours. It's a wine-fight of epic – and historic – proportions.

The festival begins with what must be one of the most bizarre religious processions anywhere: the congregation – as many as five thousand people, mostly dressed in white – comes armed not with Bibles, crucifixes and rosary beads but with an ingenious array of wine-weapons, ranging from buckets, water pistols and *bota* bags (wine-skin bottles) to agricultural spraying equipment.

The battle is thick and fast, with warring factions drenching each other with medium-bodied Rioja. In theory, the townsfolk of Haro are battling it out with those of neighbouring Miranda de Ebro, but in the good-humoured but frantic battle that rages, there are no obvious sides, and no winners or losers. Instead, the object is perfectly straightforward: to squirt, hose, blast or throw some 25,000 litres of what is presumably not vintage *vino tinto* over as many people as possible.

You won't be spared as a spectator, so you may as well join in. At the very least, come armed with a water pistol, though be warned that the locals have perfected the art of the portable water cannon, and can practically blast you off your feet from five metres. But what a way to go.

157 | Cruising through the Coto de Doñana

SPAIN The supposed site of the lost city of Atlantis, the preserve of the Duchess of Alba, Goya's muse, and a favourite hunting haunt of seventeenth-century monarchs Felipe IV and Felipe V, Andalucía's Coto de Doñana was also, up until recently, the infamous domain of malaria-carrying mosquitoes.

While many of Spain's wetland areas were drained in the fight against the disease, which put paid to many a royal and was only eradicated in 1964, the swampy triangle that is the Río Guadalquivir delta escaped with its water and wildlife intact. Five years after the area was declared disease-free, almost 350 square kilometres came under the aegis of the Parque Nacional de Doñana, Spain's largest national park. Today, the area is both a UNESCO World Heritage Site and a Biosphere Reserve, and encompasses more than 770 square kilometres. Illuminated by the hallucinatory glare of the Costa de la Luz sun, it's a place of tart air and buckled horizons, with that almost mystical lure encountered in unbroken landscapes.

Bordered by the urban centres of Seville, Huelva and Cádiz, it suffers the kind of man-made encroachments from which remoter parks are immune, so it's likely your visit will be confined to a guided tour in an incongruously militaristic 4WD bus.

Even as your driver barrels past sand dunes, sun-blind lagoons and pine stands with typically brusque abandon, however, you can rest easy in the knowledge that the flamingos, wild boars, tortoises, red deer, mongooses and vultures that reside here are otherwise left in peace.

Eking out a living alongside those creatures are small, endangered populations of imperial eagles and Iberian lynx, and the park also makes a stopping place for a rude array of migratory birds that alight in flooded marshes on their way to and from West Africa. How many of them you actually see in any one visit is liable to depend on luck, season and a good pair of binoculars; just remember to pack that repellent.

158 | Washing away the cider-house blues

SPAIN The Basques are a proud people. And, boy, do they take pride in their regional produce: they have the finest fish on the Spanish coast, the tastiest tapas across Iberia – and some of the most scrumptious cider in Europe. Prohibited under the Franco regime, cider is back with a bang. The beauty of Basque cider is that it's succulently simple. There are no must or extracts here, no gas or sweeteners; just a blend of three types of apple – bitter, sour and sweet, all lovingly combined in the perfect proportions.

The best cider is drunk on site: head out to the orchards of Astigarraga and spend the day at one of the area's many *sagardotegiak*, or cider houses, drinking the golden liquor fresh from *kupelak* (large barrels). Empty the glass each time with one quick gulp – it preserves the cider's *txinparta*: its colour, bouquet and that tangy, tantalizing taste.

159 | Big-game fishing in the Atlantic

AZORES Way out in the Atlantic, 1600km off the coast of Portugal, the string of volcanic islands that makes up the Azores is probably the only part of the European Union in which you can go big-game fishing – and for blue marlin, too, the mother of all large fish, weighing in at 150kg or more.

The islands regularly host the European and World Big Game Fishing Championships if you want to see how it's done. Alternatively, you can hire a boat and a skipper and try your own luck; the abundance of marlin in summer, as well as shark and swordfish year-round – make the Azores a game-fishers' paradise.

And while you're waiting for them to bite, be sure to keep an eye out for the dolphins and whales that frolic immediately offshore.

Fly camping along Spain's north coast in a campervan

160

SPAIN Wild, jagged cliffs, distant mountain peaks, sweeping skies over vast beaches and often-ferocious Atlantic waves – Spain's north coast does dramatic scenery in spades.

Fly camping your way along its undulating coastline, from Cantabria, through Asturias, to Galicia, in a camper van, is a great way to explore the pretty higgledy-piggledy fishing villages, golden sands and dense pine forests.

Fall asleep to the sound of the waves, rather than the snores of fellow campers, and wake up to unimpeded views of the ocean, instead of your neighbour in his PJs.

Granted, the weather can switch from Med-like sunshine and blue skies to hammering rain in the time it takes to pop up the roof, but then that's what makes the holidaymakers head south, and why you get that clifftop, that rolling meadow, that pristine beach to yourself.

Pull up, kick back, open a bottle of the local sidra, and wait for the storm to pass.

Need to know

118 For more information, visit Ⓦen.rotavicentina. com. *Casas de turismo rural* along the way are available through Casas Brancas (Ⓦcasasbrancas.pt), while there are also youth hostels in Almogarve and near Arrifana beach, and campsites at Zambujeira and near Odeceixe and Aljezur.

119 The Guggenheim is located in Bilbao's Abandoibarra district, 10 minutes' walk west of the city centre; Ⓦguggenheim-bilbao.es.

120 *Arzak*, Avda Alcalde Elosegui 273 (☎+34 943 285 593, Ⓦarzak.es).

121 The train has up to six departures in either direction daily. Tickets are sold on the day from Palma's Ferrocarril de Sóller station. See Ⓦtrendesoller.com/en.

122 For the latest updates, plus opening hours and entry fees, see Ⓦsagradafamilia.org.

123 The cable car from Funchal Bay to Monte is open daily (except Christmas Day) 9am–6pm. For more information, visit Ⓦmadeiracablecar.com.

124 Tickets sell out fast for the Concurs de Castells (Ⓦeng.concursdecastells.cat), but human towers can be seen across Catalonia during religious festivals.

125 The tourist board provides an overview of the route, with maps, on its website (Ⓦgrancanaria. com). Be sure to arrange accommodation before you set off.

126 Visit Ⓦturismodecordoba.org for festival dates. Make sure to book accommodation well in advance.

127 Several restaurants in Furnas offer *cozido*. As it takes so long to prepare, it's best to order the day before. *Canto da Doca* is on Rua Nova in Horta on Faial. 10 Fest Azores (Ⓦtaste.visitazores.com) is hosted every June by *Restaurante Anfiteatro* in Ponta Delgada, São Miguel (Ⓦefth.com.pt).

128 Tram 28 runs roughly 6am–11pm. Check Ⓦcarris .pt for fares.

129 Límitezero generally operates from Easter through to October, and is based at Av. de Portugal, 21595 Sanlúcar de Guadiana, Huelva, Spain. Call ☎+34 670 31 39 33 or visit Ⓦlimitezero.com.

130 Most mansions are restricted to exterior viewing. WOMAD (Ⓦwomad.org) takes place during the first fortnight in May.

131 For more on the São João festival, and Porto itself, go to Ⓦvisitporto.travel.

132 The Museo del Prado (Ⓦmuseodelprado.es) is on Paseo del Prado; the nearest metros are Atocha and Banco de España.

133 Opening hours and entry costs for Texas Hollywood can be found at Ⓦfortbravooficial.com, and for Mini-Hollywood at Ⓦoasysparquetematico.com.

134 Dive operators like Regal Dive (Ⓦregal-diving .co.uk) and Dive Worldwide (Ⓦdiveworldwide.com) offer holidays throughout the Azores. Peak dive season is May–Sept. Ponta Delgada is the hub for international flights and onward connections.

135 Check Ⓦmezquitadecordoba.org for up-to-date entry costs and other details.

136 For information on Semana Santa, and Seville itself, go to Ⓦvisitasevilla.es/en. The official programme is widely available from city newsstands.

137 The Alhambra is open throughout the year; make reservations as far in advance as possible (Ⓦalhambra-patronato.es).

138 Some lodges require advance reservation, others accept drop-ins: for details see *Graham's* (Ⓦgrahams-port.com), *Taylor's* (Ⓦtaylor.pt), *Ferreira* (Ⓦsograpevinhos.com), *Croft* (Ⓦcroftport.com), *Sandeman* (Ⓦsandeman.com) and *Cockburn's* (Ⓦcockburns.com).

139 Sintra (Ⓦsintraromantica.net/en) is just 45 minutes by train from Lisbon's Rossio or Sete Rios stations.

140 Guided hiking trips along the Camino Mozárabe can be arranged through Toma & Coe (Ⓦtomaandcoe. com), or by calling ☎+34 650 73 31 16

141 The Picos de Europa mountains lie around 20km inland from the northeastern coast of Spain. You can fly to Santander; good bases include Espinama (Ⓦespinama.es), Posada de Valdeon (Ⓦvaldeon.org) and Arenas de Cabrales. To plan a visit to a cave, see Ⓦfundacioncabrales.com.

142 Parque Terra Nostra is in Furnas, São Miguel (Ⓦparqueterranostra.com). The *Terra Nostra Garden Hotel* offers four-star accommodation (Ⓦbensaude .pt).

143 See Ⓦsalvador-dali.org for details of opening hours and entry fees.

144 Book tickets online and find out opening times for Palau de la Música at Ⓦpalaumusica.cat and Recinte Modernista de Sant Pau at Ⓦsantpaubarcelona. org.

145 If you'd like more information on the Parc Nacional d'Aigüestortes i Estany de Sant Maurici, visit Ⓦparcsnaturals.gencat.cat/en/aiguestortes; details of the Parque Nacional de Ordesa y Monte Perdido can be found at Ⓦordesa.net.

146 The *Parador de Cañadas del Teide* (Ⓦparador. es/en) holds comfortable rooms and a restaurant, and there's simple accommodation at the *Altavista del Teide Refuge* (Ⓦtelefericoteide.com). The Observatorio del Teide (Ⓦwww.iac.es) offers group tours on request. For more details of Starmus, visit Ⓦstarmus.com.

147 For information on La Tomatina tours, plus photos and videos of the event, see Ⓦlatomatinatours.com.

148 Visitor details for MIAC, *Jameos del Agua*, Jardín de Cactus, Mirador del Río and *El Diablo* (Montañas del Fuego) can be found at Ⓦcentrosturisticos.com, and for FCM at Ⓦfcmanrique.org; all are open daily.

149 You can book a group tour of La Geria and Masdache, including the Museo del Vino El Grifo (Ⓦelgrifo. com), through any resort hotel, or explore independently by rental car (with a designated driver) or taxi. Contact *El Chupadero* on ☎+34 928 17 73 65.

150 La Boqueria (Ⓦboqueria.barcelona) is open Mon–Sat 8am–8.30pm.

151 Jerez de la Frontera (Ⓦjerez.es) lies 85km south of Seville, with which it has regular bus connections.

152 For detailed advice on walking on Madeira, visit the island's official website, Ⓦvisitmadeira.pt.

153 *Sabores a Bacalhau* is open daily at Rua da Pimenta 47, Parque das Nações (Ⓦrestaurantebacalhau. com).

154 A *credencial* or Pilgrim's Passport, available from the monastery at Roncesvalles or via Ⓦcsj.org.uk, entitles you to free or very cheap *hostal* accommodation.

155 La Gomera lies 28km from Tenerife and is served by regular daily ferries (Ⓦfredolsen.es).

156 Haro's Wine War takes place on June 29; see Ⓦwine-fight.com for more details.

157 For details of daily bus tours from the reception centre at El Acebuche, 4km north of the coastal resort of Matalascañas, visit Ⓦdonanavisitas.es.

158 The nearest main town to Astigarraga is San Sebastián. The cider season lasts from mid-Jan to May. Devotees should check out Ⓦsagardotegiak.com.

159 The tourist board website Ⓦvisitazores.com has lots of details on the islands, including material on fishing.

160 Car ferries run direct from Plymouth or Portsmouth, UK, to Santander in Cantabria. Crossings take around 20hr or 24hr, respectively. Camping restrictions vary from region to region; check Ⓦabout-spain. net/tourism/camping.htm for more info.

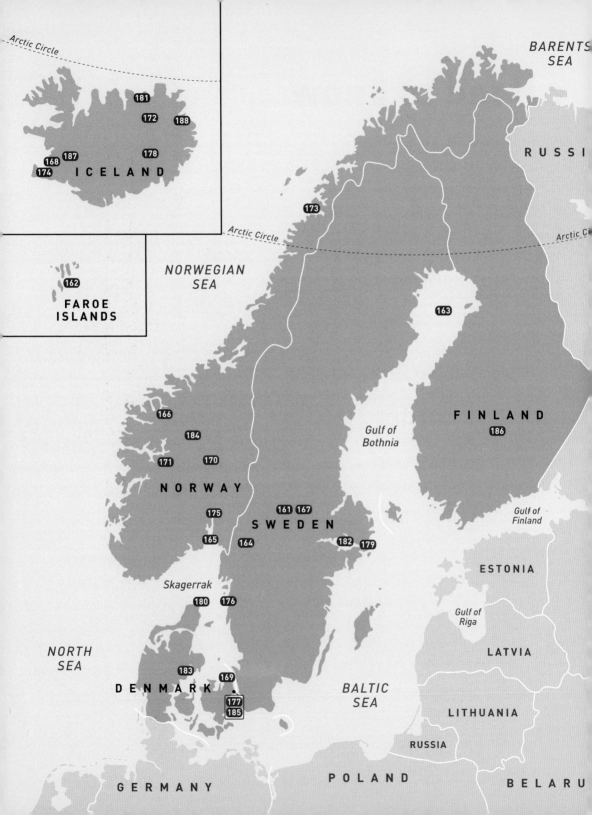

BARENTS
SEA

Arctic Circle

RUSSI

NORWEGIAN
SEA

FAROE
ISLANDS

162

181
172
188
178
187
168
174

ICELAND

Arctic Circle

Arctic C

173

163

FINLAND
186

Gulf of
Bothnia

Gulf of
Finland

166
184
171   170

NORWAY

175
165   164

SWEDEN

161 167

182   179

ESTONIA

Gulf of
Riga

LATVIA

Skagerrak

180   176

NORTH
SEA

183

169

DENMARK

177
185

BALTIC
SEA

LITHUANIA

RUSSIA

GERMANY

POLAND

BELARU

SCANDINAVIA
161–188

Cool? Absolutely, in more ways than one. Hot? Likewise. From its glacier caves and cross-country skiing routes to its wood-fired saunas and steaming hot springs, Scandinavia is a region of natural extremes – even its wildlife ranges from the tiny puffins of the Faroe Islands to the weighty whales of Iceland and elusive brown bears of Finland. So too is it a place that sets trends – innovative cities like Stockholm, Copenhagen and Reykjavik are renowned for their food, design and architecture. That Scandinavia also holds true to centuries-old traditions through events like Norway's party-hard National Day and Finland's Sámi festivals only adds to its allure.

161 Surviving surströmming

SWEDEN It's late summer and I'm drinking a beer in the garden of some Swedish friends, preparing for my first taste of *surströmming*.

"It's not that bad," one guy assures me. "It tastes much better than it smells."

Another friend tries his best not to crack a smile. "Yeah," he agrees. "But it makes your farts smell really awful."

Surströmming – or fermented herring – is a centuries-old, northern Swedish delicacy that's best eaten alfresco. Open a can of the stuff inside, I'm told, and the smell never really disappears. Even out in the open, precautions must be taken to avoid ruining the party vibe.

"Who's going to open it?" asks the host, stepping out into the garden with a can of fish in one hand and a bucket of water in the other.

"*Engelsmannen!*" the Swedes all say at once, pointing at me. *The Englishman!*

And so, as the lucky foreigner, I find myself kneeling on the grass, elbow deep in a bucket of water, trying to open a can of smelly herring. This underwater technique is supposed to stop the fishy gloop trapped inside the bulging can from spraying out and destroying your clothes with its stink.

At this point I'm still thinking *"how bad can it really be?"* and then – with a half-turn of the tin opener – it hits me. An evil smell, part fish, part death, floods out from the can. We laugh, hold our noses, and then, defying every natural impulse, sit down to eat.

It's all beautifully done: delicate pieces of slimy herring are placed onto thin slices of *tunnbröd* (Swedish crispbread) and topped with finely chopped white onion, sour cream, boiled potatoes and fresh dill. There are shots of schnapps to wash it down with, and it's all backed up by a good sing-song.

And the taste isn't *that* bad – fishy, yes, but with the sharp tang of a good blue cheese. But there's no getting away from that smell. And yes, it hangs around until the day after. A small price to pay when you've just experienced a uniquely Swedish dinner party.

Steve Vickers
has filed travel stories for newspapers around the world, including *The Washington Post*, *The Independent* and *The Observer*, plus half a dozen travel magazines. He speaks Swedish with an English accent and has worked as a correspondent in Sweden for BBC Radio 4 and the World Service.

Puffin and pantin'

162

FAROE ISLANDS It is mating season on the unspoilt Faroe Islands, about 300km north of Scotland in the windswept, weather-tossed North Atlantic. Heavy waves batter tall, chalky cliffs. Clouds of seagulls sweep through the skies, touching down on fields of purple orchids, flanked by traditional, brightly coloured houses with roofs of turf. Pairs of puffins, their feathers ruffled from the raging sea, wash up on the island, standing proud and rubbing their beaks together in displays of matrimony. The show has just begun.

For the next four months, these curious seabirds will mate, nest and raise their offspring on the towering Vestmanna cliffs. They will spend their days diving in and out of the sea, digging burrows, bringing home fish suppers and preparing for migration in late August. All of which makes for great viewing. Boats chug out here from Tórshavn, so you can gaze up at the thousands of nesting birds, hanging on to the crags of the 450m-high cliffs far above.

163

Riding the winter ice aboard an Arctic icebreaker

FINLAND Outside, in the cold winter air, a community of red-suited humans looking for all the world like miniature Teletubbies are flapping about the icebergs. Up on deck, warmly dressed passengers shudder and scan the horizon, their breath nearly crystallizing the moment it hits the air. In the distance, a slender elk springs from the shore onto the ice, darting across the frozen sea.

Breaking the silence of the Finnish Arctic is the *Sampo*, a colossal 76m-long, 3500-tonne icebreaker that rides on top of the frozen sea, bearing down on the ice and breaking it

into chunks like bits of frosty white chocolate. The jagged, fragmented shards – up to 1m thick in some parts – crash and scrape along the steel hull as the vessel cruises on past them towards the sea's deepest waters.

Built in 1960 in Helsinki, the *Sampo* plied through iced-over routes to the Arctic Sea for three decades before becoming a tourist attraction. Today, it is the only Arctic icebreaker in the world to accept passengers, leading the intrepid on four-hour cruises through the frigid waters of the Gulf of Bothnia, the only European sea to freeze every winter – which can happen as early as October.

The ship's northerly location means things get cold – as low as -40°C at water level. But this doesn't deter curious visitors from descending the ship out onto the ice, slipping into the frozen waters and floating there in the ship-issue red puffy drysuits. It's just like being 4 years old again; the only thing missing is a rubber duck.

164 | Rope rafts on the Klarälven

SWEDEN Boating is so much more satisfying when you've built the barge you're travelling in. On the Klarälven, Sweden's longest river, you can construct a raft big enough to carry six people, using just a dozen ropes and logs, and the guidance of an expert instructor.

You can put the boat together in a morning and be on the water for the afternoon, but a five- or eight-day-trip gives you the opportunity to both enjoy tranquil Värmland (Sweden's most southerly wilderness) and head onto dry land to explore the villages along the Klarälven. You can sleep overnight under canvas on your moored craft or in a tent by the river.

Rapids and whirlpools provide moments of real excitement, but much of the trip is a slow meander. This was one of the last Swedish rivers where timber was floated downstream to sawmills, and you'll be travelling at the same gentle pace, keeping an eye out for beavers and elk as the forests and marshes slip by.

165 | Getting naked on Oslofjord

NORWAY Just a short way west of central Oslo is the Bygdøy peninsula. As well as several excellent museums (hence the nickname "museum island") it's home to two sandy beaches, with glorious views across the island-studded fjord. The larger one is usually crowded and noisy, but the smaller one is peaceful. You might see a young couple strolling hand in hand along the shore, an excitable dog playing with pine cones, or a wiry old man engaging in some nude callisthenics before striding into the freezing water.

Yup, this is a nude beach.

The shock wears off quickly – clearly no one else cares about their state of undress. Once you're used to it, you might even get the urge to take a dip in the cold, clear water yourself. Keep your swimsuit on if you'd prefer, or head in *au naturel* for the full, bracing experience.

NORWAY Everything about the Geirangerfjord is dramatic, even the approach: zigzagging up through the mountains from Åndalsnes before throwing yourself round a series of hair-raising bends as you descend the aptly named Ørnevegen, or Eagle's Highway, the fjord glittering like a precious gem below.

The Geirangerfjord, a great slice of deep blue carved into the crystalline rock walls and snaking out in an "S" shape as it weaves west, is one of the region's smallest fjords and one of its most beautiful. From the pretty little village that marks its eastern end, ferries set out on the 16km trip along the fjord west to Hellesylt. On a summer's day, as the ferry eases away from the wooden pier and chugs off slowly through the passage, waterfalls cascading down the sheer walls on either side and dolphins playing in the bow waves –

as they have done since the first cruise ship found its way up here in 1869 – it's easy to see why UNESCO considered this to be the archetypal fjord, awarding it World Heritage status in 2005, jointly with Nærøyfjord.

As beautiful as it is, Geirangerfjord is just one sliver of water in a network of stunning strands, and you need to see a few fjords to appreciate their magnificence as a whole. Head south for Nærøyfjord, the narrowest fjord in the world, where you can savour the emerald-green waters close up, in a kayak. Or hop in the car and glide across on a tiny ferry, over nearby Norddalsfjord, or – to the south – glass-like Lustrafjord, the wind whipping off the water as you stand at the very bow of the boat, the imposing silhouette of Urnes' Viking stave church looming ever closer.

167 | Navigating a Swedish smörgåsbord

SWEDEN Offhand, how many different ways can you think of to prepare herring or salmon? The two fish are staples of the *smörgåsbord* and, at last count, there were well over 120 varieties being used in restaurants and kitchens across Sweden.

The Swedish *smörgåsbord* (literally "buttered table") is a massive all-you-can-eat buffet where you can sample almost anything under the midnight sun, from giant plates of fish and seafood – pickled, curried, fried or cured – to a dizzying assortment of eggs, breads, cheeses, salads, pâtés, terrines and cold cuts, and even delicacies such as smoked reindeer and caviar.

You're best off arriving early and on an empty stomach. Just don't pile everything high onto your plate at once – remember that the tradition is as much celebratory social ritual as it is one of consumption. That means cleansing your palate first with a shot of ice-cold aquavit

(caraway-flavoured schnapps), then drinking beer throughout – which as it happens goes especially well with herring, however it is prepared.

Plan to attack your food in three separate stages – cold fish, cold meats and warm dishes – as it's generally not kosher to mix fish and meat dishes on the same plate. Layer some slices of herring onto a bit of rye bread, and side it with a boiled potato, before moving on to smoked or roasted salmon, jellied eel or roe. Follow this with any number of cold meats such as liver pâté, cured ham and oven-baked chicken. Then try a hot item or two – Swedish meatballs, wild mushroom soup, perhaps *Janssons frestelse* ("Jansson's temptation"), a rich casserole of crispy matchstick potatoes, anchovies and onion baked in a sweet cream. Wind down with a plate of cheese, crackers and crisp Wasa bread and, if you can still move, fruit salad, pastries or berry-filled pies for dessert, capped by a cup of piping-hot coffee. Then feel free to pass out.

168 | Sound and light: Reykjavik's Harpa

ICELAND Shimmering like a jewel at the end of Reykjavik's pretty harbour, the Harpa concert hall, which opened in May 2011, is one of those architectural statements that has to be seen to be believed. When creating its striking facades – 43m high, and featuring 12,000 square metres of translucent glass bricks – Danish-Icelandic artist Olafur Eliasson worked to evoke the beauty of geological structures, including Iceland's own basalt columns.

The ever-shifting lightscape Harpa reflects is key to its effect: at night the bricks glow with coloured LED lights, while during the day they allow dramatic shafts of light to penetrate the vast interior. Nature saturates the building in other ways, too. The four main halls, each named after natural Icelandic phenomena – Nordurljos (northern lights), Silfurberg (translucent calcite crystal), Kaldalon (cold lagoon) and the grand concert hall, Eldborg (volcanic crater) – are accessed by long, angular ramps that zigzag through the interior, offering majestic views of the city and the sea.

As well as being the official home of the Iceland Symphony Orchestra and the Icelandic Opera, Harpa – Reykjavik's first ever dedicated concert space – hosts international and local rock, pop and electronic acts too, many of which you can catch during the city's annual music festival, Iceland Airwaves. As you'd expect from a venue that cost 1.5 billion Icelandic Krona (£90m), the acoustics are as impressive as the decor; the reverberations of each hall can be adjusted by moving canopies, and reverberation chambers are hidden behind doors. Even if you're not here for a concert, a visit is a must.

The building, which won the Mies van der Rohe Award in 2013, offers an exhibition space, a café-restaurant, design/gift store and record shop. Guided tours offer insights on how Icelandic nature has influenced its design and cover the controversy of its (somewhat costly) construction during a time of economic crisis. But Harpa's appeal is more visceral than intellectual. Simply standing inside this astonishing structure and gazing out at the sea and the mountains beyond is a unique experience.

Watching Hamlet in Kronborg Slot

DENMARK "To be or not to be: that is the question." Walking through the hallowed halls of the sixteenth-century Kronborg Slot in northeastern Denmark, you're likely to hear that famous phrase time and again. For it was here that Shakespeare's *Hamlet* was purportedly set; scores of visitors now come to marvel at this UNESCO World Heritage Site, and few can resist citing the tragic prince's most famous line. Even better, though, is if you time your visit to catch the annual Shakespeare festival in the dramatically sited castle grounds, overlooking the sea – the spine-tingling authenticity of the Bard's characters coming to life in their original setting is theatre at its finest.

169

170 | A to B by cross-country ski

NORWAY With 30,000km of marked trails, Norway is the true home of cross-country skiing, the original and most effective means of getting yourself across snowbound winter landscapes. And it's easier and less daunting to learn than the more popular downhill variety (well, more popular outside Scandinavia – here, everyone is a cross-country skier from the age of 2).

As your skills develop, you'll soon want to take on more challenging hills (both up and down) and to test yourself a little more – there are different techniques for using cross-country skis on the flat, downhill and uphill.

And once you've mastered the basics, a truly beautiful winter world will open up. Popular ski resorts such as Voss, to the east of Bergen, offer a plethora of cross-country tracks, which snake their way under snow-shrouded forests and round lowland hills, while the Peer Gynt Ski Region, north of Lillehammer, has over 600km of marked trails winding through pine-scented forests, alongside frozen lakes and over huge whaleback mountains.

It may sound blindingly obvious, but try to go in the depths of winter, for in this season the low angle of the midwinter sun creates beautiful pastel shades of lilac, mauve and purple on the deep, expansive folds of hard-packed powder, especially at the start and end of the day.

Ski trails are graded for difficulty and length so you won't bite off more than you can chew, and you'll usually find various ski *hütte* (huts) along the way, where you can stop for a warming loganberry juice. As your skills develop, you may even want to take on a multiday tour, staying overnight at cosy mountain lodges and discovering the high country of Scandinavia in marvellously traditional fashion.

171 | Plunging from mountain to fjord on the Flåmsbana

NORWAY The brakes grind then release and you're off, squeaking and squealing down a roller-coaster-like track for what might just be the train ride of your life. This is the Flåmsbana, a shiny, pine-green pleasure train that plunges nearly 1km in a mere fifty minutes. The unforgettable 20km ride takes you from the heady frozen heights of the Norwegian mountains in Myrdal right down to the edge of the icy-blue waters of the Sognefjord in the picturesque village of Flåm.

On the train, the old-fashioned carriage interior is wood-panelled and fitted with wide, high-backed benches which transport you back to the 1920s when the train was first built; it took over four years to lay the 20km track which spirals and zigzags down around hairpin bends and through twenty hand-dug tunnels during the course of its short journey. As you might imagine, the views are spectacular; to accommodate this,

enormous, over-sized windows were fitted to ensure you don't miss a thing, regardless of where you happen to be seated.

As it runs all year, the train is a lifeline in the winter months for fjord inhabitants who were previously cut off by the long frozen winters. But for the best views, stick to late spring and summer when the ice and snow-melt create majestic, crashing waterfalls (don't miss the close-range view of Kjosfossen) that seem to leap and spring from every crevice in the sheer, verdant cliffs.

The Flåmsbana offers an experience that's at the same time glamorous, hair-raising and magical. The dizzy inclines and thunderous soundtrack of crashing waterfalls will give even the most seasoned rider a shiver of excitement, and if you can't help but conjure up images of runaway trains, just remember there are five independent sets of brakes – a necessary precaution and a very reassuring feature.

172 | Soaking in Lake Mývatn's hot springs

ICELAND Most people visit Iceland in summer, when once or twice a week it actually stops raining and the sun shines in a way that makes you think, briefly, about taking off your sweater. The hills show off their green, yellow and red gravel faces to best effect, and you can even get around easily without a snowplough. But if you really want to see what makes this odd country tick, consider a winter visit. True, you'll find many places cut off from the outside world until Easter, people drinking themselves into oblivion to make those endless nocturnal stretches race by (though they do the same thing in summer, filled with joy at the endless daylight) and tourist information booths boarded up until the thaw. On the other hand, you can do some things in winter that you will never forget.

Up in the northeast, Lake Mývatn is surrounded by craters, boiling mud pools and other evidence of Iceland's unstable tectonics. Near

its northeast shore lie crevasses, flooded by thermal springs welling up out of the earth. They are too hot for summer bathing, but in winter the water temperature drops to just within human tolerance, and the springs are best visited in a blizzard, when you'll need to be well rugged up against the bitter, driving wind and swirling snow.

Clamber up the steep slope and look down over the edge: rising steam from the narrow, flooded fissure 5m below has built up a thick ice coating, so it's out with the ice axes to cut footholds for the climb down to a narrow ledge, where you undress in the cold and, shivering, ease yourself into the pale-blue water. And then... heaven! You tread water and look up into the falling snow and weird half-light, your damp hair nearly frozen but your body flooded with heat. Five minutes later, you clamber out, feeling so hot you're surprised that the overhanging ice sheets haven't started to melt.

173 | Cruising the coolest coast in Europe

NORWAY For more than 120 years, the *Hurtigruten* boat service has made the dramatic voyage from Bergen in the western fjords of Norway to Kirkenes, deep within the Arctic Circle and hard up against the Russian border. It's a beautiful trawl up the coast, past towering peaks and deep-blue fjords, the views growing more spectacular the further you go.

This is far from your average cruise. Quoits are distinctly absent from the upper deck and there are no afternoon salsa classes with the crew; entertainment comes instead in the form of the pounding ocean and some truly staggering scenery. The boat calls in at 35 ports on the way – some thriving cities steeped in maritime history, others little more than a jetty and a cluster of uniform wooden houses painted in the ubiquitous red. Joining the boat at Bodø in the far north of Norway, you're ensured a spectacular start.

Easing gently out of Bodø and into the Norwegian Sea, the boat turns to starboard for the Lofoten Islands, the soaring crags of the Lofotenveggen – a jagged wall of mountains that stretches 160km along the shore – looming ever closer. Hopping in and out of a couple of rustic fishing villages along the coast, it then squeezes through the Vesterålen Islands, almost rubbing its bows along the sheer cliff faces that line the Trollfjord, before pushing on to Tromsø, a teeming metropolis compared with the sparse settlements left behind.

From here, the boat sets off on its final leg, stopping for a couple of hours at Nordkapp, a desolate spot that marks the northernmost point in mainland Europe, before traversing the Barents Sea. Finally, six days after leaving Bergen and 67 hours from Bodø, it triumphantly chugs into the uniformly lacklustre town of Kirkenes, concrete proof – after such a journey – that it is often better to travel than to arrive.

174 | Tracking elves and trolls in the land of ice and fire

ICELAND Imagine a landscape of rolling hills, silver-grey volcanic slopes and amphitheatre-shaped mountains populated by elves and trolls, over which fairy-tale clouds and swirling sea mists blow in with regularity. Places like this are hard to find outwith the pages of a J.R.R. Tolkien saga, but journey to Borgarfjörður Eystri, on the northeastern coast of Iceland, and you can join a storytelling guide who'll have you believe in the power of mythical creatures before you can chant a wizarding spell from Harry Potter.

Today, searching for *huldufólk*, or hidden people, is treated as if a sport in Iceland, and locals approach elf- and troll-tracking without any hint of self-consciousness. You can see Álfaborg, a hill so-named because it is the residence of Borghildur, the Icelandic elf-queen. In the fields around Jökulsá farm, you can gaze on mountains from where trolls descend at night to rustle sheep, or strike out to the steeple-shaped Kirkjusteinn rock, known as the Elvish church. Should that give you reason enough

to leave, bear in mind that on the sea road out to Njardvikurskridur, you risk being surprised by Naddi, a nefarious creature with the body of a man and head of a beast.

Placed in such a scenario you'd be forgiven for thinking this was all fanciful – but the stories, legends and sagas, many of which are born from Scandinavian mythology, are as old as the mountains themselves. Storytelling in Iceland took wing for the simple reason that local desire to believe in the fictions proposed was greater than the desire to know the truth behind them. The landscape, scattered with gigantic blocks of volcanic breccia that some locals believe are elvish houses, makes that more than possible.

And this is what you come to Borgarfjörður Eystri for. It's a place that encourages you to get lost in a moment – and in that moment you can learn something new. No matter how extraordinary it may be.

175 | Joining the festivities on Norwegian National Day

NORWAY May 17 is just another day to most people, but in Oslo (and all across Norway, for that matter) it's an eagerly anticipated annual event: Norwegian National Day. A celebration of the signing of the Norwegian Constitution, National Day is a joyous and rather rambunctious affair. It has the usual parades, bands, street parties and food stalls you'd expect, plus a healthy dose of patriotic singing and flag waving. Children are allowed as much ice cream as they can ingest, and Oslo's 625,000 inhabitants come out in their droves. But the twist in Norway is all in the togs.

Walk out of your door on the big day and you'll feel as if you've accidentally stumbled onto the set of a historical costume drama, with everyone dressed head to toe in traditional dress. Women bustle about in floor-length woollen dresses in vibrant reds, greens, blues and purples, their laced-up bodices adorned with intricate embroidery. Little boys run around in plus fours and woollen waistcoats to

match their fathers while teenagers, depending on their year in school, wear traditional fishermen's overalls in fire-engine red and peacock blue. The effect is disconcerting at first and then, frankly, wonderful as everyone takes part and the city is completely transformed.

Don't worry if you've not got the gear, and certainly don't try to buy an outfit for the occasion as they cost hundreds (if not thousands) of kroner and are passed down in Norwegian families from generation to generation. Just steer clear of jeans and wear something nice and you'll blend right in. The best advice is to go with the flow: clap along with the packs of teenagers chanting traditional Norwegian songs; smile at the children strutting by, their faces scrubbed clean and hair done perfectly for the occasion; bow and nod to the waved greetings of the royal family from the balcony of the palace; and above all let yourself be dragged into the spontaneous and joyous revelry all around.

176 | Exploring the archipelago of Gothenburg

SWEDEN Sipping cold, locally brewed beer; gazing at expanses of blue sky pierced by the masts of bobbing sailboats; catching the scent of hollyhocks and lavender on the gentle breeze: this is the Gothenburg archipelago.

With just over twenty islands to discover, Gothenburg might not compare in size to its Stockholm sibling but, in terms of beauty, it more than measures up. Cafés in idyllic waterfront settings offer the perfect place to relax on a sunny afternoon, where you can enjoy a selection of fresh, locally caught seafood, home-made cakes, ice cream, strong coffee and ice-cold beer; all the Swedish favourites.

Sun-warmed smooth grey rocks pop out of the otherwise grassy, uneven terrain, often with jetties or stairs leading down into the calm, refreshing water for visitors to take a dip, even on the coldest of

days. The occasional stretch of sand can be found too, most notably Brattenbadet beach on the northeast side of Styrsö.

But swimming isn't the only attraction to these islands: seal safaris and fishing excursions are plentiful; fishing is a lifeline on the archipelago and its history is outlined in The Fishing Museum on Hönö Klåva. Woodland trails and rugged coastal paths are set out for walkers, and for any visitors who want to spend more than a day island-hopping there are some unique places to stay. You can bed down in one of Kajkanten Vrångö's traditional boathouses or sleep in a shipyard guesthouse at Brännö Varv – the perfect place to rest after dancing into the dusk, as lights begin to twinkle and the sun refuses to completely set, at one of Brännö's traditional dancing evenings, held throughout the summer.

Brushing shoulders with bears in Finland's newest national park

FINLAND In 2017, Hossa – an area of pristine wilderness with superb hiking near Finland's eastern border – became the country's fortieth national park. Nestled along the Finnish-Russian border 500 miles north of Helsinki, Hossa – even by Finland's standards – is remote. You're more likely to meet wolverines than people when wild camping here.

Like so much of Finland, Hossa is awash with lake after glorious lake. Yet, there's a mystical allure about the country's newest national park that sets it apart from its famous southern neighbours. This is one of the least densely populated regions in Europe and, as a result, it's the wildlife that rules this kingdom: countless types of trees, shrubs and plants, thousands of fish species, hundreds of birds and raptors and most famous of all, its apex predators.

The region's eco-system lends itself perfectly for species to thrive; from freshwater lakes through to peat bogs, boreal pine forests through to thick beech tree woodland. European brown bears, wolverines and Eurasian wolves all call Hossa home.

Bear sightings are common here; the region has the most European brown bears per square kilometre on the entire continent, a fact that's beginning to ignite an eco-tourism explosion in the area. European brown bears are intensely sociable animals, especially the cubs. They'll happily frolic around for hours while their mother finds food sources.

For the extra-hardy visitor, seriously cosy one-man hides are available to hire across the region. From the relative comfort of these woodland hideaways, wildlife-lovers and photography enthusiasts alike are now able to see the bears up close, with very little disturbance to the environment. Hike into the woods during the afternoon and by early evening you'll be surrounded on all sides. Alternatively, *laavu* are free-to-use shelters scattered throughout the land – predominately built by wilderness students – complete with a sleeping area, fire pit, and log shed. They make for a comfortable home-from-home after a long day's trekking through the park.

This is by far the best teddy bears' picnic you could ever have.

178 | Debunking myths in Kverkfjöll

ICELAND As you approach the entrance to the Kverkfjöll Glacier Caves, in Iceland's stark interior, you may begin to understand why local myths of trolls and mystical beings are given a surprising amount of credence. Beneath a drooping archway of ice, a shadowy cavern is partly obscured by wisps of sulphurous steam – an eerie, almost magical scene, but one entirely of nature's doing. Lurking deep beneath is a frighteningly active volcano whose intense heat melts ice from the base of the glacier, creating rivers of warm water that burrow through the ice as easily as a hot knife through butter. The tunnels and caverns etched by the rivers are enthralling frozen palaces that stretch for over 2km into the glacier.

The caves, situated along the northern edge of the Vatnajökull Glacier at the end of a rough track that passes barren lava fields and volcanic badlands, are not to be taken lightly. Falling ice, swollen rivers and toxic gases can make the caves dangerous, and it is best to explore them with an experienced guide.

Inside the air feels muggy and slightly intoxicating; given the heat, it's surprising to touch the cave walls and find them numbingly cold. Every surface is dimpled like a choppy sea, sculpted by heat and steam, but as smooth as glass. Slowly your eyes adjust to the light, and you are struck by dazzling shades of blue, from ultramarine to the deepest blue-black. As you make your way in, following tunnels that twist and turn, filtered light gives the ice an unnatural glow. Above the noise of crampons and the echo of running water you can hear the groans of the ice as it is slowly moulded by pressure and geothermal heat – the elements, not trolls, hard at work.

179 | Summer sailing in the Stockholm archipelago

SWEDEN The truly amazing thing about the Vikings was that they ever decided to leave home. With warm sunshine, cool breezes and verdant landscapes of hillocks and heather, Scandinavia boasts some of Europe's most alluring summers. Few experiences can top a week spent exploring the nooks and crannies of the Baltic, ending each day on the stern of a ship against a jaw-dropping sunset.

Splayed out across 25,000 islands, islets and skerries – only 150 of which are inhabited – the Stockholm archipelago is made up of thickly wooded inner islands and more rugged, bare and windblown atolls further out. During the day, you'll ply the waters in ferries, sailboats or kayaks, while at night you can either take to your berth or hop ashore to spend the night in a rustic inn, cottage or campsite.

Depart from Stockholm's marina and follow the day-trippers to Vaxholm, just an hour away, where an imposing sixteenth-century fortress citadel towers over a charming wharf loaded with art galleries, shops and several excellent restaurants. Another 10km on is Grinda, less crowded and great for swimming, and just next door, Viggsö, a tiny green islet where the members of ABBA penned many of their hit songs. Sail east to Sandhamn, a paradise for the yachting fraternity and home to sandy beaches that rival those of the Med.

Wend your way south of here to Fjärdlång, a 3.5km-long, pine-filled nature reserve ideal for birdwatchers, kayakers and hikers, before heading just inland to Kymmendö, a tiny rocky outcrop with just twenty residents. Strindberg called it "paradise on Earth"; you can rent a bike and pedal to his tiny cottage. Or push on further out into the sparkling waters for Björnö: it's worth the effort – small sandy cove beaches, dense reed beds, lush hillocks and undiscovered oak forests await.

180 | Seeing the light at Jutland's edge

DENMARK The fishing town of Skagen could have been torn from the pages of a Hans Christian Andersen fairy tale: half-timbered houses line the cobblestone streets and lemon-yellow daffodils bob behind white picket fences. Wander beyond the tidy hamlet, though, and the wilder side of northern Jutland reveals itself: here, the icy Baltic Sea pounds the shore, whipped up by powerful gales. At Grenen Point, you can saunter along a pale finger of sand and plant your feet in the frothy coupling of two seas, the Skagerrak and Kattegat. And just south of Skagen lies the largest migrating sand dune in northern Europe. Thanks to the strong winds, the Råbjerg Mile moves eastward at the rate of about 15m a year, collecting loose debris in its path, like a giant mop.

But it's the region's luminous skies that have long seduced artists, starting with the Skagen painters – or Danish Impressionists – who arrived in the late 1800s. Viggo Johansen, Anna and Michael Ancher, and P.S. Krøyer all immortalized the remote seaside village, capturing its everyday coastal existence – burly fishermen unloading the daily catch, women in high-necked gowns with parasols strolling the beach – amid milky-white sand dunes glowing under an incandescent light.

You can view their paintings at the Skagens Museum, founded in 1908, which features the world's largest collection of works by these great Danes. The beautifully designed space abounds with windows and skylights to maximize the natural sunlight, so you can admire their portrayals of Skagen's ethereal glow in a room that's bathed in it, and then gaze out of the window to see the real thing.

Next to the museum sits the whitewashed, country-style *Brøndums Hotel*, a favourite hangout of the bohemian artists – who enjoyed long, loose luncheons here – and still the social heart of town. Settle at one of the outdoor tables, and after a couple of Tuborgs you may also be inspired to pull out the paintbrushes and capture the bright northern skies yawning above you.

181 | Whale-watching in Húsavík

ICELAND The fact that in Icelandic the word for beached whale is the same as that for jackpot or windfall may give you some clue as to how these seaborne beasts are seen by the locals. Yes, you may well find whale on the menu in Iceland's restaurants – but thanks to a temporary IWC moratorium on whaling back in the 1980s, whalers were forced to seek alternative sources of income and at that point the whale-watching industry was born.

Sadly, Iceland recommenced commercial whaling in 2006, but stocks remain high – and consequently so do sightings. Head out to sea and across Skjálfandi Bay from Húsavík on the island's north coast, and, thanks to experienced local guides who know every centimetre of this blustery bay, your opportunities of seeing at least one gentle giant are good.

Unlike many other countries, Iceland plays host to numerous different species of whale, which makes scanning the waterline

that much more interesting. The species you're most likely to see is the (relatively) small minke whale, which favours shallow waters near the coast and is very inquisitive, often bringing its head out of the water to watch the boat. The massive blue whale (the largest animal on Earth), vast fin whale (the second largest), square-headed sperm whale and the killer whale are also often sighted, but the biggest creature you'll probably spot is the humpback. Humpback whales are famous for their entertaining behaviour and lively acrobatics, and this is the species most likely to breach, leaping out of the water to expose its whole body, often up to 17m in length.

There are also dolphins, puffins and other seabirds in this lively bay – more than enough to keep those binoculars busy, and to put a big salty smile on your face as you return to shore for dinner. Just remember to order carefully if you've fallen in love with these graceful creatures.

182 | Breakfasting with the stars at the Grand Hotel

SWEDEN Ever since the Nobel Prizes were first awarded in 1901, the winners have stayed at Stockholm's *Grand Hôtel*. And for good reason. Set on the waterfront at Blasieholmshamnen, the hotel has one of the most spectacular city views in the world. Straight ahead is the Swedish Royal Palace, the parliament building and the small island of Gamla Stan, Stockholm's old town with its narrow lanes and cobbled alleys. From the large picture windows of its fine dining room, the *Veranda*, you can watch the bustle of the promenade and the small boats ferrying people out to the islands of the archipelago.

No one of consequence visits Stockholm without staying at the *Grand*, as the signatures in the guest book attest. There is music: Leonard Bernstein, Herbert von Karajan, Bruce Springsteen, Elton John, Michael Jackson, Tina Turner and Bono. There is literature: Hemingway, Steinbeck, Beckett and Camus. And there is global politics: Dr Martin Luther King, Mandela, Churchill, Thatcher, Barack Obama and the Dalai Lama. For many it is the Hollywood connection

that makes the location special: Charlie Chaplin, Grace Kelly, Alfred Hitchcock, Ingrid Bergman and Greta Garbo are some of the stars that have stayed here.

As if the guest book weren't enough to tempt you with delusions of celebrity, the *Grand* has another secret: it serves what is probably the best breakfast in all of Europe. Naturally you can order the usual things: eggs coddled, fried, poached, boiled and served with bacon, ham, toast, muffins, crumpets, waffles and mushrooms. As well as this, there are crunchy Swedish crispbreads, fresh croissants, rigorously wholesome mueslis and porridge. Home-made pâtés, marmalades and jams moisten the palate. And then there is herring – pickled or curried in a mouth-watering number of ways – as well as cold cuts and terrines. The choice seems endless, with more than 120 hot and cold dishes to sample. Sitting at a table by the window in the glass-walled *Veranda*, you begin your day with an infusion of fine tea, crisp white linen and that subtle Scandinavian light.

183 | Passing time at the Moesgaard Museum

DENMARK In the rolling hills south of Aarhus, a wedge of grass-covered concrete rises gently from the ground. Approaching it, you might not know what you're looking at; people walk up it, stopping at the top to gaze at the sweeping view of forest and sea. Is it a lookout point? An art piece? A memorial of some kind? In fact, this is the Moesgaard Museum (MOMU), one of Scandinavia's most innovative museums.

Heading inside, you enter a huge, light-filled space. From here a broad staircase leads you through the layers of the building like an archeological dig. And above is that grassy roof: a perfect spot for a picnic or a Viking market in warm weather, and when it snows a great tobogganing slope (the museum even provides sleds).

The contents more than live up to their surroundings. Positioned along the staircase ("the evolutionary stairs") are models of stages in the evolution of humankind, usually surrounded by visitors taking selfies.

Downstairs, you can explore the story of Denmark's first immigrants, Stone Age hunter-gathers who followed reindeer herds north as the ice sheets retreated. Then you move onto the Bronze Age, the ceiling above glittering like the stars by which they navigated. Next up is the Iron Age, where you can meet the eerie Grauballe Man, a bog body so well preserved that he still has a shock of red hair, 1500 years after his death. After passing through the Viking Age – where you can sail your own ship – you reach the Medieval Christian Age, all grisly religious relics and plague doctor uniforms, under the motto "remember you will die tomorrow".

Emerging into the sunlight, watching people playing on the sloping roof and admiring the landscape around them, feels like the final exhibit, showing how the link between nature, technology and humanity is still evolving today.

Hiking the Besseggen Ridge

184

NORWAY As trekking goes, the beginning of the Besseggen Ridge is a breeze: sitting on the bow of a little tug as it chugs along picturesque Lake Gjende in central Norway's Jotunheimen National Park, you'd be forgiven for wondering what all the fuss is about – this is, after all, Norway's best-known day hike, in the country's most illustrious national park. But then the boat drops you off at a tiny jetty and you start the hike up the hill, knowing that each step takes you closer to the crest – a threadline precipice that'll turn even the toughest mountaineer's legs to jelly.

You'll need a good head for heights, but it's not a technically difficult walk: the path is generally wide and well marked by intermittent cairns, splashed with fading red "T"s. After the initial climb away from the jetty, the route levels out before ascending again across boulder-strewn terrain until – some 2hr 30min into the trek – you arrive at the base of the ridge itself.

The actual clamber up the ridge takes about half an hour, though the Norwegian youngsters who stride past, frighteningly upright, seem to do it much more quickly. It's incredibly steep and requires a lot of heaving yourself up and over chest-high ledges; in places, the rock just drops away into thin air.

But the views are some of the finest in Norway: a wide sweep of jagged peaks and rolling glaciers, and, far, far below, Lake Gjende, glinting green on sunny days but more often – thanks to the upredictably moody weather up here – resembling a menacing pool of cold, hard steel.

From there on, the going is comparatively easy, and you'll probably scamper the remaining few kilometres back to Gjendesheim, your energy bolstered by the biggest adrenaline boost you have had in a very long time.

185 | All the fun of the fair: Tivoli's fairground attractions

DENMARK Not many cities have a roller coaster, a pirate ship and an 8om-high carousel slap bang in their centre, but Copenhagen is home to Tivoli – probably the best fairground in the world. The famous pleasure gardens have dished out fun and thrills to a bewitched public since 1843 ⌐ to the deeply patriotic Danes they're a national treasure, while most foreign visitors are lured through the gates by the charming mix of old and new: pretty landscaped gardens, fairground stalls, pantomime theatres and old-fashioned rickety rides rub shoulders with brash, high-octane affairs such as the Golden Tower, which will have you plunging vertically from a height of 6om, and the Demon – a stomach-churning three-loop roller coaster.

But the rides are just the icing on the cake – whether you're grabbing a hot dog or candy floss from the fast-food stands or splashing out in one of the forty or so restaurants, eating is also part of the Tivoli experience. Music plays a big role, too, be it jazz and blues in the bandstands, rock on the open-air stage or the more stellar offerings of Tivoli Koncertshal, with its big-name international acts – anyone from Anne-Sophie Mutter to Beck. In October, the whole place is festooned with pumpkins, ghouls and witches for a Halloween-themed extravaganza, and in the weeks around Christmas, the festive spirit is cranked up with spectacular lighting displays, a Christmas Market, a skating rink by the Japanese pagoda and all sorts of tasty Christmas nibbles and warming *glögg*, while the braziers and torches help keep the worst of the Danish winter at bay.

Even if fairs usually leave you cold, you can't fail to be won over by the innocent pleasures of Tivoli. On a fine summer's night, with the twinkling illuminations, music drifting across the flowerbeds and fireworks exploding overhead, it's nothing short of magical.

186 | Feeling the heat in a Finnish sauna

FINLAND There are two million saunas in Finland – that's four for every ten Finns – and they have played an integral part in Finnish life for centuries. Finns believe the sauna to be an exorcism of all ills, and there's certainly nothing quite like it for inducing a feeling of serenity.

Always a single-sex affair in public, the sauna is a wonderfully levelling experience since everybody is naked (it's insisted upon for hygiene reasons). After first showering, take a paper towel or a small wooden tray and place this on one of the benches inside, arranged in the form of a gallery, before you sit down. This stops the benches from burning your skin. Traditionally a sauna is heated by a wood-burning stove which fills the room with a rich smell of wood smoke. However, more often than not, modern saunas are electrically heated, typically to around 80–90°C, a claustrophobic, lung-filling heat. Every so often, when the air gets too dry, water is thrown onto the hot stones that sit on top of the stove, which then hiss furiously and cause a blast of steam.

By this point you'll be sweating profusely, streams pouring off you and pooling on the ground, prompting the next stage in your sauna experience – lashing yourself with birch twigs. The best saunas provide bathers with small birch branches, with leaves still on, with which you gently strike yourself to increase blood circulation. The fresh smell of the birch in the hot air, coupled with the tingling feeling on the skin, is wondrously sensual. Traditionally, Finns end their sauna by mercilessly plunging straight into the nearest lake or, in winter, by rolling in the icy snow outside – the intense searing cold that follows the sweltering heat creating a compelling, addictive rush at the boundary of pleasure and pain.

187 | Snorkelling "the fissure"

ICELAND Few places on Earth can match Silfra for snorkelling. The setting is unique, a fissure crack running between the American and Eurasian continents, its precise location changing with the shifting of the plates each year. But it's the water – or, more accurately, the stunning clarity of the water – that makes this site remarkable.

Silfra has arguably the finest visibility anywhere in the world. Crystal is cloudy in comparison. The temperature helps, hovering at around 3°C, as does the water's glacial purity – it takes two thousand years to get here, drip-feeding its way through fields of lava. In fact, the combination creates a clarity so intense that people have been known to experience vertigo on entering the water, suspended like astronauts over a gully that seemingly drops away into the very centre of the Earth.

188 | Trekking to Door Mountain

ICELAND At the wild and sparsely inhabited eastern edge of Iceland, the granite crag of Dyrfjoll towers above the natural amphitheatre known as Stórurð (the Elves' Bowl). One edge is sharp and steep, the other a flattened tabletop, and in between, the giant square gap that earns the whole its name: Door Mountain.

Hewn by a glacier millions of years ago, the gap is 200m lower than the surrounding cliffs. Heather crowned with blueberries lines the route to Door Mountain, and there are sweeping views across the Héradsflói valley, a vast moorland plain where strands of meltwater from Europe's largest glacier shine like silver threads on a brown blanket. Few roads cross this landscape, and it remains the last great wilderness in Europe.

Need to know

161 Your chances of being invited to a *surström-mingsskiva* increase the further north you travel within Sweden.

162 Puffins are best viewed on an organized boat tour from Tórshavn; see Ⓦ visittorshavn.fo.

163 March is the best month to board, when the ice is at its thickest. Don't forget your sunglasses – the glare of the sun off snow-covered ice can be harsh – and some lip salve. See Ⓦ visitfinland.com/article/the-mighty-sampo.

164 The tour begins at Gunnerud, 95km north of Karlstad, from where you'll be taken to the raft-building site. For details visit Ⓦ vildmark.se.

165 The beach is on the #30 bus route (Ⓦ ruter.no/en) from central Oslo. Get off at the end of the line (Huk) and head left for the main beach, or straight past the snack stand for the naturist area. There is also an Oslo Bysykkel (city bike; Ⓦ oslobysykkel.no/en) stand near the bus stop.

166 Geirangerfjord is in southwestern Norway, 9hr by bus from Bergen. Naerøyfjord and Lustrafjord are 3hr and 5hr respectively from Bergen. See Ⓦ visitnorway.com.

167 Try the *smörgåsbord* at *Ulriksdals Wärdshus*, Slottspark (Ⓦ ulriksdalswardshus.se), 10min north of Stockholm in Solna.

168 For more information, see Ⓦ en.harpa.is.

169 The website Ⓦ kronborg.dk is a good port of call for information on Kronborg Slot. For the Shakespeare festival, Hamletscenen, see Ⓦ hamletscenen.dk.

170 Most cross-country ski areas offer lessons and have skis and boots available for rent. For more on Voss, see Ⓦ visitvoss.no.

171 To get to the Flåmsbana take the train from Bergen to Myrdal (via Voss). You can buy your ticket all the way through to Flåm at the Bergen train station, which means you'll be able to jump right on the train when you arrive in Myrdal. See Ⓦ visitflam.com.

172 Mývatn is about 6hr by road from Reykjavík, and 2hr from the nearest town, Akureyri. Buses run in the summer months; you'll have to rent a car during the rest of the year.

173 See Ⓦ hurtigruten.com for fares and schedules.

174 *Alfheimar*, meaning 'elf's home', is a guesthouse and restaurant run by local storyteller and hiking guide Arngrímur Ásgeirsson; Ⓦ alfheimar.com

175 Oslo's main tourist office (Ⓦ visitoslo.com) is in the centre of town, behind the Rådhus at Fridtjof Nansens plass 5.

176 All islands can be accessed by ferry with a single day pass. See Ⓦ goteborg.com/en/archipelago for more information.

177 For more information, see Ⓦ nationalparks.fi/hossa.

178 The tourist office in Reykjavík (Ⓦ inspiredbyiceland.com) has information on guides and tour companies. See also Ⓦ vatnajokulsthjodgardur.is.

179 A Båtluffarkortet pass gets you five days of unlimited ferry travel; alternatively, you can rent a sailboat from any number of outfits in Stockholm. See Ⓦ visit-

skargarden.se or, for information on the archipelago's nature reserves, Ⓦ skargardsstiftelsen.se.

180 Skagens Museum (Ⓦ skagenskunstmuseer.dk); *Brøndums Hotel* (Ⓦ broendums-hotel.dk).

181 The two main whale-watching operators are Gentle Giants (Ⓦ gentlegiants.is) and North Sailing Húsavík (Ⓦ northsailing.is). Ⓦ visithusavik.com is a useful website.

182 Menus and reservations for breakfast at the *Grand Hotel* via Ⓦ grandhotel.se.

183 The Moesgaard Museum is 30min from central Aarhus on bus #18; check Ⓦ moesgaardmuseum.dk/en for hours and prices. To explore more of south Aarhus stay at the *Helnan Marselis Hotel* (Ⓦ helnan.dk/en/marselis/hotel), right on the beach by Marselisborg Forests, and a 25min cycle from the museum.

184 Jotunheimen National Park (Ⓦ visitjotunheimen.com) is accessed via Gjendesheim, 90km southwest of Otta. The Lake Gjende boats run seasonally (Ⓦ gjende.no).

185 See Ⓦ tivoli.dk.

186 Most public swimming pools in Finland have a sauna: check out Kotiharjun (Ⓦ kotiharjunsauna.fi) on Harjutorinkatu in Helsinki.

187 Diving Iceland (Ⓦ dive.is) organizes snorkelling trips into Silfra.

188 For more information on the area, see Ⓦ east.is.

SOUTHEAST EUROPE
189–260

Southeast Europe is many things. It's a window onto the great Mediterranean past, where you can gaze wide-eyed at the ancient theatres of Greece, the fresco-splashed churches of Slovenia or the Roman ruins of Pompeii. It's a region of spectacular one-off cities, where Venice and Dubrovnik share the map with Istanbul and Athens. It's an area where the great outdoors unfurls in fine style, rolling across the hills of Tuscany, the bays of Montenegro, the islands of the Aegean and the peaks of Slovenia. Experiences here are as diverse as the region itself: go canyoning in Sardinia, bathe in Pamukkale's thermal waters, retrace Odysseus's footsteps on the Croatian island of Mljet or scale Snow White's Castle in North Cyprus.

189 Visiting the monks of Mount Athos

GREECE The ferry to Mount Athos is a serene, sedate affair. Bearded, black-clad monks and priests finger rosary beads and contemplate the steep rise of pine-covered foothills to the jagged mountain pinnacle. Here and there, pilgrims chatter on mobile phones. Athos is a peninsula, but there's a feeling of cutting away from the modern world to an island set back in time.

By pure luck, I arrive at an auspicious time – the Feast of the Transfiguration. A kindly German monk leads me, with a new friend I met on the boat, to a simple twin room. After prayers we sit at tables laden with silver-edged plates and bountiful supplies of fish, pasta, fruit, water and wine. Chanting reverberates around the room, incense swirls into my nostrils and we listen to readings from the gospels.

A stay with the monks of Athos is not to be taken lightly, but every man is welcome – unfortunately, women are not. "We get them all here," says one monk: murderers and drug addicts, millionaires and princes, saints and sinners.

On one glorious evening I stumble upon a performance. As golden light fills the western room of the Dionysius monastery, the melodious sound of a flute floats over chanting bass and tenor voices. Along a wall five Patriarchs sit on thrones – one weeps. The next day, I sit in a garden cemetery, beneath swaying cypress trees. Father Modestos, an English monk, shows me the skulls of his predecessors, dug up to make space for the next monk who "falls asleep with the Lord".

The highlight of any visit to Athos is to climb the mountain itself. I'm unprepared and have little food, but take to the foothills anyway, and my journey is supported by random acts of kindness. Towards the top of the mountain spectacular views begin to unfold. Theo, a Greek man who has shared his bread, cheese and tomatoes with me, starts to chant as we hit the summit. As we sit outside a little bunkhouse, the sun begins to set. Squealing swallows dive-bomb into the merging blue of sea and sky.

Marc Perry
is an international journalist, writer and photographer. After enlightening experiences in Afghanistan he took to humanitarian and travel writing from the safety of the Balkans and Eastern Mediterranean. He is intrigued by stories from the frontiers of change.

Something fishy in Marsaxlokk

MALTA Bobbing in the sea, staring at passers-by, the eyes of a *luzzu* appear to follow you as you walk along the promenade in Marsaxlokk – Malta's premier fishing port. Traditionally painted in red, blue and yellow, with the odd patch of green, boats line the waterfront of this otherwise small village on Malta's southeast coast.

A Maltese national symbol, the *luzzu* featured on the country's lira coins before the adoption of the euro. Originally equipped with sails, today the boats are motorized and some double as transport for tourists. Said to be the eye of Osiris, the god who protected the Phoenicians from evil, the *luzzu*'s eye is thought to save the boat's owners from the dangers of the sea.

The natural harbour at Marsaxlokk is home to over 250 registered fishing vessels, from the traditional *luzzu* to larger *skunas* and smaller *fregatinas* (rowing boats), in which you'll see men sitting, close to shore, handreels dangling over the side, hoping to take a catch in the pristine water. On a bright day, the sun dances off the water, drawing out the colours of the boats and reflecting off the fishing nets splayed out to dry.

To escape the glare of the *luzzus*' eyes, head towards the market for a spot of shopping. This was originally just a place where local fishermen could sell their daily catch, and still serves that function on Sundays especially. Other days of the week are a better bet for stocking up on souvenirs, including handmade bags constructed from recycled fishing nets and dyed a rainbow of colours.

Once you're done strolling along the promenade, duck into one of the many restaurants along the waterfront – this is, unsurprisingly, the perfect town in which to eat fish.

191

Drive like a secret agent around Lake Garda

ITALY Take to the serpentine road skirting Italy's Lake Garda and follow the tyre marks of 007. Parts of the breathtaking car chase opening the twenty-second James Bond outing – *Quantum of Solace* – were filmed on the lake's eastern shore, where the narrow road burrows in and out of the mountainside, and then round to Limone sul Garda on the western side. The 2008 film may have had its naysayers but there's no denying the edge-of-your-car-seat excitement of that opener. While the typical way to admire Lake Garda is from the water, a drive along this dramatic rock-hewn road allows you to nip between the best of the lake's unspoilt villages and quieter spots. In the summer months the lakeside route snarls up with traffic and many of the towns are swamped with tourists and day-trippers. So, consider a springtime visit (like the Bond film crew) and, needless to say, keep an eye on the speedometer.

192 | Bears and boars: trekking in the Abruzzo National Park

ITALY The Apennines stretch for some 1300km down the very spine of Italy. They are the country at its roughest and least showy. But these mountains are far from dull. In their loftiest and most rugged stretch, in the central region of Abruzzo, two hours from Rome, you'll find peaks rising up from gentle pastures, and swathes of beech woodland that roll up from deep valleys before petering out just short of the steepest ridges.

Romans come to the Parco Nazionale d'Abruzzo to walk, climb and enjoy rustic foods like wild boar prosciutto and local sheep's cheese, washed down by the hearty Montepulciano d'Abruzzo wine. Foreign visitors are rare, and you can walk for hours without seeing another person. This tranquillity isn't lost on the park's wildlife. Chamois, roe deer, martens and even wolves have found a haven here, and the park is one of the last refuges in Western Europe of the Marsican brown bear. They haven't survived by being easy to spot. After the furtive lynx – an animal which stalks its prey by night before launching an attack that can only be described as explosive – bears are among the park's most elusive creatures. You may be lucky enough to glimpse one briefly, tantalizingly exposed while crossing an open mountain ridge. You're more likely, however, to find just paw prints or rocks overturned in the hunt for moths.

The best base is Pescasseroli, a ridge-top village with a cluster of homely hotels and a park visitor centre. From here, you can hike straight into the forest and up along the long ridge that crests and falls from Monte Petroso (2247m) to the aptly named Monte Tranquillo (1830m) and on to Monte Cornacchia (2003m). Or you can take a bicycle on hundreds of kilometres of rough roads that thread through the area – by which time you'll have earned your plate of wild boar.

193 | Uncovering the Romani secrets of Šutka

NORTH MACEDONIA As you take your first steps into the Macedonian district of Šutka, you may find yourself rubbing your eyes in disbelief. In many ways, this is more like India than Europe: tradespeople cry their wares through a cacophony of parping motorbikes, livestock roam streets crisscrossed with drying laundry, and the area's houses – or at least those that have not yet collapsed – have been given coat after coat of gaudy paint.

This is one of the continent's most impoverished and dilapidated corners, but its curious charms are enticing an increasing number of foreign adventurers.

Lying just west of the North Macedonian capital of Skopje, the district of Šuto Orizari, more commonly referred to as Šutka, is home to almost twenty thousand people, the majority of whom are of Roma extraction. This makes it the world's largest Romani community. The bustling daily market disguises rampant unemployment – most youngsters dream of living abroad, and overseas remittances form a substantial chunk of the local economy. Late spring and early summer are the most popular periods for those born in Šutka to return home, and is also the best time for travellers to catch a glimpse of two of the area's prize attractions: weddings and music.

For such a small area, it's amazing how many weddings take place in Šutka – in warmer months there seems to be at least one celebration every afternoon. The most lavish celebrations take place at the district hotel, but you may find one going on in an abandoned shipping container. Big or small, all weddings feature hour after hour of exuberant Romani dancing, accompanied by braying brass and fleet-fingered guitar chords.

Šutka is one of North Macedonia's foremost centres of song and dance, and musicians from the area tend to mop up most of the national awards. Events run to no fixed schedule, but head along on a sunny afternoon and you may be in luck – just follow your ears, and enjoy the inevitably warm and welcoming Roma hospitality.

194 | Following in the footsteps of Odysseus

CROATIA According to legend, Odysseus – the hero of Homer's *Odyssey* – spent seven long years on the Croatian island of Mljet. The story goes that he was shipwrecked in a fierce storm off the island's rocky southern coast when returning from the Trojan War and swam desperately towards land, finding shelter in a cave that was later named after him. Several islands in the area also claim to have been Odysseus's residence at some point; wander through Mljet's shady pine forests and look out at the brilliant blue Adriatic and you'll find yourself wanting to stay for seven years too.

At 37km long, and a little over 3km wide, Mljet is by no means small, by Adriatic standards at least. It is, however, sparsely populated – the most recent census says there are just over 1110 inhabitants. A single road cuts and winds its way through the island's pine-carpeted interior, connecting the pretty fishing villages, such as Prožurska Luka, that line its coast. Mljet's capital is Babino Polje, a small village of around two hundred people that sits in the shadow of Mljet's highest peak, Veliki grad, near Odysseus Cave. The western third of the island is a protected national park and includes two stunning salt lakes, one of which is home to a tiny island and sixteenth-century Benedictine monastery of the same name: St Mary. The park also includes a handful of sleepy villages, including Pomena and Polače.

During the day the smell of fresh pine hangs in the air; at night, the stars still shine as bright as they did for Odysseus, almost one thousand years ago. You won't tire of the sight of the glittering Adriatic in a hurry either, which is visible from almost everywhere on the island. Mljet's crystalline waters are rich with octopi, starfish and other marine life too, making them perfect for snorkelling. Clearly marked hiking and cycling trails crisscross the island, allowing you to explore the unexplored on your own terms. Visiting Mljet is probably the closest you'll get to having your own island; one worthy of any odyssey.

195 | Going with the flow of San Gennaro

ITALY The capital of the South, Naples is quite unlike anywhere else in Italy. It's a city of extremes, fiercely Catholic, its streets punctuated by bright neon Madonnas cut into niches and its miraculous cults regulating the lives of locals almost as much as they did in Rome's pagan days. None more so than the cult of San Gennaro, Naples' patron saint, whose dried blood, kept in a vial in the cathedral, appears to spontaneously liquefy three times a year, thereby ensuring the city's safety for the months to come. It is supposed to take place on the first Saturday in May, on September 19 – San Gennaro's feast day – and also on December 16, and the liquefaction (or otherwise) of San Gennaro's blood is the biggest event in the city's calendar by far, attended by the great and the good of the city, not to mention a huge press corps.

The blood liquefies during a Mass, which you can attend if you get to the Duomo early enough (ie in the middle of the night). By the time the doors open at 9am, a huge crowd will have gathered. You're ushered into the church by armed *carabinieri*, who then stand guard at the high altar while the service goes on, the priest placing the vial containing the saint's blood on a stand and occasionally taking it down to see if anything has happened, while the faithful, led by a group of devout women called the "parenti di San Gennaro", chant prayers for deliverance. The longer it takes, the worse the portents for the city are.

If it doesn't liquefy at all... well, you will know all about it. It didn't happen in 1944, the last time Vesuvius erupted, and in 1980, when a huge earthquake struck the city, so people are understandably jumpy. Luckily, the blood has been behaving itself for the past few decades, a period which has coincided to some extent with the city's resurgence.

As the mayor of Naples commented: "It's a sign that San Gennaro is still protecting our city, a strong sign of hope and an encouragement for everyone to work for the common good." Even if you don't believe a word of it, being here amid the hype, the hope and the ceremony is an experience like no other.

196 | Living the good life in Butterfly Valley

TURKEY With over 7000km of coastline, you'd expect Turkey's tourist industry to make the most of its beaches. Along the package-holiday hub that is the Turquoise Coast, though, it's all gone a bit "fun-in-the-sun" tacky, with resorts such as Bodrum and Marmaris offering holidaymakers every home comfort (Irish breakfasts, happy hours), just with the heating cranked up to 11.

Yet one little strip of seaside stands apart. That's the beach-fronted valley locals call Güdürümsü, reachable via a short boat ride or a tricky overland adventure. Now more commonly known as Kelebekler Vadisi – "Butterfly Valley" – it was originally rechristened by Ölüdeniz hippies who, dismayed as mass tourism burgeoned around them, made the short escape here.

Pick your way down the gangway of the water taxi from Ölüdeniz into the shallows of the bay and look about you. Just back from the stony beach, orange dome tents – available to rent – are scattered among the thin tree coverage; beyond lie scrubland and vegetable patches and wooden huts (if you don't fancy camping); to left and right, valley walls leer down, craggy and ominous.

While it's only a brief trip, coming to the valley is as much of a mental displacement as a spatial one. Signage is painted flower-power style; meals are taken communally, with breakfast and dinner included in the price of a stay; and you're expected to take your plates to the cleaning station. At night: drinking, bonfires, guitars here, trance music there. It's like a hostel emptied out onto the beach.

Butterfly Valley is not entirely cut off. Tour boats and booze cruises arrive daily, blaring hits and discharging their passengers onto the beach, so that they can make the hike to the waterfall at the end of the valley, where the butterflies are supposed to be. Often there are none, and they complain. But then they're gone, and the place is yours again.

197 | Get the measure of the Medici in the Uffizi

ITALY It's a simple equation: Florence was the centre of the Italian Renaissance; the Medici were the greatest art patrons of Renaissance Florence; their collection was bequeathed to the city by the last Medici, Anna Maria Lodovica. Therefore the Uffizi Gallery – which occupies offices (*uffizi*) built for the Medici in 1560 – can boast the greatest display of Renaissance painting in the world. Which is why the Uffizi attracts more visitors than any other building in Italy – more than one and a half million of them every year.

The key to enjoying the Uffizi is to book your ticket in advance and to ration yourself; if you try to see everything you'll barely be able to skate over the surface. For your first visit, limit yourself to the first eighteen rooms or so – this will take you as far as the Bronzino portraits in the octagonal Tribuna. Arranged more or less chronologically, the Uffizi encapsulates the genesis of the Renaissance in a room of three altarpieces of the Maestà (Madonna Enthroned) by Duccio, Cimabue and Giotto. After a diversion through the exquisite late Gothic art of Simone Martini and Gentile da Fabriano, the narrative of the Renaissance resumes with Paolo Uccello's *The Battle of San Romano* and continues with Piero della Francesca, Filippo Lippi (and his son Filippino), and of course Botticelli: it doesn't matter how many photos you've seen, the *Primavera* and the *Birth of Venus* will stop you in your tracks. And there's still Leonardo da Vinci to come before you reach the halfway point.

Should you decide to make a dash to the end, you'll see a remarkable collection of Venetian painting (Giorgione, Giovanni Bellini, Paolo Veronese, Tintoretto and no fewer than nine Titians), a clutch of fabulous Mantegnas and Raphaels, and the extraordinary *Doni Tondo*, the only easel painting Michelangelo ever came close to completing. Ahead of you are fabulous pieces by Dürer, Holbein and Cranach, del Sarto and Parmigianino, Caravaggio and Rembrandt, Goya and Chardin. Wherever you stop in the Uffizi, there's a masterpiece staring you in the face.

198 | Getting lost in Diocletian's Palace

CROATIA Try imagining Pompeii as a functioning twenty-first-century city, and you'll get a good idea of what the Croatian port of Split looks like. At its heart lies a confusing warren of narrow streets, crooked alleys and Corinthian-style colonnades that looks like a computer-generated reconstruction of an archeological dig. High-street shops, banks, restaurants and bars seem stuffed into this structure like incongruous afterthoughts.

Split began life as the purpose-built palace of Roman Emperor Diocletian, who retired here after his abdication in 305 AD. When marauding Avars sacked the nearby city of Salona in 615, fleeing inhabitants sought refuge within the palace walls, improvising a home in what must have been the most grandiose squat of all time. Diocletian's mausoleum was turned into a cathedral, the Temple of Jupiter became a baptistery, and medieval tenement blocks were built into the palace walls.

Nowadays the palace's crumbling courtyards provide the perfect setting for some of the best bars in the Mediterranean. The only problem is that Split's maze-like street plan makes it head-scratchingly difficult to navigate your way back to the welcoming drinking hole you discovered the previous night. Split folk themselves possess a highly developed nocturnal radar, flitting from one place to the next without ever staying anywhere long enough to make it look as if they haven't got a better party to go to.

The best way not to get disoriented is to locate Dosud, a split-level zigzag of an alley in the southwestern corner of the palace. Here you'll find ultra-trendy *Puls*, which, with its post-industrial interior and cushion-splashed stone-stepped terrace, is an essential stop on any bar crawl; and its polar opposite, *Tri Volta*, a resolutely old-fashioned local that has long catered to neighbourhood bohemians. In between the two is *Ghetto*, a temple to graffiti art with a beautiful flower-filled courtyard that occasionally hosts alfresco gigs. History doesn't record whether Diocletian was much of a drinker, but this proudly pagan emperor would surely have approved of Split's enduring appetite for Bacchic indulgence.

199 | Shopping with style in Milan

ITALY Milan is synonymous with shopping: boutiques from all the world's top clothes and accessory designers jostle for position within a hop, skip and a high-heeled teeter from each other. The atmosphere is snooty, the labels elitist and the experience priceless.

The city has been associated with top-end fashion since the 1970s, when local designers broke with the staid atmosphere of Italy's traditional fashion home, the Palazzo Pitti in Florence. It was during the 1980s, however, that the worldwide thirst for designer labels consolidated the international reputation of home-grown talent such as Armani, Gucci, Prada, Versace and Dolce & Gabbana.

You don't need to be rich to feel part of it. These days the stores themselves make almost as important a statement as the clothes.

In-house cafés are springing up, as are exhibition spaces, and even barbers and spas.

For a handful of euros you can sip a cocktail at *Bar Martini*, in the Dolce & Gabbana flagship store; enjoy an espresso and a monogrammed chocolate at the *Gucci Café* inside Milan's famous nineteenth-century Galleria Vittorio Emanuele II; or drink prosecco at the tables outside the *Armani Caffé*, part of the four-storey temple to all things Giorgio.

And, as you're here for the experience, why not head for the ultimate in bling at *Just Cavalli Food*, where the leopardskin clad clientele floats down in a cloud-lift to the boutique's café, lined with a saltwater aquarium teeming with brightly coloured tropical fish.

200 | Stumbling through the night shadows of Old Town Rhodes

GREECE With its legendary Colossus toppled by an earthquake over two thousand years ago, Rhodes Old Town lacks immaculately preserved ancient monuments. Sometimes, however, a ramshackle maze of ruins can provide a truer flavour of the distant past. Countless peoples have left their mark on this island, from the Greeks who founded the Old Town to the Crusader knights who enclosed it within mighty walls, via the Ottoman Turks who peppered it with mosques and hammams, to the daily influx of modern-day cruise passengers. After dark, though, when the massive ships have gone and the souvenir shops are shuttered up, the few recognizable landmarks fade into the background, and the Old Town reverts to a timeless tangle of spindly dead-end alleyways and mysterious shadows.

Wander beyond its single, arrow-straight commercial street, and the centuries seem to slip away. With little light to guide you, you repeatedly stumble over unidentifiable lumps of discarded masonry. At first, the dark patches of exposed earth that constantly interrupt the backstreet lanes seem like construction sites, or simply waste ground; then you spot a solitary, overgrown wall poking up amid the weeds, or a massive stone arch, long detached from whatever structure it once supported, tottering atop a hillock of rubble. The paths dip, duck and dive, here passing above some half-buried relic, there burrowing between the columns of an abandoned temple to some forgotten god. Stealthy, skinny cats vanish into holes that might just be the tomb of a Greek warrior or medieval knight.

Your senses lulled, perhaps, by a meal of freshly grilled fish and a glass or two of retsina, you realize Rhodes has not fallen into decay – it has always been like this. After all, stray limbs from the Colossus lay strewn beside the harbour for a thousand years before they were finally sold for scrap. And night after night, strangers have lost their way in these labyrinthine lanes, wondering who lives behind each pastel-blue doorway, whose home crumbled to form that pile of stones, what once occupied this neglected site, and which looming silhouette will turn out to hold their lodgings.

201 | Paradise regained: Italy's oldest national park

ITALY Treading where once only royals and aristocrats could set foot is an everyday occurrence in Italy: formerly forbidding palaces, castles and gardens are now open to all. One of the most exhilarating such enclaves is a celebration of the sheer wonder of nature, the Parco del Gran Paradiso – a pristine alpine wilderness that lies within yodelling distance of the Swiss Alps and Mont Blanc.

King Vittorio Emanuele II donated what had been the private hunting grounds of the House of Savoy to the Italian state in 1922. The rapacious royals had managed to see off the entire population of bears and wolves, but the scimitar-horned ibex – now the majestic symbol of the park – and the park's other native mountain goat species, the chamois, survived, and now thrive in the protected environment. Even the golden eagle has been reintroduced, and currently numbers about 27 pairs, while you may also encounter cuddly-looking marmots, which, along with perky martens, are the preferred quarry of the major birds of prey.

In winter, the park is a paradise for intrepid skiers, particularly those of the cross-country variety, who embark from the enticing village of Cogne. But most visitors come in the warmer months, when the rocky heights are spectacularly pure and hundreds of species of vibrant wildflowers dazzle the eye – and when you're also more likely to spot wildlife.

The verdant valley slopes and vertiginous ridges are traversable by kilometres of walking and hiking trails of all degrees of difficulty, and these in turn link to numerous refuges where you can spend the night. There's mountaineering, too, throughout all of the ten valleys. You could try an assault on the 4000m-high summit of Gran Paradiso itself – not a particularly difficult ascent if you have the right equipment, and guides – or opt instead for the more gentle trek up to the sanctuary of San Besso, a two-hour hike to over 2000m, where the church and refuge nestle under a primeval overhanging massif.

202 | Stalagmites, stalactites and the Human Fish

SLOVENIA Of Slovenia's many show caves, none has quite the pulling power of Postojna, located in the heart of the country's beguiling Karst region. And, at more than 20km long, it is Europe's most expansive cave system. Writing about Postojna in the seventeenth century, the great Slovene polymath Janez Vajkard Valvasor remarked: "in some places you see terrifying heights, elsewhere everything is in columns so strangely shaped as to seem like some creepy-crawly, snake or other animal in front of one", an apt description for this immense grotto – a jungle of impossibly shaped stalactites and stalagmites, gothic columns and translucent stone draperies, all the result of millions of years of erosion of the permeable limestone surface by rainwater.

Although Postojna has been Slovenia's most emblematic tourist draw since Emperor Franz Josef I set foot here in 1819, the smudged signatures etched into the craggy walls suggest an earlier human presence in the caves, possibly as far back as the thirteenth century.

Visiting the cave first entails a 2km-long ride through narrow tunnels on the open-topped cave train – a somewhat more sophisticated version of the hand-pushed wagons used in the nineteenth century – before you emerge into vast chambers of formations and colours. Among them are the Beautiful Cave, which takes its name from the many lustrous features on display; the Spaghetti Hall, so-called because of its thousands of dripping, needle-like formations; and the Winter Chamber, which is home to a beast of a stalagmite called "Brilliant", on account of its dazzling snow-white colour.

Despite all this, Postojna's most prized asset, and most famous resident, is *Proteus anguinus*, aka the Human Fish. This enigmatic 25cm-long, pigmentless amphibian has a peculiar snake-like appearance, with two tiny pairs of legs – hence the name – and a flat, pointed fin to propel itself through water. Almost totally blind, and with a lifespan approaching one hundred years, it can also go years without food, though it's been known to dabble in a spot of cannibalism. Indeed, the abiding memory for many visitors to Postojna is of this most bizarre and reclusive of creatures slinking about its dimly lit tank.

203 | Seeing a Shakespeare play at the Kourion amphitheatre

CYPRUS "Doubt that the sun doth move" as it lingers over the Greco-Roman amphitheatre at Kourion while the audience gradually inhabits the semi-circular stone seating in anticipation. Then, just as the sun starts to lose its warmth for the day and begins to hug the horizon above the Mediterranean Sea, the cast appears in authentic dress to play out the starting scene of that year's chosen Shakespeare play.

The Episkopi Bay backdrop continues to shift as the sun slowly descends further, casting dramatic light on the historical structure and enhancing the performance which continues long after dark when floodlights illuminate the stage.

In 1962 The Performing Arts for Cyprus Charities first put on a show of *A Midsummer Night's Dream* at the end of June in this ancient archeological site and have continued the tradition ever since, with local producers and emerging actors giving up their time freely so all profits from the performance can be donated to local charities. Classics such as *Macbeth* and *Twelfth Night* are popular repeats, interspersed with occasional one-offs along the likes of *All's Well That Ends Well*.

Kourion was a significant kingdom in antiquity, and today holds the most impressive collection of ruins on the island. Baths, temples and churches still stand; grand, well-restored mosaics partially lacing the floors of some of the buildings, many depicting scenes of the house's given name – the most intact can be seen in the House of Eustolios. However, the *pièce de résistance* is the amphitheatre, originally built in the second century BC and extended when the rest of Cyprus was built in the second century AD, not only for its architecture but also for its magnificent views.

A night out on Independence Street

TURKEY You've had a satisfying day or two's heavy sightseeing in Istanbul's historic Sultanahmet district. You're culturally replete – but have a nagging feeling that you've missed something. The locals. Just what the hell do they do in this metropolis of thirteen million souls?

To find out, head across the Golden Horn to Independence Street (Istiklal Caddesi), the nation's liveliest thoroughfare. Lined with nineteenth-century apartment blocks and churches, and holding a cute red turn-of-the-twentieth-century tramway, this was the fashionable centre of Istanbul's European quarter long before independence, and it is now where young Istanbulites (whose home boasts the youngest urban population in Europe) come to shop, eat, drink, take in a film, club, gig and gawk, 24/7.

By day, bare-shouldered girls mingle with Armani-clad businessmen riding the financial boom, and music stores and fashion boutiques blare out club sounds onto the shopper-thronged street. At night the alleyways off the main drag come to life. Cheerful tavernas serve noisy diners wonderful meze, fish and lethal raki. Later the streets are even busier than in daylight, as blues, jazz and rock venues, pubs and clubs burst into action.

You won't see many head-scarved women here, and the call to prayer will be drowned by thumping Western sounds. But traditional Turkish hospitality survives even on Independence Street, and you may find yourself being offered a free beer or two. This is Istanbul's happening European heart; no wonder it has been heralded as "Europe's Hippest City".

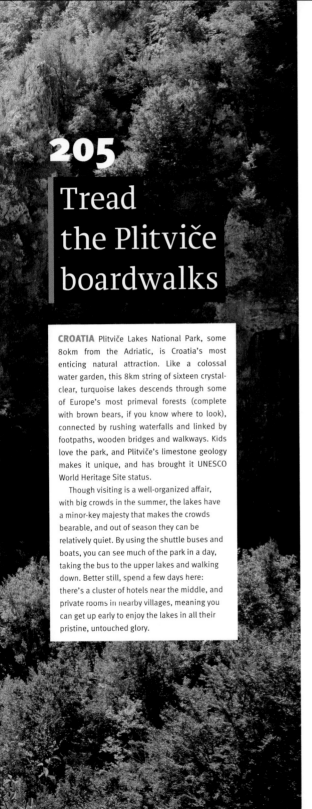

205

Tread the Plitviče boardwalks

CROATIA Plitviče Lakes National Park, some 80km from the Adriatic, is Croatia's most enticing natural attraction. Like a colossal water garden, this 8km string of sixteen crystal-clear, turquoise lakes descends through some of Europe's most primeval forests (complete with brown bears, if you know where to look), connected by rushing waterfalls and linked by footpaths, wooden bridges and walkways. Kids love the park, and Plitviče's limestone geology makes it unique, and has brought it UNESCO World Heritage Site status.

Though visiting is a well-organized affair, with big crowds in the summer, the lakes have a minor-key majesty that makes the crowds bearable, and out of season they can be relatively quiet. By using the shuttle buses and boats, you can see much of the park in a day, taking the bus to the upper lakes and walking down. Better still, spend a few days here: there's a cluster of hotels near the middle, and private rooms in nearby villages, meaning you can get up early to enjoy the lakes in all their pristine, untouched glory.

206 | The divine dancers of Calabria

ITALY Ecstasies of the cult of Dionysus, the god of divine madness, flourish still in the fishing hamlet of Gioiosa Ionica, which hugs the Ionian Sea on the instep of Italy's boot. A legacy of the ancient Greeks, the wholly incongruous excuse for this pre-Christian bacchanal is the festival of the fourteenth-century Saint Roch, who with his dog ministered to plague victims.

Every August, in the crushing summer light and heat, skimpily clad devotees throng the tiny hill town's cobbled lanes, packing around the church at the top. When his life-size effigy breaches the portal, snare drums pound a tattoo and participants roar "Roccu, Roccu, Roccu, viva Santu Roccu! Non mi toccare che non ti toccu!" ("Roc, Roc, Roc, long live Saint Roc! Don't touch me and I won't touch you!"). Suddenly everyone leaps into a frenzied *tarantella*, an ancient fertility dance, officially banned by the Church, which imitates the mating ritual of the partridge, once considered the most lascivious of creatures.

207 | This is the light: Easter celebrations in Loutró

GREECE A faint glimmer of flame behind the altar of the darkened church and the black-clad *papás* appears, holding aloft a lighted taper and chanting "Avto to Fos" – "This is the Light of the World". Thus Easter Sunday begins at the stroke of midnight in a tiny chapel in the small seaside village of Loutró, southern Crete. Minutes earlier, the congregation and entire village had been plunged into darkness.

Now, as the priest ignites the first candle and the flame is passed from neighbour to neighbour, light spreads through the church again. As the congregation pours out into the street the candlelight is distributed to every home along with the cry of "Christos Anesti" ("Christ is Risen"). It's an extraordinary experience – a symbolic reawakening of brightness and hope with clear echoes of more ancient rites of spring – and within minutes wilder celebrations begin. Firecrackers are thrown and traditional dishes devoured to break the week-long fast that the more devout have observed.

The rituals of the Greek Orthodox Church permeate every aspect of Greek society, but never so clearly as at Easter. As a visitor to the area you are inevitably drawn in, especially in a place as small as Loutró – accessible only by boat or on foot – where the locals go out of their way to include you.

After a few hours' sleep you wake to the smell of lambs and goats roasting on spits. As they cook, the wine and beer flow freely until the whole village, locals and visitors alike, joins the great feast to mark the end of Lent.

SLOVENIA A legacy of regular Turkish raids in the fifteenth and sixteenth centuries, fortified churches in Slovenia are not uncommon. The Church of the Holy Trinity in the attractive hilltop village of Hrastovlje is one such example, but while its castle-like walls are an imposing sight, its real riches lie within: every interior wall is covered with late-medieval frescoes. Painted in the fifteenth century, but concealed beneath whitewash and not rediscovered until the 1950s, the upper panels and roof tell religious stories through pictures, including biblical greatest hits such as the Passion of Christ and the Adoration of the Magi.

The church's masterpiece, however, is the work of the Istrian master painter Janez Kastav: a panorama running along the southern wall depicting the Danse Macabre, in which people of all social strata, from kings and popes to merchants and peasants, and even a young child, dance with skeletons towards their graves, beyond which Death perches waiting on a throne. This Dance of Death motif – an acknowledgement of the fact that death is life's only certainty, no matter your status – was a popular theme in both art and literature in the late Middle Ages, and examples are known to have existed across Europe, from London and Paris to Tallinn and the Balkans.

The frescoes at Hrastovlje, however, are some of the most colourful and beautiful surviving examples, featuring unique and humanizing detail in the faces and actions of the dancers, notably the gentleman attempting to bribe a skeleton into letting him live a little longer.

209 | Bomb shelters for company: hiking the Ohrid border

ALBANIA & NORTH MACEDONIA Albania and Macedonia are two of Europe's undiscovered gems. Sparsely populated lands of chunky mountains and pastoral scenery, the two countries share not just a border but a gargantuan body of water: jaw-dropping Lake Ohrid, a majestic, sea-like expanse ringed by muscular peaks. The lake itself is no secret, and the main base – gorgeous little Ohrid town, on the Macedonian side – has witnessed something of a tourist boom, but there's still plenty of room for adventure.

You can wake literally metres from the lake in Ohrid town, the bedroom ceiling ashimmer with reflected sunlight. After an early lakeside breakfast of fish and strong coffee, a bus–taxi combo will get you to the Albanian border. High up in the mountains, this crossing sees very little traffic, which makes the hour-long walk to the main Tirana road something of a pleasure: brisk winds, occasional views of the lake – and the sudden realization that horses seem larger and much scarier in the wild. Also in evidence are clusters of dome-like bomb shelters, built in their hundreds of thousands during the despotic, isolationist rule of Enver Hoxha.

On the main road, there's little option but to flag down a shared minibus known as a *furgon* for the lakeside ride to Podgradec, a pleasant town on Ohrid's southern shore. It's tempting to overnight here and catch a sunset that throws the lake into a glistening expanse of reds and yellows, but after a delicious Albanian lunch of lamb *qöfte*, yoghurt-like *kos* and Turkish coffee, it's time to start hiking once more, this time back to North Macedonia.

Despite the length of the walk – around 12km – the time flies by, with Ohrid's gentle waves lapping the shore to the left, and bomb shelter after bomb shelter to the right. Somehow, it's hard not to miss these reinforced concrete buddies once back in Macedonian territory, but on hand to mitigate any sadness is the stunning monastery of Sveti Naum, which has sat by the lake for over a thousand years, and from a distance appears to be made of gingerbread and cookies. From the monastery, occasional buses run back to Ohrid town, where there's plenty of Macedonian wine to toast the fantastic 88km route around one of the prettiest lakes in Europe.

210 | Sharing the loves of the gods at the Palazzo Farnese

ITALY One of the greatest art experiences in Italy is also one of its best-kept secrets. And for that you have to thank not the Italians, but the French, whose embassy has occupied Rome's Palazzo Farnese for the past century or so.

Inside, Annibale Carracci's remarkable ceiling fresco, *The Loves of the Gods*, was until relatively recently almost entirely off-limits, open only to scholars, VIPs and those with a proven interest in Renaissance art. Now, with a little planning, it's possible to see it for yourself on a tour. Available in English, French and Italian, these give access to perhaps the most extraordinary piece of work you'll see in Rome apart from the Sistine Chapel – and you get to view it with a small group of art lovers rather than a huge scrum of other tourists.

The work was commissioned from the then unknown Bolognese painter Annibale Carracci, by Cardinal Odoardo Farnese at the end of the sixteenth century to decorate one of the rooms of the palace. It's a work of magnificent vitality, and it seems almost impossible that it could be the work of just one man. In fact, it wasn't. Annibale devised the scheme and did the main ceiling, but the rest was finished by his brother and cousin, Agostino and Lodovico, and assistants like Guido Reni and Guercino, who went on to become some of the most sought-after artists of the seventeenth century.

The central painting, with its complex and dramatically arranged figures, great swathes of naked flesh and vivid colours, is often seen as the first great work of the Baroque era, a fantastic, fleshy spectacle of virtuoso technique and perfect anatomy. The main painting, centring on the marriage of Bacchus and Ariadne, which is supposed to represent the binding of the Aldobrandini and Farnese families, leaps out of its frame in an erotic hotchpotch of cavorting, surrounded by similarly fervent works illustrating various classical themes. Between and below them, nude figures peer out – amazing exercises in perspective that almost seem to stand alongside you in the room. Carracci was paid a pittance, and died a penniless drunk shortly after finishing the work, but the triumph of its design, and the amazing technical accomplishment of its painting, shines brighter than ever.

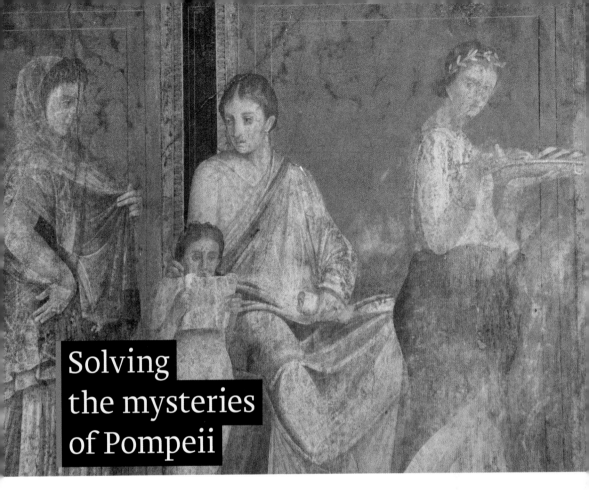

Solving the mysteries of Pompeii

ITALY Pity the poor folk picking through the rubble of the Forum in Rome. To make the most of the ruins there you have to use your imagination. In the ancient Roman resort town of Pompeii, however, it's a little easier. Pompeii was famously buried by ash from Vesuvius in 79 AD, and the result is perhaps the best-preserved Roman town anywhere, with a street plan that is easy to discern – not to mention wander – and a number of palatial villas that are still largely intact.

While crowded, not surprisingly, it's a large site, and it's quite possible to escape the hordes and experience the strangely still quality of Pompeii, sitting around ancient swimming pools, peering at frescoes and mosaics still standing behind the counters of ancient shops.

Finish your visit at the fascinating Villa of Mysteries, a suburban dwelling just outside the ancient city. Its layout is much the same as the other villas, but the frescoes that decorate its walls offer a unique insight into the ancient world – and most importantly they are viewable *in situ*, unlike most of Pompeii's mosaics and frescoes, which have found their way to Naples' archeological museum.

No one is sure what these pictures represent, but it's thought they show the initiation rites of a young woman preparing for marriage. Set against ruby-red backgrounds, and full of marvellously preserved detail, they are dramatic and universal works, showing the initiate's progress from naïve young girl to eligible young woman. Above all, they tell a story – one that speaks to us loud and clear from 79 AD.

212 | Scaling Snow White's Castle in North Cyprus

NORTH CYPRUS When the Turks seized northern Cyprus over four decades ago in a bitter and complicated struggle, there's little doubt they took the island's star region. Cocooned by its isolation for many years from the overdevelopment of the Greek south, Turkish-controlled North Cyprus – now with peace thankfully restored – sometimes feels like a time warp, maintaining an authenticity lost to other once-idyllic Mediterranean destinations. The island's charms seem more tangible here: the picture-postcard villages less commercialized; the sandy beaches more wild and remote.

And in the mighty Crusader fortress of St Hilarion, a short drive inland from Girne (Kyrenia in Greek), there's a sense of drama unmatched elsewhere across the island. Clinging to a lofty crag in the Kyrenia Mountains, St Hilarion's fairy-tale outline – all crumbling towers, grand arches and imposing battlements – is said, somewhat fancifully, to have inspired Walt Disney to create Snow White's Castle. The truth, however, is much darker.

The approach to the castle is a reminder that Cyprus remains a divided island. A gigantic silhouette of a soldier presages a Turkish army base and checkpoint, the air split by gunfire from a nearby firing range where jousting tournaments were once held. It's only when peering up from the castle's base, its hulking mass of stone blending with the sheer rock, that it becomes clear how daunting this must have seemed to early invaders.

The ascent is only for the sure-footed and not for the acrophobic. Beyond the first level, with its well-preserved remains of a Byzantine church – built in honour of St Hilarion, an ascetic hermit said in local folklore to have repelled the demons that possess the mountaintop – the path winds steeply up to the second tier, or Lower Ward, built for the Lusignan nobles who once ruled the island: a confusing warren of alleys, hidden rooms and sheer drops.

The castle saves its grizzliest tale for the final tier, accessed by steep, rough-hewn steps on an uneven, zigzagging path. Above the evocative Royal Apartments, a vertiginous climb brings you to the Prince John's Tower, where the gullible prince – falling victim to a Machiavellian plot – ordered that his faithful Bulgarian guards be hurled from the sturdy turret to their deaths on the rocks below. Guides to this day are fearful of setting foot in the tower for fear of being avenged by John's ghost.

From here it's a short scramble to the viewing platform at the summit, with vistas on a clear day beyond the sinuous coastline as far as the Turkish mainland 80km away. A wag has etched the warning: "Too high – go down". Given the swirling legends, it's best to heed their advice.

213 | Bunkering down in Durres

ALBANIA A small, rickety Ferris wheel now turns on the spot in Skanderbeg Square where Enver Hoxha's colossal gilded statue once stood. After his death in 1985, the dictator's busts were gradually removed from public view and the National Historical Museum in Tirana was "ideologically renovated". However, despite the cosmetic surgery, Albania just can't seem to shrug off one legacy of Hoxha's brutal brand of Stalinism.

The ultra-paranoid dictator covered Albania's pretty rural landscape with over 700,000 bunkers – one for every four citizens – to protect his people from invading hordes of imperialists, fascists and counter-revolutionaries. Although the enemy tanks never arrived, the bunkers were built so strongly that to this day few have been removed. These small concrete domes still occupy every possible vantage point in the rolling countryside that flanks the road between the capital and the port city of Durres on the Adriatic coast: gloomy relics of the old regime that have been reinvented to represent the spirit of the new Albania. The rusty ledge of one bunker's entrance is lined with potted flowers, while rows of tomatoes grow defiantly around it.

Inside, candles struggle to stay alight in the stale air, scarcely illuminating the table around which the family of five who call this suffocating box home are eating dinner. Other bunkers are painted with jaunty murals or emblazoned with the colours of football teams or lovers' names: unambiguous expressions of the new priorities in Albanians' lives. A young couple emerge from a solitary hilltop bunker, walk down to a beaten-up Mercedes parked by the roadside and stop for a lingering kiss before driving back to Tirana.

And at Durres, the odd imperialist tourist freshly arrived on the ferry from Italy sips beer and listens to one ABBA hit after another in the dark, slightly dank surroundings of a beachside bunker bar, as Hoxha turns lividly in his grave.

214 | The Sufi whirling dervishes of Konya

TURKEY The spellbinding displays of whirling dervishes, in transcendental thrall to the heavens above them, are known the world over. Though performances abound throughout Turkey and other Muslim nations, it's in Konya, the spiritual home of the dervish, where the Sema service is at its most traditional.

Konya, in Turkey's conservative central heartland, is the burial place of Jalal al-Din Rumi, the renowned poet who is also referred to as Mevlânâ, or the Sainted One. His followers, the Mevlevi, were once an underground sect, accepted only for their dance-like performances. Much more than pure movement, though, the Mevlevi Sema ceremony celebrates the stages these mystics go through to access God, and represents the solar system in its choreographed orbit of the ceremonial space. Added to UNESCO's list of the Intangible Cultural Heritage of Humanity in 2008, the ritual is supported by Turkey's Ministry of Culture and Tourism, and central to Anatolian heritage.

The ceremony begins with a traditional musical score played on the ney, or flute, kettledrums and Turkish lute. The haunting vocalists sing lyrics based on the verses of Rumi. Watching the ritual unfold, you almost feel like you're encroaching on a very private experience. As the dervishes begin to rotate, at the invisible request of the head dervish, they have little problem maintaining their balance and centre of gravity, even when spinning for over an hour and wearing tall brown hats and flowing white robes. Opening their arms in reverence, the right hand is held up to receive God's blessing, and the left hand turned down, to spread this benediction to everyone else. It's simply mesmerizing, and there's a hushed stillness in the audience, the like of which is rarely seen in modern auditoriums.

Bean feasts and orange fights

ITALY One of Italy's biggest and most peculiar carnival celebrations takes place in Ivrea, not far from Turin. On the Sunday before Shrove Tuesday the town fills with revellers who tuck into bowls of beans ladled out from giant cauldrons in the main square before taking part in a humongous orange fight, which starts at the same time each afternoon for the next three days. Anyone and anything is fair game here, and by the end of each day everyone is covered in pulp and drenched in freshly squeezed juice; there's nowhere to walk that's not swimming in vitamin C, and the air is full of the bitter smell of oranges. Everything finishes on Shrove Tuesday itself, with a huge procession and a celebratory bonfire in the square.

215

ITALY You'd be mad to go to Venice and never set foot in a boat. Yet many visitors do a lot of footwork up and down little bridges, and spend little time on the water. The spectacular solution is to take the splendid jaunt down the Canal Grande on the *vaporetto* water bus (forget the overpriced, touristy gondolas), but to get a real taste of Venice you've got to plunge off in search of the city's outlying islands.

As you stand at the rail of a *vaporetto* and see the city's built-up banks receding into a mirage of summer haze or winter fog, you'll start to feel the true strangeness of the place. And when your boat bumps back against the quay, and you hear the squeak of the rope tightening round the mooring posts and the distinctive rattle of the passenger gate, you may start to feel that little bit at home.

A few minutes' ride south of the city curls the Giudecca, a spine of joined-up islets whose broad, canalside *fondamente* gaze across at Venice's sun-drenched southern skirts. Set into the Giudecca are two serene churches by the great Renaissance architect Andrea Palladio, while a stone's throw away, on the island of San Giorgio Maggiore, stands his monastery church of St George, its tower offering a fine view across the water to the Palazzo Ducale.

North of Venice, the *vaporetti* forge deeper into the lagoon, stopping first at the strange, silent cemetery island of San Michele, where the tombs are shaded by tall cypresses and guarded by high brick walls. The island-complex of Murano is like a scaled-down Venice, complete with its own modest Canal Grande; it's known for its coloured glassware, which you can see being blown. Continuing north feels like steaming into Venice's past. Tiny, brightly painted Burano still has working fishing boats, while lonely Torcello preserves Venice's original cathedral, founded in the seventh century. Gazing from its campanile across the primeval mud flats and shallows, it's possible to feel afresh the miracle of Venice's emergence from the waters.

Into the lagoon: Venice's other islands

217 | Soaking weary limbs in Ischia's hot springs

ITALY For a chilled-out island holiday that's a tonic for body and soul, you can't go wrong with Ischia. Even as the ferry approaches, gliding into the horseshoe-shaped harbour of Ischia Porto, you can tell that this place is special. Rising like a mirage from the shimmering Bay of Naples, the island is topped by rugged Monte Epomeo, a craggy volcano, now dormant and blanketed in dense pine forest: a vision so lush that it could almost pass for a Central American isle, rather than a Mediterranean outcrop a short hop from chaotic Naples.

Thanks to aeons of volcanic activity, Ischia is extremely fertile: tangles of bougainvillea adorn the sun-bleached houses, cactus and prickly pear sprout along the roadside, and vineyards peppered with wild poppies bask in the sunshine. But the island is most prized for the super-strength curative powers of its thermal waters.

Each of its 103 volcanic springs is known to benefit a different ailment, from rheumatism to gout. As far back as 700 BC the first settlers here, the

Greek Euboeans, used the thermal waters to treat the wounds of injured soldiers. These days, "wellness" is a serious business: patients are referred to the island's spas by Italy's national health service.

Pick of the spa hotels is the hilltop *San Montano*, a discreetly luxurious bolthole with seven pools and a garden fragrant with lemon, lavender and jasmine, where the massages come with glorious views. Nearby *Negombo* holds a complex of thermal gardens whose fourteen pools are couched amid jungle-style foliage and exotic blooms, and dotted with contemporary sculpture.

The most memorable Ischian spa experience, though, is one you can have for free. At Il Sorgeto, a scenic cove near the village of Panza, you can wallow in volcanically heated, bubbling rocky pools just offshore. You could even do as the locals do and bring dinner to cook slowly in the simmering water – it might take a while, but with the sun setting and a cold beer in hand, you won't mind the wait.

218 | In search of İskender Kebap

TURKEY There are really only three reasons to visit Bursa: you ski, you know someone there, or you're on a pilgrimage to sample the most sumptuous meat dish Turkey has to offer. Bursa was the Ottoman Empire's first capital. But it may actually be better known as the birthplace of İskender kebap, the brainchild of native son Mehmet Oğlu İskender.

As legend – and the Kebapçı İskender brand website – has it, İskender sought a more egalitarian way of preparing lamb, which was usually cooked flat on a fire, leading to an uneven distribution of doneness and flavour across servings. By stacking meat on a vertical rotisserie, he increased the surface area coming into contact with the heat source – hot coals – ensuring equal succulence and sear for all.

Arguably, the true genius lies in the plating. Sizzling lamb is sliced from a rotating spit, layered over cubes of bread, and then

topped with a savoury sauce of sweet red pepper and tomato *salçısı* (paste). Tableside, bubbling brown butter is poured directly from hot pan to plate. Strained yogurt and tomato slices complete the dish.

Mehmet Oğlu's progeny proudly continue the now-trademarked family tradition at restaurants in Bursa and Istanbul. Look to the *Mavi Dükkan* (Blue Shop) branch of Kebapçı İskender on Atatürk Street for the "*orijinal*" experience. This quaint blue-and-white restaurant, established in 1930, is around the corner from Bursa's historic silk han and fourteenth-century mosque – and the queue out the door can stretch nearly that far. Expect to wait and share a table; it's part of the experience. Once inside, your only choice will be what to drink, as İskender kebap is the menu's single item.

219 | Wandering the golden streets of Valletta

MALTA For a capital city, Valletta is tiny – you can walk from one side to the other in ten minutes. You could have dinner looking out at the modern high-rises of Sliema, then stroll across the city for dessert with a view over the Grand Harbour. But you'll want to take your time with the walk. From the most majestic square to the narrowest of alleyways, Valletta never fails to capture your imagination.

Perhaps your interest will be piqued by the houses; though dating to many different centuries, they're all carved from the creamy sandstone which makes up the island. Wander the waterfront and you'll see old houses worn away by sea winds, sections of stone pitted like honeycomb. The homes lining the main streets have been beautifully restored, their colourful doors painted to match the boxy, wooden Maltese balconies (*gallariji*) above. And in the tapestry of tiny alleys between the two you'll see a jumble of different styles and states – but the warm, golden walls, glowing in the early evening sunlight, unite them in all their variety.

Valletta's buildings also give a fascinating insight into its history, all packed into a small space. Walking through the City Gate, you'll first see the startling

Renzo Piano-designed Parliament House; it showcases a vision of Valletta as modern and international, but its sandstone walls weave it into the fabric of the city. Just beyond is the Pjazza Teatru Rjal, the ruins of a Neoclassical Victorian opera house which have been repurposed as an open-air theatre. Commissioned during the century and a half of British colonial rule, the opera house was levelled in a World War II air raid, when Malta was of huge strategic importance. Follow the street around and you come to the sixteenth-century Church of our Lady of Victories, the very first building erected in the city, which commemorates the ending of the Ottoman siege. In about 200m, you've walked through over 400 years of history – not a bad rate.

But often, more than the grandiose auberges and churches, it's the details of everyday life which captivate in Valletta. Pavement cafés where locals sip strong coffees; laundry strung from brightly coloured *gallariji*; warped wooden shopfronts with tarnished brass signs. Though the city is small, you could lose hours strolling the steps of its golden streets, stopping to admire the saintly statues on every corner, and savouring glimpses of the Mediterranean Sea at the end of alleyways.

Conquering Mount Olympus

GREECE Work off that *moussaka* with a hike up the most monumental of the Greek mountains – Mount Olympus. Soaring to 2920m, the mountain is swathed in mysticism and majesty, mainly due to its reputation as the home of the ancient Greek gods. Reaching the peak isn't something you can achieve in an afternoon – you'll need at least two days' trekking, staying overnight in refuges or tents. You don't need to be a climber but you do need to be prepared: it's a tough climb to the summit, and requires a lot of stamina and some degree of caution. Even when the weather is stiflingly hot at the bottom, there could still be a blizzard blowing halfway up. Passing sumptuous wildflowers and dense forests on the lower slopes, the rocky, boulder-strewn terrain and hair-raisingly sheer drops of the summit are well worth the struggle. Just watch out for Zeus's thunderbolt on the way up.

221 | Braving the midday sun in rock-hewn Lecce

ITALY In a mid-August heatwave, the heel of Italy is not a place many people would choose to be. Still less standing in the centre of Lecce's Piazza del Duomo, a heat-sink square paved with burning-hot stone flags, surrounded by scorching stone buildings and overlooked by a sun that seems as hard and unrelenting as the rock itself. In such conditions the day begins at thirty degrees, and rises smoothly through the forties before topping out at a temperature that should be measured in gas marks, not degrees centigrade.

Squinting up at the towering facade of the Duomo and the bishop's palace, however, it all starts to make sense. Here, and on the surfaces of churches and palaces all over the city, the stone breaks out in exuberant encrustations, as if the very heat had caused the underlying architecture to boil over into fantastical shapes and accretions.

In fact, it wasn't the heat that caused Lecce's stone to crawl with decoration. It was a rare combination of time and place. The city lies beside a unique outcrop of soft sandstone in the razor-hard limestone that forms the tip of the heel of the Italian boot – and stonemasons' chisels take to this *pietra* Leccese like hot knives to butter. And at the very time the masons were setting to work, in the early sixteenth century, the flamboyant ornamentation of the Baroque style was taking hold in Italy. Lecce, the city they call the Florence of the South, was the fervid, sun-struck result.

222 | The peace of Paestum

ITALY The travel writer Norman Lewis called it a "scene of unearthly enchantment", and Paestum is still one of southern Italy's most haunting ancient sites. Its three Greek temples brood magnificently over their marshy location just south of Naples, where, despite the proximity of the city, there are relatively few visitors. Perhaps everyone goes to Pompeii? Whatever the reason, the site is an overgrown and romantic joy, only partially excavated and still the domain of snakes, lizards and other wildlife rather than large numbers of visitors. The splendid museum holds some fantastic finds from the site, including a marvellous mosaic of a diver in mid-plunge that is worth the price of entry alone. Afterwards you can fumble your way back through the undergrowth for a lounge and a swim on some nice nearby beaches lined by scruffy campsites.

223 | Haggle with horror in Istanbul

TURKEY The phrase "shop till you drop" might have been invented by a Turk, with Istanbul's Kapali Çarşi (Grand Bazaar) in mind, for this Ottoman-era labyrinth of shops, stalls and alleys is truly the prototype for all shopping centres worldwide – a humming magnet for consumers that boasts as many as four thousand outlets selling everything from carpets, tiles and pots to mundane household items, food and antiques. There are no prices; instead *pazarlik* (haggling) is the norm, deals being done over long sessions fuelled by tea and mock horror at insulting offers.

Don't visit hoping to snag a bargain, or necessarily even to buy anything at all – despite the many entreaties from the market traders. A lack of self-induced pressure will make you more likely to find something you like. You will certainly have a much better time.

Living it up on the Amalfi Coast

ITALY The Amalfi Coast, playground of the rich and famous, exudes Italian chic. The landscape is breathtakingly dramatic: sheer, craggy cliffs plunge down to meet the shimmering blue water and tiny secluded coves dot the coastline, accessible only by very expensive yacht. Setting off down the coastal road, you can't help but fancy yourself a bit of a jet-setter.

The drive itself deserves celebrity status; you may think you've seen corniche roads, but this one's in a class of its own, hewn into the sides of the mountain and barely wide enough for two large cars to pass comfortably, let alone the gargantuan buses that whizz between the main towns. On one side rises an impenetrable wall of mountain, on the other there's nothing but a sheer drop to the sea. Overcome the instinct to hide your head in your hands and embrace the exhilaration – this is not a ride

to miss. The road snakes its way along Europe's moneyed edge, plunging headlong into dark, roughly hewn tunnels, curving sharply around headlands and traversing the odd crevice on the way. Every hair-raising bend presents you with yet another sweeping vista.

Don't get so caught up in the drive that you forget to stop and enjoy the calm beauty of the effortlessly exclusive coastal towns. Explore the posh cliffside town of Positano or stroll the peaceful promenades and piazzas of elegant hilltop Ravello. And in more down-to-earth Amalfi, just below, readjust to the languorous pace of resort-town life at a café before heading off to enjoy the town's sandy beach. Presided over by a towering cathedral adorned with glittering gold tiles and a lush and peaceful cloister, it's the perfect antidote to the adrenaline rush of the coast road.

225 | Tackling Old Mr Three Heads

SLOVENIA It's said that every Slovene has to climb Mount Triglav, the country's highest (2864m) and most exalted peak, at least once in their lifetime. They're joined by hikers and climbers from many nations, who arrive in droves as soon as summer comes. The mountain's nickname, Old Mr Three Heads (Triglav means "Three Heads"), originated with the early Slavs, who believed that it accommodated a three-headed deity who watched over the Earth, sky and underworld.

The most difficult approach is via the north face, a stark 1200m-high rock wall that's certainly not for the faint-hearted. Most hikers opt for the route from Lake Bohinj further south; watched over by steeply pitched mountain faces, this brooding body of water is the perfect place to relax before embarking on the mountain trail ahead. Starting at the lake's western shore, you pass the spectacular Savica Waterfall, before a stiff climb over the formidable Komarča cliff, and

then a more welcome ramble through meadows and pastureland. Beyond here lies the highlight of the route: rich in alpine and karstic flora, the Valley of the Seven Lakes is a series of beautiful tarns surrounded by majestic limestone cliffs. The views are glorious, though by this stage most hikers are hankering after the simple comforts of a mountain hut.

Not only is Triglav a tough nut to crack in one day, but these convivial refuges are great places to catch up with fellow hikers as well as refuel with steaming goulash and a mug of sweet lemon-infused tea. Most people push on at the crack of dawn, eager to tackle the toughest part of the ascent, entailing tricky scrambles, before the triple-crested peak of Triglav looms into view. Once completed, according to tradition, there's just one final act for first-timers, namely to be "birched" – soundly thrashed across the buttocks with a branch.

226 | Nuts, socks and mistletoe brandy: joining the truffle train in Buzet

CROATIA Even the most committed of culinary explorers often find the truffle an acquired taste. Part nut, part mushroom, part sweaty sock, the subtle but insistent flavour of this subterranean fungus inspires something approaching gastronomic hysteria among its army of admirers. Nowhere is truffle worship more fervent than in the Croatian province of Istria, a beautiful region where medieval hill towns sit above bottle-green forests. Summer is the season for the delicately flavoured white truffle, but it's the more pungent autumnal black truffle that will really bring out the gourmet in you. A few shavings of the stuff delicately sprinkled over pasta has an overpowering, lingering effect on your tastebuds.

The fungus-hunting season is marked by a plethora of animated rural festivals. Biggest of the lot is held in the normally sleepy town of Buzet, where virtually everyone who is anyone in Istria gathers on a mid-September weekend to celebrate the Buzetska Subotina, or "Buzet Saturday". As evening approaches, thousands of locals queue

for a slice of the world's biggest truffle omelette, fried up in a mind-bogglingly large pan on the main square. With the evening rounded out with folk dancing, fireworks, alfresco pop concerts and large quantities of *biska* – the local mistletoe-flavoured brandy – this is one small-town knees-up that no one forgets in a hurry.

Buzet's reputation as Istria's truffle capital has made this otherwise bland provincial town a magnet for in-the-know foodie travellers. The revered fungus plays a starring role in the dishes at *Toklarija*, a converted oil-pressing shed in the nearby hilltop settlement of Sovinjsko Polje, whose head chef changes the menu nightly in accordance with what's fresh in the village. One of the best meals you're likely to eat is in the neighbouring hamlet of Vrh, where the family-run *Vrh Inn* serves fat rolls of home-made pasta stuffed with truffles, mushrooms, asparagus and other locally gathered goodies. With the ubiquitous mistletoe brandy also on the menu, a warm glow of satisfaction is guaranteed.

227 | Buckle up for a vintage tour of eastern Sicily

ITALY Here's an offer you can't refuse. Hire a vintage Fiat 500, or Cinquecento as the Italians call it, for a storied east coast road trip from Catania, taking in baroque history, celebrity couture and mafia movie history. How could you say no?

First buzz south to Ragusa, a magnificent cluster of honey-coloured cathedrals, crumbling ramparts and sun-dappled courtyards, reached by driving along the belly of a deep, rocky ravine. It is one of a trilogy of baroque hilltop towns (the others include nearby Noto and Modica), and each has an arsenal of sights to surprise even the most ardent of travellers.

Your Fiat 500 is also that snazziest of Italian inventions – the cabriolet – so unbuckling the leather sunroof, you make do with nature's air conditioning for the drive north. It is a slow but rewarding drive: the skies powder blue, the sunburnt fields of orange and lemon trees vast, and the smoking crest of Mount Etna, Europe's highest active volcano, in the rear-view mirror.

Next stop: Taormina, the sort of impossible town you can only find in Italy. It clings to the side of a steep rock-face, with some of the houses looking as if they're about to cascade into the aquamarine waters below. But that's just part of its appeal: it has everything you could want from storybook Italy – a medieval layout, a Greek theatre, windswept beach villas, and views of the Ionian Sea. Over the years, many famous faces have found solace in its narrow streets – Truman Capote, Oscar Wilde and Greta Garbo among them – but no one has become more associated with the town than fashion designer Domenico Dolce. He regularly returns each summer to film splashy campaigns for Dolce & Gabbana's latest collections.

These days, while Taormina is a hub of designer-label boutiques, Savoca and Forza d'Agrò to the north remain blissfully sleepy. Nearly 50 years have passed since Francis Ford Coppola and the production crew of *The Godfather* arrived in 1971, but the hilltop refuges don't look like they have changed one bit. And that's just the way the Sicilians like it.

228 | Live like a doge: a night at the Danieli

ITALY Venice has more hotels per square kilometre than any other city in Europe, and for more than 150 years one particular establishment has maintained its status as the most charismatic of them all – the *Danieli*. Founded in 1822 by Giuseppe Dal Niel, it began as a simple guesthouse on one floor of the Palazzo Dandolo, but within twenty years it became so popular that Dal Niel was able to buy the whole building. Rechristened, the hotel established itself as the Venetian address of choice for visiting luminaries: Balzac, Wagner, Dickens, Ruskin and Proust all stayed here, and nowadays it's a favourite with the Film Festival crowd and the bigwigs of the art world who assemble for the Biennale.

So what makes the *Danieli* special? Well, for a start there's the beauty of the Palazzo Dandolo. Built at the end of the fourteenth century for a family that produced four of the doges of Venice, the *palazzo* is a fine example of Venetian Gothic architecture, and its entrance hall, with its amazing arched staircase, is the most spectacular hotel interior in the city. The rooms in this part of the *Danieli* are furnished with fine antiques, with the best of them looking out over the lagoon towards the magnificent church of San Giorgio Maggiore. This is the other crucial factor in the *Danieli*'s success – location. It stands in the very heart of Venice, right next to the Doge's Palace, on the waterfront promenade called the Riva degli Schiavoni, and in the evening you can eat at the rooftop *La Terrazza* restaurant, admiring a view that no other tables in town can equal.

All this comes at a price, of course; the *Danieli* is one of the most expensive places to stay in this most expensive of cities. There are three parts to the hotel: the old Palazzo Dandolo, known as the Casa Vecchia; an adjoining palazzo; and a block built in 1948. The best rooms, with lagoon views, are in the Casa Vecchia. If your lottery ticket has come up, however, you might want to consider the delirious gilt and marble extravagance of the Doge's Suite – yours for a mere €4000 a night.

229 | Techno and turbo-folk: having a blast in Belgrade

SERBIA It is the quintessential Balkan city, a noisy, vigorous and vibrant metropolis whose nightlife is as varied as it is exciting, and whose sophisticated citizens really know how to party hard. Belgrade has every right to proclaim itself the good-time capital of Eastern Europe.

As good a place as any to start is Strahinjića bana, known as "Silicone Valley" thanks to the number of surgically enhanced women who parade up and down here. You can get the evening going with a glass of hoppy Nikšičko beer or a shot of Šlivjovica (a ferocious plum brandy) in one of the many über-hip bars packed cheek-by-jowl along this fantastically lively street. From here it's time to hit *Andergraund*, a venerable techno joint located in the vast catacombs beneath the Kalemegdan citadel. Complete with a funky chill-out zone, this vibrant place is typical of the city's clubs, and though the scene is in a constant state of flux, good dance venues are the rule rather than the exception.

To experience a different side to Belgrade's nightlife, head down to the banks of the Danube and Sava rivers which, during the summer months, are lined with a multitude of river rafts (*splavovi*), housing restaurants, bars and discos. These places can get seriously boisterous, but are popular with devotees of Serbia's infamous turbo-folk music, a brilliantly kitsch hybrid of traditional folk and electronic pop. If this type of music presses your buttons – and it is worth experiencing at least once – you can also check out one of the city's several *folkotekes*, discos specializing in turbo-folk.

Another quirky, yet somewhat more restrained, Belgrade institution is the hobby bar; these small, privately owned cafés or bars are run by young entrepreneurs ostensibly for the entertainment of their pals, though anyone is welcome to visit. The next morning the chances are that you'll be good for nothing more than a cup of strong Turkish coffee in one of the many cafés sprawled across Trg Republike – before doing it all over again in the evening.

230 | Monasteries in the air

GREECE When scouting around for a secluded refuge from the cares of the world, it's perhaps not surprising that a group of eleventh-century Greek monks should have hit upon Meteora (literally, "suspended in the air"). These otherworldly, towering sandstone pinnacles, jutting upwards from the plains of Thessaly, take the notion of remoteness to another level. In those days, access to the monasteries was by way of nets hoisted heavenwards by hand-cranked windlasses; nowadays, hard-core climbers get their kicks by making the same journey up nigh-on vertical pillars of rock with names like the Corner of Madness.

For those who prefer to take the stairs, the six monasteries are also accessible by steps hewn into the rock in the 1920s. Well-worn trails zigzag between monasteries, their rust-coloured roof tiles in cheery contrast to the desolate greyness of the wind-blasted rock. Inside, you'll find superb frescoes and late Byzantine art; outside, top-of-the-world views.

231 | Hot coals for Constantine

GREECE In a handful of sleepy farming villages in northern Greece, the fire-walking ritual is an annual celebration of a thirteenth-century miracle, when locals rescued icons from a burning church – without being burned themselves. By nightfall, the towering bonfire in the main square has dwindled to glowing embers. Every light is put out and all eyes are on the white-hot coals – and the cluster of people about to make the barefoot dash across them.

Fire-walkers limber up for the main event with rhythmic dancing, which escalates into frenzied writhing as they channel the spirit of St Constantine, believed to shield them from harm. Clutching icons for further protection, the fire-walkers step out onto the coals, stomping on the smouldering embers with gusto, as though kicking up autumn leaves. An inspection of feet after the rite reveals miraculously unmarked soles, a sign of St Constantine's divine protection – and an excuse for a slap-up feast.

ITALY Sardinia might be renowned for its scintillating sandy beaches, but the island also holds some of Italy's most dramatic mountain landscapes. The most impressive of these lie on the island's east side, where the Gennargentu National Park covers the rugged, largely uninhabited mountains and valleys of the Gennargentu range as well as the cliffy coast. Anyone taking the high and twisty SS125 road through the region will find it hard to concentrate on the road as the magnificent views unfurl on either side, not least on the stretch running above the majestic Flumineddu valley, where the eponymous river carves a mighty gash through the Gola di Gorropu far below out of sight.

One of Europe's deepest gorges – its sheer limestone walls rising more than 500m – the Gola di Gorropu presents a constantly changing scenery to anyone scrambling along its bottom, with formidable piles of gigantic boulders scattered along the route, sporadic groves of trees providing shade that are ideal for a pause or a picnic, and calm pools (*vasche*) formed by the winding river that invite a refreshing dip. Herds of wild, shaggy-haired goats along the way keep you company and, if you're lucky, you'll spot curly-horned mouflons clinging to the rock face above and golden eagles in the sky.

There are numerous access points, including tracks from the SS125 and driving routes from the villages of Urzulei and Dorgali. From the latter you can drive to a point from which it's a two-hour hike to the gorge itself. Note that in winter and spring the river can become torrential and dangerous. Proper equipment – footwear, headwear, water – is strongly recommended at any time. Even for shorter hikes, you'll need hardy shoes with a secure grip and ankle support, and preferably head protection against bumps and falls – the boulders can be extremely slippery, especially when wet. At any time of year it's a spectacular landscape, offering a fabulous opportunity to experience Sardinia's deep interior.

Canyoning in Sardinia

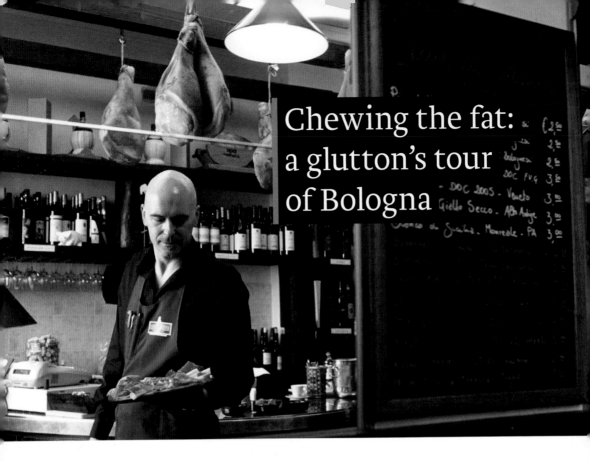

233

ITALY Bologna is "La Dotta" or "The Learned" for its ages-old university, one of the first in Europe, and "La Rossa" or "The Red" for the colour of its politics. But its most deserving nickname is "La Grassa" or "The Fat" for the richness of its food. Even fiercely proud fellow Italians will acknowledge, when pressed, that Bologna's cooking is the best in the country.

This gourmet-leaning university city doesn't expect starving students to shell out a month's rent for a fine meal, either. It's the last major Italian centre where lunch with wine barely breaks €10 a head, and €25 will buy a deluxe multicourse dinner. The only people who should be wary are vegetarians and calorie counters: dishes here are meaty and diet-busting – the Bolognese traditionally chow down on cured hams, game and creamy pasta sauces. Smells of smoked meat waft onto the pavement from the old-fashioned grocery-cum-canteen,

Tamburini, off the main square; it's staffed with old, white-uniformed men, brandishing hocks of ready-to-slice prosciutto amid a clatter of dishes at lunchtime as dozens of locals jostle around the dining room. The Via delle Pescherie Vecchie nearby is still jammed with traditional market stalls, fallen produce squishing on the street and sharp-voiced women heckling the stall holders over prices.

But Bologna's love of food is clearest through its drinks: specifically, at cocktail hour, when in bars you can load up for free on *stuzzichini*, Italy's hefty answer to tapas, for as long as you nurse that G&T. With its cream sofas, sparkly chandelier and thirty-something crowd, the *Café de Paris* serves a buffet of watermelon slices and tortilla wraps, while browsing the bars and restaurants nearby will turn up both simple snacks and fancy nibbles such as dates wrapped in ham or Martini glasses full of fresh chopped steak tartare.

234 | Taking the long view from Monte Baldo

ITALY Shimmering waters, abundant nature, fascinating villages... huge crowds. For some people, the sheer popularity of Lake Garda knocks it down a few places on the list of Italy's most desirable destinations. That does the area a great disservice, however; the crowds tend to be focused around certain well-trodden spots, and inventive travellers can find plenty of ways to go it alone.

One such option is especially appealing on a sticky summer's day: heading to the top of Monte Baldo. The mountain, on the northeast side of the lake, provides both literal and figurative breathing room, perfect for when the heat and crowds of Salò and Riva get a little too much. To get to the summit, you have several alternatives, including hiking on well-signposted paths – graded in difficulty from "touristic" to "expert hikers with equipment" – and biking.

The fastest, easiest and most popular route to the top, though, is the cable car that runs from Malcesine on the lake's shore to the natural plateau of Monte Baldo. It's also pretty fun – the cable car actually rotates through a full 360 degrees, slowly spinning on the upper leg of the trip to offer bird's-eye views of the land as it falls away beneath you.

When you get out of the cable car, 1800m above your starting point, you're faced with a truly spectacular vista. Walk just a few minutes from the station and you can have the view to yourself: Malcesine with its ninth-century church down below, Garda a glittering blue slash across the landscape, its abrupt ending to the north showing its glacial past. And all around you there's only green grass, tempting walks and the occasional bemused cow. Peace, quiet and a reminder of why you and so many other people came to Lake Garda in the first place: because it is, unquestionably, beautiful.

And if you don't fancy taking the cable car down – well, have you ever tried paragliding?

235 | Locked up in Ljubljana

SLOVENIA Fancy being banged up for the night? Well, be Celica's guest. Born from the gutted remains of a former military prison, Ljubljana's *Hostel Celica* (meaning "cell") possesses a dozen or so conventional dorms, but it's the twenty two- and three-bed rooms, or, more precisely, cells, that make it so unique.

Different designers were assigned to come up with themes for each one, resulting in a series of funky and brilliantly original sleeping spaces – one room features a circular bunk bed, for example, and in another a bunk is perched high above the door. That's to say nothing of the wonderfully artistic flourishes, such as the colourful murals and smart wooden furnishings, that illuminate many of the rooms. Surprisingly, the cells are not at all claustrophobic, though some authentic touches, such as the thick window bars and metal, cage-like doors, remain – there's little chance of being robbed here.

The hostel stands at the heart of a complex of buildings originally commissioned for the Austro-Hungarian army and which later served as the barracks of the former Yugoslav People's Army. Following Slovenia's independence in 1991, the complex was taken over by a number of student and cultural movements, evolving into a chaotic and cosmopolitan cluster of bars, clubs and NGOs collectively entitled Metelkova.

Despite repeated attempts by authorities to regulate, and even demolish, the site, the community has stood firm as the city's alternative cultural hub, with club nights, live music (everything from punk and metal to dub-techno) and performance art all part of its fantastically diverse programme. Indeed, if you don't fancy the short stroll into Ljubljana's lovely old town centre for a few drinks, this makes a lively place to hang out before stumbling back to your cell. Just don't throw away the key.

236 | Groping for groupers in the Blue Hole

MALTA Legendary oceanographer Jacques Cousteau, who said of the sea that "once it casts its spell, [it] holds one in its net of wonder forever", acquired his beloved research vessel, the *Calypso*, in Malta at the start of the 1950s. Diving as a recreational activity has come a long way since Cousteau's pioneering aquatic adventures, and the Maltese archipelago – which consists of three main islands, Malta, Gozo and Comino, plus a few uninhabited islets – is these days synonymous with excellent diving conditions and remarkable visibility.

These temperate waters are a diver's dream, with sea temperatures that vary from 14°C in winter to 28°C in summer allowing for year-round diving. Marine life is abundant; schools of barracuda, tuna and bream, moray eels, flying gurnards, octopus, groupers, stingrays, amberjacks, and the odd turtle can all be sighted. The topography of the islands allows for a rich variety of dives, ranging from easy descents around reefs busy with shoals to journeys to shipwrecks and, for thrill-seekers, myriad stunning caves and caverns.

Although it's not for the faint-hearted, and requires extra tanks, lights and other specialized equipment to ensure maximum safety, cave diving has become especially popular. So long as you can meet the technical challenge, it offers glimpses of underwater scenery and fauna seldom found elsewhere.

If you have to pick one dive, make your way to the Blue Hole in Gozo. Suitable with its protected entry for beginners and experienced divers alike, this dive follows an exciting trajectory down through the hole, an enormous natural arch, eroded in the limestone cliffs. Amid the dramatic plays of light, large groupers, dentex and amberjacks in eager pursuit of sardines are all very much in evidence, as well as the occasional conger eel.

Whatever your level or threshold, both Malta and Gozo offer dramatic drop-offs, shore and boat diving all within easy reach, while the size and proximity of the islands mean that no dive is ever further than an hour's drive or boat ride away.

237 | Land of the fairy chimneys

TURKEY An expanse of undulating, cave-pocked, tunnel-riddled rock at the centre of Turkey, Cappadocia is a landscape like no other. It's one of those rare places that can draw quality snaps from even the most slapdash photographer, with a rocky palette that shifts from terracotta through pink and honey to dazzling white, the orange fires of sunrise and sunset adding their own hues to the mix. From Uçhisar's castle to the cliff-hewn churches of Çavusin, there are heavenly views at every turn – surreal stone towers up to 50m in height pop up along innumerable valleys. Some resemble witches' hats, others are mushroom-shaped, a couple defy gravitational logic and a few are markedly phallic, but to locals they're all the *peribacalar* – or "fairy chimneys".

Although the countryside is ideal for hiking, cycling or an aimless ramble, there's no need to stay on the surface. You can delve below ground into one of many underground cities, built over 4000 years ago and once home to Christians fleeing persecution, among other groups,

or float up in a balloon to watch the sun rise over the peaks. From on high you'll also see the entrances to thousands of caves that pepper the area like Swiss cheese – some towers are honeycombed with up to twenty cave-levels, hand-hewn from the rock hundreds of years ago. Before the tourist trade, the indentations found in many caves were used to harvest pigeon dung, which was then used as fertilizer in local fields. Other caverns, particularly those lining the green Ihlara Valley, served as churches to what was once a large Christian community.

Although still host to the odd family, hermit or teashop, most of the caves lie empty, and some intrepid travellers save on costs by slinging their sleeping bags in out-of-the-way grottoes. However, in towns such as Çavusin and Ürgüp, or the relaxed backpacker capital of Göreme, a few caves have been converted into hotels and guesthouses, letting you live the troglodyte dream without neglecting all your creature comforts.

238 | Contemplating the navel of the world

GREECE Set-piece spectacle is hardly in short supply in Greece, least of all when it comes to ancient ruins. But while the Acropolis hogs the postcards and Olympia boasts a blockbuster sporting legacy, the comparatively unassuming hillside site of Delphi, three hours' drive north of Athens, has arguably the ultimate claim to renown – that of being the *omphalos*, the epicentre of known life or "navel of the world". Legend has it that Zeus released two eagles from opposite ends of the Earth, decreeing that where they met would be its midpoint. They convened here, and when you see the area's woolly mountains, towering limestone cliffs and ranging olive groves, you'd have to call it an apt choice of setting.

The fame of the UNESCO-listed site, however, is based on far more than mythical birds of prey. For more than a millennium, it served as a place of tribute and pilgrimage for leaders, dignitaries, aristocrats and warriors,

drawn here to receive the often cryptic advice of the Delphic oracle – a role filled by a succession of local women who, it was believed, acted as the gods' mouthpiece by inhaling vapours from a fissure in the Earth. Temples, treasuries and bronze statues stood here in huge numbers, a result of the offerings over the centuries, and it's the ruins of this grandeur that visitors see today.

The pillars of the oracle's main temple still stand, commanding a sweeping panorama of the green foothills of Mount Parnassus and the broad plains below. Also to be explored are Delphi's ancient athletics arena, its well-preserved amphitheatre and an excellent museum that showcases some of the votive gifts unearthed over the years. What's more, if you can come calling early in the morning or late in the afternoon – thus missing the main tour-bus slots – you may well have the site largely to yourself.

239 | The murals of Tirana's tower blocks

ALBANIA Tirana's torrid twentieth century was dominated by one colour: a Communist red so deep that the country severed ties with the Soviet Union because brutal dictator Enver Hoxha believed the USSR had turned anti-Marxist since Stalin's death. The capital's skyline is still dominated by the concrete apartment buildings thrown up in the postwar period, but under the city's wildly popular former mayor Edi Rama, who has since become Prime Minister of Albania, these bleak structures were daubed in all manner of murals, patterns and multicoloured stripes.

A painter himself, with a passion for Picasso, one of Rama's first things on taking office in 2000 was to order paint, and encourage tenants and housing cooperatives to get involved in brightening up this most maligned of cities. Tirana has been transformed into a riot of purples, yellows, greens, and yes, even a little red.

Venturing into the side streets, the injection of colour seems to have bled into the atmosphere of neighbourhoods such as Bloku. Formerly a gated area for use only by Hoxha's favoured elite, the streets now thrive 24 hours a day with slinky and swaggering cocktail bars, coffee houses serving up potent espressos (a hangover from the country's Italian occupation) and alfresco opportunities galore to people-watch with a bottle of the fine local beer, Korca.

"The city was without organs", Rama proclaimed. "My colours will have to replace those organs." After decades of all kinds of repression, the artistic impulses of this lovably chaotic city are now free to run riot, making this one of the best places in Europe to spend a weekend putting down the hammer and sickle and picking up the paintbrush and easel – or a coffee or beer – instead.

Classical drama at Epidavros

GREECE There's no better place to experience classical drama than the ancient theatre at Epidavros, just outside the pretty harbour town of Nafplio in the Greek Peloponnese. Dating back to the fourth century BC, it seats 14,000 people and is known above all for its extraordinary acoustics – as guides demonstrate, you can hear a pin drop in its circular orchestra (the most complete in existence) even if you're sitting on the highest of the theatre's 54 tiers.

It's a venue for regular performances of the plays of Sophocles and Euripedes between June and September every year. Occasionally these are in English, but whether you understand the modern Greek in which they are usually performed or not, the setting is utterly unforgettable, carved into the hill behind and with the brooding mountains beyond.

240

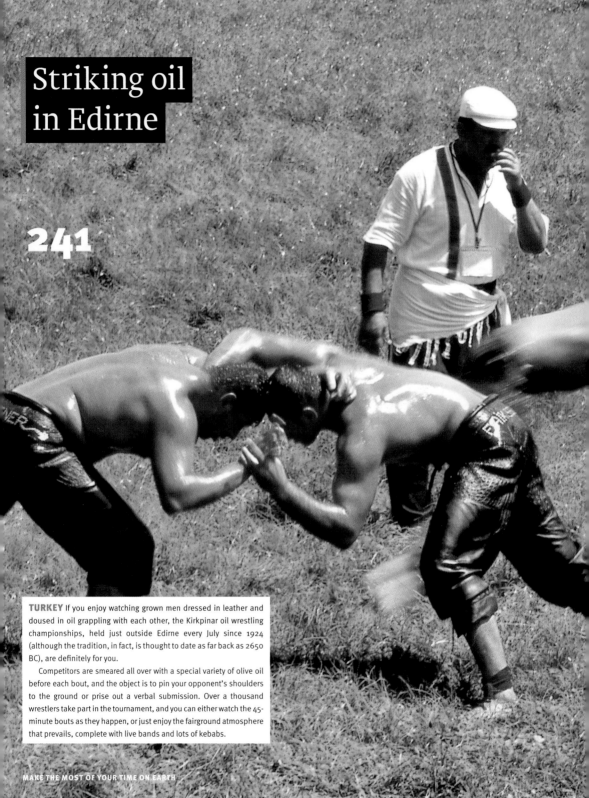

Striking oil in Edirne

241

TURKEY If you enjoy watching grown men dressed in leather and doused in oil grappling with each other, the Kirkpinar oil wrestling championships, held just outside Edirne every July since 1924 (although the tradition, in fact, is thought to date as far back as 2650 BC), are definitely for you.

Competitors are smeared all over with a special variety of olive oil before each bout, and the object is to pin your opponent's shoulders to the ground or prise out a verbal submission. Over a thousand wrestlers take part in the tournament, and you can either watch the 45-minute bouts as they happen, or just enjoy the fairground atmosphere that prevails, complete with live bands and lots of kebabs.

242 | Serbia's magic monasteries

SERBIA Serbia is ready for rediscovery. The steep wooded hills of the countryside south of Belgrade are beautiful and host a network of medieval monasteries located in deliberately out-of-the-way spots. Most boast well-preserved frescoes that the Serbs keenly tout as examples of their superior civilization before the Ottomans. But the real allure is in the locations – magical spots where the peace is disturbed only by the clinking of goat bells.

Studenica, perhaps the greatest of all, sits in a gorgeous setting 12km from the nearest town – Uscé – in the high alpine pastures of central Serbia. There's a hotel up there too, so you can experience the area at its most exquisitely peaceful. Other monasteries include Ravanica, easily accessible on a day-trip from the capital; harder-to-reach Kalenić; Sopoćani, whose frescoes are especially fine; and Mileşeva, southwest towards the Bosnian border and the last resting place of St Sava, founder of the Serbian Orthodox Church.

243 | Roam Ostia Antica

ITALY Rome's finest ancient Roman sight isn't in fact in the city, but a half-hour train ride away at Ostia, where the ruins of the ancient city's port are fantastically well preserved.

Now landlocked, Ostia was once on the coast. Though this was the beating heart of Rome's trading empire, it's relatively free of the bustle of tourists you find in the city proper. There are marvellously preserved streets with shops and upstairs apartments, evocative arcaded passages and floor mosaics, and even an old café with outside seats, an original counter and wall paintings displaying parts of the menu. There's a small theatre and a main square that would have been full of traders from all over the ancient world, with mosaics of boats, ropes, fish and suchlike denoting their trade. Afterwards, climb up onto the roofs of the more sumptuous houses and enjoy a view that once would have taken in one of the ancient world's busiest harbours.

244 | Face to face with the gods in Sicily

ITALY Gorgeous bays and smouldering volcanoes, boisterous markets and fabulous food, Sicily has the lot. But what's less well known is the fact that, amid the energy and chaos of the contemporary island, it is also home to some of Italy's oldest and most perfectly preserved classical sites, sublimely sited buildings that bring a distant era of heroism, hedonism and unforgiving gods to life.

Starting in the far west of Sicily, the fifth-century BC Greek temple of Segesta, secluded on a hilltop west of Palermo, enjoys perhaps the most magnificent location of all, the skeletal symmetry of its Doric temple and theatre giving views right across the bay – not to mention the *autostrada* snaking far below. Further east, just outside the south-coast town of Agrigento, more Doric temples, this time from a century earlier, are dramatically arrayed along a ridge overlooking the sea. They would have been the imposing setting for blood-curdling ceremonies,

yet walk a bit further and you're back in the Catholic present, at the tiny Norman church of San Biagio. Inland from here, you can view the vivid mosaics of the Villa Romana just outside Piazza Armerina – sumptuous works from the fourth century AD that show manly Romans snaring tigers, ostriches and elephants, and a delightful children's hunt with the kids being chased by hares and peacocks.

Then, on the east coast, there are the marvellous theatres of Taormina and Siracusa. The former once staged gladiatorial combats and has views that encompass sparkling seas and Mount Etna – usually topped by a menacing plume of smoke. Siracusa's Greek Theatre is one of the biggest and best preserved of all classical auditoriums; it's used every summer for concerts and Greek drama, and a starlit evening at either theatre is the perfect way to round off your classical tour.

245 | Enjoying da Vinci's Last Supper

ITALY It has always been busy, and boisterous crowds still line up around the Santa Maria delle Grazie convent in Milan, sometimes for hours in the summer. But in recent years viewing Leonardo da Vinci's *Last Supper* has been imbued with a renewed sense of wonder, mystery and, above all, conspiracy. Worn, heavily thumbed copies of Dan Brown's 2003 bestseller *The Da Vinci Code* give some indication of what's on their minds: does the image of John really look like a woman? Is there a triangle (the symbol for "holy grail") between Jesus and John? Put such burning questions aside for a moment, and use your precious fifteen minutes to focus on the real wonder inside – da Vinci's exquisite artistry.

The Renaissance master was in his forties when he painted his depiction of Christ and the twelve disciples, a mural that also served as an experiment with oil paints, a decision that led to its decay in da Vinci's own lifetime. It might be a shadow of its former self, but the epic 21-year restoration, completed in 1999, has nevertheless

revealed some of the original colours, and da Vinci's skills as a painter; his technique is flawless, the painting loaded with meaning and symbolism. Light draws attention to Jesus, who sits at the centre, having just informed his disciples that one of them will betray him. The genius of the painting is the realism with which da Vinci shows the reaction of each: Andrew on the left, his hands held up in utter disbelief; Judas, half in shadow, clutching his bag of silver; Peter next to him, full of rage; and James the Greater on the right, his hands thrown into the air.

Housed in the sealed and climate-controlled refectory of the convent, the focus on just one great work, combined with the laborious process of booking a slot and lining up to get in (25 at a time), heightens the sense of expectation. Once inside, there's usually a dramatic change in atmosphere – viewers become subdued, often overwhelmed by the majesty of the painting, and just for a second they stop looking for that elusive grail.

BOSNIA Decades on from the break-up of Yugoslavia, the Bosnian capital of Sarajevo contains few visible reminders that it was the scene of one of the most prolonged sieges in modern history. There is no central monument to the fallen, and certainly no signs leading to Snipers' Alley – the central thoroughfare that achieved international notoriety due to its vulnerability to enemy fire.

Which probably explains why the tunnel museum, 13km southwest of the centre in a tranquil garden suburb, has become such a compelling destination for locals and visitors alike. Located in the house of the Kolar family, the museum marks the southern end of the cramped underground passage that for long stretches of the siege marked Sarajevo's only link with the outside world.

From 1992 until 1995 Sarajevo was almost totally surrounded by Serbian forces, the only exception being the UN-controlled Sarajevo airport, which was out of bounds to both sides. The only way to break the blockade was to dig a tunnel beneath the airport runway. The resulting passage emerged right beside the Kolars' house – from where

a well-defended supply route ran towards Bosnian-controlled positions in the south. Three generations of Kolars were involved in constructing and maintaining the tunnel, and visiting the museum you also take an intimate voyage into one family's wartime experience. Mementos and photographs are displayed in an exhibition space that feels like a cosy living room – come in winter and you'll find one of the Kolars' cats dozing in front of the heater.

A short stretch of the tunnel has been preserved beneath the house, the first few metres of which you are free to explore. For the city of Sarajevo, this claustrophobic 1.6m-high passage made the difference between survival and surrender, bringing food and military supplies into the city, and providing an escape route for civilians and the wounded – it was used by four thousand people a day. The tunnel's 800m length doesn't sound like a great deal in terms of distance, until you gaze out across Sarajevo airport from the Kolars' back garden and realize what a slow subterranean trudge it must have been.

ITALY An exhilarating sense of triumph overtakes you as you climb the crest of a jagged, snow-laced limestone peak. From your roost above the valley floor, Cortina's campanile and the hotel where you had breakfast are barely visible. The most spectacular climbing routes in the Dolomites are within your grasp. You've suddenly joined the ranks of the world's elite Alpine climbers – or so you'd like to think. Actually, most of the credit belongs to the cleverly placed system of cables, ladders, rungs and bridges known as Via Ferrata, or "Iron Way".

These fixed-protection climbing paths were created by Alpine guides to give clients access to more challenging routes. Routes were extended during World War I to aid troop movements and secure high mountain positions. Now, hundreds of Via Ferrata routes enable enthusiasts to climb steep rock faces, traverse narrow ledges and cross gaping chasms that would otherwise be accessible only to experienced rock jocks.

With the protective hardware already cemented into the rock, you can climb most Via Ferrata routes without needing a rope, climbing shoes or the expensive ironmongery used by traditional rock climbers. With just a helmet, harness and clipping system, you fix your karabiner into the fixed cable, find your feet on one of the iron rungs and just start climbing. It's an amazingly fun way to conquer some stunning vertical terrain and quickly ascend to airy Alpine paths.

Via Ferrata climbing doesn't require polished technique, exceptional strength, balance or even prior rock-climbing experience, although the sustained ascent of several hundred vertical metres means decent aerobic fitness is a distinct advantage. Once you manage to put aside any fear of heights, you'll find secure and sure-footed excitement in this aerial playground.

ITALY The ancient hill town, with its crumbling houses and bell towers rising above a landscape of vineyards and olive groves, is one of the quintessential images of Italy, and nowhere provides more photogenic examples than the area around Siena.

The Chianti region, immediately north of Siena, has numerous pretty little hill towns. Castellina in Chianti is the obvious target for a half-day trip, but Colle di Val d'Elsa is as accessible, and while the industrial zone of the lower town mars the view a little, the upper town is a real gem.

The most famous of all the Sienese satellites, however, is San Gimignano, whose tower-filled skyline is one of Europe's great medieval urban landscapes. On the downside, in high season the narrow lanes of San Gimignano get as busy as London's Oxford Street. If you're touring in summer and don't relish the crowds, head instead to windswept, dramatically situated Volterra, whose Etruscan origins are never far from the surface. Like Pitigliano, in the far south of Tuscany, Volterra is more a clifftop settlement than a hill town – walk

just a few minutes from the cathedral and you'll come upon the Balze, a sheer wall of rock down which a fair chunk of Volterra has tumbled over the centuries.

Montalcino, 40km south of Siena, is as handsome a hill town as you could hope to find. Famed for the mighty red wines produced in the surrounding vineyards, it's also very close to the ancient abbey of Sant'Antimo, one of Tuscany's most beautiful churches. Keep going to even more handsome Montepulciano, ranged along a narrow ridge, strewn with Renaissance palaces, and home to another renowned wine, the Vino Nobile di Montepulciano.

East of here, on the other side of the river plain known as the Valdichiana, lofty Cortona is reached by a 5km road that winds up from the valley floor through terraces of vines and olives. Clinging so closely to the slopes that there's barely a horizontal street in the centre, Cortona commands a gorgeous panorama; climb to the summit of the town at night and you'll see the villages of southern Tuscany twinkling like ships' lights on a dark sea.

249
Rafting the Tara Canyon

MONTENEGRO Eighty kilometres long, and with an average depth of 1100m, the Tara river gorge is Europe's largest canyon, not to mention one of its most spectacular natural wonders. By far the most exhilarating way to get up close and personal with the Tara is to raft it, the most popular excursion being the three-hour trip between Splavište and Šćepan Polje, 18km apart.

Once you've been kitted out in boots, life jacket and helmet, and then clambered aboard the sturdy rubber boat with around ten other equally mad souls (thankfully, a steersman is included), the thrills and spills get under way. Well, sort of. The early stages of the river are characterized by a series of soft rapids and languid, almost still waters, the silence broken only by the occasional rumble of a waterfall spilling from the steeply pitched canyon walls.

But after passing beneath the magnificent Tara Bridge – a 165m-high, 365m-long, five-arched structure built in 1940 – things take a dramatic turn. The sudden increase in gradient means faster currents, which in turn means more powerful rapids. Approaching Miševo vrelo, the deepest section of the canyon, your skills at the oars are put to a severe test; the foaming waters toss the raft every which way and you bounce, shake and struggle to keep balance. If you feel vulnerable, straps on the side of the raft – somewhat unflatteringly termed "chicken lines" – are there to assist.

The river eventually relents, just in time for the home stretch. Exhausted and hungry, it's time for some Durmitor lamb, cooked in milk and prepared *ispod sača* – the traditional Montenegrin way meaning "under the coals". Served with potatoes and *kajmak* (sour-cream cheese), and washed down with a glass of local rich-red Vranac wine, it's the perfect way to round off a day on the river.

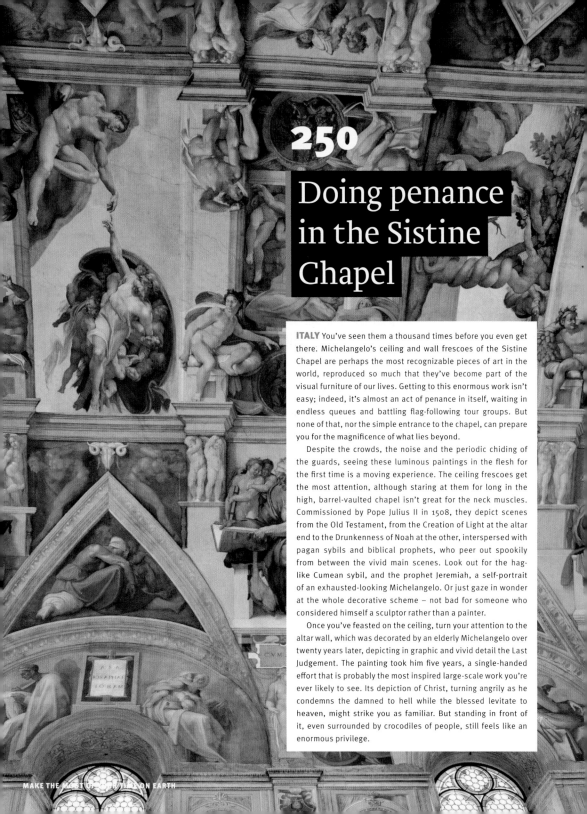

250

Doing penance in the Sistine Chapel

ITALY You've seen them a thousand times before you even get there. Michelangelo's ceiling and wall frescoes of the Sistine Chapel are perhaps the most recognizable pieces of art in the world, reproduced so much that they've become part of the visual furniture of our lives. Getting to this enormous work isn't easy; indeed, it's almost an act of penance in itself, waiting in endless queues and battling flag-following tour groups. But none of that, nor the simple entrance to the chapel, can prepare you for the magnificence of what lies beyond.

Despite the crowds, the noise and the periodic chiding of the guards, seeing these luminous paintings in the flesh for the first time is a moving experience. The ceiling frescoes get the most attention, although staring at them for long in the high, barrel-vaulted chapel isn't great for the neck muscles. Commissioned by Pope Julius II in 1508, they depict scenes from the Old Testament, from the Creation of Light at the altar end to the Drunkenness of Noah at the other, interspersed with pagan sybils and biblical prophets, who peer out spookily from between the vivid main scenes. Look out for the hag-like Cumean sybil, and the prophet Jeremiah, a self-portrait of an exhausted-looking Michelangelo. Or just gaze in wonder at the whole decorative scheme – not bad for someone who considered himself a sculptor rather than a painter.

Once you've feasted on the ceiling, turn your attention to the altar wall, which was decorated by an elderly Michelangelo over twenty years later, depicting in graphic and vivid detail the Last Judgement. The painting took him five years, a single-handed effort that is probably the most inspired large-scale work you're ever likely to see. Its depiction of Christ, turning angrily as he condemns the damned to hell while the blessed levitate to heaven, might strike you as familiar. But standing in front of it, even surrounded by crocodiles of people, still feels like an enormous privilege.

251 | Kayaking in the Bay of Kotor

MONTENEGRO Jet skis tearing through the inky bay and imposing cruise liners anchored outside medieval Kotor confirm that Europe's southernmost fjord (actually a submerged canyon) is best viewed from the water. But there's no need to sign your independence away to an Adriatic cruise – lazily kayaking around the Bay of Kotor is a wonderful way to take in the mountainous panorama that surrounds this jewel in Montenegro's increasingly popular seaboard.

Drifting towards the fortress walls and Venetian-Gothic church spires of Kotor's Old Town, in the shade of imposing Mount Lovćen, you'll feel as though you've been framed in a postcard. Idyllic villages dot the shore, while shingle beaches present tempting opportunities to rest your biceps and cool off in the sparkling water. As you glide across the calm bay aboard a kayak, finding a satisfying rhythm as your paddle slices through the sparkling water, pale stone buildings loom in and out of view and you pass restaurants selling deliciously fresh coastal specialities such as *punjene lignji* (stuffed squid) and *dagnje bouzzara* (mussels in a tomato and onion sauce).

Depending on your itinerary (and your stamina), you might stop at Risan – the bay's oldest settlement, whose intriguing Roman history is preserved in a number of extraordinary mosaics in the Villa Urbana museum.

Perched 3km further along the bay from Risan, Perast is another worthy destination where kayakers can exercise their feet. Though its diminutive size betrays little of its former significance, the town was a naval stronghold under the Venetian Empire. A fleet of around a hundred ships was based here, and the town was the site of the first nautical school in the Mediterranean, established in 1700 and the *alma mater* of many victorious Russian and Venetian naval leaders. Striking defensive towers, grand Baroque houses and palaces from Perast's maritime heyday line the waterfront, and fascinating Orthodox and Catholic churches stand along the historic streets. Returning to your faithful kayak, take inspiration from the ghosts of seafaring past as you paddle your way back through the dramatic bay.

252 | Gorging on frogs and eels in the Neretva Delta

CROATIA Nowhere along the Adriatic coast are landscape and food so closely linked as in the Neretva Delta, an hour's drive north of Dubrovnik. Standing in lush green contrast to the arid mix of limestone and scrub that characterizes much of the Croatian coast, the delta is a dense patchwork of melon plantations, tangerine orchards and reedy marsh. With a shimmering grid of irrigation channels spreading across the plain, local farmers get to their fields by boat: it's not uncommon to see a row of stone-built waterside houses with a parked motor launch bobbing up and down outside each one.

The waterways of the delta teem with frogs and eels, and hunting for these slithery creatures is an age-old local preoccupation. Together they provide the backbone of a distinctive delta cuisine, and the area is fast gaining cult gastronomic status among Croatian foodies eager to reconnect with earthy regional traditions.

The hub of the Neretva Delta is the workaday river port of Metković, but the homely *konobe* (inns) in out-of-town villages like Vid, Prud and Opuzen are the best places to eat. In these rustic establishments, frogs can fill a page or two of the menu, with the white meat of their hind legs either fried in breadcrumbs, grilled with garlic, or wrapped in slivers of *pršut*, the delicious local home-cured ham. However, it's the tangy, succulent eel that's the real delicacy, especially as the key ingredient of *brudet* – a spicy red stew often accompanied by a glossy yellow mound of polenta.

Aiding the delta's emergence as a tourist trail is the ultra-modern archeological museum in Vid, a reed-fringed village built on the ruins of the prosperous second-century Roman market town of Narona. A quick examination of the imposing statues that graced Narona's Temple of Augustus, followed by a leisurely lunch in a waterside inn, makes for the perfect delta day out.

253 | Sausages, seafood and the world's oldest vine

SLOVENIA Whether you're a food fiend, a wine-lover or a cake connoisseur, Slovenia's varied cuisine has it all. This small and modest country may only have a population of just over two million people, but it's got everything from beaches to Alpine valleys to culturally diverse cities, each with their own distinct flavours.

The history of wine in Slovenia stretches back hundreds of years; indeed the northeastern city of Maribor is the proud home of the oldest vine in the world, which has been sitting on the Drava river's edge for over 400 years. While only visitors of great importance – such as the pope or world leaders – get to savour the fruits of the Old Vine itself, you can enjoy some of the country's finest wines in the *Old Vine House*, accompanied by delectable Slovene chocolates and handmade pralines.

Just east of Maribor, the Drava Valley is the country's largest wine region, producing mainly white grapes, and is widely known as Slovenia's answer to Tuscany. Row upon row of grapevines cover the undulating green hills that rise out of the flat plains here, while many of the small farmhouses that dot the landscape display invitations to come inside and taste their nectar.

For gastro delights, the capital, Ljubljana, is the perfect place to acquaint yourself with Slovenia's 24 wildly differing cuisines, where you can sample seafood from the coast in a restaurant by the fish market, sip a rich red from the western wine regions in a locally famous bar, and devour a protected Carniolan sausage in a shop run by a watchmaker.

Taste Bosnian barbecued meat and slurp Turkish coffee beside the river, and then round it all off with some *Prekmurska Gibanica* – a layered fruit cake that's simply divine – at the top of the city's only skyscraper, all the while admiring the snow-topped Alps that beckon from beyond.

254 | Worship the cathedrals of the megalithic culture

MALTA Ggantija, Hagar Qim, Mnajdra, Ta' Hagrat, Ta' Skorba and Tarxien. Not the most recognizable names, but these Maltese locations host some of the world's most ancient buildings. Better known by their official title of the Megalithic Temples of Malta, they are jointly listed as a UNESCO World Heritage Site, and most of them date back to around 3600 BC, before even the more famous Pyramids at Giza and England's Stonehenge.

On the main island of Malta, Tarxien, the most visited of the seven sites, is considered by some to be the cathedral of European megalithic culture. Discovered in 1914 by a farmer who had grown increasingly curious about the rocks that kept ruining his plough, the temple held a

wealth of prehistoric artefacts, including the Magna Mater (or the "Fat Lady", as she's lovingly referred to by the locals). Estimated to have stood more than 2.5m tall when complete, only the lower half of the statue was found during excavations. The original is now housed in the archeology museum in Valletta, with a replica standing on the site of its discovery, but a visit to Tarxien will capture your imagination.

While the mystery of why – and how – the temples were built continues to baffle experts, the beauty of the spiral and dotted motifs that are carved into the stones, and the simple yet structurally sound building methods and intricately interwoven passageways, make that seem somehow irrelevant.

255 | Celebrating the Biennale in Venice

ITALY Several European cities hold major contemporary art fairs, but Venice Biennale has more glamour, prestige and news value than any other cultural jamboree. Nowadays it's associated with the cutting edge, but it hasn't always been that way. First held in 1895 as the city's contribution to the celebrations for the silver wedding anniversary of King Umberto I and Margherita of Savoy, in its early years it was essentially a showcase for salon painting.

Since World War II, however, the Biennale has become a self-consciously avant-garde event, a transformation symbolized by the award of the major Biennale prize in 1964 to Robert Rauschenberg, one of the *enfants terribles* of the American art scene. The French contingent campaigned vigorously against the nomination of this New World upstart, and virtually every Biennale since then has been characterized by controversy of some sort.

After decades of occurring in even-numbered years, the Biennale shifted back to being held every odd-numbered year from June to November so that the centenary show could be held in 1995. The main site is in the Giardini Pubblici, where there are permanent pavilions

for about forty countries that participate at every festival, plus space for a thematic international exhibition. The pavilions are a show in themselves, forming a unique colony that features work by some of the great names of modern architecture and design: the Austrian pavilion was built by the Secession architect Josef Hoffmann in the 1930s, and the Finnish pavilion was created by Alvar Aalto in the 1950s. Naturally enough, the biggest pavilion is the Italian one – it's five times larger than its nearest competitor.

The central part of the Biennale is supplemented by exhibitions in venues that are normally closed to the public. This is another big attraction of the event – only during the Biennale are you likely to see the colossal Corderie in the Arsenale (the former rope factory) or the huge salt warehouses over on the Záttere. In addition, various sites throughout the city (including the streets) host fringe exhibitions, installations and performances, particularly in the opening weeks. And with artists, critics and collectors swarming around the bars and restaurants, the artworld buzz of the Biennale penetrates every corner of Venice.

256 | Soldiers, monks and frescoed squid in medieval monasteries

KOSOVO When it declared independence from Serbia in 2008, Kosovo hoped for a fresh start. But breaking with the past has not been easy: the scars of war are still here, from burnt-out houses to war memorials. Of course, there is much in Kosovo's history to preserve as well as to forget: a whole string of different cultures have made their mark, from the medieval Serbian kingdoms to the Ottoman Empire. But all too often Kosovo's cultural heritage has been understood only through the prism of today's ethnic divides.

Visiting the UNESCO-listed medieval Serbian Orthodox monasteries of Gračanica in central-eastern Kosovo, or Dečani and Peć in the western corner of this diamond-shaped country, gives an instant flavour of the richness of Kosovo's inheritance. But the NATO soldiers standing guard serve as a sharp reminder of the legacy of distrust from 1998–99, when both Christian and Muslim places of worship came under fire.

The Patriarchate of Peć, framed by the mountains of the Rugova Gorge, contains splendid, 2.5m frescoes of archangels – but also silver and icons rescued from nearby churches hit

by ethnic rioting in 2004. In the candlelit chapels of Gračanica, just ten minutes' drive from the capital Pristina, a lively fresco of the Garden of Eden depicts the denizens of land and sea – including an oddly conspicuous squid – but books for sale show the damage done to Kosovo's churches in graphic detail, and fresh-faced Swedish soldiers watch from sentry boxes by the gate.

Still, there is hope that the remnants of distrust will, with time, disappear. Just 20km from Peć, at the foot of the hills that lead west to Montenegro, lies Visoki Dečani Monastery, a fourteenth-century Byzantine edifice with more than a thousand frescoes. Here, the emphasis is on what unites visitors, not what divides them. Guests attending the Thursday evensong or Sunday-morning services queue to take the Eucharist and kiss the icons, and after a leg-aching two hours with standing room only, everyone is invited for a home-made meal in the refectory. As tourists, soldiers and monks gather together to eat and drink – there's even home-made plum brandy – the differences between them seem a lot less important than the similarities.

Bathe in Pamukkale's thermal waters

TURKEY In Turkey's inner Aegean region, about 20km south of Denizli, white travertine terraces lord it over the diminutive town of Pamukkale. Sparkling turquoise and mineral-rich, the thermal waters cascade over the hillsides from a source in the cliffs high above the Çuruksu plain. The streams have created what in Turkish is a *pamuk kale*, or cotton castle – white, petrified waterfalls that puff out like hardened balls of cotton wool. Running alongside the terraces is the ancient Greek-Roman city of Hierapolis, and UNESCO World Heritage

Site status was conferred on both sites in 1988. The waters' health-boosting qualities are widely acknowledged by modern-day Turks, and Cleopatra's Pool is a swimming area that's been specially designated for visitors, filled with sunken columns, the treasures of its ancient past. Floating in the waters here, especially after the day-trippers have left, has to be one of Turkey's most invigorating experiences, particularly when there's a sunset sky above you to make the water terraces glisten and dance.

258

Meandering through Mystras

GREECE The Peloponnese may be littered with ancient sites, but arguably none is quite as evocative as Mystras, a ruined Byzantine city that dates back to the mid-thirteenth century.

It's an intriguing place to explore, strung down a steep hillside and extraordinarily intact, with crumbling mansions and tiny churches that sport monumental frescoes, as well as an ancient convent at its heart that is still inhabited by half a dozen nuns. It's not overcrowded, and you can lose yourself in its alleys and arches – which is just what you should do, maybe combining a visit with some hiking in the nearby beautiful and remote Langhada Pass between Kalamata and Sparta, said to be a route taken by Telemachus in *The Odyssey*.

259 | Opera in fair Verona

ITALY Spend a summer's night under the stars at the opera, and join a long tradition – the Roman-era Verona Arena dates from the first century AD. Today it plays host to classical opera as well as twenty-first century acts. Past and present collide in the wonderfully preserved pale-pink and white stone amphitheatre, which has welcomed big names like Elton John and Adele, as well as regularly staging established operatic favourites such as *Tosca* and *Carmen*. Tickets are released for the annual summer opera festival a year in advance, with early-bird discounts usually available. Be sure to book ahead for a cheaper seat on one of the higher tiers, where you'll be perched on stone benches – but remember to bring a cushion.

260 | Get down and dirty in Dalyan

TURKEY Stepping off the boat at Dalyan's mud baths, you'll be forgiven for wishing you'd never come. But don't be put off by the revolting rotten-egg stench of the sulphur pools – after a revitalizing day here, you'll be gagging for more.

The instructions are simple – roll luxuriously in the mud, bake yourself in the bone-warming sun till your mud cast cracks, shower off and then dunk yourself in the warm, therapeutic waters of the sulphur pool.

Not only will your skin be baby-soft and deliciously tingly, you will also revert to behaving like a big kid. A huge mud bath can mean only one thing – a giant mud fight.

Need to know

189 For more information, see Ⓦathostours.gr/en.

190 Marsaxlokk is 35min by bus from the capital Valletta. For more information, go to Ⓦmalta.com.

191 Car rental is available at nearby airports such as Verona Villafranca (15km) and Bergamo/Orio al Serio (80km); Ⓦvisitgarda.com/en/garda_lake.

192 Pescasseroli, on the single paved road through the heart of Abruzzo National Park (Ⓦparcoabruzzo.it), is served by buses from Avezzano, Naples and – in summer only – Rome itself.

193 Šutka is 30min by bus from central Skopje. Alternatively, it's only MKD100 by taxi. For general information, see Ⓦexploringmacedonia.com.

194 Mljet is reachable by catamaran from Dubrovnik, or by car ferry from Prapratno, on the Pelješac peninsula (a one-hour drive from Dubrovnik). Renting a car is highly recommended.

195 The Duomo is on Via Duomo, a 10min walk from the city's main train station.

196 To arrange a stay at *Butterfly Valley*, see Ⓦyeni-kelebeklervadisi.org, or simply take your chances and turn up on one of the five daily boats.

197 See Ⓦuffizi.com.

198 *Tri Volta*, *Ghetto* and *Puls* are officially only open until midnight, but sometimes serve later.

199 The top-name fashion stores are concentrated in the "Quadrilatero d'Oro" or "Golden Quadrilateral". *Bar Martini* is at Corso Venezia 15 (Ⓦdolcegabbana.com/martini); *Gucci Café* at Piazza della Signoria 10 (Ⓦguccimuseo.com); *Armani Caffé* at Via Manzoni 31 (Ⓦarmaniristorante.com); and *Just Cavalli Food* in Via della Spiga (Ⓦmilano.cavalliclub.com).

200 For a memorable night in Rhodes' Old Town, stay in a boutique hotel in a Crusader-era mansion, such as *Spirit of the Knights* (Ⓦrhodesluxuryhotel.com) or *Marco Polo Mansion* (Ⓦmarcopolomansion.gr).

201 Buses run regularly from the regional capital, Aosta. For more information, see Ⓦpngp.it.

202 Postojna can be accessed by bus or train from Ljubljana; see Ⓦpostojnska-jama.eu.

203 Bring a cushion as the stone seating can get uncomfortable. Each show runs for three days; see Ⓦshakespeareatcurium.com for more information.

204 From Sultanahmet take a tram to Karaköy then the Tünel funicular railway to the bottom of Independence Street; both close at around 9pm. Return to Sultanahmet by taxi after midnight.

205 Most buses between Split and Zagreb stop at the Plitvice Lakes. See Ⓦnp-plitvicka-jezera.hr/en.

206 Ⓦcomune.marinadigioiosaionica.rc.it has details on the area.

207 There are extremely popular midnight Mass celebrations on Crete, Ídhra, Corfu and Pátmos. Ferries and accommodation will be very busy; book well in advance if you want to spend Easter at Loutró.

208 Hrastovlje is best accessed by hire car or taxi. Entry can be arranged with Rozana Rihter; phone ☎+386 3143 2231.

209 To get from Ohrid town to the Albanian border, hop in a bus or shared taxi to Struga (30min), then take a 15km taxi ride to the border crossing.

210 For the current programme of tours of the Palazzo Farnese, visit Ⓦinventerrome.com.

211 Pompeii can be reached easily by train from Naples. See Ⓦpompeiisites.org for more information.

212 St Hilarion Castle (Ⓦcypnet.co.uk/ncyprus/city/kyrenia or Ⓦnorthcyprusonline.com) is open daily (April–Oct 9am–6.30pm; Nov–March 9am–3.30pm). Entry costs 9 TL.

213 Buses run regularly to Durres from Tirana, taking around an hour. See Ⓦbuscroatia.com for schedules.

214 Entry is free at the Mevlânâ Cultural Center (Ⓦmkm.gov.tr). Fly to Istanbul and take a 1hr 20min flight or 4hr 50min train to Konya – a good stop on the road to Cappadocia.

215 See Ⓦstoricocarnevaleivrea.it for more information.

216 Individual *vaporetto* tickets can be bought at most landing stages, or on board the boats, but you'd do better to buy a 24hr (€20) or 7-day (€60) pass; see Ⓦveneziaunica.it for full details. The sleek water-taxis are very expensive, but private boats can be rented through Ⓦbrussaisboat.com.

217 To reach Ischia from Naples airport, take a 30min bus or taxi journey to the port, then a 50min hydrofoil crossing. Most hotels are open April–Oct. For more details, visit Ⓦsanmontano.com or Ⓦnegombo.it.

218 *Mavi Dükkan* is located at Atatürk Caddesi No: 60 PK: 16170; open daily 11am–6.30pm; ☎+90 0224 221, Ⓦiskender.com.tr. Prices from TRY40(US$8)–TRY55(US$10), depending on portion size.

219 Valletta is on the east side of Malta, about 5km from Malta International Airport in the south; the X4 bus runs regularly between the two (see Ⓦmaltaairport.com).

220 The best map to use is Road Edition's no 31 *Olympos*, 1:50,000.

221 See Ⓦitalyheaven.co.uk/puglia/lecce.html.

222 Paestum, which is open daily, can be reached by bus from Naples and Salerno (Ⓦpaestumsites.it).

223 Istanbul's Kapali Çarşi (Ⓦkapali-carsi.istanbul) is open Mon–Sat 9am–7pm. Admission is free, and weekdays are quieter.

224 For more info, visit Ⓦamalfitouristoffice.it.

225 The tourist office in Ribčev Laz (see Ⓦbohinj.si), 20km from Mount Triglav, can offer advice.

226 The Buzet tourist office (Ⓦbuzet.hr) has details of the Buzetska Subotina festival. *Toklarija*, Sovinjsko Polje 11, ☎+385 52 663 031.

227 500 Vintage Tour offers a variety of self-drive car tours for independent travellers or escorted groups; Ⓦ500vintagetour.com.

228 *Hotel Danieli* is at Riva degli Schiavoni 4196; reservations at Ⓦdanieli.hotelinvenice.com.

229 *Anderground* is at Pariski 1a. Strahinjiča bana, Obilićev venac and Njegoševa ulica offer the greatest concentration of bars and cafés.

230 You'll need an entire day to explore Meteora (Ⓦmeteora-greece.com); the town of Kalampaka, 20min by bus, is the best bet for an overnight stay.

231 Fire-walking festivals take place towards the end of May in the villages of Langadas, Ayia Eleni, Meliki and Ayios Petros in northern Greece.

232 From Dorgali, allow 2–5 hours to explore the gorge (driving as far as S'Abba Arva); €5 entry includes helmet hire. Guides available from Dorgali tourist office (Ⓦenjoydorgali.it), or visit Ⓦgorropu.info. Wear hardy shoes with grip – the boulders can be slippery when wet. Jeep services for parts of the route available.

233 *Tamburini*, Via Caprarie 1 (Ⓦtamburini.com); *Café de Paris*, Piazza del Francia 1 (Ⓦcafedeparisbologna.it).

234 Malcesine can be reached by bus or ferry from most large towns on the lake. For cable car schedules, visit Ⓦfuniviedelbaldo.it, and for trekking information see Ⓦ360gardalife.com or Ⓦcai.it.

235 *Hostel Celica* is on Metelkova ulica (Ⓦhostelcelica.com).

236 For information on diving in Malta and Gozo, visit Ⓦvisitmalta.com/en/diving. Recommended schools include St Andrew's Divers Cove on Gozo (Ⓦgozodive.com), Planet Sea Scuba (Ⓦplanetseascuba.com), and Dive Systems (Ⓦdivesystemsmalta.com).

237 For information on Cappadocia, visit Ⓦhometurkey.com. Göreme and Ürgüp have regular bus connections to cities all over Turkey.

238 Delphi and its museum are open daily year-round. Visit Ⓦdiscovergreece.com or Ⓦwhc.unesco.org.

239 It won't cost you anything to walk around Tirana, but guided tours are available from local agency Albania Holidays (Ⓦalbania-holidays.com).

240 Epidavros is open daily. Plays are performed on Fri & Sat evenings June–Aug (Ⓦgreekfestival.gr/en).

241 For information on the Kirkpinar championships, visit Ⓦbit.ly/KırkpınarOilWrestling.

242 Buses run from Belgrade to Ravanica (see Ⓦbas.rs for schedules). Otherwise, a rental car is a better bet, although Kraljevo (200km south of Belgrade) and the nearby village of Ušće have useful bus links.

243 Ostia Antica (Ⓦostia-antica.org) is served by trains from Rome's Termini station (50min).

244 For information and tickets, contact the tourist offices at Taormina (Ⓦcomune.taormina.me.it).

245 To buy tickets, visit Ⓦcenacolovinciano.vivaticket.it.

246 The tunnel museum is 12km southwest of central Sarajevo at ul. Tuneli 1, Donji Kotorac. Tours are arranged by the tourist office (Ⓦsarajevo-tourism.com).

247 The Gruppo Guide Alpine (Ⓦguidecortina.com) offers guided day-trips, or you can stay at scenic mountain huts and go from one route to another.

248 For more info, go to Ⓦvisittuscany.com.

249 Rafting is available April–Sept; Tara Tours (Ⓦtara-grab.com) offers half-day and longer excursions.

250 Ⓦmuseivaticani.va sells Sistine Chapel tickets.

251 Kayak Montenegro (Ⓦkayakmontenegro.com) offers guided day-trips around the Bay of Kotor from Herceg Novi as well as rentals and tailored tours.

252 Metković is served by buses (1hr 20min) from Dubrovnik (see Ⓦbuscroatia.com). Family-run inns 3–4km north include both *Konoba Narona* (☎+385 20 687 555) and *Konoba Vrilo* in Prud (☎+385 20 687 139).

253 Top Ljubljana Foods (Ⓦtopljubljanafoods.com) offer food-themed walking tours of Ljubljana. For information on Slovenian wines, see Ⓦslovenia.info.

254 For more info on Malta's megalithic sites, visit Ⓦheritagemalta.org. The Fat Lady and other artefacts are in the National Museum of Archaeology, Valletta.

255 Information on tickets and other Biennale practicalities is available at Ⓦlabiennale.org.

256 Several buses depart from Skopje (2hr) each day, and Kosovo airport is served by regular flights. To reach Pejë/Peć or Deçan/Dečani from Pristina, take a bus (2hr 30min); to Gračanica/Graçanicë, take a taxi (10min).

257 Fly into Denizli, then take a bus or taxi (19km; 20min) to Pamukkale, staying in one of the small hotels at the foot of the terraces.

258 Mystras can be reached by bus from Spárti or Néos Mystrás, and is open daily (Ⓦwhc.unesco.org).

259 Arena di Verona Opera Festival runs June–September each year; Piazza Bra, Verona Ⓦarena.it/arena/en.

260 Dalyan's mud baths (Ⓦdalyanguide.co.uk/dalyan-mudbath.html) are open daily but only, with mixed bathing 11am–6pm. The pools can get busy in high season (roughly June–Aug), although there are quieter, outlying pools – ask your skipper.

FINLAND

Gulf of Bothnia

SWEDEN

Gulf of Finland

`264`
`296`

`270` `287`
`265`

ESTONIA

R U S S I A

Gulf of Riga

`279`
`263`

LATVIA

`262`
`272`
`283`

`291`

`277`

BALTIC SEA

`294`

LITHUANIA

`288`

RUSSIA

`297`

B E L A R U S

POLAND

`276`

GERMANY

`280`

`285`

`289`

U K R A I N E

`298`

CZECH REPUBLIC

`273`

`275` `292`

SLOVAKIA

`261` `290`
`282`
`286`

AUSTRIA

HUNGARY

`274`

`284`

MOLDOVA

SEA OF AZOV

SLOVENIA

R O M A N I A

CROATIA

`295`
`278`
`271`

BOSNIA-
HERZEGOVINA

SERBIA

`267` `269`

BLACK SEA

IONIAN SEA

MONTE-
NEGRO

KOSOVO

BULGARIA `281`

`266` `293` `268`

MACEDONIA
(F.Y.R.O.M.)
ALBANIA

GREECE

I T A L Y

T U R K E Y

EASTERN EUROPE
261–298

The countries of Eastern Europe – culturally complex, historically uncompromising and often spectacularly handsome – offer all manner of enduring travel experiences, from wallowing in the baths of Budapest to tracking wolves in the Carpathians and peeling back the centuries in Plovdiv. Vivacious cities like St Petersburg and Tallinn wear old-world glories with grace, while the upheavals of the twentieth century can be witnessed everywhere from Minsk to Auschwitz. It's a region where wooden churches and medieval castles share billing with Bulgarian vultures and Baltic missile bases, where horseriding might lead to an encounter with Dracula, and where the food is as hearty as the hospitality.

261 Scrubbing up in a Budapest bathhouse

HUNGARY It is ancient, peeling and smells of egg. My first impressions of Budapest's Király Baths, tucked away on a quiet backstreet to the west of the Danube, make it fairly clear that it is no standard pampering palace. Fluffy bathrobes and racks of glossy magazines are conspicuous by their absence. As I tentatively get undressed, I wonder whether coming here is a grave error. Ten minutes later I am convinced it is the greatest bathhouse in the city.

Budapest has dozens of thermal baths competing for the local and tourist forint, ranging from the ultra-modern pleasure dome to the stuck-in-time steam-house. Király falls into the latter category. People have been wallowing in the city's natural springs since Roman times, and Király dates back almost 500 years to the Ottoman era. Let me tell you now, there ain't no thermal bath like a sixteenth-century thermal bath.

Because first things first: it might be old, but it's clean. I reach the main space to find a deliciously warm octagonal pool beneath a medieval dome, its roof sprinkled with ventilation holes like a pepper pot. These tiny portholes provide the only natural light, creating a hazy, steamy environment that only adds to the sense of having stumbled into some sort of wellness netherworld.

Arranged around each side of the main pool are steam rooms and smaller baths – some of them fiercely hot, one of them yelpingly cold. Other people seem to be doing exactly as I am doing, namely dunking themselves in a succession of different baths for minutes at a time, lying back and gradually leaving the vertebrate world.

I'd paid a small extra sum on entry to receive a fifteen-minute massage. It is dispensed in a no-nonsense fashion in a small vestibule off the changing rooms and unknots me everywhere from my lower legs to my upper back. I return to the main pool afterwards in a kind of daze, then eventually prise myself back onto the Budapest streets, feeling glowingly clean and five years younger. Historical attractions don't come much more enjoyable than this.

Ben Lerwill
is an award-winning freelance travel writer based in Oxfordshire, England. His writing has appeared in more than fifty national and international titles, from *National Geographic Traveller* to *The Sunday Times*. He enjoys little-known destinations and owns far too many pens.

262

Taking a trip on the Moscow metro

RUSSIA After a few vodkas it's not unusual to hear a Russian raconteur utter two English phrases learned in a standard Soviet childhood. One concerns friendship between nations, the other, that the Moscow metro is the greatest in the world.

This second assertion isn't far from the truth. The Moscow metro was designed as an eighth wonder of the world, a great egalitarian art gallery for the proletariat, combining utility and beauty as it ferried workers around the city, beguiled them with sculpture and chandeliers, and indoctrinated them with Soviet propaganda. Even now it's hard not to believe, just a little bit, in the Soviet dream when you step out of a clean, quick underground train into the fabulously ornate stations. That's why it's easy to spot the tourists. Hard-bitten Muscovites rarely raise their eyes from their hurrying feet.

With twelve lines and over 170 stations, the problem is where to start exploring. The *Koltsevaya*, or ring, is the most distinctive and navigable metro line. Built in the 1950s, its twelve stops include

some of the finest stations, and as it's a circular line, it's hard to get lost. Park Kultury was the first station to be built on the line, and is decorated with bas-reliefs of workers enjoying sports and dancing. Travelling anticlockwise, you come to pretty, white and sky-blue Taganskaya, which is a mere prelude to Komsomolskaya, one of the most awesome stations on the whole system. Komsomolskaya connects to railway terminals for St Petersburg and Siberia, and the vast chandeliers suspended from the Baroque ceiling are designed to impress.

Novoslobodskaya is the loveliest station of all. In the light of its jewel-bright stained-glass panels, even infamously surly Muscovites seem to smile and, recalling those English phrases, you may even start believing in friendship between nations. Which takes us neatly to Kievskaya, adorned with mosaic depictions of historical events uniting Russia and Ukraine, and the last stop on your circular journey.

263 | Eccentric architecture: wandering the streets of Rīga

LATVIA Walking along Alberta iela in Rīga is a bit like visiting an abandoned film studio where a biblical epic, a gothic gore-fest and a children's fairy tale were being filmed at the same time. Imperious stone sphinxes stand guard outside no. 2, while malevolent gape-mouthed satyrs gaze down from the facade across the street. Further down at no. 11, a grey apartment block with steep-pitched roofs and asymmetrical windows looks like an oversized farmhouse squatted by a community of Transylvanian counts.

Alberta iela is the most spectacular street in a city that is famous for its eccentric buildings – products of a pre-World War I construction boom that saw architects indulge in all manner of decorative obsessions. Most influential of the local architects was Mikhail Eisenstein, father of Soviet film director Sergei. Responsible for the sphinx-house at Alberta iela 2, Eisenstein filled his designs with Egyptian , Greek- and Roman-inspired details, producing buildings that looked like extravagantly iced cakes adorning the party-table of a deranged emperor. The most famous of his creations is just around the corner from Alberta iela at

Elizabetes 10, a blue and cream confection with a scarily huge pair of female heads staring impassively from the pediment.

An imprint of equal substance was left on the city by Latvian architect Eižens Laube, who brought the folk architecture of the Baltic country cottage to the city. The apartment block at Alberta iela 11 shows his trademark, with shingled roofs and soaring gables that produce a disconcerting half-breed born of gingerbread house and Gotham City. Something of an architectural equivalent to the Brothers Grimm, Laube's creations add a compellingly moody character to the bustling boulevards of Rīga's main shopping and business districts.

Rīga's Art Nouveau-period apartment blocks seem all the more incongruous when you consider that they were built to house the stolid middle-class citizens of a down-to-earth mercantile city. Judging by the sheer number of stuccoed sprites, mythical animals and come-hither mermaids staring out from the city's facades, psychoanalysts would have had a field day analyzing the architectural tastes of Rīga's pre-World War I bourgeoisie.

264 | St Petersburg's wild White Nights

RUSSIA Imagine spending all day sightseeing, taking a shower and a restorative nap, and then looking out of the window to see the sky as bright as midday. Your body kicks into overdrive, and the whole day seems to lie ahead of you. The streets throng with people toting guitars and bottles of champagne or vodka; naval cadets and their girlfriends walking arm in arm, and pensioners performing impromptu tea-dances on the riverbank. The smell of black tobacco mingles with the perfume of lilac in parks full of sunbathers. It's eight o'clock in the evening, and St Petersburg is gearing up for another of its White Nights.

Freezing cold and dark for three months of the year, St Petersburg enjoys six weeks of sweltering heat when the sun barely dips below the horizon – its famous *Byele Nochy*, or White Nights. Children are banished to *dachas* in the countryside with grandparents, leaving parents free to enjoy themselves. Life becomes a sequence of

tsusovki (gatherings), as people encounter long-lost friends strolling on Nevsky prospekt or feasting in the Summer Garden at midnight.

To avoid disrupting the daytime flow of traffic, the city's bridges are raised from 2am onwards to allow a stream of ships to sail upriver into Russia's vast interior. Although normally not a spectacle, during White Nights everyone converges on the River Neva embankments to watch, while bottles are passed from person to person, and strangers join impromptu singsongs around anyone with a guitar or harmonium – chorusing folk ballads or "thieves' songs" from the Gulag. Those with money often rent a boat to cruise the city's canals.

The bridges are briefly lowered during the middle of the night, allowing queues of traffic fifteen minutes to race across. Keeping in lane is entirely ignored, with drivers jockeying for position as if it was a chariot race. By this time, people are stripping off and jumping into the Neva – those too prodigiously drunk to realize go swimming fully clothed.

265 | Discovering the medieval and modern marvels of Tallinn

ESTONIA Medieval yet modern, the intriguing capital of Estonia combines a picturesque old town with first-class museums, hip neighbourhoods, stylish bars and a burgeoning food scene.

Tallinn's UNESCO-listed Old Town is crammed with churches, towers and Hanseatic houses – but it's the Russian Orthodox Alexander Nevsky Cathedral that is the city's most interesting landmark. Over-the-top ornate, Nevsky is a reminder of the city's turbulent time in the Soviet Union.

Northwest from here, the hipsters' enclave of Kalamaja makes a welcome change from the souvenir shops inside the old city walls. The focal point among the disused railway tracks here is Telliskivi Loomelinnak, a "creative city" of former factories that now houses entrepreneurial start-ups, workshops, theatres and funky cafés.

The Old Town isn't short of characterful hotels either, but it's worth taking the opportunity to spend the night in a medieval merchants'

house. Or three. *The Three Sisters* hotel occupies a trio of sloping fourteenth-century warehouses and carefully combines modern decor with period features, such as exposed brickwork and ceiling frescoes.

Outside the Old Town, Tallinn's striking art museum, KUMU, is well worth a visit. It occupies a starkly modern curving block of limestone set on a bluff in Kadriorg Park. Four floors of exhibits trace the history of Estonian art from the eighteenth century to 1991, with surrealism and pop art gaining a stronger hold as the country approached independence.

And forget what you think you know about Baltic cuisine, the entire region is undergoing something of a foodie renaissance. Tallinn's *Restoran Ö* is leading the way – it's pronounced "Eugh", though the food is anything but. In a dining room done up with a forest-foraged feel, tuck into a nine-course Taste Exploration that takes in elk from Saaremaa, blackened garlic and smoked beetroot dust.

Cavorting
with the kukeri

BULGARIA When it comes to the rich folk heritage of Eastern Europe, few events carry the visceral punch of Bulgaria's annual *kukeri* processions. In archaic rites dating back to pre-Christian times, men gather to scare off the evil spirits of winter by donning shaggy animal disguises and dancing themselves into a state of exhaustion. Colourful and cacophonous, these celebrations are a world away from the sanitized folklore shows of the resorts, and are of enormous ritual significance for those who take part.

The rites are still enacted in the villages south of the Bulgarian capital Sofia, and are easy to catch if you know when and where to go. Late January is the big date in the Pernik region, where each village has a troupe of *kukeri* or "mummers", charged with cleansing the community of evil and ensuring fertility in the coming year. Costumes differ from one place to the next, although they invariably feature grotesque masks resembling demons or wild beasts. Most *kukeri* wear cowbells around their waists, throwing up a clanking wall of sound once they start jumping and gyrating around the streets. The processions can take all day to weave their way through their home villages, with participants stopping off for a round of home-brewed brandies and festive cakes in the households they bless en route.

Outsiders are welcome – although to ensure the goodwill of the *kukeri* you may have to offer sweets or small coins to the masked urchins who guard the entrance to each village. Some of the most compelling celebrations take place in the former uranium-mining village of Eleshnitsa on Easter Sunday. Dancers clad in huge sheepskin headdresses strut their way around the village square, with a thunder-like rumble of drum beats echoing off the surrounding buildings. Thousands of locals attend; you'll find it hard not to be drawn into the round of folk dancing that follows.

267 | Fiddles and flutes: Romani music in Clejani

ROMANIA You could be forgiven for wondering why on earth anyone would want to board a *personal* (read: cold, grubby and slow) train in Romania, let alone stop at the tiny *halta* that is Vadu Lat, some 40km southwest of Bucharest. A dreary 3km walk later – unless you're fortunate enough to be picked up by horse and cart, which is a strong possibility – you'll arrive at the village of Clejani, which would be the most insignificant place imaginable were it not for the fact that it is one of Romania's most famous music villages. Indeed, this is where the biggest and best Romani band in the land – Taraf de Haidouks – hail from, though there's next to no chance of seeing them here these days, so busy are they touring.

But don't let that stop you; the natives of Clejani are always happy to see the few travellers who venture this way, and groups of *lautari* (Romani musicians) – perhaps as many as seven or eight, variously armed with violins, flutes, trumpets, accordions and perhaps a double bass – will often gather before you. These musicians, nearly all of whom have been playing since they were young children, are seriously talented, their supercharged skills honed at weddings and funerals.

It's utterly joyous stuff – fiery, fast-paced and very, very loud – and you'll be hooked from the moment they launch into their frenetic, wildly improvised repertoires. It's traditional to repay the musicians with a few Lei, or better still, some beer – a small price to pay for what is effectively your own private concert.

While here, have a wander around the dusty streets. There's every chance that you'll be invited into someone's house – typically a crumbling, one-roomed abode – which will give you a sobering insight into Romani poverty. But despite – or perhaps even because of – the hardships, music is everything to the villagers, their very lifeblood. It's catching on, too – so popular is the Romani sound that the bigger names regularly play in venues around the world. Nothing, however, can beat experiencing it at source.

268 | Vulture-watching in the Madzharovo Nature Reserve

BULGARIA You are crouched in juniper bushes exuding the smell of gin when suddenly the wind shifts and a foul odour sweeps through the gorge. From their perch halfway up the cliffs, three vultures launch themselves onto the thermals before plunging into the thickets of *Salix* trees, emerging with their talons and beaks laden with rotting flesh. Refocusing your binoculars, you track them back to their nests, where they start to feed a ravenous brood of chicks.

Vulture-watching at Bulgaria's Madzharovo Nature Reserve isn't your standard ornithological experience. Vultures are ugly creatures that feed on carrion; their intestinal systems have evolved to handle any microbe nature can throw at them. The Arda Gorge is one of the few breeding grounds in Europe for Egyptian, griffon and black vultures; here twitchers can also spot eight kinds of falcons and nine kinds of woodpecker as well as black storks, bee-eaters, olive-tree warblers, and several species of bats.

All this wildlife is right on the doorstep of an ex-mining town of crumbling concrete low-rises – a juxtaposition of magnificent nature and man-made stagnation that's all too commonly seen in the Rhodope Mountains.

With its dense forests of pine and spruce, alpine meadows, crags and gorges, this is one of the wildest and most beautiful regions of Bulgaria. Travelling to the reserve through its villages, you're struck by the degrees of separation between its Christian and Pomak (Slav Muslim) inhabitants, with some villages exclusively one, others a mixture of both – signified by churches and mosques, miniskirts and veils.

With villages half-depopulated by the flight of able-bodied adults to richer nations of the European Union, and remaining subsistence farmers too poor to afford pesticides or herbicides, the land is as ecologically rich as it is economically blighted.

269 | In the footsteps of the Conducator

ROMANIA "Conducator" (Leader) and "Genius of the Carpathians" were just two of his self-styled titles. Utterly deluded he may have been, but Nicolae Ceauşescu was able to convey many of his strongest political messages through architecture, particularly in Bucharest, where you'll find some of the most haunting Communist-era structures anywhere in Europe. Returning from a visit to North Korea in the 1980s, Ceauşescu vowed to create "the first Socialist capital for the new Socialist man", declaring that it would be "a symbolic representation of the two decades of enlightenment we have just lived through". All nonsense, of course, but who would oppose such sentiments with the feared *Securitate*, or Secret Police, all around?

As large swathes of Bucharest's historical district were demolished, a whole new sector – the Centru Civic – was raised. In order to make way for this vast, concrete wasteland of high-density, utilitarian apartment blocks, several churches were uprooted and located elsewhere. The culmination of this project was the Palace of Parliament, more popularly known as the "Madman's House". The second-largest administrative building in the world, after the Pentagon, the figures are mind-boggling: 270m long and 240m wide, housing 1100 rooms and accommodating some 4500 chandeliers. So paranoid was Ceauşescu that he even had a nuclear bunker installed; a tour is not to be missed.

The many other manifestations of Ceauşescu's megalomania include the hulking Casa Radio, which the dictator had built to house his tomb, among other things – nothing so grand materialized, however, and his actual resting place ended up being a grubby little plot in a public cemetery on the outskirts. Out on the road to the airport, you'll pass the Casa Presei Libere ("Free House Press"), a Stalinist-like monstrosity in which the wheels of the state propaganda industry once turned relentlessly. If you crave more, then head out to the Balta Alba-Titan residential district in the eastern suburbs, conceived to provide homes for half a million people. A Communist paradise it was not, but the unremitting grimness is strangely compelling, offering both an insight into history and a perverse kind of nostalgia.

Beethoven in the Baltic: the seals of Malusi

270

ESTONIA Bobbing on a boat on the placid waters off Estonia's northern coast, you'll encounter a landscape of stunning bleakness and almost eerie quiet; the flat Baltic sea stretches to the horizon, peppered with 1500 islands that are nearly all uninhabited. Even in the knowledge that Malusi Island is a protected breeding ground, boasting around three hundred grey seals, the unnerving stillness means that spotting a sleek, dog-like face popping out of the water feels almost magical. And certainly the method used to attract the seals has its own surreal quality. An iPod incongruously blasts out jolly *leelo* folk tunes, catchy pop hits and classical masterpieces into the silence, echoing the days when, as far back as the nineteenth century, these curious critters would follow the boats of violin-playing sailors. Even more surprising perhaps is the seals' sophisticated musical taste – it seems living in such dramatic surroundings fosters a penchant for Beethoven.

On the Dracula trail in Transylvania

ROMANIA Few figures capture the imagination as dramatically as Dracula, the bloodthirsty vampire count from deepest, darkest Transylvania – at least that's how Bram Stoker portrayed the mythical version in his 1897 novel. The real Dracula was in fact the fifteenth-century Wallachian prince Vlad Țepeș, better known as Vlad the Impaler. Although he was never accused of vampirism, his methods of execution – spread-eagled victims were bound and a stake hammered up their rectum, then raised aloft and left to die in agony – earned him a certain notoriety, especially among his long-time adversaries, the anti-crusading Turks, who were terrified of him.

Inevitably the legend of Dracula is touted for all its worth, but finding anything meaningful associated with Vlad is tricky. Aside from his birthplace in the delightful town of Sighișoara – now a high-class if kitschy restaurant – the most played-up Dracula connection is in the small southern Transylvanian town of Bran.

Looking every inch like a vampire count's residence, the splendidly sited Bran Castle is hyped as Dracula's haunt and encompassed by an army of souvenir stalls flogging vampire tack. The more mundane reality, however, is that Vlad may have laid siege to it once.

Dracula's real castle lies in the foothills of the stunning Făgăraș mountains in northern Wallachia. Located just north of the village of Arefu, a steep hillside path – an exacting climb up 1400 steps – brings you to Poienari Castle, one of Vlad's key fortresses and where, allegedly, his wife flung herself out of a window, exclaiming that she "would rather have her body rot and be eaten by the fish of the Arges" than be captured by the Turks. Aside from some reasonably intact towers, this surprisingly small citadel is now little more than a jumble of ruins. However, its dramatic setting ensures an authentically spooky atmosphere, no doubt the sort that Bram Stoker had in mind when penning his masterpiece about the ultimate horror icon.

272 | Soviet exhibitionism in Moscow

RUSSIA For a taste of all the Soviet Union once promised and an illustration of what it has come to, there's nowhere better than the all-Russian Exhibition Centre, known by its acronym VDNKh. This enormous park in northeast Moscow is a glorious illustration of Soviet hubris, an exuberant cultural mix 'n' match vision of a world where sixteen republics join hand in socialist hand to present a cornucopia of human achievement, ranging from agricultural tools and farm animals to atomic energy.

Opened in 1939 as the All-Union Agricultural Exhibition, the grounds were extended in the 1950s to include culture, science and technology, and continued to expand until 1989. Nevertheless, the overall atmosphere is of prewar optimism, when all progress was good and man was master of the world, living in a kind of mechanized agricultural paradise where even the streetlights were shaped like ears of corn.

Set around the gaudy gold fountain of the Friendship of Nations, pavilions for the former Soviet socialist republics and areas of economic achievement make a gesture towards national building styles while remaining unmistakably Stalinist. Particularly striking are the Ukraine Pavilion, a sparkling mosaic and majolica jewelbox; the Uzbekistan Pavilion, patterned with interlocking geometric designs; and the stylish, Art Deco-influenced Grain Pavilion. Beyond, a copy of the rocket which took Yuri Gagarin into space points skywards in front of the Aerospace Pavilion. Built in 1966, the pavilion's railway-station-like hangar and glass dome are still breathtaking in their vastness.

It's a little disappointing to find the working models of hydroelectric power stations and the herds of prize cattle long gone. Happily, the famous Soviet worker and collective farm girl monument that vanished in 2003, amid rumours that it had been melted down for scrap metal, returned, restored, atop a new pavilion in 2009. The casual traders and cheap beer stands that now fill VDNKh lend the place a certain raffish charm – or at least a succinct image of today's Russia: rows of salesmen from the Caucasus selling everything from Belarusian bras to cheap Chinese trainers under the Aerospace Pavilion's unlit light bulbs.

273 | Sipping a real Bud in České Budějovice

CZECH REPUBLIC The best Czech pubs are straightforward places: tables, benches, beer mats and an endless supply of lager. And there are few more atmospheric venues for drinking the stuff in than *Masné kramy*, housed in a complex of medieval butchers' stalls in the southern Bohemian town of České Budějovice (Budweis in German).

Walk into the long central hall, sit down and place a beer mat in front of you. Soon enough a waiter will walk round with a large tray of frothing beer mugs and slap one down on your table. As you near the end of the glass, before you've even begun to worry about catching the waiter's eye, you'll have been served another. At which point it becomes clear why the Czechs don't go in for pub crawls. With table service the norm, you need serious strength of will (and a clear head) to get up and leave. Little surprise, then, that the Czechs top the world beer consumption league, downing approximately a pint a day for every man, woman and child in the country.

There's another reason why *Masné kramy* is a great place in which to quaff the amber nectar – they serve Budvar, produced by the only major Czech brewery not owned by a multinational. Instead, the brewery still belongs to the Czech state, primarily to stave off a takeover bid by Anheuser-Busch, the world's largest beer producer, responsible for the hugely inferior American Budweiser, or Bud as it's universally known. Litigation over the shared name has been going on for nearly a century, and looks set to continue well into the future. For the moment, however, Budvar is in safe hands and continues to be brewed according to traditional techniques. So enjoy the taste – smooth, somewhat hoppy, slightly bitter and with an undercurrent of vanilla – while the going's good.

274 | Get beyond goulash at the foodie fests

HUNGARY Forget what you might have heard about bland Eastern European food. Hungary, perhaps more than any other nation in this part of the world, can champion numerous culinary delights. Sure, you know all about goulash and paprika, but it's a fair bet that you haven't heard of *meggyleves* (sour cherry soup), *gesztenyepüré* (chestnut purée) or *flódni*, a delicious, sweet layered pastry.

Where better to tantalize your tastebuds than at one of the country's burgeoning food festivals? Budapest, inevitably, claims the highest-profile events. Top billing goes perhaps to the very porky Mangalica Festival, which not only celebrates the indigenous – and frankly, rather peculiar-looking – curly-haired hog from which it takes its name, but also offers an array of artisan breads, cheeses and chocolates to chow down on. The most enjoyable foodie fests, however, are out in the countryside, and these typically have some form of musical accompaniment too. The most traditional gatherings are the Szolnok Goulash Festival, with hundreds of steaming pots of the national dish, and the Békéscsaba Sausage Festival, where chefs compete to cultivate their own variety of the spicy local banger. Hungary may be landlocked, but the wet stuff (strictly river fish, of course) gets a look-in, too, courtesy of the Tisza Fish Festival, where professional and amateur chefs do battle among a phalanx of bubbling cauldrons.

Even the onion claims a festival all to itself, in the small town of Makó (which, incidentally, is the birthplace of Joszef Pulitzer). Garlic is Makó's second main commodity – so it goes without saying that this event is a particularly pungent affair. Meanwhile, the Horseradish Festival, in the tiny Uplands village of Ujleta, pays homage to the indigenous Eastern European plant, with amateur cooks competing for the esteemed title "Master of the Root".

Of course, no gastronomic gathering could be complete without an alcoholic accompaniment. Perhaps best for a tipple is Budapest's Palinka and Sausage Festival, where for every tasty sausage that tempts you there's an equally delicious spiky fruit brandy to wash it down.

275

Hiking in the Tatras

POLAND The country's traditional attractions – Warsaw's lively old town and Kraków's gorgeous squares – are worthwhile stops, but it's easy to forget that there is another Poland, a genuine wilderness of high (and often snowbound) peaks, populated by lynx and bears. The Tatras Mountains are as beautiful as any national park in Europe, and their numerous trails – from vertiginous ridge-walks to forested rambles – are enormously popular with the locals, who troop here in their thousands in summer. The hamlet of Kuźnice, just south of the resort of Zakopane, has a cable car that climbs to almost 2000m above sea level (it feels a lot higher); from here, the very heart of the Tatras, marked trails for walkers of all abilities pick their way among the pinnacles.

BELARUS For the Belarusians, World War II was a catastrophe. In all, during the brutal three-year Nazi occupation of the then Soviet republic, almost a quarter of the population died – a tragedy that has left a profound imprint on succeeding generations.

Nowhere does the nation's sense of grief retain a greater rawness than at the colossal war memorial, constructed with typical Soviet bombast, at Brest Fortress, close to the Polish border. In 1941, as today, Brest stood on a political and ideological fault line between East and West, a front-line German target during the terrifying opening assault of Operation Barbarossa. The bravery of the Soviet counter-attack became a heroic symbol of resistance for a beleaguered nation, despite the reality that the defence proved short-lived and futile, merely delaying the inevitable descent into barbarism.

It's a sombre half-hour trudge along a broad, empty boulevard out to the fortress complex on the edge of town, the eye drawn towards the monumental concrete slab carved with a giant Communist star at the entrance. As you pass through, radio broadcasts, Soviet songs and the thunder of artillery ring through the tunnel. Once inside, remains of the original fortress – much of it shelled to oblivion – are sparse.

Instead it's a massive icon of Socialist Realist art that dominates the tableau: carved into another gigantic concrete block is the head of a huge, grim-faced soldier, jutting muscular jaw set in defiance. It's a staggeringly powerful piece of work, lent added poignancy by the eternal flame that burns beneath, and the neat tiers of memorials that lead up to it, many garlanded in beautiful wreaths. A haunting choral rendition of Schumann's *Träumerei* plays on a permanent loop.

Elsewhere, it might be tempting to dismiss this oversized monumentalism as a piece of Soviet kitsch. But here, where the scars of tragedy are never deep below the surface, it's impossible not to be bowed into mournful silence.

277 | Pondering Armageddon at the Plokštine missile base

LITHUANIA It's not often you're invited to join a guided tour of a nuclear missile base, especially when you're in the middle of one of northeastern Europe's most idyllic areas of unspoilt wilderness. However, this is exactly what's on offer at the friendly tourist information centre at Plateliai, the rustic, timber-built village in the centre of western Lithuania's Zemaitija National Park.

Long popular with a happy-go-lucky bunch of Lithuanian hostellers, campers and canoeists, the park is famous for its emblematic Baltic landscape. Calm grey lakes are fringed by squelchy bogs, forests of silver birch and intricately carved wooden crosses which sprout from farmhouse gardens like totem poles. It's perversely appropriate that Soviet military planners chose this tranquil spot as the perfect place to hide a rocket base. Located at the end of a harmless-looking gravel track, the Plokštine base is virtually invisible at ground level, its low-lying domes blending sympathetically with the local landscape of stubby coniferous shrubs. There's no front door: an innocuous-looking metal panel opens to reveal a staircase, descending into an abandoned world of concrete-floored, metal-doored rooms, linked by passageways which bring to mind the galleries of an underground cave system.

Built in 1962, the installation at Plokštine was one of the first such sites in the then Soviet Union, housing four nuclear missiles capable of hitting targets throughout western and southern Europe. Closed down in 1978 and left to rot, it's now eerily empty of any signs, panels or technical equipment that would indicate its previous purpose.

Until, that is, you come to one of the silos themselves – a vast, metal-lined cylindrical pit deep enough to accommodate 22m of slender, warhead-tipped rocket. The missile itself was evacuated long ago, but peering into the abyss from the maintenance gallery can still be a heart-stopping experience. Especially when you consider that similar silos, from North America to North Korea, are still very much in working order.

278 | Riding horseback through snow in Transylvania

ROMANIA The track to the Centrul de Echitaţie takes a sharp left off the road leaving Poiana Brasov, Romania's popular ski resort in the southern Carpathian mountains. The transformation is dramatic: the noise and bustle of skis, ski-lifts and open-air cafés dies away, and suddenly you're in the rural hinterland, where horses are still crucial to agrarian life. The world of salopettes and goggles is replaced by one of stables and deep forests; fresh snow coats the tiered fields, from which just a few hardy stalks peek up, casting tiny blue shadows against the white.

The Centrul de Echitaţie is a family-run horse centre whose farm buildings huddle in the shelter of pine trees and firs. It may seem deserted, but after a few knocks at reception you'll be greeted by a member of the brood with whom you can discuss what kind of ride you'd like – either on horseback or a horse-drawn sleigh. Go for the former and you'll be led by one of the boys to the stables and then out into the glistening fields.

Sure-footed and warm, the horse gives a reassuring rhythm to the journey, and your guide will make regular checks that everything's OK. The hush that snow brings makes everything feel closer and more still; the silence only broken by the horse's breath and the crunch of hooves in snow. This relaxed, unhurried pace takes you deeper into clumps of forest – where frost sparkles on branches already weighed down by snow – and beyond onto open hillsides. As long shadows stretch out, and as the wind whips up, you'll be ready to turn back, at peace with the world and looking forward to a warming mug of hot wine.

279 | Exploring Riga's bohemian quarter

LATVIA While most visitors to Riga head straight for the architecture of the Art Nouveau district, northwest of here Miera Iela is emerging as the city's coolest quarter.

A former industrial hub of champagne and tobacco factories – only the Laima chocolate factory remains – Miera Iela has been transformed into an enclave of vintage stores, art galleries, cafés and bars. Peace Street, as it's also known, is home to Riga's creative set, with local writers and painters drawn to its bohemian vibe. It's a tranquil respite from the city centre, and well worth whiling a few hours away in.

The cobblestoned street is lined with quirky cafés and coffee shops, incuding the cosy *Mierā*, filled with potted plants and piles of old books. Excellent waffles, home-made cakes, chocolate truffles and flaky pastries are some of the items on the menu here. For an artisan coffee, *Rocket Bean Roastery* is helmed by expert baristas who are happy to share their extensive knowledge with patrons.

An eclectic array of boutique shops and antiques stores is great for a browse. The vintage design store 20. gadsimts is packed with a curated collection of restored antiques and hand-picked clothes from the 1950s and 1970s. Buteljons is a sustainable art and homeware boutique with an excellent selection of handmade mugs, glasses and decorative items, all produced using recycled wine, spirits and beer bottles.

A wave of surprising concept stores and hybrid shops are also cropping up across the area – a hairdresser moonlighting as a bookstore, a florist doubling up as a café with a focus on herbal teas.

Come evening, a young crowd flock to Miera Iela's moody bars and alternative music venues. Locally brewed Latvian beer, some infused with the likes of caraway or lingonberry, can be sampled at *Valmiermuiža Beer Embassy* and *Labietis*, while the home-made apple wine is popular at *Taka*, a dive bar with alternative classic and obscure indie music.

280 | The great escape

POLAND At first sight the area of pine forest stretching south of Żagań betrays few signs of the iconic place it occupies in popular culture. Yet this tranquil corner of western Poland was once home to an archipelago of German prisoner-of-war camps, most famous of which was Stalag Luft III. Built to intern escape-obsessed Allied airmen, the camp went on to inspire two of the best-loved tunnel-digging movies ever made.

The first of these films was *The Wooden Horse* (1950), a true story of how a group of plucky prisoners used a vaulting horse as a cover for their tunnelling activities. This was eclipsed in 1963 by *The Great Escape*, the all-star, epic retelling of a mass break-out that occurred in March 1944.

A museum at the edge of the forest recalls the history of the camps in disarmingly understated style, focusing on the fates of all of Żagań's POWs rather than the heroics of the few. Devotees of *The Great Escape* may be disappointed by the absence of any pictures of Steve McQueen attempting to cross the Swiss border on a motorcycle – but McQueen's character was in fact invented by Hollywood scriptwriters to increase American interest in the story.

The real-life Great Escape was masterminded by RAF Squadron Leader Roger Bushell, who aimed to get hundreds of prisoners out of the camp via three tunnels codenamed Tom, Dick and Harry. The first two were discovered by the Germans, but on the night of March 24, 1944, a total of 76 prisoners made their way out of Harry and into the surrounding woods.

The site of Harry is marked by an engraved boulder a half-hour's walk from the museum. It's a popular spot for laying wreaths and to reflect: only three of the great escapees ever reached the UK; of those recaptured, fifty were executed by the Germans to serve as an example to other prisoners.

281 | High on a hill with a lonely goatherd

BULGARIA Most people tend to use an alarm clock, but in rural Bulgaria you can rely on the goats to get you out of bed. In the east Bulgarian village of Zheravna, an age-old Balkan ritual is enacted daily between 6 and 7am, when the local goatherd takes the beasts to pasture, collecting them one by one from the individual households where they spend the night. Bells are clanging raucously as they pass, making for a novel dawn chorus.

With tumbledown stone houses leaning over crooked cobbled alleyways, Zheravna is a perfect example of a village whose rustic character has remained largely unchanged since the nineteenth century. Goat farming is no longer the most lucrative of industries, however, and rural depopulation has all but emptied the place of its young. Nowadays, the renovation of old houses and the development of rustic B&Bs points to a tourist-friendly future.

Zheravna is far from being the only remote community whose combination of highland scenery, historic architecture and hos-pitable landladies has made it a crucial stop-off on any village-hopping itinerary. Lying at the end of a potholed mountain road in Bulgaria's rugged southwest, Kovachevitsa is a bewitching knot of half-timbered houses and full of no-frills accommodation: just don't expect to see "vacancy" signs hanging outside gateways or tourist offices taking reservations. This is a time-lost place where you may simply be staying with a local granny who has a double bed made up and ready. Breakfast will include locally made herbal teas, and yoghurt so healthy it could add years to your life.

There's not a great deal to do when you get here, although that is undoubtedly part of the attraction. Lolling around in wildflower-carpeted meadows and meditating in the middle of a pine forest are just two of the activities on offer. If stuck for ideas, you could always follow the goats, whose taste for invigorating air and gourmet grasses will lead you up into some exhilarating wilderness areas.

Hunting for bargains in Budapest

HUNGARY Since Eastern Europe's economic transformation, shopping is no longer a voyage into the unknown. Familiar international brands fill the malls, and local crafts lie hidden behind shelves of mass-produced souvenirs. Luckily, a parallel culture of flea markets and craft fairs is still going strong, and if you happen to be in Budapest over the weekend then there's no better city in which to indulge in a rummage.

Dedicated browsers should head first for the bustling Petőfi Csarnok flea market, held in the middle of the Városliget park. With traditional porcelain sold next door to pirate DVDs and hand-operated meat-mincers, it's a bit of a mixed bag. You'll usually turn up the odd bit of folk art if you prowl the stalls for long enough: the embroidered pillowcases here are certainly better quality than those in Budapest's central souvenir shops. Fans of hammers, sickles and furry hats may be disappointed to discover that there's not as much Communist-era memorabilia on display as there used

to be, although Red Army-issue gas-mask fetishists are unlikely to walk away empty-handed.

While it's the jewel-or-junk unpredictability of Petőfi Csarnok that makes it so enjoyable, serious seekers of collectables will want to head for the Ecseri antiques market on the city's southeastern fringes. A century or so of Budapest's domestic history stands piled up in the dense bazaar-like warren of stalls. If you haven't got room to stow a hat-stand in your luggage, there are plenty of smaller items that might appeal: china, cutlery, vintage postcards and piles of magazines from the 1920s and 1930s.

Those really serious about their shopping should time their visit to coincide with the WAMP design fair, an open-air market held at least monthly on the central Erzsébet tér, which features cutting-edge work by local designers. If you're looking for something that will bring out the individual in you, then the affordable accessories on display here should help do the trick.

283

Standing at the heart of Mother Russia

RUSSIA Stand in the middle of Moscow's Red Square, and in a 360-degree turn, the turbulent past and present of Russia is encapsulated in one fell swoop: flagships of Orthodox Christianity, Tsarist autocracy, Communist dictatorship and rampant consumerism confront each other before your eyes.

Red Square, is, well, red-ish, but its name actually derives from an old Russian word for "beautiful". It might no longer be undeniably so – its sometime bloody history has put paid to that – but it continues to be Moscow's main draw. In summer, postcard sellers jostle with photographers, keen to capture your image in front of one of the many iconic buildings; but in winter, you step back in time a few decades as Muscovites, in their ubiquitous shapki fur hats, negotiate their way through piles of snow, while the factory chimneys behind St Basil's Cathedral churn out copious amounts of smoke.

It's hard to avoid being drawn immediately to St Basil's, its magnificent Mr Whippy domes the fitting final resting place of the eponymous holy fool. Should retail, rather than spiritual, therapy, be more your bag, try GUM, the elegant nineteenth-century shopping arcade, which now houses mainly Western boutiques, way out of the pocket of the average Russian, but very decent for a spot of window-shopping or a coffee, or just to shelter from the elements outside.

If you think that the presence of Versace and other beacons of capitalism would have Lenin spinning in his grave, you can check for yourself at the mausoleum opposite, where his wax-like torso still lies in state. Despite the overthrow of Communism, surly guards are on hand to ensure proper respect is shown: no cameras or bags, no hands in pockets and certainly no laughing. Putin's police officers are never far away, casting a wary eye over it all – perhaps having learned a thing or two from Lenin's bedfellows and disciples (including Uncle Joe), who are lined up behind the mausoleum under the imposing walls of the Kremlin.

TRANSDNIESTR Following independence in 1991, the Republic of Moldova has sought to modernize and shake off the shackles of its Soviet past – all except for one small corner, the self-declared republic of Transnistria, where the spirit of the USSR still holds sway. Transnistria – literally, "the land beyond the Dniestr" – is a de facto independent state within Moldova, unrecognized by the UN, which harbours designs on becoming a region of Russia.

Despite tension and a frozen but technically ongoing war with Moldova, Transnistria is easily accessible from Chisinau. A two-hour bus ride will bring you over the border, where your passport will be checked thoroughly, to the towering and almost-deserted central bus station of the capital Tiraspol. From here, it's a short walk into the centre of town, where you'll find streets named after Communist heroes such as Rosa Luxemburg, statues and busts of Lenin still standing before brutalist government buildings, and an eternal flame burning for the heroes of the Great Patriotic War, with a Soviet tank standing guard nearby. Visit in the middle of winter, when snow coats the streets and buildings, and you'll be transported to a monochrome world which feels as if 1990 never rolled around.

But go soon – even here, in this last bastion of the Soviet world, the creeping influence of consumerism is being felt. Although international brands haven't arrived yet, outlets of Moldovan restaurants have opened, as has a genuinely helpful and informative tourist office; the Transnistrian KGB, meanwhile, was disbanded in 2017.

285 | Finding Mikhail Bulgakov in Kiev

UKRAINE Of the many authors who tried to dredge some meaning from the anguish and absurdity of life in the Soviet Union, few inspire as much devotion as Mikhail Bulgakov. Though he is best known for *The Master and Margarita*, a phantasmagorical journey through 1930s Moscow, his earlier novel *The White Guard* is a sweeping evocation of Kiev, the city of his birth – and if you're keen to get to grips with its complex history, stow this book in your backpack.

Set in the winter of 1918–19, the book describes a city at the mercy of German, Ukrainian-Nationalist and Bolshevik armies. Army doctor Bulgakov was himself caught up in the events described, and his street-level portrayal of Kiev could almost be used as a guide to the Ukrainian capital of today.

No streets were more vividly evoked by Bulgakov than Andriivskyi uzviz ("St Andrew's Descent"), the cobbled alley that zigzags steeply downhill from St Andrew's Church to the city's riverside quarter of Podil. Lined with nineteenth-century buildings, this charming relic of old Kiev is nowadays the part of the city that tourists want most to look around.

Halfway down the street is the Mikhail Bulgakov museum, occupying the house in which the writer lived from 1906 to 1919. It's also the house described in *The White Guard* as the home of Bulgakov's fictional alter ego Aleksei Turbin. Blurring fact and fiction in a way that would have surely appealed to the author himself, the display sets Bulgakov's authentic possessions alongside the kind of personal effects that might have belonged to his characters. One of the rooms is entered via a wardrobe, as if to underline the fact that this is a museum of the imagination.

The museum is also deliciously disorientating in quite unintended ways. Exhibits are unlabelled, accompanying brochures are in Russian only, and even on the rare occasions when an English-speaking guide is on hand, you'll be abandoned in mid-explanation if a more important-looking group turns up for a tour. The man who wrote *The Master and Margarita* could not have wished for a more fitting tribute.

286 | Soothe your troubles at the Hotel Gellért

HUNGARY You might be impressed by the stately location of the *Hotel Gellért*, just over the "Liberty Bridge" on the western bank of the Danube, anchoring the old section of Buda. You might enjoy this picturesque scene especially after dark (and you'll certainly feel compelled to take pictures) on your way back across the bridge from a night out in Pest: the entire, rambling building, front-lit, glows like some giant Art Nouveau birthday cake at the base of craggy Gellért-hegy cliff.

You might be awed by the grand staircases leading from the lobby; charmed by the cosy, hideaway bar and its array of Hungarian liquors; spun around by the long corridors and various turns getting to and from your room (especially after a drink or two of Unicum at the aforementioned bar); satisfied by the size of the room – better still if it comes with a view of the river in front or hills behind. But none of this is by itself necessarily a reason to stay. There's a greater motivation for that.

Wake up early to find out, and pull on the robe that hangs in the closet. Go to the excruciatingly slow, caged elevator on your floor. Tip the lift operator as you reach the bottom, exit and pick your way through the milling crowd to see what they're all waiting for. Don't be embarrassed about your state of relative undress – soon you'll all be in the same boat. Then – behold the glory of the Gellért baths.

The grandeur of the vaulted entry hall, its tiling, statuary and skylit ceiling, is a worthy precursor to the pools themselves. First, the segregated areas: a dip in the 34°C waters, while admiring the magnificent mosaics and ornamental spouts; a sit-down in the aromatic sauna; a bracing splash in a tiny, freezing-cold bath; a plunge into another pool, this one 38°C... repeat the ritual again, then finish with some invigorating laps in the colonnaded central pool, the one place where the sexes intermingle. Consider doing the backstroke to enjoy best the light streaming through the retractable stained-glass roof above. And think about extending your stay another day or two.

Beavering away in Lahemaa National Park

287

ESTONIA Visitors to Lahemaa National Park, a 725-square-kilometre area of pastureland and wilderness that runs along Estonia's northern seaboard, are often frustrated by never setting eyes on the forest-roaming bears, moose and lynx that guidebooks promise. The best they can hope for is the fleeting glimpse of a deer or rabbit – hardly the thing of which travellers' tales are made. Beavers, however, are a different matter. Although they're just as elusive as many of their peers (you'd probably need infrared vision and the patience of Job to see one), evidence of them is everywhere.

You can venture into beaver-world along the Oandu beaver trail, a well-marked nature walk that begins on the eastern fringes of the park. Embracing dense forest, desolate bogs, coastal wetlands and archaic fishing villages, Lahemaa is the best possible introduction to this Baltic country's unspoilt rural character.

Leading through thick woodland, the trail crosses several streams where log-built dams and freshly gnawed tree trunks indicate the presence of a highly industrious animal. Beavers are the architects of the animal world, endlessly redesigning their environment until it meets their bark- and twig-munching requirements. The main mission of a beaver's life is to carve out a feeding area by felling trees, building a dam, and flooding an area of forest that other herbivores are loath to enter. Free of competition, it can then stuff its face with all the vegetal matter trapped in its semi-sunken realm.

These beaver-created landscapes can be found throughout the Baltic States. The Pedvale open-air sculpture park in Latvia even includes a "Mr Beaver" in its list of featured artists – a real-life furry prankster who mischievously flooded part of the grounds.

288

LITHUANIA Borscht (sour soup) comes in many forms, but arguably the most celebrated of these is Lithuanian cold borscht, or *šaltibarščiai*, the shocking-pink soup and refreshing summer staple of the Baltic States. The key ingredient is the noble beetroot, rich in vitamins and minerals, and an essential component of the North European diet. *Šaltibarščiai*'s other essentials are cucumber, a fistful of dill and lashings of sour cream. It is almost always served with boiled potatoes on the side.

To many Lithuanians a bowl brimming with the pink stuff is an essential and refreshing part of a summer's day, and you'll find it on the menu pretty much everywhere from fancy restaurants to functional canteens. It's the quintessential lunchtime choice: light, easy on the stomach and rarely slow to arrive at your table. First-timers might be put off by the soup's somewhat garish hue; it's best to just close your eyes and slurp.

Slurp Vilnius pink soup

289 | The tale and the tongue of St John of Nepomuk

CZECH REPUBLIC As you shuffle along with your fellow tourists round the chancel of Prague's main cathedral, there's not a lot to see beyond the remains of a few medieval Czech kings with unpronounceable names – Břetislav, Spytihněv, Bořivoj. That is, until you find your way virtually barred by a giant silver tomb, which looks for all the world as if it has been abandoned by a bunch of Baroque builders upon discovering it was too big to fit into one of the side chapels. Turning your attention to the tomb itself, you're faced with one of the most gobsmackingly kitsch mausoleums imaginable – sculpted in solid silver, with airborne angels holding up the heavy drapery of the baldachin. You notice the saint's rather fetching five-star sunburst halo, and, back to back with him, a cherub proudly pointing to a glass case. On closer inspection, you realize the case contains a severed tongue.

Jesuits were nothing if not theatrical, and here, in the tomb of their favourite martyr, St John of Nepomuk, the severed tongue adds that extra bit of macabre intrigue. Arrested, tortured and then thrown – bound and gagged – off the Charles Bridge, John was martyred in 1393 for refusing to divulge the secrets of the queen's confession to the king. A cluster of stars appeared above the spot where he was drowned – or so the story goes – and are depicted on all his statues, including the one on the Charles Bridge. The gruesome twist was added when the Jesuits had his corpse exhumed in 1715 and produced what they claimed was the martyr's tongue – alive and licking, so to speak – and stuck it in the glass case. Unfortunately, science had the last say, and in 1973 tests proved that the tongue was in fact part of his decomposed brain. Sadly, the object you now see on his tomb is a tongue-shaped replica.

290 | Golden mouldy: drinking Tokaj in ancient cellars

HUNGARY Eastern European wines receive few accolades. Apart from one, that is: the "wine of kings, the king of wines" was how Louis XVI described Tokaj, Hungary's most celebrated drink – indeed, so important is it to Hungarians that it's even cited in the national anthem.

Harvested among the rolling green hills of the Tokaj-Hegyalja region in northeast Hungary, the most famous variety of Tokaj is Aszú, a devilishly sweet dessert wine that owes its distinctive character to the region's volcanic loess soil and the prolonged sunlight that prevails here. More importantly, though, it's down to the winemaking techniques employed, whereby the grapes are left to become overripe, leading to botrytization – in layman's terms, decomposition (grandly termed the "noble rot"). This shrivels the grapes to raisin-sized proportions and gives them their concentrated sweetness.

Nothing beats a few hours in one of the cosy cellars lining Tokaj's narrow streets, the most venerable of which is the Rákóczi cellar, named after the seventeenth-century prince Ferenc Rákóczi. Reposed in eerily cobwebbed, chandelier-lit passages are thousands upon thousands of bottles of the region's choicest wines. No less esteemed is the cellar of the same name located in the town of Sárospatak; it was here that Rákóczi would come to smoke his pipe, indulge in his favourite tipple and plot the downfall of the Habsburgs. Hewn out by prisoners from the castle dungeons, the kilometre-long cellar, chock-full of handsome oak barrels, is thickly coated with *penész*, the "noble mould" – everything's noble where Tokaj is concerned – whose presence is integral to the wine's flavour. Whether quaffing this most regal of wines in the open air, down a cellar, or on a boat, the taste of Tokaj is something you won't forget in a hurry.

291 | Spend a night at the cells in Liepāja

LATVIA Being incarcerated in a foreign country is usually the stuff of holiday nightmares. Unless you want an insight into Latvian history, that is, in which case you're advised to buy tickets in advance.

The best place to book yourself in for a bit of rough treatment is the former naval prison in Karosta, the Russian-built port that stretches north from the seaside city of Liepāja. Built by the Tsarist Empire in the nineteenth century, Karosta subsequently served as a submarine base for the USSR, and is nowadays an enduring symbol of the half-century of Soviet occupation.

Formerly used as a punishment block for unruly sailors, the grim-looking red-brick prison is now the venue for an interactive performance/tour that involves such delights as being herded at gunpoint by actors dressed as Soviet prison guards, then interrogated in Russian by KGB officers. Dimly lit and decorated in floor-to-ceiling shades of black, the prison interior is enough

to dampen any hopes of resistance. Stay the night, of course, and things get even harder – you may well find yourself mopping the floors before bedding down in one of the bare cells, only to be brutally awoken by an early-morning call.

If the experience of being shouted at in Russian leaves you disoriented, then in a way that's the whole point: life for Latvians in the Soviet Union was a long slow process of humiliation administered by people who didn't bother to learn their language.

Once outside the prison walls, you will find that Karosta remains rich in historical resonances. A self-contained, Russian-speaking mini-city quite separate from the rest of Liepāja, it retains an onion-domed Orthodox cathedral and rows of grey housing blocks where former naval workers still live. Most poignant of all is the line of collapsing artillery bunkers behind the beach, mutely testifying to the decline of the empire that built them.

SLOVAKIA You have to see the task of finding the all-important *kl'úč* (key) as part of the experience when visiting the wooden churches of Slovakia's Carpathian foothills. Sure enough, there's nearly always a little sign (in Slovak) pinned to the wooden door, telling you which house harbours it, but finding the right one in a village without street names and only fairly random house numbers is a feat in itself. It's a sure way to get to meet the local head-scarved *babičky* (grannies), but don't expect to get to see too many churches in one day.

The churches look like something straight out of an East European fairy tale, or a Chagall painting: perched on slight hillocks by the edge of the woods, looking down on their villages, their dark-brown shingled exteriors sprouting a trio of onion domes. Most were built in the

eighteenth century when the influence of Baroque was making itself felt even among the carpenter architects of the Carpathians. Once inside, you can't help but be struck by the musty murkiness of the dark wooden interiors. At one end a vast and vibrantly decorated iconostasis reaches from the floor to the ceiling, its niches filled with saints. Elsewhere, a local folk artist allows his imagination to go wild in a gory depiction of the *Last Judgement*, with the damned being burned, boiled and decapitated with macabre abandon.

Despite the fact that the churches are often locked, they're still very much in use, mostly by the Greek Catholic Church. Should you happen upon one when there's a service, note that Mass is celebrated in Old Slavonic.

293 | Peeling back the centuries in Plovdiv

BULGARIA Plovdiv, Bulgaria's second city, is the oldest continually inhabited city in Europe. It's also one of the continent's brightest upcoming stars, and stands as a European Capital of Culture in 2019. As well as offering archeological treasures by the barrow-load, it is one of the most culturally vibrant places in southeastern Europe, with enough cultural festivals, arty neighbourhoods and cool bars to keep today's urban explorers more than happy.

Plovdiv Old Town offers arguably the best preserved collection of traditional architecture anywhere in southeastern Europe. If you want to know what Balkan towns looked like before the twentieth century, then this is the place to find out. It was here that Plovdiv's rich Bulgarian, Greek and Armenian merchants built large walled and gated houses, their overhanging upper storeys jutting out above narrow cobbled streets.

Furnished in an opulent mixture of eastern and western styles, many are now open to the public as museum houses. If you only have time for one of them, visit the ornate Kuyumdzhiev House, now home to the Ethnographic Museum.

Not every city has a Roman stadium bang in the middle of its main shopping street, and while only one end of Plovdiv's stadium is actually visible (the rest is still underground), it's still a pretty dramatic sight, with its curve of terraced seating sitting in a hollow beneath a busy pedestrian precinct. Recently relandscaped to form an attractive archeological park, it's the perfect place to start your stroll of discovery through Roman Plovdiv. A little way uphill, on the fringes of the Old Town, is Plovdiv's Roman theatre, a beautifully preserved amphitheatre that is still in use as a spectacular open-air performance venue. Roman streets and mosaics can still be seen in situ thanks to ongoing excavations around the forum, next to today's Central Post Office.

Right next to the centre but very much a self-contained world of its own, the Kapana district is where the old and new Plovdiv come so fruitfully together. Formerly the bazaar quarter, this tight web of cobbled streets still contains the kind of artisan studios and craft shops that characterize the Balkans of yore – alongside a thoroughly contemporary breed of café-bars, discos and clubs.

294 | Cycling the Curonian Spit

LITHUANIA It can come as a surprise to encounter vast sand dunes on the Curonian Spit, the delicate sliver of land that runs parallel to Lithuania's Baltic coast. The surprises don't end there. The rippling waves of sand along this giant sand bar snake their way towards dense spruce-and-pine forest, home to elk and wild boar, while the shore is studded with timeless fishing communities imbued with ancient traditions.

The best way to explore this time-lost region is to rent a bicycle in Nida, the largest village, and take the largely forested cycle path that winds its way to the bottom of the Spit. The whole path is 55km long, but the 30km stretch from Nida to the village of Juodkrantė offers a wonderful day's cycling.

Head south along the coastal road, pausing at the small graveyard beneath the pines. The carved wooden *krikštas* figures, still placed at the foot of graves today, are an enduring reminder of centuries-old pagan traditions. A tiny museum further down the road shows old photos of Nida fishermen biting the heads off crows – locals used to

eat crows in winter, the hungriest time of year – and trawling the shore waters for amber. People still find amber around here, particularly after storms. The path disappears into the forest to emerge after 5km at tiny Pervalka. Follow *žuvis* signs to a traditional smokery where you can snack on locally caught smoked fish, the most prized being the deliciously fatty *ungurys* (eel).

The path meanders to the west side of the Spit, and follows the coastline, where you can stop for a bracing dip, before a short uphill slog towards Juodkrantė. You will hear them, and smell them, before you see them: in spring and summer, the air is filled with the calls of black cormorants and grey herons whose nests cluster along the branches of the trees.

In Juodkrantė, abandon your bicycle and follow the Raganų Kalnas (Witches' Hill) trail into the forest. It's lined with enormous contemporary wooden carvings of mythological figures: from Neringa, the goddess who created the Spit, to grotesque and comic witches, devils and dwarfs.

Tracking carnivores in the Carpathian Mountains

ROMANIA Bloodthirsty vampires, howling werewolves and medieval hamlets lashed by vicious storms – welcome to the popular, and mostly mythical, image of Transylvania. This beautiful and ancient region (from the Latin for "Beyond the forest"), nestled in the breathtakingly dramatic horseshoe curve of the Carpathian Mountains, is the location for the greatest reservoir of large carnivore species outside Russia. It's home to Europe's biggest refuge for grey wolves, of which there are now an estimated 2500, while more than five thousand brown bears roam the wooded slopes. It's all a far cry from the time when Nicolae Ceaușescu, a fanatical hunter, offered bounties equivalent to half a month's salary to those who killed a wolf. Once the mad, megalomaniac president realized that Romanian bears were actually quite valuable, he afforded them protected status – albeit so that he could shoot them himself. Among the many fascinating wildlife programmes on offer in Romania, few are as popular or capture the imagination quite so much as wolf- and bear-tracking. The techniques to do this include following their prints in the soft mud or snow, sighting their droppings or looking out for telltale signs, which might include a flattened patch of grass where a bear has had an afternoon snooze, a log overturned in the frantic search for food, or a tree stump that has been scratched for ants.

Due to the vastness of the terrain and the highly elusive nature of wolves and bears, there's certainly no guarantee of a sighting, but it's the tantalizing prospect of a brief encounter that makes the exhaustive search so worthwhile.

RUSSIA The Hermitage's collections run the gamut of the ancient world and European art. Where else could you find Rubens, Matisse, prehistoric dope-smoking gear and the world's largest vase under one roof?

The museum occupies the Imperial Winter Palace and the Old and New Hermitages, added by successive tsars. To avoid the crowds, start by checking out the little-visited ancient Siberian artefacts. The permafrost preserved burial mounds that contained mummified humans and horses, even chariots, all discovered by Soviet archeologists 2500 years later. They even found a brazier encrusted with marijuana – Altai nomads used to inhale it inside miniature tents – which was still potent.

Next, luxuriate in the State Rooms, glittering with gold leaf and semi-precious stones. The Malachite Drawing Room has an underwater feel, awash with the eponymous green stone. On certain days, the English Peacock Clock spreads its bejewelled tail in the Pavilion Hall, whose decor fuses Islamic, Roman and Renaissance motifs. By this time the tour groups are thinking of lunch, making it a good time to investigate the art.

The adjacent Old and New Hermitages are stuffed with antiquities and artworks and it's difficult knowing where to turn. Old Masters are on the first floor – Botticelli, Van Dyck and twenty paintings by Rembrandt (including *Danaë*, restored after a deranged visitor slashed it in 1985) – plus works by Velázquez and Goya. If you prefer more modern art, be overwhelmed by Renoirs, Van Goghs and Gauguins – all "trophy art" taken from Nazi Germany in 1945.

The Post-Impressionist collection has a superb array of Matisses and Picassos, acquired by two Muscovite philanthropists in the 1900s. Matisse's *Music* and *Dance* were commissioned for his patron's mansion, whose owner feared that the nude flautist might offend guests, and painted out his genitals – which the Hermitage's experts have carefully restored.

Merely glancing at each item in the collection, it would still take nine years to see the whole lot. With not quite so much time on your hands, you may prefer to browse what you missed in one of the many catalogues, from the comfort of a nearby café.

297 | Getting to know Minsk

BELARUS A city of spacious avenues lined with grandiose 1940s and 1950s buildings, its immense parks studded with Socialist Realist monuments, Minsk is living testimony to the dreams and aspirations of the former Soviet Union. And yet beyond the marble of its metro, the soldiers frozen in heroic poses on plinths and the vast, uncompromising Soviet buildings, the capital of Europe's last dictatorship is a modern city, with a number of contemporary buildings, an abundance of theatres, concert halls and museums, and a dining scene that's becoming increasingly diverse.

The best way to get a feel for Minsk, in all its contradictions, is to walk a 3km stretch of the wide main thoroughfare, pr Nezalezhnastsi. Begin at pl Nezalezhnastsi (Independence Square), dominated by two astonishing examples of Stalinist architecture – the Government Building and the State University, menacingly overlooked by the KGB building, known to locals as "Amerikanka", where prisoners of conscience are held. Pass the small square Tsentralny Skver, where locals drink beer and play guitar and a tank monument commemorates

the Soviet soldiers who liberated Minsk from the Nazis in 1944. Further along, at pl Oktyabrskaya, stop by the Museum of the Great Patriotic War to appreciate the horrors inflicted by the Nazis on Belarusian Jews in World War II. A block's detour north leads you to pl Svabody (Freedom Square) where the seventeenth-century Baroque Orthodox Holy Spirit Cathedral is once again being used as a place of worship. Back on pr Nezalezhnastsi, cross the river and you reach pl Peramohi (Victory Square), where newlyweds gather by the 38m-high granite Victory Obelisk, commemorating the end of World War II.

After dark, it's worth catching a taxi north along Nezalezhnastsi to the opinion-dividing National Library, built in 2006 as the main information and cultural centre of Belarus. Illuminated at night, this remarkable rhombicuboctahedron, resembling an angular Death Star, is one of Minsk's most potent symbols. To end the day, head to flamboyant *Astara* for fragrant Azerbaijani grilled meats and a glimpse of local diplomats and film stars, and ponder at how this glitzy new wealth coexists so easily with the monumental Stalinist architecture beyond.

298 | Horrors of the Holocaust: visiting Auschwitz

POLAND One thing that will stick in your mind is the hair. Mousy, dark clumps of it and even a child's pigtail still wound like a piece of rope, all piled together like the relics from an ancient crypt. But there are no bones here. The hair in this room was deliberately, carefully, shaved from the heads of men, women and children, ready for transportation to factories where it would be turned into haircloth and socks. This is Auschwitz, the most notorious complex of extermination camps operated by the Nazis.

No one knows how many people died here: estimates range from 1.1 million to 1.6 million, mostly Jews. They starved to death, died of dysentery, were shot or beaten. And from 1941, the Final Solution, death by cyanide gas ("Zyklon-B"): 20,000 people could be gassed and cremated each day.

Auschwitz still has a chilling, raw atmosphere, as if the Nazis had simply walked away the day before. You'd think the gas chambers would be the worst place – imagining the ashy smoke billowing from the chimneys, and then inside, the agonizing struggles of the naked prisoners as the gas poisoned their blood.

But the horror of Auschwitz doesn't hit you at once, it spreads over you slowly, like an infection, so that the more you see, the sicker you feel, until you can't take any more. The camp video is loaded with images too horrible to take in: plastic-like bodies being bulldozed into pits, bags of bones with faces. It's a terrible place, full of terrible, haunting memories.

But everyone should go – so that no one will forget.

Need to know

261 Király Baths is open 9am–9pm to both sexes. You'll find it at Fő utca 84; Ⓦ en.kiralyfurdo.hu.

262 See Ⓦ mosmetro.ru for information about ticket prices and routes.

263 Alberta iela lies in the Centrs district of Rīga; see Ⓦ liveriga.com.

264 The White Nights last from June 11 to July 2. See Ⓦ saint-petersburg.com.

265 Check out *Restoran Ö* at Ⓦ restoran-o.ee/en; KUMU at Ⓦ kumu.ekm.ee/en and *The Three Sisters* at Ⓦ 3s.ee. For more information on Tallinn, check Ⓦ visittallinn.ee/eng.

266 The celebrations take place every Jan in villages including Yardzhilovtsi, Kosharevo and Banishte. The Sofia-based travel agent Lyuba Tours (Ⓦ lyuba.tours) can organize day-trips to see them. Many of Bulgaria's *kukeri* take part in the Festival of Masquerade Games (Ⓦ surva.org), usually held in Pernik every even-numbered year.

267 Trains run from Bucharest Basarab station to Vadu Lat (6 daily; 40min). For information on Taraf de Haidouks see Ⓦ facebook.com/TarafdeHaidouksOfficial.

268 From Plovdiv you can take a bus to the town of Haskovo to connect with the bus to Madzharovo. For more, see Ⓦ bulgariatravel.org and Ⓦ visitmybulgaria.com/haskovo.

269 To get to the Centru Civic, take the metro to Piata Unirii. Tours of the Palace of Parliament daily (10am–4pm, last tour 3.30pm; 25Lei; ☏ 021 311 3611; Ⓦ travelguideromania.com/palace-parliament).

270 Seal-watching trips last 2–3hr, which includes 1hr with the seals. See Ⓦ visitestonia.com for more details.

271 For Bran Castle, see Ⓦ bran-castle.com.

272 See Ⓦ vvcentre.ru.

273 České Budějovice (Ⓦ c-budejovice.cz) is 150km south of Prague, *Masné kramy* (Ⓦ masne-kramy.cz) is just off the old town square on Krajinská, and the brewery (Ⓦ budejovickybudvar.cz) is 2.5km north of the old town.

274 The Mangalica Festival (Ⓦ mangalicafesztival .hu) is held in Feb, the Palinka Festival at the start of Oct (Ⓦ palinkaeskolbasz.hu).

275 Zakopane is around 3hr by train or bus from Kraków. For more, check Ⓦ ezakopane.pl.

276 See Ⓦ brest-fortress.by.

277 Check out Ⓦ zemaitijosnp.lt for more.

278 The Centrul de Echitaţie (Ⓦ centrudeechitatie .ro) is about 2km down the road that leads from Poiana Brasov to Brasov.

279 For more information: Rocket Bean Roastery, (Ⓦ rocketbean.lv); 20.gadsimts (Ⓦ 20gs.lv); Valmiermuiža Beer Embassy (Ⓦ valmiermuiza.lv); Labietis (Ⓦ labietis.lv).

280 For more, see Ⓦ muzeum.zagan.pl.

281 See Ⓦ bulgariatravel.org and Ⓦ jeravna.com.

282 The flea market at Petőfi Csarnok (Sat & Sun 7am–5pm; Ⓦ bolhapiac.com) is in Városliget park; trolleybuses #70, #72 and #74 trundle past. Ecseri antiques market (Mon–Fri 10am–4pm, Sat 8am–3pm, Sun 9am–1pm; Ⓦ facebook.com/ecseribazar is in the southeastern suburbs. Dates for the WAMP design fair are posted on Ⓦ wamp.hu.

283 Red Square (Ⓦ whc.unesco.org) can be reached from Ploshchad Revolyutsii, Aleksandrovskiy Sad, Biblioteka Imeni Lenina and Borovitskaya metros.

284 Regular buses and marshrutkas serve Tiraspol from Chisinau's central bus station; Ⓦ getbybus. com/en/bus-from-chisinau.

285 The Bulgakov museum (Ⓦ bulgakov.org.ua) is at Andriivskyi uzviz 13.

286 *Hotel Gellért*, Szent Gellért tér, District XI, Budapest (Ⓦ danubiushotels.com/gellert).

287 Lahemaa National Park lies an hour's drive east of Tallinn. The park visitors' centre (Ⓦ lahemaa.ee) is in Palmse. See also Ⓦ visitestonia.com.

288 Almost all Vilnius cafés serve *šaltibarščiai*. For lunch with a bit of arty character try *ŠMC Kavinė*, a mildly bohemian joint in the Contemporary Art Centre at Vokiečių 2 (Ⓦ cac.lt/en).

289 For more information on St John, see Ⓦ prague. net/st-john-nepomuk. St Vitus Cathedral In Prague Castle is open daily. Charles Bridge can be visited at any time.

290 The Rákóczi cellar in Tokaj is at Kossuth tér 15 (Ⓦ tokajhetszolo.com/en); the cellar in Sárospatak is at Erzsébet utca tér 26.

291 If you don't fancy the interactive experience, you can take a simple guided tour of the prison. See Ⓦ karostascietums.lv.

292 The churches (Ⓦ whc.unesco.org) are scattered across a remote part of Slovakia – the best way to reach them is to hike or rent a bicycle.

293 For more information on Plovdiv see Ⓦ visitplovdiv.com/en.

294 Numerous passenger ferries from Klaipeda (Ⓦ keltas.lt) cross daily to Smiltynė on the Curonian Spit (15min). From Smiltynė, buses run hourly in peak season to Nida (1hr) via Juodkrantė; bicycles can be stowed in luggage compartments if there's enough room.

295 Check out Roving Romania (Ⓦ roving-romania .co.uk) for details of various wolf- and bear-tracking excursions.

296 The Hermitage (Ⓦ hermitagemuseum.org) is on Palace Square, near Nevsky Prospekt metro.

297 Most visitors to Belarus require a visa. Minsk National Airport (Ⓦ airport.by) sees flights from St Petersburg, Moscow, Prague, Warsaw, Frankfurt and Vienna. Minsk can also be reached by direct train from Vilnius or Moscow. *Astara* is at ul Pulikhova 37.

298 Auschwitz is named after the Polish town of Oświęcim, around 50km west of Kraków. Entry to the Auschwitz-Birkenau Museum & Memorial is free, though guided tours cost extra; see Ⓦ en.auschwitz.org .pl for full information.

NORTH AFRICA
299–327

Whether you're sipping tea in the sense-assaulting maze of a Tunisian medina or gazing out across the dune-filled infinity of the Sahara, bedding down in a troglodyte village or following in the footsteps of ascetic monks, it's hard not to fall under North Africa's spell. Mingling a variety of proud cultures, the region has become synonymous with vivid, authentic destinations and experiences, from ancient cities such as Fes and Kairouan to the natural sculptures of the White Desert, and from the remote dive sites of the Red Sea to the steam-fogged hammams of Marrakesh. To head off the tourist trail, you could road-trip through the remote Rif mountains, wander the UNESCO-listed core of Meknes or go meteor-hunting in the Sahara.

299 Camel trekking in the Sahara

TUNISIA I had to insist on having control of my own camel. Too many of these treks resemble a ride at the zoo with a minder walking alongside holding the bridle. Hamid saw the advantage, though. If I went solo, he could send one of his sons home and I'd stop moaning that Lawrence of Arabia drove his own beastie.

The Grinch and I have been companions for four days now. I call him Grinch because he's forever grumbling. Camels gripe a lot, a deep basso mutter whatever you ask them to do. When I enquired about his name, Hamid looked at me in surprise. Camels are for work. They don't have names any more than computers have names in my country. I must have seemed very twee. However, if I'm going to be rocking up and down on something's shoulders for seven days, I like to know whose they are.

The Grinch and I have come a long way since Douz, the trekking hub of the Sahara. We're averaging five hours a day, which is a lot of time up top if you sit "properly", ankles crossed round the hump. It's also a long time if your camel quickly deduces that you're a soft touch and that he can keep lunging down to nibble on any scrubby bit of plant that pokes up through the dunes. At first I was indulgent, but after a morning falling behind the main caravan, I toughened up. They say there are a thousand words for camel in Arabic – not all of them are pleasant.

Still, there is something wonderfully timeless about this kind of transport and a real thrill in knowing that the only way to reach our destination, the former Roman garrison of Ksar Ghilane, is on the back of The Grinch, or by far less romantic 4WD. Roads, such as they were, ran out days ago.

Best of all are the evenings sitting round the fire while Hamid's family cook, and more stars than I ever thought possible twinkle down at us.

Adrian Mourby
was a BBC producer before turning to writing and travelling full time. He has published four novels, two travel guides and a book of humour based on his award-winning BBC series *Whatever Happened To...?* In 2014 he was presented with the award for Best Travel Article in a Magazine by the Italian Tourist Board.

300
The pyramids of Giza

EGYPT The Pyramids at Giza were built at the very beginning of recorded human history, and for nearly five millennia they have stood on the edge of the desert plateau in magnificent communion with the sky.

Today they sit on the edge of the city, and it must be a strange experience indeed to look out of the windows of the nearby tower blocks to a view like this. The closest, the Great Pyramid, contains the tomb of Cheops, the Fourth Dynasty pharaoh who ruled Egypt during the Old Kingdom. This is the oldest of the group, built around 2570 BC, and the largest – in fact it's the most massive single monument on the face of the Earth today. The others, built by Cheops' son Chephren and his grandson Mycerinus, stand in descending order of age and size along a southwest axis; when built they were probably aligned precisely with the North Star, with their entrance corridors pointing straight at it.

You enter the Great Pyramid through a hole hacked into its north face in the ninth century AD by the caliph Maamun who was hunting for buried treasure. Squeezing along narrow passages you arrive at the Great Gallery, which ascends through the heart of the pyramid to Cheops' burial chamber. Chances are you'll have the chamber to yourself, as claustrophobia and inadequate oxygen mean that few people venture this far. Occasionally visitors are accidentally locked in overnight.

The overwhelming impression made by the pyramids is due not only to the magnitude of their age and size but also to their elemental form, their simple but compelling triangular silhouettes against the sky. The best way to enjoy this is to hire a horse or camel and ride about the desert, observing them from different angles: close up and looming, or far off and standing lonely but defiantly on the open sands. Seen at prime times – dawn, sunset and after dark – they form as much a part of the natural order as the sun, the moon and the stars.

301 | Living a dream in Siwa

EGYPT Siwa was once home to the feted and feared Oracle of Amun; Alexander the Great mounted an eight-day expedition here in 331 BC to ask if he was destined to conquer the world. Today this sliver of greenery exists in a dreamlike state amid the wide void of Egypt's Western Desert, surrounded by clumps of languid date palm groves and overlooked by an ancient, sagging and slumping mud-brick citadel that rises above the middle of the village. Just 50km from the Libyan border, on the edge of the Great Sand Sea, Siwa feels as remote today as it ever did.

It's a place of hidden bubbling pools reached by donkey cart rides under the palms' shady veil; a place where the furnace blast of desert sunshine slows movement down to a soporific gait. Once you've soaked in the bubbling springs that feed the fertile gardens, strolled the palm grove trails and wandered through the labyrinthine remnants of the fortress, Siwa's slow and enchanting spell will have worked its magic over your travel-weary bones.

302 | Algeria's best-kept secret

ALGERIA Timgad is the most astonishing Roman archeological site you've probably never heard of. Sitting on the northern slopes of the Aurès mountains, 480km southeast of Algiers, it was founded by Emperor Trajan in AD 100 as a military outpost against marauding Berbers. Timgad was destroyed in the fifth century and then miraculously preserved for centuries under a thick layer of sand.

Now meticulously excavated, the scale of the ruins is jaw-dropping, the sprawling gridplan as perfectly preserved as if it were built yesterday, presided over by the towering Arch of Trajan. Beyond, the remains of buildings stretch as far as the eye can see, including temples, baths, basilica and a huge theatre, still in use, with seating for over three thousand people.

Today Timgad is protected under UNESCO World Heritage as a staggering example of Roman town planning – and will take your breath away.

303 | Enjoying the view from Fishawi's

EGYPT In a small alley in the heart of medieval Cairo is the famous *Fishawi's café*, where you sit on cane chairs at marble-topped tables in the narrow mirror-lined passage. Waiters carrying brass trays dart from table to table, weaving in and out among the street hawkers who offer you everything from a shoeshine or a necklace of jasmine flowers to a woman's song accompanied by a tambourine.

Fishawi's has been open every day and night for more than two hundred years, and as you sip a thick black coffee or a sweet tea and perhaps enjoy the gentle smoke of a *narghile*, the Egyptian water pipe, you can immerse your senses in an atmosphere reminiscent of *The Thousand and One Nights*. All around you is Khan al-Khalili, a vast bazaar dating back to the fourteenth century, its shaded streets as intricate as inlay work, its shops and stalls sharp with spices, sweet with perfumes and dazzling with brass, gold and silver.

The café is within hearing of the calls to prayer rising from the minarets of the Sayyidna al-Hussein, the principal congregational mosque of the city, and of the popular nightly celebrations that take place in the square outside throughout the month of Ramadan. Opposite the square, and far older, is the mosque of al-Azhar, the oldest university in the world and the foremost centre of Islamic theology.

Naguib Mahfouz, Egypt's Nobel Prize-winning novelist, was born and raised in the neighbourhood, and it provided him with the setting of many of his novels. For Mahfouz, the streets and alleyways around the *Fishawi's* were a timeless world, which, as he wrote of Midaq Alley, a five-minute walk from the café, "connects with life as a whole and yet at the same time retains a number of the secrets of a world now past".

304 | Mopping up a Moroccan tajine

MOROCCO Robert Carrier, one of the twentieth century's most influential food writers, rated Moroccan cuisine as second only to that of France. Which is perhaps a little hyperbolic, for, outside the grandest kitchens, Moroccan cooking is decidedly simple, with only a half dozen or so dishes popping up on most local menus. But no matter where you are in the country, from a top restaurant to a roadside stall, there is one dish you can depend upon: the tajine.

A tajine is basically a stew. It is steam-cooked in an earthenware dish (also called a tajine) with a fancifully conical lid, and most often prepared over a charcoal fire. That means slow-cooking, with flavours locked in and meat that falls from the bone.

What goes in depends on what's available, but a number of combinations have achieved classic and ubiquitous status: *mrouzia* (lamb or mutton with prunes and almonds – and lots of honey) and

mqualli (chicken with olives and pickled lemons), for example. On the coast, you might be offered a fish tajine, too, frequently red snapper or swordfish. And tajines can taste just as good with just vegetables: artichokes, tomatoes, potatoes, peppers, olives, and again those pickled lemons, which you see in tall jars in every shop and market stall. The herbs and spices, too, are crucial: cinnamon, ginger, garlic and a pinch of the mysterious *ras al-hanut*, the "best in shop" spice selection any Moroccan stall can prepare for you.

There's no need for a knife or fork. Tajines are served in the dish in which they are cooked, and then scooped and mopped up – using your right hand, of course – with delicious Moroccan flat bread. Perfect for sharing.

And when you're through, don't forget to sit back and enjoy the customary three tiny glasses of super-sweet mint tea.

MOROCCO With the title of Imperial City and a UNESCO-stamped ancient medina, Meknes can rival the likes of Marrakesh, Rabat and Fes, yet it struggles to attract the same loyal following of travellers. But this scenic hilltop city has plenty to offer the curious visitor, from intricate gates to marvellous museums and mausoleums.

Meknes is made up of the old (the historic medina) and the new (the big houses and brands of the *ville nouvelle*); two distinct centres less than three miles apart but harnessing quite different vibes.

In the medina you'll find everything from specialist souks selling crafts and swathes of textiles, to souvenirs and carpets. At its heart is the twelfth-century Grand Mosque (although this is closed to non-Muslims), while teahouses in secret courtyards, ornate riads, and the odd hard-working donkey add to the atmosphere.

There's more to the medina than shopping, though. Bab el-Mansour is a big hit with visitors, and for good reason. Completed in 1732, the gate is impressive not only for its size but its original green and white *zellij* tiles, marble columns and inscriptions from the Qur'an.

The Dar Jamai Museum, a late nineteenth-century palace, now displays not only dazzling rooms and doorways but also traditional crafts, including ceramics, jewellery and costumes. Don't miss the magnificent tile work or the decorated dome ceiling on the first floor.

Elsewhere, you'll find one of the city's busiest spots, the Mausoleum of Moulay Ismail – the ornate tomb of the man who gave Meknes its imperial status. The mausoleum is open to non-Muslims (women should wear a headscarf) keen to admire the architecture, although non-Muslims can't approach the tomb directly, and it does get very busy, so go early.

305

Meknes: Morocco's best-kept secret

Down the Nile

306

EGYPT Often called "the gift of the Nile", Egypt has always depended on the river as a life source. Without the Nile, the country could not survive, and would not have nurtured the great civilizations of its pharaonic past. Snaking the full length of Egypt, it flows from south to north and boats of all varieties ply it day and night. For an authentic – and uniquely Egyptian – taste of river life, opt for a voyage on a felucca.

These traditional, lateen-rigged wooden vessels – used on the river since antiquity – are small: a group of six people will fit comfortably. Bargaining and gathering supplies before the cruise can be frenetic, but as soon as your captain guides the boat out onto open water, the bustle fades away. There's then nothing to do but lie back and soak up the atmosphere.

It's an experience that feels timeless. Drifting gently down the Nile in a traditional wooden boat, shaded from the African sun by a square of colourful cloth, watching the fields and palm groves slide past, kids waving from the banks: nothing could be more seductive. It *isn't* timeless, of course: the cloth will likely be polyester, the kids have trinkets to sell and you'll see modern Japanese cars parked in the shoreside villages – but one can dream…

307 | Unearthing Roman remains in Volubilis

MOROCCO A memory of ancient colonial empires, the ruins of Volubilis — a Roman and Berber city that rose to fame from the third century BC — rest at the bottom of a sun-baked valley. This UNESCO World Heritage Site, close to both the royal city of Meknes and the ancient medina of Fes, was the southernmost bastion of the Roman Empire in North Africa, once known as "Mauretania". Walking around the ruins of Volubilis today, you can still feel the sheer scale of this ancient city: at its maximum height in the second century, Volubilis was capital of the Kingdom of Mauretania and home to almost twenty thousand people. Its streets and buildings stretched over 42 hectares, proudly enclosed by 2.6km of fortified walls.

The Romans exploited Volubilis' surrounding bowl of fertile land to grow massive plantations of olive trees. The oil production helped fund Volubilis' impressive public buildings, which included the temple and the triumphal arch that can still be visited today. One of Volubilis' highlights, however, is the mosaic flooring found in some homes; carefully restored, they are some of best-preserved remaining in the world. Volubilis' fate changed around 285 BC, when it was occupied by indigenous tribes and never reclaimed by the Romans. The ancient capital fell into oblivion, suffering severe earthquake damage in the eighteenth century, and then looted by Moroccan rulers looking for stone.

The destiny of Mauretania's old capital seems improved under the current "rule" of UNESCO, as tourists come to admire the remains of evocative stone pillars, homes, baths and arches. After centuries, they still stand to testify how the empires of men are often destined not only to switch hands, but also to suffer the quick swings of fate.

308 | Roam without a map in Kairouan's Medina

TUNISIA Throw away your map and let the narrow lanes lead you astray. Rimmed by squat whitewashed houses, punctuated by minaret spires, Kairouan's mazey walled medina, or old city, is made for aimless wandering. A place of myth and miracles, Kairouan is Islam's fourth-holiest city and during the seventh century was the glorious North African capital of the conquering Arabs.

From the main entrance at Place des Martyrs, alleyways radiate out in random honeycombed curves. Surrender to the helter-skelter of medieval town planning and delight in skinny dead-end streets where the buildings slouch into gentle dilapidation softened by peeling paint and pastel-tinted doors.

If you must have a focus, hunt down the souqs, snuggled into the medina's womb. Here, donning your haggling hat, you can join hard-nosed customers hustling with even harder-nosed carpet dealers over toppling mountains of rugs and drinking copious tiny glasses of sweet mint tea. Even if you're too shy to play the game, it's just as much fun to stand and watch.

Elsewhere, near the central market square, you may come across the well of Bir Barouta, where pilgrims collect water that, according to local legend, is connected to Mecca's holy Zamzam spring. Winding your way north, savouring the gorgeous old doors and crumbling buildings along the way, you could encounter the high citadel-like walls of the ninth-century Sidi Oqba, or Grand, Mosque.

Particularly beautiful in late afternoon, when its ochre stone facade takes on a honey-dipped glow, this is one of the oldest mosques in North Africa, founded in 670 AD (though the current construction dates from the ninth century), and the symbol of the city. Inside the vast internal courtyard, the sea of smooth marble, arched porticos and the towering, fat minaret offer a beautiful symmetry that's in dramatic contrast to the web of doodling alleyways outside.

Resting beneath Sidi Oqba's elegant courtyard arches is the perfect, soothing end to a day wandering the mysterious lanes of the medina.

309 | Surrealism in the sand in the White Desert

EGYPT Sweeping across more than 300 square kilometres of Egypt's Western Desert, White Desert National Park (Sahara el-Beyda) is a wonderland of weird, blindingly white rock outcrops, looming over the arid landscape like icebergs that took a (very) wrong turn on their way from the Arctic.

Millennia of desert winds and ferocious sandstorms have sculpted the chalk rock here, winnowing away at soft outer layers to form fantastical pillars and pinnacles that rise out of the sand in fairy-tale shapes. The result is a natural sculpture park of epic proportions, looking for all the world like something from Salvador Dalí's sketch book. Some of the rocks have been hewn into towering mushrooms. Some are shard-like spires. Others sit like mighty cones of powdered sugar piled upon a counter of beige sand. Encountering these mammoth formations for the first time, as you drive in from the stark, barren flatlands all around, is like entering a secret door into a science-fiction world.

The desert is a popular jaunt from Baharia or Farafra Oases and, if you visit during the day, you certainly won't be the only one checking out these enchanting geological oddities. To get the full experience, you need to stay overnight. Organized safaris bed down Bedouin-style, with simple tented accommodation and campsite feasts of fresh, basic Egyptian food. Settle back to watch the pinnacles transform from gleaming white to eerie pink and orange as the sun sets, the bizarre, towering silhouettes emerging in the gloaming and taking on a spooky quality ripped straight out of the pages of a Grimm Brothers' tale.

If you forgo the tent and take your sleeping bag outside onto the sand, you will fall asleep beneath a blanket of stars. Waking at sunrise to see these dream-like vistas of rock-outcrops sparkling and shimmering under the first rays of daylight will haunt your imagination long after you have packed your bags and made the long journey home.

310 | Off the beaten track in Morocco

MOROCCO Marrakesh? Check. The souks of Fes? Been there, bought that. Jebel Toubkal? Climbed it, twice. So what's next for escaping the tourist trail?

Uncover the Roman ruins of Lixus. While most people head straight for UNESCO-listed Volubilis, the under-the-radar Lixus sits 5km up the coast from Larache. This is one of the oldest inhabited sites in Morocco, at one time also occupied by the Phoenicians and the Carthaginians – and, as legend would have it, Hercules, who is said to have stolen the Golden Apples for his last-but-one labour here. With no modern-day markings marring the landscape and barely any other people around, it's much easier to picture Lixus' Roman inhabitants packing salt at its crumbling factories, worshipping in its deserted temple sanctuaries, or baying for blood at the Upper Town's amphitheatre.

The majority of organized trekking in Morocco is concentrated on the Toubkal Massif in the High Atlas mountains, south of Marrakesh. So, to go off-grid you'll need to venture east instead, to the Jebel Saghro. While guides can be hired in several of the trailhead towns, Saghro is much less geared up for tourism. But it's worth the effort: a three-day hike will take you past weird rock formations and across a barren landscape dotted with the black nets of local nomad tribes.

Fancy a road trip instead? Morocco's forgotten mountains, the Rif see a fraction of the visitors who hike the High Atlas. Partly, the remote range lacks the accessibility provided by a big-town base like Marrakesh. And partly, the region – historically existing just outside government control and with a local economy still driven by the cultivation of cannabis, or *kif* – is altogether edgier. But it is also quite beautiful, and with a bit of common sense, perfectly fine to explore by car. Drive the scenic N2 between Chefchaouen and Al Hoceima, and you'll dip in and out of olive farms, cork oaks and cedar forests, travelling along the ridge of the mountains as they trace the Mediterranean for over 200km whilst enjoying spectacular views down towards the coast.

311 | Haggling in the souks of Fes

MOROCCO Everywhere you look in Fes's medina – the ancient walled part of the city – there are alleys bedecked with exquisite handmade crafts. Here the city's distinctive ceramics jostle for space with rich fabrics, musical instruments and red tasselled fezzes (which take their name from the city). Most of these items are made in the medina itself, in areas such as the carpenters' souk, redolent of cedarwood, or in the rather less aromatic tanneries, where leather is cured in stinky vats of cow's urine and pigeon poo, among other substances. In the dyers' souk, the cobbles run with multicoloured pigments used to tint gaudy hanks of wool, while nearby Place Seffarine, by the tenth-century Kairaouine Mosque, reverberates to the crash and clatter of metalworkers hammering intricate designs into brass.

Should you wish to buy, however, it's not a matter of "how much?", "here you go", "thanks" and "goodbye". Love it or hate it, haggling is de rigueur. These crafts are made with love and patience, and should not be bought in a rush. Rather, the shopkeeper will expect you to dally awhile, perhaps enjoy a cup of tea – sweet, green and flavoured with Moroccan mint – and come to an agreement on a price. This is both a commercial transaction and a game, and skilled hagglers are adept at theatrics – "How much? Are you crazy?" "For this fine piece of art? Don't insult me!"

Know how much you are prepared to pay, offer something less, and let the seller argue you up. If you don't agree a price, nothing is lost, and you've spent a pleasant time conversing with the shopkeeper. And you can always go back the next day to reopen discussions.

312

Touring troglodyte villages

TUNISIA When Tunisia gained its independence in 1956, its then president, Habib Bourguiba, proclaimed a new nation in which "people will no longer live in caves, like animals". He was addressing the reality that across the arid far south of the country, people did live in caves, not uncommonly with their livestock. Gradually, these people were moved into new houses put up by the government, and most of the old dwellings were abandoned.

Visit the troglodyte villages today, however, and you'll see they're enjoying a new lease of life – some even offer tourist accommodation. Many are stunningly sited. At Chenini, Douiret and Guermessa, set in a jagged prehistoric landscape, you're confronted by mountainsides riddled with cave dwellings and guarded by rugged stone forts. At nearby Ghoumrassen, three folds of a rocky spur are studded with caves, under the gaze of a whitewashed mosque. Even more scenic is Toujane, built on two sides of a gorge, with breathtaking views. Anywhere you spot oil stains down the hillside signifies caves housing ancient olive presses; visit after the olive harvest and you may well see some of these being powered by donkeys.

But the big centre for troglodyte homes is Matmata, whose people live, to this day, in pit dwellings. Signs outside some invite you to visit, and for a few dinars you can descend into a central courtyard dug deep into soft sandstone, which serves to keep the rooms – excavated into the sides – comfortably cool in summer and warm in winter. Better still, Matmata has three hotels in converted pit dwellings, including the *Sidi Driss*, which was used as one of the locations in *Star Wars* – here you can dine where Luke Skywalker once did.

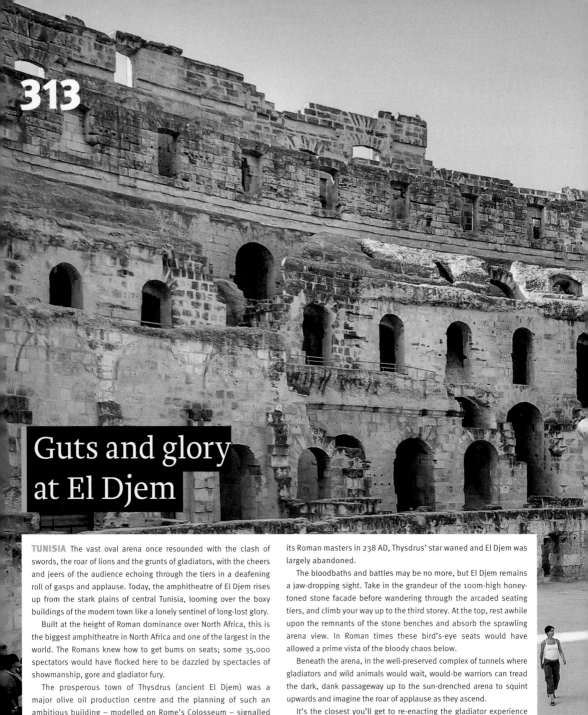

Guts and glory at El Djem

TUNISIA The vast oval arena once resounded with the clash of swords, the roar of lions and the grunts of gladiators, with the cheers and jeers of the audience echoing through the tiers in a deafening roll of gasps and applause. Today, the amphitheatre of El Djem rises up from the stark plains of central Tunisia, looming over the boxy buildings of the modern town like a lonely sentinel of long-lost glory.

Built at the height of Roman dominance over North Africa, this is the biggest amphitheatre in North Africa and one of the largest in the world. The Romans knew how to get bums on seats; some 35,000 spectators would have flocked here to be dazzled by spectacles of showmanship, gore and gladiator fury.

The prosperous town of Thysdrus (ancient El Djem) was a major olive oil production centre and the planning of such an ambitious building – modelled on Rome's Colosseum – signalled its importance to the empire. Just a couple of decades after the arena was built, however, following an unsuccessful revolt against

its Roman masters in 238 AD, Thysdrus' star waned and El Djem was largely abandoned.

The bloodbaths and battles may be no more, but El Djem remains a jaw-dropping sight. Take in the grandeur of the 100m-high honey-toned stone facade before wandering through the arcaded seating tiers, and climb your way up to the third storey. At the top, rest awhile upon the remnants of the stone benches and absorb the sprawling arena view. In Roman times these bird's-eye seats would have allowed a prime vista of the bloody chaos below.

Beneath the arena, in the well-preserved complex of tunnels where gladiators and wild animals would wait, would-be warriors can tread the dark, dank passageway up to the sun-drenched arena to squint upwards and imagine the roar of applause as they ascend.

It's the closest you'll get to re-enacting the gladiator experience – even if you only have a few fellow travellers as spectators to rain down the applause.

314 | Lose yourself in a good book at the Bibliotheca Alexandrina

EGYPT A hallmark of modern architecture, the Bibliotheca Alexandrina is a superb addition to Alexandria's cityscape. A stunning work of stone and metal, the central library features a huge, tilted glass roof reminiscent of a sundial, and the walls are carved with text from over 120 languages, ancient and modern. Its location beside the Mediterranean only emphasizes its sophisticated lines of construction. Everything is created to inspire admiration and to remind the visitor of the importance of the library's past role.

The Bibliotheca, which opened in 2003, harks back to Alexandria's role as a prominent seat of learning in ancient times. Ptolemy II of Egypt opened the original Library of Alexandria in the third century BC, from which point it grew to become the largest library in the world. While the modern incarnation does not have such high aspirations – it is still relatively small when compared with other international libraries – it is well on its way to establishing itself on the academic circuit.

But this is so much more than just a library. In addition to the central collection there are museums of antiquities, manuscripts and the history of science; galleries for temporary art displays; a planetarium; special sections just for children; and rare books that are available nowhere else in the world. You can wander around the permanent collection of Egyptian filmmaker, writer and artist Shadi Abdel Salam. Or take a seat in front of a cultural film relating the history of Egypt.

And once you've done all that, it's really not a bad place to find a quiet corner and settle down with a good book or two.

315 | Listening to Gnawa music in Essaouira

MOROCCO It's midnight in Essaouira, and a castanet-like rhythm is drifting over the ramparts on the steely Atlantic breeze.

Tucked into a courtyard is a group of robed musicians playing bass drums, reed pipes and *qaraqebs*, metal chimes which are clacked together in the fingers. Their leader, the *maalem*, plucks a three-stringed gimbri lute. Singers in tassel-topped caps weave a polyrhythmic chant into the sound. The group is surrounded by a respectful audience: some standing, some preferring to sit cross-legged.

Suddenly, the beat quickens and one of the chanters launches into a dazzling sequence of lunges, jumps and cossack-like knee-bends. Finally, he spins on the spot, his long tassel whirling like a helicopter blade. An audience member joins in and ends up collapsed on the ground, seemingly in some kind of ecstatic trance.

This is a *lila*, one of the intimate musical gatherings that take place each night during the city's annual Gnawa music festival. The Gnawas (or, in French, Gnaouas) are a spiritual brotherhood of healers and mystics whose ancestors, animist West Africans, were transported to Morocco as slaves. Their hypnotic music, a blend of sub-Saharan, Amazigh (Berber) and Arab influences, is key to their rituals.

As well as these late-night sessions, the festival offers large-scale concerts. From early evening each day, crowds of locals gather around the stages in Place Moulay Hassan and other main squares to hear bands from all over North and West Africa. But it is the starlit *lilas* that make the festival unique. And it's hard to imagine a more romantic setting for them than the rugged, windswept fortifications that protect the city from the sea.

By day, Essaouira has a different kind of romance. Seagulls soar over the sun-bleached rooftops and swoop down onto the shore, where fishermen sort their catch. The ramparts bake in the sun. This is the time for the festival's more energetic visitors to browse the souks for glass beads, leather slippers and drums. Others, meanwhile, just snooze in the cool courtyard of a riad, waiting for another evening's magic to unfold.

316 | Following in Agatha Christie's footsteps along the Nile

EGYPT The creaking charms of a wrought-iron lift; the fading gold of ornate ceilings; quaint afternoon teas in elegantly worn hotels; frozen-in-time cafés... Egypt may be in a state of flux, but the allure of its past is constant. Step back, on the banks of the Nile, to the 1930s and into Agatha Christie's shoes. Discover the places she loved: *Windsor Palace Hotel* in Alexandria, the *Gezira Palace* hotel, *Mena House* and *Fishawi's* coffee shop in Cairo, the *Winter Palace* hotel in Luxor and the *Old Cataract* in Aswan. Best of the lot, the PS *Sudan*, a 1920s, Belle-Époque-themed steamboat, still operating between Luxor and Aswan, on which the Queen of Crime herself travelled and the inspiration for *Death on the Nile*.

317 | Figuig: the end of the road

MOROCCO Few people make it to Figuig. Hard up against the Algerian frontier, in the far southeast of the country, this remote oasis is nearly 400km from the nearest signs of civilization, and since the border closed in 1994, there is only one place to go once you leave town – back where you came from. But those that do make the journey, through empty landscapes and blank red mountains, are rewarded with a genuinely charming backwater, a sleepy settlement of pink-tinged *ksour* (mud-brick houses), whose crumbling walls, studded with watchtowers, are a nod to a bygone age of raiding desert tribes. This is a place where visitors are welcomed with hot flatbread and honey, where the vast palmery is still watered in the traditional way, and where the simple late-afternoon pleasure of wandering shady alleyways never fades.

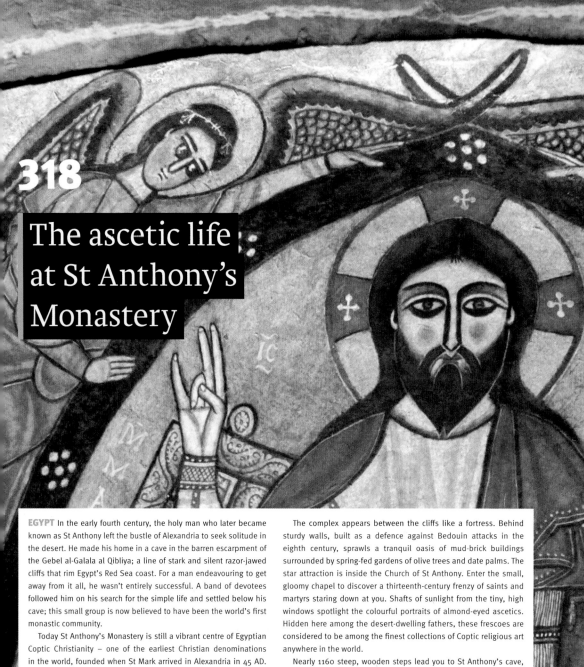

The ascetic life at St Anthony's Monastery

EGYPT In the early fourth century, the holy man who later became known as St Anthony left the bustle of Alexandria to seek solitude in the desert. He made his home in a cave in the barren escarpment of the Gebel al-Galala al Qibliya; a line of stark and silent razor-jawed cliffs that rim Egypt's Red Sea coast. For a man endeavouring to get away from it all, he wasn't entirely successful. A band of devotees followed him on his search for the simple life and settled below his cave; this small group is now believed to have been the world's first monastic community.

Today St Anthony's Monastery is still a vibrant centre of Egyptian Coptic Christianity – one of the earliest Christian denominations in the world, founded when St Mark arrived in Alexandria in 45 AD. More than one hundred monks live here, leading a simple existence devoted to prayer. A road now connects the monastery to the outside world – a long, desolate drive through unforgiving desert that doesn't deter the thousands of Egypt's Coptic Christians who make the pilgrimage here each year.

The complex appears between the cliffs like a fortress. Behind sturdy walls, built as a defence against Bedouin attacks in the eighth century, sprawls a tranquil oasis of mud-brick buildings surrounded by spring-fed gardens of olive trees and date palms. The star attraction is inside the Church of St Anthony. Enter the small, gloomy chapel to discover a thirteenth-century frenzy of saints and martyrs staring down at you. Shafts of sunlight from the tiny, high windows spotlight the colourful portraits of almond-eyed ascetics. Hidden here among the desert-dwelling fathers, these frescoes are considered to be among the finest collections of Coptic religious art anywhere in the world.

Nearly 1160 steep, wooden steps lead you to St Anthony's cave, hewn into the cliff above. Beyond the narrow entrance and tiny chapel, where pilgrims pray in front of a simple altar, is the chamber where St Anthony lived out his days. For Coptic pilgrims this beautiful wilderness is a place of devotion. For anyone else, its stark power is tangible and profound.

319 | Staying with a family in Merzouga

MOROCCO Waking up in a nomad's black-wool tent, surrounded by kilometre upon kilometre of ochre-coloured sand dunes, the first thing that strikes you is the silence: a deep, muffled nothing. The second is the cold. You'll appreciate the three glasses of mint tea served by the fireside before you help saddle up the camels for the day's trek. Notwithstanding the chilly mornings, January is the best month to visit southern Morocco's Erg Chebbi dunes. The skies are big and blue, the horizons crisp and, best of all, the hordes who descend here later in the year blissfully absent.

The *Chez Tihri* guesthouse is a rarity in a corner of the country notorious for its highly commodified versions of the desert and its people: an *auberge* run by a Tamasheq-speaking Amazigh (Tuareg) where you actually feel a genuine sense of place. Built in old-school kasbah style, its crenellated pisé walls, adorned with bold geometric patterns in patriotic reds and greens, shelter a warren of cosy rooms, each decorated with rugs, pottery and lanterns, and interconnected by dark, earthy corridors.

As well as being a congenial host, Omar Tihri, dressed in imposing white turban and flowing robe, is a passionate advocate for Amazigh traditions and culture, and living proof that tourism can be a force for good in this region. A slice of the profits from *Chez Tihri* goes towards funding a women's weaving cooperative, in addition to a small school where Tamasheq-speaking children, who are poorly catered for by state education in the area, learn French and Arabic.

320 | The Moulid of Sayyid Ahmed al-Badawi

EGYPT The Egyptian year is awash with *moulids* (festivals honouring local saints), but they don't come much bigger than the Moulid of Sayyid Ahmed al-Badawi, when the otherwise nondescript Nile Delta city of Tanta is besieged by some two million pilgrims, who converge on the triple-domed mosque where al-Badawi is buried.

Moulids are especially associated with Sufis – Islamic mystics who use singing, chanting and dancing to bring themselves closer to God. Some fifty Sufi brotherhoods put up their tents around Tanta and set to work chanting and beating out a rhythm on drums or tambourines, as devotees perform their *zikrs* (ritual dances). In the less frenetic tents, you can relax with a *sheesha* (water-pipe) or a cup of tea, while scoffing festive treats such as roasted chickpeas and sugared nuts. The atmosphere is intense, the crowds dense and pickpocketing rife (so leave your valuables at home).

Tanta doesn't have much in the way of accommodation, and most people just bunk down in the tents, but if that doesn't appeal and you can't get a room, it's near enough to Cairo to take in on a day-trip. Wherever you stay, make sure that you're here for the spectacular last-night parade, when the Ahmediya, the Sufi brotherhood founded by al-Badawi himself, takes to the streets in a colourful blur of banners.

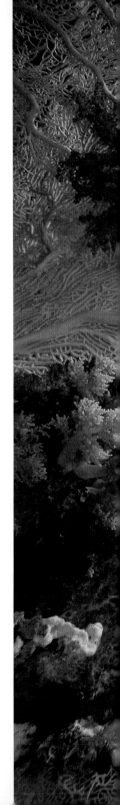

321 | Driving the route of a thousand kasbahs

MOROCCO East of Marrakesh, up over the dizzying Tizi n'Tichka pass, runs one of the oldest trading routes in history, snaking out across the Sahara and linking the Amazigh (Berber) heartland with Timbuktu, Niger and old Sudan. The gold and slaves that once financed the southern oases are long gone, but the road is still peppered with the remains of their fabulous kasbahs – fortified dwellings of baked mud and straw – and as it sprints out into the Sahara,

it passes great palmeries of dates, olives and almonds, their lush greens a vivid contrast to the barren desert. The cream of the architectural crop is at Aït Benhaddou, near the start of the route. Although most of the inhabitants have moved to the modern village across the river, it's a magical place, its stunning collection of crenellated kasbahs glowing orange in the soft light of late afternoon, among the most intricately decorated of the deep south.

322 | The pharaoh rises at Abu Simbel

EGYPT Ramses II wasn't the most modest of pharaohs. And of all the monuments he raised during his reign, the Temples of Abu Simbel are his most egocentric. The Great Temple of Ramses II here, built between 1274 and 1244 BC, is a propaganda exercise of epic proportions, dedicated to the man himself and to a colourful version of his exploits.

Originally guarding Ancient Egypt's route to Kush (modern Upper Nubia), the Great Temple was as much a warning to the people of Kush not to mess with the pharaoh as an assertion of supreme power over his own subjects. Remarkably, the entire complex was moved in the 1960s to make way for Egypt's Aswan High Dam; it now sits along the bank of Lake Nasser in a position 65m higher than the original site, aligned precisely with the original complex.

The impact of the Great Temple has not diminished across the millennia. Enter through the imposing doors, flanked by gigantic stone-cut effigies of the pharaoh glaring down upon all who pass. Inside the vast, dimly lit chamber, guarded by colossi, ferocious wall-paintings show the mighty one riding into battle, massacring all who stand in his way. Gaze upon him standing aloft on his chariot winning the Battle of Kadesh and leaving the Hittite army running for the hills.

Ramses, ever the showman, had another trick up his sleeve. The Great Temple was positioned so that once a year, on the date he ascended to the throne, the first rays of the sun would shine straight down the temple corridor, creeping forward as the sun rose until the entire 60m passage was bathed in light. The spotlight would then move up the far wall in the inner sanctuary to finally rest on Ramses' small stone statue, illuminating the god-king in a halo of light.

Nowadays, due to the repositioning of the temple, this architectural illusion – the Abu Simbel Sun Festival – takes place on February 22, one day later than in ancient times. It's a major event, pulling in crowds huge enough to gratify even Ramses himself.

323 | Mountain high: a visit to Chefchaouen

MOROCCO "So why did you come, then?" Given that Chefchaouen is renowned across Morocco and beyond for its hashish, *kif* (marijuana) and *majoun* (marijuana cake), you can perhaps forgive the local touts for their exasperation when you refuse their offerings; for why else would you come to this ancient corner of the Rif? The idea that you'd want to get high on Chefchaouen's otherworldly aura alone perhaps doesn't quite cut it in the cross-cultural stakes.

Had they rumbled his Rabbi disguise, the zealous natives might well have asked the same question of French monk Charles de Foucauld, the first Christian to breach the walls of what was then (in 1883) a militantly anti-European outpost. When the Spanish finally took control in 1920, they found not only descendants of the Muslims and Sephardic Jews they'd kicked out of Spain centuries earlier but also the medieval dialect, Haketia, the Sephardic Jews brought with them. The place is still a world apart today, and even if some of the locals automatically assume you're here to sample their wares, they'll warmly welcome you into their once-forbidden city all the same. You might even cross one of the ornate thresholds of the medina, rooted in the diaspora from Spain, with architectural echoes of al-Andalus despite the defiantly Maghrebi locale.

Washed in swathes of pastel blue, the stone passages, dead ends and doorways are more luminous and dream-like than perhaps any other old quarter in North Africa, aglow with mountain light. Aromas of baking bread, mint tea and cumin fill the air. Getting lost is a given, and a must; the medina's centuries-old momentum will deposit you into the main square in its own unhurried time. Here lies another dream-world, at least at night, when the tea shops and restaurants assume the guise of exotic grottos, twinkling and beckoning. Over it all presides the sheer rock of Jebel al-Kalaa, hanging in an electric-blue sky so crisp you can feel it crackling, across a landscape coloured with the same Indian hemp crop that has been grown here for centuries.

Dive in to Dahab

EGYPT A heady blend of sheesha pipes, trance beats and kaleidoscopic coral reefs, Dahab is the most bohemian of Red Sea resorts. Thanks to its remoteness – 100km from the nearest budget airline check-in – and some surprisingly sensitive development (even the *Hilton* blends in among the palms), it's managed to avoid the high-rise horrors of rivals Sharm el-Sheikh and Hurghada; in fact, you can almost feel the sleepy Bedouin fishing village that greeted tie-dyed travellers here in the 1970s. Despite the presence of armed checkpoints, a legacy of Egypt's current security woes, Dahab (meaning "Gold") still attracts an eclectic mix of backpackers, intrepid families and scuba junkies.

For divers the aces in the pack include the Blue Hole, a deep-violet abyss popular with hardcore freedivers, and Gabr el Bint, an extraordinary series of coral heads pulsing with neon-bright anthias and, *inshallah*, the occasional passing whale shark. Scuba tuition fees are some of the most competitive in the world, resulting in a laidback community of aspiring instructors. For those packing a board, the stiff sea breezes of the Gulf of Aqaba and a warm, waist-deep lagoon provide wind- and kite-surfing heaven. Inland, the Sinai desert is a playground for quad bikes and camel rides.

As the sun sets over the gulf, waterside restaurants glow with fairy lights and the aroma of wood-fired pizza and apple-flavoured tobacco fills the air. In Assilah, the "real" Dahab, Egyptian street-side grills fire up, knocking out delicious chicken, falafel and tahini for the price of a beer in the *Hilton*.

If you can time things right don't miss Desert Dance, a three-day pyschedelic trance "happening" that takes place in the starkly beautiful Sinai Mountains each April. In the words of the organizers, "We are one, we love, we share and dream!" – an apt tribute to Dahab's hippy heyday.

325 | A skin-smoothing scrubdown in Morocco

MOROCCO There are many fine reasons to travel to Morocco: the unforgettable fragrance of orange blossom, the ancient, maze-like medinas, the vibrant, non-stop souks… and, one of the best culturally immersive experiences to be had anywhere, a scrub-down at a local *hammam*. Every city and village throughout the country has one; cleanliness being intrinsic to Islam's five key pillars, they are often found near mosques, but ask your concierge or a taxi driver if you're finding it difficult to track one down.

Many *hammams* sell the relevant paraphernalia, such as travel-sized bottles of shampoo and soap – but it's much more fun to hunt everything down in the local souks. You'll need: "sabon beldi" (a black olive oil soap); "ghasoul" or "rhassoul" (a lava clay used to scrub the skin); a "kiis" (a loofah mitt or scrub glove) and shampoo. You should also bring a change of underwear (or shorts for men) and a towel (though some local *hammams* offer towels too). Check your *hammam* schedules:

some are exclusively for men or women only, while others have special days of the week – or certain times or evenings – set aside for each sex.

A certain amount of etiquette is required during this ritual; take care when getting changed to avoid full-frontal nudity, which is considered offensive. Men should continue, in underwear or shorts, to the steam rooms – nudity is less taboo in women's *hammams*, but it's best to wear underwear unless the locals are naked too. The rooms are usually dimly lit and in varying states of decrepitude. Fill a plastic bucket with water and, after rinsing the floor to clean away any dead skin from the tiles (some have raised marble slabs to sit and lie on) you can begin to wash yourself down. As a foreigner, you may receive curious looks at first; use the attention as an excuse to ask one of the locals to scrub your back; this is normal practice, but note that you will be expected to return the favour. And don't be surprised if you find yourself making a new friend, or even being invited to someone's house for dinner.

326 | Meteor-hunting in the Sahara

MOROCCO Ali Lamghari – 30-something stargazer, NASA geek, desert explorer – has space rocks on his mind. Clutching the handle of a metal detector, his thoughts in another galaxy, he climbs the rippling sand dune south of Agadir, probing the device from side to side as he goes. On either side of him is a whole universe of canyons and craters, dried-up river beds and hamadas, moon-like plateaus interrupted by rocks.

"When I started this as a hobby I had no idea what I was doing," he says, his shirt damp with sweat in the afternoon sun. "But I've sold around five hundred meteorites in the past decade. It's become my entire life."

Tourists don't usually venture to the far southwest corner of Morocco, but times are changing. In recent years, the country's interior has become an unlikely hub for the global meteorite trade, with space rocks chasing hands at a market value of €1,000 a gram. No one can

say for sure just how meteor-hunting took off, but nowadays you're as likely to find have-a-go hobbyists as you are researchers from Agadir's world-leading Musée Universitaire de Météorites.

Beyond the sci-fi appeal, there are reasons why southern Morocco works so beautifully as a backdrop. There is the crisp-clear air for starters, the wide-open skies, and the cloud-free weather. Then there is the geography; the empty topography and contrast of the golden sand with the blackish meteorites makes the desert trophies easier to locate. On first sight, according to Lamghari, their differing colours embody the lightness and shade of the stars themselves.

In such out-of-this-world moments, a meteor-hunting quest brings the solar system closer to us than it ever has been before. And who wouldn't want to find a piece of the universe to take home to put on their mantelpiece?

327 | Have a swell time in Taghazout

MOROCCO Ice-cream headaches, chilly wetsuits in snow-covered car parks and blown-out waves beneath leaden skies; a north European winter can make the most dedicated surfer think twice. Why bother when, in just a few hours, many landlocked surfers could access perfect right-hand points, blue skies, 16°C water and the beauty of Africa? Small wonder Taghazout is spoken of in revered tones.

The ramshackle fishing village, 20km from Agadir international airport, has come a long way. A hippy hangout in the 1960s, Taghazout – also spelled Tarhazoute or even Taghagant – is now known for great winter waves. Come late November, the first visitors arrive to join a clique of hardcore locals. By January, when low-pressure systems barrel west across the North Atlantic to lash northern countries with storm-force winds and rain, the breaks are busy with an accomplished international crew. And it's cheap, too, when double rooms sourced

from local families cost from around 450dh a week and a tajine can be had for the price of a beer back home.

It takes serious waves to lure surfers from fabled breaks like Mundaka (in Spain) or Hossegor (in France). Taghazout's edge is its bounty. As well as several minor breaks, three right-hand points break off headlands in front of the village; waves like Anchor Point, whose flawless walled rights tumble for hundreds of metres, or Panoramas, which, by happy coincidence, concludes in front of a village bar. A few kilometres either side are breaks like Killers, a powerful reef-break named for the killer whales that cruise this coast, and Banana Point, a mellow, forgiving right-hander.

Indeed, there are only two negatives to this sunny surf Utopia. One is that popular waves plus small take-off zones can equal hassle in the water; as ever, observe the rules and show respect to the locals. The other is sea urchins – so bring your wetsuit booties.

Need to know

299 Several operators specialize in camel-trekking.

300 The Pyramids are 11km west of Cairo and can be reached by bus or taxi. The site is open daily.

301 Reach Siwa by bus either from Alexandria (9hr) or Cairo (11hr).

302 You can fly into the international airport at Algiers. From there, it's around 400km to Batna town, which is close to the site.

303 *Fishawi's* is in Khan-el-Khalili and is open 24hr.

304 A variety of tajines are available from places all over Morocco, from hole-in-the-wall eateries to upmarket restaurants.

305 Meknes is widely accessible by bus and train from the major cities of Fes, Marrakesh, Tangier, Casablanca, Rabat.

306 Aswan lies 900km south of Cairo. The Aswan tourist offices in the souk and train station can recommend felucca captains and prices.

307 Many tour operators organize half-day tours from Meknes or Fes, often including a stop in the sacred town of Moulay Idriss. Renting a car makes the visit less rushed. For more info on Volubilis, visit Ⓦwhc.unesco.org/en/list/836.

308 If you're planning to visit the Sidi Oqba Mosque, make sure to wear modest clothing. Women will also need a headscarf. Non-Muslims cannot enter the prayer hall, but the door is kept open so you can peek inside.

309 White Desert safaris are easily organized at Qasr al-Farafra (Farafra Oasis) or Bawiti (Bahariya Oasis). Always inspect the vehicle and quiz the driver/guide over intended itineraries before signing up. White Desert Tours (Ⓦwhitedeserttours.com) and Helal Travel (Ⓦhelaltravel.com) are reputable local agencies.

310 For more information on travel in Morocco head to Ⓦvisitmorocco.com/en.

311 For accommodation in Fes, try the *Ville Nouvelle* or the cluster of budget places around Bab Boujeloud.

312 Accommodation ranges from Matmata's deluxe *Hôtel Diar el Barbar* (☎00 216 23 613 888; Ⓦdiarel-barbar.com) to simple guesthouses in Douiret and Toujane.

313 El Djem, a World Heritage Site, is easily visited as a day-trip from Sousse (72km north) or Monastir (63km north).

314 The Bibliotheca Alexandrina is at El Shatby 21526. See Ⓦbibalex.org for more.

315 The Festival d'Essaouira Gnaoua et Musiques du Monde (Ⓦfestival-gnaoua.net) is held annually in June. The outdoor concerts are free; there's a small fee charged for events held indoors.

316 *Gezira Palace* is now the *Cairo Marriott Hotel* in Zamalek. On a budget? Just pop in for a drink. For PS *Sudan* see Ⓦsteam-ship-sudan.com/en.

317 CTM buses run from Oujda (daily; 6hr 30min) and Er Rachidia (2 daily; 10hr). Youseff Jebbari, who speaks English, can guide you around Figuig's network of alleys (Ⓔsurvivor.afiguig@hotmail.com).

318 There is no public transport to St Anthony's Monastery. Tours are offered through hotels in Hurghada and El Gouna, or you can take a taxi from Hurghada (300km; 4hr). Monks give free tours of the monastery; you can visit the cave independently. Donations are appreciated.

319 *Auberge Chez Tihri* (Ⓦtuaregexpeditions.com) lies 2km north of Merzouga.

320 Tanta is 95km north of Cairo. The Moulid of Sayyid Ahmed al-Badawi takes place over eight days in Oct.

321 You can stay at several refurbished kasbahs along the route; the most atmospheric is *Kasbah Ellouze* (Ⓦkasbahellouze.com).

322 Abu Simbel is most commonly visited on tours from Aswan, 280km to the north, although there are a couple of hotels in Abu Simbel village. Feb 22 is an extremely popular time to visit, so booking early is recommended.

323 Chefchaouen is most easily accessed by bus from Tangier (3hr). Despite the apparent tolerance in town, be aware that cannabis possession is illegal and any foreigner caught indulging can expect the full force of Moroccan law.

324 Dahab is around a 1hr drive from Sharm el-Sheikh airport. Recommended dive companies include Ⓦblackrockdivecentre.com and Ⓦseadancedivecenter.com. Desert Dance details can be found on Facebook.

325 Entry to the *hammams* is usually around MAD5–10. If you take a massage or scrub down from a member of staff then a tip of up to MAD30 is usual, depending on how thorough they have been.

326 To find out more about joining a desert meteor-hunting trip, contact the Musée Universitaire de Météorites; Ⓦmum.uiz.ac.ma.

327 From Agadir airport there are buses to Essaouira and taxis to Taghazout. Most accommodation is with local host families; alternatively, try the surf camps (Ⓦsurfmaroc.com and Ⓦsurfberbere.com). Surf camps/surf schools offer weekly packages with board rental, lessons, travel, accommodation and meals included. You can also rent boards and wetsuits from outlets in the village.

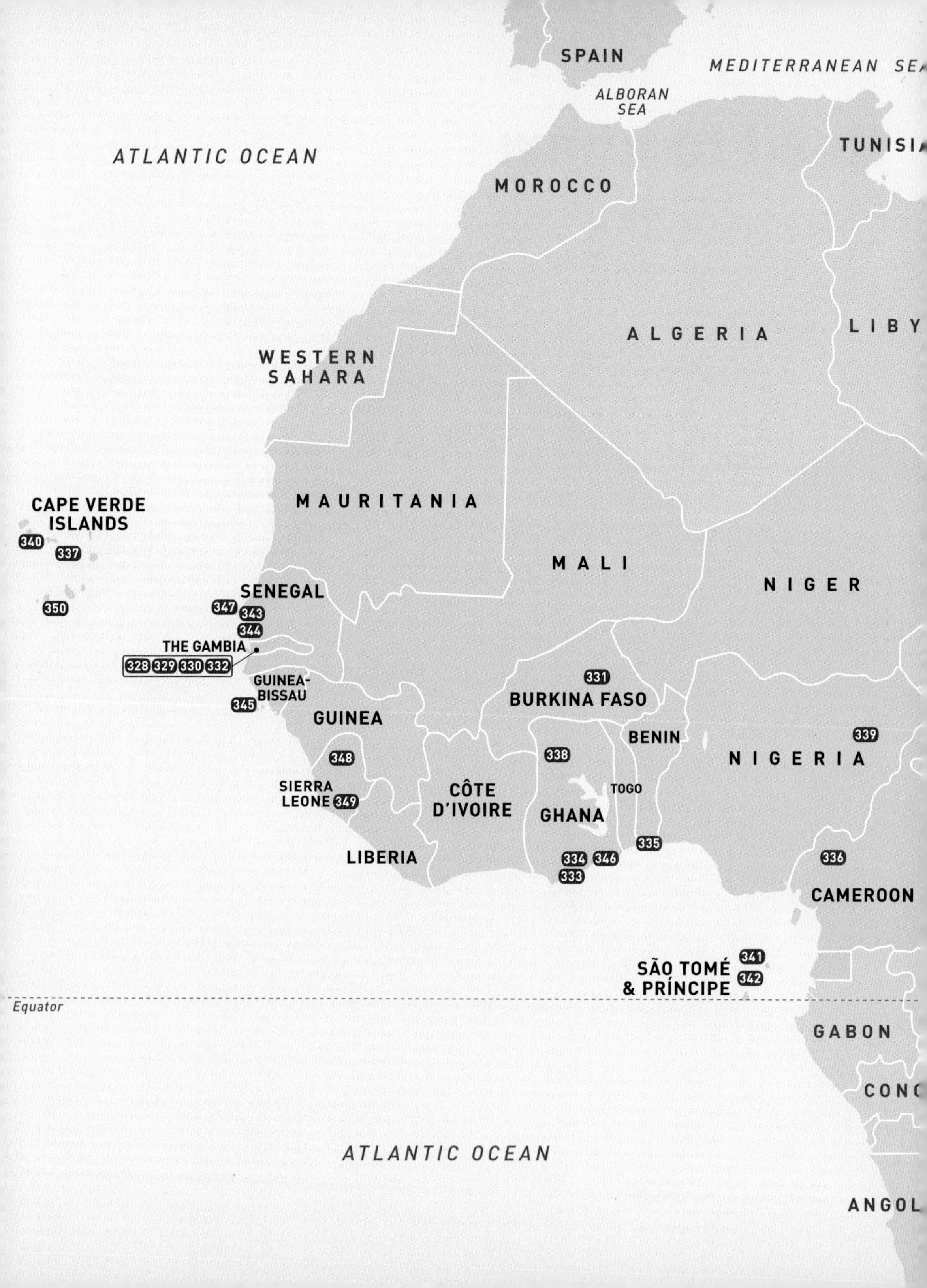

ATLANTIC OCEAN

SPAIN

MEDITERRANEAN SEA

ALBORAN
SEA

TUNISIA

MOROCCO

LIBYA

WESTERN
SAHARA

ALGERIA

MAURITANIA

MALI

NIGER

CAPE VERDE
ISLANDS

340 337

350

SENEGAL

347 343
344

THE GAMBIA

328 329 330 332

GUINEA-
BISSAU

345

GUINEA

BURKINA FASO

331

BENIN

NIGERIA

339

348

338

SIERRA
LEONE 349

CÔTE
D'IVOIRE

GHANA

TOGO

335

336

LIBERIA

334 346
333

CAMEROON

SÃO TOMÉ
& PRÍNCIPE

341
342

GABON

Equator

CONGO

ATLANTIC OCEAN

ANGOLA

WEST AFRICA
328–350

Thumping with music and simmering with energy, West Africa is a soulful, tradition-rich region, home to dense tropical landscapes and pulsating cities. Out-of-the-ordinary adventure effectively comes guaranteed, whether you're hippo-spotting in the Bijagós Islands, drinking poyo in Sierra Leone, watching island chimps in Gambia or supporting a female-led conservation initiative in Senegal. This is a welcoming and absorbing part of the world in which to travel – from volcanic Cape Verde in the west to colourful Cameroon in the east – but positively giddy with contrasts, balancing warm springs and some of the best chocolate on the planet with slave-era forts and voodoo ceremonies.

328 Admiring the catch on Sanyang beach

THE GAMBIA With pockets full of treasure – a sand dollar urchin, a cowrie, a piece of wave-bitten wood – we're padding along Sanyang beach. It's late in the day, and we hardly recognize the place, even though we were here just a few hours ago, strolling in the opposite direction. Then, in the monochrome midday heat, the shoreline was near-deserted. It's since become a boat park, a fish market, a playground for bright-eyed kids and a scavenging site for squabbling seabirds. The whole scene is a riot of colour.

A few brightly painted *pirogues* are still heading home on the incoming tide, their 12m lengths dipping into the water, heavy with the day's haul. It takes strength to manhandle them onto logs and roll them up the beach. Once ashore, prize catches such as small sharks or whip-tailed rays are held up and admired, and quick deals are struck as the quarry is divided among the crew members or offloaded to traders.

The fishermen's wives and daughters, their heads wrapped in vivid cotton *tikos*, squat beside buckets of greasy-skinned bonga fish, scraping scales onto the sand or slicing open sea snails to reveal oozing grey innards. The metallic tang of salt and blood mingles with the eye-wateringly pungent aroma of dried fish that wafts across from the smokehouses.

We're only a few kilometres from the busiest Gambian resorts. Fifteen minutes' drive and we'd be hearing a different kaleidoscope of sounds – the snap and sigh of beer bottles opening, the hairdryer-whirr of tourists getting ready for the evening ahead. But, right now, there's nothing I'd rather be listening to than these fishermen shouting good-natured jokes while the gulls wheel and call overhead.

Emma Gregg
Award-winning travel writer Emma Gregg is the author or co-author of several Rough Guides, including *First-Time Africa* and *East Coast Australia*. Emma also writes about responsible and ethical tourism, food, culture, wildlife, nature and eco-friendly adventures for national newspapers and magazines.

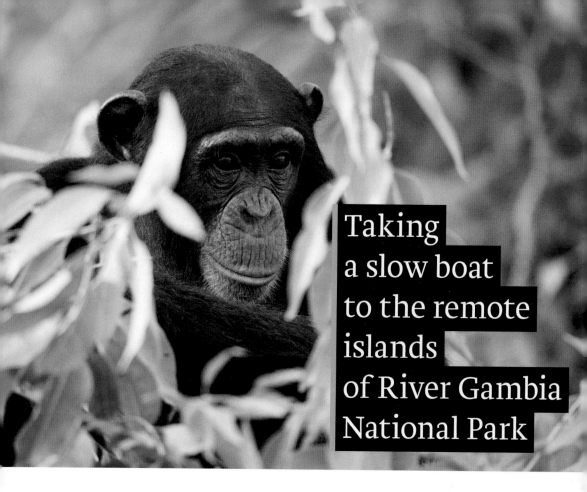

Taking a slow boat to the remote islands of River Gambia National Park

THE GAMBIA To see chimpanzees in their natural habitat is both humbling and exciting. Biologists drily inform us that we share more than 95 percent of our genes with these silky-black-haired apes, but the similarities are viscerally apparent, above all in their tendency to walk upright, and their astonishingly expressive faces.

The Chimp Rehabilitation Project was established in the River Gambia National Park in 1979, when fifty orphaned chimps, many confiscated from zoos or animal traffickers, were released onto a trio of forested islands. Thanks to an ongoing breeding programme, the islands now support a total of 104 chimpanzees, split between four communities.

Tourists can't set foot on the islands, partly for their own protection, and also to prevent the transmission of diseases common to both humans and chimps. River trips, however, offer a fantastic opportunity to see the chimpanzees up close as they groom, play, eat and squabble on the forested shore, largely indifferent to passing boats.

The lushly tropical stretch of the River Gambia protected within the park is fringed by tall palms and pristine jungle. And while chimps are the uncontested star turn, boat trips also introduce visitors to an entertaining supporting cast, including three types of monkey, some of the country's last few surviving hippos, and abundant crocodiles, as well as parrots and other colourful forest birds.

Nightfall brings more magic. Drinks and dinner are enjoyed in a rickety riverside wooden lodge, accompanied by the mysterious chatter of nocturnal frogs and insects. Accommodation is in tent-like canvas rooms, set on a breezy clifftop platform, below an African night sky undiluted by electric lighting. Morning dawns to a cacophony of birdsong and a splendid view across the canopy to the river below. Over on the island, a couple of dozen chimps clamber down from their nests. Their so-called "pant-hoot call" – a frenzied communal vocalization that builds to a spine-chilling eruptive crescendo – provides parting guests with one last unforgettable moment.

Big beaks and hasty undertakers: watching hornbills

THE GAMBIA Just like its people, the avian population of this small West African nation are a welcoming lot. There's a remarkable abundance and variety of birds to be found, and a great many are colourful, conspicuous individuals with a "look at me!" attitude – it's bird-nerd heaven. Spotting them is as easy as stepping out onto your veranda: every hotel garden is alive with jaunty little finches, doves, sunbirds and glossy starlings.

Adventurous travellers, though, will want to hire a guide and head off on the kind of walk where you get burrs in your socks and need frequent swigs from your water bottle. In some areas, you can clock up a hundred or more species in a few hours. Common wetland birds such as kingfishers, pelicans, herons and egrets, and savannah-dwellers such as vultures and rollers are practically guaranteed – and so too are many bird-watchers' favourites, the hornbills.

As endearing as they are faintly ridiculous, hornbills have beaks that seem too large for their bodies, and their flapping, gliding flight looks nothing short of haphazard. What's more, they take parental paranoia to grand extremes: during breeding season (July and August), you may see a male incarcerating his female and her brood in a nest sealed with mud, high up in a tree, where they'll stay until the young are strong enough to survive on their own.

The most lugubrious fellow of all is the Abyssinian ground hornbill. Nearly a metre tall, cloaked in black and with a beak of Gothic proportions, it strides through the open grassland with the undignified haste of an undertaker who's late for an urgent appointment. It's by far the largest – and the most impressive – of the hornbills, so if you manage to spot one, you've really scored. And before you know it, you'll be posting gloating field notes online like a true convert.

331 | Hobnobbing with Africa's film-making jet set

BURKINA FASO In an attempt to reinvent Ouagadougou, the government in Burkina Faso took the drastic decision to raze most of its centre to the ground in 2013. Apartment blocks were bulldozed and residents relocated to outlying neighbourhoods, while architects pondered how to make the Burkinabé capital the envy of West Africa. The plan was to create a gleaming new centre, although arguably Ouaga's true renaissance began when FESPACO first rolled into town forty-odd years ago.

It might not be the most likely cultural centre, but this stifling Sahelian city, known largely for its catchy name, hosts the continent's biggest film festival – one explicitly dedicated to African film-making. The biennial event is a great time to be in Ouaga. Several understated cinemas, wisely left intact by city-planners, show Africa's latest cinematographic offerings, from touching pastoral tales to riotous comedies, and festival-goers get the chance to rub shoulders with film stars and directors.

After the screenings, Ouaga's restaurants fill with people from all corners of Africa and beyond. Over glasses of French wine, lively discussions revolve around the contenders for the Étalon de Yennenga, the festival's most prestigious award, presented to the film that best symbolizes the cultural identity of Africa. And in the seething, sweaty *cabarets* (bars), local bands play as large divas dressed in vibrantly coloured *boubous* and kaftans try in vain to teach tourists to dance.

FESPACO is a democratic and unpretentious gathering, a melting pot that's the antithesis of the glitz and glamour of, say, Cannes. Forums, debates and other events offer easy access to film-makers; rather than a mere autograph, fans stand to get phone numbers, email addresses and even the chance to establish lasting friendships with the big names of Africa's silver screen. And who knows, one day Ouagadougou may even have the kind of infrastructure that wouldn't look out of place along the Côte d'Azur.

332 | Graffiti in the bush

THE GAMBIA In most respects, Galloya is a village much like any other in western Gambia. Its houses are small, well spaced and rectangular in plan, with plastered walls and corrugated-iron roofs providing a little shade on either side. Cattle and goats amble freely among the mango and cashew trees, occasionally discovering something edible in the dust. Hens scurry and peck, and the sound of children's chatter is a constant.

Galloya may stand less than 20km from Gambia's main hubs of commerce and tourism, but it's unmistakably rural. Though this is hardly the obvious place to look for something as urban as cutting-edge street art, however, that's exactly what you'll find.

Murals are everywhere. A fractured figure with a photorealistic face and a body painted bright yellow, blue and purple stares down from one facade, while an abstract portrait of an African woman with a pink eye adorns another. The end of one house is a riot of colour that spills down over the step where kids gather, making them part of the tableau.

For a couple of weeks each year, a motley assortment of leading international graffiti artists descends on Ballabu, a cluster of fourteen villages including Galloya, to make free with spray cans and brushes. Known as Wide Open Walls, the project was conceived by British-born Lawrence Williams, who owns a long-running and highly successful cultural ecotourism project nearby, called Makasutu. A passionate advocate for the transformative power of public art, he dreamed of turning the Ballabu villages into an open-air gallery – with the villagers' full consent.

Williams is also an artist himself, working with Gambian painter Njogu Touray under the name Bushdwellers. They're responsible for some of the murals, while others were created by the likes of Eelus, ROA, sheOne, Best/Ever and Remi Rough.

So what do the locals make of the paintings? "They take care of them and try to protect them as much as possible," says Lawrence. "They feel a real sense of ownership. Their children gain so much from having art in their everyday lives."

333 | The Gold Coast: sun, sea and historic forts

GHANA In 1471, Portuguese merchant seamen arrived on the palm-lined shore of the Gold Coast and built a fort at Elmina. Over the next four hundred years they were followed by British, Dutch, Swedes, Danes and adventurers from the Baltic. Gold was their first desire, but the slave trade soon came to dominate, and more than three dozen forts were established, exchanging human cargo for cloth, liquor and guns. Thirty are still standing, several in dramatic locations and offering atmospheric tours and accommodation. Here you can combine poignant historical discovery with time on the beach – a rare blend in this part of the world.

The seventeenth-century Cape Coast Castle overshadows the lively town of the same name. Just walking through its claustrophobic dungeons, where slaves were held before being shipped across the Atlantic, moves some visitors to tears – the scale of the cruelties is near-incomprehensible.

A huge harvest festival, the Oguaa Fetu – a noisy, palm-wine-lubricated parade of chiefs, fetish priests and queen mothers – takes over town in September. To be made particularly welcome, bring along some schnapps, the customary gift for traditional rulers, with whom you may well be granted an audience.

In the bustling fishing port of Elmina, the photogenic St George's Castle and Fort St Jago eye each other across the lagoon. St George's offers a worthwhile historical and cultural exhibition, and the town itself holds several intricate traditional shrines – pastel-coloured edifices of platforms, arches and militaristic figurines.

Some of the best beaches are at Busua, which has a low-key resort an easy walk from the cutely perched Fort Metal Cross. A day-trip to the far western coast, between Princes Town and Axim, brings you to an even finer stretch of beaches and sandy coves punctuated with jungle-swathed headlands.

GHANA Take the main coastal road west from capital city Accra and, after negotiating the dust and thrum of the suburbs, you'll encounter some of Ghana's choicest sights. Naturally, there are beaches – broad, surf-bashed sands – but you'll also find some striking standalone attractions. These include the riotously colourful towns of Cape Coast and Elmina – both of which hold sobering, slave-era castles – as well as the verdant slice of semi-deciduous virgin rainforest preserved in Kakum National Park. It's here you'll find a forest walk with a difference.

Elevated 40m above the forest floor, and stretching for a total of 350m, the park's treetop canopy walkway consists of vertiginous wood-and-cable bridges suspended between huge hardwood trunks. These larger trees tower above the general tree height, so you're granted canopy-level views. Platforms along the way offer spectacular, if giddying, panoramas across the park, and an

eddying soundtrack of mingled birdcalls underlines the fact that you're up in avian territory (binocular-carriers take note: Kakum is home to some two hundred bird species, as well as more than 400 butterfly types).

Although the park's 600 square kilometres also hold four-legged residents including forest elephants, giant hogs and even leopards, the density of the jungle means you're unlikely to see much evidence of them. And in truth, any animal and bird life is just a bonus. It's possible to arrange overnight camping trips (which offer good potential for elephant-spotting), but for most visitors the main draw is the walkway itself, its bridges swaying slightly as they lead you over lush West African rainforest. It's easily reached too, being close to the visitor centre. Take your time over the walk – it feels a privilege to gaze out across the canopy. And if you do happen to spy a leopard prowling through the undergrowth – well, you'll be glad you're at a different altitude.

BENIN Despite the fact that Ouidah boasts one of West Africa's most beautiful beaches, the Atlantic walkway is not its main attraction. Situated 40km west of Cotonou, Benin's de facto if not official capital, this former centre of West Africa's slave trade is the home of voodoo's eleventh supreme chief, the Daagbo (His Majesty) Tomadjlehoukpon II Metogbokandji. For visitors and locals alike, Ouidah is one of the region's most important centres of this oft-misunderstood belief.

Voodoo, Benin's official religion, isn't about sticking pins in dolls fashioned in the form of your mother-in-law or ex-boyfriend. Nor is it about the evil spells or devil worship that Hollywood makes it out to be. It's actually a faith with over fifty million followers worldwide, all worshipping a Supreme Being along with hundreds of lesser gods and spirits.

In Ouidah, the cityscape bears constant witness to its influence. Fetishes – any man-made object that has been occupied by a spirit – lurk among the faded Portuguese-style buildings and along the grassy road to the beach. You may notice them because they look

out of place in their environment, or are covered in the bloody, waxy remains of a recent animal sacrifice.

A kilometre down a dirt track from town, the Sacred Forest of Kpasse is guarded by a dozen or so statues honouring the various manifestations of the gods. Several are made from old motorcycle parts, but the most striking lies near the entrance, a metre-high horned creature with an enormous phallus, symbolizing strength and fertility. When ceremonies to the snake god Dangbé (also known as Dan) are not under way in Ouidah's Temple of the Python, visitors can creep inside its cement walls to have their photos taken with sleepy and harmless pythons slung around their necks.

The town also hosts a voodoo festival each January, and various ceremonies are held throughout the year, when costumed dancers and those "fortunate" enough to be temporarily possessed by spirits sway to the beat of drums, summoning the gods. And, if you're really lucky, you might get invited in for an audience with the Supreme Chief himself, regally perched in an imitation La-Z-Boy and sipping a Fanta. Imagine the Pope being so hospitable.

CAMEROON Straddling the fault line between English- and French-speaking Cameroon, the green, hilly Western Region is one of Africa's most verdant corners, a spectacularly beautiful bubble-wrap landscape of grassy volcanic hills, rivers, lakes and forests. The single "main road" that circles it in a 200km red-earth loop makes a perfect route for a superb week of cycling.

Start from the cacophonous, English-speaking town of Bamenda, then pedal north for an hour or two to Bafut, made famous by naturalist Gerald Durrell, whose *Bafut Beagles* recounts his visit collecting zoo animals here in the 1950s.

Durrell stayed with the traditional ruler, the Fon of Bafut, whose son, the present *fon*, encourages visits to the thatched-roofed palace complex. Come at the end of the dry season to participate in the riotous, palm wine-lubricated grass-cutting ceremony.

Further north, one or more wooden bridges on the Ring Road may well be down, so your much-mocked mode of transport (locals think it hilarious for tourists to cycle) will prove a wise, as well as fun, choice. In village markets, look out for fantastic arrays of fruit and veg – intensely flavoured, green-skinned, orange-fleshed mangoes, and avocados the size of boats. You'll also pass Lake Nyos where, one night in 1986, a freak cloud of natural carbon dioxide from the lake asphyxiated thousands of people and animals.

At Dumbo, past the lush pastures of the Grassfields, you have the option of completing the Ring Road round to Bamenda or setting off north to Nigeria, down a vertiginous escarpment of boulders, tree roots and twisting paths. If the latter takes your fancy, you can hire a porter in Dumbo for the two-day hike – he'll even carry your bike, padded and trussed up and balanced on his head.

Atlantic entreaty: stumbling upon Cape Verdean soul music

CAPE VERDE It's dim inside the little bar, cinder-black stone walls keeping the blinding island light at bay. There are no other customers, but the atmosphere is as thick as the gloom. Food and drink are served without fuss on the rough-hewn bar – a thick, heady red wine and the freshest ball of goat's cheese you've ever tasted. Suddenly the hulking, bearded bartender grabs a battered guitar from under the counter and, apropos of nothing, howls at the moon – a guttural *cri de coeur* so elemental in its pain that it takes your breath away.

It takes an instant to realize this is the rawest, most essential human song you've ever heard in your life, and all your preconceived ideas about music have been turned on their head. That this man will probably never make it to a recording studio is beside the point – in the other, mid-Atlantic world of Cape Verde, music happens in the moment. You can mourn for it when it's gone, but you can't hold on to it.

If you want a more comprehensive taste of Cape Verdean music, all the diverse strands that run through this nine-island group come together in events like the Baia das Gatas festival on São Vicente, and Santiago's Kriol Jazz Festival. There you'll hear the sounds and see the faces that Cape Verde presents to the world, legends like Titina and Tito Paris alongside younger stars such as Sara Tavares, Myra Andrade and Ceuzany. With the Atlantic Music Expo, the islands now even have their own annual world music-biz trade-bash.

It's in the archipelago's further-flung corners, however, that revelations happen on a whim – in the wastes of a lava-scape on the slopes of Fogo, or at a humble restaurant on the impossibly romantic shores of Brava, where no one gives a fig that the prime minister is sitting at the next table, and where you're slowly hypnotized away from your food by a high, keening, maddeningly sweet-and-sour siren wail that turns your digestion inside out, and which you'll still be hearing in your dreams years from now.

338

GHANA As breakfast companions go, wild five-ton bull elephants take some beating. True, they may not display much decorum, as they tear down thick branches and chomp leafy foliage, but table manners have never been too important on the savannah. And when all that separates you from an enthusiastically dining pachyderm is a few metres of undergrowth and a guide who knows his stuff, it's some thrill.

West Africa tends not to be seen as prime safari territory, but in Mole National Park – Ghana's largest wildlife refuge – you can have an up-close elephant encounter for the kind of money that would barely get you a glass of wine in the exclusive lodges of the continent's better known safari destinations. On-foot safaris always bring an extra frisson of adventure to any wildlife-spotting trip, and Mole's daily dawn walks are further boosted by the fact that the park holds a good spread of other fauna. As well as elephants, you're likely to come across bushbucks, waterbucks, kob antelopes, green monkeys, baboons and warthogs, not to mention a kaleidoscopic range of birdlife running to some three hundred species, from Abyssinian ground hornbills to red-throated bee-eaters. If your guide's on sharp-eyed form, meanwhile, your two-hour walk might also incorporate anything from hyena prints to an aardvark's den. Lions, leopards and buffalo are out there somewhere, but the reserve covers more than 4500 square kilometres, and the chances of stumbling across a teeth-baring predator in the portion of Mole that's used for walking safaris are – perhaps thankfully – slim to none. Even so, you may be relieved to hear that guides carry rifles.

Reaching the park can be something of an exploit in itself, with access along a long bumpy dirt road from the minaret-studded city of Tamale. Most visitors stay put for at least a couple of nights, and a well-priced lodge with a pool and bar adds to the appeal.

Track elephants on foot (for peanuts)

339 | Soaking in Wikki Warm Springs

NIGERIA Bathing in the near-perfect natural pool at Wikki Warm Springs, part of Nigeria's remote Yankari National Park, is one of West Africa's most gratifying experiences. Below the park lodge, down a steep path, the upper Gaji stream bubbles up from a deep cleft beneath a rose-coloured, sandstone cliff.

Twelve million litres a day, at a constant 31ºC, flood out over sparkling sand between a dense bank of overhanging tropical foliage on one side and the concrete apron that serves as a beach on the other – the one dud note in an otherwise picture-perfect environment, though the concrete helps keep the crystal-clear water clean. Floodlighting makes the springs equally idyllic at night, lending them a satisfyingly theatrical appearance, like an elaborate New Age interior design piece. A good deal larger than most swimming pools, the springs are the ideal place to wash away the frustrations of travelling in Nigeria.

Should you tire of simply drifting on your back above the gentle current, you can explore the woods around the lodge for their abundant birdlife. It's also possible to join Yankari's rangers on a guided game drive, which brings you into close contact with the park's savannah mammals, including several species of antelope, a variable population of elephants and, it's said, even lions. If, as occasionally happens, the viewing isn't up to much, returning to Wikki Warm Springs, and that delightful initial immersion, is ample compensation.

340 | Grass skirts and glitter: Carnaval in Mindelo

CAPE VERDE Mindelo's pre-Lenten carnival is inspired by Brazil's Mardi Gras – think Rio or São Paulo in miniature, with a quirky island twist. For four days, this most charming of Cape Verdean towns is engulfed by parades and concerts, modest in scale but lacking nothing in cheerful exuberance. While it's by no means the only place in the archipelago that goes crazy at this time of year, Mindelo, the capital of São Vicente, is the hottest ticket, its pretty colonial squares and colourful corniche making the perfect backdrop for an all-out party.

Elegantly laid out on a beautiful bay ringed with mountains, Mindelo is a cultured town with a breezy, cosmopolitan atmosphere. For centuries, ocean-going travellers, traders and thinkers have crossed paths here. The late, great Cesaria Evora kept a home base in Mindelo all her life, and many musicians, artists, writers and poets still do.

Gearing up for Carnaval is a lengthy affair. Troupes from each neighbourhood compete for accolades including best float and best music. People of all ages, from toddlers to grandmothers, take part, sharing out traditional roles. These always include scores of *mandingas* – young men kitted out as African tribal warriors in shiny black body paint and grass skirts, brandishing spears – and samba girls in colourful satin outfits with feathered headdresses and glittery make-up.

The parades are a visual feast and a riot of noise. *Batucadas* (drum bands) clatter through the streets and everyone dances like there's no tomorrow – this fast-paced brand of Cape Verdean music is a far cry from the slow, soulful *morna* ballads made famous by Cesaria Evora. For a dizzying overview, find your way onto a balcony overlooking Rua de Lisboa. It's fun to drop down to street level, too, to watch performers touching up their ensembles and practising their moves on the Avenida da República, or to mingle with the crowds.

Many spectators get into the swing of things by dressing up in horror masks, silly wigs or full-blown fancy dress. To join the fun, you could come prepared, or simply improvise with face paint and fripperies picked up in town.

341 | Spotting rainforest orchids in a prog-rock paradise

SÃO TOMÉ & PRÍNCIPE The island nation of São Tomé and Príncipe is Africa's second-smallest country, after the Seychelles. Marooned in the sweltering Gulf of Guinea, just 250km from the equatorial rainforests of Gabon, its size hasn't stopped it being blessed with remarkable biodiversity.

Volcanic eruptions sculpted the archipelago's landscapes into dramatic crags and made them exceptionally fertile. Both of the main islands – São Tomé to the southwest and Príncipe to the northeast – are steep-sided, their heights cloaked in humid forest. On São Tomé, mist-shrouded towers of basalt add a surreal touch. Exploring the remoter corners feels like stepping into a prog-rock album cover, or the set of a *Lord of the Rings* spin-off.

Head into the virgin rainforest of Obô National Park and you can't fail to be wowed by the sheer variety of plant species. The Jardim Botânico de Bom Sucesso, the starting point for guided tours through the park, gives you an excellent overview, with a fine array of native flora, carefully tended by local horticulturalists. Obô itself, which covers much of central and southeast São Tomé including the 2024m Pico de São Tomé, is home to giant begonias and over 150 types of tree fern – more than anywhere else in Africa. Birds and insects gravitate here: as you make your way along the mountain tracks, butterflies dance in the sunlight and African grey parrots squawk and chatter overhead.

Orchid aficionados will be in their element. Around 130 species have been identified on the islands to date, a quarter of them endemic, the descendants of plants whose seeds found their way here from the African mainland millions of years ago and have evolved in isolation ever since. Visit Obô in the rainiest months, March to April or September to December, and many of them will be in bloom. Some, such as *Cribbia pendula*, are inconspicuous, so spotting them makes a pleasant challenge. Others are more colourful: *Bulbophyllum lizae* is a delicate yellow, *Polystachya biteaui* is as pretty as lily-of-the-valley, but a delightful dusty pink.

342 | In search of the best chocolate in the world

SÃO TOMÉ & PRÍNCIPE You know you're in a country far from modernity when one of the main problems facing landowners is reforestation. São Tomé has largely been forgotten by the outside world since Portuguese colonizers packed up and left in the mid-1970s.

Away from São Tomé town – where the faded colonial-era buildings try their best to decay with elegiac ease, despite the occasional tree bursting out of a rooftop – and into the awesomely lush interior, the occasional glimpse of a long-abandoned train track is the only clue that you are about to stumble upon one of the many old plantation or roca buildings.

Built by Angolan and Portuguese slaves, these grandiose structures helped make São Tomé one of the world's leading cacao and coffee producers at the start of the twentieth century. The owner's residence of the large Augustino Neto plantation looks something like a minor Inca fortress, but, like most others on the island, it is derelict – independence and subsequent Marxist governments have brought cacao production to its knees.

There are, however, smaller signs of life elsewhere. Individual entrepreneurs are slowly arriving at this tiny island, drawn to try farming with São Tomé's exceptionally fertile soil. Italian Claudio Corallo has started a tiny cacao plantation on the even smaller neighbouring island of Príncipe, where his chocolate is so luxurious that it is bought by Fortnum & Mason in London. He'll tell you how his cottage industry has cultivated cacao species that many thought extinct; ask him nicely, and he might even give you some cocoa powder.

A tiny teaspoonful mixed with boiling water sipped on his rotting veranda in a chipped and battered mug is an explosion of rich and sumptuous flavour. This is sweetness taken straight from the raw coalface of chocolate production, and as Claudio proudly insists, "the taste is out of this world".

343 | Joining a female-led eco-initiative in Popenguine

SENEGAL I'm sitting on a crumbling old World War II-era French pillbox built on top of Popenguine's Cap de Naze, an elevated mass of volcanic rock. Below, wild Atlantic waves crash against the cliffs and scour the endless white-sand beaches, while the urban expanse of Dakar shimmers, barely perceptible, in the far distance. A lone osprey gracefully soars overhead and a pair of colourful Abyssinian rollers dart in and out of a stately baobab tree, while the acacia and tamarisk trees all around buzz and twitter with insects and birdlife.

Go back thirty years, however, and it was a very different picture: the wood in the forest had been plundered for both building materials and firewood, and the land was so degraded that it no longer acted as a viable defence from the wild ocean. That is, until a coalition of local women's groups from the surrounding villages got together with the Department of Forestry and, along with funding from a French NGO, took on the conservation of the land, naming it La Réserve Naturelle de Popenguine.

Visiting the park requires a permit and a guide, both of which are easily sought from the *Campement* next door. Guides are university-educated conservationists and speak a variety of languages, including English and French. You can also stay the night in the simple thatched huts of the *Campement* and then chat with some of the local women involved in the project as they prepare breakfast. The best time to hike in the park is dawn when the air is moist and cool, and the sun hasn't yet begun to appear from behind the hills. You might even spot a porcupine or hyena heading home from their nocturnal wanderings.

344 | Sleeping in a baobab tree in the Siné Saloum Delta

SENEGAL That treehouse you loved as a kid – did it have a creaky old wooden ladder, your very own stairway to heaven, its top rungs thrillingly high? If you were really lucky, the platform was big enough (and safe enough) for sleepouts. Did you dream of living there forever?

Deep in the northern Siné Saloum Delta, *Le Lodge des Collines de Niassam* smiles upon your childhood dreams and takes them to another level – literally. Find your way to this remote, rural eco-lodge and you can sleep in a multi-storey treehouse that hugs the elephant-hide bark of a wise old baobab tree.

Halfway up its steps you'll discover a rustic outdoor deck, wrapped in the tree's muscular embrace. Airy in the dry season, it's sun-dappled in the rainy season, between July and September or October, when the baobabs of Senegal are in leaf. Another level up, an open landing leads into a timber hideaway that holds a net-draped bed along with the simplest of furnishings. What more could anyone possibly ask for?

The lodge – which also includes Amazigh (Berber) tents, grass-thatched huts and cute little roundhouses perched on stilts over a lagoon – is satisfyingly eco-friendly. Built from local materials to blend into a knot of woodland on the sandy shore, it's powered by solar energy and cooled by Atlantic breezes. Surrounding it is a patchwork of salt flats and shallow waterways, which attracts flocks of pelicans, herons and egrets, and also draws birdwatchers by the score.

The owners, who are French, feed their guests well and encourage them to explore. You can head out on bushwalks or boat trips, visit the local market or attend a traditional wrestling match, a flurry of strength and bravado in a sandy arena. Sooner or later, though, the peace of the place will work its magic and you'll want to climb.

345

Hippo-spotting in the Bijagós Islands

GUINEA-BISSAU An acacia tree drips and keels under the sheer weight of weaverbirds' nests, an egret launches silently up into the cloudless sky, a saltwater crocodile lurks motionlessly in the marshes while leeches nearby await some tasty flesh to devour. You'll need to tread carefully through these swampy mangroves of Orango island if you want to spot a hippo. These reclusive giants languish in the lagoons of the Bijagós archipelago's largest island, surrounded by verdant undergrowth and protective of their young calves. But rumour has it that these hippos have a secret night-time hobby: surfing. The salt of the seawater acts as a disinfectant on their skin, so they head there after sunset and roll among the waves with a surprising ungainly grace. Beware, however, the jaws of the hippo are responsible for more deaths in Africa than any other large animal so you must take an experienced local guide.

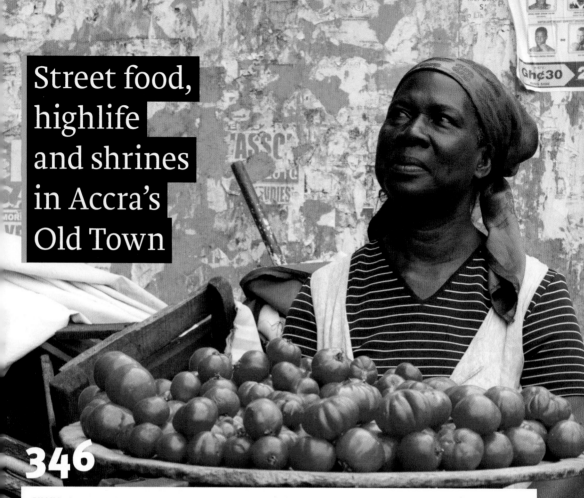

Street food, highlife and shrines in Accra's Old Town

346

GHANA If you spend most of your time in Accra's central business district around Adabraka, or in the commercial suburbs of Osu and East Ridge, you may overlook the Ghanaian capital's historic heart, the adjoining neighbourhoods of Usshertown and Jamestown. This atmospheric warren of streets and alleys lies just back from the Atlantic seafront behind the main coastal highway. Old Accra (or "Ga Mashie" to its local inhabitants) is a generally safe area to wander through alone, but you'll get more out of the visit, and greater freedom to take photos, if you're accompanied by a guide.

Beneath corrugated-iron roofs and between tinder-dry clapboard walls – hand-painted with adverts for fish and phones and often lettered with the characters of the Ga language – the district resonates with the noise of things being made, discussions about things being sold and the growl and crash of r'n'b and highlife playing from straining sound systems.

There are reminders of the Ga's pre-colonial religious and political systems here, too: look out for the Sakumo shrine by an old well on Orgle Street, where you might meet priests on the shady terrace (though you won't be allowed inside). Just around the corner, pause at the Gbese Mantse Palace, with its portrait of current *mantse* (neighbourhood chief) Nii Ay-Bonte II.

When you're tired of wandering, take a break at the small museum of slavery in Ussher Fort, on the clifftop. Nearby, Brazil House records the story of nineteenth-century Brazilian freed-slave returnees – the Tabon community (named after the Portuguese greeting "Ta bom?").

The veranda of neighbouring Franklin House is a good spot for gazing down on the busy beach, thronged with people and fishing boats. You can get street food and a cold soda on any corner: try *kenkey* (fermented, pounded maize), or *fufu* (pounded cassava, sometimes mixed with plantain), with chunks of smoked fish and scorching pepper sauce.

The best time to be in Old Accra is the second week of August, so you don't miss the Ga harvest festival of Homowo. You'll find music, drumming, men in toga-like robes, processions of twins, and what anthropologists call "suspension of behavioural sanctions" – partying.

347 | Hollow footprints in the sand

SENEGAL Though the colonial mansions that line the sandy streets of Gorée, 3.5km off Dakar, may now seem quaint, they serve as painful reminders of the island's shameful past. Between the sixteenth and nineteenth centuries, this was a trading post from which captured slaves were taken to the Americas, and the houses were home to the slave traders themselves. Some are now beautifully preserved, freshly painted in vivid hues; others have been left to crumble under the African sun.

Built by the Dutch in 1776, La Maison des Esclaves (The House of Slaves) was a holding pen where slaves might languish for three months before being shipped across the Atlantic. It has now been turned into a museum dedicated to exposing the horrors of the slave trade.

From the balcony of its second floor, where the traders actually lived, you now peer down to where buyers once scrutinized the slaves. The price of each slave depended on several factors. A child's age was determined by the quantity of teeth in his or her mouth, while young girls were valued on the state of their breasts and their virginity, and a man according to his weight. Any man weighing less than 60kg was placed in a cell to be "fattened" with beans. As a girl who fell pregnant after having sexual relations with a slave trader would be set free, it was in a young girl's best interests to try to catch the eye of a trader.

Visiting is a harrowing and emotional experience. The small galleries and cells – each no more than 2.60m by 2.60m – evoke the suffering and distress that shook the entire continent. Even more poignant is the "door of no return", through which African men, women and children left trails of footprints as they were led to the ships, knowing they would never set foot in their homeland again. Entire families were torn apart – the mother might be sent to the US, the father to Haiti, and the children to Brazil, never to see one another again.

348 | Drinking poyo fresh from the tree

SIERRA LEONE As you leave the noise and dust of Freetown behind, heading up-country along the red rural roads of Sierra Leone, you start to see them: the men carrying large yellow jerry cans slosh-full of liquid. Sometimes you pass one who's bent double, weighed down by a stick across his back, a jerry can dangling from either end. At other times you will see a cluster of cans standing sentry along the edge of remote dirt tracks, or hanging from low-branched trees, like bizarre plastic fruit.

The precious cargo they contain is not petrol, but poyo – the palm wine that is such a hugely popular drink across Sierra Leone, and regarded as a kind of home-grown nectar.

Every day, men from each village climb even the spindliest of palm trees to collect their treasure, each armed with a bucket and a wooden 'tap' implement tucked into his back pocket. Once at the top, they only have to tap the palm and out glugs the wine – pure and unfiltered. After the sap has fermented for a few hours up on the tree, jerry cans of the stuff are lowered down and sold in every imaginable location – at the roadside, on the beach, in the villages. Wherever you spot a yellow container, you can buy a mug of poyo for a small handful of Leones. The price is negligible – and a friendly stranger may even let you try before you buy. It's always worth asking around, though, to find what's considered the best poyo in the vicinity.

The liquid emerges from the can white, frothy, and none too tempting; as often as not, it's speckled with bits of bark and unidentifiable lumps. Locals like to say poyo comes "straight from God to man", but some first-timers find the taste less than heavenly. The first sip is sulphurous, the next sour, the next woody, but give it time and the taste will grow on you. Famed for its relaxing – and "romantic" – qualities, poyo is best drunk up-country, freshly tapped, not too far from the tree: the ultimate Salone sundowner as the blue sky turns black.

349 | Spotting small hippos on Big Island

SIERRA LEONE Deep in the maze of waterways, woodland and farm plots of southeast Sierra Leone lies Tiwai Island Wildlife Sanctuary, sheltering an extraordinarily rich fauna.

Tiwai means "Big Island" in the local language, and this truly is the Africa of the imagination, the air saturated with the incessant chirrups, squawks and yelps of birds, chimpanzees, tree hyraxes, assorted insects and hundreds of other creatures, all doing their thing in twelve square kilometres of rainforest. In the background, you can hear the dim rush of the Moa River where it splits to roar around Tiwai through channels and over rocks.

As you weave along paths between the giant buttress roots of the trees, park guides will track troops of colobus and diana monkeys and should know where to find the chimps. You're not likely to see the rarest and most secretive of Tiwai's denizens, however – that's the hog-sized pygmy hippo – unless you go jungle walking at night, when they traipse their habitual solitary trails through the undergrowth.

Exploring after dark with a guide is, in fact, highly recommended – take a lamp with plenty of kerosene, and a good torch. By night, the forest is a powerful presence, with an immense, consuming vigour. Every rotten branch teems with termites, and on all sides, as you stumble over the roots, you sense the organs of detection of a million unseen creatures waving at your illuminated figure. You can also take a boat tour on the Moa River in a canoe or motorboat, watching out for rare birds and butterflies and looking for turtles below the surface.

Peaking on Fogo

350

CAPE VERDE First impressions of Fogo, rising in a cone 2800m above the ocean, are of its forbidding mass, the steep, dark slopes looming above the clouds. The small plane is buffeted on Atlantic winds as you dip onto the runway, perched high on dun-coloured cliffs above a thin strip of black beach and ultramarine sea.

Fogo ("Fire" in Portuguese) is the most captivating of the Cape Verde Islands, with its dramatic caldera and peak, its fearsomely robust red wine, its traditional music and the hospitable Fogo islanders themselves.

Up in the weird moonscape of the caldera, after a slow, shared taxi ride from the picturesque capital, São Filipe, you'll be dropped on the rocky plain at a straggle of houses made of grey volcanic tufa. One of a handful of charmingly rakish-looking guides will greet you, host you in

his own home, and, early next morning, take you up the steep path to the summit, Pico de Fogo, with its extraordinary panorama. The descent is better than any theme-park ride as both guide and guided leap and tumble through the scree in an entertaining, inelegant freestyle.

Shaking out the dust and volcanic gravel at the bottom, you'll fetch up at the local social club where an impromptu band – guitar, violin, keyboard, scraper and *cavaquinho* (a four-stringed mini-guitar) – emboldened by the consumption of plentiful *vinho* and local hooch or *grogue*, often strikes up around the bar. Wind down your evening listening to Fogo's beautiful *mornas* – mournful laments of loss and longing that hark back to the archipelago's whaling past and to families far away.

Need to know

328 Sanyang beach is an easy taxi ride from Banjul and the resort towns of Kololi, Kotu, Fajara and Bakau.

329 The park is best visited on a package based out of the CRP's rustically attractive riverside camp, including accommodation, meals, boat trips and other activities. (Thurs–Sun only; 🅔 baboonislands@gmail.com).

330 Prime birdwatching areas include the Tanbi Wetlands, Abuko Nature Reserve, Brufut Woods, Marakissa and Janjanbureh. Birdfinders (🆆 birdfinders. co.uk) offers specialist tours to The Gambia.

331 FESPACO (Festival Panafricain du Cinéma et de la Télévision de Ouagadougou; 🆆 fespaco.bf) takes place in every odd-numbered year at the end of February and lasts for ten days. Book accommodation well in advance.

332 The Ballabu villages, home to Wide Open Walls (🆆 cargocollective.com/wideopenwallsgambia), lie between Brikama and the River Gambia. Plans are under way to create organized group tours – for details, contact Makasutu (🆆 mandinalodges.com) – and to build a community and visitor centre where visitors can pay an entry fee before touring independently.

333 Bus services (around 4hr) run along the main coastal highway from Accra.

334 Visit 🆆 kakumnationalpark.info for more information on Kakum National Park (closed on Sundays).

335 Ouidah is an hour's taxi ride from Cotonou. The Temple of the Python is open daily.

336 Bamenda is accessible by bus from most Cameroonian cities. 🆆 ibike.org/bikeafrica offers advice on cycling tours, and tours in Nov/Dec.

337 Baia das Gatas takes place during the Aug full moon (for exact dates, visit the Portuguese-only 🆆 facebook.com/baiadasgatas). Kriol Jazz Festival (🆆 krioljazzfestival.com), in early to mid-April, tends to attract bigger-name international stars.

338 The best time to encounter elephants is during the dry season (Sept–March). The park's accommodation, *Mole Motel* (🆆 molemotelgh.com), has options from air-con chalets to budget bunks.

339 Yankari can get crowded at weekends, especially over Christmas and Easter. The park lodge has basic rooms (🆆 yankarigamereserve.com.ng).

340 São Vicente's modern airport, ten minutes from Mindelo by taxi, is served by international flights and connections from other islands in the archipelago. Since Mindelo is a small city, it's best to book accommodation in advance, especially during Carnaval.

341 Tour operators organizing bespoke trips to São Tomé and Príncipe include Cape Verde Travel (🆆 capeverdetravel.com) and Africa's Eden (🆆 www.africas-eden. com). For more on Obo National Park and the Jardim Botânico de Bom Sucesso, see 🆆 www.obopark.com.

342 TAP (Air Portugal; 🆆 flytap.com) offers frequent flights from Lisbon to São Tomé. For more information on Claudio Corallo, visit 🆆 claudiocorallo.com.

343 Popenguine is a 25-minute taxi ride from Blaise Diagne International airport and a 40-minute drive from the coastal resort of Saly; see 🆆 rampao.org/Reserve-naturelle-de-Popenguine.html. To reserve a place at *Kër Cupaam*, call ☎ +221 3395 77251 or email 🅔 rnpopenguine@gmail.com

344 *Le Lodge des Collines de Niassam* (🆆 niassam. com) is near Palmarin, around 150km, or four hours' drive, south of Dakar. A night in a treehouse costs CFA130,00 (€200) for two, half board. The Senegal Experience (🆆 senegal.co.uk) offers packages including flights from the UK and transfers.

345 *Orango Parque Hotel*, a 10-room eco-lodge, is located in the north of Orango (🆆 orangohotel.com). For information on the region, see 🆆 ibapgbissau.org.

346 Charles Sabbiah offers street tours of Old Accra (🆆 ghana-nima-tours.yolasite.com).

347 Regular boats from Dakar take about 30 minutes to reach Gorée (see 🆆 visiting-africa.com/africa/senegal/ile-de-goree-ferry-schedule). The island is a UNESCO World Heritage Site; 🆆 whc.unesco.org.

348 Steer clear of the palm wine served in Freetown; the journey from country to city means the drink is often over-fermented, mixed with sugar or diluted with water.

349 Contact the sanctuary to make enquiries about a visit: 🆆 tiwaiisland.org.

350 The national airline TACV (🆆 flytacv.com) offers flights to Fogo.

CENTRAL & EAST AFRICA

351–391

Central and East Africa's spectacular landscapes of savannah, lake and mountains are home to some of the continent's most life-affirming sights and experiences. The wildlife is astonishing, from mountain gorillas in Rwanda and hippos in Gabon to migrating wildebeest in the Serengeti and lions in the Maasai Mara, but there's far more to the region than its safari potential. Dive off the coast of Zanzibar, hike Ethiopia's remote Bale Mountains, discover Axum's ancient stelae, climb Kilimanjaro or cycle through Hell's Gate National Park. You could even rent a private island in the Seychelles or camp out in a star bed in the Kenyan wilderness. What's keeping you?

351   Hiking the ancestral forests of the Batwa

UGANDA To me the dense jungles of southwestern Uganda look impenetrable, the thick undergrowth a solid wall of green. But to Hagumimana Kanyabikingi this is simply home, he explains, as we clamber up the steep muddy trails that wind their way across the mist-shrouded mountains of Mgahinga Gorilla National Park. Suddenly he kneels in the grass to show me a snare made of strong vines, the type once used by his people to catch small animals. "These orange berries are good to eat," he says, "and the bark from this tree can bring down a fever." Stopping at a stream, Hagumimana demonstrates how a hollow bamboo tube can carry water, enough to last a human being for days. The forest can give you everything you need, he tells me, if you only know where to look.

Hagumimana is a Batwa, or "pygmy". For millennia the forested mountains along the Congolese border were the only world his people had ever known, until in 1991 they were forced to leave to ensure the survival of one of Mgahinga's other residents, the endangered mountain gorilla. But in recent years the Batwa have returned to their ancestral forests as tour guides, sharing their unique culture with hikers like me. The Batwa Trail is a priceless glimpse of what it means to truly live in harmony with nature.

After several hours we reach Garama Cave, a sacred gathering place that was once home to the Batwa king. Hagumimana takes my hand and leads me down through the darkness, into a pitch-black world of dripping water and damp, cool stone. Suddenly the soft strains of a melody make me catch my breath, and gradually the cave fills with eerily beautiful music. When Hagumimana lights a candle I find that we are not alone; a dozen Batwa women stand in the shadows, serenading us with their ancient songs. I stand transfixed as the stone walls echo with the sounds of longing, laughter and celebration, telling the stories of an ancient way of life that may soon be lost forever.

Hilary Heuler
is a freelance journalist and travel writer. She has been writing for Rough Guides since 2007, and her adventures have taken her everywhere from the icy shores of the Baltic Sea to the most remote villages of West Africa.

352

Following the Greatest Show on Earth

TANZANIA & KENYA Imagine squinting into the shimmering Serengeti horizon and seeing a herd of wildebeest trundle into view. They're moving slowly, stopping every now and then to graze on what's left of the parched savannah. At first, they number a couple of dozen, but as you watch, tens become hundreds, and hundreds become thousands. And still they come – a snorting, braying mass, relentlessly marching north in search of food. This is the wildebeest migration, and watching it play out on the sweeping plains of Tanzania's Serengeti National Park is unforgettable.

The statistics are staggering: in May each year, over 2.5 million animals, mostly wildebeest but also several hundred thousand zebras and antelopes, set out on a three-month journey from the short-grass plains of the southern Serengeti to Kenya's Maasai Mara Game Reserve. On the way, they'll cover some 800km of open plains and croc-infested rivers, running the gauntlet of predators such as lions, cheetahs, hyenas and hunting dogs.

By June, the herds have passed deep into the park's Western Corridor and are nervously starting to cross the Grumeti River. This is the migration at its most savage – and the defining moment of countless wildlife documentaries – as the reluctant wildebeest gather at the riverbank, too scared to go any further, until the mass behind them is so intense that they spill down into the water and are suddenly swimming, scraping and fighting in a desperate attempt to get across. Many are injured or drowned in the mayhem, while huge Nile crocodiles pick off the weak and unwary.

Those that do make it are still some 65km from the Mara River, the last and brutal barrier between them and the rain-ripened grasses of the Maasai Mara. Once there, they'll have three months to eat their fill before going through it all over again on the return journey south.

353 | Sensory overload at Murchison Falls

UGANDA Murchison Falls is an unexpected sight on the smooth-flowing Nile as it makes its languid 6850km journey from the Rwandan highlands to the Mediterranean: a violent plume of thunderously frothing white water unleashed as the tropical river explodes through a 7m-wide cleft in the Rift Valley Escarpment.

The scenic highlight of Murchison Falls National Park (at 3480 square kilometres, Uganda's largest conservation area), this 43m-high waterfall is the target of a launch trip from the park headquarters at Paraa, which provides a compellingly different perspective on wildlife viewing. Gargantuan crocodiles leer menacingly from the wide sandbars just a few metres from the boat. Conferences of hippo grunt amiably in the shallows. Giraffe and antelope often come down to drink. There are few guarantees when it comes to Africa's "Big Five", but buffaloes are common along the river – and if you're really lucky you might encounter a herd of elephants drinking or swimming, or even a lion or leopard lurking stealthily on the bank.

Aquatic birds are everywhere. Eagle-eyed park guides point out stately goliath herons treading daintily along the papyrus verges, while pairs of elegant African fish eagle emit their piercing cry from the treetops, pied kingfishers hover hummingbird-like over the water, and red-throated bee-eaters and yellow-backed weavers add flashes of dazzling colour. But the undoubted star of Murchison Falls' checklist of 450-plus bird species is the shoebill, a monstrous slate-grey papyrus-dweller whose prehistoric appearance is sealed by an outlandish clog-shaped bill fixed in a vaguely unsettling smirk.

Impressive as Murchison Falls is from the launch, the full-frontal view from the water can't prepare you for the viewpoint at the top of the cascade, which can be reached by a steep footpath from a landing near the base, or by a separate road. It is here, separated from the falls by a flimsy fence, that you truly experience the staggering power with which the Nile funnels through the Rift Escarpment, and the deafening roar and voluminous spray it generates.

354 | Tracking rhinos on foot

KENYA In north Kenya's remote Sera Wildlife Conservancy – where packs of marauding wild dogs take down antelope with pin-sharp accuracy, and willowy reticulated giraffes sweep the land like diplodocus – you'll find a sheltering herd of eleven black rhino. The animals have been successfully reintroduced into the area after a thirty-year absence, and now trudge at their leisure around the 348,000-hectare reserve, hoovering up shrubs and dismantling bushes as they make this wild place their home. As such, this is one of the only places in East Africa where you can track black rhinos on foot, an experience much more visceral – and arguably more rewarding – than trundling around man-made paths in a reinforced safari vehicle.

This is how you see Africa, and its incredible creatures, up close – immersing yourself in the warning calls of a flock of red-billed oxpecker or the inquisitive gaze of a passing herd of delicate impala. Setting out early in the morning, as the dawn paints pale-pink gossamer smears across the horizon, you'll need the rangers' help to track down the

mighty rhino, scouring the ground for the broad-set, distinctive tracks of these colossal creatures and picking your way around grisly piles of bones. Tracking tech comes in the form of a basic handset that emits whirs, blips and white noise as you walk, combined with the Samburu tribesmen's traditional gear – a small, sharp knife and a rudimentary wind gauge (a sock filled with ash, jiggled occasionally to ensure you're staying downwind of any 2,300kg beasts in the vicinity).

More often than not a rhino will announce its presence by eating. The pantomime crunching of thick leaves being shredded though brick-like teeth and the comedic swaying of a bush giving away the mammoth beast sheltering among its branches. As you move closer, the crunching still audible over the squabble of guinea fowl or the screeching of eagle owls, you might spot something else in your peripheral vision: the fawn-coloured swish of a wild dog taking down a dik-dik, or the jewel eyes of a female leopard stalking through the bushes. But remember, there is just one golden rule when walking like this in the bush: never run.

355 | Hiking the rooftop of Africa

ETHIOPIA The Bale Mountains rise out of Ethiopia's scrubby Afro-alpine landscape like the jawbones of giants. This is a place where leopards roam, where packs of hyena stalk the lands and where bearded lammergeier vultures soar high above the peaks, dropping the bones of their prey before descending to gorge on the spilt marrow. Sitting in southeast Ethiopia, 400km from the capital Addis Ababa, the mountains – home to the towering Mount Tullu Dimtu – are known as the 'rooftop of Africa', and a hike here is a tough, lung-pinching affair.

But the ethereal landscape is reward enough: strewn with totem-like giant lobelia plants, jewel-coloured swathes of heather, and rock formations that look like the surface of the moon. Yet it's the wildlife that's the most remarkable thing about this place. A biodiversity hotspot, the Bale Mountains National Park is the stomping ground of the elusive russet-coloured Ethiopian wolf, the rarest canid in the world and Africa's most threatened carnivore. Decimated by habitat

loss and rabies introduced by domestic dogs, there are now fewer than five hundred of these wolves in the wild, marooned in a handful of isolated pockets in Ethiopia's mountains.

So, imagine unzipping your tent one dew-slicked morning to see two of the white-socked creatures ambling nimbly past your camp. Or making the long hike to the Sanetti Plateau (which, at an altitude of 4000m, is the highest plateau on the African continent), flanked by horsemen and your trusted guides, to be rewarded with the sight of a lone male wolf hunting giant mole-rats in the early-evening light, the sinking sun sending shafts of gold across its amber fur. These remote, beautiful mountains are an otherworldly place, giving life to one of earth's most threatened species. Most visitors' abiding memories will be sharing a few hours with an animal that's three times rarer than China's giant panda; surely one of the most privileged things you can do on this planet.

Climbing Kilimanjaro

TANZANIA The statistics are impressive. Measuring some 40km across and rising 5895m above sea level, Kilimanjaro is easily Africa's highest mountain.

But such bald facts fail to capture the incredible thrill of actually climbing it: the days spent tramping from muggy montane forest to snow-cloaked summit, pausing occasionally to admire the breathtaking views over the lush lower slopes and beyond to the dusty plains, or to scrutinize the unique mountain flora. Come evenings, a blissful few hours can be spent gazing at the panoply of stars with fellow like-minded trekkers. That's not to mention the wonderful esprit de corps that builds between yourself and your crew, a camaraderie that grows with every step until, exhausted, you stand together at the highest point in Africa.

Beguiling though the mountain may be, those contemplating an assault on Kili should consider its hazards and hardships. For one thing, though it's possible to walk to the summit, it's not easy. An iron will and calves of steel are both essential, for this is a mountain that really tests your mettle. Then there are the extreme discomforts on the slopes, from sweat-drenched shirts in the sweltering forest to frozen water bottles and wind-blasted faces at the summit. And there's the altitude itself, inducing headaches and nausea in those who ascend too fast.

Such privations, however, are totally eclipsed by the exhilaration of watching the sunrise from the Roof of Africa, with an entire continent seemingly spread out beneath you. The sense of fulfilment that courses through you on the mountaintop will stay with you, long after you've finally said goodbye to Kili.

357 | Hot air over the savannah

KENYA The day starts in the chilly pitch darkness of pre-dawn, with the soft urging of a Maasai voice outside your tent, waking you with tea and cookies. Casting your quilt and hot water bottle aside, you wash with a jug of warm water and dress quickly, adding a fleece to the usual wildlife-watching garb. You drive though the dark – the headlights picking out herds of impala, a scattering clan of hyenas and the tail end of a porcupine shuffling into the bushes – to the launch site, where a crumpled *montgolfier* smothers the savannah, like a giant butterfly just emerged from the chrysalis. A team of red-overalled mechanics swarms around the business end of the balloon as attentively as a Formula One pit crew, manoeuvring a huge fan into position. Within seconds the roaring jet of blue flame from the burner has blasted the multicoloured sack into buoyant verticality, pinioned to the ground with taut guy lines.

As the balloon tugs on its restraints, each passenger is quickly loaded. Take-off is unexpected and silent, as the guys release the guys and you're suddenly above the trees and floating south. With the sun breaking over the horizon and warming chilly faces, the perfect serenity of this mode of transport strikes everyone at once and the camera shutters rattle. Below, hippos cavort in the muddy river and vervet monkeys watch the balloon's passage from their treetop vantage points. Once it's over the plain, the balloon is ignored by the grazing herds of zebra and gazelle – but they flee its shadow and the whoosh of the burner when it flies too low. All too soon, the low-flying becomes grass-grazing and the pilot opens the vents to allow the basket to drag itself to a stop on its side, to the general hilarity of the occupants, who crawl out, elated, and settle around the breakfast tables set up on the plain. For wildlife photography, a balloon safari can't equal patient observation on the ground, but few experiences can match this one for sheer unforgettability.

358 | Dinosaur hunting by Lake Télé

CONGO Waking at dawn in the deep forest, you emerge from your tent to face clouds of tiny sweat bees and a breakfast of black coffee, tinned sardines and sticks of glue-like *foufou*, wrapped in banana leaves. The Congo Republic's official website invites visitors to this region, and even remarks on its semi-mythical attraction. But you will be a rarity at strange Lake Télé, Congo's Loch Ness, slap in the middle of 3000 square kilometres of forest, bounded by meandering creeks on three sides and logging concessions on the fourth. With no road access, and oddly missing from many maps, the almost circular lake is surrounded by thick forest – home to the biggest population of gorillas in Africa, as well as elephants, hippos, pythons and crocodiles.

But the lake's strangest denizen is an unknown quantity, an amphibious, horned monster called *mokele mbembe*, the "river dammer", often described as a living dinosaur. Colourful, mostly secondhand anecdotes, and some Japanese aerial footage of something that looks like a small motorboat creating a wake and then sinking rapidly, are about all the evidence for its existence. And yet it terrifies local people and has excited explorers and zoologists for centuries.

The lake is approached along a creek by boat, and then by a long day's hike on a difficult trail. Following your guide and porter, you're quickly deep into the forest. Shafts of sunlight illuminate the dark leaf-litter on the ground, where flickering butterflies settle on gorilla droppings. Chimps hoot somewhere in the distance. Above you, buttress-rooted forest giants soar 60m or more through the foliage towards the light. There are few locals along the way – only rarely a group of "Pygmy" hunters comes this far south – and they're as fascinated to see you as you them. With biting insects, roots to trip on, and stretches of swamp where you have to wade up to your thighs, this excursion is no picnic (except for the tsetse flies). And then suddenly the great, dark expanse of the lake is in front of you. It's hard to put your camera down, or take your eyes away.

359 | Bush and beach in Bujumbura

BURUNDI Bujumbura may not have a reputation for rest and recreation, but its fragile peace is convincing enough to short-stay visitors, and it has two fine assets. Tucked between the steep, green walls of the western branch of the Great Rift Valley, on the shores of Lake Tanganyika, little "Buj" has a national park at the edge of town – just like Nairobi. Unlike Kenya's sprawling capital, Buj's suburbs peter out onto dazzling beaches lapped by the blue waters, or occasionally thrashed by the rough waves, of Africa's deepest lake.

Coming from the airport, you don't even need to go into town: the Plage des Cocotiers, or Coconut Beach, is effectively located at the end of the runway. Although a number of resorts have opened here, if you turn up soon after sunrise, you'll find the stretch of sand near enough empty – an ideal spot for clean and safe swimming along with kite-surfing.

Later on, and especially at weekends, the bars and grilled meat stands open, the beach volleyball begins and boat rides and even the occasional local guitar band are on offer.

Taking centre stage on the sands is the surprisingly sustainable resort of *Hôtel Club du Lac* (which uses local materials and is air-cooled and partly solar-powered) – the best spot for sundowners. Just a few kilometres west of the beach, near the Congolese border, the road crosses the Rusizi River and you can drive your rented jeep or organize a river trip by pirogue downstream into the lush reedbeds and palm groves of the Rusizi National Park (notice the "Attention Crocodiles" sign at the gate).

It's just 3km to the river mouth and the lake: be sure to ask your captain to take you down the small channels on the eastern side of the estuary, where you can see hippos and plenty of birdlife, and hungry crocs waiting for fish.

360 | Visiting the Kigali genocide museum

RWANDA In 1994, while the world looked the other way, around one million Tutsis and moderate Hutus were murdered by Hutu extremists. The attempted genocide left a scar on the Rwandan nation which will be felt for generations, but the immediate wounds of that terrible three-month period have healed faster than most outsiders could have imagined. While leading *genocidaires* have faced UN trials, those who murdered their own neighbours under orders have undergone a process of reconciliation with survivors in local *gacaca* courts. The country itself has been transformed by its pragmatic government and is rapidly modernizing.

Tourism is an important part of development and it engages remarkably with recent events in Rwanda's genocide museum, the Kigali Memorial Centre, where you're likely to spend at least two very worthwhile but emotionally draining hours. On this hillside site, north of the city centre, eleven huge crypts have been constructed, the resting place for nearly a quarter of a million of the country's victims.

The semi-subterranean exhibition itself implicitly lays the blame for what happened on decades of colonial oppression, divide-and-rule policies, under-development and ultimately deliberate planning, while placing the slaughter in the context of humanity's history of genocide. Particularly poignant is the still-growing display of victims' photos, donated by their families, and the inexpressibly sad and beautiful sculptures by Rwandan artist Laurent Hategekimana. The memorial to the children who died is unbearably moving, focusing not on the huge numbers, but on fourteen individual lives, on little things like their favourite meals, and on how they were killed.

Outside, it's not always easy to be contemplative in the pretty memorial gardens, with the hum of Kigali's traffic in the background, but the sombre Wall of Names is a reminder of the arbitrariness of the genocide: although the Belgians divided people into Tutsi (owning ten cows or more) and Hutu (owning fewer than ten), the country shares one language and one culture and the division is a socially constructed one.

361 | A river-load of wildlife on the Kazinga Channel

UGANDA Africa has wildlife-viewing opportunities by the savannah-ful, but some locations are so iconic that it can be hard to find the elbow-space to point a lens, let alone appreciate the natural beauty of what's in front of you. Others are well-known locally but fly under the mainstream radar, and it's in this grouping that you'll find Uganda's Queen Elizabeth National Park.

In wildlife terms, the East African country remains best-known for the gorillas and chimps that inhabit the lush forests of the southwest. The same corner of the nation plays home to Queen Elizabeth National Park, which has been a wildlife reserve since the 1920s and still provides a thrillingly biodiverse safari experience for visitors to the region. Leopards, elephants and tree-climbing lions are among the headline draws, but it's by joining a boat trip on the Kazinga Channel that you'll appreciate the breadth of life here at its fullest. Don't imagine a gently meandering river-boat cruise, however.

The channel itself is long and wide, with trips tending to focus on the shoreline activity along one bank. And there's plenty of activity to take in. Honking pods of hippo wallow in the shallows, and warthogs skitter along by the water's edge. Crocodiles lurk offshore as elephants plod along parallel to the watercourse, tearing off branches. Buffalo gaze out stoically from beneath mighty horns, while sea eagles keep watch from the branches overhead.

That's not to mention the tropical birds that flit over the boat or the other mammals that prowl in and out of view on shore – leopards and lions can both be spotted if your luck's in. The sheer extent of it all can be bewildering, to the point where the only natural reaction is to put your camera away and resolve against trying to capture its diversity by any other means than standing and staring. Cruises last around two hours, and even if there's more than one boat astir, the scale of the channel means it won't feel crowded.

362 | A day by Lake Kivu

RWANDA Where the slopes of the Virunga volcanoes duck into the deep waters of Lake Kivu you'll find the pretty lakeside town of Gisenyi. After the emotional impact of Rwanda's genocide memorials, and the intensity of gorilla-tracking, arriving in Gisenyi – with its warm days and cool nights, tropical gardens, tan-coloured sandy beaches and shabby, European architecture – always feels like the start of a holiday. And that's what the Belgians thought, at the end of World War I, when they inherited this former military post from the Germans. Exulting in its combination of equatorial climate and 1500m altitude, Rwanda's new colonial rulers created a mini Riviera, with villas, spa-style hotels and avenues lined with palms and gum trees.

These days, Gisenyi entertains Kigali's elite crowd for weekends of water-skiing and windsurfing. But the jewel of the area lies at Rubona,

a 6km walk (or taxi ride) along the spectacular lakeside corniche, where the *Paradise Malahide* is the country's most charming hotel. Tucked in your wood-and-lava-rock cottage, you awake to the conversation of fisherpeople above the soft crash of waves. Start your day with a swim (float back and look north to see the active volcano, Nyiragongo) and then take a canoe across the bay to the local hot springs. Back on the mainland, the Belgians' old Bralirwa brewery (controlled by Heineken, who tap methane from the lake as a fuel) is behind the fishing harbour. It's just a ten-minute walk from the hotel; take a tour to see where all those huge bottles of Primus beer come from. Evenings in Gisenyi and Rubona are sedate, but look out for Intore dance shows, the sanitized but still thrilling displays of traditional royal warriorhood.

363 | In the footsteps of Franco: checking out the Kinshasa music scene

DEMOCRATIC REPUBLIC OF CONGO It all started with a guitar made from an old can, with stripped-down electrical wire for strings. The young François Luambo Makiadi – better known as Franco – was barely 11 when he was first spotted jamming on a makeshift instrument in the market district of 1940s Léopoldville, as Kinshasa was then known. Nurtured by a visionary local recording artist, Paul Dewayon, his canny blend of hard-nosed street cred and natural star quality put him straight on a path to success.

By his early twenties, Franco was the biggest star in Congolese dance music. Every night, he and his band OK Jazz would belt out a joyous blend of rippling guitars, shimmering drums and upbeat choruses – a sound that's as quintessentially African as mangoes, kola nuts and cowrie shells. He called his Cuban-influenced musical style "rumba odemba", after a favourite Congolese aphrodisiac.

Franco went on to open four nightclubs in Kinshasa, the most famous of which, the *Un*

Deux Trois club in the district of Kasa-Vubu, just south of the city centre, was his professional headquarters. Throughout the last two decades of Franco's life, the 1970s and 1980s, Kinshasa was a throbbing live-music hub. Since then, much has changed, but despite its woes, the city remains a vibrant crossroads town and a place where musicians meet.

Even now, the seedy but lively Matonge district around Rond-Point Victoire, between Kasa-Vubu and the centre, buzzes after dark. For a dose of raw-edged nightlife, head up to the rooftop terrace at the down-at-heel *Hôtel de Crèche*, near Rond-Point Victoire: live bands play here twice a week. Meanwhile in Gombe Commune, the more salubrious central district, well-heeled locals and expats pack out the dancefloor at *Chez Ntemba*, an after-midnight club. If you want to catch a big-name band, see the local press – near the Congo River, the Halle de la Gombe sometimes hosts stars such as Werra Son, Youssou N'Dour and Papa Wemba, all of whom cite Franco as a formative influence.

364 | Cycling through Hell's Gate National Park

KENYA At the entrance to Hell's Gate National Park, less than two hours' drive northwest of Nairobi, a large information board relays standard advice about opening times and ticket prices, as well as a vague map of the park's contours. At the top corner, however, there's a number, updated when needs be, signifying the number of lions spotted over the last twelve-month period – the higher the better when you're on a safari with an armed ranger, but quite alarming when you're on a bicycle, on your own.

Hell's Gate is one of very few major African national parks in which cycling is permitted, and even encouraged. It's around 16km between the two main gates, meaning that even if you bolted along as fast as possible on the bumpy dirt paths, you'd be out in the wilderness, quite unprotected, for a good hour – and even longer if the rain arrives, which it does with a frequency common to the tropics.

Lions are far from your only potential Hell's Gate hazard. Buffalo, easy to anger but often hard

to spot in the tree-shadows they occupy for much of the day, are far more numerous, while leopards and hyena are rarely too far away; even the sound of a broken twig may be enough to set the heart racing, and one can feel quite pathetically small.

Despite all of this, while riding puny bicycles through the park, visitors often get this bizarre, epiphany-like feeling that nature is somehow their friend, and that everything will somehow turn out fine – even when a herd of zebra race past at perilously close range, their hooves loud as thunder.

Eland, baboons, the odd flamingo or Thomson's gazelle... thoughts that one is in a Disney cartoon would be quite appropriate, since Hell's Gate was used as a model for the setting of *The Lion King*.

And, if you're lucky enough to commune with one of the few giraffes that don't run away at first sight of a human being, you may never take a regular safari again.

Dropping in on the churches of Lalibela

ETHIOPIA Lalibela, in Ethiopia's highlands, is a quiet, rural place. Yet in the thirteenth century it was the capital of the great Zagwe dynasty, one of whose last rulers, King Lalibela, embarked on a quest to build a Holy Land on Ethiopian soil.

Historians say he was inspired to build the town's famous rock-hewn churches after a pilgrimage to Jerusalem, while the devout claim that he was instructed by angels during a poison-induced sleep. Whatever the real reason, the town of Lalibela, built as a "new Jerusalem", leaves pilgrims and visitors alike humbled by the elegance of its churches. Gracing a rocky plateau and intricately carved, they mostly lie in two interconnected groups scattered along the "Jordan River", another biblical landscape feature that King Lalibela designed.

This major UNESCO World Heritage Site is hidden from view until you are literally upon it – a strategic design feature, offering protection from marauders. The churches are monolithic, dug deep down into the rock. As you pass through carved gullies leading from one church to the next, you can look in on caves containing the skeletons of monks, or gaze up to cubbyholes in the red rock face to see yellow-robed pilgrims reciting the Bible in Ge'ez, an archaic form of Amharic. The churches remain vibrant, their monks, nuns and priests fervently engaged with the Ethiopian Orthodox Church's demanding calendar. Every church has a hereditary guardian priest dedicated to this medieval world of incense, beeswax candles and ritual – though, incongruously, they all seem to keep sunglasses handy, protecting themselves not, this time, from marauders but from the flash photographs of camera-toting tourists.

KENYA Northern Kenya is a land apart. Vast, arid and all but ignored by the tourist industry, Kenya's forgotten half is traversed by a handful of roads, marked authoritatively on maps, but often little more than rutted, axle-crunching tracks through inhospitable plains mesmerizing in their parched emptiness.

Here you will find Lake Turkana, a sparkling green, saline expanse known as the Jade Sea. Extending over 6400 square kilometres, Turkana is so remote that it remained unknown to the outside world until 1888. Today, enclosed by the craggy Rift Escarpment, it feels primeval. Its wild and windswept shores, starkly vegetated and largely bereft of human habitation, form a breeding ground for the world's largest population of Nile crocodiles. Its surface is studded with the ragged black cones of partially submerged volcanoes. The water is barely potable; the wind so strong and steady that a lone walker might lose balance were it ever to cease blowing.

It's a long journey from Nairobi to Turkana – at least three days' hard driving, overnighting at basic village campsites. The first 250km follows surfaced roads through lush highlands, but conditions deteriorate rapidly after the road descends to the town of Isiolo into vast time-warped badlands inhabited by traditional pastoralists: the Samburu, for example, who share a language with the Maasai, and drape themselves in red blankets and beaded jewellery, and the Turkana, whose women wear a traditional combination of hide skirt, beads, dreadlocked and hennaed Mohican hairstyle, and a lower lip plug that looks deceptively like a hipster goatee.

A left turn 250km north of Isiolo leads through the Chalbi Desert, a flat expanse of cracked earth where nervous ostriches skedaddle at your approach. A handful of oases support isolated Gabbra communities, whose camel herds are almost as skittish as the ostriches.

Finally, a rutted track snakes down the rock-strewn slopes of the escarpment to the magnificent jade apparition below, and at long last you stumble out at Loiyangalani. Incredibly, this dusty village of just a thousand-odd souls is the largest settlement on Turkana's 290km-long eastern shore. The sense of isolation is absolute.

367 | A day among mountain gorillas

UGANDA Locking eyes with a mountain gorilla in the wild is one of Africa's most profoundly moving wildlife experiences. It's partly to do with their uncanny similarity to humans, from the way they cuddle and play with their young to the way they examine their fingernails. And it's partly a matter of respect.

Powerful but critically endangered, mountain gorillas were woefully abused by our species in decades past. Criminals poached them for gruesome souvenirs, while human encroachment confined them to just two patches of montane forest: Bwindi Impenetrable National Park in Uganda and the Virunga Massif on the Uganda, Rwanda and Democratic Republic of Congo (DRC) border. Thanks to concerted conservation efforts funded by philanthropy and ecotourism, their numbers are slowly rising. But they have no reason to allow us to approach. When they do, it's nothing short of humbling.

This gentle acceptance has not come about by chance. It's the result of a painstaking habituation process, whereby primatologists, wildlife vets and national park scouts and rangers spend long hours in their presence, observing their habits and winning their trust.

Uniquely, the conservation team at Bwindi Impenetrable National Park offers the chance to witness what the process entails. On their Gorilla Habituation Experience, a specialist guide takes you into the forest's knotted folds for a behind-the-scenes expedition lasting from dawn to mid-afternoon or beyond. On a regular gorilla trek, an advance party of trackers heads out to find the gorillas, which you then join for a precious hour. On a habituation trek, you're one of the advance party, and your audience could last as long as four hours.

This is wildlife-watching in the raw. Don't expect the gorillas to be lounging in a convenient spot – naturally enough, the families which have yet to be habituated are those whose ranges are least accessible. With a walking stick and a porter to assist, you'll hike up and down steep slopes, wading through waist-high foliage or tunnelling through vines so densely tangled that the scouts have to hack their way through with machetes. And when at last you find the gorillas, don't expect them to be easy to see, or totally relaxed. Protective mothers may hide in the shade, and a silverback who reckons you've overstepped the mark won't hesitate to mock-charge. But that, of course, simply adds to the thrill.

368 | Trekking in the Simien Mountains

ETHIOPIA The great mass of the Simien range – formed from one of Africa's ancient super-volcanoes – rears up in Ethiopia's remote, northern hinterland, broken into towering plateaus and peaks by a slew of rushing rivers and trailing waterfalls. In the heart of the mountains, the UNESCO Natural Heritage Site of Simien National Park is a spellbinding wilderness of fertile valleys and grassy moors, the jewel in Ethiopia's crown of natural attractions, offering one of Africa's, if not the world's, most spectacular hikes – an eight-day return trek to the snowcapped peak of Ras Dashen (4620m).

Once the fortified home of Ethiopia's Jewish community, the Simiens remain largely roadless, but are still traced by footpaths and scattered with Amhara villages. On the misty heights within the pristine national park live three large mammals unique to the region: the impressively horned and vulnerable Walia ibex (a nimble, shaggy goat that you only ever see hundreds of metres away on a sheer, high cliff face); the critically rare and beautiful red-coated Simien wolf; and the remarkable, grass-eating Gelada baboon, which you are very likely to see grazing on the steep, alpine meadows, sometimes in parties numbering hundreds.

Foot-slogging and mules are the usual transport in the Simiens, and you'll soon get used to the steady pace and moderate height gains required at these altitudes, with stunning birdlife, such as the huge lammergeier vulture, and giant African-alpine vegetation to distract you from your heaving chest and throbbing legs.

Sci-fi plants of Mount Kenya

369

KENYA The Kikuyu people venerated Mount Kenya as the dwelling place of God. They believed if they climbed to the peaks, they would find spiritual inspiration. Straddling the equator and piercing the clouds, Africa's second-highest mountain – the eroded remains of a vast, prehistoric volcano, towering 5199m from the plains – is a steeper and quicker climb than Kilimanjaro, and in terms of scenic variety and fauna and flora is perhaps the more inspirational of Africa's two giant mountains. It's certainly the less busy.

For most trekkers, the climax of seeing the sunrise from Point Lenana, among the jagged, glacier-studded peaks, is the literal high point of the experience. But try to love the climbing moments, too: on day three of the Naro Moru trail, once you've overcome the slightly daunting "vertical bog" and emerged into the high moorland, the wonders of alpine Africa's otherworldly flora, seemingly designed by some 1950s science-fiction writer, are all around you. Altitude and the equatorial location combine to nurture forms of vegetation

that exist only here and at one or two other lofty points in East Africa. When you first see them, it's hard to believe the "water-holding cabbage" or "ostrich plume plant". This is a land of giant shrubs and weeds: giant heather, giant groundsel and giant lobelia. It turns out the cabbages on stumps and the larger, candelabra-shaped, tree-like plants are the same species, known as giant groundsel or tree senecio. The intermediate stage has a sheaf of bright yellow flowers. These enigmatic plants, though frail-looking, are slow growers, and individuals may survive on these chilly, misty slopes for more than two hundred years.

The tall, fluffy, less abundant plants are a species of giant lobelia, popularly called the "ostrich plume plant", discovered by the explorer Teleki and found only on Mount Kenya. The furriness that gives this giant lobelia such an animal quality acts as insulation for the delicate flowers. It is perhaps the only plant in the world that could fairly be described as cuddly.

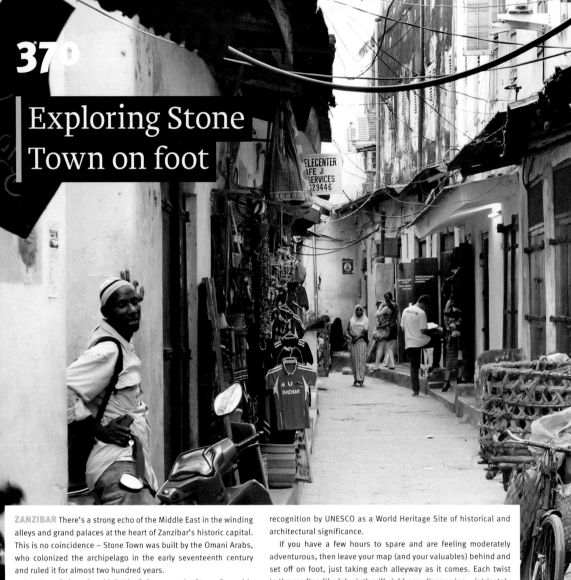

Exploring Stone Town on foot

ZANZIBAR There's a strong echo of the Middle East in the winding alleys and grand palaces at the heart of Zanzibar's historic capital. This is no coincidence – Stone Town was built by the Omani Arabs, who colonized the archipelago in the early seventeenth century and ruled it for almost two hundred years.

In 1841, Sultan Seyyid Saïd of Oman made Stone Town his capital in order to nurture lucrative trade in cloves, ivory and, most notoriously, slaves, on Zanzibar (known as the island of Unguja). Sixty thousand captives were "processed" in Stone Town every year, and the Sultan received a tax on each sale, investing a significant part of the proceeds in showy architecture.

In the late twentieth century, post independence, Stone Town neglected its clutch of mansions and palaces, leaving their hand-plastered coral limestone facades to the mercy of the punishing tropical climate. But in recent years, a wave of conservation programmes has gained momentum, spurred on by Stone Town's recognition by UNESCO as a World Heritage Site of historical and architectural significance.

If you have a few hours to spare and are feeling moderately adventurous, then leave your map (and your valuables) behind and set off on foot, just taking each alleyway as it comes. Each twist in the medina-like labyrinth will yield new discoveries – intricately carved teak or sesame wood door frames, elaborate balconies, Swahili doors studded with ornate brass knobs and souk-like curio shops piled high with textiles, beads and paintings.

To appreciate the sheer ambition of the city founders, stroll along the seafront west of the harbour. Impressive by any standards are the four-storey Old Dispensary, now restored; the Old Customs House, home to Stone Town's highly creative Dhow Countries Music Academy; the Arab-style Palace Museum, former home of the Sultans; and the famous Beit al-Ajaib or House of Wonders, a vast late-nineteenth-century palace.

371 | Losing the crowds at Katavi National Park

TANZANIA Unlike the parks of northern Tanzania, where increasingly one of the most common species is *Homo sapiens touristicus*, the remoter west of the country, close to Lake Tanganyika, feels more like central Africa, and is little visited.

The rich concentrations of wildlife in Katavi, which only gets a handful of visitors a month, include big herds of magnificent roan and sable antelope, some four thousand elephants and as many as 60,000 buffalo, among dozens of other species, supported by seasonally flooded grasslands. With flocks of waterbirds at the right time of year, and reliable numbers of hippos snorting and crocs sunning around palm-fringed Lake Katavi, it's a wonderful environment – best explored on foot, with an armed ranger you can hire on the spot.

372 | Tracking wild chimpanzees in a tropical rainforest

TANZANIA To find and follow a community of chimps in the wild, you need to immerse yourself in their world. As an adventure, it's thrilling, demanding and (at times) distinctly goofy. Aficionados call it chimping. Like all the best wildlife experiences, it starts with a waiting game. At dawn, trackers plunge into the steep, tangled forest, retracing their steps to the last place they saw the chimps the day before, then working out where they are now.

Soon, it's time to join them, hiking along dappled, leaf-strewn paths as fast as the humidity allows. That's the easy bit. Once you're close, it gets tougher. You might have to battle through creepers or scramble up a waterfall, eyes and ears straining for the first sign they're there. Sometimes a volley of pant-hoots, shrieks and tree-buttress thumps gives the game away. But – equally magically – you could simply look up and see a pair of wise, brown eyes gazing down, almost as curious about you as you are about them.

373 | Hiking Mount Nyiragongo

DEMOCRATIC REPUBLIC OF CONGO With its vast mountain ranges and thick rainforest, the DRC offers some top-notch hiking. There are lots of options in Virunga National Park, including various hikes to see the mighty mountain gorillas, but intrepid hikers will want to tackle Mount Nyiragongo. This active volcano towers over Goma in eastern DRC, emitting an eerie red glow from its bubbling lava lake as darkness sets each night.

The hike takes around six hours, climbing to 3470m through humid tropical forest, over scraggy lava rocks and past steaming geysers, before being plunged into mist at the top. At the summit, hikers camp in small huts on the crater rim, from where the boiling waves of lava can be heard crashing over each other like water in the ocean. The evening is spent gaping in awe into the molten, fiery heart of the earth, and watching as the crusted top of the lava lake rhythmically separates, revealing bolts of luminous orange liquid below.

374 | Swimming with turtles in the Indian Ocean

SEYCHELLES A cluster of granite islands enveloped in tropical vegetation and edged with blindingly white sand that's so fine it squeaks when you walk across it, the Seychelles are a near-paradisal destination. The waters of the surrounding Indian Ocean are also one of the best places to sight marine turtles, especially the hawksbill, once severely endangered by the trade in its beautifully patterned shells, which were used to make combs, spectacle frames and the like. Though the species is still threatened worldwide, with most of the Seychelles' waters now a marine reserve, hawksbill numbers have bounced back locally.

The best place to see them is on their home turf, with snorkelling and diving offering the chance to swim among these majestic creatures. Watching turtles paddling effortlessly past you is a marvellous spectacle; they're sometimes curious, sometimes indifferent, but usually wary of letting you get too close – best to catch them asleep under coral

overhangs or in shallow caves from a distance, where they can spend up to an hour dozing. If you're not prepared to get wet, time your visit during the October–February nesting season when, just after dark, you'll find females heaving themselves up the beaches to just above the high-tide line before using their hind flippers to scoop out a deep pit.

They then lay about fifty round, parchment-shelled eggs before shovelling all the sand back on top of them and making their way back down to the water. Be careful not to disturb them. The eggs incubate in the sand (the sex of the entire clutch is determined by the surrounding temperature) until the young hatch around ten weeks later. Perfect hawksbills in miniature, they dig themselves out of the nest after dark and, using the moon as a guide (hence why you should avoid shining a light near them), scuttle frenetically down the beach toward the sea like an army of wind-up bath toys.

375 | Langoué Bai: the last place on Earth

GABON The "Pygmy" tribes of the Central African rainforest gave Langoué Bai its name, but it was Mike Fay who put it on the map. When, in 1999, the American ecologist set himself the task of walking from Bomassa in Congo to Loango in Gabon, a project he called the Megatransect Expedition, he already knew that the natural riches of this challenging wilderness were diminishing fast. Together with *National Geographic* photographer Michael Nichols, his mission was to monitor the impact of human activity on this beautiful but fragile environment.

Their work revealed a hidden world where forest elephants are glimpsed, fleetingly, through thick foliage, western lowland gorillas bathe waist-deep in the cool water of marshy clearings, and chimpanzees stare in astonishment at a primate they rarely see – man. Their data inspired the government of Gabon to protect a significant proportion of

this, the second-largest rainforest in the world, through the creation of thirteen new national parks.

Langoué Bai, a large natural clearing surrounded by dense vegetation, is a jewel in the heart of one of these parks: Ivindo. Well watered and remote, the *bai* attracts a host of wildlife – not just forest elephants and endangered gorillas but also forest buffalo, antelopes (small, shy duikers and marsh-loving sitatungas) and red river hogs, whose tufty ears give them a comical, gremlin-like look. Hidden in the trees, viewing platforms built by Fay's colleagues at the Wildlife Conservation Society provide the perfect vantage point. It's a sweaty hour or two's trek from camp, but it's worth every step just to witness the spectacle of so many highly elusive species gathered together in one arena. No wonder Nichols and Fay dubbed this forest "The Last Place on Earth".

376 | Camping on a star bed

KENYA It's a simple but brilliant idea, and Loisaba, a private reserve and ranch northwest of Mount Kenya, thought of it first. It goes like this. Choose a wilderness area that's so blissfully remote that light pollution is unheard of. Build a high timber platform with rustic railings, a thatched roof and an open deck. Add a huge bed with wheels, upcycled from an old 4WD. Roll it out when it's time to sleep. Then let the African night sky work its magic.

On a clear moonless night, the term "star bed", which the people at Loisaba reckon they coined, couldn't be more apt. The dark-coloured mosquito net that drapes over your four-poster is invisible once you've climbed inside. Lie back, and you're dazzled by a dome of stars.

Loisaba has two star-bed camps – *Kiboko*, the original, and *Koija*, created later as part of a responsible tourism project that benefits the local Laikipiak Maasai community. The journey to the camps can be as rugged or as romantic as you like. You can make it the last stop on

a game drive or horse ride, or walk there from Loisaba Bush Camp, striding through open grasslands, dotted with shrubs. Or you can travel by camel, enjoying the novelty of lolloping along as the setting sun softens the hillsides to the colour of melted butter.

The camp is supremely intimate. You'll be greeted warmly by your Samburu hosts, who light a campfire and prepare pre-prandial sundowners. As you sip your drink, there may be antelopes and zebras sipping sundowners of their own at the waterhole in the valley below.

After a lantern-lit dinner, it's time for bed. For anyone who loves the idea of camping out in safari country but balks at the prospect of flinging down a bed-roll in the open, a night in a treehouse-without-the-tree, well out of reach of inquisitive lions or elephants' trunks, is the perfect solution.

The platform feels reassuringly secure, and the big, comfy mattress and snuggly blankets add a touch of luxury. The biggest luxury of all, though, is the spectacular display of constellations overhead.

Wildlife-spotting in the Ngorongoro Crater

TANZANIA The tectonic forces that created East Africa's Great Rift Valley also threw up a rash of volcanoes, one of which blew itself to smithereens 2.5 million years ago. Its legacy, the 19km-wide Ngorongoro Crater, is a place that holiday brochures like to call "the eighth wonder of the world". They're not far wrong. Ngorongoro's natural amphitheatre is home to virtually every emblematic animal species you might want to see in Africa, and the crater's deep, bluish-purple sides provide spectacular backdrops for any photograph.

The magic begins long before you reach the crater. As you ascend from the Rift Valley along a series of hairpins, the extent of the region's geological tumult becomes breathtakingly apparent. Continuing up through liana-draped forest, you're suddenly at the crater's edge, surveying an ever-changing patchwork of green and yellow hues streaked with shadows and mist.

Living in the crater's grasslands, swamps, glades and lakes is Africa's highest density of predators – lions and leopards, hyenas and jackals among them – for whom a sumptuous banquet of antelope and other delicacies awaits Glimpsing lions is an unforgettable thrill; just as memorable but far more unsettling is the macabre excitement of witnessing a kill. You'll also see elephants and black rhinos, the latter poached to the brink of extinction. Twitchers have plenty to go for, too, including hundreds of pink flamingos adorning the alkaline Lake Magadi in the crater's heart. If ogling wildlife from a vehicle doesn't do it for you, stretch your legs – and escape the crowds – on a hike through the Crater Highlands, in the company of an armed ranger and a Maasai guide.

Sustainable safaris with the Maasai

378

KENYA North of Mount Kenya, the Laikipia region, a vast sweep of rangelands, ridges and seasonal rivers, stretches out towards the northern deserts. Here, former ranches are converting to eco-tourism and conservation, and pastoral communities are setting up innovative experiments in tourist development.

Many places in Laikipia make efforts to limit their environmental footprint, and *Il Ngwesi* – owned and run by the 6000-strong Il Ngwesi Laikipiak Maasai community – has taken the lead.

The lodge, located on a remote, bush-covered ridge, is delightful. It's a birdwatcher's paradise: you awake to a jaw-dropping dawn chorus, and birds – from drongos to hornbills – fill the air all day long, crowding the footpaths and branches, and often appearing in the rooms themselves. Six huge *bandas* (artfully rustic, thatch and tree-trunk cottages) are spaced out along the west-facing slope, their open-sided fronts graced

with magnificent decks and chunky furniture made of polished branches. *Banda* number one has amazing views of the elephants that congregate around *Il Ngwesi*'s magical waterhole, and features a giant mosquito-netted four-poster bed that you can pull out onto the deck.

There's no wood burning or fossil-fuel use at *Il Ngwesi* – all electricity is supplied by solar power – and the community has a water-use association to monitor consumption and pollution, ensuring the local herds have plenty to drink and leaving enough for the lodge's beautiful infinity pool. Although strictly a private conservancy, the area swarms with wildlife, and game walks with Maasai guides and armed rangers are the norm. It's especially satisfying that all the money goes back into the community, which – among other things – has enabled them to bring back rhinos, formerly hunted out of the area, and to track and monitor at least one pack of highly endangered African wild dogs.

379 | Banana-stalk battles

ZANZIBAR Seeing in the new year with a brawl may not seem in the spirit of the occasion, but in Zanzibar it's considered a purification ritual. For the Zoroastrian new year in July, people from all over Tanzania descend upon the village of Makunduchi for the Mwaka Kogwa festival, in which the menfolk duke it out in a dusty clearing, mock-fighting each other with the stalks from banana plants. While the men settle old scores, the women don their finest outfits and conga gleefully round the fray, singing and taunting the men in an attempt to distract them. The chanting gets louder and the women pick up the pace, circling the frenzied throng in a mesmerizing dance – until all the banana stalks are snapped and everyone becomes friends again. Villagers come together to burn a specially built coconut-thatch hut, then celebrate the new year with a slap-up feast to which everyone – fighters and spectators alike – is invited.

380 | Visiting a sacred grove on Diani Beach

KENYA Before the Swahili, the original inhabitants of Kenya's coast were the Mijikenda ("Nine Tribes"). Each tribe settled in a clearing in the coastal forest, burying ritual objects and their deceased at the heart of their founding villages or *kaya*. Hundreds of years later, the villages are gone, but the sacred groves remain, some of the last stands of coastal forest in Kenya. One, Kaya Kinondo, is open to visitors, and it's a treat.

Protected by a council of Digo elders, Kaya Kinondo is an ethno-botanical treasure trove, revealed for a couple of hours by your Digo guide as you walk the sandy paths, hatless as required and wrapped in the dark shawls provided. You are asked to avoid displays of affection, but are encouraged to hug a tree and empty your cares into a forest giant.

381 | On foot in wildebeest, elephant and lion country

TANZANIA There's no such thing as a dull day in the Serengeti. Drive through the national park during migration season, and extraordinary scenes are practically guaranteed. Close-bitten grasslands as wide as a county, where endless skeins of wildebeest roam. Herds of elephants, keeping their youngsters close. Tawny-maned lions, padding into the shade of croton bushes to escape the late-morning heat. What could be more exciting?

Some would say that sights such as these, glimpsed from a vehicle, are barely the start. For Alex Walker, one of East Africa's leading safari guides, it's only when you step down from your car and out of your comfort zone that the adventure really begins.

Alex is one of just a few guides who have permission to lead walking safaris in the Serengeti, fly-camping in secret spots and exploring new areas each morning and afternoon. Fully aware of the risks, he's supported by expert trackers, rangers and camp assistants. Join them and, at first, you'll be on high alert – feeling clumsy as you

clump your way through thickets, anxious at the sight and scent of elephant dung and freshly torn bark and positively fearful as you venture into a gully where lions, leopards and hyenas have left their unmistakable pawprints in the mud. Alex understands this. He gives you time to adjust.

His trips last for several days and with each walk you clock up, you'll gain confidence. Best of all, you'll gradually tune in to the subtleties of your surroundings, from the wildflowers, insects and birds that you'd never spot from a vehicle to the after-dark dazzle of stars.

Alex's team of trackers includes Hadza Bushmen from the southern Serengeti who pace ahead, bow and arrows in hand. Brought up in the bush, they have a sixth sense for danger – you'll watch elephants and lions, for example, from a respectful distance – and for wonders, such as agama lizards, perfectly camouflaged in a tree. A few days into your trip, you'll see the Serengeti in a whole new light – complex, fascinating and truly serene.

382 | Axum's standing stones

ETHIOPIA The small town of Axum in northern Ethiopia is home to an abundance of historical artefacts: where else can lay claim to 24m-high ancient stelae, the Queen of Sheba's Palace, and the Ark of the Covenant itself? The latter may be spurious: the Ark allegedly sits inside the Cathedral of Tsion Maryam, and only the church elders are allowed access.

Happily, it's far easier to see Axum's other sights. Opposite the cathedral is the stelae field, a small area containing approximately 75 obelisks, including one positively enormous example, measuring 33m. Known as King Remhai's Stele, this vast monolith lies on the ground, cracked into five huge pieces: it's thought that its great weight – 500 tons – was such that it toppled over immediately after erection in t he third century.

The Great Stele, which at 24m is the tallest stele still standing, was returned to Axum in 2005 after spending nearly 70 years in Rome. Looted by Italian Fascist troops in the Italo-Abyssinian War of 1935, it

formed a centrepiece of Mussolini's dream of the 'new Roman Empire'. Following Mussolini's downfall, the Italian government agreed to return it, but concerns over the difficulty of transporting such an enormous and valuable artefact caused long delays. It was eventually delivered in three pieces, at the time the largest and heaviest air cargo ever transported.

Visitors to the archeological site will also find countless smaller stelae, as well as underground tombs notable for their precisely interlocking masonry. Around the corner from the stelae field is a small hut containing King Ezana's inscription, a tablet similar to the Rosetta Stone with text in Sabaean, Ga'ez and Greek, and at the other end of town is a large ruin known as the Queen of Sheba's Palace. Here history and legend blend into one: there is no scholarly basis for linking this site to the Queen of Sheba, but you will be cheerfully assured that she lived and ruled from here. Whether this is true or not, the palace is another fine example of Axum's many historical mysteries and treasures.

383 | Fulfilling fantasies on Frégate Island

SEYCHELLES They say there is pirate's treasure buried here. Pure white fairy terns nest in the branches of the tangled banyan trees. Fruit bats with metre-wide wings emerge from the forest at sunset, chattering like schoolchildren as they feast on papaya and custard apples. Giant tortoises creep among the pandanus palms, and bright green geckos perch on the trunks of the swaying bamboo. Seven beaches of purest white sand are lapped by the turquoise Indian Ocean, and just sixteen villas perch on the granite rocks that make Frégate one of the most beautiful islands in all of the Seychelles.

The island is exclusive with a capital "E". Bill Gates stayed here, and Liz Hurley jetted in to Frégate for her honeymoon. Pierce Brosnan once rented the entire island after finishing a Bond film. Every villa has its own outdoor Jacuzzi, an outdoor shower, two marble bathrooms, and bedrooms where rich teak woodwork, tropical daybeds and swathes of silk and muslin create a luxurious cocoon where anyone can hide from the real world. Sleek boats are on hand ready to take the guests out on diving excursions or to try their hand at deep-sea fishing in search of wahoo and kingfish.

Frégate Island is not your typical hotel. Privately owned, and conserved, it is home to one of the world's rarest birds: the magpie robin, rescued from the brink of extinction when there were fewer than thirty individuals. Now, the little black and white birds are breeding successfully, and mating pairs have been transported to nearby islands to help increase their chances. There are turtles, too, nesting on the soft moonlit beaches at high tide.

Neither is it your typically flat coral island. At sunset, the pink granite boulders catch the light and from the top of the island's own miniature peak, Mount Signal, the Indian Ocean is an endless expanse of blue.

384 | Reef encounter: eco-living on Chumbe Island

ZANZIBAR It's difficult to know which way to look, snorkelling in the turquoise waters off Chumbe Island. At the oriental sweetlips, bobbing in unison around a huge coral fan? At the blue-spotted stingrays, shuffling under the sand along the bottom? Or at any one of the other four hundred or so species of fish that help make the island's reef, Tanzania's first marine protected area, one of the finest coral gardens in the world?

Overlooking the reef at Chumbe's western edge are seven palm-thatched "eco-bungalows"; the rest of the island is a designated nature reserve of creeping mangroves and coral rag forest, left to the local wildlife – including the rare Aders' duiker and the endangered coconut crab, the largest land crab in the world. Everything about the bungalows shouts "green": their roofs are designed to collect rainwater, which is then filtered before running through to the shower; hot water and electricity are provided by solar power; toilets are of the composting variety; and the air-conditioning system is probably the most efficient you'll ever see – a pulley lowers the bedroom's tree-top front wall, cooling the room with a fresh sea breeze.

With a maximum of fourteen guests at any one time, Chumbe is a real honeymoon hideaway – indeed, it's often used to round off a once-in-a-lifetime safari, maybe as an ecological appeasement for all those internal flights spent whizzing from one park to another on the African mainland.

The only other visitors are schoolchildren from nearby Zanzibar, who visit the island on educational snorkelling trips. Watching them come back in off the reef, chatting excitedly about following a hawksbill turtle along the outer shelf or trying to outdo each other with the size of the groupers they've just seen, is almost as much fun as drifting above the coral yourself.

385 | Exploring the forest with the Samburu

KENYA Landing on a private airstrip in a retro 1958 Cessna at the foot of Kenya's Mathews Range offers quite an adrenaline rush. Ngelai is the last strip of parched plain in the Kenyan landscape that you encounter before heading by 4WD into the blissfully isolated mountains. Climbing steadily, you bump your way through Samburu villages where children excitedly wave as you pass and the flora becomes greener by the minute.

Your destination: Kitich Camp, an intimate spot in the heart of the forest where a scientist recently found 150 undiscovered plants; it also boasts up to 380 species of bird, and plenty of butterflies and insects. In the open-air "lounge", safari chairs topped with sheepskin overlook a floodlit glade where, if you're lucky, elephant, buffalo and bushbuck emerge from the forest at dusk to drink from the stream.

Kitich is best explored on foot. On a walking safari, you may hear the throaty call of a large male lion or the low rumble of an elephant from somewhere in the lush indigenous forest, but it's unlikely you'll have a face-to-face encounter. Escorted by native Samburu, carrying spears and a gun – just in case – you walk through the tall grass into the unknown. Your guides will be watching mainly for buffalo, which present the most danger in these parts, while you scope the landscape for Africa's other great creatures. Droppings – of all kinds – will reveal a multitude of clues: undigested fur and hoof tell you that a lion has just feasted on a buffalo; white hyena droppings shows that they've recently eaten bone.

With binoculars, a troop of baboons can be sighted in the distance. Butterflies the size of dinner plates – or as tiny as daisies – and red and black turacos swoop across your path. You'll see ancient cycads, wild orchids and a white fungs that looks like a sea-shell.

Back at camp, after an alfresco shower, sipping sundowners of Tusker beer and the local cocktail *dawa* – vodka, honey, lime and mint – by a campfire, you can examine your collection of porcupine quills and bird feathers. Treasures, indeed, from this special place.

Feasting on the spice island

ZANZIBAR Caressed by the warm waters of the Indian Ocean and cleansed by its monsoon, Zanzibar – East Africa's "Spice Island" – feels worlds apart from the Tanzanian mainland just 40km away. A millennium of trade with lateen-rigged dhows (sailing vessels) introduced numerous peoples from faraway climes, all of whom contributed to the Swahili culture and language and also brought most of the ingredients that infuse one of Africa's most distinctive, and delicious, cuisines.

There's nutmeg and cloves from the Moluccas; cardamom, rice and peppercorns from India; aromatic Sri Lankan cinnamon; and sweet basil (and hookah pipes) from Persia. Portuguese caravels carried chilli, vanilla and cassava from the Americas; Indonesians arrived with bananas, turmeric and coconuts; the Arabs introduced coriander and cumin; and Chinese fleets unloaded ginger, along with porcelain and silks for the wealthy.

A spice tour is de rigueur for visitors, but it's on the plate that Zanzibar's fragrant culinary marriage really shines. At nightfall in Stone Town's waterfront Forodhani Gardens, dozens of cooks set up trestle tables and charcoal stoves to prepare nightly banquets that would please any sultan, all in the flickering light of oil lanterns, and at bargain prices. Feast on octopus stewed in coconut sauce, along with fresh lobster, shrimp, prawns, king fish (diced and grilled), whole snappers and even shark. Cool your throat with tropical juices like coconut straight from the shell, tangy tamarind, mango, papaya, pineapple, banana and sugar cane – though you'll have to bear the banshee-like wails of an ancient iron press to sample that one.

Top off your meal with a tiny cup of Omani-style coffee laced with cardamom, and a glob of *halua*, a sticky, gooey confection made from wheat, pistachios, saffron and cardamom, and unbelievable amounts of sugar – the perfect sweet finale to a spicy feast.

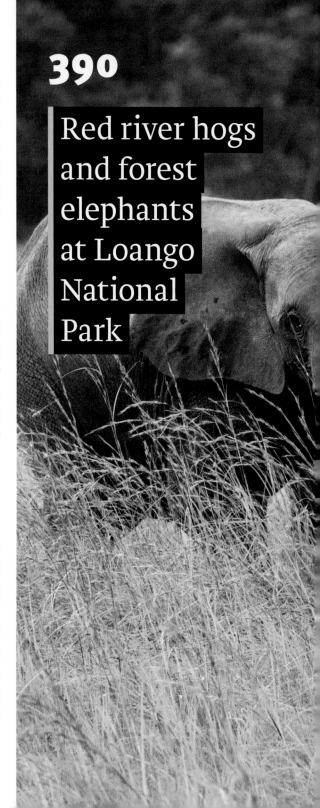

387 | Meeting the monkeys of Kibale

UGANDA It's unnerving to hear a bass drum being thumped when a) you're deep in a tropical forest and b) there is no one present to beat it. But exciting things happen in Kibale Forest National Park. And there's nothing more thrilling than when you find who it is that's responsible for the noise: wild chimpanzees.

Kibale contains the highest concentration of primates in the world; there are thirteen species in total but it is the chimps that enchant the most. After beating on flying-buttress roots with their feet, they decide on other scare tactics. Unsettling screams echo through the forest canopy – it's an exhilarating din. But the acoustics have got nothing on their terrific aerial acrobatics and displays of great ape machismo. And then they're off, moving through the branches at high speed, and it's impossible to keep up.

388 | Coming face to face with the Big Five in the wild

KENYA Coming under the mighty Big Five umbrella, Africa's elephants, rhinos, buffaloes, lions and leopards are the wild animals that every debut safari-goer wants to see. Importantly, the presence of these charismatic species indicates a healthy ecosystem. Each one is extraordinary, and you'll never forget your first glimpse.

Floundering over where to go on your first Big Five safari? The conservancies adjoining the Maasai Mara, Kenya's most famous wildlife destination, are a superb choice. This may not be the easiest place to see all five – the Mara's rhino population is small and elusive – but for the winning combination of atmosphere, romance and a forward-thinking, community-friendly ethos, it's impossible to beat.

389 | Eye to eye with Rwanda's mighty mountain gorillas

RWANDA A face-to-face encounter with a mountain gorilla in Rwanda's Volcanoes National Park is one of the most exciting wildlife experiences Africa has to offer. And locating the apes in their tangled and misty forest home is part of the thrill, an intense, high-altitude slog that has you navigating steep, muddy slopes for between one and five hours.

A guided trek high into the Virunga Volcanoes, which support more than half the world's remaining one thousand mountain gorillas, begins with a chilly dawn start at the park headquarters in Kinigi. A close-up encounter is practically guaranteed, but be warned – it can get tough, the air thinning and the anticipation building with every strenuous, slippery, step. Any exhaustion dissipates immediately, however, when you look into the liquid brown eyes of one of the magnificent bamboo-munching beasts, whose formidable bulk (up to 200kg) is complemented by a remarkably peaceable temperament – these are the archetypal "gentle giants".

390

Red river hogs and forest elephants at Loango National Park

GABON For all his shortcomings, the late President of Gabon, Omar Bongo, had a shrewd grasp of the value of his nation's mighty forests. In 2002, he successfully ring-fenced more than ten percent of Gabon's pristine wilderness from loggers, miners, hunters and farmers by creating thirteen new national parks, with one stroke of the pen.

One of the most accessible of these parks is Loango. But accessible, here, is a relative term. Getting to Loango takes time and money, whether you choose to fly or hop on a boat from Port-Gentil, the nearest town. If you're new to safaris and keen to find the quickest, easiest route to a plain teeming with zebras, lions and giraffes, then Loango isn't for you. But if you're prepared to suffer a long journey for a wildlife-watching experience that's unlike anything else Africa has to offer, it might be your kind of place.

Loango's unusual juxtaposition of habitats, including un-developed beach, savannahs and forest, makes it an out-standing place to visit. Its population of large mammals and reptiles ebbs and flows in a seasonal relay: for most of the year, there's a good chance of seeing something remarkable, be it breaching humpback whales (July to September), breeding Nile crocodiles (October to January) or nesting leatherback turtles (November to February). The park's hippos, famous for frolicking in the Atlantic surf, appear between November and January, while forest elephants patrol the shore from February to April.

Forest elephants, which are daintier than their better-known cousins, are somewhat unpredictable. They're partial to a hallucinogenic root, *ibago*, which grows wild in Loango's forests. If, as your guide drives you around the park, you come across an elephant that's under the influence, you could be in for an unnervingly close encounter. Less alarming, but just as intriguing, are the red river hogs – Loango's answer to warthogs. They're comical-looking, with very tufty ears. With care, you can creep up on them on foot as they trot through the grasslands. It's a thrilling experience in a continent where opportunities to watch unusual wildlife, out of range of dangerous predators, are rare indeed.

391

Egypt is famed for its great pyramids, but Sudan has many more. The most striking examples make up the ancient ruined city of Meroë. For nearly a thousand years from 600 BC, the little-known Kingdom of Kush prospered here alongside the Nile, once successfully repelling an attack by Alexander the Great and for centuries interring its rulers in the small but distinctively slender pyramids. Some thirty survive today, while all around small dunes in turn entomb the rubble. Meroë gets few visitors, so chances are you'll have this incredible site all to yourself.

Exploring the Meroë pyramids

Need to know

351 Mgahinga Gorilla National Park is in the Virunga mountains straddling the borders of Uganda, Rwanda and the Democratic Republic of Congo. The nearest town is Kisoro, a 10hr bus ride from Kampala. For more on the trail contact the Uganda Wildlife Authority (W ugandawildlife.org).

352 The best time to see the migration in the Serengeti is between Dec and July, for the river crossings, visit in June (Grumeti) and July or Aug (Mara).

353 The launch leaves from Paraa twice daily and takes around 3hr. There is no need to book; the trip is usually incorporated in all safaris to Murchison Falls National Park. Red Chilli Hideaway (W redchillihideaway.com) offers budget safaris from Kampala.

354 Saruni Rhino camp offers an exclusive rhino-tracking experience in the Sera Wildlife Conservancy. See W saruni.com for more details.

355 YellowWood Adventures is one of the only tour operators to run fully guided trips to the Bale Mountains. See W yellowwoodadventures.com.

356 The best times to make the ascent of Kilimanjaro are January to mid-March and June to Oct. Climbers must sign up with a trekking agency. Treks last five to nine days.

357 Balloon safaris cost around US$500 per person, including a slap-up breakfast with sparkling wine. The Maasai Mara region is the commonest venue and any camp or lodge will make a booking. Flights also sometimes operate over the Amboseli National Park and Taita Hills Game Sanctuary near Tsavo West National Park. Operators include W maraballooning.com.

358 Check security information before visiting this part of Congo.

359 Coconut Beach is a 15min taxi ride from central Bujumbura. Rusizi National Park is open daily from dawn to dusk.

360 The Kigali Genocide Memorial is open daily, except the last Sat of each month (donations accepted); for more information visit W kgm.rw). It is partnered with the UK-based Aegis Trust (W aegistrust.org), which works to prevent crimes against humanity.

361 Boat trips depart several times daily – late afternoon is always a good option wildlife-wise. The Uganda Wildlife Authority and Mweya Safari Lodge

both have boats; W ugandawildlife.org and W mweyalodge.com.

362 The *Paradise Malahide* (W paradisemalahide.com) hotel can organize most aspects of your stay in Gisenyi.

363 Kinshasa's live music venues include *Hôtel de Crèche*, Rond-Point Victoire, *Chez Ntemba*, Av. Douane, Gombe, and *Halle de la Gombe* (Institut Français), Gombe (W institutfrancais-kinshasa.org).

364 Hell's Gate National Park is just south of Lake Naivasha, accessible through the day by minibus from Nairobi (1hr 30min).

365 A four-day pass covering all eleven churches costs around US$50. Hiring a guide is worthwhile.

366 North Kenya is difficult to explore independently. One excellent option is Gametracker's overland truck trip to Turkana via the Chalbi Desert (W gametrackersafaris.com). This involves stays at village campsites and many opportunities to interact with local people.

367 Gorilla Habituation Experience permits (US$1,500) are available from the Uganda Wildlife Authority (W ugandawildlife.org) or through specialist tour operators.

368 Details on permits, preparations and guides can be found at W simienpark.org.

369 Climbing Mount Kenya is possible all year round. Many Nairobi operators and agents can offer tours, or you hike independently with a local guide. Kenya Wildlife Service (W kws.go.ke) has information.

370 Stone Town is some 7km north of Zanzibar's international airport.

371 Visit W kataviwildlifecamp.com for accommodation listings and access details.

372 Guided chimp tracking in the Mahale Mountains or Gombe Stream national parks can be booked with TANAPA (W tanzaniaparks.go.tz) or through local lodges.

373 See W nyiragongovolcano.com.

374 Many resorts offer turtle-watching trips in season; one of the easiest places to see them is Cousine Island (W cousineisland.com). Be sure not to disturb any nesting turtles or hatchlings you come across, nor shine lights as this can disorientate them.

375 Find information on Ivindo National Park at W zambezi.com/locations/ivindo-national-park.

376 Loisaba (W loisaba.com) is around 270km north of Nairobi in Laikipia, a private conservation area. The star-bed bush camps, *Kiboko* and *Koija*, each have three platforms (one double and one twin).

377 Crater safaris are easily arranged in Arusha, several hours' drive to the east.

378 *Il Ngwesi* is approximately a 90min (rough) drive from the nearest road. See W ilngwesi.com.

379 The Mwaka Kogwa festival is usually in the third week of July; the fighting is on the first of the four-day festivities, from around 11am. Check dates with a tour operator such as W zanzibarholidays.co.uk.

380 Kaya Kinondo is at the southern end of Diani Beach.

381 For details of walking safaris in the Serengeti with Alex Walker, see W serian.com.

382 Axum's historical sites are best visited with a guide; arrange with the Axum Guides Association, by the entrance to the main stelae field.

383 Frégate Island Private offers personalized services (W fregate.com). The island is a 15min helicopter hop or a 1.5hr boat trip (subject to weather conditions) from the international airport on Mahé.

384 *Chumbe Island Eco-Lodge* (W chumbeisland.com) is reached by boat from Zanzibar. Profits from the lodge go back into island conservation. Contact the office two days before your visit to check availability.

385 For details contact W chelipeacock.com.

386 Zanzibar is a 20min flight from Dar es Salaam, or under 3hr by ferry. Flights are offered daily; book on W alternativeairlines.com.

387 Kibale Forest National Park is best reached from Fort Portal, either on local buses or with organized day tours. See also W kibaleforestnationalpark.com.

388 For more information on the Maasai Mara, see W maraconservancies.org.

389 Gorilla tracking should be booked as far in advance as possible, either through an operator or Rwanda Tourism (W rwandatourism.com). Last-minute permits are occasionally available.

390 Tour operator Africa's Eden (W africaseden.com) offers safaris in Loango National Park.

391 Meroë is in northeast Sudan; the nearest town is Shendi, 50km away.

GABON

CONGO

DEMOCRATIC
REPUBLIC
OF CONGO

RWANDA

BURUNDI

UGANDA

KENYA

SOMALIA

*ARABIAN
SEA*

Equa

TANZANIA

ANGOLA

ZAMBIA

415
392
425
MALAWI
407
416
431
400
439
418
421
410
MADAGASCAR
395
437

398 438
ZIMBABWE
402
430
442
428
MOZAMBIQUE
435

411
409
412

436 443
BOTSWANA

NAMIBIA

*Mozambique
Channel*

MAURIT

RÉUNION

408

420
441

419

401
426
399

424
SOUTH
AFRICA
LESOTHO
423

394 413
417 Swaziland
434 427

403

*ATLANTIC
OCEAN*

429
406
422
440
396

393
397
414
432

INDIAN   OCEAN

433

SOUTHERN AFRICA

392-443

Combining age-old ethnic cultures with show-stopping wildlife, rolling dunes with thundering waterfalls and fishing villages with fast-moving cities, Southern Africa is an immense, diverse region. Whether you're venturing to the lion-prowelled Okavango Delta, the flamingo-speckled islands of the Bazaruto Archipelago, the black-rhino plains of Namibia or the whale-frequented waters off South Africa, very few areas of the planet can rival it for sheer natural variety. Culturally, too, it's an area of riches, from the vibrant street-art scene of Johannesburg and the traditional festivals of Swaziland to the delicious fusion cuisine of Cape Malay and the modernist architecture of Maputo.

392   Music and moonlight on the Lake of Stars

MALAWI Perhaps it was the lack of sleep from the 24-hour journey, the anti-malarials or the infectious enthusiasm of the locals, but we spent our entire weekend at the Lake of Stars festival in a state of delighted delirium. Our glee was doubtless helped by generous lashings of Chibuku Shake Shake, an infamous gloopy millet beer served in cartons and passed around with abandon, but there was something else in the air, too – a carefree atmosphere – that made our time by the southern shore of Lake Malawi so memorable.

Established by British music fan Will Jameson in 2003, Lake of Stars has grown to become a phenomenal event. A three-day party featuring bands and DJs from across Africa, it also attracts global stars and a clued-up, intrepid international audience. Over the course of 72 hectic hours we saw a huge range of Malawian acts, from local reggae legends to politicized soul funk groups via beatboxers and indie troupes, all of them laying bare the country's musical DNA. They were joined by artists from as far afield as Japan and the US; one band from South Africa had spent five days on the road for the chance to play their set. Hearing *Big Brother Africa* star Maskal offer a stirring cover of Lionel Richie's *Stuck on You* was probably the oddest moment of the weekend – until, perhaps, the arrival of the Amitofo Kung Fu collective, a crew of Malawian orphans trained by a Taiwanese monk.

Mornings began with breakfast at the lodge, tussling with monkeys for sugar sachets. We then headed out to explore – the travelling library bus and the HIV clinic, just beyond the festival site, offered a more sobering picture of life in Malawi. Evenings saw us settling back into the rhythms of the festival. Hypnotic beats pulsated across the sand while cooks tended smoking barbecues from makeshift shacks. Downing the singular sludge at the bottom of the Chibuku carton, gazing up at that wide, twinkling sky, we never wanted to leave.

Tim Chester
is a travel and culture journalist and was the editor of Roughguides.com for several years. He has explored Turkey and Myanmar for Rough Guides, and experienced a fair few festivals across the globe during his former life as a roving music journalist.

SOUTH AFRICA Think of a penguin and it's hard not to see icy wastes. Yet penguins can be found as far north as the scorched Galápagos Islands, and on family-friendly Boulders Beach, close to Cape Town, you can actually swim among them.

The African penguin population has been decimated in recent centuries, their eggs eaten by humans, who also compete for fish stocks, and habitat threatened by pollution, yet this colony of 2500 birds (one of only two groups on the African mainland) is growing.

Seeing the animals requires no tracking, no luck and no guide – just get out of your car at the Boulders Beach car park, half an hour's drive from central Cape Town, and you'll see them sunning themselves on the great granite rocks that give the beach its name, or hopping around on the beach itself. The calm, clear water, protected from the Atlantic swells and strong winds by the smooth boulders, offers glimpses of the black-and-white birds speeding through the water, using their flightless wings as efficient flippers, heading out into the mountain-encircled bay to fish. The birds are surprisingly nonchalant, and you can easily get to within a metre of them – providing a perfect photo opportunity – as they waddle their way down to the surf.

Don't expect companionship as you swim in shared waters, though. The penguins streak past at up to 25km/hr and fish way off the coast, returning to regurgitate their meals for their chicks, which you can see in the plentiful nesting sites above the beach.

The azure water may lull you into Mediterranean fantasies, but Cape Town's waters are cool even in midsummer. During the winter, especially from August to October, you might not be tempted to swim, but can still roam the beach, or stand on the boulders themselves, looking past the penguins into False Bay, where southern right whales arrive from the Antarctic every year to calve.

Swim with penguins at Boulders Beach

393

SWAZILAND Another false summit. Defeated, you lever the pack from your back and slump into the shade of a sugar bush, porcupine quills strewn at your feet like some primitive offering. Bird calls drift up from the canopy below: the chirrup of bulbuls, the growling of a turaco.

Down in the forest, the trail had been all cool, green-filtered light. Up here on the shattered slopes, the sun has you pinioned to the hillside like a beetle on a sand dune. An unseen baboon barks its alarm from the ridgetop. But the rush of the falls is a siren call. One more push?

The grandeur of Malolotja belies the bijou dimensions of Swaziland. This, the biggest park in southern Africa's tiniest nation, protects a muscular wilderness of peaks, grasslands and gorges, with vistas that stretch far beyond the country's borders. Highlights include the world's oldest iron-ore mine, the 90m bridal-veil cascade

of Malolotja Falls and the "potholes" – a terraced series of circular plunge pools that lure footsore hikers deep into an echoing ravine. Hiking trails embroider the wild ridges and forested clefts. And every stream swells the exuberant Malolotja River, which carves its way downwards and northwards until it hits the Komati and turns east for the Indian Ocean.

For birders, Malolotja means the blue swallow – southern Africa's rarest bird and just one of a fine cast of avian A-listers. Other wildlife is rich, but elusive: alert hikers might meet mountain reedbuck skittering across the rocky slopes, an otter lolloping along the riverbank or maybe a shy serval stalking the marsh. Plants, too, are prolific: orchids in the grasslands, cycads in the forests, aloes and coral trees spotting the hillsides with scarlet. It's not "Big Five" country, give or take the occasional leopard print. But whatever you find, you'll have it all to yourself.

395 | Blue beaks and beaches: birdwatching in Masoala

MADAGASCAR Welcome to Masoala National Park, an exotic finger of pristine primary rainforest in the northeast of Madagascar. Fringed by shell-white beaches and coral reefs, the area is carpeted with jungle – including precious rosewood and ebony trees – that spills vines and creepers onto the sand. This paradise is a haven for one of the world's rarest birds – the helmet vanga.

The endemic vanga family comprises fifteen different species, with a wide range of colours and unusual beaks. Blue, rufous and sickle-billed vangas are glorious enough, but none is quite as spectacular as the helmet vanga, with its predatory, bubblegum-blue beak, shaped like a half moon. That beak! Cartoon-like against black-and-russet plumage, it is, as field guides point out, "completely unmistakable". Spotting a helmet vanga is a once-in-a-lifetime prize for ornithologists, who make the intrepid journey across the choppy waters of Antongil Bay for a precious glimpse. Tourists here are few and far between, and most stay at one of the ecolodges on the beach. Rates include your own dedicated

local guide who will take you on as many day- and night-time hikes as you like, pointing out red-ruffed lemurs, long-fingered aye ayes and the world's smallest chameleon, brookesia – a perfect snack for a hungry vanga – along the way.

Nimble-footed and eagle-eyed, guides navigate the forest with ease, leading you to remote nesting sights where they mimic the helmet vanga's cascading warble. It could take minutes, hours or even days, and the walking can be tough, but the lucky few will never forget that first flash of turquoise glimpsed among the canopy. Unused to humans, the bird will view you curiously from its perch with beady eyes. Investigations complete, it will return to more important matters – gleaning tasty insects and reptiles from the dense foliage. You might even come across a multi-vanga flock, with each species exploiting its own ecological niche, or a monogamous pair carefully incubating pinky-white eggs. A "bucket list" species for birdwatchers, the helmet vanga really is the jewel of Masoala, but you don't have to be a twitcher to be blown away by its beauty.

396 | Walk with whales at the foot of Africa

SOUTH AFRICA If size really does count, then whales are the biggest attraction in South Africa. In most places on the planet you need to get on a boat to get a decent glimpse of these amazing creatures, but in South Africa they come so close to shore you can easily see them with your naked eye. One of the very best places anywhere for land-based whale-watching is the De Hoop Nature Reserve, in the Western Cape, close to the continent's southernmost tip, where in the breeding season (roughly June to November) hundreds of female southern right whales come to calve and suckle their offspring.

You can stay in cottages in the nature reserve, but the most rewarding way to come into contact with the mammals is the five-day Whale Trail, which covers the 55km from Potberg to Koppie Alleen, traversing beaches and cliff edges with terrific views from dusk to dawn. During the season, you're treated to so many whale sightings that by the end of the trail you become almost blasé. But not quite. It takes a lot to beat

the vision of a southern right blowing fine spray out of the water as it breathes or exposing its tail above the surface like some massive dark sail. Breaching, the whales create an enormous swell, leaping clear of the water and sometimes twirling in the air before returning to the deep with an enormous splash. You'll often also see seals scouting for fish and dolphins riding the surf, while on land there are some eighty mammal species, from small yellow mongooses to antelope and mountain zebras.

The hike is a "slackpacking" trail that requires only basic fitness. Your supplies and kit are taken by road to each night's accommodation – comfortable, fully equipped cottages, each one in splendid isolation. The porterage means when you're not gawking at whales, you can really enjoy the endemic fynbos vegetation, which incorporates an extraordinary diversity that includes fine-leafed heathers, minute insectivorous plants, giant proteas and orchids. And, best of all: only one group at a time is allowed on each day's section.

Cape Malay cooking in Cape Town

SOUTH AFRICA Photographers can't resist the Cape Town quarter of Bo-Kaap. Daubed in vibrant shades of pink, blue, orange, yellow and green, its cute little nineteenth-century terraced houses are always popping up in urban landscape shoots and block-colour fashion stories.

Bo-Kaap's kaleidoscope colours are a relatively recent tradition, begun at the end of apartheid, when the residents – a community of Muslims – were first allowed to buy their homes from the city council. They would splash out on a new paint job to celebrate the end of Ramadan, usually choosing whatever colours happened to be cheapest. But Bo-Kaap's distinctiveness is also expressed in longer-running traditions, such as music, dance, festivals and food.

In the apartheid era, this neighbourhood was home to the descendants of the Cape Malays, people from India, Sri Lanka, East Africa and Madagascar, imported as slaves by the Dutch in the sixteenth and seventeenth centuries. They spoke a unique dialect of Afrikaans and their days were punctuated by the call of the muezzin from Bo-Kaap's many mosques. Both can still be heard today – albeit less than before.

Increasingly, the colourful district of Bo-Kaap has been catching the eye of property investors, stirring up fears that it will soon lose its old identity forever. In central Cape Town – the freshly polished jewel of the new South Africa – such a change seems inevitable, but certain Cape Muslims are determined to keep their multifaceted culture alive.

A local cooking tour will do more than teach you to cook – it will introduce you to Cape Malay's rich culinary culture. Your food-focused morning out will probably start at the Bo-Kaap Museum, offering insights into the district's social history; you might well also stop at Atlas Trading on Wale Street, an emporium of freshly ground spices, rice, beans, coconut oil and incense, packed with pungent aromas.

From here, you'll continue to the home of your host, where, over a mug of *faloodah* (a lightly rose-scented milk drink) you'll get stuck in – learning how to blend masala spices, fold samosas and balance flavours to make a perfect Cape Malay curry. It's friendly, informal and a lot of fun. And, best of all, at the end of your masterclass, you get to scoff the lot.

Leap into Devil's Pool

ZAMBIA David Livingstone was certainly a dedicated missionary, as he regarded the magnificent Victoria Falls as an inconvenient obstacle on his journey along the Zambezi, which hurls itself down these 100m-high, 1.7km-wide falls. There is more of a sense of manic fun to the bathers who incongruously teeter across the rocks from Livingstone Island, a tiny flotsam of land amid the mist of the world's largest waterfall, to Devil's Pool, the churning infinity pool atop the streaming precipice of the falls. Standing on a boulder, take a deep breath and prepare for an up-close encounter with the spectacle known locally as Mosi-oa-Tunya, 'the smoke that thunders'. Across the misty abyss, on the far side of the chasm formed by the falls, tourists wave from a viewpoint in Zimbabwe. Be brave now, but not too bold because this is one jump you certainly don't want to miscalculate. After leaping, screaming, splashing and resurfacing with a gasp, sit on the rocky ledge known as Devil's Armchair, grinning as millions of litres of water plummet downwards.

399 | Watching the desert bloom in Namaqualand

NAMIBIA & SOUTH AFRICA Spring in Namaqualand brings the kind of miracle for which time-lapse photography was invented. After the brief winter rains, kilometre after kilometre of barren-looking semi-desert is transformed, within days, into a sea of flowers – a dazzling display that sends butterflies, bees and long-tongued flies into a frenzy.

Namaqualand, a thirsty, rocky region encompassing South Africa's northwestern corner and Namibia's extreme south, supports over four thousand wild floral species, a quarter of them endemic. It's this diversity that gives the annual display so much charm. The key lies below the surface: seeds and bulbs can lie dormant through many years of drought, and when conditions suddenly improve, the plants grow roots of differing length, so numerous species can exploit relatively small stretches of terrain.

The least showy of the plants are the succulents, some shaped like fingers, others (such as lithops) like pebbles. These cling to life on the ground, where the colour of the gravel can mean the difference between extinction and survival – a few chips of white quartz may be sufficient to lower the local air temperature by a degree or so, just enough for a plant to cope.

Intriguing though the native succulents are, it's the colourful blooms that draw the crowds. Visit on a sunny day in a good year and you'll see meadow after meadow sprinkled with aloes and lilies, daisies and gladioli, purple ruschias, golden ursinias and gaudy vermilion gazanias, as bright and tempting as hundreds and thousands on a fairy cake.

It's a photographer's dream – and a heaven for painters, too. If Claude Monet had set up his easel near Springbok instead of Argenteuil, the Namaqualand daisy would by now be every bit as famous as the Val d'Oise poppy.

400 | Paddling the great, grey, greasy Zambezi

ZIMBABWE When Rudyard Kipling wrote of an archetypal African river all set about with fever trees, he was referring to the Limpopo, which defines the southern border of Zimbabwe. Yet the Zambezi, which heads through the north of the country, is larger, grander and far more crocodile- and hippo-infested than its rival. It took Victorian missionary and explorer David Livingstone three years to travel the 2500km from its source in Zambia to its mouth in Mozambique by dugout. Today, canoeing through wilderness areas, downriver from Victoria Falls, where the spray of the plunging Zambezi can be seen 20km off, offers the rawest experience of African wildlife you will ever encounter.

Apart from your own small, guided group on the waters of the Lower Zambezi, in the Mana Pools National Park, you won't see any buildings or people for several days. You'll skim past herds of grazing buffalo and antelope as well as elephants, which stand on their hind legs to tug at delicious seed pods high up on acacia trees. And a quiet canoe can get preciously close to birdlife; vermilion carmine bee-eaters swoop in and out of nests burrowed into sandy banks, and black egrets, green-backed and goliath herons stalk the shallows for fish and frogs.

Everything is carried on your canoe, including a tent, though you may spend some nights with only a mosquito net spread over your mattress as chilling predator growls and roars split the night. Territorial male hippos, not always keen to let canoes pass through their domain, are far more frightening than the 5m crocodiles that slide into the water as you paddle by, keeping close to the river guide. The paddling itself is not strenuous and, in colonial style, canoe safaris are actually quite luxurious – meals are prepared by the camp cook, and you dine under the stars, white tablecloth and all.

The people you do meet tend to be exceptionally friendly and easy-going – the benefits of tourism are appreciated on the ground.

401 | The mining ghosts of Kolmanskop

NAMIBIA Get up early and drive 10km east from the port town of Lüderitz to watch the first fingers of sunrise reach across the desert. See them light up the sands that have piled high and inhabited every nook of this once-thriving town. The honey-toned rays reveal peeling wallpaper in empty kitchens, ceramic bathtubs waiting forlornly for a filling and empty picture frames dangling from unsteady nails.

The mining town of Kolmanskop, in southern Namibia, sprang up in 1909, a year after the first diamond, or "shining stone", was plucked out of the sand beside the Lüderitz–Keetmanshoop railway line. Within months of the discovery, the German government had established the 26,000-square-kilometre *Sperrgebiet*, or "forbidden territory", and set up mining towns all over the area. The wealth the sands concealed was beyond their wildest dreams: before the outbreak of World War I more than five million carats had been mined, and it was common for Lüderitz barmaids to be paid in sparklers. During its 1920s heyday 344 people lived in Kolmanskop. They built a bakery, a school, shops – even a ballroom. It's all still there. Metal hooks hang poignantly in the butchers, dusty skittles stand erect in the abandoned bowling alley and a splintered diving board perches over the empty swimming pool. Tour guides help unlock the town's stories, but wandering around before the bus groups arrive is far better – standing in the sand-filled doorways, you might even mistake the wind whistling through glassless windows for the distant whisper of miners' voices.

Slowly the diamond fields began to yield fewer and fewer stones. Tired of scratching at the increasingly empty sands, the miners finally abandoned the town en masse in 1956. A trio of hardy families persevered for another three years before loneliness and encroaching sands chased them away. Today, the lure of the white stone remains strong: the empty town and adjoining land are owned by NamDeb (the Namibia-De Beers mining corporation). Miners drive sturdy 4WDs into the desert, their high-tech machinery digging ever deeper, while decaying Kolmanskop watches over them enviously – a ghost town rich only in memories.

ZIMBABWE First things first: it's a caterpillar, not a worm. This revelation may or may not improve your appetite. But to many Zimbabweans – especially those living in the low-lying, mopane tree belt – this protein-packed invertebrate is a staple.

Trawl through the local markets and you'll see them by the thousand, heaped in bright plastic buckets or piled on the rickety stalls among mounds of beans and dried *kapenta* sardines. Take a closer look at one. It's grey and wrinkled; the size of your little toe. Now try a nibble. There's no real taste – it's more like dried wood than anything animal. Add a little salt, though, and you have the perfect bar snack; the insect equivalent of a pork scratching.

Those you find in the market have already been prepared, their tail ends pinched off and noxious gut contents squeezed out, then dried in the sun. For a good meal you'll need a decent portion. The vendor will scoop them up in an old tin can and wrap them in a twist of newspaper. Now you can take them home, rehydrate them in warm water, and fry them with some onion, tomato and a dash of chilli. Served the traditional way, with a portion of *sadza* (maize meal porridge), they make a cheap, tasty and nutritious dinner.

This dish – or a version of it – is eaten across a wide swathe of southern Africa, wherever the mopane tree grows. And it is on the butterfly-shaped leaves of this drought-resistant species that the emperor moth, *Imbrasia belina*, lays its eggs. When they hatch, the caterpillars work voraciously through the foliage until they are big enough to pupate, which they do underground over winter. It's at the fifth, and fattest, larval stage that local people harvest them, picking them from the leaves before drying or smoking them.

Once just a subsistence food, mopane worms now fuel a wider industry that has become vital to the local economy. OK, so they may not appeal to the first-timer. But perhaps appetite is all in the mind; after all, a bowl of prawns is hardly a thing of beauty. Forget the name and just tuck in.

402

Munch on a mopane worm

403 | Tracing Mandela's roots on the Wild Coast

SOUTH AFRICA True to its name, South Africa's Wild Coast is one of the country's most unspoilt areas – a vast stretch of undulating hills dotted with traditional African villages, lush forest and kilometres of undeveloped beaches. Arguably the best place to taste the Wild Coast is at *Bulungula Lodge*, a joint enterprise established by the people of Nqileni village and seasoned traveller and development worker Dave Martin.

Idyllically sited along the mouth of the Bulungula River, Nqileni and the lodge lie in a remote region of the former Transkei, the notionally "independent homeland" to which Xhosa-speaking black South Africans were relegated under apartheid. One consequence of South Africa's racial policies was the neglect suffered by the Wild Coast, but this also meant it escaped the intense coastal development that has ravaged many former whites-only coastal areas.

With a dearth of formal jobs, people in the Transkei still live rural lives in thatched adobe huts, growing maize, fishing, and cooking on wood fires, while young lads still herd cattle, pretty much as Nelson Mandela did when he was a boy. Wander around Nqileni and you may be invited into someone's house for a slug of traditional beer or asked to take part in everyday business, such as mud-brick making or maize stamping.

Bulungula also gives a livelihood to members of the community, who take visitors exploring on horseback or canoeing up the Xhora River to look for malachite kingfishers, or teach them how to fish with a throw net. You can meander along the beach to watch whales and dolphins or have one of the villagers take you out on an all-day expedition to beautiful Coffee Bay. At night, the skies are so clear and the shooting stars so plentiful that, according to the lodge's owner, "if you look at the sky for half an hour without seeing one, you can stay the night for free".

404 | On the trail of dead dodos and plump pigeons

MAURITIUS Island life has its upsides and its downsides. Some of the animals which washed up on the world's remotest shores in distant millennia were lucky – finding themselves in a food-rich, predator-free habitat, they thrived. On Mauritius, reptiles, birds and bats evolved into complacent creatures of considerable proportions. But their peaceful nature was their downfall. As soon as humans showed up, it was all over.

The disappearance of the dodo, the poster bird of extinct species, was total: only sketches and scraps of bone survived. Archeologists have done their best to piece together images of this metre-tall flightless pigeon from skeleton fragments found in centuries-old rubbish tips; at the Dodo Gallery of the Natural History Museum in the capital, Port Louis, you can view some of their attempts.

Dead it may be, but there's no escaping the dodo on Mauritius. It's everywhere – on tablecloths, fridge magnets and even on the passport stamp you receive at the airport. The islanders seem almost proud of being more famous for their extinct wildlife species than their living ones. But these days, they're a lot more conservation-minded than

the sixteenth- and seventeenth-century seafarers who (together with their pigs and monkeys) munched their way through the entire dodo population, or the twentieth-century settlers who nearly polished off another Mauritian endemic, the pink pigeon.

On Ile aux Aigrettes, a small woodland reserve in a lagoon off the southeast coast, the Mauritian Wildlife Foundation is taking great pains to protect the few pink pigeons which remain. The pigeon, *Columba mayeri*, is naturally plump and reluctant to fly: their population had plummeted to under a dozen in the early 1990s before naturalists, including the Durrell Wildlife Conservation Trust, stepped in to intervene.

You can visit Ile aux Aigrettes by motorboat, a short trip from Pointe Jerome across stunning turquoise waters. Once ashore, a guide leads you along paths lined with rare flora: little by little, rangers are replacing non-native species with endemics thanks to funds raised from tours such as these. You'll almost certainly spot some pink pigeons, sunning themselves in a clearing with the smugness of a bird that knows it's on to a good thing.

405 | The shifting spectacle of the Seven Coloured Earths

MAURITIUS The Seven Coloured Earths is a swirling kaleidoscope of multicoloured sands in southwestern Mauritius. This geological curiosity sees seven layers of volcanic earth in different hues – red, brown, violet, green, blue, purple and yellow – combine to create rainbow-like sand dunes; the colourful alter-ego of the rugged Chamarel Plains. Interestingly, if you sieve a handful of all the different strands through your hands, they'll eventually reform into their distinct colours – although the science behind it isn't entirely understood.

While many of the Instagrammed images of the spectacle are filtered into oblivion, the actual colours are softer variations of these unrealistically vivid shades – pink-tinted pastel hues stark against the wall of emerald trees that wraps around the dunes. The remote site is 4km southwest of Chamarel, a traditional Mauritian village

283m above sea level, and is a bit of a journey from the more well-trodden parts of the island – Port Louis is 50km north. A visit is best combined with a picturesque twenty-minute hike through the dense forest to the Chamarel Waterfall, which cascades 90m over a cliff face into a shallow pool where you can bathe.

A twenty-minute drive will take you to the Black River Gorges National Park, home to nine endemic species of bird, including the elegant white Paille-en-queue and endangered varieties like the Mauritius kestrel and Kermit-green echo parakeet. A huge population of flittering giant fruit bats shares the skies. Herds of deer and wild boar can often be seen among the ebony trees, along with macaque monkeys that also cavort up by the Black River Peak viewpoint, from where you can take in one of the best views of the island.

406 | Tracking cheetahs in the Karoo

SOUTH AFRICA Mountain Zebra National Park, established to protect the rare Cape mountain zebra, covers 280 square kilometres of raw Karoo semi-desert on the northern slopes of the Bankberg range. Around 800km from Johannesburg and Cape Town, the park offers a special activity to attract visitors down the long and dusty roads to its gate.

Continuing the conservation ethos of its 1000-plus Cape mountain zebra population, which has grown from a founder herd of six, the park has reintroduced cheetahs, brown hyenas and lions since 2007. Taking advantage of the big cats' GPS and radio collars, used by rangers and researchers to monitor their health, habits and prey, you can sign up to track cheetahs in the reassuring company of a gun-toting guide. It's possible to get within 10m of the spotted felines,

which, despite being the fastest land animals, are now regarded as a vulnerable species. *Gorillas in the Mist* this ain't, but most people are unlikely to have bumped into the Asiatic cheetah, which reaches over 100km/hr and suffocates prey by biting its throat, in their local park.

The thrill of the experience also lies in the finer details, which always make a drive or, better yet, a walk in the African bush an adventure, whatever you see. For starters, you get to spend the morning with a khaki-clad ranger, deciphering their Afrikaans-flecked English and using terms such as 'spoor' while you scan the rocks with your binos. As you bump along the gravel roads and leave the safety of your safari vehicle, you'll also learn about everything from sweet thorn acacia to the cheetahs themselves, which were introduced before the fiercer lions so they didn't compete for food.

407 | Witnessing a blizzard of bats

ZAMBIA Think African wildlife migration, and chances are you'll picture wildebeest and zebras pounding across the Serengeti or risking life and limb in the crocodile-infested Mara River.

Featuring galloping herds of 1.5 million or more, East Africa's Great Migration is certainly impressive. But Africa has another mass movement of mammals that's simply gigantic. Estimates vary wildly, but it's thought the Kasanka migration outnumbers the Serengeti-Mara by a factor of between four and seven.

Chances are you won't have heard of it. The species concerned has a bit of an image problem compared to those reliably charismatic and comical zebras and wildebeest, and their route is well off the beaten track. They're bats – straw-coloured fruit bats, to be precise – and each year between October and November anything up to ten million of them fly from Central Africa to Zambia, converging on a particular group of trees in the 400 square kilometres of well-watered woodland and grassland that is Kasanka National Park.

Their target is a patch of mushitu swamp forest measuring little more than one square kilometre. Somehow, roughly as many bats as there are people living in Singapore, London or Lagos manage to squeeze themselves in. With a wingspan of up to 80cm, these migrants are hardly minute, so it takes a miracle of tolerance, endurance and skill for them to cram onto the branches, which regularly collapse under their weight.

The attraction is a rare abundance of ripe loquats and waterberries – a highly nutritious seasonal food source. Head into the forest in the late afternoon to stake out the papyrus beds or climb into a treetop hide, and, as dusk falls, you can watch dense clouds of bats fill the skies as they head out for their nightly feast. Even better, if the idea of walking through a pitch-black African forest that's squelchy underfoot doesn't unsettle you too much, set an alarm to wake you before dawn. There's nothing to match being up in a hide as thousands of bats, full and happy, come in to land, silhouetted against the sunrise.

408 | Sailing a dhow in the Bazaruto Archipelago

MOZAMBIQUE The helicopter journey from Vilanculos to the Bazaruto Archipelago takes fifteen minutes across the teal-blue Mozambique Channel, swirled with pink sandy shoals. So transparent is the water that you can see manta rays moving serenely below, and the flash of silvery dolphin as they leap clear of the surface.

Dhows ply the maze of tidal channels, their pointy sails slicing the aqua shallows like shark fins. Traditional Arab-style dhows are a dime a dozen in these straits. Small creaking wooden vessels with slanting triangular sails of merikani cotton, they're atavistic hold-overs dating back centuries to a time when Mozambique's coastline was a precious dominion of Arab ivory, pearl, spice and slave traders. Though their lateen-rigged design has remained unchanged for more than a thousand years, these days they're used mainly by locals for fishing, and for idyllic island-hopping excursions for travellers.

The Bazarutos – an archipelago of six tiny isles strung like pearls and haloed by jaw-droppingly beautiful beaches – lie off Vilanculos, a slow-paced coastal town a 90-minute flight from Maputo, the tranquil

and non-threatening capital. Hotels hereabout all arrange adventure excursions by dhow. These vessels are authentically rustic: the beam, mast and sail-yard are made from less-than-straight tree trunks, lashed together with coconut coir rope. So, don't expect luxury. And don't panic when the crew starts to bail out your dhow while at sea.

Rough-hewn affairs, they're still caulked in traditional manner by hammering cotton into the gaps between the hand-adzed planks. When wet it forms a tight seal. But all dhows leak. The creaking of timbers, the crack of the wind in the billowing sail, and the crisp slap of the dhow scything the water are pure music.

You'll step ashore on Bazaruto and Benguerra islands to look for crocodiles and climb massive dunes spilling into the Indian Ocean, with flats speckled pink by flamingos. You'll swim in crystal waters teeming with angelfish, Moorish idols, and blackspotted sweetlips so close you can almost kiss them. And a gourmet picnic lunch is usually served on a blazing white beach while your boatmen play mancala in the talcum sand.

NAMIBIA With a population density of fewer than three people per square kilometre, much of Namibia feels very empty indeed. But few parts of the map look as blank as eastern Otjozondjupa. To reach the Ju/'hoansi town of Tsumkwe, you turn off the Grootfontein to Rundu highway onto a bone-white ribbon of gravel that slices through 220km of arid bush, with barely a turn-off to distract you.

Like the other San Bushman communities of southern Africa, the Ju/'hoansi were once hunter-gatherers leading entirely nomadic lives in the harsh Kalahari desert. These days, they're largely settled or semi-settled, but they're increasingly keen to keep their traditions alive. Several groups of Ju/'hoansi invite visitors to join them in the bush for anything from a few hours to several days, to see the Kalahari through their eyes and learn a little bushlore.

Before you meet your Ju/'hoansi guides, they'll have changed from their everyday clothing into traditional dress – loincloths made from soft antelope skin and, for the women and children, necklaces of glass and ostrich-egg beads. Barefoot, they assemble at a meeting place, a collection of grass huts built for the purpose.

At first, it's natural to wonder whether you've signed up for an artificial encounter in which everything will feel staged and contrived, but such concerns soon fade when, with little preamble, the Ju/'hoansi lead you into the bush, fully focused on the genuine task of reading the landscape and explaining, through an interpreter, what they see.

With a society founded on principles of modest, non-competitive cooperation, the Ju/'hoansi move with ease as a group, stopping every so often to pick and share fruit or demonstrate something of interest. You'll be shown which plants provide the most nutritious berries or water-rich tubers, and which leaves, when crushed, are stimulants or have other medicinal uses. Some shrubs harbour neurotoxic grubs, used by hunters to tip their arrows, and others have roots which, when burned, make a powerful lion repellent. This benign-seeming sandy woodland holds much of value – and harbours plenty of unseen dangers, too.

409

Learning about Kalahari bushlore from the Ju/'hoansi San

Tsingy's bread-knife forest

MADAGASCAR Some of the butterflies are so large they hardly look able to get off the ground. But the lemurs and hairy crabs aren't interested in them, nor are the lime green parrots. They're too busy fussing through the *tsingy*.

These serrated limestone rock formations, sharp as bread-knives, cut up through the landscape of western Madagascar, creating baroque grottos and pinnacles. Dry and seemingly inhospitable, they are home to extraordinary wildlife. Even fat baobabs manage to grab hold in this alien environment. But astonishing beauty is also found in the detail: miniature red ants and tiny jewelled orchids dazzle against jagged bone-coloured stone.

410

411 | Camping out in desert elephant country

NAMIBIA Eking out an existence in a region that receives barely any rainfall for all but a couple of weeks in the year is hard at the best of times – but when you're competing with elephants, it's considerably harder. Kunene, in Namibia's northwest corner, is a remote and starkly beautiful region of rugged mountains scored by sandy seasonal river gorges that snake their way down towards the Atlantic coast. To the region's desert-adapted elephants, these dry-looking gorges serve both as highways and as crucial sources of water. The feet of desert elephants, which are larger than those of savannah elephants, are sensitive to the tiny vibrations that signal there's a subterranean watercourse somewhere below. If the signal is strong enough, they dig with their tusks, and drink.

For the Himba and Herero people of Puros, a village close to the Hoarusib River in the heart of Kunene, dealing with large, thirsty wild animals is a daily headache. But the elephants also bring benefits.

In times past, women had to trek down to the dry riverbed to draw water from a well, but the presence of elephants made this hazardous and unhygienic. An appeal was launched, funds were raised and a new, elephant-proof well was built within the village. Another benefit of the pachyderms' presence is that visitors, intrigued by the fact that elephants exist in these unlikely surroundings, make the trip to Kunene for a chance to see them. *Puros Campsite*, created and run by the villagers, provides a welcoming base, with fees going directly into community funds.

This simple but immaculate site is set in a shady grove of camelthorn trees on the Hoarusib's sandy bank. Unfenced, it is a place where elephants make their presence felt. You're likely to see their big, broad footprints in the sand, and there's usually a heap or two of dung scattered about. Very occasionally, the mighty beasts stroll close to the tents, so it's crucial to stay alert. But it's more common to see them at a distance, passing peacefully by in small family groups – a glorious vision on a unique camping adventure.

412 | Tricky topography: the Okavango Delta

BOTSWANA The vast Okavango River flows for 1600km through three countries, yet never reaches the sea. Instead, it hits the ultra-flat plain of arid nothingness that is northern Botswana. It's like a strange contest – desert versus river – and here the desert wins. With no gradient to guide it, the water spreads out over 15,000 square kilometres, then gives up and seeps away or evaporates in the heat. Nothing quite like it happens anywhere else on Earth. The river simply disappears.

The Okavango Delta is a birder's paradise and a cartographer's nightmare. No one seems able to decide if it should be green or blue on a map. The waters rise and fall in tune with distant rainfall patterns, creating a bewildering maze of islands, waterways and lagoons, much of which disappears underwater during floods, only to reappear in a quite different arrangement when the waters recede.

The best way to see the delta is in a *mokoro*, the local variety of canoe; a poler will guide you, often along waterways that are precisely the width of a hippo's body, for the simple reason that they have been formed by the daily migration of hippos from the lagoons, where they bask during the day, through the reeds to the shore, where they graze all night.

The water is utterly clear, with hundreds of tiny fish darting just below the surface. The hippo-made waterways snake and curve through the tall reeds, which seem to glow in the low, bright African sun, occasionally opening out into wide lagoons, each of which is only the most minuscule fraction of this endless, mysterious landscape of not-quite-land, not-exactly-water. The only sound is the swish of the pole in the water, and the croak of frogs, happily proclaiming that they have found frog heaven.

413 | Mid-century cool in Maputo

MOZAMBIQUE In the mid-twentieth century, the top layer of Lourenço Marques' unequal society was as glamour-hungry as Monaco's or London's, and futuristic architecture was all the rage. Today, thanks to the cold-storage effect of Mozambique's slow, late route to independence and a fifteen-year civil war, this laidback Indian Ocean city – renamed Maputo in 1975 – is peppered with idiosyncratic classics: concrete villas, a church shaped like a lemon squeezer, and tower blocks embellished with bold modern art. Setting out on foot or by *chopela* (tuk-tuk taxi) with a local architecture, art and design enthusiast is an exciting way to explore. There's plenty to discover, from the striking facades created by Tropical Modernist architect Pancho Guedes to the kind of cafés, galleries and studios where the characters of cult TV drama *Mad Men* would look perfectly at home.

414 | Wine tastings with a view

SOUTH AFRICA As travel surprises go, the Cape Winelands are hard to beat: travellers touch down in Cape Town expecting a wild slice of Africa and are instead met by a pastoral vision of vineyard-fringed mountains. Around the refined towns of Stellenbosch and Franschhoek, respectively established by Dutch and French Huguenot winemakers in the late seventeenth century, a patchwork of Cape Dutch estates climbs the mountain passes. With their trademark gabled and thatched manors, there are literally hundreds of these grand wine estates, most open for reasonably priced tastings and pairings with a view. The area is known for Pinotage, a robust cross of red Pinot Noir and Cinsaut grapes, but other than that it's a case of choosing your own adventure, as the tourist-savvy wineries offer extras from gourmet picnics to art galleries.

415 | Cycling through the Nyika Plateau

MALAWI Now the going gets tougher. The red dirt track has narrowed, and your wheels crunch as you enter the dense miombo woodland of the Rukuru Valley. Splintered branches strewn across the track tell of recent elephants. The Chisanga Falls are somewhere below: a chance to wash the dust off jolted limbs. But beyond them lies a climb of 40km, back onto the escarpment where camp awaits.

Just thirty minutes earlier you had been on top of the world – or at least on top of the Nyika Plateau, which must feel pretty similar. Grazing zebra had lifted their heads to stare as you'd passed them on your two-wheeled steed. Eland antelope, ever cautious, had filed away along the distant ridge. They're still filing now, 5km behind you, silhouetted against a towering cloudscape.

"It doesn't look like Africa", comes the refrain from first-timers. Certainly, the undulating treeless terrain up top can be more suggestive of the moors than the tropics. But what do you expect at 2500m? The logbook at *Chelinda Lodge* tells of a young couple who, only last week, cycled around a corner to find a leopard lying on the track. That was certainly enough "Africa" for them.

There's a final day's hard pedalling ahead, but tonight will be spent at a campfire beneath the stars with a continent laid out below you: Zambia to the west, Tanzania to the north and, lying far below like a darkened pool, Lake Malawi to the east.

416

Winging it over Luangwa

ZAMBIA "Over there," bellows the pilot into your headphones, "that's part of the original course." He indicates a sun-cracked crescent of clay down to your left. "Hang on, I'll show you."

You hold your breath and clutch your camera as the microlight makes a low pass over the river. Its angular shadow sweeps ahead, scrambling crocs from the bank and sending hippos snorting through the shallows. A saddle-billed stork hangs for a second in your flight path before lurching away with ponderous wing beats.

Then suddenly you're whisked up again and the valley rolls out in pin-sharp detail, buffalo filtering through the mopane woodland like ants through broccoli. Down below, the Luangwa snakes to the horizon in contours of sand, its dry-season flow reduced to a broken chain of pools and channels that wink at the dawn. Such is the clarity of light that you could swear the distant escarpment walls – yesterday just a smudge of heat-haze blue – have advanced across the valley floor overnight.

South Luangwa is Zambia's premier national park. You can explore its rugged terrain on foot and by vehicle, scouring the rutted plains and thorny thickets for game. But this aerial perspective is a revelation, the park arrayed in an exquisite model-railway mosaic of oxbows, palm stands and forest islands. Imagine if Livingstone had seen it like this.

You're losing height – and a glimpse of thatched roofs beside the riverbank reveals *Tafika*. This is your camp, an intimate base where each chalet comes with its own alfresco shower. Beyond is the red-earth airstrip where you took off fifteen minutes earlier, parked Land Rover at one end, elephants ambling across the other.

But you're not done yet. Your pilot is pointing again and you follow his gaze to a line of golden shapes emerging from the thickets, casting exaggerated feline shadows across the sand. Lions. A big male brings up the rear, massive head swinging from side to side. He stares up at the microlight as you pass – now low enough to see the tufted tail and narrow haunches – then trudges onward towards the river.

Warriors and maidens: The Reed Dance of Ludzidzini

417

SWAZILAND Seen from the rugged heights of Hangman's Rock, the scale of the pageantry is breathtaking. Column upon column advances across the cattle-cropped sward onto the parade grounds of Ludzidzini, the Queen Mother's royal village, before dissolving into the pulsating mass of bodies already assembled there. Panning out towards the horizon, the group continues to swell as more and more people arrive, snaking like huge, multicoloured millipedes over the contours of the Ezulwini Valley. The noise laps against the escarpment, drifting towards your elevated perch like the roar of distant surf.

Soon you are down among the spectators on the valley floor, where at close quarters it all becomes rather more real. Ranks of dancers bear down from all sides. Bare-breasted girls stamp and sway in step, anklets rattling, as the confusion of colour and flesh blurs into a chanting kaleidoscope. Details flash past: the oranges impaled on ceremonial knives; the crimson headdresses of turaco feathers marking out those of royal descent. Ahead of each column strides its warrior escort, adorned with cow tails and clutching knob-stick and

shield. His glance is contemptuous of cameras, although the girls behind him seem to be taking things less seriously: there is giggling in the ranks, flashed smiles and shared jokes. It's Swaziland's biggest holiday, and after seven days of tramping the hillsides, cutting reeds and camping out, they're determined to enjoy the party.

Cultural historians will tell you about the origins of the Umhlanga (or Reed Dance): how the maidens have travelled from across the kingdom to cut reeds at various sacred locations, then marched to the Queen Mother's *kraal* – carrying their bundles – in a symbolic celebration of chastity and tribute; how the date varies from year to year according to ancestral astrology. They might also marvel at how the event's popularity defies the apparent decline of traditional culture elsewhere in the region.

On the ground, though, who can tell what's really happening? Understanding and description are overwhelmed by a sea of colours, faces and voices. It's dusty, noisy, chaotic and utterly thrilling: celebration at its most African.

418 | Diving with manta rays in the Quirimbas Archipelago

MOZAMBIQUE You have to be fairly wealthy to holiday in the Quirimbas Archipelago in northern Mozambique, but it's not a place for spoilt, petulant types with exacting demands and trolleyloads of luggage. The islands are home to a handful of lodges specializing in back-to-basics barefoot luxury, with the emphasis firmly on the "barefoot". No need for designer heels here – but a good pair of fins will definitely come in handy.

From the mainland town of Pemba, a light aircraft carries you and your single bag (the most you're permitted to bring) over a wilderness of dazzling beaches and intricate reefs. From above, the archipelago has a pristine, faraway charm that's irresistible. By the time you touch down, you're itching to sink into the soft sand.

Even more alluring is the prospect of exploring offshore. The islands are surrounded by the vivid turquoise waters of the Quirimbas National Park, created in 2002 on the recommendation of the WWF. Thanks to the cooperation of local communities and lodge-owners, the park, which includes 1500 square kilometres of ocean and island habitats, is one of the best, and least exploited, scuba-diving destinations in southern Africa.

While the coral gardens teem with colourful fish, manta rays are without a doubt the star attraction. These balletic megafish are the subject of extensive studies elsewhere in Mozambique; take the plunge, and you might be lucky enough to encounter one face to face. Though related to sharks, they're filter-feeders and harmless to humans: in fact, some appear positively friendly. Flowing through the blue with easy sweeps of their wings, which can measure up to 6m in span, they may approach close enough for you to check out the cleaner wrasses hitching a ride on their bellies. And if you meet one that's supremely relaxed, or just plain curious, it may circle you as you hover in the water – a truly captivating moment.

419 | Find a tiny slice of heaven on Nosy Ve

MADAGASCAR Trekking through Madagascar's backcountry and paddling its interior is a wonderful way to spend your time, but sooner or later you'll want to rest your aching muscles and swap your well-worn hiking boots for a pair of makeshift flip-flops. And there are few better places to do it than the unspoilt tropical beaches and aquamarine waters of the Mozambique Channel.

Situated a few kilometres south of the Tropic of Capricorn, on the southwestern shores of Madagascar, lies the picturesque fishing village of Anakao. Accessible only by boat, it sits by a crescent-shaped white-sand beach, nestled between spiny forests and rolling dunes and guarded by an armada of brightly coloured pirogues and herds of wandering goats. This tiny slice of heaven is dotted with a string of bungalows, cooled by gentle trade winds and lapped by the calming surf.

A trip to this remote locale is not complete until you've hired a fisherman to take you by pirogue to the nearby island of Nosy Ve.

Rumoured to have been a former pirates' haunt in the seventeenth century – some say their bones are still scattered about – it's deserted now, and offers superb snorkelling among schools of colourful angelfish, parrotfish and tangs that dart through the small offshore coral. The beach, strewn with seashells of every conceivable shape, size and colour, is a stunning place for a stroll – you can return with your pockets full to a mouthwatering meal of freshly caught lobster and fish grilled on a makeshift barbecue by your captain.

As the late afternoon winds pick up speed the captain signals, and it's time to return. An hour or so later you'll be back at your bungalow in time to witness another spectacular sunset framed over the waters that separate you from Africa. Lazing in your low-slung hammock, you'll be lulled to sleep by millions of flickering stars and that wafting offshore breeze.

420 | Hunkering down among the Big Five

SOUTH AFRICA Kruger National Park offers what most others don't: the chance for a DIY safari. Many of Africa's national parks are only open to those with the thickest wallets, but thanks to its comparatively low fees and reliable network of roads – feasible in even the most civilized of rental cars – Kruger is accessible to all. Within its boundaries you'll find the Big Five, which are so abundant that you could cross them off your list by lunch, as well as African wild dogs, cheetahs, hyenas and plenty more besides.

There are 24 fenced rest camps, with accommodation ranging from simple thatched *rondavels* (huts) up to luxurious bungalows. *Skukuza*, for instance, has a wide range of accommodation as it is the park's headquarters and feels almost like a small town, while *Satara*, based in big cat country, is smaller and has a high proportion of huts.

Very few offer a more authentic experience of the African bush than *Tamboti*, set within a chain-link fence overlooking the dry Timbavati River on the park's western boundary. Here you'll find a series of rustic canvas tents with wooden decks mounted on stilts, flanked on either side by thick patches of scraggly trees and with a wave of yellowing grass out front – it's unlikely that you'll get much more than a glimpse of your neighbours.

There is nothing more South African than a *braai* (grill over an open fire) and as night falls you can pile yours high with wood and set it alight. Wrap potatoes in tin foil and toss them in the hot ash, and grill some spicy *boerewors* (meat sausage) or *sosaties* (kebabs) as you sip a glass of Amarula (South African cream liqueur) and watch the large-spotted genets creeping around camp.

Just make sure you keep a close eye on any barbecued leftovers – baboons and honey badgers are regularly spotted and will snatch any unattended food. Still, you'll find it's easy to get distracted when the lions roar somewhere in the darkness beyond the fence.

When nature calls, you'll have to grab your torch and make the notoriously spooky walk along the dirt track to the communal bathrooms. Shine your light into the vegetation on either side and it's likely you'll see several sets of orange eyes flashing back – just try not to think about the rumours of the resident leopard.

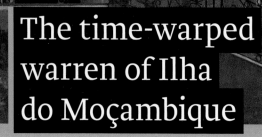

The time-warped warren of Ilha do Moçambique

MOZAMBIQUE The oldest European settlement in subequatorial Africa? Not Cape Town, as you might assume, but the altogether more modest Ilha do Moçambique, set on the tiny crescent-shaped island of the same name, floating in the Indian Ocean off the Mozambican mainland. True, it is too lived-in and rough around the edges to become a beach destination *à la* Ibiza or Zanzibar – but why worry about that when there are so many idyllic beaches elsewhere along Mozambique's Indian Ocean coastline? This quirkily old-world urban island is one of Africa's great undiscovered travel gems.

Capital of Portuguese East Africa for almost four centuries, it's an intriguing place. While the timeworn facades that line the narrow alleys look distinctly Iberian, the townspeople are almost entirely Afro-Arabic – descendants of the Islamic merchants and shipbuilders who were forced to relocate to the mainland during the centuries-long Portuguese occupation, but who drifted back after Lourenço Marques (now Maputo) became the Mozambican capital in 1898.

A backwater throughout the twentieth century, Ilha do Moçambique avoided modernization and its historic core remained intact. It also became seriously run down, not helped by the civil war in the 1970s and 1980s. However, since being designated a UNESCO World Heritage Site in 1991, the island has been granted a fresh lease of life. Derelict colonial mansions have been rehabilitated as hotels and hostels, and old fortresses and palaces have been renovated as museums.

The most impressive historical landmark is the sixteenth-century Fortaleza São Sebastião, whose immense buttresses protect the southern hemisphere's oldest surviving European construction, the modest Chapel of Nossa Senhora Baluarte, built in 1522. Elsewhere, the alleys that connect the island's two Indian Ocean waterfronts are lined with whitewashed old churches and grandiose palaces, while the Fortress of São Lourenço is perched improbably on a mushroom-shaped coral outcrop that you can wade to at low tide.

Unpretentious local restaurants are dotted throughout the time-worn alleys. Here you can feast on freshly caught local seafood and tangy peri-peri chicken, along with chilled Mozambican 3M beer and Cape wines, as the warm Indian Ocean breeze wafts by.

422 | Exploring Johannesburg: the graffiti capital of Africa

SOUTH AFRICA You may be surprised to think of Johannesburg as the graffiti capital of Africa – I certainly was. The city's image is still defined by its troubled history, but the vibrant street-art scene actually emerged from the city's degeneration in the eighties and nineties. Faced with soaring unemployment and a dearth of opportunities, many young Joburgers used the landscape of abandoned buildings around them to express their frustrations. Scrubbing out street art was hardly a priority, so the scene was mostly left alone, maturing over the years.

By now there are even government-commissioned murals. As we walk through Maboneng Precinct on a Past Experiences street-art tour, our guide Jo Buitendach points to two giant figures embracing, rendered in simple black, white and red. "This piece is by a French artist, Kazyusclef. It was actually commissioned by Maboneng Precinct – you can tell it was commissioned because of the scale, you couldn't do that on the fly."

Not all the bigger pieces are government-commissioned, though. We pass some vibrant pink-and-orange gates painted by Johannesburg artist Ryza – he's even done the padlock to match. Jo explains that local businesses and residents who need a wall smartened up might offer it to an artist: one gets a free paint job, the other a free canvas. It's hard to miss the huge brown eyes staring down from a warehouse off Fox Street, a Falko mural commissioned by Adidas for their "I Art Joburg" project.

I had expected the street art in Johannesburg to be unrelentingly political, confronting the city's fraught history. But while there's plenty of politicism there, the artists are also looking forward to the city's bright future, and creating some truly beautiful work along the way.

I think back to an imaginative piece we saw earlier: a looming portrait of Dutch colonialist Jan van Riebeeck swathed in modern African wax-print fabric ("Africa's colonizing him right back," Jo said with a wry smile) by Gaia and Freddy Sam. Standing there, craning my neck to gawp at the stunning piece, I felt that, more than exploring the past or looking to the future, Johannesburg's street art is most meaningful as an ever-changing public gallery, capturing the present moment.

423 | Pony-trekking in the mountain kingdom

LESOTHO Landlocked within South Africa, the mountain kingdom of Lesotho is an impoverished but magical place.

A lot of the magic is encapsulated in those two words – mountain kingdom. Lesotho is one of Africa's few surviving monarchies, proud of its distinctive history, and the whole country lies above an altitude of 1000m, its highest peaks soaring into a distinctly un-African realm of mists and dank cloud.

Back in the nineteenth century, the dominant figure in the country's history, King Moshoeshoe (pronounced Mo-shweh-shweh) acquired a pony stolen from a farm in the Cape. Its suitability for Lesotho's hilly terrain was soon clear, and the people, the Basotho, quickly became a nation of horse riders. They remain so today. Few of the scattered villages of the mountains are reached by any road, tarred or otherwise.

Everywhere is connected by paths, and to get anywhere you need to walk or ride.

Pony trekking isn't really an "activity", something to do instead of canoeing or birdwatching; get atop a horse here and you're participating in Basotho life. There's nothing prim about it either; no one will comment on your posture or how you hold the reins, and given that the paths only go uphill or downhill, you'll do a lot more plodding than prancing.

You'll greet passing locals, breathe mountain air, village woodsmoke and the scent of clammy horse sweat, and hear the ringing shouts of barefoot children rounding up goats on the hillside – accompanied, all the while, by the steady clip-clop of your sure-footed pony picking its way along the path.

424 | Coming to terms with history in Johannesburg and Soweto

SOUTH AFRICA Buy a ticket to Johannesburg's Apartheid Museum and it will classify you, at random, as white or non-white. There are separate entrance gates for each. It's a gimmick, but it hits home.

The museum is the showpiece of a growing number of cultural sites that aim to distil the history of the apartheid era into a coherent narrative. Before the advent of democracy in 1994, non-whites were barred from South Africa's museums, which recorded just one strand of history. But since then a new generation of curators, artists and sculptors has found its voice, telling stories, uncovering histories and healing wounds.

Tackling the full arc of the story, the Apartheid Museum documents the era through heart-rending images and testimonies. It also presents a lucid biography of Mandela, revealing how listening to tribal council meetings in the Eastern Cape as a teenager taught him the value of empathy and constructive negotiation.

Smaller museums narrow the focus. At Constitution Hill, site of Johannesburg's notorious Old Fort prison, you can pore over Mandela's diaries and correspondence in the cell that housed him in 1962. To continue the story, head across to Liliesleaf, former hideout of the military wing of the ANC. The Mandela House Museum in Orlando West, Soweto, was Mandela's home for 44 years, for much of which he was a fugitive or prisoner. The area has been gentrified, but the house has a poignant atmosphere, enhanced by recordings of interviews with Mandela's daughters.

The Hector Pieterson Museum, also in Soweto, pays tribute to one of the many Sowetan schoolchildren who, on June 16, 1976, joined a peaceful protest over the quality of education for blacks. The march ended in confrontation, the police fired, and Pieterson was one of the first to die. He was only 12 years old. Regina Mundi Church, which some students used as a refuge, still bears the scars of battle – bullet holes in windows, broken marble on the altar. And above the whole ensemble are the stained-glass windows, centring on a portrait of Mandela addressing a crowd in a blaze of colour and hope.

425 | Counting fish in Lake Malawi

MALAWI On satellite images of the Rift Valley, Africa's third-largest lake looks like a long, dark gash in a crumpled curtain. But visit Lake Malawi on a bright day, and it's luminous. The turquoise waters stretch way beyond the horizon. It's as vast as a sea but benign, its sandy shore lapped by the gentlest of waves.

Explore beneath the water's surface and you'll soon be drifting through granite archways among clouds of brilliantly coloured cichlids. These small fish, prized by aquarium-keepers, are abundant in Lake Malawi. Scientists have counted over 1500 endemic species; as evolutionary hotspots go, the lake is almost as fascinating as Madagascar or the Galápagos.

If you're new to diving, it's a dream. It's far more fun to work through your drills on the sandy bottom of a warm lake than on the cold, hard tiles of a swimming pool. As you practise flooding your mask and clearing it again, the fresh, clear, chlorine-free water won't sting.

The lake has advantages over the ocean, too. There are no awkward currents or underwater menaces to spook you, no moray eels, jellyfish or sharks. You'll need less weight on your belt to help you sink. And once you're back on dry land, there's no salt to rinse off your gear – just head down to the campfire where, after dark, you can swap stories under the stars.

426 | Hiking the Fish River Canyon

NAMIBIA Africa's biggest ravine and one of southern Africa's great hiking trails, the Fish River Canyon is a mega-rent in the Earth's crust more than 0.5km deep, 20km wide and 150km long, snaking south to vent its river into the mighty Orange River. The Grand Canyon may be bigger, but Fish River, ranked second in the world, is still unfathomably vast, the result of tens of millions of years of erosion, and on a scale that is more accessible. The area's astounding natural beauty and the ease with which you can walk – it takes five days to traverse the canyon – and camp here, together with the birdwatching opportunities, have made it one of Namibia's greatest outdoor attractions.

427 | Birding by Lake St Lucia

SOUTH AFRICA Safari in South Africa is not all about lions, leopards and laughing hyenas. The Greater St Lucia Wetlands has its hippos and its crocs, but it's the staggering number of birds that makes this northeastern corner of KwaZulu-Natal so special.

Over five hundred species pass through each year, drawn by the park's unique cocktail of world-class wilderness: dune-backed beaches, tidal estuaries, coastal forest, swamps, saltwater marshes and dry thornveld, all bordering the 360-square-kilometre Lake St Lucia, one of South Africa's most important waterbird breeding areas.

On the lake's western shore, a number of self-guided trails lead off through the vegetation. African broadbills chase butterflies through the forest, southern banded snake eagles circle overhead, and Neergaard's sunbirds flit between succulent bunches of weeping boer-beans. In the Greater St Lucia Wetlands, small really is beautiful.

Mulanje: more than just a mountain

MALAWI If variety's the spice of your life, a trip to Malawi is hard to beat. You might luxuriate at the glassy lake or spot an elephant or three, but you should not neglect the country's iconic western highlands. Rising out of the plain, emerald-green tea estates sprawling at its feet, Mount Mulanje is a stunning massif that offers something for everyone.

Extreme sports fans can coincide their visit with the Porters' Race, which takes place every July – a 25km scramble up to the central plateau, along and down again, completed in just over two hours by the winners. The cerebral can sit at its base with Laurens van der Post's *Venture to the Interior*, in which he describes a harrowing encounter with the mountain and the death of one of his companions. Naturalists can hunt out the endemic Mulanje cedar trees, their branches festooned with strands of pale green lichen so long you could knit with them, and serious rock climbers can attempt the sheer west face of Chambe, one of the longest climbing routes on the continent.

The average visitor, though, is someone with a modicum of fitness and two or three days to spare. There are numerous starting points located all around the massif, with guides and porters for hire at each. Three to four hours' slow plodding (all the ascents are steep) takes the hiker up narrow, winding paths, through patches of forest populated with rare blue monkeys, and on to the 2000m plateau where there are a number of simple wooden huts.

Each hut has a watchman who will light a fire for you to cook your meal on, and heat water so that you can wash away the day's exertions. After a night tucked into your sleeping bag, you can go on to conquer one of the peaks – many go for Sapitwe, at 3002m the highest in South-Central Africa – or continue across the plateau through swathes of montane grassland to a different hut, admiring the endless panorama of peaks and vistas that unfolds along the way.

Visit the house of the spirits

SOUTH AFRICA It's art, myth and archeology, it's visually stunning and you can reach back through the millennia and immerse yourself in its marks and contours. South Africa's rock art represents one of the world's oldest and most continuous artistic and religious traditions. Found on rock faces all over the country, these ancient paintings are a window into a historic culture and its thoughts and beliefs. In the Cederberg range alone, 250km north of Cape Town, there are some 2500 rock art sites, estimated to be between one and eight thousand years old.

The paintings are the work of the first South Africans, hunter-gatherers known as San or Bushmen, the direct descendants of some of the earliest *Homo sapiens* who lived in the Western Cape 150,000 years ago. Now almost extinct, their culture clings on tenuously in tiny pockets of Namibia, northern South Africa and Botswana.

If you're looking to dig deeper, the easy-going Sevilla Trail gives you the opportunity to take in ten rock art sites along a stunning 4km route. The animals that once grazed and preyed in the fynbos (literally "fine bush") vegetation of the mountainous Cederberg are among the major subjects of the finely realized rock art paintings, which also include abstract images and monsters as well as depictions of people and therianthropes – half-human, half-animal figures. You'll see beautifully observed elephants, rhinos, buffaloes, oryx, snakes and birds, accurately portrayed in sinuous outline or solid bodies of colour – often earthy whites, reds and ochres. Frequently quite small, they're dotted all over rock surfaces, sometimes painted one over the other to create a rich patina.

Archeologists now regard many of the images as metaphors for religious experiences, one of the most important of which is the healing trance dance, still practised by the few surviving Bushman communities. The rock faces can be seen as portals between the human and spiritual world: when we gaze at Bushman rock art we are gazing into the house of the spirits.

430 | Puzzling over the past at Great Zimbabwe

ZIMBABWE How can a medieval settlement as significant and sizeable as Great Zimbabwe be so shrouded in mystery, five hundred years after it was abandoned? It's thought to have been home to around 18,000 people in its heyday. Thanks to accounts recorded in the sixteenth century, we know they grew rich on gold and ivory, but precious few details of their rise and fall survive.

The name Zimbabwe, in Shona, means Houses of Stone. Easily the largest stone-built settlement in southern Africa, Great Zimbabwe is also one of the oldest, dating back to the eleventh century. Today, these once formidable buildings are reduced to a collection of atmospheric, intricately built dry-stone walls surrounding grassy enclosures.

Nature had been reclaiming these mighty walls for at least four hundred years when, in the early 1900s, British-American archeologist David Randall-MacIver set about excavating parts of the site. Until then, historians had been reluctant to accept that Africans could have built a citadel to rival the wonders of Ancient Greece and Phoenicia.

But Randall-MacIver's discoveries forced a rethink. Pottery fragments and soapstone artefacts offered compelling evidence that the ruins had once been a Shona stronghold.

Now a UNESCO World Heritage Site, the 200-acre ruins of Great Zimbabwe are open to the public, with three complexes to explore – the fragmented Valley Complex, mighty Great Enclosure and intriguing Hill Complex.

With its massive walls, narrow, roofless passages and mysterious tower, the elliptical Great Enclosure is the most iconic of the three, while the Hill Complex, thought to have been a royal residence, feels every bit the perfect military stronghold. Perched on a granite hilltop, it can only be reached via a steep path that winds tightly between massive boulders. One of its most haunting features is a cave-like echo chamber. Crouch inside it and yell, and you'll hear the sound bounce back at you from the Great Enclosure far below like a message from the past.

431 | Busanga: the plains truth

ZAMBIA The slimline feline slinks away through the sea of grass, all seesaw shoulders and switching tail. Two elegant wattled cranes, picking at a patch of burnt ground, pay no heed – but a rummaging warthog breaks off to stare, poised rigid for flight.

You're itching to follow. A cheetah is a rare sight, especially in Zambia. But the terrain is treacherous. Only your guide can tell where the firm ground gives way to swamp, and once already this morning he's had to dig you out of trouble. With no other vehicle on the horizon, no shade to speak of and – judging by the abundant tracks – only the local lion pride to keep you company, this is no place to get stuck.

You take a swig from your water bottle and check out the surroundings. The map, which shows Busanga Plains smuggled discreetly into the remote northwest corner of central Zambia's Kafue National Park, gives little sense of scale. But perched out here in the middle, the grasslands seem limitless, their irregular punctuation of palm islands and termite mounds simply emphasizing the immensity. A binocular sweep reveals animals in all directions: not vast herds, but a wall-to-wall scattering of grazers – puku, lechwe, wildebeest – all munching their way across the great salad bowl. Many more will join them as the dry season begins to bite.

To the south a low line of miombo woodland shimmers in the heat haze, reminding you of the vast hinterland and yesterday's battles with the tsetse flies as you'd lurched and jolted your way here. To the north you can see where the grassland gives way to water, each flash of blue littered with the white forms of egrets, storks and pelicans.

"Zambia's Okavango", they call this place. Out on the water this afternoon, drifting among the grunting hippo pods, the comparison will seem even more apt. But for now you're happy to soak in the one big difference. No people.

432 | Climbing Table Mountain

SOUTH AFRICA If the skies are clear on your first day in Cape Town, drop everything and head straight for Table Mountain. It's an ecological marvel, and a powerful icon for the entire African continent. What's more, the views from the top are unmissable – as long as the celebrated "tablecloth" of cloud stays away.

For Capetonians, Table Mountain is a backdrop and an anchor, both physically and spiritually. Close to the South African coast, it was one of the beacons that Nelson Mandela and his fellow inmates fixed upon during their incarceration on Robben Island, just offshore.

The mountain's famous plateau is part of a short upland chain that stretches from Signal Hill, just west of the city centre, to Cape Point, where a lighthouse marks the meeting of the Indian Ocean and the Atlantic. The obvious, and most popular, route to the top is to take the aerial cableway – a sizeable cable car that, thrillingly, gently rotates on the ascent. But if you'd rather work a little harder, you can tackle one of the hiking trails that snake their way up the cliffs.

Visit in the South African spring or summer and the fynbos vegetation, unique to the Cape, will be in full bloom. You'll see plenty of pretty daisies and heathers in the tussocky wilderness, while proteas, sundews and watsonias add splashes of red, white and pink. Botanists have identified over 1470 plant species on the mountain – there's more floral diversity here than in the entire United Kingdom. The wildlife scores top marks for entertainment value, too. Stars of the show are the dassies, placid creatures that look a bit like monster guinea pigs and are more than happy to pose for photos.

And then there's that view. You may only be 1000m up, but gaze out over the city to the ocean beyond and you'll feel like you're standing on top of the world.

433 | Swigging the most remote beer on Earth

TRISTAN DA CUNHA The *Albatross Bar* does a rather decent lobster quiche as a bar snack. The lager isn't bad either. It's a good job really, because there's nowhere else to get a drink or a bite to eat for 2815km. This is the only pub on the most remote inhabited island on Earth.

Tristan da Cunha is one of the far-flung hotchpotch of islands that make up what's left of the British Empire. None, however, is as isolated as this. Situated in the middle of the notoriously rough patch of the South Atlantic Ocean known as the Roaring Forties, its closest landmass is southern Africa, some 540km nearer than South America. The island has no airport and can only be reached by fishing vessel from Cape Town; a trip that can take upwards of six days, with no guarantee of being able to dock in the island's tiny harbour because of the often torrid weather.

The sole settlement is the evocatively named "Edinburgh of the Seven Seas" which is where, in a motley collection of tin-roofed bungalows, the 260 or so resident islanders live and work, mainly farming and fishing;

Tristan's number one export is crayfish. Everything is dwarfed by the volcano that rises over 1700m above sea level. It is rarely climbed by locals, and there are signs everywhere of the 1962 eruption, not least the huge pile of volcanic debris that still lies just outside the village. In the wake of the eruption, the islanders were evacuated to the UK, where they spent two unhappy years before being allowed to return.

With no mobile phones, one shop, one school, one policeman and one available TV channel, many things about Tristan remain unchanged by the twenty-first century. The accent spoken is a curious, and almost incomprehensible, dialect of early eighteenth-century seafaring English; everyone's birthday is celebrated by a party in the Prince Philip Hall next to the *Albatross*; and absolutely nobody seems to have any desire to leave their epically remote home. "People think we're stranded here," the barman says over yet another slice of quiche. "But it's not true. We're happy, and we're here because we want to be."

434 | Frog safaris in Zululand

SOUTH AFRICA The South African bush looks different by torchlight. Reed beds and acacia branches stand out in sharp relief, a mesh of clean lines and crisp angles. Beyond the beam, the middle-distance is unimaginably black. Your eyes strain to make out the details, then give up. Your ears take over.

Frogging is all about tuning in. Across wetland regions throughout the tropics, frogs greet the seasonal rains with a nightly symphony in which different species perform distinctive roles. Experienced listeners can isolate and identify each one. Of South Africa's 115 known species of frog, some, like the delightfully perky-looking tinker reed frog, emit a metallic, staccato sound, while others trill like a mobile phone. Bullfrogs belt out a full-throated belch. You can probably guess what kind of noises the chirping frog, the clicking stream frog and the snoring puddle frog make.

All this vocal exhibitionism is, as you'd expect, part of a mating game. The males are the protagonists, laying noisy claim to territory

and females. In the Amazulu Private Game Reserve, KwaZulu-Natal, voyeurs can witness their moves at close quarters by joining an after-dark walking safari, led by an expert guide.

African walking safaris are, by definition, thrilling; setting out by night adds an unforgettable extra dimension. Leave your trekking sandals behind – wellington boots are the footwear of choice. You will squelch through the mud around rain-soaked waterholes, watching as your guide's torch beam traces a variety of clinks and chirrups to the source. There can be much searching: amplified by its balloon-like vocal sac, the racket made by even the most minuscule of frogs can cover a considerable range.

Some individuals choose prominent perches and are conspicuous enough to be spotted, and blasé enough to be observed very closely. It's important to try not to touch their delicate, permeable skin, which doubles as a breathing membrane. Instead, aim the beam of your torch onto their jewel-bright colours, and prepare to be dazzled.

435 | Up the Tsiribihina in a dugout canoe

MADAGASCAR The early morning daylight filters through the tent and slowly warms your aching body. You awaken to the muffled sounds of roosters crowing and the echo of beating drums from a neighbouring village. A faint whiff of smoke entices you out of your slumber and onto the sandy riverbank to join the guides and a few curious onlookers around a crackling campfire. Together, you share fried eggs, fresh fruit, stale baguettes and a cup of strongly brewed coffee. Another day on the Tsiribihina River has begun.

After breakfast, the guides pack camp and load the wooden pirogues. Within minutes, you're drifting down the muddy waters and into the heartland of Madagascar. Exploring this fascinating country is not complete until you've experienced a few days on this remote waterway, meeting local villagers, paddling alongside impressive landscapes and discovering Malagasy folklore.

The sun burns overhead as you glide past thatched-hut villages, where excited children bound into the waters waving and screaming

"bon voyage". Gradually, the landscape transforms from low-lying flood plains lined with green rice paddies to sparsely covered rolling hills and thick forests, the river slicing through deep gorges before widening once more as it drains into the Mozambique Channel. Along the way, you make chance encounters with wildlife: Verreaux's sifaka forage high in the canopies and enormous flying foxes flutter by while river crocodiles lurk in the murky waters below. Hundreds of exotic birds vie for your attention: metallic-coloured kingfishers dart along the shoreline, white egrets hitch a ride on floating mats of hyacinths and a majestic harrier hawk wheels on the horizon.

At the end of a long day's journey, you reach camp on the shores of yet another sandbank, arriving just in time to witness a spectacular sunset framed against a rugged mountainous backdrop. While dinner is prepared, you set up the tents and begin to wind down for the evening. Dancing fireflies and singing katydids give way to a night sky filled with flickering stars.

Exploring the Skeleton Coast

436

NAMIBIA There's a good reason why Namibia's extreme northwest is called the Skeleton Coast. Its treacherous conditions have scuppered ships – the beach is littered with rusting iron and weathered timbers from long-abandoned wrecks – and whales, too, have met their end here, their massive vertebrae bleaching on the shore, lapped by the tides.

As a visitor, you'll need an eye for detail to appreciate the allure of this bleak and barren place, where the chilly Atlantic meets mountainous dunes and endless, grey-white gravel plains, and distant wind-sculpted rocks cast unearthly shadows. Look carefully and you'll begin to realize that the desert is not as devoid of life as it might seem. Walking through the rugged landscapes with a guide, you'll learn how beetles, lizards and sidewinder adders

survive on the moisture brought by the early morning mists. You may begin to distinguish the different lichens – delicate smudges of black, white and ginger which decorate slabs of quartz and basalt. Drought-resistant succulents like the bizarre, pebble-like lithops and the ragged, ancient-looking *Welwitschia mirabilis* cling to life in the gravel. Among the few mammals hardy enough to survive in this environment are black-backed jackals and noisy, malodorous colonies of Cape fur seals, the latter a potential target for hungry lions, which very occasionally can be seen prowling the shoreline. Perhaps the best way to enjoy the desert's strange beauty is from the air. Soar over the landscape in a light aircraft and you feel like an astronaut over an alien world, the scene below mottled and textured like a vast abstract painting.

437

Jungle operatics: the lemurs of Andasibe-Mantadia

MADAGASCAR Close your eyes and imagine the haunting song of a humpback whale. Add heat, humidity and air infused with the aroma of damp vegetation and moss that tingles your nasal passages. Sounds improbable, doesn't it? Now open your eyes: you're in a Madagascan rainforest listening to a group of indri, the largest of the island's lemurs, proclaiming rights to their territories like arboreal opera singers.

This is the sound of Madagascar. In the early mornings, the forests of Andasibe-Mantadia National Park ring out with the indri's eerie, wailing chorus. It wafts through the canopy in wave after glorious wave, sending shivers down your spine and making every nerve-end jangle.

A number of indri family groups here have become thoroughly accustomed to people. With the help of a local guide, they're easily seen, and their cute teddy-bear looks, striking black-and-

white coats and comically inquisitive manner make them hugely endearing – most people fall for them immediately.

When you first come upon them, the indri are likely to be high in the canopy, shrouded by a veil of foliage, but it pays to be patient and wait (something many people don't do), as they regularly descend to lower levels and are quite happy to sit and munch their leafy breakfasts while you watch in wonder from close by.

Eleven other lemur species live in the national park, and there's a good chance of seeing several of these, too. One of the most remarkable is the diademed sifaka, its orange and silver fur contrasting vividly with the dark recesses of the forest. You can see both indri and diademed sifakas many, many times, and remain fascinated: these are arguably the most beautiful primates on the planet.

438 | Rafting the Stairway to Heaven

ZAMBIA Ever thought it might be fun to be trapped inside a giant washing machine as it switches from rinse to spin? Perhaps not. But after a dozen drenchings and umpteen mouthfuls of river water, you might just find yourself tumbling headlong down the Stairway to Heaven, yelling like a maniac, high on the thrill of just staying alive.

Dropping 8m over a 10m distance, the Stairway is one of the steepest of the world-class rapids that churn up the mighty Zambezi just below Victoria Falls. But it's by no means the scariest. The names the rafters give the toughest runs – Gnashing Jaws of Death, Overland Truck Eater, Double Trouble, Oblivion – say it all.

The Lower Zambezi rafting route begins in one of the most dramatic midriver locations on Earth. You paddle across the foam-marbled water of the Batoka Gorge – the steep-sided ravine that receives the full fury of the 1.5km-wide, 100m-high falls. Behind you, water crashes against water and hurtles into the heavens as spray. It's a nerve-jangling display of natural energy.

The first three rapids come hard and fast, then there's a sharp left turn as the gorge zigzags downhill. Before you know it, you're tackling Morning Glory, the first big challenge, where a "hole" almost as wide as the river threatens to swallow you in one gulp.

Survive this and, thanking the river gods for their kindness, you can prepare for the Stairway. But you'll never be truly ready for Rapid 18: Oblivion. This one eats rafts for breakfast – the chances of making it through its three monster-sized waves without your raft being flipped are only one in four. They say that a baptism in the Zambezi purifies the soul: one tussle with Oblivion and you'll be praying for mercy.

439 | Giving something back at Guludo Beach Lodge

MOZAMBIQUE Translucent turquoise water swarming with rainbow-coloured fish, sand the colour and consistency of finely ground pearls, a hinterland of irrepressible tropical greenery... it sounds like paradise. But for the inhabitants of this remote stretch of the Mozambique coast, still licking its wounds after four decades of civil war, life isn't a beach. Infant mortality runs at one in three, and – thanks to rampant malaria, a shortage of clean water and poor sanitation – average life expectancy struggles to exceed forty years.

It was exactly this glaring juxtaposition of beach idyll and grinding poverty that inspired a team of young British entrepreneurs to establish a tourist resort with a difference on the deserted seashore near Guludo village, just north of the Quirimbas National Park. But instead of carving out an exclusive enclave, the primary aim of the project was to provide a sustainable means of alleviating hardship in the neighbourhood: some seventy local people work in the tourist lodge, and one day they'll run the place entirely.

Guludo Beach Lodge was designed to have minimal impact on the environment. Its "rooms" are thatched, tented shelters, or, with raised inner platforms, private, but open to the sea breezes and views, and equipped with luxurious beds, mozzie nets and alfresco bathrooms. All the wonderful food is sourced locally, and all waste is recycled.

Far from being screened from local conditions, guests are actively encouraged to visit Guludo village, patronize handicraft businesses there, play in the weekly locals-versus-staff football match, and generally get involved in the development projects financed by the resort.

Five percent of the lodge's profits are channelled directly into schemes such as well excavation, health and sanitation workshops, support and training for midwives and – most ambitiously – the construction of new schools for the village.

440 | On a swing and a prayer: through the Tsitsikamma forest canopy

SOUTH AFRICA Skip back a few millennia and we were all arboreal primates. We'll never know for sure what those ancestors of ours looked like. But in Tsitsikamma National Park, you can discover the primate within by swinging through the canopy – 30m up.

In fact, whizzing is a better word, for instead of bombing through the forest on the end of a vine, Tarzan-style, you're strapped into a high-tech harness and sent careering along a steel cable that's strung between two trees. But you can yodel as much as you want.

Each cable slide – there's a circuit of eleven – leads to a timber platform high up in a mighty outeniqua forest. Here, as you catch your breath, a guide sorts out your karabiner clips, gives you a few nature notes and gets you ready for the next slide.

The platforms and slides may stir up childhood memories of monkeying around in tree houses, but in fact they're state of the art. Cleverly engineered using tensile forces, leverage and rubber blocks instead of bolts to keep the trees as pristine as possible, the whole circuit is based on a system designed by ecologists working in the Costa Rican rainforest. They used their cables to collect specimens and data. Trust the adventure-mad South Africans to use theirs just for fun.

The longest and steepest slides are the best: with a good shove, you can hurtle along at up to 50km/hr, hyped with excitement. But on the gentler ones, there's more time to enjoy the scenery: the light and shade playing on the foliage above, the intricate forms of the giant ferns below, the passing birds and staring monkeys. Or you can just soak up the rich, unfamiliar smells – the musty whiff of decaying vegetation mixed with the damp freshness of new growth – and the heart-pounding sensation of exploring a new domain.

SOUTH AFRICA Two weeks ago, it would have been just another pile of poo. But now, a fortnight into your ranger-training course, this tower of dung is so much more than that. Now, it means elephants have passed through here recently, maybe within the last few hours. It means that the herd is heading west, looking for fresh foliage. And it means that if you swing your Land Rover around and take the dusty track behind you, you'll have a good chance of beating them to the waterhole. And the guests in the back of your 4WD will have yet another great tale to tell the folks back home.

The ranger-training course in the mighty Kruger National Park is the epitome of "hands-on" learning. You'll spend long days in the bush, discovering how to take a game drive effectively, learning to understand animal behaviour, brushing up your tracking skills, and getting used to handling a high-calibre rifle. You'll drive along rutted roads, you'll sit up-front in the tracking seat to scan the undergrowth for the rustling movements of antelope – and you'll have one of the most marvellous months of your life.

442 | Majete: Back from the brink

MALAWI A few years ago, wildlife-watching in Malawi meant counting fish in its eponymous lake. This small landlocked country had a handful of reserves along its western fringe but nothing to compare to the mighty parks of Kenya and Tanzania. The once-plentiful Majete, at the tail end of the Great Rift Valley, had been decimated by poachers in the 1980s and 90s, and by 2003 just a handful of baboons were left in the 173,000-acre reserve. But fast forward a decade and Majete is back. The original species have been steadily reintroduced – a warthog here, an eland there – and now more than 2500 animals call the reserve's miombo woodlands and granite-topped hills home. And with the return of lions in late 2012, Majete has become the country's only Big Five reserve. It's a tantalizing combination: iconic wildlife without the crowds, and in a beautiful setting, the Lower Shire Valley – though you're more likely to spot hartebeests than hobbits here.

443 | Tracking rhino in Damaraland

NAMIBIA The endless scrub of northern Namibia's Damaraland is the only place in the world where you can find free-roaming black rhino. But you've got to know where to look. And the trackers from the aptly named *Desert Rhino Camp* – a luxurious canvas community set amid the grassy plains and light bush of a million-acre private reserve – know exactly where to look. Noticing a stack of steaming spores is week-one stuff at safari guide school; spotting an acacia bush that's been recently crumpled by the hooked lips of a browsing black rhino is much tougher, and it's that sort of proficiency that pretty much guarantees that you'll be sneaking up on one just a few hours after leaving camp. Black rhinos are immense yet beautiful, and you'll probably get close enough to these BMW-sized beasts to make out the oxpecker birds picking insects off their backs. Just remember to stay down wind.

Need to know

392 Lake of Stars takes place in Sept at *Sunbird Nkopola Lodge* in Mangochi by Lake Malawi, about a 5hr drive from Lilongwe airport. Head to Ⓦ lakeofstars.org for more information and to buy tickets.

393 Boulders Beach is on the itinerary of every Cape Peninsula tour and is easy to reach in your own car. Sanccob (Ⓦ sanccob.co.za) is dedicated to the preservation of African penguins. For accommodation in the area, see Ⓦ simonstown.com.

394 Malolotja Nature Reserve is 30min drive from the capital, Mbabane, and 90min from Manzini airport. See Ⓦ sntc.org.sz for more information.

395 Air Madagascar flies from Antananarivo to Maroantsetra (Ⓦ airmadagascar.com). The park office can help you organize a multiday camping trek (guides for Masoala are obligatory). Alternatively, the park's ecolodges (Ⓦ tampolodge.marojejy.com, Ⓦ masoala-forestlodge.com, Ⓦ arol-ecolodge.com) can arrange a 3hr speedboat transfer, guide and accommodation.

396 In the whale season, booking is essential, preferably a year ahead. CapeNature's website (Ⓦ capenature.co.za) has information about the Whale Trail, including booking details.

397 Andulela (Ⓦ andulela.com) offers a half-day Cape Malay Cooking Safari, including a walking tour, cooking workshop and traditional meal, for R660.

398 A tour of the falls can be organized in Livingstone (Zambia) and Victoria Falls (Zimbabwe) and departs from the *Royal Livingstone* hotel by Anantara (Ⓦ victoria-falls-hotels.net/royal-livingstone).

399 Since rainfall and temperatures vary from year to year, it's impossible to be sure when and where the show of flowers will be at its peak, but the best displays are usually from mid-Aug to mid-Sept.

400 Visit in April–Nov, outside the rainy season, and use a reputable river safari company: try Ⓦ natureways.com or Ⓦ zambezi.com.

401 Permits to visit Kolmanskop (8am–1pm) can be bought at the gate or from Lüderitz Safaris & Tours (Ⓣ +264 (0) 63 20 27 19). These give you the option of a tour and photos are allowed. A photographer's pass is required for sunrise visits.

402 Dried mopane worms are sold at markets across Zimbabwe, as well as parts of South Africa, Namibia, Zambia and Botswana. You can also buy them tinned – usually in brine or tomato sauce – in supermarkets.

403 *Bulungula Lodge* (Ⓦ bulungula.co.za) has dorms, private rooms, luxury tents and camping space.

404 The Natural History Museum is in Port Louis. Excursions, which include a tour of Ile aux Aigrettes (see Ⓕ facebook.com/IleAuxAigrettes or Ⓦ www.mauritian-wildlife.org), can be booked at several hotels.

405 The Chamarel 7 Coloured Earth Geopark is open year-round: summer 8.30am–5.30pm; winter 8.30am–5pm. Tickets cost MUR250 (£5.60/US$7.30); Ⓦ chamarel7colouredearth.com.

406 Cheetah-tracking, which costs R429 (£21/US$28) per person for the three- to four-hour tour, should be booked in advance through Mountain Zebra National Park (Ⓦ sanparks.org/parks/mountain_zebra).

407 The Kasanka Trust (Ⓦ kasanka.com) provides simple guest accommodation and meals at *Wasa Lodge*, close to the roost, and offers guided batwatching walks.

408 For the most memorable Bazaruto Archipelago experience, stay at a boutique island lodge, such as *Azura Benguerra* (Ⓦ azura-retreats.com) or *Anantara Bazaruto* (Ⓦ anantara.com).

409 Tsumkwe is around 740km northeast of Windhoek in the Otjozondjupa region of Namibia. In town, Ju/'hoansi bushwalks can be booked through the Nyae Nyae Conservancy office (Ⓣ +264 (0) 67 24 40 11).

410 Anjajavy, a useful base for exploring the *tsingy*, is a very remote spot that's realistically only accessible by air – the *Anjajavy Hotel* (Ⓦ anjajavy.com) runs a regular transfer from the capital, Antananarivo.

411 You can visit *Puros Campsite* on a guided camping safari with Conservation Safaris (Ⓦ kcs-namibia.com.na), a community-owned company that specializes in authentic and professionally guided wildlife and cultural experiences in northwest Namibia.

412 Most lodges in the Okavango Delta run *mokoro* safaris. Visit Ⓦ okavangodelta.com for more.

413 Walking tour company Maputo a Pé (Ⓦ maputo-a-pe.com) offers guided tours of Maputo on a variety of themes, including local architecture, art and design.

414 Visit the wineries in a hire car (try Ⓦ aroundabout-cars.com); on a tour (check out Ⓦ wineflies.co.za); or in the Franschhoek Wine Tram (Ⓦ winetram.co.za). Tastings typically cost around R70 (£4/US$5).

415 Nyika Plateau National Park lies 350km north of Malawi's capital, Lilongwe. It's a long slog by road to the top, or a short flight to Chelinda, the park headquarters, where there's a camp and an upmarket lodge run by Wilderness Safaris (Ⓦ wilderness-safaris.com).

416 Microlight flights over South Luangwa National Park are available between May and Oct from *Tafika Camp* (Ⓦ remoteafrica.com). The 15min flights can be arranged on site. Other top Luangwa safari operators: Ⓦ robinpopesafaris.net and Ⓦ timeandtideafrica.com/norman-carr-safaris.

417 The Umhlanga is held in late Aug or early Sept, the precise date varying from year to year. There is plentiful accommodation in the nearby Ezulwini area and admission to the festivities is free – though you will need a permit for photography. Find out more at Ⓦ thekingdomofeswatini.com.

418 Excellent bases for diving in the Quirimbas include *Medjumbe Island Resort* (Ⓦ anantara.com/en/medjumbe-island), *Vamizi Island* (Ⓦ vamizi.com) and, on the mainland, *Guludo Beach Lodge* (Ⓦ www.guludo.com).

419 Anakao is accessible from the city of Toliara, in the south of the island, via a 55km rough dirt road or by boat. Most hotels provide a transfer by land and sea – be prepared for an extremely bumpy ride. Contact Safari Vezo at Ⓦ safarivezo.com for travel to and accommodation in Anakao.

420 Accommodation sells out quickly in Kruger, so you'll have to book well in advance (Ⓦ sanparks.org/bookings). Note that you will also need to pay a daily conservation fee.

421 Ilha do Moçambique is linked to the mainland by a causeway. The easiest way to get there from Maputo, Mozambique's capital, is to fly to Nampula and then travel by *chapa* (bus) 200km (4hr) or so east.

422 Past Experiences offers street-art walking tours of Maboneng Precinct; Ⓦ pastexperiences.co.za.

423 *Malealea Lodge* (Ⓦ malealea.co.ls), a 1hr drive south of the capital, Maseru, can arrange treks.

424 Admission charges apply at all sites, including the Apartheid Museum (Ⓦ apartheidmuseum.org), Liliesleaf (Ⓦ liliesleaf.co.za), Constitution Hill (Ⓦ constitutionhill.org.za), the Mandela House Museum (Ⓦ mandelahouse.com) and Regina Mundi Church (Ⓦ reginamundichurch.co.za).

425 You can dive in Lake Malawi all year round, but be wary of bilharzia (schistosomiasis): avoid reedbeds in calm water close to shore.

426 Hiking along the canyon is only allowed May–Sept, to avoid flash floods. Numbers are limited: book as far in advance as you can at Ⓦ nwr.com.na.

427 For details of trails and local accommodation, check Ⓦ stluciasa.co.za.

428 The nearest large town is Blantyre, where trips to Mulanje can be arranged. For information, try the Mountain Club of Malawi (Ⓦ mcm438.wordpress.com).

429 You don't need to book to walk the trail, but you do need a permit, which can be obtained from *Traveller's Rest Farm* (Ⓦ travellersrest.co.za), which also has accommodation.

430 Great Zimbabwe is 30km from the town of Masvingo, around a 3hr drive from Harare or Bulawayo via main roads. For Z$5400 (US$15), you can explore the site and its small museum. Guided tours are available on request.

431 Access to Busanga Plains is by air from Lusaka or Livingstone, or by road through the park (4WD only). Wilderness Safaris (Ⓦ wilderness-safaris.com) lodges are closed during the wet season (Nov–May), when the region is inaccessible by road.

432 To make the most of Mount Mulanje, book a place on one of Hoerikwaggo Trails' guided hikes (Ⓦ sanparks.org/parks/table_mountain/tourism/hoerikwaggo_trail.php).

433 Fishing vessels leave around nine times a year from Cape Town to Tristan da Cunha. To enquire about permission to visit the island, go to Ⓦ tristandc.com.

434 KwaZulu-Natal's *AmaKhosi Safari Lodge* (Ⓦ amakhosi.com) offers frog safaris from Nov–March as part of the activity programme included in its full-board rate. Good bases for do-it-yourself frog watching elsewhere in eastern South Africa include Chrissiesmeer in Mpumalanga province.

435 Gassi Tours (Ⓦ gassitours.com) offers river tours.

436 A package trip includes guided nature walks and 4WD excursions. For accommodation, try the *Hoanib Skeleton Coast Camp* (Ⓦ wilderness-safaris.com), a luxury tented camp reachable by air.

437 Try Ⓦ papyrustours.co.uk, Ⓦ wildlifeworldwide.com or Ⓦ theultimatetravelcompany.co.uk.

438 The river is at its lowest (and calmest) between mid-July and mid-Jan. Safari Par Excellence (Ⓦ safpar.com) runs trips out of Livingstone.

439 For more on *Guludo Lodge* see Ⓦ guludo.com.

440 A Tsitsikamma Canopy Tour is available with Stormsriver Adventures (Ⓦ stormsriver.com).

441 For more details on wildlife ranger training, see Ⓦ ecotraining.co.za and Ⓦ tinyurl.com/kruger-river.

442 Robin Pope Safaris (Ⓦ robinpopesafaris.net) run the luxury *Mkulumadzi Lodge* in Majete.

443 *Desert Rhino Camp* is run by Wilderness Safaris (Ⓦ wilderness-safaris.com).

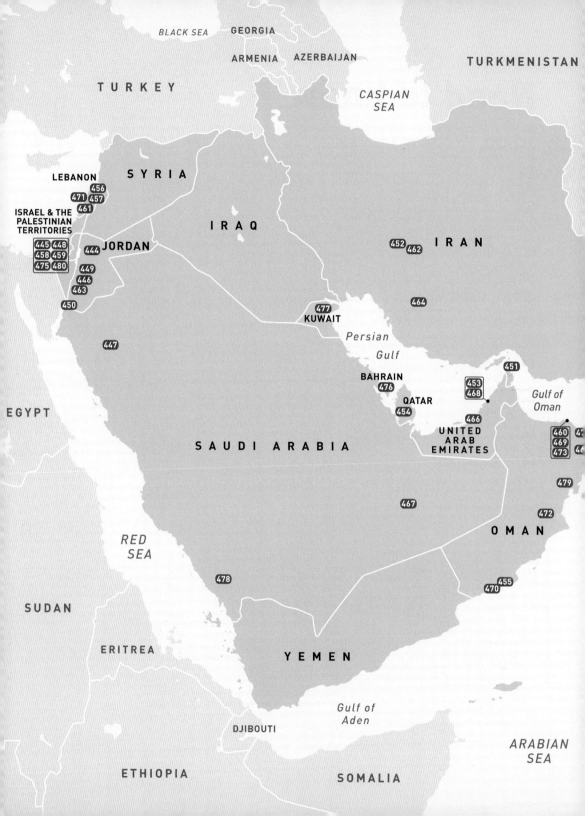

BLACK SEA

GEORGIA

ARMENIA   AZERBAIJAN

TURKMENISTAN

TURKEY

CASPIAN
SEA

LEBANON
471 456
457
461

SYRIA

ISRAEL & THE
PALESTINIAN
TERRITORIES
445 448
458 459
475 480

444 JORDAN

449

446
463

450

447

IRAQ

452 462

IRAN

464

477
KUWAIT

Persian

Gulf

451

EGYPT

BAHRAIN
476

QATAR
454

453
468

Gulf of
Oman

460
469
473

479

UNITED
ARAB
EMIRATES

466

SAUDI ARABIA

467

472

OMAN

RED
SEA

478

470 455

SUDAN

ERITREA

YEMEN

ETHIOPIA

DJIBOUTI

Gulf of
Aden

SOMALIA

ARABIAN
SEA

THE MIDDLE EAST

444-480

What activity best sums up the reality of travel in the Middle East? Trekking in Oman? Diving in Jordan? Taking tea in Iran? Setting out into the Saudi Arabian desert? It might be a contender for the planet's most complex region, but its blend of millennia-old heritage, shiny modernity and humbling hospitality makes the Middle East an endlessly beguiling place to visit.

Whether you're drifting through the babbling hubbub of Jerusalem's Old Town, perusing the art of the new Louvre Abu Dhabi or pitching a tent on Oman's sculpted dunes, this is a part of the world that confounds many of its clichés.

444 Getting acquainted with Arabic sweets

JORDAN Whenever I go back to Jordan (which is often), my first appointment is in downtown Amman. There, up an unpromising-looking alleyway alongside a bank building, is a hole-in-the-wall outlet of Habiba, a citywide chain devoted to *halawiyyat* (literally "sweets", or sweet pastries and desserts). I join a line – there's always a line – and, for the equivalent of a few cents, I get a square of *kunafeh*, hot and dripping with syrup, handed to me on a paper plate with a plastic fork. It is a joyous experience: for the Ammanis hanging out and wolfing down the stuff, it's everyday; for me, it's like coming home. Habiba's *kunafeh* is worth crossing continents for.

Kunafeh is the king of Arabic sweets. Originating from the Palestinian city of Nablus, it comprises buttery shredded filo pastry layered over melted goat's cheese, baked in large, round trays, doused liberally with syrup and cut up into squares for serving. It is cousin to the better-known *baklawa*, layered flaky pastry filled with pistachios, cashews or other nuts, also available widely.

However, you're rarely served such treats in Arabic restaurants: there's not a strong tradition of postprandial desserts. Instead, you'll need to head to one of the larger outlets of Habiba, or their competitors Jabri or Zalatimo, patisseries with a café section. Glass-fronted fridges hold individual portions of *Umm Ali*, an Egyptian milk-and-coconut speciality, sprinkled with nuts and cinnamon, and *muhallabiyyeh*, a semi-set almond cream pudding, enhanced with rosewater: comfort food, Arab-style. Choose one to go with a coffee and perhaps a water-pipe of flavoured tobacco.

Or get a box of assorted sweets – *baklawa*, *maamoul* (buttery, crumbly, rose-scented cookie-style biscuits), *burma* (nut pastries baked golden brown), *basma* (delicate lacy pastries filled with cashews) and other delectably sticky and aromatic varieties – the perfect gift if you're lucky enough to be invited to someone's home. Forget, too, about Western-bred inhibitions: in the Arab world, as far as *halawiyyat* are concerned, consumption is guilt-free!

Matthew Teller
writes and broadcasts on the Middle East for media outlets around the world, from CNN, the BBC and *The Times* to *Wanderlust, National Geographic* and *Condé Nast Traveler*. He has been a Rough Guides author for twenty years.

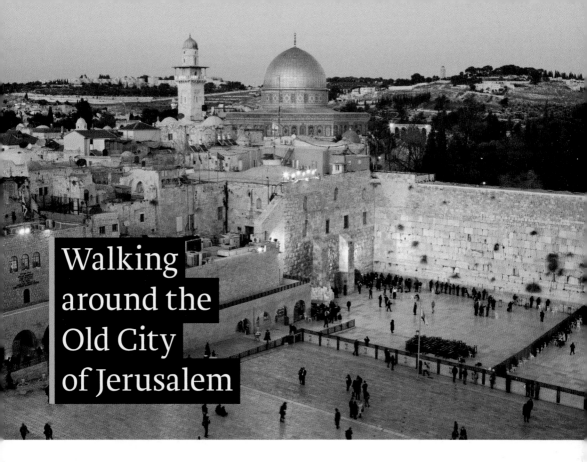

Walking around the Old City of Jerusalem

ISRAEL & THE PALESTINIAN TERRITORIES For a place so dear to so many hearts, and so violently fought over, the walled Old City of Jerusalem is not as grandiose as you might imagine; it's compact and easy to find your way around, though you'll stumble at almost every turn over holy or historic sites. The streets hum with activity: handcarts, sellers of religious artefacts, Jews scurrying through the Muslim quarter to pray at the Wailing Wall, and Palestinian youths trying to avoid the attentions of the Israeli soldiers patrolling the streets.

The three biggest attractions are the major religious sites. The Church of the Holy Sepulchre is a dark, musty, cavernous old building, scented by incense, and home to the site of the crucifixion. Pilgrims approach the church by the Via Dolorosa, the path that Jesus took to his execution, observing each Station of the Cross and not infrequently dragging large wooden crosses through the narrow streets, where local residents pay them scant attention.

Heading through the heart of the Old City, past a meat market, piled high with offal and sheep's heads, you emerge blinking into the sun-drenched esplanade that fronts Judaism's holiest site, the Western ("Wailing") Wall, last remnant of the ancient Jewish Temple that was originally built by King Solomon and later rebuilt by Herod. From here, you can nip into the Western Wall Tunnels that run under the city's Muslim Quarter; with subterranean synagogues, underground gateways and ancient aqueducts, they're fascinating to explore.

Around the side of the Wailing Wall, up on Temple Mount, is the Dome of the Rock, Islam's third-holiest site. This is the spot where Abraham offered to sacrifice his son to God, and where Mohammed later ascended to Heaven upon a winged steed. The perfect blue octagon topped with a golden dome is a fabulous gem of Ummayad architecture, immediately recognizable as the symbol of Jerusalem.

The wealth of sights in this ancient, entrancing city is overwhelming, so don't forget to make time on your wanderings for more mundane pleasures: a cardamom-scented Turkish coffee at the café just inside the Damascus Gate, or hummus at *Abu Shukri's*, arguably more divine than the relics that surround it.

Roadtripping along the Path of Kings

JORDAN Ancient path of kings, caliphs, Crusaders and conquerors, the King's Highway scythes its way in languorous loops across the Great Rift Valley's ridge from the city of Madaba to the ancient settlement of Petra. Passing important historical sites, backed by stark skyscraper cliffs and yawning views across rippling ochre rocks that tumble down to the Dead Sea basin below, this is the most scenic drive in the Middle East and makes a wonderful one-day road trip.

Heading south out of Madaba – home to the Byzantine mosaic map of the Holy Land, famed for its geographical accuracy – you come to the church-capped summit of Mount Nebo, where Moses first saw the Promised Land. Beyond, the road dips and turns, offering panoramic views of the great rip in the Earth's surface spooling out below. The lonely flat-topped peak of Mukawir, where St John the Baptist is said to have lost his head, rises up over the barren countryside. Further along, 33km south, is the turn-off for the UNESCO World Heritage Site of Umm ar-Rasas, where dazzling Byzantine mosaics sit amid the stubby fields.

The most famous landmark along the route is the Crusader castle of Kerak, with its imposing, honey-toned fortifications. From here you can take the dizzying descent down to the Dead Sea, stopping for a dip in the waters where it's impossible to sink, or carry on south for 92km to Dana Nature Reserve. Swooping over a chunk of the Great Rift Valley, tumbling from 1200m to 100m below sea level, the reserve encompasses semi-arid forest slopes, subtropical valleys and stark sand-dune plateaus. If you want to stop for the night, this is the place to do it.

Dipping away from the ridge, the highway rolls on through the sweeping, arid plains to Showbak Castle – another Crusader stronghold – ending amid the magnificent rock canyons of the Wadi Arabah. Here the ancient Nabataean capital of Petra, the astonishing rose-red city carved out of colossal cliffs, is a fitting finale for a epic road trip that reveals Jordan in all its historic and scenic magnificence.

447 | Discovering Mada'in Saleh

SAUDI ARABIA Rocky, remote and allegedly accursed, Mada'in Saleh, deep in the Arabian Desert, is the location of the magnificent Nabataean city known in ancient times as Hegra. With its great rock-cut facades carved from warm golden sandstone, this city was once an important stop on the powerful Arabian tribe's incense trail.

Built in the first century AD on the fringes of Nabataean territory, Hegra lay at a junction of trade routes. Camel caravans travelling north from the incense towns of Arabia would stop here; animals would be rested, merchants would do business, taxes would be collected. With the constant traffic and trade, Hegra prospered, and the ruins here are suitably grand.

Roaming Mada'in Saleh you'll discover all the styles typical of Nabataean architecture, set against a breathtaking backdrop of desert landscapes. Ornate, classically influenced tombs are carved into the looming cliffs, displaying impressively intricate workmanship; their extraordinary detailing, preserved in the dry desert air, remains crisp and sharp.

Standing beneath these towering funerary edifices, you'll feel the heavy, silent heat pressing down upon you. The Nabataean people, who were conquered by the Romans and slid into obscurity after the trade routes shifted, maintain a ghostly presence.

448 | Drumming in the Sabbath in Tel Aviv

ISRAEL & THE PALESTINIAN TERRITORIES As the Sabbath arrives on a Friday afternoon in Tel Aviv, many people, following centuries of tradition, head homewards, to the synagogue, or to family dinners clutching bottles of kosher wine and freshly baked challah bread. Some, however, choose a more secular ritual to welcome in Shabbat: drumming on the beach as the sun goes down.

Tel Aviv's seafront is divided into beaches that cater for all comers: families, teenagers, Matkot-players, sun-worshippers and posers can all find a place to call their own. The drumming contingent is found on the so-called Drum Beach, at the southern end of the seafront promenade.

A few hours before the sun starts to set, people begin to arrive, many of them carrying drums, bongos, guitars or flutes. You will find all sorts here, from middle-aged hippies to passing tourists to trendy Tel Aviv twenty-somethings. Quite why, no one knows, but revellers have been coming to this spot for twenty years – jamming and tapping out their disparate rhythms that soon merge into an enormous, joyous, hypnotic sound.

Capoeira artists and jugglers add to the festivities. Picnics are eaten, and there's plenty of alcohol to be had; it's even been known for bottles of Gold Star beer to act as temporary percussion instruments. For some it's a spiritual experience, for others just a chance to dip their toes in the surf, listen to great music and unwind for the weekend.

When not struck dumb by the magic of it all, you'll find yourself tapping away, talking to perfect strangers – and maybe even getting up to dance. You won't be alone – plenty of spectators take their place in the middle of the circle, shaking their hips, clapping along to the beats that continue for hours as the sun slips into the Mediterranean sea.

If the beach is the heart of Tel Aviv, the Friday-night drum circle is its pulse: perhaps nowhere else is the life and irrepressible energy of Israel's most vibrant city more vividly felt.

449 | Blazing a trail at Dana Biosphere Reserve

JORDAN When you think of eco-friendly travel, the Middle East might not immediately spring to mind. In environmental terms, the region is a disaster, characterized by a general lack of awareness of the issues and poor – if any – legislative safeguards. But Jordan is quietly working wonders, and the impact in recent years of the country's Royal Society for the Conservation of Nature (RSCN) has been striking: areas of outstanding natural beauty are now under legal protection and sustainable development is squarely on the political agenda.

The RSCN's flagship project is the Dana Biosphere Reserve, the Middle East's first truly successful example of sustainable tourism. Until 1993, Dana was dying: the stone-built mountain village was crumbling, its land suffering from hunting and overgrazing, and locals were abandoning their homes in search of better opportunities in the towns.

Then the RSCN stepped in and set up the reserve, drawing up zoning plans to establish wilderness regions and semi-intensive use areas where tourism could be introduced, building a guesthouse and founding a scientific research station. Virtually all the jobs – tour guides, rangers, cooks, receptionists, scientists and more – were taken by villagers.

Today, over eight hundred local people benefit from the success of Dana, and the reserve's running costs are covered almost entirely from tourism revenues. The guesthouse, with spectacular views over the V-shaped Dana Valley, continues to thrive, while a three-hour walk away in the hills lies the idyllic *Rummana* campsite, from where you can embark on dawn excursions to watch ibex and eagles.

But the reserve also stretches down the valley towards the Dead Sea Rift – and here, a memorable five-hour walk from the guesthouse, stands the *Feynan Ecolodge*, set amid an arid sandy landscape quite different from Dana village. The lodge is powered by solar energy and lit by candles; it's a bewitchingly calm and contemplative desert retreat.

450 | Diving in the Gulf of Aqaba

JORDAN Tucked between the arid lands of northern Africa and the Arabian Peninsula, the Red Sea is one of the world's premier diving destinations, and leading off from its northern tip the Gulf of Aqaba boasts some of its best and least-damaged stretches of coral. The long Egyptian coastline is filled with brash, bustling and rather commercial resorts, and Israel's slender coast around Eilat can get uncomfortably crowded, but the unsung Jordanian resort of Aqaba offers a tranquillity and lack of hustle that, for many, makes it top choice in these parts.

Diving from Aqaba is simple and rewarding: the reef begins directly from the shallows and shore dives are the norm; only 100m offshore you can explore coral walls and canyons, shipwrecks and ethereal undersea gardens.

The water here is nearly always warm and the reefs exquisite. Wide fields of soft corals stretch off into the startlingly clear blue gulf, schools of anthias shimmering over the various fans, sea fingers and sea whips. Huge heads of stony, hard corals grow literally as big as a house, their limestone skeletons supporting an abundance of marine life, including turtles, rays and moray eels. Endless species of multicoloured fish goggle back at you from all sides. Seabass, lionfish and groupers patrol the fringing reef of First Bay, while shoals of barracuda circle the sunken Lebanese freighter *Cedar Pride*. The views along the sheer wall of the Power Station are worth the dive alone – and, if the fates are really smiling on you, you might be lucky enough to spot a shark circling in the depths below.

451 | Bobbing about on the Musandam Fjords

OMAN The scenery is majestic: towering mountains plunge like runaway rock into the turquoise water 2000m below, and crystal-clear waterways knife their way through craggy cliffs.

These are fjords all right, but not as most visitors know them. There are no snowcapped peaks around here, no gushing waterfalls or fertile slopes. Instead, a heat haze hangs over the Hajar, and the waters are plied not by 3000-tonne ferries but by the occasional fishing dhow, bobbing its way towards Khasab harbour with a bounty of grouper and spiny lobster. Welcome to the Musandam Peninsula, an isolated entity, cut off from the rest of Oman by the United Arab Emirates and jutting out into the Strait of Hormuz. This is a strikingly rugged region, dominated by the Hajar Mountains, which, having snaked across the UAE, topple off into the Gulf of Oman.

Such grandeur is best appreciated from below, from one of the sheltered fjords, or *khors*, that riddle the peninsula. What better way to start the day than by setting sail from Khasab in a traditional wooden dhow, maybe a *landj*, a *batil* or the larger *mashuwwah*? And what more relaxing way to spend it than by propping yourself up among the Persian carpets and thick, lolling cushions, and gazing out at the tiny villages that cling to the cliff face, and at the humpback dolphins that cavort alongside your boat.

Taking time in Isfahan

IRAN You could easily devote a day to exploring Isfahan's great Naqsh-e Jahan, a vast rectangular space dotted with gardens, pools and fountains and ringed by arcades, above which rise the domes of the adjacent mosques. Separate from the bustle of this cultured city, it has even managed to cling onto its original polo goals, though the game hasn't been played here for centuries.

The square is always buzzing. It spreads south from the sprawling Bazar-e Bozorg, packed with shops offering hand-woven Persian carpets. As you stroll the square you may well find yourself engaged in conversation by an eminently courteous Iranian with impeccable English, who turns out to have a brother/uncle/cousin with a carpet shop – where, of course, there's no charge for looking…

Even if you're able to resist the charms of the carpet bazaar, you won't be able to ignore the square's exquisite seventeenth-century Islamic architecture. To the south is the Masjid i-Imam mosque, its portal and towering dome sheathed in glittering tiles of turquoise and blue, while to one side, the smaller Sheikh Lotfollah Mosque – marked by an attractive dome of cream-coloured tiles which glow rosy pink in the afternoon sun – is, if anything, even more stunning, with fine mosaics and a dizzyingly decorated interior. Opposite, the Ali Qapu Palace – an ex-royal residence – boasts a sensational view over the square from its high terrace.

Either way, be back at one of the terrace teashops as sunset approaches. The square fills with Isfahani families strolling or picnicking on the grass, and you get a grandstand view over the scene, sipping *chay* (tea) as floodlights turn the arcades, domes and minarets to gold.

Shopping in the City of Gold

453

UNITED ARAB EMIRATES Dubai's nickname, the "City of Gold", is well earned: gold jewellery is sold here at some of the world's most competitive prices, and shopping among the constant flow of customers, many here for their marriage dowries, is an exceptional experience.

The Gold Souk is a fascinating warren of tiny shops and stalls clustered together in the old quarter of Deira. Visit in the cool of early evening when the souk is at its best, with lights blazing and window-shoppers out in force. Every corner is crammed with jewellery of every style and variety; spotlights pick out choice pieces and racks holding dozens of sparkling gold bangles and chains dazzle the eye.

Buying is a cagey but good-natured process: treat it as the chance to have a friendly chat with the shopkeeper, talking about family, work, life – anything but the item you've got your eye on. Then ask to see a few pieces, while surreptitiously assessing quality and sizing up your adversary, before lighting on the piece you knew you wanted from the start.

When the time comes to discuss money, bear in mind that the gold price fluctuates daily – and every shopkeeper in the souk knows the current price to several decimal places. Whereas in the West gold jewellery is sold at a fixed price, in Dubai the cost of each item has two separate components: the weight of the gold and the quality of craftsmanship involved in creating it. The former is fixed, according to the daily price-per-gram (listed in the newspaper) set against the item's purity; the latter is where bargaining comes into play, with you and the shopkeeper trading prices – always with a smile – until you reach agreement.

It takes a cool head, amid all that glittering gold, not to be dazzled into paying over the odds, but the experience is more than worth it.

454 | Sand-skiing in the dunes

QATAR Skiing in the desert? You don't have to go to Dubai's super-cooled ski dome to experience it. Launching yourself down the slopes under a scorching desert sun is possible in Qatar, a small Gulf country midway between Kuwait and Dubai – but forget about snow machines and fake icicles. Here, the ski slopes are all natural.

Jaded ski bums looking for a new thrill should take a 4WD trip to Khor al-Adaid – known as Qatar's Inland Sea. This is a saltwater inlet from the blue waters of the Gulf which penetrates far into the desert interior and is surrounded on all sides by monumental formations of giant, silvery sand dunes.

These are almost all crescent-shaped barchan dunes. Both points of the crescent face downwind; between them is a steep slip face of loose sand, while the back of the dune, facing into the breeze, is a shallow, hard slope of wind-packed grains.

This formation lends itself particularly well to sand-skiing or, perhaps more commonly, sand-boarding, both of which are almost identical to their more familiar snow-based cousins – without the woolly hats but with a softer landing for novices. The 4WD delivers you to the top of the dune, whereupon you set off down the loose slip face, carving through the soft sand to the desert floor; friction is minimal, and this kind of dry, powdery sand lets you glide like a dream.

And Khor al-Adaid comes into its own as sunset approaches. With low sunshine illuminating the creamy-smooth slopes and glittering light reflected up off the calm surface of the *khor*'s blue waters, a surreal, almost mystical quality settles on the dunes.

This is après-ski with a difference – and not an experience to be missed.

455 | Tawi Attair: the singing sinkhole

OMAN At the edge of an emerald highland plain patrolled by Jabali tribesmen and their herds of camels and cattle lies the opening to Tawi Attair ("the Well of Birds"), one of the largest sinkholes in the world. A massive, gaping limestone cavity 150m in diameter and 211m deep, the well was formed eons ago when a cave roof collapsed into itself; today, it could house half the Empire State Building. Thousands of visitors come here each year to witness numerous bird species swooping in and out once the torrential *khaleef* (monsoon) has drenched the Omani plains.

Work your way through the marshy grasses towards the edge of the pit and gaze down: bedecked with specks of green foliage amid crumbling mounds of dirt and the occasional falling rock, the craggy walls are alive with hundreds of birds – raptors, swifts and rock

doves – their warbles and chirps welling up in a harmonious flurry of sound. From the side of the opening, carefully follow the stony path down to the small platform for better views of the deep abyss 80m below – you'll need a powerful torch to see all the way down to the bottom, where an aquamarine pool funnels into a complex and intertwined system of sub-aquatic caves.

The platform is the best vantage point to hear the famed bird calls of the well's diverse residents – exotic, isolated species such as the Yemen serin, Bonelli's eagle and African rock bunting, among many, many others.

Once the birds embark on their flight towards the sky, their coos hushed, the silence down here is uncanny, trumping even that of the vast desert above.

456 | Forests, frescoes and hermitages in the Qadisha Valley

LEBANON There's a timeless quality to Lebanon's Qadisha Valley. This fertile slash in the northernmost reaches of the Mount Lebanon Range is home to the country's Maronite Christian community, whose strand of Christianity dates back to the seventh century and whose many churches remain a major pilgrimage destination. Most visitors associate Lebanon with the glitz and glamour of party-town Beirut; trekking amid the valley's lush forests, between chapels clinging to clifftops and up to villages spilt higgledy-piggledy across the ridge, reveals a very different picture.

Much of Lebanon's old Ottoman character – long bulldozed away in other parts of the country – remains here. Visit the impossibly pretty village of Bsharri where stone-cut Ottoman houses cling to the ridge, connected by winding cobblestone roads where the only traffic jams are caused by chugging farm tractors. Kahlil Gibran (1883–1931), the country's most famous writer, grew up here: his museum and tomb, where you can see examples of his artwork and writing, sit just above the village in an old hermitage.

Below Bsharri, the yawning gash of the Qadisha Valley is at its most dramatic. Within the lush forests below is a jumble of Maronite chapels and monasteries connected by paths. Deir Mar Elisha, which dates back to at least the fourteenth century and where in 1695 the first official Lebanese Maronite Order was founded, is still a functioning monastery. From here a 6km hike through a gorgeous slice of Lebanese countryside – carpeted in wildflowers and surrounded by orchards and vegetable plots terraced into the steep cliff slopes – brings you to the fresco-filled chapel of Deir Qannoubin, one of the oldest churches in the valley. Its lonely position gives it an air of beautiful serenity.

Afterwards, history lovers should make a beeline to Hamatoura Monastery, which hangs precariously from the cliff face by the town of Kousba, 35km west of Bsharri. Climbing the narrow uphill path to the monastery affords fantastic views; stop off to admire the fragments of tenth-century frescoes in the cave-cut chapel before feasting your eyes on the dizzying drop down to the valley floor below.

457 | From ski suit to swim suit in a single day

LEBANON The best things come in small packages, but few small packages contain quite as much as Lebanon. In a single day you can swish your way down the slopes in the morning before losing the salopettes and donning your shades at the seaside in the afternoon.

Though boasting neither the altitude nor the acreage to qualify as a major international resort, Lebanon's skiing is great fun. Best of all, the resorts lie within a day's trip by car from Beirut, meaning you don't have to risk long and expensive journeys for nothing. The best plan is to check out the resort's snow conditions in advance then head out early the following morning – either taking a rental car along the boisterous roads or travelling with a tour company – to catch the snow before Lebanon's Levantine sun turns it all to mush.

The pick of the bunch, with the most-developed infrastructure and facilities, is Mzaar, northeast of Beirut, with the powder-friendly Cedars,

southeast of Tripoli, close behind. Many resorts also offer cross-country skiing and snow-shoeing, and there's a good variety of pistes, though most are short. The most important thing to remember is that in Lebanon looking good is almost as important as skiing.

To work on your tan, head to Lebanon's best beaches, which can be found south of Tyre and near Byblos. In Beirut the well-maintained private beach clubs are generally your best bet – they have heated pools (in case you find the winter sea chilly) and are home to much shimmying and strutting. After a day on the slopes, there's no better way to unwind, and there's still time for a spot of shopping in Beirut's boutiques, a beer followed by fresh fish at one of the city's bars or restaurants and more shimmying and strutting at the booming nightclubs. Best of all, you'll return from your skiing trip with a perfect tan, much to the chagrin of your panda-eyed Alpine friends.

458 | Haggling in Mahane Yehuda

ISRAEL & THE PALESTINIAN TERRITORIES Chaotic, colourful, pungent – Mahane Yehuda in Jerusalem is the market of markets. Go for a couple of loaves and perhaps a few fishes and you'll come away laden with spices, olives, baklava, fruit teas and furry slippers – maybe even a live owl, should your shopping spree run away with you.

There's been a market on this site since the late nineteenth century, and not much has changed since then. More than 250 vendors try to out-heckle and out-display each other in this tight grid of narrow lanes, making for a full-on sensual assault. You can sample the rich, silky sweetness of Turkish Delight, breathe in the earthy aroma of cinnamon and glide your hands over rainbow silks as vendors yell in Hebrew about their wares. Watch out for the boys scurrying through the crowds with trays of sweet treats held over their heads.

There are two main thoroughfares: Eitz HaChaim street, which is covered; and Mahane Yehuda street, which is open to the sun. Between these runs a ladder of smaller lanes named after different fruits. Make

your way up this ladder, sampling sesame-flavoured halva and sticky pastries along the way. Some pushing and shoving may be required; this is no genteel tourist market, but the shopping centre of choice for many Jerusalemites – hence the jostling crowds on a Friday in the run-up to the Sabbath.

By day, Mahane Yehuda is a place to take pictures. Each corner reveals a new kaleidoscope of goods just begging to be snapped. At night, however, the market becomes a trendy venue for young Jerusalemites to drink beer, listen to live music and – most importantly – eat. Mahane Yehuda is fast becoming the city's foodie hotspot, dotted with tiny restaurants where no reservations are taken and you eat elbow to elbow. All palates are catered for – you can choose from shwarma stands, boutique wine bars, Ethiopian cafés, hip Middle Eastern restaurants, pasta joints, even a fish and chip bar. Come with a thick wallet and an empty stomach – after a hard day's haggling, you're going to need a good feed.

459 | Exploring the Holy Land along the Jesus Trail

ISRAEL & THE PALESTINIAN TERRITORIES For hikers who love history, the Jesus Trail is one of the Middle East's most fascinating treks. This three- to five-day, 65km-long walk, traversing the rugged countryside where Jesus began his ministry, is not just for pilgrims. The ruins and archeological sites along the way illuminate everything from Rome's mighty dominance over the area to the glorious heyday of the Byzantine period, while the jagged cliff ridges and pastoral countryside reveal the Holy Land's ancient natural beauty. More than that, this is a snapshot of the modern Holy Land, passing through places that connect Judaism, Christianity and Islam.

Beginning in Nazareth – Jesus' birthplace – with its mazey Old Town souk and clutch of stately, pilgrim-packed churches, the trail soon leaves the camera-clicking crowds behind and sets out across the peaceful countryside. Explore the ruined Talmudic city and intricate Byzantine mosaics in Zippori National Park, and walk on to the village of Cana where (tradition states) Jesus performed his first miracle by turning water into wine.

Beyond Cana the route is at its most viscerally beautiful, with wide valley panoramas opening up as you descend from the ridge to hike through forest trails to Kibbutz Lavi. The next day, you can climb the craggy rock outcrop known as the Horns of Hattin where in 1187 the Crusaders launched into battle with the Muslim Ayyubid dynasty. From here you reach the fertile shores of the Sea of Galilee and the churches and monasteries of Tabga, marking the spot where Jesus is said to have performed the miracle of loaves and fishes. Next comes the Mount of Beatitudes, capped by a domed Franciscan church that is traditionally thought to be the location of the famous Sermon on the Mount. The trek ends at the shoreside ruins of Capernaum, where pilgrims gather to pray at the site where Jesus preached.

This chunk of countryside is a place of miracles and myth, where many of the events recorded in the New Testament are said to have occurred. Walking the Jesus Trail is an unsurpassed way to connect the dots through this region's staggering history.

460 | Frolicking with dolphins off Muscat

OMAN Lightly wedged along a coastal strip between the Hajar Mountains and the blue waters of the Gulf, Muscat has been called the Arabian Peninsula's most enigmatic capital for its bewildering mixture of conservative tradition and contemporary style. Muscat itself – the walled, seafront quarter that hosts the Sultan's Palace – is one of three towns comprising the city. Inland lies the busy modern area of Ruwi, while a short walk along the coast from Muscat is Muttrah, site of the souk and daily fish market. But the city's unmissable attraction is the astonishing display of marine acrobatics to be seen daily just offshore.

Dolphins are the star performers, dancing and pirouetting on the water in the sparkling sunlight. From various points along the coast near Muscat, tour operators run dolphin-watching trips, departing around 6.30 or 7am. The early start is worth it, as each morning numerous pods of dolphins congregate beside the little boats, including common, bottlenose and the aptly named spinner dolphins, which delight in somersaulting out of the water with eye-popping virtuosity, directly under your gaze. Adults and youngsters alike take part, seemingly showing off to each other as well as the goggling humans; nobody knows why they spin, but they do it every morning, before sliding off into deeper waters. Whales have also been sighted close to shore in the winter months (Oct–May), among them humpbacks and even killer whales.

And if that's not enough, you can return at sunset for more dolphin-watching, or alternatively even take to the water yourself for a closer look: kayaking with the dolphins, morning or evening, is a real treat. Paddling a short distance into the midst of the frolicking beasts brings you close enough to interact with them, their squeaks and clicks filling the air as they come and investigate who or what you might be.

461 | Feasting on Lebanese meze

LEBANON Lebanese food is one of the great pleasures of travel in the Middle East, and the mainstay of this cuisine is meze. This array of dishes, served simultaneously on small plates as a starter or main, has spread around the world. But to get a real sense of it, it's worth going to the source.

The concept extends far back into history: the ancient Greeks and Persians both served small dishes of nuts and dried fruits with wine as an appetizer, a tradition which continued (with a non-alcoholic beverage) throughout the medieval Arab period.

Today, good restaurants might have thirty or forty choices of meze on the menu, ranging from simple dishes of herbs, olives and pickled vegetables, *labneh* (tart yoghurt), and dips such as hummus and *baba ghanouj* (aubergine), up to grander creations like *kibbeh* (the national dish of Lebanon, a mixture of cracked wheat, grated onion and minced lamb pounded to a paste, shaped into oval torpedoes and deep-fried), *tabbouleh* (another Lebanese speciality: parsley and tomato salad with cracked wheat), *shanklish* (spiced goat's cheese) and *warag aynab* (stuffed vine leaves). *Kibbeh nayeh* (lamb's meat pounded smooth and served raw) is perhaps the most celebrated of all meze, while mini-mains such as lamb or chicken shish kebabs, charcoal-roasted larks and even seafood are also common. Everything is always accompanied by unlimited quantities of hot, fresh-baked flatbread, used for scooping and dipping.

Meze exist to slow down the process of eating, turning a solitary refuelling into a convivial celebration of good food and good company. Sitting at a table swamped in colours and aromas, and eating a meal of myriad different flavours and textures, is nothing short of sensuous delight – as, indeed, it's intended to be.

462 | Trawling over the hidden sand dunes that buried a sinful civilization

IRAN From afar, they emerge from the flat, rocky desert around the village of Varzaneh like the golden humps of giant camels. "Legend says that once upon a time, a father fell in love with his own daughter," says Sina, the bespectacled manager of *Negaar Varzaneh Guesthouse* in Varzaneh. "He announced his wicked decision to the rest of his village and got their consent. Little did they know that, by granting his unholy wish, they had infuriated the Gods. A shower of sand came from the sky, covering all the sinners under the beautiful dunes you see today."

Sina's story may have a base of truth: in fact, between Varzaneh and Isfahan – the more famous Iranian city 105km to the west – there's a lot of rocky nothingness, but not a grain of sand. The legend rings even truer when one proceeds 25km east of the dunes, and finds the Gavkhouni wetland, a paradise for birdwatchers that defies the topography of any desert. It's set in the shadow of a black magma mountain, and next to a salt lake.

These days, the odd sand dunes fill up quickly with Iranian tourists keen to marvel at the rippling landscape. They cross the country's central wasteland to slide on surfboards or ride noisy buggies over the sandy slopes. But it just takes a good sun hat and a bit of patience to walk farther down the road, and find solitary dunes that are as empty as they are stunning. Sina also mentioned that archeologists had found earthenware and pots buried beneath these dunes, adding even more weight to his mysterious tale.

On the way back to Varzaneh – which has its own share of secluded mosques, an ancient pigeon tower, and an arched bridge which rivals Isfahan's – one can see old, bearded men singing to their bulls. It's the only way to get them to operate an age-old system of stone mills – and one last quirk to make God-fearing local lore sound even more plausible.

463

Walking the Siq to Petra

JORDAN Tucked away between parallel rocky ranges in southern Jordan, Petra is awe-inspiring. Popular but rarely crowded, this fabled site could keep you occupied for half a day or half a year: you can roam its dusty tracks and byways for kilometres in every direction. Petra was the capital of the Nabataeans, a tribe originally from Arabia who traded with, and were eventually taken over by, the Romans. Grand temples and even Christian-era church mosaics survive, but Petra is best known for the hundreds of ornate classical-style facades carved into its red sandstone cliffs, the grandest of which mark the tombs of the Nabataean kings.

As you approach, modern urban civilization falls away and you are enveloped by the arid desert hills; the texture and colouring of the sandstone, along with the stillness, heat and clarity of light, bombard your senses. But it's the lingering, under-the-skin quality of supernatural power that seems to seep out of the rock that leaves the greatest impression.

As in antiquity, the Siq, meaning "gorge", is still the main entrance into Petra – and its most dramatic natural feature. The Siq path twists and turns between bizarrely eroded cliffs for more than 1km, sometimes widening to form sunlit piazzas in the echoing heart of the mountain; in other places, the looming walls (150m high) close in to little more than a couple of metres apart, blocking out sound, warmth and even daylight.

Just when you think the gorge can't go on any longer, you enter a dark, narrow defile, opening at its end onto a strip of extraordinary classical architecture. As you step out into the sunlight, the famous facade of Petra's Treasury looms before you. Carved directly into the cliff face and standing 40m tall, it's no wonder this edifice starred in *Indiana Jones and the Last Crusade* as the repository of the Holy Grail – the magnificent portico is nothing short of divine.

477 | Celebrating on Liberation Day

KUWAIT Few travellers have Kuwait on their bucket lists, but the country is certainly worth visiting in late February, when its entire population goes into carnival mode to celebrate the end of Iraqi occupation. This came in 1991, at the end of the first Gulf War, and on each anniversary Kuwait City's coastal road witnesses a little conflict of its own. The main instigators are local youths, who arm themselves to the teeth with water bombs and high-calibre water pistols, then wait by the roadsides for passing vehicles. These are easy to spot, since the whole of the seafront road becomes a huge, very wet traffic jam, with the occupants of many cars – and, even more ominously, minivans – armed in a similar manner. In this usually sombre land, it's quite wonderful to witness everyone letting their hair down for the day.

478 | Hanging out in Habalah

SAUDI ARABIA Appearing to dangle from a 250m cliff face over a deep valley, the deserted village of Habalah is an astonishing vision and a truly unique settlement. It takes its name from "habl", meaning "rope" – a reference to the ladders that the long-gone inhabitants used to descend to their dwellings from the plateau above.

These days getting up and down is a little easier. A cable car runs visitors down to the village, offering outstanding views over the dramatic Arabian landscape along the way. Built out of the rock on which they stand, the houses offer a fascinating insight into traditional Saudi life.

Visiting this time-lost place gives a whole new meaning to the phrase "living on the edge".

479 | Trekking the desert mountains of Wadi Halfayn

OMAN In the last few decades Oman has leapt from medieval times into the modern world. Tiny mountain villages are now linked by paved roads, so everyone drives. The villagers love it, and so do hikers keen to explore the old paths that once provided vital trade links over steep ridges into neighbouring valleys. They're now deserted but for the occasional goat herder and a few – very few – hikers.

Craggy peaks, long views and isolation make trekking here an appealing prospect, but coping with minimal water quickly synchs you with the rhythm of the desert. Between villages you have to rely on random pools, and dinner and breakfast may be just dates and crackers washed down with a slug of bottled water. A small oasis the next day makes a great spot for a rehydrating lunch out of the scorching midday sun.

One particularly spectacular three-day loop starts up the Wadi Halfayn valley, where broken irrigation channels and abandoned terraces attest to Oman's rapid urbanization. Sporadic flashes of paint on rocks mark a tortuous route up into the mountains, over a pass then down to the small village of Al Manakhir. A thin smattering of gnarled pines partly shades the route onwards to the palm-fringed village of Hadash, heralded by a lone tower which once fortified this route. The guidebook talks of a route from Hadash into Wadi Bani Rawahah, but an almost sheer 600m-high ridge of mountains blocks the way. It seems highly improbable, but up the route goes – with a few stretches of airy ledges and a couple of rickety tree trunks that have been fashioned into primitive ladders for scaling the steeper sections. From the col it is a 1400m descent down Wadi Bani Rawahah and back to the road. A restorative Coke will never be more welcome.

A far easier option is the three-hour Balcony Walk, which threads its way along an easy but spectacular path into a deep canyon on Jebel Shams, Oman's highest peak at just over 3000m. It ends at a tiny cluster of rough houses tucked under a massive overhang. Until thirty or so years ago people eked out a living directing a single small spring across precipitous terraces. They may have upped sticks for the cities, but the now-untended trees still bear fruit.

480 | Treading in Abraham's footsteps along the West Bank

ISRAEL & THE PALESTINIAN TERRITORIES There are hiking trails, and there are hiking trails. The Abraham Path is a remarkable long-distance route, not least for the fact that it exists at all. Regions don't come much more troubled than the so-called Holy Land, so when the last stretches of a full seventeen-day path through Palestine's West Bank were completed in late 2013, it marked an achievement of rare magnitude. Leading through plummeting canyons, remote villages, holy cities and hillside olive groves, the path makes use of local homestay accommodation and is an astonishing way of getting a feel not only for the region's hospitality but also for its day-to-day realities.

The overall initiative is extraordinary. When fully complete, it's hoped that the Abraham Path will stitch a continuous route through Turkey, Syria, Jordan, Palestine and Israel (there are currently sections open in Turkey, Jordan and Palestine). The trail loosely retraces the on-foot journey made by Abraham himself – a major figure in Christianity, Islam and Judaism – some four thousand years ago, although the thinking behind the modern-day path is focused on comradeship and not on religion.

One of the aims of this non-profit, non-religious and non-political project is to build enduring connections between travellers and the local people whom they meet along the route, and certainly the West Bank trail – which can be walked in stages as short or long as desired – throws up no shortage of enduring encounters. The various staging points, from the storied but troubled city of Hebron to the beer-brewing Christian town of Taybeh, are eye-opening enough, but it's likely to be the walking itself that stays with you.

The landscapes are hilly, tough and stirring, with far-reaching views – a single panorama might encompass a sacred mountain range, an Israeli settlement, the outcrops of Jordan and the banks of the Dead Sea. And underpinning it all is the regional gift for heartfelt hospitality, which sees walkers being accosted by sweet mint tea one hour and waylaid by syrup-thick cardamom coffee the next. By any standards, this is far more than just a hiking trail.

473 | Sipping kahwa with the frankincense sellers

OMAN The bayside urban village of Muttrah is in many ways the true heart of Muscat. Backed by the crumpled Hajar mountains and fronted by sparkling sea, this is the old commercial capital where, for centuries, fish have been hauled in, deals struck and goods from distant continents exchanged. Situated at a crossroads between China, India, East Africa and Europe, Muttrah's impressive natural harbour is one of the most ancient trading places in the Arab world.

After a stroll along the Mediterranean-style corniche you should make a beeline for the souk – the most famous covered marketplace in Oman. Locals come here for fresh produce and household essentials, but for tourists, it's a mine of souvenirs – perfumes, embroidered textiles, chunky silver jewellery, decorative daggers. Always a hive of activity, it's busiest in the evenings.

As you step into the dimly lit labyrinth, you'll immediately catch the dark, resinous scent of stalls burning chunky crystals of frankincense or scoops of *bakhoor* – a blend of oil-soaked woodchips, oud (agarwood),

sandalwood and attar – over charcoal. Frankincense has been harvested in the Dhofar region for milliennia and is emblematic of Oman. Presented in a little casket, it makes a popular souvenir, so you can expect plenty of enthusiastic beckoning from the stallholders.

To encourage you further, they may invite you to try a beaker of aromatic *kahwa*, hand-blended coffee with a hint of cardamom and a camel's kick. To offer *kahwa* is the classic Omani gesture of hospitality, and there's a certain ritual to accepting. It's not done to add milk or sugar; instead you sip it with a juicy local date or a chunk of sweet, rose-scented *halwa*, the Omani answer to fudge. As fast as you finish your cupful, you'll be poured another, unless you shake your beaker between thumb and forefinger to signal you're done.

There's no obligation to buy after this, but if you do, look for *hojari* or *fusoos*, exquisite varieties of frankincense with an intense, citrus note. The paler and larger the chunks, the better. And, yes, should you wish, you can buy gold and myrrh in the souk, too.

474 | Swimming the Wadi Shab

OMAN If Adam and Eve had carried Omani passports, they'd probably have bitten into their poison apple somewhere in the waters of Wadi Shab. Arguably the country's most enchanting destination, the edenic Wadi Shab ("Gorge of Cliffs" in Arabic) runs full of water for much of the year thanks to a series of flash floods and torrential rains. Here, the region's barren rocky desert plains give way to a heavenly oasis decorated with natural, shallow pools of aquamarine water, verdurous plantations and cascading waterfalls, with caverns, grottoes, crevices and sheer rock faces providing a haven from the beating sun.

From the fishing village of Quriyat, follow the bumpy coastal track alongside stretches of white beach to arrive at the *wadi*, bordering a lake. Hop in one of the small rope-pulled ferries to traverse the lagoon, plying your way through the oleander and brush, from where you'll enter a steep, rifted valley, overgrown and shaded with trees,

grasses and date palms. Lazily wade through the azure waters – which should only come up to your knees – before making your way up for a hike along the craggy, winding hills, during which you might even come upon an Omani family, ready to offer traditional dates and coffee. After a good two hours of medium-intensity trekking, you'll arrive at a cave that drops down to a shimmering pool of water. Perch yourself on the ladder and climb down for a well-earned swim while iridescent kingfishers flash past.

Now the tricky part: you'll need to swim through a small keyhole opening in the cavern rock to access a small subaquatic channel. But it's a worthy endeavour, as the channel leads to a second cavernous pool that empties into the mouth of the *wadi* itself, where the idyllic, sandy Fins Beach is adorned with fishing boats and makes a perfect spot for a picnic – assuming you've remembered to waterproof your packed lunch.

475 | Masada: Herod's hilltop palace

ISRAEL & THE PALESTINIAN TERRITORIES The steep cliffs rising out of the Judean Desert look like an unlikely place for a fortress, but there, 400m up, overlooking the Dead Sea, sits the legendary stronghold of Masada. Masada was first fortified in the first century BC by Herod, so scared his people would revolt that he built this virtually impenetrable fortress. There's a cable car for those who don't fancy taking one of the paths that lead up the hill, but for the best experience opt for the ancient snake path, which winds its unsheltered way up the eastern side – an exhausting forty-minute walk. Your reward is an archeological site that appears to dangle over the edge of the precipice, and tremendous views across the desert and the Dead Sea.

476 | Pearl diving in the Persian Gulf

BAHRAIN The largest of their kind in the world, Bahrain's 650 square kilometres of oyster beds have attracted divers since ancient times. Before oil was discovered, the country's economy was dependent upon these little sea treasures, which provided riches where the desert landscape could not.

Pearl diving in those days was an act of great bravery and skill, done without any equipment – divers descended on a weighted rope and spent only one minute under water at a time. Though no longer the industry it was, visitors can now dive this coast themselves – with the benefit of equipment, of course – and unlike the divers of long ago, those lucky enough to find a pearl today are allowed to keep it.

Spot an Arabian Unicorn

OMAN Unicorns do exist. They're alive and thriving in the Arabian desert. The beast, the so-called "Arabian Unicorn", is actually an antelope species: the Arabian oryx, a magnificent white creature whose elegant horns appear to fuse as one when viewed in profile. Unlike the mythological white one-horned unicorn, the hardy antelope has indeed risen from extinction. And that's no fable. The last Arabian oryx in the wild was shot in 1972. A captive-breeding program to save the species was so successful that in 1982 a small population was reintroduced to a protected area, designated as Oman's Arabian Oryx Sanctuary. Today, almost 750 oryx roam the renamed Al Wusta Wildlife Reserve, a remote pristine desert environment inland of the coastal town of Duqm, about 435km south of Muscat. A guided tour with a member of the Harsusi tribe offers your best chance of spotting the Sultanate's national animal in the wild.

471

Sample Beirut's cutting-edge culture

LEBANON It's the most happening place in the Middle East. In Beirut, you can lean over the shoulders of some of the Arab world's most exciting artists, take in thrilling gigs and explore a decidedly hip bar and club scene.

Start your day with a tour of the city's politically charged street art. The roads around the American University, as well as east Beirut, are home to ever-changing images. Expect to see Banksy-style stencil art advocating revolution, the end of religious politics, or LGBTQ rights. It's passionate, often experimental and always controversial.

As well as visual art, there are varied live music shows every night, with even the more popular bands often playing in tiny, packed-out bars for free. You might hear Arabic rhythms over the top of a saxophone, electronic soul in French and Arabic, or funky and impassioned Palestinian hip-hop.

To plan your night you'll need to pick up some of the flyers dumped at the entrance to *T-Marbouta* in Hamra or at the *Art Lounge* bar in Karantina. Then head across town to walk up the hilly Monot Street, home to the city's see-and-be-seen crowd. But Monot is losing its edge to Gemmayze, at the bottom of the hill, a change kick-started by a red-neon-lit bar called *Torino Express*. With a DJ pressed up against the window, it maintains its exclusivity by its sheer size – only a lucky few can squeeze in to this little Lebanese legend.

The bars start emptying out after midnight, when queues start to form at *BO18* and *Sky Bar* – clubs which attract superstar DJs including Judge Jules and Fred Baker. *BO18* is in a converted bunker, and when the sun rises over the Mediterranean, the roof peels back and the party steps up a gear. *Sky Bar*, meanwhile, is patronized by Armani-clad, Hummer-driving playboys. It may all feel a little too cool for school, but on a good day Beirut can rival London or New York.

468 | Finding the real Dubai on a dhow

UNITED ARAB EMIRATES Glamorous, fast and flash, Dubai excites admiration and contempt in equal measure. In a frenzy to find new, post-oil industries fast, the diminutive emirate has turned to tourism, buying, borrowing or stealing the world's most popular attractions. It boasts a ski dome where you can take to the slopes in the sweltering heat of summer, pristine golf courses that unfurl across the desert like great green carpets, dozens of tropical islands fashioned Creation-like from the sand and the sea, and a Venice complete with canals and gondoliers.

If you're looking for culture and traditions under the high-rises and Vegas-style attractions, charter a dhow for a cruise along the city's historic Creek. A piece of history in itself, the dhow has linked the Gulf with Asia and Africa for millennia. Built upon its bows are the fortunes not just of its daring merchant seamen, but also of their city. Unmistakable for its squat shape and distinct, lateen sail, the beautiful boat still plays a key role, transporting the spices, fish,

fruit and vegetables of olden times alongside TVs, fridges, air-conditioners, power-showers and bootlegged liquor.

A cruise up the Creek takes you right through the city's history. Stone, Bronze and Iron Age settlements sprang up on both its sides, living off rich fishing waters. Later came the *barasti*, the famous mud and palm-frond huts of the early pearl divers, who risked their lives until 1929, when the Wall Street Crash and the introduction of the Japanese cultured pearl devastated the industry. On both sides of the Creek rise neat grids, the buildings of the oil boom rising like giant chess pieces: offices, hotels and private residences, each more lavish than the last. Around them, in low-rise sprawls, are the quarters of the Asian immigrants who built them, with their temples, shrines, fabric shops, flower markets and teahouses. Drifting past the sights, smells and sounds of this city, you might just rediscover the one thing Dubai's accused of losing but can never buy: its soul.

469 | Dazzled by the Sultan Qaboos Grand Mosque

OMAN Gazing up into the central dome of Muscat's Grand Mosque is like staring into a giant kaleidoscope. The vortex of the pattern is a chandelier so dazzling you'll have to give your eyes time to adjust before they can take in the rest – a web of intricately inlaid arches and columns of blue and white marble, flanked by timber ceilings, carved and painted in classic Omani style.

This opulent space feels steeped in tradition, but is, in fact, contemporary. The mosque, commissioned and funded by Sultan Qaboos bin Said as a gift to the nation, opened in 2001, the culmination of a design and construction process that lasted almost a decade. Created by the veteran Iraqi architect Mohamed Makiya, it takes traditional Islamic sacred architecture and strips it down to its purest elements. This allows areas of elaborate detail, such as the 50m-high dome in the main *musalla*, or prayer hall, to shine that much more brightly.

Back to the chandelier. It's hard to keep your eyes off this magnificent construction – 14m high, with 600,000 glittering

crystals lit by more than one thousand bulbs – and the smaller (that is, slightly less gigantic) chandeliers that hang like satellites around it, lighting a space large enough to accommodate 6600 worshippers. But if you cast your eyes down, you can admire another of the *musalla*'s miracles – a hand-knotted prayer carpet that's the largest of its type in the world. Measuring 4343 square metres, it took four hundred women from the Iranian province of Khorasan four years to weave its intricate swirls of flowers and foliage in deep red, navy and gold.

Elsewhere in the mosque, you can glide along cool marble cloisters surrounding the inner and outer *sahns*, or courtyards, peer up at the minarets, which symbolize the five pillars of Islam, or visit the relatively modest women's prayer hall, where men are welcome outside prayer times, heralded by the distinctive call of the muezzin. The walls, built of pale Indian sandstone, gleam beautifully in the sun. Whether or not you're a believer, the entire complex, spacious and serene, lends itself perfectly to peaceful contemplation.

470 | On the incense trail in Arabia Felix

OMAN In antiquity, the Romans knew southern Arabia – the area of modern Yemen and the far southwestern tip of Oman – as Arabia Felix, meaning fortunate. This rugged land was so named for its fabulous wealth, derived from trade in exotic goods such as spices, perfumes, ivory and alabaster (most of them brought from India) and, above all, locally cultivated frankincense and myrrh.

The incense trail was followed, in ancient times, by camel caravan from Salalah, regional capital of Oman's Dhofar region and traditionally regarded as the source of the world's finest frankincense, to Petra in Jordan. Plunging into the alleys of Salalah's souk is a heady experience. Here, hemmed in by coconut groves, stalls and shops are crammed tightly together, offering everything from snack foods to textiles and jewellery. The air is filled with the cries of hawkers, the sweet smell of perfumes and the rich, lemony scents of frankincense and myrrh.

Prohibitively expensive commodities in the ancient world, frankincense and myrrh were offered by two of the wise men as gifts to the newborn Christ. They were also essential to religious ritual in every temple in every town. Buying them today is a fascinating business: shopkeepers will show you crystals of varying purity, sold by grade and weight; most people sniff each crystal before choosing. Coals and an ornate little pottery burner complete the fascinating purchase.

After Salalah, you can follow your own incense trail. However, if, as is highly likely, spending several months on a camel to Petra doesn't appeal, perhaps head for the "lost" city of Ubar, the legendary centre of Arabia's frankincense trade, reputed to lie near Shisr, where a permanent water source irrigates Oman's most highly prized groves.

SAUDI ARABIA The Empty Quarter is well named. Covering an area the size of Belgium, Holland and France combined, it is almost entirely devoid of life. With its constantly changing colour, vast, ever-shifting dunes and eerie silence, it's quite simply the most mesmerizing desert in the world.

Since ancient times, frankincense and spice caravans – sometimes in the form of hundreds of plodding camels – risked sandstorms, quicksand, tribal wars and vast well-less stretches. European explorers dreamt of conquering this challenging terrain, and wrote of whole raiding parties swallowed by the sands.

Once home to the fascinating Bedu, who regarded the dunes with reverence, the desert today hosts the Arabian oryx, endemic to the region and one of the most beautiful creatures on Earth, around two dozen species of plants (many of which lie dormant beneath the surface, ready to spring to life on the slightest suggestion of rain) and hundreds of species of insects.

Visiting the Empty Quarter requires serious preparation. With few if any useful maps, very little chance of meeting another human being, and extremely low chances of survival in the case of stranding, you need to travel well prepped and well equipped. Most visitors choose to join a tour run by any of several reputable local tour companies. Knowledgeable and experienced, they can also organize the many permissions and passes required for a foray into the Empty Quarter. Guides, tents and even camels can also be arranged.

When you're in the midst of the sands, the desert's Arabic name, Rub al-Khali (the "Abode of Silence"), seems utterly apposite. Devoid of bird song, the sound of grazing or the slightest sign of human habitation, it is instead the 55°C heat which seems to hum. Darkening as the day grows long, the sand dunes turn a deep crimson at dusk, resembling a giant damask cloth thrown from heaven across the Earth.

The Abode of Silence: the most beautiful desert on Earth

464 | Carving a path through Persepolis

IRAN You begin to feel the historical weight of Persepolis as you drive down the tree-lined approach, long before reaching the actual site. Here, on the dusty plain of Marvdasht at the foot of the Zagros Mountains, the heat is ferocious, but nothing can detract from the sight before you: a once-magnificent city, looming high above the plain on a series of terraces.

You enter through the massive, crumbling stone Gate of All Nations, adorned with cuneiform inscriptions that laud the mighty Persian emperor whose father built the city across a gap of 2500 years, "I am Xerxes, king of kings, son of Darius…". Walking between great carved guardian bulls standing to attention on either side of the gate, you come out on a vast terrace, stretching almost 500m along each side.

It's not the scale, though, but the details – specifically the carvings – that make Persepolis special. Wherever you look, they indicate what went on in each area: in private quarters, bas-reliefs show servants carrying platters of food; in the Hall of Audience, Darius is being borne aloft by representatives of 28 nations, their arms interlinked. Everywhere you can trace the intricately worked details of curly beards and the even more impressive expressions of body language that show the skill of the ancient artists.

The centrepiece is the ruined Apadana Palace, where you come nose to nose with elaborately carved depictions of the splendours of Darius the Great's empire – royal processions, horse-drawn chariots and massed ranks of armed soldiers. Look closer and you'll spot human-headed winged lions, carved alongside esoteric symbols of the deity Ahura Mazda. Begun around 518 BC by Darius to be the centrepiece of his vast empire, Persepolis was a demonstration of Persian wealth and sophistication – and it shows.

465 | Wild camping on the Arabian Peninsula

OMAN The traditions of the Bedouin nomad lie at the heart of the Omani culture, and making temporary shelter wherever you need comes as part of the deal. Wild camping, or pitching a tent on public land, is an extension of this and legal in Oman. The sheer variety of terrain – the sculpted dunes of the desert sands, the jagged drama of the towering mountains – means you're spoilt for choice.

A trip into the eastern desert is unmissable. Travellers can use the *Bidiya Desert Camp* as orientation, but do strike off into the depth of the dunes, to set up camp. Oman has some of the highest dunes in the world, with the largest recorded at 455m, and they reveal their magic as the sun slides down behind the golden peaks. Don't be fooled into thinking the sweeping sands are barren of life; scarab beetles scuttle beneath a spangled swathe of midnight sky, while desert foxes skulk at a distance looking for scraps.

Remote beaches don't come more inaccessible than Bar al Hikmān, perched on the edge of a peninsula on the country's east coast. Travelling here, past mirage-like salt flats, their harsh glitter as prelude of the sea to come, is almost as good as your arrival. Here you can pitch your tent on the spit of white sand between the sea and a lagoon, complete with a flamboyance of flamingos. It's easy to spend a few days, swimming in the warm sea, birdwatching and even turtle spotting. If you're lucky you can buy or barter fish to barbecue from local fisherman.

The best way to finish your trip is with a tour into the Jebel Akhdar mountains, part of the Al Hajar range which spans much of the country from east to west. Despite the angular peaks it's easy to find the flat plateaus on which to make a camp. Sitting outside your tent watching the sunrise soar above a sheer canyon that plummets down 3000m is a destination you'll be hard-pressed to match.

466 | Discovering the 'other' Louvre

UNITED ARAB EMIRATES Where the world's largest art museum in Paris is all Mona Lisa drama and contemporary pyramidal architecture, its Middle East counterpart celebrates the wider region's Islamic heritage, from ancient civilization to lesser-known Arab pieces. Rumours persist that it cost £3 billion to build, but as it's constructed half on land, half floating above the Arabian Gulf, it needs to be seen to be believed.

Oil-rich Abu Dhabi excels at beyond-five-star hotels, out-of-this-world theme parks and grandstanding architectural schemes, and the much-hyped, much-delayed Louvre Abu Dhabi is that very thing. It opened in November 2017 as the centrepiece of the work-in-progress Saadiyat Cultural District, which will eventually welcome the Guggenheim Abu Dhabi (designed by Frank Gehry) and Zayed National Museum (envisioned by Sir Norman Foster). The idea is this art-lover's Xanadu is intended to be a regional catalyst for cultural metamorphosis, with the Louvre's galleries presenting a pantheon of three hundred pieces on loan from the original in Paris. After that, the hope is the museum will have purchased enough of its own treasures at auction.

Despite the hyperbole, a visit should be compulsory – no matter how long your stay in the capital of the Emirates. Start under the museum's star-spangled dome, created by French architect Jean Nouvel. Light rains down through its starry latticework, creating ever-variegated, arabesque patterns on the concrete floor and it's more than a distraction before you can continue your art tour into the bitesize, medina-like galleries.

Here, globetrotting highlights include works by Jackson Pollock and Mark Rothko and masterpieces by Henri Matisse and Pablo Picasso. As your journey continues, look out for Vincent van Gogh's *Self-Portrait*, Da Vinci's *La Belle Ferronnière*, Claude Monet's *The Saint-Lazare Station*, and Chinese provocateur Ai Weiwei's Tower of Babel-like crystal fountain, one of several pieces specially commissioned for the museum. Plan for a good half-day to get even just a hint of its vast aspirations.

Need to know

444 Habiba (W habibahsweets.com), Jabri and Zalatimo (W zalatimosweets.com) have numerous stores across Amman.

445 *Abu Shukri*'s is at the fifth Station of the Cross on the Via Dolorosa, near the Damascus Gate.

446 Although the Middle East has a reputation for chaotic traffic and a lack of road rules, outside the city of Amman the small population and well-maintained road system make driving in Jordan (W visitjordan .com) relatively pain-free.

447 For more information see W whc.unesco.org. A limited number of tourist visas are issued each year to groups travelling to Saudi Arabia on organized tours (W saudiembassy.net).

448 Drum Beach is next to the large structure that used to be the Dolphinarium, beside Banana Beach and about halfway between Tel Aviv and Jaffa.

449 Check out W rscn.org.jo.

450 Tour operators around the world have diving packages to the Red Sea, and dive centres in Aqaba offer PADI and other international diving courses. Try W aqabadivingseastar.com or W diveaqaba.com.

451 Khasab Travel and Tours (W khasabtours.com) runs cruises on the Musandam Fjords; otherwise, try Shaw Travel (W shawtravel.com), who include the Musandam Fjords in some of their Oman itineraries.

452 The I-Imam Mosque, Sheikh Lotfollah Mosque and Ali Qapu Palace are all open daily. Always check the latest safety advice before travelling to Iran.

453 Most shops in the Deira Gold Souk follow similar hours (Sat–Thurs 10am–10pm, Fri 4–10pm). See also W definitelydubai.com.

454 Khor al-Adaid lies 75km south of Doha, the Qatari capital. No roads run even close. The only way to get here is in a 4WD vehicle organized by any of several tour companies: try W gulf-adventures.com. For more information see W auth.qatartourism.gov.qa.

455 Tawi Attair is located in southwest Oman. You'll need a 4WD to access the area, which you can rent in nearby Salaha. See also W omantourism.gov.om.

456 Bsharri, with the most accommodation options in the Qadisha Valley, is the best place to base yourself while exploring. Although a car is handy, regular buses zip between the villages.

457 Lebanon's ski season runs late Dec–early April. For information on runs, resorts, weather conditions and lift prices, check out W skileb.com.

458 The stalls at Mahane Yehuda (Sun–Thurs 8am–7pm, Fri 8am–3pm; W machne.co.il/en) are closed for the Sabbath on Saturday, but many restaurants remain open. The market can be reached on the Jerusalem Light Rail – it has its own station, three stops from the Damascus Gate.

459 The Jesus Trail (W jesustrail.com) is fully waymarked. A guidebook, and topographical map, are available online and in bookshops in Nazareth and Jerusalem.

460 A number of operators offer dolphin-watching trips; try W zaharatours.com.

461 The country's finest meze restaurants are in the town of Zahlé, just over an hour's drive east of Beirut.

462 Buses to Varzaneh leave from Isfahan's Jey terminal (1hr 30min; IRR50,000). Walking to the dunes is possible, but a taxi is the most cost-effective way to cover most of Varzaneh's sights in a day. To book *Negaar Varzaneh Guesthouse*, see W negaarhouse.com.

463 Petra (daily 6am–sunset) is 240km south of the Jordanian capital, Amman. The adjacent town of Wadi Musa has restaurants and hotels. Check out W petranationaltrust.org.

464 All visitors to Iran require a visa. Persian Voyages (W persianvoyages.com) can organize a trip.

465 You can pick up everything you need in Muscat. Noman Tours W nomadtours.com can organize all equipment, guides and a 4WD. It's recommended that you don't go into the desert alone – local guides are on hand to orientate you. For info on *Bidiya Desert Camp*, see W bidiyah-desert.com.

466 Check W louvreabudhabi.ae for opening hours and ticket prices.

467 A small number of tourist visas are issued each year for visitors to Saudi travelling on organized tours only. Check out W saudiembassy.net.

468 A number of Dubai travel companies run dhow cruises, including Al-Boom Tourist Village (W alboom .ae), which offers various cruises.

469 The Sultan Qaboos Grand Mosque (W sultan-qaboosgrandmosque.com), in Ghubrah, Muscat, is the only Omani mosque that both Muslims and non-Muslims are routinely permitted to visit (Sat–Thurs 8–11am). Respectful behaviour is expected and arms and legs covered. Women should also cover their hair.

470 Salalah is 1000km southwest of Muscat, served by regular worldwide flights.

471 *T-Marbouta* is on Hamra Square, *Art Lounge* is opposite the Forum de Beyrouth in the Karantina area (a 10min taxi ride from Achrafiyeh), *Torino Express* is in the heart of Gemmayze, *BO18* is near the Forum de Beyrouth (you'll need a taxi to find it) and *Sky Bar* (W skybarbeirut.com) is in the BIEL centre, downtown.

472 The Sultanate of Oman Ministry of Tourism can help you plan a visit to Al Wusta Wildlife Reserve. See W bit.ly/OmanMinistryTourism.

473 Muttrah Souk (Sat–Thurs 8am–1pm & 5–9pm, Fri 5–9pm) is on the Muttrah corniche (Al Bahri Rd), northeast of central Muscat.

474 Wadi Shab is near the coast between Muscat and Sur and requires a 4WD vehicle to access.

475 Buses run to Masada (W whc.unesco.org) from Jerusalem, Tel Aviv, Beersheba and Eilat.

476 For more on visiting Bahrain, see W bahrain.com.

477 Liberation Day falls on 26 Feb each year; since it's mainly a local affair, it's usually easy (though never cheap) to find a hotel room.

478 Habalah is about 75km from Abha, near Saudi Arabia's southwestern tip. A limited number of non-business visas are issued to groups travelling to Saudi on organized tours. See W saudiembassy.net.

479 The trekking season runs Dec–Feb. Bus services are limited, so renting a car works better. *Adventure Trekking in Oman*, by Anne Dale and Jerry Hadwin, is the best guide, with reasonable maps.

480 The Abraham Path website gives details of the thinking behind, and the various stages of, the route (W abrahampath.org). The Siraj Center (W sirajcenter .org) arranges guided walks in the West Bank.

RUSSIA

ARCTIC
OCEAN

Arctic Circle

ALASKA

BERING
SEA

502

505

510

514

Gulf of Alaska

Hudson
Bay

C A N A D A

487
MAINE

VERMONT

WASHINGTON

499

526

OREGON

MONTANA

NORTH
DAKOTA

508

MINNESOTA

509
521

NH
495

537

504

WISCONSIN

488

MICHIGAN

NEW
YORK

539
MA
CT

RI

IDAHO

SOUTH
DAKOTA

501

PENNSYLVANIA

497

534
538

511

WYOMING

IOWA

DELAWARE

NJ

525

NEBRASKA

ILLINOIS

INDIANA

482

OHIO

484

WEST
VIRGINIA

VIRGINIA

506
MARYLAND

540

485
520
517

493

494

NEVADA

UTAH

527

515

541

COLORADO

KANSAS

496

MISSOURI

KENTUCKY

519

NORTH
CAROLINA

522

CALIFORNIA

531

512
536

523

492

ARIZONA

NEW
MEXICO

489

530

ARKANSAS

503

TENNESSEE

513

OKLAHOMA

MISSISSIPPI

ALABAMA

533

507

GEORGIA

483

SOUTH
CAROLINA

ATLANTIC
OCEAN

UNITED STATES
OF AMERICA

PACIFIC
OCEAN

TEXAS

518

529

LOUISIANA

528
532

FLORIDA

490

524

500

491
535

Gulf of Mexico

CUBA

M E X I C O

PACIFIC
OCEAN

486

498

HAWAII

481

BELIZE

HONDURAS

JAMAICA

CARIBBEAN
SEA

GUATEMALA

EL SALVADOR

PANAM

PACIFIC OCEAN

COSTA
RICA

USA

481–541

The Land of Opportunity. Uncle Sam. The Home of the Brave. Call it what you will, no single nickname could ever encapsulate the full depth of the US – any nation that can marry cities as life-filled as New York, San Francisco, LA and Chicago with landscapes as breathtaking as those of Alaska, Arizona and Hawaii is beyond easy summary. Its rewards come in droves, from all-American icons like baseball, blues and bourbon to the unbridled spectacles of Mardi Gras, Burning Man or showtime Las Vegas, and the vibrant traditions of its native peoples. That's not to mention extraordinary experiences like a moose safari in Maine, camping in the mighty Yellowstone and walking among giants at Sequoia National Park. As a travel destination, its possibilities stretch to the far horizon.

481 Sidestepping ash and lava on Kilauea

HAWAII Hawaiian islands are the summits of volcanoes rooted 20,000ft below the Pacific. The youngest of these volcanoes, Kilauea on the Big Island, has been erupting continuously ever since 1983. Mark Twain described its crater as a dazzling lake of fire, but the action these days is lower down its flanks, where molten lava explodes directly into the ocean.

I parked my car where the Chain of Craters Road, which winds from the crater down to the sea, was abruptly blocked by fresh black lava. No path set off beyond; instead I picked my way through broken slabs, and stepped across mysterious cracks, dodging the vapours that hissed from gashes in the rock. I finally found myself ten feet above the crashing waves, on a precarious "bench" of lava. Down at sea level, a sluggish river of incandescent rock churned into the water, amid plumes of steam and evil-smelling gases. Other hikers prodded at the eggshell crust with sticks, to see if they could break through to the river beneath their feet and set the wood ablaze.

Once the sun went down, the molten glow of the lava was the only light. A small cone of fine ash had formed at the seafront. As I climbed it, my feet sank deep with every step, and sent a fine powder slithering down. From the top I looked down into a fiery orange pool that gently bubbled and popped, sending up phlegmy strings of rock. There were three or four people nearby, silhouetted against the orange clouds.

A sudden thud from below, solid as a hammer stroke, made my knees buckle. As I turned, the volcano nonchalantly spewed a shower of rocks high into the air. Now I felt entitled to run, though wading through thick volcanic ash felt more like a slow-motion nightmare. I struggled to speed up, all too aware that it was a matter of pure luck whether any of the lumps overhead would hit me.

As it turned out, a glowing boulder larger than my head thumped down six feet away. I crept back to examine it, bright orange on the black moonscape, then stumbled away through the night.

Greg Ward
has written sixteen travel, history and music books for Rough Guides as sole author, and has contributed to many more. He has also written and edited books for several other publishers.

INDIANA "Start your engines!" With that, the crowd noise roars to a deafening crescendo, and 33 cars line up to await the start of the most thrilling speedway race in the world. The numbers boggle the mind: two hundred tension-filled laps, speeds topping off around 230mph, more than 300,000 spectators, $14-million-plus in prize money. The Indy 500 is an electrifying experience, not to mention the event that best embodies the American obsession with getting somewhere *fast* – in this case, right back where you started.

Visitors come for the glitz and glamour as well as the star-power of legends like Mario Andretti, hailed as the greatest driver of all time, who conquered Indy in 1969 and has since watched his sons, grandson and nephew compete. But the race is not without its homespun midwestern charm: rather than a champagne spray, the winner's celebratory libation is … milk, a tradition since 1937,

after three-time winner Louis Meyer chugged a glass of buttermilk in Victory Lane the year before. The garage area is still referred to as Gasoline Alley, even though the cars run on methanol, and the final practice race is known as "Carb day", despite the switch to fuel-injection systems.

If the ear-splitting noise and heart-stopping speeds don't provide enough of a rush, pivoting your foot on the accelerator of a real 600 horsepower V-8 Nascar certainly will. The Richard Petty Driving Experience allows you to experience first hand the thrill of Indy-car racing on the actual Indy track. After being kitted out in racing suits, each class of around twenty aspiring Andrettis is given a crash course in safety, driving instructions and an introduction to the philosophy of "trust the car" before competing for the fastest average lap speed. If your blood's not racing when you step out of the car, you must be made of stone.

Hitting the track at the Indianapolis 500

482

483 | Strolling through downtown Savannah

GEORGIA When an intrepid British Utopian named James Oglethorpe founded Savannah in 1733, he thought he could tame the local marshes and alligators without the aid of slaves or even hard liquor. The latter ban fell by the wayside less than twenty years later, and Savannahians have been devoted to immoderation ever since. Any walking tour of the three-square-mile downtown historic district should, for tradition's sake, be accompanied by a cold beer in a perfectly legal "to-go cup". (The traditional local tipple, Chatham Artillery Punch, is more safely appreciated sitting down, however.)

One element of Oglethorpe's vision that did stick was the city's layout – a patchwork of grids and squares that has become 21 miniature parks, each offering a different proportion of dappled shade, fountains and monuments. The squares are most alluring in the spring, when the azalea, dogwood and honey-rich magnolia trees are in full bloom. But even in the thick of an August heat wave, when the air is like a sauna and the greenery is growing wildly up the cast-iron balconies, the squares offer a respite from the untamed mugginess. The sunlight shimmers through craggy oak boughs and Spanish moss, the cicadas drone and cars motor laconically around the cobblestone streets. The stately homes that face each square represent all of the most decadent styles of the eighteenth and nineteenth centuries: Neoclassical, Federal, Regency, Georgian, French Second Empire and Italianate.

"The Belle of Georgia", as the city is known, hasn't always been so; for much of the twentieth century, decadence had slipped into outright decay. But in 1955, seven elderly ladies banded together against developers to prevent the 1821 Davenport House from being turned into a parking lot, and the Historic Savannah Foundation was born. Fortunately, no such effort is required of today's casual visitor – you can just stroll, sip your drink and watch the centuries roll by.

484 | In high spirits on the Bourbon Trail

KENTUCKY What is the spirit of the United States? Ask an average citizen or, worse, a politician, and you may get a rambling metaphysical reply longer than the Bill of Rights. Ask a seasoned bartender, however, and you'll get that rarest of responses, the one-word answer: bourbon.

The country's sole native spirit and, thanks to a congressional declaration, its official one as well, bourbon is a form of whiskey. Technically speaking, the grain used to make bourbon must be at least 51 percent corn, and it must be aged for a minimum of two years inside charred, white-oak barrels – though both the percentage and years are typically much greater.

And while bourbon can be produced elsewhere, the spirit of the spirit resides in Kentucky, which is not only home to the finest distilleries, but also, according to local legend, its birthplace. Late eighteenth-century settlers in Bourbon County are said to have combined their extra corn harvests with local iron-free water to make the fabled whiskey.

The best place to find out more is along the Bourbon Trail, a meandering route through the rolling hills of central Kentucky that links several distilleries and historic towns. Must-sees include Loretto, where you can watch the deliciously smooth Maker's Mark being produced in a picture-perfect setting laced with green pastures and well-preserved nineteenth-century buildings like the Master Distiller's House, and the Jim Beam Distillery an hour's drive away in Clermont, whose pedestrian main brand is augmented by several "small batch" potions, like the fiery Knob Creek and silky Basil Hayden's, which can be sampled on-site.

Tucked in between the two is friendly Bardstown, the state's second-oldest city, which is home to the Oscar Getz Museum of Whiskey History and September's lively Bourbon Festival. Book a bed at the *Old Talbott Tavern*, whose former guests have included Abraham Lincoln and Daniel Boone, and you'll only have a few steps to walk after an evening spent using your new-found knowledge comparing local bourbons at the bar.

485 | Spending a weekend in Wine Country

CALIFORNIA With its rolling green hills, bucolic landscapes and small towns heavy on antique charm, California's Wine Country, centring on Napa and Sonoma valleys, is among the most beautiful places in the West. Beyond touring the wineries – Beringer, Silver Oak, Stag's Leap, Robert Mondavi and many more, all of which allow you to sample the goods – there's no shortage of things to see and do. Come here for a weekend retreat (preferably not at the peak of summer, when the hordes descend), and your first instinct might be to pack in as much as possible. But in a place where the main point is to relax, indulge and melt away the stresses of modern life, that's the last thing you should do.

Instead, aim for just a few choice tastes of the good life. Start with a spot of nature, either driving the Silverado Trail (parallel to Hwy-29), taking in the mountains and vineyards along the way, or enjoying a peaceful walk through the woods in Jack London State Historic Park, once ranchland owned by the famed naturalist writer. Next, rest your aching bones and revitalize your senses by checking into one of the luxury spa resorts near Calistoga. At Dr Wilkinson's Hot Springs, dip yourself in a mix of heated mineral water and volcanic ash, or, at Mount View Spa, enjoy the mud baths and herbal applications, as well as aromatherapy, hydrotherapy and other refined New Age treatments that pamper both the body and the soul.

Round out your experience with a great, even legendary, meal at one of the region's many gourmet restaurants; these days the area is known as much for food as the vino. Foremost among these is Thomas Keller's *French Laundry*, an icon of California Cuisine known for its blend of fresh local ingredients and creative, spellbinding presentation. It won't come cheap and you'll have to reserve months in advance, but it's reason enough to visit.

Finding paradise on Kauai's north shore

HAWAII Kauai is the Hawaii you dream about. Spectacular South Seas scenery, white-sand beaches, pounding surf, laidback island life – it's all here. While the other Hawaiian islands have the above to varying degrees, none has quite the breathtaking beauty nor sheer variety of beguiling landscapes of Kauai. And none has a shoreline as magnificent as the Na Pali Coast ("the cliffs" in Hawaiian), where lush valleys are separated by staggering knife-edge ridges of rock, some towering almost 3000ft tall and all clad in glowing green vegetation that makes them resemble vast pleated velvet curtains.

The one road that circles Kauai peters out on the North Shore. Shrinking ever narrower to cross a series of one-lane wooden bridges, it finally gives up where lovely Ke'e Beach nestles at the foot of a mighty mountain. Swim out a short distance here, and you'll glimpse the mysterious, shadowy cliffs in the distance, dropping into the ocean.

Now deserted, the remote valleys beyond the end of the road once supported large Hawaiian populations, who navigated the fearsome waves between them in canoes. The only way to reach the valleys these days is on foot. One of the world's great hikes, the eleven-mile Kalalau Trail is a long, muddy scramble: one moment you're perched high above the Pacific on an exposed ledge, and the next you're wading a fast-flowing mountain stream. Your reward at the far end – an irresistible campsite on a long golden beach, where you can breathe the purest air on Earth, explore the tumbling waterfalls of Kalalau Valley and then gaze at the star-filled sky long into the night – is a little slice of heaven.

On a moose safari in Maine

MAINE You don't need a Maine Moose Calling Championship winner to tell you the Great North Woods in the northeast of New England are special. But it does help to have one like Chris Young – a veteran who's spent 35 years tracking the creatures – guide you.

Firstly, he can introduce golden ponds and fairy-tale hemlock forests, taking you to rarely visited backcountry for fishing and hunting. But, more importantly, he leads spine-tingling canoe and walking safaris to track moose, because a thriving population of 25,000 live in the woods outside his hometown, Greenville.

What helps Young locate the elusive beasts is his almost unheard-of bushcraft. At first the moose remain invisible, but after hearing the guide's aggressive calls – ranging from a looping grunt to a throaty bark – they slowly appear from the shadows. And as you eyeball a 800lb bull with an antler rack as wide as a bus, the realization hits you: how could you ever think Maine was so tame?

488 | Getting hooked on Michigan's historic Fishtown

MICHIGAN There's a certain surreality to Fishtown, a waterfront resort and historic village in Leland, Michigan. Unlike living history museums, where actors parade around in period costumes and have somewhat stilted interactions with twenty-first-century visitors, in Fishtown, establishments dating back to the early 1900s are more likely to be manned by teens in hoodies and jeans. Modern commercial fishing still takes place from these weathered docks, with vintage vessels, the *Janice Sue* and *Joy*, bringing in more than 50,000lb of fish annually.

The juxtaposition of old and new is most pronounced in the wooden shanties and boardwalk lining the rather miniscule Leland River. Their silvered boards reveal decades of exposure to Michigan's notoriously harsh winters and heavy use as net-mending shacks and icehouses. But crossing the threshold into one of these rustic structures will quickly extinguish that line of nostalgic reverie. Under the auspices of the non-profit Fishtown Preservation Society, these fishermen's shacks have been reincarnated as retail space and eateries. The former offers everything from T-shirts to assorted tchotchkes (trinkets); the latter are likely of greater interest to the intrepid global traveller.

First stop: *Carlson's Fish*. An offshoot of the Carlson family's commercial fishing business, which was established in 1904, this shop serves up maple-smoked jerky and a highly addictive whitefish paté, both made using Fishtown's still-operational smokehouses. Head to the *Village Cheese Shanty* for one (or more) of twenty made-to-order sandwiches. Anything on a pretzel bun is recommended, and all sandwiches cost $6.75. The award-winning shop also sells craft brews, regional wines and local products made from cherries, a major Michigan agricultural crop. Sit-down restaurants tend toward the casual, with seafood-centric menus, waterfront views and maritime-inspired decor.

Leland's past-present *pas de deux* normalizes outside the cluster of waterfront shanties, giving way to a quaint downtown-ish area that is timeless Middle America. Along North Main Street, painted-brick retail spaces house quirky boutiques and galleries. The white clapboard Old Art Building, constructed as a community centre in 1922, delivers art classes and exhibitions. From Leland, you can also venture further afield to the North and South Manitou Islands, administered by the National Park Service, via Manitou Island Transit. Traverse City, home to the National Cherry Festival, and the Leelanau Peninsula Wine Trail are both within an hour's drive of storied Fishtown.

489 | Chasing storms in Tornado Alley

KANSAS, NEBRASKA & OKLAHOMA The central plains may not seem the likeliest of places to find a weather wonder, but every long, hot summer these cornfield-flat states play witness to some of the most powerful storms on Earth.

In fact, Mother Nature gets so aggressive around here, and with such consistency, that the area – along with Texas – has been dubbed "Tornado Alley" thanks to the record number of funnel and wedge tornadoes that batter its turf each year.

This is ideal twister-tracking territory. Behind every great storm is an even greater equipped team of daredevil stormchasers who specialize

in stalking tornados across the central plains from vans loaded with the latest in GPS systems, Doppler radars, satellites and lightning-detector sensors.

You can join these professionals on the hunt, keeping an eye on the skies as they try to anticipate growing storms. With every cloud-gathering there is a tingle of expectation, and the hope that this is the one they're looking for: a supercell.

The holy grail of high winds – capable of spreading as far as a mile wide and reaching up to 300mph – this is the biggest and baddest of them all.

490 | Scoping out the scene on Miami's Ocean Drive

FLORIDA At sundown, the main promenade of Miami's hedonistic South Beach was like a gigantic movie set, where several different films were being shot simultaneously.

A 1978 Mustang pulled up outside the *Kent Hotel* and three Latino men, designer shirts unbuttoned almost down to the navel and sporting heavy gold chains, stepped out in what could have been a scene from *Scarface*. A bronzed male rollerblader in a "Gold's Gym" tank top wove between the pedestrian traffic that crept past the thoroughfare's swanky cocktail lounges, thrusting his hips from left to right, a gasping Pomeranian struggling to keep up. Crossing the road in the direction of the beach brought the area's famed Art Deco buildings perfectly into view – a strip of pastel yellows, blues and oranges bathed so dramatically in the fading sunlight that you could have been standing in the middle of a Disney cartoon.

As sunbathers gradually left the beach, a couple of real-life Barbie dolls with tiny waists and enormous chests lingered on the sand to be filmed for some such internet site. The poolside at the *Clevelander* began to fill up with Spring Break schmoozers and the latest movers and shakers. Electronic music that earlier had drifted gently from hotel lobbies was now being pumped out in energetic beats, heralding the transformation of twilight's languorous Ocean Drive into night-time's frenetic strip of revelry – clubbers flashed synthetically manufactured smiles as they hurried to the latest place to see and be seen in. Young hostesses talked to passers-by who paused to have a look at the expensive restaurant menu they were touting, and the waitress at the *Kent* scribbled her number on a napkin when one of the three Latinos from the Mustang asked her about the new club she was heading to after her shift.

Just another day in the neighbourhood.

491 | Celebrating Fantasy Fest in Key West

FLORIDA The saucy climax of Key West's calendar, capping the end of hurricane season in October, is a week-long party known as Fantasy Fest. The old town is transformed into an outdoor costume bash, somewhat tenuously pegged to Halloween; really, it's a LGBTQ-heavy take on Mardi Gras, with campy themes (past ones have included "Freaks, Geeks and Goddesses" and "TV Jeebies") and flesh-flashing costumes.

The week is punctuated with offbeat events, like the pet costume contest where dogs and their owners dress the same, and a sequin-spangled satire of a high-school prom. On Saturday, the final parade slinks down the main drag, Duval Street, on a well-lubricated, booze-fuelled route.

It's not surprising that such an irresistibly kitschy shindig should have emerged and endured in Key West. Save San Francisco, there's nowhere in America more synonymous with out and proud LGBTQ life than this final,

isolated, all-but-an-island in the Florida Keys – the town's been a byword for homocentric hedonism since the sexually liberated 1970s.

In many ways, though, Key West's queer reputation is misleading. Sure, it's still a LGBTQ hotspot, as the thong-sporting go-go boys, who wield their crotches like weapons in bars along Duval Street, attest. But what drew the gay community here in the first place was the town's liberal all-inclusiveness; be who you want to be, the locals say, whatever that is. It's all summed up by the town's official motto: "One Human Family". Indeed, Key West welcomes everyone, from President Truman, who holed up in the so-called Little White House here in the 1940s, to an oddball bar owner like "Buddy" today, who built his ramshackle café-pub, *B.O.'s Fish Wagon*, out of piles of junk. After a few days, these kinds of visual quirks seem quite standard – except maybe that pet costume contest.

492 | Snakes and ladders in the desert Southwest

NEW MEXICO Until recently, visitors to the Southwest were encouraged to puzzle over the mystery of the so-called Anasazi. Supposedly, these early native Americans vanished a thousand years ago, leaving only enigmatic ruins like the "cliff palaces" of Colorado's Mesa Verde and Arizona's magnificent Canyon de Chelly.

Now the word itself has disappeared. The Anasazi have been restyled as the "Ancestral Puebloans", on the indisputable basis that today's Pueblo peoples are their direct descendants. Nowhere is the continuity between ancient and modern more apparent than at Puyé Cliff Dwellings in New Mexico. Around 1250 AD, migrants from Mesa Verde settled here, close to the Rio Grande. Three centuries later, just after the first Spanish explorers arrived, they made one final shift, moving slightly nearer the river to establish Santa Clara Pueblo.

Santa Clara Indians now lead tours of their people's former home, a rare opportunity to visit an ancient site with members of the very group who built it. It's a dramatic spot, set against cliffs of volcanic stone so soft

that individual "apartments" were hollowed out using only wooden tools. Here and there, personalized figures above the doorways, some carrying bows and arrows, seem to denote who lived in each dwelling; it's so vivid, you almost expect to find them still there. The apartments are stacked in parallel tiers, strung along narrow ledges and linked by ladders. A note of tension is added by the rattlesnakes that stretch across the ledges to catch the sun, turning visits into a real-life game of snakes-and-ladders.

As you climb the cliff face, the guide picks up pottery sherds and stone blades, explaining how and why they were made. You hear tales of conflict and cooperation with first the Spanish and then the Americans, and of how traditional beliefs and spiritual practices have adapted over the centuries, forming a new synthesis with Catholicism. Finally you reach the mesa-top, to find the ruins of a massive circular dwelling. Looking out across the spectacular valley, side by side with a descendant of its earliest inhabitants, you feel as though you're seeing it with new – or rather, timeless – eyes.

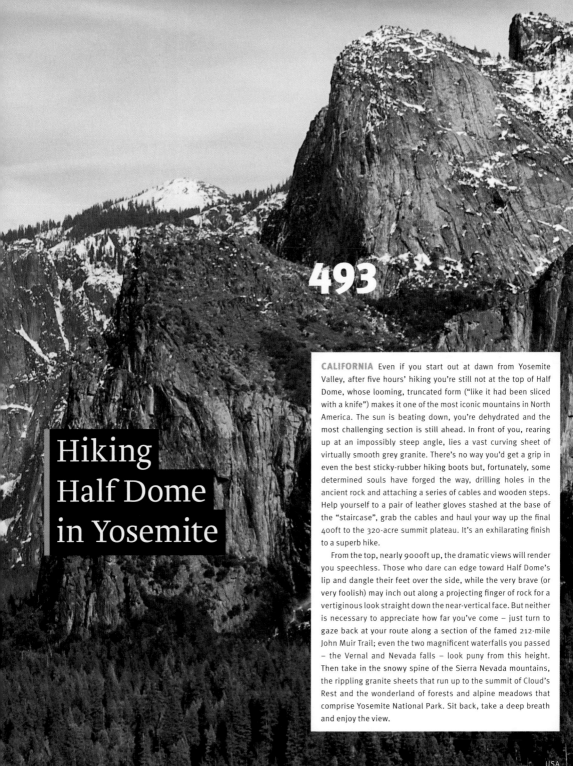

493

Hiking Half Dome in Yosemite

CALIFORNIA Even if you start out at dawn from Yosemite Valley, after five hours' hiking you're still not at the top of Half Dome, whose looming, truncated form ("like it had been sliced with a knife") makes it one of the most iconic mountains in North America. The sun is beating down, you're dehydrated and the most challenging section is still ahead. In front of you, rearing up at an impossibly steep angle, lies a vast curving sheet of virtually smooth grey granite. There's no way you'd get a grip in even the best sticky-rubber hiking boots but, fortunately, some determined souls have forged the way, drilling holes in the ancient rock and attaching a series of cables and wooden steps. Help yourself to a pair of leather gloves stashed at the base of the "staircase", grab the cables and haul your way up the final 400ft to the 320-acre summit plateau. It's an exhilarating finish to a superb hike.

From the top, nearly 9000ft up, the dramatic views will render you speechless. Those who dare can edge toward Half Dome's lip and dangle their feet over the side, while the very brave (or very foolish) may inch out along a projecting finger of rock for a vertiginous look straight down the near-vertical face. But neither is necessary to appreciate how far you've come – just turn to gaze back at your route along a section of the famed 212-mile John Muir Trail; even the two magnificent waterfalls you passed – the Vernal and Nevada falls – look puny from this height. Then take in the snowy spine of the Sierra Nevada mountains, the rippling granite sheets that run up to the summit of Cloud's Rest and the wonderland of forests and alpine meadows that comprise Yosemite National Park. Sit back, take a deep breath and enjoy the view.

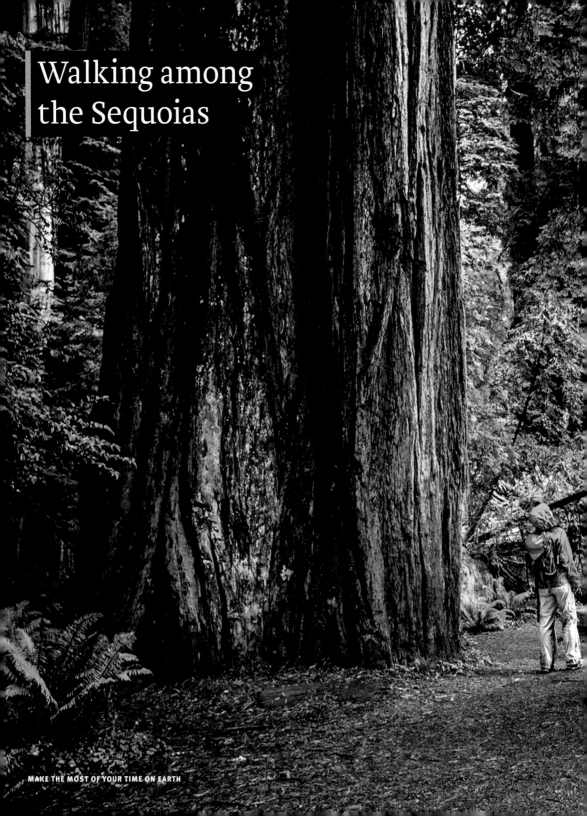

Walking among the Sequoias

CALIFORNIA *Sequoiadendron giganteum*, a redwood conifer species in the cypress family, is the world's largest living thing, though not its tallest (its coastal cousin, *Sequoia sempervirens*, is taller but narrower). Renowned naturalist and explorer John Muir called it "the king tree… the very god of the woods." Walking beneath these looming giants – some as tall as a 30-storey building – is humbling, to say the least.

The experience is made more awe-inspiring by the trees' age (very old) and remote, severely wintry setting. Giant sequoias grow exclusively between 4000ft and 8000ft on the western slopes of California's rugged Sierra Nevada mountain range, where they spend six months a year blanketed in cosseting snow. Known as the High Sierras, the region is a realm of breathtaking grandeur scythed with glacier-carved canyons beneath bare granite peaks, at their most spectacular in Yosemite National Park. The Mariposa Grove – home to more than five hundred giant sequoias – was a major reason the park was created.

While Yosemite gets the limelight, the majority of these majestic trees are found further south in lesser-known Sequoia and Kings Canyon National Parks.

Of the 75 sequoia groves in the world, forty are found here, including the Giant Forest which boasts more big-league sequoias than anywhere else. So, lace up your hiking boots and prepare to feel dwarfed on the two-mile-long Congress Trail, which leads past the major giants.

Start with an informative visit to the Giant Forest Museum, then take the park service shuttle to the General Sherman Tree trailhead. Named for US Civil War general William Sherman, this titan is the biggest Brobdingnagian of all. Craning to see the 275ft-high tippy top will give you neck ache. Just trying to comprehend its other statistics – a 36.5ft diameter and 106ft circumference – could induce dizziness.

Following the trail is like strolling a vast vaulted cathedral supported by stalwart columns, including the McKinley Tree honouring president William McKinley; the General Lee Tree (named for General Robert Edward Lee, commander of the Confederate Army of Northern Virginia); and the President Tree, at 3200 years old, the most ancient known living redwood. They're still growing and won't typically die of disease or old age: they simply grow too big and topple over.

A night at the lobster pound

495

MAINE You're seated at a picnic table at the *Lobster Shack at Two Lights*, which has to be one of the most picturesque spots in the country: an unassuming clapboard restaurant with a storybook lighthouse to the left and craggy cliffs pummelled by an unruly sea to the right. Maine's slogan is "The Way Life Should Be", and here, along its gorgeous corrugated coastline, you can't help but agree. That is, of course, if you're able to think of anything other than the red, hot challenge in front of you – one freshly steamed Maine lobster, waiting to be cracked open.

Eating Maine lobster is a culinary rite of passage for visitors to the state. It requires tools (nutcracker, teeny-tiny fork), patience and enough hubris to believe that you can look cool even while wearing a disposable bib. It's smart to bring along an experienced lobster slayer; your first lobster can be intimidating, and it's nice to have a bit of guidance (as well as someone to take that requisite

embarrassing photograph). When you're ready to begin, crack the claws in half, pull out the meat with your little fork and dip it in the melted butter. Lobster meat comes well defended, so be wary of sharp points along the shell. The tail follows the claws: tear it from the body, pushing the meat from the end. Finally (if you're feeling emboldened), pull off the legs to suck out the last bit of flesh. There is no other meat like lobster – tender, sweet, elusive – and in Maine, where lobster is king, the crimson crustacean is celebrated with parades, festivals and an energetic devotion that's shared by everyone.

At its best, a lobster dinner should be an all-around sensory experience. Breathe in the salty ocean breezes. Listen for the booms coming from the lighthouse. Finally, lick the butter off your fingers, remove the bib and give your dining partner a high five – you've just taken part in a Maine institution.

496 | Burnt ends and barbecue in Kansas City

MISSOURI & KANSAS Don't be fooled by appearances – the best barbecue in Kansas City is cooked up in lowbrow joints that flourish on word-of-mouth popularity, often with little more than a no-frills counter service, formica tables and fluorescent lighting. Just breathe in the woody fragrance of roasting meats, pick up a tray, choose your burnt ends and sides, slather with sauce and get stuck in.

Barbecue is serious business in Kansas City. According to legend it was introduced around 1908 by one Henry Perry, a native of Tennessee, who served up his slow-cooked ribs on newspaper in the flourishing African-American neighbourhood where jazz legend Charlie Parker was born in 1920. Charlie Bryant, who worked for Perry in the early days, took over his restaurant in 1940, and passed it to brother Arthur in turn six years later. Today, despite being one of America's most lauded barbecue joints, *Arthur Bryant's* remains surprisingly low-key. It's no tourist trap either, with locals outnumbering visitors and long lines at peak times.

Beef and ribs are smoked to perfection, but the real secret is the sauce: in original, sweet or rich and spicy varieties. Equally beloved is *Gates Bar-B-Q*, founded in 1946 by George Gates and chef Arthur Pinkard, who had also cut his stripes working for the illustrious Henry Perry.

So what makes Kansas barbecue so good? First, Kansas City meats are slow-smoked with a combination of aromatic hickory and oak wood. Then there are "burnt ends", a particular Kansas speciality – tasty chunks of meat cut from the charred end of a smoked beef brisket (and smothered with sauce, of course). Indeed, barbecue sauce is an integral part of the Kansas City experience. Most sauces are tomato-based, often with sweet and spicy variations. *KC Masterpiece* has become the most successful brand of Kansas City sauces, sold in supermarkets around the world, though Arthur Bryant's addictive original sauce is more vinegary and peppery than sweet. The ingredients? You've more chance of winning the lottery than of finding that out.

497 | Witnessing power in action on Capitol Hill

WASHINGTON DC Dominated by massive monuments, museums, war memorials and statues, Washington DC represents the purest expression of political might. But the seat of government of the world's greatest superpower is a surprisingly accessible place – it's by the people, for the people, after all – and though certain security measures may seem an obstacle, no visitor should miss the chance to see the corridors of power, and maybe even catch a glimpse of the action.

Wherever you go in DC, it'll be hard to avoid the looming, cast-iron dome of the US Capitol building. From its marvellous Rotunda (styled after Rome's Pantheon) to the stately figures of National Statuary Hall, you won't be disappointed (and may be slightly awed) by the country's centre of legislative power – pick up a ticket for a free tour at the kiosk on the building's southwest side. For an up-close look at the angry speech-making and partisan posturing of

Congress, however, you'll need to get a special pass in advance of your trip.

Although the president and his advisors stay well out of the public eye, you can still tour the White House; make reservations in advance to check out the richly draped, chandeliered East Room, the silk-trimmed and portrait-heavy Green Room, the oval, French-decorated Blue Room and a glittery display of presidential china.

Perhaps the most rewarding spot to see the American government at work is the US Supreme Court. The building itself is stately enough, with its grand Greek Revival columns and pediment, but the real sight is all nine justices arrayed behind their bench, meticulously probing the lawyers making their arguments. From these arguments the Court writes its opinions, affirming or striking down existing laws and at times making history before your very eyes.

498 | Jumping through hoops to see the hula

HAWAII In a state filled with some of the country's most lavish resorts, where you generally go to sleep late and relax on the beach, it's well-nigh perverse to camp in a park, rise before sunset and head on a bus to the top of a mountain – normally off limits to the general public – for the ceremonial beginning of a hula festival.

Of course, coming to Molokai in the first place, the Hawaiian island best known for its former leper colony, seems somewhat perverse, too. But everything here is so refreshingly unpretentious and uncommercialized that the appeal is soon obvious. And it's here that it's thought the art of hula was born. The sound of the conch shell signals the start of the festival, Ka Hula Piko. The dancers' movements steadily increase in intensity. The celebration continues under the trees at Papohaku Beach Park, beside a beautiful strand of golden sand abutting crashing crystal-blue waters; that pre-dawn wake-up call becomes a distant memory.

499 | Castles of sand: acting like a kid at Cannon Beach

OREGON Dreaming of a forum for your long-repressed artistic abilities? Hoping to construct a life-size sand-version of Elvis, Jesus or someone else close to your heart, then have it washed away with the afternoon tide?

Every June, the annual Sandcastle Day in Cannon Beach offers just the opportunity – along with the chance to have your creation gawked at by thousands of onlookers, in America's oldest sandcastle-building competition. Others may have surpassed it in size since its debut in 1964, but there's something to be said for taking part in the original.

The field is limited to 150 entrants, so you may have some qualms about taking the place of an expert, but don't worry too much; unless you've won in a comp before, you won't be eligible for the "masters" competition – where the local architects get serious with their sand.

500 | Bed, barracuda and breakfast: Jules' Undersea Lodge

FLORIDA Named after intrepid aqua-explorer Jules Verne, *Jules' Undersea Lodge* began life as a research lab off the coast of Puerto Rico in the 1970s. Subsequently moved to the Florida Keys, it was converted to its current use in 1986 by a pair of diving buffs and budding hoteliers.

A pod that sits a few feet above the lagoon floor, the lodge has just two smallish guest bedrooms, fitted out with TVs, VCRs, phones and hot showers, plus a fully equipped kitchen and common room. All very ordinary – except, of course, that you are 21 feet below the sea. Expert scuba divers can spend up to 22 hours exploring the marine habitat each day – safety regulations permit no longer than that; first-timers, meanwhile, need only take a three-hour tutorial on the basics of underwater swimming and survival before they can duck down for check-in.

(Fitful types will sleep with the fishes far more restfully knowing that there's 24-hour safety monitoring from land nearby.)

Guests – or "aquanauts" as the lodge-owners call them – must swim down to reach the lodge, which, shaped like a figure of eight, has a small opening on the base in the centre. Your first point of arrival is into a wet room; the disconcerting sensation is much like surfacing from a swimming pool, except, of course, that you're still underwater. Compressed air keeps the sea from flooding in.

Once ensconced in this enclave, most guests spend their time gazing out of the enormous, 42-inch windows in the lodge's hull: these vast portholes make a spectacular spot to spy on its surroundings. *Jules' Undersea Lodge* is anchored in the heart of a mangrove habitat, the ideal nursery for scores of marine animals, including angelfish, parrotfish and snapper; meanwhile, anemones and sponges stud the sea floor. Anyone too busy fish-spotting to whip up a spot of dinner needn't worry, as there's a chef on hand who can scuba down to prepare meals; or, for late-night munchies, a local takeaway joint offers a unique delivery service – perfectly crisp, underwater pizza.

501 | Checking the progress of the Crazy Horse Memorial

SOUTH DAKOTA Angered by the completion of the presidential portraits on Mount Rushmore in 1941, a group of Lakota Sioux chiefs led by Henry Standing Bear asked sculptor Korczak Ziolkowski to build a monument to the Native American legend known as Crazy Horse: victor of the Battle of the Little Big Horn; a leader who never signed a treaty; and a warrior who never surrendered. Mount Rushmore, just seventeen miles down the road, was big – this had to be bigger. As Henry Standing Bear put it, "we want to let the white man know we have heroes too."

The first thing that hits you when you gaze upon the memorial, deep in the Black Hills of South Dakota, is indeed its colossal size. While the images of Mount Rushmore were carved onto the existing rockface, Ziolkowski reshaped an entire mountain, blasting, drilling and carving, slab by slab, an image of the revered warrior atop his horse, his arm stretched over the land that he fought to defend

in the 1870s. The modern Orientation Center is over a mile from the 563ft peak, so initially you won't even grasp the memorial's true dimensions, but take a bus to its base and you're guaranteed to be utterly mesmerized.

It's not just the proportions that are overwhelming. The audacious, seemingly hopeless, timescale of the project makes the great Gothic cathedrals of Europe seem like prefabs. When Ziolkowski died in 1982, his family continued the work he had begun 34 years earlier; Crazy Horse's face, with its finely shaped nose and eyes, measures 87ft tall and was completed as recently as 1998. Today, his horse is gradually taking shape through a series of blasted-out ridges, but it's impossible to estimate when everything will be finished. No matter, though: time seems to have little significance here, as the construction work – careful, reverential – has become almost as sacred as the monument itself.

502 | Angling for brown bears at Brooks Falls

ALASKA If you've ever seen a photo of a huge brown bear standing knee-deep in rushing water, poised to catch a leaping salmon in its mouth, there's a 95 percent chance it was taken at Brooks Falls, a stalling point for the millions of sockeye salmon that make their annual spawning run up the Brooks River. Each July, at the height of the migration, bears flock in to exploit the excellent feeding possibilities, and with viewing platforms set up a few feet from the action, watching them is both exhilarating and slightly nerve-racking. It's easy to feel as though you're right in the middle of a wildlife documentary.

At any one time, you might see a dozen or more jockeying for position. Such proximity causes considerable friction among these naturally solitary animals, but size, age and experience define a hierarchy that allows posturing and roaring to take the

place of genuine battles. Fluffy and defenceless babies are highly vulnerable to fatal attacks from adult males, so the mothers go to great lengths to ensure they're secure, sending their cubs to the topmost branches of nearby trees and then fishing warily close by. Daring juveniles like to grab the prime fishing spot atop the falls, but become very nervous if bears higher up the pecking order come close – successfully holding pole position might mean moving up the rankings, but the youngster risks a severe beating. Some older and wiser bears prefer wallowing in the pool below the falls: one regular visitor dives down every few minutes and always seems to come up with a flapping sockeye in his mouth. Come the end of the salmon run, the bears head for the hills, only to return in September for a final pre-hibernation gorge on the carcasses of the spent fish as they drift downstream.

MISSISSIPPI The ceilings are often made up of half-rotted wood, half plastic sheeting, and rain-drops are collecting in buckets on the stained carpet floor. If you want a drink, your choices are simple: beer or whiskey served in a plastic cup. From the outside on a weekend night these places often look abandoned, with assorted junk piled up against the front wall. But open the door after 10pm, and you'll find one of the most influential musical genres of the past century in full swing, with a hard-drinking, hard-partying crowd grooving and shaking to some of the Delta's finest bluesmen – who are usually stuffed into a corner with their battered guitars and primitive PAs, but making enough noise to be heard three zip codes away.

The blues originated in the early 1900s in the cotton fields of the Mississippi Delta, and juke joints flourished as the only places where black people could gather and hear this new music, first created by black workers in the sordid working conditions of the fields.

Rough shacks with few amenities, sporadic opening times and often far from the centre of town, many of the joints still operating today have changed little from the times when the likes of Robert Johnson, the king of the Delta blues singers, performed in the 1930s.

Live music is guaranteed on weekends and could come from gnarled white country boys with one battered slide guitar, dungarees and a ZZ-Top-esque beard, or from nattily attired black bluesmen armed with electric guitars, drums and bass.

The Delta is still a racially divided area – the poorest region of the poorest state in the US. *Red's,* on the outskirts of Clarksdale in a residential area straight out of *The Wire*, and *Po'Monkey's,* located in a field a few miles from Merigold, are patronized by an eclectic mixture of predominantly local characters. Expect to embrace conversation with music lovers, beer-swillers and tall-tale tellers, all of whom need little excuse to hit the dance floor. A visit to a juke joint remains one of the most grittily authentic nights out in the States – just be sure to avoid hitting those buckets as you dance.

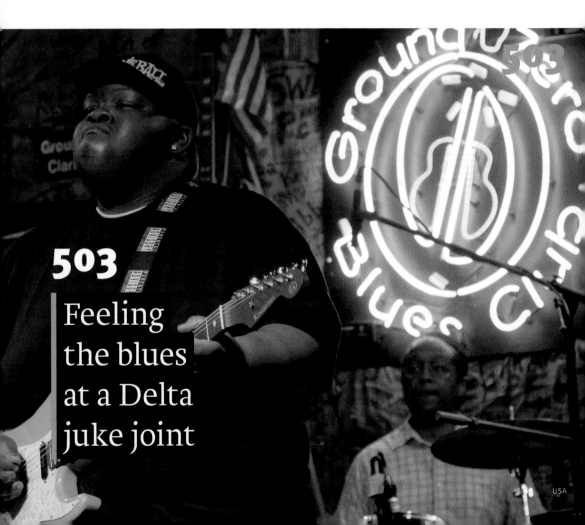

503

Feeling the blues at a Delta juke joint

504

Pitching your tent in Yellowstone National Park

WYOMING, MONTANA & IDAHO Famously referred to as "America's best idea", Yellowstone became the world's first national park when it was founded in 1872. Within its borders lies a primeval pocket of American wilderness, spanning almost 9000 square kilometres between Wyoming, Montana and Idaho. And it won't take you long to discover why it inspired an entirely new breed of conservation: inside the caldera of an active volcano, its geothermal areas seem almost otherworldly.

Over half of the world's geysers are found here, set amid billowing fumaroles, churning mud pots and thousands of colourful hot springs, which stain the landscape with a rainbow of seemingly unnatural hues. Any of these features would justify Yellowstone's status as the country's foremost national park, but it's equally blessed with an astonishing array of wildlife. More than sixty species of mammals roam its fertile plains and subalpine forests, including vast herds of bison and elk as well as healthy populations of moose, bears, mountain lions and wolves.

From its inception, it took Yellowstone just under eighty years to top a million annual visitors, and today over four million make the trip each year. The ever-growing popularity of the park has put pressure on its infrastructure and environment, and its major sights – among them

Old Faithful geyser, Grand Prismatic Spring and the Grand Canyon of the Yellowstone – are frequently overrun with tourists during the peak summer season. But it would be a mistake to dismiss Yellowstone entirely on the basis of this.

Vast areas of the park remain untouched, and are easily reached via its extensive network of picturesque hiking trails, and there are hundreds of campsites for those hoping to make even better use of the great outdoors. In fact, camping may well be the best way to truly experience the park, so long as you stick to the designated campgrounds.

For starters, strap on your pack and head for one of the plots facing Shoshone Lake, the largest lake in the park's backcountry. As the sun descends over the mountains and the crowds beat a hasty retreat for the hotels, pitch your tent amid grazing elk and watch for ground squirrels emerging from their burrows or moose creeping along the forest edge. After toasting marshmallows over the campfire, you can spend time stargazing or listening out for the exhilarating howls of Yellowstone's wolves from the safety of your sleeping bag – they'll sound much closer than they really are. This is it: an authentic, uncrowded experience of America's most famously crowded park.

505 | Sea kayaking in Prince William Sound

ALASKA As you manoeuvre your way towards the towering face of one of Alaska's many tidewater glaciers, the gentle crunch of ice against the fibreglass hull of your kayak sounds faintly ominous. It's nothing, though, compared to the thunderclap that echoes across the water when a great wall of ice peels away from the glacier and sends waves surging toward you. Your first reaction is quite naturally a jolt of fear, but no need to panic: if you're at least 500 yards away from the glacier face (as any sensible paddler is), the danger will have dissipated by the time whatever's left of the waves reaches you.

Watching glaciers calve while paddling round a frozen margarita of opaque blue water and brash ice is an undoubted highlight of sea kayaking in Prince William Sound. Perhaps better still are the opportunities for viewing marine life here. Seals often loll around on icebergs close to glaciers, while sea otters swim in the frigid waters, protected by the wonderfully thick fur that made them prized by the eighteenth-century Russian traders who partly colonized Alaska. In deeper water, look for pods of orcas cruising the waterways in search of their favourite food, seals (no wonder they hang back on the icebergs). You might even spot a few humpback whales, which congregate in small groups and breach spectacularly on occasion. Keep a splash-proof camera handy at all times.

Even if you miss out on a great action photo, there is considerable pleasure in just gliding around the generally calm waters of the fjords, where cliffs clad in Sitka spruce and Douglas fir rise steeply from the depths.

For full atmospheric effect, stay in a simple Forest Service cabin or camp out on a small beach or at a designated campsite in one of the state marine parks; it's a wonderfully relaxing way to while away a few days – falling sheets of ice aside, of course.

506 | Making a mess with Maryland crabs

MARYLAND Hands stained red with Old Bay seasoning, fingers so slick with crab fat you can hardly clutch your beer, maybe a few stray bits of shell stuck in your hair or to your cheek – that's the sort of dishevelled look which you should be aiming for at a Maryland crab feast.

"Picking" hard-shell steamed blue crabs is a sport Marylanders attack with gusto from May to October – though anyone will tell you that the heaviest, juiciest number-one "jimmies" are available only near the end of the summer. That's when the most popular crab restaurants up and down the bay have lines out of the door, and every other back yard in Baltimore seems to ring with the sound of wooden mallets smacking on crab legs.

It's simplicity itself: a bushel or two of crabs in the steamer with some beer and lashings of spicy Old Bay, and yesterday's newspaper laid out on a big picnic table, along with a few rolls of paper towels. What else? Only more beer (cold this time), some corn on the cob, a hot dish or two ... nothing to distract from the main attraction.

Then it's down to business. The process starts with yanking what can only be described as an easy-open pull tab on the crab's under-shell. From there, dig out the yellowish fat called "mustard", as well as the gills, then snap the hard-back shell in half and proceed to scoop out the sweet, succulent flesh. Soon you'll be whacking the claws just so with a wooden mallet and gouging the meat out with a knife.

It's easier than it sounds, and the crabmeat is certainly a powerful motivator for thorough picking (and fast learning). In the process, you can't help but marvel at man's cleverness when it comes to eating critters with the prickliest of defences. But maybe that's just the beer talking.

507 | Leaving it all behind on the Appalachian Trail

GEORGIA–MAINE Hiking the Appalachian Trail, the epic trek that stretches 2186 miles from the peak of Springer Mountain in Georgia to the top of Mount Katahdin in Maine, changes your perspective on life, whether you want it to or not. When your house weighs a pound, your job involves walking from sunrise to sunset and your nights are filled with strangers' stories round roaring campfires, the mundane routines of the modern world are replaced with the realities of survival: water, gear, aching joints and the insatiable rumbling in your stomach.

A popular saying on the AT is that the only thing that separates a hiker from a hobo is a thin layer of Gore-Tex. So why do so many choose to spend upwards of four months walking a distance that could be covered by a car in two days? As you plan your route across the snowcapped peaks of the Smokies at the end of winter, then the indigo waves of the Blue Ridge Mountains in early spring, the grassy green mounds of the Shenandoahs in the heat of mosquito season and finally the striking profiles of the Presidentials in early fall, you find there's a sublime satisfaction in mapping out your future, one mountain at a time. (Most through-hikers walk from south to north, to catch the best weather.)

But the trail is really about those countless days when you walk twenty-five miles through three thunderstorms and over six mountains, and arrive at your campsite feeling exhausted yet triumphantly alive.

That and the sleepy towns to which you hitchhike for supplies, where welcoming locals ply you with pitchers of beer at the local bar and blueberry pancakes for breakfast and offer lifts to buy new shoes for the next leg of your trip.

508 | Ice fishing on Gunflint Lake

MINNESOTA On the edge of the Superior National Forest in the north of the state sits Gunflint Lake – the invisible border with Canada slicing horizontally through its centre. Tents are dotted across the frozen surface, bright flares of reds and yellows flapping in the wind, in contrast to the blinding expanse of glaring white that stretches as far as the eye can see.

Just try to relax as you step on to the ice, and don't think about the sharp cracks that zigzag across the frozen surface, or the unforgiving deep blackness below – nor the anecdotes doing the rounds in these remote parts involving inquisitive bears.

Smoke from small makeshift chimneys protrudes from the sides of the tents, busily chuffing into the freezing air, connected to wood burners inside. Cosy might be stretching it, but the warmth from the burning logs definitely takes the edge off the January chill. At -23°C outside and dropping, it's nippy.

Once under canvas, the fishing guide drills a hole down through the thick layer of ice, which, reassuringly, turns out to be around 14 inches thick. As the cold inky water whooshes up to the surface, you fix the bait, drop a line down and then, well, wait. You may as well get comfortable, for the wait could be a long one. This is when you're glad there's a stool for your backside and something warming in a flask.

This is not an activity for adrenaline-rush seekers, although you may feel a frisson when you feel a tug on the line and you pull out your first fat lake trout or gleaming smallmouth bass. No, the enjoyment comes from the muffled quiet of soft snow – on the lake and in the surrounding Narnia-like forest of spruce and fir trees. It's when you spot a moose gently sniffing the sharp air along the lake's edge before disappearing back into the forest. It's in the solitude and the sense of timelessness, and in the unhurried chat with your fellow anglers. And, of course, it's when you tuck into the fish dinner that evening.

509 | Leaf-peeping along Route 100

VERMONT Route 100 is beautiful year-round – winding its way through quintessential New England scenery, it skirts tidy chocolate-box villages dotted with white-steepled churches, clapboard houses and home-made sweet shops, all nestled beneath the Green Mountains. But from late September to early October, when the leaves start to change colour, the road is transformed into a 200-mile, skin-prickling display of arboreal pyrotechnics; it's as if the entire state has been set ablaze. Even the most die-hard cosmopolitan will find it hard not to be seduced by the spectacular scenery, as dizzying peaks give way to a conflagration of vermilion sugar maples, buttery aspens, scarlet sourwoods and acid-yellow ashes.

This yearly riot of colour can be appreciated whether you choose to leave your car or not. Gliding along a winding stretch of open road, crawling through an impossibly picturesque nineteenth-century town, or off-roading along serpentine country lanes, the explosion of unreal-looking leaves is utterly inescapable – and unadulterated (no billboards or malls are allowed along the route).

For the ultimate up-close look at these colourful scenes, pull off Route 100 and head into Green Mountain National Forest to walk a section of the 265-mile Long Trail, which has countless leaf-peeping opportunities alongside rugged, mountainous terrain, flowing streams and placid ponds.

510 | Cruising the Inside Passage

ALASKA There's little better than sitting on deck and nursing a warm nightcap sometime around 11pm, as the sun slowly dips towards the horizon and you cruise past mile after gorgeous mile of spruce- and hemlock-choked shoreline. If you're lucky, whales will make an appearance; perhaps just a fluke or a tail but maybe a full-body breach. This is Alaska's Inside Passage, flanked by impenetrable snowcapped coastal mountains and incised by hairline fjords that create an interlocking archipelago of over a thousand densely forested islands.

Gliding into port at successive small settlements, you can't help but think these towns insignificant after the large-scale drama of the surrounding landscape. They cling to the few tiny patches of flat land, their streets spilling out onto a network of boardwalks over the sea. Shops, streets and even large salmon canneries are perched picturesquely along the waterside on spruce poles.

Everything is green, courtesy of the low clouds that cloak the surrounding hills and offer frequent rain. The dripping leaves, sodden mosses and wispy mist seem to suit ravens and bald eagles. You'll see them everywhere: ravens line up along the railings overlooking the small boat harbours while bald eagles perch, solitary and regal, in the trees above.

The next stop is Glacier Bay National Park, a vast wonderland of ice and barren rock where massive tidewater glaciers push right into the ocean. The ship lingers a few hours as everyone trains their eyes on the three-mile-wide face where walls of ice periodically crumble away and crash into the iceberg-flecked sea. The schedule is pressing and it is time to move on; the moment you turn away, the loudest rumble of the day tells you you've just missed the big one.

Grazing with the black sheep at Burning Man

511

NEVADA Picture a nudist miniature golf course, an advanced pole-dancing workshop and a bunch of neon-painted bodies glowing in the night, and you may be getting close to imagining what Burning Man is all about. Every year during the last week of August, several thousand digerati geeks, pyrotechnic maniacs, death-guild Goths, crusty hippies and too-hip yuppies descend on a prehistoric dry lakebed in the Nevada Desert to build a temporary autonomous "city" – one that rivals some of Nevada's largest in size and leaves no trace when it disbands. Known as Black Rock City, it's not the ideal place to consume a heady cocktail of alcohol and drugs – temperatures are scorching – but the thousands of anarchists, deviants, techno-heads, trance-dancers and freakish performance artists who arrive here from all over the world give it their best shot.

Art and interactivity are at the very core of the Burning Man ethos. Basically, this is the most survivalist, futuristic and utterly surreal show on Earth, where the strangest part of your alter ego reigns supreme.

Faceless Pythia give advice in oracle booths, flying zebras circle, caged men in ape suits pounce and motorized lobster cars tool about. Some of Burning Man's participants see the event as a social experiment and others a total free-for-all. But the main goal is the same: you're there to participate, not observe. Burning Man allows all the black sheep of the world to graze together, so the more experiential art you share, gifts you give, bizarre costumes you wear or free services you provide, the better.

The highlight of the week is the burning of a 50ft-tall effigy of a man, built from wood and neon and stuffed with fireworks. After all the laser-filled skies, electroluminescent wired bodysuits and fire-breathing mechanical dragons that illuminate the skies every evening for the rest of the week, it's almost an anticlimax, but it's still certainly a sight to behold. If you fancy making a smaller-scale statement, you can choose whatever alter ego or fantasy you desire. Just pack your (animal-friendly) non-feathered boas, body paint and imagination, and you're all set.

512

Going native in the land of the blue-green water

ARIZONA A stunning Shangri-la of turquoise waterfalls and lush vegetation, little-known Havasu Canyon lies deep in the heart of the Grand Canyon. It doesn't belong to the national park, however, for the simple reason that it's the ancestral home of a small group of Native Americans. One anthropologist called this "the only spot in the United States where native culture has remained in anything like its pristine condition."

Havasu Canyon receives virtually no rain, but every drop of water that falls for miles around funnels into this narrow gorge, to feed the year-round torrent of Havasu Stream. Known as the "people of the blue-green water", the Havasupai have farmed here for centuries. Now, though, they depend as much on tourism as agriculture, ferrying visitors on horseback down the demanding eight-mile trail from the nearest road, and running a simple lodge and campground. Their village, Supai, is a bedraggled affair that has been repeatedly battered by flash floods; the reason to visit lies a few miles deeper into the canyon, in the glorious succession of waterfalls. These too are frequently reshaped by flooding; thus Navajo Falls disappeared in 2008, to be replaced by two brand-new cascades.

Towering Havasu Falls survives, however. Here the stream foams white as it hurtles over a 170ft cliff to crash into shallow terraces filled with clear turquoise water. Bizarre rock formations all around are formed from travertine – the same stuff that clogs the inside of domestic kettles – which also coats the riverbed and gives the water its astonishing blue-green glow.

Weary hikers can swim here and at the base of the even taller Mooney Falls, which you descend via footholds chiselled into the rock, while clutching a precarious iron chain. Splashing beneath these mighty cascades, knowing you're in a remote oasis at the bottom of the Grand Canyon, is a quite extraordinary thrill.

513 | Touring Graceland

TENNESSEE As pilgrimages go, touring Graceland isn't the most obvious religious experience. The Memphis home of legendary rock 'n' roll star Elvis Presley doesn't promise miraculous healing or other spiritual rewards. But for those who perceive truth in timeless popular music – as well as in touchingly bad taste – a visit to the home of "the King" is more illuminating than Lourdes.

From Elvis's first flush of success (he bought the house in 1957 with the profits from his first RCA hit, "Heartbreak Hotel") to his ignominious death twenty years later, Graceland witnessed the bloom and eventual bloat of one of America's biggest legends. Just as he mixed country, gospel and rhythm and blues to concoct the new sound of rock 'n' roll, Presley had an "anything goes" attitude towards home decor. The tiki splendour of the Jungle Room, which has green shag carpeting on the floor and the ceiling, is only steps from the billiards room, where the couch and the walls are covered in matching quilt-print upholstery. In the living room, a 15-ft-long white sofa sets off a glistening black grand piano. (The audio-tour commentary, from Lisa Marie Presley, is understandably preoccupied with her father's impetuous shopping habits.)

Amid all the glitz, though, you can still glimpse an underlying humility. A modest windowless kitchen was one of the King's favourite rooms, and the blocky colonial-style house itself is nothing compared to today's mega-mansions, especially considering he shared the place with his extended family for decades. The quiet, green grounds are a respite from the less-than-attractive patch of Memphis outside. And even after passing through a monumental trophy room and a display of Elvis's finest jewel-encrusted jumpsuits, you can't help but think that this was a man who hadn't strayed too far from his rural Mississippi roots.

Serious pilgrims pay their respects at Elvis's grave, which is set in the garden at the side of the house. Around the mid-August anniversary of the singer's death, tens of thousands flock here to deposit flowers, notes and gifts – a homage to a uniquely American sort of saint.

514 | Trusting in Tusty on the Alaska Marine Highway

ALASKA It's America, but not as you know it. There are no malls, ball games, Tex-Mex or frappuccino lights. Indeed, there are scarcely any shops at all, which is why, when the *Tustumena* – the Alaska Marine Highway's state ferry from Bellingham, Washington, to Dutch Harbor in the Aleutian Islands – calls four times a year, the locals surge towards the docks with delight.

She's no luxury liner: a few of the 174 passengers manage to book berths and the rest just pitch tents on the deck or lay sleeping bags on the floor among the snoring bodies of strangers. But because the "Trusty Tusty" – as locals call her – is small, she can squeeze through narrow passageways that cruise ships can't, and visit communities that no dressed-for-dinner passenger could ever hope to see.

In Chignik (population: 80), midway down the south coast of the Alaska Peninsula, passengers flock to *Janice's Donut Hole* for pastries – she's been baking since 6am on this lucrative day – while the locals of this restaurant-less community rush to the ferry to buy cheeseburgers that the ship's chef has cooked up especially for them. At King's Cove, 270 miles west, passengers feast on fresh salmon chowder. Between stops, the onboard naturalist points out a colony of sea otters here, a humpback whale there, and relates the history of this remote territory: in 1942, the Japanese invaded the Aleutian Islands of Attu and Kiska.

As the days pass – it takes three days and four nights to travel between Homer and Dutch Harbor – the scenery becomes more dramatic: flower-filled meadows turn to rugged outcrops before emerald-green hills until, on the final evening, the *Tustumena* passes the three volcanoes of Unimak island: Roundtop, Isanotski and Shishaldin. Southwest Alaska's weather is famously moody, but if you're lucky, you'll see them capped with snow, basking against a brash, tangerine-coloured sky.

515 | Adrift in the desert – the San Juan River

UTAH Many rivers in the desert Southwest – the Colorado, for one – are renowned for whitewater rafting. If you're more of a chill-seeker than a thrill-seeker, though, it's hard to beat the gentle but glorious float down the San Juan River.

Flat-bottomed inflatable boats set off each morning from Bluff, Utah, and take out in the afternoon thirty blissful miles downstream. They may have to turn on the engine now and then, but mostly you're simply drifting. You don't even have to stay in the boat; when the desert sun starts to scorch, you can just jump into the river and bob along in your lifejacket.

The San Juan flows along the northern edge of the Navajo Indian Reservation. Many river guides are themselves Navajo, keen to point out bighorn sheep as they emerge from the tamarisk to snatch a drink or pick their way along the jagged crest of the skyline. An indolent heron flaps ahead to find a new perch as the boat approaches; golden eagles circle above. Sheer cliffs of golden sandstone tower above the water during the early stretches; for a mid-morning break, you haul the boat onto a sandy beach, and hike up to investigate an immaculately preserved thousand-year-old ruin. A snake pictograph suggests it was originally home to a migrating group of Hopi.

Although the river only drops a few hundred feet, the Comb Ridge anticline through which it cuts is so tilted that the day corresponds to a stunning voyage through geological aeons. During the afternoon, the banks turn to a colourful extravaganza of crumbling shale, striped in extraordinary zigzag patterns and topped with a striking yellow layer that marks the presence of oil. In one vivid formation, sharp red strata appear to outline a figure plunging into the water.

The Navajo, who gather here in family groups each evening to cool off in the stream, call this the Diving Boy. Finally, a large flat rock on the hillside, balanced sombrero-like atop a smaller boulder, catches your attention – this is Mexican Hat, namesake of the nearby town, and it's time to return to the twenty-first century.

516 | Make a transatlantic sailing

NEW YORK Cruising has its detractors, and it takes a particular sort of traveller to be drawn to some of the more garish, culture-slim cruises on the market. Some routes, however, just have cachet. Crossing the Atlantic from Southampton to New York on Cunard's *Queen Mary 2* is very much a sailing that doesn't fit the usual mould. This is partly because of its history, which is bound up in a more glamorous time, and partly because of the length of the crossing. A week at sea without so much as an island stop to break the journey? That's a proper trip.

With the possible exception of the Trans-Siberian Railway, there can't be a passenger journey on Earth that grants quite so much time to reflect on getting from A to B. And in a world constantly jostled along by smartphones and deadlines, who wouldn't want to spend seven enforced days of leisure on the vessel once memorably described as "a watertight container of cask-aged nostalgia"?

The ship is a colossus, travelling the globe more or less constantly. Its Atlantic crossings, though bookable separately, generally form part of much longer round-the-world cruises. And as is the way with these sorts of things, on board are cabins, restaurants and bars that vary from the very posh to the not-so-posh. Passenger numbers are generally in excess of 2400 – but crucially, everyone makes the same transatlantic journey.

The vessel has the features you'd expect from a 150,000-ton ocean liner – blustery decks, long corridors, epauletted crew – while showcasing a particularly British brand of on-board hospitality. Expect entertainment to come in the form of everything from Jane Austen plays and cream teas to foxtrot tutorials and art classes. It's said that the vessel accounts for 1.35 million teabags a year.

These are mere details. Cunard's liners have been crossing the Atlantic since the 1840s. And as the hours become days, your mind lulls and you begin appreciating the variations in the ocean swells and wave patterns: blues, greys and indigos. After a week of this, the Manhattan skyline arrives like something from a dream. And in travelling from the UK to the USA, the liner also provides something that no hotel on the planet can match: an extra hour's sleep each night, as it slips from one time zone to another.

517 | California in a convertible: driving the length of Highway 1

CALIFORNIA Highway 1 starts in little Leggett, but most people pick it up in San Francisco, just after it has raced US-101 across the Golden Gate Bridge and wiggled its way through the city. Roll down the rooftop on your convertible – this is California, after all – and chase the horizon south, through Santa Cruz and misty Monterey and then on to Big Sur, one of the most dramatic stretches of coastline in the world, where the forest-clad foothills of the Santa Lucia Mountains ripple down to a ninety-mile zigzag of deeply rugged shore.

You could easily spend a week in one of the mountain lodges here, hiking in the region's two superb state parks or watching grey whales gliding through the surf, but SoCal's sands are calling. Gun the gas down through San Luis Obispo and swanky Santa Barbara until you hit Malibu, from where – as the Pacific Coast Highway – the road tiptoes around Los Angeles, dipping in and out of the beachside suburbs of Santa Monica, Venice and Long Beach.

Highway 1 eventually peters out at San Juan Capistrano, but most people pull off a few miles shy, finishing their journey in Los Angeles. Leaving Malibu's multi-million-dollar condos behind and easing gently into the downtown LA traffic, it'll suddenly dawn on you that the hardest part of the journey is still to come – at some point soon, you're going to have to say goodbye to the convertible.

518 | Going batty in Austin

TEXAS Every evening from mid-March to early November, Austin plays host to one of urban America's most entertaining natural spectacles. Just after sunset, Mexican free-tailed bats emerge from the deep crevices of the Congress Avenue Bridge, flapping and squeaking in a long ribbon across the sky. An eclectic mix of townies and tourists watches from the south bank of Town Lake, from boats, from blankets at the *Austin American-Statesman*'s observation centre, and from the bridge itself.

Picturesque from any spot, the bats' game of follow-the-leader is most impressive when you stand beneath the ribbon and look up – that's when the sheer number of these creatures hits home.

During the summer, the best viewing season, more than 1.5 million bats reside here, making it the largest urban bat colony in North America. Caves elsewhere in Texas host larger colonies, but in Austin there is a certain wonder in watching natural and man-made worlds collide harmoniously.

519 | Paying homage to country music

VIRGINIA Along a highway disguised as a rambling country road in the town of Hiltons, the Carter Family Fold showcases acoustic mountain music in a place where time seems to simply stand still. Here it might as well be 1927, the year of the "Big Bang" in country music, when the original Carter family sang about hard times and wildwood flowers.

The children of Sara and A.P. Carter constructed and nurtured this unique structure, building it right into the hillside. An on-site museum in A.P.'s old grocery store contains snapshots of "Mother Maybelle", a lock of Sara's hair and the clothes that June Carter Cash and Johnny Cash wore when they entertained at Richard Nixon's White House.

During the weekly concerts, the site still evokes a direct connection to June and Johnny, to their famous forebears who are honoured here, and to all of the music that came from these mountains.

520 | Biking the Golden Gate Bridge

CALIFORNIA Like a bright-orange necklace draped across the neck of San Francisco Bay, the Golden Gate Bridge is said to be the most photographed man-made structure in the world, and no wonder: you can snap a postcard-worthy picture of it from almost any hilltop in the city. But to really experience the span, you need to get close. You need to feel it. And the best way to do that is by biking it. The eight-mile trip from Fisherman's Wharf over the bridge to Sausalito is truly spectacular and, just as important, truly flat.

Rent some wheels at the base of Hyde Street Pier, then cruise through manicured Aquatic Park. It's a short climb to Fort Mason Park, where you can catch eerie glimpses of Alcatraz through the thick cypress trees. Swoop down to Marina Green, past the legions of kite flyers and the small harbour, and you'll soon be gliding past Crissy Field, replete with newly planted sea grasses, sand dunes and the occasional great blue heron.

Grab a grass-fed beef hot dog from the popular *Let's Be Frank* cart, then press on to the end of the path, where at historic Fort Point you'll find you can peer up into the awesome latticework underbelly of the bridge.

You'll have to double back a few hundred yards to the road up to the bridge approach. But the steep ascent is worth it as you serenely pedal past mobs of tourists and onto the bike and pedestrian path. As the crowds thin out, you can contemplate the bridge's stunning Art Deco lines and mind-boggling scale. The towers rise 65 storeys and contain 600,000 rivets apiece. The 3ft-wide suspension cables comprise 80,000 miles of pencil-thin steel wire. More darkly, over a thousand people have jumped to their deaths from this very trail.

There's one last viewing platform on the Marin County anchorage, after which it's time to drift downhill along the twisting road to the quaint town of Sausalito, where you can catch the ferry back to San Francisco. Though it hardly seems possible, the view from the ferry landing may be the most magnificent of the whole journey, especially at sunset, when the white lights of the city glow against the darkening bay.

521 | Death by ice cream at Ben & Jerry's

VERMONT In the late 1970s, a couple of hippy dropouts decided they'd like to make ice cream for a living. They took a $5 correspondence course, bought a cranky ice-cream machine and opened a scoop shop on the concourse of a shabby gas station in Burlington, Vermont. Ben Cohen and Jerry Greenfield had a talent for mixing tasty stuff into their ice cream – chunks of real chocolate, cashew nuts and cookies all went into the blender.

Today, Vermont is known for its green hills, ski slopes and picture-perfect clapboard villages. Yet the state's most popular attraction is Ben & Jerry's manufacturing plant just outside the sleepy town of Waterbury. To be sure, it's an intriguing enterprise; a quirky video describes the unlikely origins of the venture and, even though it's now a division of Unilever, the company is proud of its small size, eco-friendly philosophy and community involvement. But there's really only one reason everyone comes here; that super-chunk, fudge-soaked, biscuit and marshmallow choco-rich ice cream that is the most addictive product ever sold (legally) in the US.

Guided tours run above the factory floor where machines turn cream, sugar and other natural ingredients into over fifty flavours, but does anyone really care about output levels and local dairy farms? The real highlight is the free taster at the end – rare or brand-new flavours are dished out here. Think coconut double-chocolate chip and peanut butter cookie dough. Nirvana for ice-cream addicts.

The shop outside presents a real opportunity to indulge. Don't feel self-conscious and order that single scoop; you'll soon observe seniors and six-year-olds alike walking out with plates stacked high with multi-flavoured dollops of ice cream and toppings. Before you leave, waddle over to the Flavor Graveyard to mourn the likes of Tennessee Mud, Rainforest Crunch and the short-lived Cool Britannia (strawberries and shortbread).

One fact is sure to boggle your mind as you drive away; each employee can take home a tub of ice cream every day, for free. Most do not – apparently, there really is a limit on how much ice cream you can eat.

522 | Hang-gliding the Outer Banks

NORTH CAROLINA There are few coastal spots in America as magnificent as Carolina's Outer Banks. Your main goal here should be contemplating the fragility of the shifting sands and unique ecosystems, hitting deserted beaches along the southern portions of the barrier islands, in Cape Hatteras, Ocracoke Island and largely undeveloped Cape Lookout. Getting off – and above – beach level is an experience not to be missed: there's a hang-gliding school in Jockey Ridge State Park where you can soar over the largest sand dunes in the eastern US, in Nags Head. Once airborne, you may well consider what fired the imagination of Orville and Wilbur Wright, who launched their historic flight just a few miles north.

523 | Travelling the Turquoise Trail

NEW MEXICO A stunning 52-mile stretch of Highway 14 – known as the Turquoise Trail – links Santa Fe and Albuquerque. It's a day-tripper's delight: start with a bit of ghost town charm in Cerrillos, where you'll be greeted by little more than tumbleweed, dirt roads and empty western storefronts complete with hitching posts.

Continue south, taking in golden hills, desert meadows and miles of startling blue sky, and head to the mining town-cum-artist enclave Madrid. Here you can shop for turquoise jewellery, check out local art and visit the Old Coal Mine Museum. Top off your trip with a beer at the *Mine Shaft Tavern*, an old roadhouse-style saloon that boasts the longest bar in New Mexico.

524 | Up close with alligators on the Anhinga Trail

FLORIDA Stepping onto the concrete Anhinga Trail, you can't help but doubt its reputation as serious gator territory. Leading straight from a car park and with a friendly little visitor centre at its head, the half-mile circular pathway smacks of the type of "nature trail" on which you'd be lucky to catch sight of a sparrow. But don't judge it hastily – the Everglades is full of surprises.

Located way down in Florida's tropical south, the Everglades National Park covers 1.5 million acres of sawgrass-covered marshland and swamp, the largest subtropical wilderness in the United States and the perfect home for the American alligator. So as you stroll along admiring the exotic birdlife, don't let your guard down: all around you, massive carnivorous reptiles are lurking in the shallows, blending effortlessly into their surroundings. Almost comically prehistoric-looking, they sunbathe inches from the path or sometimes even stretched across it, motionless and slit-eyed, with seemingly hundreds of long, pointed teeth glinting in the hot Florida sun.

The sheer number of lazing alligators is remarkable, but your effortless proximity to them is even more incredible. In fact, you nearly forget you're in the wild – it all seems far too zoo-like (or even museum-esque, since the animals don't stir); and then, almost before you realize it, and with truly incredible speed, an alligator moves – and the enjoyable awe and excitement you were feeling morphs into sheer terror. When they take to the water and adopt that classic alligator pose – only eyes, teeth and powerful, ridged tail visible as they glide quietly and quickly towards their prey – it's nigh-on impossible to stop yourself from leaping away down the path, burning to tell someone of your near-death experience.

525 | Skiing at Snowbird and Alta

UTAH Squeezed side-by-side at the upper end of Little Cotton-wood Canyon, the Alta and Snowbird resorts first linked their lifts in 2002, and ever since, their nearly five thousand combined acres have added up to the finest downhill skiing experience in North America. Like two brothers forced to share a bedroom, the resorts have learned to co-exist while maintaining their distinctive characters.

Alta, an old silver mining town, opened its slopes in 1939. Not much has changed since then, and therein lies Alta's charm: while other resorts loudly embrace all things modern, anachronistic Alta tenaciously holds onto its old-world lodges, creaky double-chair lifts and ban on snowboarding, prizing tradition over convenience at nearly every turn. Opened forty years later, brash Snowbird next door welcomes boarders and any other daredevils willing to ride the thrilling aerial tram zipping nearly 3000 vertical feet up to the crest of Hidden Peak. Steep-and-deep is the quickest way to describe the riding here, where a ski-it-if-you-can ethos prevails.

Granted, you won't find a hip village like nearby Park City or the glitzy crowds that flock to Aspen and Vail in Colorado at either resort. Instead you'll encounter laidback downhillers happy to spend their time exploring a spine-tingling collection of chutes, cirques, cliffs and knee-knocking steeps that can leave even the most hardcore enthusiast humbled. Softening the inevitable spills, an epic 500 inches of yearly snowfall forms light, fluffy pillows. So much snow can dump at once, in fact, that breakfast is often accompanied by the deep, pleasing boom of World War II-era howitzers blasting away at fresh drifts, readying the slopes for a morning filled with first tracks through heavenly bottomless powder.

526 | Kooky city – exploring Chuck Palahniuk's Portland

OREGON Underground tunnels, quirky museums, swingers' sex clubs, crackpots, ghosts and geeks. These aren't the stories you find in the official history of Portland. Long overshadowed by West Coast hotspots San Francisco and Seattle, Oregon's biggest metropolis is increasingly matching its rivals in the hipster cool stakes, with booming arts, culinary, coffee and microbrew scenes, and an alternative, outdoorsy culture lampooned in cult TV show *Portlandia*. As writer Chuck Palahniuk put it in his offbeat 2003 travel guide to the city, *Fugitives and Refugees*: "Every corner has a story... from axe murders to penguins with a shoe fetish." Even then, things were already changing, but don't worry – Portland still retains healthy doses of the weird and wacky.

One of Palahniuk's top picks is now Portland's last true burlesque/drag show. Attend the *Darcelle XV Showplace*, and you'll be regaled by the veteran "empress of Portland" Walter Cole (aka Darcelle), still performing nightly to adoring fans. Expect hilarious stand-up comedy – prepare to be insulted – lip-synced Broadway hits and the obligatory *Rocky Horror* tribute. Fans can get a fuller fix of *The Rocky Horror Picture Show* at the Clinton Street Theater, which has put on an "interactive" showing at midnight every Saturday since 1978.

For something a little less risqué, wander around Kidd's Toy Museum. Its dusty rooms, akin to a Victorian curio shop, hold the eccentric collection of one Frank Kidd, including everything from cast-iron 1840s piggy banks to stuffed bears and bicycle emblems.

At another Palahniuk favourite, local institution *Hippo Hardware*, you can stroll the aisle admiring the decor as much as the merchandise – "kids have counted more than 300 hippos hiding in the store".

Portland also boasts an unfeasibly large number of "brew'n'view" cinemas; take in a show at the *Hollywood Theatre* and you can munch on Atomic Pizza and slurp six beers on tap while you watch. Then reconnect with nature at Mill Ends Park, officially the smallest park in the world: it's the size of a large dinner plate, a small patch of green in the middle of Naito Parkway that Palahniuk dubs, without irony, as one of his "gardens not to miss".

Riding the Slickrock in Moab

UTAH The allure of the small town of Moab, 238 miles southeast of Salt Lake City and 325 miles from Denver, lies not in the inspiring desert landscape that surrounds it, nor the stunning moonscape of ochre rocks, deep folded canyons, mesas or spires. Nor is it the spectacular landforms in nearby Arches National Park, the gurgling Colorado River, which swoops past town, or the landscape of mesas and buttes that stretch out before a backdrop of the snowcapped La Sal Mountains. No, what makes the place really remarkable is the incredible grip offered by the sandpapery surfaces of a group of contorted sandstone rocks near town – the location of the exceptional Slickrock mountain-bike trail.

From a distance these rocks look smooth, their neat shapes resembling a giant basket of eggs, but up close they offer bikers

traction that's positively unreal, and with it a powerful sense of possessing superhuman skills. You'll be able to glide across areas where you'd usually expect the bike to slip out from under you and astonish yourself with the grades you can climb and descend – all adding up to a mind-blowing roller-coaster ride in wonderful desert surroundings.

It's all so extraordinary that the trail – little more than a series of dots daubed on the rock to form a 10-mile loop – has become the most famous ride in the mountain-biking world. But perhaps best of all, it doesn't really matter how experienced a mountain biker you are: the Slickrock experience is accessible to anyone who can ride a bike, thanks to a 2.5-mile practice loop that never strays more than a half-hour's walk from the parking lot.

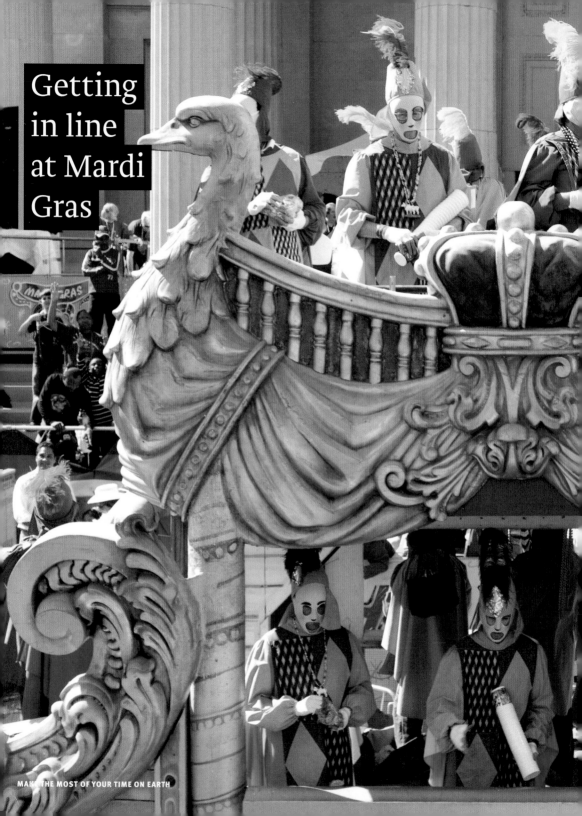

Getting
in line
at Mardi
Gras

LOUISIANA America's most over-the-top and hedonistic spectacle, Mardi Gras in New Orleans reflects as much a medieval European carnival as it does a drunken Spring Break ritual. Behind the scenes, the official celebration revolves around exclusive, invitation-only balls; for such an astonishingly big event, it can seem to put on more for locals than the raucous crowds who descend on the town, but you'll hardly be wanting for entertainment or feeling left out.

Over a period of several weeks, culminating on Mardi Gras itself, the Tuesday before Ash Wednesday, more than sixty parades wind their way through the city, snaking around but not into the historic French Quarter on routes of up to seven miles long. Multi-tiered floats crawl along the streets, flanked by masked horsemen, exuberant high-school marching bands, stilt-walking curiosities, *flambeaux* carriers brandishing flaming torches, and, of course, second liners – dancers who informally join the procession. It's even more fun to participate than it is to simply look on.

As each parade goes by, spectators gleefully vie to catch "throws" – strings of beads, souvenir "doubloons", knickers, fluffy toys – hurled into the crowd by the towering float-riders, who, milking it for all it's worth, taunt and jeer the watchers endlessly. Meanwhile, along Bourbon Street, women bare their breasts and men drop their trousers in return for baubles and beads.

The whole celebration is set to one of the greatest soundtracks in the world: strains of funk, R&B, New Orleans Dixie and more stream out of every bar and blare off rooftops – no surprise, of course, considering the city's status as the birthplace of jazz.

You might have thought that all of this madness would have been curtailed in the wake of Katrina, but like New Orleans, the party carries on in the face of long odds; indeed, the year following, many of the weird and wonderful costumes were made from the bright blue tarps that swathed so much of the city in the immediate aftermath of the storm.

529 | Eating barbecue in Texas Hill Country

TEXAS If you think barbecue is a sloppy pulled-pork sandwich or a platter of ribs drowned in a sticky, sweet sauce, a Texan will happily correct you. In the rolling hills around Austin – where pecan trees provide shade, pick-up trucks rule the road and the radio is devoted to Waylon, Willie and Merle – you'll find barbecue as it should be: nothing but pure, succulent, unadulterated meat, smoked for hours over a low wood fire. In fact, at one veteran vendor in Lockhart, *Kreuz Market*, the management maintains a strict no-sauce policy, so as not to distract from the perfectly tender slabs of brisket. Your meat, ordered by weight, comes on butcher paper with just crackers to dress it up.

Thankfully, this austerity applies only to the substance – not the quantity – of the meat. Gut-busting excess is what makes barbecue truly American, after all, especially at places like the legendary *Salt Lick*, southwest of Austin near the town of Driftwood. The all-you-can-eat spread here includes heaps of beef brisket, pork ribs and sausage, all bearing the signature smoke-stained pink outer layer that signifies authentic barbecue. On the side, you get the traditional fixin's: German-style coleslaw and potato salad, soupy pinto beans, sour pickles, plain old white bread and thick slices of onion.

So whether you visit *The Salt Lick*, *Kreuz Market* (those anti-sauce hardliners in Lockhart), *Black's* (another Lockhart gem, which has conceded to a light sauce), *Louie Mueller Barbecue* (in an old wood-floor gymnasium in Taylor), *City Market* (in Luling) or any of the other esteemed purveyors a local barbecue fetishist points you to, don't ever forget: it's all about the meat.

530 | Rediscover small-town America on Route 66 in Oklahoma

OKLAHOMA You get a taste of what's to come at *Waylan's Ku-Ku Burger*, a classic burger stand in the northeastern Oklahoma town of Miami. This is American nostalgia at its finest: you park beneath a buzzing neon sign unchanged since 1965, and chomp on giant cheeseburgers and waffle fries smothered with chili, cheese and green onions. It's a greasy, cheesy delight.

Expect a lot of this sort of thing cruising Route 66 in Oklahoma, a 400-mile stretch of the iconic road that's rich in Americana, neon-clad diners and quirky historic sights.

Long superseded by interstate highways, Route 66 is mostly two-lane and relatively traffic-free here, a ribbon that cuts through the state from its northeast to southwest corners. It's a landscape of rolling farmland and flat, grassy fields with lonely red-roofed barns, small towns and the odd Harley rider. Folks here are straightforward, friendly and say "fixin' to" a whole lot.

Outside Catoosa, you pull over at the Blue Whale, a wacky 80-foot sculpture, and stroll through its gaping mouth – kids sometimes cool off in the adjacent lake. A few miles on, outside Tulsa, you can walk under the legs of a mammoth statue of an oil worker, the 76ft-tall "Golden Driller." By the time you reach Stroud you're ready to eat again. Here the *Rock Café* has been knocking out alligator burgers (with real alligator) and German *jagerschnitzel* since 1939. Eating in this small stone-clad diner, with its all-wood, shack-like interior, is like travelling back to the 1950s.

At Chandler, you can learn more about the road at the Route 66 Interpretive Center, a fort-like sandstone armoury where you lounge in replica motel beds and vintage cars watching videos.

Half an hour outside Oklahoma City, the crimson dome of Arcadia's Round Barn looms over the roadside hedges. The 1898 landmark and museum, made of curved oak timbers and topped with shingle tiles, never seems busy, while its spritely volunteer staff look as if they've been here since the beginning.

Still hungry? Nearby lies *POPS*, a modern homage to 1950s diners, fronted by – what else? – a giant 66ft-tall soda bottle.

531 | Paddling in the Pacific

CALIFORNIA Despite being just an hour north of LA by boat, the Channel Islands National Park feels a world away. Whether you're enjoying a hiking trail along the islands' rugged contours or dipping into the waters for a look at some of the two thousand marine creatures on view, the natural splendour of this 250,000-acre preserve is an unexpected delight. Spoiled for choice, you can fish or scuba dive in the crystal-clear Pacific waters, take a close-up look at intriguing caves, coves and shipwrecks or, in the late winter and early spring, watch the world's largest pod of migrating blue whales cavorting offshore.

Part of the fun is sailing between each of the islands: volcanic outcrops whose cliffs and crags were carved by glaciers during the last Ice Age. On most tours, one-mile-square Anacapa will be your first stop and you'll make your entrance past dramatic Arch Rock – a 40ft-high, wave-cut natural bridge. With rocky headlands and steep promontories over the sea, Anacapa also has an attractive beach near Frenchy's Cove (a good base for scuba divers and snorkellers).

To the west, the much larger Santa Cruz is the largest and highest of the islands, rich in its fauna – from bald eagles and scrub jays to native foxes – and diverse landscapes, with forbidding canyons and lush green valleys. It's a fine place to hike or camp, as is Santa Rosa further west, with its alluring grasslands and steep ravines.

Off Santa Rosa's northwest tip, San Miguel is most notable for being crowded with barking elephant seals and sea lions. Only for the most gung-ho nature explorers, the place is frequently foggy and windy, and its surrounding rocks make for a white-knuckle sailing trip (park-approved boat tours only).

South of the main group, little Santa Barbara has its own sea lions, kestrels, larks and meadowlarks. A beautiful, lonely outpost, it almost makes you forget the teeming metropolis a short hop away.

532 | Lunching on Creole cuisine in New Orleans

LOUISIANA New Orleans is a gourmet's town, and its restaurants are far more than places to eat. These are social hubs and ports in a storm – sometimes literally, in the case of the French Quarter kitchens that stayed open post-Katrina, dishing out red beans and rice to the stubborn souls who refused to abandon their beloved city. Above all, they are where New Orleans comes to celebrate itself, in all its quirky, battered beauty. And no restaurant is more quintessentially New Orleans than *Galatoire's*, the grande dame of local Creole cuisine.

Lunch, particularly on Friday and Sunday, is the meal of choice; set aside an entire afternoon. Reservations aren't taken for the downstairs room – *the* place to be – so you'll need to come early and wait in line. In true New Orleans fashion, this bastion of haute Creole style sits on the city's bawdiest stretch, Bourbon Street. Picking your way through the morning-after remnants of a Bourbon Saturday night – plastic cups floating in pools of fetid liquid, a distinctive miasma of drains and stale booze and rotting magnolias – brings you to a display worthy of a Tennessee Williams play. Seersucker-clad powerbrokers puff on fat cigars, dangling dainty Southern belles on their arms; immaculately coiffured women greet each other with loud cries of "dawlin'!" Inside – or downstairs at least – it's like time has stood still: brass ceiling fans whir overhead, giant old mirrors reflect the lights cast by Art Nouveau lamps, and black-jacketed waiters, who have worked here for ever, crack wise with their favourite diners.

It's the same century-old menu, too: basically French, pepped up with the herbs and spices of Spain, Africa and the West Indies. Lump crabmeat and plump oysters come with creamy French sauces or a piquant *rémoulade*, a blend of tomato, onion, Creole mustard, horseradish and herbs; side dishes might be featherlight soufflé potatoes or fried eggplant. To end with a kick, order a steaming tureen of potent *café brûlot* – jet-black Java heated with brandy, orange peel and spices – prepared tableside with all the ceremony of a religious ritual.

533 | Tracing civil rights history in Montgomery

ALABAMA The struggle for African-American civil rights – one of the great social causes of American history – played out all across the South in the 1950s and 1960s. To gain a grasp on its legacy, and a sense of how the fabric of the country has changed as a result, make your way to Montgomery, Alabama, the culmination of the so-called Selma-to-Montgomery National History Trail.

Start at the state capitol building (which looks like a cross between the US Capitol and a plantation mansion), where you can almost hear Dr Martin Luther King Jr in 1963 declaring at the end of the four-day Selma-to-Montgomery civil rights march, "however difficult the moment, however frustrating the hour, it will not be long, because truth pressed to earth will rise again."

To experience more of King's spirit, take in a passionate Sunday service at the Dexter Avenue King Memorial Baptist Church, where today's ministers use King's example to inspire both parishioners and visitors. The basement holds a mural depicting scenes from King's life, as well as his desk, office and pulpit. His birthplace, for those interested, is in the Sweet Auburn district of Atlanta, Georgia.

The Rosa Parks Museum honours the Montgomery event that started it all. Parks's refusal in 1955 to accept a seat at the back of a Montgomery bus in essence sparked the civil rights movement; her inspiring story is told through photographs and dioramas, and you can step onto a replica of that city bus.

Most poignant, though, is the Civil Rights Memorial, centred on a black-granite table designed by Maya Lin and inscribed with the names of forty activists killed by racist violence from 1954 to 1968. The events described on the table provide as telling an overview of the era as you're likely to find.

534 | Taking the A-train through Manhattan

NEW YORK It may be just a dirty, run-of-the-mill inner-city commuter train, but ever since 1941 when Duke Ellington's band immortalized the A-train – the subway from Brooklyn through the heart of Manhattan and into Harlem – the route's been associated with jazz, the Harlem Renaissance and the gritty glamour of travelling through New York. The iconic tin-can carriages – long a favourite location for TV cop dramas – rattle along on this express route, taking you to some of Manhattan's most varied neighbourhoods.

Wherever you choose to board the train, getting out at Jay Street in Brooklyn Heights, and stopping at one of the cafés on leafy Montague Street for a long, lazy brunch starts the day in true New York style. From here, the Brooklyn Bridge beckons; cross on foot and enter downtown Manhattan, taking in the spectacular views of the skyline as you traverse the sparkling East River, the Statue of Liberty just visible to your left.

Rejoin the A-train at Park Place and head up the line. Jump off at West 4th Street and browse the boutiques alongside funky West Villagers; stop at Columbus Circle, emerging at the southwest corner of Central Park for a leafy stroll. From here it's a nonstop express trip whizzing under the Upper West Side – sit in the front carriage for a driver's-eye view of the glinting tracks as they disappear beneath the train.

Your final stop is Duke Ellington's own journey's end: 145th Street for Harlem's Sugar Hill. High above the city, with hazy views back along Manhattan's straight avenues, this was the more upmarket part of the neighbourhood during the Jazz Age. Today, well into its second renaissance, the area's art and music scenes thrive, nowhere so much as in its classic jazz clubs. Stick your head into *Showman's Jazz Club* to hear some live jazz and blues – Duke would definitely approve.

On the trail of the perfect Key Lime Pie

535

FLORIDA The only portrait of "Lee" Ida Mae Neil hangs on the wall of the old Customs House in Key West. She faces sideways, dressed in white, her veiny arms the only sign of decades of lime squeezing; making key lime pie is very hard work. Neil moved to Key West in 1944, eventually becoming the undisputed "Queen of Key Lime Pies", and today, the beloved pie is the Florida Keys' best-known culinary export, made from the tiny, green citrus fruits that every local seems to grow in their back yard.

Highway 1 connects the Florida mainland with Key West, a spectacular ribbon of causeways and bridges that soars above sandy bars, mangroves and channels thick with giant manta rays and sharks. It's also your route to the best key lime pies in the country. Aficionados are divided: graham-cracker or pastry crust? Meringue on top or whipped cream? The one thing that everyone can agree on is that adding green food colouring is taboo. Authentic key lime pie is always light yellow.

The gluttony begins in Key Largo, where the *Key Lime Tree* offers thick, piquant creations made with condensed milk. Heading south, Tavernier is home to the *Blond Giraffe Key Lime Pie Factory*, renowned for its classic fluffy meringue toppings and whipped cream. Marathon holds *Porky's Bayside Restaurant*; skip the barbecue and go straight for the coronary-inducing, deep-fried key lime pie. This time it's the batter that's top secret. Key West, at the end of the road, is pie central. The *Key West Key Lime Pie Co* dishes up all sorts of fancy, custard-like, frozen versions, including mango, pineapple and coconut. *Kermit's Key West Key Lime Shoppe* serves pie with a consistency somewhere between gelatin and cake, a perfect blend of sugary and tart, but the insider's choice is the *Rooftop Café*: the top layer of meringue and the gooey graham-cracker base sandwich a tangy core made with fresh lime juice and traces of melted butter. It's easy to get hooked, but at least you're never far from the Keys, where kayaking, swimming and snorkelling offer a chance to burn off those calories.

536 | Lost for words at the Grand Canyon

ARIZONA If a guidebook tells you that something is "impossible to describe", it usually means the writer can't be bothered to describe it – with one exception. After pondering the Grand Canyon for the first time, the most spectacular natural wonder on Earth, most visitors are stunned into silence.

Committed travellers hike down to the canyon floor on foot or ride on a mule, spending a night at *Phantom Ranch*, or hover above in a helicopter to get a better sense of its dimensions. But it is still hard to grasp. The problem isn't lack of words. It's just that the canyon is so vast and so deep, that the vista stretches so far across your line of vision, up, down and across, giving the impression of hundreds of miles of space, that it's a bit like looking at one of those puzzles in reverse – the more you stare, the more it becomes harder to work out what it is or where you are. Distance becomes meaningless, depth blurs, and your sense of time and space withers away.

The facts are similarly mind-boggling: the Grand Canyon is around 277 miles long and one mile deep. The South Rim, where most visitors go, averages 7000 feet above sea level, while the North Rim, eleven miles away as the crow flies but 215 miles by road, is over 8000 feet high – its alpine landscape only adding to the sense of the surreal.

On the canyon floor flows the Colorado River, its waters carving out the gorge over five to six million years and exposing rocks that are up to two billion years old through vividly coloured strata. It's this incredible chromatic element that stays with you almost as much as the canyon's size, with the various layers of reds, ochres and yellows seemingly painted over the strangely shaped tower formations and broken cliffs.

Think of it this way: the Grand Canyon is like a mountain range upside down. The country around the top is basically flat and all the rugged, craggy elements are below you. The abruptness of the drop is bizarre and, for some, unnerving. But the Grand Canyon is like that: it picks you up and takes you out of your comfort zone, dropping you back just that little bit changed.

537 | Snowshoeing on Sawtooth

IDAHO Tucked beneath the serrated peaks of the Sawtooth Range – part of the Rocky Mountains, and as far removed from the haunt of the Hollywood stars down the road as it's possible to imagine – you'll discover perfect snowshoeing trails, for all levels of ability, snaking their way through Idaho's silent winter forests.

For millennia, Native Americans used snowshoes as a means of getting around in winter – the tennis-racquet-like extensions to your feet spread your weight, allowing you to move through deep snow that would otherwise swallow you to the knees or beyond. Modern snowshoes are lightweight, and it takes seconds to fasten the bindings to your boots before you're all set to head off and explore. There's not really any special technique – just lift your feet slightly higher than normal. Marked routes on the scenic North Valley Trails can be accessed from Galena Lodge, north of Ketchum. The Cowboy Cabin Trail is perfect for first-timers; dazzling views of the surrounding icy mountains and meadows unfold on Pioneer Cemetery Loop; or for something a bit more heart-pumping, challenge yourself on Tilt a Whirl or Psycho Adventures. You can take a guide, but pretty much anyone can enjoy snowshoeing here under their own steam and renting shoes for the day is far cheaper than skiing.

The palpable silence of the forests will occasionally be broken by a soft "whump" as a pillow of snow slips from a tree branch, or by the gentle tick of snowflakes landing on your shoulders, but despite this almost eerie lack of noise there is still plenty of life here. Look out for the tracks of squirrels, rabbits, hare and deer and listen for the occasional tweet of winter wrens and mountain bluebirds, which are tough enough to survive winter in the mountains.

At the end of the day, there's nothing quite like heading back to civilization, icy dusk descending and a well-earned hot bath awaiting. Pity those poor squirrels who are out there all night, though...

538 | Gospel truth in Harlem

NEW YORK The church is overflowing, humming with whispers. Smartly dressed ladies with wide-brimmed hats, neat dresses and flowers, men in immaculate suits, and little boys and girls sparkling in their best clothes. The choir, dressed in deep red and gold robes, fills the raised platform above the altar, facing the congregation and backed by vivid stained glass. The pastor enters, and the service begins.

There are prayers, and a sermon of course, but it's the choir that drives worship here; entrancing, invigorating music that soon has the whole congregation clapping, whooping and praising the Lord. Soloists belt out hymns and spirituals, moving some to tears, before the tempo picks up and a chorus of voices joins in. Sometimes they hum, softly, building up to a crescendo of sound and rhythm that seems to envelop the whole church; the singers clap and dance, and the congregation joins in, everyone on their feet.

Make no mistake, this is a religious service not a show, but the quality on display is astounding – every member of the choir is a powerful artist, and the soloists hold everyone spellbound. As the waves of music blast the congregation, hats slide, suits are loosened and everyone seems uplifted – even the tourists jump and clap.

Harlem is chock-full of churches and almost every one features Gospel music on Sundays. The choir at Abyssinian Baptist Church, the second-oldest black congregation in the US, is the city's finest, and attracts steady streams of curious visitors. The Abyssinian started to become the religious and political powerhouse that it is today when it moved to Harlem in 1920. Under charismatic pastors such as Reverend Adam Clayton Powell, Jr (1937–70), the first black Congressman from New York, it became the largest Protestant congregation in the US and remains a hugely influential centre of African-American spirituality and activism.

Gospel tours are big business, but entry is free and you can easily visit alone – get there early. Just remember this is a place of worship, so you should dress accordingly: shoulders should be covered before entering, and no flip-flops, shorts or tank tops are allowed.

539 | At home with Emily Dickinson

MASSACHUSETTS Wandering through the Homestead, the Amherst birthplace and residence of poet Emily Dickinson, is a haunting experience. It's quiet: clocks tick, birds chirp outside and only the odd car or hushed tones of tour guides remind you of the twenty-first century. The elegant Greek Revival-style home has been furnished to match its 1860s appearance, when Dickinson began to write stark, witheringly beautiful poetry. The wooden desk in which her poems were found after her death lies as if Emily has just left to make a cup of tea, her rooms scrupulously restored with authentic floor coverings, furniture and wallpaper.

The guides who give tours of the house – now the Emily Dickinson Museum, together with the grander Evergreens next door, home of Emily's brother Austin and his family – are passionate about her life and work. As you file into the main, rather cold and stiff parlours, they'll quote Dickinson poems – rain that "sounded till it curved" and "loosened acres, lifted seas". Fading photos and oil paintings, porcelain teacups, rugs and simple wooden Empire chairs evoke Emily's reclusive existence.

Born in Amherst in 1830, Dickinson attended nearby Mount Holyoke College, but loneliness drove her back home without finishing her studies, and she soon embarked upon a life of self-imposed seclusion.

Emily's bedroom, repainted in its nineteenth-century mustard tones, is especially poignant, containing reproductions of her writing stand and bureau. The tour guides seem genuinely moved – the small window with a view of billowing trees and the Holyoke Range, the humble bed. This was her safe haven, a creative space into which she could escape, perhaps where she "felt a funeral in my brain, and mourners, to and fro."

Tours also take in the small library, where Emily spent hours poring over musty tomes. With palpable sadness, guides explain that despite her literary hyperactivity, Emily published fewer than a dozen poems, and was completely unknown when she died in 1886. Her work was collected and published in 1890 by her sister, but she wasn't widely read until the 1950s. Dickinson is now regarded as one of the greatest American poets.

540 | Riding high on the Blue Ridge Parkway

VIRGINIA & NORTH CAROLINA Slicing through some of the most stunning scenery in the country, the Blue Ridge Parkway winds its way along the crest of the Appalachian Mountains, from Shenandoah National Park in Virginia to Great Smoky Mountains National Park between North Carolina and Tennessee. Originally it was dotted with the isolated frontier communities where bluegrass was born. Today you'll still find such traces of the region's history as old gristmills, abandoned wooden barns and ramshackle diners scattered along the road, but in truth much of what has been preserved is aimed squarely at the tourist trade. What the parkway is best for is simply a heavy dose of nature at its finest.

The first part of the drive cuts through northern Virginia, and here the ridge is very apparent, sometimes narrowing to a ledge not much wider than the road. The central section is much less dramatic – the land is heavily farmed and the road busier with local traffic, especially around Roanoke. But the lower highway, which snakes through North Carolina, is the most spectacular part. There's plenty of kitschy development here (the town of Blowing Rock is a full-scale resort, with shopping malls and themed motels), but the views are astonishing – at nearby Grandfather Mountain, on Hwy-221 one mile south of the parkway, a mile-high swinging bridge hangs over an 80ft chasm with 360-degree views.

Further south, near Mount Pisgah, the road reaches its highest point. As you ascend towards it you'll have numerous chances to stop at overlooks, or just pull onto the shoulder, for breathtaking vistas: hazy blue ridges, smothered in vast stands of hickory, dogwood and birch, and groves of mountain ash bursting with orange berries.

541 | Reconsidering the Wild West in Monument Valley

ARIZONA & UTAH When you think of the American West, it's hard to conjure a more iconic image than Monument Valley, with its awesome mesas, spires of jagged sandstone and arid, desert-like plains. This is the Wild West of popular culture – a vast, empty landscape that dates back to antiquity and can make you feel at once tiny and insignificant and completely free and uninhibited. These qualities have made it the perfect location for Westerns, which is perhaps why it seems so familiar: *Stagecoach*, *The Searchers* and *How the West Was Won* are among the numerous movies that have been filmed here.

But while Hollywood favours heroic cowboys on stallions, you won't be restaging the gunfight at the OK Corral while here (head south to Tombstone, Arizona, for that). Instead, this is sacred native American country managed by the Navajo Nation, and to visit the area today is to experience the West through their eyes.

From the Ancestral Puebloan petroglyphs in Mystery Valley to the traditional hogans still inhabited by Navajo, every rock here tells a story. The valley's most famous formations – like the twin buttes of the Mittens, with their skinny "thumbs" of sandstone, and the giant bulk of Hunt's Mesa – can be seen from a circular, seventeen-mile track that's usually smothered in red dust. Navajo guides, who fill you in on local history and culture, lead 4WD rides around the track, as well as longer, usually overnight, expeditions by foot. These may start before dawn, allowing you to reach the top of a mesa before it gets too hot and watch the sunrise across a land where sand and rock stretch endlessly before you to the horizon.

Need to know

481 Kilauea is part of Hawaii Volcanoes National Park (Ⓦ nps.gov/havo).

482 The Indianapolis 500 (Ⓦ indianapolismotorspeedway.com) is held over Memorial Day weekend at the Indianapolis Motor Speedway. For details of the Richard Petty Driving Experience, visit Ⓦ drivepetty.com.

483 Walking tours cover everything from local architecture to legends; visit Ⓦ visitsavannah.com.

484 For Bourbon Trail info, visit Ⓦ kybourbontrail.com.

485 Dr Wilkinson's Hot Springs, 1507 Lincoln Ave, Calistoga (Ⓦ drwilkinson.com); Mount View Spa, 1457 Lincoln Ave, Calistoga (Ⓦ mountviewhotel.com); Jack London State Historic Park, Glen Ellen (Ⓦ jacklondonpark.com); *The French Laundry*, 6640 Washington St, Yountville (Ⓦ frenchlaundry.com).

486 Direct flights connect Lihue with Honolulu, San Francisco, Los Angeles, Phoenix and Seattle (see Ⓦ airports.hawaii.gov/lih). Visit Ⓦ hawaiistateparks.org for info on hiking in the Na Pali Coast State Park.

487 The Great North Woods are best accessed from Greenville. Young's Guide Service can arrange moose safaris (Ⓦ youngsguideservice.com). For more information, see Ⓦ visitmaine.com.

488 *Carlson's Fish* is located at 205 W. River, Fishtown in Leland, Michigan; Ⓣ +1 231 256 9801. Additional resources: *Village Cheese Shanty* (Ⓦ villagecheeseshanty.com); Manitou Island Transit (Ⓦ manitoutransit.com); Leelanau Peninsula Wine Trail (Ⓦ lpwines.com); National Park Service (Ⓦ nps.gov/slbe/planyourvisit/the-manitou-islands.htm).

489 Experienced stormchasing operators include Storm Tours (Ⓦ stormtours.com).

490 South Beach occupies the southernmost part of Miami Beach; Ocean Drive runs south–north for 10 blocks.

491 For more information on Fantasy Fest, check out Ⓦ fantasyfest.com.

492 Puyé Cliff Dwellings stand on the Santa Clara Pueblo Indian Reservation, 30 miles northwest of Santa Fe. Tours run daily (Ⓦ puyecliffs.com).

493 The round-trip hike to the top of Half Dome is 17 miles (9–12hr; 4800ft ascent). For more information on Yosemite, visit Ⓦ nps.gov/yose.

494 The contiguous Sequoia and Kings Canyon National Parks are open year-round, but winter storms often close access roads temporarily. Visit Ⓦ nps.gov/seki.

495 Lobster Shack at Two Lights, 225 Two Lights Rd, Cape Elizabeth (5 miles south of Portland); Ⓣ +1 207/799-1677).

496 Both *Arthur Bryant's*, 1727 Brooklyn Ave (Ⓦ arthurbryantsbbq.com), and Gates Bar-B-Q, 3205 Main St (Ⓦ gatesbbq.com), are open daily. For Kansas City information visit Ⓦ visitkc.com.

497 US Capitol (Mon–Sat 8.30am–4.30pm; Ⓦ visitthecapitol.gov); White House (Ⓦ whitehouse.gov/about/tours-and-events); Supreme Court (Oct–April arguments 10am & 1pm; Ⓦ supremecourt.gov).

498 Ka Hula Piko (Ⓦ kahulapiko.com) takes place in May on the western tip of Molokai. Admission is free.

499 See Ⓦ cannonbeach.org for more info.

500 *Jules' Undersea Lodge*, Key Largo Undersea Park, 51 Shoreland Drive, Key Largo (Ⓦ jul.com).

501 The Crazy Horse Memorial (Ⓦ crazyhorsememorial.org) is in South Dakota's Black Hills, on Hwy-16/385.

502 Brooks Falls (Ⓦ nps.gov/katm) is a 20min walk from Brooks Camp, which can be reached by flying from Anchorage to the town of King Salmon, then taking a short float-plane flight.

503 Juke joints don't tend to have websites, phones or set opening hours. For up-to-date information on what's

on in the Delta, contact the Cat Head music and crafts store in Clarksdale (Ⓦ cathead.biz).

504 Camping in Yellowstone is only permitted in designated sites, and some require reservations in advance. There are twelve serviced campgrounds in Yellowstone National Park and a further 300 basic sites in the backcountry. See Ⓦ nps.gov/yell/planyourvisit/campgrounds.htm for more information.

505 Alaska Sea Kayakers (Ⓦ alaskaseakayakers.com), in Whittier, rents sea kayaks and runs guided day-trips and multi-day tours.

506 Annapolis's *Cantler's Riverside Inn*, 458 Forest Beach Rd (Ⓦ cantlers.com), or *Costas Inn*, 4100 Northpoint Blvd (Ⓦ costasinn.com), in Baltimore, will do the trick.

507 Visit Ⓦ appalachiantrail.org for more info.

508 Gunflint Lake is a three-hour drive from Duluth airport; six from Minneapolis–St. Paul airport. Local places offering ice-fishing packages and accommodation include *Gunflint lodge* at 143 S Gunflint Lake, Grand Marais, MN 55604 (Ⓦ gunflint.com).

509 Early Oct is prime leaf-viewing time. Visit Ⓦ foliage-vermont.com for updates.

510 Companies that run cruises through Alaska's Inside Passage include Celebrity (Ⓦ celebritycruises.com), Holland America (Ⓦ hollandamerica.com) and Un-Cruise Adventures (Ⓦ un-cruise.com).

511 For ticket info, photos and a helpful "First-Timers' Guide", visit Ⓦ burningman.com.

512 For all details, see Ⓦ havasupaireservations.com. Visitors pay $35 entrance fee, plus $17 to camp, or $175 for a lodge room. Getting from the road to the village costs $175 by horse; hiking is free.

513 Graceland, 3734 Elvis Presley Blvd, Memphis (Ⓦ graceland.com).

514 For more information on the Alaska Marine Highway, go to Ⓦ dot.state.ak.us/amhs.

515 Bluff and Mexican Hat are in the southeastern corner of Utah, close to Monument Valley; both hold hotels and restaurants. As well as one-day-trips, Wild River Expeditions (Ⓦ riversandruins.com) also offer longer float trips, camping beside the river for up to nine nights.

516 Cunard offers numerous westbound transatlantic crossings every year, from Southampton to New York (Ⓦ cunard.co.uk).

517 To experience life on the road in true Golden Statestyle, rent a convertible; you can slip behind the wheel of a Chevrolet Corvette with San Francisco-based Specialty Rentals (Ⓦ specialtyrentals.com).

518 The *Austin American-Statesman* Bat Observation Center is on the southeast side of Congress Avenue Bridge.

519 Concerts take place every Saturday night at the Carter Family Memorial Music Center (Ⓦ carterfamilyfold.org).

520 Blazing Saddles Bike Rentals & Tours is at 2715 Hyde St at Beach, and six other San Francisco locations (Ⓦ blazingsaddles.com).

521 Frequent half-hour tours are offered daily at the factory, on Rte-100 in Waterbury Center, one mile north of I-89 (Ⓦ benjerry.com/about-us/factory-tours). Ice cream is manufactured Mon–Fri only.

522 Jockey's Ridge State Park, US 158 Bypass, mile marker 12. Kitty Hawk Kites (Ⓦ kittyhawk.com) provides instruction and equipment.

523 For information on both the Old Coal Mine Museum, at 2814 Hwy-14 in Madrid, and the *Mine Shaft Tavern*, alongside at 2846 Hwy-14, visit Ⓦ the mineshafttavern.com.

524 The Everglades (Ⓦ nps.gov/ever) are best visited during the dry season (Nov–April).

525 Visit Ⓦ alta.com and Ⓦ snowbird.com for full details on lift tickets, accommodation and transport.

526 The *Darcelle XV Showplace* takes place on Wed, Thurs, Fri & Sat at 208 NW Third Ave (Ⓦ darcellexv.com). Kidd's Toy Museum is at 1301 SE Grand Ave (Ⓦ facebook.com/Kidds-Toy-Museum-113578118676868); Hippo Hardware at 1040 E Burnside St (Ⓦ hippohardware.com); the Hollywood Theatre at 4122 NE Sandy Blvd (Ⓦ hollywoodtheatre.org); and Clinton Street Theater at 2522 SE Clinton St (Ⓦ cstpdx.com). For more information, visit Ⓦ travelportland.com.

527 Local stores offering bike rentals, tours and shuttles to trailheads include Rim Tours (Ⓦ rimtours.com) and Poison Spider (Ⓦ poisonspiderbicycles.com). The best seasons to visit are spring and autumn.

528 For a full schedule, visit Ⓦ mardigrasneworleans.com.

529 In Lockhart: Kreuz Market, 619 N Colorado St (Ⓦ kreuzmarket.com); *Black's Barbecue*, 215 N Main St (Ⓦ blacksbbq.com). In Luling: City Market, 633 E Davis St (Ⓦ lulingcitymarket.com). Near Driftwood: *The Salt Lick*, 18300 FM 1826 (Ⓦ saltlickbbq.com). In Taylor: *Louie Mueller Barbecue*, 206 W 2nd St (Ⓦ louiemueller-barbecue.com).

530 Useful sites for travellers heading down Route 66 in Oklahoma include Ⓦ oklahomaroute66.com; Ⓦ visit-tulsa.com; Ⓦ rockcafert66.com; Ⓦ route66interpretivecenter.org; and, for POPS, Ⓦ pops66.com.

531 For information on transportation and outfitters, visit Ⓦ nps.gov/chis. The National Park Service also operates a visitor centre at 1901 Spinnaker Drive in Ventura on the nearby California coast. Camping permits cost $15 per night.

532 *Galatoire's*, 209 Bourbon St (Ⓦ galatoires.com). Jackets required for men after 5pm and all day Sunday.

533 Alabama state capitol, 600 Dexter Ave (Ⓦ alabama.gov); Dexter Avenue Church, 454 Dexter Ave (Ⓦ dexterkingmemorial.org); Civil Rights Memorial, 400 Washington Ave (Ⓦ splcenter.org/civil-rights-memorial); Rosa Parks Museum, 252 Montgomery St (Ⓦ troy.edu/rosaparks).

534 The A-train runs from Queens through Brooklyn and Manhattan to Inwood–207th Street.

535 Key Largo: *Key Lime Tree* (Ⓣ +1 305/853-0378). Tavernier: *Blond Giraffe Key Lime Pie Factory*, 92220 Overseas Hwy (Ⓦ blondgiraffe.com). On Marathon: *Porky's Bayside Restaurant*, 1410 Overseas Hwy (Ⓦ porkysbaysidebbq.com). In Key West: *Key West Key Lime Pie Co*, 511 Greene St (Ⓦ keylimepieco.com); *Kermit's Key West Key Lime Shoppe*, 200 Elizabeth St (Ⓦ keylimeshop.com); *Rooftop Café*, 308 Front St (Ⓦ rooftopcafekeywest.com).

536 The South Rim remains open all year; winter snows preclude access to the North Rim, which is usually open from mid-May to mid-Oct. See Ⓦ nps.gov/grca for more information.

537 Snowshoes can be rented at *Galena Lodge* (Ⓦ galenalodge.com), four hours' drive from Boise airport.

538 Visitors are only welcome at the Abyssinian Baptist Church's Sun 11am service, at 132 Odell Clark Place (Ⓦ abyssinian.org). Mount Nebo Baptist Church, 1883 Adam Clayton Powell, Jr Blvd (Ⓦ mountneboh.org), is less touristy.

539 The Emily Dickinson Museum, 280 Main St, Amherst, is open Wed–Sun only, between March and Dec; see Ⓦ emilydickinsonmuseum.org.

540 The Blue Ridge Parkway (Ⓦ nps.gov/blri) starts at Rockfish Gap near Waynesboro, Virginia, just off I-64, and ends 469 miles later at Cherokee, North Carolina.

541 Monument Valley (Ⓦ navajonationparks.org) is off Hwy-163, near the Arizona/Utah state line.

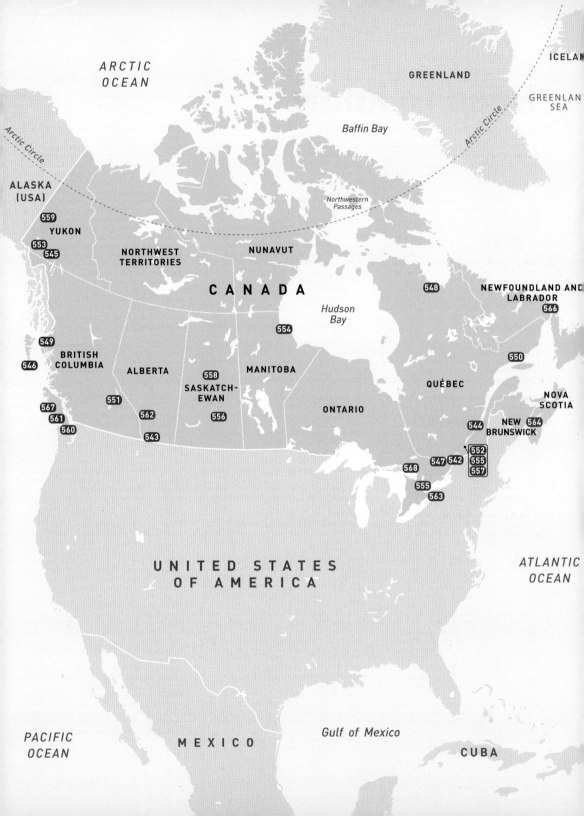

ARCTIC
OCEAN

ICELAN

GREENLAND

Baffin Bay

GREENLAN
SEA

Arctic Circle

Arctic Circle

ALASKA
(USA)

559 YUKON

553
545

NORTHWEST
TERRITORIES

NUNAVUT

*Northwestern
Passages*

CANADA

548

NEWFOUNDLAND AND
LABRADOR

566

*Hudson
Bay*

554

549

546

BRITISH
COLUMBIA

ALBERTA

558

MANITOBA

QUÉBEC

550

NOVA
SCOTIA

567
561

560

551

562

SASKATCH-
EWAN

556

ONTARIO

544

NEW
BRUNSWICK

564

543

568

547 **542**

552
555
557

555

563

UNITED STATES
OF AMERICA

ATLANTIC
OCEAN

PACIFIC
OCEAN

MEXICO

Gulf of Mexico

CUBA

CANADA
542-568

Things are big in Canada. The heftily proportioned wildlife, the temperature extremes, the lens-filling scenery, the unending road trips. The globe's second-largest country offers a powerful set of contrasts, from primordial landscapes to the pageantry of the Calgary Stampede, and from the elegant beauty of Québec's historic Old Town to the passion of Ontario's ice hockey infatuation. Whether you're searching for spirit bears in British Columbia, or going off-grid in northern Saskatchewan – it's all about pushing yourself outside your comfort zone. The remains of ancient cultures and remote islands are ripe to be explored, and when you factor in such immense natural landmarks as the Niagara Falls, the Rocky Mountains and Hudson Bay, the destination's full-sized appeal becomes more ample still.

542 Getting Gaelic: the Glengarry Highland games

ONTARIO I spent most of my first ever day at my first Glengarry Highland Games recovering from one hell of a hangover, brought on by something only the devil himself or someone with two minutes' illicit access to his parents' liquor cabinet could concoct. I was 16. As a boy growing up in eastern Ontario's Glengarry County, the trip to Maxville, the home of the games, was a rite of passage – albeit one that was more about drinking and dancing than appreciating Scottish heritage.

It was only years later, when visiting the games as an adult – older, wiser and just a little less keen on partying – that I discovered the games I know and love today, the games that have seen tens of thousands of people flood into Maxville (population 800) every August since 1948. Watching knots of kilted pipers, cheeks puffed and fingers working up a lilting drone, practising all around me, I learned that the games were the home of the North American Pipe Band Championships, and the largest gathering of pipe bands outside Scotland. Later I watched in awe as a packed grandstand cheered on brawny giants tossing 8m cabers and shotputting 12kg field stones as if they were straws and marbles. In another corner, Highland dancers sprung into the air, a gravity-defying tartan whirlwind. And then there was the whisky tasting and the gloriously rumbustious two-stepping to local bands. And the tattoo, a spectacular headlined by Celtic music superstars. All this in little old Glengarry, almost 5000km from Scotland, an area settled in the eighteenth century by Scots fleeing the American War of Independence and, later, the Highland Clearances.

As the massed bands closed the games with a sunset rendition of *Amazing Grace,* the sight and sound of a lone piper playing the first notes before being joined by more than one thousand other musicians sent shivers down my spine. This time I had truly soaked up the living heritage of a people who are always ready with a warm *Ceud Mìle Fàilte* – a hundred thousand welcomes.

Harry Wilson
is a former Rough Guides editor who now lives in Ottawa, where he's the senior editor at *Canadian Geographic* and *Canadian Geographic Travel* magazines. His Scottish credentials don't extend to having attempted the caber toss, but he does own a kilt.

543

Go wild in Waterton

ALBERTA Good things come in small packages. No – *great* things come in small packages. That's certainly true of Waterton Lakes National Park, which at 505 square kilometres is the smallest of its kind in the Canadian Rockies.

While its behemoth siblings to the north – Banff, Kootenay, Yoho and Jasper – trumpet their credentials with towering crags and great slabs of glacial ice, tiny Waterton, nestled into the southwest corner of Alberta, seems to fly under the radar. But it has a trump card to play.

And what a card. Waterton is located at a point where multiple ecological regions meet, creating a melange of habitats and climate that yields a diversity of flora and fauna unmatched by any of Canada's other western national parks. Want gently rolling prairie grasslands studded with wild rose and sagebrush? Waterton's got 'em. Looking for picturesque peaks where bighorn sheep and hikers roam? There they are, lower and more irregular than those in Banff, but just as captivating, dramatically emerging from the prairie. Yearning to get your feet wet? There are about eighty lakes and ponds, including the park's largest and namesake body of water, as well as more than 100km of rivers and streams, making Waterton a dream for everyone from paddlers to birdwatchers. Look out for waterfowl, in particular, including the trumpeter swan, once nearly extinct in North America. With such variety packed into an easily accessible and compact area – compact for Canada, that is – it's easy to feel as if you're in command of the park, especially in summer, when moving around is a breeze.

Winter, however, offers a different perspective. Visitors slow to a trickle, but those who do come know there's a special kind of peace to be found here, whether along the snowshoe trails that snake through evergreen forests or on the windswept shores of Waterton Lake. Perhaps it's the stillness that comes with a thick blanket of freshly fallen snow or the distant boom of a backcountry avalanche, but Waterton in winter brings the profound understanding of what's actually true in any season – it's not the park that's small, it's us.

544 | Getting lost within the walls of Vieux-Québec

QUÉBEC You'd be forgiven for mistaking Canada's most graceful downtown for somewhere in the middle of Europe. As you amble the cobbled streets of a centuries-old walled city, where the views encompass castle turrets and battlefields – and the main language spoken is French – it's easy to feel you've left North America far behind. Founded by the French in 1608, Québec City was taken in 1759 by the English in a historic battle on the Plains of Abraham, just outside the city walls; the victory also won them control of Canada. The fortifications survive today (making it North America's only walled city) and mark the boundaries of the old town, or Vieux-Québec. Its lovingly maintained, chaotic tangle of streets holds a treasury of historic architecture, fine restaurants and tiny museums. Pottering around its pedestrianized precincts – which are virtually untouched by minimarts, chain stores and fast-food restaurants – is the chief pleasure of a visit here.

The lower town, particularly the Quartier Petit-Champlain – a beautiful warren of narrow lanes and hidden staircases lined with carefully restored limestone buildings – is a good place to begin an aimless wander. It's easy to idle away hours soaking up the historic charm, listening to buskers and browsing refined boutiques, antique shops and studio-galleries where artists are often at work, before being tempted by the aromas that drift from the doorways of the many old-fashioned restaurants.

Luckily, the climbs up and down the steeply sloping streets and staircases around the town help justify indulging in rich, multi-course meals. After a feast of local duck, rabbit or wild game and creamy local cheeses, you'll need to hit the streets again to walk it all off.

545 | Following the Yukon Quest

YUKON At the start of the Yukon Quest dogsledding race, a din has broken out. Dogs are barking, whining and howling as they're hooked up to their lines. They leap high in the air, hauling forward with all their might, trying to shift the weight that anchors them. Their ears are pricked, their tails wag, their tongues loll, their wide mouths grin. Anyone who suggests that sled dogs run against their will has never witnessed this – these dogs can't wait to get going.

The course of the Yukon Quest crosses 1600km of inhospitable winter wilderness between Fairbanks, Alaska, and Whitehorse in Canada's Yukon Territory. In temperatures that can drop into the −50°C range, mushers and their dogs negotiate blizzards and white-outs, sheer mountains, and frozen rivers and overflow ice that snaps and cracks under paws and sled. Checkpoints are far apart (the more famous Iditarod race has twenty-five, but the Yukon Quest has just ten), with more than 300km between some of them, and teams have to camp beside the trail. Mushers must be able to care for themselves and their dogs no matter what the elements throw at them and, except at the race's halfway point in Dawson City, they're allowed to accept no outside help.

As the days progress, spectators observe the mushers' eyes go bloodshot and rheumy. Their hair becomes matted; their posture stoops. These men and women are enjoying little sleep. They may stop to rest their dogs for six hours in every twelve but by the time they've massaged ointment into their team's feet, melted snow for water and fed the dogs – who burn ten thousand calories a day when racing – and themselves, only a couple of hours remain. The curious spectator might wonder what could motivate these people to endure such hardship. But then darkness falls, the moon rises and the northern lights weave a tapestry of green and red against the night sky and the answer is clear: it's the world's most beautiful racetrack.

546

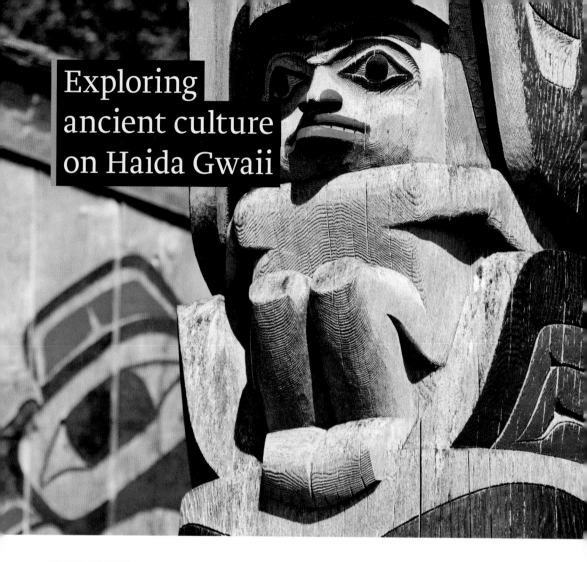

Exploring ancient culture on Haida Gwaii

BRITISH COLUMBIA Soaking in natural hot springs on a rainforest island while a pod of humpback whales swims past... suddenly the "Canadian Galápagos" moniker, occasionally used to describe the remote archipelago of Haida Gwaii, doesn't seem so far-fetched.

Cast some 150km off the west coast of British Columbia, Haida Gwaii is a place where the world's largest black bears forage on deserted beaches, black-footed albatross show off their enormous wingspan, and sea stars the size of coffee tables and the shades of disco lights sprawl languidly on rocks.

Only two thousand people a year make the journey to the pristine national park in the southern portion of the islands. Here, it takes eight people to hug a thousand-year-old cedar tree, months to kayak around the 1750km of coastline and a lifetime for an archeologist to uncover artefacts left untouched by a 10,000-year-old civilization. There is an underlying eeriness to this place that was, until recently, home to thousands of Haida – the most sophisticated and artistically prolific of British Columbia's aboriginal peoples.

These days, moss-covered beams of longhouses and decaying totem poles are the lingering remains of the ancient Haida villages, whose populations left after being drastically reduced in an 1880s smallpox epidemic. The most haunting and remote of the deserted villages is SGang Gwaay, a mist-shrouded UNESCO World Heritage Site on the southernmost tip of the park, where the world's largest collection of Haida mortuary poles stare defiantly out to sea.

Looking up at this forest of tree trunks – expertly carved with the wide-eyed features of bears, frogs, beavers, eagles, ravens and whales – is to gaze into the weather-beaten face of history. However, as is the wish of the Haida, there is little attempt at preserving the totems. Some day soon the poles will lean, fall, rot and – like everything else here – return to nature.

CANADA

Skating on the world's largest ice rink

ONTARIO Yes, Paris has the elegance of the Seine. Fine, London has the bustling Thames. And OK, Rome has the historic Tiber. Great waterways all, no doubt about it – but none of them is a match for what you can do on the ribbon of snow and ice that is Ottawa's Rideau Canal in winter.

Because when the chill hits, an 8km stretch of water running through the heart of the city freezes and becomes the world's largest natural ice-skating surface, the size of ninety Olympic-sized ice rinks. This is the signal for hearty Ottawans to bundle up, strap on their skates and head out onto the ice to play, glide past the sights of the nation's capital and even commute to work. It's all part of an annual ritual that has become a favourite winter pastime.

Completed in 1832, the whole of the Rideau Canal is actually much longer than the segment you can skate on in Ottawa. Its 202km-length connects the capital with Kingston, to the southwest, via a series of canals, rivers, lakes. In winter, though, the canal is best experienced in Ottawa during the annual Winterlude Festival, held during the first three weekends of February.

In the crisp bright of a Canadian winter the canal is a hive of activity. Thousands glide – and sometimes totter – about, a quick game of pond hockey breaks out on a more isolated stretch, figure skaters spin, speedskaters skim by, all metronome-like consistency, and everybody vies for a glimpse of world-renowned sculptors carving masterpieces from blocks of snow and ice.

As daylight gives way to an even chillier darkness, floodlights light up the canal and the icy spectacle becomes cosier and even more magical. Children – overbalanced either by lack of practice or thick winter clothing – zip precariously along, steaming cups of hot chocolate are sipped, kisses are exchanged and BeaverTails (don't worry – they're the fried, sweet pastry variety) are eaten. Everyone, it seems, is totally oblivious to the subzero temperatures. Who needs a beach when you can have this much fun on ice?

548 | Bedding down in an igloo

QUÉBEC Tucked away between rolling hills and vast stretches of craggy tundra in a remote corner of northern Quebec lies a series of igloos. These domed shelters were built by sealskin-clad Inuit elders, who carved huge snowblocks from windswept snowdrifts, using home-made snow knives and traditional skills passed on from their ancestors.

Igloos have long played a vital role in the lives of the Inuit people across northern Canada, where generations have gathered to share food, sing, dance and socialize while seeking refuge from the unforgiving elements of the Arctic winter. Today, igloos continue to safeguard hunters even as they also become the latest travel trend for adventure seekers.

To enter an igloo, you crawl through the narrow tunnel that leads to the large domed enclosure. Sunlight, streaming in from a window fashioned from a block of clear river ice, fills the room to reveal a raised sleeping platform of snow, covered with willow mats and caribou skins, which occupies the back half of the structure. Here, you sit back, remove your heavy parka and take it all in. Children giggle and play with a husky pup, while an elderly woman tends to the flame of her *qulliq*, a crescent-shaped lantern carved from soapstone and fuelled by seal blubber.

A short while later you join the others around a plastic bag placed on the igloo floor where dinner is served. On the menu tonight: caribou stew and frozen Arctic char, eaten raw and considered a delicacy in this icy corner of the world.

After dinner and a round of cards you lie back in your sleeping bag and stare up at the spiralling blocks of snow while listening to muffled laughter and chatter from the elders. Within minutes the sounds of the kids throat-singing and the gentle flicker of the burning *qulliq* lull you to sleep. This experience offers a fascinating insight into the lives of the Inuit people and a chance to battle the elements – even if just for the night.

549 | Searching for spirit bears

BRITISH COLUMBIA The Great Bear Rainforest, in the central wilds of British Columbia, is a bewitching place. A place where orcas glide through the channels, where coastal wolves den their pups, and where the haunting screech of bald eagles fills the mist-laden air. But most beguiling of all are the mighty spirit bears that stand shoulder-to-shoulder with huge grizzlies in these lands, fishing the same waters for salmon and scouring the moss-draped forests for food.

While the spirit bear is actually a sub-species of the North American black bear, there's only one of these white-furred creatures in every 40–100 black bears on the British Columbia mainland coast, with the most concentrated population found on certain islands in the Great Bear Rainforest. The ghostly animal is so elusive, the local First Nations peoples (who call the animals *mooksgm'ol*) believe they have supernatural powers and should never be hunted. Although these spirit bears share the mist-shrouded fjords and densely forested islands with grizzlies, wolverines and humpback whales, you'll need patience to spot one – keeping your eyes peeled for the telltale vanilla fur in a sheltered daybed at the foot of a towering red cedar, or the flash of a white bear poaching an egg-heavy salmon from a foam-lipped eddy.

Many tourists travel to this forest and never even catch a glimpse of the elusive creature, having to make do with the sight of a colossal humpback whale breaching just feet from the forest; or a sitka deer swimming across a deep channel, its magnificent antlers balanced like a trophy above it. But when it comes, the experience is awe-inspiring and almost spiritual: the heavy forest curtains parting to reveal a biscuit-coloured paw, and the thick, fuzzy length of a limb, followed by the dazzling hulk of this rare creature – one that very few people will ever have the privilege of seeing.

550 | Sea kayaking in the Mingan Archipelago

QUÉBEC On the map, the Mingan Archipelago, stretching 150km from Longue-Pointe-de-Mingan to Aguanish, looks like a trail of biscuit crumbs scattered in the Gulf of St Lawrence. But from the vantage point of your sea kayak, cruising through the channels that separate this collection of forty uninhabited islands and nearly a thousand islets and reefs, it's a very different story. First, it's impossible to miss the tall rock monoliths that guard the bays. The sea has worn the rock into smooth curves and, from a distance, these towering hunks of stone look very much like people; from closer to shore, they resemble abandoned flying saucers placed one on top of the other. Second, much of what you're paddling around to see actually lurks beneath the surface. The waters here are a feeding ground for the largest mammal on Earth, the blue whale, as well as for minke, fin, beluga and humpback whales – keep your eyes trained on the horizon, looking for the telltale puff of water vapour blown by a whale as it surfaces. But don't ignore what's right around you: seals pop their heads through the waves, like periscopes, no more than a few strokes away. Their big brown eyes set in moustachioed faces stare at you curiously before the animals disappear back into the deep with a flash of silver underbelly.

Beneath your paddles the water is so clear that it magnifies the seabed. Bright orange sea stars, deep red urchins and lime green kelp crust the sea floor, the rock worn into underwater monoliths or crazily paved ledges. As sunset stains the sea pink and purple, you'll need to pick an island and a beachside campsite. Civilization feels a galaxy away as you laze around the campfire or scramble up a clifftop for a last gaze out at sea, hopeful of spotting a whale silhouetted against the sinking sun.

551 | Ski from the sky in the Rockies

BRITISH COLUMBIA The small town of Golden, between Glacier and Revelstoke national parks near the British Columbia-Alberta border, doesn't seem like much as you pass through. But descend on to a snowy peak in the area from a helicopter, skis in tow, and you're likely to form a totally different opinion.

Heliskiing got its start in the Rocky Mountains of BC, and this is still one of the best places on Earth to take part in this terrifically expensive, fairly dangerous and undeniably thrilling activity. It's a pristine mountain wonderland filled with open bowls and endless tree runs, all coated in a layer of light and powdery snow. Accessing these stashes by helicopter, with its odd mix of mobility and avian fragility, only intensifies the feeling of exploration and isolation. From the air, you'll eagerly envisage making your signature squiggles and carve lines in the untouched powder fields. And once the helicopter recedes into the distance, leaving you alone atop the mountain, you'll feel every bit the pioneer.

After you've adjusted to the rhythm and bounce of skiing or riding this light powder, you might find yourself on a good day descending twice the typical distance as at a top ski resort.

You're also likely to discover that the deeper the snow and steeper the grade, the more exhilarating the run. Cornices and drop-offs that seemed foreboding from the helicopter will be a daring enticement; trees that from a distance looked impossibly dense reveal tempting paths; you'll drop into pitches that would have been unthinkable on harder snow, plunging in and out of chest-deep powder again and again. But be warned: all this may be enough to transform you into one of the many diehards who sign up for their next heliskiing adventure the moment they reach base.

552 | Cycling on the P'tit Train du Nord trail

QUÉBEC After a day of pedalling, a long downhill coast is a moment to be savoured. On either side the forest is a blur of green tinged with gold and the breeze ruffling your hair smells faintly of pine and earth. The treetops almost form a tunnel around the trail but in the glimpses of sky loom crinkled mountains, and off to the right, screened by foliage, roars the frothing fury of the Rivière Rouge, the Red River.

In the silence of the forest it's hard to imagine that fume-belching locomotives once thundered along the same route as your bicycle tyres. The P'tit Train du Nord was a busy railroad for eighty years, carrying Montréalers to the resorts of southwest Québec's Laurentian region before closing in 1989. But instead of abandoning the route to the forest, the rail bed was transformed into a magnificent cycling trail that winds for 230km through wooded splendour, especially beautiful in the autumn. Many of the original railroad station houses have been converted into cafés, information booths and facilities for cyclists, their decorative wooden gables and shady terraces restored with vibrant paint and blooming baskets.

The northern half of the trail is wild and remote, crossing numerous rivers dyed chestnut-brown by minerals and passing blue-black lakes close enough to wet your wheels. Small villages full of silver-steepled churches and impossibly cosy cottages cluster around the southern half of the trail. But whichever part you choose to ride (if not the whole course), nearly every bend holds an inviting picnic spot to laze in or a shady pool to revive sore feet and aching muscles.

553 | Rafting the Tatshenshini

YUKON The morning sunlight streams over the mountaintops, casting its warm rays on your wilderness campsite. Moments later you awaken to the calling of white-crowned sparrows as the thunderous crash of icebergs calving from nearby glaciers ricochets across the valley. A whiff of smoke entices you out onto the pebbled shore for breakfast around a crackling campfire. You take a deep breath and stretch – another day of rafting on the famed Tatshenshini River is about to begin.

These silt-laden waters are a paddlers' paradise, with the most magnificent portion coursing 213km through the heart of the St Elias Mountains, which extend from the southern Yukon across to northern British Columbia and on into the Gulf of Alaska. But long before anyone shrugged on a waterproof jacket, stowed their pack and grabbed a paddle, the river and surrounding region were home only to the Champagne and Aishinhik aboriginal peoples and wildlife – lots of wildlife.

There's still no shortage of things beaked, toothed and clawed here, and the inevitable sightings and full-on encounters are thrilling: grizzly bears lumber along gravel river beds, hoary marmots scramble up scree slopes and schools of glinting salmon swim in the murky waters below. Meanwhile, rufous hummingbirds hover overhead, swallows dart along the shoreline and a pair of bald eagles tend to their chicks atop a towering spruce tree.

Putting in at tiny Dalton Post, Yukon, for the start of a ten-day expedition that ends at Dry Bay, Alaska, you'll soon be floating through the same territory prospectors did during the late 1800s Klondike gold rush, when the river was a busy thoroughfare. Yet you'd barely know anyone had ever been this way – the whole region remains gloriously untouched, surrounded as it is by BC's Tatshenshini Provincial Park, the Yukon's Kluane National Park and Wildlife Sanctuary and the US Glacier Bay National Park. Journeying through these, you'll pass through steep-sided mountain canyons, negotiate rapids, drift past razor-sharp cliffs and thick stands of pristine wilderness and come within touching distance of 10,000-year-old icebergs – the river system, after all, passes through the largest non-polar ice field in the world.

At the end of another long and rewarding day's paddle, you glide up to the riverbank in time to witness the spectacular sunset framed against a backbone of majestic peaks. And later, after a hearty meal and a round of trading tales with your companions, you crawl into your tent, bone-tired but already dreaming about what the river holds in store for you tomorrow.

Tracking down polar bears in Churchill

554

MANITOBA Signs warning "Polar Bear Alert – Stop, don't walk in this area" dot the city limits of Churchill, Manitoba. Beyond them lie wide expanses of the bleak and often frozen Hudson Bay or the treeless, endlessly flat tundra. It's this location on the threshold of two forbidding environments that makes the town the unchallenged "polar bear capital of the world".

Local polar bears spend most of their lives roaming the platform of ice covering Hudson Bay to hunt seals. But by July the ice melt forces the bears ashore to subsist on berries, lichen, seaweed, mosses and grasses. This brings the animals close to your doorstep; indeed, during the summer Churchill's "Polar Bear Police" typically remove over a hundred bears from the town. It's challenging and very dangerous work: although cuddly-looking, these creatures are also the largest land carnivores in existence. They can run at 50km/hr and a single whack of their 0.3m-wide clawed paws can kill. Being unaccustomed to humans, they'll also quickly size you up as potential prey.

It's better to wait until later in the year, and from the relative comfort of a tundra buggy (a converted bus that rides high above the ground on giant balloon tyres), to do your bear-watching. At the beginning of October, around two hundred polar bears gather near town to wait for the bay to freeze. With temperatures beginning to drop below zero and winds gusting up to 60km/hr, the prime viewing season begins.

Lean and mean from the meagre summer diet, male polar bears spend the autumn sparring with one another for hours, standing on their hind legs to launch fierce swipes and rather more gentlemanly (for a polar bear, anyway) chest-punches. Females steer clear of these shenanigans, particularly when with cubs, and spotting a mother lying back on a snowbank nursing her offspring – making tenderness and brute force temporary bedfellows – is a surprisingly touching scene.

Seeing old rivals in an ice-hockey game

ONTARIO & QUÉBEC Saturday is known, on TV at least, as "Hockey Night in Canada" – pretty much all you need to know in terms of the country's fanaticism for one of its national games (lacrosse is the other one, but it has a long way to go before arousing the same level of passion that hockey does).

Perhaps it's the nature of the game itself. You'll have to focus hard to track the movement of the puck and the hurried but fluid way the teams shift players – frequently – in the middle of it all. And with those skaters hurtling around at 50km/hr and pucks clocking speeds above 160km/hr, this would be a high-adrenaline sport even without its relaxed attitude to combat on the rink. As an old Canadian adage has it, "I went to see a fight and an ice-hockey game broke out".

To maximize your exposure to the madness – and the bone-crunching body checks that send players smashing into the rinkside Plexiglas – try to get a seat near the ice during a game matching old rivals. Any of the six Canada-based teams will do, but when the Montréal Canadiens, the most successful team in hockey history, and the Toronto Maple Leafs meet – mirroring the country's Francophone and Anglophone divisions – you'll get a real feel for the electricity a match can generate. You may even see a hockey game break out.

556 | Float on Little Manitou Lake

SASKATCHEWAN In the minds of most Canadians, Saskatchewan is the heart of the rather plain prairies: a land of vast skies and dull Trans-Canada Highway drives. But within easy reach of the highway lies a lake with world-class therapeutic waters that must rank as the province's, if not the country's, best-kept secret. Little Manitou Lake and the adjacent *Manitou Springs Resort* offer a no-frills spa experience where you come out heavily coated with minerals and feeling much the better for it.

The lake's magnesium and iodine-rich waters are good for the skin, glands and joints, and overall a dip in the water is said to promote healing and be an effective treatment for some dermatological problems. But reasons to soak here go well beyond skin therapy, the relief of aches and pains or even the many claimed cures attributed to the waters: in short, it's just a whole lot of fun. The water has three times as much salt as seawater does and is denser than that of the Dead Sea, which means you'll find yourself bobbing on the surface, feet up. This unique sensation of effortless floating is as close as you'll likely get to the weightlessness of space; it brings with it all sorts of acrobatic possibilities, or just the chance to drift about on your back and comfortably read a newspaper.

The waters have long been celebrated, first by the aboriginal peoples who camped on its shores and named it for its healing properties, later by homesteaders who spread the news of the mineral-rich lake, and of course by the Manitou Mineral Water Company, which shipped it as a product across North America. But things have quietened down from its spa town heyday, so for once there are few to rebuke you for time spent aimlessly adrift.

557 | Lighting up the sky in Montréal

QUÉBEC Summer is a celebratory time in Montréal. After the winter hibernation, Montréalers spill onto the street terraces and fill the parks at the first sign of fine weather. Keen to milk it for all it's worth, the city lays on all sorts of colourful outdoor parties – the calypso-tinged Carifiesta and the world's pre-eminent jazz festival – that keep you tapping your feet. But the constant crowd-pleaser just requires you to look skywards: to the spectacular firework displays, staged throughout July, which pay tribute to balmy nights in a normally frigid city.

Montréal's International Fireworks Competition has become synonymous with summer in the city and sees music and dazzling pyrotechnics synchronized to tell a story, creating an ephemeral, somewhat surreal fantasy world. Fireworks companies representing different countries let off their arsenals at La Ronde – an amusement park on an island in the middle of the St Lawrence River – and the shows are stunningly artistic.

The thousands upon thousands of wheels, candles, fountains and rockets that light up the sky are intended to be viewed with the accompanying musical score (broadcast live on local radio). It's not too far a leap to imagine a profusion of red stars and comets set to the soundtrack of *Born Free* to be the rising African sun. Then again, you could just turn off the radio, tilt your head skyward and be thankful that summer has arrived.

558 | Going wild in northern Saskatchewan

SASKATCHEWAN There's an old Canadian joke that only in Saskatchewan can you visit your grandparents and spend three hours waving goodbye when you leave. And it's true: mercilessly flat, the Wheat Province can seem a little monotonous. But only in the south. Strike north, beyond the wide-open prairies, and it's a very different story.

Two hours' drive north of the lively city of Saskatoon, a dense tract of vibrantly coloured aspen woodland heralds the rugged terrain of Prince Albert National Park, with a landscape as changeable and endlessly surprising as the erratic weather that sweeps these parts. Blanketed with thick boreal forest and cut by vast lakes, interweaved with stands of ethereally beautiful spruce bog, this is paradise for nature-lovers, ripe for thrilling encounters with wildlife. Bears are an ever-present hazard, while the park's western grasslands thunder with the hooves of plains bison — one of the few herds roaming their historic range. Autumn nights are pierced by the Ringwraith-like bugle of bull elks, while muffled by snow, the forest trails take on a magical otherworldliness in winter.

Yet the national park represents only the start of an epic, glacier-carved wilderness that stretches up to the Arctic north. By the time the tarmac runs out and the ancient rocks of the Canadian Shield hove into view, 400km out of Saskatoon just beyond the remote, dusty town of La Ronge – home to a trading post where hunters still hawk their pelts – you'll begin to feel you're in frontier country.

In Lac La Ronge Provincial Park, Woodland Cree First Nations communities still cling on to their traditional way of life, teaching survival skills and hunting methods to their youngsters that are lost to their prairie counterparts further south. For the few intrepid visitors that make it this far, the pristine lakes and waterways of the immense Churchill River system provide endless possibilities for adventure, from white-knuckle kayaking trips – following the trailblazing routes of the voyageurs – across fast-flowing rapids, to excursions to remote fishing outposts that are accessible only by floatplane. Camping out on the shore, with only the gentle lap of the water disturbing the silence, you'll feel you're on the edge of the known world.

559 | Striking it lucky in Dawson City

YUKON In the late 1890s, rumour spread that the streets of Dawson City were paved with gold. In the most hysterical gold rush stampede the world has ever known, tens of thousands of fortune-seekers packed their bags and headed north for this former patch of moose pasture just below the Arctic Circle. By the time they arrived, most of the claims had been staked, and the brothels, dance halls and theatres of this burgeoning city were busy mining every last cent from the dejected prospectors.

More than 120 years on, the streets of Dawson City are still not paved with gold. In fact, they're not paved at all, and you need not bother panning for the few flakes of the yellow stuff left in the creeks just outside town. Instead, make the trek to appreciate the rough-and-tumble feel and gold-rush-era charm of which Dawson City still has plenty.

With its historic wooden false-fronted buildings, dirt streets, creaking boardwalks and midnight sun, it's easy to see how Dawson City inspired literary titans such as Jack London and Robert Service – not just to write about the place but to live here too.

As for striking it lucky, your best chance is at Diamond Tooth Gertie's Gambling Hall, Canada's oldest legal casino, where women in breathtaking corsets and ruffle skirts hustle up drinks while you bet your way to boom or bust. Having doubled your chips at the roulette table, it's customary to celebrate at the *Sourdough Saloon*, in the *Downtown Hotel*, where the house tipple is the sour-toe cocktail – a drink that includes a real pickled human toe in a shot of alcohol (local charitable frostbite victims keep the bar well stocked). As the rule goes: you can drink it fast or drink it slow, but your lips must touch the toe.

560 Taking afternoon tea in Victoria

BRITISH COLUMBIA Silver cutlery tinkles against Royal Doulton china as piano music wafts over idle chatter. "Would you like one lump or two?" enquires the waitress politely as she pours the piping-hot tea. You'll take two, you say, and sink back into the floral sofa, taking in this most splendid view of Victoria's Inner Harbour from the *Empress Hotel*. Rudyard Kipling once took afternoon tea in this very room and described Victoria as "Brighton Pavilion with the Himalayas for a backdrop". You can't help but agree with him.

Indeed, this provincial capital on the southern tip of wild and windy Vancouver Island is doing its bit to keep the "British" in British Columbia. Vancouver itself may have embraced lofty glass condominiums and coffee, but across the Georgia Strait, Victoria has clung steadfastly to its English heritage, preserving its late-1800s and early 1900s-era architecture and keeping alive the age-old tradition of afternoon tea.

There are many quaint places in Victoria to indulge this whim – small, suburban teahouses surrounded by royal family memorabilia, or amid the floral finery of the Butchart Gardens – but none can match the palatial *Empress Hotel* for grandiosity or price. Shirley Temple, John Travolta and Queen Elizabeth II have all been spotted ingulging their sweet tooth here.

The multi-course ritual starts off innocently enough: seasonal fruit topped with Chantilly cream with a choice of eight types of tea. Then a three-tiered plate arrives, heaving with cucumber and smoked salmon sandwiches, raisin scones slathered with jam and clotted cream and, on top, a glorious selection of irresistible pastries. If you're too self-conscious to indulge in the very un-English practice of stuffing yourself silly, you could always fall back on the distinctly North American custom of asking for a doggy bag. It's all too good to just leave behind.

561

BRITISH COLUMBIA Between raging Pacific gales and steady rainforest downpours, chances are you're going to get wet. Very wet. But it's the rain that has made the primordial landscape of the West Coast Trail, a 75km hike along a remote and rugged stretch of western Vancouver Island, almost magical for its lushness. Deep shades of green colour much of what grows here, from thick stands of evergreen trees and giant ageless cedars to the smooth rocks dappled with emerald moss and billowing kelp strands floating just beneath the water's surface.

Though in high season only a limited number of people each day are permitted to embark on the trail, you won't be alone as you wade across rivers, negotiate log bridges and climb up and down ladders. Expect to catch glimpses of seals, sea lions, great blue herons, bald eagles and migrating grey whales. Just don't expect to stay dry.

Hiking the wet and wild West Coast Trail

CANADA

Reliving the Wild West at the Calgary Stampede

ALBERTA For ten days each year, in July, the usually conservative city of Calgary loses its collective head (or finds a new cover for it, at least). Virtually everyone turns out in white Stetsons, bolo ties, blue jeans and hand-tooled boots. Indeed, everything seems, well, more western – which for a city like Calgary means shifting gears into serious cowboy overdrive. It's all a signal that the self-proclaimed "Greatest Outdoor Show on Earth" – the Calgary Stampede – has begun.

For Canada's rural folk – who often live on isolated farms or in tiny communities – this is the opportunity to bring their culture into the big city and really let rip. For the half-million visitors from elsewhere, it's a chance to witness the ultimate Wild West carnival, said to be North America's roughest rodeo.

Many activities, both kitschy and quite serious, vie for your attention. The main event is the daily rodeo competition, featuring the likes of bronco and bull riding, wild-pony racing, calf-roping, steer-wrestling and barrel-racing. But what sets the Stampede apart from other rodeos is the presence of the ludicrously dangerous, hugely exciting, chuck-wagon races: several teams of horsemen pack a stove and tent into these covered wagons, then hurtle around the dirt track at breakneck speeds.

The non-rodeo action takes place at the festival's focal point, Stampede Park. Top attractions include a First Nations tepee village where you can try traditional foods; the world-class marching bands; and an Agricultural Building that's home to many a handsome cow and bull.

Finish each day with a dash of Stampede nightlife, yet another world unto itself. The drinking, gambling and partying at various bars and mega-cabarets goes on into the small hours, sustained by a seemingly endless supply of barbecued meat and baked beans.

563 | Form a lasting impression at Niagara Falls

ONTARIO In 1860, thousands watched as Charles Blondin walked a tightrope across Niagara Falls for the third time. Midway, the Frenchman paused to cook an omelette on a portable grill and then had a marksman shoot a hole through his hat from the *Maid of the Mist* tugboat, 50m below. Suffice to say, the falls can't be beaten as a theatrical setting.

Like much good theatre, Niagara makes a stupendous first impression, as it crashes over a 52m cliff shrouded in oceans of mist. It's actually two cataracts: tiny Goat Island, which must be one of the wettest places on Earth, divides the accelerating water into two channels on either side of the US-Canadian border. The spectacle is, if anything, even more extraordinary in winter, when snow-bent trees edge a jagged armoury of freezing mist and heaped ice blocks.

You won't just be choosing sides – note that the American Falls are but half the width of Canada's Horseshoe Falls – but also how best to see the falls beyond that first incredible impression. A bevy of boats, viewing towers, helicopters, cable cars and even tunnels burrowing into the rock-face behind the cascade ensures that every angle is covered.

Two methods are especially thrilling and get you quite near the action: the *Maid of the Mist* boats, which struggle against the cauldron to get as close to the falls as they dare; and the tunnels of the "Journey Behind the Falls", which lead to points directly behind the waterfall. Either way guarantees that your first impression won't be the last one to register.

564 | Watching the tide roll away in the Bay of Fundy

NOVA SCOTIA & NEW BRUNSWICK There's an eeriness to the Bay of Fundy, never more so than when the banking fogs that sweep in off the Atlantic shroud its churning waters, rendering its sea cliffs and coves barely visible in an all-pervasive gloom. Tourist brochures would lovingly call this "atmospheric", which it is. But what they tend to play up more are the bay's impressive stats: this is where the highest tides in the world come crashing in – there is up to 16m difference between high and low tide; in some places, the tide retreats 4 to 5km as it ebbs.

But you don't need numbers; you just need your own eyes. Stand on the steps at Evangeline Beach in Grand-Pré and see young boys pedalling bicycles across far-reaching mud flats, then return a few hours later to find the beach deserted, the water 3m high and rising still. You could build a giant IMAX movie screen on the mud flats at low tide and it would be completely submerged by water at high tide, just six hours later.

The effect comes in part from the bay's shape. At its mouth it is 100km wide, but it gradually narrows and shallows, producing a funnelling effect when the water comes in. Many of the rivers that lead off the upper bay are sites of tidal bores – basically the name for what occurs when the water rushes against the current. This is what people come to see.

When you first spot it from a distance, it may be subtle: just a faint line across a wide section of water. But as the river narrows and the water closes in, seeming to pick up speed, it's more like a moving wall – one that submerges islets, rides up high on floating docks and provides plenty of challenge for those foolish enough to break out surfboards or inflatable Zodiac boats.

565 | Newfoundland's extraordinary cod-kissing ceremony

NEWFOUNDLAND "Repeat after me: to behold the charter of ordinary Newfoundlanders, I promise to drink 'screech' every Sunday for a fortnight. And to honour and respect me cod-fathers and me cod-mothers until the day I die."

So begins Newfoundland's traditional 'screech-in' ceremony – a time-honoured, if bamboozling, ritual that involves a willing newcomer reciting a limerick, drinking a shot of branded Screech Rum, kissing a codfish on the lips and dancing a jig to become an honorary member of the Newfoundland and Labrador community.

Experiencing a screech-in first-hand is hard work – every step is supervised by a native Newfoundlander – but to take part is an unforgettable experience. Picture the scene: all eyes in the town pub fall on you as you recite the verse, stumbling over local vernacular from the piece of paper handed to you. The shock of the throat-burning moonshine then takes your breath away, before you feel you have a point to prove, so end up dancing on the bar to win the respect of the whooping crowd. Better not think about the morning after, either.

Despite such unusual ceremony, there's plenty of tradition to justify it. Historically, this swearing-in is thought to date back some two centuries to when Newfoundlanders had to import alcohol from the Caribbean in the midst of prohibition. Illicit boats full of liquor sailed the coastal waters under the cover of darkness and as fishing communities turned to Jamaica for supplies of rum, so Jamaicans asked for salted cod fish in return. The ceremony, according to folklore, was then born when traditional seal-hunters played tricks on newcomers, before going out onto the ice to hunt.

That explains the ritual, rum and codfish, but only hints at a measure of the friendliness – and great fun – of the Newfoundlanders. They have a reputation for openness, humour and hospitality, so if taking part in a 'screech-in' sounds a bit much, then remember this: it's just as much fun to watch.

NEWFOUNDLAND & LABRADOR Stuck out in the Labrador Straits, the jagged knot of granite that is Battle Harbour feels like it's perched at the end of the world. Established in the 1770s, the island soon became one of North America's busiest saltfish, salmon and sealing ports. Today the fishing boats are long gone; only a red-roofed church and a clutch of clapboard cottages dot the hillside above the rickety wharf. Just offshore, shimmering blue-white icebergs float gently southwards, slowly melting into bizarre shapes and twisted pillars. Humpback whales chase herring and capelin right up to the rocky shoreline, their gaping jaws bursting out of the water, full of fish; minke whales bask a little further out, while killer whales sometimes glide just off the docks.

Spending the night here is a magical experience; the island's natural beauty is complemented by its equally evocative human elements – cottages and creaking bunkhouses equipped with oil lamps and wood stoves, a spa built from old, salt-stained warehouses and friendly locals who seem to have stepped straight out of *Moby Dick*. Accents have changed little since the first settlers arrived from England's West Country in the 1800s; children ask their mothers "Where's me father to?", and old fishermen look at the sky and say "ee look like rain, don't ee?".

In its prime Battle Harbour was the scene of Robert E. Peary's first news conference after he reached the North Pole in 1909. Long-term decline began in the 1930s and most residents were relocated to Mary's Harbour on the mainland in the 1960s. Many of those still work here as guides, boatmen and volunteers, all of them part of an epic heritage project that has resulted in the smattering of historic buildings currently open to the public; stay the night in one of the artfully restored cottages and you'll have little more than the cracking of ice and the splashing of whales for company.

567 | Catching a wave on Vancouver Island

BRITISH COLUMBIA For some of the wildest surfing in the world, head to the shipwreck-strewn west coast of Vancouver Island, also known as "the graveyard of the Pacific". Flanked by the lush temperate rainforest of the 130km-long Pacific Rim National Park, the waters here are ferocious. Swells reach up to 6m, and epic storms uproot trees, sending drifting logs down the face of waves. Whales have been known to sneak up on unsuspecting surfers, diving under their boards and lifting them clean out of the water. As if that weren't enough abuse, barking, territorial sea lions often chase these thrill-seekers from the ocean back to shore. On land, it's just as wild – bald eagles soar between giant trees, and wolves and black bears forage for food amid piles of sun-bleached driftwood.

Even in summer, when swells ease to a gentle 1–2m, the water remains bone-chillingly cold, hovering around 13°C. Still, plenty of wannabe wave riders flock to the chilled-out surf centre of Tofino to practise their "pop-ups", but a thick skin – or a thick wetsuit – is required to keep the chill at bay.

Come winter, the waves start pummelling in from the Pacific with all the force of a boxer's knock-out punch. The wind whips off the snowcapped mountains, the ocean cools down to a shocking 8°C and hardy surfers hit the waves wearing 5mm-thick wetsuits as well as boots, gloves and protective hoods. For the novice, this is the time to peel off the wetsuit and watch the waves roll in from the blissful confines of a seaside hot tub.

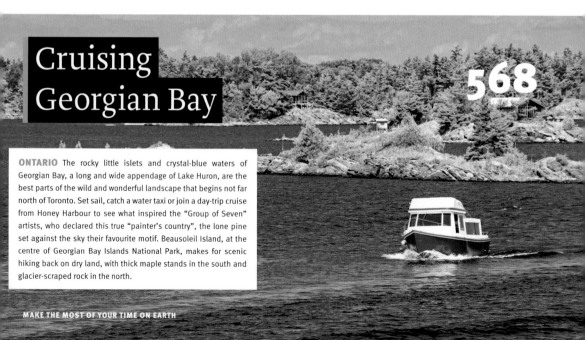

Cruising
Georgian Bay

568

ONTARIO The rocky little islets and crystal-blue waters of Georgian Bay, a long and wide appendage of Lake Huron, are the best parts of the wild and wonderful landscape that begins not far north of Toronto. Set sail, catch a water taxi or join a day-trip cruise from Honey Harbour to see what inspired the "Group of Seven" artists, who declared this true "painter's country", the lone pine set against the sky their favourite motif. Beausoleil Island, at the centre of Georgian Bay Islands National Park, makes for scenic hiking back on dry land, with thick maple stands in the south and glacier-scraped rock in the north.

Need to know

542 The Glengarry Highland Games (Ⓦglengarry highlandgames.com) take place during the first long weekend in Aug. There is some accommodation in Maxville and the nearby communities of Alexandria, Moose Creek and Hawkesbury, but many visitors choose to camp at the games.

543 Waterton Lakes National Park is 270km south of Calgary, which is the site of the closest international airport. There are several hotels and restaurants located in Waterton village, along with stores selling camping supplies and groceries. For more details see Ⓦpc.gc.ca/waterton.

544 See Ⓦquebecregion.com for information.

545 The race's official website (Ⓦyukonquest.com) has past and future race details.

546 For information on travelling to Gwaii Haanas National Park Reserve and Haida Heritage Site, see Ⓦpc.gc.ca/gwaiihaanas.

547 The National Capital Commission (Ⓦncc-ccn.gc.ca) maintains the Rideau Canal and has information on ice conditions and events; the canal is usually open for skating from January to March. You can rent skates at kiosks along the canal.

548 Spending a night in an igloo can be arranged in any Nunavik or Nunavut community – see Ⓦnunavik-tourism.com or Ⓦnunavuttourism.com.

549 For more information visit Ⓦhellobc.com.

550 See Ⓦpc.gc.ca/mingan for more information.

551 Contact CMH Heli-Skiing (Ⓦcmhski.com).

552 The P'tit Train du Nord trail starts in Saint-Jérôme and ends in Mont-Laurier (Ⓦlaurentides.com).

553 Tatshenshini Expediting in Whitehorse (Ⓦtatshenshiniyukon.com) has details on package tours.

554 You can book all-inclusive bear-spotting packages with Wildlife Adventures – see Ⓦwildlifeadventures.com.

555 Tickets need to be bought in advance for nearly all matches; check the club websites via links at Ⓦnhl.com.

556 Little Manitou Lake lies beside the small town of Watrous. The *Manitou Springs Resort* (Ⓦmanitou springs.ca) is adjacent to the lake.

557 See Ⓦsixflags.com/larondeen/linternational-des-feux/overview for schedule and ticket details.

558 For more information on planning a trip, contact Ⓦtourismsaskatchewan.com.

559 Dawson City (Ⓦdawsoncity.ca) is a 1hr 15min flight from Whitehorse. *Diamond Tooth Gertie's Gambling Hall* is at 4th Ave and Queen St; the *Sourdough Saloon* (Ⓦdowntownhotel.ca) is at 2nd Ave and Queen St.

560 Afternoon tea starts at 11.30am at the *Empress Hotel*, 721 Government St (Ⓦfairmont.com/empress).

561 See Ⓦpc.gc.ca/pacificrim for more details on planning a trip and general information on the trail.

562 Plan at least a year in advance for the annual Stampede, which is held in July: see Ⓦcalgarystampede.com.

563 The *Maid of the Mist* runs from May to early Nov – see Ⓦmaidofthemist.com.

564 Truro, Moncton and Saint John are all good bases for trying to watch a tidal bore – see Ⓦpc.gc.ca/fundy.

565 Screech-in ceremonies usually take place once a week in summer only. Ask at your hotel for more information, or contact Ⓦnewfoundlandlabrador.com.

566 See Ⓦbattleharbour.com.

567 See Ⓦwestsidesurf.com and Ⓦsurfsister.com for lessons.

568 Go to Ⓦvisitgeorgianbay.com for information.

UNITED
STATES OF
AMERICA

ATLANTIC
OCEAN

570
BAHAMAS

569
580
594
600
578

599

CUBA

CAYMAN
ISLANDS 592

583

DOMINICAN
REPUBLIC

571   577
        597

PUERTO
RICO

589   586

BRITISH VIRGIN
ISLANDS

598

ANGUILLA
ST MARTIN/SINT MAARTEN

575 590
596 584

JAMAICA

HAITI

572
593

574
588

ST KITTS & NEVIS

ANTIGUA

585
587

MONTSERRAT

GUADELOUPE

HONDURAS

CARIBBEAN
SEA

576
595

DOMINICA

NICARAGUA

MARTINIQUE

579
581

601

ST LUCIA

ST VINCENT

BARBADOS

COSTA
RICA

ARUBA
582

CURAÇAO

GRENADA

591
BONAIRE

TOBAGO

573 TRINIDAD

PANAMA

VENEZUELA

GUYANA

PACIFIC
OCEAN

COLOMBIA

BRAZIL

THE CARIBBEAN
569–601

People who have never been to the islands tend to picture the Caribbean as little more than a sun-sand-and-sea bolthole. To define it by its exclusive resorts and rum-punch happy hours, however, would be a travesty – from the rich art scene of Cuba and the challenging hiking trails of Dominica to the festival clamour of Trinidad and the reggae vibe of Jamaica, this is a culturally dynamic region with much for travellers to enjoy. Yes, you'll find beautiful beaches with ease, but places such as Puerto Rico, Haiti, Martinique and the Dominican Republic help the Caribbean offer so much more, whether you're into horseriding or heritage-delving.

569 Breaking the ice in a city frozen in time

CUBA "We don't complain," says the young Cuban, draining his rum and turning to applaud the salsa band. "I wouldn't want to be anywhere else."

The next bar beckons. The intense sunlight that has baked lime, cigars and sweat into the flavour of this Havana salsa hall is beginning to fade. The sun is departing and, however much I would like to stay, we have to see it off properly before our next Caribbean stop.

Saying our goodbyes to the tourists struggling with salsa steps, the barman who has denied the existence of any cocktail other than his *mojito*, and one of the multiple Celia Cruz impersonators, we step out into the street.

Banners celebrating sixty years of glorious revolution hang from decaying Art Deco houses, rusted saloon wagons are haphazardly parked along the decaying street. Architectural flourishes on building facades are discernible despite the tropical moss that clings to them, remnants of the Havana that used to be, when the city was a capital within Spain's empire.

Havana today is a city frozen in the moment that communism came to town. For visitors, Cuba offers a stark insight into the realities of life under communist rule. A country of bittersweet beauty, where the stunningly decadent *Hotel Nacional* won't accept Cuban nationals as guests. The *mojito*-fuelled Havana nights that ordinary Cubans can't afford.

Spending time in Cuba is a unique experience, a taste of life in another incarnation. A mentality and culture that can only be understood first-hand.

Back on Havana's seafront, as the setting sun spills its dusky colours over the seawall, through a trick of the light the crumbling city is transformed. Through eyes altered by the lessons of this living museum, it seems brand new once again.

Alasdair Baverstock
Rough Guides writer Alasdair Baverstock is a travel writer and journalist specializing in Latin America.

570

Doing Junkanoo

BAHAMAS The country's most important and spectacular party, Junkanoo is a blast to the senses. It's organized pandemonium, held in the pre-dawn hours on two days each year – December 26 and New Year's Day. Its roots can be traced back to Africa, and it's reminiscent of New Orleans' Mardi Gras and Rio's Carnival, but really, Junkanoo is distinctively Bahamian. There is no other festival like it – not in the Caribbean, not anywhere.

Parades flood the streets of Nassau in a whirling, reeling mass of singing and dancing chaos, as competing groups or "crews" rush out to meet the dawn, moving toward one another from all directions rather than following each other in the semi-organized fashion of the modern parade. Various groups and societies compete to have the biggest and loudest floats, which means you'll see stilt-dancers, clowns, acrobats, goatskin drummers and conch and cowbell players, all blaring out their tunes in an awesome celebration of life that could only have come together in the Caribbean.

When the distant beats of Goombay drums indicate that the paraders are shifting into formation, that's your cue to join the spectators jockeying for the best views, climbing trees and spilling onto balconies and the verandas of stores, hotels and houses. Under the Christmas lights, the crowds reach a frenzy of anticipation. The first cowbells are heard soon after, everyone swigs from bottles of rum and fireworks crackle in the background. Behind, in Nassau Harbour, the looming cruise ships form an almost surreal counterpoint to the phantasmagoric crowds, who are now stamping and clamouring in time to the music. Then, as if from everywhere and nowhere, Junkanoo crews – some numbering a thousand – flood the streets in a swirling, kaleidoscopic mass of singing and dancing.

In search of the Citadelle

HAITI High in the hills above the northern plains sits an imposing fortress, an architectural marvel that would be among the Caribbean's top destinations were it not for the grave lack of tourists in Haiti. Constructed in the early 1800s following the successful revolt of Haiti's massive slave population, the Citadelle La Ferriere was designed to house and protect the new black royal family of Henri Christophe and 5000 soldiers for up to a year in the event of a French retaliatory attack, which never came.

Travelling to the Citadelle is an adventure in itself, taking nearly an hour to traverse 20km of motorway riddled with craterous potholes, pedestrians and roadside repairs. In the peaceful town of Milot visitors can expect to be descended upon by a horde of would-be guides. Although the Citadelle is easy enough to get to, guiding is important to the local economy and each visitor will end up with one, like it or not. Some offer sad horses that look as though you should carry them up the hill, rather than vice versa.

During the two-hour ascent you'll be immersed in a day in the life of Haitian rural poverty – families living in one-room shacks without running water. A lively entrepreneurial spirit thrives along this cobblestone trail, with vendors and kids selling fresh fruit, handmade dolls and artefacts. There is a small *vodou peristyle*, or temple, along the way and anybody hanging about will be happy to show you the sacred space for a small donation.

Once you enter the Citadelle, via massive doors through nearly 10m-thick walls, the cavernous interior reveals moss-covered staircases, chambers and cisterns, topped by panoramic views of Haiti's sadly deforested yet strikingly beautiful landscape. Hundreds of cannons of all shapes, sizes and nationalities, salvaged from shipwrecks off the treacherous coast, are aimed toward unseen enemies, while thousands of rusting, unused cannonballs remain stacked in pyramids, a testament to the ultimate triumph of the revolution.

572 | Join a baseball crowd in Santo Domingo

DOMINICAN REPUBLIC The Dominican Republic has been besotted with baseball ever since American ships – and, more pertinently, their bat-and-ball-carrying crews – began to frequent this part of the Caribbean in the late 1800s. The sport has grown to become a full-blown national infatuation – the Dominican Republic has consistently provided the US's Major League with more players than any other foreign nation on the planet. Indeed, of the Most Valuable Player awards handed out from 2002 to 2009 (in what, it's worth pointing out, is one of the world's highest-profile sports leagues), precisely half went to players of Dominican origin – an improbable return from a country 15 times smaller than Texas.

The country's single-sport obsession makes attending a professional match in the capital, Santo Domingo, a high-octane experience. Evening games at the Estadio Quisqueya are colourful, frenetic, boozy affairs, particularly when the city's two leading teams – Tigres del Licey and Leones del Escogido, who share the stadium – square up to each other.

Rum and coke flow freely, girls gyrate on dugouts and drummers pelt out hour-long rhythms. As an insight into how a nation lets its hair down, it's a deeply entertaining spectacle. You may even see a few future Major League stars in action.

The domestic league runs from late October to January. Just six professional teams take part – in addition to the two Santo Domingo clubs, there are outfits in Santiago, San Pedro de Macoris, La Romana and San Francisco de Macoris. While baseball here has had its controversies – including scandals over steroid use and falsified ages, both products of the desperation to reach the hallowed playing diamonds of America – it remains an absolute cultural fixation.

Sammy Sosa, one of the greatest Dominican players of all time, achieved US Major League glory after growing up using sugar canes for bats, old milk cartons for mitts and taped-up socks for balls, and his story remains symbolic of how, across the nation, the sport still shapes dreams.

573 | Getting on bad on Carnival Sunday

TRINIDAD Trinidadians are famed for their party stamina, and nowhere is this dedication to good times more evident than in their annual Carnival, a huge, joyful, all-encompassing event that's the biggest festival in the Caribbean, and one which quite possibly delivers the most fun you'll ever have – period. And as Carnival here is all about participation, rather than watching from the sidelines à la Rio, anyone with a willingness to "get on bad" is welcome to sign up with a masquerade band, which gets you a costume and the chance to dance through the streets alongside tens of thousands of your fellow revellers.

Preceded by weeks of all-night outdoor fetes, as parties here are known, as well as competitions for the best steel bands and calypso and soca singers, the main event starts at 1am on Carnival Sunday with Jouvert. This anarchic and raunchy street party is pure, unadulterated

bacchanalia, with generous coatings of mud, chocolate, oil or body paint – and libations of kick-ass local rum, of course – helping you lose all inhibitions and slip and slide through the streets until dawn in an anonymous mass of dirty, drunken, happy humanity, accompanied by music from steel bands, sound-system trucks and the traditional "rhythm section" band of percussionists. Once the sun is fully up, and a quick dip in the Caribbean has dispensed with the worst of the mud, the masquerade bands hit the streets, their followers dancing along in the wake of the pounding soca. This is a mere warm-up for the main parade the following day, however, when full costumes are worn and the streets are awash with colour. The music trucks are back in earnest and the city reverberates with music, becoming one giant street party until "las lap" and total exhaustion closes proceedings for another year.

574 | Riding the sugar train to Brimstone Hill Fortress

ST KITTS Today the Caribbean is perhaps most famous for its beaches, but in the past it was sugar that the islands were known for. Railways were built to carry the sugar cane; however, today, only one has survived.

Often referred to as 'The last railway in the West Indies', the St Kitts Scenic Railway is now one of the best ways to discover the island. Filled with bottle-green volcanic peaks, palm-fringed beaches and vast plantations, its epic landscapes are best discovered aboard the old sugar train. The railway was built between 1912 and 1926 to transport sugar cane from the fields to the mill in Basseterre.

The three-hour journey passes through the island's most spectacular scenery – on narrow bridges over lush gorges and deep canyons, past undulating fields of sugar cane, and along the jagged coastline, where the waves crash below. On board, visitors are plied with rum punch and regaled with traditional Caribbean beats, while

enjoying the views of the mist-shrouded Mt Liamuiga, the highest point on the island. One of the highlights of the trip is seeing the impenetrable black walls of the huge UNESCO-listed Brimstone Hill Fortress rise out of the landscape.

Nicknamed 'the Gibraltar of the West Indies', the fortress is noteworthy for being one of the best examples of seventeenth- and eighteenth-century military architecture in the Caribbean. Set atop a volcanic hill, it overlooks the Caribbean Sea and was designed by the British for defence purposes. During a month-long siege in 1782, the French took Brimstone Hill from the British; however, it was returned to them a year later in the Treaty of Paris.

Fortifications and better defence systems were added, ensuring its walls were never breached again. You can't see inside the fortress while on the sugar train, but it's well worth a separate visit to explore further and see inside the central Fort George.

575 | Grooving at Reggae Sumfest

JAMAICA As you might expect from Jamaica's flagship music festival, Sumfest is one of the best reggae shows in the world. If you're expecting a bacchanalian free-for-all of campfires on the sand, you'll be sorely disappointed – it's a four-day series of concerts and sound-system jams. But if you're interested in seeing the hottest names in Jamaican music past and present, with a few international R&B or hip-hop acts thrown in for good measure, then you're in for a serious treat.

It's best to arrive in Montego Bay a week or so before the event – held in late July or early August – and head for the beach to rid yourself of that fresh-off-the-plane pallor, and to attend pre-festival events: the Blast-Off beach party on the Sunday before the festival starts, and the Monday street party with DJs and outdoor jams.

Once the festival is under way, the island's stage shows start late, carry on until dawn and involve some serious audience participation – or lack of it, if a performer fails to please the famously fickle local crowd. And it's doubtful you'll find a better high than standing under the stars in a grassy bowl by the Caribbean with the music echoing out over the bay.

576 | A walk you'll never forget: the Boiling Lake hike

DOMINICA Demanding treks aren't what you typically associate the Caribbean with, but the eight-mile (return) Boiling Lake hike ranks as one of Dominica's most challenging. Starting in Laudat by the entrance to Titou Gorge and heading towards Breakfast River, the trail winds into Morne Trois Pitons National Park through rainforest and ravines.

The Boiling Lake certainly tests you as you climb up to the summit of Morne Nicholls, with views across to Morne Watt, before going down and then back up through the atmospheric Valley of Desolation. You then, finally, reach the holy grail: the world's second-largest boiling lake.

Technically, the Boiling Lake is a flooded fumarole, a crack in the Earth's crust. And it really does boil. With a direct link to the molten layers of the Earth below, vents pump scorching gases and steam into the water; think of it as a fast-boil kettle, albeit one that's about 76m wide (for obvious reasons, no one knows how deep this boiling vat is). There's a slightly acrid smell of sulphur in the air as you take in the misty, steamy views over this truly spectacular natural phenomenon while tucking into a packed lunch.

Take time to appreciate the suitably sombre-sounding Valley of Desolation, a seemingly barren wasteland home to bubbling pools and sulphur springs – the mud here is nutrient-rich and some guides encourage a quick 'face mask' stop. But don't be fooled by the water: this place is hot, hot, hot.

Start early in case the trek proves a little more challenging than expected; it can take anything from five to eight hours and anyone with a good general level of fitness can do it, although some parts are quite steep. A slower hike allows the guide to point out interesting fauna and flora, too, and leaves time at the end for a well-earned soak in the waters of Titou Gorge. But every ache and pain is, retrospectively, if not at the time, worth it to lay eyes on this otherworldly sight.

Kiteboarding in Cabarete

DOMINICAN REPUBLIC Kiters from around the world come in droves to the broad, archetypally Caribbean cove of Cabarete off the north coast of the Dominican Republic. Some never leave, hanging out on the beach in a state of perpetual kite-slacker bliss, like lotus-eaters from Homer's *Odyssey*. Others shuttle in at weekends between stints at investment banking firms and crash at the high-end condos on the edge of town. All seem perpetually chilled, except for those moments when they're riding the Caribbean trade winds like a hundred little neon-coloured insects trained to do circus tricks for the nearby beach loungers. Life is good here.

And why not? Cabarete's bay seems engineered by a benevolent god of kiteboarding. Steady trade winds blow east to west, allowing easy passage out to the bay's offshore reefs and then back to the sand. Downwind, the waters lap onto the sardonically named Bozo Beach, which catches anybody unfortunate enough to have a mishap. The offshore reef provides plenty of surf for the experts who ride the waves here, performing tricks and incredible jumps. The reef also shelters the inshore waters, ensuring that they remain calm on all but the roughest of winter days. During the morning the winds are little more than a gentle breeze, and this, coupled with the flat water, makes the bay ideal for beginners, especially in summer when the surface can resemble a mirror. Then, as the temperature rises, the trades kick in big-time and the real show starts.

Increasingly, the kiteboarding community has left the built-up main village to the windsurfers and retreated west to so-called Kite Beach. Here you can experience Cabarete as it was fifteen years ago, a kiteboarder's paradise filled with fellow wind worshippers and a lively outdoor nightlife scene, including bonfires along the beach into the wee hours.

578 | Cigars and horses in Viñales Valley

CUBA Far from the intoxicating salsa beats, slick cigar rooms and dilapidated glamour of Havana, the rustic and remote Viñales valley feels like another world. This prehistoric landscape formed during the Jurassic era, 160 million years ago, when underground rivers and rainfall eroded the high bedrock to create the massive gorges that now make up Cuba's most impressive limestone karst valley.

Bizarre, hulking limestone towers, known as *mogotes*, interrupt serene flatlands of vivid green, peppered with tall palm trees, pointy thatched tobacco-drying houses and terracotta-stained ploughed earth. As you gaze around, life seems to slow down; farmers and their oxen amble through neat leafy rows of tobacco, banana and coffee crops, while old men doze on shady porches in little villages.

Staring at the dramatic scenery and surrendering to the gentle pace of life might be enough to tempt you here, but the landscape begs to be explored: sheer cliff faces dare to be climbed, cave systems yawn mysteriously open, and the steep hillsides are perfect for cycling down. Yet the best way to see it all is on horseback.

Mounted on a sturdy horse, following a local *guarijo* (mountain man), you can truly appreciate this stunning landscape. Trot along narrow muddy paths that open out into wide flat stretches of lush fields, splash through small clear lakes and pick your way across wobbly bridges that sway over winding streams – forever overlooked by the magnificent, bulbous *mogotes*. Leave your horse beneath the shade of a tree and duck into a tobacco drying house to escape the blazing midday heat and ease your aching muscles. As you sit on a rickety wooden chair in the darkened room, sipping a concoction of rum, honey and coconut milk from a hairy coconut husk, a lithe cat winds its way around your shins, and a farmer rolls cigars from tanned, crinkly tobacco leaves. Close your eyes and let it all sink in. This, not the polished mahogany cigar boxes, or the crushed-ice *mojitos* in thumping salsa bars, is the heart of Cuba.

579 | Sugar cane, saltfish and tranquil Soufrière

ST LUCIA Lazing on one of St Lucia's manicured beaches, it's easy to forget that the island has a rich and turbulent history. Fought over by the French, Spanish and English, there's plenty of heritage squashed in between the dense jungle slopes and five-star resorts.

To really get away from the tourist trail you need to drive south, bypassing the capital Castries, into the sun-baked Roseau Valley, a swathe of billowing sugar plantations. Beyond here, the road drops down to Anse La Raye, a totally unspoilt St Lucian village, nestled between green headlands on the edge of a pristine bay. The streets are crammed with weathered clapboard cottages, some brightly adorned in gingerbread style, all with corrugated iron roofs and neatly tended gardens. Fishing shacks and small boats line the beachfront, while schoolkids play football on the sand.

Just inland, the island's colonial legacy is on view at La Sikwi Sugar Mill, which was built in 1876 and is now in a state of refined decay. The casual tours take in lush, blossom-strewn gardens humming with butterflies, trees laden with cacao pods, coconuts and bananas, and the old weather-beaten, vine-smothered ruins themselves. Inside you'll find the original sugar kettles, huge cauldrons of iron where cane juice was boiled for hours before turning into crumbly brown sugar.

Back on the coast road, *La Plas Kassav* is an essential St Lucian food experience; little more than a small shack, perched high above the sea, it produces traditional cassava breads in a variety of flavours (such as saltfish and yam). You can also watch the baking process, where cassava root is pounded and the dough cooked in a huge cauldron over an open wood fire.

Keep driving south and you'll end up at Soufrière, dating from 1746 and the oldest town in St Lucia. It's a tranquil place today, filled with an appealing blend of modern houses and clapboard huts. The town faces a sharply defined bay at the end of a jungle-smothered valley, and the views from the coastal road as you enter are utterly spectacular – a world away from those cocktails and beach umbrellas.

580 | State of the art in Havana

CUBA Havana has been bursting with creative energy for centuries, but finding a platform for your artistic expression in a totalitarian state that sought to control everything hasn't always been easy – in recent times, though, some of that tethered creativity has been unleashed. Now, under new laws, small, makeshift but captivating artists' studios and galleries abound in the bustling neighbourhoods of Old Havana. They occupy the front rooms of creaking colonial and neocolonial apartment buildings; their quirky sculptures, magical photography, and wildly expressionistic paintings further animating the already-boisterous backstreets of the city's pedestrian-friendly core. Seek out these kerbside workshops and make direct contact with the artists in their own environment.

581 | High adventure on Gros Piton

ST LUCIA High adventure in the Caribbean usually comes in the form of charter flights between islands, but not so on St Lucia. Standing sentinel on the southwestern coast are the twin peaks of the Pitons, two of the tallest and most striking mountains in the West Indies.

Gros Piton, the taller at 798m, makes a challenging and dramatic day-hike, its steep trail winding past a former cave hideout of slave freedom fighters and through a dense tropical landscape home to colourful birds and butterflies. Set out early to avoid climbing in the stifling midday heat, and at the summit you'll be rewarded with breathtaking views of Petit Piton and the azure Caribbean below.

ARUBA Massive boulders, towering cacti, ancient petroglyphs, abandoned gold mines and secluded limestone grottoes dot the hilly interior. There are glitzy beaches a few short kilometres away, but Arikok National Park, a bizarre desert-like landscape in the northeastern corner of resort-heavy Aruba, has little in common with the rest of the island save the blazing tropical sun. Indeed, walking its dirt paths can feel more like wandering the Australian outback.

As you traverse some of the 34km of self-guided trails, you gain a sense of the untamed beauty of the area. Patches of reddish-orange rocky outcrops interspersed with gnarled divi-divi trees and herds of wandering goats give way to rolling sand dunes and a rugged shoreline sprinkled with white sandy coves ideal for a picnic retreat from the midday desert heat. Nearby, limestone caves are adorned with Arawak rock drawings and beautiful flowstone formations, while burrowing owls, rattlesnakes and lizards guard the ruins at the Miralamar gold mine.

In the stifling afternoon heat you find yourself at the base of Cerro Arikok (176m), the second-highest peak on the island. A 1.5km pathway guides you through an example of what the typical Aruban countryside would have looked like in the nineteenth century. Along the way, you'll pass aloe plants growing alongside other endemic thorny shrubs, large diorite boulders and a petroglyph of an ancient bird left behind by indigenous communities.

Halfway through your trek you come across a partially restored *casa di torta* farmhouse, a small traditional country home constructed with dried cactus husks and glued together with layers of mud and grass. A short stroll uphill brings you to the peak and a stunning panoramic view of the surrounding park and its unique natural treasures.

583 | Land of the midnight son

CUBA It's a sweltering Saturday night in Santiago de Cuba, and the entire *barrio* seems to be packed into *La Casa de las Tradiciones*. A mist of rum, beer and sweat fills the air of the much-loved club, while dozens of pairs of feet pound the flexing plywood floors. The wail of a trumpet rides above the locomotive percussion – maracas, congas and *guiros* all chugging along in rhythmic, rumba unison.

The *cajón* player raises his hand, silencing the band and the room. From somewhere among the revellers, a reed-thin voice salvages the melody, this time with less urgency but more emotion. The aged *cantor* takes the stage, his voice bolstered by an upright bass, violin and *tres*. Momentary transfixion melts into sinuous shuffle-steps as the audience swoons to his rousing *son*. The rest of the band joins in again, and soon the crowd is echoing the singer's refrains as his voice soars with the vigour and vibrato of someone half his age.

As dawn steadily approaches and the performance winds down, word arrives of a nearby wedding reception. Eager celebrants spill outside and navigate the barely lit streets between tiny houses, cement bunkers with corrugated tin roofs and the flickering eyes of stray dogs. Along the way, party-goers rush into their homes and emerge clutching bottles of bootlegged *ron* and a cornucopia of musical instruments.

Arriving at the scene, they're welcomed with cheers and the neighbourhood fiesta surges with renewed energy. One man hammers away at a *bata* drum while a teenage girl plonks a pair of wooden *claves*. An older fellow raises an ancient trumpet to his lips; it's dented, with only the memory of a sheen left, but sits in his hands as if he's held it since birth. Then he wades into the roiling *descarga*, horn crowing wildly as morning begins to glow at the edges of the sky.

584 | Gourmet coffee in the Blue Mountains

JAMAICA For most people, Jamaica is synonymous with reggae, Rastas and beach-bound relaxation. Yet the island is also a paradise for coffee lovers, its Blue Mountain beans some of the most sought-after – and delicately flavoured – in the world.

Only coffee grown above a certain altitude can claim the coveted trademark, and there's now a clutch of guesthouses and quality hotels where you can experience this high, rugged landscape – and a fresh daily brew – first hand. *Strawberry Hill Hotel* is traditionally chosen by the international glitterati, while *Forres Park* is a lower-key B&B below a coffee plantation, but there's no better option than the magnificent *Lime Tree Farm*. This small and luxurious family-run hotel, built high upon a remote ridge, is only accessible by a perilous track local villagers politely refer to as a road. The slopes descend on three sides, a beautiful panorama stretching past vast terraces of red coffee berries, interspersed with eucalyptus, fuchsias, begonias and orchids. Hummingbirds flutter about, while the murmur of coffee pickers is just audible as they call to one another across the hillsides. In the distance, the glint of white surf is the only indication you're near Caribbean waters.

The cool, moist climate here – the mountains rise up to 2256m – is a far cry from the dogged heat of the coast. This is a reliably friendly and unhurried land, and excitement comes in the form of hiking trails through plantations and forest, and staggering views every few minutes. Guided walks teach you about the planting and picking of some of the world's finest coffee bushes, while a tour of the Jablum coffee factory, perched on the mountainside at Mavis Bank, demonstrates the process from berry to cup, its several million beans drying out in the sunshine.

The vast majority of Blue Mountain coffee is sold to Japan, leaving its price in Europe and North America sky high – all the more reason to pick up a few bags at source. Known for its rich aroma, smooth silky feel in the mouth and a total absence of the bitter aftertaste so common in standard blends, it's no wonder people save these beans for a special occasion.

Exploring Nelson's jungle dockyard

ANTIGUA Long before his famous victory at Trafalgar, a fully limbed Horatio Nelson cut his teeth in the Caribbean. He wasn't there on holiday; the 27-year-old captain arrived in Antigua in 1784 and stayed for three years, ruffling feathers and generally having a miserable time, claiming he was "most woefully pinched" by mosquitoes. Determined not to get soft, he drank a quart of goat's milk a day, and had six pails of salt water poured over him at dawn.

Like most islands in the Caribbean, Antigua is best known these days for its picture-perfect beaches, but the island offers more than windsurfing and sunbathing. Thanks to the Royal Navy, it's home to the only working Georgian-era dockyard in existence, a rare window into the world of Nelson that dates back even earlier, to the 1720s. This southeastern corner of Antigua is unusually rugged, which made it an excellent refuge from Caribbean storms, French privateers and freeloading pirates, and Nelson's Dockyard is now a national park in sheltered English Harbour, hemmed in by lush jungle slopes.

The dockyard is a sleepy, languid place, hosting the odd beach escapee and plenty of yachties from the nearby marina. Wander down to the water after a drink at *Admiral's Inn*, a pitch and tar store erected in 1788 that's now a gorgeous hotel and restaurant. The restored colonial buildings along the way mix classic Georgian architecture with the Caribbean: thick stone blocks, wooden shutters and plenty of palm trees. The 1769 sawpit shed is the oldest part of the Dockyard, while the joiner's loft, boathouse, blacksmith's workshop and the copper and lumber store all date from the late eighteenth century. The cordage and canvas store is marked with graffiti, said to have been left by the future King George V when he was here in 1884; disappointingly, the young royal simply wrote: "A Merry Xmas and a Happy New Year 2 You All".

Finally, the Dockyard Museum, once an officer's house, tells the story of English Harbour from its original Arawak inhabitants to the 1950s. Inside, "Nelson's Room" holds a life-sized portrait of the great commander, and what's said to be his bed – minus mosquito net.

586 | Swim the light fantastic at Puerto Mosquito

PUERTO RICO Tucked away on the south coast of Vieques, an unspoilt tropical island best known for its beaches, the placid waters of Puerto Mosquito look fairly ordinary by day, fringed by scrubby hills and thick mangroves. But when night falls everything changes. You have to see it to believe it: fish, boats and kayaks leave ghostly trails in the darkness, water falling like sparks of light from paddles and trailing arms. If you get a chance to swim, things become even stranger; as you splash around in the warm lagoon, bodies are engulfed by blue-green luminous clouds, while droplets spill off hands and hair like glittering fireflies.

Thanks to harmless microscopic creatures known as dinoflagellates, Puerto Rico is home to the truly spellbinding phenomenon of bioluminescent bays. It's hard to believe, but CGI is not involved; the natural effect is produced when the little creatures release a chemical called luciferin, which reacts with oxygen to create light (experts are divided on why this happens; it's either a defence mechanism or an attempt to attract food). Dinoflagellates are found all over the tropics, but the lagoon at Puerto Mosquito has a particularly intense concentration: it's shallow, has a narrow mouth that acts like a valve, the salinity is perfect (with no freshwater source or human contamination) and the mangroves provide a crucial nutrient boost. Though you can visit the bay on your own, it's much more enriching to use one of the local tour operators.

Tours usually begin with an introductory talk, followed by a bone-shaking bus ride through the scrub to the waterside. From here enthusiastic guides take small electric pontoon boats for one-hour loops around the lagoon, providing a non-stop commentary on local history and botany. If it's a dark night, you'll already see signs of luminescence, but it's when the boat stops for a twenty-minute swim in the middle of the bay that things really get weird. Don't be shy; jump in and prepare to be amazed.

587 | A hike with a difference up Antigua's Green Castle Hill

ANTIGUA Green Castle Hill's emerald-green slopes are peppered with bizarre rock formations. For a hike with a difference, hire a guide to take you up to the megaliths at the summit of the hill, 20km northwest of English Harbour. There's no conclusive evidence to show when or how these cone-shaped rocks formed. It's possible they are man-made and were once used in ancient rituals by indigenous peoples, though it's more likely the result of volcanic activity. Wear long trousers and sturdy shoes, as the lemongrass has invaded the area and you'll need to fight through the sticky leaves (which grow up to 2m tall) to get to the top, a lofty 170m above sea level. Don't let that put you off, though – it's worth the climb; the sweeping views of southwest Antigua are jaw-dropping, with green arable land leading to dark hilly mounds and the bright blue of the ocean.

588 | Sucking up the killer bees

NEVIS *Sunshine's Bar and BBQ* is a ramshackle hut with just a couple of picnic tables on Pinney's Beach, but once you've tasted the signature rum drinks and burned your lips on the spicy charred shrimp you won't care what it looks like. The owner himself serves up the syrupy "killer bee", a special rum punch made from a secret and lethal recipe (though its name hints at the inclusion of honey among the closely guarded ingredient list) – sip it slowly while you wait for the food. Then, sitting under the shade of a palm-frond umbrella or in the steeply shelving sand, take your first, delicious bite. In the heavy, humid air of the West Indies the sharp heat of the shrimp, straight from the fire pit, hits you first and then intensifies as the insanely hot spices sear your tastebuds. Cool your toes in the gently lapping water and soothe your burning mouth with a long gulp of ice-cold rum punch – now you're living like an islander.

589 | Sugar and spice: touring rum-makers

PUERTO RICO Rum is history on this island. Track down its greatest rum-making dynasties and you might meet Fernando Fernandez, heir to the family that has been making Ron de Barrilito since 1880. His office lies inside the shell of a graceful windmill built in 1827, surrounded by aged photographs of his grandfather and dusty bottles of what many believe to be the world's finest rum. The rambling *hacienda* contains cellars crammed with white-oak barrels of rum, once used to mature Spanish sherry, the air thick with the burnt, sweet aroma of sugar molasses. Workers bottle the rum by hand, slap on labels and then pile them, delicately, onto trucks for distribution.

Real connoisseurs drink Barrilito on ice – a spicy, rich spirit that goes down like fine Cognac – but the top rum-maker in Puerto Rico is Don Q. The brand was created by the Serrallés family, who started selling rum in 1865 in the southern coastal city of Ponce.

Then there's Casa Bacardí. Visit this slick tourist centre inside the "cathedral of rum", the vast Bacardí distillery across San Juan Bay, and you'll enter another world – Cuba, to be precise. The Bacardí family started making rum in Santiago de Cuba in 1862, and now utterly dominate the world market. Hand-held audio devices and enthusiastic guides help you navigate the seven sections of the centre. Special barrels allow you to "nose" the effects of wood barrelling, ageing and finishing, as well as the various Bacardí brands on offer: sweetly scented apple and melon flavours and the rich, addictive aroma of coconut-laced rum – *piña colada* in a bottle. Mercifully, there are two free drinks waiting for you at the end of the tour.

Bacardí abandoned Cuba in 1960 and now has its headquarters in Bermuda, but while you can argue about where it came from or who made it first, there's no doubt that today the home of rum is Puerto Rico.

590 | Finding inspiration at Goldeneye

JAMAICA It has been the scene of many an iconic James Bond moment, from the London double-decker bus chase through the palms to Ursula Andress emerging goddess-like from the sea. And though the island doesn't make a huge deal of its connection with Bond creator Ian Fleming, who wrote most of his famous novels on Jamaican soil, there are a few places where you can pick up 007's trail. Named by the Spanish for the golden light that bathes the area, the village of Oracabessa, on the island's north coast, was chosen by Fleming as the site for his Jamaican home, Goldeneye.

These days, his classy bungalow forms the centrepiece of one of Jamaica's most beautiful and exclusive hotels, a homage to all things chic and a far cry from the bowing obsequiousness of the all-inclusive "tourist prisons". Swathed in lush greenery, the property sits atop a bluff overlooking the Caribbean, with its own private beach and a teeming reef within paddling distance.

Whether you bed down in Fleming's old pad, with its luxurious outdoor bathroom and his old Remington typewriter still on his desk, or go for seclusion at Naomi Campbell's fabulous cottage right on the water, it's pretty much guaranteed that as you sip a sundowner, you'll find the same inspiration as Fleming himself: "Would these books have been born if I hadn't been living in the gorgeous vacuum of a Jamaican holiday? I doubt it."

591 | Snorkelling with turtles in a hidden cay

BONAIRE After months of planning and years of dreaming, you've finally arrived at a small, uninhabited cay off the coast of Bonaire. Beneath the crystal-blue waters awaits a spectacle unparalleled in the marine world. Immense schools of tropical fish in every conceivable shape, size and colour swim alongside sea turtles and dolphins in and around the most impressive coral and sponge gardens in the Caribbean.

The waters surrounding this tiny boomerang-shaped island, 80km north of Venezuela, were made a marine park in 1979. Here, deep ocean currents carry nutrient-rich waters to the surface, nourishing the magnificent reef communities. These same currents bring minimal rainfall to Bonaire, which in turn reduces surface run-off to create the clearest waters imaginable.

Once underwater, you immediately hear the continuous grinding of parrotfish grazing on the algae that grows on top of coral heads. Within seconds, a dazzling spectrum of reef fish comes out of hiding from the delicate stands of soft and hard corals. Schools of brightly coloured butterflyfish, angelfish and damselfish swim in and out of the crevices and between colonies of elkhorn and staghorn corals. Several metres below, purple sea fans and the tentacles of anemones sway back and forth as the swift current pushes you along. You take a deep breath through your snorkel and submerge to the sea floor where you peek into nooks and crannies to spy on wrasse, tangs and other fish. You spot the slender body of a trunkfish, carefully hidden amid the branches of sea rods, patiently waiting for its prey to drift by. A lunging moray eel emerges out of hiding, warning you not to get too close, while a triangular-shaped boxfish hovers nearby.

Before you realize it, the captain signals it's time to return on board. As you prepare to board the craft, you take one final glance at your underworld surroundings – just in time to spot two hawksbill turtles cruising by through the magical sea.

592 | Diving Bloody Bay Wall

LITTLE CAYMAN The reeftop is fairly flat and relatively shallow – around eight metres deep – but when you swim to the edge it's like you are looking into the abyss, 2000m straight down a vertical wall of coral.

Bloody Bay Wall is over 3km long and dotted with coral arches, chimneys and sand chutes. Giant barrel sponges as tall as a man cling to the wall, while barracuda, Nassau groupers and turtles patrol the wall. The crystalline waters around Little Cayman are among the clearest in the Caribbean, and possibly the world, and floating over the drop-off is a unique experience – as close to skydiving underwater as you can get.

593 | Going underground in Santo Domingo

DOMINICAN REPUBLIC Originally used by the indigenous Taino people for religious ceremonies, this massive, multi-level underground cave now attracts those who worship a different type of deity – the DJ. In a city full of hot clubs, La Guacara Taina, or simply "The Cave", is Santo Domingo's best, attracting world-class musicians and hordes of ravers. Decadence awaits as you descend into the club, passing bars, stalactites and scantily clad, well-to-do locals. If the intricate lightshow and three throbbing dance floors don't pull you out into the crowd, you can pass the evening sipping your Presidente in one of the smooth rock alcoves in the back.

CUBA First-time visitors to Havana can feel they are in a dream, coasting through a fantastic cityscape of colonial fortifications, Art Deco towers and Fifties hotels, uncluttered by advertising but punctuated by the bold colours and lines of painted propaganda. Part of their character comes from their decay, from the peeling layers of lemon-yellow and sea-green paint, chipped tiles and tumbling plaster.

Yet not everything is rundown. Designated a UNESCO World Heritage Site for its architecture, the historic district of La Havana Vieja has in parts been well restored and forms a wonderful walkable grid of narrow streets, graceful squares and wide avenues lined with pastel mansions.

Check out the Catedral de San Cristóbal, its wide facade decorated with the restrained swirls and classical columns of the Cuban Baroque style, and the Art Deco Bacardí building, which looms over the district's west side like a wild Gotham City creation, its trademark bat adorning everything from the brass door handles and cracked light fittings to the Gothic sculpture that crowns the roof.

West from La Havana Vieja lies Vedado, bounded to the north by the long line of the sea wall (*malecón*), the city's promenade and the focus of its nightlife. Here you'll find the bulky *Hotel Nacional* with its twin arched towers, and the shell-like form of concrete *Coppelia*, the city's enduringly (and endearingly) popular ice-cream parlour. In contrast, Havana's lavish pre-Revolutionary decadent era is recalled in the Fifties *Riviera* building, built by the Mob as a casino hotel and still with its original sculptures, furniture and fittings miraculously intact.

Like the Italian cities which survived unblemished only because of centuries of poverty and neglect, Havana is a time capsule, one that makes life hard for locals who can't afford repairs each time hurricanes batter their homes. The limited conservation work shows how Havana could be restored in a blaze of glory – for now, it remains a fascinating hotchpotch.

594

A taste of Havana's battered glamour

595 | Unleashing your sense of adventure in Dominica

DOMINICA More than just white-sand beaches and clear waters, the enigmatic Dominica is ripe for adventure.

Discover the mysterious depths of the island with a boat trip down the Indian River, which was a set location for *Pirates of the Caribbean II: Dead Man's Chest*. Within minutes, the river narrows, trees close in overhead, the light dims, and the only sound is of birdcall. The swirling tree roots hug the shoreline, intertwined in fantastic patterns – like something from a fantasy world.

At Bubble Beach, you can go swimming in water that's literally bubbling (hence the name). Here, by Soufrière in the island's southwest, the sea shallows are warmed by hot sulphuric gases trickling into the water in tiny bubbles.

Dominica is also the only country where you can see sperm whales year-round (though Nov–March is best). Boats track the whales with underwater audio devices (played aloud on board), so staff can tell how many whales are communicating, and how far away they are.

596 | Getting real on Treasure Beach

JAMAICA In countries whose main income is from tourism, holidaying can be a somewhat surreal experience – and Jamaica is no exception. The big resorts are dominated by fenced-off all-inclusive hotels, the best bits of beach are pay-to-enter, and most visitors' only interaction with Jamaicans is ordering a beer or a burger. It's easy to see why savvier tourists are heading away from the white sand and gin-clear waters of the resort-packed north to the black sand and breakers of the south.

In Treasure Beach, sustainable, community-based tourism is the order of the day. Locals have taken control of development, opening low-key hotels and guesthouses instead of selling up to the multinational chains, ensuring that the tourist dollar goes into the community rather than some corporate bank account. Instead of themed restaurants and bars selling flavoured margaritas and bongs of beer, you'll find laidback,

locally run outfits where you can feast on Jamaican home cooking, learn the art of dominoes Caribbean-style or sip a white rum while the regulars teach you the latest dancehall moves. And thanks mostly to community group BREDS – named after "bredrin", the patois term for friend – tourism has had a tangibly positive effect: funds raised by visitor donations and an annual triathlon and fishing tournament have, among many other achievements, bought an ambulance (essential in a place where few have a car and the nearest hospital is 24km away), upgraded the local school and given financial aid to low-income families whose lives were ripped apart by 2004's Hurricane Ivan.

A cheering thought as you hop in a fishing *pirogue-cum-tour* boat to head up the coast to the *Pelican Bar*, a rickety shack built on a sandbar a kilometre or so out to sea – easily the coolest drinking spot in Jamaica, with not a flavoured margarita in sight.

597 | Whale-watching in Samaná

DOMINICAN REPUBLIC No Caribbean experience can top sitting on a seaside veranda in the sleepy town of Samaná, sipping a *cuba libre servicio* – two Cokes, a bottle of aged rum and a bucket of ice – as you watch a series of massive humpback whales dive just offshore. Thousands of whales – the entire Atlantic population – flock to the Samaná waters each winter to breed and give birth. And no matter how long you relax there, looking out at the swaying palms backed by a long strand of bone-white sand, you never cease to be surprised as one whale after another sidles up the coastline and emerges from the tepid depths of the Samaná Bay before coming back down with a crowd-pleasing crash.

Samaná, on the northeast coast of the Dominican Republic, is refreshingly free from package tourists. The modest expat community is almost all French, and they've set up a series of laidback outdoor restaurants and bars along the main road. A lot of the native

Dominicans are from the United States originally – free black men and women who moved here in the early nineteenth century when the country was a part of Haiti, the world's first black republic.

Samaná also once held an allure for Napoleon, who envisioned making its natural harbour the capital of his New World empire. While he never carried out his grand plans, look out over Samaná today and you can still imagine the great Napoleonic city destined to remain an emperor's dream: a flotilla of sailboats stands to attention behind the palm-ridged island chain, and in place of the impenetrable French fortress that was to jut atop the western promontory is a small, whitewashed hotel.

For now, though, Samaná remains passed over, which means you can have its natural beauty, tree-lined streets and, above all, its spectacular whale population, pretty much all to yourself.

598

Bath time in Virgin Gorda

BRITISH VIRGIN ISLANDS In the extreme southwest of Virgin Gorda, a bizarre land- and seascape of volcanic boulders known as The Baths offers a prehistoric twist on the archetypal Caribbean beach. These granite rocks, some the size of houses, stretch from the wooded slopes behind the sands right on into the clear aquamarine sea, forming a series of striking grottoes, pools and underwater caves through which you can swim, snorkel or just bob around in. The usually calm waters and sun-streaked private nooks can help make a day at the beach seem like a visit to the largest, most outlandish bathtub imaginable.

599 | Kick back in a casa particular

CUBA By far the best option for accommodation in Cuba is to stay in a *casa particular* (private house), always abbreviated to "*casa*". It's also the best way to meet the country's famously gregarious and charming people: you can sip a *mojito* while getting a good dose of gossip from the owner, as well as the lowdown on the best nearby music venues, bars and festivals.

There are thousands of *casas* across the country. You'll find them in Viñales in the west, where simple village homes are backed by lush tobacco fields and tall limestone stacks; in angular tower blocks and historic homes in Havana; and in the paradisal seaside town of Baracoa in the far east.

Perhaps the pick of them all is *Hostal Florida Center*, an airy nineteenth-century mansion located in urbane Santa Clara, burial place of Che Guevara. Beyond the private rooms at the entrance to the house, owner Angel will take you to the open courtyard with its Art Deco tiled floor and luxuriant orchids, fruit trees and ferns, around which are high-ceilinged rooms for visitors. One of these is in Thirties style, featuring a fabulous antique black-lacquered bed and dressing table; the other is colonial, with ornate mirrors, wrought-iron beds and delicate miniatures on the walls.

Dinner is served in the candle-lit courtyard: abundant home-cooked Cuban food at its simple but tasty best – organic chicken, corn on the cob, shredded beef or river prawns. After dinner you could take a stroll to the main square to see its colonial theatre and palaces, and the mint-green *Santa Clara Libre* hotel, pockmarked with bullets from the Battle of Santa Clara, a decisive victory for Castro's forces in 1958. Or just stay in Angel's verdant courtyard, pick a book from his shelves and order yourself another *mojito*.

600 | Trekking through Cuba's only eco-community

CUBA Cuba's only true eco-community is a simple idyll tucked between the palm trees on the slopes of the Sierra del Rosario mountain range. The community was founded over forty years ago to restore the biodiversity of an area badly deforested for coffee plantations and other prerevolution agriculture. Locals lavished care and attention onto the rich red soil, returning it to full fertile health, managed a huge reforestation project which covered some fifty square kilometres and earned the region UNESCO Biosphere Reserve status in 1985. The self-sufficiency of the area continues today, and from the fruit of their labours springs an abundance of bananas, sugar cane, citrus fruits and tobacco alongside an ecology-education programme.

Hiking here is a pure pleasure. The surrounding rainforest is a wonderland with panoramic viewpoints, natural springs and local flora. Several of the waterfalls that cascade down the hillsides are swimmable. It's also a birdwatcher's paradise, with some seventy or so notable species, including the breathtakingly beautiful multicoloured Cuban trogon (or tocororo) and no fewer than three types of hummingbird. Other hidden delights include eerie ruins of several abandoned coffee plantations for which the area was once famous. At the end of a day's trekking join the locals at the Baños de Bayate stretch of river, which twists through the forest at the foot of the valley. The scenery – and temperature – will take your breath away.

For evening respite, the best place to breathe in the peace of the hills is the *Hotel Moka* that overlooks the Terrazas lake. White arches with hillside vistas, a graceful colonnade and red-tiled roofs create a picturesque spot for a sundown *mojito*. Much of the produce served here and in the homespun *paladar* restaurants in the area is grown locally, and, unusually for Cuba, one of them, *El Romero*, is exclusively vegetarian and vegan. However, the defining factor is far and away the indigenous trees around which the complex is entwined – one gargantuan trunk even grows straight through the central lobby.

601 | Climbing into the clouds on the Route de la Trace

MARTINIQUE It may be blessed with fabulous beaches, enticing ruins and fine cuisine, but Martinique can seem more like a suburb of Nice than a Caribbean island to new arrivals. Traffic is painfully congested in and around the capital, Fort-de-France, resorts line the southern beaches and hordes of tourists hop from one (admittedly superb) rum distillery to another as if on a Rhône Valley wine tour. To escape the crowds, rent a car and head north into the hills; the Route de la Trace (aka N3) runs through increasingly lush slopes like a winding ribbon, ending at the far more tranquil north shore.

The road was created by Jesuits in the eighteenth century, so it's fitting that the first major sight en route is the Sacré Cœur de Balata, a smaller, weather-beaten version of its famous namesake in Paris. From here the road snakes through steep valleys and dripping forests of bamboo, tree ferns and mahogany, passing the Jardin de Balata, a sweet-smelling botanical garden.

Hiking trails lead off from car parks all along the road, yet the most rewarding comes at the end of the Route, beyond the town of Morne-Rouge. The vast dome of Mont-Pelée, the infamous volcano that destroyed the town of St-Pierre in 1902, looms over the whole island, asking to be climbed; it's an exhilarating hike to the top, the cool winds and tranquillity a million miles from the coastal resorts.

The volcano is still active, but carefully monitored and safe to climb. The walk begins from a small car park and café at the end of the Morne-Rouge road. You'll need at least four hours, for although the trail is not long it cuts a very steep path up to the rim. Once at the 1397m summit you'll literally be on top of the island, with a precipitous drop on one side and the rocky slope on the other. You can wander along the rim, soaking up the mesmerizing views of the Caribbean, but remember that the peak is often shrouded in clouds; even if it's sweltering on the beach, it's a different world up here.

Need to know

569 For more information, visit ⓦgocuba.ca. While US nationals are not officially allowed to visit Cuba, Cuban officials do not stamp passports, so they can enter the country without fear of repercussions. Note however that US bank cards do not work in Cuba.

570 To find more information about Junkanoo, visit ⓦbahamas.co.uk.

571 From the northern city of Cap Haitien you can take a private taxi or the public bus to the town of Milot, where you'll start your ascent to the Citadelle.

572 LIDOM (Liga de Beisbol Profesional de la Republica Dominicana) has a Spanish-language website with fixtures, results and relevant news at ⓦlidom .com.

573 The main parades in the capital, Port of Spain, take place on the Monday and Tuesday before Ash Wednesday. Visit ⓦgotrinidadandtobago.com for more details.

574 Visit ⓦstkittsscenicrailway.com to reserve train tickets (prices vary); those on a cruise can buy tickets on board. For information about the fortress visit ⓦbrimstonehillfortress.org.

575 The official festival website (ⓦreggaesumfest .com) has full details.

576 The trail begins by Titou Gorge; start early and finish in daylight. Ask your accommodation to recommend a guide or visit ⓦdominicaadventures.com.

577 The international airport at Puerto Plata is 20km west of Cabarete. All the major windsurfing and kiteboarding equipment manufacturers have schools and equipment rental along the town's main strip. You can find more information at ⓦactivecabarete.com.

578 Yoan and Yarelis Reyes, who run *casa particular Villa los Reyes*, organize various activities around the Viñales valley, including 1–5hr horseriding tours. For more information visit ⓦvillalosreyes.com or email ⓔjoanmanuel2008@yahoo.es.

579 Visitor information on St Lucia can be found at ⓦstluciauk.com. To tour the island you need to rent a car; there are outlets at the airport, Castries and Rodney Bay, and most of the larger resorts.

580 The galleries of Adrian García Garrido at Muralla 166 e/ Plaza Vieja y Cuba; Inti Alvarez Hauville at Cuarteles 118 e/ Ave. de las Misiones y Habana; and Leo D'Lázaro at O'Reilly 501 esq. Villegas are all in Old Havana.

581 The Pitons Tour Guide Association (ⓣ+1 758 459 9748) leads hikes of Gros Piton from the Interpretive Centre in Fond Gens Libre, near Soufrière.

582 Arikok National Park (ⓦaruba.com) lies 20km east of the capital city of Oranjestad.

583 *La Casa de las Tradiciones*, between Rabí no.154 and Princesa y San Fernando, Santiago de Cuba, features live *son* and other varieties of Cuban music.

584 *Lime Tree Farm* (ⓦlimetreefarm.com), *Forres Park* (ⓦforrespark.com) and *Strawberry Hill Hotel* (ⓦislandoutpost.com) offer tours as well as accommodation.

585 Nelson's Dockyard is open daily; see ⓦnational parksantigua.com). The national park also includes the fortifications at Shirley Heights and the multimedia centre at Dow's Hill.

586 Island Adventures offers boat tours of Puerto Mosquito. Tours usually begin at their office, west of Esperanza on PR-996, daily 8–10pm. Avoid heading down on a full moon, when it's impossible to appreciate the effect. Vieques is connected to Puerto Rico by plane and ferry; visit ⓦdiscoverpuertorico.com.

587 For more information on Green Castle Hill, see ⓦnationalparksantigua.com/visiting/parks/green-castle-hill.

588 *Sunshine's* is on Pinney's Beach, on the northwest corner of the island. During high season, mid-Dec to mid-April, it's open seven days a week for lunch and dinner.

589 To visit the makers of Ron de Barrilito, call (ⓣ+1 787 785 3490). The Casa Bacardí Visitor Center lies across San Juan Bay (ⓦbacardi.com/casa-bacardi).

590 To book at *Goldeneye*, visit ⓦislandoutpost.com.

591 ⓦinfobonaire.com has lots of information on snorkelling.

592 For more info, check ⓦvisitcaymanislands.com.

593 *La Guacara Taina*, Av Mirador del Sur, Santo Domingo (ⓣ+1 809 995 5853).

594 You won't need any transport to get you around Old Havana, and it's possible to walk to Vedado along the *malecón*. Otherwise, look for a metered taxi near one of the large hotels. You can visit the bar in the Bacardí building for a drink, and ask at reception to be taken up the tower for the views.

595 Discover Dominica offers a range of packages and tours of the island; ⓦdiscoverdominica.com/en.

596 For info on Treasure Beach, visit ⓦtreasurebeach.net. For more on BREDS, see ⓕfacebook.com/ BredsTreasureBeachFoundation.

597 Fly into Puerto Plata's international airport, from where it's a 4hr bus ride to Samaná village. Check with Victoria Marine (ⓦwhalesamana.com) for a whale-watching boat tour.

598 Check ⓦbvitourism.com for more information on the British Virgin Islands.

599 For accommodation ideas, see ⓦcubacasas.net. Well-known *casas* like *Hostal Florida Center* (ⓦhostalfloridacenter.com) are dogged by touts, who pretend the *casa* is full and try to take visitors elsewhere. Don't be put off – if you have a booking, make sure you get through the front door. If you haven't booked ahead, look for the blue symbol outside the establishment that shows it's legal.

600 Las Terrazas is around a three-hour drive west from Havana. *Hotel Moka* (ⓦhotelmoka-lasterrazas. com); a double room is CUC128.

601 For more info on Martinique, go to ⓦmartinique .org; for the Jardin de Balata check ⓦjardindebalata. fr. Avis, Budget, Europcar and Hertz have offices at the airport and in Fort-de-France.

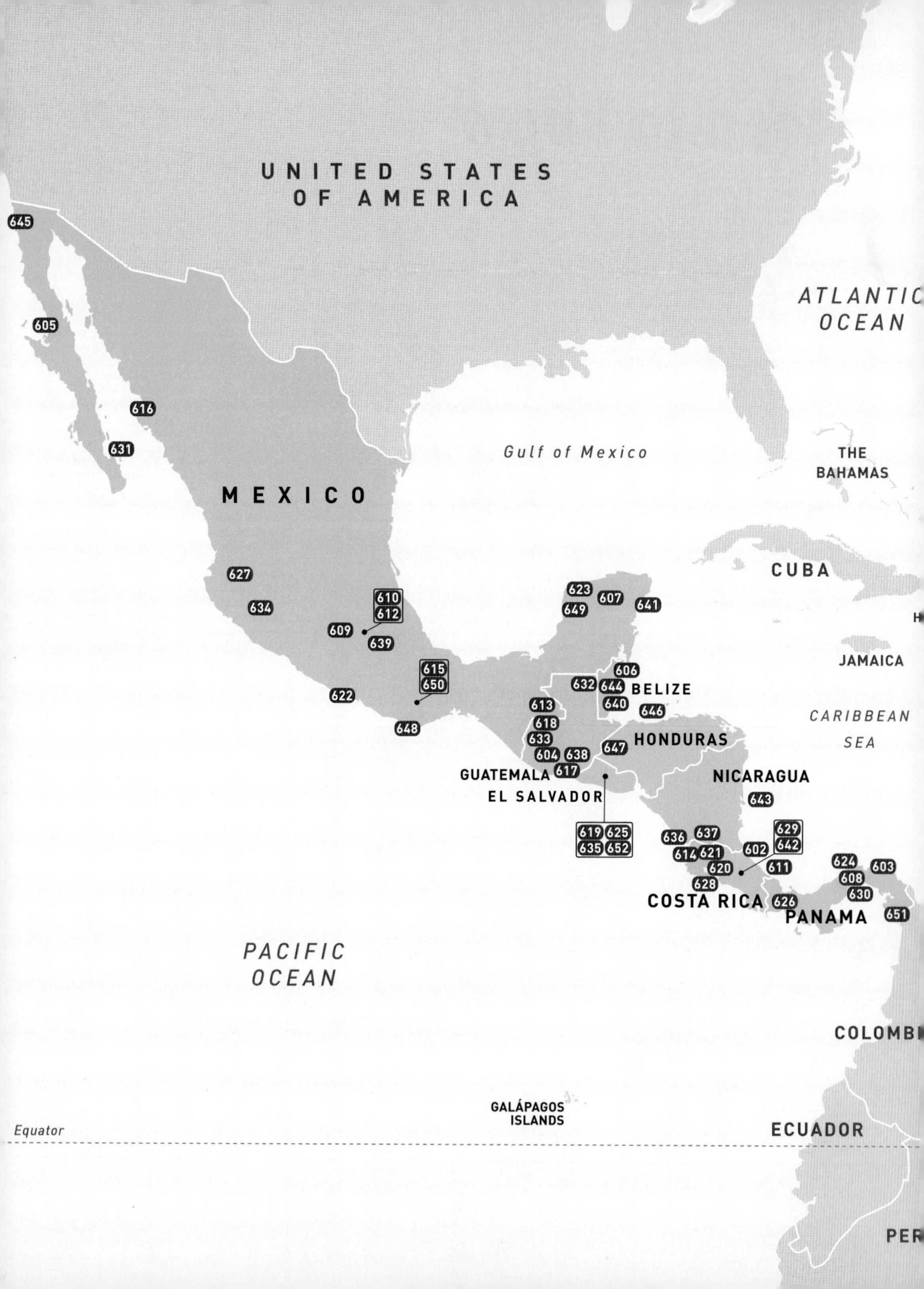

UNITED STATES
OF AMERICA

ATLANTIC
OCEAN

645

605

616

631

MEXICO

Gulf of Mexico

THE
BAHAMAS

CUBA

627

634

609

610
612

639

623
649

607

641

JAMAICA

615
650

606

632
644

BELIZE

CARIBBEAN

622

640

SEA

648

613

646

618

633

647

HONDURAS

604

638

NICARAGUA

617

GUATEMALA

643

EL SALVADOR

629
642

619
635

625
652

636

637

602

624
603

614
621

611

608

620

630

628

651

COSTA RICA

626

PANAMA

PACIFIC
OCEAN

COLOMB

Equator

GALÁPAGOS
ISLANDS

ECUADOR

PER

MEXICO & CENTRAL AMERICA
602-652

Mexico and Central America offer fertile potential for adventure. Lost cities tower over jungle canopies, cloudforests abound with exotic species, and jangling chicken buses steer their way across lush tropical landscapes. The region throws up all manner of escapades, whether you're swimming in underwater Maya caves in Belize, cheering on the death-defying cliff divers of Acapulco, rafting Costa Rica's Río Pacuare or learning to surf in Nicaragua. Full-throttle entertainment is rarely far away – Guatemala's fiestas and the Yucatán's street parties are testament to that – while activities from turtle-watching to railroad-riding offer gentler types of fun.

602 Turtle-watching in Tortuguero

COSTA RICA It's a clear, moonless night when we assemble for our pilgrimage to the beach. I can't understand how we are going to see anything in the blackness, but the guide's eyes seem to penetrate even the darkest shadows. We begin walking, our vision adjusting slowly.

We've come to Tortuguero National Park, in northeast Costa Rica, to witness sea turtles nesting. Once the domain of only biologists and locals, turtle-watching is now one of the more popular activities in ecotourism-friendly Costa Rica. As the most important nesting site in the western Caribbean, Tortuguero sees more than its fair share of visitors – the annual number of observers has gone from 240 in 1980 to over fifty thousand today.

The guide stops, points out two deep furrows in the sand – the sign of a turtle's presence – and places a finger to his lips, making the "shhh" gesture. The nesting females can be spooked by the slightest noise or light. He gathers us around a crater in the beach; inside it is an enormous creature. We hear her rasp and sigh as she brushes aside sand for her nest.

In whispers, we comment on her plight: the solitude of her task, the low survival rate of her hatchlings – only one of every five thousand will make it past the birds, crabs, sharks, seaweed and human pollution to adulthood.

We are all mesmerized by the turtle's bulk. Though we are not allowed to get too close, we can catch the glint of her eyes. She doesn't seem to register our presence at all. The whirring sound of discharged sand continues. After a bit the guide moves us away. My eyes have adapted to the darkness now, and I can make out other gigantic oblong forms labouring slowly up the beach – a silent, purposeful armada.

Jean McNeil
is the author of ten published books, including five novels and several editions of *The Rough Guide to Costa Rica*. She teaches on the Masters in Creative Writing at the University of East Anglia and lives in London.

Encountering Guna culture

603

PANAMA It's often said that there's an island for every day of the year in the San Blas archipelago. In fact, there are slightly more than that in this chain of coral atolls that stretches for 375km along the Caribbean coast of Panama. This is Guna Yala, the autonomous homeland of the Guna Indians, one of the most independent indigenous cultures in Central America. Even if you haven't heard of the Guna before, you've probably seen them, in particular, the women in their patterned headscarves, gold nose rings and colourful traditional costumes. With palm-fringed beaches and coral reefs, Guna Yala is the stuff of Caribbean dreams, but it is the Guna themselves, with their rich cultural traditions, that most people come here to see.

In some ways, visiting Guna Yala gives a feel of what the Caribbean must have been like before European colonists arrived. No outside development is allowed – non-Guna cannot own land or property on these islands. You'll need to ask permission of a community's headman, or *sahila*, if you wish to visit an inhabited island in the least touristed central and eastern groups. Around forty of the islands are inhabited; some are home to several thousand people, while others are narrow sandbanks sheltering only a few families.

Despite the regulations, you can still explore Guna culture and your natural surroundings pretty widely. Travelling by motorized dugout canoe, your guide will take you to pristine beaches and reefs where you can swim and snorkel, as well as to other island communities.

You may even be lucky enough to witness a traditional religious ceremony or to join a fiesta in a communal hall (*casa de congreso*). Here, as you listen to poet-historians sing myths and legends from their hammocks, you will be left with an unforgettable impression of the Guna heritage.

604

Circling Lago Atitlán

GUATEMALA Ever since Aldous Huxley passed this way in the 1930s, writers have lauded the natural beauty of Lago Atitlán. Ringed by three volcanoes, the lake is also surrounded by a series of Maya villages, each with its own appeal and some still quite traditional, despite the influx of visitors. A week spent circumnavigating Atitlán is the ideal way to experience its unique blend of Maya tradition and bohemian counterculture.

Start at the main entry point, Panajachel, which was "discovered" by beatniks in the 1950s and remains the most popular lakeside settlement. The hotels and shopping (especially for textiles) are excellent, even if the place has become something approaching a resort.

By contrast, Santiago Atitlán remains close to one hundred percent Tz'utujil Maya and has a frenetic and non-touristy market that fires up early each Friday morning. It's a riot of colour and commerce as a tide of highlanders overloaded with vegetables and weavings struggles between dock and plaza. Elsewhere, drop by the textile museum, the parish church and the shrine of the Maya pagan saint Maximón, where you can pay your respects with offerings of liquor and tobacco.

Neighbouring San Pedro is another Tz'utujil village, but in the last decade or so has become Guatemala's countercultural centre, with a plethora of language schools and cheapo digs for backpacking bong-puffers and bongo drummers. Even if this puts you off, you can content yourself with the village's wonderful restaurants and a hike up nearby San Pedro volcano.

It's a short hop to San Marcos, for New Age vibes at the renowned *Las Pirámides* meditation-cum-yoga retreat. Last stop is Santa Cruz, where a few great guesthouses make the ideal base for days spent idling in a hammock and admiring the perfect lake views.

605 | Whale-watching in Baja California

MEXICO Whale shapes are picked out in fairy lights; whalebones are hung on restaurant walls and garden fences; posters, flyers and sandwich boards depict whales outside every shop and bar – even the name of the supermarket here, La Ballena, means whale.

If you didn't already know, you might guess that Guerrero Negro, a flyblown pit stop halfway down the long, spindly peninsula of Baja California, is the main base for whale-watching in Mexico. Every November, California grey whales leave Alaska en masse and migrate south to calve, arriving in the warm waters of Mexico in January and February. The lagoon close to Guerrero Negro is where most end up – and the tour to see them, with a guaranteed sighting at close quarters, is one of Mexico's most unforgettable experiences. And it goes like this. By the time the small boat reaches the middle of the glassy-smooth lagoon and the captain switches off the engine, all its excitable passengers have been silenced. Someone spots a distant, cloudy spray – then a great grey body, studded white with barnacles, rises out of the water and curves back in with a deep, resounding splash, leaving a trail of smooth rings across the surface of the water. The little boat rocks and shakes, and curious whales come closer.

Round and round they swim, 9m of pure elegance twisting, flipping, rolling and spouting, their brand-new offspring gliding alongside. And the whales are often joined by dolphins, aquatic bodyguards swimming in perfectly synchronized pairs to protect the whale calves, and by sea lions, their cheeky whiskered faces nearly stealing the show.

Then just as suddenly as the mammals arrived, they disappear back into the deep. The lagoon settles and, moved to silence or even tears, a boatload of awestruck tourists motors back to shore.

606 | In search of grilled rodent

BELIZE The petite coastal country of Belize brings to mind sandy islands, oiled tans and tropical drinks with little paper umbrellas. What doesn't come to mind is grilled rodent. But, gibnut is one of Belize's traditional dishes – and it reveals an intriguing side to a nation known more for its cays than its cuisine.

Gibnut (also called "paca" elsewhere in Central and South America) is a nocturnal rodent that's hunted in the northern and western jungles of Belize. It's then grilled, carved up and plated as a local delicacy. Belizeans, particularly those with rural roots, have been dining on it for years – but gibnut first came into the international spotlight when it was served to Queen Elizabeth II at a state dinner in Belize. When news reached the UK that the Queen had been served rat, the press corps were apparently scandalized (plus, the headline sold plenty of newspapers), and gibnut got its nickname, "Royal Rat". So, what does it taste like? On the plate, gibnut looks like pork – slightly fatty, and often tender enough to cut with the side of a fork; in the mouth, its wild nature comes through, with a pungent, earthy gameyness. In fact, as many chefs report, when hunters haul in gibnut to the kitchen, the odour is so powerful and rank that it has to be dunked in a vat of lime juice for the day.

Tracking down gibnut is also part of its appeal. Most tourist-geared restaurants don't offer it, but just asking around will bring huge grins to the faces of Belizeans – and directions to the nearest family restaurant that serves it. Dig in to gibnut and ease into the Caribbean night at the one-room *Nerie's II*, in Belize City. The setting is wonderfully Belizean traditional: chalkboard menu; plastic table covers; an out-of-date calendar hanging askew on the wall; Belizean reggae spilling out of crackly speakers; a sticky bottle of Marie's hot sauce next to your plate; and a chilled Belikin beer cracked open for you as soon as you drain your previous one. Spend a while here, and you may even be in the mood for a second helping of gibnut.

607 | Taking a dip in the Yucatán's cenotes

MEXICO The Yucatán Peninsula can be unpleasantly muggy in the summer. At the same time, the low-lying region's unique geography holds the perfect antidote to hot afternoons: the limestone shelf that forms the peninsula is riddled with underground rivers, accessible at sinkholes called cenotes – a geological phenomenon found only here.

Nature's perfect swimming spots, cenotes are filled with cool fresh water year-round, and they're so plentiful that you're bound to find one nearby when you need a refreshing dip. Some are unremarkable holes in the middle of a farmer's field, while others, like Cenote Azul near Laguna Bacalar, are enormous, deep wells complete with diving platforms and on-site restaurants.

The most visited and photographed cenotes are set in dramatic caverns in and around the old colonial city of Valladolid. Cenote Zací, in the centre of town, occupies a full city block. Half-covered by a shell of rock, the pool exudes a chill that becomes downright cold as you descend the access stairs. Just outside town, Dzitnup and neighbouring Samula are almost completely underground. Shin down some rickety stairs, and you'll find yourself in cathedral-like spaces, where sound and light bounce off the walls. Both cenotes are beautifully illuminated by the sun, which shines through a hole in the ceiling, forming a glowing spotlight on the turquoise water.

Even more remarkable, however, is that these caverns extend underwater. Strap on a snorkel or scuba gear, and drop below the surface to spy a still, silent world of delicate stalagmites. Exploring these ghostly spaces, it's easy to see why the Maya considered cenotes to be gateways to the underworld. The liminal sensation is heightened by the clarity of the water, which makes you feel as if you're suspended in air.

Isla Barro Colorado: the appliance of science

PANAMA Semi-hidden in the thick forest floor, a nervy agouti is on the forage for food. It stops to nibble on some spiny palm fruit, sandwiching each bite with anxious glances into the surrounding undergrowth. Less than 5m away from the unsuspecting rodent, and closing the gap with every stealthy stride, an ocelot moves in for the kill. The agouti enjoys its last few drips of sweet palm juice, and then...pounce. The cat gets the cream.

In the surrounding rainforest, several scientists from the Smithsonian Tropical Research Institute (STRI) monitor the moment, another important step in piecing together the relationship between ocelot and agouti, predator and prey. Further south, more scientists observe the family behaviour of white-faced capuchins; to the west, the evolution of Baird's tapirs is the focus. Welcome to Isla Barro Colorado, the most intensely studied tropical island on Earth.

Sitting plum in the middle of man-made Gatún Lake, roughly halfway along the Panama Canal, Barro Colorado is a living laboratory, 15 square kilometres of abundant biodiversity – more than a thousand plant species, nearly four hundred types of bird and over a hundred species of mammals – that the island owes to the canal itself. Flooding the area to facilitate its construction chased much of the wildlife in the surrounding forests on to higher ground. The one-time plateau became an island, and the island became a modern-day Noah's Ark, the animals coming in two by two dozen to seek refuge in its dense rainforest covering.

The Smithsonian has run a research station on Barro Colorado since 1946, and they now open their doors to tourists. Hiking through the rainforest in the company of expert guides, the jungle canopy abuzz with screeching howler monkeys and ablaze with red-billed toucans, is an incredible experience, even if the Hoffmann's two-toed sloths, hanging lazily from the trees, seem distinctly underwhelmed by it all.

609

Honouring the dead in Janitzio

MEXICO Mexicans believe that the thin veil between the land of the living and the world of the spirits is at its most permeable on the night of November 1, as All Saints' Day slips silently into All Souls' Day. This is the one time each year, it is said, when the dead can visit the relatives they have left behind. Mexicans all over the country aim to make them feel welcome when they do, though nowhere are the preparations as elaborate as on the island of Janitzio in Lago Pátzcuaro.

Market stalls laden with papier-mâché skeletons and sugar skulls appear weeks in advance; the decorations and sweets go on shrines set up in people's homes. Dedicated to the departed, the shrines come complete with a photo of the deceased and an array of their favourite treats – perhaps some cigarettes, a few *tamales* and, of course, preferred brands of tequila and beer.

When the big day comes, you don't want to arrive too early at the cemetery – it isn't until around 11pm, as the witching hour approaches, that the island's indigenous Purhépecha people start filtering into the graveyard. They come equipped with candles, incense and wooden frames draped in a riot of puffy orange marigolds. Pretty soon the entire site is aglow with candles, the abundantly adorned graves slightly eerie in the flickering light. So begins the all-night vigil: some observers doze silently, others reminisce with friends seated at nearby graves. It is a solemn, though by no means sombre, occasion. Indeed, unlike many cultures, Mexicans live with death and celebrate it.

By early morning the cemetery is peaceful, and in the pre-dawn chill, as sleep threatens to overtake you, it is easier to see how the dead could be tempted back for a brief visit, and why people return year after year to commune with the departed.

610 | Lucha libre: wrestling in Mexico City

MEXICO With its masks, muscles, comedy and high drama, *lucha libre* is glitzy, over-the-top and uniquely Mexican. Distinctively costumed heroes and villains – with names like Blue Demon, El Terrible and Virus – ham it up in the ring, parading around in sequinned tights and lycra, enacting action-packed, mock battles to the delight of besotted fans.

Legendary 1940s *luchador* "El Santo" raised the profile of Mexican wrestling, appearing in countless films and comic books during his five-decade-long reign over the ring, and it remains one of the country's classic spectator sports, with thousands heading to the capital's Arena México stadium each week for a chance to cheer on their champions. Inspired by professional wrestling in the US, *lucha libre* sets itself apart with its colourful masks and anonymous stars – *luchadores* are fiercely protective of their true identities and some even keep up the mystery by hiding behind their masks outside the ring. Unmasking an opponent is the ultimate no-no and usually spells instant disqualification – unless the *luchador* is about to retire or adopt a new persona.

Often representing bygone warriors, saints, politicians or superheroes, the good guys (*técnicos*) spring into the ring flexing their toned biceps before performing a series of high-flying acrobatic kicks, designed to crush their foe and defend the public. *Técnicos* play fair, and alongside their athleticism use skill and intelligence to defeat their opponents. Their rivals – the underhanded baddies (*rudos*) – are thuggish by comparison. They stand for corruption, brutality and dishonesty and take gleeful pleasure in rule-breaking.

Three or four rounds peak with a final almighty bout. Excitable fans, fuelled by a steady supply of beer, become increasingly raucous in the face of this extravagant farce, which involves lots of theatrical shoving, tantrums and full-blown clashes. Performers regularly get knocked or slip out of the ring, driving the front row wild and baying for blood. Yelling and hurling insults, the audience eggs the drama on and, boosted by the attention, wrestlers respond with even more exaggerated and daring moves. Of course, the good guys tend to come out on top – but only after a repeated bruising by their snarling arch-enemies.

611 | Soundwaves on the Caribbean's secret shore

COSTA RICA At the southeastern end of Costa Rica's Caribbean coast, a tiny spur of rainforest and golden sand butts into the warmth and verdant wetness of Panama. This is the little-visited and low-key Gandoca-Manzanillo Wildlife Refuge. Unlike in Costa Rica's more visited national parks, there are no shrieking scarlet macaws, no ringing three-wattled bellbirds, no volcanoes, no pounding Pacific surf – and not many tourists either. You can bask on the expansive arc of Manzanillo beach, sheltered by its massive green wall of coastal rainforest, and hardly see or hear another person.

What you will see – and hear – are animals: everywhere. On the beach, every footfall disturbs sapphire-blue land crabs, scurrying to hide in their sandy holes. In the shallows, you might spot a jumping devil ray, its wings spread like a menacing angel before it splashes back into the water. On the forest trails you'll hear the eerie shrieks of howler monkeys

– which inspired Christopher Columbus to name the adjacent headland Punta Mona, or "Monkey Point"; you may glimpse the improbably bright chestnut-mandibled and keel-billed toucans too. At night, guides take you to see leatherback turtles; torches can hardly illuminate the expanse of the carapace, but sit quietly beside a laying female and you'll hear the gentlest popping as she lays her eggs.

The inshore coral reefs offer fine snorkelling and diving (there are some sleepy local dive centres), and fishermen can take you in search of the local dolphins – bottlenose, Atlantic spotted or the rare, tiny tucuxi. Once the boat's engine is cut, there's nothing to hear but the surge of the dolphins' leaping or the sudden insuck of blowhole air as they surface. Ask the boatman why dolphins breach like this and you might get a truly Caribbean reply: "him jus' jump up and taalk to I". It's the best kind of conversation.

612 | Floating through Xochimilco

MEXICO Spend a few days in the intoxicating, maddening *centro histórico* of Mexico City, and you'll understand why thousands of Mexicans make the journey each Sunday to the "floating gardens" of Xochimilco, the country's very own Venice.

Built by the Aztecs to grow food, this network of meandering waterways and man-made islands, or *chinampas*, is an important gardening centre for the city, and where families living in and around the capital come to spend their day of rest. Many start with a visit to the beautiful sixteenth-century church of San Bernadino in the main plaza, lighting candles and giving thanks for the day's outing. Duty done, they head down to one of several docks, or *embarcaderos*, on the water to hire out a *trajinera* for a few hours. These flat, brightly painted gondolas – with names such as *Viva Lupita*, *Adios Miriam*, *El Truinfo* and *Titanic* – come fitted with table and chairs, perfect for a picnic.

The colourful boats shunt their way out along the canals, provoking lots of good-natured shouting from those wielding the poles. As the silky green waters, overhung with trees, wind past flower-filled meadows, the cacophony and congestion of the city are forgotten. Grandmothers unwrap copious parcels and pots of food, groups of friends open bottles of beer and aged tequila; someone starts to sing. By midday, Xochimilco is full of carefree holidaymakers.

Don't worry if you haven't come with provisions – the *trajineras* are routinely hunted down by vendors selling snacks, drinks and even lavish meals from small wooden canoes. Others flog trinkets, sweets and souvenirs. And if you've left your guitar at home, no problem: boatloads of musicians – mariachis in full costume, marimba bands and wailing ranchera singers – will cruise alongside or climb aboard and knock out as many tunes as you've money to pay for.

613 | A glimpse of the murals at Bonampak

MEXICO For almost a century, scholars studying ancient Maya culture believed the Maya to be pacifists, devoted to their arcane calendar and other harmless pursuits. It wasn't until 1946, when a few Lacandón Maya led an American photographer to a ruined temple at Bonampak, deep in the Chiapas jungle, that they had any reason to think differently.

As the party entered the narrow building perched at the top of the temple and torchlight played across its interior, the ancient Maya flickered into living colour. A series of murals covered the walls and ceilings of three rooms, depicting the Maya in fascinating detail. Lords paraded in yellow-spotted jaguar pelts and elaborate headdresses, while attendants sported blue-green jade jewellery.

More remarkable was the quantity of bright-red gore splashed on scenes throughout the rooms: severed heads rolled, prisoners oozed blood from mangled fingers, sacrifice victims littered the ground. On one wall, the eighth-century king Chan Muan glowered mercilessly

at writhing captives, while on another his soldiers engaged in a frenzied battle.

The artistry of the murals was undeniable: even the most gruesome images – such as the king's wife threading a thorn-studded rope through her tongue – were balanced by lush colours and captivating precision. But the discovery, while offering unparalleled insight for anthropologists and Maya experts, must have been somewhat unsettling, too: to see Chan Muan poised to lop the head off a prisoner was astounding.

Visiting the Bonampak murals is slightly easier now than it was when they were found seventy years ago, but only just. They remain buried far enough in the humid Lacandón forest that you can still feel – when you step into the dimly lit rooms – a sense of drama and revelation. If you can't make it to Chiapas, check out the reproductions in the National Museum of Anthropology in Mexico City, where the colours are brighter but the ambience lacking.

614 | Galloping through Guanacaste

COSTA RICA This is not the Costa Rica you may have imagined: one glance at the wide-open spaces, the legions of heat-stunned cattle or the mounted *sabaneros* (cowboys) trotting alongside the Pan-American Highway reveals that Guanacaste has little in common with the rest of the country. This is ranching territory: the lush, humid rainforest that blankets most of the country is notably absent here, replaced by a swathe of tropical dry forest. It's one of the last significant patches of such land in Central America.

Given the region's livelihood, it's only fitting that the best way to tour Guanacaste is astride a horse. Don't be shy about scrambling into the saddle – many of the working ranches in the province double as hotels, and almost all of them offer horseback tours, giving you a chance to participate in the region's *sabanero* culture. From your perch high above the ground, the strange, silvery beauty of the dry forest appears to much

greater advantage – in the dry season, the trees shed their leaves in an effort to conserve water, leaving the landscape eerily bare and melancholy. You'll be able to spot all kinds of wildlife, from monkeys and pot-bellied iguanas to birds and even the odd boa constrictor (though the horses may not be impressed by this one).

For a different sort of scenery, head to the area around still-active Rincón de la Vieja, where you can ride around bubbling mud pots (*pilas de barro*) and puffing steam vents, all under the shadow of the towering, mist-shrouded volcano.

Some of the region's ranches-cum-hotels even let guests put in a day's work riding out with the ranch hands, provided their fence-mending and cattle-herding skills are up to scratch. Regardless of your level of equestrian expertise, once you've had a gallop through Guanacaste, you'll never look at sightseeing on foot the same way again.

615 | Market day in Oaxaca

MEXICO Oaxaca is pure magical realism – an elegant fusion of colonial grandeur and indigenous mysticism. From the Zócalo, the city's main square, streets unfold in a patchwork of Belle Époque theatres, romantic courtyards and sublime churches.

While the city's colonial history reaches its zenith in the breathtaking Iglesia de Santo Domingo, pre-Hispanic traditions ignite in its kaleidoscopic markets. The largest of these is the bustling Mercado de Abastos, which bombards the senses with riotous colours, intoxicating aromas and exotic tastes.

Indigenous women dressed in embroidered *huipiles*, or tunics, squat amid baskets overflowing with red chillis and *chapulines* (baked grasshoppers), weaving *pozahuancos*, wrap-around skirts dyed with secretions from snails. Stalls are piled with *artesanía* from across the region. Sandals, or *huaraches*, are the speciality of Tlacolula; made from recycled tyres, they guarantee even the most intrepid backpacker a lifetime of mileage.

Hand-woven rugs from Teotitlán del Valle, coloured using century-old recipes including pomegranate and cochineal beetles, are the most prized. The shiny black finish on the pottery from San Bartolo Coyotepec gives it an ornamental function – a promotion from the days when it was used to carry mescal to market.

Street-smart vendors meander the labyrinthine alleyways, offering up the panaceas of ancient deities – *tejate*, the "Drink of the Gods", is a cacao-based beverage with a curd consistency and muddy hue. (A more guaranteed elixir is a mug of hot chocolate, laced with cinnamon and chilli, from Mayordomo, the Willy Wonka of Oaxaca.) The stalls around the outer edges of the market sell shots of mescal; distilled from the sugary heart of the cactus-like maguey plant and mixed with local herbs, it promises a cure for all ailments. With a dead worm at the bottom as proof of authenticity, it's an appropriately mind-bending libation for watching civilization and supernaturalism merge on a grand scale.

MEXICO As the countryside – by turns savage, pristine, lush – flashes past the windows of the *Chihuahua-Pacific Express*, Mexico reveals a side of itself that is both spectacular and unexpected.

"El Chepe", as the train is known, traverses the country's most remote landscape, a region of rugged splendour called the Copper Canyon. Spanning six prodigious canyons and a labyrinth of some two hundred gorges, this natural wonder is four times the size of the Grand Canyon. Harsh, inaccessible and thoroughly untamed, the canyons are sparsely populated only by the Rarámuri, an indigenous agrarian people.

El Chepe's journey commences on Mexico's Pacific coast, in Los Mochis, then trundles through 75km of arid, cactus-strewn wasteland to placid El Fuerte, the gateway to the canyons. From here, the track climbs, the air cools and the scenery shifts: for the next six hours you roll past one incredible vista after another. In a continual skyward ascent, El Chepe plunges in and out of tunnels, rattles over bridges and makes hairpin turns.

Colossal stone cliffs, folds of rock and serpentine rivers flicker by. Above you, mountains rise like fortified cities, while gaping chasms open on either side. Then, all at once, the stone corridor yields to a sweeping plateau of pine-scattered towers and stratified monoliths.

At El Divisadero, 300km from Los Mochis and 2000m above sea level, three canyons converge to form an astonishing panorama. The train makes a brief stop here, giving you time to snap some pictures and breathe in the ozone and pine. Creel, another 60km along, is the place to stop for extended excursions – forests, gorges, waterfalls and hot springs all lie within easy reach.

The 655km expedition concludes on the desert plains of Chihuahua, though it feels as if you've travelled further. Stepping off the train, you're as likely to feel humbled as you are exhilarated.

616

Hopping aboard the Copper Canyon Railway

All aboard the chicken buses

617

GUATEMALA *Camionetas* ("chicken buses") start their lives as North American school buses, Bluebirds built to ferry under-8s from *casa* to classroom. Once they move down to these parts, they're decked out with gaudy "go faster" stripes and windshield stickers bearing religious mantras ("Jesús es el Señor"). Comfort, however, is not customizable: bench seat legroom is so limited that gringo knees are guaranteed a bruise or two, and the roads have enough crater-sized potholes to ensure that your gluteus maximus will take a serious pounding. But you choose to hop aboard in Antigua anyway, just to say you've ridden one if for no other reason.

Pre-departure rituals must be observed. Street vendors stream down the aisles, offering everything from *chuchitos* (stuffed maize dumplings) to Bibles. Expect a travelling salesman-cum-quack to appear and utter a heartfelt monologue testifying how his elixir will boost libido, cure piles and insomnia. Don't be surprised to find an indigenous family of delightful but snotty-nosed kids on your lap and a basket of dried shrimp under your feet; on the chicken bus, there's no such thing as "maximum capacity". A moustachioed driver jumps aboard, plugs in a tape of the cheesiest merengue the marketplace has to offer, and you're off. The exhaust smoke is so dense even the street dogs run for cover.

The trip from Antigua to Nebaj doesn't look much on a map – around 165km or so – but the route passes through four distinct Maya regions, so you look out for the tightly woven zigzag shawls typical of Chichicastenango and the scarlet turban-like headdresses worn by the women of the Ixil. Considering the way the bus negotiates the blind bends of the Pan-American Highway, you'll find anything to divert your attention.

With some luck, after five hours you arrive in Nebaj, a little shaken, slightly bruised, but with many stories to tell.

618 | Dancing drama with the Maya

GUATEMALA Every Maya village in Guatemala celebrates its patron saint's day with a life-affirming fiesta – a riot of colour, music, dance, alcohol, religion and tradition. You'll find the village square packed with trinket-selling traders, a fairground with dodgy-looking rides, festival queens wearing exquisite *huipiles* (blouses made from hand-woven textiles) paraded on floats and an endless array of machine-gun-style firecrackers and *bombas* (eardrum-splitting fireworks which provoke all the stray dogs in town to bark at the moon – night or day).

Alongside standard-issue bands (complete with a strutting lead singer) belting out the latest Latino hits, traditional dances are performed. These enact a custom of history-telling through dance drama. Masked performers wearing fantastical plumed headdresses and elaborate and gaudy costumes skip to the beat of the *marimba* (a kind of xylophone), flute and drum. The *Baile de la Conquista* (Conquest Dance) recounts the struggle between the Spanish and Maya. Tecún Umán, the K'iche king, confronts the conquistadors but is killed in battle and the Maya are converted to Christianity. Though the drama narrates a tragedy for the Maya, the dancers manage to inject humour into the tale as the arrogance of the invaders is ridiculed. By performing this dance the spirits of their defeated ancestors are released.

In some areas of the western highlands, even more arresting spectacles take place. The most astonishing of all, the *Palo Volador*, is performed in Cubulco, Chichicastenango and Joyabaj. Men climb to the top of a 20m pole, then swallow-dive to the ground, with only a cord tied around both feet to break their fall, spiralling slowly down in ever-increasing circles. This ritual is said to signify the descent of the hero twins into hell to fight the Lords of the Underworld in the Maya creation epic.

As a spectacle, Maya fiestas are a total assault on the senses as dance and custom, noise and costume combine in an orgy of celebration, which is as much about honouring highland ritual as it is about having one hell of a party.

619 | Tracking down the perfect pupusa

EL SALVADOR Every nation has at least one simple culinary speciality, described longingly, defended avidly and eaten proudly – and to excess – by the locals. The US has the hot dog, Mexico has the taco, Peru has ceviche and little old El Salvador has the *pupusa*. This is street food at its finest: small tortillas made fresh from thick cornmeal, served piping hot and stuffed with melted cheese (*queso*), beans (*frijoles*), pork crackling (*chicharrón*) or all three – all for less than an American dollar. You can ask for *pupusas* with spicy sauce, tomato juice and/or *curtido*, a blend of pickled cabbage, beetroot and carrots. For aficionados, it's the *curtido* that really makes the experience – the tangy, kimchi-like pickle is the perfect foil for the *pupusa*'s hefty cheese-and-carb punch.

Pupusas have been made in El Salvador by the Pipil and Maya people for at least two thousand years, though the modern explosion in popularity only really got going in the 1960s. Today they are served everywhere, from ramshackle streetside stalls to posh sit-down restaurants, and competition is fierce. Most *salvadoreños* will tell you the best *pupuserías* can be found in Olocuilta, a small town on the road between San Salvador and the international airport. Here you'll find more than fifty stalls pumping out their own version of the national dish – many of them specializing in using rice flour rather than cornmeal – made to order and served with giant plastic jugs of *curtido*. Closer to the capital, in Los Planes, rustic *Pupusería Paty* serves some of the best and biggest *pupusas* in the country. You really need a car to sample these rural *pupuserías*, but non-drivers can trawl plenty of top-notch spots without leaving the capital. Downtown, no-frills *Pupusería Doña Isabel* is a local favourite, while workers in the Zona Rosa hang out at *Comedor y Pupusería Shadaii*, little more than a series of shacks on a backstreet. With its outdoor tables and cheap beer, *Shadaii* knocks out some of the tastiest *pupusas* you'll find – just don't tell that to the folks in Olocuilta.

620 | Things that go bump in the night

COSTA RICA The thick cloud hangs heavily among the branches, leaving a trail of moisture as it swirls slowly through the dense foliage of Monteverde Cloudforest Reserve. The blurry silhouette of a creature gradually emerges through the fine mist, advancing down the track towards you. As more figures appear, you recognize their outlines – a swarming group of greatly spotted tourists.

Ever since *National Geographic* declared that Monteverde might just be the best place in all of Central America to see the resplendent quetzal – a striking emerald bird, revered by the Aztecs and Maya alike – the neat trails of this vast reserve have been swamped with ecotourists and twitchers intent on catching a glimpse of a shimmering tail feather. Visitor numbers are limited, but at times you could be forgiven for thinking that most of the wildlife is of the camera-toting kind. There is one excellent way, however, of escaping the crowds.

Each night, when a hush has fallen on the forest, a small group sets out from the reserve office to walk the deserted trails with just an expert guide – and a flashlight or two – for company. In the dark, your sense of hearing peaked by the inky blackness, you can almost hear the jungle breathing. Many of Monteverde's animals are nocturnal, and as the guide scans his torch across a pair of toucans, their beaks nestled firmly in their feathers for the night, his beam lands on the furry face of a cuddly-looking kinkajou, a comic-book member of the racoon family, steadily navigating the lower branches. As it heads off on the forage for food, you stand stock-still to soak up the silence. The only sound is the crunching of leaf litter as a rather hefty tarantula makes its way across the forest floor. By morning, it'll be safely hidden out of sight, as the tour groups arrive to take over the trails once more.

621 | Hiking through darkness in the Bajo del Tigre forest

COSTA RICA Hiking blanketed in darkness through a place known as Bajo del Tigre – or "below the tiger" – sounds both a magical and a rather foolhardy decision. The tigers here may well be mythical, but there are plenty of other eyes looking down on you as you pass through the reserve's forested depths.

Monteverde's Bajo del Tigre is just one slice of Costa Rica's largest nature reserve: the Bosque Eterno de los Niños – this name, however, is much less misleading. Translated as the Children's Eternal Rainforest, this enormous swathe of protected area really did come about thanks to the efforts of children. A group of Swedish primary-school students first sparked the conservation efforts through a fundraising project in the late 1980s; now, children from over forty countries have contributed donations to protect this biodiverse sweep of wilderness.

The hike through the Bajo del Tigre begins just after sunset. Standing on the edge of the reserve, hikers gather to watch as the glowing sun slinks below the horizon, casting streams of colour across the sky. As the darkness encroaches, it's time to make your slow, fumbling descent into the blacked-out forest. With your vision gone, a current of acute awareness sparks through your other senses: the rustle of the wind through the trees; the unnerving squeal of two swaying branches rubbing against each other; a light mist of almost-rain settling on your brow, the whisper of a cobweb catching across your neck.

But your eyes do gradually adjust to the darkness, and one by one, the sights of the forest reveal themselves. Nestled high into tree-nooks are fluffed-up slumbering birds and, far below them, frogs cling to the undersides of leaves – tiny specs of creatures barely the size of a fingernail. Even more unexpected is the discovery of a scorpion, an unreal, luminescent glow caught beneath a flash of the torchlight. Intermittently, the canopy clears enough to reveal a glimpse of sky pinpricked with scattered stars that radiate out from a low-slung moon. Yet most spellbinding of all are the forest's fireflies. Mirroring the night's sky within the canopy itself, this mesmerizing drift of flickering lights is just the magic you were came looking for.

622 | The death-defying cliff divers of Acapulco

MEXICO Acapulco is a great survivor. Beloved of Elizabeth Taylor and the Kennedys and sung about by Sinatra, this is a city of vintage mid-century glamour. Sadly, its reputation among international visitors has been damaged in recent years by a surge in cartel-related violence. This rarely affects tourists, however, and domestic visitor numbers continue to rise, drawn in their droves to the perfect beaches, glamorous hillside hideaways and stunning coastal landscapes of Acapulco Bay.

Nothing better illustrates the twin pillars of Acapulco's character – courageous and enduring on the one hand, an incorrigible show-off on the other – than its *clavadistas*. These death-defying cliff divers have been launching themselves off the edge of La Quebrada, a rocky outcrop on the fringes of the old town, five times a day since the 1920s. The practice was formalised in 1934, since which time the crowds have gathered once an afternoon and four times each evening to experience a breathtaking display of bravery and athleticism.

Just as impressive as the diving itself is what comes first. Beginning in the sea, the divers climb the rocky 25m-high cliff face by themselves, and at remarkable speed, queuing up beside a shrine to Our Lady of Guadalupe (*El Virgen de Guadalupe*). After a while spent geeing up the crowd – and revelling in the adoration – they are ready to dive. They jump alone or in pairs, often incorporating synchronized pirouettes and somersaults, or – equally impressively – remaining as straight as an arrow. The final diver goes even further than the others, following the path to the highest point of the cliff and, after one final sign of the cross, launching himself off from a 35m summit. All this must be timed to meet an incoming wave – otherwise there's not enough water in the narrow channel to stop them crashing against the rocks.

For a full appreciation of the cliff divers, visit twice: once during the day, when you can better see what's going on, and again for the final night dive, when the last diver makes his jump holding flaming torches in each hand – as if it wasn't spectacular enough already.

623 | Dancing in the streets: Mérida's parties

MEXICO Almost every day of the week, the graceful old colonial city of Mérida, capital of Mexico's steamy Yucatán Peninsula, comes alive with music and dancing. Largely attended by locals, Mérida's parties have a vibrancy that reflects the city's creative streak, and are so inclusive that even as a visitor you will be welcomed with open arms.

On Mondays, check out the *Jarana Yucateca* folk dances, which are performed in front of the Palacio Municipal to the raucous sound of a wind instrument-led band, with the women wearing beautifully embroidered traditional white dresses. On Saturday evenings, the *noche Mexicana* showcases music and dancing from all over the country, filling the Paseo de Montejo with a festival atmosphere; grab a *taco chicharrón* (pork-rind taco) from a vendor and perch on a plastic chair while watching the flurry of skirt twirling and foot stamping.

The highlight of the week, however, is Sunday, when the historic city centre is closed to traffic and market traders set up in the streets around the cathedral and the Plaza Grande. Alongside stalls selling traditional dresses, colourful shirts and panama-style hats, food carts serve overstuffed *tortas* (sandwiches), cinnamon-sprinkled *churros* and fresh tropical fruit, cramming so tightly into Calle 60 that you have practically no choice but to stop and eat. With every plaza occupied by a different band or dance troupe, music fills the streets along with the crowds, an infectious, vivacious Yucatan soundtrack that will have you toe tapping your way through the city. Perhaps the most enjoyable parties are those you stumble across, led by curiosity to follow a wave of excited applause or lured by the enthusiastic shout of a trumpet playing a rhythmic *mambo*.

Sitting in a tree-shaded square in the afternoon sun, clapping in time to the music, brings with it a wonderful sense of belonging. It's hard to resist joining the crowds that throng the stage and giving yourself up to the Latin beats, before stumbling back to your hotel, half-drunk on the irresistible mix of live music, sunshine and a vibrant, shared experience.

From sea to shining sea: cruising the Panama Canal

624

PANAMA The Panama Canal, a narrow channel surrounded by virgin jungles teeming with toucans and white-faced capuchin monkeys, takes only a day to traverse. But during that day you'll experience an amazing feat of engineering and cross the Continental Divide. Politically fraught from its inception and burdened by the death of nearly 30,000 workers during its construction, the 77km canal, opened in 1914, is a controversial yet fascinating waterway which offers safe passage to over 14,000 vessels per year.

Your trip begins in the Caribbean near the rough-and-tumble town of Colón, which prospered during the canal's construction but has since declined, its ramshackle colonial buildings and hand-painted signs frozen in time. Once on board, ships enter the narrow Gatún locks; the canal rises over 25m above sea level as it crosses the Panamanian isthmus, so you start and end your journey in a series of locks, which elevate and then lower you from the ocean on either end.

On the far side, the enormous, sparkling Gatún Lake was formed by a flooded jungle valley and serves as an intersection for shipping freighters, cruise ships, local pleasure boaters and environmentalists, drawn by the lake's isolated islands – basically the tops of mountains that remained above water level. They and the surrounding rainforest are home to thousands of species of wildlife, including monkeys, sloths, lizards and a variety of tropical birds, all of which you'll see from the boat. With the lake behind you, you enter the narrowest part of the canal – the Gaillard Cut. Blasted out of solid rock and shale mountainside, this channel is so perilously close that it's impossible for two large ships to pass; as you enter, your clothes stick to your skin in the hot, heavy equatorial air, and the rainforest feels very close by. Listen for the calls of the myriad birds, loud and distinct above the engine's low-speed hum, and scan the banks, where you'll pick out crocodiles floating menacingly in the shallows.

After nearly 14km of slow, careful progress, you emerge at the Miraflores Locks, beyond which lies the Pacific. As you exit the final chamber and pass under the Bridge of the Americas at Balboa, the bright lights and skyscrapers of Panama City appear on your left. From the timeworn streets of Colón to the bustling metropolis ahead, you have truly travelled from one side of the world to the other.

Suchitoto: El Salvador's colonial treasure

EL SALVADOR Suchitoto perches like a weathered crown on a ridge high above a tranquil lake, an unspoilt cluster of single-storey adobe houses with red-clay roof tiles. There's a tangible sense of history in this sleepy, time-lost place, where creaking machines in smoky Spanish bakeries pump out corn tortillas, dozy cattle are herded along cobbled streets and salsa rhythms waft through cracked wooden doorways.

Just one hour east of San Salvador, this enchanting Spanish colonial town lies between the mountains and Lago de Suchitlán. Stroll around the main plaza to soak up the languid atmosphere, and pop into the whitewashed Iglesia Santa Lucía, which boasts a particularly atmospheric interior of peeling walls, painted altars and timber pillars. Shady Parque San Martín, meanwhile, a couple of blocks northwest of the church, commands eye-popping views across the azure waters of the lake. Take time to wander down to the lakeshore itself, where you can swim in the clear cool waters or hang out in one of the simple bars, doing like the locals do and sipping a refreshing Pilsner lager. From here you might take a boat or hike along the shore to the Cascada Los Tercios, where a mountain stream tumbles over unusual hexagon-shaped basaltic columns. You could also jump on the small tourist boat that chugs around the lake. It sometimes visits the Isla de los Pájaros, where you can spy a range of fish-eating bird life squawking in the trees or wading amid great beds of floating lilies.

Back in town, an evening cocktail at one of the little plaza cafés is very welcome, or you could head over to the elegant *Posada Suchitlán*, where a terrace draped in blossoms (and the odd parrot) affords intoxicating views of sunset and the lake shimmering far below.

626 | Taste the world's best coffee in the cloud forests of Boquete

PANAMA Driving west from Panama City, you'll notice the temperature drop and the topography become lush as you ascend into hill country. The Chiriquí highlands might be less well-known than neighbouring Costa Rica, but Panama has a thriving coffee scene and some of the best plantation lodges to spend a few days. In this land of cloud forests and hummingbirds, the climate is perfect for the coffee bean to thrive. Volcanic ash from the looming Barú Volcano enriches the soil, while the 1000m-plus elevation offers cool mountain air.

A small town in itself, Boquete is inhabited by Panamanians, the indigenous Ngöbe-Buglé, and North American expats, who know a thing or two about the best places on Earth to spend their golden years. And, like many of the people who make it to Boquete, they're always looking for that perfect cup of joe. Coffee's a serious business, and some of the plantation tours last for several hours, restricting visitors from wearing anything that might affect the delicate aroma of the beans, or jeopardize the sensitive nose of the coffee-tasters – go easy on the perfumed soap that day, be warned.

Boquete's famed for its geisha coffee. A clear, light brew, geisha is to coffee what champagne is to wine. Though originating in Ethiopia, the geisha bean arrived in Panama in the 1960s, and these Central American coffee farmers haven't looked back. A number of plantations, from Hacienda La Esmeralda to Finca Lerida, have been developing their brand, offering tours, tastings and other hands-on experiences. The bean is a feather in Panama's cap, winning prizes internationally and selling for staggering amounts at coffee auctions. In recent years it's dominated the scene, scoring higher than all other varieties at Boquete's international coffee tastings. With judges from as far as Japan and South Korea, they're all agreed on the superior quality of this magnificent little bean.

Staying on a plantation gives you the inside track on how coffee is grown and harvested. You'll probably also have a hammock on your terrace, for afternoon naps amid that mountain greenery. And when the aroma drifts up from the café there's no need to hit snooze – you'll be raring to hit the road again.

627 | Being serenaded by mariachis in Guadalajara

MEXICO Saturday night in downtown Guadalajara, Mexico's second city: the Plazuela de los Mariachis, squeezed into a corner of the colonial heart of the city, reverberates with the sounds of instruments being tuned. You'll no doubt recognize the violins, trumpets and guitars; more exotic to the ear – and unique to the music you're about to hear – are the *vihuela*, a small plinky guitar with a bowed back, and the *guitarrón*, a large bass guitar. For time-honoured tunes, you're in the right spot: Guadalajara, the most traditional of Mexico's cities, is also the birthplace of mariachi, the country's famous musical export.

A smartly dressed couple – he with hair slicked back and she in her best dress – start the festivities with a request for an old love song. The mariachis line up around their table, forming a wall of *charro* (nineteenth-century cowboy) outfits: large bow ties, gleaming belt

buckles, jackets and trousers decorated with embroidery and silver fastenings. A trumpeter raises his instrument to his lips, and the first familiar notes of *Cielito Lindo* ("Ay, ay, ay, ay, canta y no llores") float over the square. Another song follows, then another. The couple get to their feet and begin to waltz slowly between the packed café tables. Several troupes join the fray, serenading elderly couples, students, young lovers, fascinated travellers. Each group competes to be louder and more flamboyant than the next, and the noise – a melodious cacophony – is ear-splitting.

Fittingly, the evening winds down with several howled rounds of one of the most popular mariachi tunes: "Guadalajara, Guadalajara, tienes el alma de provinciana, hueles a limpia rosa temprana" ("you have the soul of the provinces, you smell of fresh early roses").

628 | Trekking in Corcovado National Park

COSTA RICA The road to Corcovado National Park was once paved with gold – lots of gold – and although most of it was carried off by the Diquí, miners still pan here illegally. These days, though, it's just a rutted track that fords half a dozen rivers during the bone-rattling two-hour ride from the nearest town, Puerto Jiménez, and which runs out at Carate, the southern gateway to the park.

The journey in doesn't make an auspicious start to a hike in Corcovado – and it gets worse. Trekking here is not for the faint-hearted: the humidity is one hundred percent, there are fast-flowing rivers to cross and the beach-walking that makes up many of the hikes can only be done at low tide. Cantankerous peccaries roam the woods, and deadly fer-de-lance and bushmaster snakes slip through the shrub.

But you're here because Corcovado is among the most biologically abundant places on Earth, encompassing thirteen ecosystems,

including lowland rainforests, highland cloudforests, mangrove swamps, lagoons and coastal and marine habitats. And it's all spectacularly beautiful, even by the high standards of Costa Rica.

Streams trickle down over beaches pounded by Pacific waves, where turtles (hawksbill, leatherback and olive ridley) lay their eggs in the sand and where the shore is dotted with footprints – not human, but tapir, or possibly jaguar. Palm trees hang in bent clumps, and behind them the forest rises up in a 60m wall of dense emerald vegetation.

Corcovado has the largest scarlet macaw population in Central America, and the trees flash with bursts of their showy red, blue and yellow plumage. And after the first sighting of the birds flying out from the trees in perfectly coordinated pairs, the long journey to reach Corcovado seems a short way to come.

629 | Rafting the Río Pacuaré

COSTA RICA Costa Rica is renowned as a white-water paradise. Precipitous mountains. Prodigious rainfall. It's a perfect combo, resulting in some of the most spectacular river runs on the continent. No wonder rafting in Costa Rica is a popular and world-class outdoor activity. The exhilarating Dom Pérignon of whitewater is the Río Pacuaré, which cascades from the Talamanca Mountains and makes a plummeting descent to the Caribbean lowlands through a tropical *fantasia* teeming with wildlife. Ranked among the world's top ten whitewater runs for its ultimate combination of natural beauty and thrills, this class III-IV river will intoxicate you with sheer delight.

Local operator Ríos Tropicales specializes in the Pacuaré and offers one- to three-day trips. Beginning your run near the town of Turrialba, you'll pass through several life zones as you tumble through canyons overhung with dense virgin rainforest. Monkeys and toucans screech in the canopy. Parrots and macaws rocket by overhead. And you're sure to spot agoutis, deer, sloths and neotropical otter, while sightings of anteaters, ocelots and even jaguars are possible. Sections of the 30km upper run of challenging cascades drop some 30 metres per mile. Steep drops produce big waves. In general, the most exciting times are May to June, and September to October (with June and October preferred), when the rainy season serves up the most potent rapids. The adrenaline-charged whitewater sections are interspersed with calms, with waterfalls and warm pools the colour of celadon, that allow for swimming and peaceful contemplation with nature.

Trips include transport, meals and (on multiday options) deluxe riverside accommodation at *Río Tropicales Lodge*. The company supplies large rubber dinghies and bilingual guides, plus life vests and helmets. These are paddle trips: you and your raft-mates will power through the rapids while your guide controls things from the rear. You're guaranteed to get drenched – half the fun. All you'll need is a set of dry clothes, plus a swimsuit, shirt and water sandals with toe protection while on the river. And don't forget plenty of sunscreen – you'll be out in the open all day.

630 | Birdwatching on the Pipeline Road

PANAMA The logbook at Parque Nacional Soberanía's headquarters reads like a "who's who" of exotic bird species. There are mealy Amazons, purple-throated fruitcrows, shining honeycreepers and red-capped manakins; ocellated antbirds make a regular appearance, alongside grey-headed chachalacas, thick-billed motmots and the diminutive tropical pewee. Each entry is more gushing than the last – someone had almost torn through the page describing their chance encounter with a rufous-vented ground cuckoo – but if there's one place on Earth that's guaranteed to send twitchers into a feathery frenzy, it's the 24km-long trail at the heart of Soberanía: a dirt track they call the Pipeline Road.

During World War II, the US government built a pipeline along the Panama Canal to transport fuel from the Pacific to the Atlantic in the event the waterway was attacked. The backup was never needed and the "road" constructed to maintain the pipeline barely used. Over time, it was swallowed by the rainforest. But nature's gain was also man's, and the thin stretch of track now provides some of the finest bird-spotting on the planet, with over four hundred recorded species.

The Pipeline Road, or Camino del Oleoducto, runs through a range of habitats, from second-growth woodland to mature rainforest. A network of side tracks, creeks and rivers can be followed into the surrounding forest, but the road itself is a rich hunting ground, especially in the soft light of dawn or the cool hours around dusk, when activity is at its greatest. Army ant swarms attract birds by the hundred, while the trail is a popular location for leks – an incredible avian dance-off where males gather at the same spot each season for the purposes of elaborate (and very competitive) courtship displays. Just don't be surprised if you find yourself rushing back to HQ, pen at the ready.

631 | Kayaking in the Sea of Cortés

MEXICO Standing on the east coast of Baja California, surveying the peninsula's near-lifeless ochre landscape, it's hard to imagine that a frenzy of nature lies just steps away. But launch a sea kayak into the glistening surf of the Sea of Cortés and you'll find yourself surrounded by rich and varied wildlife – a veritable natural aquarium.

The remote and ruggedly beautiful Baja coastline has become a favourite destination for sea kayakers – and for good reason. The calm waters of the Sea of Cortés make for easy surf launches and smooth paddling. Hundreds of unexplored coves, uninhabited islands and kilometres of mangrove-lined estuaries play host to sea lions, turtles and nesting birds. Just the shell of your kayak separates you from dolphins, grey whales, coral reefs and more than six hundred species of fish as you glide through placid lagoons, volcanic caves and natural arches.

It's a good idea to keep your snorkelling gear handy – should you ever tire of the topside scenery, you can make a quick escape to an even more spectacular underwater world. Rookeries of sea lions dot island coasts, and if you approach them slowly, the pups can be especially playful, even mimicking your underwater movements before performing a ballet of their own.

Back on land, as you camp on powdery white-sand beaches and feast on freshly made ceviche under the glow of a glorious sunset, you'll have time to enjoy some peace and quiet before pondering your next launch.

Watching the sun rise at tikal

GUATEMALA The dense jungles of northern Guatemala, once the heartland of the Maya civilization, were home to dozens of thriving cities during Classic Maya times (250–909 AD). Tikal was arguably the greatest of them all, controlling an empire of vassal states and trade routes between the southern highlands and the Caribbean. The symbols of its dominance – six great temples – still stand.

Impressive at any time of day, Tikal shows itself to full advantage in the hours around sunrise. Because of the nature of the terrain – the extreme humidity of the forest usually shrouds the sun's early rays – it's rare actually to see the sun come up over the jungle. But even without a perfect sunrise, as the ruins of this Maya city come to life around you, dawn is still a magical time.

As day breaks, head for the top of Temple IV or Temple V. An ocean of green unfurls before you, the jungle canopy broken only by the chalk-white roofcombs of the other pyramids, soaring over the giant ceiba and zapote trees. The forest's denizens gradually begin to appear, emerging from their night-time resting places. Flocks of green parakeets career over the temple tops and keel-billed toucans hop along bromeliad-rich branches. Howler monkeys are at their most vociferous at dawn, their roars echoing around the graceful plazas and towering temples. Many of the animals that live in Tikal have become accustomed to seeing humans, so you're virtually guaranteed to come across packs of playful racoon-like coati snuffling through the undergrowth or the startling blue-chested ocellated turkey strutting around in search of its first feed of the day. As the sun climbs higher in the sky and the heat increases, things begin to calm down. By 9am, when the large tour groups roll in, nature's activity has all but faded away – until the jungle awakes the next morning.

Heading to market in the Guatemalan highlands

633

GUATEMALA The market town of San Francisco el Alto adopted its suffix for good reason. Perched at 2610m atop a rocky escarpment, it looks down over the plain of Quetzaltenango to the perfect volcanic cone of Santa María that pierces the horizon to the southwest.

But on Friday mornings, few of the thousands that gather here linger to take in the view; instead, the largest market in Guatemala's western highlands commands their attention. Things start early, as traders arrive in the dead of night to assemble their stalls by candlelight and lanterns, stopping periodically to slurp from a bowl of steaming *caldo* broth or for a slug of *chicha* maize liquor to ward off the chilly night air.

By dawn a convoy of pick-ups, chicken buses and microbuses struggles up the vertiginous access road, and by sunrise the streets are thick with action as blanket vendors and tomato seekers elbow their way through lanes lined with shacks. There's virtually nothing geared towards the tourist dollar, unless you're in desperate need of a Chinese-made alarm clock or a sack of beans, but it's a terrific opportunity to experience Guatemala's indigenous way of life – all business is conducted in hushed, considered tones using ritualistic politeness that's uniquely Maya.

Above the plaza is the fascinating animal market, where goats, sheep, turkeys, chickens and pigs are inspected as if contestants at an agricultural show. Vendors probe screeching porkers' mouths to check out teeth, tongues and gums, and the whole event can descend into chaos as man and beast wrestle around in the dirt before a deal can be struck.

634 | Meeting the monarchs in Michoacán

MEXICO Early morning in the mountains of Michoacán. There's a stillness in the wooded glades and a delicate scent of piny resin in the air. Mostly oyamel firs, the trees are oddly coated in a scrunched orange blanket – some kind of fungus? Diseased bark? Then the sun breaks through the mist and thousands of butterflies swoop from the branches to bathe in the sunlight, their patterned orange and black wings looking like stained-glass windows or Turkish rugs – the original Mexican wave. The forest floor is carpeted with them. Branches buckle and snap under their weight. And there's a faint noise, a pitter-patter like gentle rain – the rarely heard sound of massed butterflies flapping their wings.

The annual migration of hundreds of millions of monarch butterflies from North America to this small area of central Mexico – no more than 96 square kilometres – is one of the last mysteries of the scientific world. For years, their winter home was known only to the locals, but in 1975,

two determined American biologists finally pinpointed the location, and now visitors (mainly Mexican) flock here during the season to witness one of nature's most impressive spectacles. In the silence of the forest sanctuary, people stand stock-still for hours at a time, almost afraid to breathe as millions of butterflies fill the air, brushing delicately against faces and alighting briefly on hands.

No one is entirely clear why the butterflies have chosen this area. Some say it's the oyamel's needle-like leaves, ideal for the monarch's hooked legs to cling onto; or that the cool highland climate slows down their metabolism and allows them to rest and lay down fat before their arduous mating season. The Aztecs, however, had other ideas, believing that the butterflies – which arrive in Mexico shortly after the Day of the Dead on November 1 – were the returning souls of their fallen warriors, clad in the bright colours of battle.

635 | Travelling the lesser-known Maya route

EL SALVADOR Around 1500 years ago, a small Maya village in Central America faced disaster. Black smoke had been spewing from a nearby volcano for several days, and violent tremors shook the ground. In desperation the villagers, simple farmers, fled, abandoning virtually everything they owned. Shortly afterwards the village was buried under more than 6m of volcanic ash.

Today the archeological site of Joya de Cerén, an hour north of San Salvador, isn't quite the "Pompeii" it's hyped up to be, but it does form part of El Salvador's rich and often ignored Maya heritage. It also offers a totally different perspective to all the other great Mesoamerican ruins. What remains of sites like Copán and Tikal is spectacular but ceremonial – there's very little evidence in these ruined cities of how people actually lived. At Joya de Cerén you can see the beautifully preserved homes of Maya farmers, excavated from the ash and dirt, *in situ* – small, rectangular structures with raised earth bases, wattle-and-daub walls, doorways and raised benches for sleeping. A few structures stand out, such as a solid-

looking *temascal* or sweat lodge, with a partly intact domed roof and a stone hearth (for creating steam) in the centre. Neatly constructed cane frames, exposed in collapsed walls, look as if they were made yesterday. Everyday objects excavated here included petrified beans, maize, utensils, ceramics and even the skeleton of a duck – all on show in the site museum.

A few kilometres southwest, in an open field surrounded by farms and dense jungle, lies the ceremonial centre of San Andrés, originally supporting a population of about twelve thousand. Seven crumbling, enigmatic structures include the Acrópolis, a simple three-tiered pyramid of heavy stones, its platforms smothered in grass. Currently off-limits, the tallest pyramid ("La Campana") rises above the plots and terraces like an overgrown volcano.

El Salvador's most obviously impressive Maya site is Tazumal, 80km northwest of the capital, a vast fourteen-stepped ceremonial pyramid with its own powerful charm – perhaps best of all, however, like all the sites in El Salvador, on most days you'll have the ruins to yourself.

636 | Learning to surf in San Juan del Sur

NICARAGUA The laidback Nicaraguan town of San Juan del Sur, with its wave-lashed coastline, powerful Pacific swell and three hundred days of offshore wind a year, has become the destination of choice for an adventurous generation of surfers. And in contrast with the development that characterizes so many other surfing hotspots, this old fishing settlement has also retained an easy-going Caribbean vibe. Strung along a palm-fringed bay, its pastel-hued houses have been gradually taken over by a cheery assortment of hostels, board-shops and backpacker bars. It's a particularly welcoming place for beginners, too. No surprise, then, that many surfers linger here far longer than intended.

The best waves are a short ride out of town. Nearby Remanso Beach, a small cove with gentle surf, a thin strip of sand and a thatch-roofed beach bar, is the ideal spot for amateurs. Lessons start with ungainly

"pop-up" tutorials on dry land, as students practise standing on the board before they paddle out into the bay. New riders will also need to discover if they're "goofy" – more comfortable standing with their right foot forward – and learn how to duck-dive under oncoming waves. Old wives' tales say that the trick is to wait for the seventh and largest wave, but in truth perfecting the perfect surf stance takes hard work and time. Even with no previous experience, however, most people can proudly be propelled to shore on two feet after just one day's instruction.

Perhaps the real joy of learning to surf in San Juan del Sur is at sundown, when troupes of surfers heave their battered and bronzed bodies back into town. There are few experiences more satisfying than nursing a glass of Nicaragua's famous Flor de Caña rum (and some bruises) as a magical sunset unfolds along the horizon, your hammock swinging lightly in the evening breeze.

637 | Solentiname: peasant painters and revolutionary poets

NICARAGUA Breached by extinct and not-so-extinct volcanoes, haunted by vampire bats and frequented by some of the most dangerous sharks in the world, the opaque waters of Lake Nicaragua, southeast of the capital Managua, offer some of the more adventurous destinations in the country's fast-emerging tourist industry. The bow-tied island of Ometepe may get much of the press, but it's the Solentiname Archipelago, clustered in the lake's southeastern corner, which really offers a trip off the edge of Central American civilization.

You won't find a regular and convenient ferry crossing from the mainland, so it's worth chartering a private boat; you wouldn't really want to hang around much on the mainland at all, given that the point of departure is the down-at-heel port of San Carlos. If you're lucky, your arrival might coincide with the twice-weekly boat, a mere 15km whizz across the lake to a series of untouched islands which, lo and behold, are more famous for their art than their beaches or budget PADI courses.

For, back in the day, Solentiname was home to a community of peasant painters and nascent revolutionaries headed by poet-priest Ernesto Cardenal, himself once a pivotal figure in the country's iconic socialist movement, the Sandinistas.

The simple church on Mancarrón where Cardenal preached is a touching monument to the primitivist art he pioneered, and though he left in the late 1970s the creative community remains, earning a crust from the life-affirming colour and guileless lines of their canvases. The reality of the landscape they portray isn't quite so dreamlike – how could it be? – but it is untamed and teeming with life, both aquatic and avian, much of which other artisans stylize in wood carvings: willowy egrets and barking parrots, wily caimans and vibrant fish. It's likewise a landscape more pristine even than the most undeveloped corners of the Caribbean; the islands that are inhabited have few conventional tourist facilities to speak of.

638 | Bean there, done that

GUATEMALA Above Guatemala's crumbling colonial cities lie mist-cloaked highlands where rumbling volcanoes, colourful wildlife and a string of magnificent lakes attract visitors to get off the beaten track. There's another lure here, too: coffee, which has been planted in this gentle tropical climate and these rich, high-altitude soils since the 1800s. Guatemala is one of the world's top coffee producers, and visiting a *finca* is a highlight of any trip to this beguiling nation.

In the shadow of Volcan Agua and Volcan Acatenango, north of Guatemala's architectural set-piece, Antigua, lies Finca Filadelfia. This rambling 250-acre plantation, which has been farming coffee since 1869, today runs tours that trace the drink from bean to brew and outline their own evolution from small farm to modern coffee producer and resort. Morning visits start in the shade of the fields, where you discover the difference between the Arabica plant, predominantly planted in the Americas, and the less sophisticated Robusta, which is mostly used to make instant coffee. Depending on

the time of year, guides might pluck a hard, round coffee cherry from the bush; its blush deepens from rose-hip pink to a vivid cardinal red as they ripen. Tear away the outer casing and you can nibble one of the two sweet but slimy green coffee beans hidden inside the fruit. Next, as the morning chill starts to shake off, you'll be led into the *finca*'s sun-drenched courtyard, where they have been drying coffee beans for nearly 150 years. Several weeks of baking see the beans parched to an ivory colour; after the outer layer of parchment is removed, machines sort them by size before they're roasted.

Tours end in the "lab" with a cupping session – the wine-tasting equivalent of the coffee world. Guides pour out small cups of different roasts and grades, filling the room with a tantalizing fragrance. Start with a long inhale to identify the aromas, which might include caramel, fruit and chocolate. Then, when the coffee has slightly cooled, take a sip to analyze the mouth feel and assess the length of the finish. Once you've tasted coffee this nuanced, you'll never see your morning brew in the same way again.

639 | A taste of mole poblano in Puebla

MEXICO Visitors to Mexico may find some of the country's culinary offerings a bit odd – not only do fried grasshoppers, baked maggots and raw ant eggs occasionally appear, but the national dish, *mole poblano*, combines two flavours, chilli and chocolate, to a sweet yet fiery effect. *Mole* (or *mólli*), a Nahuatl word, means "mixture", of which there are actually dozens in Mexico; *mole poblano*, the most revered, comes from Puebla.

A rich sauce normally served with turkey or chicken, *mole poblano* can boast upwards of thirty ingredients; the most cherished recipes are guarded like state secrets. Fruits, nuts and spices are toasted over a fire, ground by hand and mixed into a paste. The chocolate, added at the last minute, is in its traditional unsweetened form, powdered cacao seeds.

The dish was created in the seventeenth century in the kitchens of the Convento de Santa Rosa for a banquet. It's still made for special occasions: no wedding in Puebla is complete without the women spending days preparing their *mole poblano* in huge black cauldrons. Among Cholulteca families, a live turkey is considered the guest of honour at wedding receptions; the bird is slaughtered the next day to serve as the base for the newlyweds' first *mole*.

The dish stars on various menus across the city on May 5, or Cinco de Mayo, a national holiday that celebrates the defeat of Napoleon's invading army in Puebla in 1872. After the festivities, join the crowds and top off the night by feasting on the city's savoury speciality.

640 | Searching for jaguars in Cockscomb Basin Wildlife Sanctuary

BELIZE Looking for tigers? Head to India. Lions or cheetahs? You'll want to be in southern Africa. If it's jaguars you're after, though, few places are more spectacular than the rainforests of Belize.

Here, in the Cockscomb Basin Wildlife Sanctuary, the enormous, elusive wildcats roam freely through 400 square kilometres of pristine jungle.

According to local guides, sunrise is the best time to glimpse jaguars. Almost every day, eager cat-spotters set out in the small hours from Maya Centre, an indigenous Mopan Maya community and the hub for trips into the reserve. In the half-light, the rainforest teems with wildlife. The trees form a cavernous canopy above your head; in combination with the thick undergrowth, the vegetation can overwhelm – and the atmosphere is intensified by sightings of red-eyed tree frogs, tarantulas, bats and iguanas. Gibnuts – small, rat-like creatures – rustle through the scrub. Keep an eye out for the four other species of wildcats that also call the reserve home, including margay, who favour the canopy, and pumas, who slink through the surrounding mountains. As the forest warms up, four thousand species of flowering plants spring into bloom, and toucans, king vultures and scarlet macaws flit through the trees.

You've come for the jaguars, though, and as the sun climbs in the sky, you still haven't seen one. Let's be honest – you're far more likely to see the eyes of a gibnut shining from the undergrowth than you are the glamorous yet camera-shy felines. It's the hunt that makes Cockscomb so special. You know they're there, and they know you know it – if your paths happen to collide you'll be rewarded with a sight very few people are lucky enough to witness. In the meantime, don't forget to enjoy the natural wonderland around you.

641 | Diving at Palancar Reef

MEXICO The view from the boat is beautiful, with the variegated blues and greens of the Caribbean stretching toward the Yucatán coast on one side, and palm trees bowing over Cozumel's pearly-white beach on the other.

From the surface, though, you'd never know that the most stunning sight of all is directly beneath you: Palancar Reef, a 5km stretch of some of the globe's richest coral beds, and the kind of vivid world people tend to imagine only with the aid of hallucinogens. Teeming with marine life, Palancar is just one small part of the Mesoamerican Barrier Reef, which stretches from Mexico to Honduras, but it is in a prime position to flourish. Just off the southwest corner of the island of Cozumel, and part of a larger ring of coral around much of the island, it is washed by slow, steady currents that keep the water clear and bear nutrients from nearby mangrove swamps.

Bumped by clumsy snorkellers, battered by hurricanes and boiled by freakish spikes in water temperature, Palancar not only survives but prospers as a fascinating and complex ecosystem. Any diver, novice or expert, could explore this reef for hours – or, if you're Jacques Cousteau, who put this place on divers' maps in the 1960s, years. Lobsters pick their way delicately along outcrops, feelers blown by the current, while blue-green parrotfish gnaw at the coral with their beaky mouths. (Their digestive system produces the powdery sand that slopes away into the deep-blue distance.) Striped clownfish hide in the protective tentacles of an anemone, immune to its toxic sting; mellow turtles graze on algae; a graceful ray glides by. All this happens as if in a dream, in near-complete silence – the only audible sound is the rush of your own breath. Lovely as the surface world is, when you come up for air, it will all seem impossibly drab.

642 | A river runs to it: Pacuare Lodge

COSTA RICA Standing outside your palm-thatched river-view suite, its wooden doors opened on to the terrace to reveal a vast canopy, king-size, Egyptian-cotton sheets ruffling in the breeze, *Pacuare Lodge* seems like the archetypal luxury hideaway. But there's one big difference: you're dripping wet and are kitted out in a life jacket and helmet.

At some hotels, you arrive by limo; at *Pacuare*, you (and your guide) can paddle there in a raft, negotiating several kilometres of the raging Río Pacuare in order to bed down for the night in your own private piece of paradise. Surrounded by rainforest, the lodge perches on a bend in the river and has to be one of the few five-stars in the world where you can truly say that getting there is half the fun.

The Río Pacuare's adrenaline-inducing mix of open canyons and narrow passages has made it one of the best whitewater-rafting rivers on Earth – when rapids are called "Double Drop" and "Upper Pinball" you know they've earned their names – but the journey is as much about the scenery as the scintillation. Thundering waterfalls cascade down overhanging rocks, and the lowland tropical forest that borders the river spills right down to the water's edge, its thick undergrowth providing refuge for monkeys, sloths and an astonishing array of birdlife.

There's more nature when you step out of the raft. A lot of so-called ecolodges pay lip-service to the environment, but *Pacuare* wears its credentials on its sleeve: it part-funds a nearby jaguar research project and has started its own conservation effort by reintroducing howler monkeys into the surrounding area.

Hopefully, the howler monkeys won't disturb you too much in the night – you'll need as much sleep as you can get for that thrilling return journey.

Corn of plenty

NICARAGUA Some 70km off the coast of Nicaragua, a far-flung Caribbean world away from film stars and offshore bank accounts, lies one of the Atlantic's most endearingly ramshackle outposts: the Corn Islands. You need neither an expense-account flight nor a million-pound yacht to get here, nor an inheritance to pay for your stay. You do need the nerve to board a single-prop Cessna plane – either that or the stomach for a potentially rough five- to ten-hour ferry crossing. Once you've arrived, though, the mere prospect of a return journey may well seem unthinkable, as it must have done to the pirates, slaves and Miskito people who once took refuge here.

While construction has brought a patina of modernity to Big Corn – the larger of the two islands – there's a definite end-of-the-English-speaking-world feel to the place, English-speaking because Britain once exercised a modicum of control over this often lawless corner of the Caribbean. They likewise left their mark on the architecture, straggling past the main drag and out into kilometres of palm-stitched coastline.

If you want an impression of how Big Corn must have once appeared minus its airport, electricity and island-round road, though, you need only hop aboard a boat for the high-seas scoot across to Little Corn, just over two square kilometres of traffic-free rainforest that surely can't retain its "best-kept Caribbean secret" cliché for much longer. Enjoy the peace and tranquillity while it lasts.

Though travel writers have only recently begun raving over it, this hideaway-within-a-hideaway has drawn divers and dreamers for years, some of whom have stayed and set up businesses like *Farm Peace and Love*, a biodynamic farm offering an array of tranquil accommodation for those who've made the effort of a cross-island trek to get there.

Then there's the ocean itself, magnifying the pearl-white sand, bottle-green mangroves and bleached-blue firmament in a tie-dye riot of eagle rays, nurse sharks and parrotfish, all massing on one of Central America's most pristine reefs. Islands in the (main) stream these are not.

644 | Descend into the Maya Underworld

BELIZE To the ancient Maya, the caves that pepper their homelands were entrances to Xibalba – "the place of fright", home to the Lords of Death. Modern travellers find them scary too, but the twin prospect of underground adventure and mysterious relics is irresistible to any Indiana Jones wannabe. Actun Tunichil Muknal, or ATM, stands deep in the Belizean rainforest. Really it's more of a tunnel than a cave, through which the aptly named Roaring Creek burrows for five long kilometres. Only Maya shamans were permitted to pass this way, leading sacrificial victims on their terrifying final journeys. And while the shamans came back out, their victims are still here, lying unburied beneath the mountains.

You enter the cave by stepping through an hourglass-shaped hole atop a waterfall, then swim across a cool pool of still water. As you look back towards the upper world, the rocky cave mouth seems to silhouette a mighty Maya warrior. Next you wade for thirty minutes upstream, squeezing between jagged outcrops in the dark. The water is neck deep;

at one point the way is so narrow you can only pass through sideways, holding your chin at the necessary haughty angle.

Eventually you clamber up from the riverbed, contorting to position feet and hands on successive slippery ledges. Emerging into a vast cathedral-like chamber, you pass massive pottery vessels embedded in the calcified floor. The guide's torch picks out eerie human-shaped stalagmites – one perhaps a princess, crowned by an intricate headdress – that appear to march in procession beside you. Finally you climb a ladder to reach the ultimate sacrificial chamber, where you're confronted by the sudden dreadful spectacle of the complete skeleton of a young woman, crusted with limestone and set spreadeagled into the rock. A brutal reminder of the stark reality of her death lies alongside – the stone axe with which she was probably killed. Nearby, another grinning skull, shattered when a clumsy tourist dropped his camera, bears a stark white hole. All cameras are now banned from ATM. Even without a souvenir photo, though, it's not a place you'll forget.

645 | Sampling fish tacos in Ensenada

MEXICO The *taco de pescado* – Baja California's gift to locals, dust-caked off-road explorers and cruise-boat day-trippers alike – exemplifies the simple pleasures that make the peninsula so appealing.

Constructed by piling freshly fried pieces of white fish on two warm corn tortillas and topping with shredded cabbage, a little light mayo, a splash of hot sauce and a squirt of lime, the *taco de pescado* is Mexican food at its most basic and delicious. Like all great street food, fish tacos taste better when served somewhere devoid of any atmosphere – most choice locations lack proper flooring, ceiling, walls or any combination thereof. The quality of the tacos corresponds directly to the length of time it takes for the cook to get them to you, then for you to get them into your mouth.

Ensenada, a large fishing centre on the peninsula's northwest coast, is one of the best places to sample the *taco de pescado* – it's said that the dish was first concocted here by Japanese fishermen. Fifteen minutes inland from the port and the Mercado Negro fish market lies a well-established street vendor, *Tacos Fenix*. The outfit operates from the pavement: one person preps the ingredients, a second mans the frying pan and the third handles the money and drinks. You don't have to know much Spanish (beyond *por favor* and *gracias*) to order; just listen and watch the people in front of you. And don't worry about the juices running down your hand after the first bite – getting dirty is part of the fun.

646 | Spotting whale sharks near Utila

HONDURAS The island of Utila, off the coast of Honduras, isn't your ordinary scuba-diving base. Sure, there's plenty of stunningly beautiful marine life to be seen. It isn't the beautiful, though, that draws many diving enthusiasts here. Rather, it's the exotically monstrous – Utila is one of the few places on Earth that the whale shark, the world's largest fish, can be spotted year-round.

Whale sharks, which are harmless to humans, remain elusive creatures – relatively little is known about them, and their scientific name (*Rhincodon typus*) wasn't even established until 1984. Measuring up to 15m (and twenty tonnes), they are filter feeders, sieving tropical seas for nutrients and migrating across oceans and up and down the coast of Central America. Oceanic upswells close to Utila consistently sweep together a rich soup of plankton and krill, making them a prime feeding ground for the immense creatures.

Most mornings, dive boats scour the seas north of Utila between reef dives looking for "boils": feeding frenzies created by bonito tuna rounding up huge schools of baitfish, or krill. Hungry sharks home in on the boils, gliding just below the surface, mouths agape as they scythe through the sea. Their blue-grey upper bodies are sprinkled with intricate patterns of white spots (which appear electric blue from a distance in the sunlight), interspersed with chessboard-style markings.

Often, they feed upright, an astonishing sight – watch as the great fish manoeuvre themselves into a vertical position, bobbing up and down and gulping sea water into 2m-wide mouths. If you like, you can slip into the water with them. But do it while you can – the chance to swim among them is usually fleeting, as the boils disintegrate rapidly and the sharks disappear as quickly as they came.

647 | Stelae stories of Copan

HONDURAS It's hot, the air is thick with fragrant tropical aromas and the undergrowth is wrapping its verdant claws around everything in sight. It's a wonder, then, that Copan's 700-year-old stelae are still standing and that the tangled jungle hasn't completely taken over these intricately carved stone slabs that line the processional walkways between Copan's decaying pyramids.

The carvings on the stelae may at first simply look like big-beaked birds and stylized plants amid swirls and scrolls, but a closer investigation reveals these to be Maya hieroglyphs that tell the detailed stories of this long-gone civilization. Each depicts the illustrious King Waxak Lahun Ubah K'awil (also known as Eighteen Rabbit), the most powerful of Copan's leaders, in a variety of guises including his apotheosis as several Maya gods. He is remembered for his patronage of the arts and for sourcing some of the best craftsmen the Maya world had ever seen.

648 | Sea turtles and sailfish: cast away in Mazunte

MEXICO After a few days spent sinking into soft sand and being playfully flipped and tumbled by the waves in Mazunte – a relaxed fishing village on Mexico's Pacific Coast – the urge to skim across and explore the choppy waters slowly takes hold. Early morning is the best time to set off; local boats steer small groups out to spot – or snorkel with – colourful fish, sea turtles and leaping dolphins, or to try their luck at deep-sea fishing. The sparkling blue ocean is swarming with dorado and tuna, but the ultimate prize is the huge sailfish. It takes strength to reel in these high-speed 2m stunners, followed by the thrill of getting back to land without being toppled by crashing waves. Locals gather on the beach, waiting to admire the day's haul before it's sliced open and sold – take your own catch to a beach restaurant and they will happily serve it up for lunch.

649 | Magicians and man-eating snakes at Uxmal

MEXICO It's not hard to imagine the sense of wonder the first explorers would have felt, stumbling across the crumbling Maya ruins of Uxmal for the first time. As you climb in the sweltering tropical sun to the top of the Grand Pyramid, lizards scuttling away at the sound of your feet, the Pyramid of the Magician – an astonishing sight with its rounded sides and elliptical base – rises out of the lush jungle below. Uxmal features arguably the finest and most atmospheric ruins in the Yucatán, if not the entire country. Thought to have been built between 800 and 1000 AD, its imposing structures are decorated with elaborate, occasionally grisly, motifs – check out the feathered rattlesnake devouring a warrior, for example. The site is quiet and contained enough to evoke a real sense of the ancient city, and those brooding pyramids still cast a spine-tingling sense of mystery and enchantment.

Unravelling the mysteries of Monte Albán

650

MEXICO Rising like a giant fist above the valleys of Oaxaca, magical, mystical Monte Albán is above all a statement of power. The Zapotecs built their city far from the valleys and without any natural water supply (water was carried up by hand and stored in vast urns). This wasn't a mistake – they wanted to emphasize their dominance of their people, and nature itself. Founded around 500 BC, most of the city was abandoned by 950 AD, and though the Mixtecs later used it as a burial site, the main structures were only cleared and restored in the 1930s.

Approaching from the city of Oaxaca, the narrow road snakes its way through a series of terraced hillsides, now all overgrown scrub but once home to a thriving population of almost 20,000. What remains today is just the very centre of the site – the religious and political heart – and until you reach the top it's impossible to appreciate the sheer audacity of this place; a whole mountaintop was effectively levelled by hand to create this massive, man-made plateau on which the Zapotecs constructed soaring pyramids, astronomical observatories and palaces.

You enter by the Plataforma Norte, but won't appreciate the true dimensions until you reach the Gran Plaza, the ceremonial focus of the city, lined by sombre stone platforms. The best place to get your bearings is on top of the Plataforma Sur, a mighty square pyramid offering a fine overview of the site and mesmerizing panoramas of the surrounding countryside; the Oaxaca Valley is clearly visible, often shrouded by mist (or smog, sadly), as well as the rugged hinterland to the northwest. The building of Los Danzantes may offer a better insight into how all this was possible; the carved "dancers" here are actually nude male figures that may represent prisoners or, more likely, sacrificial victims. If you have time, explore the tombs to the northeast of the main site, linked by rough paths across the scrub – here, among the stone memorials to Zapotec rulers long forgotten, Monte Albán's sense of lingering mystery is most palpable.

PANAMA Enveloped in the thick blackness of night, the sounds of the rainforest assail your senses: against a chorus of cicadas and crickets, a panoply of other nocturnal creatures chirps, trills, squeaks and rustles in the undergrowth. Tucked under a mosquito net 4m off the ground, on the floor of a traditional wood-and-thatch house on stilts, you slide into your first night's sleep in the Darién jungle.

Comprising vast swathes of near-impenetrable tropical wilderness straddling the border between Panama and Colombia, the Darién has achieved near-mythical status with its potent allure of outstanding natural beauty, inaccessibility and danger: from deadly pit vipers to guerrillas and paramilitaries, and vampire bats to drug-traffickers, the rainforest commands respect. A magnet for nature-lovers, boasting a staggering array of wildlife, it is also home to several thousand indigenous Emberá. Once semi-nomadic hunter-gatherers, adept at pursuing their prey with poison-tipped arrows and blowpipes, the scattered communities of the Emberá now lead a more settled existence,

welcoming tourists, sharing their traditional culture and knowledge, and even their homes. Learn about the intricacies of basketry and wood-carving, for which they are world-renowned; try fishing from a *piragua* – a wooden dugout canoe, keeping an eye out for crocs and caimans; or have your body painted with the indigo dye of the jagua fruit, providing a temporary two-week tattoo and convenient natural insect repellent.

Engage a guide to venture into the rainforest itself – preferably at dawn when the dazzling birdlife is at its most active and the heat tolerable. Several villages have trails leading to harpy eagle nests, where a patient stake-out may be rewarded by a sighting of arguably the world's most powerful raptor; instantly recognizable by its imperious slate-grey cloak and regal crest, it boasts a 2m wingspan and talons the size of a grizzly bear's claws. Like the endangered harpy eagle, the Emberá way of life is under threat; sensitively managed ecotourism may help preserve their culture and guarantee future visitors a rich and unforgettable experience.

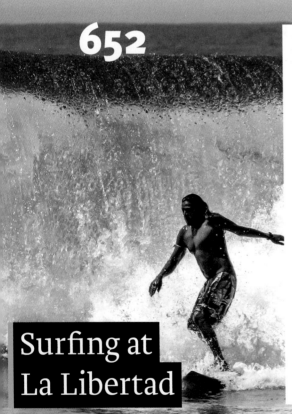

652

Surfing at La Libertad

EL SALVADOR It's not surprising that the beach in La Libertad is packed on Sundays. The port town is less than an hour's drive from the choked capital of San Salvador, its oceanfront restaurants serve the finest *mariscada* (creamy seafood soup) in the country and, of course, there's *el surf*.

The western end of the beach here has one of the longest right point breaks in the world, prosaically called *punta roca* (rocky point). On a good day – and with year-round warm water and consistent and uncrowded waves there are plenty of those – skilled *surfistas* can ride 1000m from the head of the point into the beach. Amateur surfers, meanwhile, opt for the section of gentler waves, known as *La Paz*, that roll into the mid-shore.

It's rare to walk through the town without seeing one of the local boys running barefoot, board under arm, down to the sea or hanging outside the Hospital de las Tablas while a dent or tear is repaired. Some, like Jimmy Rotherham, whose American father kick-started the expat surf scene when he arrived in the 1970s (witness the psychedelic surfboards on the walls of *Punta Roca* restaurant), have become semi-professional.

If you're looking for quieter, cleaner breaks, join the foreign surfers who head west to beaches such as El Zonte, now a backpacker heaven. The point break here used to be a secret among locals and students from Santa Tecla. The village's best surfer, El Teco, was inspired to jump on a board after watching *Hawaii Five-O*, later polishing his technique by observing pelicans surfing the waves. Even if you miss out on *olas de mantequilla* (waves like butter) or suffer too many *wipeadas*, there's always the Zonte scene: at weekends the capital's hip kids come to party amid bonfires, fire dancers and all-night drumming.

Need to know

602 Tortuguero National Park (Wcosta-rica-guide. com/nature/national-parks/tortuguero) is 3–4hr north of Limón by boat. Independent travellers must buy tickets for the park and arrange for a certified tour guide.

603 Daily flights leave Panama City for several islands in Guna Yala as well as a cheaper daily 4WD road transfer to Cartí.

604 Frequent *lancha* boats buzz across Lago Atitlán between each village.

605 Guerrero Negro is easily reached by bus from Tijuana or La Paz. Numerous operators offer whale-watching tours in Guerrero Negro and the town of San Ignacio, 150km to the south. W allaboutbaja.com is a useful resource.

606 Gibnut is served at traditional Belizean restaurants around the country. In Belize City, try *Nerie's II*, on Queen St at Daly St (Wneries.bz); it's offered seasonally.

607 Cenote Zací in Valladolid is in the block formed by *calles* 34, 36, 37 and 39. Dzitnup and Samula are 7km west of Valladolid on Hwy-180. There are also cenotes along the Caribbean coast.

608 To visit Barro Colorado, contact the Smithsonian Institute in Panama City (Wstri.si.edu).

609 The town of Pátzcuaro, on the shores of Lago Pátzcuaro, is the main staging point for boat trips to Janitzio; boats run throughout the night. You should book accommodation for the Day of the Dead at least six months in advance.

610 Fights in Mexico City usually take place at the Arena México (Warenaciudaddemexico.com). Tickets are sold on the door – it's worth paying extra for seats towards the front.

611 The refuge lies 12km south of Puerto Viejo. Kayaks, surfboards and nature guides can be hired through ecoresorts in the forest or budget places in Manzanillo village.

612 Xochimilco is 28km southeast of Mexico City; it's accessible from Tasqueña station.

613 Bonampak is a short hike from the village of Lacanjá Chansayab. You can also ride directly to the site in a Lacandón-run van from the Frontier Highway.

614 There are frequent buses to Liberia, the capital of Guanacaste province, from elsewhere in Costa Rica, along with regular flights (Wnatureair.com and Wfly-sansa.com).

615 Sat is the biggest market day in Oaxaca. Mercado de Abastos is on Periférico.

616 Train services depart daily from Los Mochis and Chihuahua. For more, see W chepe.com.mx.

617 Antigua's main bus terminal is next to its market; set off for Chimaltenango, from where a *directo* leaves to Nebaj.

618 See Weverfest.com/lists/guatemala for information about fiestas in Guatemala. To find the most traditional fiestas, head for the western highlands.

619 In San Salvador you'll find *Pupusería Doña Isabel* at 9A Ave Nte (Mon–Sat 7am-6.30pm, Sun 7am-noon) and *Comedor y Pupusería Shadaii* at 77A Ave Sur (Mon–Fri 7am–3pm).

620 Monteverde Cloudforest Reserve is 190km from San José and is run by the Center for Tropical Science (W cloudforestmonteverde.com). The centre's night walks leave every day.

621 The Bajo del Tigre is part of the Bosque Eterno de los Niños. Night hikes take place daily at sunset; for more information, see W acmcr.org.

622 The *clavadistas* dive at 1pm, 7.30pm, 8.30pm, 9.30pm and 10.30pm. Watch them from the opposite viewing platform or *Hotel Mirador*'s restaurant (Wmiradoracapulco.com).

623 Mérida lies in the northwest of the Yucatán; the airport (13km from the city) is served by domestic and international flights. The free parties are held Sat–Thurs; see W yucatanliving.com.

624 Panama Canal Tours (Wpmatours.net) and Canal and Bay Tours (Wcanalandbaytours.trekksoft.com) offer full and partial transits of the Panama Canal.

625 Local "chicken" buses run from San Salvador's Terminal de Oriente to Suchitoto (every 15min; 1hr 30min); taxis will make the trip for around US$40–50 one-way. See Welgringosuchitoto.com or Wlaposada.com.sv.

626 Boquete is manageable by road from the capital (around 6hr 30min), or take a trip from the beaches at Bocas del Toro (around 5hr, including ferry), or across the border from Costa Rica (via private shuttle or public bus from Puerto Viejo de Talamanca; around 9hr).

627 Every Sept, Guadalajara hosts performers from all over the world for the Festival de los Mariachis (Wmariachi-jalisco.com).

628 It's best to visit Corcovado during dry season (Dec–March). For more, see W osawildtravel.com and W corcovadofoundation.org.

629 Children as young as 12 can raft the Pacuaré December–May, but the minimum age is 14 June–November. See W riostropicales.com for more information.

630 Parque Nacional Soberanía (Wvisitpanama. com/destino/soberania) is a 45min drive from Panama City or 2km hike from the town of Gamboa, which is served by regular daily buses from the capital.

631 Tour operators in Loreto and La Paz offer outfitting, guided expeditions and accommodation, with La Paz providing more rental options for independent kayakers.

632 Tourist minibuses run from every hotel in El Remate and Flores to Tikal National Park (Wtikalpark .com). There are three hotels in the park, and both towns also have plentiful accommodation.

633 San Francisco el Alto is 1hr by bus from Quetzaltenango.

634 The best place to see the butterflies is in the sanctuary near the village of El Rosario (mid-Nov to late March). There are frequent buses from Mexico City.

635 To visit all three Maya sites (usually Tues–Sun 9am–4pm) it's best to rent a car or taxi or take a tour from San Salvador. For more, see Wfundar.org.sv.

636 Numerous operators in San Juan del Sur run daily lessons, including Wsanjuandelsursurf.com; see Wcoconutsurf.com for longer surf camps.

637 There are daily flights from Managua to San Carlos with La Costeña (Wlacostena.online.com.ni). If your arrival doesn't coincide with the boat to Solentiname and you can't find a private ride, it's worth taking a side-trip down the San Juan River to El Castillo.

638 Coffee tours at *Finca Filadelfia* (Wfiladelfia.com .gt) run daily at 9am, 11am and 2pm, with pickups available from Antigua.

639 Puebla's best restaurant is *Mesón Sacristía de la Compañia*, 6 Sur 304 (Wmesones-sacristia.com). You can buy *mole* paste at the Mercado 5 de Mayo.

640 All buses between Dangriga and Punta Gorda pass Maya Centre. Wcockscombmayatours.com can arrange trips into the reserve.

641 Cozumel has many dive operators who will take you to Palancar Reef; Deep Blue (Wdeepbluecozumel .com) is recommended.

642 *Pacuare Lodge* (Wpacuarelodge.com) is near the town of Siquirres, southeast of San José. Two-night packages, including (if desired) rafting in and out, start from US$1300.

643 La Costeña (Wlacostena.online.com.ni) flies daily to Big Corn (Maíz Grande) from Managua and Bluefields. If the weather permits, the water taxi from Big Corn to Little Corn also runs twice daily.

644 ATM is roughly 120km southwest of Belize City, and only accessible on guided tours. Recommended operators in the closest town, San Ignacio, 28km northwest of the caves, include Mayawalk Tours (Wmayawalk.com), who charge around US$110 for a full-day tour, and also offer overnight trips.

645 There are regular bus services to Ensenada from Tijuana. *Tacos Fenix* is on Calle Espinosa.

646 Utila has several daily flights and a daily ferry connection with La Ceiba on the mainland. Utila Dive Center (Wutiladivecenter.com) is recommended.

647 The nearby town of Copán Ruinas, a 15min walk from the ruins, has plenty of accommodation.

648 Boat trips usually leave at 8am, last 3hr, and cost around M$180 per person, including snorkelling equipment. Your accommodation can help you to book, or simply speak to one of the fishermen on the beach to organize.

649 Uxmal (daily 8am–5pm; M$85) lies 80km south of Mérida in the Yucatán; the drive from the city takes 1hr 15min.

650 Monte Albán (Wwhc.unesco.org) is 9km southwest of Oaxaca – most visitors make day-trips by bus from the city.

651 The safest way to travel to Darién is on a tour, although it is possible to travel independently; more of your money goes to the indigenous population that way. Contact the Darién National Park office (T507 299 4495; Wbiosferadarien.com).

652 Puerto La Libertad is 34km south of San Salvador; there are frequent buses. For rooms, try *Punta Roca* (Wpuntaroca.com.sv).

SOUTH AMERICA
653-730

A land of music and mountains, football and fiestas, passions and politics, South America convulses with life and variety. The golden glow of the pre-Columbian era still has a profound presence, thanks in part to stunning archeological remains from Machu Picchu to the Easter Island statues. The region also has more than its share of super-sized natural wonders, from the dramatically sparse Patagonian wilds to the wildlife-rich Pantanal wetlands in Paraguay, from the chatteringly dense Amazon rainforest to the kaleidoscopic colours of Rainbow Mountain in Peru. Urban intensity comes courtesy of zeal-charged cities like Rio, Cartagena and Buenos Aires – and if you fancy a local pick-me-up, be it a glass of Mendoza wine or a caipirinha, you'll be spoilt for choice.

653 The incredible Inca Trail alternative

PERU You can't feel too scared on a hike where there's an emergency horse trotting behind you. My kind of hike: challenging, rewarding, beautiful – and reassuring.

This is the Salkantay Trail, one of several ancient Incan routes in the Sacred Valley surrounding Cusco. It's quiet, there are few other hikers and, as it's the end of rainy reason, the trail is as green as it gets. The peaks of the Andes tower over and around us as we hike through fifteen ecosystems, from cloudforest to river valleys, over six days. This is what I call a great hike.

My guide Wilfredo is as knowledgeable about the flora and fauna as he is about the history of the Incas, the people who carved these trails through these not-so-easy-to-navigate mountains. His anecdotes provide the perfect context for the holy grail: Machu Picchu, a place that becomes even more wondrous when you've grasped the sheer audacity of building such a citadel in such a remote place – so remote that the Spanish invaders didn't even find it.

While the Salkantay Trail doesn't lead directly into the citadel, it's proving a popular alternative to the more crowded Inca Trail – the fact you can overnight in community-run lodges (with hot tubs, massages and gourmet dinners) certainly appeals to this reluctant, fair-weather camper.

At 74km long, it's longer than the Inca Trail but, as it's hiked over six days, the pace is manageable. Sure, some of the climbs are challenging, particularly the ascent to the trail's highest point, the 4600m-high Salkantay Pass – but you always know the horse is right there. How I'll ever hike without an equestrian friend behind me, I'm not quite sure.

But it's easy to forget your aches and pains: the Peruvian highlands are one of the most beautiful landscapes I've seen. Bright purple lupin flowers, the brilliant blue of Lake Humantay, lush green jungle and the soaring peak of Mount Salkantay all compete for my favourite view. But I just can't choose.

Meera Dattani
is a freelance travel journalist, guidebook author and co-editor of Adventure. com. Nature, wildlife and hiking feature in most of her travels, often to emerging destinations, where she often finds their cultural and historical context as interesting as the sights.

Natural rejection in the Galápagos Islands

654

ECUADOR The utter indifference (some call it fearlessness) that most of the animals of the Galápagos Islands show to humans suggests that they knew all along they'd be the ones to change humanity's perception of itself for ever. It was, after all, this famous menagerie of accidental inmates, washed or blown from the mainland across 1000km of ocean and cut off from the rest of their kind, that started the cogs turning in Charles Darwin's mind. His theory of natural selection changed humankind's understanding of its place in the world, and by extension, some might say, its place in the universe.

Peering out to shore from your cabin, you little suspect that the neon sea and coral beaches mark not the fringes of paradise, but of hell solidified – a ferocious wasteland of petrified lava lakes, ash-striped cliffs, serrated clinker tracts and smouldering volcanoes. Even so, as you walk through this scarred landscape, you find that life abounds, albeit peculiar life, the product of many generations of adaptation to a comfortless home. A marine iguana flashes an impish grin at you and, unlike its more familiar ancestors on the continent, scuttles into the sea to feed. On a rocky spur nearby, another one-of-a-kind, a flightless cormorant, which long ago abandoned its aerial talents for ones nautical, hangs its useless wing-stumps out to dry. With each island, new animal oddities reveal themselves – giant tortoises, canoodling waved albatrosses, lumbering land iguanas and Darwin's finches, to name but a few – each a key player in the world's most celebrated workshop of evolution. And except for the friendly mockingbirds that pick at your shoelaces, most life on Galápagos is blank to your existence, making you feel like a privileged gatecrasher, one who's allowed an up-close look at a long-kept secret: the mechanics of life on Earth.

MAKE THE MOST OF YOUR TIME ON EARTH

ECUADOR Just about every traveller is struck at some point by the panic-inducing realization that there are people back home expecting to be lavished with exotic gifts from faraway lands. If you happen to find yourself in Ecuador at this anxiety-ridden moment you're in luck: Otavalo's spectacular indigenous *artesanías* market is one of the largest crafts fairs on the continent and one of the most enjoyable alfresco shopping experiences to be had anywhere.

Up for grabs are handicrafts of every description – ceramics, jewellery, paintings, musical instruments, carvings and above all a dazzling array of weavings and textiles, for which the Otavalo Valley has long been famous. Looms in back rooms across the countryside clatter away to produce chunky sweaters, hats, gloves, trousers and tablecloths, while weavings of the highest quality, indigenous ponchos, blouses, belts and tapestries are still made by master-craftsmen using traditional means in tiny village workshops. Come Saturday, when the crafts market combines with a general produce, hardware and animal market to create a megabazaar that engulfs much of the town, people stream in from far and wide for a day of frenzied trading.

The Plaza de Ponchos is the epicentre of the crafts melee, a blazing labyrinth of makeshift passageways and endless ranks of tapestries, jumpers, hammocks, cloths and shawls, amid which Otavaleños dressed in all their finery lurk at strategic points to tempt potential customers. But hard sell isn't their style; gentle, good-natured coaxing is far more effective at weakening the customer's resolve. Even the most hardened skinflints will soon be stuffing their bags with everything they never knew they needed and plenty else besides. The only tricky part is deciding who back home should get the 2m rain-stick and who should get the sheepskin chaps.

655

Retail at Otavalo crafts market therapy

656 | Wildlife-spotting in the Beni wetlands

BOLIVIA It's just a forty-minute flight from La Paz to the tropical lowlands of Beni, but the contrast couldn't be greater. From a window seat you'll see the snow-covered Andes give way to a dark green shadow of rainforest, before disembarking to the sweltering humidity of Rurrenabaque and rapidly shedding your high-altitude layers of clothes. This laidback town sits in a shimmering heat haze on the banks of the Beni River, framed by shrub-covered hills. It's a fine base for trips into the lush wetlands of Bolivia's Amazon Basin, popular with travellers who idle in hammocks under palm-thatched canopies before visiting the jungle.

Local operators take small groups into the wetlands on three-day excursions, the knowledgeable guides pointing out wildlife as well as plants used by locals as remedies for fever, colds and flu. Tours glide down the Yacuma River's overgrown waterways in low-bottomed boats, eyes peeled for inquisitive yellow skull monkeys and magnificently plumed birds, and wade through sticky, swamp-like mud in search of anacondas. Accommodation is basic: you'll spend your nights on mattresses shrouded in mosquito nets within a wooden hut on stilts. But the boat quickly becomes your breezy second home as you cruise along vegetation-lined channels, past graceful, long-necked herons and sunbathing turtles. In the shady shallows between tangles of tree roots, you can hook piranhas on home-made fishing rods using cubes of raw meat as bait. Further upstream you can swim with playful river dolphins, coloured an improbable shade of dusky pink.

Douse yourself in repellent to watch the sky burn brightly as the sun sets over the flat pampas. Once night falls, glowing fireflies provide intermittent light; shine a torch into the murky, shrub-covered riverbanks and you'll catch the sinister white glint of unblinking caiman eyes. At dawn, the wetlands echo with the eerie rumble of howler monkeys waking up, and the clouds form perfect reflections on the calm, mirrored surface of the water.

657 | Glitz and golden sands on Punta del Este

URUGUAY The continent's most exclusive beach resort by some distance, Punta del Este is Uruguay's answer to St-Tropez. There's a certain level of celebrity that's achieved simply by being here: if you don that outrageously expensive Sauvage swimsuit, act like you belong and hit the beach, chances are you may end up in the pages of a South American glossy mag. Punta is largely about glitzy casinos, all-night parties, designer sushi and fashionistas sipping frozen *mojitos*.

It's the kind of place where you might spot Naomi Campbell and Prince Albert of Monaco on the same evening – though probably not in the same Ferrari convertible. Every January half a million visitors – mostly Argentines and Brazilians – cram themselves in between surfers' paradise Playa Brava and family-friendly Playa Mansa, so you can easily lose yourself in the crowds.

But there's another side to Punta. Leave the Quiksilver-clad funboarders and world beach-volley tournaments behind and head for one of the infinite golden *playas* way beyond Punta Ballena, on the River Plate side of things. In Chihuahua, where you can sunbathe among the enormous straw-hued dunes, take cover in the secluded pine groves and venture into the tepid waters.

At night, drive across the landmark roller-coaster bridge to La Barra and race past the windswept ocean strands to José Ignacio. Here you can dine in discreet style right on the seafront, enjoying simply barbecued squid and chilled Sauvignon Blanc, as the breakers crash onto the sand and the Atlantic breeze ruffles your hair. The shutterbugs will be busy snapping the heir to the Spanish throne at some heaving cocktail bar in Punta: they're welcome to their prize.

658 | Itaipú: plugging the world's biggest dam

PARAGUAY & BRAZIL Colossal, gargantuan, mammoth, gigantic – it's difficult to find the right adjective to capture the sheer magnitude of the Itaipú Dam. The joint property of Paraguay and Brazil, it has been voted one of the seven wonders of the modern world by the American Society of Civil Engineers (who should know what they're talking about), and is arguably man's greatest ever feat of practical engineering, meeting the energy needs of most of Paraguay as well as a large chunk of southern Brazil. You don't need to be mechanically minded to appreciate it, however: the introductory video about the finer details of electricity generation might not hold your attention, but the sheer awe-inspiring scale of the structure certainly will.

It took sixteen years to build the dam, a project that was begun in the dark days of Paraguayan dictator Alfredo Stroessner's rule and finally completed in the early years of democracy; its inception created a reservoir so deep and wide that it completely flooded the Sete Quedas, a set of waterfalls comparable in size to those at nearby Iguazú. The dam is 8km long and 195m high, so standing next to it and looking up is as dizzying as you might expect. But to really feel insignificant, make a visit to the inside of the structure and the extraordinary 1km-long machine room.

It's like the inside of an anthill, with workers scurrying around, dwarfed by the sheer scale of their surroundings. Itaipú is at its most impressive when water levels are at their peak during the rainy season, when torrents of water rush down the chutes and the roar can be deafening. Whenever you're here, though, it's an amazing sight – and one that for once does justice to even the highest expectations.

COLOMBIA There's a certain sense of nervous excitement that comes with leaving for a hike at dawn. Shoelaces are double-tightened, extra snacks are jammed into backpacks, waterproofs are grabbed, just in case. Set in Colombia's lush coffee-growing region, the hike to the Valle de Cocora is worth every ounce of that excitement.

A short jeep ride from the colour-splashed village of Salento, the hike begins in a broad valley crumpled at its edges by mountains. Soon the slopes envelop the route as it twists upwards through mountainous cloudforest, the pathway intermittently broken by rickety bridges that swing over gurgling streams. The incline becomes increasingly torturous but there are plenty of distractions: a waterfall's distant rumble; iridescent flashes of hummingbirds; glimpses of the view through low-slung mist. And, then, the moment that everyone treks for, the descent into the Valle de Cocora. Finally you enter a prehistoric-looking valley, cloaked in undulating green and speckled with wax palms – the world's tallest species of palm tree – which soar and pierce the sky around you.

659

Hiking among giants in the Valle de Cocora

BRAZIL What could be simpler than a *caipirinha*? Made with just *cachaça* (a rum-like spirit distilled from fermented sugar-cane juice), fresh lime, sugar and ice, the *caipirinha* (literally "little peasant girl") is served at nearly every bar and restaurant in Brazil. Neither insipidly sweet nor jarringly alcoholic, it's one of the easiest and most pleasant cocktails to drink.

Therein lies the problem: because it's so smooth, it's all too common to lose count of just how many you've quaffed. And as lots of bars mix the cocktail with the cheapest *cachaça*, chances are that the next day you'll have to deal with a thumping headache, scarcely a just reward for a hard day at the beach. So a true aficionado will only accept the cocktail made with *cachaça* that's good enough to sip neat.

There's no better place to find this than at Rio de Janeiro's *Academia da Cachaça*. Opened in 1985, when Brazil's aspirant whisky-drinking middle class tended to dismiss *cachaça* as the drink of the poor, the *Academia* has many varieties on offer, and the bar's friendly owners and staff enjoy nothing more than offering tasting hints to their customers.

As you enter you may well wonder what all the fuss is about. The green and yellow Brazilian-flag-themed decor is utterly unremarkable and the music inaudible. But the shelves on the walls of the tiny bar, lined with a bewildering selection of bottles, remind you why you've come.

The *caipirinhas* are everything one might hope for, with just the right balance of alcohol, tang and sweetness. After one or two, you may even feel ready to forgo the sugar, lime and ice and start downing shots. Choosing a label is easy: if you don't listen to the house recommendations, the regulars around you will intervene to suggest their personal favourites. The spirit inspires debates, not unlike those over the finest single malt whiskies. The perfection of the *caipirinha*, on the other hand, is undebatable.

660

Downing caipirinhas in Rio de Janeiro

661 | Silence and solitude: the ruins of Trinidad

PARAGUAY It's an odd feeling to have a UNESCO World Heritage Site all to yourself. But hop on a bus in Encarnación, Paraguay's second-largest city, and within thirty minutes you could be standing in the middle of the finest Jesuit ruin in South America. And chances are you won't have to share it with a single soul.

Set on a hilltop in a borderline bulge in the far southeast of Paraguay, some 400km from the capital city of Asuncíon, the former Jesuit-Guaraní mission of Trinidad feels relatively remote in this small, little-visited country. Paraguay boasts seven of the Jesuits' *Treinta Pueblos*, the thirty towns they built across the continent as they sought to spread Catholicism during the seventeenth and eighteenth centuries, and Trinidad was the most important of them all. It is also the most complete today, providing the best sense – not just in Paraguay but in all of South America – of how life would have been for the inhabitants.

Like all Jesuit missions, Trinidad, or La Santísima Trinidad de Paraná to give it its full name, was a self-sufficient town, a miniature city-state that was independent of colonial Spanish rule and established with the ideal of educating the indigenous communities rather than enslaving them. Built in 1706, it boasted a central square, a school, workshops, cemeteries and housing for the local Guaraní people. The brick skeletons of these survive, and there's a magic in walking the moss-covered courtyards and peering through long-gone windows across rolling agricultural land to the simple painted wooden houses of rural Paraguay. But it is the impressive Iglesia Mayor, the cathedralesque church at Trinidad's centre, that steals the show, with its fantastically ornate stone carvings, including a famous frieze of angels stretching around the altar. Standing here, in your open-air congregation of one, you'll wonder why more people don't make the journey down to Trinidad – and feel guiltily glad that they don't.

662 | Fill up in the world's pie capital

URUGUAY Prince Charles ate it as a child. It's considered as British as drizzly rain and disappointing cricket results. Allied soldiers chomped it by the truckload during both world wars. Yet the mighty Fray Bentos range of foods has its home in a charmingly elegiac corner of Uruguay.

Once known as "the kitchen of the world", and employing more than a quarter of the town's population, Fray Bentos, in the cattle fields of Uruguay, made a perfect location for the German- and British-owned Liebig Extract of Meat Company to build a vast factory in 1863. Every day thousands of cows and lambs were slaughtered in the abattoir to make corned beef and pies that went into tins and were exported to the UK and the rest of Europe. Such was its popularity that British soldiers during World War I referred to anything good as being "Fray Bentos".

Outdated equipment and a declining export market led to the factory being closed down for three decades until a Brazilian company started operating out of the town again in 2008 and began exporting the pies to the US for the first time. The new plant is much smaller, leaving the original abattoir vacant – it's now been converted into the Museum of the Industrial Revolution, where tours explore the vast, spookily empty slaughterhouses and retro admin offices, untouched since the 1970s.

The rest of the town seems trapped in time, its central bandstand gathering dust. Sightseers might venture into a museum dedicated to the locally born artist Luis Solari, who made bizarre sketches of humans with animal heads.

It's not a trip to recommend to vegetarians – the tour guide seems to relish telling macabre tales of cows' ear hair being exported to Europe to make brushes, and the pies on sale in the town are cheap enough to encourage some serious binge eating. But providing you're not planning a diet anytime soon, this is a fascinating, and highly eccentric, way to explore the centuries-old trading links between this quiet corner of one of South America's least-known nations and the rest of the pie-loving world.

663 | Rubber busts and top hats: opera in the Amazon

BRAZIL A noisy concrete forest of tower blocks and brightly lit malls, the remote Amazonian capital and duty-free zone of Manaus throngs with shoppers braving the hot, humid streets to buy cheap electronic goods. Glittering in the twilight and visible above the chaos and heat of downtown is a large dome whose 36,000 ceramic tiles are painted gold, green and blue, the colours of the Brazilian flag. The palatial building it presides over is a grand pink and white confection of Belle Époque architecture, the Teatro Amazonas.

Nothing could seem more out of place. Built in the late nineteenth century during the height of Brazil's rubber boom, the lavish opera house was designed by Italians to look Parisian (indeed, almost all the materials were brought over from Europe). Abandoned for many years when the rubber industry died and Manaus could scarcely afford its electricity bill, the theatre is now funded by a large state budget and hosts regular performances of jazz and ballet, though nothing is quite so singular as its staging of top-quality opera in the middle of the jungle.

The surreal experience begins the moment you enter the foyer and step onto a floor covered in gleaming hardwood; walls are lined with columns made from the finest Carrara marble and ornate Italian frescoes decorate the ceiling. Hundreds of chandeliers hang in falling crystal formations. It's as if you've been transported to a European capital. You're ushered through red velvet curtains by men dressed in tailcoats and top hats. The orchestra, the Amazonas Philharmonic, pick up instruments that have been specially treated to cope with the humidity of the jungle, and the chatter dissipates abruptly. The conductor raises his baton, and the first familiar notes of Wagner's *Ring Cycle* fill the auditorium, then seep out languidly into the steamy night.

664 | Spend lazy days at Parque Tayrona

COLOMBIA You'll have to hike through thick jungle to reach Colombia's best beaches, tucked away in a paradisal national park on the Caribbean coast. Parque Tayrona, an hour by bus from the mellow port city of Santa Marta, is famed for its vast swathes of verdant forest, swaying palms and pristine beaches, and enjoys a legendary status among locals and travellers.

Arriving at secluded bays so impossibly pretty you feel as if you're on a film set, you won't begrudge the arduous trudge to reach them. After forty minutes' march and muddy scrambles over rocks under a woodland canopy, the moment you first stumble upon a stunning vista of glistening turquoise sea and white sand is unforgettable. Arriving at Arrecifes, you'll find a wide stretch of sand and plenty of accommodation, from spartan *cabañas* to pricey "EcoHabs" with fancy restaurants. Most people camp or string up a hammock, the cheapest and most picturesque option.

It's worth walking on to discover the park's other beaches – not least because rip tides at Arrecifes make swimming dangerous. Nearby La Piscina is a natural swimming pool of limpid water in a sheltered cove, and at El Cabo San Juan del Guía coconut-laden palms lean over two perfect sandy bays. Beyond lies a long, semi-deserted nudist beach, where you can work on your all-over tan and cool off in the vigorous waves.

Your most arduous choices in Tayrona will be deciding which beach to lounge on and what time to crack open a beer. There's a ruined indigenous village at El Pueblito, a ninety-minute uphill hike from El Cabo, but most people are content just to swim, sunbathe and snooze in a hammock.

Stay as long as you can and congratulate yourself on finding this relaxed, tropical idyll.

665 | Hike out to the Inca ruins of Choquequirao

PERU The endlessly photogenic presence of Machu Picchu – today, arguably the biggest single draw in South America – may loom large over travel to Peru, but in fact the site represents just one of the country's extraordinary collection of Inca ruins. At its height, during the fifteenth and early sixteenth centuries, the Inca Empire was the largest realm in pre-Columbian America, spanning modern-day Peru and Bolivia and also incorporating much of what are now Ecuador and Chile. After its demise in the mid-1500s, it left behind a huge number of archeological settlements.

One of the very best is Choquequirao, a spectacular mountain citadel that's long been talked about as the next big thing in Peruvian tourism but for now remains a little-visited gem. This is largely down to its remote location – high above the mighty Apurímac Canyon and best reached via a two-day hike from Cachora, a rural town three hours' drive from Cusco. But while it draws only the merest fraction of visitors that Machu Picchu attracts, Choquequirao is increasing in popularity, and there have even been mentions of a plan to construct a cable car (which would be able to bring 150,000 visitors annually), so now's definitely the time to go.

The hike itself features momentous mountain scenery and a heart-quickening 75m rope-bridge crossing of the Apurímac River. You'll see hummingbirds and parakeets as you ascend. And then, on arrival – having negotiated a tough, high-altitude climb to 3050m above sea level, some 600m higher than Machu Picchu – you're treated to your own deserted Inca city. On a clear day the view stretches for some 65km, with the snowcapped peaks of the Vilcabamba Range rampaging into the distance.

It's estimated that only around thirty percent of the city, which covers some six square kilometres, is visible today – the rest remains hidden in the jungle. There's still a grand sense of scale, however, with broad ceremonial plazas, aqueduct-fed water shrines and dozens of stone terraces, some inlaid with ornamental llama designs.

The Incas did not use the written word, and historians know very few firm facts about Choquequirao's role and importance. When you're one of the few souls wandering the ruins of this isolated Andean refuge, however, the enigma only adds to the allure.

666 | Watching the sun rise in the Valley of the Moon

CHILE The bracing early-morning air of the Atacama Desert rouses you from your stupor as you leave your *residencial*. Gradually your eyes adjust to a darkness illuminated softly by a crescent moon, and you make out the well-trodden dirt road just ahead. Leading out from the village of San Pedro, the track wends its way 14km to your destination, the surreal Valle de la Luna – the Valley of the Moon. It's about ninety minutes before sunrise and time to get moving, which is just as well – your chattering teeth are doing little to warm you. Driven in equal measure by a need to generate body heat and the joy of embarking on an otherworldly mountain-bike ride, you start pedalling west.

Though the prospect of seeing the sun rise in the Valle de la Luna is what lured you out of bed, there is more than a bit of truth in saying that the journey is the destination. Enveloped in silence and without another soul in sight, you ride across the Atacama with a stunning panorama for a backdrop – flat arid fields punctuated by jagged age-old boulders give way to red crested dunes and valleys layered in a thin orange and white crust. It's easy to see why NASA chose here to field test their Martian rover, but surely they didn't have as much fun as you are with your two knobbly tyres and a suspension that is thankfully forgiving.

When dawn breaks, the sky springs to life in fiery hues, from blood-red to burnt amber. Taking it in from the perch of one of the higher crests, you gaze upon the lunar landscape that surrounds you – a perfect vantage point to see how far you've come and to plot your course back to the comforts of San Pedro.

Walking on ice: the Perito Moreno Glacier

ARGENTINA Fed by one of the planet's largest freshwater reserves – the Southern Patagonian Icecap – the Perito Moreno Glacier is the world's biggest ice-cube dispenser. It looks like a gigantic frozen Blue Lady, thanks to centuries of compression which has turned the deepest ice a rich shade of *curaçao*, whose sapphire veins can be tantalizingly glimpsed through plunging fissures. This icy leviathan of a cocktail is one to linger over, surveying its infinite cracks and curves from the viewing platform across the Lago Argentino. One of the few advancing glaciers in the world, it does move, but at, well, glacial speed. It's noisy, too, squeaking and whining and sporadically exploding, as every few minutes a wardrobe-sized chunk splashes into the lake's chilly waters and bobs away as an iceberg.

But the spectacular event you'll be hoping to see, the *ruptura*, when Perito Moreno lunges forward, forms a dam of ice and then violently breaks, happens only every four to five years.

A great way of getting to know this icy beast is to go for a walk on it. Standing on the glacier, you can see every crack and crevice, every tiny pinnacle. Even on a warm summer's day, the glacier remains chilly, so wrap up well. Protect your eyes and exposed skin from the immense white glare with sunglasses and a high-factor sunscreen. The ice can be slippery, but it's not dangerous as long as you stick to sensible footwear and snap on the crampons issued by all the tour companies offering glacier-treks. And when you've walked far enough, you'll be glad to know that most treks end up with a tumbler of whisky on the rocks – made with ice-cubes chipped out of the glacier, of course.

668 | Making a pilgrimage to Isla del Sol

BOLIVIA Set against the parched grasslands of the Altiplano, where agriculture is dependent on irrigation and capricious rain, the deep, sapphire-blue waters of Lake Titicaca offer the promise of life and fertility. The Incas believed the creator god Viracocha rose from the waters of this lake, calling forth the sun and the moon to light up the world from an island in its centre now called the Isla del Sol – the Island of the Sun.

Claiming their own dynasty also originated there, they built a complex of shrines and temples on the island, transforming it into a religious centre of enormous importance, a pan-Andean pilgrimage destination once visited by thousands of worshippers annually from across their vast empire.

Modern visitors can follow the same route as the pilgrims of Inca times, travelling by boat from the port town of Copacabana – itself a pilgrimage centre for the now nominally Christian population of the Bolivian highlands – through the waters of the world's highest navigable lake.

With no roads or cars on the island, the only way to visit the Inca ruins is on foot, trekking through the tranquil villages of the indigenous Aymara, who raise crops on the intricate agricultural terraces left by the Incas and still regard Lake Titicaca as a powerful female deity capable of regulating climate and rainfall.

The ruined temples themselves are small in comparison with Inca sites elsewhere in the Andes, but the setting more than makes up for this. The great rock where the sun and moon were created looks out on all sides across the tranquil expanse of the lake, which is in turn surrounded by mighty, snowcapped mountains, each of which is still worshipped as a god in its own right. Serene and beautiful, Titicaca's sacred Andean geography makes it easy to believe it could indeed be the centre of the universe.

669 | Mountain biking the world's most dangerous road

BOLIVIA The reputation of the road linking La Paz with the tropical lowlands of Bolivia is enough to put most travellers off. But for downhill mountain bikers and all-round thrill-lovers, it's an irresistible challenge. The World's Most Dangerous Road, as this byway is colloquially known, is a stunning ride through some of the most dramatic scenery South America has to offer, and with a vertical descent of around 3500m over just 64km, it's one of the longest continuous downhill rides on Earth. A bypass, which most cars and trucks now use to avoid the steepest stretch, means the old road is now quieter for cyclists, although the route has got no less precipitous.

Starting amid the icebound peaks of the Andes at over 4000m above sea level, the road plunges through the clouds into the humid valleys of the Upper Amazon basin, winding along deep, narrow gorges where dense cloudforest clings to even the steepest of slopes. The descent is an intense, white-knuckle experience, not made easier by the sight of so many stone crosses marking where buses and trucks have left the road. The surface is so bad that in most countries it wouldn't even be classified as a road. On one side, dizzying precipices drop down hundreds of metres to the thin, silver ribbon of a river below; on the other, a sheer rock wall rises into the clouds. In the rainy season, waterfalls cascade across the road, making its broken surface even more treacherous. At every hairpin bend, there's a risk a heavy lorry may lurch round the corner, leaving very little room for manoeuvre on a track only 3m wide.

By the time you're sipping beer and resting aching limbs by the pool in the tropical heat of Coroico, the resort town at the end of the ride, your only fear will be the bus ride back up to La Paz.

670 | Flying close to the wind in the Bolivian Amazon

BOLIVIA Thirty minutes into a ninety-minute flight and you're wishing that you hadn't drunk that final beer. Even the sight of skyscraper-tall thunderheads and tantalizing glimpses of snaking silt aren't enough to distract you. When the toilet-free Fairchild Metro touches down in Trinidad and you hit the loo after a doubled-up sprint, the elation is all-consuming.

Welcome to the jungle, where flooded roads are virtually impassable for months at a time, and planes are pretty much the only way to go. In the region's remoter outposts, the "airport" may well consist of a single trestle table with a basin of fly-blown *empanadas* and a hut serving as check-in; security is non-existent. The only other passenger is an old woman who's never flown before and whom you end up having to belt in. She crosses herself then covers her entire head with her shawl – maybe she knows something you don't about the route's safety record.

You remind yourself that such crashes are rare, though perhaps invoking divine protection is not such a bad idea. Especially if you opt for an "air taxi" – tiny, often antiquated planes that take impromptu short hops in the most remote regions. You may even be press-ganged by a silver-tongued local scouring the bus stops for unsuspecting gringos to share the cost. In a cramped shed with an overgrown back garden of a runway, a gaggle of characters load chickens and God knows what else into the fuselage of a single-prop Cessna.

A gruff, uniform-less pilot arrives and barks at you to get in the front seat alongside him. With growing anxiety you take in the tiny cockpit: dirty, cracked dials and taped-up steering handlebars – *puta-madre*, is he expecting you to co-pilot? No, you're just along for the ride, though every instinct is telling you to get out. Too late, you're in the air, your heart in your mouth, exhilarated, dazzled by fear and the breathless sight of the mighty Amazon basin stretching away to every horizon.

Now *this*, you conclude in a momentary release from the trauma, really is air travel.

Trek to the Lost City

671

COLOMBIA It's a challenging three-day trek through dense jungle to the Ciudad Perdida, the fabled ruins of a lost city hidden deep in the mountains of northern Colombia – and then another three days back. But the strenuous hike along steep trails sticky with mud is worth it just for the time you spend in the tranquil, unblemished cloudforest of the Sierra Nevada de Santa Marta, washing beside waterfalls in bracingly fresh pools and mastering the art of sleeping soundly in a hammock. Indiana Jones-style moments abound, from wading across the fast-flowing River Buritaca to inching along narrow ledges at the path's whim.

The only other people you'll encounter along the way are a few bemused Kogui tribesmen standing outside their circular thatched huts and youthful soldiers guarding occasional military outposts. Gaps in the trees afford glimpses of rolling peaks carpeted in vegetation, filling the landscape in every direction. It's easy to fixate on where you're placing your feet, but remember to pause to admire the view. After a day or two you'll start to distinguish the jungle's infinite textures and

shades of green and appreciate the subtly contrasting hues of twisted vines and delicate leaves.

Walking six hours each day can be exhausting, but the group camaraderie carries you up the most gruelling slogs. Even the fittest trekker will be effortlessly outstripped by the nimble guide in wellies. Darkness descends around 6pm, so evenings are spent chatting as fireflies flicker. The dramatic climax to your journey involves hauling yourself out of the river to climb 1200 worn, moss-covered and perilously slippery steps hacked out of the rock.

Little remains of the Ciudad Perdida bar grass-covered plateaus edged with rocks. But you can picture how it looked before Spanish-brought illnesses devastated the Tayrona people, and marvel at their resourcefulness at establishing a thriving community in such a remote location. By day, sunlight dapples the paths, lending the place a fairy-tale aura; things become more eerie when the damp white mist rolls in at night. Colombia's precolonial history is largely unknown, and in this ancient site your imagination is free to conjure up the mysterious past.

672 Carnival in colonial Olinda

BRAZIL From Olinda's Alto da Sé, a languid, curving hilltop plaza, Brazil's future seems framed by its rich Portuguese past. In the distance Recife's skyscrapers shimmer in the sun, a forest of steel and glass pillars, while in the foreground lie the weathered convent towers, lush gardens and tropical trees of one of the largest and most beautiful colonial towns in Brazil.

Founded by the Portuguese in 1535, Olinda is a maze of cobbled streets, brilliant white churches, pastel-coloured houses, Baroque fountains and elegant plazas. The ensemble of colonial architecture here is the finest in all Brazil: the Convento de São Francisco, established in 1577 as the first Franciscan church in the country, is a prime example. Most of what you see today was rebuilt in the eighteenth century, and though the interior is exquisitely maintained there is enough peeling wall and crumbling plaster to convey its great age.

Olinda is perhaps most renowned, though, for its *carnaval*. Generally considered to be one of the three greatest in Brazil (with those of Rio and Salvador), Olinda's *carnaval* has a style and feel all its own: much of it takes place in the old town, where giant puppets known as *bonecos* (papier-mâché figures of folk heroes, or savage caricatures of local and national figures) parade through the winding streets, and small squares resound with blistering brass *frevo* music and thundering *maracatu de nação* (Afro-Brazilian drummers, singers and dancers). Best of all, everyone takes part in the parades and parties; *carnaval* in Olinda is not a spectator sport. The streets will be jam-packed, so be prepared to go with the flow (you'll really have no choice), grabbing a cold beer or ice-cold coconut from wandering vendors when you can. You'll be swept up by processions of *maracatu* drummers and dancers, stumble onto impromptu dance parties, get hosed down by kids on rooftops and sprayed with multicoloured paints (leave the designer gear at home). And don't be surprised if you end up receiving a big kiss from Superman, Cat Woman and other assorted superheroes.

673 Rafting on sacred waters in the Urubamba Valley

PERU Snaking along from the Andes out to the Apurímac in the Amazon basin, the mighty Urubamba is the main artery pulsing through the Inca heartland. Winding between many of the most revered Inca sites, the river itself is sacred. Not all the Urubamba is negotiable by craft, but one section, not far from the start of the Inca Trail, is perfect for a bit of gentle whitewater rafting.

On the first stretch, a serene meander through the Urubamba Valley, novice rafters will have the chance to get used to the feeling of having nothing but inflated plastic between them and some fairly sharp rocks. This is a chance to enjoy the superb views of the snowy peaks of the Andes in the distance on one side, and the wooded slopes of the valley stretching up hundreds of metres on the other, where Quechua-speaking llama herders ply the steep trails of their ancestors and the distinctive black and white forms of condors can be seen wheeling far above. Blink and you'll miss the rows of ancient Inca grain stores, carved from rock and piled impossibly high on the emerald-green banks.

Don't be lulled into thinking this is naught but a pleasure boat, though. The roar of the rapids quickly gets louder as the raft moves faster. Following the instructor's command, you'll paddle harder and duck lower as the raft shoots down increasingly larger and faster falls. However secular you are, you may find yourself praying to the ancient spirits of the Incas as you go rushing down the final and biggest drop along this beginner's stretch. There are scarier, more dangerous river rapids in Peru for experienced rafters – the excellent class V rapids of the Colca Canyon, for instance – but none can rival the beauty and majesty of the sacred river of the Incas.

Finding Eden on the Altiplano's edge

674

BOLIVIA You can't buy a ticket to the Garden of Eden, but if you could, your final destination would almost certainly be the Middle East. Colonial Spain begged to differ; according to Eduardo Galeano's *Open Veins of Latin America*, one contemporary account located the biblical garden in the heart of the Amazon basin. It's the conquistadors who were nearer the mark, though, finding their own Eden further west in Sorata, Bolivia. Here, after an endless and desolate plain, the Altiplano jigsaws down into the kind of valley routinely trumped up in fairy tale and myth. That it's seemingly hidden from the world goes without saying, but it's the topography that dazzles, a cosmic wedge of terraces falling into mist, so ravishingly green after the whey-brown Altiplano they seem like, well, the hallowed allotments of Eden, if not quite the garden itself.

At the heart of it all, below the lottery of bijou maize plots and heaven-scented eucalyptus, sits Sorata, a beginning-of-the-world outpost populated by diggers, dreamers, eccentrics and entrepreneurs, its colonial piles crumbling contentedly under the gaze of almighty Illampu. At over 6300m tall, this ice-crowned mountain deity shadows every cobbled corner of town, its glacial heights all the more fantastical amid the bucolic setting, and one reason why the place remains popular among climbers and trekkers.

Yet Eden or no, once upon a time Sorata was itself a gateway to the heart of Amazonian darkness; Victorian explorer Colonel Fawcett, who inspired Conan Doyle's *The Lost World*, passed this way more than once on his journey to oblivion, while the town's predominantly German merchants made a killing on quinine and rubber hauled up from the jungle. These days adventurous travellers can still head east down the old trails, assuming they can tear themselves away from Sorata's sequestered cafés and glorious climate, an eternal spring with blissfully warm days and cool, quiet nights. Those nights will be spent in a peerlessly eccentric choice of psychedelic cabin, time-warped colonial chamber or haunted Art Deco hotel. You might not find Eden but you will find a cure for modernity.

Looking down on Kaieteur Falls

675

GUYANA From the vantage point of a Cessna, the great expanse of Guyana's rainforest interior looks like billows of green cloud. The little plane drones over the soft canopy, almost low enough that the passengers could blow and the trees would disperse like smoke, revealing whatever mysteries lie hidden beneath. About an hour out of Georgetown, just as the unbroken jungle scenery starts to get monotonous, the plane banks sharply to the right, losing roughly half of its altitude in a couple of seconds, and heads down towards a gorge bordered by thick forest. As the plane descends farther, a waterfall soon comes into view, cascading down the middle of the gorge, not in tumultuous rumbles of white foam, but in a single, rapier-like gush of water that seems to come from nowhere.

Enjoying the kind of splendid isolation that Niagara Falls can only dream of, Kaieteur Falls is five times as high as its North American rival, and infinitely more enigmatic. The narrow band of water that runs off the side of the Kaieteur Gorge plunges 226m past nesting swifts to the bottom, making the falls here among the highest single-drop waterfalls in the world. Flying close enough to hear the water's roar blend menacingly with the sound of whirring propellers, it all seems dark and forbidding down below. Passengers may start to worry about those hardy souls who opted to walk through the rainforest for several days in order to reach the falls, getting their first glimpse of Kaieteur dropping on top of them – a somewhat intimidating experience when compared with the exhilaration of flying in, but no less awesome.

676 | Canoeing the Rio Negro while fireflies light up the darkness

BRAZIL The Meeting of the Waters in Manaus is the point where the Amazon river, or Rio Solimões, meets the Rio Negro – but the two don't mix. The confluence of the dark waters of the Negro and the sandier, lighter Amazon runs for several kilometres without merging, due to differences in density, flow and temperature. And while most travellers head for the larger of the two rivers, it's a different, quieter experience on the Negro.

Leaving the sweat and the hubbub of Manaus, the last trading post and biggest city on the Negro's course, behind you, you're on the largest left tributary of the Amazon River. More acidic than the Amazon, the blackwater river means fewer mosquitoes. What it does have in abundance, though, is another insect that's going to light up your life.

At night your guide will want to take you alligator-spotting, leaving the comfort of your hammock on the small houseboat and stepping into a motorized dugout canoe. It's best to turn off the motor; the dark stillness the best way to creep up on desolate riverbanks. It's not for the faint-hearted, and you might find yourself wishing you were elsewhere as the shadowy foliage and narrowing branches of the river suggest all manner of untold threats.

But what your guide may not have told you is that on the way back from searching for tiny red eyeballs peering above the surface, you're in for a magical experience. Moving silently through the water, what was once gloomy and threatening becomes a fantasy backdrop, as the dark jungle's hostility melts away into something akin to a Wes Anderson movie.

Myriad twinkles of light begin to form in the inky blackness, as an unassuming invertebrate that goes by the Latin name *lampyridae* begins its nightly show. Fireflies are actually beetles, about the size of a regular paper clip. Thriving in humid, temperate environments, these lightning bugs are just waiting for night to fall so they can start their spectacular seduction, glowing for prospective mates. We might do it by candlelight, but these clever little critters use their in-built luminescence.

677 | Star-gazing at Mamalluca

CHILE In the northern half of Chile, the driest place on Earth, clouds are virtually unknown and the skies are of the brightest blue. At night, far away from the lights of major settlements, you can look up at a dark vault simply shimmering with stars. The near-perfect visibility almost every night of the year makes the region ideal for observing the universe – indeed, there are more astronomical observatories here than anywhere else on Earth – but you don't need to be an astronomer to get a great view.

Some of the world's most powerful computerized telescopes sit here, among the plains and hills, but you can also catch sight of constellations such as the Southern Cross and familiar heavenly bodies like Jupiter or Mars at more modest observatories, such as Mamalluca. Set aside one evening, resist that extra *pisco sour* and book one of the regular stargazing tours that depart after dark. These take you high up on Cerro Mamalluca, where the darkness is absolute and the air is crisp.

There's the classic visit – a short talk giving you a grounding in basic astronomy, followed by a few minutes looking through a telescope – or the Andean Cosmovision tour, in which guides explain how the pre-Columbian peoples interpreted the night sky, and perform native songs, with flutes and drums accompanying mystic verses, speaking of a local cosmology dating back thousands of years.

678 | Exploring Quichua culture in Ecuador's volcanic highlands

ECUADOR You're at an altitude of 3900m, shivering in the cold as the sun rises behind you. Below, a saw-edge precipice encircles a still, emerald-green lake 3km in diameter. Lower still, fertile plateaus creased with deep, shadowed valleys are picked out by the golden dawn light and, beyond, snowcapped peaks fringe the horizon.

This is the dormant volcano of Quilotoa, high in the Andes' central highlands. In the late 1940s, its altitude, beauty and proximity to the equator led a young American here who believed himself to be a reincarnation of John the Baptist. He called himself Johnny Lovewisdom and stayed on the lake shore for a year, pursuing his belief that it's possible to live on rarefied air and sunlight alone.

There is an undeniable spirituality about this beautiful place, something partly fostered by the culture of the Quichua people, who lead a traditional farming life, and have dotted the landscape with tiny shrines. Their religion is Catholicism blended with indigenous beliefs: the Virgin Mary is identified with Pachamama, the female Earth deity with whom a drop of any drink is shared by pouring it on the ground. A public bus is the best way of exploring the local area and culture on the Quilotoa Loop, a string of Quichua villages a half-day trip from Quito. If you can stomach the twists and turns as it hurtles along the bumpy hillside tracks, the views are much better from the roof. Anyway, inside the bus it's probably more comfortable.

If you take a bus to the top of the pass, Quilotoa can be tackled as a challenging day-walk down to the villages in the valley below. The trail starts along the crater rim, winding between wild lupins and grasses, descends past farms and fields, plunges down a precipitous canyon and finally ends up by a handful of hostels in the sleepy village of Chugchilán.

The walk's not particularly long, but it tells on the lungs, and the steep slopes are hard going. It's at this point that staying at the *Black Sheep Inn*, a beautiful ecolodge, pays dividends: it boasts a home-made, wood-fired sauna and a hot tub to ease your aching limbs.

679 | The road to ruins: Machu Picchu

PERU There's a point on the Inca Trail when you suddenly forget the accumulated aches and pains of four days' hard slog across the Andes. You're standing at Inti Punku, the Sun Gate, the first golden rays of dawn slowly bringing the jungle to life. Down below, revealing itself in tantalizing glimpses as the early-morning mist burns gradually away, are the distinctive ruins of Machu Picchu, looking every bit the lost Inca citadel it was until a century ago.

The hordes of visitors that will arrive by mid-morning are still tucked up in bed; for the next couple of hours or so, it's just you, your group and a small herd of llamas, grazing indifferently on the terraced slopes. That first unforgettable sunrise view from Inti Punku is just the start: thanks to its remote location – hugging the peaks at 2500m and

hidden in the mountains some 120km from Cusco – Machu Picchu remained semi-buried in the Peruvian jungle until Hiram Bingham, an American explorer, "rediscovered" them in 1911. Which means that, descending onto the terraces and working your way through the stonework labyrinth, you'll discover some of the best-preserved Inca remains in the world.

Sites such as the Temple of the Sun and the Intihuatana appear exactly as they did some six hundred years ago. The insight they give us into the cultures and customs of the Inca is still as rewarding – the former's window frames the constellation of Pleiades, an important symbol of crop fertility – and their structural design, pieced together like an ancient architectural jigsaw, is just as incredible.

680 | The southernmost town on Earth

CHILE At the southern tip of South America the continent fragments into an archipelago of sparsely populated islands, islets and rocky outcrops: Tierra del Fuego (Land of Fire). This isolated region is divided between Argentina and Chile, and while the former has the biggest city – Ushuaia – the latter boasts the southernmost town on earth.

On the edge of Navarino Island, facing the Beagle Channel and backed by the jagged Dientes de Navarino mountain range, Puerto Williams is less than 1000km north of Antarctica. The only significant human settlements south of here are the tiny fishing village of Puerto Toro, also located on Navarino Island and currently only accessible by boat, and the international research stations on Antarctica itself.

Founded as a military outpost in 1953 and named after John Williams Wilson, a nineteenth-century British-Chilean naval commander and politician, the town is home to around three thousand people. Most of the population are navy officers and their families, but there is also a community of around one hundred Yámana people. Once one of the largest indigenous groups in Tierra del Fuego, the Yámana

were virtually wiped out by waves of nineteenth-century European settlers, who came in search of gold or to work on the region's vast sheep ranches.

Today few travellers make it to this windswept, low-rise and rather desolate town, but those who do discover a remarkably friendly place. Conditions in the winter are harsh, but days during the short-lived summer can be surprisingly pleasant, with highs of 16 or 17ºC in January and February. This is the best time to attempt one of South America's most spectacular – and challenging – hikes, the 70km Dientes de Navarino circuit. Less strenuous activities include boat trips along the Beagle Channel, where sightings of sea lions, dolphins and whales are common, and a visit to the town's excellent anthropological museum, which charts the history of the Yámana and Tierra del Fuego's other indigenous peoples.

But Puerto Williams's biggest attraction is its end-of-the-world feel and the sense that you've travelled just about as far as you can in South America.

681 | Parrot-watching at the world's biggest macaw lick

PERU Crawling out of a mosquito-netted bed and into a canoe an hour before dawn isn't everyone's idea of a good time. But, in this verdant corner of the Amazon, it gives you the chance to reach one of nature's great sights – the spectacle of hundreds of exotic birds arriving at a remote island in the Tambopata river for breakfast.

This island, not far from the Bolivian border, is just metres away from the world's biggest macaw lick – a place where flocks of bright parrots come most days to eat clay and minerals which aid their digestion of otherwise inedible jungle fruits. Usually, at least one group of ecotourists or birdwatchers can be found sitting quietly in a row of deckchairs, their binoculars, telescopes and cameras pointing towards the 30m-high river cliff well before the sun rises.

The jungle is quiet except for the constant drone of insects, the occasional bull frog call and water lapping along the river's edge. Then, the first flock will be heard, perhaps the high-pitched squawks

of a squadron of some sixty blue-headed parrots, flying and working together, patrolling the area around the cliff to make sure there is no danger from predators like spider monkeys. If the coast appears clear, other parrots start to gather. By the time day arrives, several pairs of scarlet or chestnut-fronted macaws will follow. Within an hour the entire cliff is studded with brilliant colour. The birds use their strong beaks to peck away at the soft cliff face, holding on fast with their sturdy feet. If the highly sensitive parrots become aware of their audience or any threat they fly off en masse, a ribbon of rainbow in the deep blue sky.

By 8 or 9am, groups usually head back to the lodge, eager to get their own breakfast. And while the parrots may be the highlight of your trip, there's plenty more on offer. By day, you can see monkeys, sloths, wild boar and deer; after dark, guides take visitors on the river to look for caimans, flying fish and tarantulas.

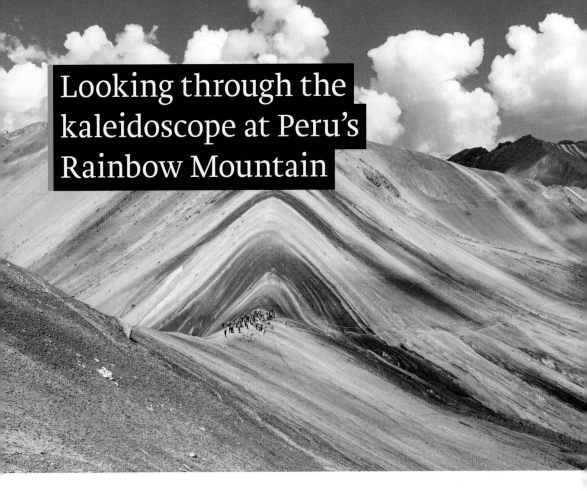

Looking through the kaleidoscope at Peru's Rainbow Mountain

682

PERU Like a giant slab of cake, Rainbow Mountain is striped with shades of lavender, maroon, turquoise and gold that could be straight from bottles of icing colouring. This multicoloured mountain, known as Vinicunca to locals, is a spectacle of shifting colours found in the Peruvian Andes, 100km southeast of Cusco.

The geological phenomenon is thought to be down to sediment from mineral deposits building up over millions of years: rust mixtures causing the rose hues, iron sulphide creating the yellow tones and chlorite responsible for the green. The mountain was originally cloaked in snow but when the ice melted, the banded peaks materialized and people started taking notice. Peruvians believe Vinicunca to be holy and every year thousands of pilgrims head to the Andes for Quyllurit'i, a native celebration of the stars.

Hiking is the best way to see the extraordinary rock formation, although the long distance and high altitude (over 6,000m above sea level) make it notoriously challenging. Many of the multiday routes start in Ocongate,

wending around the edge of Ausangate, and take between three and six days; some incorporate horseriding along parts of the route. A string of campsites is dotted along the journey. Alternatively, a three-hour drive from Cusco takes you to a trailhead for a demanding three-hour climb to the attraction. The best time to visit is either right after sunrise or just before sunset; avoid times of the year with a high chance of rain or snow, as poor weather dulls the colours and worsens hiking conditions.

While the tourism industry has ploughed money into the local Pampachiri community, there are concerns that Vinicunca will join the growing crop of attractions that are a victim of their own allure, with worries over the environmental impact of the daily 1,000 visitors. Hopefully, the surge of wider sustainability endeavours in Peru will provide inspiration on tackling the issue.

Although Photoshopped images on social media can stretch the limits of believability, this is one of the natural wonders that really does take your breath away – and not just because of the altitude.

683 | Savouring ceviche in Lima

PERU Located on the edge of the barren Atacama Desert, Lima is among the driest cities on the planet, with kilometres of hot red rocks stretching inland beyond its limits. You'd be forgiven for assuming its residents eke out a scorched, *Road Warrior*-style existence, but, as descendants of the Inca, innovators of irrigation systems and aqueducts, Peruvians have made their capital surprisingly verdant.

Lima's foliage finds sanctuary in manicured parks, as should you: they're perfect venues for picnicking with old travelling friends or new *limeño* acquaintances. Savoury *anticuchos* and spicy *papas a la Huancaína* make a marvellous menu, but if you can pull together a few kitchen utensils and an ice-filled cooler, nothing completes the feast better than a freshly made *ceviche*.

Something like fish salad, *ceviche* is "cooked" in an acidic bath of lemon and lime juice with diced onion, tomato, coriander and *ají* pepper, leaving the fish soft, moist and cool. Peruvians are proud of their national dish, and its preparation is a familiar ritual. Though other countries have tried to claim it, *peruanos* know it's as unique to their heritage as Machu Picchu and the Nazca lines. They've even mythologized it: *leche de tigre*, the bracingly sour "tiger's milk" that remains after the fish has been devoured, is known as a potent aphrodisiac.

So find a shady spot – one with a picnic table is best – and don't forget the *choclo* (boiled, large-kernel corn cobs) and sweet yams, *ceviche*'s traditional accompaniments. Once the work's been divvied up and completed, sit back for a couple of hours while the fish marinates. Savour the afternoon light, the warm chatter of nearby families, perhaps a slight breeze off a man-made pond. Take an icy sip of a *pisco sour*, and try to remember those desert dunes you heard about, now so very far from this lush oasis.

684 | Treasure, trinkets and trash in Neruda's casa

CHILE One morning Pablo Neruda looked out of the window and spotted a chunk of driftwood being tossed about in the Pacific Ocean. He walked down to the beach behind his home, Casa de Isla Negra, and waited patiently for the surf to carry it to the shore. This "present from the sea" was turned into the desk on which many of the poems that earned him the 1971 Nobel Prize were written.

The desk remains in the study of his wonderfully eccentric house, a few hours' drive west of Santiago, which was turned into a museum after his death. While his other homes were ransacked by supporters of General Pinochet shortly after the military coup, Casa de Isla Negra survived largely unscathed. When soldiers arrived late at night to search the house, Neruda reputedly remarked: "Look around. There's only one thing of danger for you here – poetry."

Today, the house has the feel of a treasure-trove. An inveterate hoarder, Neruda crammed the place with bric-a-brac, kitsch collectables and bits of junk that he had picked up on his travels – including coloured glasses, seashells, Hindu carvings, a full-size model horse, African masks and ships in bottles. The house perfectly sums up Neruda's tangle of contradictions, and offers as good an insight into the man as any of his poems. He was fascinated by the sea – Casa de Isla Negra was built to resemble a ship, with narrow hallways, porthole-like windows and low ceilings – but could not swim, and rarely ventured onto a real ship. Similarly, he loved to collect musical instruments, but was unable to play any of them.

On September 23, 1973, Neruda died of cancer, two weeks after the coup that claimed the life of his great friend, and the elected President of Chile, Salvador Allende. Alongside his poetry, Casa de Isla Negra survives as lasting tribute to a man considered Chile's, and arguably South America's, greatest poet. His most famous work, the melancholic and erotically charged *Twenty Love Poems and a Song of Despair*, is the perfect accompaniment to a visit here, with a line from "Poem 20" particularly appropriate: "Love is so short, forgetting is so long."

685 | Brave the devil's throat at Iguazú

ARGENTINA & BRAZIL Upon first seeing Iguazú Falls, all Eleanor Roosevelt could manage was "Poor Niagara". Every year, tens of thousands of visitors from around the world try to evaluate the sheer dimension of this natural miracle – a collection of more than two hundred cascades thundering over an 80m cliff – and usually fail. However you spell it – Iguazú, Iguaçu or Iguassu – the Guaraní name, translating as "Big Water", is something of an understatement. Situated on the border of Brazil, Argentina and Paraguay, the falls are surrounded by lush tropical forest that's home to more than 2000 species of flora, over 500 bird species and approximately eighty different mammals.

Many marvel at these massive falls from the relative dryness of the Brazilian side, but you are advised against looking down at them from a Brazilian helicopter for ecological reasons. Armchair travellers might watch these gushing waterfalls rival Robert De Niro and Jeremy Irons for the leading role in the 1986 epic film *The Mission*.

But the true way to experience the rapids, or *cataratas* as the locals call them, is to land right in the action and get soaked to the skin. Leave your digital camera and your iPod in your hotel room; think twice before wearing that new crimson top that might run or the T-shirt that gets transparent when wet; don't even bother with the waterproof gear the guidebooks tell you to bring. Just give the boat crew the kick they never tire of: take a soothingly tepid bath in the world's biggest open-air shower, the ominously named Devil's Throat, the most majestic of Iguazú's many cascades.

686 | Giving thanks to Gauchito Gil

ARGENTINA Argentines are a superstitious lot – taxi-drivers religiously garland their rear-view mirrors with rosaries; busmen faithfully display images of the Virgin over their dashboards; nearly everyone routinely tucks a banknote under their plate of gnocchi at the end of each month in the hope of better financial fortunes. But all this pales in comparison to their fervent dedication to the people's saint, Antonio – or "Gauchito" – Gil.

Blood-red monuments of all shapes and sizes punctuate roadsides throughout this vast country. Sometimes you'll see ragged crimson flags flapping from a tree. Others are more elaborate, with a figurine of the Gauchito in a shelter decorated with bunting, the waxy vestiges of vermilion candles and all manner of offerings.

Antonio Gil was essentially a nineteenth-century Robin Hood. One tale tells that he died from stab wounds in the 1870s along the highway near Mercedes. A cross, later known as the Curuchú Gil, was erected by the roadside and, so the legend goes, became a place of cult worship. In the mid-twentieth century, as part of the resistance to Argentina's military regime, folklore became a vehicle for progressive ideas. Building on literature that glorified the *gaucho* – the cowboy of the Pampas – but emphasizing his independent spirit, the resistance movement adopted Gauchito Gil as a hero. A new version of the story told how Gil, about to be executed by the military for an unknown crime, told his executioner that he would later find his son sick, but that he would be cured. This turned out to be true; many Argentines believe that he was a miraculous faith healer.

The national mega-shrine dedicated to Gauchito Gil stands a few kilometres west of the tradition-steeped Corrientes market town of Mercedes, up towards the northern border with Paraguay. It's almost a township, complete with shanty-style shacks, souvenir stalls and makeshift restaurants. At weekends people flock to pay tribute and leave a gift for their long-departed hero. Fortunes are told, *choripanes* (chorizo hotdogs) are munched and revellers dance to local *chamamé* folk music. It's clear that superstition, perhaps more than conventional religion, is alive and well in today's Argentina.

687 | Chasing condors in the Colca Canyon

PERU The rays of the morning sun begin to evaporate the mist that shrouds the depths of Peru's Colca Canyon. You've come out in the early hours to see the condor, or Andean vulture, in action, and as the mist dissipates, you can see hundreds of others have done the same. Many cluster at the mirador or Cruz del Condor. Others perch above pre-Inca terraces embedded into walls twice as deep as the Grand Canyon. Audacious visitors clamber to the rocks below to see the condor, but a short hike along the rim of the canyon allows for a viewpoint that is less precarious and just as private.

Wrapped up against the cold, you whisper excitedly and wait for the show to begin. Suddenly, a condor rises on the morning thermals, soaring like an acrobat – so close you think you could reach out and touch its giant charcoal wings. It scours the surroundings, swooping lower and then higher, then lower again, in a roller-coaster pursuit of food. Soon it is joined by another bird, and another, in a graceful airborne ballet.

Eventually, the birds abandon the audience in their hunt for sustenance, and the mirador becomes home to a less elusive species. Peruvian women, brightly dressed in multilayered skirts, squat on their haunches, hawking food, drinks and souvenirs – everything from woolly Andean hats to purses embroidered with the condor.

The panpipe sounds of *El Condor Pasa* are played so often in Peru that they become the theme tune for many trips. Simon and Garfunkel might have made the song famous with their cover version, but it's the eponymous bird that deserves a place in your Peruvian holiday.

688 | On the trail of Butch Cassidy and the Sundance Kid

BOLIVIA No one really knows how Butch Cassidy and the Sundance Kid spent their final days. Rumours still abound, enhanced by the 1969 Hollywood classic starring Paul Newman and Robert Redford. But this much is true: the outlaws pulled their last heist, stealing the $90,000 payroll of a mine company, in Bolivia. To pick up their trail, start in the easy-going southern Altiplano town of Tupiza, set in a lush valley that slices through striking desert. It was in the leafy main square that the gunslingers devised their plan to overtake the payroll transport, and locals can show you where they lived – in a house just behind the mansion of the mining family they were to rob. From there, take a scenic jeep tour 100km northwest to the dusty village of San Vicente, where Butch and Sundance, the military hot on their heels, sought shelter. It is here, according to the prevailing belief, that the pair met their end inside a simple adobe home after a gunfight with a small military patrol.

689 | Seeking heat in the Chapada Diamantina

BRAZIL If it weren't for the *forró* band playing in its tiny plaza, Lençóis, at the heart of Brazil's vast Parque Nacional da Chapada Diamantina, could be an outpost in the American Southwest. Then again, a cold *caipirinha* and a crispy chicken *picadinho* aren't so easily found in Arizona. The dry, rugged *sertão* of northeastern Brazil offers something unique: a Martian landscape of rifts and ridges, ideal for hiking or bouldering and dotted with modest but vibrant villages still scraping by since the days this area was mined for diamonds. Climb the 300m-high, vaguely camel-shaped mesa called Morro do Pai Inácio – named for a legendary lover who threw himself from its edge – or watch a stream make a similar plunge from the top of Cachoeira Glass, the country's tallest waterfall. When the sun reaches its apex, take cover in any of several grottoes that puncture the plain. Whatever you do, bring plenty of liquids, for the heat – like the otherworldy terrain – is mind-altering.

690 | Microbrews and beerfests in Blumenau

BRAZIL Lederhosen, oompah bands, sauerkraut, long blond plaits and foamy mugs of weissbier being quaffed by hordes of boozy beer drinkers are probably the last things you'd expect to find in Brazil, but Blumenau's Oktoberfest delivers all that authentic Munich madness and more. Held since 1984, usually over eighteen days in October, the biggest German festival in South America regularly attracts more than 500,000 revellers to its vast beer tents, folk dances, shooting matches and German singing contests.

Blumenau's German roots go deep. Picturesquely located on the banks of the Rio Itajaí, the town was founded in 1850 by Hamburger Dr Hermann Blumenau and a handful of mostly Pomeranian immigrants, enticed to settle in Brazil by the promise of fertile land and a balmy, subtropical climate – as late as the 1920s, two-thirds of the population spoke German as their first language. That changed after World War II, but Blumenau still retains aspects of its Teutonic past, most notably when it comes to beer.

Blumenau's microbreweries have blossomed in the last ten years, with several top-notch beer makers adhering to the Reinheitsgebot (the German beer purity law that has been regulating ingredients since 1487) and offering tours and tastes within easy reach of the city centre. The most successful has been Cervejaria Eisenbahn, which produces fourteen kinds of beer, including "Lust", made by the same method that's used to create French champagne.

Sample it at the *Bar da Fábrica* at the Eisenbahn brewery; they'll even drive you back to your hotel for free. Tours of the factory are also available if arranged in advance. Competitor Cervejaria Bierland offers a range of German but also Belgian- and North American-style ales, while relative newcomer Cervejaria Wunder Bier knocks out a tasty range of artisanal weizen, pilsen, and even wein bier ("wine beer", where red wine grapes are added during the brewing process). You can visit the factory and sample the suds in their tap room – inevitably dubbed the *Wunder Bar*.

691 | Taking a ringside seat at the Península Valdés

ARGENTINA "SHWOCK!" Or should that be "SHWAP!"? It's difficult to pin down precisely the slapping sound that emanates when six tonnes of blubbery wet flesh collides, but while you are still working out if perhaps it actually isn't more of a "SHWACK!" than either, the two huge bull elephant seals thunder together again, sending gallons of sea water flying in their titanic battle.

The object of their affection, a fertile female with a twinkle in her coal-black eyes, has spent the last twenty minutes preening her coat to the height of seductive softness but is now far more concerned with keeping her month-old pup well clear of the thriving mass.

This is October on the Península Valdés, a scrubby blob of land clinging to the side of Argentina's Atlantic coast that, other than being the only continental breeding ground for southern elephant seals, also happens to be one of the world's most significant marine reserves. The strip of sand on which the seals try proving their prowess is also crammed with some of the area's 20,000-strong sea lion population.

Along the coast, a colony of Magellanic penguins have pocked the rugged hillside with their burrows, coming ashore each afternoon to make their comical but arduous waddle up the hill and home, while up to half of the world's southern right whales frolic in the peninsula's sheltered waters.

At the shingle spits of Caleta Valdés, and around wild Punta Norte, further up the coast, the sight of ominous black dorsal fins cruising just offshore is the precursor for one of nature's most incredible sights: killer whales storming the shingle banks, beaching themselves at up to 50km/hr in an attempt to snap up a baby sea lion or young elephant seal.

Back at the beach, though, mother and pup are still dodging the fighting fatties. Behind them both – and both as impressed with her perfect pelt – two more gigantic males square up, clashing with such force that the sand shakes. And this time, there's no doubt that it's a "SHWACK!"…

692 | The frenzy of Boi Bumba

BRAZIL One of South America's greatest parties, Boi Bumba is a riot of colour, dancing, pageantry and parades on Parintins Island, deep in the Amazonian jungle, and as remote as any major festival, even in Brazil, gets – if you don't fly, it's a two-day boat journey from "nearby" Manaus. Surrounded by more than 1000km of rainforest on all sides, the isolated location is key to making the festival special. Whereas party-goers in Rio or Salvador gather for the parades and disperse anonymously into the city afterwards, in Parintins the sixty-thousand-plus crowd is contained by the Amazon itself – over the three-day frenzy, the festival becomes a private party of familiar faces and dancing bodies.

The origins of the event, which takes place every June, lie in the northeastern Bumba Meu Boi festival (it was introduced to Parintins by emigrants from the state of Maranhão), telling the story of Pai Francisco, his wife Mae Catarina and their theft of a prize bull from

a wealthy landowner. But it tells it on a huge scale, in a purpose-built forty-thousand-seat stadium called the Bumbódromo. Here, two competing teams, Caprichoso and Garantido, parade a series of vast floats made up of giant statues and animal heads, some 30m tall. Serpents, jaguars, macaws and other rainforest creatures switch places like actors in a play, wheeled on by troupes dressed in traditional costumes and surrounded by one-hundred-strong drum orchestras and scores of scantily clad dancers.

Against this spectacular backdrop, a whole host of characters tell the story, led by the beautiful feminine spirit of the rainforest, the Cunhã-Poranga, and a shaman, both of whom emerge in a burst of fireworks from the mouth of a serpent or jaguar on the most extravagant and dramatic of the floats. Fans of each group are fiercely partisan and roar their encouragement from the stadium stands throughout.

693

Summiting at sunrise on Volcán Cotopaxi

ECUADOR A shard of sunlight cracks open the horizon, spilling crimson into the sky and across the last icy crest, glittering like a crown of diamonds above you. Your exhausted legs can barely lift your snow-encrusted boots and the crampons that stubbornly grip the ice, but you're almost at the top. Gasping in the thin air, you haul yourself from the chilly shadow of night into the daylight. As the sun bursts across your face, a spectacular dawn spreads out before you.

The perfect cone of Volcán Cotopaxi, regarded by early explorer Alexander von Humboldt as "the most beautiful and regular of all the colossal peaks in the high Andes", at 5897m is one of the highest and most magnificent active volcanoes in the world. From the refuge at 4800m, tucked just below a girdle of ice and snow encircling the peak, it's around seven gruelling hours to the summit on a route that picks its way between gaping crevasses and fragile seracs, over ladders and up vertical ice. For some it's just as well that much of this steep climb is done unseen at night; hopefuls must rouse themselves from a fitful and breathless slumber at midnight to climb before the heat of the day makes the glacier unstable.

The payback is arriving at the summit just as the sun rises, when you're treated to mind-blowing views of Cotopaxi's yawning crater, the giant peaks of the Andes in the distance, and through the clouds, glimpses of Quito sleeping far below.

694 | Celebrate Qoyllur Riti

PERU Most visitors to the ancient Inca capital of Cusco in southern Peru are drawn by the extraordinary ruined temples and palaces and the dramatic scenery of the high Andes. But the only true way to get to the heart of the indigenous Andean culture is to join a traditional *fiesta*. Nearly every town and village in the region engages in these raucous and chaotic celebrations, a window on a secret world that has survived centuries of oppression.

Of all the *fiestas*, the most extraordinary and spectacular is Qoyllur Riti, held at an extremely high altitude in a remote Andean valley to the south of Cusco. Here you can join tens of thousands of indigenous pilgrims, both Quechua and Aymara, as they trek up to a campsite at the foot of a glacier to celebrate the reappearance of the Pleiades constellation in the southern sky – a phenomenon that has long been used to predict when crops should be planted.

At the heart of the *fiesta* are young men dressed in ritual costumes of the Ukuku, a half-man, half-bear trickster hero from Andean mythology, and if you're hardy enough, you can join them as they climb even higher to spend the night singing, dancing and engaging in ritual combat on the glacier itself. Be warned, though, that this is an extreme celebration. Some years, pilgrims have died during the night, having frozen or fallen into crevasses, and when the pilgrim-celebrants descend from the mountain at first light, waving flags and toting blocks of ice on their backs, they bear the bodies, the blood sacrifice at once mourned and celebrated as vital to the success of the agricultural year ahead.

695 | Head to the end of the Earth at Cape Horn

ARGENTINA & CHILE Patagonia is a fabled wilderness, a windswept land of towering mountains, water channels and grassy plains. The region has always appealed to a certain, hardy kind of traveller, and the huge archipelago at its foot – Tierra del Fuego, divided between Chile and Argentina – is quintessential Patagonia in its remote, raw beauty.

It's not a straightforward place to visit under your own steam, but on an expedition cruise from Punta Arenas in Chile to Ushuaia in Argentina you'll get rare views of the peak-ringed bays, glacier-fed waterways and birdlife-rich islands that lured everyone from Francis Drake to Charles Darwin. Here you will find the fabled Straits of Magellan, the Beagle Channel and Wulaia Bay – the mountain-flanked natural harbour where HMS *Beagle* controversially abducted three native children for "education" back in Britain. Best known of all, however, is the gust-blown island that marks Tierra del Fuego's southernmost tip: Horn Island, home to the sloping headland of Cape Horn and sitting some 120km from the nearest settlement of note. Notorious among seafarers, it has been the site of some eight hundred shipwrecks over the ages, largely due to the savage, swirling currents offshore; today, when conditions are favourable (on around 70 percent of sailings), you can disembark and explore the legendary island yourself.

It's a strange sensation standing on the planet's last belch of land before Antarctica and watching the Atlantic meet the Pacific in a pitch and toss of waves and wind. A striking albatross-shaped memorial to stricken vessels pays tribute to the mariners of the past and the perils they faced when rounding the cape. Today the island serves as home to a lighthouse and a tiny church, and is manned at any one time only by a Chilean naval officer who, having been vetted for mental and physical fortitude, serves a twelve-month posting with family before handing the baton on to a colleague. It is, quite literally, one of the world's wildest jobs.

696 | Coming face to face with jaguars

PARAGUAY A maze of waterways wiggles like capillaries through some 210,000 square kilometres of flat, tropical wetlands called the Pantanal – the largest of its kind in the world. It falls mostly into Brazilian territory, but knows no boundaries, crossing into Bolivia and Paraguay. Neither do its rivers, which burst in the rainy season, absorbing this bucolic landscape into a deluge six metres in height.

Vast swathes have been lost to dust and cattle ranches, but conservationists are keeping these intruders at bay. Its pristine lands have the highest concentration of wildlife in South America, with 650 species of bird, plus eighty mammals, including the "big three": the giant anteater, giant armadillo and giant otter. It is after these animals that the 15,000-hectare reserve and lodge in the Paraguayan Pantanal, *Tres Gigantes*, is named.

You arrive by speedboat along the Río Negro. Chasing you upriver are the throaty groans of yacare caiman, camouflaged on thick, buoyant islands of aguapé that obstruct the boat's passage. Along the banks, jabiru storks with thick, crimson throats throw themselves precariously into the air seconds before you pass.

A simple lodge is your base. Every morning, you awake to a dawn chorus issued from the branches of the 10m-high wax palms lining the riverbank, where shrill monk parakeets are joined in bass by howler monkeys' guttural roars.

The reserve's rangers are facilitators, not guides, and so you are left to your own devices – and, in dry season, to wander the Pantanal alone. Three short trails for this purpose have been hacked into the dense, low undergrowth surrounding the lodge. Your first steps along them are tentative, apprehensive; the quiet is unsettling. But you're quickly joined by a rare rufous nightjar that flits in front of you like a dappled shadow, before a curious family of dusky titi monkeys peer at you from the canopy above.

You hope that the trails will lead you to the beasts that leave tantalizing footprints in the mud of a nearby waterhole, that every step brings you closer to the fleeting swish of a jaguar's black and golden tail. Very soon, this stark wilderness begins to feel hospitable, unthreatening – although you don't realise this until the choked laughter of the caiman sends you back on your way downriver.

Visiting the last Panama hat weavers

697

ECUADOR Panama hats, as any Ecuadorean worth their salt will tell you, don't come from Panama. Authentic Panamas – or *sombreros de paja toquilla*, as they call them locally – are only woven in the Andean country, from the straw of the toquilla plant, which grows in the swamps near Ecuador's central coast. The origin of the misnomer comes from the hat's widespread use by the workers who built the Panama Canal from 1904 to 1914. Toquilla hats have been woven in Ecuador for at least five hundred years, but in the face of cheap Chinese competition, lower demand and the massive emigration of young Ecuadoreans, the traditionally woven Panama is now an endangered species.

It's well worth seeking out the last few artisans who create the very best *superfinos*. Most tourists on the trail go to Cuenca, a weaving centre in the southern highlands. A better option is to head west to Montecristi, which is to Panama-hat lovers what Havana is to cigar aficionados. It's no showroom: the dust-and-concrete town is an inauspicious centre for the production of some of the most expensive headgear in the world. But ask around for a local *comisionista* (middlemen who travel around villages and buy hats from weavers) and arrange a trip to meet the weavers in nearby villages such as Pile.

The time to arrive is just after dawn, when the light is atmospheric and the heat and humidity are perfect for weaving. The contrast between the beautiful hats – the finest of which are woven so tightly they look like off-white cotton – and the conditions in which they are produced is stark. The weavers, who spend up to four months weaving each hat, live in ragged red-brick dwellings with rusting corrugated-iron roofs, linked by degraded dirt streets patrolled by strutting chickens and shuffling pigs. Be sure to visit the straw-cutters, too, and accompany them on a hike to see the plants growing. The more you see of the hats and the weavers, the better equipped you'll be to buy your own.

Watching a football match

698

ARGENTINA & BRAZIL Few sporting events rival the raucous spectacle of a football match in South America, from a small, local but enthusiastically supported game in the Andes to a clash of the titans in one of the great cathedrals of the sport in Brazil or Argentina. Even those who can't tell a goal kick from a penalty kick won't fail to be impressed by the colour and passion – both on the pitch and in the stands.

Fans of the sport can look forward to fast, attacking football, individual star turns, lots of goals (especially in the Brazilian league; things tend to be tighter in Argentina), red cards aplenty and quite possibly a pitch invasion.

The bigger the team, the bigger the stadium, and the louder the roar of the crowd. Choose Rio's Maracanã, one of the world's largest, São Paulo's Art Deco Pacaembú, or Buenos Aires's Bombonera ("chocolate box", for its shape) for a full-on assault of the senses – particularly if you time your visit for a local derby such as São Paulo v Corinthians or Boca Juniors v River Plate.

As well as their teams' jersey, fans will go armed with ticker tape, flags, flares, horns and drums. Don't be surprised if you can hardly see the players through the resulting clouds of red, blue or yellow. You certainly won't be able to miss the supporters' loud and decidedly colourful singing before, during and after the match, whether their team wins or loses, accompanied by entire brass bands and battalions of drummers. The frenetic, all-standing terraces (*popular* in Argentina, *geral* in Brazil) are the noisiest part of the stands, but first-time attendees are advised to head to the relative calm of the seating area (*platea* or *arquibancada* respectively). After a big game, follow the (winning) crowds to the boisterous after-match street parties.

699 | Tackling the Fitz Roy massif

ARGENTINA From the sandstone canyons of La Rioja to the granite peaks of Patagonia, Argentina's superb network of national parks form the backdrop to some of the continent's most diverse trekking. Most visitors, however, head south to the Andes, and the legendary Parque Nacional Los Glaciares, the northernmost section of which – the Fitz Roy massif – contains some of the most breathtakingly beautiful mountains on the planet.

At the centre of the massif, puncturing the wide Patagonian sky, is the 3405m incisor of Monte Fitz Roy, known to the native Tehuelche as El Chaltén, "The Mountain that Smokes", in reference to the wisps of cloud that almost continually drape from its summit. Alongside Fitz Roy rise Cerro Poincenot and Aguja Saint-Exupéry, while set back from them is the forbidding needle of Cerro Torre, a crooked finger standing in bold defiance of all the elements that the Hielo Continental Sur, the immense icecap that lurks behind the massif, can hurl at it. A series of excellent trails crisscross the massif, several of which can be combined into the Monte Fitz Roy/ Cerro Torre Loop, a three-day jaunt done under the perpetual shadow of these imposing peaks.

700 | Birdwatch and be watched

SURINAME The strap of your binoculars chafes the back of your neck and the mosquitoes, constant companions in this nature reserve, form a pesky aura around your head. Yet you can't tear yourself away from what's locked in your sight: a flock of bright orange cocks-of-the-rock stripping a tree of Suriname cherries. A flurry of feathers to your left signals the arrival of a pair of sparrow-sized antbirds. They peer intently at your hiking boots, which are parked right in the marching path of their black, crawling prey. Leaving the little feasters to their work, you press deeper into the jungle until you're stopped dead by the piercing "whee-oo!" of an ornate hawk-eagle. With the discreetness of an Apache helicopter it lands on a branch and seizes you in its fierce glower – you must have ventured too near its nest. It's a funny thing they call it birdwatching, when you're so often the one being watched.

701 | Chowing down on churrasco in Porto Alegre

BRAZIL The state of Rio Grande do Sul is at the heart of Brazil's *gaucho* (cowboy) culture. No surprise, then, that this is also the home of *churrasco*, the sumptuous Brazilian barbecue tradition that involves a mind-boggling array of dino-sized steaks, chicken hearts, juicy sausages and crispy chicken legs grilled to perfection over wood or charcoal. Brazilians typically visit *churrascarias* to indulge in a gut-busting *rodízio*; waiters glide around the restaurant, slicing meats directly onto your plate until you can eat no more. The booming state capital of Porto Alegre is famed for its *churrascarias*, with *Gambrinus*, founded back in 1889 inside the elegant Mercado Público, one of the grandest. Connoisseurs prefer *Na Brasa*, a swish, modern place, though for atmosphere it's hard to beat *Galpão Crioulo*, a rustic barn-like space with a bewildering selection of meats, foot-tapping *gaucho* music and traditional dance performances most evenings.

702 | Traversing the Salar de Uyuni

BOLIVIA Driving across the immaculate white expanse of the Salar de Uyuni, you'd think you were on another planet, so alien and inhospitable is the terrain. Some 3650m above sea level in the remote Andes of southwest Bolivia, the Salar is the largest salt flat in the world, a brilliantly white and perfectly flat desert that stretches over 10,000 square kilometres.

In some places the salt is over 120m deep, saturated with water, its thick surface crust patterned with strange polygons of raised salt crystals that add to the unearthly feel. When dry, the salt shines with such intensity you'll find yourself reaching down to check that it's not ice or snow. After a heavy rainfall, meanwhile, the Salar transforms into an immense mirror, reflecting the sky and the surrounding snowcapped peaks so pristinely that at times the horizon disappears and the mountains seem like islands floating in the sky. The best views are from Isla del Pescado, a rocky island at the centre of the Salar that's home to an extraordinary array of giant cacti that somehow manage to thrive in this harsh saline environment.

To appreciate the scale and surreal beauty of the landscape, it's worth taking the full four-day tour, travelling right across the Salar in a 4WD and sleeping in rudimentary huts and shelters on the shores of the lake; you can even stay in a hotel made entirely from salt. These trips also take in the Eduardo Abaroa Andean Fauna National Reserve, south of the Salar, a windswept region of high-altitude deserts, ice-bound volcanoes and mineral-stained lakes where you can see an unlikely variety of wildlife, including flocks of flamingoes and herds of vicuña, the delicate and rare relative of the llama.

703 | Thermal springs and the devil's poncho: a Patagonian odyssey

CHILE The Carretera Austral – Chile's Southern Highway – begins nowhere and leads nowhere. Over 1000km in length, it was hewn and blasted through the wettest, greenest and narrowest part of the country. This sliver of Patagonia is a majestic land of snowcapped volcanoes, Ice Age glaciers, emerald fjords, turquoise lakes and jade-coloured rivers, set among lush temperate forest where giant trees seem to drip with rain the whole year long. The Carretera was built with the very purpose of settling this damp, secluded sliver of territory, but the only way to reach it from the rest of Chile is by boat or plane or overland from Argentina. Few roads can feel more remote.

Although some rickety buses ply the route, they are irregular, unreliable and can't take you everywhere you'll want to go. It's far more rewarding to rent a 4WD pick-up truck, pack a can of fuel and plentiful supplies and drive yourself. The slippery, loose-gravel surface demands the utmost respect, so don't expect to average more than 50km/hr. As the locals will tell you: hereabouts, if you hurry, you never arrive! Lashing rain, gales and passing vehicles – albeit few and far between – are the only likely hazards.

The pleasures, however, are many and varied: make pit stops to wallow in the thermal springs at Cahuelmó after the bone-rattling ride, enjoy the warm hospitality and delicious cakes at *Casa Ludwig* in Puyuhuapi, or feast on roast Patagonian lamb by the fireside at *El Reloj* in Coyhaique. Most of the route affords fantastic views of the Andean cordillera, and along the way you'll see dense groves of southern beech and immense lakes like miniature seas, as well as the amazing "hanging glacier" in the Parque Nacional Queulat and the Capilla de Mármol, a magical grotto carved into the blue and white limestone cliffs looming from Lago Carrera. But the best bit is the feeling of driving through utterly virgin lands – especially the southernmost stretch that leads to pioneering Villa O'Higgins, completed only in 2002. The road seems to fly over the barren crags to the place where, according to local legend, the devil left his poncho.

704 | Catching a launch at the Centre Spatial Guyanais

FRENCH GUIANA Completed in 1968, the Centre Spatial Guyanais (CSG) could form the backdrop to countless Bond films. Rocket launch towers, futuristic silos and other state-of-the-art technology poke out above the trees in the rainforest surrounding Kourou. Once a quiet, nondescript village in the French overseas *département* – and former penal colony – of Guyane (French Guiana), it was discovered that Kourou was the only place in the world where both polar and equatorial synchronous orbits could be achieved. Over the course of a few years, French Guiana was transformed from a Hell-on-Earth for France's hapless convicts (the penal colony was finally abolished in 1947) to the centre of the European Space Agency's satellite-launching operations.

Nowadays Kourou is bustling with technicians in jumpsuits scurrying about with clipboards in hand, and occasionally the French Foreign Legion patrols the perimeters, protecting the CSG from spies and other such threats. This isolated, surreal and, it must be said, slightly sinister space centre in the jungle outdoes anything that NASA's Florida-based Kennedy Space Center has to offer, at least as far as sci-fi-fantasy-meets-reality is concerned. *Ariane 5* rockets have been blasting off from the CSG since 1996, carrying payloads consisting mainly of satellites.

Launches take place in the early evening, just after the sun has set and the enigmatic, nocturnal sounds of the rainforest draw attention to the eerie coexistence of extreme technology and extreme nature. Hundreds, sometimes thousands, of people gather to watch lift-off. With an almighty roar, the rocket lifts into the sky, leaving a great plume of white smoke and a blinding sheet of fire in its wake that lights up the trees and warms the faces of the starry-eyed onlookers.

ARGENTINA When it first emerged in the city's brothels and slums sometime in the 1890s, the world's sexiest ballroom dance, the tango, horrified the genteel residents of Buenos Aires.

Some of the city's more liberal-minded upper-class youths fell in love with tango, though, and brought it to Paris, where the dance's characteristic haunting melodies, seductive gazes and split skirts took the capital of passion by storm. By the 1910s tango's popularity had gone global, but Buenos Aires was and remains the spiritual and professional home of both the music form and dance.

If you want to keep a low profile, head to a tango show where you can enjoy being a spectator. Aimed squarely at tourists, these events are glitzy, polished, expensive affairs where the dance is performed on stage by professionals. More earthy and authentic – and worth seeking out – are the *milongas*, or tango gatherings, where everyone takes part. These range from stately mid-afternoon affairs in the city's exquisite Art Deco tea salons to smoky, late-night events behind unmarked doors deep in the suburbs and youthful tango-meets-techno *milongas* in the city's trendy districts. Be sure to check out the hip Parakultural events in Palermo.

For those who want to take part, some *milongas* are preceded by a tango lesson – you'll need several of these, and, if you're a woman, a killer pair of heels before you can master the basics of the fairly complex dance. It's also perfectly acceptable to turn up, albeit smartly dressed, and simply enjoy the music while watching the dancers glide with apparent ease across the floor. Beware, though: the music and the locals may have you under their spell – and in their arms – faster than you may have anticipated.

Swept off your feet in Buenos Aires

COLOMBIA The great riches that flowed through Cartagena during colonial times must have made the pirates and privateers that roamed the Caribbean salivate. Founded nearly five centuries ago as Cartagena de Indias – the Carthage of the Indies – this was one of the most strategically vital points in the Spanish empire. It was here that the galleon fleets would gather before making the perilous return journey to Spain, their holds laden with the gold and silver looted from the great civilizations of the Americas. Here, too, was the empire's main slave market, a clearing-house for the ill-fated Africans whose blood and sweat underwrote the entire colonial venture.

Though the Spanish have long since departed, Cartagena's colonial heritage is inescapable. The narrow, winding streets of the old walled city are still lined with grand mansions painted in the vibrant pastel hues of the Caribbean, with overhanging balconies draped in flowers and arched doorways that lead into cool courtyard gardens. Its nightclubs and rum shops pulsate with salsa, *cumbia* and reggaeton – African rhythms little changed from those brought over in the first slave ships. As you wander down these almost fantastical, decaying streets, it's easy to understand how this city inspired Colombia's greatest author, Gabriel García Márquez, to create his masterpieces of magical realism.

Stop for a coffee in the rundown artisans' neighbourhood of Getsemani, or cool off with a freshly blended tropical fruit juice by the docks, and you could be rubbing shoulders with Marxist guerrillas plotting against the government, cocaine traffickers planning their next shipment, emerald smugglers cutting a deal or just a local hustler cooking up his latest scam. In the country of dreams, as the locals call it, anything is possible.

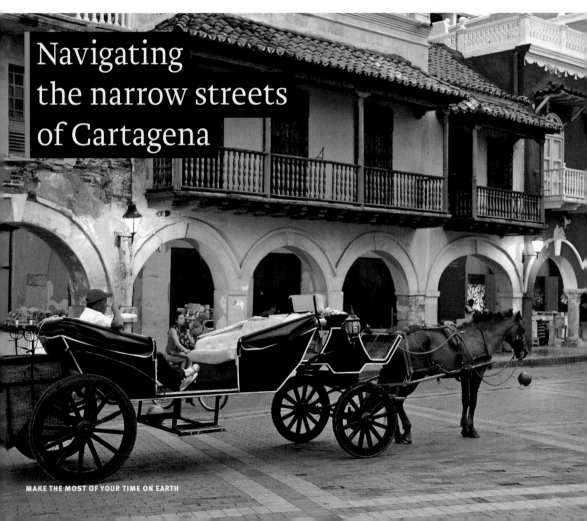

Navigating the narrow streets of Cartagena

707 | Going downhill in the Andes

ARGENTINA Skip the beach this year. Instead, embrace winter in July and get a tan on the sunny slopes of the Andes in the middle of Argentina's Lake District at Bariloche, a laconic town turned major South American skiing destination. Surrounded by spectacular forests, pristine rivers and lakes, rift valleys and towering alpine peaks, and with average seasonal temperatures around 4°C, it's no wonder that this is prime ski country for South Americans. Luckily, since the rest of the world hasn't quite caught on, you won't spend a fortune on rentals and lift tickets, or wait a lifetime in line.

Start by hitting the slopes at Cerro Catedral, the oldest, largest and most developed ski resort in South America, which features a vertical drop of 1070m and over 100km of marked trails, gullies and chutes – the longest run is 6.5km long – to say nothing of the off-piste possibilities, with backcountry riding that can rival anything in the French Alps or Colorado. Skiing is a lot less common in South America than elsewhere in the world, and mid-level skiers will find themselves in plenty of good company here. On the other hand, if you're a superstar on the snow, the more challenging pistes are much less crowded and yours for the shredding.

Unlike the massive resorts of US and European ski centres, Argentina's mountain destinations are decidedly more low-key in terms of their sprawl, though don't think for a moment that this means there is less going on. Argentines are well known for their indulgence in the refined institution of après-ski, and Bariloche's off-slope adventures include dozens of discos, casinos and wine bars, with ample restaurants for savouring Argentina's scrumptious cuisine. After all, what would a week (a month? an entire season?) on the slopes be without exploring the excellent winter nightlife?

708 | Show no restraint in Rio

BRAZIL Brazil might not have a monopoly on exhibitionism, but it comes pretty damn close. There's no other country on the planet where the unbridled pursuit of pleasure is such a national obsession, transcending race, class and religion. Brazilian bacchanal reaches its apogee during Carnaval, when the entire country enters a collective state of alcohol-fuelled frenzy.

Rio is home to the most glitzy and outrageous celebration of them all, an X-rated theatre of the absurd and the greatest spectacle of flesh, fetish and fantasy you are ever likely to see. For this five-day blowout before Lent the streets of the Cidade Maravilhosa are overrun with Amazonian-sized plumed headdresses, enormous floppy carrots, cavorting frogs, drag queens and head-to-toe gilded supermodels clad in impossibly tiny tassels, sequins and strategically applied body paint, challenging the ban on complete nudity.

The centrepiece of Carnaval is the parade of the samba schools (a neighbourhood association, there's nothing academic about it) down the kilometre-long parade strip of the colossal Sambódromo (a specially constructed parade stadium). Samba schools often hail from the poorest communities and spend nearly the entire year preparing a flamboyant allegory of their chosen theme, which is dramatized through a highly choreographed display of impassioned songs, wild dances, gigantic papier-mâché figures, lavish costumes and pulsating percussion.

It doesn't take long for such organized celebrations to erupt with infectious delirium as the whole city voraciously indulges in sensual pleasure at every turn – Rio's denizens, also known as *cariocas*, have never been known for their temperance. The neighbourhood *blocos*, or parades, are the most accessible, authentic and impromptu way to immerse yourself in the city's sexually charged atmosphere. This is a freewheeling fantasy land in which trucks are converted to moving stage sets with bands and loudspeakers and anything goes. Even the most rigid of hips will gyrate freely as the night unravels.

709 | Enjoying isolation at the Puyuhuapi Lodge

CHILE It can take you days to reach the *Puyuhuapi Lodge* – but then getting there is all part of the fun. One of the most remote hideaways in the world, the luxurious lodge-cum-spa sits halfway down Chile's Carretera Austral, or "Southern Highway", a 1000km, mostly unpaved road that threads its way through a pristine wilderness of soaring mountains, Ice Age glaciers, turquoise fjords and lush temperate rainforest. The most exciting way to travel down it is to rent a 4WD – you'll rarely get above 30km/hr, but with scenery like this, who cares?

Separated from the *carretera* by a shimmering fjord, the lodge is unreachable by land. Instead, a little motor launch will whisk you across in ten minutes. It's hard to imagine a more romantic way to arrive, especially during one of the frequent downpours that plague the region, when guests are met off the boat by dapper young porters carrying enormous white umbrellas.

The hotel is made up of a series of beautifully designed low-lying buildings, constructed from local timber with lots of glass, that blend in handsomely with their surroundings. Having come quite so far to get here it would be a shame not to splash out on one of the shoreside rooms, with their mesmerizing views across the fjord. Inside, it's all understated luxury: flickering log fires, bare wooden floors, sofas to sink into, light streaming in from all directions.

You can take to the wilderness in a number of ways: go sea-kayaking (with dolphins, if you're lucky); learn to fly-fish in rivers packed with trout and salmon; take a hike through the rainforest to a nearby glacier. And afterwards soak your bones in the hotel's *raison d'être*, its steaming hot springs, channelled into three fabulous outdoor pools – two of them right on the edge of the fjord, the other (the hottest of all) enclosed by overhanging ferns. Lying here at night, gazing at the millions of stars above, you'd think that you were in heaven. And really, you'd be right.

Exploring Colonia del Sacramento by scooter

URUGUAY Perched on a peninsula at the confluence of the Río Uruguay and Río del Plata, Colonia del Sacramento is perhaps the most picturesque town in all of Uruguay. One of the best ways to explore it is by scooter, zipping past the brightly coloured homes, tiny bars and craft stores that line the perfectly preserved maze of cobblestone streets in the Barrio Histórico. Cut through the lovely Plaza Mayor, where parakeets screech in the trees, and head for the town's lighthouse, El Faro, which sits next to the ruins of a former convent. Take a break from your scooter here, and ascend to the top of this still-operating beacon to see a stunning panorama of the surrounding city and shoreline. Be sure to make it down before dusk, though, as you'll want to head to the sloping Calle de los Suspiros (Street of Sighs) to watch the sun sink slowly into the silver water of the rivers – the street has some of the best views of sunset in the city.

711 | Hear gaucho tales in the beastly Pantanal

BRAZIL Weary travellers twist in their hammocks as the sun rises; no one has slept much. All night long, the small campsite glade has resounded with the noise of snuffling, snorting and bashing through the undergrowth, broken only by a hideous high-pitched yelling and the sound of thrashing in the water. And then, the deafening squawking of the dawn chorus.

"The snuffling?" says one of the *gaucho*-cum-guides over *cafezinho* and toast. "That's the peccaries. It's normal." And the thrashing in the water? "Ah, you were lucky. That was an anaconda killing a cow in the stream over there." The stream the group waded through last night on a so-called torchlit adventure? "Yes." And the birds? "Parrots – possibly. Parakeets. Or toucans. Storks. Roseate spoonbills. Kingfishers. Snowy egrets. Red-crested cardinals . . ."

Some 650 species of bird inhabit the Pantanal, the world's largest freshwater wetland, alongside 3500 plant species, 250 types of fish, 110 kinds of mammal and 50 different reptiles. And when the waters of the Paraguay River recede in April, its grassy plains resemble nothing other than a vast, cageless zoo. Caimans, capybaras and giant otters wallow in the murky lagoons and rivers, jaguars and ocelots prowl the long grass, armadillos and anteaters forage for insects. And eight million cows graze.

The *gauchos* who roam the Pantanal on horseback comprise most of its human population, and make the most knowledgeable guides. They'll track down flocks of magnificent hyacinth macaws, roosting in trees and preening their violet feathers. They'll wrestle a crocodile out of the water for close-up viewing or point out the jabiru stork, as tall as a man, picking its way around the edge of a lily-choked pond. And in the evening they'll invite their visitors to sit round a blazing fire while they play accordions, pass round *yerba maté* and tell tales of life on the plains of the Pantanal.

712 | Tapati: fun and games on Easter Island

CHILE Rapa Nui – Easter Island – is shrouded in mystery. How did its people get there? Where did they come from? How did they move those gigantic statues? Some of that enigma comes to life during January's fortnight-long Tapati, a festival that combines ancient customs, such as carving and canoeing, with modern sports, such as the triathlon and horse racing.

First, the islanders form two competing teams, representing the age-old clans, so if you want to participate, it's best to get to know one of the captains. The opening ceremony kicks off with Umu Tahu, a massive barbecue, followed by a parade of would-be carnival queens wearing traditional grass skirts.

Most of the sports events are for men only: one breathtaking highlight is the bareback horse race along Vaihu Beach. If you fancy your chances against the proud locals, be prepared to wear little more than a bandana, a skimpy sarong and copious body paint. Another event, staged in the majestic crater at Rano Raraku, has contestants – including the odd tourist – paddling across the lake in reed canoes, running round the muddy banks carrying two handfuls of bananas and finally swimming across, with huge crowds cheering them on.

Meanwhile, the women compete to weave the best basket, craft the most elegant shell necklace or produce the finest grass skirt; visitors are welcome to participate. Little girls and venerable matriarchs alike play leading roles in the after-dark singing and dancing contests. They croon and sway through the night until the judges declare the winning team, usually around daybreak.

But the true climax is Haka Pei, in which three-dozen foolhardy athletes slide down the steep slopes of Maunga Pu'i Hill – lying on banana trunks. Top speeds reach 80km/hr, total chaos reigns and usually a limb or two is broken, but the crowds love it. Should they ask you to take part, learn two vital Rapa Nui words: "mauru uru", "no thanks".

713 | Life on the quiet side: homestays on Lake Titicaca

PERU Set against a backdrop of desert mountains, the shimmering waters of Lake Titicaca have formed the heart of Peru's highland Altiplano civilizations since ancient times, nourishing the Pukara, Tiawanaku and Colla peoples, whose enigmatic ruins still dot the shoreline. More than seventy of Titicaca's scattered islands remain inhabited, among them the famous *islas flotantes*, floating islands created centuries ago from compacted reedbeds by the Uros Indians.

In recent decades, such attractions have made the lake one of Peru's top visitor destinations; as a consequence, only in the most remote corners can you still encounter traditional settlements that aren't overrun with camera-toting outsiders.

Yet merely by visiting such isolated places, aren't travellers running the risk of eroding the very ways of life they've come to see? Not in distant Anapia, a cluster of five tiny islets near the border with Bolivia, whose ethnic Aymara residents – descendants of the Altiplano's original inhabitants – make a living from subsistence agriculture and fishing, maintaining their own music, dance, costume and weaving traditions.

A group of Anapian families have got together to create their own homestay scheme. Each takes it in turn to host visitors, in the same way they've traditionally rotated grazing rights. Accommodation is simple, but clean and warm: you get your own room and bathroom but share meals with the host family on tables spread with brightly coloured homespun cloth. Potatoes are the staple, and if you're lucky they'll be prepared *huatia*-style, baked in an earth oven with fresh fish and herbs from the lake shore.

Walking, fishing, sailing and rowing trips fill your time. Your hosts can also take you to the uninhabited island of Vipisque, where the Aymara rear vicuñas – small, cinnamon-coloured cousins of the alpaca, prized for their fine wool. From the hilltop at the island's centre, the view extends across Lake Titicaca to the icy peaks of Bolivia's Cordillera Real – one of South America's most magnificent panoramas.

Capoeira up close

714

BRAZIL There's not meant to be any physical contact in this age-old, ritualistic melding of martial arts and breakdancing. Your instructor probably explained that, though unless you happen to speak Portuguese you probably didn't understand (and if you did, would you trust it to be true?). But you're ready to give it a whirl; who knows, you may even get to sing or play an instrument to help keep the beat – tambourine, drum, some kind of gourd with strung beads. Probably not the *berimbau*, a stringed bow struck while positioned against your stomach; that looks more difficult. In fact, it all looks difficult: how can the dancer-combatants fly and spin with such grace, spending as much time on their hands and airborne as on their feet? Maybe you should just passively observe, or head back to any number of street corners in Salvador, where *capoeiristas* cartwheel and kick encircled by onlookers. And save your own handstand prowess for another day.

715 | Going to church in Chiloé

CHILE Never mind that just a short flight or a thirty-minute ferry ride separates Isla Grande from mainland Chile. You sense it with your first step onto the principal island of the Chiloé archipelago: this is a land wholly unto its own. Though centuries-old legends of trolls and witches haunting its forests and secluded coves still linger, there's more to Chiloé's identity than mythical underpinnings. With its rural way of life and sleepy fishing villages of *palafitos* – wooden houses built on stilts above the sea – it's often regarded as a curiosity even among Chileans, but there's no better way to get to know Chiloé than by going to church.

Over 150 reverently maintained eighteenth- and nineteenth-century timber churches dot the islands, with the greatest concentration on Isla Grande. Start your journey in the north at Ancud, where the red- and orange-tiled Iglesia Pio X makes for an excellent introduction to the distinctive style – bold colours, arched porticoes and striking hexagonal bell towers – first created by Jesuit missionaries and the local indigenous population and later enhanced by Franciscan monks. As you make your way south, you'll pass delicate roadside shrines and quiet side roads that lead to solitary churches standing in an open field or presiding over breezy plazas. Though few of these aspire to the grandiose design of the yellow and eggshell blue of Iglesia San Francisco in Castro, the island's capital, they each shed light on the essence of Chiloé in their own way. The trick is to take your time exploring, and when you're done gazing upon the churches, be sure to turn around and take in what lies before them. Chances are it's the sea.

716 | Wine tasting with a view at the world's highest cellar

ARGENTINA Given its location at 3700m above sea level (masl) in Jujuy's legendary Quebrada de Humahuaca canyon, an altitudinous wine-tasting at Bodega Claudio Zucchino's Mina Moya cellar will actually take your breath away. First the vintner shows you around his tiny bodega, before inviting you to clamber into his 4WD to zigzag 11km up through the clouds, a bone-shaking drive dotted with cardon cacti and alpaca clans. The first stop takes in Finca Moya at 3329 masl, a green oasis nestled among mountains where Malbec and Merlot vines battle to survive the extreme climate. Taste Claudio's Uraqui Minero 2016, a Malbec/Syrah/Merlot blend, inside the cellar – a disused mine where his father used to work – or in the bright sunlight, looking down at the vibrant red and yellow hues of La Pollera mountain opposite. The most breathtaking wine-tasting experience of your life.

717 | Ice climbing in the Cordillera Real

BOLIVIA You're halfway up a sheer ice wall in the high Andes, with crampons on your feet, an ice axe in each hand and your stomach quavering somewhere around knee level, when you sense that there are some things humans were not meant to do. Yet if you don't mind the odd moment of panic, the Cordillera Real, strung across Bolivia between the barren Altiplano and the Amazon basin, is a wonderful place to begin mountaineering. For one thing, it's substantially cheaper than Europe or North America. More importantly, this harsh landscape, with its thin air, intimidating peaks and snow-covered ridges, is unforgettable.

718 | Taking time over maté

URUGUAY The process is long, the preparation meticulous. The *matecito*, a wooden, hollowed-out gourd, is stuffed with yerba herb. A *bombilla*, a straw-shaped tube of silver, is thrust into the leaves, then water – very hot but not boiling – trickled down its side, slowly, carefully, wetting the yerba from below.

"¿Como lo tomás?" the *cebador*, the *maté*-maker, asks you. "Amargo", you reply. Without sugar. The connoisseur's choice. You take a suck. Long and smooth. And bitter – a shock to first-timers, who are far better off taking it *dulce* (sweet). You pass it on, with your right hand, and clockwise, as tradition dictates.

A little more yerba, a little more water. The *matecito* is emptied, the process started afresh.

719 | Fly fishing in Tierra del Fuego

ARGENTINA It may seem a long way to come to cast your line, but down in the toe of Argentina's boot the rivers run with gold. Well, with brown and rainbow.

The waters of the Río Grande boil with trout. Back, flick, cast, catch. Back, flick, cast, catch. It's like taking candy from a baby. And some fairly hefty candy at that, as the river is home to some of the most super-sized sea-running brown trout in the world, whose forays into the nutrient-rich ocean help them swell to weights in excess of 14kg.

Back, flick, cast, catch. The fly barely has time to settle on the surface before another monster gobbles it up and is triumphantly reeled up onto the bank.

720 | Walking with giants at Serra da Canastra

BRAZIL The mist has cleared and the wind is in your favour. You hold your ground – and your breath – as the outlandish animal ambles steadily closer. Her long nose breaks into view, parting the shivering grass heads. Now you can see her pickaxe front claws and the 1m-long glory of her shaggy tail. And, best of all, her passenger: a myopic mini-me clinging tighter to mum's back with every bump in the trail.

At 5m – just as you're looking nervously to your guide – she stops. The wind has changed. Her outrageous hooter swings up, combing the breeze for your scent like some animated vacuum-cleaner nozzle. And then she's off, turning tail and harrumphing away down the hillside. You breathe again.

Among South America's menagerie of the weird and wonderful, few creatures come stranger than the giant anteater. And nowhere do you have a better chance of making its acquaintance than among the high, rolling grasslands of Serra da Canastra National Park.

Here, perched on a plateau in Minas Gerais Province, the beleaguered animals are safe from the hunters, traffic and loggers that have reduced their numbers across the continent and thus are more inclined to wander about in broad daylight. Just find an elevated spot and scan the slopes; sooner or later you'll spot that distinctive profile working a distant hillside. Every termite mound is scarred with their excavations.

It's not only anteaters that make Canastra special. This park marks the birthplace of the mighty São Francisco River, which gurgles up from a fern-choked hollow on the plateau to cross the grasslands and cascade off the escarpment into the forests below. Hike the river's upper reaches and you may meet a rare maned wolf – a fox on stilts, decked out with a mane and tail – stalking elegantly through the long grass. Pick your way along the lower river and you might spy a party of Brazilian mergansers, one of the world's rarest ducks, bottle-green heads glinting as they bob and plunge among the rapids.

For now, though, you unwrap a sandwich and pull on another layer as the mist comes rolling back. Brazil is not all tropical rainforest and sun-kissed beaches. But that anteater might just be worth a little samba.

721 | Equatorial differences in Quito

ECUADOR If you find yourself in Quito, a visit to the equator is more or less obligatory – the middle of the Earth is only about a thirty-minute drive north from the Ecuadorean capital. As you get closer, the highland vegetation gives way to sandy plains punctuated by uninspiring brown hills. The "Mitad del Mundo" monument itself is even less exciting: a low-level metal-and-stone affair, it sits at the point determined by a French scientific expedition in 1736 to be latitude 0° 0′ 0″. The real treat here is to stand on the red-painted equator line, with one foot in each hemisphere. Doing so is more than just an unmissable photo opportunity: you can't help but be struck by a sense of reverence.

It all seems a bit unreal – and it may be: about 150m north, a short walk up the highway, is a rival museum, Intiñan, which claims that it sits on the location of the real equator line, a point well known to mystics from Ecuador's indigenous Quichua peoples since pre-Columbian times. There's no monument and everything has a very home-made feel, but you do get to interact with the magnetic forces at work here. A sink is produced, filled and then emptied of water to show you that instead of swirling, water at the equator runs straight down the plug. You can also balance an egg on a nail, since the forces of gravity are weaker. The passion of the guides involves more than the position of the equator line: Intiñan is about honouring traditional knowledge as much as scientific accuracy.

Ultimately, a visit to the equator would be incomplete if you didn't go to each of the sites, tipping your hat to the achievements of both early modern science and ancient heritage. Rather than transcendental cosmic awe, you're more likely to be somewhat comforted by the kitschiness of it all, as if the Earth is having the last laugh.

COLOMBIA There's something at once romantic and rugged about riding, *gaucho*-style, past great rivers and waterfalls to ancient statues, your feet in iron stirrups. The locals in this mountainous region above the Río Magdalena in Colombia's Andean south claim the statues represent chiefs and shamans, as well as jaguars, eagles that communed with the sun and frogs that represented fertility. Some show grinning mothers presenting their newborn children to the gods for sacrifice.

The statue builders themselves remain shrouded in mystery. They disappeared in the fifteenth century, and are referred to as San Agustinas purely because all five hundred statues were found near the town of San Agustín. They were not patriarchal, selecting men and women as their chiefs and shamans, and carved wild-eyed figures holding containers of coca leaves and lime, suggesting intoxicants were used in search of esoteric knowledge. Yet no writings or buildings have yet been uncovered in this vast necropolis. The likelihood is that the Agustinas lived here for thousands of years before being carried off during an Inca invasion in search of slaves – and that they buried their sacred statues before they were captured. They lay there, silent and overgrown, for three hundred years, until Spanish missionaries arrived in the area and began uncovering the remnants of a long-dead civilization.

Over a hundred of the statues are found within an archeological park 2km above San Agustín. Most are less than 1.5m tall, caricatured figures with huge heads created by bold deep cuts into grey tufa. Often their teeth are filed into points and sometimes they support masks on heavy poles that reach down to the ground. We know that originally they would have been painted in red and yellow with white teeth and black eyes. The two statues accessible by horseback at La Pelota, a wooded hillside to the north of the archeological park, have traces of their original colour and stare angrily out at us. We can only guess at the lost world they represent.

The silent statues of San Agustín

7²³

Braving the wind at Torres del Paine

731 Losing track of time on the Trans-Siberian

CHINA TO RUSSIA On the fourth day I stop caring about time. Well, I thought it was the fourth day, in fact it is the third. Beijing is a receding memory, Moscow impossibly distant. I have slipped into the habit of sleeping for four hours and then getting up for four hours, it doesn't matter whether it is light or dark. Life inside the train bears no relation to the outside world – Siberia – barrelling past, cold, unwelcoming and as predictable as wallpaper: birch trees, hills, birch trees, plains, birch trees.

"I hate those trees," says an elderly German. "I want to cut them all down."

Occasionally we pass an untidy village of wooden cabins but mostly the only human touch to the epic landscape is the telegraph poles at the side of the track.

My first Russian is a young guy in a shell suit with a moustache and an anarchy tattoo. "The Beatles," he says, on hearing I am British.

"The Rolling Stones," I counter. He nods, "The Doors."

"Pearl Jam?" I enquire. "Nirvana," he parries.

"Napalm Death."

Once or twice a day the train stops and I emerge for air, dizzy and blinking, onto a platform swarming with frenzied shoppers. Traders stand in the carriage door and the townsfolk, who have waited all week for two minutes of consumerism, riot to get to them. To save time, the traders throw money over their shoulders to be collected by colleagues. They sell World Cup T-shirts, plastic jewellery and Mickey Mouse umbrellas. Even the man from the dining car has a cupboard of trainers, which is perhaps why he can only offer gherkins and soup in his official capacity.

I play cards then sleep, battleships, sleep, charades, sleep. It becomes a long, slow, comfortable delirium. But on the seventh day when grey housing blocks start to appear and Moscow is imminent, I suddenly feel nostalgic for that easy sloth. When I finally get off, something feels terribly wrong; it takes me a while to figure it out – oh yes, the ground isn't moving.

Simon Lewis

As well as writing or contributing to the *Rough Guides to China*, *Beijing* and *Shanghai*, Simon Lewis is a screenwriter and novelist. He wrote the sci-fi feature film *The Anomaly*, released in 2014, followed in 2015 by two feature thrillers, *Tiger House* and *Jet Trash*.

CENTRAL & NORTHERN ASIA

731–799

Few regions feel so resolutely *different* as Central and Northern Asia. Even today, much of it remains a genuine enigma, from the otherworldly plains of Siberia to the ritualistic festivals of East Asia. This is a part of the globe where the ancient tangles with the futuristic, where the aeons-old spice routes of the 'Stans complement the cutting-edge cityscapes of Shanghai and Hong Kong, and where Tibetan temples vie for attention with Japanese bullet trains. There may be a colossal amount to take in – the fertile vineyards of the Caucasus are far removed from the rigid towers of North Korea, in more ways than one – but it's adventure heaven. Experiences abound for intrepid types, from running the Pyongyang Marathon to defying gravity at China's dizzying Hanging Temple and wildlife-watching in Japan's green heart.

BARENTS
SEA

KARA
SEA

LAPTEV SEA

Arctic Circ

757

RUSSIA
731

SEA OF
OKHOTS

7
7

UKRAINE

KAZAKHSTAN

756

790

787

MONGOLIA

764

792

744
776
795

791

746

797

GEORGIA

UZBEKISTAN

783

KYRGYZSTAN

774

733
771
789

766

749

ARMENIA

AZERBAIJAN

779

770

781

NORTH
KOREA

741
743
750
754
763
772
785
793

74
74
75
75
76
77
78
79

TURKEY

735
768

784
798

TURKMENISTAN

762

739

740
758

751

JAPAN

IRAQ

IRAN

TAJIKISTAN

CHINA

778

782
745

SOUTH
KOREA

759

AFGHANISTAN

732

769

748
760

765

PAKISTAN

786

775

736

TAIWAN

EGYPT

SAUDI
ARABIA

OMAN

737
796

761

734
752

780
799

SUDAN

INDIA

MYANMAR

LAOS

YEMEN

ARABIAN
SEA

BAY OF
BENGAL

THAILAND

PACIFIC
OCEAN

CAMBODIA

ETHIOPIA

VIETNAM

THE PHILIPPINES

Equator

SOMALIA

SRI LANKA

MALAYSIA

KENYA

INDIAN OCEAN

INDONESIA

PAPUA N
GUINE

The external boundaries of India as shown on this map are neither correct nor.

Need to know

653 March–Dec is the best time, with Cusco the start point for most operators. Currently, the only lodge-to-lodge trek is with W mountainlodgesofperu.com.

654 See W galapagos.org.

655 The Plaza de Ponchos market in Otavalo is open every day, but is most impressive on Sat.

656 Fly with Amazonas (W amazonas.com) or take the 20hr bus from La Paz. Tour companies operate from La Paz and Rurrenabaque; try W indigenatour.com. Avoid the flood-prone, insect-packed rainy season (Nov–March).

657 Punta del Este's airport is only around 30min from Buenos Aires' Aeroparque Jorge Newbery. Nov and March are best for avoiding crowds.

658 Visits to the dam are by tour only. For more, check W turismoitaipu.com.br.

659 Jeeps (called "willys") travel between Salento's main square and the start of the trail. The trek takes around 6hr, so catch the earliest jeep from Salento.

660 *Academia de Cachaça*, Rua Conde Bernadotte 26, Leblon, Rio de Janeiro (W academiadacachaca.com.br).

661 The Trinidad ruins are open daily; the entrance ticket also covers the Jesuit ruins at Jesús del Tavarangue.

662 Tours of the old Fray Bentos factory take place daily (W welcomeuruguay.com).

663 The Teatro Amazonas, which hosts an annual opera festival in April, can be visited on guided tours.

664 Officially a yellow fever vaccination is required to enter Parque Tayrona.

665 Cusco trekking companies include Choquequirao Trek (W choquequiraotrek.com). You can also trek from Choquequirao to Machu Picchu – an unforgettable nine-day walk. Try KE Adventure (W keadventure.com).

666 You can see the Valley of the Moon on a tour from San Pedro – there are lots of operators.

667 The nearest town to the glacier is El Calafate; W losglaciares.com and W elcalafate.gov.ar are useful resources.

668 Boats to Isla del Sol depart every morning around 8.30am and in the afternoon at 1.30pm from the town of Copacabana (for details see W bolivianlife.com).

669 One-day bike trips are easy to arrange in La Paz; the original and best operator is Gravity Assisted Mountain Biking (W gravitybolivia.com).

670 Airlines in the Bolivian Amazon include Amazonas (W www.amazonas.com), BOA (W boa.bo) and Aerocon (W alternativeairlines.com/aerocon). For air taxis, ask locally; costs are usually split with other passengers.

671 Tours depart for the Ciudad Perdida from Taganga and Santa Marta – check W laciudadperdida.com.

672 For more information visit W olinda.pe.gov.br.

673 The rapids are Class III and suitable for beginners. Trips can be arranged in Cusco; try W sastravelperu.com.

674 Sorata is served by buses from La Paz (4hr). In June–Aug, climbers arrive en masse and it's worth booking ahead.

675 Wilderness Explorers (W wilderness-explorers .com), in Georgetown, offers tours. The falls are at their most dramatic in the wet season (April–Aug).

676 Fly into Manaus from Rio or Recife, and join a local guide on a small houseboat trip to keep it simple.

677 The installations at Mamalluca are accessible from the city of Vicuna (W munivicuna.cl).

678 Rainbow Mountain tours daily from Cusco at 3–3.30am, costing around PEN100 (£23/US$30); W rainbowmountaintravels.com. It is recommended staying in Cusco for two days pre-hike to acclimatize.

679 You can only hike the Inca Trail on a tour or with a licensed guide. In Cusco, try SAS (W sastravelperu .com) and United Mice (W unitedmice.com).

680 There are regular flights between Puerto Williams and the Chilean city of Punta Arenas. Boats also run to/

from Ushuaia, Argentina (see W turismoshila.cl).

681 Rio Tambopata is accessible from lodges in the Puerto Maldonado region. Try Rainforest Expeditions (W perunature.com).

682 For more information, visit W rainbowmountain-peru.com.

683 *Country Club el Bosque* (W elbosque.org.pe) has picnic tables, tennis courts and a pool.

684 *Casa de Isla Negra* (Tues–Sun) is 110km west of Santiago. For more, visit W fundacionneruda.org.

685 The best close-up experience to be had is in the Parque Nacional, outside Puerto Iguazú (Argentina). The rainy summer season (Nov–March) is the best time to go. For more, consult W iguazuargentina.com.

686 On Jan 8 every year some 300,000 believers, mostly from Buenos Aires, converge on the Mercedes shrine, camping along the main road.

687 Most Colca Canyon trips leave from Arequipa, approximately 5hr away. See W colcaperu.gob.pe

688 Tupiza Tours, inside the *Hotel Mitru* (W tupiza tours.com), can organize trips to San Vicente.

689 Lençóis is 6hr by bus from Salvador da Bahia. Try Lentur (W facebook.com/lentur1990) for park day-trips.

690 Blumenau can be reached by bus or plane from Curitiba, Florianópolis and Joinville; W oktoberfestblumenau. com.br.. Microbreweries include Cervejaria Bierland (W bierland.com.br), Cervejaria Eisenbahn (W eisenbahn.com. br) and Cervejaria Wunder Bier (W wunderbier.com.br).

691 Elephant seals are at their most active Sept–Nov.

692 Boi Bumba takes place for three days every June. Visit W boibumba.com for more information.

693 Volcán Cotopaxi is in the Cotopaxi National Park, accessed from the Panamericana 41km south of Quito. Fully qualified guides are available through operators in Quito or Riobamba.

694 Qoyllur Riti happens in the middle of every year. You can arrange transport to the start of the trek near the town of Ocongate with tour companies in Cusco.

695 Chilean cruise company Australis (W australis .com) is the only operator licensed to navigate the region, running cruises between Sept and April.

696 The *Tres Gigantes* (W facebook.com/lostresgigantespantanal) arranges basic, overnight stays in their lodge, with food, for around PYG110,000 (£15) per person, per night. A speedboat from Bahía Negra costs around PYG745,000 (£100/US$129).

697 Montecristi is about 3hr by road from Guayaquil, Ecuador's biggest city.

698 The football year runs late July–early June, with a break in Dec and Jan. Tickets are available on match days, but buy ahead for the big games.

699 The national park information centre is open daily (W losglaciares.com).

700 Find information on the Central Suriname Nature Reserve on W whc.unesco.org.

701 *Galpão Crioulo*, Parque Maurício Sirotsky Sobrinho; *Na Brasa*, Av. Ramiro Barcelos 389, Floresta (W nbsteak. com.br); *Gambrinus* (W gambrinus.com.br).

702 Expeditions to the Salar by 4WD can be arranged with local tour operators in Uyuni, 12hr from La Paz.

703 Jan and Feb are the best months to drive the route. See also *Casa Ludwig* (W casaludwig.cl) and *El Reloj* (W elrelojhotel.cl).

704 Visit W www.cnes-csg.fr for launch dates.

705 Venues and times of *milongas* are constantly changing, so seek local advice; a good place to start is W hoymilonga.com. See also W facebook.com/Confitería-Ideal-114137994827 and W parakultural.com.ar.

706 It's much easier to fly to Cartagena than take the bus; military roadblocks can cause lengthy delays.

707 Ski season lasts from late May until early Oct, with the peak season from mid-July to early Aug.

708 Carnival starts the Fri before Ash Wednesday. For more, see W rio-carnival.net.

709 *Puyuhuapi Lodge & Spa* (W puyuhuapilodge.com) offers transfers from Balmaceda airport.

710 "Moto Rent" shops are abundant in the Barrio Histórico; golf carts and bicycles are also available.

711 The Pantanal's dry season (April–Oct) is the best time to spot wildlife; a dozen lodges offer tours with *gaucho* guides, or try W ecoverdetours.com.br.

712 Tapati begins every year at the end of Jan. Lan Chile (W latam.com) makes the 5hr flight to Easter Island several times a week from Santiago.

713 Homestays on Anapia can be arranged at the jetty in Puno, a 2hr boat ride from the island, or as a package; try Insider Tours (W insider-tours.com).

714 The Associacao de Capoeira Mestre Bimba is Salvador's foremost dance school; check their classes on W capoeiramestrebimba.com.br.

715 Ferries depart daily every 30min from Pargua in the Lake District to Chacao at Isla Grande's northern tip. For more, see W chile.travel.

716 Drive to *Bodega Claudio Zucchino*, near Uquía, Jujuy; T +549 1137 943667. Drink plenty of water and don't exert yourself, to avoid altitude sickness. Wine-tasting ARS2,650 (US$70), reservations only.

717 The Cordillera Real is a few hours' drive from La Paz – guides and equipment can be organized here or in Sorata.

718 W welcomeuruguay.com has more about *maté*.

719 Fishing licences are available in Río Grande, from the Asociacíon de Pesca con Mosca (W aapm.org.ar).

720 The Serra da Canastra National Park (W serrada canastra.com.br) lies some 8km from Sao Roque de Minas and about a 5hr drive from Belo Horizonte – the nearest airport. Access is best during the dry season (April–Oct).

721 For more, see W www.mitaddelmundo.com and W museointinan.com.ec.

722 Travel the Unknown (W traveltheunknown.com/ tours) offers Colombian excursions.

723 Guided treks run to Torres del Paine (W torresdel paine.com) from Puerto Natales, or you can travel to the park by bus or Zodiac.

724 Lago Budi can be reached by rental car from Temuco, 95km east. The Llaguepulli community (W lagobudi.cl) organize overnight *ruka* stays from CLP60 (US$88/£68).

725 Visitors are admitted to *terreiros*, with "mass" generally beginning in the early evening. Trousers and long skirts should be worn, preferably white. For more information on ceremonies in Salvador, contact the Federação Baiana de Culto Afro-Brasileiro (W bahia .com.br). Another useful site, W terreiros.ceao.ufba.br, has a map showing the *terreiros de candomblé*.

726 Tren de la Costa runs from Olivos, Buenos Aires, and pulls in at the edge of Tigre, near the Puerto de Frutos; W trendelacosta.com.ar.

727 Oruro gets extremely crowded during carnival, so you should book your room well in advance. W oruro carnival.com is a comprehensive resource.

728 Don Bosco Roga is at 289 Cedar and Ecuador, Lamaré. For information on similar projects, contact the Servicio Voluntario Menonita (W mennonitemission.net).

729 *Bodega Catena Zapata* is in Luján de Cuyo (W catena wines.com). See W greatwinecapitals.com/capitals/mendoz for more.

730 The Witches' Market is on Calle Linares. Ask before taking photos and think twice before buying animal products – some are endangered species.

728 | On a mission in Asunción

PARAGUAY Asunción, the capital of Paraguay, is one of the oldest cities in South America. But where time has endowed places like Buenos Aires and Rio de Janeiro with a tangible cultural history and a feast of architectural landmarks, it has been less kind to *Asunció*. Indeed, the memories most visitors take home are of woebegone buildings, flaking and forgotten, and of a frightening number of street children. An estimated fifteen thousand young people live rough on the capital's streets, shining shoes, sifting rubbish in the city's dumps, peddling penny sweets to survive. Or worse.

They are driven here by poverty, abandoned by families who can no longer afford to look after them, are in jail or who have had to find work in Brazil; or by violence, rural runaways escaping a back story of abuse and deprivation. And that's where the projects come in – the orphanages, shelters and schools that have sprung up across Asunción in response. These are not your everyday run-of-the-mill volunteer programmes, the kind where you part with a good deal of money for a week of "pitching in" before skipping off on a holiday around the rest of the continent. At somewhere like Don Bosco Roga, a Salesian mission in Greater Asunción's Lambaré district, you'll need to commit at least six months, living in a small room while tutoring a group of street-hardened teenage boys, helping with their homework and, most importantly, providing the care and support so often absent from their childhood.

It's a challenge, physically and emotionally, but then big challenges bring big rewards. That could be watching a boy learn a vocational skill, such as plumbing or welding, or it might be something as simple as seeing him get a good night's kip at last – it can take most of the young people who walk through Don Bosco's doors about six months to shed their fear and learn how to sleep soundly again. Tough to work at but even tougher to leave, the mission will probably change your life. And when was the last time you could say that about a holiday?

729 | Wine-tasting in Mendoza

ARGENTINA One of the world's "Great Wine Capitals", putting it alongside more famous regions like Napa and Bordeaux, Mendoza is the main reason Argentina has become one of the top wine-producing countries across the globe. The area attracts top-flight vintners from around the globe, but arguably the finest wines in the region are those of Argentine Nicolás Catena. Even if you've already had the bacchanalian pleasure of uncorking one of his US$100 bottles, nothing can match the excitement of visiting his otherworldly winery, Bodega Catena Zapata, where the grapes are harvested from February to April.

Rising like a Maya pyramid from the dusty flatlands that surround Mendoza, the adobe and glass structure stands against the breathtaking backdrop of 6962m Aconcagua, the highest peak in the Americas. Descend through a pathway of stone arches into the building's cool, dimly lit cellar, where the wine barrels are stored, and a long oak table is set with a sampler to quicken your pulse. It's the perfect setting for a taste of Mendoza's signature red grape, Malbec, which has prospered like no other in this dry, high desert *terroir*. For decades after being brought over from Europe by Italian immigrants like Catena's grandfather, the ruby-coloured grape was deemed too robust for all but the beefy Argentine palate. Now widening curiosity among wine consumers and more consistent growing techniques have made this fruity and full-bodied nectar a stalwart of the wine world.

With hundreds of tasting rooms within reach – many in the traditional bodegas are still free – there's no shortage of places to visit. So get an early start, and unless you want to topple over in a sun-kissed, drunken haze, abide by the sommelier's golden rule: swirl 'n' spit.

730 | Armadillos and amulets: sampling a witch's brew

BOLIVIA At first glance, the bustling market seems much like any other in Bolivia: there are neat piles of fruit and vegetables, baskets of *empanadas* and alpaca-wool hats, jumpers, ponchos and socks for sale. But take a closer look at the stalls and a strange picture emerges. Among the everyday items are shrivelled llama foetuses, dried frogs, birds, armadillos, porcupines and turtles, boxes of herbs, remedies and potions, smouldering multicoloured candles, soapstone figures, and collections of amulets, charms and talismans.

The Witches' Market (the Mercado de Hechicería or Mercado de las Brujas) sits on a cobbled street a few blocks back from Plaza San Francisco in La Paz, the world's highest capital city at more than 3800m above sea level. Although the conquistadors and missionaries brought Catholicism to Bolivia, they failed to completely supplant the indigenous population's traditional religious practices, such as the worship of Pachamama (Mother Earth). Instead, the two sets of beliefs blended together and today continue to find their expression in rituals that require an evocative array of ingredients.

At the market, the smell of incense hangs in the air, while the low hum of whispered requests from locals mingles with the excited chatter of foreign tourists. The stallholders or "witches", generally Aymara women clad in traditional Andean dress – long woven skirts, bright shawls and small black or brown bowler hats (known locally as *bombín*) – claim to cure almost any malady, and the methods they use have barely changed in hundreds of years.

Llama foetuses are buried under the foundations of most Bolivian homes as an offering to Pachamama, apologizing for digging into her. Armadillos, meanwhile, are believed to dissuade burglars, while frogs bring wealth. There are amulets and potions for people hoping for a happy marriage, to conceive or reinvigorate their sex life. Others promise good luck in business or protection against illness.

For anyone with more complicated problems, or just a healthy sense of curiosity, there are even *yatiris* (spiritual healers) to be consulted – a memorable experience regardless of personal beliefs.

The weird and the wonderful: the Oruro Carnival

BOLIVIA It might not have the glamour of Rio, but the Andean outpost of Oruro can lay claim to the most outlandish carnival in all of Latin America, a fiesta where the devil really is in the detail. This is a place where roots run deep, far below the city streets, where the pre-Columbian god of the underworld, Huari, holds jealous dominion over a mine-shaft labyrinth. When the week before Lent rolls around, Oruroños bring that kingdom to life with an unparalleled eye for the satirical and the grotesque, lolloping through the crowds amid a cacophonous siren of Ben Hur-scale brass bands.

If the bulging, bloodshot eyes and slavering tongues of the *morenada* dancers – representing African slaves forced into lung-searing labour in the city's silver mines – affect a comic-book suffering, you can be sure the guy propping up the costume's incredible weight is suffering in turn, and will even have paid for the privilege. You can't take your eyes off the slow, hypnotic stomp of the choreography, but even this pales next to the *diablada*, the showpiece showdown between Lucifer – a riot of demonic kitsch with antenna-like horns and Medusa hairdo – and the Archangel Michael, accompanied by packed ranks of no-less-outrageous demons and libidinous she-devils.

Small wonder UNESCO has designated the spectacle a "Masterpiece of the Oral and Intangible Heritage of Humanity", but even that doesn't hint at the sheer scale of the thing: tens of thousands of dancers, crowds getting on for half a million and enough water-bombs to fill several reservoirs. Tourists are particularly juicy targets, yet while long-gone colonial overseers are wonderfully sent up in the bow ties and long noses of the *doctorcitos* parade, for a price and months of practice gringos can actually join in: you too can don a whip and a pair of jingle-jangle boots and high-step your way through the Afro-Bolivian *caporales* dance, or strut your stuff in a bouffant mini and jaunty bonnet. With a route of no less than four raucous kilometres, though, almost 4000m above sea level, be prepared to pant.

724 | Spending a night in a traditional Mapuche ruka

CHILE Until 25 years ago, the Mapuche of southern Chile inhabited earthquake-proof dwellings, known as *ruka*. Vertical coigüe trunks meet slender lengths of luma and temú to form a frame, which is thatched with reeds plucked from marshes along the coast.

Inside, the wood is infused with the smoke of the countless fires that have warmed its hearth over the years and that keep it waterproof, even in the heaviest of downpours. It is the ultimate eco-home, and an apt representation of this indigenous culture whose name means "People of the Earth" and whose existence is interwoven with the ground on which they live.

The eighty-family community of Llaguepulli on the shores of Lago Budí now have twenty *ruka* available for curious tourists to stay in overnight. These oval-shaped buildings have vaulted roofs and just one entrance: a door opening out to the east. The word "door" in their native tongue, Mapudungun, means "where the sun enters"; indeed, the Mapuche position their beds and buildings facing east, believing that they then wake filled with positive energy.

But staying in a *ruka* is an experience beyond sleeping in an ancestral house. This Mapuche community wish to introduce outsiders to their culture, which survived centuries of persecution at the hands of the Spanish. Tours of their smallholding, where medicinal plants are grown to cure everything from heartache to liver disease, are followed by lunches of heavy but delicious *catutos* – slices of Mapuche wheat grain bread dipped in sticky home-made honey.

After sundown, the evening is spent huddling around the smoky warmth of the *ruka*'s fire. Community elders explain Mapuche cosmovision, a belief system grounded in time as cyclical, not linear, and in man existing in equilibrium with the fertile, rolling hills and pastures of his home.

When you finally retire to bed, the lodgings are cosy, with simple, wooden beds lining the back wall. They smell earthy, natural and of thousands of years of history. As the rays of the sun pour in through the door the next morning, don't be surprised if you rise imbued with new positivity.

725 | Honouring the Orixás in Salvador

BRAZIL Along the "Red Beach" of Salvador da Bahia, worshippers dressed in ethereal white robes gather around sand altars festooned with gardenias. Some may fall into trances, writhing on the beach, screaming so intensely you'd think they were being torn limb from limb. Perhaps in more familiar settings you'd be calling an ambulance, but this is Salvador, the epicentre of the religion known as *candomblé*, in which worshippers take part in *toques*, a ritual that involves becoming possessed by the spirit of their Orixá.

A composite of Portuguese Catholicism and African paganism, *candomblé* is most fervently practised in Salvador, but it defines the piquancy and raw sensuality of the Brazilian soul throughout the entire country. In this pagan religion, each person has an Orixá, or protector god, from birth.

This Orixá personifies a natural force, such as fire or water, and is allied to an animal, colour, day of the week, food, music and dance. The ceremonies are performed on sacred ground called *terreiros* and typically feature animal sacrifices, hypnotic drumming, chanting and

convulsing. Props and paraphernalia are themed accordingly; the house is decorated with the colour of the honorary Orixá, and usually the god's favourite African dish is served.

Ceremonies are specialized for each god, but no matter which Orixá you are celebrating, you can be sure that the experience will rank among the most bizarre of your life. If you attend a ritual for Ossaim, the Orixá of leaves, for example, chances are that you will be swept from head to foot in foliage.

If pyrotechnics are your thing, better pay homage to Xango, god of fire, whose ceremony reaches a rather hazardous climax as bowls of fire are passed, head to head, among the participants. While animal sacrifice, one central aspect of the ceremony, may not be for the faint-hearted, music and feasting provide a more universally palatable denouement to the public "mass".

After you enter the realm of *candomblé*, you may view Salvador, and indeed Brazil, through an ethereal prism that challenges your accepted reason.

726 | The subtropical river system just outside Buenos Aires

ARGENTINA Just outside Buenos Aires, Argentina is one of South America's most unexpected landscapes – the Paraná Delta. Barely 35km northwest of the city centre and part of the continent's second largest river system, this subtropical tangle of tea-coloured waterways and lush islands is reminiscent of the Amazon or the Everglades.

The gateway to the delta is the island-town of Tigre : imagine a cross between an undeveloped Venice and a subtropical Henley-on-Thames, and you're halfway there. One of the great pleasures of Tigre is the journey from Buenos Aires. Although you can catch a commuter train, most travellers opt for the far more atmospheric Tren de la Costa, a toy train that runs the 30-minute waterfront journey from the suburb of Olivos.

The highlight of Tigre is a boat, canoe or kayak trip into the delta. At first you pass island-hotels, sports clubs, houses raised up on wooden stilts,

and the rusty, semi-submerged skeletons of abandoned boats. Most people content themselves with a short cruise, but to really get away from it all you need to head deeper into the delta, staying overnight in a remote cabin and hiking or horseriding through the forests. Wildlife-spotting opportunities abound here: the region is awash with hummingbirds, pygmy owls, cormorants, colocolos (small wild cats) and marsh deer.

Viewed from above this labyrinth of waterways, islands and rainforests – which spans almost 22,000 square kilometres – looks like the veins of a giant heart. Down on the water, as the signs of habitation steadily disappear, the wilderness closes in on you. Birdsong, the electric hum of cicadas, and the dull drone of mosquitoes fill the air.

It seems inconceivable that one of the largest cities in Latin America is only 30 minutes away.

CHILE You have to keep your head down. Despite the spray-laden wind, it's tempting to lift it above the rim of the boat and look ahead, so you can see the foam-capped waves racing past as the Zodiac inflatable roars upstream. Soon, in the distance, a towering peak of rock rises up. As you get closer you see shattering precipices and giant towers dusted with snow.

This is Torres del Paine, the citadel of Chile's epic south and one of the wildest national parks in the world. When the inboard of the Zodiac inflatable is finally switched off, all you can hear is the fury of the wind. The waves die down and the water reflects the massif in a pool as perfect as you could imagine, fringed by gnarled trees and blasted by bitter winds. Close by is a huge glacier, an offshoot of one of the largest ice fields in the world.

Then you set off walking, shifting the weight of your pack to get comfortable. There are other hikers around you, too – this isn't deserted wilderness by any means – but the largeness of the landscape can more than accommodate everyone. High up to the east, and overlooking the scrub and blasted forest, are the unnaturally sculpted Paine Towers themselves, and in front of you, dark-capped, are the weird sculptures of the peaks of the Cuernos del Paine. If you're lucky you'll stumble across some guanacos, wild relations of the llama, or even a shy ñandú, the South American ostrich. But perhaps the best experience to be had here is simply to inhale the air, which is so crisp and thin that breathing is like drinking iced water.

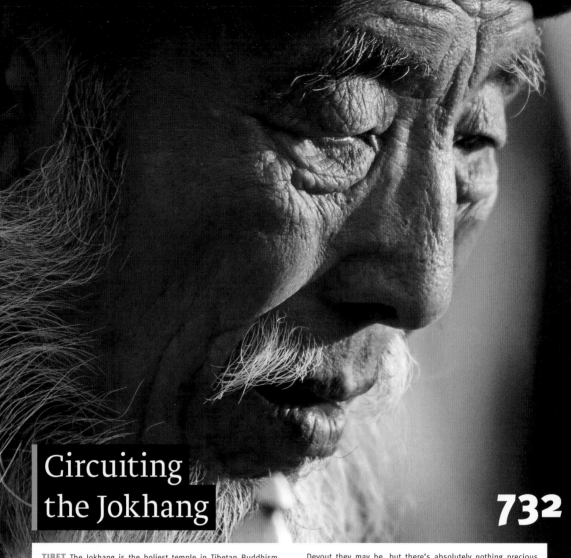

Circuiting the Jokhang

732

TIBET The Jokhang is the holiest temple in Tibetan Buddhism, and what it lacks in appearance – a very shabby facade compared with the nearby Potala Palace – it makes up in atmosphere. It's in the cobbled lanes of the Barkhor district, Lhasa's sole surviving traditional quarter, and there's an excited air of reverence as you approach, with a continuous throng of Tibetan pilgrims circuiting the complex, spinning hand-held prayer wheels and sticking out their tongues at each other in greeting. A good many prostrate themselves at every step, their knees and hands protected from the accumulated battering by wooden pads, which set up irregular clacking noises. Most of the pilgrims are wild-haired Tibetan peasants reeking of yak butter and dressed in thick, shabby layers to protect against the cold; especially tough-looking are the Khampas from eastern Tibet, who almost always have one arm exposed to the shoulder, whatever the weather.

Devout they may be, but there's absolutely nothing precious about their actions, no air of hushed, respectful reverence – stand still for a second and you'll be knocked aside in the rush to get around. Inside, the various halls are lit by butter lamps, leaving many of the wooden halls rather gloomy and adding a spooky edge to the ensemble of close-packed saintly statues clothed in multicoloured flags, brocade banners hanging from the ceiling, and especially gory murals of demons draped in skulls and peeling skin off sinners – a far less forgiving picture of Buddhism than the version practised elsewhere in China. The bustle is even more overwhelming here, the crowds increased by red-robed monks busy topping up the lamps or tidying altars. Make sure you catch the Chapel of Jowo Sakyamuni at the rear of the complex, which sports a beautiful statue of the 12-year-old Buddha, and the Jokhang's flat roof, where you can look out over the rest of the city.

CHINA The Great Wall is one of those sights that you've heard and seen so much about that you know reality is going to have a tough time living up to the hype. But having made it all the way to Beijing, it seems perverse to ignore this overblown landmark, so arm yourself with a thermos of tea and catch a bus north from the capital to Simatai, one of several sections of this 4800km-long structure which has been restored.

It's easy to find bad things to say about the Great Wall, the work of China's megalomaniac first emperor Qin Shi Huang. Over a million forced labourers are said to have died building the original version, around 250 BC, and this 7m-high, 7m-thick barrier didn't even work. History is littered with "barbarian" invaders who proved sophisticated enough to fight or bribe their way around the wall's 25,000 watchtowers, most notably the Mongols in the thirteenth century, and the Manchus – who went on to become China's final dynasty – in 1644. Indeed, the Manchus were so unimpressed with the wall that they let the entire thing fall into ruin.

And yet, you'll be blown away. Not even swarms of hawkers and crowds of tourists can ruin the sight of this blue-grey ribbon snaking across the dusty, shattered hills into the hazy distance, beyond which one end finally runs into the sea and the other simply stops in northwestern China's deserts. You can spend hours walking between battlements along the top – in places, following the contours of the hills up amazingly steep inclines – until restorations give way to rubble. Even then you can't quite believe that such a solid, organic part of the scenery is only an artefact, built by simple human endeavour. If ever proof were needed of Chinese determination, this is it.

Blown away by the Great Wall

733

734 | Paying homage to the Queen of Heaven

TAIWAN First come the police cars and media vans, followed by flag-waving and drum-beating teams, along with musicians and performers dressed as legendary Chinese folk heroes, their faces painted red, black and blue, with fierce eyes and pointed teeth. Finally, carried by a special team of bearers, comes the ornate palanquin housing the sacred image of the Queen of Heaven. The whole thing looks as heavy as a small car: the men carrying the Queen are wet with perspiration, stripped down to T-shirts with towels wrapped around their necks. Ordinary pilgrims follow up behind.

Every year, tens of thousands of people participate in a 300km, nine-day pilgrimage between revered temples in the centre of Taiwan, in a tradition that goes back hundreds of years. The procession honours one of the most popular Taoist deities, a sort of patron saint of the island: the Queen of Heaven, Tianhou, also known as Mazu or Goddess of the Sea. In true Taiwanese style, the pilgrimage is as much media circus

as fervent religious experience, with the parade attracting ambitious politicians and even street gangs who in the past have ended up fighting over who "protects" the Goddess during the procession.

Becoming a pilgrim for the day provides an illuminating insight into Taiwanese culture – you'll make lots of friends and eat like a horse. The streets are lined with locals paying respects and handing out free drinks and snacks, from peanuts to steaming meat buns. At lunch, you'll get a huge bowl of sumptuous noodles from a gargantuan, bubbling vat managed by a team of sprightly old ladies. As well as a constant cacophony of music and drums, great heaps of firecrackers are set off every few metres. Whole boxes seem to disintegrate into clouds of smoke as everyone goes deaf and is dusted with ashy debris. No one cares – the noise drives off ghosts and evil spirits, ensuring that the Queen can pass in spiritual safety, and in any case, it's all part of the fun.

735 | The birthplace of State Christianity

ARMENIA When an Armenian noble called Gregory stopped by Khor Virap in the late third century, he probably wasn't expecting to stay there for thirteen years – and certainly wasn't planning to spend his time there imprisoned in a 6m-deep pit. Unfortunately, Gregory's father had recently assassinated King Khosrov I, and Khosrov's son, Tiridates, wanted revenge, which took the form of Gregory's captivity in a dungeon.

Gregory – a devout Christian – attributed his survival to the power of faith, which had inspired a local Christian widow to regularly drop a loaf of bread into his pit. Eventually, in the year 301, he was released from the dungeon in order to cure King Tiridates II from a fit of madness brought on after a betrayal by the Roman emperor Diocletian. Once Tiridates was restored to his senses, he ordered a halt to the ongoing massacre of Christians in his kingdom, and accepted conversion to Christianity by Gregory.

Tiridates then made history: he adopted Christianity as Armenia's state religion, making Armenia the first country in the world to do so.

Gregory became the Patriarch of Armenia and established the still-extant cathedral at Echmiadzin, and, after his death, was canonized as St Gregory the Illuminator. The site of his imprisonment at Khor Virap, meanwhile, became a monastery, and has remained an important pilgrimage site ever since.

Today, Khor Virap makes a fascinating day-trip from Yerevan. Nestled atop a small hill overlooked by the mighty Mount Ararat – the alleged final resting place of Noah's Ark – it's an attractive, typically Armenian church structure, blessed with a stunning backdrop. Archeological excavations of King Tiridates' former capital are underway nearby, but perhaps the biggest draw for tourists and pilgrims alike is Gregory's terrifyingly claustrophobic pit.

It can still be accessed by a precipitous ladder and now forms a shrine to the man who, for the first time, brought Christianity to a whole nation.

736 | Village life in Zhaoxing

CHINA In a damp and misty corner of southwest Guizhou, not far from the town of Congjiang, the valleys are dotted with distinctive villages that are home to the Dong people. Covered "wind-and-rain" bridges span fast-flowing streams and provide shelter from the region's execrable weather. Octagonal drum towers with dramatic nine-tier roofs act as informal meeting houses, with men gathering around games of Go and children playing hide-and-seek behind the many pillars. Open-air stages with extravagantly upturned eaves still host occasional performances by melodious Dong choirs.

The village of Zhaoxing was once five distinct clan villages separated by the rivers that tumble down from the surrounding hills, each village with its own wind-and-rain bridge, drum tower and playhouse. Today, the five settlements have merged, covering the floor of this lush, terraced valley with rain-stained cedar-wood houses and grey slate roofs, the village skyline punctuated by pagoda-like drum towers.

Women weave and dye their own indigo cloth, sitting in the streets as they fold and hammer the bolts of fabric to a lacquered sheen. Men build their families' houses by hand and work in the surrounding fields growing sticky rice and vegetables. This everyday buzz of activity makes the small village an excellent, fascinating place to wander along the stone-flagged lanes and slip into the rhythms of rural life.

The Dong are heirs to a long tradition of expert forestry and carpentry – the timber that Admiral Zheng He, the Ming-dynasty mariner, used for his fleet was said to have come from Dong-maintained forests. On the lush wooded slopes above Zhaoxing, offerings are still laid at the foot of the largest and oldest trees, which the animistic Dong revere as possessing magical properties. Once up in the hills, it's possible to walk from each pretty village to the next along muddy footpaths, sustained by invitations from one hospitable local family after another to join their lunches.

Hill tribes and fine teas: Trekking the Burmese border

CHINA It's not what you expect from China. Right at the country's southernmost edge, by the Burmese border, you'll find an amazing subtropical Southeast Asian landscape – rolling hills covered in virgin forest – and an astonishing set of cultures. This lush region is home to minority peoples, each with a culture, language and even building style so distinct that walking from one village to the next (the only way to get around) is like crossing into another country.

Bulang women wear black turbans decorated with shells, and the men sometimes have fierce facial tattoos; the shy, hill-dwelling Hani are polytheistic and the women sport spectacular coloured headdresses; the plains-dwelling Dai, close relatives to the Thai people, have a reputation for being cultured and easy-going, though they are said to look down on other minorities as they have a written form to their language; and while the animist Wa might have given up headhunting they still maintain their reputation as crafty trackers.

Each group has a separate set of festivals, and if you're very lucky you'll get to see one – expect a colourful pageant and plenty to drink. It's rather easier to time your trip to coincide with one of the weekly markets held in the larger communities, when people come down from the hills, dressed in all their finery, to trade.

As you walk in the forest between villages, you're overwhelmed by a glut of visual detail, with brilliant colour provided by iridescent butterflies that fly tantalizingly just ahead, then close their wings the moment you get your camera out. In cultivated areas, you'll see a lush cubist terrain of rice terraces sliced into the hillsides, and plenty of tea plantations – this is the source of fine teas such as the half-fermented *pu'er cha*.

You meet Burmese jade-dealers, men hunting with home-made crossbows, teenage monks, and curious children. It's an absolutely fascinating region, rich in culture and environment. Get there fast, before the forest is cut down for rubber, and the people fall prey to the pressures and enticements of modernity.

738

Trekking through the Valley of the Geysers

RUSSIA Penetrating Kamchatka's remote and rugged terrain to discover one of the world's most restless regions of seismic hyperactivity has never been easy. With no roads or nearby settlements, the spectacular Valley of the Geysers wasn't discovered until 1941. Not even Russians were permitted to travel to this far-eastern peninsula until after the fall of Communism. Today, a trek through the Kronotsky Reserve on the peninsula's eastern edge leads you into this land of fire and ice, and brings you face to face with the full range of Kamchatka's volcanic phenomena.

You'll be dropped into the heart of the 2.5-million-acre bioreserve by helicopter, cruising over several of Kamchatka's 29 active volcanoes along the way. Your trek involves ten days and 130km of moderately strenuous hiking through coastal mountains, forests, bush thickets and some forest-less highlands. As you navigate this landscape down to the Pacific shore you'll circuit active glacier-flanked volcanoes and encounter piping fumaroles, belching mudpots and bubbling cauldrons.

Through forests of Siberian pine you'll descend into the Uzon Caldera, a marshy depression scattered with scalding lakes, warm streams and over a thousand hot springs. Steaming waterfalls cascade into rivers running with red salmon, migratory birds find green vegetation in April and bears coming out of hibernation warm themselves by simmering mud cauldrons.

From a forested ridge you descend into the Valley of the Geysers along the steamy banks of the River Geyzernaya, one of dozens of rivers that bisect the reserve en route to the Pacific shore. You don't immediately sense what's going on underfoot, as dozens of tributaries feed a concentration of hot springs below the surface.

Over twenty major geysers fill the narrow valley, each performing on its own timetable: some erupt every ten minutes, while others take 4–5 hours between show times. Some pulse in an erect column while others surprise you with a side shot – stick to the boardwalk or you might be nailed by an unexpected burst of scalding water.

Your onward descent to the Pacific shore leads through bushy and mossy tundras to an abandoned fur-trading outpost where, if all goes according to plan, your helicopter awaits for the return ride. Kamchatka's never-ending volcanic display is a reminder that Earth's creation is a work in progress.

739 | Faces from the past: Xi'an's Terracotta Army

CHINA Qin Shi Huang, China's first emperor, never did anything by halves. Not content with building the Great Wall, he spent his last years roaming the fringes of his empire, seeking a key to immortality. When (with inevitable irony) he died on his quest, his entourage returned to the capital near modern-day Xi'an and buried his corpse in a subterranean, city-sized mausoleum whose ceiling was studded with precious stones and where lakes and rivers were represented by mercury.

Or so wrote the historian Sima Qian a century after a popular uprising had overthrown Qin Shi Huang's grandson and established the Han dynasty in 206 BC. Nobody knows for sure how true the account is – the tomb remains unexcavated – but in 1974 peasants digging a well nearby found Qin Shi Huang's guardians in the afterlife: an army of over ten thousand life-sized terracotta troops arranged in battle formation, filling three huge rectangular vaults.

Make no mistake, the Terracotta Army is not like some giant schoolboy's collection of clay soldiers lined up in ranks under a protective modern hangar. The figures, some of which are occasionally on show in special exhibitions around the world, are shockingly human; every one is different, from their facial features to their hands, hairstyles, postures and clothing. They are so individual that you can't help feel that these are real people, tragically fossilized by some natural disaster – more so in places where excavations are incomplete, leaving their half-buried busts gripped by the earth. Even their horses, tethered to the remains of wooden chariots, are so faithfully sculpted that the very breed has been established.

At the end, there's just one burning question: will they find a statue of Qin Shi Huang leading them all? A realistic statue over two thousand years old of China's first emperor – now that surely would be immortality.

740 | Walking among Silla royalty

SOUTH KOREA In the centre of Gyeongju lies a gently undulating series of mysterious, grass-covered bumps. Though smaller and much softer to the eye, these mounds serve a similar purpose to the great Egyptian pyramids: tombs for great leaders from an ancient civilization, the impressive Silla dynasty, which ruled southeastern Korea for nearly a millennium, more than a millennium ago.

For some, the feeling of ancient power becomes quite palpable when walking through Tumuli Park, Gyeongju's district of burial mounds. Though close to the city centre, there's surprisingly little intrusion from the modern world – Gyeongju's more recent rulers chose to impose a cap on the height of buildings and encouraged the use of traditional roofing, all of which fosters a natural, relaxed feeling hard to come by in other Korean cities. As you walk around the park, you'll pass gentle green humps on your left and right – the larger the bump, the more important the occupant. The largest is a double-humped mound belonging to a king and queen, and it's even possible to enter a slightly smaller one to see a cross-sectioned display of the surroundings of deceased Sillan nobility. These tombs have yielded wonderful treasures from the period, most notably an elaborate golden crown.

Gyeongju's pleasures do not start and finish with its tombs. Bulguksa, a temple dating from 528 AD and viewed by many as the most beautiful in the country, lies nearby to the east. It exudes vitality, and is surrounded by some staggering mountain scenery. Delving into the mountains on a meandering uphill path, you'll eventually come across a grotto known as Seokguram. Here you'll see a stone Buddha that has long fixed his gaze over the East Sea – a perfect place to enjoy the sunset at day's end.

741 | Better than Disneyland: the Ghibli Museum

JAPAN Move over Mickey Mouse: in Japan it's a giant cuddly fur-ball called Totoro who commands national icon status. This adorable animated creature, star of *My Neighbour Totoro*, is among the pantheon of characters from the movies of celebrated director Miyazaki Hayao and his colleagues at Studio Ghibli – Japan's equivalent of Disney.

Just like Walt, Miyazaki had an ambitious vision that his movies could come alive in real life. The result – Ghibli Museum, Mitaka – is an opportunity to step into a world that, true to Miyazaki's words, "is full of interesting and beautiful things". On a far more intimate scale than Mickey's sprawling theme park across Tokyo Bay, this candy-coloured, stained-glass-decorated fantasy on the edge of western Tokyo's leafy Inokashira Park provides an unparalleled experience – a chance not only to learn about the art of animation but also to glimpse the genius of an Oscar-winning director.

You don't need to be familiar with Ghibli's movies, such as *Spirited Away*, *Howl's Moving Castle* and *Ponyo*, to enjoy the museum. Every little detail has been thought of – from the rivets on the giant robot soldier from *Castle in the Sky* on the roof to the straws, made of real straw, served with drinks in the *Straw Hat Café*.

Amazingly detailed dioramas and Technicolor displays evoke the many steps needed to make an animated movie, and a child-sized movie theatre screens original short animated features, exclusive to the museum.

To make this charming experience even more special, only a limited number of tickets are available daily, meaning everyone can move around the compact galleries comfortably – and kids won't feel crowded when romping around the giant cuddly cat bus, reading a book in the library or rummaging through the quirky gift shop.

742 | A floral wave of cherry blossoms

JAPAN The arrival of the *sakura*, or cherry blossom, has long been a profound yet simple Japanese lesson about the nature of human existence. For centuries, poets have fired off reams of haiku comparing the brief but blazing lives of the flowers to those of our own – a tragically fragile beauty to be treasured and contemplated.

In Japan, spring sees the country gradually coated in a light pink shade, soft petals slowly clustering on their branches as if puffed through by some benevolent underground spirit. The *sakura-zensen*, or cherry blossom front, flushes like a floral wave that laps the country from south to north; this is followed ardently by the Japanese, who know that when the advancing flowers hit their locality, they'll only have a week or so to enjoy the annual gift to its fullest. This desire is most commonly expressed in the centuries-old form of countless *hanami* parties – the word literally means "flower viewing" in Japanese – which take place in the rosy shade of the *sakura-zensen* throughout the entire duration of its course.

The existential contemplation is often over in seconds, before the party's real *raison d'être*: consumption. Female members of the group are expected to provide the food, and then, of course, there's alcohol – *hanami* are often convenient ways for grievances to be aired in highly conservative Japan.

Hanami are typically friends-and-family affairs, often taking place in a park or on a river bank. Some of the most popular places are illuminated at night, and many are atmospherically decorated with red-and-white paper lanterns. Of course, the coming of the blossom can be enjoyed in any way you see fit; among the best places to go are Kiyomizu-dera, a gorgeous temple in Kyoto, Tokyo's Ueno Park or the castles in Osaka or Himeji, all of which are lent a dreamlike air by the arrival of the blossom each spring.

A *hanami* party may even be possible in your own country – hunt down some sake, roll up some rice balls and become as one with the nearest flowering cherry tree.

743 | Discovering Nara, Japan's hip merchant district

JAPAN As Japan's first permanent capital, Nara is most famous for its temples and Buddhist sculpture dating back as early as the eighth century – not to mention its sacred herds of tame deer, who will bow and obligingly pose for a photo in exchange for a *shika senbei* (deer cracker). But this charming city has much more on offer for inquisitive travellers willing to venture beyond the UNESCO World Heritage Sites.

If all the bronze Buddhas and towering pagodas are beginning to blur into one, wander over to Naramachi. Once home to merchant families and bustling warehouses, it's now been transformed into a warren of tiny museums, restaurants and craft shops. *Shika no Fune* – a sort of artisan canteen, deli and visitors' centre rolled into one – is an excellent place to start. Fortify yourself with one of their delicious set lunches before heading to Kosho-no-Ie, a replica of a traditional townhouse.

A few streets away, slip off your shoes and climb onto the tatami mats at Nara Mechanical Toy Museum, where adult visitors seem just as enamoured as the children with the ingenious *karakuri*, handmade

Japanese toys. Visitors are encouraged to handle and play with the exhibits, which are rotated regularly. Nearby is the little Naramachi Museum, crammed with artwork, antiques and amulets. Of course, lovingly crafted souvenirs can also be found practically everywhere throughout the district's narrow lanes.

Keep an eye out for Nara's distinctive 'scapegoat monkeys', designed to be hung outside houses to protect the inhabitants from misfortune. While Naramachi has its share of sacred sites too – most importantly Gangoji, one of the earliest Buddhist temples in the country – what really sticks in the visitor's memory is its atmosphere of quirky creativity and warmth. Top off a day of exploration and rest your weary feet with a trip to Harushika Sake Brewery, where for just 500 yen you can sample a flight of five rice wines. Each is surprisingly different and staff provide verbal tasting notes and explanations of the sake-brewing process as you sip. Our favourite was a sparkling 'champagne-style' sake, which came with an unusual smoked squash pickle.

744 | Sampling the age-old wines of the Caucasus

GEORGIA A popular folktale in the Caucasus neatly encapsulates Georgia's passion for wine. When God was distributing land to the various peoples of the world, goes the story, the Georgians were too busy pouring drinks and raising toasts to pay any attention. Incensed, the Almighty threatened to grant the revellers nothing, before being invited to join the feast. When he experienced the local wine and hospitality for himself, he responded with the ultimate honour: granting Georgia the scenic plots of land he'd kept aside as his own.

The tale says much not only about the handsomeness of Georgia's countryside – a verdant spread of mountains and water meadows – but also the quality of its wine. This might not be the best-known wine-producing region on the planet, but many experts point to the country as being the oldest. Viticulture here is known to date back at least 6000 years – some put the figure closer to 8000 – and, what's

more, it's still going strong. Many of its wines are still fermented in the age-old manner, in underground clay urns called *kvevri* – in 2013, UNESCO even saw fit to place this method on its List of Intangible Cultural Heritage.

You'll find some enjoyably full, fruity local wines for sale in capital city Tbilisi, but for anyone wishing to investigate the country's wine culture further – and frankly, why wouldn't you? – the rolling Kakheti region in the east is the most obvious place to tour. Assorted wineries welcome visitors for tastings, ranging from small traditionally run vineyards to larger international exporters, while in addition local families often have their own home-made varieties to hand. Homestays, in fact, make a fantastic way to get to the nub of the region: Georgia sat for centuries on a key Silk Road *spice* route, drawing in influences and flavours from East and West, so the food is something special too.

Step aerobics: climbing Huang Shan

745

CHINA The Chinese would say that "Where there is yin, there is yang"; Westerners would more prosaically opine "No gain without pain". At Huang Shan, Anhui province's Yellow Mountains, this means ravishing scenery tempered by steps, steps and more steps. All 15km of the path to the top of Huang Shan are cut into steps and paved in stone, which has been quarried, carried up here and laid by hand in an amazing human endeavour. It has also made the mountain accessible to generations of the country's greatest painters and poets, whose impressions have turned Huang Shan into a national icon of natural beauty, today attracting cartloads of tourists.

The mountain's scenery of clouds, soaring granite monoliths and wind-contorted pine trees at first gives the impression of a Chinese garden writ large. You soon realize, however, that the experience of visiting Huang Shan is what those gardens' designers were trying to capture and fit into some rich patron's back yard, where it could be appreciated without the physical strain of eight hours of relentless step aerobics.

In winter, when there are very few people, the mountain is overlaid with another layer of grandeur, but it's far easier to enjoy in spring or autumn – colourful times when nature is in compelling transition. The crowds are worse (though not as bad as they are during summer), but at least you can collectively share your pain while gasping ever upwards. The toughest moment of all is on finally reaching the "top", only to find there's no real summit, rather a plateau ringed in by little peaks which bring Huang Shan's height to within a whisker of 1900m. The finest sight here is watching the sun rise out of or set into a sea of clouds, alongside hundreds of other onlookers, all momentarily hushed by the incredible spectacle.

Cruising the singing dunes of the Gobi

MONGOLIA Climbing one of the world's largest sand dunes is hard work – every step towards the top involves a tiny slide back down – but reaching the crest is an extraordinary experience. The wind suddenly roars in your face and, 800m below, rows of tiny dunes stretch off to the horizon. It takes your breath away, so you duck back down, and lie in the calm of the crest of the dune. Sand trickles around you as it's blown from the top, and the mountain hums – a low, sonorous bass that reverberates inside your chest.

The massive Khongor sand dunes, also known as the "singing dunes", are about the deepest you're likely to reach in the Gobi Desert on a typical week-long round trip from Ulaanbaatar. This can be a punishing journey: the vast majority of the country is empty wilderness, and hurtling off-road at 65km/hr in a Soviet-era van in the dusty heat can be trying on your patience and your backside.

The rewards, though, are breathtaking. The landscape that unfolds outside the dusty windows is extraordinarily varied. There are plains of red gravel, dotted with camels and the rusting remains of unknown machinery; green, rolling grassland carpeted with herbs and coloured heathers; and outcrops of red rock in bizarre, wind-sculpted shapes. You'll pass the huge crimson canyons of the "flaming cliffs" of Bayanzag, as well as a long natural canyon, Yolin Am, which is so narrow and so deep that ice remains here even in the height of summer.

The daily routine of relentless driving between these major sites is broken into small moments that are equally memorable. Although the Gobi is a wilderness, you're never more than thirty minutes' drive away from a nomadic family's yurt, and you're likely to meet quite a few locals.

The people here are friendly, and though English is rarely spoken, it's not a barrier to interaction: sitting around a fire under the vast starry sky, handing round enormous measures of vodka, brings a sense of togetherness that transcends the cultural gap.

747 | Getting naked in Inazawa

JAPAN Old men start to scream as the crush of naked flesh becomes so intense that steam is rising from the enormous crowd. It's only lunchtime and everyone's liver is saturated with sake. The chants of "*Washyoi! Washyoi!*" ("enhance yourself") rise to an ear-rupturing crescendo from the nine thousand men, all dressed in giant nappies, or *fundoshis*. Finally, just when it seems that the entire town of Inazawa is about to be ransacked by the baying mob, the Naked Man appears.

Dating back 1200 years, the Naked Man festival was originally a call to prayer, decreed by Emperor Shotoku in order to dispel a plague that was sweeping the region. The plan worked, so at a date determined by the lunar calendar each year (usually around February or March) men of all ages, though particularly those who are 25 and 42, which are considered *yakudoshi* or unlucky ages, gather in the narrow lane that leads up to the town's Shinto temple in order to touch the Naked Man and get rid of their own personal curses. On the day of the festival, the volunteer Naked Man, minus even a *fundoshi*, must run through the crowd, all of whom are hoping to touch him in order to transfer all their bad fortune and calamity.

The ordeal is terrifying. The crowds punch, kick, drag and crush anyone in sight in order to get near. The Naked Man himself disappears under the tidal wave of nakedness. It is only twenty minutes later that he emerges at the end of the temple lane: his nose broken and with scars all over his body.

The spectacle is intense, frightening and utterly unique. Only a handful of Westerners have ever been brave enough to compete. It's strongly suggested that you watch from the sidelines – an exhilarating enough experience, and one that is more likely to leave you in full possession of your teeth and sanity.

748 | Dawdling along Doodle Street

CHINA At face value, it can be difficult to decode China's contemporary personality, with its traditional buildings, stern-looking edifices and looming portraits. But a visit to Doodle Street, in the southwestern Chongqing municipality, doesn't just let you get beneath China's surface – you become completely absorbed in it.

Spanning 1.25 kilometres and covering 50,000 square metres, *Tuya Lu* (as it's locally known) is the largest collection of street art in China, and once held the world record for it, too. The art trail starts at the Huangjueping Railway Hospital and ends at the 501 Art Repository. There's a distinct bohemian vibe here, which is unsurprising as it's home to the prestigious Sichuan Fine Arts Institute (SFAI). In the early 2000s, the neighbourhood had become rundown and was eyed up for redevelopment, but Luo Zhongli, president of the SFAI, stepped in and enlisted the help of over eight hundred students, artists and workers to transform Huangjueping into the riotous explosion of art you can see today: there's no missing the flower- and zebra-printed apartment blocks, neon-coloured cartoon figures on the crumbling sides of shop buildings, and haunting, following eyes on brick walls.

It maintains its status as a cultural hub of activity with its independent coffee shops, art galleries and sculptures. In the park, elderly locals gather to play Mahjong against a backdrop of painted wall murals. Doodle Street is a slice of China's personality – a playground for artists – where artists share their ideas and messages on just about any space they can find. Chongqing may be one of the fastest-growing cities in the world, but Doodle Street is delightfully different from the rest of the area.

Be sure to take a pencil and paper with you: after you've finished the trail, it won't be long until you realize you're doodling away yourself.

749 | Eyeballing soldiers in the "scariest place on Earth"

NORTH & SOUTH KOREA Your bus leaves central Seoul. The buildings soon start to decrease in size, before disappearing completely. Then, just ninety minutes from the capital, you see it – a barbed-wire fence that runs, in parallel to its spiky northern twin, from sea to sea across the Korean peninsula, separating South Korea from the hermit-like North, capitalism from communism, green from red. Between these jagged frontiers stretches a 4km-wide demilitarized zone (DMZ), across which the two countries aim undefined weapons at each other; bang in the middle of this is the village of Panmunjeom, where it's possible, under the escort of American infantry, to see now-nuclear North Korea at first hand, and even take a few precious steps inside it.

This is the most heavily fortified border in the world, a fact that prompted a visiting Bill Clinton to describe it as "the scariest place on Earth". While he had the advantage of knowing the full scope and power of the surrounding weaponry, as well as what might happen should the fuses be lit, many visitors are surprised by the tranquillity of the place – there's birdsong among the barbed wire, and the DMZ is home to two small farming communities, one on each side of the Military Demarcation Line.

Your soldier-guide will take you by bus from Camp Bonifas – home to a single par-3 golf hole – to the DMZ itself, and before long you'll be in the Joint Security Area, where the two nation's soldiers stand almost eyeball to eyeball. Three small, sky-blue buildings here are shared by both sides, and by entering one and circumnavigating its central table you'll technically be able to straddle, walk across and take pictures of the border. Rumour has it the microphones on the table are left on, so whatever you say can be heard by the North Korean military; but there's no need to guard your words, as your guide himself will be a young pup, full of stories and propaganda – don't hesitate to ask questions.

The scariest place on Earth? Visit and see for yourself.

747 | Getting naked in Inazawa

JAPAN Old men start to scream as the crush of naked flesh becomes so intense that steam is rising from the enormous crowd. It's only lunchtime and everyone's liver is saturated with sake. The chants of "*Washyoi! Washyoi!*" ("enhance yourself") rise to an ear-rupturing crescendo from the nine thousand men, all dressed in giant nappies, or *fundoshis*. Finally, just when it seems that the entire town of Inazawa is about to be ransacked by the baying mob, the Naked Man appears.

Dating back 1200 years, the Naked Man festival was originally a call to prayer, decreed by Emperor Shotoku in order to dispel a plague that was sweeping the region. The plan worked, so at a date determined by the lunar calendar each year (usually around February or March) men of all ages, though particularly those who are 25 and 42, which are considered *yakudoshi* or unlucky ages, gather in the narrow lane that leads up to the town's Shinto temple

in order to touch the Naked Man and get rid of their own personal curses. On the day of the festival, the volunteer Naked Man, minus even a *fundoshi*, must run through the crowd, all of whom are hoping to touch him in order to transfer all their bad fortune and calamity.

The ordeal is terrifying. The crowds punch, kick, drag and crush anyone in sight in order to get near. The Naked Man himself disappears under the tidal wave of nakedness. It is only twenty minutes later that he emerges at the end of the temple lane: his nose broken and with scars all over his body.

The spectacle is intense, frightening and utterly unique. Only a handful of Westerners have ever been brave enough to compete. It's strongly suggested that you watch from the sidelines – an exhilarating enough experience, and one that is more likely to leave you in full possession of your teeth and sanity.

748 | Dawdling along Doodle Street

CHINA At face value, it can be difficult to decode China's contemporary personality, with its traditional buildings, stern-looking edifices and looming portraits. But a visit to Doodle Street, in the southwestern Chongqing municipality, doesn't just let you get beneath China's surface – you become completely absorbed in it.

Spanning 1.25 kilometres and covering 50,000 square metres, *Tuya Lu* (as it's locally known) is the largest collection of street art in China, and once held the world record for it, too. The art trail starts at the Huangjueping Railway Hospital and ends at the 501 Art Repository. There's a distinct bohemian vibe here, which is unsurprising as it's home to the prestigious Sichuan Fine Arts Institute (SFAI). In the early 2000s, the neighbourhood had become rundown and was eyed up for redevelopment, but Luo Zhongli, president of the SFAI, stepped in and enlisted the help of over eight hundred students, artists and

workers to transform Huangjueping into the riotous explosion of art you can see today: there's no missing the flower- and zebra-printed apartment blocks, neon-coloured cartoon figures on the crumbling sides of shop buildings, and haunting, following eyes on brick walls.

It maintains its status as a cultural hub of activity with its independent coffee shops, art galleries and sculptures. In the park, elderly locals gather to play Mahjong against a backdrop of painted wall murals. Doodle Street is a slice of China's personality – a playground for artists – where artists share their ideas and messages on just about any space they can find. Chongqing may be one of the fastest-growing cities in the world, but Doodle Street is delightfully different from the rest of the area.

Be sure to take a pencil and paper with you: after you've finished the trail, it won't be long until you realize you're doodling away yourself.

749 | Eyeballing soldiers in the "scariest place on Earth"

NORTH & SOUTH KOREA Your bus leaves central Seoul. The buildings soon start to decrease in size, before disappearing completely. Then, just ninety minutes from the capital, you see it – a barbed-wire fence that runs, in parallel to its spiky northern twin, from sea to sea across the Korean peninsula, separating South Korea from the hermit-like North, capitalism from communism, green from red. Between these jagged frontiers stretches a 4km-wide demilitarized zone (DMZ), across which the two countries aim undefined weapons at each other; bang in the middle of this is the village of Panmunjeom, where it's possible, under the escort of American infantry, to see now-nuclear North Korea at first hand, and even take a few precious steps inside it.

This is the most heavily fortified border in the world, a fact that prompted a visiting Bill Clinton to describe it as "the scariest place on Earth". While he had the advantage of knowing the full scope and power of the surrounding weaponry, as well as what might happen

should the fuses be lit, many visitors are surprised by the tranquillity of the place – there's birdsong among the barbed wire, and the DMZ is home to two small farming communities, one on each side of the Military Demarcation Line.

Your soldier-guide will take you by bus from Camp Bonifas – home to a single par-3 golf hole – to the DMZ itself, and before long you'll be in the Joint Security Area, where the two nation's soldiers stand almost eyeball to eyeball. Three small, sky-blue buildings here are shared by both sides, and by entering one and circumnavigating its central table you'll technically be able to straddle, walk across and take pictures of the border. Rumour has it the microphones on the table are left on, so whatever you say can be heard by the North Korean military; but there's no need to guard your words, as your guide himself will be a young pup, full of stories and propaganda – don't hesitate to ask questions.

The scariest place on Earth? Visit and see for yourself.

750 | A sea-fronted desert paradise

JAPAN The Japanese archipelago seems to have it all where natural geography is concerned, but the existence of a vast vista of sand dunes surprises many.

Head to the hidden corner of Tottori prefecture to see the 131-hectare Tottori Sand Dunes. Standing atop any one of the dunes grants you with a breathtaking view – tiny figures of fellow walkers are the only thing to help judge the huge expanse of sand and the endless blue of the neighbouring Sea of Japan.

Unlike the arid climate of the desert, the Tottori Sand Dunes are blessed by a cool sea breeze and more temperate weather, allowing for many outdoor activities. Strong winds permit the adventurous to paraglide, the more calm-minded can partake in sand yoga, or you can travel in style with a camel ride.

This natural wonder, 100,000 years in the making, is formed from sediment deposits carried from the Chūgoku Mountains via the Sendai River. After marvelling at its grandeur and natural beauty, head to the Sand Museum just across the road to see some man-made designs – an art gallery dedicated to sand sculptures with the theme of "Travel Around the World in Sand". With each year focusing on a different country, the annual exhibitions are sure to transport visitors to another world.

Stop by for a breather at *Sunaba Coffee*, its name a tongue-in-cheek reference to the Japanese nickname for Starbucks: 'Sutaba'. With its name literally translating to "sandpit coffee", enjoy another example of Japan's penchant for sticking to themes, while also supporting the local economy.

751 | Getting steamy in a jjimjilbang

SOUTH KOREA Although the word "sauna" may have certain connotations, the family-oriented Korean subspecies represents one of the most distinctive ways – and certainly the cheapest – to spend a night in the country, as almost all are open 24 hours a day.

Your *jjimjilbang* journey starts at the reception desk. After handing over some cash, you'll receive nightclothes and a locker key, then be directed to the single-sex changing areas; these are commonly accessed by lift and on separate floors, populated by Koreans in varying states of relaxation and undress. Your own clothing sacrificed and locked away, you're free to head to the pool area; here you'll find several pools and steam rooms, but it's exceptionally bad form to jump into either without a preliminary shower – free soap is provided. After this, it's up to you: there are usually

several pools, ranging from icy to skin-boiling, and some are even infused with giant tea-bags.

On exiting the pool area you'll find a towel and a free-to-use array of hairdryers, cotton buds and scents on the way back to your locker. Don the kindergarten-style T-shirt and shorts given to you earlier (often pink for women and baby blue for the gents) and head to the large, unisex common area; these usually contain televisions, internet terminals, water dispensers, massage rooms and snack bars. A cushioned mat will serve as your bed, and though you're free to sleep pretty much wherever you want, you'll usually be able to track down a sensible little corner, and can doze off with the knowledge that you've just enjoyed a quintessentially Korean experience.

752 | Filling up on little eats

TAIWAN Crowded alleyways, blaring scooter horns and a mix of Mandopop and Nokia tunes may not sound like an appealing night out, but there's a reason why Taiwan's night markets pack people in – they offer some of the best food in Asia.

The Taiwanese love food so much, they've perfected what's known in Chinese as "little eats" (*xiaochi*), tasty snacks served in small portions – think Chinese takeaway meets tapas. The places most associated with *xiaochi* are night markets held all over the island; most get going in the evening and don't typically close till after midnight. Each stall has a speciality, a "little eat" it likes to promote as food fit for an emperor. But royal lineage is unimportant, as is language: just point, pay and devour.

At Shilin, Taipei's best and biggest night market, a typical evening starts with a few warm-up laps, perhaps grabbing a couple of appetizers along the way: a sugar-glazed strawberry, fried pancake with egg, or succulent Shilin sausage served with raw garlic and eaten with a cocktail

stick. Suitably inspired, it's time for a little more chopstick work: many stalls own a cluster of plastic tables and chairs where you can slurp and munch while seated. Classic dishes include slippery oyster omelettes covered in luscious red sauce, and addictive *lu rou fan*, juicy stewed pork on rice. Still hungry? Try some celebrated regional specialities: *danzi mian* from Tainan (noodles with pork, egg and shrimp), or deep-fried meatballs from Changhua.

Serious connoisseurs – or more likely those with adventurous palates – can opt for the really scary stuff. Most infamous are *chou doufu*, cooked in pig fat and better known as stinky tofu, the smell of which sickens newcomers but the taste of which is sublime (the fried, crispy outer layer perfectly balances the fluffy tofu underneath), and *lu wei*, a savoury blend of animal guts, simmered in broth, and often eaten cold. Try this, washed down with a cold Taiwan beer, and you're certain to win the respect of the incredulous Taiwanese sitting next to you.

Bathing with snow monkeys

JAPAN Should you choose to imagine a monkey, for whatever reason, it's likely to be surrounded by tropical vines or thick jungle, trading screams with the parrots or chowing down on a banana. Snowy peaks would not usually be on the agenda, but Japan is home to a particular breed of macaque that positively revels in the stuff. These clever monkeys share a number of common bonds with human beings – they're one of the only two animals known to wash their food before eating it, and no other primates live further north. Also, like their occasionally more intelligent two-legged cousins, many macaques counter the winter cold by hunting down a source of warmth; in Japan, you're never far from a hot spring, and one of the country's most magical winter sights is the view of a horde of apes silhouetted in the mist of an outdoor pool.

With a number of hot springs and other hydrothermal features – though most have been straddled by resorts and cut off from the outside world by a ticket booth – Japan offers its snow-loving macaques a place to escape the freezing temperatures. The winter coincides with the mating season, and it's hard to say what's more amusing – monkeys engaging in poolside trysts, or the Japanese pretending not to notice.

Tourists head to places such as Jigokudani in Yamanouchi to catch glimpses of the bathing apes, especially the lovable baby macaques. The monkeys are usually the first to arrive, their faces standing out against the snow – pink Easter Island statues in balaclavas of fur. Bear in mind that though their eyes may appear dispassionate, it's unwise to look directly into them for too long, lest it be taken as a sign of aggression. In contrast, their postures can be eerily human as they plonk themselves into the water, slouched over the poolside in contented silence, and then perch on an outer stone to cool off.

JAPAN To stand before one of the oldest living trees in the world, in one of the oldest evergreen forests, is a humbling experience. This tiny island of Yakushima, only 27km wide, is tucked into the warm southern waters of Japan – an otherworldly mix of pearl-white beaches, misty mountains and humid rainforests pulsing with life. It's not uncommon to find a monkey or ten sunbathing at the roadside, nor herds of indigenous deer treading softly among the moss.

At the heart of this subtropical landscape stands one of Yakushima's greatest lures: Jōmon Sugi. This knotted and gnarled cedar, rising like a colossal stone giant from the spongy earth, is thought to be among the largest and oldest trees in the world, with a circumference the length of four cars. To reach it takes some determination – first you must take a ferry to the island then embark on a ten-hour, round-trip hike that loops and weaves through one of the wettest climates on the planet.

Nowhere does a forest feel more alive than here. As you follow the trail past stormy rivers and fairy-tale tree roots, it's as if the branches of the ancient sugi are beckoning you deeper into their fold — your senses engulfed by the wet soil, warm air and songs of a million invisible insects. You can even spend the night at the wooden Takatsuka hut, near Jomon Sugi, if you feel brave enough.

Hiking to one of the oldest trees in the world

755 | Relaxing in tropical Taketomi-jima

JAPAN On tiny Taketomi-jima the traditional bungalow homes are ringed by rocky walls draped with hibiscus and bougainvillea. From the low-slung terracotta-tiled roofs glare *shiisa*, ferocious, bug-eyed lion figures. The only traffic is cyclists on rickety bikes negotiating the sandy lanes, and buffalo-drawn carts hauling visitors to the beaches.

This is Japan – but not as you might know it. Taketomi-jima is one of the hundred-plus subtropical islands of Okinawa that trail, like scattered grains of rice, some 700km across the South China Sea. Cultural influences from China, Southeast Asia and the US, who occupied Okinawa until 1972 following WWII, have all seeped into the local way of life, providing a fascinating counterpoint to the conformity and fast-paced modernity of mainland Japan.

Fringed by soft, golden beaches, the islands are popular with Japanese looking for some R & R. Taketomi-jima especially is often besieged with day-trippers, as it's just a short ferry ride from the mountainous Ishigaki-jima, the main island of the Okinawan sub-collection known as the Yaeyamas. The trick is to stay on after the masses have left. Take up residence in one of the many family-run *minshuku* – small guesthouses with tatami mat floors, futons and rice-paper shoji screens. After a refreshing bath, slip into the *yukata* (cotton robe) provided and dig into a tasty dinner of local delicacies, and then wander down to the beach to watch the glorious sunset.

On returning to the *minshuku*, it's not unusual for a bottle or two of Okinawa's pungent rice liquor *awamori* to appear. Locals strum on a *sanshin* (three-stringed lute) and lead guests in a gentle sing-along of Okinawan folk favourites. As the *awamori* takes effect, don't be surprised if you also learn a few local dance moves.

756 | Visit the Berlin of the Steppes

KAZAKHSTAN Astana beggars belief. This new city, thrown up with a mix of determination and flair last seen when Peter the Great forged St Petersburg out of a Baltic swamp, is the second-coldest capital in the world, after Ulaanbaatar in Mongolia. Why did newly independent Kazakhstan want to build its new capital on steppe-land where temperatures plummet to -40°C in winter? True, the old capital, Almaty, 1000km to the south, was prone to earthquakes and lacked space for expansion, but some suspect the real reason was to bring ethnic Kazakhs up to the north of the country so that its Russian-speaking population didn't form an enclave.

The city is the project of President Nursultan Nazarbayev, who has ruled Kazakhstan since the fall of the Soviet empire. A gilded imprint of his hand rests on the top of the Bayterek, a spiky space-age tower representing the poplar tree in which, according to legend, the magic Samuruk bird laid its egg. Visitors are encouraged to place their hand in his and make a wish, whereupon the Kazakh national anthem plays.

Yet this is only one of a number of statement buildings across this extraordinary city. Astana's planners have claimed they want to create a new Eurasian capital of culture rather than a purely administrative capital like Ottawa or Canberra.

Other recent buildings include a glowing glass Pyramid of Peace designed by Norman Foster, which incorporates an opera house. Conspiracy theorists believe it is actually a piece of Masonic symbolism designed to herald a new world order. Others reckon it was constructed on its artificial hill so that President Nazarbayev has something to look at from his huge blue-domed marble palace. Foster also designed Khan Shatyry, a 50m-high "royal tent" that encloses an entertainment complex, while the distinguished Japanese architect Kisho Noriaki Kurokawa was brought in to design the airport and much of the town planning.

Money seems to be no object in Astana. As long as the petrodollars keep flowing in, this is a city that can genuinely say "Make it so".

757 | White nights on the world's edge

RUSSIA The inhabitants of Russia's far north have a hard time of it in the winter months, seeing just two hours' daylight in December, but the summer more than makes up for it, with sunlit days stretching into magical "white nights".

St Petersburg's White Nights festival is an established tourist draw, but more adventurous travellers can head north towards the Arctic Circle and the remote Solovetsky Archipelago in the Karelia region. Situated in the White Sea, in the uppermost part of the world's biggest country, these islands seem close to the tipping point of the world.

Whether you are walking along the sand beaches of the White Sea, dawdling by the shores of the hundreds of lakes dotting the islands, or taking a boat trip to spot white whales, the sense of space and timelessness is incredible.

From the Middle Ages till the Bolsheviks seized power, monks sought out this place for solitary contemplation; when the Soviet Union fell, they returned, and today the exquisite monastery on the main island, pure white with silver onion domes, is again a site of active worship.

But there were darker times in the interim. The Soviet authorities saw the potential of the islands' remote location, and in 1923 created a Camp of Special Significance, where political opponents could be subjected to the near-constant winter darkness, isolation and bitter cold. Solovetsky became, as the great dissident Aleksandr Solzhenitsyn put it, "the mother of the gulag".

Today, the camp is remembered in a museum inside the Kremlin on the main island. On top of Sekirnaya Gora ("Hatchet Mountain") you can also see the Church of the Ascension, which was used for solitary confinement – an incongruously picturesque spot a pleasant 12km walk from the monastery.

However you spend your days on the archipelago, one impression is liable to linger long after you've left: the otherworldly, eerie feel of days that last 22 hours and nights than never fully fall.

758 | Buddhist boot camp at Haeinsa temple

SOUTH KOREA It's 2.30am on Sunday. Your head is spinning, and you feel like you might fall over, or even throw up. No, this is not another night out in one of Seoul's rowdy bars – it's an ordinary evening at Haeinsa, one of South Korea's most beautiful and famous Buddhist temples. Unlike other temples, where foreigners are introduced to "Buddhism lite", Haeinsa – meaning "Temple of Reflection on a Smooth Sea" – is not for the faint-hearted. It is a kind of Buddhist university, or rather Buddhist boot camp, for trainee monks and game foreigners.

On a typical weekend trip, you arrive on Saturday afternoon and immediately cast off your worldly attire – and all your worldly cares – in favour of baggy, grey replacements. Then it's straight into temple etiquette and meditation practice. No unnecessary talking, no unnecessary touching, no unnecessary thinking – just clear your mind and adhere to the rules. Bedtime is at 9pm. That's for a good reason, as

you have to get up at 3am. After waking up and donning your grey outfit in a daze, it's out into the cold night for morning rituals.

First you head to the main dharma hall, where you're expected to perform 108 bowing moves, an effort that takes almost an hour. That's a lot of kneeling and standing in the middle of the night – not easy for unpractised backs and heads. Then, at 4am it's time to walk down a quiet mountain path to a marble meditation area. Here, you sit on the edge of what looks like it should be a pond, legs crossed. Clearing your mind is much easier in this environment. Staying awake is not. But luckily monks are on hand to nudge slumping backs.

After meditation, you head back to the dharma hall for a simple breakfast before watching the rising sun illuminate this beautiful temple. Your body may be battered and exhausted, but your soul definitely feels lighter.

759 | Sail to the Galápagos of the East

JAPAN The Ogasawara Islands are not your everyday archipelago. Only reachable by a 24-hour ferry ride, 1000km south of Tokyo, the thirty-plus islands have never been joined to another landmass. Their unique flora and fauna includes 441 endemic plant species, 379 types of insect and 134 land-snails, as well as a disconcertingly large flying fox, regularly spotted at dusk.

Weekly ferries arrive at the largest island, Chichijima, where the small port makes a good base for cyclists and walkers. One scenic yomp leads through the valley scenery of the Nakayama Pass to John Beach, where improbably large hermit crabs trace patterns in the sands.

Activities include snorkelling trips and, between February and April, whale-watching cruises, in search of playfully breaching humpbacks. You can even take a night tour, to see glow-in-the-dark mushrooms – not endemic, but remarkable nonetheless – and other nocturnal oddities.

760 | Surviving a hotpot dinner in Chongqing

CHINA As red-faced patrons cluster around each table, there's no way of knowing whether their faces are flushed from the beer they're drinking or from the steaming, chilli-spiked broth that's the real focus of their attention – Chongqing is renowned throughout China as the home of the country's spiciest hotpot.

Simply dip bite-sized chunks of meat and vegetables into your cauldron of soup, wait for them to cook and then dunk each morsel in a soothing sesame-based sauce. Daring diners can order a *málà guōd* – a whole pan of oily, crimson soup, the effect of which is intensified by an infusion of mouth-numbing Sichuan pepper – but you may prefer to opt for a *yuānyāng guō*, divided into hot and mild halves.

Whichever you choose, you'll definitely need plenty of icy beer to clear your palate, all of which will leave you as red-faced and happy as the diners at the table next door.

761 | Trekking through Tiger Leaping Gorge

CHINA "A stony path winds up to cool hills", or so goes a Chinese poem. Well, it was never truer than at the spot where a youthful Yangzi channels violently through Tiger Leaping Gorge in Yunnan province.

The stony path in question winds up to the foothills of an ash-grey, spiky range – though the peaks, at over 5000m high, spoil the comparison by actually being mountains. Of course, poetry also doesn't mention anything as mundane as what it's like to lug a backpack around for three days at this altitude: rather tiring. Nor does it explain the 100m-wide gorge's dramatic name: "A tiger was being chased, and it leaped across the river to escape" is the villagers' well-rehearsed answer.

Altitude and names aside, though, trekking along the high path through the gorge is fantastic. The Chinese don't usually have a romantic view of nature; instead they see the Great Outdoors as being frighteningly empty, unless livened up by tour groups, cable cars, stone staircases, strategically placed pavilions, souvenir hawkers and noodle stands. But here there is nothing – just the mountains, the path, the gorge and a huge, blue sky. Occasionally you'll see a farmer or some goats; every few hours' walking throws up a couple of houses. You sleep along the way at small villages, and can sit outside under a gloriously luminous Milky Way while an unlikely number of satellites race in straight lines across the night.

Conquering the Pamirs

TAJIKISTAN Standing at a skyscraping crossroads – the Himalaya, Karakoram, Hindu Kush and Tien Shan ranges meet here – the magnificent Pamirs remain one of the most unexplored places on the planet. Known as Bam-i-Dunya ("Roof of the World"), this vast, rugged stretch of Central Asia boasts astounding crested peaks and stretches of undulating fields. Visitors can camp with nomads and ride bareback across the steppe – and hike and climb a unique land.

While many of Tajikistan's hundred-odd mountains have never been scaled, you can climb Peak Lenin (also known as Ibn Sina Peak), at 7134m the third-highest mountain in the former Soviet Union. The summit is one of the world's easiest mountains over 7000m to climb due to its easy access and sixteen relatively uncomplicated routes.

As the classic ascent has few steep sections, ropes, harnesses and extensive high-altitude experience are not necessary – though several exposed ridges and glaciated areas make winter mountaineering experience and use of an ice axe and crampons essential.

Although you can reach base camp by helicopter, it's better to acclimatize yourself culturally by trekking from village to village in the lower altitudes, where Sunni Muslim shepherds tend sheep, goat and yak, and traditional families live unfathomably isolated existences (if anyone offers you the local delicacy, sheep lungs soaked in yak milk, say yes without hesitation and swallow very quickly). Situated on a raised meadow of alpine flowers between two steep river valleys on the Tajik–Kyrgyz border, the lush green edelweiss meadows of base camp lead to a heavily glaciated ascent towards several steep, exposed stretches of ridge that open south towards the Hindu Kush.

The climb to the summit traverses a range of terrain, including wide and steep snow-covered spurs and icy, crevassed slopes, while above, barren shards of rock shoot off sheer into the sky. The summit is crowned by a number of plaques, including one of Lenin himself, and offers unsurpassed views across the Pamirs, beyond which stretch China's Muztag Ata peak and the Karakoram range linking Pakistan to Ladakh in northern India and the Tibetan border.

Hanging out in super-cool Shinjuku

JAPAN Shinjuku isn't for the faint-hearted. But if you're new to Tokyo and want a crash course in the frenetic pace of life, it's the first place you should come to. Sure, Asakusa has more history and Roppongi has better nightlife, but neither can compete when it comes to dealing out high-voltage culture shocks.

On the west side of Shinjuku station, which heaves with commuters and the smell of strong espressos, things are typically well ordered. This shimmering business district is home to some of Japan's tallest skyscrapers (as well as more than 13,000 bureaucrats) and there are enough high-rise megastores to have you craning your neck in disbelief. It's a hardworking part of the city, where success is measured by the number of hours you spend at the office, and exploring it for the first time feels like stumbling through an ultra-efficient city of the future. But cross to the other side of the train tracks, and things couldn't be more different.

Here, chaos rules. Under the hot neon lights of Kabukichō, in the eastern part of Shinjuku, you'll find stand-up noodle bars snuggled next to strip joints and love hotels. Huge video screens pump noisy adverts into roadside bars, *Blade Runner*-style, and street hawkers skulk in the shadows by jazz clubs and theatres. To escape these guys, who'll try anything to get at your yen, head to an all-night karaoke bar where you can croon until your sake-soaked vocal cords feel like they're on fire. Or squeeze down the oddball alleyways of the Golden Gai district, which attracts artists, musicians and filmmakers with a ramshackle heap of more than 250 bars – each with its own unique theme. Chances are, you'll still end up singing the night away.

When the morning sunlight starts to extinguish Shinjuku's nocturnal glow, you can take a stroll through the cherry blossom trees of Shinjuku Gyoen – Tokyo's finest park – and give yourself a well-earned pat on the back. Consider yourself initiated.

MONGOLIA For Mongols, life has always been portable – homes, families and livelihoods are all carried on horseback. There's no better conveyance for this rolling grassy terrain than their well-trained steeds, and certainly no other way to immerse yourself in this last great nomadic culture. To enlist in this itinerant life you'll saddle up for the grassy steppe of the Darhat Valley, where horsemen and herders find prime summer pastures.

From an encampment on the shores of Lake Khovsgol, a day's horse trek across the Jigleg Pass leads through forests of Siberian larch trees laced with magenta fireweed before descending into the Darhat Valley – but this is just the beginning. Throughout your days on horseback you will come upon isolated encampments dotting the grassy expanse, each with several *gers*, the traditional lattice-framed, felt-covered homes of nomadic herders. Mongols are quick to invite you inside, where you'll witness their shamanistic rituals

as they call for rain or predict the future from the shoulder bone of a sheep. As you sit on the felt-lined *ger* floor, they'll reach for a leather bag and pour you a bowl of *airag*, a fermented horse-milk beverage – think fizzy sour milk with a kick. It's an acquired taste, but it quenches thirst and a swig will help wash down that morsel of roasted marmot you've been gnawing. Evenings will be spent in comfortable *ger* camps and in tents with all the accoutrements of catered camping.

As you approach the southern skirt of the valley you can expect to encounter the Tsaatan, a tribe that both rides and herds reindeer. The Darhat Valley is their favoured home for summer grazing before they retreat to the more protective forest highlands in the winter.

With fresh horses, you'll leave the Darhat through mountainous birch woods, bringing you back to Lake Khovsgol – the conclusion of your passage into a vanishing, but still vigorous, way of life.

Horsing about with the Mongols

764

765 | Thangha painting monks in Tongren

CHINA As your eyes get used to the dim light of the prayer hall, wall paintings picked out in gold leap in the candlelight. Fierce *dharmapalas* dance atop the bodies of demons, beatific bodhisattvas float on lotus flowers, and scenes from Buddha's life flicker like images in a zoetrope. In this rural corner of eastern Qinghai, just outside the town of Tongren, two small monasteries in the village of Wutun have fostered a rich tradition of *thangka* painting, one that has left a repository of sublime Tibetan religious art on their walls.

The thirty monks of Upper and Lower Wutun Monasteries spend their days painting – at least until their eyesight gives out, which usually happens around the age of forty. When they are no longer able to work, these masters teach younger monks how to draw and paint the vivid characters of the Tibetan pantheon, using methods that have changed little through the centuries. Ground mineral pigments are mixed with glue and water, creating colours that grow richer with time. Silk or cotton fabric is stretched and sewn taut over a wooden frame, which the monks tie up near a window while they work cross-legged, their noses hovering just centimetres above the cloth.

Lower Wutun Monastery houses several aged *thangka* panels that were covered with newspaper to hide and protect them during the Cultural Revolution, when the monastery buildings were converted to grain stores. Kept properly in dry conditions (and out of reach of Red Guards), a *thangka* can last for centuries. A few minutes' walk down the road, Upper Wutun Monastery houses a 30m-wide *thangka* that is kept rolled up at the back of the prayer hall for most of the year. This vast painting is unfurled on a nearby hillside at sunrise on festival days, during Saga Dawa or Shoton, to allow the first light of the morning to shine upon the Buddha's face.

766 | Running the Pyongyang Marathon

NORTH KOREA Nobody in the history of the universe has ever run a marathon without bragging a little bit to their friends afterwards, but those 42 kilometres will feel even more special if you've chalked them up in Pyongyang, capital of one of the world's most isolated countries. The Pyongyang Marathon has been held since 1984, but was of limited international interest until recent years; it's now one of the country's most popular drawcards, and comes with the added bonus of – you know – visiting North Korea.

The run starts with a colourful opening ceremony, involving a lap of the Kim Il-sung Stadium. After bursting out of the ground, you'll pass the Arch of Triumph, which is like a brutalist version of the Arc de Triomphe, but (of course) a little taller. From here the course heads north, then makes a sharp turn southwest to hit the Potonggang, a small river where your first sights will be *USS Pueblo* – an American ship captured by North Korea in 1968 – and one of the country's many bombastic war museums.

From there it's a quick pant east to Kim Il-sung Square, which you may recognize from the stock footage played whenever North Korea makes the international news (the goose-stepping solders, the missile parades... and now you, sweating profusely). After that, the course follows the Taedong river south to a turning point, then heads back towards the stadium. Here you'll be greeted by thousands of cheering North Koreans – whatever time you post, this may be as close as you'll ever get to feeling like an Olympic athlete.

767 | Communing with the sun goddess

JAPAN Nestled amid the mist-shrouded mountains of eastern Kyushu, Takachiho has the unmistakable air of an age-old sanctuary. It is revered in Shintoism as the spot where gods first walked the Earth, after Ninigi – grandson of the sun goddess and great-grandfather of Japan's first emperor, Jimmu – descended from the heavens to pacify the land.

Wandering the green paths around Takachiho's stunning gorge and waterfall gives a taste of the spine-tingling mysticism at the heart of Japanese cultural life, but the walk to Ama no Iwato Jinja, a cave shrine to the sun goddess Amaterasu, is even more compelling. You follow a gently winding trail beside a small river, through ancient woods, until eventually it widens and, surrounded by piles of pilgrim-stacked stones, you emerge into a clearing by the cave itself.

Despite its immense significance, this place is not stuffy. You can pray at the small shrine in the cave, or simply take photos by the *torii* (stone gate) and admire the stunning surroundings, then head back for a bowl of the local speciality, chicken *nanban*, and a cool beer.

Such prosaic pleasures are appropriate for this holiest of holy places – it was the site of the party that saved the world, after all. Legend has it that in a fit of restlessness Susano'o, Amaterasu's brother and god of storms, went on a bizarre rampage in which he destroyed her rice fields and threw a dead horse at her, killing an attendant. Understandably angry, and ashamed of his wayward behaviour, Amaterasu hid in this cave.

After trying everything to get her to come out again, the other gods resorted to a strange stratagem: they had a party. Another goddess danced in front of the cave, and the drunken applause and laughter outside made Amaterasu so curious that she peeked out. The gods grabbed her and sealed the cave, thereby ensuring that the sun kept shining.

As the light filters down through layers of deep green leaves to reach the clear-running water, reflecting in ripples across the roof of this unassuming cave, you'll be glad that they went to so much trouble.

768 | Slurping a Turkish coffee in Yerevan

ARMENIA The break-up of the Soviet Union gave the world an impressive array of new capitals. Some have since become familiar fodder on travel itineraries – think Tallinn's Baltic charm, Kiev's bulbous cathedrals and Riga's cultural riches. Others, for better or worse, remain something of a mystery.

Step forward Yerevan, capital of Armenia, a city swaggering into a new era, and making a mockery of the usual Soviet stereotypes of drab, grey skies and drab, grey architecture. Lofty and landlocked, Yerevan is one of the sunniest of the ex-Soviet capitals, and for most of the year the azure-blue firmament is punctuated only by the awe-inspiring shape of Mount Ararat. This fabled 5137m peak is where Noah's floating zoo is said to have come to rest after the floods, and although it now lies just across the border in Turkish territory, the fact that it can be seen from so many parts of Yerevan makes it one of the main symbols of the city.

One other unmissable feature here is the liberal, almost ubiquitous use of duf, a sumptuously coloured stone used in the construction of the vast majority of Yerevan's buildings. Its precise hue shifts from peach to pink to rose depending upon the weather and time of day, though the fiery tones that emerge under the rising and setting sun are particularly magnificent.

Nowhere is this more apparent than on Northern Avenue, a sleek pedestrianized thoroughfare in the very centre of the city. Half a kilometre of soft, pinkish stone regularly inset with the cafés and boutiques of a burgeoning middle class, it would look stylish in any European city, and makes a grand place to people-watch over a coffee, served Turkish-style from a conical metal pot. The same could be said of most of Yerevan – indeed, on a summer afternoon it can seem as if the whole city is out, dressed for a fashion shoot, getting a caffeine fix.

769 | Riding by bus to Dêgê

CHINA Ticked off western Sichuan's pandas, pristine blue lakes, raw mountain scenery and Tibetan monasteries? Well then, for what is likely to prove one of the most adrenaline-packed eight hours of your life, ride the public bus from Ganzi to Dêgê. You start 3500m up in a river valley at the foot of the Que'er Shan range, Ganzi's dusty sprawl of tiled concrete buildings disappearing abruptly around a corner behind you, the bus packed to capacity with raucous crowds of Tibetans.

The road – like all roads here, if you're riding west towards the Himalayan Plateau – heads ever upwards, crossing a wide pass festooned with prayer flags at the head of the valley, at which point the Tibetans all cheer and hurl handfuls of paper prayers out the windows like clouds of confetti. At the halfway town of Manigange, beyond, the passengers get out and (despite their Buddhist leanings) consume vast quantities of meat dumplings and butter tea – the latter revolting as tea but satisfying if thought of as soup.

Back on the bus, the journey continues past brown glaciers hemming in the holy lake of Yilhun Lhatso and boulders carved in Tibetan script with "*Om Mani Padme Hum*", and the valley reaches a rounded conclusion beneath some particularly wicked-looking, spiky, snow-bound peaks. Unfortunately, the road goes on, winding back on itself as it climbs up... and up... and up. The Tibetans are no longer so boisterous; several are blatantly chanting prayers, thumbing rosaries with their eyes screwed up tight. Up among the peaks now, the bus is suddenly exposed to the wind as the road wobbles through the narrow, 5050m-high pass and around a corner so tight that at night you'd be over the edge before you even knew that there was a corner to turn.

On the far side, the road slaloms down a virtually vertical rock face to the valley far below, and then, after all that excitement, your heart rate can settle on the unadventurous final stretch to Dêgê, just an hour away.

770 | Mud walls and silk carpets in Khiva

UZBEKISTAN Sturdy mud walls encapsulate a town that seems plucked from the Middle Ages, when a healthy stream of Silk Road traders would tramp in through fortified gateways from the dusty desert, their camel trains in tow. Here you will find scant evidence of modernity. Few cars enter the Old City, and children play freely in the narrow streets, their laughter dampened by the mud-brick and adobe facades.

While ochre dominates the palette, the monotony is split by brilliant lapis lazuli and turquoise tiles decorating the chunky minaret of Kalta Minor, the cupolas of poet Pakhlavan Mahmoud's mausoleum and the fronts of madrassahs. Further mud fortifications within the city walls belong to Itchan Kala, protecting Kuhna Ark, a vast twelfth-century citadel, and complete with an arsenal, harem and camel stables.

These magnificent Silk Road dinosaurs cluster round open plazas, unchanged in centuries. The same can be said for the pace of life. Women in colourful shawls press roundels of dough onto the heated insides of tandoor ovens on the street outside their homes; a slice of domesticity among the historic exhibits.

Silk carpets are still woven by hand in Khiva. Pass through ageing, carved wood doors into courtyards filled with completed works that took months to complete. Here, around the courtyard, are rooms filled with silk, dyed a myriad of colours using natural pigments. Others contain tall looms where the threads are woven in complex patterns by teams of skilled artisans.

Exploring the 798 art district

CHINA In a country where censorship rules, few people gave the idea much of a chance. In little more than a decade, however, the 798 Art District, which occupies a former military zone on the northeastern edge of Beijing, has grown to become a genuine creative hub for contemporary art.

The story begins in the 1950s, when huge brick factories were thrown up around the Chinese capital to help satisfy the army's growing demand for communications technologies. When manufacturing techniques moved on, these Bauhaus-style buildings were left abandoned. And by the early 2000s artists had moved in, attracted by low rents and the high-ceilinged spaces that gave them room to work on, and show off, their paintings and sculptures. With few other places for local artists to express themselves, and the empty factories effectively a blank canvas, news began to spread.

Today, the vast 500,000-square-metre complex teems with bookshops, galleries and art stores. Bright sculptures (think lipstick red and lime green) add colour to the traffic-free streets, while hipsters from Beijing, Shanghai and beyond rummage through trailers stacked high with ceramics and old cameras.

It's hard to spot much in the way of politically charged art, though you might glimpse the odd cartoonish doodle of a tank or gunman, and the shops do a good line in "Obamao" T-shirts. Away from the glossy commercial galleries, multimedia installations and corporate-sponsored exhibitions, though, there are still traces of the area's edgier beginnings. Old factory walls shimmer with graffiti, and lone photographers snap at the handful of tumbledown industrial buildings and rusting pipelines that have yet to be torn down or redeveloped.

On its journey from niche art hangout to major tourist attraction – a transition that has caused rents to spiral, and thus priced out many artists – the district has picked up its share of critics. But then, if an art district like this wasn't bringing in the money, it might not have been tolerated for so long.

772

JAPAN A sleek, space-age train glides into the station precisely on time. When it pulls to a stop the doors align exactly in front of each orderly queue of passengers. The guard, wearing immaculate white gloves and a very natty peaked cap, bows as you climb aboard. Where but Japan could a train journey start in such style?

Japan's high-speed Shinkansen, popularly known as the "bullet train", is the envy of the world, and while it's not cheap, it's something you just have to experience once. The Tokaido–Sanyo line runs from Tokyo west to Kyoto and Hiroshima – 900km – and the fastest *Nozomi* trains cover this in just four hours. In places, they reach 300km per hour, yet the ride is as smooth as silk.

It's only by looking out of the window that you get a sense of speed; neat rows of houses flicker by, gradually giving way to rice fields, woods and the occasional temple, as you leave Tokyo's sprawling metropolis behind. If the weather's clear, you'll catch Mount Fuji's iconic, snowcapped cone.

Meanwhile, inside the train all is hushed calm. People sleep, punch messages into mobiles (calls are forbidden except in designated areas), or tuck into *eki-ben*, takeaway station meals that are an art form in themselves. Before you know it, you're pulling in to Kyoto's monumental station – eyesore or emblem, depending on whom you ask. No time for the city's myriad temples now, though. The doors swoosh shut and you're off again. Osaka brings yet more urban sprawl, but after Kobe the tracks run along the coast, offering glimpses of the island-speckled Inland Sea as you near Hiroshima.

In a country where cutting-edge design coexists alongside ancient traditions and courtesies, the bullet train is a shining example of the extraordinary attention to detail and awesome teamwork that lies at the heart of Japanese society. Far more than a mere journey, riding the Shinkansen provides a glimpse into what makes Japan tick.

Space-age travel
riding the Shinkansen

JAPAN In many ways, the Fuji Rock festival will be familiar to any seasoned Western festival-goer. Major international acts like Franz Ferdinand and Arcade Fire headline stadium-scale stages, and smaller local bands play anything from Japanese drumming to experimental electronica at fringe locations. There's unexpected downpours and mud baths, and impossibly early mornings as the sun turns your tent into an oven. But all of this comes wrapped with the charms of Japanese culture, both softening and enriching the experience.

The night before the official first day, the festival kicks off with a *bon-odori* folk dance. The happy crowd honours the ancestors by stomping in a circle around a drummer, raising and lowering their hands. When the festival proper gets under way, food and drink stalls line all the main routes between the stages, but there's more sushi than burgers on the menus. There's alcohol, of course, but as well as beer stands, there are sake stalls where you can sample a variety of rice wines you'd never see outside Japan. Despite all the drinking, there's no aggression, and a warm welcome for the occasional foreigners. Above all, people are here because of their passion for music: many choose to quietly stand and watch, and moshing is carried out enthusiastically but with due regard for others. Most impressively, the entire site is rubbish-free: there are bins for sorting and recycling waste everywhere, including dedicated chopstick bags.

Pristine portaloos fully stocked with toilet paper are an extraordinary sight, and if the main areas feel a touch hectic you can get a cable car up the mountain, leaving the rockers and ravers far below, to enjoy noodles or ice cream at the top. But the on-site *onsen* is perhaps the most delicious local detail. It's a common form of relaxation that's popular throughout Japan: a large, natural hot-tub fed by volcanic springs. Sitting with your head just above the water and gazing at a small Zen garden of artfully arranged rocks and gravel, you can watch your hangover drift away with the steam into the cool mountain air.

773

Have a sake party at FujiRock

774 | Defying gravity at the vertiginous Hanging Temple

CHINA There are more temples in China than one could ever count, so it takes something rather special for one to stand out – step forward Xuankong Si, southwest of Datong, which may haunt the nightmares of those afflicted by vertigo. Its name roughly translates as the "Temple Suspended in the Void", but in tourist literature it's usually referred to as the "Hanging Temple", on account of its jaw-droppingly precarious position.

There has been a place of worship here since the Northern Wei dynasty (386–535), though its buildings were often ravaged by the flooding of the Heng River, causing the temple to be rebuilt higher and higher each time. While the river has long since been tamed by a dam upstream, the temple's pretty, golden-roofed buildings now sit on a near-vertical cliff face, propped up on a series of wooden poles set into the rock.

Even before the entrance to the compound, you're likely to be wowed by the first sight of the Hanging Temple. Things take an even more spectacular turn once you're inside the rickety, claustrophobic, atmospheric structure: tall, narrow stairs and plank walkways connect its six halls, in which shrines exist to Confucianism, Buddhism and Taoism. Ground level suddenly seems a startlingly long way down, and you'll most likely be relieved by the sight of some unobtrusive modern cables and the like, there to support the aforementioned wooden poles.

The Hanging Temple is an easy day-trip from Datong, a city that also deserves a mention. Once famed for its ever-present stench of coal, it has done a remarkable job of tidying itself up in recent years, and its rebuilt, almost tourist-free city walls are even more photogenic – especially around sunset – than the more famous ones further south in Xi'an.

775 | Exploring Punakha, a valley lost in time

BHUTAN Visiting Punakha might be the closest you can get to time travel. This narrow valley, tucked into the folds of the Himalayas at the heart of Bhutan, is a place of bows, arrows and nomadic yak herders, where traditional dress is still the norm, and more cows wander the roads than people. On arrival, you might be struck by the isolation — a four-hour, zigzagging drive from the international airport, surrounded on all sides by towering mountains. Or you might notice the lack of tourists. The government strictly limits visas to Bhutan, which means that in rural places like Punakha, you can go for days without seeing another visitor.

Certainly, you'll notice the scenery: a patchwork of rice and chilli fields dotted with red-roofed houses, sliced by two wide silver rivers. At the confluence of these waterways stands the fortress-like Punakha Dzong, considered one of the most beautiful buildings in Bhutan. This majestic red and white structure, laced in gold and fronted by purple jacaranda trees, is the winter home of a retinue of one thousand monks.

Punakha was Bhutan's capital until 1955, before it moved to the city of Thimpu, a three-hour drive away. Despite the power shift, you can sense the important role Punakha still plays, with some of the country's most prized monasteries dotting the hillsides. The famed Chimi Lhakhang 'fertility temple', for example, is somewhat of a pilgrimage for couples across the Himalayas. Visiting this ornate white and gold monastery might leave your inner child giggling: built in 1499, it's decorated in an extraordinary number of phalluses, representing hope and good fortune for all those who wish to conceive.

Less eyebrow-raising but equally eye-catching is the pagoda-like Khamsum Yulley Namgyal Chorten, built by the Queen Mother in 2004 to symbolize prosperity and wellbeing for Bhutan. It stands on a tall hill above the valley, requiring a 40-minute ascent on foot over rickety bridges lined with prayer flags and through woodlands speckled with avocado trees. From the top, 360-degree views extend over Punakha's jigsaw of rice fields and to the snow-capped Himalayas beyond.

776 | Svaneti – the hidden heart of the Caucasus

GEORGIA The isolated Svaneti region of northern Georgia is as beautiful as it is remote. True to the traditions of the Caucasus, its inhabitants have always been independent-minded, and for centuries frustrated outside attempts at control with the help of the sturdy defensive towers that still punctuate its hillsides. Yet today Svaneti is a place with a sense of peace that is a far cry from the breakaway Russian republics of Chechnya and Dagestan to the northeast. Locked under snow for much of the year, in summer defiant green hillsides emerge as if new-made by the thaw, and the bright white meadow flowers echo and amplify the snows on the peaks of the Greater Caucasus mountains all around.

The village of Ushguli, sitting at the head of the Inguri gorge, with Georgia's highest peak, Mount Shkhara, as the backdrop, claims to be Europe's highest inhabited spot, at 2300m above sea level. Actually a collection of four tiny villages, Ushguli is home to just seventy families. It is reachable only by 4WD – it's two hours from Mestia, the town where most visitors stay, which is two hours from Zugdidi, where the overnight train from Tbilisi stops. Svan drivers

take bends at high speed, and the roads are lined with shrines. But the journey is one worth braving.

Walking, biking, or horseriding out from Ushguli or Mestia gives stunning views of alpine valleys, deep gorges and distant peaks. The walk from Mestia to the Ushba glacier is particularly memorable: starting in gentle alpine forest, you pass guards inspecting passports on the route north to Russia, and end by scrambling over a post-apocalyptic landscape of raw black rock before finally arriving at a unique picnic spot – a crack in the rock and ice that is deep enough to sit in, sited just below the final scramble to the mouth of the glacier.

Svaneti's welcoming homestays offer unstinting hospitality, including enormous meals of home-made delicacies like *khinkali* (light meat dumplings in pleated dough), home-made yogurt and honey, and aubergine with walnuts. Crammed round the family table with visitors from around the world, it is easy to feel like travellers from an earlier century thrown together in some untouched spot. For now, that is just what this small corner of the Caucasus remains.

RUSSIA Still and white at the far northeastern tip of Siberia, Chukotka is nine time zones and nine hours by plane from Moscow. It's so remote that locals call the rest of Russia "the mainland". The territory is almost the size of Britain and France combined, but has only around 50,000 inhabitants. No highways connect their few communities. To travel out from Anadyr, Chukotka's capital, you must charter a boat, helicopter or plane – or in winter, you can wrap up in boots and parka, and travel across the tundra by snowmobile.

The only sounds you'll hear as you cross this bitter yet beautiful land are the thrum of the snowmobile's engine and the occasional flapping of pure-white ptarmigan, alighting in small flocks from tundra shrubs. While humans are few here, wildlife is plentiful. Chukotka is home to snow sheep and wolves; Wrangel Island, off its northern coast, is the world's largest polar-bear breeding ground. And then there are the reindeer. In this incredibly remote region, they outnumber humans by three to one.

The thermometer reads -20°C: the snowmobile's heated handlebars keep your hands warm but breathe on your helmet's visor and the moisture freezes, a veil of tiny ice crystals obscuring your view. For hour after hour, you fly over frozen hummocks and hurtle across solid turquoise lakes.

Drive for a few days, past a coastal Eskimo village where you're offered whale to eat and a rusting Cold War radar station that still points towards Alaska, past tumbledown gulag buildings where political prisoners perished under Stalin's Terror, and you'll find the reindeer and their herders. The reindeer provide the Chukchi with clothing, tents and food as they move from pasture to breeding ground. These people aren't used to tourists; they don't speak English and they've no souvenirs to sell you. Instead, they offer steaming tea, hunks of boiled reindeer meat and fresh, salty cakes of bread they've just baked over the fire.

Back on your snowmobile, heading towards civilization, you feel that some tiny part of you has changed. The journey has been long and hard, and you're happy to be heading to home comforts – yet you feel a wrench as you leave the tranquillity of the tundra, one of the few true wildernesses left on earth.

777

Visit
the reindeer
herders
of Siberia

778 | Beaten and bruised at Wudang Shan

CHINA If in your travels around China you hope to find a place where bearded mystics totter around mountain temples, unwinding after performing amazing feats of martial prowess, then head for Wudang Shan ("Martial Mountain") in Hubei province. Mythologized versions of this place can be seen in big-screen martial-arts epics such as *Crouching Tiger, Hidden Dragon*, which made such a significant impression in the West; if domestic critical response was more muted, it's only because people here were already used to this sort of thing. But there's no doubt that kung fu is a growth industry in modern China, not least because of the need for security: crime rates have mirrored the explosion in personal wealth with today's more capitalist-driven, free-market society, and the demand for bodyguards has increased too. Students can study kung fu privately, at martial art academies (where many hope to become film stars), and even at Wudang Shan, which is one of the homes of traditional Chinese kung fu.

There is a catch, however. Firstly, to study full-time at one of Wudang's temples you have to become a Taoist monk, which – what with the accompanying sexual abstinence, spartan living conditions and religious doctrine – might not appeal.

Secondly, these people are serious. Not necessarily vicious, but you'll have to get used to being hit with fists, fingers, palms, feet, sticks and an escalating number of weapons. Turn up casually, however, and you'll probably find people willing to spend an hour or two teaching you some basics of their systems without involving too much hand-to-hand combat.

And even if you're not in the slightest bit interested in getting into a scrap, the mountain and its temples are a rare treat, with stone paths rising through thin woodland to the magnificent spectacle of the summit of the mountain, completely ringed by a fortress-like stone wall, a group of gold- and green-tiled temples rising within.

779 | Staring into the inferno

TURKMENISTAN It's like standing on the edge of hell. Huge flames leap out from a massive crater and fire balls explode, sending rocks cascading down the sides to the unseen pit, the jagged edges threatening to give way and send onlookers there too.

Here, in the middle of the desert in northern Turkmenistan, lie nine craters formed when the Soviet gas explorers came searching for energy. Some bright spark had the idea of setting one alight, and for the last two decades it has burned continuously, creating an orange glow that can be seen from far away at night and smelled from just slightly closer. There can be few attractions stranger than these Darvaza gas craters, and that's saying something considering the idiosyncracies of Turkmenistan, home to one of the world's most bizarre personality cults.

Setting up camp in the desert, your party looks out for giant zemzen desert lizards and waits for night to fall. Once the sky descends into inky darkness, the guide revs his 4WD, ready to crash through the dunes. Banging into sand walls and dropping into sand holes, you career through the emptiness towards the craters. As you get closer, the glow becomes brighter and the heat and smell hit you as soon as you get out of the car. Beholding this burning, furious pit in the middle of all the nothingness, you'll have a more vivid understanding of the saying "a snowball's chance in hell".

780 | Breakfast of champions

CHINA Every morning – but particularly on Sundays – Hongkongers descend on the city's dim sum restaurants. Stacks of steamers are pushed around on carts or balanced precariously on trays, steam billowing from beneath each bamboo lid. Diners abandon their newspapers and crowd around each new dish as it emerges from the kitchen. Families argue light-heartedly over who should eat the last *siu mai* and debate which dish was best. *Yum cha* or "drinking tea", as the Cantonese call a leisurely meal of dim sum washed down with plenty of tea, is a local love affair.

To sample a decent selection of the small dishes – which range from foreigner-friendly favourites like *char siu bao* (fluffy steamed dumplings filled with unctuous honey-sweet barbecued pork) and crispy prawn wontons to more exciting orders like stewed chicken feet – it's best to eat with a crowd. Delicately dip translucent prawn *har gau* in soy sauce,

crunch your way through crispy spring rolls, and test your chopstick skills on *ma lai gou*, a soft steamed sponge cake, sipping tea throughout. Dim sum may be delicious, but it's also full of calories, and drinking tea is believed to help digest all those dumplings.

Chinese diners like their restaurants "hot and noisy" and full of atmosphere. That's something that communal family-style eating encourages, and that many traditional dim sum joints excel in producing. There are hundreds of restaurants to choose from across Hong Kong, from simple street stalls to the elegant 1930s-style dining room at *Luk Yu* and the grandeur of City Hall's chandelier-hung ballroom. Wherever you go, be prepared to work up an appetite in the line. Queuing for good food is another classic Hong Kong pastime, as the hordes of people waiting patiently outside dim sum favourite *Tim Ho Wan* (purportedly the world's cheapest Michelin-rated restaurant) will attest.

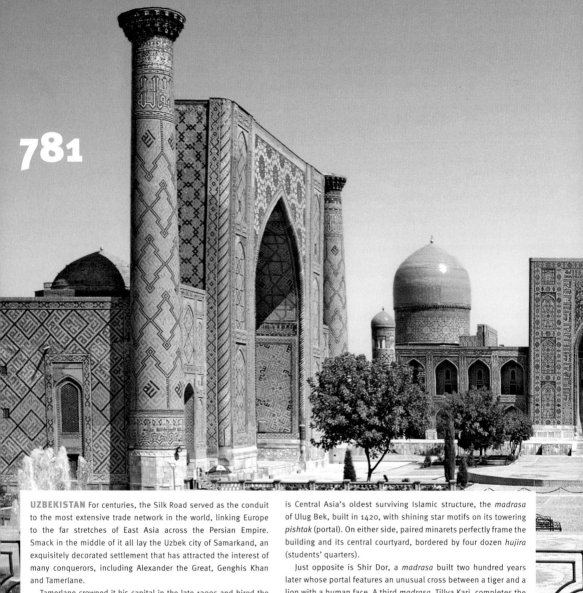

781

UZBEKISTAN For centuries, the Silk Road served as the conduit to the most extensive trade network in the world, linking Europe to the far stretches of East Asia across the Persian Empire. Smack in the middle of it all lay the Uzbek city of Samarkand, an exquisitely decorated settlement that has attracted the interest of many conquerors, including Alexander the Great, Genghis Khan and Tamerlane.

Tamerlane crowned it his capital in the late 1300s and hired the world's best craftsmen to construct the imposing and impossibly beautiful Registan, a Persian term meaning "City of Sand". If that sounds poetic, it's worth bearing in mind that the sand was reportedly sprinked on the ground to soak up the blood in the central square after Tamerlane's victims' heads had been set on spikes.

Amid the dusty, somewhat grungy downtown of modern Samarkand, the jaw-dropping, elephantine Registan lies at the terminus of six main roadways, its grand central plaza bounded by a triumvirate of *madrasas* (Islamic theological colleges) covered in bright, geometrically patterned tiles. The greatest of the three is Central Asia's oldest surviving Islamic structure, the *madrasa* of Ulug Bek, built in 1420, with shining star motifs on its towering *pishtak* (portal). On either side, paired minarets perfectly frame the building and its central courtyard, bordered by four dozen *hujira* (students' quarters).

Just opposite is Shir Dor, a *madrasa* built two hundred years later whose portal features an unusal cross between a tiger and a lion with a human face. A third *madrasa*, Tillya Kari, completes the ensemble, with rich gilding on its dome, facade and mihrab; the interior is completely covered in gold leaf, which was applied by attaching the leafing to animal skins and beating it into the walls with a mallet.

The courtyards of each *madrasa* are now occupied by vendors selling carpets, crafts and souvenirs – and, if you're lucky, cold drinks. Further traders can be found puttering about the grounds, intermingled with devout Muslims, praying to Allah and searching for inspiration in one of the most evocative, gorgeous structures ever built by human hands.

Touring Tamerlane's bloody city of sand

782 | Look down on the city of the future

CHINA Gaze at Shanghai's avant-garde architecture, tangled flyovers and massive new shopping and housing districts, all of which seem to have sprung up with magical haste, like mushrooms after rain, and you can see the city of the future. The best place to view all this is from above – from very high above, on the observation deck at the top of the World Financial Center, to be precise. This blunt, tapering tower with a hole near the roof – locals nickname it "the bottle opener" – is, at 492m, the fourth-tallest building in China, and its 100th-floor observation deck is the second highest in the world.

Though Shanghai is often compared to *Blade Runner*'s dystopian city, the journey up the tower is more reminiscent of the space station in *2001*, as greeters usher you along hushed corridors to the pod-like lift. Emerging a minute later, with your ears well and truly popped, you are confronted with a 360-degree view of the urban sublime. Space is at a premium in Shanghai, so the city has built up rather than out – by population it's four times denser than New York.

Those claustrophobic streets and jostling showcase buildings make for an astonishing cityscape.

To the south is Pudong: 25 years ago this was mostly paddy fields, but today it's new-build as far as the eye can see, with the unreal sheen of an architectural model. Right next to you you're looking down on one of the most beautiful modern buildings in Asia, the pagoda-like Jinmao Tower; the neighbouring Shanghai Tower overtook the World Financial Center in 2014 to become China's tallest building. Below, barges ply the Huangpu River, an example of the trade that is the source of the city's wealth. Across the water are the fusty colonial-era buildings of the Bund, where Art Deco classics such as the *Peace Hotel* show why the city was once nicknamed the Paris of the East.

One caveat, though – this is no place for the nervous. Hardened glass tiles in the floor allow you to look right down beneath your feet and, rather disconcertingly, a sign asks you not to jump on them.

783 | Experiencing the nomadic life

KYRGYZSTAN Sleeping in a yurt is akin to sleeping in a sheep's stomach. It's warm but damp, smells of wool and is filled with strange gurgling noises. Staying at the lush lakeside summer residence of Krygyz nomads – a row of round woollen tents with an open cauldron for cooking and a pen for the goats – there's little to do but enjoy this itinerant style of life.

Spending time in a *jailoo* (pasture) in Son Kul, a bone-jarring eight-hour drive in an old Soviet truck from the capital Bishkek into the centre of Kyrgyzstan, is like stepping back into the past to the days when life was simple, as long as Genghis Khan wasn't around.

Kyrgyz families have been moving around these sweeping pastures with their yurts for centuries, folding up the rugs and the walls and carting the huge circular roof frame from meadow to meadow, taking their animals to greener fields to graze or simply opting for a change in summer scenery.

Inside the yurt, traditional Krygyz *shyrdak* rugs hang from the walls as colourful insulation. The spokes in the wooden wheel-like roof ascend to the apex of the cone, while a little hat sits on top of the cone on the outside, flung on or off for ventilation or warmth.

Arriving at night, you'll settle on the handmade felt rugs of the central yurt and enjoy a magnificent feast of flat Kyrgyz bread, chunky soup, *plov* (rice and meat), *laghman* (noodles) and endless glasses of vodka, each one preceded by an elaborate toast.

The next morning, saddled up on awaiting ponies, you can explore the hills beyond the camp, riding up through the hushed valleys to imposing peaks overlooking the glacial lakes and galloping across the wide pastures back to the yurts. Along the way you can buy *kymys*, fermented mare's milk, from farmers sporting traditional high, peaked woollen hats. The fizzy beverage nips the back of your throat – the perfect way to quench a Kyrgyz pasture thirst.

784 | Feeling the magic of carpets in Baku

AZERBAIJAN In a business where antiquity is a mark of quality, it is fitting that Baku's carpet-sellers ply their trade in the Old City. These narrow lanes and winding streets, enclosed within medieval fortress walls, used to be the sum total of Baku. But during the first oil boom in the mid-nineteenth century, the city started to ooze out of its confining inner walls and the Outer City was born. In its heyday, the Old (or "Inner") City had 707 shops for its seven thousand inhabitants, but nowadays it is much quieter. The carpet-sellers remain, their colourful rectangles with intricate and beautiful patterns draped over the ancient walls as they sit drinking tea on the lookout for business.

"Welcome! No charge to look. Welcome!" And you are being led down a narrow flight of stairs into a grotto piled high with rugs from Iran, Afghanistan, Pakistan and several other 'stans of the Caucasus and Central Asia – not forgetting Azerbaijan itself, which has a long and proud tradition of carpet making. More tea is poured and the merchant's

son rolls out carpets woven a generation or two ago. Each piece tells its own story. The missing tassels on one might have been caused by the burning coals of a water pipe, knocked over during the wild festivities at an Azeri wedding. And maybe the faded patch in the middle of another was the result of a million prayers to Allah.

The merchant's keen eye notices you giving one piece a lingering look. With the passion and authority of a curator at a museum he launches into a vivid description of a carpet nearly a century old, coloured with dyes from octopus, saffron and pistachio, and made with only the finest sheep's wool and camel's hair. The merchant's son holds the carpet high above his head while the customer, gazing at the soft, deep hues, is overcome by a gentle feeling of happiness. A carpet does not have to fly to be magic, and eventually you emerge from the grotto back onto the cobbled streets of the Old City carrying an old rug which is about to begin another chapter in its chequered life.

JAPAN Everyone knows about Japan's futuristic skyscrapers, zen temples and speeding bullet trains. But startlingly few people know of the country's natural beauty and incredible wildlife – and just how easy it is to explore it.

Barely an hour from Tokyo on a bullet train, Karuizawa couldn't feel further from the bustling, buzzing metropolis. Almost three-quarters of Japan is mountainous, and here you're surrounded by forested peaks, dotted with *onsen* (hot spring) towns, upscale resorts and remote villages. After the city, it's a breath of fresh, pure air.

Many people come here to lounge in an *onsen* resort or to hike, but you really don't have to choose. Nestled at the base of Mount Asama is *Hoshinoya Karuizawa*, a luxurious and restorative base for your exploration of the area. Rather than one monolithic building which looks like it's been dropped into the landscape, *Hoshinoya* is made up of several "guest pavilions" spread out generously, giving the whole place the feel of a (very chic) village. No matter how relaxing the resort, though, soon the verdant mountains will start calling you. You can head out solo for a hike, but if you want to spot wildlife you should go with an expert guide.

Picchio has been running nature tours for almost thirty years, as well as doing vital bear conservation work, which helps local communities and the area's black bears to coexist safely and happily. Though you might be lucky enough to spot bears on your Picchio nature walk, there's so much more to see. Perhaps you'll encounter shy, nocturnal flying squirrels, graceful sika deer, or strangely beautiful Japanese serows, which look something like a cross between an antelope and a goat. You'll certainly see several of Karuizawa's eighty-odd bird species – the area is one of just four national wild bird forests in the country. Whatever you spot, the guides' knowledge of, and love for, the environment will make a strong and lasting impression.

Shintoism, Japan's native religion, holds that all of nature is imbued with spirits, and that the forest is a deeply holy place. As you walk over the wooded slopes, your guide leading you along ancient trails and migratory routes, you'll find it hard to disagree. And long after you've returned home, you'll find your mind wandering back along those winding paths, feeling grateful that you got a glimpse of the green heart of Japan.

785
Wildlife-spotting in the green heart of Japan

Catching your breath at Lake Nam-tso

786

CHINA Wind whips across the expanse of electric blue water, white-capped waves break on the rocky shore, and a long-haired yak – immune to the cold – paddles in the shallows. Huge, high and holy, Nam-tso is Tibet's largest lake and, at 4720m above sea level, the highest saltwater lake in the world. Bordered to the south by the snowy wall of the Nyechen Tanglha mountains, while the vast Changtang plateau stretches away to the north, the lake has, thanks to its isolated beauty, attracted pilgrims in search of spiritual succour for countless generations.

In spring the icy edges of the lake melt and the wide swathes of grassland that surround it return to life. Come the brief summer, the spider-like black tents of nomads appear on the lakeshore and rare black-necked cranes fly in to nest. Most of these temporary inhabitants disappear when temperatures drop in autumn, leaving the freezing lake in magnificent solitude throughout the winter. Heinrich Harrer and Peter Aufschnaiter crossed the Nyechan Tanglha not far from here in January 1946 on their way to Lhasa, a journey Harrer recounted as "the worst trek of all" in *Seven Years in Tibet*.

Devout Tibetan pilgrims spend eighteen days walking the 200km perimeter of the lake, but most visitors settle for visiting prayer-flag-festooned Tashi Dor, a rocky peninsula that juts into the lake's eastern end. Two lumpy natural pillars mark the start of a clockwise *kora* or ritual prayer circuit around the peninsula. Red-cheeked Tibetans spin handheld prayer wheels as they go, stopping at the shrines that line the path, their rock worn smooth by thousands of fervent prostrations. Those less piously inclined can pose for photos astride a shaggy yak, sample the nomads' home-made yogurt or puff their way to the top of Tashi Dor for staggering views along the scalloped lakeshore.

787 | Ice fishing on Lake Baikal

RUSSIA The fabled Siberian winter freeze-frames the north Asian landscape in spectacular desolation. Nothing, however, quite prepares you for the sight of Lake Baikal, the world's deepest inland body of water, in solid form – a dazzling white slash in the Earth's crust, ringed by Siberia's nameless peaks. And as you approach the world's most plentiful source of freshwater across the tracks of the Trans-Siberian Railway at Slyudyanka, you're confronted by the even more incongruous spectacle of a cluster of 4WDs parked wagon-train style about half a kilometre out on the metre-thick ice. What on earth would inspire anyone to drive a two-tonne Land Cruiser onto a crust of ice? The answer – fish.

Siberians are mad about fish, especially the *omul*, a salmon-like inhabitant of Lake Baikal's bottomless blue depths that colonizes restaurant menus in shoals across Siberia. Weathered babushkas offer this greasy snack foil-wrapped to passengers at Trans-Sib stations hereabouts, the fishy pong adding an unwelcome tang to the stale air of the carriage as you round the lake's dramatic southern shore. Between December and April, though, Baikal protects its scaly inhabitants with a steel-hard shield of ice, the strange groans and booms of which punctuate the snow-muffled still of the Siberian winter. However, angling *homo-Sibericus* is a determined sort.

At first you are wary of stepping on the ice. Fissures and faults riddle the surface. In places the ice is unnervingly crunchy underfoot; in others, kilometre-long cracks have opened up then frozen over to create sharp-edged ridges. Once you forget about the 100m of water and certain death below, and draw near to the icy car park, you begin to encounter local menfolk squatting over 30cm-wide holes, miniature rods in hand. Handing over a contraption resembling a mammoth corkscrew, the assembled anglers watch in amusement as you attempt to make even the slightest impression on the Baikal's resilient crust. With help, you break through, scooping out the slush with a kitchen ladle. A celebratory vodka shot later, you are bobbing a line into the black circle of water, hoping for that sudden tug of success.

788 | On the temple trail in Shikoku

JAPAN Japanese temples have an air of magic about them. Though somewhat austere in comparison to those of other Asian nations, less has long been more in Japan. A good sunset can draw simmering shades of gold from the bareness, while dusk can make white flashes of paint hover against dark, brooding backgrounds – like an anime come to life. Paper doors and windows play similar optical tricks within the buildings, filtering the light of the outside world into a soft, mind-cleansing cream.

While the former capital, Kyoto, is arguably home to the most ornate temples in the country, some of the most atmospheric are located in the nooks and crannies of small towns or farming communities. Those truly in the know head to Shikoku – this smallest and most bucolic of Japan's four main islands is home to a mammoth 88-temple pilgrimage, which takes a couple of months to complete on foot. The overwhelming majority follow the route in a car or on a bus tour, but in warmer months you're sure to see staff-wielding pilgrims, or *henro-san*, pacing the route, as well as hikers who don traditional white costumes along with their backpacks.

Few will have the time or inclination necessary to complete the whole pilgrimage, but the number of temples on it – only a fraction of the total number on the island – means that opportunities for shorter treks are plentiful.

Though each temple has its merits, one of the most commonly visited is Zentsu-ji, the birthplace of Kobo Daishi, in whose memory the pilgrimage is made. Despite its official status as number 75 on the clockwise course, the temple is one of the first you'll come upon after crossing the Seto Ohashi, a series of bridges slung across the spectacular island-peppered sea between Shikoku and the main Japanese island of Honshu. From there, green Shikoku and its temples are yours to discover.

789 | Jostling for a taste of Beijing duck

CHINA Beijing 1985: Mao has been dead for nine years but China is still reeling from the effects of his restrictive policies, which have held the country's economy back at almost pre-industrial levels. People shuffle around dispiritedly in blue Mao suits, bicycles outnumber cars about a thousand to one, the air is heavy with the smell of charcoal burning in braziers and the most modern buildings are functional, grey, Communist-inspired concrete blocks. The only shops selling anything other than daily necessities are the "Friendship Stores", full of imported luxuries such as televisions and the locals that dream about earning enough money to own one. Restaurants serving anything other than bland, uninspiring food are extremely thin on the ground, with one very notable exception: the *Quanjude Roast Duck* restaurant, founded in 1864 and resurrected after being closed down during the Maoist era.

For Chinese and foreigners alike it's a free-for-all, where only the quick and strong get fed. The dining hall is so crammed with tables that there's barely room to fit the chairs in, and that's a big problem because all available room – every centimetre of space – is occupied by salivating customers hovering like vultures beside each chair, waiting for the person sitting down to finish their meal and begin to get up. The ensuing moments of hand-to-hand combat, as three people try to occupy the half-empty seat, end with the victor knowing that they are about to enjoy a cholesterol-laden feast.

First comes the duck's skin, crispy brown and aromatic; next the juicy meat, carefully sliced and eaten with spring onion slivers, all wrapped inside a thin pancake; and lastly, a soup made from duck bones and innards. There are other branches of *Quanjude*, but this is the original and still the best.

790 | Meeting the throat singers of Tuva

RUSSIA The southern Siberian republic of Tuva is a revelation for those few determined travellers who brave the white-knuckle bus ride across the Yergaki Mountains. Its remote location and lack of transport links to the Russian mothership give this little-known country a real "Seven Years in Tibet" feel.

In Kyzyl, the ramshackle capital, the must-have local experience is to hear traditional throat-singing, an eerie and outlandish style that's famed among world music aficionados. The country's – indeed, the planet's – top throat-singing ensembles perform and rehearse at the brand-new Centre for Tuvan Culture in central Kyzyl.

While the various growling, burping styles are impressive enough, it's the technique known as Sygyt, consisting of a high whistle produced at the back of the mouth – and resembling the sound of a wet finger being rubbed around the rim of a wine glass – that provides a lingering soundtrack to unforgettable trips across Russia's exotic underbelly.

791 | Scrubbing up in Almaty

KAZAKHSTAN Straddling the cultural crossroads between Europe and Asia, Kazakhstan is an intriguingly cosmopolitan place. Almaty, its biggest city, may have ceded capital status to its flashy young rival, Astana, but it remains the country's cultural and financial centre, and custodian of the Kazakh soul. Spectacularly set beneath the snow-capped peaks of the imperious Zailysky-Alatau mountains, it's the sophisticated, modern hub of a booming petro-economy for sure, but one with enough surprises to make Almaty a highlight of any visit to Kazakhstan.

Perhaps Almaty's one truly unmissable experience, the Arasan Baths complex is the most elaborately styled bathhouse in the region, built in the 1980s as a grand statement of late Soviet ambition. Pick up a towel, slippers and conical felt *shapka* (hat) and leave your modesty behind in the changing room.

There's a Finnish sauna and a marble Turkish hammam but they're invariably empty – you'll find your fellow bathers in the ferociously hot Russian *parilka* (steam room), vigorously thrashing each other with *vyeniki* (bundles of oak or birch leaves), a wince-inducing ritual said to improve circulation.

The masochism doesn't end there though: once out of the *parilka*, it's de rigueur to upturn a pail of gasp-inducingly cold water over yourself. Finish up with a refreshing dip in the cool plunge pool, beneath a domed atrium so grand it wouldn't feel out of place in imperial Rome. Surprising, indeed.

792
Cracking the Ice Festival

CHINA Getting out and about when the temperature dips to forty below may seem a little crazy, but that doesn't stop the thousands of visitors who every January don thick coats, hats and gloves and head to Harbin.

That's when an army of builders from China, Russia, Europe, Asia and even Australia descend on the capital of the wintery, northeastern province of Heilongjiang, fire up their chainsaws, axes and chisels and kick off the month-long Winter Ice Festival.

All sorts of extraordinary sculptures appear in the city's parks, shaped from ice blocks cut from the Songhua River. A surreal cityscape of cathedrals, pyramids, Thai palaces and Chinese temples rises in Zhaolin Park: most of the replicas are built to a reduced scale but are still so large you can wander through them, though some – including a section of the Great Wall, which inevitably puts in an appearance – are life-sized.

And as if a parkful of transparent, fairy-tale castles weren't enough, at night everything is lit up splendidly in lurid colours by light bulbs embedded in the ice, drawing huge crowds despite the intense cold.

Across the Songhua River, Sun Island is another park populated, this time, by snow sculptures. Some follow traditional Chinese themes – you'll usually find a giant Guanyin, the Buddhist incarnation of mercy – but most are contemporary cartoon characters, overblown mythical creatures or fantastical inhabitants of the sculptor's mind. Amid such bizarre companions, the occasional straightforward bust of a famous celebrity, or perhaps a life-sized sculpture of a rearing horse, stands out for its sheer ordinariness.

Sitting ringside at a Sumo tournament

793

JAPAN Forget the comical Western stereotype of gargantuan men in nappies slapping each other around – sumo is serious business. Few sports have as long a pedigree; sumo has been around for a millennium. The basic object of the fighters is to force their opponent out of the ring, or get them to touch the ground with any part of their body other than their feet. The enormous body mass involved ensures that fights are brief but blazing, though these guys are no mere spheres of flesh – to see a *rikishi* hoist up to 200kg of squirming human by the belt and carry it out of the ring is nothing short of astonishing.

Six tournaments, or *basho*, take place across the year – one every other month – and last for fifteen days. Good *rikishi* progress though the ranks to *makuuchi*, the highest level; here, the top 42 wrestlers

fight once per day, their main aim the posting of a positive tournament record of at least eight wins. The very best rise to *yokozuna* level and national superstardom, before a ceremonial cutting of their top-knotted hair on retirement.

Your ticket entitles you to nine hours of fight-time and hundreds of bouts; since many spectators only come for the *makuuchi* fights at the end, it's often possible to pinch a first-class seat for much of the day. Keep in mind that ringside seats come with an element of risk. Arriving early also increases the chances of sharing your train journey in with a wrestler or two; many are more than willing to chat, though the super-formal dialect drilled into them at their training "stable" can be impenetrable even for Japanese-speakers. One certainty is that you won't be able to miss them.

794 | Discovering subcultural sisters Nakano and Kōenji

JAPAN What if the nerd mecca of Akihabara and the voguish thrift-shop paradise of Shimokitazawa were populated by discerning locals instead of tourists and only a stone's throw away from each other? Enter Nakano and Kōenji, the trendier, cheaper, more authentic alternatives. Wandering around these adjacent neighbourhoods makes for a relaxed yet stimulating afternoon, and their unique yet compatible personalities illustrate the richness of Tokyo's subcultures.

From Nakano station, head to Nakano Broadway, a shopping arcade that's the place to stock up on *otaku* souvenirs. Anime figurines, games, manga and Japanese idol merchandise abound, along with an amusement arcade and eateries. Don't neglect the alleyways on the side of the complex where traditional wooden *izakaya* (bar with light bites), maid-cafés and gloriously geeky themed bars can be found (*Bar DIO* and *Daikaiju Salon* are worth a visit).

Where Nakano's tribe is *otaku* (computer nerds), Tokyo's bohemians flock to Kōenji. As with Nakano, Kōenji's shopping street, PAL Arcade, and the adjoining Look Street make for an inviting centrepiece. Here you have a fighting chance of scoring the best vintage-clothing find of your life, and afterwards there's an excellent choice of good-value international cuisine to celebrate (try *KHANA* for curry or *Baan-Esan* for Thai).

When you tire of shopping, the two neighbourhoods have a great offering of independent music and art. In local venues you can find hidden gems of creative and atmospheric excellence, such as Heavy Sick Zero in Nakano and Sound Studio Dom in Kōenji. Exhibiting quintessential Tokyoite space-saving innovation, many bars and coffee houses are multipurpose, such as the ridiculously cool CLOUDS ART + COFFEE, an art space which also serves some of the best coffee in Tokyo.

795 | The church in the clouds

GEORGIA Silhouetted on a remote hilltop against snowy Mount Kazbegi, the fourteenth-century Gergeti Trinity Church, also known as Tsminda Sameba Church, is considered one of Georgia's most iconic images. This sacred church is modest in scale and built like a small fortress. Indeed, during dangerous times in the past, treasures from the cathedral at Mtskheta were hidden here.

The majestic alpine setting above the town of Stepantsminda, high in the Caucasus mountain range close to the Russian border, has a solemn yet irresistible charm. The weather can change at any moment – from clear blue skies to dense fog – but each dramatic meteorological moment provides another stunning view. The church frequently appears to be floating on clouds. Orthodox Christianity, the main religion of Georgia, dates from the first century and is highly revered – even today few locals pass a church without stopping to cross themselves. Respectful attire is also taken very seriously and both men

and women must cover their legs, and women also their heads, before entering an Orthodox church. At Gergeti Trinity Church, even women in trousers must cover themselves in one of the cloth wraps provided at the side entrance.

Once inside, the atmosphere is dark, subdued and often draughty. Candles flicker beneath icons and religious murals depicting St Nino, the woman who spread Christianity in fourth-century Georgia, and St George, the dragonslayer and country's namesake, both looking sternly down upon worshippers and visitors alike. Many pilgrims leave jewellery beneath the icons in the hope that their prayers will be answered, and it's fascinating to peruse the eclectic range of gold, silver and plastic rings and bracelets. Outside, the church has some intriguing exterior stone carvings of dinosaur-like beasts and pagan-like human images. It's an easy day-trip from the capital Tbilisi and the area is also a popular place for hiking, horseriding and paragliding.

796 | Hiking along the Tea Horse Road in Yunnan

CHINA For centuries, caravans trudged from the peacock-filled jungles of southern Yunnan to the arid heights of the Tibetan plateau – an arduous, six-month journey – simply in order to deliver a caffeine fix to Tibetan tea-lovers. Leaves plucked near the Burmese border were dried, steamed and compacted into bricks before being loaded onto mules for their long journey. These mule trains then navigated the deeply corrugated eastern edge of the Himalayas and negotiated their way across the churning waters of the Yangtze, the Mekong and the Salween rivers using a collection of trails that the Chinese know simply as the "Tea Horse Road".

Today, much of the route and its romance have been overwritten by modernization. While caravan stops elsewhere in the region have become modern market towns and dirt trails have morphed into highways, in northwest Yunnan a few fragments of the Tea Horse Road remain more or less intact. In the valleys around Dali, a series of small towns have managed to hang on to their heritage. In Shaxi,

100km north of Dali, a weathered Qing-dynasty playhouse sits at the centre of a network of cobbled lanes, the stones worn smooth by horses' hooves and farmers' boots, and faded Maoist slogans flake from whitewashed houses. In Weishan, 60km south of Dali's own old town, the historic centre is still a lively part of local life. Noodle shops and hairdressers are housed in timeworn fifteenth-century buildings, and old men play Chinese chess in the shade of the imposing Gongchen Lou, an ornate Ming city gate.

Excitingly, it's not just the architecture that has survived – sections of the trails themselves still snake across the forested hills, linking diminutive Yi and Bai villages with the larger towns, and offering a glimpse of what the epic journey would have been like. Spend a day walking through the pretty Shaxi Valley, or set out on the multi-day hike from the tea groves of Fengqing to Weishan, and dream of continuing over the cloud-draped mountain passes to Lhasa.

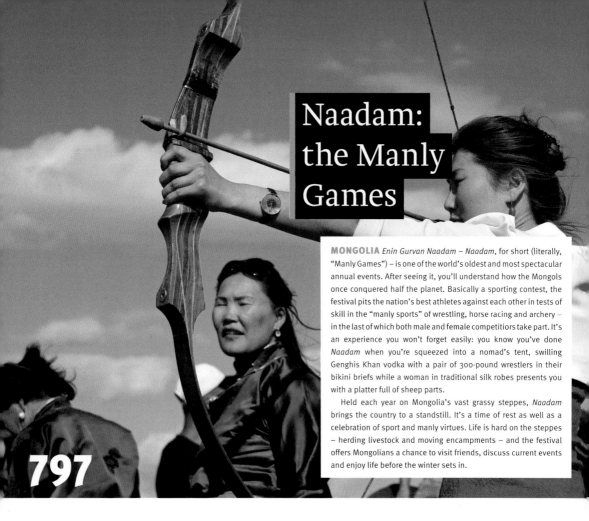

Naadam: the Manly Games

MONGOLIA *Enin Gurvan Naadam – Naadam*, for short (literally, "Manly Games") – is one of the world's oldest and most spectacular annual events. After seeing it, you'll understand how the Mongols once conquered half the planet. Basically a sporting contest, the festival pits the nation's best athletes against each other in tests of skill in the "manly sports" of wrestling, horse racing and archery – in the last of which both male and female competitiors take part. It's an experience you won't forget easily: you know you've done *Naadam* when you're squeezed into a nomad's tent, swilling Genghis Khan vodka with a pair of 300-pound wrestlers in their bikini briefs while a woman in traditional silk robes presents you with a platter full of sheep parts.

Held each year on Mongolia's vast grassy steppes, *Naadam* brings the country to a standstill. It's a time of rest as well as a celebration of sport and manly virtues. Life is hard on the steppes – herding livestock and moving encampments – and the festival offers Mongolians a chance to visit friends, discuss current events and enjoy life before the winter sets in.

797

798 | A lilliputian library

AZERBAIJAN The winding yellow-brick streets of Baku's Old Town hide many offbeat museums, but none as quirky as the Museum of Miniature Books.

Just around the corner from the Palace of the Shirvanshahs, the museum itself is appropriately small – just one room – but exhibits a remarkable 5800 tiny editions of world literature, from the Qu'ran to the works of Beatrix Potter. One cabinet in particular will draw your attention, containing four of the world's smallest books, one of them a mere 0.75mm by 0.75mm. This minuscule masterpiece consists of twenty-two pages of intricate illustrations of Japanese flowers, and is best read with the help of a magnifying glass.

Other fascinating exhibit cases feature a variety of works more accessible to the naked eye, including forty volumes of a 33mm by 40mm *Complete Works of William Shakespeare*, the collected works of the twelfth-century Azeri poet Nizami, and numerous histories of the Olympic Games.

799 | Roaring on dragon-boat races

CHINA Hong Kong's dragon-boat races commemorate the aquatic suicide of an upright regional governor, Qu Yuan, who jumped into a river in central China in 278 BC rather than live to see his home state invaded by a neighbouring province's army. Distraught locals raced to save him in their boats, but were too late; later on, they threw packets of sticky rice into the river as an offering to his ghost.

There are festivities all over China each year on the national holiday held to remember the uncompromising Qu Yuan, but the race in Hong Kong's Stanley Harbour is one of the best, with huge quantities of sticky rice consumed and some fierce competition between the dragon-boat teams, who speed their narrow vessels across the harbour to the steady boom of pacing drums. To soak up the best of the buzz, go down to the waterside with a cold beer and take in the festive atmosphere – you'll need to get up early to catch the dedication ceremonies of the dragon-head prows. The celebrations carry on through the evening, with firecrackers and traditional dragon dances.

Need to know

731 See Ⓦ transsiberianexpress.net for information.

732 The Jokhang is part of the Potala Palace complex (Ⓦ whc.unesco.org). As with all Tibetan temples, circuit both the complex and individual halls.

733 Many sections of the Great Wall (Ⓦ whc.unesco .org) are accessible as day-trips from Beijing.

734 The Mazu festival is held in April or May each year.

735 Khor Virap is a one-hour drive from Yerevan; if travelling by bus, take an Ararat-bound service, get off at Pokr Vedi, and walk.

736 Zhaoxing is a 5hr bus journey from Guizhou's provincial capital, Guiyang. A less direct but more interesting way to get here is from Guilin via the Dragon's Backbone Rice Terraces.

737 You'll need a guide, which you can find by asking in the backpacker cafés in Jinghong, the nearest city.

738 For more details, see Ⓦ kronoki.ru.

739 The Terracotta Army (daily 8.30am–5.30pm; Ⓦ terracottawarriorsmuseum.com) is 28km east of Xi'an and can be reached on buses #914, #915 or #306.

740 Gyeongju (Ⓦ whc.unesco.org) is served by buses running daily every hour from Gimhae Airport and trains from all over Korea (for schedules see Ⓦ info. korail.com).

741 The Ghibli Museum (Ⓦ ghibli-museum.jp/en) is in Mitaka, Tokyo. Book well in advance via the website.

742 Though the exact dates vary each year, the *sakura* usually blossoms in late March or early April.

743 Naramachi is a short walk from either Kintetsu Nara or JR Nara railway station. Most museums are free to visit.

744 For information on accommodation, wine routes and more visit Ⓦ georgia.travel/en_US/kakheti/.

745 For more details, see Ⓦ huangshantour.com.

746 There are tour operators in Ulan Bator. The more expensive alternatives include a tour guide, driver, and yurt (or hostel) accommodation; the cheapest option is to hire your own van and driver and take a tent.

747 The Naked Man festival (Ⓦ www.japan.travel/en/ spot/910) generally falls between Jan and March.

748 To get to Doodle Street, take the metro to Yangjiaping station (line two) then a taxi, or two short bus rides, to Huangjueping.

749 Several tour companies run tours of the DMZ. The best is KORIDOOR Tours; see Ⓦ koridoor.co.kr.

750 Tottori Sand Dunes can be reached via buses or taxi from Tottori station. For more, visit Ⓦ www.japan. travel/en/spot/949.

751 There are several *jjimjilbang* in every Korean city of note; any tourist office or taxi driver can direct you.

752 Shilin Night Market is opposite Jiantan MRT station, and is open daily. For more information, see Ⓦ shilin-night-market.com.

753 You can see snow monkeys throughout Japan, but your best chances are in Jigokudani, or "Hell's Valley" (Ⓦ jigokudani-yaenkoen.co.jp).

754 Daily passenger and car ferries arrive at Yakushima from Kagoshima. Daily flights also operate through JAC (part of Japan Airlines). Visit Ⓦ yesyakushima.com for more information.

755 Taketomi-jima is reached by ferry from Ishikagi on Ishikagi-jima.

756 Ⓦ airastana.com flies direct to Astana from many Asian and European airports, including London.

757 There's regional information at Ⓦ pomorland.travel. See also Ⓦ whc.unesco.org. Take cash and warm, waterproof clothes.

758 For more, check Ⓦ eng.templestay.com.

759 Ogasawara Kaiun Co has information on the islands, and timetables for weekly sailings, at Ⓦ ogasa-warakaiun.co.jp/english. Chichijima holds several guesthouses.

760 Hotpot chain *Little Cygnet* is popular with locals, but for a unique experience head to *Brigade General Hotpot*, where the walls are covered in revolutionary memorabilia and waitresses are dressed like Red Guards – there are eight branches around Chongqing.

761 The full trek takes at least two days, though three is recommended. Spring and autumn are the best months for walking as summer can be wet, with potentially dangerous landslides.

762 Central Asian climbing is best July–Sept. Ⓦ asiamountains.net organizes expeditions to Peak Lenin.

763 Shinjuku's railway station is served by the Tokyo Metro, Toei Subway, and several inter-city lines.

764 The best time for horse trekking is late June to mid-Sept. Ⓦ boojum.com offers trips.

765 A small *thangka* will cost a very reasonable ¥300, but larger versions – which often take well over a month to paint – will set you back at least ten times that amount.

766 The Pyongyang Marathon Ⓦ pyongyangmarathon. com) is held each April, and this being North Korea you'll have to join a tour – Koryo Tours (Ⓦ koryogroup. com) offers several packages.

767 Takachiho (Ⓦ takachiho-kanko.info) can be reached from Fukuoka on the Nishitetsu and Miyazaki Kōtsū buses. *Yokagura* dance performances of the myths at Takachiho shrine take place in winter, and you can take a boat down the gorge in good weather.

768 Yerevan is accessible by plane, bus or overnight train from the Georgian capital, Tbilisi. The Turkish border, just 20km from the city, has been closed since 1993 but this may change.

769 Buses (8hr) run daily from Ganzi to Dêgê.

770 Tickets bought at the West Gate give access into all the important buildings in Khiva, although the city's streets are themselves the main attraction.

771 For more information on the 798 Art District, visit Ⓦ 798district.com. The fastest and most convenient way to reach it from central Beijing is by taxi.

772 The Japan Rail Pass (Ⓦ japanrailpass.net) must be bought before arriving in Japan; it's only available to foreign visitors.

773 Fuji Rock (Ⓦ fujirock-eng.com) is in July each year.

774 The Hanging Temple is around 80km from Datong – city hotels can organize day-trips by minibus, though private taxis are quite affordable.

775 Punakha Valley is a four-hour drive from Bhutan's only international airport, located in Paro. Visit Ⓦ bhutan.travel or Ⓦ traveltourtobhutan.com for information on visas and compulsory tour operators.

776 You can get to Svaneti from Tbilisi by plane, train or minibus. For more, see Ⓦ gnta.ge.

777 Chukotka is remote, there is virtually no infrastructure for independent tourists and, if you get it wrong, the temperatures are deathly. You also need a special permit on top of a Russian visa. For more information, including details of tours, see Ⓦ arcticrussiatravel. com/chukotka or Ⓦ russiadiscovery.com/regions/ chukotka.

778 Wudang Shan is in northwestern Hubei; from the nearest train station at Shiyan (25km west), catch a bus to Wudang town at the bottom of the mountain

and then a minibus to Nanyan temple, about halfway up. A tiring 2hr track leads from Nanyan to the summit.

779 Getting to the craters is a difficult, bumpy ride across sand dunes. Check Ⓦ turkmenistan.embassy-homepage.com for details on travel restrictions and visas.

780 Sunday morning is the busiest time at most restaurants – save waiting time by heading for dim sum on a weekday. Many restaurants stop serving dim sum in the early afternoon.

781 Visit at dusk, when the buildings are bathed in amber and locals crowd the plaza.

782 The World Financial Building (Ⓦ swfc-shanghai .com) is in Pudong, near the Lujiazui subway station.

783 For more on yurting, see Ⓦ cbtkyrgyzstan.kg.

784 Haggling is recommended. No matter what a carpet-seller might tell you, an export certificate (or "carpet passport") is required to take antique carpets out of Azerbaijan. Certificates are available from the Azerbaijan Carpet Museum (Ⓦ azcarpetmuseum.az) or the seller.

785 Karuizawa is accessible from Tokyo on the Hokuriku shinkansen, and by bus. You'll need to book well in advance for *Hoshinoya Karuizawa* (Ⓦ hoshinoya.com/ karuizawa/en), and for the Picchio nature tours (Ⓦ wildlife-picchio.com).

786 Nam-tso can be seen at breakneck speed on a day-trip from Lhasa, 300km away. More satisfying, however, is to stay overnight in Damxung, 60km southeast of Nam-tso, or in one of the ultrabasic guesthouses at the lake itself.

787 For more information about Lake Baikal, visit Ⓦ bww.irk.ru or Ⓦ lakebaikal.org. Irkutsk, the nearest large city, is a major halt on the Trans-Siberian Railway.

788 There's a total of 1400km between the 88 temples on the Shikoku pilgrimage route. Zentsu-ji is outside the small port of Marugame, in the north of the island.

789 *Quanjude Roast Duck* restaurant, 32 Qianmen Dajie, Beijing.

790 The only way to reach Kyzyl is by road from Abakan. The Centre for Tuvan Culture hosts daily appearances of the Tuvan National Orchestra (Ⓦ tuvannationalorchestra.com). For more information on the Republic of Tuva visit Ⓦ russiatrek.org/tuva-republic.

791 See Ⓦ thepeak.com.hk.

792 See Ⓦ icefestivalharbin.com.

793 Tokyo's Ryogoku Kokugikan arena has tournaments in Jan, May and Sept. The March, July and Nov *basho* take place in Ōsaka, Nagoya and Fukuoka, respectively. Schedules are listed on Ⓦ sumo.or.jp.

794 Nakano and Kōenji are one and two stops, respectively, on the JR Chūō Line from Shinjuku station. For more information on Nakano Broadway visit Ⓦ nbw.jp.

795 *Rooms Kazbegi* (Ⓦ roomshotels.com/kazbegi) has an excellent viewing deck and is also a great place for lunch or staying overnight.

796 Northwest Yunnan's rainy season falls between July and Oct – it's still possible to visit, but many trails will be reduced to mud. For more information, visit Ⓦ climbdali.com.

797 Naadam is held annually in July. Ⓦ boojum.com runs tours.

798 The Museum of Miniature Books is round the corner from the Palace of the Shirvanshahs in Old Baku; Ⓦ minibooks.az/index_en.html.

799 Check Ⓦ dragonboat.org.hk for more details, particularly of the date, which varies each year.

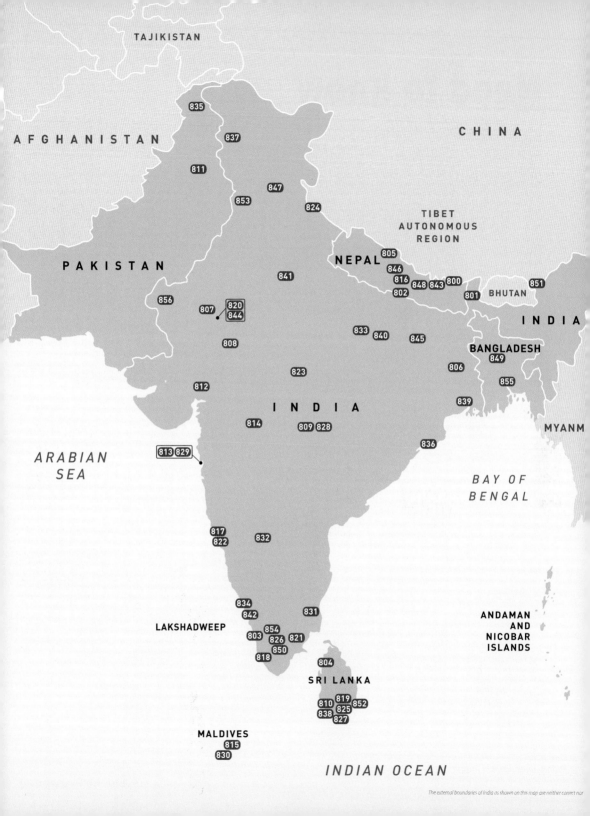

TAJIKISTAN

AFGHANISTAN

CHINA

PAKISTAN

835

837

811

853

847

824

TIBET
AUTONOMOUS
REGION

NEPAL

805
846
816
802

848 843 800

801 BHUTAN

851

INDIA

841

856

807

820
844

808

833 840

845

BANGLADESH

849

806

823

855

812

INDIA

839

814

809 828

MYANM

813 829

836

ARABIAN
SEA

BAY OF
BENGAL

817
822

832

ANDAMAN
AND
NICOBAR
ISLANDS

834
842

831

LAKSHADWEEP

854
803 826 821
850
818

804

SRI LANKA

810 819 852
838 825
827

MALDIVES
815
830

INDIAN OCEAN

The external boundaries of India as shown on this map are neither correct nor

THE INDIAN SUBCONTINENT

800-856

Rainbow-hued and rambunctious, India and its neighbours are like nowhere else on the planet. The cities are more clamorous, the day-to-day contrasts more vivid, the encounters often more extraordinary. With elephants and leopards, spice-charged foods and kaleidoscopic festivals, lofty temples and loftier treks, the Subcontinent offers a vast range of travel experiences. Whether you're gazing at the ruins of Hampi, searching for sloth bears in Sri Lanka, or paragliding in Pokhara, the region is deeply memorable – where else do tea plantations and cricket matches rub shoulders with Sufi mystics and mountain ashrams?

800 Everest the easy(ish) way

NEPAL The road to Everest Base Camp starts with a 5am wake-up call in the *Kathmandu Guesthouse*. I heave myself off the thin mattress and am soon climbing the steps of a rickety-looking Twin Otter plane bound for Lukla, aka "the scariest airport in the world". Ears stuffed with cotton wool against the noise, I eventually spot a minuscule mountain runway through the cockpit window. As the pilot pushes into a dive, I close my eyes and don't open them until we've come to a juddering halt.

Lukla, a chilly one-street town with a fake *Starbucks* and an airport the size of a yak pat, is now the main gateway to the roof of the world. Back in the days of Hillary, Tenzing and co, you had to trek your way up here from Kathmandu, a week-long marathon of logistics now covered in a thirty-minute flight. Pushing past a rowdy welcome party of porters touting for work, I'm engulfed in a Gore-Tex-clad snake of trekkers and walking poles.

Three days in, the crowds thin out and we're rewarded with a first look at Chomolungma or the "Mother Goddess of the World". The unmistakable black summit sends a jolt of excitement down my spine. After negotiating a few Indiana Jones-style rope bridges, Namche Bazaar, the Sherpa capital (3440m), heralds the arrival of altitude sickness, a mixture of brain-throbbing headaches and insomnia. The local cure – vampire-strength garlic soup – soon kicks off every teahouse meal.

Beyond Namche we press on to the Mordor-esque Gorak Shep (5140m), last stop before Base Camp. "Jam Jam!" – Nepali for "Let's go!"– comes a voice through the plywood door. The trail narrows to shoulder width. Distant avalanches announce themselves with a crack and a rush of powdery snow. After a few nervy steps across deep blue ice, we reach some battered tents and flapping prayer flags: our final goal, a mind-altering 5364m above sea level. The rising sun illuminates the scene – a perfect panorama of Everest, Lhotse and Nuptse. All the aches, pains and garlic soup melt in the memory.

Andy Turner
Andy's first travel memory is messily eating a Twix on a flight to Canada aged two. A few hundred thousand air miles later, he's a freelance travel writer and editor, still eating chocolate and continually planning his next adventure.

Toy trains and tight curves: the Darjeeling unlimited

801

INDIA It was the Brits who laid the foundational tracks of the Indian railway system, whose lines today comprise the largest locomotive network in the world: nearly 65,000km of track, 7172 stations and 1.3 million staff. The most romantic – and affordable – way to explore India is by train, venturing into a bygone world of steam locomotives and dilapidated rail cars, and chugging past rural villages that have hardly changed for hundreds of years.

One of the least-known – and most adventurous – routes is the Darjeeling Himalayan Railway, a tiny, steam-driven locomotive that more than deserves its nickname "The Toy Train". The string of narrow-gauge railway cars plies the hilly Himalaya of West Bengal, from New Jalpaiguri north of Kolkata up to Darjeeling, an early nineteenth-century station near the Nepali border, established for workers and servants of the East India Company.

Built in 1881 and ascending some 1800m of narrow-gauge track, the 82km route takes around seven hours, rarely exceeding 16km/hr.

Past Siliguri Junction, the train climbs slowly (and noisily) at a steady gradient. The rail cars switchback, zigzag and, on several occasions, cross the very track they have just veered off after making 180-degree hairpin turns. In the most nail-biting section of the journey, the aptly named Agony Point outside Tindharia, the train wraps around one of the tightest track curves in the world.

Beyond the carriage windows stretch tea plantations, rainforests and endless plateaus of green and umber fields: Sukna, where the landscape morphs from flat plains to wooded lower slopes; Rangtong, where a deciduous forest sprawls off into the distance; Kurseong, with its colourful, bustling bazaar stalls; and Ghum (2258m), the summit of the line and the highest railway station in the Indian Subcontinent.

Finally, as the train reaches Darjeeling station, you enter a relaxed new world: clean, alpine air, a colonial setting of convent schools and palaces and – in the distance – the soaring Himalayan peak of Kanchenjunga, at 8586m the third highest in the world.

NEPAL Once a big-game hunting reserve and playground for foreign aristocrats – King George V slaughtered a staggering 39 tigers and 18 rhinos here in 1911 – Chitwan National Park, in the foothills of the Himalayas, is these days a wildlife sanctuary that's a must-see destination for intrepid travellers.

Combining riverside grasslands with rich tropical and subtropical forests, Chitwan is best known as one of the few remaining bastions of the single-horned Asiatic rhinoceros, but it's also home to the Bengal tiger (at last count there were 120 breeding adults), as well as gharial crocodiles, gaur (Indian bison), and more than five hundred species of birds, and acts as an important migratory corridor for elephants. Thanks in part to the tourism dollar, the national park has bounced back since the troubles of the early twenty-first century, with a successful conservation drive that has seen a dramatic drop in poaching.

While hanging off the back of a jeep as it bumps across the plains can be a pretty big thrill, joining the daily flock of battered vehicles as they jostle for a prime spot alongside a solitary rhino may not always appeal, and you can opt instead for a more serene guided walk, jungle trek or canoe trip. While elephant rides are a popular attraction for tourists here, for animal welfare reasons Rough Guides doesn't want to encourage this practice. If you're feeling adventurous, go on foot – turning your back on civilization certainly makes you feel daring.

Guided safaris also include a hushed exploration of the Sauraha area's rivers by dugout canoe. Along the way, guides point out the lesser-known species that inhabit the park's enchanting hills, lakes, rivers and lowlands, and it's an indescribably magical and scary moment when you track down a truly wild beast roaming its natural habitat.

Come ideally in February or March, when the climate is cooler and locals from nearby villages cut back the long grass for thatch, making it easier to spot elusive wildlife.

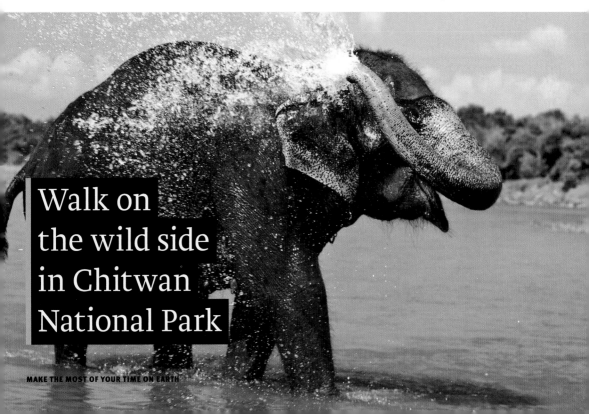

Walk on the wild side in Chitwan National Park

803 | Touch the past in Fort Cochin

INDIA The Keralan city of Kochi consists of three parts: traffic-clogged, modern Ernakulam; the old Jewish district of Mattancherry; and Fort Cochin, an atmospheric grid of streets at the tip of the peninsula that juts into Lake Vembanad. Thanks to its multi-layered history, lakeside position and elegantly decaying mansions, it's Fort Cochin that's the most immediately appealing. This is a place like nowhere else in India – crammed full of colonial buildings drawn from not just the British but also the Portuguese and Dutch eras, yet nonetheless unmistakably Indian.

The Portuguese erected their first citadel in Fort Cochin at the turn of the sixteenth century, to protect their interests in the spice trade, while India's first church had been built just a stone's throw away long before that, possibly as early as 52 AD. This desirable port was, of course, eagerly taken over by each ruler in turn, thereby leaving the peninsula with a fascinating mishmash of Indo-European architecture.

Fort Cochin is at its most alluring at dusk, when the crowds have dispersed, the tour signs have been put away, and the setting sun casts the Chinese fishing nets fixed to the shoreline into striking silhouettes against the orange sky. Said to have been introduced by traders from the court of Kublai Khan, these huge but surprisingly graceful contraptions need at least four men to operate their combination of levers and weights. Improbable as it may seem, they're still very much in use today.

Behind the fishing nets, the quiet charm of the peninsula's streets is hard to resist. A leisurely wander allows you to stumble across beautiful relics of colonial history – some in notable disrepair, others rescued from ruin and turned into luxury hotels – and dip into cool, fan-spun interiors for a little respite from the heat and a lime soda. It all feels like stepping back in time, though it's not so much that Fort Cochin remains an unchanging monument to its history, as that the past seems always tangible here.

804 | Searching for sloth bears in Wilpattu National Park

SRI LANKA Wilpattu National Park, a 1316-square-kilometre sprawl of forests and lakes in Sri Lanka's north, has history. It was forced to close in 1988, after a horrific Civil War-era attack in which its wildlife rangers were lined up and shot. It reopened again from 2003 to 2007, before further trouble saw it close its gates again until 2010. Today it stands as Sri Lanka's largest national park by area, but draws a mere fraction of the visitors that descend on spots like Yala in the south. Those travellers that do visit have rewards in store.

The park's wildlife was affected terribly over the Civil War years – partly by poaching – but has since been left to restore itself naturally. You don't need to spend long here before concluding that it's done so with some success. Rumble along its rutted roads on a game drive and, as well as the usual rainbow menagerie of birds, monkeys and deer, you might spot anything from crocodiles in the swamps to leopards in the undergrowth.

And if you're really lucky: it's one of the best places in the country to spot the sloth bear, a shambling black bundle with shaggy paws and a large, pale face muzzle. It's a rare animal – estimates suggest that in Sri Lanka there are fewer than a thousand left in the wild – but a thrill to witness first-hand, ambling along the forest floor and hoovering up unfortunate termites.

It is, however, emphatically no teddy bear. The creature is no relation to the sloth, despite its name, and can use its long claws to deadly effect if provoked. It has poor eyesight and poor hearing, but a razor-sharp sense of smell – coupled with its ursine strength – that makes it an animal not to be trifled with.

As in so many places, the fruitfulness of a game drive in Wilpattu is always hard to predict. Birds and animals often cluster at the *willus*, the water-filled natural depressions from which the park takes its name, while other trails lead through wooded areas that at times appear to yield little. Yet all it takes to lift the experience into something sublime is for a shuffling dark shape to materialize among the trees.

805 | Dodging the crowds on the Sikles Trek

NEPAL If you've ever longed to hike the land of the yak and yeti, but lack the endurance of hardened adventurers such as Sirs Edmund Hillary and Ranulph Fiennes, there's a trek out there just for you. Mid-West Nepal's five-day Sikles trip is an ideal eco-trekking route and an excellent alternative to the famed – and far too overtouristed – Annapurna Circuit. Exploring an untrampled corner of the Annapurna Conservation Area, it offers beguiling views of the peaks of Annapurna II, III and IV, Manaslu and the dozen summits of the monolithic Lamjung Himal.

Leaving from the erstwhile hippy base of Pokhara, a rickety tin bus jounces trekkers north for several hours, across blacktop highway and potholed byroad, alongside the Mardi Khola River towards the thickly forested ridges of highland Nepal. Foot hits ground in a succession of terraced fields that quickly steepen towards the tiny hillside settlement of Ghalekharka. From this base, a steep, dense jungle of orchids, rhododendrons and the occasional bloodsucking leech leads towards

Sikles's most demanding ascent – the slog up to the wooded col of Tara Top, a plateau with dusk and dawn views of most of the Annapurna massif and the Himalayan foothills that drop to the Ganges and the plains of India. At an elevation of just over 3000m, the views of the snowy Eastern Annapurnas from this small knoll are rarely bettered, even on more formidable treks.

From here, follow the river's west bank down to a ridge above the trek's namesake village of Sikles (1980m), one of Nepal's largest Gurung settlements and home to many families of Gurkha soldiers. Up here are magical scenes: uniformed schoolgirls with red ribbons in their hair skipping down the hillside; giant oxen trailing them; and guides and porters, heads bowed, praying silently in front of the jagged peak of Machhapuchhre, considered sacred by locals. As day draws to a close, kick back as impossibly tall mountains unveil themselves against a clear blue sky, dotted with cushions of puffy white cloud, bands of setting sunlight slicing across their summits.

806

INDIA As you travel by train across rural Bengal, it's not unusual for your carriage to be boarded by troupes of musicians with matted hair and straggling beards, dressed in flowing saffron or white robes and turbans. Their manner will be peaceful and respectful, while the easy, percussive rhythms and soaring melody lines of their songs, played on traditional Indian drums and stringed instruments, may well induce reverie as you gaze through the window at the rice paddies and reed-thatched villages of the Ganges floodplain.

These are no ordinary buskers. They're Bauls – meaning "mad" or "possessed" in ancient Sanskrit – members of loose religious sects who spend their lives travelling around rural Bengal, playing their soulful, melancholic music at fairs and markets, on riverbanks and under shady banyan trees in the middle of nowhere. Their purpose is less to solicit alms (though many survive on donations) than to attain, and inspire, a state of spiritual ecstasy – to get closer to the divinity they refer to as "Moner Manus", the "Ideal Being" or "Man of the Heart".

As with the Sufis of Islamic tradition and adherents of Bhakti cults in Hinduism, this longing is often phrased in terms of earthly love, which is perhaps why the music of the Bauls remains so popular among Bengalis the world over. Finding it isn't always easy. The Bauls lead an itinerant life, wandering between wayside shrines, temples, mosques and monasteries. Each December, however, during the feast of Makar Sankranti, over the new-moon nights of the winter solstice, thousands of Baul musicians gather at Kenduli village beside the Ajoy River to sing and dance in honour of the twelfth-century poet Joydev, who was born here.

While the Bengali government erects special stages for performances of Joydev's most famous work, it's after hours, in huge riverbank encampments, that the real action takes place. As the sun sinks below the horizon of bleached river sand, Bauls congregate around campfires to smoke ganja, gossip and sing together, continuing through the night, wrapped in their trademark multicoloured patchwork shawls – a scene unchanged in centuries.

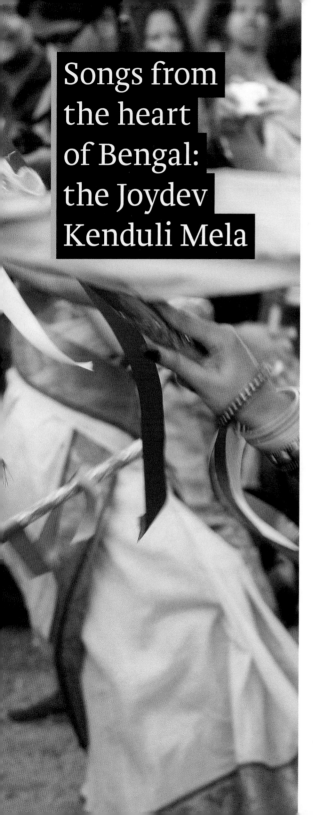

Songs from the heart of Bengal: the Joydev Kenduli Mela

807 | Sounds for the soul: the World Sufi Spirit Festival

INDIA Although primarily renowned for their flamboyant Rajput-Mughal architecture, the great fortress-palaces of Rajasthan were, in their heyday, also repositories of sophisticated music and dance traditions. Their fabulous glass mosaic apartments, candle-lit courtyards and domed pavilions hosted the Maharaja and his court or consorts during evenings of poetry and dalliance, when the finest musicians in the land would play until dawn.

Each year in late February, these same exotic venues reverberate once again to the strains of spiritually uplifting music, as performers from diverse Sufi traditions across the world converge on Jodhpur's Mehrangarh Fort and the Ahitchatragarh Fort in Nagaur. Whether Gnawa bands from Morocco, Aramaic singers from Syria or a local Manganiyar folk troupe from the Thar desert, the one thing the participants all share is a desire to inspire transcendental experience in their audiences – a goal the sublime settings complement to magical effect.

808 | Walking with leopards in Jawai

INDIA Reports of violent encounters between leopards and humans are all too common in Indian newspapers these days, as conurbation eats away at the wild fringes of towns and cities. In one remote and beautiful region of Rajasthan, however, big cats and people coexist in a unique state of mutual tolerance.

The reason: the leopards were for centuries protected by a ban on hunting imposed by the local Maharajas, who paid compensation for all livestock killed. The tradition, maintained today by the Indian Forest Service, has enabled the feline population to swell to the point where virtually every hillock rising from the mustard and chickpea fields is inhabited by one, if not two or three, leopards.

For the Rabari people who graze their flocks in the shadow of the eroded granite outcrops, the cats' watchful presence is a fact of everyday life. As the herders, dressed in scarlet turbans and white cotton tunics, lead their animals home each evening, they routinely see leopards crouched low on rock slabs or hunched under euphorbia bushes flanking the pathways, waiting to snatch a straggling sheep, grab a goat, pounce on an unwary peacock or make off with one of the silver-furred langur monkeys that congregate on the boulder tops. In the mornings, their pugmarks follow the same sandy tracks that the village children take to school.

Outsiders can now experience this extraordinary phenomenon at close quarters. Guests at the Jawai Leopard Camp are taken on twice-daily safaris by experts who have spent years tracking and watching the cats, and know their every den and lookout point. Most outings are by Jeep, but you can also don a turban and join Rabari herders as they accompany their animals.

Stay at least a couple of nights, and leopard sightings are almost guaranteed. It's not unusual to see two or more together; a family of five is the current record. Even after a few days, the experience of watching a wild cat emerge from a hollow on a granite kopje and creep towards a flock of Rabari goats is never less than exhilarating.

INDIA With nail-biting cricketing action in twenty-over innings and teams owned by Bollywood royalty and business tycoons, the Indian Premier League adds a dramatic and showy twist to a decidedly traditional sport.

From the day the event is announced to its spectacular opening ceremony and much-hyped finale, the IPL completely dominates the Indian psyche. The drama unfolds with a high-powered auction, in which international stars can reach over two million dollars as the IPL lives up to its cash-rich reputation in style.

Some fans may grumble that money has become the name of the game, but the appeal of seeing promising young guns in the midst of big money and big names sweeps the vast majority along. Each franchise – teams include the Kolkata Knight Riders, Delhi Devils and Rajasthan Royals – can include up to four non-Indians in their eleven, and passionate fans scream advice to brothers-in-arms who would otherwise face off as members of opposing international sides.

Once the games begin, the pent-up excitement becomes palpable. The first thing that strikes you is the rush of sound – loud cheering from the crowds and the latest Bollywood melodies. This is cricket shorn of some of its subtleties, but with the spectacle ramped up to the max. Matches seem like one big party, high-risk cricket, cheerleading, celebrities and slow-motion replays ensuring that things never let up.

Celebrations reach their peak as the teams take up their different positions on the field, and every wicket, six or boundary is followed by sheer revelry in the stands. Even the riotously hued players aren't immune to the merry-making, and some can be seen shaking a leg between innings.

A trip to the IPL is like a trip through India. The excitement, colour, chaos and non-stop drama offer a vivid insight into the Subcontinent and the flights of fancy that run through its veins. The eager crowd – men, women and children – can't get enough.

Glitz, leather and willow: the IPL

809

810 | Climbing to the Sacred Footprint

SRI LANKA Adam's Peak is quite possibly Sri Lanka's most recognizable landmark, with its iconic curved crest piercing the clouds high above the forested hills of the central highland region. It has been a pilgrimage site for over a thousand years, and this is thanks to an unusual depression on its summit known as the Sri Pada or "Sacred Footprint", which has inspired a host of tales over the years. Buddhists believe the footprint was left by the Buddha, while Hindus claim it was created by Shiva, and Christians and Muslims attribute it to Adam after he was cast out of heaven. Still, the peak is predominantly a Buddhist place of worship.

Thousands of people make the gruelling climb to see the footprint every year, and you shouldn't take it lightly – at 2243m, Adam's Peak is Sri Lanka's fifth-highest mountain. Tradition dictates that you start around 2am to reach the temple at the top by sunrise, when the view is less likely to be obscured by clouds and you're in with a better chance of seeing the mountain's inexplicably triangular shadow. During peak

season, between December and May, you'll find teashops and a string of lights illuminating the way – at other times, you'll just have to bring snacks and a reliable torch.

The easiest route is the 7km-long track from the village of Dalhousie, which starts with a gentle incline through tea estates and past Buddhist shrines. From there, around 5500 stone steps begin in earnest, culminating in a near-vertical section towards the top where you'll have to haul yourself up using the handrails. Still, all thoughts of exhaustion or jellied knees will fade once you reach the temple compound: the sweeping views down across the tea plantations and dense cloudforest, enhanced by the soft light of sunrise, are simply out of this world.

No technical ability is needed for the climb, and you also won't need a guide, unless you're particularly wary of making the trip out of season. Still, it's easy to pick up a companion: slip one of the local dogs a biscuit at the bottom and he'll follow you all the way up.

811 | Cycling the Karakoram Highway from Pakistan to China

PAKISTAN A sky the colour of wild sapphires wraps around the tips of an interminable series of jagged, ash-gray mountains like you've never seen elsewhere on Earth. The "Cones" — or "Cathedrals", as some call them — rise from the ground like a dragon's fangs right outside the village of Passu in northern Pakistan.

This mountain range is just one of the many highlights to be found along the Karakoram Highway, once a challenging high-altitude passage connecting the Chinese part of the Silk Road with Hindustan. Today, the Karakoram Highway is a perfectly sealed road maintained by the joint efforts of the Chinese and the Pakistani governments. It connects the cities of Islamabad and Kashgar, boosting Chinese investment and trade with Pakistan, and snaking through some of the world's most stunning mountain scenery. The best bit starts right before Gilgit, the main centre of the Gilgit-Baltistan region, where the Himalaya, the Karakoram and

the Hindu Kush ranges meet. Karimabad, with its ancient Baltit and Altit forts, and the viewpoint at Eagle's Nest, is a three-hour cycle ride north. Sit on a rock and enjoy the sun as it sets beyond a bowl of 7000m-plus-high mountains like Rakaposhi — the peak with the sharpest rising rock face in the world.

And it's not just the mountains that will steal your breath: riding along a bit further north, the startlingly turquoise Attabad Lake beckons like an ethereal eye opening in the midst of grey high-altitude deserts. Born in 2010 out of Gilgit-Baltistan's worst floods, it has turned into one of the region's main tourist hotspots — visit soon, as it's slowly shrinking, year after year. If you manage to drag yourself away from Passu's magnetic beauty, you'll ride for another day through Khunjerab National Park until the village of Sost and the Chinese frontier — at 4880 metres, it's the highest land border in the world.

812 | Visiting Gandhi's peaceful ashram

INDIA A peaceful plot on the western bank of the Sabarmati River in Gujarat, on the edge of Ahmedabad, holds an evocative tribute to a man who changed the course of history. Mohandas Karamchand Gandhi, born in Porbandar in western Gujarat, led the campaign for Indian independence and will forever symbolize nonviolent protest.

The Mahatma ("Great Soul") established the Sabarmati Ashram in 1917, bringing together people who went on to work to secure India's freedom. Symbolically located between a jail and a crematorium – Gandhi believed a *satyagrahi* (someone engaged in passive resistance) inevitably ended up in one of these two places – the ashram soon became the centre of the Indian independence movement.

Although no longer in operation, it's now a pilgrimage site that draws hundreds of thousands of visitors each year. In keeping with Gandhian philosophy, it's a modest place, but one with unmistakable authority. The simple, single-storey whitewashed buildings and neatly tended gardens have a serene air that invites contemplation, in stark contrast

to the crowded, pollution-choked city outside. Many come here simply to sit and think in the peaceful grounds, but there is also an auditorium for talks and film screenings, a photo gallery, library and archive, and an appropriately pared-back museum. Among the exhibits is a letter from Gandhi to Hitler urging him to avoid war, and an emotive collection of personal possessions, including wooden shoes, pristine white clothes and a pair of round spectacles.

The ashram was the starting point for the famous Dandi March on March 12, 1930. Gandhi led 78 people on a 388km walk to the Gulf of Cambay in protest against the British Salt Law, vowing not to return to the ashram until India was free. Although the country gained independence on August 15, 1947, Gandhi was assassinated before he could set foot in the ashram again.

Today, the Sabarmati Ashram commemorates the great achievements of the past, but in a state that has suffered bitter violence in recent years, it also stands as a potent symbol of hope.

813 | Dining with the locals on Chowpatty Beach

INDIA For all the gloss and glamour of its recent development, the real highlight of a trip to Mumbai remains the same as ever – the street food. Mention the city to anyone who calls him or herself a foodie, and the chances are they'll be salivating within moments – from the crisp filled shells of *pani puri* to the soft spicy rolls of *pao bhaji* and the refreshing drinks served up by Mumbai's innumerable juice bars, this is the stuff of a food-lover's fantasy.

If you find the idea of street food appealing but the practice a little daunting, opportunities abound to sample tasty offerings in more "hygienic" surroundings. *Elco Pani Puri Centre* is the place to try *pani puri* – feather-light little *puris*, filled with a spicy mix of potato, chickpea, coriander and tamarind – while on the lookout for Bollywood stars in the fashionable Bandra neighbourhood. Or hunt out *pao bhaji*, a Portuguese-style bread roll, served alongside a spicy vegetable stew, that's ubiquitous enough to appear on hotel menus.

However, no place epitomizes Mumbai's street-food culture better than Chowpatty Beach. Though this stretch of sand is unlikely to win any awards for its looks, it has an undeniable charm, especially towards sunset when families descend en masse to walk, play – and, most importantly, eat.

Chowpatty is synonymous with *bhel puri*, a mouth-tingling combination of crunchy *sev* (spiced, fried chickpea-flour noodles) and puffed rice, soft potato, tangy fresh onion and tamarind sauce, plus just enough spice to give your mouth a bit of a challenge. Grab a polystyrene plateful from one of the stalls – as with all street food, the best is freshly prepared in front of you – and join the locals to seek out a spot on the sand to watch the smoggy dusk-orange sky descend into night. As the lights of the city begin to twinkle around you and a soft breeze blows in from the sea, you'd be hard-pressed to find a better seat for dinner.

814 | Picturing a lost civilization at Ajanta

INDIA Even now, with the approach road marred by postcard stalls and car parks, the Ajanta Caves in northern Maharashtra retain the aura of a lost world. Hollowed into the sides of a horseshoe-shaped ravine, deep in an arid wilderness that has always been forbiddingly remote, the complex remains hidden from view until you're almost directly beneath it. When Lt Alexander Cunningham of the 16th Bengal Lancers stumbled on the site during a tiger hunt in 1813, the excavations had lain forgotten for more than a thousand years – their floors a midden of animal bones and ash from aboriginal hunting fires, their exquisite frescoes blackened by soot.

These days, the worn, rock-cut steps to the caves are fitted with metal handrails, and electricity has replaced the candles used by Cunningham's party, but from the instant the guide first swings his arc light over the murals that adorn the walls you're plunged into another time. It's a moment few visitors forget. Once your eyes have adjusted to the swirls of earthy red, yellow, blue and black pigments, scenes of unimaginable sophistication emerge from the gloom: sumptuous royal

processions; elaborate court and street scenes; snowcapped mountains; sages; musicians; stormy seascapes and shipwrecks; marching armies; and a veritable menagerie of animals, both real and imagined.

But it's the intimacy of the art that really captivates. The beautifully fluid tableaux seem to glow with life. Kohl-rimmed eyes light up; well-toned torsos, draped with jewellery, still look sexy; dance poses ooze sensuous grace, humour and vitality; and you can almost smell the aroma of a lotus blossom being raised by the smiling Bodhisattva Avalokitesvara in Cave 1 – India's own Mona Lisa.

For the long-vanished pilgrims who originally filed past these sacred Buddhist treasures, the art would have fired the imagination with a power equivalent to that of modern cinema. These must have been the Bollywood movies of their era, complete with resplendently bejewelled heroines and strong, compassionate heroes, backed by a supporting cast of thousands – and if the images are anything to go by, the soundtrack would have been amazing too.

815 | Dive in the Indian Ocean, with reef sharks and wrasse

THE MALDIVES The white-sand beaches and luxurious resorts are undoubtedly special places to unwind, but many people make the long journey to the Maldives with a snorkelling mask in their suitcase and PADI certification card in their wallet. The brilliantly turquoise waters hold over two thousand species of fish, including serpent-like moray eels, bulbous napoleon wrasse and huge, elegant manta rays.

With visibility of up to 40m, diving in this remote archipelago, 700km southwest of Sri Lanka, is big business. Dive centres at most resorts offer reef and drift diving, as well as the opportunity to dive at night – which promises intrepid divers intimate encounters with sharks and rays.

Reef sharks are one of the main attractions in the Maldives, and are reassuringly unlikely to be aggressive towards divers. Often sighted gracefully skimming the edges of the reef, the grey reef shark, distinguished by a lighter strip on its dorsal fin and a black flash across the edge of its tail, can reach up to 2m in length. Once

immediate thoughts of *Jaws* have been banished, gliding through the sparkling Indian Ocean only metres from a great predator as it slinks its way around the coral is thrilling.

If you'd rather stay closer to the shore, snorkelling over the threshold of the shallow water is also a spectacular experience. As you swim out from an immaculately sandy beach, with the sun warming your back and your breath whispering through your snorkel, the reefs suddenly and dramatically drop away to reveal shoals of tropical fish and vividly coloured coral, while the chattering sound of feeding parrotfish resonates under water.

At an average of only 1.5m above sea level, the 1190 islands of the archipelago barely peer above the surface of the Indian Ocean. Sadly, as water levels rise, the islands' future is increasingly threatened – and the extraordinary underwater world lying beneath the sand banks is likely to be easily accessed for only a few more decades. Plan your reef-shark rendezvous soon.

NEPAL The bustling lakeside town of Pokhara is dwarfed by the towering Annapurna and Manaslu ranges of the Himalayas. Beyond the forest-clad hills that surround its criss-crossing streets, some of the world's highest mountains rise snowcapped to the north, providing a breathtaking contrast to the dense jungle-like vegetation of Pokhara itself.

Many visitors rise early, and gather at viewpoints like Sarangkot to watch the sun illuminate the peaks. On a clear day, though, when the mountain tops reach into a blue-sky abyss, the best way to enjoy panoramic views of mountains, lake and town alike has to be from beneath a parachute canopy, soaring with the eagles.

The green slopes that climb within a short drive of Pokhara make the perfect launch spot for the hundreds of paragliding enthusiasts who travel here each year. Some are coming for the first time, others are returning, and there are those who have never left, remaining captivated by the slow pace of life and incredible mountain scenery. Launching on a tandem flight, harnessed to the front of an experienced flier and with the parachute laid neatly on the ground behind you, you'll need faith in the laws of physics to allow the wind to lift you into the air – a truly thrilling and liberating experience.

For the ultimate freedom, spend a few days paratrekking through the valley, soaring for up to three hours away from Pokhara to sleep in the mountains, and returning by parachute the following day. From the skies, the small villages, rice paddies and people below become miniatures, the landscape stretches for ever, and the only sound is the wind as thermal pockets lift the canopy higher. With just the company of the eagles above you, there are unobstructed views of the impressive Machhapuchchhre ("Fish Tail") and Annapurna peaks. Finally you come back to land beside the deep-blue lake, dwindling back to human scale beneath the grandeur of the Himalayas.

816

Soaring with the eagles in the Himalayas

INDIA Though a cable winch (or a modern boat) would be more efficient, the Goan fishermen of Benaulim bring in their catch the old-fashioned way and, if you're strolling by, they'll probably wave you over to help. Two long ropes stretch all the way up the beach, with heavy branches attached at intervals; on the other end is their net, sometimes floating 500m from the shore and visible only as a massive swirl of water and seabirds. You and a dozen fishermen brace your backs against the branches and take straining steps in reverse toward the line of palms.

The old wooden fishing boat that rests on the sand, with the Portuguese name *Bom Jesus* painted on its prow, is both a reminder of the tiny state's colonial past and evidence of its peculiar culture. Like most of India, Goa had a sophisticated indigenous society for more than a millennium before Europeans arrived, but its modern character is the result of spice-hunter Vasco da Gama's arrival here at the turn of the fifteenth century. Though the Indian army finally drove the Portuguese out in the 1960s, Goans today are proud of their unique identity: partly Lusophone, largely Catholic and with an intriguing and delicious fusion of Portuguese and Indian cuisine. These traits have attracted travellers to Goa for decades, as much to admire its cathedrals and colonial architecture as to throw massive raves on its famously lovely beaches.

It's not party time in Benaulim, though; the sand slips out beneath your feet and you must be conceding 3m for every one you gain. Either the waves don't want to give up their bounty so easily, or the fish aren't keen on being dinner. Groaning, yelling, laughing and grimacing, your team could keep at this for hours until the net is hauled in, though by this point you may have turned over your position to someone else. Stick around, though, and you'll see what's likely to end up on your plate that evening in a fish curry.

Hauling in dinner in Goa

818 | The Andaman Islands: India's far-flung string of pearls

INDIA The long emerald necklace of the Andaman Islands, lying over 1000km out in the Bay of Bengal, is unlike anywhere else in India.

The only point of entry is the capital, Port Blair, from where the requisite free special permit is granted, which delineates the areas and islands you are allowed to visit. Most visitors then make a beeline for Havelock, a 12km-long mix of forested hills, verdant farmland and white sandy beaches, a couple of hours away on a fast catamaran. Although some would say Havelock is on the verge of becoming spoilt, it remains the only island to offer a wide range of eating and sleeping options. Plus it has the majority of diving operations and boasts the splendid arc of Radhnagar (aka #7). Havelock's diminutive neighbour, Neil, has started to take some of the overspill and is preferred by many for a longer stay.

Many people make the mistake of sticking solely to Havelock and maybe Neil, but there are a lot more places to be explored.

For a relaxed and relatively isolated refuge, one of the best options is Long Island. On the boat route from Havelock north to Rangat, it contains a low-key little bazaar, just one or two accommodations, and the possibility of a fine hike across to the island's best beach, which you are likely to have entirely to yourself.

Best of all, however, is Little Andaman, the southernmost island in the group and paradoxically quite large. Much of the island is reserved for the Onge tribe and thus off-limits, but a sizeable chunk of the northeast is included on your permit. Just establishing itself on the traveller trail, Little Andaman is home to a handful of small guesthouses and extremely laidback, inexpensive beach hut operations strung along the coast between Hut Bay and Netaji Nagar, behind a magnificent 8km strand. You can also admire the tranquil White Surf Waterfalls, whose name gives away the fact that Little Andaman boasts excellent surfing conditions.

819 | Browsing English veg in the Asian hills

SRI LANKA Sri Lanka has many unexpected sights, but few are as surreal as early morning in Haputale. As dawn breaks, the mists that blanket the town for much of the year slowly dissipate, revealing the huddled shapes of Tamils, insulated against the cold in woolly hats and padded jackets, hawking great bundles of English vegetables – radishes, swedes, cabbages and marrows – while the workaday Sri Lankan town slowly comes to life in the background, with its hooting buses and cluttered bazaars.

As the mists clear and the sun rises, the tangled ridges of the island's hill country come slowly into view to the north, while to the south the land falls dramatically away to the lowlands below, with the far-off coast and its sweltering Indian Ocean beaches faintly visible in the distance. As an image of Sri Lanka's unexpected juxtapositions, Haputale has few peers, and to stand shivering on a hilltop within a few degrees of the equator, watching a scene reminiscent of an English market town crazily

displaced in time and space, is to understand something of the cultural and physical paradoxes of this fascinatingly diverse island.

The contradictions continue in the countryside beyond Haputale, as the road twists and turns up into the sprawling British-era plantations of the Dambatenne Tea Estate, whose antiquated factory is filled with the ingenious Victorian mechanical contraptions which are still used to process the leaves brought in from the surrounding estates. For the British visitor particularly, there is always the faint, strange nostalgia of seeing the legacy of one's great-great-grandparents preserved in a distant, tropical island.

But there is also the subversive awareness that the hillsides of Haputale, once colonized by the British, have now reached out and quietly conquered distant parts of the world in their turn, filling the teabags and chai shops of countries as varied as England, Iran and India, with a taste that is purely and uniquely Sri Lankan.

820 | Crowd-watching at Kartik Purnima

INDIA In this era of "Readymade Suitings and Shirtings", traditional Indian dress is definitely on the decline. There is, however, one place where you're still guaranteed to see proper old-fashioned finery at its most flamboyant. Each year, during the full-moon phase of Kartika month, tens of thousands of Rajasthani villagers hitch up their camel carts and converge on the oasis of Pushkar, on the edge of the Thar Desert, to bathe in the town's sacred lake, whose waters are said to be especially purifying at this time. As well as a redemptive dip, the festival also provides an opportunity to indulge those other great Rajasthani passions: trading livestock, arranging marriages, and generally strutting one's stuff.

Kartik Purnima has since been rebranded by the region's dynamic tourist office as the Pushkar Camel Fair, and the vast sea of neatly clipped beige fur undulating in the dunes around town during the festival does indeed present one of India's most arresting spectacles. But it's the animals' owners who really steal the show. Dressed in kilos of silver jewellery, flowing pleated skirts and veils dripping with intricate

mirrorwork and embroidery, the women look breathtaking against the desert backdrop, especially in the warmer colours of evening, when the sand glows molten red and the sky turns a fantastic shade of mauve. The men go for a more sober look, but compensate for their white-cotton *dhoti* loincloths and shirts with outsized, vibrantly coloured turbans and handlebar moustaches waxed to pin-sharp points.

Traditional Rajasthani garb looks even more wonderful when set against the sacred steps, or *ghats*, that are spread around Pushkar. For the full effect, get up before dawn, when the drumming, conch-blowing and bell-ringing starts at the temples, and position yourself on one of the flat rooftops or peeling whitewashed cupolas overlooking the waterside. When the sun's first rays finally burst across Nag Pahar ("Snake Mountain") to the east, a blaze of colour erupts as thousands of pilgrims gather to invoke Brahma, the Supreme Creator Being of Hindu mythology, by raising little brass pots of sacred water above their heads and pouring them back into the lake. It's a scene that can have changed little in hundreds – even thousands – of years.

821

INDIA Rising from the surrounding plains of tropical vegetation like man-made mountains, the great temples of the Chola dynasty utterly dominate most major towns in Tamil Nadu. For sheer scale and intensity, though, none outstrips the one dedicated to the fish-eyed goddess, Shri Meenakshi, and her consort, Sundareshwara, in Madurai. Peaking at 46m, its skyscraping *gopuras* stand as the state's pride and joy – Dravidian India's Empire State, Eiffel Tower and Cristo Redentor rolled into one. The towers taper skywards like elongated, stepped pyramids, their surfaces writhing with an anarchic jumble of deities, demons, warriors, curvaceous maidens, pot-bellied dwarfs and sprites – all rendered in Disney-bright colours, and topped with crowns of gigantic cobra heads and gilded finials.

Joining the flood of pilgrims that pours through the gateways beneath them, you leave the trappings of modern India far behind. A labyrinth of interconnecting walkways, ceremonial halls and courtyards forms the heart of the complex. Against its backdrop of 30,000 carved pillars unfolds a never-ending round of rituals and processions. Day and night, cavalcades of bare-chested priests carry torches of burning camphor and offerings for the goddess, while musicians blast out devotional hymns on Tamil oboes. Shaven-headed pilgrims prostrate themselves on the greasy stone floors as women clutching parcels of lotus flowers, coconuts and incense squeeze through the crush to the innermost sanctum.

Perhaps the most amazing thing of all about the Meenakshi Temple is that these rituals have taken place in the same shrines, continuously and largely unchanged, since the time of ancient Greece. Nowhere else in the world has a classical civilization survived into the modern era, and nowhere else in India do the ancient roots of Hinduism remain so tangible. It's as if Delphi or the Acropolis were still centres of active worship in the dot-com era.

India's Acropolis:
a shrine to
the fish-eyed goddess

INDIA Goa tends to be where most people head when they fancy a relaxing beach break in India. There is, however, one special little town a couple of hours further south down the coast, where you can hit the sands without feeling like you've left the country entirely behind.

As the site of one of India's most revered Shiva shrines, Gokarna has been an important Hindu pilgrimage destination for thousands of years. Like a lot of India's religious centres, it's locked in a charismatic time warp: worn and dilapidated, but full of old-world atmosphere. Brahmin priests still saunter around bare-chested, swathed in white or coral-coloured *lunghis*, and the main market street is always thronged with stray cows and bus-loads of pilgrims squelching their way from the town's sacred beach to the temples after a purifying dip in the sea.

A lone Rama temple, overlooking Gokarna's seafront from the edge of a headland wrapped in waxy green cashew bushes, marks the start of a path to an altogether different kind of beach scene. Backed by coconut groves and forested hills, the series of beautiful bays to the south is where the hardcore hippy contingent forced out of Goa by the 1990s' charter boom regrouped and put down roots.

Of all of them, Om Beach, where a pair of twin coves and their rocky outcrops replicate the sacred Hindu symbol for "Oneness and Peace", is the most famous. Further south, the path continues beyond steep, grassy clifftops dotted with miniature palms and red laterite boulders to a string of even more gorgeous side coves with names like "Full Moon" and "Paradise". This far away from civilization, the jungle descends right to the sand line, while the sea crashes in wild and clean. Fish eagles patrol the foreshore and dolphins regularly flip out of the waves.

Admittedly, the kind of ersatz Indian behaviour beloved in these hideaways isn't for everybody. But if the ostentatious chillum-smoking, yoga posing and mantra-chanting does start to grate, rest assured you can always slip one of the local fishermen a fifty-rupee note and have him whisk you back to town to watch the real thing.

822

Walking to paradise at Gokarna

823 | Tracking tigers in the jungles of India

INDIA With so many fabulous tourism draws across the country, it's easy to forget that the steamy jungles of India are home to more than half of the world's remaining Bengal tigers. Amazingly, there's no better time to spot them in action. A true conservation success story, India's tiger numbers are actually increasing for the first time in over a century – its tiger population jumping from a measly 1706 to 2226 in a 2014 census. Despite ongoing threats to tiger habitats – from poaching to habitat destruction – that figure is expected to surpass three thousand when new data is released in 2019.

Fiercely territorial and mostly nocturnal, India's Bengal tigers enjoy (relatively) safe havens within fifty designated tiger reserves across the nation. At its heart, the state of Madhya Pradesh is the core of tiger country, with five reserves accessible within several hours of its heritage-rich capital, Bhopal, which doubles as a hub for safari operators. Arguably the most famous reserve is Bandhavgarh. Sanskrit for Brothers' Fort (don't miss the stunning ancient fort perched on a cliff in the park) Bandhavgarth is known for its rich biodiversity, with possible safari sightings including several species of deer and antelope, wild boar, Indian bison, wild dog, leopard, Indian fox, sloth bears and, of course, tigers. It's also the last place a white tiger – the big cats' distinct colouring due to an autosomal recessive trait – was spotted in the wild, more than 60 years ago.

South of Bandhavgarh, the Satpura, Pench and Kanha tiger reserves arc southwest of Bhopal. Despite the fact that Rudyard Kipling never visited Madhya Pradesh, it's widely thought the English author set *The Jungle Book* collection in the district of Seoni, on the outskirts of what is now Pench National Park, home to tigress Collarwali Baghin – the star of BBC documentary *Tiger: Spy in the Jungle*. The large open meadows of Kanha bode particularly well for big-cat spotting, and while Satpura's striped residents are more elusive, it's the only Indian tiger reserve where walking safaris are permitted in its core, offering a more immersive wildlife-spotting experience.

824 | Trekking to the source of the Ganges

INDIA Of all the holy rivers of India, Hindus consider the Ganges – or "Ganga" as it's known in Sanskrit – to be the holiest. And of all the sacred sites along its course, the most sacred is the spot, high in the Garhwal Himalaya, where its waters first see the light of day.

Aside from bringing you much spiritual merit (a mere wind-borne droplet of Ganga water is believed to purge the body of a hundred lifetimes of sin), the pilgrimage to the source of the river provides the fastest possible route into the heart of the world's highest mountain range. Winding through rhododendron and deodar cedar forests, a paved road runs nearly all the way from the Indian plains to Gangotri, at an altitude of 3200m.

From here on, you have to join the ragged procession of pilgrims and ash-smeared sadhus as they cover the final 20km leg: a long day's walk over a moonscape of grey dust and scree. Laden with sacks of offerings and supplies, many chant the 108 honorific titles of the river as they walk: "Imperishable", "A Sun Among the Darkness and Ignorance" or "Cow Which Gives Much Milk". And for once, the earthly splendour of the surroundings still lives up to its mythology.

As you cross a rise on the valley floor, the full glory of the Gangotri Glacier is suddenly revealed, snaking away to a skyline of snow peaks. A 400m vertical wall, grey-blue and encrusted with stones, forms the awesome snout of the ice floe – Gau Mukh, the "Cow's Mouth".

For the community of sadhus who live semi-naked in this freezing spot year-round, nearly 4000m above sea level, nowhere on Earth is more uplifting. Come here at dawn, and you'll see them plunging into the icy water that surges from the foot of the glacier, wringing it out of their long dreadlocks, and settling down on the eroded rocks of the river bank to meditate or practise yoga. Even without the magnificent mountain backdrop the source would be one of the most enthralling places on the planet. But with the crystal-clear mountain light, the rituals and the vast amphitheatre of rock and ice rising on all sides, the effect is nothing short of transcendental.

825 | Watching elephants go wild in Uda Walawe

SRI LANKA It's a hazy dawn in Uda Walawe National Park, and the thirty orphans at the Elephant Transit House are waking up to a day that will see seven of them spend their last few hours here. Each year, dozens of baby elephants from Sri Lanka's 4000-strong population get separated from their herds, or fall into wells or ditches. The transit house nurses them back to health and provides the care they need to overcome the trauma. Release days – which occur roughly once a year – are special events, with government ministers in attendance, orange-robed Buddhist monks honouring the occasion and a crowd of tourists and locals looking on.

On this occasion, the first of the radio-collared youngsters to go into the truck, five-year-old Baby Blue – found living in a buffalo herd – complains noisily at being pushed on board. His carer pats his trunk and murmurs in his ear, while funnelling milk into his mouth. Once he's aboard, four other young males and two females follow more willingly. They're all given leafy sugar-cane tops to keep them busy. A dusty half-hour ride takes the orphans to the release site, where a lurching water truck pulls up alongside and hoses them down with a shower of water mixed with elephant dung, to rid them of their human odour.

The release, when it comes, is quick but strangely moving. Baby Blue barges forward through his peers and stomps off into the bush, shaking his ears at onlookers and shrieking with delight. The less experienced orphans follow, uncertain what to do in a place with no apparent barriers. After a minute they find a gap in the thick bush and follow each other further into the park. The radio-tracking Land Rover sets off down the nearest bush road in pursuit. The next morning, the trackers report the elephants have walked 4km and are still in one group. Within weeks, most of them have integrated into the park's herds. It's all over for another year, when the next batch of youngsters will be ready to brave a new life in the bush.

826 | Cruising the Keralan backwaters

INDIA Kerala's Kuttinad backwaters region is, in every sense, a world apart from the mainstream of Indian life. Sandwiched between the Arabian Sea and the foothills of the Western Ghat Mountains, its heart is a tangled labyrinth of rivers, rivulets and shimmering lagoons, enfolded by a curtain of dense tropical foliage. This natural barrier screens Kuttinad from the roads, railways and market towns that dominate the rest of the coastal strip, making it blissfully tranquil for such a densely populated area.

Innumerable small vessels glide around Kuttinad, but easily the most romantic way to explore it is in a *kettu vallam*, or traditional Keralan rice barge. Hand-built from teak and jackwood and sporting canopies made from plaited palm leaves, they're beautiful craft – whether propelled along gondolier-style using long poles or by less environmentally friendly diesel engines.

Views constantly change as you cruise along. One minute you're squeezing through a narrow canal clogged with purple water hyacinth; the next, you're gliding over luminous, placid lakes fringed by groves of coconut palms. Every now and then, a whitewashed church tower, minaret or temple finial reveals the presence of a hidden village. Some settlements occupy only the tiniest parcel of land, barely large enough for a small house. Others have their own boatyards, vegetable gardens and ranks of cantilevered Chinese fishing nets dangling from the river bank.

Dozens of *kettu vallam* cruise firms compete for custom in towns such as Alappuzha and Karunnagapalli, some offering top-of-the-range rice barges complete with designer cane furniture, gourmet kitchens and viewing platforms scattered with cushions and lanterns. Alternatively, you could eschew such luxury in favour of a more authentic mode of transport: one of the stalwart municipal ferries that chug between Kuttinad's major towns and villages. Aside from saving you the equivalent of the average annual wage of most of your fellow passengers, arriving in one of these oily beasts won't provoke the frenzied response from local kids that can shatter the very tranquillity that makes Kuttinad so special.

827 | Scooting through elephant territory

SRI LANKA The coast road that runs east from Galle across the south of Sri Lanka can, at times, be a perilous place to take a moped. It's never long before the terrifying but universally accepted "triple overtake" comes into play, and a huge truck overtakes another bus that's already overtaking someone else, on a single-carriage two-way road. On the plus side, at least it's impossible to get lost, with beautiful vistas of the Indian Ocean on your right, and countless potential stop-offs along the way, in little beachside fishing villages that become increasingly remote and luxurious the further east you go. The road eventually breaks off inland to approach Yala National Park, home to over three hundred elephants, along with the highest density of leopards in the world.

Take a jeep tour at dawn or dusk, and you'll see herds of elephants nuzzling each other in the bush, water buffalo lazing around in the muddy waterholes, monkeys leaping through branches and peacocks parading their splendour. You might even get lucky, and glimpse the spots of one of those magnificent, and usually solitary, big cats – leopards.

Journeys down the B35, which cuts right through the western side of Yala, are often interrupted by intriguing traffic obstacles: wild elephants. You zip through to the front of the traffic to see an adult bull standing 50m away, right in the middle of the road, and frozen with terror. You wish people wouldn't toot their horns, and wonder whether he'll charge. After perhaps half an hour, the cars and trucks lose patience. One by one they begin to risk it, and simply drive around him. A scooter suddenly seems like an alarmingly tiny, vulnerable, ridiculous machine. You look at the size of the bull and notice his panicked eyes. You wait it out. A long hour in, and at last the bull has had enough; slowly, majestically, he walks away from the road and disappears into the bushes.

828 | Criss-cross the country with Indian Railways

INDIA It's just enough to wake you: a small voice, further along the carriage, murmuring a quiet mantra. "Chai, coffee?", it asks, stepping over the parcels and suitcases that have tumbled out into the aisle during the night. "Coffee, chai?" Now and then, there's a pause as passengers get out of bed, followed by the clinking of coins and the slow, bubbling sound of paper cups being filled to the brim. And then, suddenly, it's your turn.

"Chai, coffee?" demands the man, much louder now that only a thin curtain separates him from your sleeping compartment. You poke your head out into the aisle. Tired smiles are swapped, more coins change hands, and milky-sweet chai pours into a cup. And so begins another day aboard Indian Railways, one of the world's biggest and most befuddling train networks, which has somehow managed to retain a strange sense of romance.

Criss-crossing the Subcontinent on these ageing, juddering, chronically overcrowded trains can test a traveller's patience. Unless you've been lucky enough to book a bed in one of the air-conditioned sleeper compartments, you may spend the entire journey wishing the train would just arrive. But no other mode of transport provides a better snapshot of India – of its wealth, its poverty, and its tapestry of people and faiths. A glance at the dusty departure boards at any big station, replete with exotic-sounding services like the Darjeeling Mail, the Gujarat Express and the delightfully named Mysore Arsikere Passenger – rest assured, the name has nothing to do with the quality of the seats – is enough to set the imagination alight.

Securing a comfy spot on an Indian train – or in fact any seat at all – usually calls for forward planning, form filling, a working knowledge of railway jargon, unlimited amounts of patience and a sprinkling of good luck. Sometimes, the process runs smoothly. Often, it derails. When you finally get yourself a bed aboard a sleeper train, though, and awaken to the distant voice of the *chai wallah*, you'll forget that it ever felt like hard work.

829

Bollywood glamour at the Mumbai Metro

INDIA If you've never seen a Bollywood movie, think John Travolta and Olivia Newton-John in *Grease*, then pump up the colour saturation, quadruple the number of dancing extras, switch the soundtrack to an A.R. Rahman masala mix and imagine Indo-Western hybrid outfits that grow more extravagant with every change of camera angle.

Like their classic forerunners of the 1970s and 1980s, modern Bollywood blockbusters demand the biggest screens and heftiest sound systems on the market, and they don't come bigger or heftier than those in the Metro BIG in Mumbai, the *grande dame* of the city's surviving Art Deco picture houses. The palpable aura of old-school glamour that still hangs over the place is at its most glittering on red-carpet nights, when huge crowds gather in the street outside to glimpse stars such as Shah Rukh Kahn or Ashwariya Rai posing for the paparazzi in front of the iconic 1930s facade.

A sense of occasion strikes you the moment you step into the Metro BIG's foyer, with its plush crimson drapery and polished Italian marble floors. A 2006 revamp transformed the auditorium into a comprehensive multiplex, complete with six screens, lashings of chrome and reclining seats, but the developers had the good sense to leave the heritage features in the rest of the building intact. Belgian crystal chandeliers still hang from the ceilings, reflected in herringbone-patterned mirrors on the mid-landing, and original stucco murals line the staircases.

While the Metro may have had a makeover, the same quirky conventions that have styled Indian cinema for decades still very much hold sway – in spite of Bollywood's glossier modern image and bigger budgets. So while the waistlines have dropped and cleavages become more pronounced, the star-crossed hero and heroine still have to make do with a coy rub of noses rather than a proper kiss.

Down in the stalls of the Metro BIG, meanwhile, the change of decor did nothing to subdue behaviour in the cheaper seats. Shouting at the screen, cheering every time the hero wallops someone, and singing along with the love songs are still very much part of the experience – even if overpriced popcorn has supplanted five-rupee wraps of peanuts.

Surf boats on the southern seas

THE MALDIVES Imagine a series of perfect tropical reef breaks populated by parrotfish, turtles and manta rays, over which crystalline waves roll with regularity. Surf conditions like these are generally hard to find, but charter a surf boat in the Maldives and you can anchor off the break of your choice early in the morning, with such waves there for the taking. When the late risers paddle out, simply clamber back onto your floating hotel and enjoy a leisurely breakfast while you sail away to more distant, isolated areas.

A two-week trip here in peak surf season (July/August) may net you fourteen consecutive days of head-high surf. You'll never need to wear more than board shorts, a rash vest and plenty of sun cream, and it's easy enough to get in five sessions a day, since you're literally living next to the breaks. Downtime can be spent snorkelling the reefs, chilling out on deck with a book or snoozing in the sea breeze.

831 | Eating a banana-leaf lunch in Chidambaram

INDIA "Step in!", reads the sign. "For: idly-wada-dosai-utthapam-appam-pongal . . . and rice plate!". Even if you don't know what any of these promised gastronomic delights may be, the aromas of freshly cooked spices, smoky mustard oil, simmering coconut milk and sandalwood-scented incense billowing into the street are enticement enough to do just as the sign says.

In the temple towns of Tamil Nadu, where regional cooking styles have been refined over centuries in the kitchens of the great Chola shrines, "meals" or "rice-plate" restaurants are where most working men – and travellers – eat. Some are swankier than others, with air-conditioning instead of paddle fans, but none serves tastier or more traditional south Indian food than *Sri Ganesa Bhawan*, in the shadow of the famous Nataraja Temple in Chidambaram.

Space for lunch in the old-fashioned dining room is always at a premium – you'll probably find yourself squeezing onto a table of pilgrims, hair neatly oiled and caste marks smeared over their foreheads, who'll greet you with a polite wobble of the head. Once you're seated, a boy in a grubby cotton tunic unrolls a plantain leaf, on which you sprinkle water. This acts as a signal for a legion of other boys, older and less grubby, to swing into action, depositing ladles of rice, fiery *rasam* broth and lip-smacking curries onto your plate.

The dishes are always consumed in the same set order, but chances are you won't have a clue what that is – much to the amusement of your fellow diners, who will by now be watching you intently. Mixing the various portions together with the rice, yoghurt, buttermilk and sharp lime pickle, and then shovelling them into your mouth with your fingers, requires a knack you won't get the hang of straight away. Not that it matters. Underscored by the tang of tamarind, fried chilli, fenugreek seeds and fresh coconut, the flavours will be surprising, delicious and explosive regardless of how you combine them.

832 | Exploring Hampi, the ruined city of Vijayanagar

INDIA Step into Hampi and you're immediately immersed in an otherworldly landscape of decayed beauty. This city of rubble was once the prosperous capital of the powerful Vijayanagar empire, but a crushing defeat and subsequent plundering by invading Muslim armies in 1565 left it in such a state of ruin that you'd be forgiven for thinking the monuments are much older than they actually are. Now its giant granite boulders, lush banana plantations and crumbling monuments, scattered over 26 square kilometres around the banks of the sacred Tungabhadra River, offer profound echoes of its medieval heyday.

Clamber across the atmospheric remains on foot to appreciate the extraordinary size and sophistication of the city. With the sun beating relentlessly down, you can almost picture the dusty scene four or five hundred years ago when this was the lucrative heart of South India – a thriving market with the scent of cardamom, turmeric and pepper in the air, filled with roaring traders peddling everything from gold, ivory and diamonds to rose petals and Persian horses.

There's plenty of mystery and adventure to capture the imagination and keep visitors here for weeks on end, enchanted by the near-magical quality and pure vastness of the site – head to the city's royal monuments and you can't fail to be wowed by its sheer scale and ambition. A steady stream of tourists and worshippers continues to flock to the main Virupaksha Temple – one of South India's holiest centres of pilgrimage, dedicated to Lord Shiva. Best of all is the ornate Vitthala Temple, a UNESCO-protected highlight of Vijayanagar architecture, with its splendid stone chariot and monolithic musical pillars – each, when tapped, sounds a different note of the classical Indian scale. For a spectacular sunrise, wind your way up to the summit of Matanga Hill, just east of Hampi Bazaar, and gaze down at the early morning golden boulders unfolding beneath you.

833 | Sadhu-spotting at the Kumbh Mela

INDIA At first it looks like a severed head, smeared with cow dung, ash and sandalwood paste. But then the eyelids flutter open. A murmur of amazement ripples through the crowd. Buried up to his neck, dreadlocks coiled into a luxurious topknot, the sadhu begins to chant. Around him, smoke curls from a ring of smouldering camphor lamps, fed periodically by saffron-clad acolytes who hassle the crowd for baksheesh.

"How many days is Baba-ji sitting in this way?" comes a voice.

"Eight years, more than," is the reply.

Of all the extraordinary sights at the Maha Kumbh Mela – India's largest religious festival, held every twelve years around the confluence of the Ganges, Jamuna and (mythical) Saraswati rivers, near Allahabad – the penances performed by these wandering Hindu holy men make the most visceral impact.

Popular self-inflicted tortures include standing on one leg, holding an arm in the air until it withers, sticking skewers through the genitals, and dangling heavy bricks from the penis. Most sadhus who gather at the Kumbh, however, gain celestial merit in less ostentatious ways. The simple act of bathing at the confluence during the festival is the fastest possible track to liberation from the cycle of rebirth.

The monastic orders, or Akharas, to which they belong erect elaborate tented camps ahead of the big days. Watching each proceed to the river banks in turn, led by their respective pontiffs enshrined on gilded palanquins and caparisoned elephants, is the great spectacle of the Allahabad Kumbh. Stark naked, their bodies rubbed with ash and vermilion, the lines of dreadlocked sadhus march military-style through the early-morning mist, brandishing maces, spears, swords and tridents.

When they finally reach the waterside, the shivering ranks break into an all-out sprint for the shallows, ecstatically shouting invocations to Shiva and Rama. Arguments over pecking order often erupt between rival Akharas, and those traditional weapons are sometimes put to traditional uses, turning the foreshore into a bloodbath. Onlookers should avoid getting too close.

834 | Theyyam: Temple trance rituals in Kerala

INDIA The wild nocturnal temple trance rituals known as *theyyam* are far more raw, energetic and exciting than Kerala's better-known dance tradition of *kathakali*. They are also somewhat more elusive and tricky to track down. First of all, there is no fixed location, other than they take place in the vicinity of Kannur at the less touristic northern end of the state. Indeed, the best way to witness a ritual is to hole up for a few days on the stunning Malabar Coast, a stretch of swaying palms and uncrowded beaches, and wait for word of an event, which spreads like the breeze whispering through the fronds. Think the British rave scene of the early 90s and you'll be on the right track.

When news does come, you'll be whisked in the dead of night to a temple buried deep in the rural interior, where you join the locals in a *kaavu* (clearing) next to the shrine and sip a steaming glass of chai in anticipation of the proceedings. Although more travellers are starting to find their way up here, it is still quite possible you'll be the only foreigner in the crowd. Things usually start off quite sedately with the *thottam*, whereby the performers recite songs in a small red headdress, then the pace picks up with the *vellattam*. At this point the movements and poses become more complex, as the drumming builds up in rhythm. Uniquely, the dancers are always low caste and, instead of just portraying the gods, they actually become a manifestation of their chosen deity.

It is during the climatic *mukhathezhuttu* that all hell breaks loose. Now the performers, completely possessed by the spirit of the deity being invoked, appear in full regalia and dance manically around the clearing. One may sport a 6m-long wooden headpiece, held in place by a slat running the length of his back, and gyrate for minutes on end in divine trance. Another might appear in an iron contraption with firebrands attached to it and run round in circles, the flames licking all over his bare chest. This can continue all night, leaving you sleepless and emotionally shattered by the end, but replete with unforgettable images.

835 | Get high on mountain polo

PAKISTAN The highest and most isolated polo tournament in the world, the Shandur Polo Tournament is staged every July in the Shandur Pass, in the far north of Pakistan, between six teams from each end of the pass. It's a fantastically remote place for a sporting event, 3700m up and nine hours' rocky and precipitous drive from Chitral to the west or thirteen hours from Gilgit in the east – you have to be either a keen polo fan, or a determined traveller, to make the journey.

But around ten thousand people do so every year, including the Pakistani president. Whether or not you like polo, the trip is unforgettable, and the tournament, surrounded by some spectacular mountain scenery, completely unique.

836 | The juggernauts of Puri

INDIA There are chariot festivals in other parts of India, but as the home of Lord Jagannath and one of the most significant stops on the Hindu pilgrimage trail, the one held in Puri, in the state of Orissa, is by far the biggest. They build three vast chariots from scratch here every June, garishly painted and draped with coloured cloth, and a crowd of thousands pulls them from the Jagannath Temple to the outskirts of town and back again – a magnificent, devotional procession that is joined by thousands more.

Orissa may be one of India's poorest states, but by any standards this is one of the country's greatest events – and just for good measure, the passion of its followers and the size of the chariots has bestowed on the English language the word "juggernaut".

Finding perfect powder in Kashmir

INDIA The subject of a bitter and long-standing territorial dispute between India and Pakistan, Kashmir was dubbed "the most dangerous place on Earth" after a particularly heated period during the 1990s involving not-so-veiled nuclear threats between the two countries. While a few other places have since clinched that dubious title, talk of the region largely continues to focus on its politics, and thereby obscures the fact that Kashmir, with its verdant valleys and towering mountains, makes the Alps look like nothing more than a cheap film set.

It's on the mountains that perhaps its biggest secrets – at least to snowboarding junkies – can be found. Although the Himalayas that jut into Kashmir from Nepal boast light, dry powder in absurd quantities, all too few visitors are around to take advantage of it. Its remoteness means that, without a plane ticket, you might have to travel for days on a combination of trains, buses and Jeeps filled with chickens to see for yourself.

Thankfully it doesn't disappoint. Kashmir, or rather the small ski town of Gulmarg, seems set to explode onto the ski-resort radar. At just shy of 4000m, its gondola Is the fourth highest in the world, while the powdery terrain that spreads out before it is limitless and untracked. From the top, head to Apharwat's high northwest and southeast shoulders, before descending the mountain's multiple ridges, faces and bowls. Or drop down the backside of the mountain on a 1700m run that takes you through forests dotted with snow-leopard and hill-fox tracks.

Topping it off are some very unresort-like qualities: you'll ride a pony back to a hot shower and a warm bed, and pick a chicken from the yard for dinner. The secret won't keep for long.

Exploring Galle Fort's Dutch heritage

838

SRI LANKA Battled over for centuries by South Indian kingdoms and European powers, Sri Lanka's palm-fringed coastline is studded with a network of sturdy colonial fortresses. Constructed by the Portuguese, expanded by the Dutch and later occupied by the British, many are off-limits, occupied by the military; others lie in picturesque decay. One citadel, however, remains splendidly preserved, having survived invasion and tsunami alike, with its mighty bastions and pepperpot towers enclosing a maze of tranquil streets virtually unchanged since its days as the town's Dutch quarter.

Perched between bustling Galle and the glittering Indian Ocean, the soot-blackened, moss-covered walls of Galle Fort loom into view the moment you leave the city's chaotic bus and train stations. Enter via the tunnel-like Old Gate, inscribed with the date (1669) and crest (VOC, said to be the world's oldest logo) of the Dutch settlers. Once inside, a historic vista unfurls like a movie set. An aimless wander through the backstreets will take you past dozens of gorgeous ornate-gabled houses, often still fronted by pillared verandas, with windows protected by heavy louvred shutters. The crumbling facades of traditional family dwellings, their ochre paint stripped by sea breezes, stand cheek by jowl with beautifully restored mansions, many belonging to wealthy Western immigrants, Galle's new invaders.

A five-minute walk from the Old Gate lies the Muslim quarter, where many residents, clad in long white robes and hand-woven skullcaps, are descended from Arab traders, though a few Hindu families live alongside. Climb to one of the delightfully homespun rooftop cafés hereabouts for spectacular views across the fort's huddle of red rooftops, above which the stumpy spire of St Andrew's Church and gleaming white dagoba of the Buddhist temple stand prominent. It's a beautiful panorama; Sri Lanka's ethnic mix in microcosm.

From here it's a short amble to the fort's slender British-built lighthouse, the starting point for a circuit of the ramparts, best savoured in early evening when the townsfolk turn out en masse to enjoy the spectacular reddish-purple ocean sunsets. A carnival scene of gossiping locals and street peddlers, young lads playing cricket and courting couples sheltering coyly beneath umbrellas, it's one of the happiest sights in Sri Lanka.

839 | A taste of Kolkata, India's foodie capital

INDIA India's most underrated city, Kolkata (formerly Calcutta) is a far cry from its negative stereotypes: it's friendly, attractive and home to some of the best – and most diverse – food in the country.

Kolkata's ultimate street food is the *kati* roll: a paratha flatbread stuffed with chicken, mutton, paneer, egg or spiced potato, then spiked with chilli and fresh lime juice. Sometimes referred to as a "kathi roll", these inexpensive snacks are sold from humble stands across the city.

Bengali cuisine is one of the tastiest in India, but among the least known internationally. Mustard oil, *panch phoran* (a blend of fenugreek, cumin, nigella, mustard and fennel seeds), coconut, seafood, and fresh and saltwater fish all feature heavily. The best place to try Bengali cuisine is in a family home, but if you can't score an invite, Kolkata has a growing crop of restaurants specializing in the region's traditional cooking. Among the best is *Kewpie's Kitchen*, a private home with an attached restaurant: several lavish *thalas* (multicourse meals) are on offer, featuring dishes like *daab chingri* (spicy coconut prawns).

During the Raj, the city had a significant Chinese community. In north Kolkata a bustling Chinatown developed, filled with restaurants, temples, markets and shops. Little remains of this world today – most of Kolkata's two thousand Chinese residents have decamped to the Tangra district – but a few echoes remain. In an unprepossessing location off Ganesh Chandra Avenue, above a petrol station and up a gloomy flight of steps, is the family-run *Eau Chew*, one of the city's oldest Chinese restaurants. Its tasty, generous "chimney soups", which are cooked slowly around a metal coal-burning container, are particularly good.

Bengalis have a famously sweet tooth, and there are plenty of places in Kolkata in which to indulge. Perhaps the most famous sweetshop is Ganguram, which has branches scattered throughout the city. Don't miss the *rosogulla* (syrupy cottage cheese-and-semolina dumplings), *sandesh* (a sugary, creamy sweetmeat), or the *mishti doi* (a thick, sweetened yoghurt often flavoured with cardamom and served in earthenware pots).

840 | City of Light: on the Ganges in Varanasi

INDIA The sun has barely risen above the river banks, but already the cremation *ghats* are hard at work. Four corpses, tightly bound in cotton and still soaked from their final cleansing dip in the Ganges, are laid out on wood pyres, ghee and garlands of orange marigolds piled on top of them. While gangs of small, dark, muscular men feed the flames, grieving relatives look on, murmuring prayers with palms pressed together and heads bowed. The surrounding buildings are black with soot.

Varanasi – or Kashi ("City of Light"), as it was known in ancient times – is Hinduism's holiest city. Infamous for its squalor, its old core is a teeming warren of narrow alleyways, where intricately carved doorways open onto hidden, high-walled courtyards and shrines. Wander for long enough and eventually you'll emerge at the *ghats*, or sacred stone steps, which spread around the mighty bend in the river. From dawn until dusk, they present an animated canvas of bathers, sadhus, tourists, hawkers, stray cows and priests plying their age-old trade under ragged parasols – all set against a magnificent backdrop of crumbling temples and palaces.

To enjoy the spectacle at its best, jump in a rowing boat at Asi Ghat, in the south of the old city, just before sunrise. Paddling north as the first rays of sunlight infuse the riverfront with a reddish glow, you glide past the dark stupas of Buddha Ghat, the distinctive leaning towers of Rewa Ghat, and the candy-striped steps of Vijayanagar Ghat. Manikarnika, the cremation *ghat*, is where the boatmen generally turn around.

Out on the river, visitors are insulated from the hassle of guides and trinket sellers, but not necessarily from Varanasi's still less savoury aspects. Poor Hindus who can't afford enough wood for their pyres will often have their charred remains shoved unceremoniously into the water – it's not unusual to find your boat bumping into a bloated body part, or even something eating one.

The *ghats* themselves are at their most atmospheric immediately before dark. As you watch the cane lanterns of the priests flicker to life and mingle with the reflections of the afterglow, Kashi feels every inch the mystical "Threshold of Eternity" that for Hindus it has always been.

841 | Visiting the Taj by moonlight

INDIA When it comes to viewing the Taj Mahal, there's no such thing as an unflattering angle or wrong kind of weather. Even the Dickensian smog that rolls off the Jamuna River in midwinter only heightens the mystique of the mausoleum's familiar contours. The monsoon rains and grey skies of August also cast their spell; glistening after a storm, the white marble, subtly carved and inlaid with semi-precious stones and Koranic calligraphy, seems to radiate light.

The world's most beautiful building was originally commissioned by Mughal Emperor Shah Jahan in the 1630s as a memorial to his beloved wife, the legendary beauty Arjumand Bann Begum, or Mumtaz Mahal ("Elect of the Palace"). Inconsolable after she died giving birth to their fourteenth child, Shah Jahan spent the final years of his life staring wistfully through his cusp-arched window in Agra Fort at her mausoleum downriver.

The love and longing embodied by the Taj are never more palpable than during the full-moon phase of each month, when the Archeological Survey of India opens the complex at night. For once, the streams of visitors flowing through the Persian-style Char Bagh Gardens that lead to the tomb are hushed into silence by the building's ethereal form, rising melancholically from the river bank.

Shah Jahan's quadrangular water courses, which flank the approaches, are specially filled for full-moon visits, as they would have been in Mughal times. The reflections of the luminous walls in their mirror-like surfaces seem positively to shimmer with life, like the aura of an Urdu devotional poem or piece of sublime sitar music. At such moments, it's easy to see why the Bengali mystic-poet Rabindranath Tagore likened the Taj Mahal to "... a teardrop on the face of Eternity".

INDIA While most visitors make a beeline for the famous backwaters of Kerala, a region far less travelled – and far more adventurous – is the Godavari Delta on the eastern coast of Andhra Pradesh.

The mighty Godavari, second only in length to the Ganges, traverses central India from its source near the holy city of Nasik in the Western Ghats, finally issuing in the Bay of Bengal after its almost 1500km journey. A good base from which to explore the fascinating region is Rajahmundry, which sprawls along the east bank of the river just at the point where it makes its first major split into the mouths of the vast estuary. As you would expect for the last major town on India's second holiest river, this area is lined with temples, shrines and bathing ghats – a splendid spot to take in Hindu practices at work.

The best tour from here is the trip north up the main trunk of the Godavari to the hills of Papikondalu, best taken as an overnight stay. Having been transported some 50km by road along the west bank of the narrowing river to a small jetty at Polavaram, you board a double-decker motor boat and are fed a typically South Indian breakfast of *idli*, *vada*, sambar and coconut chutney. This vessel then chugs sedately upstream, as the river snakes through a mixture of agricultural and wooded land, fringed with more thickly forested hills.

There are a couple of stops, one for *puja* at a small riverside Shiva temple and later a quiet Ramakrishna hermitage. A tasty veg lunch is also provided on board. If you choose to stay overnight, there's a choice between the very basic *Kolluru Bamboo Huts*, only accessible by boat, and a slightly more comfortable hotel at *Bhadrachalam*, which has an impressive Sri Rama temple and is connected by road, so the tour can actually be used as a means of transport, much like the famous Kollam to Alleppey trip in Kerala.

There's no doubt the more romantic option is to stay at *Kolluru*. The huts certainly have no frills, or even doors, but the location on a hillock between the Godavari and a picturesque side stream, surrounded by the high Papikondalu Hills, is exquisite.

843 | Bungee jumping the Bhote Koshi

NEPAL The worst part is the wait. Standing on a footbridge spanning a spectacular Himalayan gorge, it's impossible not to glance down at the churning Bhote Koshi River, which races down from the nearby Tibetan border. Every so often a cheer – or a scream – sounds, as someone plummets towards the water on the end of a disconcertingly thin rubber rope. The locals gathered at the far end of the bridge exchange wry looks, before returning to their conversations.

Operated by The Last Resort, a tented camp and adventure sports centre, this 160m bungee jump is one of the highest in the world – to put it into context, the Statue of Liberty only measures 93m from its base to the tip of the flame. When your turn comes, a reassuringly thorough member of staff checks, and double-checks, the safety harness, then ushers you towards the jumping-off point. With a final nervous wave at the cameraman (who has been recording your comments for posterity), and perhaps a quick prayer, you shuffle to the edge, vainly attempt to compose yourself, and jump as high as you can.

The mountains ahead appear briefly in your line of vision, before vanishing as you plunge down at what feels like an impossible speed. The river and the valley walls become little more than a blur, giving the strange sensation of both dramatic speed and slow-motion travel. For a few terrifying, exhilarating moments you feel as though you're flying. Finally, the rope goes taut and the bounces slow to a stop, leaving you twirling gently above the water. A long pole is hoisted up from the river bank for you to clasp, and you're pulled down onto a bed to wait for the adrenalin rush to subside. As your heart rate slowly returns to normal, a sense of elation prevails – particularly when you realize the camp bar is just a short stumble away.

844 | Discover your inner veggie in Pushkar

INDIA Meat may be off the menu in the holy town of Pushkar, but there's no shortage of animals to go round. Skinny white cows swish through the narrow streets, untroubled by the swirling exhaust fumes, the frantic rat-tat-tat-tat of temple drums, or the packs of pilgrims wrapped in sequined saris. Hungry piglets too pick their way through the crowds, hoovering up rose petals dropped by wandering Brahmins, and ducks flock to the town's glistening lake – a welcome resting place in this sun-scorched region of Rajasthan.

Fringed by bone-white temples and concrete bathing ghats, this reflective body of water has a special significance for Hindus. Legend has it that when the Creator, Brahma, dropped a lotus flower from the sky, separate lakes appeared in the desert at the site where each petal landed. The largest such lake is still at the centre of daily life in Pushkar, and remains one of the most important pilgrimage sites in all India. Out of respect for Brahma, meat, alcohol and even eggs are forbidden within the town.

Naturally, diehard carnivores can find plenty of ways to get around the ban, and plenty of guesthouse owners willing to help them break the rules – for a small commission, of course. Respecting the local customs, on the other hand, might just provide the perfect opportunity to discover your inner vegetarian. Even the cheapest of street-side restaurants offer steaming heaps of delicately spiced vegetarian curries, serving tangy banana *lassis* in terracotta cups to sweeten the deal.

As more and more tourists discover Pushkar, the eating options have expanded far beyond the classic veg thali. Restaurants serve up steaming bowls of fresh veg, sometimes with brown rice and tofu, and sometimes just with a sticky fig sauce that makes the taste-buds tingle. If a quick snack is all you need, head to the nearest street corner, where you're sure to find a wooden cart warping under the weight of juicy red pomegranates and waxy green apples. Who needs meat, anyway?

INDIA In 528 BC, Prince Siddhartha Gautama settled under a bodhi tree and – after withstanding threats of flood, fire, thunder and lightning from the evil Mara, as well as the temptations of Mara's beautiful daughters – found enlightenment. He later became known as the Buddha, and the Mahabodhi Temple, which marks the spot of his deliverance, has since become the world's most significant Buddhist pilgrimage site.

Bodhgaya, the town that has sprung up around the temple, maintains a wonderfully serene air, despite being located in Bihar – India's poorest state – an anarchic place, riven with caste conflict. Between November and February, large communities of exiled Tibetans – including, from time to time, the Dalai Lama – join red-robed monks, pilgrims and curious travellers here, giving the site a truly cosmopolitan feel. Devotees have built a number of elaborate, sometimes incongruous, modern temples and monasteries in various national styles, among them Thai, Japanese, Bhutanese and Tibetan. The site includes innumerable meditation centres, a 25m-high Buddha statue set in an ornamental garden, and an increasing array of hotels, ranging from austere monastic guesthouses to luxury five-star establishments.

The focal point of it all is the imposing Mahabodhi Temple, a sixth-century construction with an elegant single spire surrounded by a collection of smaller stupas and shrines. At the heart of the temple complex is the bodhi tree itself, a distant offshoot of the original, which was destroyed by Emperor Ashoka before his conversion to Buddhism. Beside the tree, which is festooned with multicoloured threads and encircled with Tibetan butter lamps, is the *vajrasana* (thunder seat), a sandstone block on which the Buddha reputedly sat. Many people come to meditate, but the spot invites quiet contemplation whatever your religious beliefs, particularly as the afternoon draws to a close, when the crowds disperse, the sun descends and ritual chants drift over on the breeze.

Finding enlightenment in Buddhism's birthplace

Paragliding in Pokhara

846

NEPAL A favourite backpackers' haunt since the hippy trail opened up South Asia to Western eyes in the 1960s, Pokhara remains one of the jewels in Nepal's crown. In the laidback Lakeside neighbourhood, bustling cafés are alive with the chatter of intrepid trekkers, rewarding themselves with a well-earned slice of apple pie after weeks exploring the Annapurna Circuit. Each evening, the whole place seems to briefly stop in its tracks to watch the sun go down over Phewa Tal, Pokhara's famous mirror to the Himalayas. Brightly coloured boats bob on the shore, sending gentle ripples across the surface of the water. The reflected peaks of the Annapurna massif flicker and refract, then finally extinguish as the evening light dims.

Trekking aside, Pokhara offers spectacular opportunities to get a different perspective on the Himalayas. Sarangkot, a high ridge overlooking the mountains, is Pokhara's premier viewpoint, and one of the world's most picturesque places to paraglide. As the first rays of the dawn sun catch the peaks, they seem to hesitate for a moment, before finally throwing themselves over to bathe the mountainsides in pink and gold. The view is dominated by Machhapuchhre, with its craggy, fishtail-shaped peak; sacred to Hindus as one of the mythical abodes of Shiva, the mountain has never been climbed.

A ride in an old Tata pick-up takes you to a grassy clifftop plateau, where parachutes are fanned out like technicolour jellyfish marooned on a beach. After a brief introduction to your instructor, you're trussed up in a harness like a giant baby before making the wholly counterintuitive move of running at full pelt to the edge of a rocky cliff and jumping into the void. Everything is silent. Machhapuchhre looms in the background, looking more massive than ever. A huge Himalayan griffon vulture hangs in the air before you; you follow it into a thermal column and soar, effortlessly, Phewa Tal glittering into nothingness beneath you.

847 | Journeying over the roof of the world

INDIA & TIBET "Unbelievable is it Not!" reads a road sign at Tanglang La, which at 5360m is the highest point on the Manali–Leh highway. As you look north from the thicket of prayer flags that flutter above the pass, you'll probably find yourself agreeing. Between you and the white line of the Karakorams in the distance stretches a vast, bone-dry wilderness of mountains and snow-dusted valleys – not a view you'd normally expect from a bus window.

The 485km route from Manali in Himachal Pradesh to Leh in Ladakh is the great epic among Indian road journeys. With an overnight stop at altitude under a makeshift parachute tent en route, it takes two days to cover, carrying you from the foothills of the Himalayas to the margins of the Tibetan Plateau. Weather conditions can be fickle – blizzards descend even in mid-summer – while facilities along the way are rough and ready, to say the least. But the privations pale into insignificance against the astonishing scenery.

The first and most formidable obstacle to be crossed is Rohtang La, "Pile of Bones Pass". Straddling one of the most sudden and extreme climatic transitions on the planet, Rohtang overlooks lush green cedar woods and alpine meadows on one side, and on the other a forbidding wall of chocolate- and sand-coloured scree, capped by ice peaks trailing plumes of spindrift. Once across, settlements are few and far between. Nomadic shepherds and their flocks may be the only signs of life on gigantic mountainsides streaked purple, red and blue with mineral deposits. Packed under snow for most of the year, the road surface deteriorates as you gain altitude, crumbling to loose shale and dizzying voids.

You cross lofty Tanglang La late on the second afternoon, and reach the first Ladakhi villages soon after. Swathed in kidney-shaped terraces of ripening barley, each is surveyed by its own fairy-tale Buddhist monastery, with spinning prayer wheels and golden finials gleaming from the rooftops in sunlight of an almost unearthly clarity.

848 | Meditating in the Himalayas

NEPAL People have looked to the mountains for spiritual consolation for millennia. "I will lift up mine eyes unto the hills," say the Psalms, "from whence cometh my help." For Nepalis, the link is especially powerful. The Himalayas are where the Hindu gods go to meditate and replenish their *tapas*, or spiritual "heat", and the Buddhist peoples of Nepal's Himalayan regions regard many of the highest peaks and lakes as sacred.

Many trekkers come to Nepal to make personal pilgrimages. When you stand on a ridge festooned with colourful prayer flags torn ragged by the wind, or look down on the luminous, glacial blue of a Himalayan lake, or when with aching lungs, cracked lips and a spinning head you come to the top of the highest pass yet, it's hard not to feel your own spiritual store hasn't been warmed just a little. Of course, you can always just emulate the gods: find a high place, fix your eyes on the Himalayas, breathe and begin the search for mindfulness.

For spiritual discipline, perhaps the richest possibilities are found in the Kathmandu valley, Nepal's heartland in the Himalayan foothills. The valley has been described as a living *mandala*, or spiritual diagram – its very geography mapped out by temples, devotional stupas and holy caves and gorges. Pashupatinath, where Kathmandu's dead are burned beside the river, attracts pilgrims from across India. Many Western travellers make for neighbouring Boudha, the vibrant Tibetan quarter, where the painted Buddha eyes on the great white dome look out across throngs of Buddhist monasteries, and where, at dawn and dusk, the violet air echoes with the sounds of horns and bells, and the murmured mantras of the faithful.

849 | Get swept away at Durga Puja

BANGLADESH Hindus constitute just eight percent of the population of Bangladesh, but the Durga Puja in Dhaka is at least as gripping as its Indian counterparts. Indeed, a consciousness of minority status seems to amplify the devotees' passion, and the close-knit Hindu enclaves concentrate the celebrations, creating a rarefied, otherworldly atmosphere. But the enclaves are not ghettos, and the Puja is not exclusively for Hindus: instead it is at once a religious event and a vibrant carnival.

The centrepieces of the individual *pujas* – religious rituals that show respect to Hindu gods and goddesses – are the beautiful, exquisitely painted clay effigies of Durga, best seen in Shankharia Bazaar, the largest Hindu quarter in Old Dhaka, where the drama of street life at Puja time is intense. A canopy of saffron drapes filters and softens the light, bathing the entire bazaar in an amber glow, and the numerous sites of worship, the market stalls, the artisans, the creaking wooden Ferris wheels, the troupes of singers, musicians and dancers – sometimes performing on a bamboo dais under which you walk – all of this gives the impression of a fantastic elongated temple having opened its doors to a throbbing street fair.

On the evening of the tenth day, the Puja erupts into frenzied activity. Galvanized by the eerie fanfare of conch-shell horns and the rolling thunder of ceremonial drums, columns of chanting devotees swarm towards Sadarghat, carrying their effigies aloft. Tens of thousands of people line the river bank, and crowd around the *ghat* as a relentless succession of Durgas arrives at the water's edge, where priests superintend their consecration and anoint their bearers with smears of sandalwood ash. The goddesses are then loaded aboard diminutive boats that pitch and roll violently as the accompanying men dance and punch the air. In mid-stream the precious cargo is given to the water; the sodden appearance of the returning men – delirious as they clamber up the steps of the *ghat* – hints at the mayhem beyond the reach of the light.

850

INDIA There is no more rewarding way to taste a Keralan *thali* of spiced potatoes and vegetable masalas than after a sweaty few hours in the *Haritha Farms* kitchen. On his late father's farm in the heart of Kerala, Jacob Matthew opens his home to visitors in pursuit of real Indian flavour – not just in the food but also in life. During the practical and challenging cooking classes – involving lessons on how to treat different seeds and spices, what each one is used for and what to do when it all goes wrong – even for a seasoned cook there are new lessons to be learned and challenges to meet.

While *Haritha Farms* markets itself as a cooking holiday, there's much more to a stay here than hovering over a hot stove. Sprawled on the slopes of the Maniyanthadam hills in Kerala, 55km inland from Kochi, the farm is an eco-haven – with its solar power and home-grown coffee and fruit. The nearest town, Kadalikad, isn't exactly on the backpacker trail but it feels like a relaxed, honest town, refreshingly undisturbed by the tourist industry so prevalent elsewhere in this green and humid region of southern India.

Jacob is well connected, so makes it his mission to show a side of Indian life that all too few visitors experience. He'll introduce you to the people who make your favourite Indian snacks, from banana chips to the sweet Keralan *madhura seva*, and spend an entire morning chatting with the men who paint those famously psychedelic cargo lorries that honk along all Indian roads.

And after bartering for your own ingredients at the colourful roadside vegetable stall, the hours of chopping, stirring and frying will culminate in an explosion of flavours, in dishes from a simple *dhal* to an egg masala, and you can finally indulge as your hard work is laid out in front of you for some well-deserved consumption.

Cooking the Keralan way

851 | Cross the Himalayas to your own Shangri-la

INDIA In the far northeast of India, lodged between Tibet and Bhutan in the tiny state of Arunachal Pradesh – "the land of dawn-lit mountains" – lies a lonely valley. Here, high on a spur, is Tawang Gompa, India's largest Buddhist monastery. Although you can get here by helicopter, the most rewarding way to reach Tawang is by joining the locals and wedging yourself into a *sumo*. These shared Jeeps – packed to bursting point with people and possessions – shuttle along the 345km road to the city of Tezpur in Assam, an exhausting journey that takes anything from 12 to 24 hours, depending on the weather.

Along this winding route of orchid groves, primeval forests, glacial streams and ice-blue lakes, darkly humorous road signs with phrases like "Be gentle on my curves" and "Overtaker, meet undertaker" warn drivers to take care at the wheel. The numerous military bases strewn along the route are potent reminders that the region remains a bone of contention between India and China – the latter occupied the area

during the 1962 Chinese-Indian war and still lays claim to it. At the breathtakingly high (4300m) Sela Pass, the *sumos* stop at a tiny wooden hut, the *Tenzing Restaurant*, where passengers crowd round a wood-fired stove and drink cups of salted yak-butter tea.

From here, the road curls down into an isolated valley, and eventually Tawang itself, a sleepy end-of-the-road town filled with Buddhist prayer wheels and flags. A few kilometres beyond is the actual monastery. A colourful fortified complex that was the birthplace of the sixth Dalai Lama, it remains home to around five hundred monks, as well as a priceless collection of Buddhist texts and historic manuscripts.

The monastery is most atmospheric in the late afternoon, when the setting sun bathes the place in a rich orange light. As you gaze down at the valley below, with its isolated *ani gompas* (nunneries), tiny hamlets, glistening lakes and sheer mountain slopes, it's hard to escape the feeling that you've found your own Shangri-la.

852 | The hidden forest hermitage of Kudimbigala

SRI LANKA The air of serenity is suffused with a slight sensation of danger as you enter the secluded forest hermitage of Kudimbigala through the massive boulders that mark its entrance. In the remote southern corner of the east coast, the hermitage is an ancient Buddhist complex of hundreds of caves believed to have been occupied by meditating *bhikkhu* (Buddhist monks) since the first century BC.

These days, a few orange-robed monks live here as custodians, tending to the altars and keeping the narrow forest paths immaculately swept for the small trickle of visitors that find their way here from the popular surfing town of Arugam Bay, usually on their way to Kumana National Park or the Hindu temple at Okanda. At dusk, wild leopards and elephants roam the massive rocks and sloth bears meander through the forest. This is why it's not a good idea to wander alone or stay there late in the afternoon, when unusual sounds start to emerge from the surrounding jungle and the trees rustle in the wind, or something else moves.

The hermitage is spread over a 50-square-kilometre unspoilt area hugging the northern edge of Kumana. Once past the entrance to Kudimbigala, the forest path leads to the Sudarshana Cave, a tranquil white shrine tucked beneath a large boulder. From here, two pathways continue to the complex's most spectacular sites. The left fork takes you up to Madhya Mandalaya ("Plain of Ruins"), where a small dagoba and some monastic ruins nestle between rocky slabs. This is where the LTTE – Liberation Tigers of Tamil Eelam – hid out during Sri Lanka's long civil war. The hermitage provided shelter and expansive views.

The best vantage point is from the dagoba at the summit of Belumgala – take the right fork from the cave and follow the steps carved into the boulders. At the steepest points, chains provide support as you climb high above the forest canopy. The reward is an uninterrupted view that stretches from the far hills of Monaragala in the northwest to the glimmering Indian Ocean in the east.

853 | Sikhs, sabres and a giant canteen: the Golden Temple

INDIA The gates of Sikhdom's holiest shrine, the Golden Temple in Amritsar, are open to all. Given the desecrations inflicted on the complex by the Indian army in 1984 and 1987, this is an extraordinary fact, and vivid testament to the spirit of inclusiveness and equality that lies at the heart of Sikhism.

Originating in the sixteenth century, the youngest of India's three great faiths drew its converts mainly from the oppressed and disenchanted underclasses of Islam and Hinduism. Philosophically and stylistically, it's very much an amalgam of the two, and nowhere is this hybrid nature more apparent than in the architecture of the shrine that forms the nerve centre of the temple.

Seeming to float on a serene, rectangular lake, the temple's centrepiece, the Harmandir, is adorned with a fusion of Mughal-style domes and Hindu lotus motifs. Smothered in gold leaf, it looks at its most resplendent shortly after dawn, when sunlight begins to illuminate its gilded surfaces and the reflections shimmer in the lake. Before approaching it, pilgrims bathe and then perform a ritual *parikrama*, or circumambulation of the gleaming marble walkway

surrounding the lake. En route, returning Sikh expats in sneakers and jeans rub shoulders with more orthodox pilgrims wearing full-length *shalwar-camises*, beehive turbans and an armoury of traditional sabres, daggers and spears. Despite the weaponry on display, the atmosphere is relaxed and welcoming, even dreamy at times, especially when the temple musician-priests are singing verses from the Adi Granth, Sikhism's holy text, accompanied by tabla and harmonium.

Perhaps the most memorable expression of the temple's open-hearted spirit, though, is the tradition of offering free meals at the Guru-ka-Langar, a giant communal canteen next to the temple entrance. Foreign tourists are welcome to join the ranks of Sikh pilgrims and the needy from neighbouring districts who file in and sit together cross-legged on long coir floormats. After grace has been sung, the massive job of dishing up thousands of chapatis and buckets of black-lentil dhal begins. By the time all the tin trays have been collected up and the floors swept, another crowd will have gathered at the gates for the cycle to begin again.

INDIA With India's population ever on the rise, its few remaining pockets of wilderness are under increasing threat. None more so than the mountains that separate Kerala from Tamil Nadu in the far southwest – the so-called Western Ghats. Stripped of their native forest by the British during the nineteenth century, to make way for tea groves, they're now besieged by domestic tourists in search of cool air and abundant greenery.

The peaks themselves, however, remain aloof from the commotion. Access to the high ground is prohibited by the Forest Service and the large corporations that own it, with only a handful of carefully managed honeypots open to the public. Yet chinks in the protective cordon do exist, if you know where to look. The most delightful is a mountain hut on the Kolukkumalai estate, ninety minutes' drive from the Keralan tea town of Munnar, where an entrepreneurial crew from Cochin has converted a block of "pluckers' lines" (tea pickers' quarters) into a kind of boutique bunkhouse for walkers.

Resting on a hidden balcony on the south side of a staggeringly beautiful valley, 2175m (7130ft) up and enfolded on all sides by tea bushes and high, jagged peaks, Kolukkumalai is the world's highest tea plantation. A trickle of day-trippers bumps up the track to the estate in Jeeps for a tour of the Heath-Robinson-esque factory, unchanged since the 1930s.

To savour the views at their most sublime, though, with the tropical sun low on the serrated horizon and mist lapping like a pale orange sea against the foot of the mountains, you have to spend the night in one of the hut's avocado-coloured rooms. That way you're in prime position for an early-morning ascent of Meeshapulimalai (2640m), peninsular India's second-highest summit. Leading through tea gardens and patches of fragrant shola forest to the grassy ridges beyond, the route affords extraordinary panoramic views over the spine of the Western Ghats – an area where elephants, and even, it's said, the odd tiger, still roam free.

855 | Riding the Rocket across the Ganges Delta

BANGLADESH Merging 60km west-southwest of Dhaka, the arterial Ganges and Jamuna feed hundreds of subsidiary rivers that radiate across the vast Ganges Delta, dissecting the land into a series of contiguous islands. This is the final stage in the odyssey of divine water, infused with an essence of the Subcontinental millions who have used and venerated it along its courses.

A Conrad-esque journey aboard one of the Rocket service's paddle-wheeled boats lets you join the flow of life on this awesome network of waterways. Your odyssey begins in the evening at Sadarghat, Dhaka's teeming main hub for river traffic, approached through the labyrinthine Old Quarter. From the *ghat* – perhaps the most compelling location in the capital – you can take in the panorama of bustling activity playing itself out on land and water against the backdrop of the striking cityscape on the far bank. It's an intoxicating blend of the old and the new: people bathe among beds of

water hyacinth, swarms of gondolier-like craft weave amid wallowing cargo vessels, and the call of the muezzin mingles with the ferment of voices rising from the riverside market.

Night descends fast, and your first proper sight of rural Bangladesh is likely to come the next morning. The verdant fields that unfurl along the river bank, the brightly dressed women, and the children cavorting in the shallows join with fishermen, dolphins and a thousand other ingredients to form a truly mesmerizing canvas.

Rocket boats are not pleasure cruisers that cocoon their passengers, but working parts of the transport infrastructure. During its nine stops between Dhaka and Khulna, the boat comes alive with the transfer of people, animals and goods. It offers the rare privilege of close-up views of riverside habitations that range from clusters of huts nestled in pockets of jungle to the port of Mongla with its towering cranes and ocean-going freighters.

856 | Exploring the Thar Desert by camel

INDIA In defiance of its old Rajasthani name, Marusthali – Land of Death – the Thar is the most densely populated of the world's great deserts. From the cities on its fringes all the way to the India–Pakistan border, the vast sand flats spreading across the northwest of the Subcontinent are dotted with myriad tiny mud-and-thatch villages, most of them many kilometres from the nearest stretch of tarmac. A train line and national highway wind in tandem to Jaisalmer, the Thar's most remote and beautiful citadel town, but from there on, the only way to reach the desert's more isolated settlements is by camel.

Riding out into the scrub, 2m off the ground, with the honey-coloured ramparts and temple towers of Jaisalmer fort receding into the distance, you enter another kind of India – one of wide, shimmering vistas, endless blue skies and, when the rolling gait of your camel ceases, profound stillness. The landscape, though, is no great shakes: apart from a few picture-book dunes blistering up here and there, the Thar is monotonously flat.

Instead, it's for the flamboyance of the desert settlements that most visit this stark borderland. Perhaps as compensation for the sandy drabness of their world, the villagers adorn their children, their animals, houses, carts, shrines – and themselves – in elaborate style. Adobe walls are enlivened with elegant ochre and red geometric patterns, kitchen utensils with green and blue lacquerwork, moulded mud interiors, clothes and furniture with fragments of sparkling mica, cowry shells or embroidery.

Packs of jubilant children scamper out of every village as soon as a line of camels hoves into view. And the same pack follows you out again afterwards, which perhaps explains why trekking camps tend to be in the middle of nowhere, well beyond foraging range. At sunset, saddle sore and a little sunburnt, you can sit back and reflect on the day's encounters as the desert glows red in the dying light. Sprawled on a rug beside a flickering campfire, with a pan of smoky dhal and rice bubbling away under the starriest of skies, the Thar feels a lot less like a "Land of Death" than a wholesome, blissful retreat.

Need to know

800 The best time to tackle the Everest Trek is between Sept and Nov. Operators include Intrepid Travel (W intrepidtravel.com) and Nepal-based Bold Adventures (W boldadventuresnepal.com).

801 For details of the Toy Train, visit W dhrs.org. The ride also forms part of larger luxury excursions, with operators such as Cox & Kings (W coxandkings.com).

802 For more information on Chitwan National Park, visit W chitwannationalpark.gov.np. To reach it from Kathmandu, fly to nearby Bharatpur (20min) or take a minibus or bus to the village of Sauraha (5–7hr), which holds most of the park's budget accommodation.

803 Fort Cochin's international airport is at Nedumbassery, 26km north of Kochi. For more information, visit W keralatourism.org.

804 Numerous operators offer game drives of Wilpattu National Park, and there are various accommodation options close by. The park sits around four hours north of Colombo.

805 Encounters Nepal (W encountersnepal.com) offers a six-day Sikles Trek, while Intrepid Travel (W intrepidtravel .com) runs a Nepal Adventure trip that includes a five-day trek to Sikles.

806 The Joydev Kenduli Mela – aka "Poush Mela" – takes place at Kenduli, 30km west of Bolpur in West Bengal. The most convenient base is the guesthouse of Visva-Bharati University (W visvabharati.ac.in/Guest-House.html), on the northern outskirts of Bolpur.

807 The programmes extend over separate weekends in late Feb. Go to the festival website (W worldsufispirit-festival.org) for full details.

808 Book the eight luxurious canvas tents in the Jawai Leopard Camp, midway between Jodhpur and Udaipur in southern Rajasthan, via W sujanluxury.com.

809 Matches in the IPL (W iplt20.com) run through April and May each year, with the auction in Feb.

810 *Slightly Chilled* (W slightlychilledhotel.com) is one of the best places to stay in Dalhousie, with bright, comfortable rooms overlooking Adam's Peak.

811 Although Pakistan's security situation has improved significantly since 2017, using a local tour operator can help to secure the hard-to-get visa and to stay safe. Recommended Pakistani/Australian company Karakoram Bikers (W karakorambikers.com) rents motorbikes and organizes guided rides.

812 The Sabarmati Ashram is open daily 8.30am–6.30pm (W mkgandhi.org/gandhiyatra/sabarmati.htm).

813 Recommended *bhel puri* stalls on Chowpatty Beach include *Badshah's* and *Sharmajee's*. *Elco Pani Puri Centre* is at 2/A Elco Market, 46 Hill Rd, Bandra West.

814 The Ajanta Caves are open daily except Mon (Ellora caves are additionally closed on every Tues; W ajantacaves.com). Most visitors base themselves in the city of Aurangabad, 108km southwest, travelling by bus or Jeep taxi.

815 For a list of dive spots in the Maldives, visit W www.divesitedirectory.co.uk. The water is clearest Dec–March, but May–Sept is the best time to see manta rays, as a rise in plankton attracts them to the reefs.

816 Agents in Pokhara offering tandem flights include Bluesky Paragliding (W paragliding-nepal.com), Sunrise Paragliding (W sunrise-paragliding.com) and Paranova Paragliding (W facebook.com/paraglidingnepal).

817 Benaulim is 15min by public bus from Margao, Goa's "second city".

818 Return flights to Port Blair from Chennai or Kolkata can cost well over £200 during the peak winter season. Boat crossings from the mainland cost as little as £20. Road and sea transportation between the islands is very inexpensive, while the cheaper accommodations only cost £5–10 per night.

819 Haputale can be reached by train from Colombo (9hr) and Kandy (5hr 30min). Accommodation is limited

to a handful of guesthouses: try the excellent *Amarasinghe Guest House* (T +91 (0) 57 2268175).

820 Kartik Purnima is usually held in early Nov. Check W tourism.rajasthan.gov.in for the exact dates.

821 For more information about the temple, visit W maduraimeenakshi.org.Fly to Madurai from Mumbai (3hr 20min) or Tamil Nadu's capital, Chennai (1hr).

822 Gokarna is most easily accessible via the Konkan Railway (W konkanrailway.com), which connects Mumbai with Kerala.

823 Oct–April are generally considered optimum tiger-viewing months in India. Set up to monitor the operators working in Indian nature reserves, TOFTigers (W toftigers.org) is a great resource for selecting a responsible tiger-safari operator.

824 Gangotri is accessible from May to Oct. Most visitors stay in the dorm of the state-run Tourist Bungalow (no phone), in Bhojbasa, 5km from the glacier.

825 Uda Walawe National Park lies south of the island's central hill country. You can find more information on the park at W dwc.gov.lk.

826 *Kettu vallam* cruises can be arranged through most upscale hotels in Kerala.

827 Many guesthouses and shops in southern Sri Lanka, including the *Blue Corals Guesthouse* near Matara, rent scooters to visitors carrying international driving licences. Daily Jeep tours set off to Yala National Park (W yalasrilanka.lk) from Tissamaharama, 27km south; the park closes each year from Sept to mid-Oct.

828 For more information on travelling by train in India, visit W indianrailways.gov.in.

829 Mumbai's Metro BIG Cinema is at Dhobi Talao Junction, at the top of Azad Maidan, a short taxi ride from CST (VT) Station. For more details, see W www .bigcinemas.com.

830 You should be a good intermediate or advanced surfer with experience of surfing reefs, as there are no beach breaks in the Maldives.

831 *Sri Ganesa Bhawan*, on West Car St (no phone), serves lunch between 11.30am and 2.30pm.

832 For more information, visit W hampi.in. Frequent buses from the nearby transportation hub of Hospet terminate close to the site's main street, Hampi Bazaar, which holds the best selection of places to stay and eat, as well as offering the easiest access to Hampi itself.

833 Kumbh Mela takes place every three years, by rotation, at Haridwar, Allahabad, Nashik and Ujjain. The next Maha Kumbh Mela in Allahabad will be in 2025.

834 Kannur is well connected by train, bus and plane, with Kannur International Airport serving the district (W kannurairport.aero). *Costa Malabari* (T +919 4477 75691) is a great place to stay. Info on *theyyam* at W theyyamcalendar.com.

835 The Shandur Polo Tournament (W shandur.com) takes place every year during the second week of July. A tent village is set up at the pass during the tournament.

836 *Z Hotel*, near the beach on CT Rd (W zhotelindia .com), is a decent backpacker's hostel in Puri.

837 For details on Gulmarg's ski resort, which is a 2hr, 200km taxi ride from Srinagar, visit W gulmargskiing. com. Dec–April is the best time to visit, but check the security situation with your foreign office.

838 Galle is a picturesque 3hr journey along the coast by road or rail from Colombo. Fun to explore at any time, the fort is at its most animated during the annual Literary Festival (W galleliteraryfestival.com) in late January, when global literati descend on the town and all accommodation is booked well in advance.

839 To find out more, see W roughguides.com/ article/a-taste-of-kolkata.

840 Boat rides on the Ganges at Varanasi may cost anything from INR200 to INR2000 per person, per hour, depending on demand and your ability to haggle.

841 The Taj Mahal is open daily except Fri from sunrise to sunset (W tajmahal.gov.in). Over the four days of a full moon (except on Fri and during Ramadan), you can also visit between 8pm and midnight; tickets must be booked a day in advance at the Archeological Survey of India office, 22 Mall Rd (W asi.nic.in).

842 Konaseema Tourism offers tours along the Godavari up to Papikondalu (W konaseematourism.com).

843 The Last Resort (W thelastresort.com.np) is a 3hr drive northeast of Kathmandu.

844 Pushkar is easily reached by bus. At the train station in Ajmer, which is served by trains from New Delhi, cross the footbridge out front and wait at the roadside, where buses to Pushkar pull in.

845 The Mahabodhi Temple is open daily. The town of Gaya, 13km north, is the nearest transport hub, with an international airport, railway station and bus connections to elsewhere in Bihar. For more information, see W bihartourism.gov.in.

846 A number of operators offer paragliding trips from Pokhara's Lakeside tourist district; the original is Sunrise Paragliding (W sunrise-paragliding.com).

847 The Manali–Leh highway is only open between late June and mid-Sept, although buses tend to run as long as the passes remain free of snow.

848 *Gompas* (monasteries) such as Boudha's Shedrub, the "White Monastery" (W shedrub.org), and nearby Kopan (W kopanmonastery.com) run teachings on Tibetan Buddhism in English, as well as meditation courses. For serious Hindu meditation, try the Osho Tapoban Forest Retreat Centre (W tapoban.com) and Nepal Vipassana Centre (W dhamma.org).

849 The Durga Puja falls in Sept or Oct, depending on the lunar cycle – check W tourismboard.gov.bd.

850 Rates for cooking holidays at *Haritha Farms* (W thepimenta.in) include accommodation, food, drink and transport.

851 The Tawang Gompa is open daily. The best times to visit are during Losar – the Buddhist New Year, in Feb or early March – and Jan's Torgya Festival, when dancing and celebrations ward off evil spirits and disasters. Foreign visitors require Protected Area Permits; see W arunachaltourism.com.

852 To arrange a jeep from Arugam Bay to Kudimbigala contact W ecowave.lk or W ceylonwalkingtours.com. The hermitage opens at dawn and you must exit by 5pm.

853 Both the Golden Temple and Guru-ka-Langar are open 24hr (W sgpc.net). Although meals are served free of charge, small donations are welcomed.

854 Rooms at the Kolukkumalai hut can be booked at W kolukkumamali.info or W rithudmc.com; rates include meals. The nearest transport hub is Munnar.

855 Operated by the Bangladesh Inland Water Transport Corporation (W biwtc.gov.bd), the Rocket service, covering the 354km route between Dhaka and Khulna, runs all year.

856 Camel treks can be arranged through any Jaisalmer hotel or tourist office, but try to avoid those that use touts; try Adventure Travel (W adventurecamels .com) and Sahara Travels (W saharatravelsjaisalmer. com). Early Dec–end Jan is the best time to go.

SOUTHEAST ASIA
857-913

Southeast Asia stirs serious wanderlust. Bubbling with mesmeric cities like Hanoi and Chiang Mai, fringed with powder-soft beaches from Indonesia to the Philippines, home to the relics of ancient civilizations and blessed with some of the planet's most craved cuisines, this temple-studded region draws everyone from culture-curious backpackers to jungle-bound adventurers. Its history is an attraction in its own right, shaped by looming figures as diverse as Ho Chi Minh and Pol Pot, while its spread of mountains, bays, islands and rainforests can have you meeting the orang-utans in Sumatra one week and floating past Burmese pagodas the next.

857 Up close with a manta ray

INDONESIA The engine of our boat coughs and stops and we bob on an indigo sea beneath sheer cliffs. We've arrived at Manta Bay on the southwest coast of Nusa Penida. I've already drift-dived over coral gardens and watched turtles melt away into the oceanic haze off neighbouring island Nusa Lembongan. But it's the chance of seeing manta rays that has brought me here, 30km east of mainland Bali. With a wingspan up to 6m, mantas are a star attraction of the Indonesian diving scene, but their intelligence and curiosity – they have the biggest brain-to-size ratio of any fish – also makes them easy prey for fishermen. Populations are dwindling.

So it was welcome news in February 2014 when Indonesia declared itself a manta sanctuary. The hunting and export of rays within its 5.6 million square-kilometre sea area, previously home to some of the world's largest ray fisheries, is now outlawed. A populist step, certainly, but also a pragmatic one – manta tourism earns Indonesia far more than the fishing industry. For conservationists and divers, however, the economics are irrelevant. The opportunity to witness a manta in the wild is beyond price. And the accreditation of Nusa Penida and Nusa Lembongan as a Marine Protected Area has catapulted the islands into a premier-league Southeast Asian dive destination; depending on who's counting, there are fifteen to twenty sites within an hour of your base on Lembongan.

Back at Manta Point, I drop beneath the surface, the only sound the rumble and hiss of my breathing through the regulator. Carousels of fish whirl around coralheads in the plankton-rich waters, but for once I struggle to engage. Then a sharp metallic clang: my guide tapping her tank. I turn and see a ghostly grey diamond. It banks effortlessly towards us then soars above through our exhaled bubbles – a flash of white belly in the splintered sunlight – before flapping away into the gloom like an outré spaceship. I'm ecstatic. And I want more.

That's the only disadvantage with manta ray diving. Seeing one is never enough.

James Stewart
A travel and activities journalist specializing in scuba, surfing and sailing, James Stewart learned to dive in the Cayman Islands while researching a magazine article and has since dived worldwide in the name of "work".

The hills are alive: tribal trekking

THAILAND Exhilarating though the ridgetop views often are, it's not the scenery that draws travellers into the hills of northern Thailand, but the people who live in them. There are some four thousand hill-tribe villages in the uplands of Chiang Mai and Chiang Rai provinces, peopled by half a dozen main tribes whose ancestors wandered across from Burma and China. They have subsistence-farmed up here for two hundred years and continue to observe age-old customs and beliefs; visiting the villages makes for a fascinating, and popular, trip.

The trekking between villages is moderately taxing – you're in the hills, after all – but the trails are well worn and a good guide will bring the landscape alive, pointing out medicinal plants and elusive creatures along the way. The highlights, though, are the villages themselves, clusters of stilted bamboo huts close by a river, invariably wreathed in wood-smoke and busy with free-ranging pigs and chickens. Village architecture varies a little between the communities, particularly where animist shrines and totems are concerned, for each group lives by distinct traditions and taboos. But the diverse costumes are more striking: the jangling headdresses of the Akha women decorated with baubles hammered out of old silver coins; the intricately embroidered wide-legged trousers worn by the Mien; and the pom-poms and Day-Glo pinks and greens favoured by the Lisu. Many hill-tribeswomen make their living from weaving and embroidering these traditional textiles, and buying direct is a good way of contributing to village funds.

Insensitive tourism has caused problems in hill-tribe villages, and exploitation by travel companies is widespread, so choose your operator wisely; Eagle House and the Trekking Collective are reputable options.

859

VIETNAM If you're looking for a classic Southeast Asian scene, Vietnam's Mekong Delta, south of Ho Chi Minh City, will do the trick. This is an area of vivid green rice paddies, conical-hatted farmers and lumbering water buffaloes, of floating markets and villages built on stilts. Lush orchards overflow with mangoes, papayas and dragonfruit; plantations brim with bananas, coconuts and pineapples. And through it all wind the nine tributaries of the Mekong River, which nourish this fruitbasket of Vietnam, the waters busy with sampans, canoes and houseboats. It is the end of the run for Asia's mighty Mekong, whose waters rise over 4000km away in the snows of the Tibetan plateau and empty out here, into the alluvial-rich plains fringing the South China Sea.

For the fifteen million people who live in these wetlands, everything revolves around the waterways, so to glimpse something of their life you need to join them on the river. Boat tours from the market town of My Tho will take you to nearby orchard-islands, crisscrossed by narrow palm-shaded canals and famous for their juicy yellow-fleshed sapodilla fruits. At Vinh Long, home-stay programmes give you the opportunity to sample the garden produce for dinner and spend the night on stilts over the water.

Chances are your host-family catch fish as well – right under their floorboards in specially designed bamboo cages, so the daily feed is simply a matter of lifting up a plank or two. Next stop should be Can Tho, the delta's principal city, to make the ride out to the enormous floating market at Phung Hiep.

Here at the confluence of seven major waterways, hundreds of sampans bump and jostle early each morning to trade everything from sugar cane to pigs – and of course mountains of fruit.

Feeling fruity in the Mekong Delta

860 | Dawn over Kelimutu in Flores

INDONESIA There's something magnificently untamed about Flores. As with almost every island in this part of the Indonesian archipelago, Flores is fringed by picture-postcard beaches of golden sand. But to appreciate its unique charms you have to turn away from the sea and instead face the island's interior. Despite its relatively small size (a mere 370km long and, in places, as narrow as 12km), only the much larger Indonesian landmasses of Java and Sumatra can boast more volcanoes than this slender sliver of land.

Unsurprisingly, Flores' jagged volcanic spine has played a major part in the island's development. The precipitous topography contributes to torrential wet seasons, which in turn provide a tropical countenance – not for nothing did the Portuguese name this island "Cabo das Flores", the Cape of Flowers. The rugged peaks have also long separated the tribes on the island – an enforced segregation that has ensured an inordinate number of languages and dialects, as well as many distinct cultures.

The highest volcanic peak on the island is the towering Gunung Ranaka, at a lofty 2382m, while its most volatile is the grumbling, hot-headed Ebulobo on Flores' south coast. But the prince among them is Kelimutu. Though just 1620m high, the volcano has become something of a pilgrimage site.

Waking at around 4am, groups of trekkers pile onto the back of an open-sided truck for the thirty-minute ride up the volcano's slopes, from where a short scramble to Kelimutu's barren summit reveals the mountain's unique attraction: three small craters, each filled with lakes of startlingly different colours, ranging from vibrant turquoise to a deep, reddish brown.

With the wisps of morning mist lingering above the water's surface and the rising sun bouncing off the glassy waters creating an ever-changing play of light and colour, dawn over Kelimutu is Indonesia at its most beguiling.

861 | Sand and spice on Ko Samui

THAILAND Ko Samui is perhaps an unlikely spot to learn the art of Thai cooking. Given the choice between lapping up rays on a patch of sand, palms and waterfalls in the Gulf of Thailand or arming yourself with a sharp cleaver to take on a mound of raw pork and fiery chillies, most people will surely opt for the former – especially when the best plate of food you're likely to have in your life costs about a buck at the local market.

Yet the packed schedule at the Samui Institute of Thai Culinary Arts suggests otherwise. The school focuses on central Thai food, considered the classic style among the country's four regional cuisines, with its coconut-milk curries and flavoursome balance of hot, sour, salty and sweet. The classes begin with a discussion of the ingredients (and substitutes for those hard to find outside Southeast Asia), work up to wok skills and end with a feast of your own making, an array of tempting and delicious stir-fries, curries and soups.

Walk into the school's unassuming shophouse just off Samui's Chaweng Beach and you may wonder whether you've been shanghaied into a tropical *Iron Chef* gone awry. A sea of tiny bowls bursting with cumin seeds, tamarind, coriander root, galangal and shrimp paste lie scattered across the prep tables, and you've got a little more than two hours to whip up three dishes. But before panic sets in, the lead chef calmly explains how to chiffonade a kaffir lime leaf, and soon enough, you're grinding out a proper chilli paste with a mortar and pestle with the steady hand of a market lady who's been at it for fifty years.

It can't be this easy, can it? You chop a few more chillies, toss in an extra dash of fish sauce, swirl the wok with a flourish and – *aroy mak* – you've just duplicated that delicious *tom yum kai* (spicy shrimp soup) you saw at the market. So what if it cost a few dollars more? It's worth it.

862 | Partying at the Ati-Atihan festival

THE PHILIPPINES You need serious stamina for the three days and nights of non-stop dancing that mark the culmination of Ati-Atihan, the most flamboyant fiesta in the fiesta-mad Philippines. No wonder the mantra chanted by participants in this marathon rave is *hala bira, puera pasma*, which means "keep on going, no tiring". If you plan on lasting the course, start training now.

Ati-Atihan, which takes place during the first two weeks of January in Kalibo – an otherwise unimpressive port town on the central Philippine island of Panay – actually lasts for two weeks. But it's the final three days that are the most important, with costumed locals taking to the streets in a riot of partying, music and street dancing. And it's this the tourists come for – 72 sleepless hours of alcohol-fuelled, intoxicating mayhem acted out to the deafening anks of massed drums.

Don't expect to just stand by and watch – the locals have an unwritten rule that there are no wallflowers at Ati-Atihan – and if you don't take part, they'll make you. Even if all you can muster is a drunken conga line, you can take the edge off your nerves with a few glasses of *lambanog*, a vigorous native aperitif made from leftover jackfruit or mango fermented in cheap containers buried in the earth – the "zombie flavour" is especially liberating.

Ati-Atihan is still partly a religious festival, held to celebrate the child Jesus (Santo Niño). In recent years it has morphed into a delightful hodgepodge of Catholic ritual, indigenous drama and tourist attraction. It's the one time of the year when Catholic Filipinos aren't afraid to push the boat out, especially for the final-day fancy dress parade that sees thousands of people in costumes so big and brash they almost block the street.

If you're feeling a little rough after all this, do what many others do and head up the coast to the beautiful little island of Boracay, where you can sleep off your hangover on one of the finest beaches in the world.

863 | Conquering Southeast Asia's highest peak

MALAYSIA It's a hell of a slog up Malaysian Borneo's Mount Kinabalu, but every year thousands of visitors brave the freezing conditions and altitude sickness to reach the 4095m-high summit. The reward is a spectacular dawn panorama across granite pinnacles rising out of the clouds below you, and the knowledge that you've conquered the highest peak between the Himalayas and New Guinea.

Your two-day expedition up the southern ridge begins at Kinabalu Park headquarters, where you meet your obligatory guide and gulp at the multiple jagged peaks ahead. You need to be equipped as for any mountain hike, prepared for downpours and extreme chill at the summit, but Kinabalu's appeal is that any averagely fit tourist can reach the top. The steady climb up to the Laban Rata mountain huts is a five-hour trek along a well-tramped trail through changing forest habitats. Beyond 1800m you're in dense cloudforest, among a thousand species of orchids, 26 types of rhododendron and a host of insect-hungry pitcher plants. By 2600m most of the vegetation has given up, but you stagger on to 3300m and the long-awaited flop into bed. Day two starts at 2.30am for the final push across the glistening granite rock face to Low's Peak, Kinabalu's highest point. It's dark and very cold; for three hours you can see no further than the beam of your headtorch and, despite the handrails and ropes, the climb is tough; some have to turn back because of pounding altitude headaches.

But when you finally reach the summit, your spirits will rise with the sun as the awesome view comes into focus, every horizon filled with the stark grey twists of Kinabalu's iconic peaks, and the deep chasm of infamous Low's Gully at your feet.

864 | Meeting the relatives: orang-utans in Sumatra

INDONESIA Sandwiched between the raging Bohorok River and the deep, silent, steaming jungle, the Bukit Lawang Orang-utan Sanctuary, on the vast Indonesian island of Sumatra, offers the unique opportunity of witnessing one of our closest and most charming relatives in their own backyard.

Having crossed the Bohorok on a precarious makeshift canoe, your first sight of these kings of the jungle is at the enclosures housing recent arrivals, many of whom have been rescued from the thriving trade in exotic pets, particularly in nearby Singapore. It's here that the long process of rehabilitation begins, a process that may include learning from their human guardians such basic simian skills as tree-climbing and fruit-peeling.

Most of these activities are done away from the prying cameras of tourists, but twice a day park officers lead visitors up to a feeding platform to wait, and to watch. The sound of rustling foliage and creaking branches betrays the presence of a rangy, shaggy silhouette making its languid yet majestic way through the treetops.

Orang-utans literally force the trees to bend to their will as they swing back and forth on one sapling until the next can be reached. Swooping just above the awestruck audience, they arrive at the platform to feast on bananas and milk, the diet kept deliberately monotonous to encourage the orang-utans – all of whom have been recently released from the sanctuary – to look for more diverse flavours in the forest.

Once the ape has proved that it's capable of surviving unaided, it will be left to fend for itself in the vast, dark forests of North Sumatra. Its rehabilitation will be considered complete. Sadly, at Bukit Lawang there never seems to be a shortage of rescued apes to take its place.

865 | Diving the Tubbataha Reef

THE PHILIPPINES If you're looking for some of the most adventurous and thrilling scuba diving in the world, Tubbataha Reef Marine Park in the Sulu Sea is the place to start. Well out of sight of land and almost 200km southeast of Puerto Princesa in Palawan, this World Heritage Site is only accessible on live-aboard boats when seas are favourable between March and June. Its very isolation means it's not overrun by package-tour divers, and even during these peak months you'll probably be on one of only a handful of small boats in the area. The reef – actually a grouping of dozens of small reefs, atolls and coral islands covering more than 300 square kilometres – is one of the finest in the world, with daily sightings of the big pelagics that all divers dream of.

Rise at dawn for a quick dive among the turtles and small sharks before breakfast. Afterwards there's time for a visit to Shark Airport, where sharks "take off" from sandy ledges like planes, before it's back to the boat for lunch and a snooze. You can do deep dives, night dives, drift dives, all kinds of dives. Or you can simply fossick gently along some of the shallower reefs, home to so many varieties of coral and fish that it's hard to know where to look next.

For a real buzz, dive deep over one of the many coral walls that seem to plunge into infinity, and hang out for a few minutes with giant manta rays, black-tip reef sharks and, just possibly, cruising hammerheads. You also stand a good chance of getting up close and personal with a whale shark, the harmless gentle giants of the sea known in the Philippines as *butanding*.

Of course, there's life beyond diving at Tubbataha. For a change of scene, you can snorkel around some of the atolls, picnic on the beach at the ranger station, or just kick back on deck and watch dolphins and tuna perform occasional aerial stunts.

LAOS The pace of life is deliciously slow in Luang Prabang, but if you opt for a lie-in you'll miss the perfect start to the day. As dawn breaks over this most languorous of Buddhist towns, saffron-robed monks emerge from their temple-monasteries to collect alms from their neighbours, the riverbanks begin to come alive and the smell of freshly baked baguettes draws you to one of the many cafés. It's a captivating scene whichever way you turn: ringed by mountains and encircled by the Mekong and Khan rivers, the old quarter's temple roofs peep out from the palm groves, its streets still lined with wood-shuttered shophouses and French-colonial mansions.

Though it has the air of a rather grand village, Luang Prabang is the ancient Lao capital, seat of the royal family that ruled the country for six hundred years until the Communists exiled them in the 1970s. It remains the most cultured town in Laos (though it's not exactly a hard-won accolade), and one of the best preserved in Southeast Asia – as recognized in its World Heritage Site status. Chief among its many beautiful temples is the entrancing sixteenth-century Wat Xieng Thong, whose tiered roofs frame an exquisite glass mosaic of the tree of life and attendant creatures, flanked by pillars and doors picked out in brilliant gold-leaf stencils. It's a gentle stroll from here to the graceful teak and rosewood buildings of the Royal Palace Museum and the dazzling gilded murals of neighbouring Wat Mai.

When you tire of the monuments, there are riverside caves, waterfalls and even a whisky-making village to explore, and plenty of shops selling intricate textiles and Hmong hill-tribe jewellery. Serenity returns at sunset, when the monks' chants drift over the temple walls and everyone else heads for high ground to soak up the view.

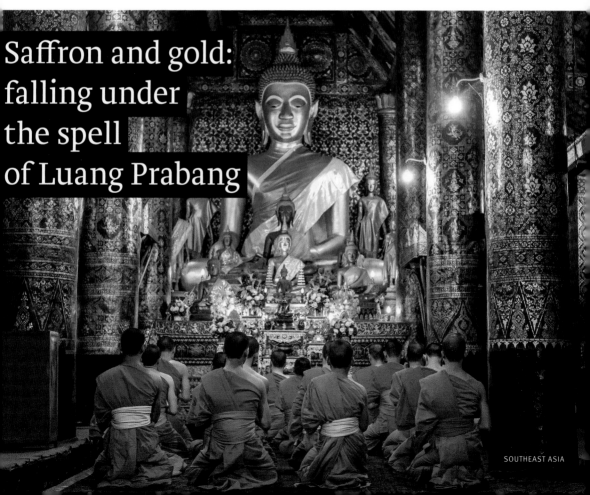

Saffron and gold: falling under the spell of Luang Prabang

SOUTHEAST ASIA

867 | Fight night in Bangkok

THAILAND The Thai people are predominantly Buddhist, and through much of their country Siddhartha's spirit is palpable. Even in the noisy and overcrowded capital city, even the most hard-faced of nationals will soften their features and treat visitors with a respect given all living creatures. The exception that proves the rule is the brutal national sport of *muay thai* or Thai boxing – where knees batter ribs while gamblers wager their salaries on who will fall, and when.

Vendors surround Bangkok's Lumpinee Stadium three nights out of seven, peddling wares and heated snacks to patrons streaming into a theatre of controlled violence. Past the ticket booth is a mere hint of a lobby, its walls pierced with numbered archways too small for the seating areas behind them. A rhythmic thudding from deeper inside triggers a bottleneck at the edges of the arena, the narrow entryways imparting a final suggestion of order before releasing spectators into the clamour beyond. In the ring the pre-fight display has already begun. Like many of the martial arts, *muay thai* has its roots in national defence, and the fighters perform awkward dances before the bell in honour of a kingdom which was never at any point conquered by foreign invaders.

Drums pulse behind tense woodwind sounds as the early rounds get under way, each fighter cautiously feeling for weakness in his opponent's defence. The crowd is equally patient, watching carefully for an advantage they can use against the bookmakers. At the end of the second round all hell breaks loose. In the stands men are waving and shouting, signalling with contorted hands the amounts they're willing to lose. Within two minutes the fighters must retake the ring, and when they meet there are no more feints or dodges. Each attack is without pause. The music quickens. Blows are harder now, exchanged at a furious rate. The crowd raises its voice at every strike. Against the shin, into the ribs. Ferociously. Relentlessly. And then a step backward and to the left reveals enough space to slip an instep up to the loser's jaw. Patrons make good on their markers while a stretcher carries away the unconscious also-ran. With ten fights a night, there's simply no time for compassion.

868 | Joining the party at an Iban longhouse

MALAYSIA It's always polite to bring gifts to your hosts' house, but when visiting a Sarawak longhouse you should make sure it's something that's easily shared. Longhouses are communal, and nearly everything gets divvied up into equal parts. This isn't always an easy task: typically, longhouses are home to around 150 people and contain at least thirty family apartments, each one's front door opening on to the common gallery (hence the tag "a thirty-door longhouse" to describe the size). These days not everyone lives there full time, but many of Sarawak's indigenous Iban population still consider the longhouse home, even if they only return for weekends.

Many longhouses enjoy stunning locations, usually in a clearing beside a river, so you'll probably travel to yours in a longboat that meanders between the jungle-draped banks, dodging logs being floated downstream to the timber yards. Look carefully and you'll see that patches of hinterland have been cultivated with black pepper vines, rubber and fruit trees, plus the occasional square of paddy, all of which are crucial to longhouse economies.

Having first met the chief of your longhouse, you climb the notched tree trunk that serves as a staircase into the stilted wooden structure and enter the common area, or *ruai*, a wide gallery that runs the length of the building and is the focus of community social life. Pretty much everything happens here – the meeting and greeting, the giving and sharing of gifts, the gossip, and the partying. Animist Iban communities in particular are notorious party animals (unlike some of their Christian counterparts), and you'll be invited to join in the excessive rice-wine drinking, raucous dancing and forfeit games that last late into the night.

Finally, exhausted, you hit the sack – either on a straw mat right there on the *ruai*, or in a guest lodge next door.

869 | Karst and crew: overnighting on Ha Long Bay

VIETNAM Spend a night afloat among the limestone pinnacles of Ha Long Bay, and you'll witness their many moods as their silhouettes morph with the moonlight, mist and midday sun. Scores of local boat companies offer this experience, for the spectacularly scenic bay is a World Heritage Site and Vietnam's top tourist destination.

Regularly referred to as the eighth natural wonder of the world, the 1500 square kilometres of Ha Long Bay contain nearly two thousand islands, most of them uninhabited outcrops that protrude from the Gulf of Tonkin. Their intriguingly craggy profiles have long inspired poets, wags and travel writers to wax lyrical about Italianate cathedrals, every type of creature from fighting cocks to bug-eyed frogs, even famous faces, but the bay's creation myth is just as poetic. "Ha Long" translates as "the dragon descending into the sea": legend tells how the islets were scattered here by the celestial dragon as a barrier against invaders.

Even the most imaginative visitor might tire of interpreting the shapes for a full two days, so overnight trips offer different angles on rock appreciation. As well as lounging on island beaches by day and swimming the phosphorescent waters by night, there are plenty of caves and floating villages to explore, and endless fresh seafood to enjoy. Some tours allow you to paddle yourself around in a kayak, while others feature forest treks and cycle rides on Cat Ba Island, the largest in the bay.

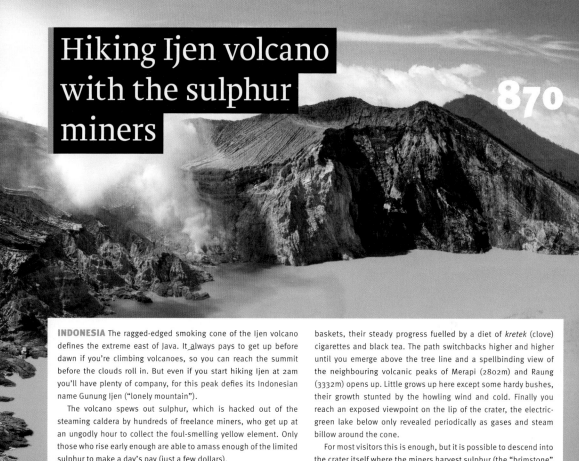

Hiking Ijen volcano with the sulphur miners

INDONESIA The ragged-edged smoking cone of the Ijen volcano defines the extreme east of Java. It always pays to get up before dawn if you're climbing volcanoes, so you can reach the summit before the clouds roll in. But even if you start hiking Ijen at 2am you'll have plenty of company, for this peak defies its Indonesian name Gunung Ijen ("lonely mountain").

The volcano spews out sulphur, which is hacked out of the steaming caldera by hundreds of freelance miners, who get up at an ungodly hour to collect the foul-smelling yellow element. Only those who rise early enough are able to amass enough of the limited sulphur to make a day's pay (just a few dollars).

Starting from the isolated national park post at Pos Paltuding, a steep trail ascends the shoulder of the mountain, passing through tropical forest that's home to gibbons and patrolled by eagles. You'll pass a steady stream of miners, who joke and chatter as they balance loads of up to 100kg across their backs in bamboo baskets, their steady progress fuelled by a diet of *kretek* (clove) cigarettes and black tea. The path switchbacks higher and higher until you emerge above the tree line and a spellbinding view of the neighbouring volcanic peaks of Merapi (2802m) and Raung (3332m) opens up. Little grows up here except some hardy bushes, their growth stunted by the howling wind and cold. Finally you reach an exposed viewpoint on the lip of the crater, the electric-green lake below only revealed periodically as gases and steam billow around the cone.

For most visitors this is enough, but it is possible to descend into the crater itself where the miners harvest sulphur (the "brimstone" of biblical times), which is mainly used by the cosmetics industry, and is added to fertilizer. Be warned: the vapours can be overpowering. Ijen miners wear no more than cotton scarves to protect themselves from the noxious fumes, but you might want to arm yourself with a mask.

871 | Sampling Baba-Nyonya cuisine in Malaysia

MALAYSIA The delicious hybrid cuisine of Malaysia's Baba-Nyonya is one of southeast Asia's finest. Like the community from which it takes its name, the cooking style is a unique hybrid of Chinese and Malay culture – a legacy of marriages between Chinese immigrants and native Malaysians in Melaka during the fifteenth and sixteenth centuries.

At this time Melaka was an important Portuguese and Dutch trading route, and the quest for spices resulted in a European community with large plantations growing cloves, pepper and nutmeg. Eager to benefit from these riches, and hoping to escape famine and poverty during Manchu rule, Chinese merchants and entrepreneurs flocked to Melaka. The Chinese settlers, who were largely male, intermarried with Malay women, and so the Baba-Nyonya community was born.

Their cuisine marries Chinese wok cooking styles with Malay ingredients and condiments, such as candlenut, Vietnamese coriander and fermented shrimp paste, relying on sour sauces and coconut milk. Added in the mix are Indian and Middle Eastern spices, Javan vegetables such as *buah keluak* (black mangrove tree nuts) and *ulam* (a plant native to Asian wetlands), resulting in a truly distinctive cuisine that bursts with flavours. Nyonya cooking simultaneously tastes sweet, sour, salty and spicy.

Some of the best dishes include *laksa nyonya* (curry noodles with coconut milk), *ayam pongteh* (Nyonya stewed chicken), *udang masak lemak nenas* (curry prawns with pineapple) and *ayam buah keluak* (chicken with "black nuts").

Paddling into secret lagoons

THAILAND The first time you enter a *hong* you're almost certain to laugh with delight. The fun begins when your guide paddles you across to the towering karst island and then pilots your canoe through an imperceptible fissure in its rock wall. You enter a sea cave that reeks of bats and gets darker and darker until suddenly your guide shouts, "Lie back in the boat please!" Your nose barely clears the stalactites and you emerge, with your toes first, into a sunlit lagoon, or *hong*, right at the very heart of the outcrop.

Hong ("rooms" in Thai) are the *pièce de résistance* of southern Thailand's Phang Nga Bay. Invisible to any passing vessel, these secret tidal lagoons are flooded, roofless caves hidden within the core of seemingly solid limestone islands, accessible only at certain tides and

only in sea canoes small enough to slip beneath and between low-lying rocky overhangs. Like the islands themselves, the *hong* have taken millions of years to form, with the softer limestone hollowed out from the side by the pounding waves, and from above by the wind and the rain.

The world inside these collapsed cave systems is extraordinary, protected from the open bay by a turreted ring of cliffs hung with primeval-looking gardens of inverted cycads, twisted bonsai palms, lianas, miniature screw pines and tangled ferns.

And as the tide withdraws, the *hong*'s resident creatures – among them fiddler crabs, mudskippers, dusky langurs and crab-eating macaques – emerge to forage on the muddy floor, while white-bellied sea eagles hover expectantly overhead.

873 | Puzzles at the Plain of Jars

LAOS After three hours trudging along steep forest paths, you come to a surreal sight. Hundreds of megalithic stone jars, large enough for someone to crouch inside, are strewn all around. This group of 416 jars is the largest at the aptly named Plain of Jars, where thousands of jars are found in scores of clusters, along with a number of jar-making sites. They were made by a vanished civilization and their presence indicates that the mountains were prosperously settled at the time. Today the Xieng Khoung province is on the rise again, this time as a tourist hub.

Little is known about the jar-makers, except that the plateau was a strategic and prosperous centre for trade routes extending from India to China. Nearly two thousand years ago, possibly earlier according to new evidence, these jars functioned as mortuary vessels: a corpse would be placed inside the jar until it decomposed down to its essence, then cremated and buried in a second urn with personal possessions. Now all that remain here are the empty jars, set in clusters on the crests of hills, an imposing and eerie legacy.

At Phukeng, you can see where the jars were made. Dozens of incomplete jars lie on the mountainside where they were abandoned after cracking during construction. It's a sight that evokes the magnitude of the effort: after many weeks spent gouging a jar from a boulder with hammer and chisel, the creators then had to haul the load of several tonnes (the largest jar weighs six tonnes) across the undulating, grassy, pine-studded landscape to the "cemetery" 8km away. How the jars were transported is another puzzle that serves to deepen the enigma that pervades the Plain of Jars.

874 | Unearthing the medieval Spanish heart of Manila

THE PHILIPPINES If walls could talk. Long before Manila was crowned by flash skyscrapers and apartment blocks, the city's most imposing sight was Intramuros, a walled fortress hidden within the modern city. As history shows, Spanish Conquistadors led armies into Manila in the sixteenth century to defeat the incumbent ruler, the Sultan of Brunei, and their first task was to build an administrative centre from where they ruled for more than three centuries. Today, the lasting result is a boxed-in grid of cobbled lanes, Madrid-style squares and the imposing cannon-mounted Fort Santiago.

In keeping with the colonial vibe, the fort's backstreets are best explored by bamboo bike, and it's a modern-day rite of passage to rent one from Bambike, a sustainable start-up that makes bicycle frames from a hybrid knit of bamboo and abaca twine. Remember you're in the tropics, so rent one in the morning before it gets too hot.

First pedal to Plaza de Roma, where you'll find the eighth reincarnation of Manila Cathedral, a church that simply refuses to die. First built in 1571 from bamboo, wood and nipa palm, it's been damaged by fires, ravaged by typhoons and earthquakes, and became a major World War II casualty during the Battle for Manila in 1945. Against the odds it still stands, and is a symbol of the dogmatic Christian spirit of the Filipinos. As a quick reminder you're still in the present day, the world's most peculiar Starbucks is nearby, tucked inside a disused prison cell built into the old city walls.

From here, cut past the Palacio del Gobernador, or Governor's Palace, to Fort Santiago for the backstory on former prisoner and national hero José Rizal, who successfully led the rally for Spanish independence. As tributes go, it's a little dilapidated, but far better is Rizal Park, a green lung to the south that is home to ornamental gardens, fountains and statues.

875 | Meeting sun bears and orang-utans in Borneo

MALAYSIA A dark shape moves high in the leaves, climbing towards the jungle canopy with the grace of a large cat. An ursine face pokes through the undergrowth; the sleek, black sun bear raises herself on her hind legs next to a tree trunk and proceeds to sharpen her long, capable-looking claws. Though it easily rivals the panda in the cuteness stakes, little is known about the world's smallest bear, named for the distinctive white mark on its chest that resembles the sun. Seriously endangered, sun bears live throughout Asia, but Borneo is their last stronghold.

Like orang-utans, the sun bears face drastic threats. Their habitat is shrinking as the rainforest is converted to palm oil plantations, and the danger of being shot by farmers, hunted by poachers or taken as babies from their mothers to be sold as pets is very real. The Borneo Sun Bear Conservation Centre in Sepilok, next to the Sepilok Orang-utan Rehabilitation Centre, is the first of its kind. Both centres aim to educate people about these wonderful animals, to rehabilitate and teach life skills to orphaned and injured mammals before releasing them into the wild, and to provide a long-term home to those that can't be rehabilitated. It's precious indeed to be able to spend time with two of Borneo's most fascinating creatures in one day.

Visiting the orang-utans at feeding times, keep your eyes on the fruit-strewn platform, connected to the trees with thick ropes. A murmur runs through the crowd as a large, powerful simian covered in shaggy red hair swings down in leisurely fashion, picks up a banana with his foot and starts to eat. Within moments another "wild man of Borneo" arrives at the platform – though this one is in fact a "wild woman", with a tiny, big-eyed baby on her hip. She sits and reaches for the fruit, swatting at any scavenging macaques who dare come too close. Witnessing these graceful animals go about their lives, there can be no doubt that the efforts directed towards their survival are more crucial than ever.

876 | Hanging out with the hornbills

CAMBODIA Deep inside the Cardamom Mountains in Cambodia's southwest Koh Kong province is the Wildlife Release Station. Run by the much-respected Wildlife Alliance, this brilliant set-up in the heart of the jungle is reached by a rather bumpy motorbike ride from the nearest town, Chi Phat, itself a community-tourism project set up by the Alliance.

At the station, dedicated gamekeepers care for endangered animals, most of which have been rescued from the illegal wildlife trade in Cambodia (animal trafficking is rife here). Visitors can shadow the keepers, see their work and enjoy the tranquillity of this still-pristine environment, with all profits going towards the project. There's also the chance to stay overnight in simple but comfortable thatched bungalows.

The idea is to rehabilitate and eventually release the animals back into the wild. A night here might be the first time you see a pangolin, one of the most threatened creatures in the country, hunted for its meat and scales (believed by some to possess medicinal properties). Be amazed as the creature's long sticky tongue hoovers up thousands of ants during a night-time feeding session. Or you might offer a banana to an adorable bearcat (binturong) and observe the quirky-looking hornbill. Activities can vary: you could be helping gamekeepers to track wildlife after release, or setting up camera traps in the nearby forest – slow loris, leopard cats, bearcats and deer have all been spotted. Guests can also help to feed the resident sun bears, monkeys and birds or just-released animals who still need supplementary food.

The Wildlife Release Station is also a place to appreciate nature, take gentle hikes through the forest along old logging trails, swim in natural pools, spot small fauna and flora, and learn about Cambodia's fragile ecosystem. It's a place to hang out on hammocks by the communal hut where staff prepare delicious Khmer food, and chat to the friendly gamekeepers over a cold beer or glass of rice wine, next to the evening campfire. It's also a place that restores your faith in humanity.

877 | Going underground in Puerto Princesa

THE PHILIPPINES The Philippines' 7000-plus islands are filled with natural wonders, from conical volcanic peaks to ancient rice terraces, hidden beaches, and lagoons fringed by towering limestone karsts.

One of the most unique of these wonders is the Puerto Princesa underground river and ancient cave system on Palawan, the Philippines' westernmost island. The world's longest navigable underground river, it measures 8.2km and winds its way beneath the Mount St Paul, before pouring out into the sea. Both a UNESCO World Heritage Site and voted as one of the New 7 Wonders of Nature, the river comprises a unique ecosystem, home to some species that can be found nowhere else on the planet. Visitors are limited to just 900 per day to try to protect the unique habitat.

The tour begins with a stunning twenty-minute boat ride from the town of Sabang along the coast, before reaching the Puerto Princesa Subterranean River National Park. From here, it's a short hike through the emerald-green jungle, where monkeys peer down at you from the trees and giant monitor lizards slink their way through the undergrowth.

Once at the mouth of the river, small boats take visitors on a 4km journey, paddled by a single guide and lit by just one head torch. Once inside, the light and sounds of the outside world slowly slip away. All you can hear are the hollow, echoing drips of water and the soft flapping bats and swallows flying high above your head. In near-silence, your boat enters vast cavernous rooms: natural cathedrals of towering rock formations, stalagmites and stalactites. In the gloomy light, your eyes begin to pick out shapes – giant candles and huge bulbous mushrooms.

Further down into the darkest depths past the 4km mark, the river holds even more secrets, which most visitors never get to see – the 20 million-year-old fossil of a manatee, spaces so narrow you have to swim through, a hidden room covered in shimmering crystals.

878 | Visiting the Tuol Sleng Genocide Museum

CAMBODIA Everyone over the age of 45 in Cambodia has lived through the Khmer Rouge era. The friendly woman who runs your guesthouse in downtown Phnom Penh; your Angkor temples tour guide; the waiter at the seaside café in Sihanoukville. At the Tuol Sleng Genocide Museum you'll learn something of what that means.

A former school on the outskirts of Phnom Penh, Tuol Sleng, code-named S-21, was used by the Khmer Rouge to interrogate perceived enemies of their demented Marxist-Leninist regime. During the Khmer Rouge rule, from 1975 to 1979, some fourteen thousand Cambodians were tortured and killed here, often for the crime of being educated: for being a teacher, a monk, or a member of the elite; for wearing glasses; for being a discredited cadre.

We know this because the Khmer Rouge were meticulous in their documentation. When the Vietnamese army arrived at S-21 in January 1979 they found thousands of mugshots of former prisoners, each of them numbered, along with reams of typed "confessions".

Those black-and-white photographs fill the downstairs walls of the museum today. There are rows and rows of them: men, women, children, even babies. Only seven prisoners survived S-21; one of them, Ung Pech, became the museum's first director. When the museum opened to the public in 1980, thousands of Cambodians came here to look for evidence of missing relatives.

The interior of the prison has in part been left almost as it was found. There are old tiled floors, classrooms crudely partitioned into cramped cells, shackles, iron bedsteads and meshed balconies. Elsewhere, a handful of graphic paintings by another of the survivors, Vann Nath, depicts the torture methods used to extract confessions.

Once they'd been coerced into admitting guilt, prisoners were taken to the Choeung Ek Killing Fields and murdered. Choeung Ek, 12km southwest, is now the site of another memorial, incongruously set amid peaceful countryside.

Padding round the golden rock

879

MYANMAR Every year, between November and March, barefoot pilgrims flock to Kyaiktiyo – the Golden Rock – high up in the Eastern Yoma mountains. Crowned with a slender gold stupa, the Rock is a huge granite boulder perched rakishly on a natural stone plinth that Burmese Buddhists believe has been held in place by a few extra-strong strands of Buddha's hair through centuries, cyclones and earthquakes.

While the most devout pilgrims will walk barefoot up the rocky 11km trail from the small town of Kinpun, the majority of visitors opt to take a converted truck up the roller-coaster road that curls to the mountaintop. Whether you choose the steep, sweaty hike or the white-knuckle ride, the journey to the summit is likely to leave you feeling decidedly more spiritual by the time you arrive. Activity around the shrine peaks at sunrise and sunset – the midday heat drives all but the most determined (and thick-soled) visitors into the shade. Join the pilgrims' dawn vigil amid clouds of incense and fervent prayers, or linger in the evening as the sunset throws the otherworldly scene into Technicolor and swifts swoop through the warm air.

By rocking the boulder gently to and fro, it's allegedly possible to pass a hair (even an ordinary human one) between the rock and its base. (Note that only male visitors can get close enough to try – women aren't allowed to enter the sanctuary immediately surrounding the Rock.) Most people settle for sticking small squares of gold leaf (sold at the site) to the already thick layer that covers the bare granite. Once you've paid your respects, head for the surrounding hills, which are crisscrossed with quiet, sandy trails leading to other strange rock formations, waterfalls and unexpected wayside shrines. Or take the 2km trail to the far side of the mountain, where you will find a peaceful contrast to the reverential bustle that surrounds the main attraction.

880 | Islands far from any sea

LAOS It feels a lot like paradise. Palm trees whisper in the hot shimmer of the tropical sun, neon-blue butterflies play kiss-chase along the shoreline, and warm water laps at sand so soft that it swallows your toes. But there are no oceans eating away at the islands of Si Phan Don. And the closest sea is hundreds of kilometres to the east.

As the Mekong River oozes through southern Laos towards the Cambodian border, its coffee-brown stream is split by a maze of low-slung atolls – most of them uninhabited. With a longtail boat and a guide navigating the labyrinth, you can see ferocious waterfalls and endangered Irrawaddy dolphins, or the rusting remains of the French colonial railway project that tried (and failed) to bridge these islands to exploit the region's vast natural resources. Or you could, of course, just kick back in your hammock for a while. With lazy days like these, who needs the ocean?

881 | Candles in the wind: the Loy Krathong Festival of Light

THAILAND In the days leading up to Thailand's annual Loy Krathong Festival of Light, pretty little baskets fashioned from banana leaves and filled with orchids and marigolds begin to appear at market stalls across the country. On festival night everyone gathers at the nearest body of water – beside the riverbank or neighbourhood canal, on the seashore, even at the village fishpond. Crouching down beside the water, you light the candle and incense sticks poking out of your floral basket, say a prayer of thanks to the water goddess, in whose honour this festival is held, and set your offering afloat. As the bobbing lights of hundreds of miniature basket-boats drift away on the breeze, taking with them any bad luck accrued over the past year, the Loy Krathong song rings out over the sound system, contestants for the Miss Loy Krathong beauty pageant take to the stage and Chang beer begins to flow.

MAKE THE MOST OF YOUR TIME ON EARTH

Be dazzled at Bangkok's Grand Palace

THAILAND As befits a former royal residence, there's bling aplenty at the Grand Palace, whose main temple, Wat Phra Kaeo, dazzles with its shimmering walls and gables covered all over in gilt and coloured glass mosaics. Join the hundreds of Thai pilgrims and step inside to pay homage to the teeny Emerald Buddha, the holiest icon in the country. The figurine is just 60cm high, elevated atop a towering golden pedestal, and is dressed according to the season: a golden shawl in winter, a monk's robe for the monsoon and a crown for summer. Things get even more surreal in the colonnades that encircle the temple, where an exuberant kilometre-long mural depicts the complicated ups and downs of the Ramayana story, an ancient epic tale of good versus evil, whose cast includes a monkey king, a demon with ten heads and otherworldly airborne creatures.

883 | Paradise islands in azure seas

CAMBODIA Sixty Cambodian islands dot the azure Gulf of Thailand. Easily accessible from the mainland, they may not have roads, ATMs or mains electricity, but that's a small price to pay for squeaky-white beaches, warm translucent seas and an escapist vibe. Controversially, a number of these islands have been leased to developers, mooted for super luxury resorts, so it's anyone's guess as to how long this rustic tranquillity will continue. Time is of the essence if you want to experience them in their humblest form.

You might start with Koh Totang, a tiny dolphin-shaped island in the Koh S'Dach archipelago. Just a handful of people, plus roosters and dogs, live on this wooded isle, along with the owners and guests of the Crusoe-esque *Nomads Land*, an idyllic retreat on its sand-swept eastern shores. If you're looking for utter tranquillity, a chance to channel your inner yogi, or to spend a day beachcombing on deserted sands, it's ideal.

That said, many assert that Koh Rong, with its 43km of paradisiacal snow-white beaches, aquamarine ocean and twilight phosphorescence,

is the one to beat. Its southeastern shores are the go-to spot for young party-loving backpackers, but it's easy to find your own patch of paradise along these undeveloped sands. The verdant interior is also ripe for trekking; join Gil at *Paradise Bungalows* on his guided nature walks and you may even discover new species.

It's not all about hedonism and hiking, though. At the small island of Koh S'Dach – with more than two thousand inhabitants, the largest community across the Koh S'Dach archipelago – fishing is king and the prosperous village is unaffected by tourism. Shallow Waters, a British marine NGO, offers numerous volunteering opportunities, from surveying coral reefs to collecting data and getting involved in community projects. The serene mangrove-ringed island of Koh Thmei, meanwhile, within Ream National Park, is a fabulous base for birdwatchers – the island boasts around 155 bird species, including the endangered Brahminy kite. There's just one very low-key eco-conscious venture, the *Koh Thmei Resort*, along with shell-sprayed beaches to stroll, a coral reef to snorkel, and the uninhabited Koh Ses Island within a kayak's reach.

884 | Budget beach-chic

THAILAND Old-school travellers complain that Thailand has gone upmarket, swapped its cheap sleeps for identikit villas and sacrificed the beach-shack-and-hammock vibe for apartments with swimming pools. They've got a point. Thailand is prospering: new boutique hotels entice you with minimalist curves and luxurious fabrics, and at $200 a night, a five-star suite can seem like an affordable indulgence.

But the rudimentary bamboo beach huts still exist and arguably there's no better way to experience the pleasures of Thailand's gorgeous strands. With over 3000km of coastline and scores of accessible islands you've got plenty of beaches to choose from, the

default option being squeaky white sand and luminous turquoise water. Staying in a wooden hut you're often all but camping: you'll see the sand beneath your feet through the slats of the wonky planked floor; you'll hear the waves lapping the shoreline just a few metres from your ill-fitting front door; and there's no need for a fan when you prop open the woven rattan shutters and let the breeze waft through.

Make your own shell mobiles, hang your sarong as a door curtain and string up your hammock to rock to and fro. It's your very own eco home and worth every bit of the modest daily sum that buys you residency.

885 | Appeasing the spirits with Balinese theatrics

INDONESIA On the island of Bali, a Hindu enclave in the Muslim majority nation of Indonesia, the gods and spirits need regular appeasing and entertaining. Offerings of rice and flowers are laid out twice a day in tiny banana-leaf baskets and on special occasions there is ritual music and dancing. Temple festivals are so frequent here that you've a good chance of coming across one, but there are also dance performances staged for tourists at the palace in Ubud, the island's cultural hub. Even though the programme has been specially tailored, there is nothing inauthentic about the finesse of the palace performers. And the setting – a starlit courtyard framed by stone-carved statues and an elaborate gateway – is magnificent.

Every performance begins with a priest sanctifying the space with a sprinkle of holy water. Then the gamelan orchestra strikes up: seated cross-legged either side of the stage, the 25 musicians are dressed in formal outfits of Nehru jacket, traditional headcloth and sarong. The light catches the bronze of their gongs, cymbals

and metallophones, the lead drummer raises his hand, and they're off, racing boisterously through the first piece, producing an extraordinary syncopated clashing of metal on metal, punctuated by dramatic stops and starts.

Enter the dancers. Five sinuous barefooted young women open with a ritualistic welcome dance, scattering flower petals as an offering to the gods. Next, the poised refinement of the Legong, performed by three young girls wrapped in luminous pink, green and gold brocade, the drama played out with gracefully angled hands, fluttering arms and wide flashing eyes.

Finally it's the masked Barong-Rangda drama, the all-important pitting of good against evil, with the lovable, lion-like Barong stalked and harassed by the powerful widow-witch Rangda, all fangs and fingernails. With typical Balinese pragmatism, neither good nor evil is victorious, but, crucially, spiritual harmony will have been restored on the Island of the Gods.

886

Great dates and temple ceremonies

INDONESIA It's mid-afternoon and you're sitting in an outdoor café when suddenly the street is closed to traffic and a procession of villagers comes streaming by. Women with delicate frangipani blossoms woven into their hair balance lavish offerings of food, fruit and flowers on their heads and walk with grace and poise, while men march by playing musical instruments or sporting ceremonial swords. All are making their way to one of the village temples to honour its gods and celebrate the anniversary of its dedication.

Bali is home to over 10,000 temples of varying sizes, each one of which has a dedication ceremony at least once during the course of the Balinese year of 210 days. Each anniversary celebration, known as an *odalan*, is carried out on an auspicious date set by a local priest and usually lasts three days. In preparation the temple is cleaned, blessed and decorated with flowers, silk sarongs and colourful umbrellas. Women spend hours weaving elaborate headpieces and decorations from palm leaves while men carve ornate objects from wood. Streets leading to the temple are lined with vivid flags, banners and long, decorated bamboo poles (*penjors*) that arch overhead with woven garlands of dried flowers and ornaments fashioned from young palm leaves. Worshippers from around the island arrive en masse to celebrate with prayer, ceremonial dance, drama, musical performances and food to entice the gods and spirits.

Celebrations take place inside the temple walls: fragrant hair oils and smoke from sandalwood incense fill the air as the chimes of bells and the shimmering sounds of the gamelan orchestra electrify the atmosphere. In one corner worshippers kneel before an altar filled with offerings to recite prayers and be blessed with holy water and rice, while in another spectators are treated to an elegant dance of girls in golden costumes. Shadow-puppet performances recount ancient tales while barong dances ward off evil sprits. All this activity competes with the sizzling smells of saté being grilled over coconut husks and the laughter of lads gambling with cards.

887
Shopping at Chatuchak Weekend Market

THAILAND Want to feel like a local on a weekend in Bangkok? Then you need to go shopping. Specifically, you need to go to Chatuchak Weekend Market and spend a day rifling through the eight thousand-plus stalls of what some claim to be the world's biggest market. It's certainly a contender for the world's sweatiest and most disorientating, with a quarter of a million bargain-hunters crammed into an enormous warren of alleyways, zones, sections and plazas. The maps and occasional signs do help, but much of the pleasure lies in getting lost and happening upon that unexpected must-have item: antique opium pipe, anyone?

Alongside the mounds of secondhand Levi's and no-brand cosmetics you'd expect to find in Southeast Asia's most frantic flea market, there's also a mass of traditional handicrafts from Thailand's regions. Fine silk sarongs from the northeast, triangular cushions and mulberry-paper lamps from Chiang Mai, and hill-tribe jewellery and shoulder bags are all excellent buys here. But what makes Chatuchak such a shopaholic's dream is its burgeoning community of young designers. Many of Asia's new fashion and interior design ideas surface here first, drawing professional trend-spotters from across the continent.

The clothing zone is the obvious beacon, with its hundreds of mini-boutiques displaying radical-chic outfits and super-cute handbags, while the lifestyle zone brims over with tasteful ceramics and sumptuous furnishings.

Need a break from the achingly fashionable? Then wander through the pet section, perhaps lingering to watch Bangkokians' poodles getting their weekly grooming treatments, before enjoying a blast of natural beauty among the orchids and ornamental shrubs. You can treat your tastebuds for a handful of change at any number of foodstalls specializing in everything from barbecued chicken to coconut fritters, and there's even a tiny jazz café for that all-important chillout between purchases. And don't let aching feet call a premature end to the day: simply get yourself along to the foot-massage stall for a sit-down and a pamper.

888 | Breakfast in a Burmese teahouse

MYANMAR Eager tea boys dodge between the tables, slopping sweet tea into saucers and serving up sinful deep-fried snacks. Patrons air kiss loudly – as is the custom in Myanmar – to attract the staff's attention, keeping their eyes on the Premier League football on TV and their minds on teahouse gossip. Myanmar's teahouses are institutions, from the traffic-choked streets of Yangon to the dusty lanes of the smallest villages. Much as in London's eighteenth-century coffeehouses, locals rely on these simple cafés to catch up on the latest news and to discuss everything from Manchester United's most recent performance to national politics, all while relaxing over a cuppa.

Burmese people take their tea sweet and thick with condensed milk, and a special vocabulary has grown up to describe exactly what you want. *Paw cha* (strong and not too sweet), perhaps? Or *cho hseint* (sweet and milky)? Drinking black tea without sugar is not an option, although unsweetened thermoses of green tea from Myanmar's Shan State are placed on each table for free. Coffee drinkers have a choice between the ubiquitous mix – instant coffee, creamer and tooth-rotting amounts of sugar in a handy sachet – and *Bamar kaw-fi*, locally grown ground coffee served black with sugar and a fresh wedge of lime on the side, delicious and unexpectedly refreshing.

Once you've taken your seat, a tea boy will bring a selection of snacks to your table unasked. Fellow diners tear chunks off *cha kway* (Chinese-style deep-fried dough sticks) and dunk them in their tea, or slurp up bowls of Myanmar's national dish, *mohinga* (rice noodles in a savoury fish soup). Each teahouse has its own specialities and, given the rarity of English on the menus, once you've sampled the snacks on your table the best bet is to point-and-order whatever else takes your fancy.

When you air kiss for the bill, you'll only pay for what you've eaten or drunk. A table full of food and drink will set you back just pennies, making a serious *cha kway* and tea addiction alarmingly easy to sustain.

889 | Spotting the world's smallest primate in Tangkoko National Park

INDONESIA Shaped like a letter "K" wedged between Borneo and the Moluccas, the island of Sulawesi is a well-known paradise for wildlife-lovers. One of its best reserves is Tangkoko National Park, just a couple hours east of Manado, set next to a black-sand volcanic beach that marks the end of Sulawesi's northeastern tip. But the park's remote, stunning location isn't its main draw card.

The local star is the tarsius, or the world's smallest primate, which comes alive at dusk after lazy daylight hours spent sleeping inside hollow tree trunks. A prodigiously tiny mammal, it's a mix between a cute alien with huge, round eyes, and a mini-monkey that would fit into the palm of your hand. This highly endangered species survives only in Tangkoko and a few other Southeast Asian islands. Tiny tarsius awaken as soon as the sun goes down, zooming through the thicket like a bullet to chase their favourite diet of live insects. Don't fear if a hungry tarsius swivels its head 180 degrees to stare you in the eye: they don't eat humans, it's just the way their neck swings.

The tarsius isn't Tangkoko's only endemic superstar: your guide should be able to find a pack of long-faced macaca nigra, or black-crested macaques — from the clump of fuzzy hair sprouting at the top of their heads. It was one of these cheeky monkeys who shot the infamous "monkey selfie", starting the world-famous lawsuit that British photographer David Slater and PETA fought over the intellectual property of wildlife.

So keep your cameras around your necks, especially because there may be some bear cuscus ogling at you with piercing grey eyes from up above in the thicket. Tangkoko also has tropical birds galore, and a very swimmable volcanic beach — a postcard-perfect spot to start or end any visit to this incredibly diverse Indonesian island.

890 | Sniffing out the corpse flower

INDONESIA When the English naturalist Joseph Arnold smelled rotting flesh during an 1821 expedition to the steamy jungles of Sumatra, he must have feared the worst. Back then, this was cannibal country. Blood-thirsty local tribes were known to capture their most hated enemies, tie them to a stake, and start feasting on their roasted body parts. So imagine his surprise when he learned that the stench was coming not from a dead explorer, but a plant that produces the world's biggest flower. *Rafflesia arnoldii* (named after Arnold and Sir Stamford Raffles, who led the expedition) can produce blooms up to 1m across – and they carry the stink of death.

No surprise then, that Arnold's find has been nicknamed the "corpse flower" by those who've caught a whiff of it. There aren't many who can say they have, though – this is one of Southeast Asia's most endangered species. And despite each flower weighing in at around 11kg, they're notoriously difficult to come across.

They're parasitic, for one thing, and can only take root beneath the dark green tendrils of undisturbed grape vines. And even when a plant does begin to thrive, its meaty-red flower lasts just days. If you want to see one in bloom, you'll have to learn to follow your nose.

But why would a plant evolve to smell like rotting meat? Well, here in Sumatra, where the race for survival is tough, it pays to be ingenious. Flies are lured into the corpse flower's spongy interior by the promise of somewhere to lay their eggs, only to find they've been deceived.

When they eventually get bored, they'll take off in search of somewhere better. And maybe, just maybe, they'll drop pollen from one plant onto another. When you consider how unlikely this is to happen, you'll realize that your chances of seeing the corpse flower are pretty slim. But what better excuse to go sniffing around one of the last great rainforests?

891 | Yoga with a view – and then some

NEPAL Nepal and yoga seem to go hand in hand: with yoga's beginnings linked to Hinduism and over 80% of Nepalese identifying as Hindu, it's only natural that Nepal yoga retreats have become extremely popular. And that's without mentioning the stunning mountain scenery that immediately helps visitors feel detached from the hustle and bustle of everyday life. Whether you're a beginner or pro yogi, want a quick immersion or an extended stay, Nepal has some of the best yoga retreats around the world on offer.

One of the huge draws to Nepal is the opportunity for trekking and hiking in the Himalayas. For small hikes or going all out to Everest Base Camp, the snow-capped ragged peaks are among one of the greatest sights and most compelling experiences in the world. So, naturally, trekking and yoga came together.

Pokhara, Begnas Lake and even the Himalayas have a wide-range of yoga retreats available, while still allowing you to immerse yourself in these great surroundings. Whether you want to hike, swim, visit local coffee farmers or more, the plethora of retreats around the country allow you to make the most of your time in Nepal.

One yoga retreat allows you to trek the Everest region's sacred peaks and then practice yoga with a view over them, giving it an added spiritual element. The retreats up in the Himalayas can be some of the most challenging, too, as the high altitude affects your breathing – but it's worth it when you can see Everest while you're practising your warrior pose.

892 | Floating down the Irrawaddy reading Burmese Days

MYANMAR The Ayeyarwady River languidly curls its way down from the humid, rainforest-cloaked hills that range across the southern edge of the Himalayas. The river unfurls past the pagodas of Mandalay, curves around the temples of Bagan and slips south through Myanmar's arid heartland before dividing into thousands of smaller streams in the lush lands of the delta, finally spilling its silt-filled waters into the Andaman Sea.

Myanmar's most important waterway, the Ayeyarwady – better known abroad by its old Anglicized name, the Irrawaddy – is plied by a diverse range of craft, from stylish luxury steamers with teakwood decks and sumptuous cabins to uncovered and leaking longtail boats with throbbing engines. Unhurried, clanking government ferries – descendants of the Irrawaddy Flotilla Company's colonial-era steamboats – ply the river for most of its length, passengers setting up camp on the deck for the duration of their long, slow journeys. For those with less time on their hands, long thin motorboats also chug up- and downstream, their soundtrack of Burmese pop music echoing on the breeze long after they've passed.

While the stretch of river between Mandalay and Bagan attracts the most visitors, it's the upper reaches of the river between Bhamo and Katha (the latter being the inspiration for the fictional "Kyauktada" in George Orwell's Myanmar must-read, *Burmese Days*) that provide the best opportunity to mingle with local people and the most interesting glimpses of traditional Burmese village life. The gently rolling landscape makes a wonderful backdrop for the scenes that play out along the banks; children shout and splash in the chocolate-coloured water, elephants heave teak logs onto barges, and fishermen throw out their nets, which briefly catch the sunlight before sinking to the turbid depths.

Those same nets have contributed to a drop in the Ayeyarwady's most reclusive residents, the Irrawaddy dolphins. A 70km-long stretch of the river between Katha and Mandalay has now been set aside for their protection – keep your fingers crossed and your eyes peeled, and you may yet chance to see one…

893 | Climbing the stairway to heaven in Banaue

THE PHILIPPINES Lay them out end-to-end and they'd stretch from Scandinavia to the South Pole. No wonder the tribes of Ifugao province, in the beautiful northern Philippines, call the Banaue rice terraces their stairways to heaven.

The terraces are one of this country's great icons, hewn from the land two thousand years ago by tribespeople using primitive tools, an achievement that ranks alongside the building of the pyramids. Cut into near-vertical slopes, the water-filled ledges curve around the hills' winding contours, their waters reflecting the pale green of freshly planted rice stalks.

And unlike other old wonders of engineering, the terraces are still in the making after two millennia. Employing spades and digging sticks, generations of Ifugao farmers have cultivated rice on thousands of these mountainside paddies. Constantly guarding them against natural erosion, the farmers have fortified the terraces

with packed-earth and loose-stone retaining walls, supporting an elaborate system of dykes.

A few kilometres up the road from Banaue town is a popular lookout point that offers a sweeping vista down a wide valley with terraces on both sides. It's a great view, but it's not the only one. The only way to really get to know the landscape is on foot. Dozens of narrow paths snake their way past thundering waterfalls into a dazzling green hinterland of monolithic steps.

If you're looking for rural isolation and unforgettable rice-terrace scenery, the 15km trek from Banaue to the remote tribal village of Batad shouldn't be missed. Batad nestles in a natural amphitheatre, close to the glorious Tappia Waterfall. Accommodation here is basic, but it doesn't matter. In the semi-dark, after a long trek and a swim in the falls, you can sit on your veranda, listening to the the squawk of giant bats, transfixed by the looming silhouettes of the mountains.

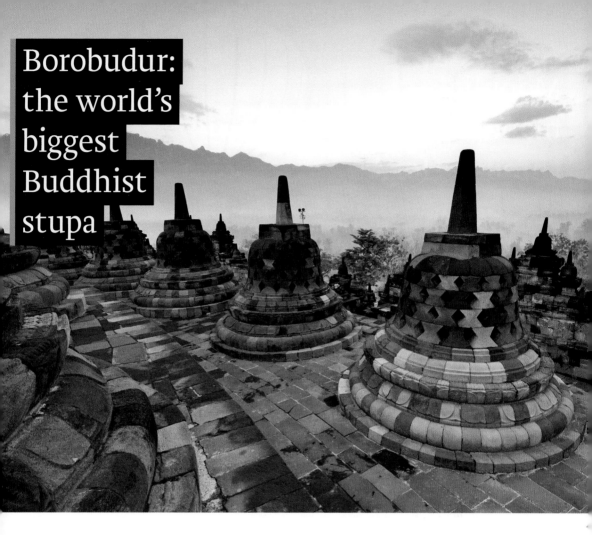

Borobudur: the world's biggest Buddhist stupa

894

INDONESIA On one level, the Buddhist monument at Borobudur is just one huge stone comic strip: the life of the Buddha told in a series of intricate reliefs carved around a gigantic stupa-shaped structure rising from central Java's fertile plains. But it's also a colossal representation of the Buddhist cosmic mountain, Meru. Built sometime around the ninth century AD by the short-lived Saliendra dynasty, occupying some 200 square metres of land and incorporating 1.6 million blocks of local volcanic rock, it is the largest monument in the southern hemisphere.

Much of Borobudur's appeal, however, comes not from its huge size but from the little details: the delicately sculpted reliefs, eroded down the generations but still identifiable and alive with warriors, maidens, the devout and the debauched, as well as elephants, turtles and other creatures. Beginning at ground level, pilgrims would walk clockwise around the monument, studying the frieze as they went, before moving up to the next level. Borobudur can be viewed as one enormous 34.5m-high educational tool: a complete circuit would take the pilgrims and monks, most of whom would have been illiterate, through the life of the Buddha.

Starting from his earthly existence, represented by the friezes on the first four tiers, it ends with his attainment of Nirvana (or "nothingness") at the tenth and top level, here represented by a large, empty stupa. The friezes on the first four "earthly" tiers are, on an artistic level, the most remarkable, but it is the upper five galleries that tend to linger in the memory, as the outside walls disappear, allowing you to savour the views over the lush Javanese plateau to the silent, brooding volcanoes beyond.

Moonlit manoeuvres through Hoi An

895

VIETNAM Once a month, on the eve of the full moon, downtown Hoi An turns off all its street lights and basks in the mellow glow of silk lanterns. Shopkeepers don traditional outfits; parades, folk opera and martial arts demonstrations flood the cobbled streets; and the riverside fills with stalls selling crabmeat parcels, beanpaste cakes and noodle soup. It's all done for tourists of course – and some find it cloyingly self-conscious – but nevertheless this historic little central Vietnam town oozes charm, with the monthly Full Moon Festival just part of its appeal.

Much of the town's charisma derives from its downtown architecture. Until the Thu Bon River silted up in the late eighteenth century, Hoi An was an important port, attracting traders from China and beyond, many of whom settled and built wooden-fronted homes, ornate shrines and exuberantly tiled assembly halls that are still used by their descendants today. Several of these atmospheric buildings are now open to the public, offering intriguing glimpses into cool, dark interiors filled with imposing furniture, lavishly decorated altars and family memorabilia that have barely been touched since the 1800s. Together with the peeling pastel facades, colonnaded balconies and waterside market, it's all such a well-preserved blast from the past that UNESCO has designated central Hoi An a World Heritage Site.

The merchant spirit needs no such protection, however: there are now so many shops in this small town that the authorities have imposed a ban on any new openings. Art galleries and antique shops are plentiful, but silk and tailoring are the biggest draws. Hoi An tailors are the best in the country, and for $200 you can walk away with an entire custom-made wardrobe, complete with Armani-inspired suit, silk shirt, hand-crafted leather boots and personalized handbag. And if you've really fallen under Hoi An's spell, you might find yourself also ordering an *ao dai*, the tunic and trouser combo worn so elegantly by Vietnamese women.

896 | Stalking the creatures of the night

SINGAPORE Darkness engulfs the sky, blanketing trees, the path and those out walking. From the mysterious shadows, sounds of people – breathing, treading on twigs, murmuring in the distance – filter through. Then suddenly an intimidating roar penetrates the din. Welcome to Singapore Zoo's night safari, the world's first nocturnal zoo.

Walk one of four trails – Fishing Cats, Wallabies, Leopards and East Lodge (African and Asian) – or jump on a tram and travel two road loops to catch oblivious nocturnal creatures going about their usual business. You might find the shadowy corners of the trails a little disorientating, especially when you look up to find yourself face to face with a giant flying squirrel. Unlike other zoos, where animals laze around waiting for a keeper to bring them their meal,

here you'll witness them actually prowling around hunting for their supper – this is about as close to a real safari as you can get within the confines of a zoo.

The safari park is broken into seven geographical zones, home to more than one thousand animals. In addition to the zones, there's an animal show, various shops and places to eat, and cultural performances (including highlights from Borneo tribal dancers).

Many of the walk-through exhibits are likely to get your heart pumping faster: in addition to the larger animals, the zoo is home to flying lemurs, owls and tree shrews, so if you're at all uneasy about having a creature flapping within centimetres of your face, this is not the place for you.

897 | Motorbiking the northwest loop

VIETNAM Vietnam's most spectacular mountain scenery is in the extreme north, shadowing the border with China. It's an astonishing landscape of evergreen mountains, plunging river valleys, high passes and hill-tribe villages. The bad news is that public transport is woefully inadequate and car rental costly, so two wheels are your best option. Main roads are virtually all paved, though there are rough sections.

The classic route begins in the featureless lowland town of Lao Cai, which is connected to Hanoi by highway and train. From here it's a three-hour run to Bac Ha, a lonely mountain village that hosts one of the best hill-tribe markets in Vietnam each Sunday. The stars of the show are the Flower Hmong women, who wear incredibly intricate hand-woven clothes made of Technicolor textiles.

The next leg of the trip entails a return journey to Lao Cai followed by a steep climb up to Sapa via some towering rice-paddy terraces. Sapa is a graceful old French hill station, replete with colonial architecture

and good restaurants. It sits on a high ridge overlooking a valley, and on clear days the views are sublime. Moving west from Sapa involves a precipitous climb up to the Tram Ton Pass (1900m), the high point on this journey, where you're virtually guaranteed a soaking from the rain clouds that permanently cling to the peaks.

On the western side of the pass the weather usually improves, and as the road descends in altitude you'll probably find yourself peeling off layers as the sun comes out. Eventually you'll reach a flat-bottomed valley where the villages are famous for their rice wine.

The next stretch to Dien Bien Phu is magnificent, as the road clings to the banks of a river valley, which narrows to squeeze through a limestone gorge in sections. Dien Bien Phu, where the Viet Minh inflicted an epochal defeat on the French in 1954, has some intriguing museums and battle monuments and is a great place to recharge and get your bike checked over, before heading back to Hanoi.

898 | Sailing the world's least-trawled seas by schooner

INDONESIA "Look to the left… whales!" says one of the crewmen as a pack of short, black fins emerges from the sea surface, just metres from the boat. We are aboard *Tiger Blue*, a luxury pinisi wooden schooner with blood-red sails. It was entirely custom-built by master ship-makers in Bira, adhering to the century-old Makassarese boat-making tradition of South Sulawesi, an intangible UNESCO heritage since 2017.

Not even fifteen minutes later, a curious dolphin leaves its pod to zoom ahead of the vessel's bow. Swimming fast, it rushes forward as if it wanted to show who's the real king of these forlorn seas. And for a good reason: the stretch of Pacific Ocean between Waigeo — better known as Raja Ampat, West Papua's most incredible collection of dive sites — and the northern Moluccas is still one of the least-visited in the world. This collection of sparse, scarcely populated islands hasn't changed much since the nineteenth century, when adventurer and scientist Alfred Russel Wallace braved these harsh seas. Doomed by

interminable doldrums, it took him over a month to reach his home-away-from-home in Ternate. Wallace had studied the colourful dance of the birds of paradise and collected specimens of the region's flora and fauna for years.

This knowledge helped him write the letter that pushed his good friend Charles Darwin to step off his feet in England and present the joint lecture that forever changed natural science as we know it. Today, charter vessels like *Tiger Blue* repropose the routes and the wild sea exploration of pioneers like Wallace. Whether sharing the deep waters with manta rays, or observing giant fruit bats fly from one empty isle to the other against a velvet-pink dusk, the feeling is that our planet still has plenty of power to amaze us.

Disembarking in volcanic Ternate, once a crucial spice-growing sultanate in the former East Indies, the cloves and nutmeg — and zero tourists — keep up the oceanic spell.

Sea-gypsies, turtles and frogfish

MALAYSIA Every diver who comes to Sipadan will see something that they haven't seen before. Famous for its large resident population of green and hawksbill turtles as well as healthy numbers of reef sharks and magnificent coral, Sipadan is Malaysia's only oceanic island. Sitting in the Sulu Sea off the northeastern coast of Borneo, it's also a great base for exploring the nearby shoals of Kapalai and the island of Mabul, well suited for voyeurs who are tantalized by the mating habits of mandarin fish and frogfish and other cryptic reef dwellers like sea-wasps. Above water, on Mabul you'll also meet the indigenous "sea-gypsies" – the Badjao – who live either in stilt-houses perched over the lagoon or on their tiny fishing boats which ply the Sulu Sea as far as the Philippines.

899

900 | All aboard the Eastern & Oriental Express

SINGAPORE–THAILAND First, tea is served. In a fancy teapot, with biscuits, by a butler dressed in pristine white uniform. You gaze lazily out of the window as porters labour in the crushing afternoon humidity, blissfully cool in your air-conditioned cabin. Then the train eases out of the station: the skyscrapers of Singapore soon fall away, and you're across the Straits of Johor and into the lush, torpid palm plantations of Malaysia.

This is the *Eastern & Oriental Express*, the luxurious train service that runs between Singapore and Bangkok, the last remnant of opulent colonial travel in Southeast Asia – evoking the days of the posh British administrators, gin-sloshed planters and rich, glamorous dowagers whom you might see on the set of a Merchant Ivory movie.

To be fair, you're more likely to meet professionals from San Francisco or Hong Kong on the train today. There are a few stops to break the three-day journey – a night-time stroll through Kuala Lumpur station, a rapid but absorbing tour of colonial Georgetown on Penang Island, and an evocative visit to the infamous bridge over the River Kwai – but it's the train itself that is the real highlight of this particular trip.

If you feel the need to stretch your legs, you can head for the observation car, which offers a 360-degree panorama of the jungle-covered terrain. And then there's the elegant dining car. Eating on the train is a real treat, with superb haute cuisine and Asian meals prepared by world-class chefs. Many travellers choose to wear evening dress to round off the fantasy and after dinner retire to the bar car, where cocktails and entertainment await, from mellow piano music to formal Thai dance. A word of warning: after all this, reality hurts. Standing on the chaotic platform of Bangkok's Hualampong station, you might long to get back on board.

901 | Volcanic activity: sunrise on Mount Bromo

INDONESIA It's not the most famous, the most active or the biggest volcano in the world, but Indonesia's 2392m-high Mount Bromo is one of the most picturesque – in a dusty, post-apocalyptic sort of way. The still-smoking and apparently perfectly symmetrical cone rises precipitously out of a vast, windswept, sandy plain. This is the Sea of Sand, actually the floor of an ancient crater (or caldera), stretching up to 10km in diameter and with walls towering some 300m high.

Though the locals will try to persuade you to take their horse, it's an easy enough walk to the summit, with no climbing ability required. Setting off an hour before sunrise, you follow a path across the Sea of Sand to the foot of Bromo's vertiginous cone. A small matter of 249 concrete steps up, past crowds of others with the same idea – it's one of Java's most popular attractions – leads to the crater rim and a view down onto the fumaroles belching noxious sulphuric fumes. But the rewards of climbing Bromo are not olfactory, but visual: if the gods of climate and cloud cover are on your side, a flamboyant golden sunrise awaits, casting its orange glow over the vast emptiness of the sandy basin, with Java's lush green landscape stretching to the horizon beyond.

902 | Diving the Four Kings

INDONESIA On Christmas Day 1857 Victorian naturalist Alfred Russel Wallace sailed through the islands off Papua New Guinea in a wooden outrigger *prau* and was stunned by the sight before him: "Few European feet had ever trodden the shores I gazed upon: limestone pinnacles rose from the depths and the sea ranged from emerald to lapis lazuli. I was in a new world, and could dream of the wonderful productions hid in those rocky forests and azure abysses."

Today these remote "azure abysses" offer some of the finest diving in the world. Centred around the islands of Raja Ampat (meaning the "The Four Kings" in Indonesian) is a vast patchwork of reefs unrivalled in its quality and diversity. Packing in more than 1700 species of fish (among them bizarre walking sharks and pygmy seahorses) and 600 types of coral, the area pulses with life and iridescent colour.

Instead of a humble bamboo-decked outrigger, modern travellers arrive in air-conditioned comfort on live-aboard boats bristling with state-of-the-art scuba kit. Trips take around twelve days to sample the pick of the dive sites, from manta cleaning stations where these ocean giants are groomed of parasites by tiny wrasse and butterfly fish, to challenging drift dives in the Dampier Strait, a vortex of nutrient-rich water attracting whale sharks and barracuda (beginners are advised to earn their fins somewhere calmer first).

Topside, you'll discover some of the most paradisiacal islands in the Seven Seas. At Wayag, Misool and Arborek those bleached white beaches, swaying palms and razor-sharp cliffs jutting from the sea resemble nothing as much as movie sets from *King Kong*. A day spent paddling a kayak in their turquoise lagoons will reveal baby reef sharks and shimmering schools of sweetlips and surgeon fish darting below you.

Look up and you might find neon-green honeyeaters flitting through the air and sea eagles soaring above. Just remember to pack a pair of binoculars along with your dive mask.

903

Island-hopping in the Bacuit archipelago

THE PHILIPPINES If you thought Alex Garland's tropical-island classic *The Beach* was inspired by Thailand, think again; it was the Philippines, particularly the spectacular islands and lagoons of the Bacuit archipelago in Palawan. It's not hard to see why Garland was so bewitched by this place: 45 stunning limestone specks rise from an iridescent sea. Most have exquisite palm-fringed beaches, so you shouldn't have too much trouble finding your own piece of paradise for the day. All you need to do is pack yourself a picnic, hire yourself an outrigger boat – known locally as a *banca* – and ask the boatman to do the rest.

Start by chugging gently out to Miniloc Island, where a narrow opening in the fearsomely jagged karst cliffs leads to a hidden lagoon known as Big Lagoon, home to hawksbill turtles. A couple of minutes away, also at Miniloc, is the entrance to Small Lagoon,

which you have to swim – or kayak – through, emerging into a natural amphitheatre of gin-clear waters and the screech of long-tailed macaques.

Other islands you shouldn't miss? Well, take your pick. Pangalusian has a long stretch of quiet beach; Tres Marias has terrific snorkelling along a shallow coral reef; and Helicopter Island (named after its shape) has a number of secluded sandy coves where your only companions are monitor lizards and the occasional manta ray floating by.

The culmination of a perfect day's island-hopping should be a sunset trip to Snake Island, where you can sink a few cold San Miguels (take them with you in an ice box) and picnic on a slender, serpentine tongue of perfect white sand which disappears gently into shallow waters that are ideal for swimming.

904 | The buzz around Chiang Mai

THAILAND The motorbikes of Chiang Mai are beautiful things. Renting them is easy and cheap, and they let you get around like a local, even if you have a poor sense of direction. Pick a morning, strap on your fisherman pants from the night market and, if you're brave, make room for a friend. Fly east to hilltop Wat Doi Saket to have your mind blown by trippy murals teaching Buddhist morality – illustrated with traffic signs. Buzz back along the "Handicraft Highway" to visit paper, celadon, wood and silk workshops. South of the city, get lost among the ancient *chedis* of Wiang Kum Kam, then rocket north to canoodle with baby elephants and watch their mothers make modern art at Mae Sa Elephant Camp.

Once you've got the hang of all this, zibp west up Doi Suthep mountain for lovely views of the countryside. If the bike's motor hasn't turned your legs to jelly, climb the three hundred stairs to Wat Phra That Doi Suthep, ding the bells in the courtyard for good luck – and beware speeding *songthaew* buses on the way back down.

905 | Long live the emperor: the imperial mausoleums of Hué

VIETNAM The broad, peaceful outer courtyard sweeps you past an honorary guard of immaculate stone mandarins towards the first of a series of elegantly roofed gateways, through whose triple doorways you get a perfectly framed view of Emperor Minh Mang's mausoleum complex. Archways look wistful in peeling ochre paint; slatted lacquer-red shutters offer tantalizing angles on lotus ponds, pavilions and artfully placed bonsai trees; and ceramic rooftop dragons add a touch of kitsch in pastel pinks, greens and yellows. Look carefully and you'll see the Chinese character for "longevity" picked out in blue, red and gold – Minh Mang, who designed his own mausoleum, left nothing to chance.

906 | Vietnam by night train

VIETNAM Known as the Reunification Express, Vietnam's north–south line was built by the French when the region was part of French Indochina. Badly damaged by constant bomb attacks during the Vietnam War, it reopened in 1975 after the fall of Ho Chi Minh City (then Saigon) – and now I'm using it to navigate Vietnam's coastal towns.

The first leg of my trip is from Ho Chi Minh to Nha Trang. After a night in a four-bed cabin, I wake at 7am, just in time to stumble off the sleeper train at the popular resort town. Backed by mountains, Nha Trang borders a wide sandy bay and bursts to the brim with backpackers. After two days' exploring, it's back on the train and northwards to Hué, with its old citadel walls wrapping around a vast complex of temples, shops and museums.

After a brief interlude in UNESCO-listed Hoi An, I'm back on a train to Hanoi. Here, I explore the dizzying ancient quarter, a knot of lanes lined with craft shops selling everything from bamboo baskets to paper lanterns. Heading south of here, I swap the commotion for the relative calm of Hoàn Kiem Lake, where people go to exercise, play chess or relax.

And 726kms later, my journey is over – but my love of Vietnam has just begun.

907 | Discovering the City of Victory

LAOS Your eyes narrow as you step out of the caves and into the skin-warming glow of the early morning sun. Up ahead, ribbons of mist gradually melt away, revealing a maze of sheer limestone walls, tangled with knotted vines and scarred by something unnatural. And then you hear jet engines: the terrifying sound of the sky being ripped in half.

For the leaders of the Communist Pathet Lao and their supporters, who used these caves as their base, this sound meant imminent danger. For nine years during the USA's secret war in Laos they were bombed here – day in, day out – in what became one of history's heaviest aerial bombardments.

Join the stirring, sound-effect-filled audio tour of these vast caves, near the Vietnamese border in northeast Laos, and you'll get a powerful sense of what life was like for the people who sheltered here during the late 1960s and early 1970s. The deep, almost impregnable limestone caves provided protection from the American assaults and allowed everyday life to continue – albeit in a most unusual fashion.

In one cave, you'll see where Pathet Lao's politburo gathered for talks. Then there's the ultra-austere office of Kaysone Phomvihane (who later became prime minister), still protected from the outside world by a super-thick concrete blast wall.

But it wasn't only high-ranking leaders who used the caves. Around twenty thousand soldiers and staff were based in the area during the American onslaught. Local people farmed the surrounding fields at night and cooked under the cover of darkness, hiding pots and pans in small caves afterwards for fear they'd be spotted. The caves were eventually expanded to house printing presses, hospitals, schools, a cinema and an enormous hall for weddings and parties.

When the air raids eventually stopped, in 1973, American boasts about bombing the enemy "back to the Stone Age" held a bitter irony. By hiding out like cavemen, the Pathet Lao had managed to hold back the most powerful nation on Earth. And after the conflict, the Communist stronghold was given a new name: *Vieng Xai*, City of Victory.

908 | A night in the rainforest

MALAYSIA You probably won't get much sleep on your first night in Taman Negara National Park – not because there's an elephant on your chalet doorstep or the rain's dripping through your tent, but because the rainforest is unexpectedly noisy after dark. High-volume insects whirr and beep at an ear-splitting pitch, branches creak and swish menacingly, and every so often something nearby shrieks or thumps. Taman Negara is a deceptively busy place, home to scores of creatures including macaques, gibbons, leaf monkeys and tapirs, as well as more elusive tigers, elephants and sun bears. Not to mention some three hundred species of birds and a huge insect population.

Many rainforest residents are best observed after dark, either on a ranger-led night walk or from one of the tree-house hides strategically positioned above popular salt licks. But a longer guided trek also offers a good chance of spotting something interesting and will get you immersed in the phenomenally diverse flora of Taman Negara, which supports a staggering 14,000 plant species, including 75m-high tualang trees, carnivorous pitcher plants and fungi that glow like lightbulbs. The rewarding six-hour Keniam–Trenggan trail takes you through dense jungle and into several impressive caves, while the arduous week-long expedition to the cloudforests atop 2187m-high Gunung Tahan involves frequent river crossings and steep climbs.

With minimal effort, on the other hand, you can ascend to the treetops near park headquarters, via a canopy walkway. Slung some 45m above the forest floor between a line of towering tualang trees, this swaying bridge offers a gibbon's perspective on the cacophonous jungle below.

909 | Mopeds and magic

THE PHILIPPINES The islands of the Philippines are so friendly and laidback that independent travel is a breeze. A moped is ideally suited to exploring a place where so much life is lived outdoors. Pick a smaller island like Siquijor and you don't even need a map, and although there aren't many filling stations, you're never far from a village store where you can buy soft drinks, snacks and huge Pepsi bottles full of petrol.

Cruising around at a leisurely pace, it's hard not to smile back at the succession of children yelling greetings, as the sun gently warms your back and the wind cools your face. Between villages on the coastal road you'll pass green fields and drive over carpets of rice that have been laid out to dry on the hot road surface. Everywhere, you'll see jeepneys: artistically decorated buses, covered in chrome and neon, and packed with schoolchildren, farmers, businessmen, and sacks crammed with food.

Head into the jungled interior, and it gets much quieter. Here, the dark tunnels of vegetation and trees that you drive through suggest a hint of Siquijor's reputation throughout the Philippines as a centre for witchcraft and healers (it's possible while you're here to arrange a session with a shaman to consult on anything from bad luck to kidney problems).

You'll also find unexpected panoramic views of the sparkling sea. And near the unfortunately named village of Poo, there's a sequence of waterfalls where you'll have to negotiate your way between local children somersaulting into the plunge pools.

Siquijor is pleasantly quiet, and has wonderfully clear beaches. But it also has just the right amount in common with other places: at the end of the day, there's always an opportunity to watch the sun set from a bar, sipping a cold San Miguel beer, with your toes in white sand.

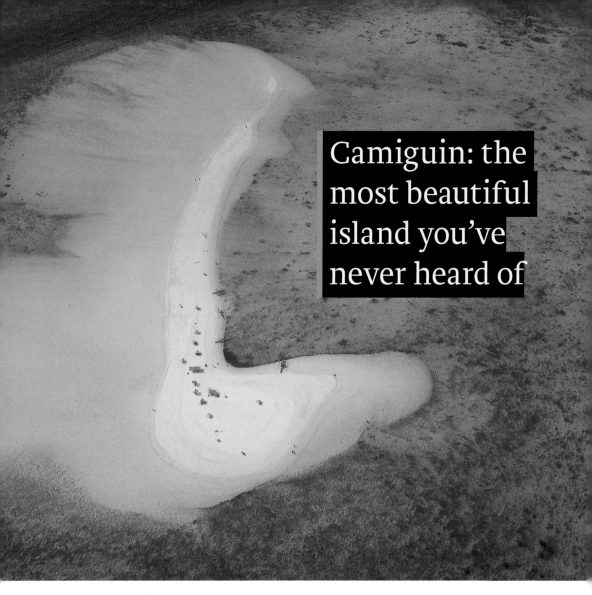

Camiguin: the most beautiful island you've never heard of

910

THE PHILIPPINES The peaceful, unruffled island of Camiguin, located around 20km off the north coast of mainland Mindanao, is one of the country's most appealing beach escapes. That it's under the radar, a world apart from the bumper-to-bumper resorts of Boracay and Alona Beach, is reason enough to put it at the top of your travel list. Camiguin offers the best of the Philippines in a microcosm: ivory-white beaches, bubbling hot springs, jungle cascades, perma-grinning islanders and quirky festivals. There's also no shortage of adventure, with unbeatable scuba diving (you can spot sharks, turtles, giant clams, even a sunken, underwater cemetery within metres of the shoreline) and bucket-list volcano trekking. In particular, don't miss summiting Mount Hibok-Hibok, a 1332m-high cone that offers spellbinding views across the island.

911 | Take a slow boat down the Mekong

LAOS Cargo-hold hell used to be the order of the day for travellers taking the slow boat through Laos, squashed between chickens and sacks of rice. But the ride's become so popular that there are now specially designed backpackers' boats running the 300km route from the Thai border east to Luang Prabang. They even have proper seats and a toilet – both pretty handy when you're spending two long days on the river. It's still a cramped, bottom-numbing experience, though, with over a hundred passengers on board, and an average speed that's very slow indeed.

In truth you wouldn't expect a trip on Southeast Asia's longest and most important river to be plain sailing. Here in northern Laos, approximately halfway down the river's 4000km journey from its source on the Tibetan plateau to its delta in southern Vietnam, the Mekong is dogged by sandbanks and seasonal shallows. It can be tough to navigate, as passengers in the hurtling, accident-prone speedboats often discover. Better to take it slowly: bring a cushion and enjoy the ride.

Little about the river has changed over the decades. The Mekong has always been a lifeline for Laos, Southeast Asia's only land-locked nation, and villagers continue to depend on it for fish, irrigation and transport, even panning its silt in search of gold. Limestone cliffs and thickly forested hills frame its banks, with riverside clearings used for banana groves, slash-and-burn agriculture and bamboo-shack villages. The largest of these, Pakbeng, marks the journey's midpoint, where everyone disembarks for a night on dry land.

A ramshackle place for such an important river port, Pakbeng offers an unvarnished introduction to Laos, with rudimentary guest-houses, basic restaurants and patchy electricity. Roll on the civilized comforts of Luang Pragang, a mere eight hours downriver.

912 | Finding a beach of your own in Dawei

MYANMAR For much of the last fifty years Tanintharyi, Myanmar's southernmost region, was a tricky place to get to. Foreign travellers were restricted to flying in and out of the three main towns (Dawei, Myeik and Kawthaung), and day-trips anywhere else required a sheaf of permits from Yangon or the capital Naypyidaw. Tantalizing rumours of the Myeik Archipelago's islands leaked from the handful of visitors who made it that far on Thai dive tours – James Bond-esque tales of island military bases, crony-owned casinos and semi-aquatic sea gypsies – but the mainland beyond was largely unknown.

In 2013 these official travel restrictions were relaxed. Between Myeik and Kawthaung you still need to take one of the motorboats that scud over the Andaman Sea (passing palm-edged islands and scaring up shoals of flying fish – a rare instance of official restrictions being anything other than an inconvenience), but elsewhere you're free to explore.

Skip the Myeik Archipelago, the area's best-known destination, and head north to the area around the laidback town of Dawei. The coast here is beautiful, varied, and (as yet) completely undeveloped – there are no hotels, no beach bars and few other people. Beaches range from 11km stretches of sand to tiny coves where palm-thatched fishing villages run right down to the water. With a motorbike, a full tank of petrol and a sense of adventure you can beach-hunt at will.

The only shadow on the sun-drenched horizon is the question of how long Dawei's alluringly untouched coastline will remain intact. Local people tell of mysterious businessmen buying up swathes of the shore for a pittance in preparation for a future property boom. Myanmar's government has grand plans for Dawei itself, too, with a vast deep-sea port planned just north of the town.

For now, however, while the port project is mired in financial trouble and the property boom has yet to materialize, it's still possible to rent a fishing boat and cruise from beach to beach, lose yourself down sandy tracks, and sit alone at seaside pagodas, gazing at the sky-blue sea.

913 | The revolting kings of Komodo

INDONESIA There are few expeditions more disquieting than visiting Indonesia's Komodo Island. Approaching by boat, it appears staggeringly beautiful – the archetypal tropical hideaway. But doubts about the wisdom of what you're about to do surface as soon as you step ashore and discover that you're sharing the beach with the local deer population: if they're too frightened to spend much time in the interior, is it entirely wise for you to do so?

Your unease only grows at the nearby national park office, as you're briefed about the island's most notorious inhabitant. From the tip of a tail so mighty that one swish could knock a buffalo off its feet, to a mouth that drips with saliva so foul that most bite victims die from infected wounds rather than the injuries themselves, Komodo dragons are 150kg of pure reptilian malevolence.

They are also – on Komodo at least – quite numerous, and it doesn't take long before you come across your first dragon, usually basking motionless on a rock or up a tree (among an adult dragon's more unpleasant habits is a tendency to feed on the young, so adolescents often seek sanctuary in the branches).

So immobile are they during the heat of the day that the only proof that they're still alive is an occasional flick of the tongue, usually accompanied by a globule of viscous drool that drips and hangs from the side of their mouths. Indeed, it's this docility that encourages you – possibly against your better judgement – to edge closer to the creatures, until eventually those of sufficient nerve are almost within touching distance.

And it's only then, as you crouch nervously on your haunches and examine the loose folds of battle-scarred skin, the dark, eviscerating talons and the cold, dead eyes of this natural-born killer, that you can fully appreciate how fascinating these creatures really are. There genuinely is no animal as utterly, compellingly revolting on this planet.

Need to know

857 Nusa Lembongan dive centres such as Big Fish Diving (Ⓦ bigfishdiving.com) and World Diving (Ⓦ world-diving.com) offer half-day two-tank dives for around IDR600,000 (US$35–40). Manta rays are present at specific sites year-round, but dive destinations will be dictated by sea conditions.

858 Insensitive tourism has caused problems in hill-tribe villages, and exploitation by travel companies is widespread, so choose your trekking operator wisely. Recommended outfits in Chiang Mai include Eagle House (Ⓦ eaglehouse.com) and the Trekking Collective (Ⓦ trekkingcollective.com).

859 My Tho is a 90min bus ride from Ho Chi Minh City. Homestays can be arranged at local tourist offices.

860 Regular flights from Bali serve Flores' three main airports: Labuan Bajo, Maumere and Ende.

861 Classes are held twice daily at SITCA (Ⓦ go2westernaustralia.com/sitcanet), on Soi Colibri.

862 Kalibo is a 1hr flight south of the Philippine capital, Manila. Hotels are usually full for Ati-Atihan, so book well in advance.

863 Kinabalu Park is a 2hr bus ride from Kota. Book accommodation in advance. The Park headquarters (Ⓦ sabahparks.org.my) issues permits and organizes guides and porters.

864 Bukit Lawang (Ⓦ bukitlawang.com) is a 3hr bus journey from Medan. The sanctuary is only open to visitors; entry fee IDR150,000 (£8/US$11).

865 Philippines-based dive operators such as Dive Buddies (Ⓦ divephil.com) organize trips out of Puerto Princesa.

866 Luang Prabang is served by flights from Bangkok, Chiang Mai and Vientiane. You can also reach it by bus and boat from Vientiane and by boat from the Thai–Lao border at Chiang Khong/Houayxai.

867 For more on Lumpinee Stadium, see Ⓦ lumpinee-muaythai.com.

868 Contact (Ⓦ sarawaktourism.com) to arrange a stay in a longhouse.

869 Most people arrange all-inclusive tours of Ha Long Bay (Ⓦ whc.unesco.org) from Hanoi, about 150km away. April–Oct is the best time to visit.

870 Banyuwangi is the nearest large town to Ijen. The tourist board (Ⓦ eastjava.com) can organize trips in a 4WD. The path is easy to follow; it takes around 2hr to reach the summit.

871 The restaurant of the *Casa del Rio Hotel* in Melaka is open to non-guests and serves traditional sweet and savoury Nyonya dishes in pretty tiffin boxes at high tea (noon–4pm); see Ⓦ casadelrio-melaka.com.

872 Phang Nga Bay covers 400 square kilometres of coast between Phuket and Krabi. A reputable operator is Ⓦ johngray-seacanoe.com.

873 Daily public buses connect Luang Prabang and Vientiane with Phonsavan.

874 Bamboo bikes are available for rent from Bambike's fair-trade workshop on Plaza San Luis. Guided tours of Intramuros run regularly; Ⓦ bambike.com

875 Frequent buses run to Sepilok from the town of Sandakan (around 45min–1hr) on Borneo's northeastern coast. Both the Borneo Sun Bear Conservation Centre (Ⓦ www.bsbcc.org.my) and Sepilok Orangutan Rehabilitation Centre (Ⓦ orangutan-appeal.org.uk/about-us/sepilok-rehabilitation-centre) are open daily. Orang-utans are most frequently seen during the dry season (April–Nov).

876 Book a tour and/or stay and pick-ups at Ⓦ wildlifealliance.org/wildlife-release-koh-kong. You can also ask the CBET Visitor Centre in Chi Phat.

877 The easiest way to visit is to book a tour from Puerto Princesa. Independent travellers should take a bus to Sabang and buy a permit well in advance.

878 The Tuol Sleng Genocide Museum (Ⓦ tuolsleng.gov.kh/en; daily 8am–5pm) is off Street 113 on the southern fringes of Phnom Penh.

879 Kyaiktiyo, in the mountains 200km east of Yangon, is inaccessible during the rainy season; visit between Nov and March. You'll need to stay on the mountain if you want to catch sunrise or sunset – the trucks from Kinpun only run between 6am and 6pm. Try the *Mountain Top Hotel* (Ⓦ mountaintop-hotel.com).

880 Three islands have significant tourist facilities. The largest, Don Khong, is served by combined bus-and-boat services from Pakse and Champasak. From there, local boats run to the other islands. For more information on Laos, see Ⓦ tourismlaos.org.

881 One of the best places to experience Loy Krathong is in Sukhothai, the first Thai capital, 400km north of Bangkok, where the ruins of the ancient capital are lit up by fireworks.

882 Wat Phra Kaeo, or the Grand Palace, is open daily (8.30am–3.30pm). See Ⓦ bangkok.com.

883 See Ⓦ koh-thmei-resort.com, Ⓦ paradisebungalows.com and Ⓦ nomadslandcambodia.com.

884 Thailand's best old-style beach huts are *KP Huts*, scattered through a shoreside coconut grove on Ko Chang (☎ +66 84 077 5995); *Island Hut* on Ko Mak (☎ +66 87 139 5537); and *Bee Bee Bungalows* on Ko Lanta (☎ +66 81 537 9932, Ⓦ diigii.de).

885 Dance performances are staged nightly at Ubud Palace, about 30km from Bali's international airport.

886 Foreigners are invited to attend temple ceremonies; however, you must respect local customs and ensure you are appropriately dressed with a sarong, headpiece and footwear.

887 Chatuchak Weekend Market (Ⓦ chatuchak.org) is in north Bangkok.

888 A cup of tea or coffee in a Myanmar teahouse will cost just 500 *kyat* (US$0.50), a *cha kway* 200 *kyat* (US$0.20) and a bowl of *mohinga* 600 *kyat* (US$0.60).

889 The easiest way to reach Tangkoko is by private car, taxi or rental motorbike. Most hotels in Manado offer day-trips, but the tarsius is most active at dusk. There are several budget accommodations around park headquarters, where you pay 100,000 rupiah per person for a guided 3hr walk into the forest.

890 Tourists can hire a guide to point out the corpse flower from the office at the Batang Palupuh reserve, 12km north of Bukittinggi.

891 With Kamzang Journeys, you can trek the Everest region's sacred peaks and then practice yoga with a view over them, giving this yoga retreat an added spiritual element. Visit Ⓦ kamzangjourneys.com/nepal-journeys for more information.

892 At the time of writing, foreigners were not allowed on the stretch of river north of Bhamo. The best time to visit is during Upper Burma's brief winter and spring (Nov–Feb). For more information on the government's IWT ferries, visit Ⓦ iwt.gov.mm/en.

893 It's a bumpy 7hr bus ride from Manila to Banaue, where guides for treks can be hired.

894 Borobudur (Ⓦ borobudurpark.com) is served by frequent buses from Yogyakarta, 40km southeast, and can be visited as a day-trip. An overnight stay, however, allows you both to watch the sunset and to visit early the next day before the crowds arrive.

895 Hoi An is around 700km south of Hanoi. The nearest airport and train station are in Da Nang, a 30km taxi ride away.

896 For further information on Singapore Zoo's night safari, check out Ⓦ wrs.com.sg/en/night-safari.

897 Rent a bike in Hanoi: Off Road Vietnam (Ⓦ offroadvietnam.com) is highly recommended.

898 Tiger Blue (Ⓦ tigerblue.info) organizes all-inclusive sea-safari packages, with departures from different East Indonesian islands.

899 For more information on diving Sipadan, check Ⓦ visitborneo.com.

900 The train ride from Singapore to Bangkok costs around US$3500 one way – see Ⓦ belmond.com/eastern-and-oriental-express.

901 Mount Bromo is the main attraction of East Java's Bromo-Tengger-Semeru National Park. Many people stay in the nearby village of Cemoro Lawang, a 2hr bus drive from Probolinggo on Java's north coast.

902 Original Diving (Ⓦ originaldiving.com) offers trips to Raja Ampat year-round. The nearest airport is Sorong on the tip of West Papua (2775km east of Jakarta). Direct flights to Sorong are available with Garuda Indonesia from Makassar Airport on Sulawesi, which connects in turn with Singapore, Jakarta and Manado. See Ⓦ garuda-indonesia.com for schedules and more.

903 ITI offers daily flights from Manila to El Nido, departure point for the archipelago (Ⓦ itiair.com).

904 The nearest international airport is on Cebu island; the trip to Siquijor can be done in a day, by getting a bus to the south of Cebu, and then taking a ferry from Cebu to Siquijor. The best months to visit are Dec–May, outside the typhoon season.

905 The Minh Mang mausoleums are part of Hué's imperial city (Ⓦ whc.unesco.org).

906 Book train tickets in Vietnam at Ⓦ vietnamimpressive.com, and find timetable and fares information at Ⓦ vr.com.vn/en.

907 Around a dozen caves are open to the public. You can only visit them on a guided tour run by the Caves Visitor Centre in Vieng Xai (☎ +85 66 431 4321; daily 9am & 1pm; 2hr).

908 Taman Negara (Ⓦ wildlife.gov.my) is 250km from Kuala Lumpur and can be reached by bus or, more enjoyably, by train and boat.

909 Queen Bee (Ⓦ queenbeetours.com) in Chiang Mai has reliable motorbikes and insurance coverage.

910 Visit in October to see the Lanzones Festival, an insanely brilliant tribute to the local fruit, with revellers dressing up Rio Carnival-style.

911 Slow boats leave around 11am every day or when full, running between Houayxai on the Thai–Lao border and Luang Prabang. There is only one slow boat per day and in high season up to two boats.

912 For more information on Tanintharyi visit Ⓦ southernmyanmar.com. As long as you have your own transport Dawei is the most convenient place to stay.

913 Most trips to Komodo (Ⓦ komodonationalpark.org or Ⓦ komodo.tours) are organized from Labuan Bajo, on the coast of neighbouring Flores.

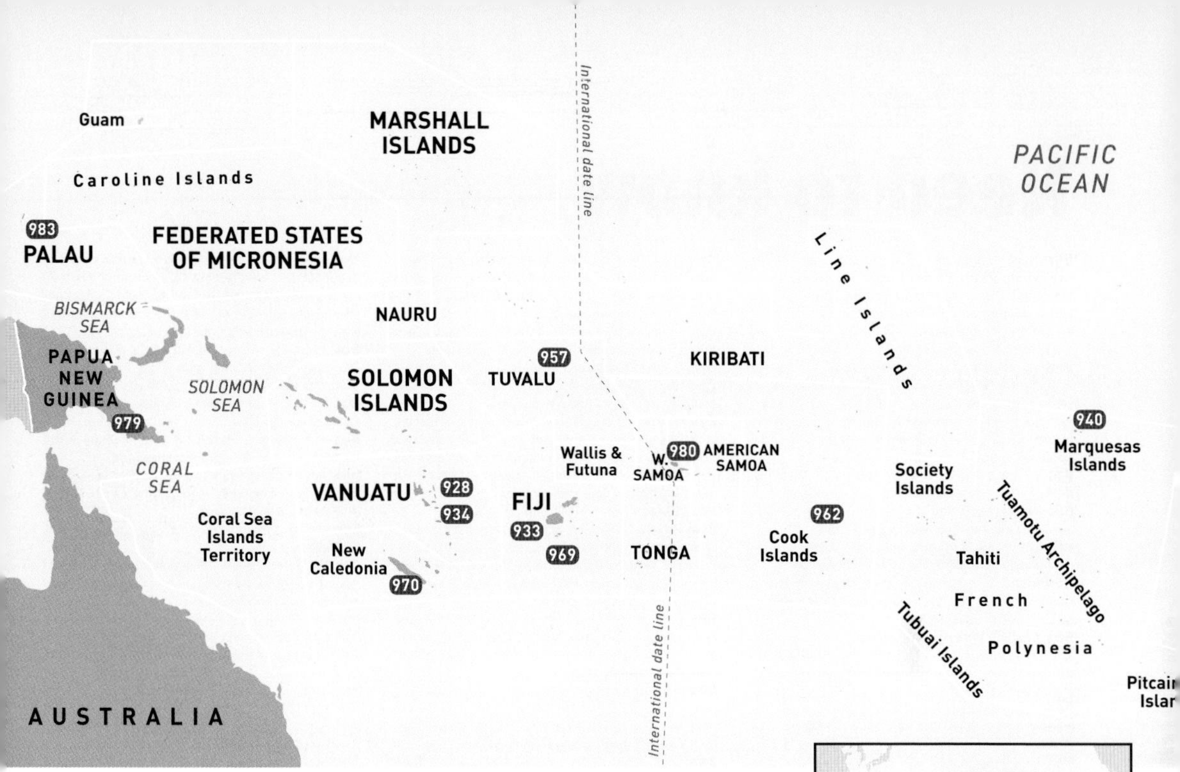

Guam

MARSHALL
ISLANDS

Caroline Islands

PACIFIC
OCEAN

International date line

983
PALAU

FEDERATED STATES
OF MICRONESIA

Line Islands

BISMARCK
SEA

NAURU

PAPUA
NEW
GUINEA

SOLOMON
SEA

SOLOMON
ISLANDS

TUVALU

957

KIRIBATI

940
Marquesas
Islands

979

CORAL
SEA

Wallis &
Futuna

980
W.
SAMOA

AMERICAN
SAMOA

Society
Islands

Tuamotu Archipelago

VANUATU

928

934

FIJI

Coral Sea
Islands
Territory

New
Caledonia

933

969

TONGA

962

Cook
Islands

Tahiti

French

AUSTRALIA

970

Polynesia

Tubuai Islands

Pitcair
Islar

PACIFIC
OCEAN

International date line

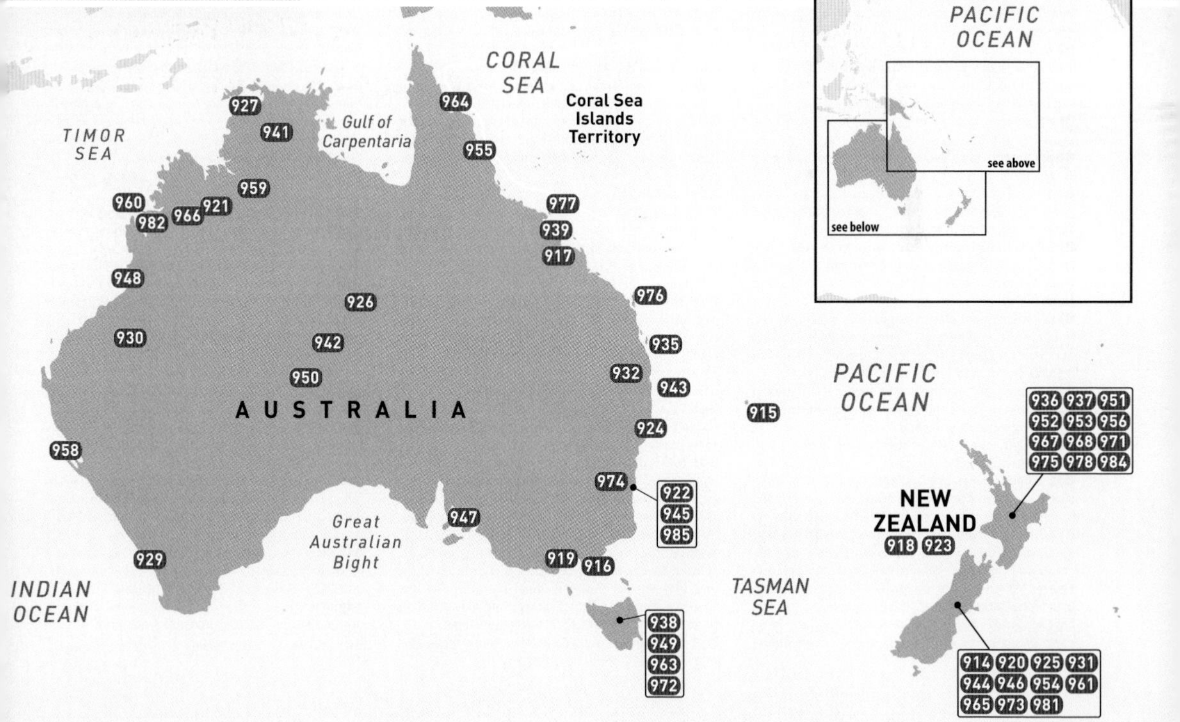

CORAL
SEA

Coral Sea
Islands
Territory

927

964

TIMOR
SEA

941

Gulf of
Carpentaria

955

see above

959

977

960

982

966

921

939

see below

948

917

926

976

930

942

935

PACIFIC
OCEAN

950

AUSTRALIA

932

943

936 937 951

924

915

952 953 956

958

Great
Australian
Bight

947

974

922

945

985

NEW
ZEALAND

967 968 971

975 978 984

929

919

916

TASMAN
SEA

918 923

INDIAN
OCEAN

938

949

963

972

914 920 925 931

944 946 954 961

965 973 981

AUSTRALIA, NEW ZEALAND & THE SOUTH PACIFIC

914-985

They've certainly got a good thing going Down Under. Proud ancient cultures and rousing widescreen landscapes provide a momentous backdrop, but they're just two central parts of a wider story – you'll also find cosmopolitan coastal cities, ready adrenaline kicks and a menagerie of weird and wonderful indigenous critters. From the snowcapped peaks of New Zealand's South Island to the tropical dive sites of Fiji, the sun-baked outback trails of Australia's Red Centre to the lush national parks of New South Wales, and the avant-garde art scene of Tasmania to the age-old Maori customs of Northland, there's a huge amount to love.

914 Getting high on the Gillespie Pass

NEW ZEALAND As I cling to the sheer cliff, with a 15kg pack pulling on my back, I know that I can't afford to put a foot wrong: one slip on the scree and I plummet 500m. Forget bungee jumping and speedboats – if you want white-knuckle New Zealand, climb the Gillespie Pass. Below me, the steely grey crags of the Young Basin are shrinking, while far above the almighty 2200m bulk of Mount Awful is looming ever larger. When it comes to names, the Kiwis certainly know how to pick 'em.

After a series of tight switchbacks, I finally reach the Gillespie Pass: a rocky saddle speckled with brilliant wildflowers and random patches of snow. The tremendous panorama of the Southern Alps spreads out in front of me, their peaks piercing the sky. Up here, only the shrill squawk of a lonesome kea shatters the silence. The feeling of being alone above the world is beyond words and a million miles away from New Zealand's more populated hikes. This is hardcore. As if to prove my point, a bitter wind blows across from Mount Awful, where threatening storm clouds are gathering. A hostile reminder that Siberia lies ahead.

The Siberia Valley is aptly named. Even when you're cocooned in a high-tech sleeping bag, the chill creeps in and grips you with its icy claws. Outside, the moon illuminates both the near-frozen river and the summit of Mount Dreadful (presumably Mount Awful's little brother).

Shivering and sleepy, the final test of my mettle is the uphill climb to Crucible Lake the next morning. The boulder-strewn trek is tough, but the lake is awesome: a glacier-gouged crater filled with turquoise water and chinking icebergs. It looks like an alpine pasture struck by a meteorite. New Zealand boasts many great walks, but if you're seeking the real deal, this has got to be it.

Kerry Christiani
is an award-winning travel writer and the author/co-author of more than a dozen guidebooks. She specializes in Europe, Morocco, hiking and adventure travel.

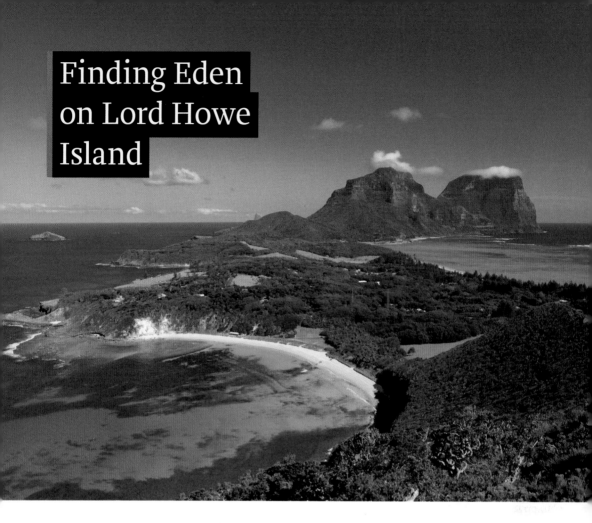

Finding Eden on Lord Howe Island

915

AUSTRALIA From the summit of Mount Gower, Lord Howe Island lies before you – a Pacific paradise of swaying palms and turquoise lagoons that feels more Polynesian than Australian, despite being part of New South Wales. Wonderful as they are, the views don't come easy. The early botanists who first scaled the peak took several days to machete their way up to the 875m summit, and the route is now a strenuous guided walk. You'll understand why you need a guide when you see the track – an unlikely slice across a cliff face with nothing but air between you and rocks far below. Once you've clambered your way to the top you'll be pulsing with adrenaline, even if the thought of the return journey can make lunch up here a quiet, contemplative affair.

Many visitors are perfectly content to skip the tough ascent of Mount Gower in favour of snorkelling among the fish and sponges of the world's southernmost coral reef, or strolling along the island's Malabar Cliffs, where red-tailed tropicbirds ride the thermals. Another nature show is on offer at Ned's Beach Marine Reserve. At low tide you can stand knee-deep amid a seething mass of metre-long king fish, which come in to be fed each afternoon. For a closer look, grab a mask and fins from the beachside shack where you drop a few dollars in the honesty box – on this island everyone knows everyone's business and no one locks their car or even takes the key out of the ignition.

After a sundown beer overlooking the lagoon, everyone returns to Ned's Beach at dusk to watch ungainly muttonbirds crash out of the sky, land at your feet, then waddle off unconcerned to their burrow in the woods. That kind of innocence chimes nicely on this slice of Aussie Eden.

916 | Walking with wombats in "The Prom"

AUSTRALIA Victoria is hardly short of spectacular places to while away a day or three. The self-styled Garden State packs in a tantalizing array of coastal panoramas, mountain ranges and wildlife-rich forests, all of which serve as slow-moving counterpoints to the cosmopolitan thrum of Melbourne. The likes of Phillip Island and the Great Ocean Road are firmly established on tour-group itineraries, but one place that sneaks under most travellers' radars is Wilsons Promontory, the fauna-rich national park that continues to attract more than ten times as many locals as it does overseas visitors.

Almost universally referred to as "The Prom", the 120,000-acre reserve sits some three hours' drive southeast of Melbourne, occupying the southernmost tip of the Australian mainland. What brings people here? The diverse landscapes are a big draw – combining beach-scalloped headlands, rainforest glades and purpled cliffs – and so too is the wildlife. Emus strut through grassland, wallabies hop across dunes, cockatoos wheel overhead.

If the park has a poster-boy, however, it's the humble wombat, a rotund barrel of fur and muscle combining teddy-bear looks with a keen nose for a bush-camp barbecue. The Prom is among the best places in Australia to encounter these dumpily lovable creatures, and while their habit of emerging at the smell of a grilling sausage makes them near-unavoidable in the main Tidal River campsite, you'll be better rewarded by spotting them on one of the park's excellent walking trails. The reserve has been repeatedly battered by storms over the years, so it's testament to its natural powers of restoration that it remains such a fantastic place to hike.

If you have the time (and the gear), the three-day Circuit Trail takes in swimming spots, remote headlands and a series of beautiful rocky outcrops. Those on a tighter schedule can opt instead for a two-hour round-trip climb of Mount Oberon or the three-hour hike out to secluded Millers Landing. For anyone with an interest in Australia's rightly famed wildlife and birdlife, there's a huge amount to enjoy.

917 | On the lookout for the duck-billed platypus

AUSTRALIA When the first dried, stuffed platypus specimens reached Britain from Australia, early in the nineteenth century, they were promptly dismissed by scientists as being a badly executed hoax, clearly made from bits of other animals sewn together. In fact, the truth was even weirder: not only do platypus genuinely look like a cross between a duck and an otter, but they lay eggs, an anomaly that required a whole new order of mammals – monotremes – to be created.

All the more reason, then, to head up to Queensland's Eungella National Park and make a point of tracking one down. Platypus live in rivers and are reasonably common, but as they're extremely timid, vanishing at the slightest movement, you'll need a lot of patience to see one – dusk and dawn are the best times to try.

A tried-and-tested tracking method is to follow the trail of mud rising off the bottom of a stream, caused as their rubbery bills rummage along the bottom in search of shrimps and beetles. Once they've found a beakful they bob to the surface to eat, lying flat on their fronts with their webbed feet splayed as they chew and glance nervously around – then it's a swift roll headfirst down to the bottom again.

Platypus are less than 30cm long, so your first reaction may be "they're not as big as I thought". In winter you might see a courting pair chasing each other in tight circles; after mating, the female walls herself into a burrow, dug into the bank above the water line, to wait for the young to hatch. If you're lucky, you might see them following her in a line, each holding the tail of the one in front.

918 | Witnessing the power of the haka

NEW ZEALAND Few spectacles can match the terrifying sight of the All Blacks performing a haka before a test match. You feel a chill down your spine 50m away in the stands; imagine how it must feel to face it as an opponent. The intimidating thigh-slapping, eye-bulging, tongue-poking chant traditionally used is the Te Rauparaha haka, and like all such Maori posture dances it is designed to display a mix of fitness, agility and ferocity.

This version was reputedly composed early in the nineteenth century by the warrior Te Rauparaha, who was hiding from his enemies in the sweet potato pit of a friendly chief. Hearing noise above, and then being blinded by the sun when the pit covering was removed, he thought his days were numbered. As his eyes became accustomed to the light, however, he saw the hairy legs of his host and was so relieved he performed the haka on the spot. It goes:

Ka Mate! Ka Mate! (It is death! It is death!)
Ka Ora! Ka Ora! (It is life! It is life!)

Tenei te ta ngata puhuru huru (This is the hairy man)
Nana nei i tiki mai whakawhiti te ra (Who caused the sun to shine)
A upane, ka upane! (Step upwards! Another step upward!)
A upane, ka upane! (Step upwards! Another step upward!)
Whiti te ra! (Into the sun that shines!)

Over the past decade or so, descendants of tribes once defeated by Te Rauparaha took umbrage at the widespread use of this haka at rugby matches, and consequently a replacement, the Kapa o Pango (Team in Black) haka, was devised. Numerous Maori experts were consulted over what form the haka should take, but controversy still surrounds the final throat-slitting gesture, which is supposed to symbolize the harnessing of vital energy. The Kapa o Pango and traditional Te Rauparaha haka are now used roughly equally, the uncertainty over what they'll be exposed to further unsettling the All Blacks' opponents. But whichever you manage to catch, both versions still manage to elicit that same spine-tingling response.

919 | Pamper your tastebuds at Queen Victoria Market

AUSTRALIA A visit to Queen Victoria Market, or "Vic Market", located on the northern fringe of the city centre, makes a superb introduction to Melbourne's vibrant food culture. Into the bargain, it will have you rubbing shoulders with everyone from government ministers to the city's best chefs. Established in 1878 and still going strong, it's one of the oldest markets in Australia, at its liveliest at weekends when buskers compete with spruiking stallholders for your attention.

Follow your nose to the deli section, characterized by its pungent smells and shops that sell such regional specialities as Jindi Triple Cream Brie and Milawa's tasty goat's cheese, as well as lesser-known fusions like kangaroo biltong (South African-style dried meat). Arrive hungry, and you'll find the free tastings will put a stop to the pangs just as fast as they tempt you to lighten your wallet. Greek, Italian, French and Polish stalls stock everything from marinated octopus to juniper sausage, while speciality butchers sell emu and crocodile.

If you're looking for more traditional meat offerings, head to the Meat and Fish Hall. Here, competition is fierce, with dozens of butchers supplying prime cuts from legs of lamb to Japanese-style Wagu beef, and fishmongers' stalls groaning under an impressive array of seafood that ranges from northern Australian wild barramundi to Victorian crayfish and fresh Tasmanian oysters.

Reflecting the shifting seasons, the fruit and vegetable market is dominated by root vegetables in winter and stone fruits during the summer – the proximity of Southeast Asia means exotic fruits like mangosteens, rambutan and the pungent-smelling durian are also available to buy.

If you're after something less epicurean, however, you can always venture over to the German Bratwurst shop to sample a sauerkraut and mustard-covered sausage, or head for the American Doughnut Van, which serves up irresistible bags of jam-filled indulgence for a few dollars.

920 | Supping wine in sun-drenched Marlborough

NEW ZEALAND When Marlborough's Cloudy Bay Sauvignon Blanc hit the international wine shelves during the late 1980s, its zingy fruitiness got jaded tongues wagging. All of a sudden New Zealand was on the world wine map, with the pin stuck firmly in the north of the South Island. While half a dozen regions now boast significant wine trails, all roads still lead back to Marlborough, which remains the country's largest grape-growing area, protected by the sheltering hills of the Richmond Range, and blessed with more than 2400 hours of sunshine a year.

Cellar doors around the region are gradually becoming more sophisticated, with their own restaurants and specialist food stores, but the emphasis is still mainly on the wine itself. And tasting it. To squeeze the very best from the area, start by visiting Montana Brancott,

the biggest and most established operation hereabouts. Take their winery tour to get a feel for how wine is made nowadays, then stick around for a brief lesson on wine appreciation. Even visitors familiar with the techniques will learn something of the qualities Marlborough winemakers are trying to achieve.

Next visit Cloudy Bay. Of course you'll want to try the famous Sav, still drinking well today and available for tasting. Somehow it always seems that little bit fresher and fruitier when sampled at source out of a decent tasting glass.

Come lunchtime, head for Highfield Estate, with its distinctive Tuscan-style tower, and dine in the sun overlooking the vines. A plate of pan-seared monkfish is just the thing to wash down with their zesty Sauvignon Blanc.

921 | Buzzing over the Bungle Bungles

AUSTRALIA If you've never been in a helicopter then a flight over Purnululu National Park – or the Bungle Bungles, as most people know it – makes a great initiation. This mass of orange and black striped beehive-like domes is amazing enough at ground level, but leaning out of the doorless cockpit, your foot on the landing rail, you'll have a grin as wide as the Fitzroy River as you swoop and soar over the maze of 200m-deep chasms between the "bungles". At one point you launch low off the plateau and in an instant the ground disappears, sending your stomach spiralling after it.

Each dome ranges from 10 to 40m high, but in total they cover only a small proportion of the park's 25,000 square kilometres of lightly wooded hills and pockets of grassland. While Purnululu has been a sacred site to local Aboriginal people for millennia, the wonders of this remote region of northwestern Australia were only fully acknowledged during the 1980s, when a TV crew came across it while filming a documentary.

Recognizing these curious rock formations to be geologically unique, Purnululu National Park was created in 1987, with access deliberately restricted to small aircraft or high-clearance vehicles able to negotiate the twisting 53km access track.

The origin of the domes is still unclear. The theory that a meteor impact shattered the rock into the now-weathered segments takes a knock when one sees mini-bungle formations elsewhere in the Kimberley. A more mundane, but all the more likely, explanation is that they're the result of deposition, uplifting and subsequent erosion. The banding, on the other hand, clearly illustrates aeons of alternating sediments: the orange deposits (iron oxide) are not porous, while the rock above and below holds water and supports the fragile-looking crusts of black lichen.

And "fragile" may well describe your knees as you climb out of the helicopter and wobble across the launch pad. Now you've seen them from the air it's time for a closer inspection on foot.

Walking on the wild side at the Sydney Mardi Gras

922

AUSTRALIA Sydney is probably the world's most LGBTQ-friendly city, and its annual Gay & Lesbian Mardi Gras Parade is a huge red- (or should that be pink?) letter day, drawing a bigger crowd than any other annual event in Australia. In essence, it's a full-on celebration of LGBTQ culture, and a joyous demonstration of pride; but it's also enjoyable for people of any sexuality, provided partial nudity, G-strings, wild unleashings of inhibitions and senseless acts of kindness don't offend.

The parade route runs from Hyde Park, through the city's gay quarter, to Moore Park. Pumped-up marshals, searchlights, flares, fireworks, strobes and dance music from all the nearby clubs bring the throng to a fever pitch of anticipation – a perfect build-up to the gleaming Harley-Davidsons of the Dykes on Bikes, who have heralded

the start of the parade for many years. Vast floats, effigies and marching troupes follow in their wake – everything from two hundred drag Madonnas in cowgirl hats, to three hundred Barbara Cartlands in pink-sequined evening gowns, or mist-enshrouded boats carrying Thai princes and princesses. Up to half a million spectators of every age and gender line the route as the ten thousand participants float, shimmy or line dance their way past.

Afterwards, Australia's biggest parade is followed by Australia's biggest party at Moore Park Entertainment Quarter. Tickets sell out fast, and touts will ask exorbitant prices. Whatever your sexuality, it's a pretty decadent affair, and – how can we put this? – voyeurs are not encouraged. But even if you can't get in, just wander along the gay strip and the chances are you'll find every bar is jumping, and just as much fun as the last.

923 | Tucking into a hangi

NEW ZEALAND A suitably reverential silence descends, broken only by munching and appreciative murmurs from the assembled masses – the hangi has finally been served. Pronounced "hungi", this traditional Maori meal, similar to the luau prepared by the Maori people's Polynesian kin in Hawaii, is essentially a feast cooked in an earth oven for several hours. It can't be found on restaurant menus – but then again a hangi is not just a meal, it's an event.

First of all, the men light a fire. Once that has burned down, carefully selected river stones that don't splinter are placed in the embers. While these are heating, a large pit is dug, measuring perhaps 2m square and 1.5m deep. Meanwhile the women are busy preparing lamb, pork, chicken, fish, shellfish and vegetables (particularly kumara, the New

Zealand sweet potato). Traditionally these would have been wrapped in leaves and then arranged in baskets made of flax; these days baking foil and steel mesh are more common.

When everything is ready – the prep can take up to three hours – the hot stones are placed in the pit and covered with wet sacking. Then come the baskets of food, followed by a covering of earth that serves to seal in the steam and the flavours.

There's a palpable sense of communal anticipation as hosts and guests mill around chatting and drinking, waiting for the unearthing. Eventually, a few hours later, the baskets are disinterred, to reveal fall-off-the-bone steam-smoked meat and fabulously tender vegetables with a faintly earthy flavour. A taste, and an occasion, not easily forgotten.

924 | Visiting the Port Macquarie Koala Hospital

AUSTRALIA Few Australian animals are more endearing than a koala, wedged into a eucalyptus tree, blissfully asleep. You'll always find plenty in exactly this pose at the Port Macquarie Koala Hospital, thereby enabling you to compare their size, colouring and general fluffiness, and perhaps guess at their personalities. What makes the encounter truly poignant, though, is the fact that almost all are survivors of illness, road accidents or dog attacks.

Founded in 1973 and run by experienced koala carer Cheyne Flanagan, along with five eucalyptus-leaf collectors and a squadron of volunteers, the Koala Hospital has a treatment room, intensive care units and rehabilitation yards in which recovering koalas can brush up their climbing skills. Every area is beautifully kept and viewable, either through windows or fences.

In New South Wales, unlike in Queensland, state laws forbid members of the public to handle koalas, no matter how huggable they may seem. However, at certain times of day, volunteers hoick amenable individuals down from their snoozing places and carry

them over to the waiting visitors, so you can see the little battlers up close.

While it's a wonderful privilege to be able to stare into the sleepy eyes of such a reclusive animal, it's tragic that the hospital is so badly needed. Every year, it treats between 200 and 250 koalas, many of them orphans. Rehabilitation is always the aim, but some, inevitably, don't make it.

Local support for the hospital runs high: in 2014, Port Macquarie launched a Cow-Parade-style sculpture trail, called Hello Koalas, to celebrate the town's koala connections. Each of the fifty fibreglass koalas on the trail was decorated by a celebrity or a community group. Visiting the hospital costs nothing, though if you want to keep it ticking along, you're welcome to make a donation. The volunteers also run a tree-planting fund. For every A\$15 paid in, they plant a tallowwood, swamp mahogany or forest red gum tree – all favourite koala food sources – in the hope that, in time, more koalas will have the chance to live safer lives, far from roads and dogs.

925 | Tramping the Milford Track

NEW ZEALAND You're going to get wet on this tramp. In fact it would be disappointing if you didn't. When the heavens open it seems like the hills are leaking; every cliff face springs a waterfall, and the rivers quickly become raging torrents.

The Milford Track lies in Fiordland National Park which gets at least 5m (yes, metres) of rain a year, making it one of the wettest places on Earth. But unless you are really unlucky it won't rain the whole time. Blue skies reveal a wonderment of magical scenery, which explains why this four-day hike (or "tramp", as the locals call it) has become the most popular in the country.

The highest point, in terms of both altitude and views, comes at the 1073m Mackinnon Pass. Deep glaciated valleys drop steeply away on both sides while weather-worn mountains rear up all around. It's a great place to eat your lunch, always keeping a wary

eye out for kea, New Zealand's cheeky alpine parrot, which will be off with your sandwiches given even a quarter of a chance.

From the pass, it's possible to see most of the Milford Track route. Behind you lies the valley of the Clinton River, along which you've just spent a day and a half tramping, after being dropped off by a small launch on the shores of Lake Te Anau. Ahead is the Arthur River, where the rain puts on its best display with two spectacular waterfalls. The story goes that when blazing the route in 1880, explorers Donald Sutherland and John Mackay came upon one magnificent fall and tossed a coin to decide who would name it, on the understanding that the loser would name the next one. Mackay won the toss but rued his good fortune when, days later, they stumbled across the much more famous and lofty Sutherland Falls, at 580m the tallest in New Zealand.

926 | Getting to grips with Aboriginal art

AUSTRALIA You don't need in-flight entertainment when you're flying across Australia because the view from the plane is always diverting. The endless, barely inhabited Outback spreads before you like a vast natural canvas: ivory-coloured saltpans merge into clumps of grey-green scrub; sienna, ochre and russet sands expand to the horizon, broken only by the occasional dead-straight line of an oil exploration track or the wiggle of a long-dried watercourse. It's like one enormous abstract picture and, in part at least, that's what informs many Aboriginal artworks, particularly the so-called dot paintings.

Practices for surviving in the extreme conditions of the Outback, and the need to pass on this knowledge to descendants, lie at the heart of many Aboriginal traditions. Historically, one way to do that has been to draw a map in the dust, detailing crucial local features such as sacred landmarks, waterholes and food sources. These sand paintings are elaborate and take days to create; they are also sacred and to be viewed only by initiated clan members before being destroyed. In the early 1970s, however, a teacher at Papunya, northwest of Alice Springs, began to encourage young Aborigine kids to translate their sand-painting techniques onto canvas. In fact it was the elders who took to the idea – without divulging culturally secret information, of course – and a new art form was born.

Those early Papunya artists have been superseded by painters from throughout the central desert, the most successful of whom use innovative abstract and minimalist styles in their bid to woo international collectors. Alice Springs now has two dozen art galleries devoted to Aboriginal art, with paintings priced between Aus$40 and Aus$40,000. Browsing these galleries is one of the highlights of a visit to Alice; even if you don't bring a picture home, you'll come away with a different perspective on the Outback.

927 | Getting to know Darwin

AUSTRALIA Tucked away in the "Top End", closer to Indonesia than Sydney, Darwin is the least known of Australia's regional capitals – stunningly remote, buffeted by extreme weather, and with an atmosphere like nowhere else in the country.

Thanks to its proximity to Asia, Darwin is rich in culinary diversity; head to the Parap Village and Mindil Beach Sunset markets to find everything from Vietnamese *pho* to crocodile-tail sushi. Its nightlife is also lively, from popular drinking spot Stokes Hill Wharf to the club-lined Mitchell Street.

More than 25 percent of the people in the Northern Territory are from aboriginal communities. Visit the Tiwi Islands, some 80km off the coast of Darwin, to learn about the Tiwi people and their culture, or travel 150km to Kakadu National Park to see some ancient aboriginal rock art.

Located 100km south of Darwin, Litchfield National Park is home to dramatic waterfalls, innumerable giant termite mounds, and plenty of designated swimming holes; a great place for a spot of bushwalking.

Darwin is fast-growing, youthful, multicultural – and ripe for discovery.

928 | Diving the Coolidge

VANUATU There is no other wreck on Earth like the *SS President Coolidge*. This 210m-long ship is so huge that you could dive here for a year and not see the half of it. Built in the 1930s as a luxury liner, the *Coolidge* was converted to carry troops in World War II. She met her end at Espiritu Santo in Vanuatu when the captain ran her aground and abandoned ship after hitting mines intended for the Japanese. All but two of the crew of five thousand disembarked safely, but the ship listed and slipped off the reef, flipping onto her side to lie 20m below at the shallowest point.

You start the dive by finning down the guide line into the deep blue, ending at the stern; from there, it's over the hull to where a hatch has been cut in the side. You're in darkness, following torchlight beams and rising bubbles along claustrophobic corridors. Slowly, your vision adjusts and the lights come back on. Down past dials, panels and machinery – the engine room – then there's a flash of grey and blue and you're on the sand outside the wreck, 60m down with half your air left. Time for a mellow ascent to the surface.

929 | Pure indulgence in Perth's Valley of Taste

AUSTRALIA Early in the nineteenth century, botanist Thomas Waters noted that the climate of the Swan Valley, 15km northeast of Perth, would be perfect for planting vineyards. Two centuries later, the area has become something of a gastronomic theme park, known, thanks to its 150-plus wineries, breweries and gourmet food outlets, as "The Valley of Taste".

While bus tours are available, the best way to explore the valley is by bike. Once you have acclimatized to the heat – and swallowed your first mouthful of flies – the scenic 32km trail offers plenty of wiggling detours to keep you entertained between the gluttony. And what gluttony! Where else in the world would you be inclined to cut short your time in a chocolate factory in order to check out the nearby nougat factory, ice creamery or honey house?

Despite all the impressive food offerings, it's alcohol that rules the roost in the Valley of Taste. Wineries range from the *uber*-exclusive – all artisan merchandise and lavish dining rooms – to the more rustic, where the sommelier running the tasting session has been out picking grapes that same morning.

At the higher end of the spectrum, both Houghton and Sandalford offer extensive tasting menus and well-polished service. In the smaller establishments, such as Ambrook and Lancaster, the lower price tags tend to correlate with greater charm, and more often than not you'll also get a hearty wedge of cheese to accompany each wine tasting.

Beer aficionados are catered for, too. Home to a series of mammoth 1200-litre beer containers, hipster-hangout Mash has an impressive range of IPAs, ciders and lagers, while the Feral Brewing Company down the road brews what is quite possibly the best beer in West Australia – the fragrant, fruity Hop Hog pale ale.

If you do explore by bike, use the proffered spittoons and drink plenty of water – otherwise you may end up taking a "wrong turn" into the Swan River, like so many locals in the past.

930

Canyoneering in Karijini

AUSTRALIA Canyoneering through Karijini National Park is an Indiana-Jones-style adventure through a rarely seen world of towering red rock canyons, trickling waterfalls and hidden pools. Be prepared for half a day of walking then crawling, wading then swimming, climbing along ledges and up waterfalls and jumping into freezing pools. The trails are graded by how extreme the terrain gets. Most people can handle classes 1–3; classes 4–6 are where the real excitement lies, and should be tackled onlywith a qualified guide.

One of the best is the "Class 4" Knox Gorge. Descending the steep track into the ravine, you have little idea of what waits ahead. Paths and ledges peter out and you're forced to swim across a couple of pools until the walls narrow suddenly into a shoulder-wide slot that never sees sunlight. You enter the chasm, bridging over jammed boulders, deafened and disoriented by water running through your legs until it seems there is no way ahead. There is, but to continue you must hurtle blindly down the "do-or-die" Knox Slide into an unseen plunge pool below.

Later, pumped with adrenaline and teeth chattering from the icy water, you look up to see tourists pointing and staring at you from a viewpoint, wondering how on Earth you got down there.

931

Paddling through Abel Tasman National Park

NEW ZEALAND Some people hike along the coast of Abel Tasman National Park, others cruise through its glassy waters, but by far the best way to explore New Zealand's smallest and most intimate national park is by sea kayak. The sheltering arm of Farewell Spit ensures the waters are seldom rough, so even inexperienced paddlers can head out for several days in relative safety.

Above all, this type of trip is about enjoying yourself at a relaxed tempo. Not only can you take to the shore at your own pace, but the kayak will carry all the wine, beer and tasty delicacies you'd want to bring along. A wide choice of golden beaches with designated camping spots is at your disposal for pit stops – spend the afternoon lazing on the sand, explore rock pools or take a dip. Pack a mask and snorkel and you'll be able to watch the shoals of fish weaving among the rocks and kelp beds.

One essential stop is the Tonga Island Marine Reserve, where the rocks come slathered with seals. These playful creatures have been known to come up to swimmers and cavort for a while before speeding off as fast as they arrived.

When you crave something a little more sophisticated than dinner cooked over a camp stove, wend your way up the delightful estuary of the Awaroa River, where a few lodges inhabit patches of private land. Stop in for a sandwich and an espresso or a beer on the deck; if you're feeling flush and hankering for white linen you can stay the night. A perfect finale to a glorious few days of relaxation.

932 | Paragliding over the paddocks

AUSTRALIA Early starts are required if you want to get the best out of paragliding over the vast farmland behind Mount Tamborine in Southern Queensland. The cool morning air, calm and still, gradually heats and begins to show signs of releasing every free-flyer's addiction – thermals. Bubbles of rising warm air lift the lucky ones clear off the ground and reward them with breathtaking views out over the plains towards the Great Dividing Range.

Once at cloud base, the hopeful pilots take in the view of rich green pasture intersected by old red dusty scars and wait for 2pm, checking their watches anxiously until the strong coastal breeze hits like a wall and accelerates them and their gliders towards the horizon.

933 | Knocking back kava

FIJI If you want to get to the heart of Fiji, drinking *kava* makes a good place to start. First, you'll be invited to join a group, languidly assembled around a large wooden bowl. Then, a grinning elder will pass you a coconut shell, saying "*tovolea mada*" – "try please". You take a look – the muddy pool in the shell looks like dirty dishwater, but what the hell, you sip anyway.

And then the taste hits you, a sort of medicinal tonic tinged with pepper. Resist the urge to spit it out and you'll gain the respect of your hosts. Passing the cup back you exclaim "*maca!*", which loosely translates as "thanks". Keep drinking, and you'll start to get numb lips, feel mildly intoxicated and, if you're lucky, end up as tranquil as your new friends.

934 | A volcanic trip up Mount Yasur

VANUATU The walk up to the continuously erupting Mount Yasur on Tanna Island takes about ninety minutes. A notice at the bottom warns against approaching the crater when there's a particular level of activity; usually it's safe to move on. The climb goes through tropical forest: rainwater trickles down every tree, then gushes down the path. Suddenly the forest gives way to a grim desert of rock and mud that extends to the summit. The temperature drops markedly; a cool, dank mist blows in from the sea.

Yasur announces itself the closer you get. Every few minutes, there's a loud boom, then a few lesser booms. Just below the summit, a battered letterbox proclaims itself the world's only Volcano Post – it's quite literally a chance to send postcards from the edge.

At the rim, a pleasant waft of heat rises up and drives the mist away. But booms accompany tremendous eruptions of red-hot rocks – pyroclasts – that crash into the edge of the crater, and either fizzle or explode. The louder eruptions cause the ground to shake. Often the balls of fire soar high into the air; you'll have to guess where they're going to land. Most people, it seems, get lucky.

935 | Zen and the art of relaxation, Byron Bay

AUSTRALIA Back in the early 1970s, longboard surfers and yoga-loving hippies in "save the whale" T-shirts discovered Byron Bay, elevating it from a sleepy backwater to the coolest hangout on Australia's East Coast. It hasn't looked back since.

Today, the counterculture that made Byron's name continues to blossom. But things have changed: while the town is still stuffed with quirky vegetarian cafés and shops selling windchimes, crystals and sarongs, chic resorts with elegant spas have started to outnumber the scruffy hippy hangouts. Byron Bay is now a playground for backpackers and cashed-up city escapees alike. Aussie soap and sports stars have become a common sight, and you may even spot the odd A-lister; squeaky-clean Olivia Newton-John runs a wellness centre nearby. So if you like the idea of tapping into your nature-loving, spiritual side but balk at the thought of going right back to basics, Byron Bay may be just your sort of place.

Sign up for a yoga and surf retreat, and you'll experience Byron at its best. With the services of professional yoga, meditation, pilates and wave-riding gurus on tap, you can divide your time as you choose. Byron's teachers cater for all comers: if you've never tried to keep your balance on a longboard or bend your body into a cobra before, you'll be in safe hands. It's a superb way both to relax and to tone up – and the in-house cooks will rustle up enough healthy macrobiotic treats to fuel you through your exertions, however hard you choose to push yourself.

To get each day off to an invigorating start, you can be the first to greet the Australian dawn by heading down to Byron's lovely, long, sandy beach for a series of sun salutations on the shore, coordinating your breathing with the rhythmic roar of the surf. It certainly beats a sweaty studio with an ocean-wave soundtrack on the stereo.

936 | Taking a trip to hell on Earth

NEW ZEALAND You'll smell Rotorua before you even reach the city limits. It isn't known as the "Sulphur City" for nothing, and the unmistakable bad-egg aroma gets everywhere. Thankfully you get used to it after an hour or so. The whole city sits on a thin crust of earth that's underlain by a seething cauldron of waters and superheated steam that seem desperate to escape. As you walk around you'll see puffs of vapour rising out of people's backyards, and stormwater drains venting sulphurous jets. Mausolea predominate in the cemeteries as graves can't be dug into the ground, while on the shores of Lake Rotorua gulls are relieved of the chore of sitting on their nests – the earth is warm enough to incubate without assistance.

A dozen or so dramatic geothermal wonders lie close to town. Tourists have been coming for over a century to see the Pohutu Geyser,

which regularly spouts to 20m; around the turn of the millennium it performed continuously for an unprecedented 329 days. It still spouts several times a day, a spectacular show that's heralded by the smaller Prince of Wales Feathers geyser (10m). Mineral deposits turn lakes wild shades of orange and green, and steam forces its way to the surface to form boiling mud pools patterned with myriad concentric circles.

Weary bones are also well catered for in Rotorua – just about every motel and campsite has a hot pool in which to soak. Make a point of seeking out genuine mineral ones that are filled by therapeutic geothermal waters, whether it be hydrothermal pampering in sophisticated resorts or back-to-basics natural pools out in the woods under the stars.

937 | Getting hands-on at Wellington's Te Papa

NEW ZEALAND Spend any time in the Kiwi capital and you can't help but notice the bold, angular building amid the yachts and seagulls of the waterfront. This is Te Papa, which translates as "Our Place", the Museum of New Zealand. Universally known by its Maori name, it was created in partnership with the nation's *iwi* (tribes) and presents a uniquely bicultural view of the country.

A far cry from the stuffy glass cases of the old museum that it replaced, Te Papa exudes a radical modern approach, not just in the design of the building but in the way the exhibits invite interaction and involvement. Like any good museum it works on several levels, and yet, despite its size, it never feels overwhelming. You can easily waltz through in a couple of hours and get a comprehensive overview of what makes New Zealand tick. To make the most of your visit, linger over the superb Maori section with its robustly carved war canoe, traditional houses, collections of fearsome war clubs and intricately worked jade jewellery. Displays showcase how people have migrated to New Zealand, first using the stars to navigate the Pacific in double-

hulled canoes, later in sailing ships, and more recently as immigrants from east Asia. And you shouldn't miss the *marae*, a Maori meeting place that is dramatically different from the red, black and white wood carvings you'll see elsewhere. Here semi-mythological figures are fashioned from warped plywood and shaded in an eye-catching array of pastel tones.

With more time on your hands, there's plenty to keep you occupied – drawers reveal smaller artefacts, a gallery showcases the best in Kiwi painting and sculpture, and "sound posts" encourage you to tune into wide-ranging views about the ongoing debate on New Zealand's founding document, the Treaty of Waitangi.

Te Papa is a great place for kids too, offering all kinds of interactive, hands-on displays, the chance to feel the shudder of New Zealand's most powerful earthquake, and even some high-tech rides.

More than a decade after its opening, over a million people pass through Te Papa's doors every year. Not bad, considering the country only has a population of four million.

River deep, mountain high: bushwalking the Overland Track

938

AUSTRALIA Tasmania's Overland Track is one of the world's greatest long-distance walks. Stretching from the island's highest peak to Australia's deepest lake, you cross a magnificent alpine wilderness, unbroken by roads and adorned by brooding lakes, glacier-carved cirques and thundering waterfalls.

Stormy skies are frequent on Tassie, but even on the ground there's no shortage of drama. Features named after their classical Greek counterparts – Mount Eros, the Acropolis and Lake Elysia – provide a fitting backdrop to the Olympian landscape. And though much of the 65km trail is boardwalk with bridged creeks, there's no escaping several muddy interludes – be prepared to get wet.

This is Tasmania, so fresh drinking water is plentiful and need not be carried; the daunting task is to lug enough food and stove fuel for the duration. Once you accept that, the exhilaration of wandering completely self-sufficient through the mountain wilderness fills you with a sense of deep satisfaction. Up above, raven-like currawongs and eagles cut through the skies, while below you quolls – cat-like relatives of the famous Tasmanian devil – and wallabies abound.

It takes about a week to tramp across the Overland's stirring range of landscapes. You'll want to add a day or two, however, for side trips to waterfalls, lakes and scrambling up peaks such as Mount Ossa, Tasmania's highest at 1617m, overlooking forests of King Billy pines and carpeted in fragrant wildflowers in early summer. Even then you're sure to have rain and even snow at some point, and eventually you'll stagger aboard the Lake St Clair ferry, aching, mud-caked but happy, for an uncelebrated return to civilization.

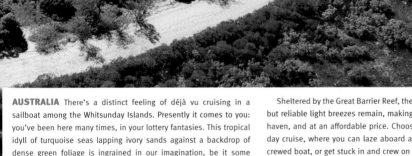

Island dreaming: sailing the Whitsundays

939

AUSTRALIA There's a distinct feeling of déjà vu cruising in a sailboat among the Whitsunday Islands. Presently it comes to you: you've been here many times, in your lottery fantasies. This tropical idyll of turquoise seas lapping ivory sands against a backdrop of dense green foliage is ingrained in our imagination, be it some Jungian folk memory or saturation advertising. *The Beach* before it all turned sour. Paradise.

Just over 1200km north of Brisbane, this compact archipelago of seventy-odd islands lies just off Airlie Beach, a small resort described by locals as "a drinking town with a sailing problem". From here you can pick from a delectable menu of islands, including Hayman, which offers resorts so posh staff scurry unseen along tunnels. Others like Long Island are more affordable, or you might prefer the Molle Islands, home to little more than a couple of basic campsites.

Sheltered by the Great Barrier Reef, the Pacific swell is dampened, but reliable light breezes remain, making the Whitsundays a sailing haven, and at an affordable price. Choose between a sedate three-day cruise, where you can laze aboard a spacious and comfortable crewed boat, or get stuck in and crew on a huge racing "maxi yacht" catering for partying backpackers.

Either way, life becomes sybaritically simple. By day you commune with turtles, dolphins and even whales – up from the Antarctic to give birth before heading south again. Or go snorkelling on the lookout for morays and parrotfish (the northeastern tip of Hook Island is best). Come sunset, you moor in one of the many unnamed bays while the chef prepares a fresh seafood meal. A shower is as simple as diving into the surrounding water, and your bed is the deck of the boat or the sand on the beach.

940 | Catch a freighter to the Marquesas

FRENCH POLYNESIA The Marquesas Islands are the most remote island group on Earth: the furthest from any continent. No coral reefs protect these Polynesian islands – 1200km northeast of Tahiti – from the full force of the Pacific. Copper-coloured cliffs loom out of the sea and pile up to piercing volcanic heights. The breathtaking landscapes, the heavenly scents, and the statuesque beauty of the islanders have enticed sailors, artists and writers for centuries. In *In the South Seas* Robert Louis Stevenson recalls his two months here in 1888. French post-Impressionist artist Paul Gauguin spent his last two years painting on Hiva Oa. And American novelist Herman Melville jumped ship on Nuku Hiva in 1842, believing he'd found paradise. Who wouldn't want to jump ship here?

The link between the islands and the outside world is the *Aranui 5*: an offbeat freighter that every three weeks departs Papeete on a 14-day, 2500km circuit to the Marquesas Islands. Albeit a working freighter, the lady is no tramp steamer. She comfortably accommodates up to 250 passengers in four classes of air-conditioned cabins. There's a swimming pool, library and lounge, along with a dining room serving copious food, washed down with free-flowing wine.

You'll visit all six of the inhabited Marquesas Islands, beginning with Nuku Hiva, beautiful as a movie creation. You'll explore ashore while the Polynesian crew load and unload the cargo, often carrying huge bags of copra (dried coconut flesh) on their shoulders through the surf. On Nuku Hiva you'll hike to ancient ceremonial sites with large scowling stone statues called tikis, half-screened by masses of foliage. More climbs on other islands open to spectacular vistas: the pinnacles of Ua Pu clawing the sky like witch's fingers; the emerald basalt spires guarding Fatu Hiva's Bay of Virgins. After dinner, showered and sweet-smelling, and with white flowers tucked behind their ears, the Polynesian sailors entertain guests with ukuleles and Marquesan ballads in the heat of the tropical night.

941 | Canoeing Nitmiluk Gorge

AUSTRALIA The town of Katherine is generally seen as little more than a convenient pit stop on the long road trip between Darwin and Kakadu in the north and Uluru to the south. While there's plenty to recommend it in its own right, however, including hot springs and a fine Aboriginal centre, best of all is the set of supremely dramatic river gorges that sit twenty minutes' drive east of town in Nitmiluk National Park.

Known as both Katherine Gorge and Nitmiluk Gorge, the 12km river chasm is hemmed in by sheer ochre cliffs. Freshwater crocodiles are a regular sight on the banks – the non-traveller-eating kind, if you're wondering – and when you find yourself alone on a cool, hushed stretch of river, with red rock faces towering high above you and no sounds but the breeze in the gum trees and the soft splash of a croc tail to disturb the silence, it's an utterly magical place.

Sections of rapids split the whole gorge into thirteen parts. It's possible to explore the first on a pleasure cruise or a dinner sailing, but the scenery really starts to ramp up when you reach the second. Full-day exploration by canoe – the only realistic way to get this far – is highly recommended. Depending on what you arrange with the hire outlet, you can either carry your canoe and equipment along the short, rocky walk between the first and second gorges, or simply switch to a waiting canoe.

The paddling can be hard work, particularly against the wind, so don't expect to get anywhere near the "thirteenth" in a day – and bear in mind that however far you go, you ultimately have to return to the first gorge. If you're keen to reach the end, you'll need overnight gear (there are designated campsites at the fifth, sixth, eighth and ninth gorges) and the energy to do a fair amount of canoe-carrying over boulders. Needless to say, it's worth it.

942 | Hiking the rim of Kings Canyon

AUSTRALIA If you dream of feasting your eyes on a spectacular panorama of the Outback, there's an alternative to scaling Ayers Rock – a climb that's set to close in October 2019. After much debate, the decision to ban the Uluru climb was made to respect the wishes of local Aboriginal groups and protect the spiritual nature of climbing the sacred monolith. But there's another option. Three and a half hours' easy drive northeast of the Rock, Kings Canyon offers vistas every bit as spellbinding, even if it doesn't attract as much attention. Few visitors may arrive in Australia with the express intention of coming here, but hiking in Kings Canyon provides an unforgettable experience for those who make the effort.

Victorian explorer Ernest Giles, who in 1872 became the first outsider to clap eyes on the canyon, was taken aback to encounter a mountain range looming out of the flatness. He christened the wonderfully verdant gorge between the peaks after Fieldon King, his expedition's chief sponsor, and what the canyon lacks in terms of a rightful apostrophe it gains through an appropriately regal title. Today it forms part of the protected Watarrka National Park, which,

much like Uluru, covers an area of profound cultural importance to local Aboriginal communities.

For walkers, however, that's where similarities between the two end: to hike into Kings Canyon is to embark on a journey that has much more to do with connecting than conquering.

By far the main draw is the roughly U-shaped Rim Walk, a 6km trail that begins with five hundred rocky, uneven steps leading up to the shelf of the canyon, where sheer walls of sandstone look down onto a green creek bed far below. While the grandstand long-range views are the headline attraction – you'll see both into the canyon and out across the Outback – the trail leads past stunning natural features, from erosion-formed, beehive-like domes to the shaded cliff-top chasm known as the "Garden of Eden". Close-at-hand details en route, such as the ancient marine fossils embedded in the sandstone, serve to underline the age-old majesty of the canyon.

It's a walk to take your time over, lingering at the stupefying lookouts and stopping to consider the feet that have walked these red buttresses and crags in times gone by.

943 | Learning to surf on the Gold Coast

AUSTRALIA Mastering the art of riding a wave is not as tricky as it looks, and the southernmost coast of Queensland is one of the best surfing nurseries on the planet. Here the swell along the 40km beach from Coolangatta to South Stradbroke Island is untamed by wave-dampening atolls of the Barrier Reef further north. Between those two points you can't miss the high-rise blight of Surfers Paradise, Australia's domestic holidaymaking "Costa", but as far as you're concerned it's the reliable and easy surf that matters.

With tropical cyclones animating the Pacific swell, summer is the season to watch the surfing pros, while the temperate winter is the time to learn. From April to October the regular waves break safely over sand here, and the warm, waist-deep water makes things all the more pleasurable. If you've got a good sense of balance, you'll be at an advantage; though most surf schools promise to have you at least

standing on the board by the end of a typical two-hour session, and surfing properly in a day or two.

It mostly boils down to being in the right place at the right time. Learning to predict the break of a wave and positioning yourself in front of it can be most easily learned on a short boogie board. The next big step on a full-sized board is getting from prone to on your feet in the blink of an eye – easy enough to practise on dry land but a lot trickier in the water. Soon enough, though, you'll be heading beachwards while adopting the classic surfer stance, even if the wave's only halfway up your shin. Get it right and you'll experience a taste of the bigger rush, the raw surge of adrenaline which is what surfing's all about. But everyone's got to start somewhere, and for the novice surf junkie the beaches around Surfers Paradise couldn't be more aptly named.

944 | Coast to coast with the TranzAlpine

NEW ZEALAND New Zealand's South Island is split vertically by the Southern Alps, a snowcapped spine of 3000m mountains. Only three road passes breach this barrier, and just one rail line – the TranzAlpine. Slicing 225km across the South Island from Christchurch, the island's biggest city, to the small west-coast town of Greymouth, this unassuming train offers one of the most scenic rail journeys in the world.

Don't come looking for a luxury experience. This certainly isn't the *Orient Express*, but any shortcomings of the train itself will fade into the background when you take a look out of the window – the scenery is mind-bogglingly spectacular, especially in winter, when it's at its most dramatic with the landscape cloaked in snow.

As the train eases out of Christchurch, urban back gardens give way to the open vistas of the Canterbury Plains, acre upon acre of bucolic sheep country. After an hour the rail line cuts away from the

main highway to chart its own course past the dry grasslands of the Torlesse Range, gradually climbing all the while.

The west of the South Island gets huge amounts of rain, the east very little. Here you're in a transition zone, and you'll notice the character of the vegetation change with every kilometre. Subalpine tussock gives way to damp beech forests before heading into the dripping west-coast rainforest, thick with rampant tree ferns. Step onto the open-air viewing carriage for an even more intimate experience; photo opportunities abound.

At the little alpine community of Arthur's Pass you enter the 8km Otira Tunnel, burrowing under the high peaks and emerging at the former rail town of Otira. After losing height quickly along the cascading Taramakau River, the train cuts to the tranquil shores of Lake Brunner before its final run down to Greymouth – just four and a half hours but a world away from Christchurch.

945
Sydney harbour-mastering

AUSTRALIA For foreign visitors, taking the public ferry across Sydney Harbour always seems to awaken the urge to emigrate to Australia. The views from the deck not only encompass the city's two biggest icons – the Sydney Harbour Bridge and the Sydney Opera House – but also the very stuff of daily Sydney life.

Who wouldn't want to live in a harbour-view apartment, drop by one of the countless sandy beaches on the way home from work, or learn to sail? Best of all, you could be taking this ferry on your daily commute from downtown Sydney to a home in Manly (12km north), a suburb that has not one but two beaches of its own. One faces the harbour, the other overlooks the high-rolling surf of the Pacific.

Fittingly, the Manly ferry sets off from alongside Sydney's oldest neighbourhood, The Rocks, site of the first permanent European settlement in 1788 and now, with its preserved homes, museums and twee cafés, a sort of neighbourhood theme park. A few minutes later the ferry chugs within waving distance of the bridge, and all eyes swivel right for captivating views of the shell-shaped Opera House, with sea-sparkle in the foreground.

Want a different perspective of the harbour? Sign up for the Bridge Climb, a three-and-a-half-hour tour that takes you onto the girders of Sydney Harbour Bridge itself, and up to its summit, 134m above the water. Once primed and prepped, you're clad in a regulation steel-grey jumpsuit and clipped on, steeplejack-style, to the railings, as you negotiate ladders and catwalks in the footsteps of your tour leader. Aside from awesome high-level vistas, you get to learn about the construction of its mammoth 503m-long arch, completed in 1932.

Eighty-plus years on, and the Harbour Bridge is still the enduring symbol of the Sydney good life, linking the city's energetic business and historical districts with those oh-so-desirable North Shore suburbs across the water.

MAKE THE MOST OF YOUR TIME ON EARTH

Cruising the Milford Sound

NEW ZEALAND From the water, dwarfed beneath the forest-clad mountains that soar to either side, it's hard to comprehend just how tiny you are in comparison to the sheer size of Milford Sound. That the fiord makes even the most cumbersome and colossal cruise ship look small is an indication of just how impressive the scale is here.

Known to the Maori as Piopiotahi, Milford Sound is the most northerly fiord in New Zealand's Fiordland. Home to dolphins, seals and penguins, its dark blue waters stretch for some 15km between towering emerald-green cliffs. Though it might sound crazy to hope for rain on holiday, while the Sound is undeniably beautiful in all weather, it's in the rain, when mist haunts the water and waterfalls descend from every cliff face, that it becomes truly magnificent. Fortunately, with over 180 rainy days per year (averaging a massive 7m of rain in total), you're in with a pretty good chance of a soggy encounter.

Milford Sound is not a place to admire from solid ground. Only getting out on the water will give you a true sense of its majestic beauty. To really get up close, and access spots that no cruise ship could ever reach, head out on a kayak.

There's something undeniably exhilarating about exploring somewhere so immense from so close to the water – feeling the spray of a waterfall on your face, coming within arm's reach of a surfacing dolphin, with only the sound of your paddles breaking the stillness of your surroundings. That said, if you prefer a more sedate water adventure, taking a cruise around the fiord still enables you to appreciate this glacial beauty. Head through the mirror-like waters towards the dramatic 1692m-high Mitre Peak, and you're guaranteed to feel just a little bit smaller than before you got on the boat.

Riding the Ghan to Darwin

947

AUSTRALIA In 2004, roughly a hundred years behind schedule, the Adelaide–Darwin *Ghan* train finally reached its destination. Constructing a reliable rail link between the two towns took up most of the twentieth century; around the start of the new millennium, the government decided to plug the final 1500km gap from Alice to Darwin, and complete a legendary transcontinental rail journey.

For most of the three-day, two-night northbound ride, the train passes through uninhabited Outback that most people only see out of a plane window. Just a couple of hours out of Adelaide and you're already lost on the vast Nullarbor Plain. Night falls, and bleached saltpans glow eerily in the moonlight as you tuck yourself in to your comfy four-berth cabin.

Next morning, the view from the dining car reveals classic Outback colours: clear blue skies, grey-green scrub and rich orange sand. While you stare, doze or read the train passes close to the geographical centre of the continent, and squeezes through the West MacDonnell Ranges by lunchtime. Soon the driver's whistle heralds your arrival at the likeable desert town of Alice Springs, where you're allowed a couple of hours' break.

Beyond Alice, the *Ghan* works its way through the ranges before spilling out onto the featureless 1000km Tanami Desert. The sun sets as you near Wycliffe Well roadhouse, famous for UFO sightings. You peer keenly into the blackness but see only your reflection in the glass. Dawn delivers you to the tropical Top End. Trees reappear for the first time since Adelaide, interspersed with countless 2m-high termite mounds. The town of Katherine marks another first on this epic journey – the only flowing river for over 2000km – and then it's just an hour or two to journey's end in Darwin.

Sure, you could have flown here in a few hours, or driven and arrived feeling like week-old roadkill. But by rolling into town on the *Ghan* your carbon footprint is the size of a possum's front paw. And that is something to feel good about.

948 | Swimming with whale sharks at Ningaloo Reef

AUSTRALIA Once a year, the world's largest fish makes an appearance at the Ningaloo Reef fringing Western Australia's North West Cape. Its arrival is strategically timed with a moonlit night in late summer when coral polyps spawn en masse, ejecting millions of eggs into the tropical waters. Guided by some arcane instinct, the hungry whale sharks are ready and waiting, mouths agape.

More whale than shark, this 15m-long gentle giant is twice the size of the great white of *Jaws* fame, but entirely harmless to humans. It survives by cruising the world's oceans ingesting all the krill and plankton that its metre-wide mouth can scoop in. For the whale shark, the weeks that follow the coral spawning are equivalent to being locked up in a sweetshop for a night.

Not surprisingly, the North West Cape has become the world's prime destination for diving and snorkelling with whale sharks. Spotter planes

search for the telltale shadows and radio the boats below, which race into position ahead of the shark. After what may have been many hours of waiting, suddenly it's all action as you hurriedly don your kit. On the boat's rear platform they give the signal and you leap in, fins kicking hard, following the lead diver.

As the bubbles clear, a solitary grey silhouette looms out of the murk, its back speckled with white spots. With lazy sweeps of its tailfin, this oceanic behemoth glides slowly by, and for a couple of minutes, using your own fins, you do your best to keep up. This silent encounter with a shark longer than the boat you just jumped off should trigger alarm bells. Strangely, though, as you swim alongside, you're mesmerized by its benign bulk until it dives effortlessly down into the abyss. You rise to the surface elated at having crossed paths with the biggest shark on the planet – and lived to tell the tale.

949 | Confront the new in Tasmania's anti-Tate

AUSTRALIA Not so long ago, Tasmania's tiny capital Hobart was derided as backward. So how come its latest gallery is not just the toast of the art world but has been named the premier cultural sight in Australia, pipping some old opera house in Sydney? It's all down to David Walsh, mathematician, professional gambler, vineyard owner and mastermind of the Museum of Old and New Art – a man whose tale is as extraordinary as the personal art collection he's put on show.

Emerging as a geeky misfit from a poor Hobart suburb, Walsh could have been just another computer nerd. Instead he devised gambling systems and became, first, a multi-millionaire, then an art obsessive, cherrypicking everything from Greek and Egyptian antiquities to iconoclastic modern works. In 1995, he bought a wine estate on the River Derwent, and began an ambitious building project that culminated when he unveiled MONA in 2011. Some in the art establishment cheered, others reeled in shock – it was impossible to be neutral.

Styled like a pharaoh's tomb, lit like a Berlin nightclub, this subterranean gallery, hewn from the sandstone, rips up the rulebook.

It's the antithesis of the usual white box. While the above-ground spaces are all crisp glass-walled modernism, descending the escalator into the gallery itself you feel as though you're penetrating the bowels of an Egyptian pyramid. Displays have no explanatory captions. Old and new are juxtaposed to unite or confront. And Walsh's exhibitions venture deep into the badlands of modern art: previous installations have included sculpted vaginas and rotting cows; "Bit.Fall", a waterfall of droplets of the most-Googled words of the day; and, infamously, "Cloaca Professional", a digestive machine that is fed and excretes daily.

Although Walsh has described MONA as a "subversive adult Disneyworld" and his "anti-Tate", it's more than just the shockjock of modern art. Whether displaying Roman coins or the purported remains of a suicide bomber covered in chocolate, everything is beautifully presented and thoughtfully curated.

Locals speculate that MONA was intended to scandalize the state's traditional prudish sensibilities. If so, Walsh has failed utterly – most Tasmanians love the place.

950 | A walk around Uluru

AUSTRALIA As you cruise westwards along the Lasseter Highway, you get your first glimpse of Uluru over cinnamon-red dunes while still 50km distant. Slowly the ochre-coloured monolith invades the empty horizon; it's hard to look at anything else. Then, just past the Uluru-Kata Tjuta National Park gates, you turn a bend, and suddenly it fills your field of vision.

The Rock means different things to different people. To the Pitjanjarra people who have lived in its shadow for 20,000 years, "Uluru" is the name of a seasonal waterhole near the summit, formerly revealed only to initiates of the Mala wallaby clan during secret ceremonies. To them this iconic image of the Outback is no Mecca-like shrine, but a vital, resource-rich landmark at the intersection of various trails in the region. These "songlines" criss-cross the desert and any conspicuous natural features found along them were put into songs celebrating the "Dreaming" or Creation, to help memorize the way and so "learn the country". Despite its spiritual significance,

many tourists still inappropriately see Uluru – or Ayers Rock, as explorer William Gosse named it in 1873 – as a climb to conquer, or a radiant landmark to photograph en masse from the Sunset Viewing Area. This is set to change in October 2019, however, when it will no longer be possible to climb the sacred monolith.

A far better way to honour the spirit of the place, in fact, is to take the 9km walk through waist-high grass around its base. The massif is a series of near-vertical strata that thrust inexplicably upwards. Looking like a weathered loaf of sliced bread, its grooves and cliffs vary with perspective. Approaching the "slices" end-on reveals smooth gullies in the rock that feed waterholes like Mutijulu Springs, shaded by groves of casuarina oaks. A few kilometres on, the steep flanks harbour caves and bizarre scalloped formations, some of them protected sacred sites: every bend in the track offers another startling profile. When you're back at the start, hot and sticky from exertion, you can be satisfied that you've experienced the Rock, and not merely stood on top of it.

951 | Dig your own spa on Hot Water Beach

NEW ZEALAND Hot springs are dotted all over New Zealand, but the two natural thermal springs that course up from under a North Island beach are unique. Easily accessible by car, just over two hours' drive east from Auckland, the Coromandel Peninsula separates the Hauraki Gulf from the Pacific Ocean and is an explosion of mountains, rainforest, coves and stunning coastal scenery. Visitors in the know head east of the ragged Coromandel range towards the bucolic coastline of the northeast tip, and above all to Hot Water Beach, near Whitianga.

Although the beach offers great surfing, strong rips and currents make swimming dangerous; the real attraction here comes during the two hours either side of low tide, when anyone can dig their own personal spa beside the rocky outcrop partway up the beach. Depending where you dig, the thermal water can be scalding hot – the two fissures issue water as hot as 64°C at a rate of up to fifteen litres per minute.

Best to test a few areas before you begin to excavate in earnest; aiming to channel an additional dose of cool seawater into your pool is all part of the fun.

In summer, Hot Water Beach is liable to be overrun, with visitors and locals jostling for the best spot. You can avoid the crowds by turning up in the pre-dawn hours, armed with a torch – just be sure to check the tide times! That way, you can have the place to yourself while you wait for the sun to break over the horizon. It's also worth bearing in mind that the climate hereabouts is mild in winter: lying back and immersing yourself in the sultry geothermal water is almost better when it's chilly, especially when you're enveloped by steam as the hot water hits the cool air.

When the tide finally rolls in, the waves break over the manmade pools and return the white-sand beach to its perfect natural state, ready for the next influx of spa seekers.

952 | Exploring Maori culture in Auckland

NEW ZEALAND Despite centuries of colonialism that have had a devastating effect on the traditional indigenous way of life, Maori culture in New Zealand is experiencing a resurgence.

For generations, schoolchildren were taught that New Zealand was "discovered" in 1642 by Dutch explorer Abel Tasman but, in fact, around eight hundred years earlier, a famous Polynesian explorer named Kupe first reached the shores of Aotearoa ("long white cloud"). In one Maori legend, Kupe followed an octopus from his homeland of Hawaiki, while in others it was a whale. Maori history was passed down through storytelling and each tribe has its own narrative – there was no written language until Pakeha (foreign) settlers arrived. By the twentieth century, Maori culture and language was in danger of being lost.

Maori are *tangata whenua* (people of the land), and when many Maori moved to urban areas they felt alienated: the heartbreaking film *Once*

Were Warriors opened the eyes of cinema-goers around the world to the generational trauma of cultural bereavement.

Today, Maori is an official language of New Zealand; the All Blacks rugby team perform their amazing *haka*; and there's a resurgence of *ta moko* (Maori tattoo art), *whakairo* (wood carving), *raranga* (weaving) and *kapa haka* (group performance). Spend a little time in New Zealand and you come to realise that although Maori make up just fifteen percent of the population, their culture is integral to Kiwi identity.

You'll discover the focus of New Zealanders on environmental issues is influenced by the traditional Maori symbiosis with land: Maori are *kaitiaki* (guardians) who protect the earth and its *taonga* (treasures) for future generations. An excellent collection of *taonga* fills the Auckland Museum, while Maori artworks form part of the fabric of the Auckland Art Gallery building. Maori culture is finally getting the recognition it deserves.

953 | Taking in the views on the Tongariro Crossing

NEW ZEALAND Alpine tundra, barren volcanic craters, steaming springs and iridescent lakes – the sheer diversity on the Tongariro Crossing makes it probably the best one-day tramp in the country. The wonderful long views are unimpeded by the dense bush that crowds most New Zealand tracks, while from the highest point you can look out over almost half the North Island, with the lonely peak of Mount Taranaki dominating the western horizon.

The 16km hike crosses one corner of the Tongariro National Park – wild and bleak country, encompassing the icy tops of nearby Mount Ruapehu, which at 2797m is the North Island's highest mountain. Catch the Crossing on a fine day, and it's a hike of pure exhilaration. The steep slog up to the South Crater sorts out the genuinely fit from the aspirational, then just as the trail levels out, Mount Ngauruhoe (2291m) invites the keen for a two-hour side-trip up its scoria slopes. Ngauruhoe famously starred as Mount Doom in the *Lord of the Rings* films, and you

can live out your hobbit fantasies as you look down its gently steaming crater. Getting back on track is a heart-pounding, hell-for-leather scree run back down the mountain – in just fifteen minutes you cover what took an hour and a half to ascend.

The gaping gashes and sizzling fissures around Red Crater make it a lively spot to tuck into your sandwiches and ponder the explosive genesis of this whole region. From here it's mostly downhill past Emerald Lake, its opaque waters a dramatic contrast to the shimmering surface of Blue Lake just ahead. With the knowledge that you've broken the back of the hike, you can relax on the veranda of Ketetahi Hut, and gaze out over the tussock to glistening Lake Taupo in the distance. Rejuvenated, you pass the sulphurous Ketetahi Hot Springs on the final descent, down to the green forest and the welcome sight of your bus. Tired but elated, you settle back in the seat, dreaming of a good feed and the chance to relive the events of the day over a couple of beers.

954

Jet-boating on the Shotover River

NEW ZEALAND Nowhere does adrenaline quite like Queenstown, the "Adventure Capital of the World". Careering in a little jet boat through the narrow river gorges of the South Island is truly a heart-in-mouth experience.

The original Hamilton Jet boat was developed in New Zealand during the 1960s, to navigate the shallow waterways around Canterbury, but not surprisingly the Kiwis couldn't pass up the opportunity for a bit of high-speed fun, and jet-boat rides have become big business. Even in water depths of a mere 10cm, the boats can reach speeds of over 80km/hr; when two jet engines combine to produce more than 700 horsepower, the acceleration really does make it feel as though you're flying.

Courtesy buses take visitors 5km north from Queenstown to the scenic departure point of Arthur's Point, where you walk down to the grey pebble beach and strap on lifejackets. At this juncture, it's reassuring to know that more than three million passengers have been safely shuttled through the canyons since 1970, by industry-regulated professionals.

Passing perilously close to the sheer rock face, negotiating rapids, skimming jagged boulders and being soaked by spray as the boat is spun more than 360 degrees: the twenty-minute trip over the glacial-blue waters is the high-speed ride of a lifetime. Yes, the "big red" jet boat really is manoeuvrable, and yes, the driver has nerves of steel... but as the undeniably beautiful valley flashes past, with the vessel spinning indiscriminately, you're more likely to be focusing on your own mortality, gripping tight onto the handrail and screaming at the top of your lungs. It's one of those all-time great outdoor activities where you end up back on dry land with shaky legs, a face-splitting grin and a real sense of achievement.

While of course a video recording of your trip is available for purchase, these days you can also take hands-free photography gear onboard, to record the thrills – and hopefully not spills – for yourself.

955 | A torchlight tour of Queensland's critters

AUSTRALIA If you're spending the night in rural Queensland, spotting nocturnal wildlife is as easy as picking up a powerful torch and pointing it at a tree. You have to know which kind of tree to choose, to some extent – but in favourite wildlife-watching areas such as the Daintree rainforest, Eungella National Park or Fraser Island, almost any tree will do.

Trees that are fruiting or in flower are a particularly good bet. Shine your spotlight into one of these, and at least one pair of eyes may shine back at you. Possums and flying foxes are common in forested areas, and you may see sugar gliders – some of Queensland's smallest, cutest and most aerodynamic marsupials – feasting on eucalyptus sap or planing from tree to tree with limbs outstretched.

In grassy areas, a distant dark shape on the ground may turn out to be a pademelon or kangaroo. Some of these endearing herbivores are so accustomed to humans, and even to torch beams, that you can watch them at close quarters – only when truly alarmed will they break off their nibbling to bounce away to safety.

For one of Queensland's most sublime after-dark wildlife experiences, join a guided canoe trip on Lake Tinaroo, near Yungaburra, in the Atherton Tablelands. On a clear night, you'll be paddling under a dome of stars, the sound of cicadas filling your ears. Having crossed the smooth, dark water, you can trace your way along the rainforested banks where, if you're quiet, you'll spot bandicoots and brushtail possums.

With a little luck, your torch beam may even pick out a Lumholtz's tree kangaroo. These rare creatures are climbers, not bouncers: perching in the rainforest canopy, they can easily be mistaken for monkeys, making them perhaps the most intriguing marsupials of all.

956 | Scuba diving the wrecks at Poor Knights Islands

NEW ZEALAND Jacques Cousteau championed the Poor Knights Islands as one of the top ten dive sites in the world. And with their warm currents, crystal-clear visibility and a host of undersea attractions his judgement is understandable.

Dive boats spread themselves over fifty recognized dive sites that jointly cover New Zealand's most diverse range of sea life, including subtropical species such as Lord Howe coralfish and toadstool grouper, found nowhere else around the coast. Near-vertical rock faces drop 100m through a labyrinth of caves, fissures and rock arches teeming with rainbow-coloured fish, crabs, soft corals, kelp forests and shellfish. Blue, humpback, sei and minke whales also drop in from time to time, while dolphins are not uncommon.

A typical day might include an hour-long cruise out to the islands followed by a drift dive through a sandy-bottomed cave populated by stingrays and lit by shafts of sunlight. After lunch on board, and perhaps some time paddling one of the boat's kayaks, you'll head around the coast to a second dive spot, maybe working your way along a technicolour wall of soft corals and a few nudibranchs.

As if that weren't enough, the waters north and south of the reserve are home to two navy wrecks, both deliberately scuttled. The survey ship *HMNZS Tui* was sunk in 1999 to form an artificial reef, and proved so popular with divers and marine life that the obsolete frigate *Waikato* followed two years later. These form part of a Northland wreck trail that also includes the remains of the Greenpeace flagship *Rainbow Warrior*, bombed by French government agents in 1985, just before it set out to campaign against French nuclear testing in the Pacific. In what seems a fitting end to its quest to protect the ocean, it's now colonized by new life.

957 | To the ends of the Earth

TUVALU "Going sightseeing?" asks the guesthouse owner. Sure, what's to see? "Well, you can go that way... or you can go that way." Welcome to Tuvalu, a country like no other, parked more or less squarely at the end of the Earth. Bar a supply boat which docks every few months (if the sea-gods agree), Tuvalu's only connection with the rest of the world is a twice-weekly flight from Fiji – and not even Fiji's main airport.

With just under 11,200 inhabitants, Tuvalu is the least populous country in the United Nations. Around half of its citizens live on Funafuti, an atoll whose super-skinny habitable section is shaped like a distorted boomerang. Funafuti, also being the capital of the island nation, contains all of the country's facilities – one hotel, one farm, one embassy (to Taiwan, who funded the hotel and the farm), one bank (with no ATM), one hospital (with one qualified surgeon catering to the whole nation), two restaurants (both Chinese) and two very small nightclubs. One of those clubs booms music out each night over the airport runway,

the only flat, large-ish space in the country, and thus where people go for recreation. It's unofficially divided into eight segments – one each for the nation's component atolls – and most of the day there are eight separate games of football or rugby going on. At the eastern end of the runway stands a mound of earth – a full five metres above sea level, it's the country's highest "mountain".

Lying so close to a sea that keeps rising, Tuvalu may well not last much longer than a few decades; people here are understandably reluctant to discuss what will happen then. For now, it's an honour to be able to visit this simple South Sea strip of palms and jackfruit trees: a just-about-functional country that can run out of flour, onions and even eggs for months on end. There's nothing to do, and yet everything to do – swims at the north beach, fishing, boat trips to outlying islands, or simply a whole lot of doing nothing. Just be sure to check in the required four-and-a-half hours before your flight back out, or you may get stuck in this bizarre paradise for longer than you'd expected.

958 | Sea kayaking around Shark Bay

AUSTRALIA The Peron Peninsula in Shark Bay, on the northwest coast of Western Australia, is well known for its regular dolphin visitations, and a beachside resort at Monkey Mia has grown around the spectacle. There's much more to this UNESCO-listed reserve than meeting Flipper and the family, however. Thanks to its sheltered conditions, the Shark Bay area is ideal for a sea kayaking adventure.

Paddling in a bay named after the ocean's deadliest predator may sound as sensible as skinny-dipping in Piranha Creek. Sure, there are tiger sharks out in the depths, but the abundant sea life ensures that they're fed well enough not to bother you in the shallows. Besides the pleasures of gliding serenely across bottle-green waters and camping beneath paprika-red cliffs on whichever deserted beach takes your fancy, marine-life spotting adds a "sea safari" element to your trip. Don't be surprised if before long a green turtle passes under your kayak, followed by rays the size of a tablecloth. And where there are rays there are usually sharks, but only frisky babies less than a metre long, maturing in the shallow nurseries before heading out to sea.

As you battle the winds around Cape Peron, there's a good chance you'll encounter dugongs grazing in the seagrass meadows, while flocks of cormorants, terns and pelicans will take to the air when you cruise down the sheltered side of the peninsula.

Finally, if you've not seen any already, bottlenose dolphins are a guaranteed sight at Monkey Mia, which is also a great place for basically a day paddle.

959 | Spend a night in a swag bag under Outback open skies

AUSTRALIA With a reputation for creepy-crawlies, Australia's Outback might not be your first thought when deciding on a location for a week of open camping. You'd be wrong, though. From the Northern Territory across to Western Australia's remote Kimberley region, the great, red sandy wilderness just begs for a few nights around a campfire. Join any number of Outback specialists and you'll be in good hands – they know the best spots, and will have basically swept the place for snakes and dingo tracks long before you show up.

That pioneering jolly swagman, who sat by a billabong, knew what he was doing – find a bit of shade beneath a tree by day, and roll out your bedding by night. Better than a tent, swag bags are really mobile mattresses, with all of the snuggly comfort you'd associate with a childhood single bed. Rugged canvas envelopes, filled with pads, blankets and soft duvets, they roll up every morning ready for the next adventure. To be honest, though, the rolling bit is easier said than done. You need to fling yourself at it every morning, body pitched over the top, then get it all tied up fast, before it starts to unravel. But the satisfaction of chucking your swag on the top of the 4WD as dawn breaks is worth the sweat and tears. You'll have earned your billy of tea.

Night-time cooking by campfire is one of the joys of the Outback – and being on a well-organized tour means you get to enjoy a hearty meal, accompanied by a tinny or glass of something local. With the group's swag bags circling what's left of the fire, you'll soon be safely ensconced in yours, cocooned by blankets as the temperature drops. There's not much room for manoeuvre, but you won't want to move a muscle, with nature's greatest show unfolding above your head. Australia's dark skies mean there's no better place for stargazing. Now who'd want a tent getting in the way of all that?

960 | Ocean to ocean, cape to cape: across Australia by 4WD

AUSTRALIA You're only going to do this once, so do it right. Driving from Cape Leveque, Western Australia, to Cape York on Queensland's northern tip is a two-month, 8000km odyssey; make sure you've packed your sense of adventure.

Broome, on the dazzling turquoise Indian Ocean, is a fantastic place to start, right beside the pearly sands of Cable Beach. The journey kicks off with the suspension-mashing 700km Gibb River Road. Starting near Derby, it cuts through the Kimberley region's untamed ranges, known as Australia's "Alaska". Turn-offs along the way tempt you to idyllic waterfalls, like the Bell Creek Gorge where water rolls off a series of ledges into shallow inviting pools.

The Gibb finally spits you out at Kununurra township, where you can stock up on provisions and, hopefully, team up with another vehicle for the stretch ahead. Now comes the lonely 1500km all-desert stage into the Territory and down to Alice Springs, notable for the only traffic lights en route until Cairns.

Exploring Alice's hinterland and weaving among the majestic ghost gum trees along the shady Finke River track to Uluru (Ayers Rock) is an adventure in itself. Moving on from the Rock, scoot eastwards to the solitary Mount Dare homestead; fill up here and then head out across the dune fields of the Simpson Desert to join the pilgrimage to the legendarily remote *Birdsville Hotel*, Australia's best-known bush pub.

Have a drink, then head any which way northeast across Queensland's flat dusty interior. Finally, it's time to get ready for the 1000km creek-crossing climax of your journey: the "Trip to the Tip". Between you and the Pacific lies one of the most ecologically diverse habitats on the planet: creeper-draped rainforest teeming with tombstone anthills and day-glo snakes.

Watching the sunset over Cape York, your journey is complete; the red dust is now in your blood and what you've missed of the Australian Outback is a very short list indeed.

961

Heading south for the winter in Queenstown

NEW ZEALAND Queenstown is definitely the place to savour winter in the southern hemisphere. Always popular with Kiwis, the Southern Alps also draw Australians and ski addicts from north of the equator who can't get enough action in their own season.

As for the slopes, they're bald. None of your slaloming through trees here: this is all open vistas (and high winds when it blows). With more than 400 vertical metres of skiing and the longest pedigree of any Kiwi skifield, Coronet Peak is probably the more popular of the two fields. The Remarkables maxes out at 500 vertical metres and has its adherents, as much for the fine off-piste terrain as for the forgiving groomed slopes.

For the freshest powder, you'll need to jump on a helicopter. Heli-skiing has a long heritage in Queenstown and was first developed here in the 1970s. Today it offers a shortcut to over twenty 3000m-plus peaks, ranging from remote razorback ridges to the majestic focal point of the Southern Alps, Mount Cook.

Back in town, the après-ski is second to none. The restaurants are easily the match of those in Auckland and Wellington, while the nightlife ranges from lively dance clubs to chic joints where you need to know the doorman to get in.

The season typically runs from early June into October, but the best time to come is for the Queenstown Winter Festival in the last week of June – a real riot with heaps of activities, crazy stunts and, of course, plenty of carousing.

Double-crossed in the South Seas

962

RAROTONGA The Cook Islands are not exactly synonymous with hiking. Nor would you expect them to be; that's not why people make the journey to these South Sea idylls – snorkelling, diving and the castaway lifestyle tend to top the list. But the cross-island walk in Rarotonga is well worth packing your boots for.

Most hikers head out on a guided walk, not least because the trek is demanding. It certainly is if you decide to go it alone and tackle it in the wrong direction: the chances of taking a wrong turn are much greater on the south–north route. That might look like the quickest way on the map, but it does involve ignoring the prominent sign that reads, "It is advised you start the cross-island walk from the other side" – heed this advice and head from the north coast to the south coast, via the 413m-high Te Rua Manga (Needle), following the orange track markers carefully.

Not long after the starting point, the trail leads through tall, subtropical forest where tree roots have fashioned themselves into stairs. It's like walking through a carved tunnel in an old cathedral. Soon, however, you find yourself scaling sheer slopes, using any available tree root or liana for leverage. The vegetation gets pricklier and sparser; still, power on and climb to the top of the ridge, where the Needle stands. From here you can see the island's tallest peak as well as the golden beaches below, while the infinite crystal sea stretches away in every direction. The views make the calf-shredding hike worthwhile and, from here, the long descent to the south coast is a whole lot easier than the ascent.

963 | Tasting notes from a small island

AUSTRALIA The judges' comments read like an appreciation of Scotland's finest: they identify hints of caramel and honey, a whiff of campfire smoke, a smooth, buttery feel in the mouth and a peppery finish. Yet Sullivans Cove single malt French Oak Cask comes not from Scotland but from Tasmania. Among a slew of other accolades, in the World Whiskies Awards of 2014, it was judged the best whisky on Earth.

Surprised a small Aussie state half a world away from the Old Country could snatch the accolade from Scotland or Japan? Don't be. The wonder is it took so long.

A sparsely populated island in the Roaring Forties, Tasmania is a sort of Scotland max. It has officially the purest air in the world – the next landmasses upwind are Patagonia and Antarctica – so some of its purest rainwater, which flows in soft mountain streams. Add highland peat bogs and a cool climate, and you have a terroir tailor-made for whisky.

Bill Lark thought so as he sat with a dram while trout fishing in the Tasmanian highlands in 1988. Puzzled by the lack of home-grown whisky, he discovered that the distilling of spirits was banned in the young colony by puritanical state governor Sir John Franklin in 1838, prompted by his wife Lady Jane's comment that "I would prefer barley be fed to pigs than it be used to turn men into swine".

Thanks to Bill's legal challenge 150 years later, Lark Distillery opened in 1992. Eight more have followed. Most are in southern Tasmania, and all are open for tastings and a yarn about whisky. Some, like Overeem or Belgrove – which distils rye harvested outside the back door – are tiny family affairs. Others, such as Sullivans Cove or Hellyers Road near Launceston, are rising international stars.

What unites them is the use of quality island ingredients and a handcrafted approach that's refreshing given the corporate creep of Scottish whisky. At around A$130 (£72) for a typical bottle – and hovering around the A$1050 (£600) mark for French Oak Cask – Tassie whiskies certainly aren't cheap. Given their sublime taste, however, it's money well spent.

964 | Four-wheeling through croc country: Cairns to Cape York

AUSTRALIA You may ordinarily have little use for 4WDs, but in a particular corner of Australia these all-terrain machines can provide the sort of adventure they were truly built for. Cape York, Australia's northernmost point, is over 1000km from Cairns, a challenging drive that will demand all your concentration as you gingerly inch across tidal creeks inhabited by crocodiles.

From Cairns, head out along the scenic Captain Cook Highway to Cooktown, the last settlement of any size on your "Trip to the Tip". Choose either the coastal route via Cape Tribulation, where Cook's *Endeavour* nearly sank in 1770, or, for a real adventure, the infamous "CREB Track" out of Daintree. Here's your chance to play with the transfer levers as you run along the CREB's tyre-clawing gradients to the *Lion's Den Hotel*, a classic "bush pub" dating back to 1875.

Past Cooktown, the Lakefield National Park is Queensland's answer to Kakadu, with "magnetic" anthills aligned north–south to avoid overheating in the noonday sun, 180 species of birds and a rich colony of flying foxes.

But there's more. A tough, creek-ridden diversion leads east to the Iron Range National Park, where the creeper-festooned rainforests don't recede until Chilli Beach campsite on the Coral Sea. Ecologically this extraordinary park has more in common with New Guinea, and it's famed for the nocturnal green python and brilliant blue-and-red eclectus parrot.

Back on the main road, die-hards avoid the newer bypasses to follow the Old Telegraph Track's numerous creek crossings. Eventually you arrive at Twin Falls, with its safe swimming holes, before reaching the 100m-wide Jardine River, a once-demanding crossing now made easier by the nearby ferry. Then suddenly the road runs out near a rocky headland overlooking the Torres Straits. A sign marks the tip of mainland Australia and the end of your journey.

965 | Heli-biking Ben Cruachan

NEW ZEALAND The helicopter drops you high on a mountaintop and swoops back down into the valley. Patches of snow lie on the ground, clouds hang low overhead and the air has a crisp, alpine bite. In every direction thrusting peaks stand in ranks around you, punctuated by fertile green valleys. As you watch the helicopter diminish into a speck, you take a deep gulp of alpine air before donning helmet, gloves and body armour. Pointing your front tyre downhill, it's time to let gravity take care of the rest.

Ben Cruachan, a 2000m peak tucked behind the Remarkables, the mountain range that flanks the picturesque resort of Queenstown, is a favourite of many backcountry mountain bikers. It's no surprise why: it offers 1600m of pure downhill adrenaline. And that's after the rush of flying up to the top.

The trail follows a rough 4WD road down the ridgeline from the summit. Littered with loose shale, it demands both balance and patience to navigate. After a few kilometres the route veers left onto a vertiginous single track snaking 6km down a steep valley. The upper reaches here are fast and fun; further down, shallow streams cut across the trail and you need to concentrate hard to avoid flying over the handlebars when your tyres come to an abrupt halt in a muddy bog.

Two hours after you alight on the mountain's summit, the crunch of gravel signals the final stretch into the Gibson wine valley. The race to the finish is on: a fast loose blast with the odd pothole and small jumps to negotiate. Once you get your breath back you'll want to do it all over again – that or recover over a tasty Pinot Noir.

966 | The last frontier: working on a cattle station

AUSTRALIA Director Baz Luhrmann did his best to make cattle droving look dramatic, even sexy, in the epic film *Australia*. But if you yearn to pull on your riding boots and start rounding them up like Hugh Jackman or Nicole Kidman, you may be in for a reality check. Working on a real Kimberley cattle station is as tough as it gets: hot, sweaty, hard graft for long hours and low pay. You'll be sharing a bunkhouse and meals with rangy stockmen, and things like TV, telephones, the internet and even the radio are luxuries you'll have to learn to live without.

But when it's over and the aches have subsided, you'll look back with satisfaction. Instead of following the hordes along the usual backpacker trail you'll have participated in an iconic Australian activity. Apart from honing your riding skills, you'll learn how to brand a bull, build up plenty of muscle and experience life in the fabled "Nor'west".

The Kimberley is Australia's last frontier, a place where cattle stations run to a million acres and are on the margins of manageability. The rugged landscape and climate (which in turn floods then burns) make this some of the toughest cattle country on the planet. But eager hands are always sought so you'll be welcomed, particularly if you've an aptitude for working with horses or motorbikes. With a bit of luck you'll be part of the annual muster, when cattle are tracked down and driven in from the four corners of the property for transport to market. As well as horses, dirt- and quad bikes are used, all coordinated from above by helicopters equipped with radios, but you'll be just as useful on foot, coaxing the nervy beasts into mobile yards or triple-trailer roadtrains.

After working in a tight-knit team, you may find it tough to leave at the end of your stay, and while the *Australia* fantasies may have faded you'll have plenty of real memories to savour.

967 | Fresh breaks and fresh beans: surfing utopia at Raglan

NEW ZEALAND The laidback town of Raglan, about 150km south of Auckland, is loved by in-the-know surfers for both its legendary left-handers and its bohemian vibe. Lines of perfect breakers appear like blue corduroy along the shore here, watched over by the majestic Mount Karioi or "Sleeping Lady".

For beginners, the best place to paddle out is sandy-bottomed Ngarunui Beach, 5km out of town. Seasoned surfers, though, seek out the wildest rides at Manu Bay, around 8km from Raglan, which starred in the cult 1960s surf flick, *Endless Summer*. Manu's exposed point break provides one of the longest and most consistent waves on the planet and it regularly hosts pro surfing competitions. Ideally, it's best sampled at low tide when there are offshore, southeasterly winds, but you'll find it packed with grinning, wet-suited locals whatever the weather.

Once you've stashed your board and washed the salt from your hair, check out Raglan's artist-run galleries or its vibrant craft market, held twice a month. For a caffeine hit, follow the smell of freshly roasted beans to tiny *Raglan Roast*, squeezed next to a surf shop down tiny Volcom Lane. If your stomach begins to rumble, grab some fish and chips down at the wharf or head to one of the cafés and pubs lining palm-shaded Bow Street. There's usually a band playing at one of them – don't miss local reggae legends Cornerstone Roots if they're in town.

If you find you can't drag yourself away from Raglan, check in at the *Solscape Eco Retreat* on Manu Bay. This sustainably run hostel offers accommodation in teepees and converted train carriages, provides its own solar water heating and lighting and, of course, rents boards and runs a surf school.

968 | Kiwi-spotting in Trounson Kauri Park

NEW ZEALAND They're elusive creatures, these kiwi. In fact, New Zealand's national bird is so rare that it's almost never seen other than at the half-dozen places where guided night safaris raise the odds considerably. As you head out on foot, you may hear the piercing cry of the male cutting through the inky darkness, closely followed by the husky female reply, but you wonder whether either will see fit to show its pointy face. The eeriness of the situation is enhanced by the vast walls of kauri trees that close in around you, and the thick understorey of tree ferns that blocks out the stars.

You sense the kiwi are nearby, but these things can't be rushed. Not so long ago you'd have been lucky to hear them at all, as introduced stoats, rats, possums and feral cats and dogs had decimated numbers. But Trounson is one of several "mainland islands" where this diminutive relative of the ostrich is being brought back from the brink of extinction, with intensive trapping

and poisoning keeping predator numbers low enough to allow indigenous species to flourish. And it's not just kiwi that benefit. Your guide will introduce you to the ruru – a native owl known as the "morepork" for the sound of its haunting call – as well as the palm-sized, carnivorous kauri snail and the scary-looking, grasshopper-like weta, which can grow up to 10cm long. They're not dangerous, but no one wants to get too close.

Finally, a gentle scuffling in the leaf litter comes closer and you get your first glimpse of a North Island brown kiwi, its slender beak probing the ground for food. Seemingly unconcerned by your presence, it wanders closer, its shaggy pelt looking more like fur than feathers. Then someone makes an unexpected move and the kiwi takes fright, skittering off into the darkness. Initial disappointment soon fades as another makes itself visible. That's it for the night, but even two sightings seem a rare privilege.

Life beyond the beach in Melanesia

969

FIJI For many visitors, Fiji begins at the poolside bar and ends somewhere near the third sunlounger on the right. Yet the archipelago's largest island Viti Levu, or "Big Fiji", provides much more than tropical sun and coconut cocktails. Turn your focus inland and you'll find dramatic mountain scenery, exhilarating hikes and a fascinating indigenous culture, all accessible by simply renting a 4WD and hitting the dirt roads.

A few hours from Nadi, Fiji's tourism hub, the baking-hot sugar-cane fields give way to the misty rainforest of the Nausori Highlands. Back in the 1860s, these mountains were inhabited by cannibal tribes; today, crater-sized potholes and the odd speeding truck are the main hazards to watch out for.

Following the bone-shaking earth roads, and asking directions as you go, you'll find your way to Navala, the most stunning village in Fiji. All the homes here are *bures*, thickly thatched huts built with woven

bamboo walls. Brightly coloured washing hangs between the huts and palm trees, the only traces of modernity supplied by the concrete church and school building. Given the idyllic setting, it's tempting to stay the night and there's accommodation close by at *Bulou's Eco-Lodge*, a family-run homestay that offers en-suite *bures* as well as a small dorm.

Bulou's son Tui will introduce you to the village elders at Navala, and with luck you'll be invited to sup *kava*, Fiji's national drink, with the chief. Now accepted as a guest, it's up to you how you spend your time. With river trips on traditional *bilibili* rafts, jungle treks along ancient hunting trails, or the ascent of Mount Tomanivi (Fiji's highest mountain at 1323m) on offer, there's little chance of getting bored. Returning to *Bulou's*, the smell of home-cooked Fijian food will welcome you back, and the lure of the beach resort will be far from your mind.

From prison to paradise on l'Île des Pins

NEW CALEDONIA If you have to go into exile somewhere, it might as well be the South Pacific, and this blob of an island at the southern end of French New Caledonia is a particularly bearable spot. Measuring just 14km by 18km, the Île des Pins – "Island of Pines" – was a penal colony in the nineteenth century, the last stop for many dissidents from the Paris Commune in the 1870s. It's interesting to share the impressions of one of the convicts transported here. Having acknowledged that he had ended up in a paradise, he immediately adds, with obvious bitterness, "but I saw nothing of its beauty".

The modern-day visitor comes to the island by choice, of course, and can hardly fail to notice the natural beauty of the destination: stunning coastlines, with hot, white sand, and warm, limpid water, pale blue as far as the reef, and a deeper blue beyond. The classic South Sea paradise. The most obvious place to test the water has to be the island's "piscine naturelle", or natural swimming pool, where the sea enters a shallow bay through a narrow defile between jagged rocks and creates a calm, pristine pool, lined by sun-baked sand. You can wallow in safety while listening to the waves breaking in the distance.

But one thing stops it all from becoming a cliché: the araucaria pines that so struck Captain Cook when moored offshore that he named the island after them. Although there are plenty of swaying palms as well, it's these dark, spindly posts, soaring bolt upright into the sky, and adorned by minimal vegetation, that define and distinguish this place. And their forbidding, stark rigidity, in marked contrast to the friendly sway of the palms, creates a certain ambivalence. Do they really belong in paradise?

Before you leave, take in the island's ruined prison and monument and be thankful that you get to come and go as you please.

971 | Exploring the eerie underground world of Waitomo

NEW ZEALAND Waitomo, a tiny town in rolling sheep country, sits on a veritable Swiss cheese of limestone, with deep sinkholes, beautifully sculpted tunnels and wild organ pipes of stalactites all lit up by ghostly constellations of glow-worms.

Their Harry Potter-esque scientific name is *Arachnocampa luminosa*, a reference to the almost magical bioluminescence which they use to hunt and attract mates. More prosaically, you learn that they are not worms at all but the larvae of a humble insect, the fungus gnat. But the silk-like threads they produce to catch insects, hanging like fine gossamer from the stony roof, are nothing less than beautiful.

The traditional way to see all this is on a gentle stroll through some of the shallower caverns, where Victorian explorers named the rock formations after animals, mythical creatures and household items. Coloured lights pick out the salient features before you take an otherworldly ride in a dinghy across an underground lake, the green pinpricks of light above your head resembling the heavens of some parallel universe.

Ever the adventure pioneers, New Zealanders have also created another method of exploring the caves – blackwater rafting. Decked out in wetsuit, helmet and miner's lamp, you head underground with a truck inner tube, then sit in it and float through the gloom (just remember not to watch *The Descent* beforehand). The few rapids are gentle and safe, but the blackness gives that extra *frisson* of uncertainty.

For an extra thrill you can try a 100m-long abseil, waterfall jumps and even a little subterranean rock climbing. With small groups there's a genuine feeling of exploration as you negotiate tight squeezes and find your way into pristine chambers, with that reassuring glow far up above.

972 | River of no return: rafting the Franklin

AUSTRALIA Determine when you come and the river decides how long you'll stay. You're going to be soaked to the skin, cold and challenged by rapids with names like The Cauldron, Thunder Rush and Jawbreaker. And that's exactly why you're here.

The plan: you and nine others, including two all-knowing river guides, are to spend a week paddling, pinballing and peacefully drifting more than 100km through southwest Tasmania, one of the wildest and remotest parts of Australia. All the gear's provided: two inflatable rafts, camping equipment, wetsuits, helmets (to be worn at all times), waterproof-paddling jackets (unflatteringly called "cags") and, most importantly, lifejackets. The rest is up to the river.

Rafting the Franklin is one of the world's last true wilderness experiences, not least because the river has such a fearsome reputation. Its banks are so steep and its catchment so vast that any rain upstream (and it's plentiful in Tasmania) can cause river levels to rise 10m overnight, turning benign rapids into life-or-death obstacles for all but the most experienced river-travellers (that's where the guides come in). Sometimes the team will even be forced to carry the fully laden rafts and gear along precarious, cliff-hugging tracks that skirt the most dangerous sections of river.

The good news is that no matter what the conditions – high water, low water or somewhere in between – you're in for the ride of your life. Most of the whitewater is Grade 3 and 4, but there are plenty of still and silent pools where you might spot a platypus or drift past stately 2000-year-old Huon pine trees.

It's humbling to spend days in such a place, travelling along the river by day and camping on its fringes at night. And in losing track of time and the days of the week, you gain something else – something bigger: that rare relief of being nobody of consequence in true wilderness.

973 | Delivering the mail with dolphins

NEW ZEALAND The deep blue waters of Pelorus Sound are calm, the scenery along the sinuous waterways is wonderful and there's a fair chance of spying dolphins riding the boat's bow wave. But that's only part of the story. The real pleasure in riding the Pelorus Mail Boat is simply watching the day drift by as you chug between bush-clad hills around the waterways at the northern tip of the South Island.

There has been a mail service around the sounds since 1869, and while thirty-odd tourists a day help keep the business afloat, the *Pelorus Express* still plays a vital role. Apart from the mail itself, it supplies a reassuring link to the outside world for this isolated group of small homesteads. It's a mixed bunch living here far from roads and shops – artists, retirees, entrepreneurs playing the stock market and even families whose kids receive their correspondence school papers by mail boat.

The mail run is a much anticipated event, and at most wharves skippers are greeted by at least one local. They always have a few minutes to stop and shoot the breeze and pass on local gossip. Dogs wait eagerly at wharf end awaiting a treat from Val's boxes of biscuits. There's often a little bartering: a few tomato seedlings from the garden centre back in town might be traded for a bag of oranges from a laden tree up by the homestead.

The waters of Pelorus Sound are also known for a gastronomic treat – the green-lipped mussel, which grows here to epic proportions. Almost every bay has its mussel farm, and you'll usually spot a tender hauled up alongside while the deckhands winch up the ropes and slough off the juicy bivalves.

When it is time for home, the passengers scan the water for those elusive dolphins while looking forward to a seafood feast back at the marina.

974 | Learning the ancient art of bush medicine

AUSTRALIA In a country where a small spider can kill you, it's reassuring to know Mother Nature has a softer side. Hidden in the prehistoric valleys of the Blue Mountains National Park in New South Wales are hundreds of plants used by Aboriginal peoples to cure everything from earache and fevers to snake bites and colds. The best chance you have of spotting them, and learning about the art of bush medicine, is to delve deep into the forest with an expert guide. Walking ancient hunting tracks used by indigenous peoples, far from the car parks and crowded viewpoints, you will discover a different side of this wonderful national park.

One of the first things that strikes you as you descend into the chiselled gorges of the park is the smell – an astringent mix of eucalyptus and tea tree, a result of the oils evaporating from these plants that also gives the air its blue haze. While you might think of tea-tree oil being used to zap the odd spot, Aboriginals used it widely, inhaling the infused oil to cure coughs and stuffing the raw leaves into

cuts to prevent infection. Colonial settlers soon learned about this miracle plant, and tea-tree oil was even issued to Australian soldiers during World War II.

Descending further, the hum of cicadas gets louder and the air becomes humid as you enter the moss- and lichen-encrusted cloudforest. While you concentrate on the barely distinguishable path, your eagle-eyed guide will point out everything from bush pears, an ancient Aboriginal snack, to the aptly named headache vine, once crushed and rubbed directly into the skin to treat migraines. As the gradient steepens, you're glad of the guide ropes attached to the slippery stone walls. Most visitors end up nonetheless with an impromptu mud pack on their lower half before they reach the bottom of the creek. As the air grows warmer and your spirits start to flag, your ears will welcome the hiss of the nearby Wentworth Falls, signalling both the end point of the hike and the prospect of an invigorating swim.

975 | Waitangi: reliving the birth of a modern nation

NEW ZEALAND The birth of New Zealand as a modern country can be traced back to a small patch of landscaped grass, just across the Waitangi River from Paihia in the Bay of Islands. On February 6, 1840, representatives of the British Crown and several dozen northern Maori chiefs met in a marquee here to sign the Treaty of Waitangi. To this day it remains debatable whether the Maoris knew they were signing away their sovereignty, but sign they did, and the Treaty became not just New Zealand's founding document, but the cornerstone of the country's race relations to this day.

Arriving at the Treaty Grounds, you walk straight out onto that hallowed lawn, with its views out over the Bay of Islands, and the historic flagpole where Maori and British flags still fly. Curious foreign visitors, and Kiwis in search of their heritage, gravitate towards the 1834 Treaty House, all neat white weatherboards and rooms containing material on the early colonial period.

Most of the Maoris who came for the signing arrived by canoe, but few canoes would have been as big as *Ngatoki Matawhaorua*, now in residence down by the shore. The world's largest wooden war canoe, it stretches more than 35m from prow to gloriously carved sternpost and took over two years to carve from a pair of massive kauri tree trunks. Eighty warriors are needed to paddle it during its annual outing on the anniversary of the signing of the treaty.

Lolling-tongue carved figures with iridescent seashell eyes greet you at the *whare rununga*, or Maori meeting house, up beside the lawn – the only pan-tribal meeting house in the country. For a deeper understanding of the significance of the *whare rununga*, return in the evening for the stirring Night Show. Through heartfelt dance, song and storytelling you'll get a primer in the richness of Maori legend and history, and learn a good deal about modern Maori life and how the Treaty remains so essential to it.

976 | Dodging planes on Fraser Island

AUSTRALIA Wipe the dust from your rear-view mirror and keep one juddering eyeball fixed on the sky behind you. At any moment a plane could drop down, flinging hot sand into your paintwork, and you'll be expected to give it enough space to land. On Fraser Island's 75 Mile Beach, you see, the highway doubles up as a runway – and pilots have priority. But nearly everywhere else on the world's largest sand island, you're better off in a 4WD.

Fraser Island is Australia at its most rugged, and a tarmac-free zone. From the moment you roll off the ferry and start to trundle down the steamy forest trails of the interior, you can expect to have your driving skills tested to the limit. As your tyres begin to slip into the powder-fine sand, and the cabin to fill with the tangy smell of burnt clutch, you'll also need to look out for fallen trees, deep creeks and the resident population of hungry,

pure-blood dingoes. It's not all slow and steady, though; when you hit the beach highway you can floor the accelerator, sending high-pitched tyre squeals through the rickety roll cage. The key to beach driving is to look out for treacherous patches of wet sand and remember not to panic when you hear the "pop-pop-pop" of washed-up jellyfish being squashed under the wheels.

On a good day, it's possible to dash between multicoloured sand dunes, Aboriginal reserves and sparkling freshwater lakes in a single afternoon. But you won't see all of Fraser Island in a day, no matter how good your driving is, and that's why most visitors camp here overnight. So when you see a plane taking off, do give it plenty of room, but don't start to wish you were on board. After all, it's down here on the ground, with the dingoes and the dust, that you'll feel every jolt of the island.

What lies beneath: snorkelling at the Great Barrier Reef

AUSTRALIA "It's like being in another world!" may be the most predictable observation following a close encounter with the Great Barrier Reef, but only when you've come face to face with the extraordinary animals, shapes and colours here do you realize that you've truly entered a watery parallel universe. And as a curious thick-lipped potato cod nudges your mask, you might also wonder, "who exactly is watching whom?"

The Great Barrier Reef follows Australia's continental shelf from Lady Elliot Island, in southern Queensland, 2300km north to New Guinea. Its northern reaches are closer to land, so while it's 300km to the main body from Gladstone, Cairns is barely 50km distant, making this the best place for reef day-trips. Scuba diving may get you more quality time down below, but a well-chosen snorkelling location can reveal marvels no less superb without all the bother of training, equipment and lengthy safety procedures. Though commonly called the world's biggest life form, the Great Barrier Reef is more an intricate network of patch reefs than a single entity. All of it, however, was built by one animal: the tiny coral polyp that grows together to create modular colonies – corals. These in turn provide food, shelter and hunting grounds for a bewildering assortment of more mobile creatures.

Rays, moray eels and turtles glide effortlessly by, while fish so dazzling they clearly missed out on camouflage training dart between caves to nibble on coral branches, and slug-like nudibranchs sashay in the current. It all unfolds before you one breath at a time, a never-ending grand promenade of the life aquatic.

NEW ZEALAND It may seem odd to drive for hours on end just to look at a bunch of old trees, but the kauri forests of New Zealand's North Island are special. To start with, the kauri trees are staggeringly, sensationally large. The tallest, Tane Mahuta (God of the Forest), towers some 50m above the earth; it's the same height as Nelson's Column in London's Trafalagar Square.

Its long, straight trunk soars neck-achingly upwards, a smooth, brown cylinder unhindered by branches. Then, from near the top, spiky boughs spray outwards, covered in thousands of tiny, dark-green, oval leaves. The thin, gnarly branches look feeble compared to the massive trunk, and they betray the tree's age like the wrinkles etched onto an old man's face. But this tree is older than any man by far. It's reckoned to have started life some two thousand years ago; humans wouldn't even land here for another thousand years.

A walk through this protected sanctuary – European loggers and the gum trade greatly thinned the kauri ranks – takes you from Tane Mahuta to Te Matua Ngahere (Father of the Forest). This tree isn't as tall as Tane Mahuta, but it is phenomenally fat, more than 16m wide. Personality oozes from every crack in its ancient bark. How many people before you walked beneath its branches? Which now-extinct birds rested on its boughs? The tree replies with a far-distant rustle of leaves and continues its millennia-long watch.

979

Hike through history on the Kokoda Trail

PAPUA NEW GUINEA As you trek along Papua New Guinea's Kokoda Trail, winding north 96km from Owers' Corner to Kokoda, it can feel like every step has its own story. During World War II, Australian troops used the route to prevent the Japanese, who had landed on the northern beaches, from taking Port Moresby on the southern coast. Though the trail's military pedigree attracts both war buffs and nostalgics, it's also justly famous for some of the most rugged and remote terrain in the region. Climbing up to 2200m as it tops the Owen Stanley Range, the path traverses orchid-decked jungles, lush river valleys and the settlements of the Koiari and Orokaiva tribes. Like the help these people gave Allied troops during the war, the smiles you share with the villagers won't easily be forgotten.

980 | Travelling back in time in Samoa

SAMOA Ever wanted to travel back in time? It's surprisingly easy in the Samoas, where you can board a tiny plane in April, then land twenty minutes later, suddenly back in March again. This little trick is made possible by the fact that the Samoan archipelago straddles the International Date Line: to the west of this invisible tangent lies an independent nation aligned towards Asia and Australia, and to the east a territory of the United States. However, visiting the two will get you that time-travel feel in more ways than one, since these charming slices of the South Pacific are refreshingly undeveloped. All the way around their coasts, you'll spot countless *fales* – tiny, wall-free traditional structures consisting of little but a thatched roof, a wooden platform and a few posts.

Samoa, or the Independent State of Samoa, is made up of two main islands, 20km apart and linked by ferry. To the west, Savai'i is the larger of the two; it's also less populous and more appealing – the best thing to do here is rent a scooter for a five-hour ride around the island. The north coast features a string of great beaches where you can snorkel or kick back with a coconut, as well as some spectacular lava fields (one of which courses merrily through a now-empty church); the south coast features more watery attractions, including the extremely powerful Alofaaga Blowholes, and a pleasing waterfall. The eastern island, Upolu, is home to Apia, the country's bustling little capital, and the To Sua sinkhole, a turquoise swimming hole surrounded by sheer jungle walls.

You'll need to head to a small airstrip near Apia to board the flight to American Samoa, on a plane so small that you'll feel every updraft, and merely need to crane your neck to get a pilot's view of the landing. After twenty minutes, you'll be a full day behind, thus confusing the hell out of your smartphone's calendar app. The people in American Samoa may look similar, but the vibe is quite different – basketball shirts abound, the Stars and Stripes flutter here and there, and the closest ATM to the airport is a twenty-minute walk away, in a McDonald's. The island also rises very steeply from the sea, and it's tempting to climb up into the national park for a sky-high view of the cute little capital, Pago Pago (and another McDonald's). After staying a night or three at a beachside *fale*, and eating some great seafood, it'll soon be time for your return trip back to the future.

981 | Taking the plunge with A.J. Hackett

NEW ZEALAND Ever since speed skiers and general daredevils A.J. Hackett and Henry van Asch invented commercial bungee jumping, New Zealand has been its home, and Queenstown its capital. So, if you're going to bungee, what better place than here? And if it's the classic experience you're after, then the original Kawarau Suspension Bridge is your spot. At 43m it's only a modest jump by modern standards, but you're guaranteed an audience to will you on and then celebrate your achievement.

Diving off tall towers with vines tied around your ankles has been a male rite of passage in Vanuatu for centuries, but modern bungee started with the nutty antics of the Oxford University Dangerous Sports Club in the 1970s. The next leap forward was A.J. Hackett's bungee off the Eiffel Tower in 1987. He was promptly arrested but soon started commercial operations in Queenstown.

So are you going solo or double? Dunking or dry? Shirt on or shirt off? Decisions made, you stroll out onto the bridge (looking oh so casual) while pumping rock or hip-hop starts to build the adrenaline. Wrapping a towel around your ankles for protection, they'll attach the cord while feeding you some jocular spiel about the bungee breaking (it won't) or not being attached properly (it will be). You'll then be chivvied into producing a cheesy grin (or more likely rictus) for the camera before shuffling out onto the precipice for the countdown.

Three. Two. One. Bungee!

982 | Slip into Broometime

AUSTRALIA The laidback, romantic appeal of Broome stems partly from its uniqueness along the west Australian coastline. In many thousands of kilometres, no other town matches its alluring combination of beautiful beaches, relative sophistication and a still resonant "frontier town" charm.

From its earliest days, Broome has been home to an ethnically diverse population: Timorese, Malays and Chinese came in their thousands to get rich quick when the pearl industry boomed here in the late 1800s. The world's largest oysters prospered in the tidal waters and shells were originally shovelled off the beach. With the invention of the diving helmet, Asian divers kept the supply going, but along with frequent cyclones the newfangled technology caused many deaths, as a stroll around the town's different ethnic cemeteries reveals. Pearl farming continues today offshore, from securely guarded pontoons, and Broome remains the best place to buy these treasures, particularly along Dampier Terrace.

The old Chinatown has been tastefully renovated. Its once grubby tin-shack bordellos are now trendy boutiques, while a kilometre or two away the former master pearlers' bougainvillea-shrouded villas house galleries and coffee shops. Nearby, the 1916 Broome Picture House, the world's oldest open-air cinema, is still going strong. Bats flutter across the latest release on screen as you watch under starlight from communal canvas benches; the newer air-con cinema round the corner just misses the point.

Nature has further blessed Broome with heavenly Cable Beach, 22km of palm-swaying indolence named after the telegraph cable that ran from here to Singapore. The classic vista from Gantheaume Point lays red cliffs over ivory sands and a sea so hypnotically turquoise it should carry a health warning. Occasionally a watery illusion is created by the moon rising over the low-tide mudflats. Dubbed the "staircase to the moon", it sounds better than it looks, but you don't mind, you're on Broometime after all.

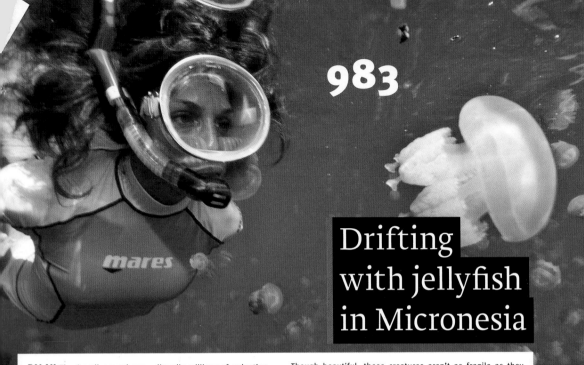

983

Drifting with jellyfish in Micronesia

PALAU They're all around you – literally millions of pulsating golden mastigia, like a swarm of squishy tennis balls in zero gravity. As you move your limbs to keep yourself afloat in this warm lake on one of Palau's Rock Islands, the jellyfish brush softly against your skin, then waft away as endless others take their place. They can barely sting – aeons spent in this saltwater lake without a single predator have weakened their defences – so there's no need to avoid them, and you couldn't even if you tried.

Though beautiful, these creatures aren't as fragile as they look; the depths where they spend the night contain high levels of hydrogen sulphide, which is toxic to humans. Scuba diving is banned for this reason, but a mask and snorkel are all you need to explore the lake's upper reaches. Along with the mastigia, you'll also spot tiny gobies and cardinal fish hiding among the mangrove roots, while up above, kingfishers perch imperiously on their branches.

984 | Where art meets nature – Waiheke Island

NEW ZEALAND Artists, writers and craftspeople have long flocked to Waiheke Island, which lies 35 minutes from Auckland by ferry. It may be the relative isolation that appeals, or perhaps it's the captivating combination of sandy beaches, verdant native bush, neatly rowed vineyards and alluring restaurants. Whatever the reason, creative types thrive in this laidback environment, and there's ample opportunity to view the fruits of their labour.

The best place to start is Connells Bay Sculpture Park. Here, a 2km guided walk through bush and farmland takes you past a medley of stark sculptural works by renowned New Zealand sculptors that amalgamate effortlessly with the surrounding lush vegetation. There are lovely views of the Hauraki Gulf along the route.

Pieces range from outlandish carbon-fibre structures to wood-carved monoliths reminiscent of Easter Island statues. With all of this framed by awe-inspiring vistas of the Hauraki Gulf beyond, it's a true union of art and nature.

985 | Hiking Sydney's Spit to Manly Walkway

AUSTRALIA Sydney's 10km harbour-side hike, running through bush above ragged cliffs and via sandy beaches, is surely the world's most scenic city walk. You begin at Spit Bridge, which spans the Middle Harbour, and end, an exhilarated three hours later, at the ferry wharf in Manly. Officially known as the Manly Scenic Walkway, the route is well signed and dead easy to navigate – just keep the sea on your right and let your eyes feast on the scalloped sandstone coastline and the enviable colonial homes that get this view day in and day out.

If you're not quite ready for a dip at Clontarf Beach, just 1500m into the walk, you'll surely be tempted when you reach secluded little Washaway Beach, once an official nudist spot and still attracting the odd bare-buttocked bather.

Tramping up to Grotto Point and later on to Dobroyd Head, through the thick woodlands of Sydney Harbour National Park, provides a different view – the fabulous panorama of the harbour and its ocean jaws, the North and South heads.

Need to know

914 To hike the Gillespie Pass in the Mount Aspiring National Park, you need to be fit and have a head for heights. For further information, contact the Makarora Visitor Centre (Ⓦ doc.govt.nz).

915 Lord Howe Island (Ⓦ lordhoweisland.info) is a 1hr 50min flight from Sydney (Ⓦ qantas.com). The Mount Gower walk takes 8–10hr.

916 Parks Victoria gives information on walks, campsites and other activities at Ⓦ parkweb.vic.gov.au. You'll also find updates on any trail closures.

917 Platypus safaris in Eungella National Park are offered by Ⓦ reeforest.au.

918 To find schedules of upcoming matches, visit Ⓦ allblacks.com.

919 Queen Victoria Market is open Tues & Thurs–Sun;see Ⓦ qvm.com.au for details.

920 Visit Ⓦ marlboroughtours.co.nz or Ⓦ winetours-bybike.co.nz for more information.

921 Purnululu National Park (Ⓦ parks.dpaw.wa.gov.au) is open April–Dec, weather permitting. Helicopter flights are offered by Ⓦ helispirit.com.au.

922 Sydney Gay and Lesbian Mardi Gras takes place mid-Feb to early March, see Ⓦ mardigras.org.au for full details.

923 If you're not lucky enough to be invited to a private hangi, contact Rotorua (Ⓦ rotoruanz.com), which provides the widest range of commercial hangi nights.

924 The Port Macquarie Koala Hospital and Study Centre, in the Macquarie Nature Reserve on Lord Street, Port Macquarie, New South Wales, is open daily (Ⓦ koalahospital.org.au).

925 For more details, visit Ⓦ doc.govt.nz/parks-and-recreation; for guided hikes try Ⓦ ultimatehikes.co.nz.

926 One of the best Aboriginal art galleries in Alice Springs is run by the Central and Western Desert Art Movement: Ⓦ papunyatula.com.au.

927 For more information on Darwin and its attractions, see Ⓦ australia.com/en-us/places/darwin-and-surrounds/guide-to-darwin.html.

928 Vanuatu's tourism website (Ⓦ vanuatu.travel) lists dive operators that offer trips to the *Coolidge*.

929 For more information on the Valley of Taste, visit Ⓦ swanvalley.com.au. Cycle rental is available from Brookleigh Bike Hire, 1235 Great Northern Hwy (Ⓦ brookleigh.com.au).

930 West Oz Active (Ⓦ westozactive.com.au) offers tours into remote parts of Karijini.

931 Most visitors rent kayaks in Marahau; try Ⓦ abeltasmankayaks.co.nz or Ⓦ kahukayaks.co.nz.

932 To get an early start on Mount Tamborine, book in at the cosy *Polish Place* (Ⓦ polishplace.com.au).

933 Most resorts offer *kava* tasting sessions, while local tour operators are listed on Ⓦ fiji.travel.

934 For links to tour operators that offer trips up Mount Yasur, visit Ⓦ vanuatu.travel.

935 *The Byron at Byron* (Ⓦ thebyronatbyron.com.au), a luxury lodge, offers daily yoga sessions and can arrange surfing lessons with local experts, while *Escape Haven* (Ⓦ escapehaven.com) runs full-board yoga and surf retreats for women only.

936 For more information, visit Ⓦ rotoruanz.com.

937 Te Papa (Ⓦ tepapa.govt.nz) is open daily; admission is free.

938 The best time to walk the Overland Track (Ⓦ overlandtrack.com.au) is during Feb and March.

939 Whitsundays Sailing Adventures (Ⓦ whitsailing.com) offers outings on classic tall ships; Southern Cross (Ⓦ soxsail.com) has tours on fast yachts.

940 The *Aranui 5* departs year-round. For more information, visit Ⓦ aranui.com.

941 Nitmiluk Tours (Ⓦ nitmiluktours.com.au) offer single and double canoes for full-day, half-day and overnight rental. The best time for canoeing is early in the dry season, from May to July; book ahead.

942 For more information on Watarrka National Park, visit Ⓦ parksandwildlife.nt.gov.au. The Rim Walk occasionally closes in summer due to excessive temperatures. Avoid the midday heat, and if possible hike in the afternoon rather than the busier morning.

943 For lessons, try Cheyne Horan School of Surf (Ⓦ cheynehoran.com.au) or Gold Coast Surf School (Ⓦ surfinparadise.com.au).

944 The TranzAlpine (Ⓦ greatjourneysofnz.co.nz) operates daily from Christchurch to Greymouth and back.

945 For ferry times, visit Ⓦ transportnsw.info; for information on harbour bridge ascents, see Ⓦ bridgeclimb.com.

946 Milford Sound (Ⓦ milford-sound.co.nz) is on the west coast of New Zealand's South Island, and well served by coach; though it's fabulous year-round, winter (June–Sept) is the best time to visit.

947 The *Ghan* (Ⓦ gsr.com.au) leaves Adelaide for Darwin every Sun at 12.15pm, and also on Wed at 12.10pm between June and late Aug. The journey takes 48hrs.

948 The best time to see whale sharks is between April and July. Licensed operators include Three Islands (Ⓦ whalesharkdive.com) and Exmouth Diving Centre (Ⓦ exmouthdiving.com.au).

949 MONA is open Wed–Mon (daily in January) at 655 Main Rd, Berridale (Ⓦ mona.net.au), and can be accessed by bus from central Hobart or a gallery catamaran from Brooke St pier.

950 For more information, visit Ⓦ parksaustralia.gov.au/uluru.

951 Hot Water Beach is 15km southeast of Whitianga, or just over 30km by road; there's also accommodation nearby, and the local surf shop rents out spades. Check tide timetables at Ⓦ niwa.co.nz.

952 For opening times and more information on Auckland Museum see Ⓦ aucklandmuseum.com.

953 The Tongariro Crossing typically takes 6–8hrs and requires a good level of fitness. See Ⓦ doc.govt.nz for updates on track conditions.

954 Trips depart from Queenstown's Shotover Jet Beach daily (Ⓦ shotoverjet.com), with a typical cost of NZ$155 for adults, NZ$89 for children. Wear sunglasses, and, in winter, warm clothes including hat and gloves.

955 *Kingfisher Bay Resort* (Ⓦ kingfisherbay.com) on Fraser Island offers night-time wildlife walks in the surrounding forest. *On the Wallaby* (Ⓦ onthewallaby.com), a budget lodge in Yungaburra, runs nocturnal canoe trips on Lake Tinaroo.

956 The Poor Knights Islands Marine Reserve is 25km off the east coast of Northland. For more information, visit Ⓦ diving.co.nz.

957 Fiji Airlines flies from Suva to Tuvalu, and then straight back, on Tuesdays and Thursdays (3hr).

958 Visit Ⓦ sharkbay.org for more information.

959 Join a specialist tour operator like Kimberley Wild (Ⓦ kimberleywild.com.au) from Broome, Darwin or Alice Springs for the best Outback wilderness experience.

960 For a long trip, you're best buying a 4WD bushcamper. Visit Ⓦ exploreoz.com for more advice on Outback four-wheeling.

961 Harris Mountains Heli-Ski (Ⓦ heliski.co.nz) offer heli-skiing and heli-boarding around Queenstown, Wanaka and Mount Cook. The season runs June–Oct.

962 To do the trek properly, arrange a hike with Pa's Treks (Ⓦ pastreks.com). For more on the Cook Islands, see Ⓦ cookislands.travel.

963 Find a range of distillery locations and hours at Ⓦ taswhiskytrail.com. Tasmanian Whisky Tours runs day tours from Hobart to three or four distilleries (Ⓦ tasmanianwhiskytours.com.au). Bookings can be made in the UK via Tasmanian Odyssey (Ⓦ tasmanian-whiskytours.rezdy.com).

964 You can rent a fully equipped 4WD bushcamper in Cairns via Ⓦ apollocamper.com or Ⓦ britz.com.au; allow at least a fortnight for the return trip. Travel is only possible out of wet season from May to Nov.

965 Heli-biking trips up Ben Cruachan are run by Vertigo Bikes (Ⓦ vertigobikes.co.nz) in Queenstown.

966 For more information on work opportunities, visit Ⓦ outback-australia-travel-secrets.com.

967 More information on Raglan (including surf cams) is available at Ⓦ raglan.net.nz. For details of Solscape *Eco Retreat*, check out Ⓦ solscape.co.nz.

968 Guided kiwi-spotting tours depart nightly, weather permitting, from the *Kauri Coast Top 10 Holiday Park* (Ⓦ kauricoasttop10.co.nz).

969 Four-wheel drives can be rented at Nadi Airport. To book *Bulou's Eco-Lodge*, contact Ⓔ stuinakavadra@gmail.com or Ⓣ 679 628 1224.

970 To stay on the island, contact the *Nataiwatch* bungalows (Ⓦ nataiwatch.com).

971 Waitomo caving trips with glow-worm watching are run by Ⓦ glowworm.co.nz and Ⓦ waitomo.com/black-water-rafting.aspx.

972 Rafting trips on the Franklin begin and end in Hobart. Guides are recommended: contact Ⓦ tasmanian-expeditions.com.au or Ⓦ franklinrivertasmania.com.

973 The *Pelorus Mail Boat* (Ⓦ mail-boat.co.nz) runs from Havelock Nov–April daily and May–Oct Mon, Wed & Fri. There's a different route each day, taking 7–9hrs. Bring your own lunch.

974 Blue Mountains bushwalks are offered year-round by The Blue Mountains Adventure Company (Ⓦ bmac.com.au), based in Katoomba, Blue Mountains National Park.

975 The Waitangi Visitor Centre and Treaty House are open year-round (Ⓦ waitangi.org.nz). You can book the Night Show through Culture North (Ⓔ culturenth@xtra.cp.nz).

976 Fraser Island (Ⓦ fraserisland.net) is a 25–40min ferry ride from Hervey Bay, in the southern part of Queensland. Fraser Magic 4WD Hire (Ⓦ fraser4wdhire.com.au), based in Hervey Bay, offers a range of self-drive options.

977 For more information, visit Ⓦ travelonline.com. For snorkel tours, try Ⓦ seastarcruises.com.au.

978 Waipoua Kauri Forest is 50km north of Dargaville; Footprints Waipoua (Ⓦ footprintswaipoua.co.nz) runs excellent walks to the kauri trees from Omapere.

979 The website Ⓦ kokodatrackauthority.org has lots of information on the Kokoda Trail.

980 Apia and Pago Pago are connected by several daily Samoa Airways flights (20min; plus or minus one day time difference).

981 A.J. Hackett Bungy (Ⓦ bungy.co.nz) operates individual and tandem bungee jumping, and also ziplining, at Kawarau Suspension Bridge near Queenstown.

982 For more information on Broome, see Ⓦ broomevisitorcentre.com.au.

983 See Ⓦ pristineparadise.com for more details, and links to Palau diving operators including Neco Marine (Ⓦ necomarine.com), Fish'n'Fins (Ⓦ fishnfins.com) and Ocean Hunter (Ⓦ oceanhunter.com).

984 Connells Bay Sculpture Park offers tours by appointment only – contact Ⓦ connellsbay.co.nz.

985 You can pick up a map of the walkway from the Manly Visitor Centre (Ⓦ manlyaustralia.com.au).

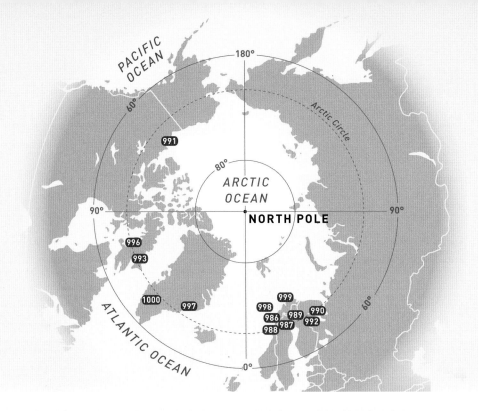

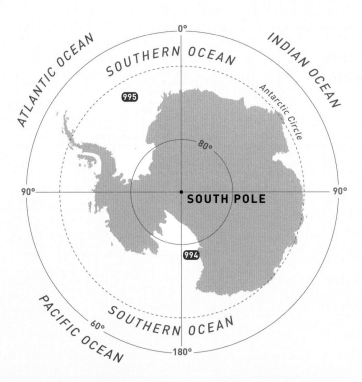

THE POLAR REGIONS

986–1000

The extremes of the Earth are just that: extreme. Travel in the polar regions is the stuff of grand spectacle, whether you're gazing at the ethereal dance of the northern lights in Arctic Sweden, sailing among pods of whales in the bays of Antarctica, or exploring unchartered fjords in wild East Greenland. Forever bound up in tales of intrepid explorers like Ernest Shackleton, Robert Peary and Roald Amundsen, these are beautiful regions of limitless horizons, raw wilderness and climate-hardened wildlife – places, in short, where the word "awesome" can be used literally.

986 White nights in Arctic Norway

NORWAY It is midnight when I adjust my sunglasses and begin to climb the mountain. Around me stretches a blanket of green Arctic hills and mirror-calm waters. Wildflowers nod in the night-time breeze. The higher I hike, the further the view opens out – far out at sea, I can see birds circling a trawler. And above the horizon, as it has done for at least a fortnight, the sun keeps blazing.

I've come to the small coastal village of Sommarøy, a herring-fishing settlement around an hour's drive from Tromsø, and so too has the season of white nights. Sommarøy sits more than 300km north of the Arctic Circle, at around 70° latitude. Being so far north means that, over the winter months, the region is prime territory for admiring the northern lights.

When summer comes around, however, its appeal takes on a different shape. Northern Norway at the height of midsummer is a remarkable place to visit, not least because the sun never sets. Wake up at 3am to pop to the loo and you'll be dazzled by the light pouring in through the window. There's an almost sedative calm as "night" arrives, and something genuinely stirring about being surrounded by so much light and nature in the small hours. When you're somewhere like this, who needs sleep?

Happily, I find the daytimes are special too. One afternoon I rent a boat and drift around the fjord, spotting puffins and sea eagles, then arrive back into the village for the freshest halibut dinner I'm ever likely to eat (food miles: approximately 75 metres). And hours later, I sit in the hotel hot tub watching the sun colour the landscape, then get up to plunge into a lake. It is way past my bedtime, but I'm not sure I've ever felt more wildly alive.

Ben Lerwill
is an award-winning freelance travel writer based in Oxfordshire, England. He's been writing about travel since 2003 and continues to work with a broad range of magazines and newspapers, as well as Rough Guides. He's passionate about the outdoors, good food and biros that don't leak.

987

Behold the northern lights

SWEDEN They appear as shimmering arcs and waves of light, often blue or green in colour, which seem to sweep their way across the dark skies. During the darkest months of the year, the northern lights, or aurora borealis, are visible in the night sky all across northern Sweden. Until you see the light displays yourself, it's hard to describe the spectacle in mere words – try to imagine, though, someone waving a fantastically coloured curtain through the air and you've pretty much got the idea.

What makes the northern lights so elusive is that it's impossible to predict when they're going to make an appearance. The displays are caused by solar wind, or streams of particles charged by the sun, hitting the Earth's atmosphere. Different elements produce different colours, blue for nitrogen, for example, and yellow-green for oxygen.

The best place to view these mystical performances is north of the Arctic Circle, where temperatures are well below freezing and the sky is often at its clearest – two conditions that are believed to produce some of the most spectacular sightings.

For the quintessential northern lights experience, pack a couple of open sandwiches topped with smoked reindeer meat and a thermos of hot coffee to keep out the chill, then take a snow-scooter tour deep into the forests of Lapland – Kiruna, Sweden's northernmost city, is the best base. Park up beside a frozen lake and train your eyes on the sky. Try this between mid-December and mid-January, when there's 24-hour darkness north of the Arctic Circle, and the chances are you won't have to wait too long for your celestial fix.

Living the quiet life in Lofoten

988

NORWAY Draped across the turbulent waters of the Norwegian Sea, far above the Arctic Circle, Norway's Lofoten Islands are, by any standard, staggeringly beautiful.

In a largely tamed and heavily populated continent, the Lofoten are a rare wilderness outpost, an untrammelled landscape of rearing mountains, deep fjords, squawking seabird colonies and long, surf-swept beaches. This was never a land for the faint-hearted, but, since Viking times, a few hundred islanders have always managed to hang on here, eking out a tough existence from the thin soils and cod-rich waters. Many emigrated, while those who stayed came to think they were unlucky: unlucky with the price of the fish on which they were dependent, unlucky to be so isolated, and unlucky when the storms rolled in to lash their tiny villages.

Then Norway found tourism. The first boatloads turned out to be English missionaries bent on saving souls, but subsequent contacts proved more financially rewarding. Even better, the Norwegians found oil in the 1960s, lots and lots of oil, quite enough to extend the road network to the smallest village, and thereby end rural isolation at a stroke. The islands' villages have benefited from this road-building bonanza and yet kept their erstwhile charm, from the remote Å i Lofoten in the south through to the beguiling headland hamlet of Henningsvaer, extravagantly picturesque Nusfjord and solitary Stamsund.

Today, the Lofoten have their own relaxed pace. For somewhere so far north, the weather can be exceptionally mild: you can spend summer days sunbathing on the rocks or hiking around the superb coastline. When it rains, as it does frequently, life focuses on the *rorbuer* (fishermen's huts), where freshly caught fish are cooked over wood-burning stoves, tales are told and time gently wasted. If that sounds contrived, in a sense it is – the way of life here is to some extent preserved for the tourists. But it's rare to find anyone who isn't enthralled by it all.

998 | Snorkelling with orcas

NORWAY As you slide quietly over the side of the boat and put your face in the freezing water, it's hard to breathe – not just because your teeth are chattering, but also because there, below you in the blue, are six or seven killer whales that seem as curious about you as you are about them.

Tell your friends that you're going snorkelling with "killer whales" north of the Arctic Circle in winter, and they're likely to think you're a few minnows short of a school. While orcas, as they're more properly known, have been known to eat prey larger than humans, however – including seals, dolphins, sharks, and even other whales – the ones in northern Norway mainly eat fish.

Prime orca-viewing time is between October and January, when migrating shoals of herring lure hundreds of orcas to Tysfjord in northern Norway. You might even have a chance to see them feed. Norway's orcas have perfected a fishing technique called "carousel feeding": they herd the unsuspecting herring into a tight ball using air bubbles as a net, slap the ball with their tails to stun ten to fifteen fish at a time, then scoff them one by one.

Sure it's cold (winter water temperatures hover around 4ºC), but there's plenty of gear to keep you warm: dry suit, warm inner suit, mask, snorkel, gloves and booties. And yes, you might feel a tad vulnerable drifting on the surface of the North Atlantic surrounded by a bunch of five-tonne marine mammals, with a small rubber dinghy as your only back-up. But all that's forgotten as soon as you spot a dorsal fin breaking the surface – and you realize you didn't just become dinner.

999 | Whale-watching from a tiny RIB

NORWAY Like submarines, they'll glide effortlessly through the icy water towards you, difficult to pick out in the murky twilight of the polar night. In the self-styled Arctic capital of Tromsø, 400km north of the Arctic Circle, the sun hardly rises over the mountains between November and February. But this is peak season for the whales, who arrive each winter to chase the shoals of herring in the long, narrow inlets of the Norwegian fjords.

The waters around Kvaløya (or "Whale Island"), just over 20km from Tromsø, have long been known as a hotspot for cetaceans, with humpbacks, orcas and even fin whales making an appearance. The best way to experience a feeding frenzy is to go by RIB, or rigid inflatable boat, as you'll be almost level with the water and, at times, close enough to smell them.

You'll speed out into the fjords, passing snow-capped peaks and fishing trawlers inundated with gulls, feeling the icy wind against your cheeks and every bump as your dinghy hits the crest of each wave. And then you'll see the whales, perhaps twenty of them, working as a team to herd the shoals of herring into tighter and tighter balls, forcing them towards the surface. The whales won't be afraid of the RIB, and will glide past you and dive underneath you in their efforts to corral the herring. Humpbacks will eventually rise up as a group to swallow their prey, but the orcas have a different tactic: watch closely, and you'll see them tail-slapping the herring to stun them.

The whales have been known to leave the area around Kvaløya for years at a time, depending on which routes the herring decide to follow. Most recently the whales took a decades-long hiatus from the fjords around the island, and only returned to these waters around five years ago. There's no telling when the herring will once again lead them elsewhere, so if you're keen to see the whales, the time to go is now.

1000 | Walking on the ice cap

GREENLAND Get your head round this: the Greenland ice cap (also called the inland ice) is 2400km long – that's to say, it's the length of the journey from Greenland's east coast to London. It contains 2.85 million cubic kilometres of ice (that's more than a billion Olympic swimming pool; if the whole lot were to melt, most of the world's coastal cities would vanish under water, and several island nations would be wiped out. It covers a land area more than three times the size of France, and the oldest bits of ice are a staggering 250,000 years old.

The super-hardy like to ski from one side to the other, but for the rest of us, a simple summer stroll out onto the ice will do, for the ice cap is astonishingly accessible. Its edge lies just a 25km drive from Greenland's international airport at Kangerlussuaq. And there's a road that leads right there.

You leave the huddle of squat buildings that makes up Kangerlussuaq and drive out through spectacular rolling tundra. Small groups of musk oxen, with their stooped posture and strangely cute upturned horns, stand a short distance away and stare; occasionally a reindeer grazes, or an Arctic fox trots out in search of smaller prey. Then, as you round a bend in the road, you see it: a cliff of bluish-white ice in the distance soaring ever upwards. Drawing closer, you discern its spiralling peaks and diving crevasses, and the streaks of grey that smear the surface. And then you're there, walking out over this rugged, frozen mass of ice. There's no easy trail – the ice cap rolls and dips like an Alpine landscape in miniature, and you have to pick your own path. And if a comfy bed doesn't matter to you, pitch your tent on the edge of the inland ice, and wake in the morning to the thunderous calving of glaciers.

995 | Taking the Polar Plunge

ANTARCTICA An expedition cruise to the Antarctic Peninsula throws up more giddying thrills than you could ever hope to count. What with the glaciers and the whales, the mountains and the million-strong penguin colonies, the sunsets and the elephant seals, the scale and beauty of the place can be genuinely overwhelming. Literally the most breathtaking tradition of all, however, has to be the opportunity to dunk yourself into the Southern Ocean for as long as you can bear. If you've never taken a dip in sub-zero Antarctic waters, rest assured that it's a bracing experience.

The very idea may sound like madness, and some travellers choose to give the so-called "Polar Plunge" a wide berth, but it's not so reckless as it might seem. By their very nature, cruises to the continent have to take place during the warmer portion of the year, when the seas aren't frozen

solid. So while it's cold, teeth-chatteringly so at times, the temperature's not so icy as to seriously endanger health.

Cruise operators generally offer the Plunge as an optional extra during one of the shore landings towards the end of an itinerary. If, like most people, you only immerse yourself for a few seconds, you're far more likely to be left with a life-affirming, all-over skin-tingle than a bad case of the sniffles. That said, you'll have new respect for the hardy penguins that somehow cope with darting around beneath the chilly waves all day.

Any trip to Antarctica is inevitably dominated by the landscapes and the wildlife. So in a sense, stepping into the Southern Ocean and sinking into its cold, clear waters – however briefly – is not so much about rising to a challenge as giving yourself a short, sharp shock that enables you to appreciate the fullness of your surroundings.

996 | Stumbling upon a polar oasis

CANADA Travelling by skidoo, you and your Inuit guide venture onto the sea ice off the coast of Baffin Island in Canada's eastern Arctic for a day's outing. Three hours later you spot a small body of water completely surrounded by ice and shrouded in mist. Nestled between two rocky islands, this mysterious marine "lake" is teeming with life – hundreds of eider, long-tailed ducks and guillemots dive for food while in the distance a ringed seal keeps a close watch. Fresh tracks of an Arctic fox circle the perimeter of the ice edge where only days earlier a local hunter had spotted a wandering polar bear. You have stumbled upon a polynya.

Polynyas are areas of open water bordered by thick sea ice that recur year after year in the same location. There are a few dozen scattered throughout the Arctic Archipelago, ranging in size from less than 100m across to a massive 40,000 square kilometres. A combination of wind and strong ocean currents keeps these areas free of ice year-round. Although they account for less than five percent

of the entire surface area of the Arctic Ocean, their presence is crucial to the survival of countless marine organisms.

As the spring sun glares down onto the reflective icy surface and penetrates deep into the water, billions of microscopic plankton suddenly burst to life, thanks to incoming solar radiation. This influx of energy triggers a chain of events many naturalists describe as one of the greatest spectacles in the Arctic. Millions of migratory seabirds and ducks join bowhead whales and large pods of narwhals and belugas to feed in the nutrient-rich waters.

Standing at the edge of the ice, and surrounded by a symphony of sound and colour, you begin to scan the horizon for more signs of life. A flock of at least three hundred king eiders flutters by while the tell-tale spray from a pod of belugas signals their return to the surface. This flurry of activity almost distracts you from spotting the 2m spiralled ivory tusk of a narwhal as it pierces through the calm waters of this remarkable polar oasis.

997 | Explore uncharted fjords in wild East Greenland

GREENLAND Remote East Greenland should be scored by an orchestra. The barnacle-encrusted humpback whales that break the surface of the glassy waters look like they should come with a low oboe soundtrack. The cathedral-sized icebergs that sparkle like giant geodes definitely deserve their own string section. Because this really is a place for the senses, where wind-whipped landscapes speak to your very soul. Unlike the more populous west coast of Greenland, you won't find many locals on the wild east side. In fact, you can travel for days, even weeks, before you spot another human being.

The waters of Scoresbysund – the largest fjord system on the planet; roughly the size of Iceland – are best navigated on a small ship safari. There's nothing quite like weaving your way through tapestries of electric-blue icebergs, under coral-coloured skies that stay bright throughout the summer; or taking to a Zodiac to get closer to the polar

bears you've spotted on shore – a mum suckling her cubs on the fast ice, or a huge male feasting on a seal carcass with glee.

But what's most beautiful about this place is when nothing much happens at all. When all is still. Huge forts of ice floating quietly through the doldrums, clusters of basalt columns and red-tinged cliffs stretching upwards, and monstrous lion's mane jellyfish hanging bloated just beneath the water's surface. But inland, the tundra is a hive of life, home to mighty musk oxen, Arctic fox and the remains of Inuit settlements some 800 years old. Look closely and you'll see the ground is littered with ancient artefacts: carved arrowheads, tools made from mandibles, and intricate bone knives that all hold beguiling secrets of the people who lived here centuries before we ever set foot here. You can imagine them engulfed by deafening silence, watching the aurora borealis dance in the night sky as they clustered around their crackling fires.

992 | Husky driving along the Russian border

FINLAND Outside in the frosty whiteness of the Arctic your team of three dozen harnessed huskies – gleaming in the late afternoon sunlight with their piercing blue eyes and sleek coats of fur – is busy howling, yelping, snarling and barking. The campfire lunch over, you're off again, thrashing through a magical northern scenery of Boreal taiga forest and swamp, then speeding across frozen lakes and fells. The only sound to break the eerie silence of the North is the *swish swish* of the sled's runners as they break the clumps of snow, and the howls and pants of excitement emanating from the front of the pack.

Driving a sled of huskies – four-paw-drive – is probably the best way to experience the sights, sounds and smells of the Arctic winter. Venturing out some 40km each day, you'll traverse the deep woods that run to the Russian and Norwegian borders, where tall pines drip blankets of snow onto trails that glisten a brilliant, blinding white. You'll be at the helm of your own dog sled, and though a guide will give tips on how to drive and tend to the dogs, it's up to you to learn how to work as a team. Come evening, you'll be taming, harnessing, rigging, feeding, watering and prepping the pack for the following day's mush; these friends and companions need to be shown who is boss and should be treated, in the words of one husky trainer, "as you would a hyperactive 5-year-old".

After a day's sledding, there's time for sauna and dinner at a wilderness lodge in a traditional lakeside Finnish log cabin, but then it's early to bed and early to rise; by day, concentration, alertness and peripheral vision are key. Still, it'll pay off: one thing that's nearly guaranteed is a unique wind-in-your-face exhilaration just about every moment you're out in the snow.

993 | Trekking across the Arctic Circle

CANADA As you bounce along in a wooden *kamotik*, a traditional Inuit sled pulled by a snowmobile, you might find yourself having serious doubts as you think of what lies ahead: polar bears, hypothermia, avalanches and blizzards. You may question your sanity on the strenuous trek all the way to the Arctic Circle Marker in Auyuittuq National Park on Baffin Island. But in the end, you won't regret it for a moment.

Home to ten-thousand-year-old glaciers, towering granite mountains and awesome icy landscapes, Auyuittuq (pronounced "I-you-we-took") is an extraordinary place to explore on foot. Most visitors come during the summer to trek 97km through the scenic Akshayuk Pass, a corridor that has been used by Inuit for thousands of years.

The guide drops you on the frozen shores at the Overlord Warden Station, the southern gateway to the park. Dwarfed by rugged snow-covered mountains, you're left alone to battle the elements. Within minutes the loud drone of the snowmobile disappears. Adrenaline pumping, you begin the 15km trek to the Arctic Circle, along the glacier-scoured terrain of the Weasel River Valley.

Guided by *inuksuit*, stone markers built by Inuit to navigate the land, you cross the turquoise-blue ice of braided streams, along the base of sheer cliffs a kilometre high and over boulders of every conceivable shape and size. Nearly five hours after starting out, you'll catch the first glimpse of the holy grail in the distance atop a gravel bed: a lonely *inukshuk* bearing a simple sign with the words "Arctic Circle" written in English, French and Inuktitut. Without fanfare or a welcome party you have reached your destination. A few moments surrounded by the great Arctic stillness is all the reward you'll need.

994 | Scrambling up Observation Hill

ANTARCTICA Ice-locked into the France-sized Ross Ice Shelf lies Ross Island, a primary base for the British expeditions to Antarctica of a century ago. Many reminders of their efforts remain, including a stirring monument at the summit of the 230m Observation Hill, or "Ob Hill", so named because it was used as a lookout for ships returning to the ice; today station residents climb it for a view of their utterly alien, white surroundings.

The first third of the extinct volcano consists of loose scree, which you have to scramble up until you reach a road that winds partially around the hill to a decommissioned nuclear power plant. Here, most climbers turn to look for the first time at their temporary home – much like a new Manhattanite walks to the middle of the Brooklyn Bridge before gazing back at the city's towers. McMurdo Station, America's chief Antarctic research facility, looks like a small mining town from this vantage point, with curls of steam puffing from each building.

Ob Hill's next two thirds must be bounded up, billy-goat-style, over large, haphazardly strewn rocks. Roughly 75m from the top, a small, boulder-topped peninsula flattens out in front of the climber, offering the chance to take a breather and peer out at the frozen McMurdo Sound and, further off to the left, the imposing Royal Society mountain range. To the right looms the smoking cone of Mount Erebus, the world's southernmost active volcano.

Not until you nearly reach the top do you see the solid wooden cross which stands as a memorial to Captain Scott and his men. The stout cross is inscribed with a line from Tennyson's *Ulysses*, which serves as a sobering reminder of the sacrifices made so that climbers can stand here today: "To strive, to seek, to find, and not to yield".

989 | Herding reindeer across the tundra of Lapland

FINLAND Ask most people to free-associate with the word "reindeer", and you're likely to get "Christmas", "Santa" or "Rudolph" in response. For Finland's nomadic Sámi people, however, the reindeer has been a fundamental figure in their existence for centuries. The Sámi eat and sell reindeer meat, use the skin and fur for clothing and blankets, and fashion their antlers into handicrafts and housewares. Semi-wild, reindeer are free to roam in large herding districts, and easily outnumber Lapland's human population. Each spring, Finland's seven hundred remaining Sámi herdsmen help thousands of these handsome beasts make their 200km migration from Finnish Lapland's central woodlands towards the mountainous regions of the northwest. Sign up to assist them, and you'll be in for an unforgettable adventure.

Each morning, you'll venture out by ski, sledge or *kelka* (snowmobile), racing through sun-dappled forests of birch and fir towards the fells, their trees marooned with snowdrifts the size of large igloos, fox tracks trailing off in the whiteness. Dressed to the hilt in warm clothes – it's cold 400km north of the Arctic Circle – you'll be working hard throughout the day, herding, counting, labelling, feeding, petting and listening to the distinctive low bellowing of reindeer hungry for dinner. Come evening, as the sun sets, kick back for a brief moment and relax as your Sámi driver speeds you onwards towards a local wilderness cabin for warm coffee – even by Scandinavian standards the Sámi drink a vast amount – and an evening meal of thick slabs of skillet-grilled reindeer sausage.

Though it's often the reindeer themselves who decide exactly where you'll end up each evening, herders and their apprentices can pitch the traditional Sámi *katas* (tents) anywhere. Once your bed is made, there's little to do besides huddle around a fire, share stories and gaze up at the sky as it morphs from deep amber to midnight blue to black, then settle in for a crisp, cold night of Arctic silence.

990 | Diving under the ice in the White Sea

RUSSIA How to go ice diving? 1. Fly to Moscow. 2. Board a 28-hour train north to Chupa, a polar station in the northernmost stretches of the European continent. 3. Head out by Chinese jeep to *Polar Circle Lodge* in the remote wilderness of northern Russia. 4. Zoom from the lodge out over the frozen White Sea by snowmobile. 5. Saw through the 1.5m-thick ice. 6. Jump in.

Once the colder months settle in and the unforgiving landscape freezes over, Russia's far north is a landscape of wonder and wandering, and ice diving in the White Sea – an open body of water that freezes over completely in the wintertime – is probably the most memorable time you'll ever spend underwater. Although the winter air temperature in the Arctic can drop to an extremity-shrivelling –25°C, the water in the sea is thankfully a bit balmier: just below 0°C at ice level and only a few degrees colder towards the bottom.

Wearing base layers, undersuit and dry suit, the only part of your body to get cold will be your face – that, though, will be numb within seconds. Connected to the world above via a single safety rope, use your underwater torch to follow your guide down past ice hummocks, rifts, cavities and caves, minnowing under tall arches and vertical rocks overgrown with sea anemones and sponges.

Underwater rocks vanish into the pitch-black depths of the sea's deepest parts, while kelp sways gently atop kelp gardens and sea urchins flutter about. You'll even come upon pieces of shipwrecked fishing and patrol boats, while up above – visibility can reach a crystal-clear 50m – the masses of surface ice appear as glowing green castles bobbing atop the air bubbles. After you surface, let yourself be guided along the frozen land by the glimmering northern lights as you retire to a Soviet-era cottage for some real Russian hospitality, comradeship and – if you're lucky – a sauna in the buff.

991 | The ice road from Inuvik to Tuktoyaktuk

CANADA Tuktoyaktuk is an Inuit community on the shores of the Beaufort Sea. In the summer, its thousand inhabitants can access the outside world only by air or water.

During the dark Arctic winter, though, one aspect of life becomes easier for the people of Tuk. They can drive to their nearest town, Inuvik in Canada's Northwest Territories, along the seasonal, 194km ice road that's carved into the surface of the Mackenzie River, and across the frozen ocean itself – and visitors can rent a jeep to visit them.

"You've gotta go slow", the manager of the car-rental firm advises first-timers. "Remember, it's all white out there". The cautious visitor chugs tentatively onto the ice. The road is wide, smooth and gleams like a figure-skating rink. Its route weaves with the meanderings of this waterway that has featured in the writings of explorers such as Mackenzie, Franklin and Stefansson.

Early in the journey, spindly trees poke out to either side of the river's banks. Once you pass the tree line, they vanish. It's utterly silent – just the occasional thrum of a car resonates through the still air – but it's not entirely white. As your eye adjusts you'll pick out the buttery yellow of low sunlight on ice; the inky-blue shadows thrown by mounds of snow; the pink tinge in the sky as the weak sun dips. It's not all flat, either. Pingos – mounds of earth pushed up by frozen water trapped beneath the permafrost – loom like giant molehills and, as the road leaves the river and strikes out across the ice of the Beaufort Sea, the landscape is detailed in tiny, icy peaks and troughs, coloured palest violet and washed-out denim blue.

At last, the lone driver sees dark specks on the horizon: this is the settlement of Tuk, but even though it's visible to the eye, there's still some way to go. This is a vast canvas and perspective has been sucked away into the white, icy air at the very top of the world.

Need to know

986 The Midnight Sun season in the Sommarøy region lasts from around late May to mid-July. See Ⓦ visitnorway.com for further details.

987 In Kiruna, stay at the comfortable *Camp Ripan* (Ⓦ ripan.se/en).

988 The Lofoten Islands (Ⓦ lofoten.info) can be reached by car ferry, passenger boat and plane from Bodø, in northern Norway.

989 For more information on joining the herd, visit Ⓦ visitinari.fi. Bundle up; the weather outside can range anywhere from −1º to −34ºC, and the blustery wind – and occasional heavy snowfall – won't make things any warmer.

990 Ice diving is at its best Feb–April. Some caution should be taken, such as acclimatizing your equipment to water temperature before beginning a descent.

991 The ice road is usually only open Feb–April – see Ⓦ inuvik.ca for the latest information.

992 Tinja Myllykangas operates Siperia Lapponica (Ⓦ siperia.eu), a local company near Inari that raises and trains huskies, and leads regular husky safaris across Lapland during the colder months. You can also find information at Ⓦ visitinari.fi. There are regular flights from Helsinki to Ivalo airport, 40km south of Inari.

993 You can get more infomation on Auyuittuq National Park at Ⓦ pc.gc.ca. All visitors must register with Parks Canada.

994 Visit Ⓦ polarcruises.com to find cruise operators that currently offer trips to Ross Island.

995 The cruising season to Antarctica extends between Nov and Feb. Hurtigruten (Ⓦ hurtigruten.com) and Quark Expeditions (Ⓦ quarkexpeditions.com) sail from Ushuaia in Argentina, and offer the Polar Plunge.

996 There are numerous polynyas in Canada's Arctic, and each village has outfitters who can arrange trips. Ⓦ nunavuttourism.com lists operators that offer snowmobile visits.

997 Natural World Safaris offers a variety of exclusive small ship expeditions to the High Arctic, including East Greenland. See Ⓦ naturalworldsafaris.com for more details.

998 The local Tysfjord tourist office runs snorkelling safaris between Dec and Feb, for 2200kr per person (Ⓦ tysfjord-turistsenter.no).

999 Norwegian (Ⓦ norwegian.com) runs direct flights from London to Tromsø. Due to the warming effect of the Gulf Stream, winter temperatures rarely drop below -5ºC.

1000 Air Greenland (Ⓦ airgreenland.com) flies six days a week from Copenhagen to Kangerlussuaq in summer. From Kangerlussuaq, you can take a guided tour to the ice cap with Albatros Travel Greenland (Ⓦ albatros-travel.dk). Visit Ⓦ greenland.com for more information.

SMALL PRINT
INDEXES

AUTHOR CREDITS

001 Samantha Cook
002 Sophie Middlemiss
003 Lucinda Hallett
004 James Smart
005 Paul Gray
006 Sophie Middlemiss
007 Lucinda Hallett
008 Paul Whitfield
009 Ben Lerwill
010 Rebecca Hallett
011 Chris Scott
012 Brendon Griffin
013 Robert Andrews
014 Edward Aves
015 Mike MacEacheran
016 Robert Andrews
017 Dave Dakota
018 Annie Shaw
019 Hayley Spurway
020 Mark Robertson
021 Tom Smith
022 Polly Thomas
023 Donald Reid
024 William Sutcliffe
025 Rebecca Hallett
026 Caitlin Fitzsimmons
027 Sarah Eno
028 Martin Dunford
029 Mera Dattani
030 Georgia Stephens
031 Mark Ellingham
032 Paul Gray
033 Helena Smith
034 James Smart
035 Polly Evans
036 Alf Anderson
037 Keith Drew
038 Paul Gray
039 Paul Whitfield
040 Annie Shaw
041 Rob Coates
042 Diana Jarvis
043 James Smart
044 Dave Dakota & Paul Gray
045 Donald Reid
046 Mark Ellingham
047 Tim Elcott
048 Paul Whitfield
049 Alf Anderson
050 Georgia Stephens
051 Norm Longley
052 Katy Bell
053 Norm Longley
054 Al Spicer
055 Paul Sullivan
056 Helena Smith
057 Neville Walker
058 Martin Dunford
059 Brendon Griffin
060 James Stewart
061 Martin Dunford
062 Shafik Meghji
063 Sophie Middlemiss
064 Ross Velton
065 Ben Lerwill
066 Matthew Teller
067 James Stewart
068 Sarah Eno
069 Keith Drew
070 Paul Sullivan
071 Lucy White
072 Mike MacEacheran
073 James McConnachie
074 Chris Straw
075 Matthew Teller
076 Adrian Mourby
077 James Stewart
078 Ben Lerwill
079 Kevin Fitzgerald
080 Keith Drew
081 David Abram
082 Martin Dunford

083 Keith Drew
084 Neil McQuillan
085 Martin Dunford
086 Jan Dodd
087 Alice Park
088 Martin Dunford
089 Paul Sullivan
090 Ross Velton
091 Paul Sullivan
092 Nick Woodford & Tim Beynon
093 Martin Dunford
094 Eleanor Aldridge
095 Ben Lerwill
096 Kerry Walker
097 Emma Thomson
098 Stephen Keeling
099 Michelle Bhatia
100 Paul Sullivan
101 Stephen Keeling
102 Martin Dunford
103 Ross Velton
104 James McConnachie
105 Greg Ward
106 Ross Velton
107 Martin Dunford
108 Jan Dodd
109 Stephen Keeling
110 AnneLise Sorensen
111 Paul Sullivan
112 Natasha Foges
113 Andy Turner
114 James McConnachie
115 Stephen Keeling
116 Emma Gibbs
117 Emma Gibbs
118 Neil McQuillan
119 Brendon Griffin
120 Brendon Griffin
121 Ben Lerwill
122 Brendon Griffin
123 Steven Vickers
124 Lottie Gross
125 Ben Lerwill
126 Esme Fox
127 Emma Gregg
128 Matthew Hancock
129 Amanda Tomlin
130 Brendon Griffin
131 Matthew Hancock
132 Brendon Griffin
133 Brendon Griffin
134 James Stewart
135 Brendon Griffin
136 Brendon Griffin
137 Brendon Griffin
138 Amanda Tomlin
139 Matthew Hancock
140 Mike MacEacheran
141 Samantha Cook
142 Emma Gregg
143 Brendon Griffin
144 Esme Fox
145 Brendon Griffin
146 Emma Gregg
147 Dave Dakota & Damien Simonis
148 Emma Gregg
149 Emma Gregg
150 AnneLise Sorensen
151 Brendon Griffin
152 Matthew Hancock
153 Matthew Hancock
154 Brendon Griffin
155 Christian Williams
156 Martin Dunford
157 Brendon Griffin
158 Keith Drew
159 Martin Dunford
160 Michelle Bhatia
161 Steven Vickers
162 Kate Thomas

163 Roger Norum
164 Richard Hammond
165 Rebecca Hallett
166 Keith Drew
167 Roger Norum
168 Paul Sullivan
169 Nikki Birrell
170 Alf Anderson
171 Sarah Eno
172 David Leffman
173 Keith Drew
174 Mike MacEacheran
175 Sarah Eno
176 Sian Marsh
177 George Turner
178 Felicity Aston
179 Roger Norum
180 AnneLise Sorensen
181 Helen Ochyra
182 Tim Ecott
183 Rebecca Hallett
184 Keith Drew
185 Caroline Osborne
186 James Proctor
187 Keith Drew
188 Tim Ecott
189 Marc Perry
190 Megan McIntyre
191 Monica Woods
192 James McConnachie
193 Martin Zatko
194 Tom Fleming
195 Martin Dunford
196 Neil McQuillan
197 Jonathan Buckley
198 Jonathan Bousfield
199 Lucy Ratcliffe
200 Greg Ward
201 Jeffrey Kennedy
202 Norm Longley
203 Sian Marsh
204 Terry Richardson
205 Martin Dunford
206 Jeffrey Kennedy
207 Martin Dunford
208 Owen Morton
209 Martin Zatko
210 Martin Dunford
211 John Fisher
212 Edward Aves
213 Ross Velton
214 Nori Jemil
215 Martin Dunford
216 James McConnachie
217 Natasha Foges
218 Ruth Terry
219 Rebecca Hallett
220 Lucy White
221 James McConnachie
222 Martin Dunford
223 Martin Dunford
224 Sarah Eno
225 Norm Longley
226 Jonathan Bousfield
227 Mike MacEacheran
228 Jonathan Buckley
229 Norm Longely
230 Natasha Foges
231 Natasha Foges
232 Robert Andrews
233 Mark Ellwood
234 Rebecca Hallett
235 Norm Longley
236 Emma Mattei
237 Martin Zatko
238 Ben Lerwill
239 Rob Crossan
240 Martin Dunford
241 Martin Dunford
242 Martin Dunford
243 Martin Dunford
244 Robert Andrews
245 Stephen Keeling

246 Jonathan Bousfield
247 Greg Witt
248 Jonathan Buckley
249 Norm Longley
250 Martin Dunford
251 Lucy Cowie
252 Jonathan Bousfield
253 Lottie Gross
254 Megan McIntyre
255 Jonathan Buckley
256 Sophie Middlemiss
257 Nori Jemil
258 Martin Dunford
259 Monica Woods
260 Martin Dunford
261 Ben Lerwill
262 Lily Hyde
263 Jonathan Bousfield
264 Dan Richardson
265 Keith Drew
266 Jonathan Bousfield
267 Norm Longley
268 Dan Richardson
269 Norm Longley
270 Olivia Rawes
271 Norm Longley
272 Lily Hyde
273 Rob Humphreys
274 Norm Longley
275 James Smart
276 Edward Aves
277 Jonathan Bousfield
278 Ruth Hedges
279 Joanna Reeves
280 Jonathan Buckley
281 Jonathan Bousfield
282 Jonathan Bousfield
283 Alison Murchie
284 Owen Morton
285 Jonathan Bousfield
286 Andrew Rosenberg
287 Jonathan Bousfield
288 Jonathan Bousfield
289 Rob Humphreys
290 Norm Longley
291 Jonathan Bousfield
292 Rob Humphreys
293 Jonathan Bousfield
294 Anna Kaminski
295 Norm Longley
296 Dan Richardson
297 Anna Kaminski
298 Stephen Keeling
299 Adrian Mourby
300 Michael Haag
301 Jessica Lee
302 Gavin Thomas
303 Michael Haag
304 Mark Ellingham
305 Kirsten Henton
306 Matthew Teller
307 Marco Ferrarese
308 Jessica Lee
309 Jessica Lee
310 Keith Drew
311 Dan Jacobs
312 Dan Jacobs
313 Jessica Lee
314 Juliana Barnaby
315 Emma Gregg
316 Matt Norman
317 Keith Drew
318 Jessica Lee
319 David Abram
320 Dan Jacobs
321 Keith Drew
322 Jessica Lee
323 Brendon Griffin
324 Andy Turner
325 Paul Sullivan
326 Mike MacEacheran
327 James Stewart
328 Emma Gregg

329 Philip Briggs
330 Emma Gregg
331 Ross Velton
332 Emma Gregg
333 Richard Trillo
334 Ben Lerwill
335 Eliza Reid
336 Richard Trillo
337 Brendon Griffin
338 Ben Lerwill
339 Richard Trillo
340 Emma Gregg
341 Emma Gregg
342 Rob Crossan
343 Diana Jarvis
344 Emma Gregg
345 Diana Jarvis
346 Richard Trillo
347 Kiki Deere
348 Clare Foges
349 Richard Trillo
350 Richard Trillo
351 Hilary Heuler
352 Keith Drew
353 Philip Briggs
354 Lizzie Pook
355 Lizzie Pook
356 Henry Stedman
357 Richard Trillo
358 Richard Trillo
359 Richard Trillo
360 Richard Trillo
361 Ben Lerwill
362 Richard Trillo
363 Emma Gregg
364 Martin Zatko
365 Beth Wooldridge
366 Philip Briggs
367 Emma Gregg
368 Richard Trillo
369 Richard Trillo
370 Emma Gregg
371 Richard Trillo
372 Emma Gregg
373 Harriet Constable
374 David Leffman
375 Emma Gregg
376 Emma Gregg
377 Jens Finke
378 Richard Trillo
379 Natasha Foges
380 Richard Trillo
381 Emma Gregg
382 Owen Morton
383 Tim Ecott
384 Keith Drew
385 Sally Beck
386 Jens Finke
387 Nick Maes
388 Emma Gregg
389 Philip Briggs
390 Emma Gregg
391 Chris Scott
392 Tim Chester
393 Barbara McCrae
394 Mike Unwin
395 Alison Roberts
396 Tony Pinchuck
397 Emma Gregg
398 James Bainbridge
399 Emma Gregg
400 Barbara McCrae
401 Emma Thomson
402 Mike Unwin
403 Tony Pinchuck
404 Emma Gregg
405 Joanna Reeves
406 James Bainbridge
407 Emma Gregg
408 Christopher P. Baker
409 Emma Gregg
410 Nick Maes
411 Emma Gregg

412 William Sutcliffe
413 Emma Gregg
414 James Bainbridge
415 Mike Unwin
416 Mike Unwin
417 Mike Unwin
418 Emma Gregg
419 Claus Vogel
420 Georgia Stephens
421 Philip Briggs
422 Rebecca Hallett
423 Donald Reid
424 Emma Gregg
425 Emma Gregg
426 Richard Trillo
427 Keith Drew
428 Gill Harvey
429 Tony Pinchuck
430 Emma Gregg
431 Mike Unwin
432 Emma Gregg
433 Rob Crossan
434 Emma Gregg
435 Claus Vogel
436 Emma Gregg
437 Nick Garbutt
438 Emma Gregg
439 David Abram
440 Emma Gregg
441 Keith Drew
442 Keith Drew
443 Keith Drew
444 Matthew Teller
445 Matthew Teller
446 Jessica Lee
447 Matthew Teller
448 Clare Foges
449 Matthew Teller
450 Matthew Teller
451 Matthew Teller
452 Matthew Teller
453 Matthew Teller
454 Matthew Teller
455 Roger Norum
456 Jessica Lee
457 Frances Linzee Gordon
458 Clare Foges
459 Jessica Lee
460 Matthew Teller
461 Matthew Teller
462 Marco Ferrarese
463 Matthew Teller
464 Matthew Teller
465 Fiona McAuslan
466 Mike MacEacheran
467 Frances Linzee Gordon
468 Frances Linzee Gordon
469 Emma Gregg
470 Matthew Teller
471 Sakhr Al-Makhadhi
472 Christopher P. Baker
473 Emma Gregg
474 Roger Norum
475 Marie Houghton
476 Emma Gregg
477 Martin Zatko
478 Matthew Teller
479 Paul Whitfield
480 Ben Lerwill
481 Greg Ward
482 Caroline Lascom
483 Zora O'Neill
484 Stephen Timblin
485 JD Dickey
486 Greg Ward
487 Mike MacEacheran
488 Ruth Terry
489 Keith Drew
490 Ross Velton
491 Mark Ellwood

492 Greg Ward
493 Paul Whitfield
494 Christopher P. Baker
495 Sarah Hull
496 Stephen Keeling
497 JD Dickey
498 Andrew Rosenberg
499 Andrew Rosenberg
500 Mark Ellwood
501 Stephen Keeling
502 Paul Whitfield
503 Rob Crossan
504 Georgia Stephens
505 Sarah Lieber
506 Zora O'Neill
507 Sara Lieber
508 Michelle Bhatia
509 Caroline Lascom
510 Paul Whitfield
511 Cali Alpert & Brad Olsen
512 Greg Ward
513 Zora O'Neill
514 Polly Evans
515 Greg Ward
516 Ben Lerwill
517 Keith Drew
518 Madelyn Rosenberg
519 Madelyn Rosenberg
520 Shea Dean
521 Stephen Keeling
522 Andrew Rosenberg
523 Megan Kennedy
524 Sarah Eno
525 Stephen Timblin
526 Stephen Keeling
527 Christian Williams
528 Sean Harvey
529 Zora O'Neill
530 Stephen Keeling
531 JD Dickey
532 Samantha Cook
533 JD Dickey
534 Alice Park
535 Stephen Keeling
536 Stephen Keeling
537 Alf Anderson
538 Stephen Keeling
539 Stephen Keeling
540 Stephen Keeling
541 Stephen Keeling
542 Harry Wilson
543 Harry Wilson
544 Christian Williams
545 Polly Evans
546 Janine Israel
547 Claus Vogel
548 Claus Vogel
549 Lizzie Pook
550 Felicity Aston
551 Christian Williams
552 Felicity Aston
553 Claus Vogel
554 Christian Williams
555 Christian Williams
556 Christian Williams
557 Ross Velton
558 Edward Aves
559 Janine Israel
560 Janine Israel
561 Steven Horak
562 Christian Williams
563 Phil Lee
564 Melissa Graham
565 Mike MacEacheran
566 Stephen Keeling
567 Phil Lee & Anna Roberts Welles
568 Phil Lee
569 Alasdair Baverstock
570 Gaylord Dold & Natalie Folster
571 Chris Hamilton
572 Ben Lerwill
573 Polly Thomas

574 Esme Fox
575 Polly Thomas
576 Meera Dattani
577 Sean Harvey
578 Olivia Rawes
579 Stephen Keeling
580 Matt Norman
581 Steven Horak
582 Claus Vogel
583 Seph Petta
584 Rob Coates
585 Stephen Keeling
586 Stephen Keeling
587 Helen Abramson
588 Sarah Eno
589 Stephen Keeling
590 Polly Thomas
591 Claus Vogel
592 Tim Ecott
593 Megan Kennedy
594 Helena Smith
595 Helen Abramson
596 Polly Thomas
597 Sean Harvey
598 Andrew Rosenberg
599 Helena Smith
600 Fiona McAuslan
601 Stephen Keeling
602 Jean McNeil
603 James Read
604 Iain Stewart
605 Polly Rodger Brown
606 AnneLise Sorensen
607 Zora O'Neill
608 Keith Drew
609 Paul Whitfield
610 Mani Ramaswamy
611 James McConnachie
612 Polly Rodger Brown
613 Zora O'Neill
614 Jean McNeil
615 Caroline Lascom
616 Richard Arghiris
617 Iain Stewart
618 Iain Stewart
619 Stephen Keeling
620 Keith Drew
621 Olivia Rawes
622 Daniel Stables
623 Emma Gibbs
624 Lily Fink
625 Stephen Keeling
626 Nori Jemil
627 Polly Rodger Brown
628 Polly Rodger Brown
629 Christopher P. Baker
630 Keith Drew
631 Gregory Witt
632 Iain Stewart
633 Iain Stewart
634 Polly Rodger Brown
635 Stephen Keeling
636 Eleanor Aldridge
637 Brendon Griffin
638 Eleanor Aldridge
639 Polly Rodger Brown
640 Rob Coates
641 Zora O'Neill
642 Keith Drew
643 Brendon Griffin
644 Greg Ward
645 Jason Clampet
646 Iain Stewart
647 Diana Jarvis
648 Mani Ramaswamy
649 Emma Gibbs
650 Stephen Keeling
651 Sara Humphreys
652 Polly Rodger Brown
653 Meera Dattani
654 Harry Adès
655 Harry Adès
656 Melanie Kramers
657 Andrew Benson
658 Paul D Smith
659 Olivia Rawes

660 Oliver Marshall
661 Keith Drew
662 Rob Crossan
663 Polly Rodger Brown
664 Melanie Kramers
665 Ben Lerwill
666 Steven Horak
667 Andrew Benson
668 James Read
669 James Read
670 Brendon Griffin
671 Melanie Kramers
672 Stephen Keeling
673 Rosalba O'Brien
674 Brendon Griffin
675 Ross Velton
676 Nori Jemil
677 Andrew Benson
678 Seb Bacon
679 Keith Drew
680 Steph Dyson
681 Dilwyn Jenkins
682 Joanna Reeves
683 Seph Petta
684 Shafik Meghji
685 Andrew Benson
686 Andrew Benson
687 Hannah Hennessy
688 Steven Horak
689 Seph Petta
690 Stephen Keeling
691 Keith Drew
692 Alex Robinson
693 Harry Adès
694 James Read
695 Ben Lerwill
696 Steph Dyson
697 Hal Weitzman
698 Rosalba O'Brien
699 Keith Drew
700 Seph Petta
701 Stephen Keeling
702 Keith Drew
703 Andrew Benson
704 Ross Velton
705 Rosalba O'Brien
706 James Read
707 Roger Norum
708 Caroline Lascom
709 Melissa Graham
710 Megan Kennedy
711 Polly Rodger Brown
712 Andrew Benson
713 David Abram
714 Andrew Rosenberg
715 Steven Horak
716 Sorrel Moseley-Williams
717 James Smart
718 Keith Drew
719 Keith Drew
720 Mike Unwin
721 Hal Weitzman
722 Adrian Mourby
723 Richard Danbury
724 Steph Dyson
725 Caroline Lascom
726 Shafik Meghji
727 Brendon Griffin
728 Keith Drew
729 Joshua Goodman
730 Adrian Mourby
731 Simon Lewis
732 David Leffman
733 David Leffman
734 Stephen Keeling
735 Owen Morton
736 Jo James
737 Simon Lewis
738 Greg Witt
739 David Leffman
740 Martin Zatko
741 Simon Richmond
742 Martin Zatko
743 Jenny Reddish
744 Ben Lerwill

745 David Leffman
746 Seb Bacon
747 Rob Crossan
748 Aimee White
749 Martin Zatko
750 Arthur Reiji Morris
751 Martin Zatko
752 Stephen Keeling
753 Martin Zatko
754 Olivia Lee
755 Simon Richmond
756 Adrian Mourby
757 Sophie Middlemiss
758 Anna Fifield
759 Ben Lerwill
760 Jo James
761 David Leffman
762 Roger Norum
763 Steven Vickers
764 David Leffman
765 Jo James
766 Martin Zatko
767 Rebecca Hallett
768 Martin Zatko
769 David Leffman
770 Paul Stafford
771 Steven Vickers
772 Jan Dodd
773 Seb Bacon
774 Martin Zatko
775 Olivia Lee
776 Sophie Middlemiss
777 Polly Evans
778 David Leffman
779 Anna Fifield
780 Jo James
781 Roger Norum
782 Simon Lewis
783 Anna Fifield
784 Ross Velton
785 Rebecca Hallett
786 Jo James
787 Marc di Duca
788 Martin Zatko
789 David Leffman
790 Marc di Duca
791 Edward Aves
792 David Leffman
793 Martin Zatko
794 Julia Mascetti
795 Sally McLaren
796 Jo James
797 Martin Dunford
798 Owen Morton
799 Martin Dunford
800 Andy Turner
801 Roger Norum
802 Rachel Mills
803 Emma Gibbs
804 Ben Lerwill
805 Roger Norum
806 David Abram
807 David Abram
808 David Abram
809 Megha Gupta
810 Georgia Stephens
811 Marco Ferrarese
812 Shafik Meghji
813 Emma Gibbs
814 David Abram
815 Lucy Cowie
816 Lottie Gross
817 Seph Petta
818 Nick Edwards
819 Gavin Thomas
820 David Abram
821 David Abram
822 David Abram
823 Sarah Reid
824 David Abram
825 Richard Trillo
826 David Abram
827 Helen Abramson
828 Steven Vickers
829 David Abram
830 Alf Anderson

831 David Abram
832 Mani Ramaswamy
833 David Abram
834 Nick Edwards
835 Martin Dunford
836 Martin Dunford
837 Flip Byrnes
838 Edward Aves
839 Shafik Meghji
840 David Abram
841 David Abram
842 Nick Edwards
843 Shafik Meghji
844 Steven Vickers
845 Shafik Meghji
846 Daniel Stables
847 David Abram
848 James McConnachie
849 Richard Wignell
850 Lottie Gross
851 Shafik Meghji
852 Sally McLaren
853 David Abram
854 David Abram
855 Richard Wignell
856 David Abram
857 James Stewart
858 Lucy Ridout
859 Lucy Ridout
860 Henry Stedman
861 Lucy Ridout
862 David Dalton
863 Lucy Ridout
864 Henry Stedman
865 David Dalton
866 Lucy Ridout
867 Sean Mahoney
868 Lucy Ridout
869 Lucy Ridout
870 Iain Stewart
871 Kiki Deere
872 Lucy Ridout
873 Victor Borg
874 Mike MacEacheran
875 Anna Kaminski
876 Meera Dattani
877 Esme Fox
878 Lucy Ridout
879 Jo James
880 Steven Vickers
881 Martin Dunford
882 Lucy Ridout
883 Emma Boyle
884 Lucy Ridout
885 Daniel Stables
886 Claus Vogel
887 Lucy Ridout
888 Jo James
889 Marco Ferrarese
890 Steven Vickers
891 Kirsten Powley
892 Jo James
893 David Dalton
894 Henry Stedman
895 Lucy Ridout
896 Megan Mcintyre
897 Iain Stewart
898 Marco Ferrarese
899 Tim Ecott
900 Stephen Keeling
901 Henry Stedman
902 Andy Turner
903 David Dalton
904 Christina Markel
905 Lucy Ridout
906 Heidi Fuller-Love
907 Steven Vickers
908 Lucy Ridout
909 Seb Bacon
910 Mike MacEacheran
911 Lucy Ridout
912 Jo James
913 Henry Stedman
914 Kerry Christiani
915 Paul Whitfield
916 Ben Lerwill

917 David Leffman
918 Paul Whitfield
919 Chris Scott
920 Paul Whitfield
921 Alec Simpson
922 Chris Scott
923 Paul Whitfield
924 Emma Gregg
925 Paul Whitfield
926 Chris Scott
927 Shafik Meghji
928 David Leffman
929 Greg Dickinson
930 Alec Simpson
931 Paul Whitfield
932 Scott Stickland
933 Stephen Keeling
934 Peter Chapple
935 Emma Gregg
936 Paul Whitfield
937 Paul Whitfield
938 Chris Scott
939 Chris Scott
940 Christopher P. Baker
941 Ben Lerwill
942 Ben Lerwill
943 Martin Dunford
944 Paul Whitfield
945 Chris Scott
946 Emma Gibbs
947 Chris Scott
948 Lucy Ridout
949 James Stewart
950 Chris Scott
951 Rachel Mills
952 Rachel Mills
953 Paul Whitfield
954 Rachel Mills
955 Emma Gregg
956 Paul Whitfield
957 Martin Zatko
958 Paul Whitfield
959 Nori Jemil
960 Chris Scott
961 Paul Whitfield
962 Diana Jarvis
963 James Stewart
964 Alec Simpson
965 Holly Wallace
966 Chris Scott
967 Catherine Le Nevez
968 Paul Whitfield
969 Andy Turner
970 Peter Chapple
971 Paul Whitfield
972 Chris Scott
973 Paul Whitfield
974 Andy Turner
975 Paul Whitfield
976 Steven Vickers
977 Chris Scott
978 Polly Evans
979 Seph Petta
980 Martin Zatko
981 Paul Whitfield
982 Chris Scott
983 Seph Petta
984 Nikki Birrell
985 Lucy Ridout
986 Ben Lerwill
987 James Proctor
988 Phil Lee
989 Roger Norum
990 Roger Norum
991 Polly Evans
992 Roger Norum
993 Claus Vogel
994 Hunter Slaton
995 Ben Lerwill
996 Claus Vogel
997 Lizzie Pook
998 Louise Southerden
999 Georgia Stephens
1000 Polly Evans

PHOTO CREDITS

(Key: T-top; C-centre; B-bottom; L-left; R-right)

INDEX BY COUNTRY

YOUR TAILOR-MADE TRIP
STARTS HERE

Tailor-made trips and unique adventures crafted by local experts

Rough Guides has been inspiring travellers with lively and thought-provoking guidebooks for more than 35 years. Now we're linking you up with selected local experts to craft your dream trip. They will put together your perfect itinerary and book it at local rates.

Don't follow the crowd – find your own path.

HOW ROUGHGUIDES.COM/TRIPS WORKS

STEP 1

Pick your dream destination, tell us what you want and submit an enquiry.

STEP 2

Fill in a short form to tell your local expert about your dream trip and preferences.

STEP 3

Our local expert will craft your tailor-made itinerary. You'll be able to tweak and refine it until you're completely satisfied.

STEP 4

Book online with ease, pack your bags and enjoy the trip! Our local expert will be on hand 24/7 while you're on the road.